For reference

Not to be taken from the room.

P9-DCQ-923

Encyclopedia
of the
American Constitution

Original 1986 Editorial Board

Henry J. Abraham

Charles L. Black, Jr.

Robert H. Bork

William J. Brennan, Jr.

Henry Steele Commager

Martha A. Field

Ruth Bader Ginsburg

Erwin N. Griswold

Gerald Gunther

Harold M. Hyman

Philip B. Kurland

Alpheus T. Mason

Paul L. Murphy

C. Herman Pritchett

Harry N. Scheiber

Martin Shapiro

Encyclopedia
of the
American Constitution

SECOND EDITION

Edited by
LEONARD W. LEVY
and
KENNETH L. KARST

ADAM WINKLER, Associate Editor for the Second Edition

DENNIS J. MAHONEY, Assistant Editor for the First Edition
JOHN G. WEST, JR., Assistant Editor for Supplement I

MACMILLAN REFERENCE USA
An imprint of the Gale Group
New York

Copyright © 2000 by Macmillan Reference USA

All rights reserved. No part of this book may be reproduced or
transmitted in any form or by any means, electronic or mechanical,
including photocopying, recording, or by any information storage and
retrieval system, without permission in writing from the Publisher.

Macmillan Library Reference USA
1633 Broadway
New York, NY 10019

Printed in the United States of America

Printing Number
10 9 8 7 6 5 4 3 2 1

Library of Congress Cataloging-in-Publication Data
Encyclopedia of the American Constitution / edited by Leonard W. Levy and Kenneth L.
Karst.—2nd ed. / Adam Winkler, associate editor for the second edition.
   p. cm.
  Includes bibliographical references and indexes.
  ISBN 0-02-864880-3 (hard cover : alk. paper)
    1. Constitutional law—United States—Encyclopedias. I. Levy, Leonard Williams,
1923– II. Karst, Kenneth L. III. Winkler, Adam.
KF4548 .E53 2000
342.73—dc21
    00-029203

This paper meets the requirements of ANSI-NISO Z39.48-1992 (Permanence of Paper).

QUERN v. JORDAN
440 U.S. 332 (1979)

This case held that SECTION 1983, TITLE 42, UNITED STATES CODE, does not abrogate the states' ELEVENTH AMENDMENT immunity from suit in federal court. The amendment therefore precludes retroactive damage awards against states. States, however, may be forced to bear the costs of future compliance with the Constitution and state officials may be enjoined to comply with the Constitution.

THEODORE EISENBERG
(1986)

QUIRIN, EX PARTE
317 U.S. 1 (1942)

In 1942 President FRANKLIN D. ROOSEVELT issued a proclamation subjecting enemies entering the United States through the coastal defense zones to trial by military tribunal and denying them access to the civil courts. Seven German saboteurs, who had been set ashore in the United States from submarines and who had subsequently been captured, were tried under the terms of the proclamation. The saboteurs petitioned for a writ of HABEAS CORPUS, arguing that, so long as the regular courts were open and operating, they were entitled to TRIAL BY JURY, and citing as PRECEDENT the CIVIL WAR case EX PARTE MILLIGAN.

The Supreme Court, then in summer recess, met in extraordinary session to hear the petition. An 8–0 Court, speaking through Chief Justice HARLAN F. STONE, upheld the constitutionality of military trial for offenses against the law of war. But the Court also insisted upon the right of the civil courts to review the constitutionality or applicability of Roosevelt's proclamation in individual cases.

DENNIS J. MAHONEY
(1986)

(SEE ALSO: *Cramer v. United States; Haupt v. United States.*)

Bibliography

BELKNAP, MICHAL R. 1980 The Supreme Court Goes to War: The Meaning and Implications of the Nazi Saboteur Case. *Military Law Review* 89:59–95.

QUOCK WALKER CASES

See: *Commonwealth v. Jennison*

QUOTAS, RACIAL

See: Racial Quotas

R

RABINOWITZ, UNITED STATES v.

See: Search Incident to Arrest

RACE AND CRIMINAL JUSTICE

Racial minorities have long sought equal application of the rights the Constitution provides to people accused of crimes. They have needed the protection of these rights because the CRIMINAL JUSTICE SYSTEM has at times seemed vehemently biased against them. The result of this quest for justice is that the Supreme Court has often addressed whether particular law enforcement practices are unconstitutional because of racial concerns. The Court has interpreted the Constitution as prohibiting the most obvious and blatant forms of RACIAL DISCRIMINATION, such as excluding racial minorities from juries. There are, however, some practices such as racially skewed application of the CAPITAL PUNISHMENT and race-based assessments of suspicion, where thus far the Court has declined to order constitutional relief.

Historically, the Constitution has had a limited role in regulating the criminal justice system. Most criminal law originates with, and is enforced by, the states. The principle of FEDERALISM has limited the ability of the federal government to intervene, even in cases in which states have applied, or not applied, the criminal law in egregiously unfair ways. The FOURTEENTH AMENDMENT promises the "EQUAL PROTECTION OF THE LAWS" to all persons, but infamous cases like HODGES V. UNITED STATES (1906) and SCREWS V. UNITED STATES (1945) demonstrated the tenuous nature of this protection. In *Hodges*, whites were prosecuted by the federal government for vicious physical attacks against African Americans. The Court overturned the convictions, on the ground that the federal government exceeded its authority by making a federal case out of what should have been, in the Court's view, state charges. Thus, in the same manner that federalism provided constitutional justification for Southern states to establish de jure SEGREGATION, the Court allowed the principle to foster separate and unequal application of the criminal law to minority and white accused persons. *Hodges*, in which the Court held that the THIRTEENTH AMENDMENT gave Congress the power to reach only acts that closely resembled enslavement, was later OVERRULED by JONES V. ALFRED H. MAYER CO. (1968).

In other cases, however, the Court has been less reticent about insuring a strong role for the federal government in protecting the criminal justice rights of people of color. In fact, many of the best known decisions of constitutional CRIMINAL PROCEDURE involved African American or Hispanic litigants. These cases include POWELL V. ALABAMA (1932), which established the RIGHT TO COUNSEL in capital cases; BROWN V. MISSISSIPPI (1936), which held that coerced confessions violate DUE PROCESS; and MIRANDA V. ARIZONA (1966), which established the right of defendants to be informed about their Fifth Amendment RIGHT AGAINST SELF-INCRIMINATION. In its opinions, the Court referred to race tangentially, if at all, but the facts of the cases often arose in a context in which it was clear that racial bias infected the state's criminal justice process, and would not be remedied by the state itself. In these cases, accused persons of color vindicated rights that are now enjoyed by all Americans.

The Court has also confronted the issue of explicit bias

against racial minorities in the criminal justice system. It has been most protective of minority rights in cases in which the law has permitted discrimination on the basis of race. These cases have often arisen in the context of the right to trial by an impartial jury. Even after the Fourteenth Amendment affirmed their CITIZENSHIP, African Americans were often routinely excluded from juries. In STRAUDER V. WEST VIRGINIA (1879), the Supreme Court reversed the conviction of a black man who had been found guilty of murder by a jury from which blacks were legally excluded. The Court ruled that the Fourteenth Amendment provides "a positive immunity, or right, most valuable to the colored race—the right to exemption from unfriendly legislation [and] exemption from legal discriminations." *Strauder* represents the first time that the Fourteenth Amendment was interpreted to apply to government racism.

Even though *Strauder* guaranteed African Americans the legal right to serve on juries, they still often were excluded through the practice of PEREMPTORY CHALLENGES. In a criminal trial each side may exclude a limited number of jurors even if there is no reason to think that jurors are biased. In SWAIN V. ALABAMA (1965), the prosecution peremptorily challenged all the African Americans in the jury pool. After the defendent was convicted he charged that the government's race-based exclusion of potential jurors violated the equal protection clause. The Court disagreed, upholding the conviction. The Court emphasized the historic importance of peremptory challenges, and ruled that race-based selection of jurors, absent a pattern of discrimination, was permissible in a particular case if it was part of the government's strategy to win the case. Twenty-one years later this aspect of *Swain* was overruled by the Court in BATSON V. KENTUCKY (1986), where the Court ruled that the equal protection clause prohibits the government from using race as a consideration in jury composition, even in a single case. In GEORGIA V. MCCOLLUM (1992), the Court prohibited defendants from using race-based challenges as well.

The Court has been more reticent in finding equal protection violations when the discrimination is not admitted by the government. In MCCLESKEY V. KEMP (1987), the Court considered statistical evidence that the Georgia death penalty was applied in a race-conscious manner (a sophisticated study found that race of the victim was a significant factor in jurors' determination whether convicted killers should be sentenced to death). The Court declined to invalidate the death penalty under the Fourteenth Amendment because it believed that the statistics did not demonstrate purposeful discrimination in the particular case. Under equal protection jurisprudence an intent to discriminate must be proven. In *McCleskey*, the Court emphasized the importance of discretion in the

criminal justice system and stated that "exceptionally clear proof" was required before it would find an abuse of discretion. The Court also noted that "because of the risk that the factor of race may enter the criminal justice process, [it has] engaged in 'unceasing efforts' to eradicate racial prejudice from our criminal justice system." Since it found that because the statistical evidence showed at most "a discrepancy that appears to correlate with race," the requisite showing had not been advanced.

The requirement of purposeful discrimination has also confounded constitutional challenges to racially selective prosecution and punishment for noncapital offenses. In *Ah Sin v. Wittman* (1905), the defendant complained that the government's prosecution of gambling offenses was limited to Chinese people. The Court refused to reverse the conviction, establishing a standard of "certainty to every intent" before it would invalidate a conviction on grounds of selective prosecution. Likewise, in *United States v. Armstrong* (1996), the Court declined even to allow discovery in a case in which there was a claim of selective prosecution of African Americans for offenses involving crack cocaine. The Court required the defendant to show that similarly situated individuals of a different race were not prosecuted, but did not explain how this showing could be made in the absence of court-ordered discovery of prosecutors' files.

Despite constitutional challenges, the Court continues to permit law enforcement officers to consider race when determining suspicion of criminal activity. In *United States v. Martínez-Fuerte* (1976), the Court found no constitutional violation in Border Patrol officers' using Mexican ancestry as part of their determination of whom to stop for investigation of violation of IMMIGRATION laws. The Court's analysis was that the FOURTH AMENDMENT requires government SEARCHES AND SEIZURES to be reasonable, and that it was reasonable to think that people of Mexican ancestry were more likely to have violated the immigration laws. Some commentators have argued that race-based assessments of suspicion violate the Fourteenth Amendment's equal protection clause, but the Court has not so ruled. The use of racial profiles remains one of the most controversial practices by police departments, and one of the few instances in which the Court has approved official race-consciousness by government actors.

PAUL BUTLER
(2000)

Bibliography

ARMOUR, JODY DAVID 1997 *Negrophobia and Reasonable Racism: The Hidden Costs of Being Black in America.* New York: New York University Press.
BRIGHT, STEPHEN B. 1995 Discrimination, Death, and Denial:

The Tolerance of Racial Discrimination in the Infliction of the Death Penalty. *Santa Clara Law Review* 35:433, 453–454.

BUTLER, PAUL 1995 Racially Based Jury Nullification: Black Power in the Criminal Justice System. *Yale Law Journal* 105: 677–725.

COLE, DAVID 1999 *No Equal Justice: Race and Class in the American Criminal Justice System.* New York: New Press.

DAVIS, ANGELA J. 1996 Benign Neglect of Racism in the Criminal Justice System. *Michigan Law Review* 94:1660–1686.

DEVELOPMENTS IN THE LAW 1988 Race and the Criminal Process. *Harvard Law Review* 101:1472–1641.

JOHNSON, SHERRI LYNN 1983 Race and the Decision to Detain a Suspect. *Yale Law Journal* 93:214–258.

—— 1985 Black Innocence and the White Jury. *Michigan Law Review* 83:1611–1708.

KENNEDY, RANDALL 1997 *Race, Crime, and the Law.* New York: Pantheon Books.

MILLER, JEROME G. 1996 *Search and Destroy: African-American Males in the Criminal Justice System.* New York: Cambridge University Press.

SKLANSKY, DAVID A. 1995 Cocaine, Race, and Equal Protection. *Stanford Law Review* 47:1283–1322.

TONRY, MICHAEL H. 1995 *Malign Neglect: Race, Crime, and Punishment in America.* New York: Oxford University Press.

RACE AND SEX IN ANTIDISCRIMINATION LAW

Over the past few decades, federal courts have developed fairly well-defined legal frameworks for the adjudication of RACIAL DISCRIMINATION claims and SEX DISCRIMINATION claims. But what if a plaintiff asserts that her employer discriminated against her based on both her race and her sex? What constitutional framework applies: a race discrimination framework, a sex discrimination framework, or something else? Are discrimination claims combining race and sex even constitutionally cognizable? Consider the following hypothetical case.

Mary Lo, a single mother, is an Asian American female employee of the California Department of Water Resources (CDWR), an entity of the state of California. Mary has a master's degree in civil engineering, and she has been employed as a CDWR engineer for eight years. Within the past three years, Mary has applied for promotions to supervisory positions three times. Each time Mary responded to a notice listing the opening after determining that she met the stated qualifications for the job.

After interviewing for the position, Mary was denied the promotion on each occasion. The first time, an Asian American man was promoted. The two subsequent openings were filled by white women. All three had either less work experience or fewer certifications than Mary. In addition to not receiving these promotions, Mary has been disciplined on several occasions for arriving at work late

and for taking unauthorized sick days when her children were ill. The only other employee to suffer such reproach is another Asian American female. However, there is no evidence of explicit animus against Mary or other Asian American females.

According to Mary, CDWR's denial of her promotion was discriminatorily motivated. More specifically, Mary's contention is that CDWR did not promote her because she is an Asian American woman. As a general matter, the law requires a plaintiff like Mary to think about her discrimination as arising from her (perceived) national origin, her status as a woman, or her race as an Asian American. However, Mary wants to argue that CDWR does not view her as either a female or as an Asian American or as a foreigner. She is convinced that all three of these aspects of her identity (her race, her gender, and her perceived national origin) shape CDWR's interaction with her.

Broadly speaking, there are two legal routes Mary can take to challenge her employer's decision to deny her promotion—one statutory, the other constitutional. First, she can claim EMPLOYMENT DISCRIMINATION under Title VII, a federal statute prohibiting private and public employment discrimination. Second, Mary can claim that the state has denied her EQUAL PROTECTION OF THE LAWS in violation of the FOURTEENTH AMENDMENT. This second option is available to Mary because her employer is a governmental entity. Let us first examine Mary's claim under Title VII; Title VII jurisprudence includes a small body of opinions that directly address the question of whether a plaintiff like Mary may bring a combined race-and-sex employment discrimination claim.

Courts initially viewed claims alleging race-and-sex discrimination brought under Title VII as distinct and independent claims. For example, in *Degraffenreid v. General Motors Assembly Division* (1976), the U.S. District Court for the Eastern District of Missouri held that plaintiffs may argue race discrimination and sex discrimination separately or in the alternative, but they may not argue race-and-sex discrimination as one claim. In *Degraffenreid*, a group of black female employees invoked Title VII to advance a disparate impact theory of discrimination. They alleged that General Motors's seniority system disproportionately affected black women. Prior to 1964, General Motors did not hire any black women at all. Those who were hired after 1964 all lost their jobs as part of a workforce reduction by General Motors. Because black women were the last to be hired, they were the first to be fired.

The *Degraffenreid* court granted summary judgment for the defendants. It explained that although the black female plaintiffs could argue that General Motors discriminated against them based on their race (i.e., the fact that they are black) or based on their sex (i.e., the fact that they are women), they were not permitted to argue that General Motors discriminated against them based on their race *and* sex (i.e., the fact that they are black women). The court reasoned that

> The legislative history surrounding Title VII does not indicate that the goal of the statute was to create a new classification of "black women" who would have greater standing than, for example, a black male. The prospect of the creation of new classes of protected minorities, governed only by mathematical principles of permutation and combination, clearly raises the prospect of opening the hackneyed Pandora's box.

There are at least two ways to understand the court's analysis here. The court might be suggesting that Congress did not contemplate that black women could be discriminated against as black women. Alternatively, the court could be saying that even to the extent that black women experience discrimination that neither black men nor nonblack women experience, Congress did not intend to protect them. Either way, the court's conclusion is that plaintiffs may not aggregate their race and sex discrimination claims. Having reframed the plaintiffs' case as alleging separate claims of race discrimination and sex discrimination, the court found evidence of neither. Black men were not discriminated against, which undermined the notion that there was race discrimination, and white women were not discriminated against, which undermined the notion that there was sex discrimination.

Unlike the plaintiffs in *Degraffenreid*, Mary, our hypothetical plaintiff, would be asserting a disparate treatment, as opposed to a disparate impact, theory of discrimination. Her argument is not that CDWR employs neutral employment criteria that disproportionately burden Asian American women. Rather, her contention is that she is being treated differently (hence the term "disparate treatment") because she is an Asian American female. Under the *Degraffenreid* standard, Mary's claim would not survive the defendant's motion for summary judgment. To establish a prima facie case of discrimination under a disparate treatment theory, Mary would have to establish that (1) she belongs to a group protected by Title VII, (2) she applied and was qualified for a job for which the employer was seeking applicants, (3) despite her qualifications, she was rejected, and (4) after her rejection the position remained open and the employer continued to seek applicants among persons having the plaintiff's qualifications. Should Mary succeed in establishing a prima facie case, the burden would shift to her employer to set forth a legitimate, nondiscriminatory reason for not promoting her. If CDWR makes this showing, the burden shifts back to Mary to prove that CDWR's articulated reason was a pretext for discrimination.

Mary would likely succeed in establishing a prima facie

case of discrimination. Both race and gender are protected categories under Title VII, and Mary was more than qualified for the position she applied for. However, it is generally not very difficult for employers to articulate a "legitimate" reason for not promoting particular employees. In Mary's case, CDWR might point to Mary's tardiness and her unauthorized sick days. Mary will have a hard time proving that these justifications are a pretext for discrimination. Why? Because CDWR promoted white women and an Asian American man.

One of the problems with *Degraffenreid's* antidiscrimination framework is that it fails to address what might be referred to as compound discrimination. All of us have "compounded identities" comprised of our race, our gender, our SEXUAL ORIENTATION, and so on. How we experience discrimination is shaped by the way in which our identities are compounded. Black men and black women do not experience race discrimination in the same way, because of their gender difference. White women and black women do not experience sex discrimination in the same way, because of their racial difference. Yet, under *Degraffenreid*, black women are entitled to Title VII protection only to the extent that their discriminatory experiences comport with the discriminatory experiences of either white women or black men. The court's failure in *Degraffenreid* to acknowledge that black women experience compound discrimination based on their race and sex together results in an antidiscrimination framework that privileges the experiences of white women and black men.

In some sense, the employment of the concept "compound discrimination" is problematic. It suggests that our identities and the discrimination we experience are additive. This is not exactly true. Think again of our hypothetical plaintiff, Mary Lo. She is subject to discrimination based on stereotypes that attach to Asian American women. These stereotypes are different from those that attach to Asian men and different from those that attach to white women. Nor are the stereotypes that Asian American women face the sum of Asian American male and white female stereotypes. The "compound discrimination" metaphor is employed here to convey the idea that the discriminatory experiences of women of color— including Asian American women—are shaped by the interaction (not addition) of racism and sexism and that the *Degraffenreid* antidiscrimination framework fails to take this into account.

The *Degraffenreid* approach to antidiscrimination has not gone unchallenged, however. One of the first decisions to the contrary was *Jefferies v. Harris County Community Action Association* (1980). In *Jefferies*, a black woman made claims of race-and-sex discrimination arising out of the defendant's failure to promote her and its decision to terminate her. The positions for which she applied were

RACE AND SEX IN ANTIDISCRIMINATION LAW 2091

filled by black men and nonblack women. When the trial court dismissed her claims, she appealed, arguing that the court had erred in refusing to consider her claim of compound discrimination based on race *and* sex. The U.S. Court of Appeals for the Fifth Circuit agreed. In accepting Jefferies's compound discrimination claim, the Fifth Circuit adopted the "sex-plus" analysis established by the Supreme Court in *Phillips v. Martin Marietta Corporation* (1971). In *Phillips*, the Court held that the disparate treatment of a subclass of one sex can violate Title VII. The term "sex-plus" refers to situations in which employers discriminate by coupling a nonprotected factor (in the *Phillips* case, having preschool-age children) with a protected one (sex). The Court held that this type of discrimination was actionable under Title VII even if women in general and men with preschool-age children were not discriminated against.

The *Jefferies* court analyzed the plaintiff's "sex-plus-race" claim by characterizing her as a woman who, because of a secondary consideration, race, was treated differently. The court recognized that "discrimination against black females can exist even in the absence of discrimination against black men or white women." Title VII provides a remedy for such discrimination, the *Jefferies* court reasoned, because of the wording of the statute and its legislative history. Title VII forbids discrimination on the basis of an employee's "race, color, religion, sex, or national origin." Because Congress used the word "or," the court reasoned that it intended to include discrimination based on any or all of the listed characteristics. Moreover, Congress explicitly rejected a revision to the statute which would have added the word "solely" before the word "sex." The court viewed this rejection as signifying an intention to allow plaintiffs to aggregate their claims.

Although the sex-plus framework improves on the *Degraffenreid* race or sex framework, it nevertheless presents several important problems. First, it requires plaintiffs to argue that their race is a subordinate reason for discrimination based on gender. The sex-plus analysis treats discrimination as being drawn purely on gender lines but operating to discriminate against a certain subset of women.

Second, the sex-plus analysis equates race discrimination with other "pluses" such as marital or familial status. Equating race with other pluses ignores the fact that race itself, unlike marital or familial status, is a classification explicitly protected under Title VII.

Third, the sex-plus framework limits the number of characteristics a plaintiff can allege as contributing to her employer's discrimination. Specifically, plaintiffs are permitted to add only one "plus" to their sex discrimination claim. Thus, in Mary's case, if she alleges discrimination based on her race as a "plus" to discrimination based on her sex, she cannot add factors such as (perceived) national origin, single motherhood, or both.

A recent decision of the U.S. Court of Appeals for the Ninth Circuit takes a small step toward eliminating some of these difficulties. In *Lam v. University of Hawai'i* (1994), the plaintiff, an Asian American woman, invoked Title VII to allege race, sex, and national origin discrimination after she was turned down twice for a job as a law professor at the University of Hawaii. The Ninth Circuit explicitly rejected the district court's separate treatment of race and sex, arguing that an antidiscrimination framework that examines racism "alone" or sexism "alone" is impoverished. Significantly, the Ninth Circuit's compound discrimination approach is not based on *Jefferies*'s sex-plus analysis. *Lam*'s move away from (or noninvocation of) the sex-plus framework creates a jurisprudential window for plaintiffs to base their discrimination claims on the aggregation of several aspects of their identity. Still, it remains to be seen what impact *Lam* will have on future Title VII litigation.

Having looked at how Mary's sex-and-race compound discrimination claim would be adjudicated under Title VII, let us now turn to the Constitution. Mary would base her constitutional claim on the equal protection clause of the Fourteenth Amendment. Unlike plaintiffs claiming discrimination under Title VII, plaintiffs asserting an equal protection violation have only one path available to them; they must prove that the government is engaged in intentional discrimination. Intentional sex-based discrimination by the government is unconstitutional unless it passes what is referred to as "intermediate scrutiny." Sex-based discrimination survives intermediate scrutiny if it is substantially related to an important governmental objective. The government is not absolutely barred from discriminating against individuals based on sex, then, but it must justify that discrimination by reference to an important objective.

The Constitution regulates racial discrimination in a similar, though stricter, way. Intentional race-based governmental discrimination is unconstitutional unless it passes what is referred to as STRICT SCRUTINY. Race-based discrimination passes strict scrutiny if it serves a COMPELLING STATE INTEREST and is narrowly tailored to meet that interest.

This is the constitutional framework Mary would face should she decide to bring an equal protection discrimination claim against CDWR. This framework invites us to think about at least the following three questions: (1) Would Mary succeed in establishing a case of intentional discrimination based either on race or sex? (2) Would Mary's race-and-sex compound discrimination be constitutionally cognizable? (3) If Mary were permitted to assert a race-and-sex compound discrimination claim and she ultimately established the claim, what level of judicial scrutiny would apply: intermediate scrutiny (which applies to sex discrimination), strict scrutiny (which applies to race discrimination), or something else?

With respect to the first question, it is unlikely that Mary has enough evidence to prove intentional discrimination based either on sex or race alone. The CDWR was not overtly racist or sexist in denying Mary the promotion. Nor does CDWR have an express policy of sex or race discrimination. In the absence of such "smoking gun" evidence, it would be very difficult for Mary to convince a court that CDWR intentionally discriminated against her. The case would come down to circumstantial evidence. At this point, the court is likely to look at the people who were promoted. And if Asian American men fared well and white women fared well, the court may decide that there is no triable issue of fact—that is to say, grant summary judgment for the defendant.

But what if Mary asserted a race-and-sex compound discrimination claim? First, would such a claim be constitutionally cognizable? And second, would she be able to prove it? The answer to the first question is unclear. The issue has arisen—at least implicitly—in context of section 1983 litigation. SECTION 1983, TITLE 42, U.S. CODE is a federal statute that provides civil and criminal remedies for violations of constitutional and certain federal statutory rights. Plaintiffs bringing a section 1983 claim must demonstrate that (1) a person acting under the COLOR OF LAW (2) committed an act that deprived her of some right, privilege, or immunity protected by the Constitution or federal law. Since Mary is arguing that her constitutional rights were violated, she may invoke section 1983. Significantly, Mary still has the burden of establishing the underlying constitutional deprivation; namely, that CDWR violated her right to equal protection.

There are few judicial opinions adjudicating compound discrimination claims under section 1983. One reason is that redress under section 1983 for equal protection violations is limited to plaintiffs whose employers are state agencies (or, can show STATE ACTION) and those who can meet the burden of proving intentional discrimination.

Despite the dearth of published opinions analyzing compound discrimination claims under section 1983, two district court opinions offer plaintiffs some hope. In *Anthony v. County of Sacramento* (1995), a federal trial court, relying on *Lam*, implicitly suggested that plaintiffs advancing an equal protection argument under section 1983 may combine their race and sex discrimination claims. And in *Tennie v. City of New York Department of Social Services of the New York City Human Resources Administration* (1987), a federal trial court refused to certify a class that included whites, blacks, and hispanics of both sexes. The court reasoned that female minority women—when compared to white women and men of color—had different discrimination claims under both Title VII and the equal protection clause because of their vulnerability to racism and sexism.

Tennie and *Anthony* notwithstanding, the ability of plaintiffs to bring constitutional race-and-sex compound discrimination claims under the equal protection clause remains unclear. The Supreme Court has not spoken definitively on this issue. Moreover, at least one federal appeals court opinion, *Lowe v. City of Monrovia* (1985), decided before *Tennie* and *Anthony*, suggested that in order to prevail under a section 1983 claim alleging race and sex discrimination, the plaintiff "must first prove that the defendants purposefully discriminated against her either because of her race or her sex."

Assuming that compound race-and-sex discrimination claims are constitutionally cognizable, does Mary have a viable claim? Probably not. She would not be able to point to sufficient evidence to demonstrate that CDWR intentionally discriminated against her because she is an Asian American woman. Is there any evidence that CDWR might have discriminated against Mary? Recall that Mary was reprimanded for taking sick days and for tardiness, and that the only other employee to suffer such reproach is another Asian American female. These facts are certainly probative of discriminatory intent, but, without more, they do not demonstrate that CDWR denied Mary the promotion because she is an Asian American woman.

A final equal protection issue raised by compound race-and-sex discrimination claims is the applicable level of scrutiny. Some commentators have suggested that the Supreme Court's decision in UNITED STATES V. VIRGINIA (1996) has effectively nudged the STANDARD OF REVIEW for sex discrimination toward strict scrutiny. Irrespective of this consideration, however, a strong argument can be made that at least strict scrutiny should apply. In other words, should the government engage in compound race-and-sex discrimination against, for example, black women, such discrimination would be deemed unconstitutional unless it served a compelling state interest and was narrowly tailored to meet that interest. At least two theories could be advanced to support this argument: (1) a "double bind" theory of discrimination—that black women, because they occupy at least two subordinate identities (women and blacks), experience a double-discrimination (sexism and racism), and (2) a "DISCRETE AND INSULAR MINORITY" theory—that black women have historically been discriminated against, subject to pervasive stereotypes, and denied meaningful access to the political process.

Of course, neither of these theories renders uncontroversial the notion that black women should be treated as a distinct class in equal protection analysis. There are "slippery slope" concerns: If black women are deemed a cognizable class for equal protection purposes and are entitled to strict scrutiny protection, there may be no stopping point. As it turns out, however, the slope is not nearly so slippery as it might appear to be. There is a limiting principle: a group seeking strict scrutiny protection based on a compound theory of discrimination could be required to demonstrate historical discrimination, discreteness and insularity, and political powerlessness. This limiting principle is already a part of our equal protection jurisprudence. To the extent that other compound identities, for example, Mexican American women, are able to satisfy this test, there is no good reason to deny them strict scrutiny protection.

DEVON W. CARBADO
(2000)

Bibliography

CARBADO, DEVON W. 1999 Introduction. *Black Men on Race, Gender, & Sexuality: A Critical Reader.* New York: New York University Press.

CRENSHAW, KIMBERLÉ 1989 Demarginalizing the Intersection of Race and Sex: A Black Feminist Critique of Antidiscrimination Doctrine, Feminist Theory and Antiracist Politics. *University of Chicago Legal Forum* 1989:139–142.

TRENT, JUDY SCALES 1989 Black Women and the Constitution: Finding Our Place, Asserting Our Rights (Voices of Experience: New Responses to Gender Discourse). *Harvard Civil Rights–Civil Liberties Law Review* 9:23–27.

RACE AND VOTING

Controversies over race and voting stem from the fact that citizens belong to racial and ethnic groups with different and often conflicting interests, and as group members they tend to vote for candidates representing those interests. What should be done when their group's preferred candidates are consistently prevented from winning election?

The question became urgent after passage of the VOTING RIGHTS ACT OF 1965. In the South, most newly enfranchised blacks were unable to elect black candidates. Racially polarized voting was the main culprit: In electoral venues where whites outnumbered blacks—and in the 1960s this was almost always the case—white votes overwhelmed black ones.

The paucity of majority-black venues resulted primarily from racial GERRYMANDERING; white legislators refused to draw majority-black districts in single-member-district systems or adopted majority-white multimember-district ("at-large") systems. Suits by black and other minority voters—particularly Hispanics—attacked racial gerrymandering as illegal efforts to dilute minority voting strength. On this theory, the FOURTEENTH AMENDMENT guarantees racial minorities the opportunity to participate equally in the political process by electing candidates of their choice, and the guarantee is abridged by ELECTORAL DISTRICTING that denies minorities this opportunity. The Supreme Court adopted the theory in *White v. Regester* (1973), and Congress in 1982 then added vote-dilution protection to groups covered by the Voting Rights Act. *Thornburg v. Gingles* (1986) simplified the criteria for proving dilution, and the U.S. Department of Justice, charged with administering the Voting Rights Act, required states redistricting after the 1990 Census to draw majority-minority districts whenever feasible. Consequently, from the middle 1970s to the early 1990s the number of black and Hispanic officials in the South and Southwest, respectively, increased sharply.

This trend was reversed in the mid-1990s. In SHAW V. RENO (1993), white plaintiffs in North Carolina, a state that is 22 percent black, challenged aspects of the 1990s REAPPORTIONMENT, which had resulted in the election of the first two African American members of Congress from that state since RECONSTRUCTION. The plaintiffs claimed that the shape of one of the safe black districts was "so extremely irregular on its face that it rationally can be viewed only as an effort to segregate the races for purposes of voting, without regard for traditional districting principles and without sufficiently compelling justification." The Court majority agreed that such a claim was justiciable. In MILLER V. JOHNSON (1995) the Court emphasized that the harm to voters was not determined by the shape of the district, but by whether the district had been created predominantly for racial purposes. This new cause of action is said to derive from a theory of "expressive harms," as distinct from either vote denial or vote dilution.

Shaw caused various safe black and Hispanic congressional districts to be replaced with majority-white ones. Vote-dilution challenges by minority plaintiffs diminished, and suits were filed challenging safe minority districts below the congressional level.

Critics of vote-dilution litigation welcomed these developments. Among their reasons, all arguable, are that racial gerrymanders as remedies for vote dilution violate the principle of "the colorblind Constitution"; that creating safe minority districts both cuts the Democratic margins among elected officials and diminishes the substantive REPRESENTATION of minority voters; and that the probable decline in the number of minority elected officials resulting from *Shaw* encourages consideration of proportional representation schemes that are allegedly superior to winner-take-all, single-member-district plans.

In response, those who favor the theory of minority vote dilution argue that, whatever the trade-offs between electing minority officeholders and furthering the substantive representation of minorities, minority voters lose an important kind of access to the polity when white bloc voting constrains (and in some locales prohibits altogether) minority officeholding. This argument, in turn, raises the issue of how intense racially polarized voting is today, particularly in the South and Southwest. Systematic research suggests that it is still quite intense there, although the degree of intensity is disputed among political scientists.

In the nation's polity as on the Court, three views on race and voting presently vie for supremacy: race neutrality in districting, which rejects the theory of minority vote dilution altogether; racial pluralism, which advocates protecting the right of minority groups to elect their candidates of preference using race-based districting; and proportional representation, through the replacement of district systems with such plans as limited or cumulative voting. None of these views has yet gained ascendancy.

CHANDLER DAVIDSON
(2000)

Bibliography

DAVIDSON, CHANDLER and GROFMAN, BERNARD, eds. 1994 *Quiet Revolution in the South: The Impact of the Voting Rights Act 1965–1990.* Princeton, N.J.: Princeton University Press.

GUINIER, LANI 1994 *The Tyranny of the Majority: Fundamental Fairness in Representative Democracy.* New York: Free Press.

ISSACHAROFF, SAMUEL; KARLAN, PAMELA S.; and PILDES, RICHARD H. 1998 *The Law of Democracy: Legal Structure of the Political Process.* Westbury, N.Y.: Foundation Press.

KOUSSER, J. MORGAN 1999 *Colorblind Injustice: Minority Voting Rights and the Undoing of the Second Reconstruction.* Chapel Hill: University of North Carolina Press.

LUBLIN, DAVID 1997 *The Paradox of Representation: Racial Gerrymandering and Minority Interests in Congress.* Princeton, N.J.: Princeton University Press.

SWAIN, CAROL M. 1993 *Black Faces, Black Interests: The Representation of African Americans in Congress.* Cambridge, Mass.: Harvard University Press.

THERNSTROM, ABIGAIL 1987 *Whose Votes Count? Affirmative Action and Minority Voting Rights.* Cambridge, Mass.: Harvard Univesity Press.

RACE-CONSCIOUSNESS

It was once widely believed that BROWN V. BOARD OF EDUCATION (1954, 1955) had removed the last vestiges of race-consciousness from the Constitution. Many observers saw the *Brown* decision as a vindication of Justice JOHN MARSHALL HARLAN's lone dissent in PLESSY V. FERGUSON (1896). Harlan's critique of the majority's SEPARATE BUT EQUAL DOCTRINE was summarized in these famous words: "Our Constitution is color-blind, and neither knows nor tolerates classes among citizens. In respect of civil rights, all citizens are equal before the law." In the years between *Plessy* and *Brown*, the ideal of a "color-blind" Constitution served as one of the central tenets of liberal CONSTITUTIONALISM.

Today, however, some leading liberal constitutionalists argue that adherence to the ideal of a color-blind Constitution was a mistake. It has been only recently discovered that "color-blindness" was all along a "myth" or, at best, a "misleading metaphor." The principal reason for the volteface on the part of liberal activists is summarized by Laurence H. Tribe, who writes that "judicial rejection of the "separate but equal' talisman seems to have been accompanied by a potentially troublesome lack of sympathy for racial separateness as a possible expression of group solidarity." Indeed, it seems to be true that the expression of racial or ethnic group solidarity does require something like the old—and once justly decried—"separate but equal doctrine." Tribe's tergiversations indicate, however, that it is not yet entirely fashionable to speak openly about the desirability of returning to separate but equal. Attacks on the idea of a color-blind Constitution, on the other hand, are legion.

A curious feature of the *Brown* decision is that it did not make a comprehensive condemnation of racial classifications or entirely overrule the *Plessy* decision. Only racial classifications that were said to produce "feelings of inferiority" were deemed to violate EQUAL PROTECTION, and from the psychological evidence adduced by the Court, this was "proven" to be the case only in the context of grammar school education. Presumably, racial SEGREGATION that did not stigmatize one race or ethnic group as inferior would survive the test adumbrated in *Brown*. Thus, *Brown* did not overrule all racial classifications—or treat them as SUSPECT CLASSIFICATIONS—but left open the possibility that under certain circumstances racial classifications could be "benign" if the classification were designed to produce racial class remedies rather than racial class injuries. Resort to the doctrine of STRICT SCRUTINY in the *Brown* case would probably have effectively foreclosed the future use of race as a legitimate classification.

Perhaps the best expression of the new understanding of "separate but equal" was made by Justice HARRY A. BLACKMUN in his separate opinion in REGENTS OF UNIVERSITY OF CALIFORNIA V. BAKKE (1977): "I suspect that it would be impossible to arrange an affirmative-action program in a racially neutral way and have it successful. . . . In order to get beyond racism, we must first take account of race. There is no other way. And in order to treat some persons equally, we must treat them differently." Justice Blackmun could have used the word "separately" in lieu of "differently" without changing his meaning in the slightest. Indeed, it has been the advent of affirmative action that has generated the greatest controversy about race-consciousness and the Constitution. At its inception, the proponents of affirmative action assured a skeptical world that it was only a temporary measure to be employed in the service of equality of opportunity. But now, some twenty-odd years after its appearance, affirmative action is looked upon unabashedly by its supporters as a means of securing racial class entitlements.

Inevitably, the test of racial class entitlements—and RACIAL DISCRIMINATION—is the concept of racial proportionality. This idea assumes that, absent discrimination, the races will freely arrange themselves in the various aspects of political and private life in exact racial proportionality and that when they do not, there is a prima facie evidence of discrimination (or underrepresentation) that eventually must be rectified by any number of coercive remedies. This situaion, of course, presents the alarming spectacle of a nation one day looking upon all civil rights as nothing more than racial class entitlements. But any nation with the slightest concern for the lessons of history would never self-consciously allow itself to regard the rights of individuals as nothing more that the by-product of racial class interests. Even though we may be assured that the ultimate ends of such programs as affirmative action are "to get beyond racism," those who advocate such policies simply have not thought out the likely consequences, believing, no doubt, that a means can never become the end itself.

The constitutional doctrine that most contributes to race-consciousness is that of DISCRETE AND INSULAR MINORITY. The underlying premise of this doctrine is that there are certain racial and ethnic minorities that are permanently isolated from the majoritarian political process and therefore cannot vindicate their racial class interests by merely exercising the vote. The concept of the discrete and insular minority assumes that American politics has always been dominated by a monolithic majority that seeks only to aggrandize its own racial class interests at the expense of the various discrete and insular minorities. Thus, the moral authority of the majority—indeed, of majoritarian politics itself—must be questioned, if not undermined. In fact, some legal scholars argue that the only way that the rights of discrete and insular minorities can be absolutely guaranteed is in those instances where legislation disadvantages or injures the majority. Thus, one could argue that the Constitution not only permits affirmative action but requires it. It is only where the majority suffers a positive disadvantage that one can be certain that discrete and insular minorities are not harmed by the operation of the majoritarian political process. Fortunately, the Supreme Court has never accepted this negative version of the categorical imperative.

A bare acquaintance with history shows the impossibility of such a simplistic view of American politics. Could such a monolithic majority bent on the exclusive aggrandizement of its own racial class interests approve the Declaration of Independence and the Constitution? Ratify the Bill of Rights? Fight the Civil War to overturn the DRED SCOTT V. SANDFORD (1857) decision? Ratify the THIRTEENTH AMENDMENT, FOURTEENTH AMENDMENT, and FIFTEENTH AMENDMENT? Pass the CIVIL RIGHTS ACT OF 1964 and the VOTING RIGHTS ACT OF 1965? These great events (and a host of others) in American constitutional history make it incredible that learned people—including the Justices of the Supreme Court—could believe that the concept of discrete and insular minorities was in any way an accurate reflection of American political life. American life is too subtle and complex to be understood exclusively in terms of racial class interests.

The Framers of the Constitution knew that class politics, in whatever guise it appeared, was incompatible with constitutional democracy. The whole thrust of JAMES MADISON's belief in the "capacity of mankind for self-government" was his conviction that under a properly constructed constitution, majorities could be rendered capable of ruling in the interest of the whole of society rather than in the interest of the part (i.e., in the interest of the majority). The structure of society itself, with its multiplicity of interests and accompanied by a constitutional structure informed by the SEPARATION OF POWERS, held the prospect that majorities could act in a manner consistent "with the rules of justice and the rights of the minor party." Madison called these majorities *constitutional* majorities as distinguished from *numerical* majorities. Many legal scholars today, however, simply proclaim that every majority is ipso facto a special-interest group and that majorities cannot therefore be trusted to rule in the interest of the whole. Some even conclude that courts should be cast in the role of virtual representatives of discrete and insular minorities, because judges are isolated from the majoritarian political process and can therefore "rule" in the interest of the whole of society. Others, however, have not forgotten such infamous decisions as *Dred Scott, Plessy v. Ferguson*, LOCHNER V. NEW YORK (1905), and *Korematsu v. United States* (1944) and are quick to recognize this scheme as a form of judicial oligarchy. Virtual representation is an idea that is incompatible with republican government.

It has become something of an orthodoxy among legal scholars to ridicule the moral imperative of racial neutrality as the driving force of the Constitution. They retort that race has always been a factor in American political life and it is simply unrealistic to think that it will not be so for the foreseeable future. Because race-consciousness will inevitably be part and parcel of constitutional calculations, it is more honest to advocate them openly than to seek a deceptive refuge in the ideal of a color-blind Constitution. It is true that America's constitutional past is all too replete with race-consciousness. After all, the Constitution itself gave support to SLAVERY. The toleration of slavery in the Constitution was a product of political necessity. The Constitution itself—and thereby any prospects of ending slavery—would never have been accepted without compromise on the issue of slavery. But most of the Framers of the Constitution looked upon that compromise as a necessary (but temporary) departure from the principles of the regime that had been enunciated in the Declaration of Independence. The best they could do under the circumstances was to fix those principles in the Constitution so that the Constitution could one day provide the basis for emancipation. The American founding was incomplete, but the Constitution looked forward to its completion by putting, in ABRAHAM LINCOLN's words, "slavery on the ultimate road to extinction." Lincoln always interpreted the Constitution in light of the principles of the Declaration. In doing this, he was following the lead of the Framers themselves.

In 1857, Lincoln gave an account of the aspirations of the American polity and the role the Declaration played in fixing constitutional aspirations. He noted that the authors of the Declaration "did not mean to assert the obvious untruth, that all were then actually enjoying equality, nor yet, that they were about to confer it immediately upon them." In fact, Lincoln noted, they had no power to "confer such a boon," had they been inclined to do so. Rather, "they meant simply to declare the *right*, so that the *enforcement* of it might follow as fast as circumstances should permit. They meant to set up a standard maxim for free society, which should be familiar to all, and revered by all, constantly looked to, constantly labored for, and even though never perfectly attained, constantly approximated, and thereby constantly spreading and deepening its influence, and augmenting the happiness and value of life to all people of all colors everywhere." With the Constitution viewed as the means of implementing the "standard maxims" of the Declaration, the nation has made tremendous progress since the Civil War and Reconstruction.

Yet, at almost the eleventh hour, liberal constitutionalists want to abandon those principles that have been the source of progress. Surely the progress came too slowly and advanced by fits and starts, according to the political circumstances of the day. But no one can deny that progress occurred and that it resulted directly from our "ancient faith" that the Constitution should be race-neutral. Now we are told that progress in race relations has not gone far enough or fast enough and it is time to return to a race-conscious Constitution to implement a newer, more certain view of racial progress. The return to race-

consciousness also means that sooner or later we will have to pronounce the principle of equality "an empty idea." The reason is simple: equality is a principle that is incompatible with group rights and preferential treatment. One prominent author has argued that because it cannot comprehend the "rights of race," "equality is an idea that should be banished from moral and legal discourse." Indeed, group claims—including racial group claims—are not claims of equality, but claims of inequality, and they necessarily rest upon some notion of "separate but equal." Class claims deny the principle of equality because they ascribe to individuals class characteristics that are different—and necessarily unequal—from those of individuals occupying other classes. If there were no inequalities implicit in class distinctions, such distinctions would be superfluous and there would be no need to substitute group rights for individual rights.

Almost the whole of American constitutional history has been a history of the nation's attempt to confine the genie of race by powerful constitutional bonds; yet the most sophisticated constitutional scholars today advocate the release of the racial genie once again, this time to act as a benign, rather than destructive, force. This is dangerous advice because this time the genie will not be restrained by the moral principle that "all men are created equal."

EDWARD J. ERLER
(1992)

Bibliography

ERLER, EDWARD J. 1989 Equal Protection and Regime Principles, Pages 243–283 in Robert L. Utley, Jr., ed., *The Promise of American Politics*. Lanham, Md.: University Press of America.

STRAUSS, DAVID A. 1986 The Myth of Colorblindness. *Supreme Court Review* 1986:99–134.

TRIBE, LAURENCE H. 1988 *American Constitutional Law*, 2nd ed. Pages 1474–1480. Mineola, N.Y.: Foundation Press.

WESTEN, PETER 1982 The Empty Idea of Equality. *Harvard Law Review* 95:537–596.

RACE, REPRODUCTION, AND CONSTITUTIONAL LAW

Race has always influenced the meaning of reproductive freedom in America. Scientific racism explained the domination of whites over blacks as the natural social order: blacks were biologically destined to be slaves and whites to be their masters. For three centuries, courts and legislatures carefully defined race according to amount of black ancestry and enforced the rule of white racial purity. One of America's earliest laws was a 1662 Virginia SLAVERY statute that gave the children born to slave mothers and fathered by white men the status of slaves. Laws against MISCEGENATION, designed to keep the races from intermingling, were not declared unconstitutional by the U.S. Supreme Court until 1967. Even today, Americans' continued understanding of race as an inherited trait profoundly connects reproductive policy to racial politics.

Regulating black women's reproductive decisions has been a central aspect of racial oppression in America. Slavemasters had a financial incentive to exploit slave women's reproductive capacity to replenish the enslaved labor force. During the Depression, the alliance between the emerging BIRTH CONTROL movement and eugenicists paved the way for public birth control clinics aimed at reducing the birthrates of poor blacks in the South. It was discovered in the 1970s that thousands of black women had been coercively sterilized annually under government welfare programs. Federally funded programs had similarly sterilized more than one-third of women of childbearing age in PUERTO RICO and one-fourth of Native American women.

Although contemporary reproductive health policies are not so blatantly racist, many coercive policies have a disparate effect on minority women and are arguably designed to curb the birthrates of minority mothers on welfare in particular. Many states have enacted child exclusion policies, or "family caps," that deny additional benefits for children born to women already receiving public assistance. Politicians have proposed even more coercive measures, such as mandating that mothers on welfare be implanted with the long-acting contraceptive Norplant. In the 1980s prosecutors across the country initiated a punitive response to the problem of drug use during pregnancy. Although the problem cuts across racial and economic lines, the vast majority of more than two hundred women prosecuted for prenatal crimes were poor black mothers who smoked crack cocaine. Recently the Supreme Court of South Carolina upheld the conviction of a black woman whose fetus was exposed to crack, ruling that a fetus is a child for purposes of the state's child abuse statute.

There are two types of constitutional challenges to reproductive health policies that threaten RACIAL DISCRIMINATION. First, the EQUAL PROTECTION clause of the FOURTEENTH AMENDMENT prohibits any law regulating reproduction that explicitly classifies citizens on the basis of race or that disproportionately affects a racial or ethnic minority where invidious purpose can be shown. Such claims are rarely successful, for government officials today are unlikely either to make explicit racial distinctions or to express racial motivation in enacting reproductive policies. The U.S. Supreme Court has upheld reproductive health laws that disproportionately burden minority women. Federal and state laws denying Medicaid reimbursement for ABORTIONS and other regulations that make it difficult for poor women to obtain abortion services, for example, disproportionately affect minority women, but were held constitutional in cases such as HARRIS V. MCCRAE (1980) and PLANNED PARENTHOOD V. CASEY (1992).

A second constitutional challenge combines the equal protection mandate with the protection of reproductive decisionmaking under the DUE PROCESS clause. These two provisions support a constitutional prohibition of invidious government standards for childbearing that reinforce white supremacy. SKINNER V. OKLAHOMA (1942) acknowledged the threat to racial equality posed by government interference in the right to procreate. *Skinner* invalidated the Oklahoma Habitual Criminal Sterilization Act authorizing the sterilization of persons convicted two or more times for "felonies involving moral turpitude." The Court found that the statute treated unequally criminals who had committed similarly culpable offenses: chicken thieves like Mr. Skinner were sterilized while embezzlers were not. Applying STRICT SCRUTINY under the equal protection clause, the Court concluded that the government failed to demonstrate that the statute's classification was justified by eugenics or the inheritability of criminal traits.

The *Skinner* Court's reason for choosing strict scrutiny is especially pertinent to the constitutionality of racial discrimination in reproductive health laws. Declaring the right to bear children to be "one of the basic civil rights of man," the Court recognized the significant risk of racial discrimination inherent in state intervention in reproduction. "In evil or reckless hands," Justice WILLIAM O. DOUGLAS wrote, "[the government's power to sterilize] can cause races or types that are inimical to the dominant group to wither and disappear." The state's discriminatory imposition of sterilization against certain types of criminals was as invidious "as if it had selected a particular race or nationality for oppressive treatment." Thus, the Court acknowledged the potential for racist governmental regulation of procreation even in the absence of explicit racial classifications.

LOVING V. VIRGINIA (1967) also deployed the constitutional guarantee to strike down a discriminatory law involving reproduction. *Loving* invalidated a Virginia statute that banned interracial marriage, resting the decision on both the equal protection and the due process clauses of the Fourteenth Amendment. The Virginia federal judge who convicted Mr. and Mrs. Loving explicitly endorsed scientific racism as an explanation for antimiscegenation laws, reasoning that "[t]he fact that [Almighty God] separated the races shows that he did not intend for the races to mix." The Court held that, "as measures designed to maintain White Supremacy," the laws had no legitimate purpose independent of invidious racial discrimination. Citing *Skinner*, the Court further concluded that the anti-miscegenation statute unjustifiably deprived the Lovings of their freedom to marry guaranteed by the due process clause.

Would the current Supreme Court invalidate, as "measures designed to maintain White Supremacy," reproductive regulations that disproportionately penalize minority women's childbearing, or whose popularity hinges on a widespread perception that they have such an effect? Probably not. Present equal protection doctrine requires a stronger showing of discriminatory purpose. Nonetheless, *Skinner*'s warning about the dangers of racist restrictions on procreation and *Loving*'s condemnation of laws that protect racial purity emphasize the constitutional importance of equality in reproductive decisionmaking. Laws that effectively single out black mothers to deter or punish their decision to have children impose a racist government standard for procreation. They function to preserve a racial hierarchy that essentially disregards black humanity. They evoke the specter of racial eugenics, especially in light of the history of sterilization abuse of women of color. Government policies that perpetuate racial subordination through the denial of reproductive rights, thereby threatening both racial equality and SUBSTANTIVE DUE PROCESS should be subject to the most exacting judicial scrutiny.

DOROTHY ROBERTS
(2000)

Bibliography

DAVIS, ANGELA Y. 1983 *Women, Race, and Class.* New York: Vintage.

DAVIS, PEGGY COOPER 1997 *Neglected Stories: The Constitution and Family Values.* New York: Hill and Wang.

FRIED, MARLENE GERBER, ed. 1990 *From Abortion to Reproductive Freedom: Transforming a Movement.* Boston: South End Press.

GORDON, LINDA 1976 *Woman's Body, Woman's Right: A Social History of Birth Control in America.* New York: Grossman.

ROBERTS, DOROTHY 1997 *Killing the Black Body: Race, Reproduction, and the Meaning of Liberty.* New York: Pantheon.

RACIAL BALANCE

The idea of racial balance is a product of the DESEGREGATION of public schools in the years since BROWN V. BOARD OF EDUCATION (1954–1955). The term refers to the racial distribution of students in particular schools in relation to the racial distribution of school children in an entire district. If a district's children are seventy percent white and thirty percent black, then a hypothetically perfect balance would produce these same percentages in each school. By extension, the notion of racial balance may be used in discussing other institutions: a housing project, a factory's work force, a state university's medical school. (See AFFIRMATIVE ACTION; RACIAL QUOTAS.)

In the school cases, the Supreme Court has held that racial balance is an appropriate "starting point" for a lower court to use in fashioning a remedy for de jure SEGREGATION. (See DE FACTO/DE JURE; SWANN V. CHARLOTTE-MECKLENBURG BOARD OF EDUCATION.) However, even where segregation has been deliberately caused by school board actions, there is no constitutional requirement of racial balance throughout the district's schools. Although one-race schools are presumptively to be eliminated, the school board will be allowed to prove that the racial distribution in those schools results from something other than the board's deliberate policy. SCHOOL BUSING over very long distances, for example, would not be required under this approach; distance alone would be a racially neutral explanation for the board's failure to remedy racial imbalance.

In the absence of previous legislation commanding or authorizing school segregation, or school board actions with segregative intent, the fact of racial imbalance in a district's schools, standing alone, does not amount to a constitutional violation. However, intentional acts of segregation by the board in the remote past, coupled with current racial imbalance, will place on the board an almost impossible burden of proving that it has dismantled its "dual" (segregated) system. (See COLUMBUS BOARD OF EDUCATION V. PENICK.)

The term racial balance is sometimes used in a different sense. Some discussions of school segregation use the term to describe a school that includes a "critical mass" of students from each race. Social scientists disagree over the educational value to minority students of having a significant number of white students in the classroom. The suggestion that minority students learn better in the company of whites has roots in the Supreme Court's pre-*Brown* decisions on graduate education. (See SWEATT V. PAINTER.) And where segregation is imposed by official action, *Brown* itself takes the view that the resulting stigma impairs minority students' ability to learn. But the abstract proposition that minority students cannot learn effectively outside the presence of whites is more than a little patronizing. And the notion of racial balance in this sense is immensely complicated in a multiethnic community: is a school integrated if it contains significant numbers of both white and minority students, or should the category of minority students be broken down into its black, Hispanic, and other components? Merely to ask this question is to understand why the Supreme Court has avoided speaking of racial balance in this latter sense and has used the idea in its mechanical racial-percentages sense only as a "starting point."

KENNETH L. KARST
(1986)

Bibliography

FISS, OWEN M. 1975 The Jurisprudence of Busing. *Law and Contemporary Problems* 1975:194–216.

RACIAL CLASSIFICATION

See: Benign Racial Classification; Invidious Discrimination; Racial Discrimination; Suspect Classification

RACIAL DISCRIMINATION

The nation was founded with the enslavement of blacks as an established and ongoing institution, and though we were not particularly proud of the institution, we were prepared to live with it. The Constitution did not mention the word "slave," and contemplated the eventual closing of the slave trade (referred to simply as the "importation of persons"), but, through similar circumlocutions, also created obligations to return fugitive slaves, and included a proportion of the slaves within the population base to be used for the apportionment of representatives and taxes. In DRED SCOTT V. SANDFORD (1857) the Supreme Court viewed slaves as property and declared that the right of slaveholders to take their slaves to the territories was protected by the DUE PROCESS CLAUSE of the Fifth Amendment.

The CIVIL WAR brought SLAVERY to an end and reversed the basic commitment of the Constitution toward blacks. The law sought equality rather than enslavement, and it was through the elaboration of this egalitarian commitment that the concept of racial discrimination emerged. Prohibiting racial discrimination became the principal strategy of the American legal system for achieving equality for blacks. The laws against racial discrimination typically protect all racial minorities, not just blacks, and yet, for purely historical reasons, the development of those laws would be unimaginable apart from the struggle of blacks for equality in America. That struggle has been the source both of the achievements of antidiscrimination law and of its recurrent dilemmas.

The three amendments adopted following the CIVIL WAR constitute the groundwork of this branch of the law, although only one—the FIFTEENTH AMENDMENT—actually speaks of racial discrimination. It provides that "the right . . . to vote shall not be denied or abridged . . . on account of race, color, or previous condition of servitude." The other Civil War amendments are not cast in terms of racial discrimination. The THIRTEENTH AMENDMENT prohibits slavery and involuntary servitude, and the FOURTEENTH AMENDMENT, in relevant aspect, prohibits states from denying "the EQUAL PROTECTION OF THE LAWS." But the Supreme Court has interpreted both these amendments to prohibit racial discrimination. With respect to the Thirteenth Amendment, the Court reasoned in JONES V. ALFRED H. MAYER CO. (1968) that racial discrimination is a badge or incident of slavery. (See BADGES OF SERVITUDE.) Similarly, in interpreting the Fourteenth Amendment, the Court, as early as STRAUDER V. WEST VIRGINIA (1880), declared racial discrimination to be the kind of unequal treatment that constitutes a denial of equal protection of the laws. Indeed, over the years, racial discrimination came to be seen as the paradigmatic denial of equal protection, and supplied the standard against which all other equal protection claims came to be measured, even when pressed by nonracial groups such as the poor or women. They too had to show that they were discriminated against on the basis of some impermissible criterion such as their wealth or sex. The promise of equal protection was thus transformed into a promise not to discriminate.

It was, moreover, through the enforcement of the Fourteenth Amendment that the prohibition against racial discrimination achieved its greatest prominence. Antidiscrimination was the instrument that finally put to an end the system of white supremacy that emerged in the late nineteenth and early twentieth centuries and that worked by separating whites and blacks—Jim Crow. The discrimination appeared on the very face of Jim Crow laws and a principle that condemned racial discrimination easily brought those laws within the sweep of the Fourteenth Amendment. All that was needed was an understanding of how the separatism of Jim Crow worked to the disadvantage of blacks; that was the burden of BROWN V. BOARD OF EDUCATION (1954) and the cases that followed. As the principle controlling the interpretation of the Fourteenth Amendment, antidiscrimination was a limitation only upon the actions of states, but once the step entailed in *Brown* was taken, the federal government was, in BOLLING V. SHARPE (1954), made subject to an identical prohibition by a construction of the due process clause of the Fifth Amendment. Racial discrimination was deemed as inconsistent with the constitutional guarantee of liberty as it was with equal protection.

Statutes, too, have been concerned with racial equality. In the years immediately following the Civil War, Congress passed a comprehensive program to protect the newly freed slaves, and defined the conduct it sought to prohibit in a variety of ways. In the CIVIL RIGHTS ACT OF 1866 Congress promised that blacks would enjoy the same rights as whites; in the FORCE ACTS (1870, 1871) it guaranteed all citizens the rights and privileges arising from the Constitution or laws of the United States. In the decades following *Brown v. Board of Education,* however, when the antidiscrimination principle of the Fourteenth Amendment received its most strenuous affirmation and the nation embarked on its Second Reconstruction, Congress cast the substantive standard in terms of a single idiom—do not discriminate. (See CIVIL RIGHTS ACT OF 1964; CIVIL RIGHTS ACT OF 1968; VOTING RIGHTS ACT OF 1965.)

During this period, Congress introduced new mechanisms to enforce the equal protection clause; for example, it authorized the attorney general to bring injunctive school desegregation suits, required federal administrative agencies to terminate financial assistance to segregated school systems, and provided for criminal prosecutions against those who forcibly interfered with desegregation. Congress also broadened the reach of federal antidiscrimination law beyond the scope of the Fourteenth Amendment by regulating, in the name of racial equality, activities of private agencies (for example, restaurants, employers, or landlords), which otherwise would not have been covered by that amendment because of its "state action" requirement. In each of these measures, Congress used the language of antidiscrimination. So did the President in promulgating EXECUTIVE ORDER 11246 (1965), which regulates government contractors. Many state legislatures also intervened on behalf of racial equality during the Second Reconstruction, and these enactments were also couched in terms of prohibiting discrimination.

Sometimes Congress and the state legislatures exempted certain discriminatory practices from the laws they enacted. One instance is the federal open housing law, which exempts discrimination by small residences ("Mrs. Murphy's roominghouse"); another is the federal fair employment statute, which exempts from its coverage small businesses (at first businesses with fewer than twenty-five employees, later reduced to fifteen). Apparently Congress viewed the interest in associational liberty present in these settings as sufficiently strong to justify limited exemptions to the ban on racial discrimination. Yet, putting these exemptions and a handful of others to one side, it is fair to say that today, primarily as a result of the Second Reconstruction, the prohibition against racial discrimination is all-encompassing. It has both constitutional and statutory bases and is the subject of an executive order. It is a pervasive feature of both federal and state law and calls forth a broad array of civil and criminal remedies. It almost has the status of a moral imperative, like the norm against theft or killing. The issue that divides

Americans today is thus not whether the law should prohibit racial discrimination but what, precisely, doing so entails.

The antidiscrimination norm, as already noted, was largely fashioned at a time when the nation was swept by the SEPARATE BUT EQUAL DOCTRINE of Jim Crow and when blacks were disadvantaged in a rather open and crude manner. In such a context, the principle of antidiscrimination invites a color blindness: When allocating a scarce opportunity, such as a job or a place in a professional school, the decision maker should not prefer a white candidate over a black one on the basis of the individual's color or race. Here antidiscrimination requires that individuals be judged independently of race. This much is settled. Interpretive problems arise, however, when the social context changes—when we have moved beyond Jim Crow and blacks have come to be disadvantaged primarily in ways that are hidden and systematically entrenched. Then we confront two issues. One arises from the exclusion of blacks on the basis of a seemingly innocent criterion such as performance on a standardized test; the other from the preference given to blacks to correct for longstanding unequal distributional patterns.

To clarify the first issue, it should be understood that the appearance of innocence might be misleading. Although a black scores higher than a white on a test, the employer might manipulate or falsify the scores so that the white is given the job. In this case, the apparent use of an innocent criterion is simply a mask for racial discrimination. The decision is still directly based on race and would be deemed unlawful. The most straightforward remedy would be to set aside the decision and allow an honest application of the test.

There are, moreover, situations when a test is honestly administered and yet the very decision to use the test in the first place is based on an illegitimate concern, namely, a desire to exclude blacks. A highly sophisticated verbal aptitude test might be used, for example, to select employees for manual work because the employer, wanting to maintain a predominantly white work force, assumes that fewer whites than blacks will be screened out by the test. Here again, the "real" criterion of selection is race; a court would disallow the use of the irrelevant test, and require the employer to choose a criterion that serves a legitimate end. In both of these cases—the dishonest application of legitimate criteria and the honest application of illegitimate criteria—the appearance of color blindness is a sham and a court could use the simple, colorblind form of the antidiscrimination norm to void the results.

The more troublesome variant of the first issue arises when (1) the facially innocent criterion is adopted in order to serve a legitimate interest; (2) the criterion in fact furthers that interest; and (3) the application of the criterion disadvantages the racial minority in much the same way as would the use of race as the criterion of selection. The job may in fact require sophisticated verbal skills and the test that measures these skills may screen out more blacks than whites. The test is job-related but has a disparate adverse impact on blacks. The question then is whether an employment decision based on the test violates the antidiscrimination prohibition. This is a question of considerable difficulty because while the law, strictly speaking, prohibits distinctions based on race, this particular decision is based on a criterion other than race.

One school of thought answers this question in the negative. This view stresses process, and interprets antidiscrimination in terms of the integrity of the selection process: A selection process based on race is corrupt and cannot be allowed. A selection process free of racial influence might redound to the benefit of the racial minority, since it would allow them to compete on equal footing with other groups and thus give them a chance to alter the distributional inequalities that occurred under a regime such as Jim Crow, where they were penalized because of their race. Any actual effect on their material status as a group, however, would represent just an agreeable byproduct, or a background assumption, not the purpose of antidiscrimination law. According to this school, the aims of antidiscrimination law are fulfilled when the process of selection is purified of all racial criteria or motivations.

Another viewpoint stresses results or effects, not process; it would find the use of the innocent criterion unlawful even if it serves legitimate ends. What is decisive, according to this school of thought, is the actual disadvantaging of blacks, not the way the disadvantage comes about. If the application of a criterion has a disproportionately adverse impact on the racial minority, in the sense that it excludes substantially more blacks than whites, the criterion should be treated as the functional equivalent of race.

At the heart of this interpretation of antidiscrimination is a concern for the social status of blacks. It is motivated by a desire to end all practices that would tend to perpetuate or aggravate their subordinate position. Admittedly, the costs of this program are real, for it is stipulated that the contested criterion serves some legitimate end; the test is job-related. But these costs are seen as a necessary price of justice. Only when the costs become extraordinarily large or achieve a special level of urgency, as when the criterion serves some "compelling" (and not just a "legitimate") interest, will the use of the criterion be allowed.

The theorist who so emphasizes effects rests his argument principally on the Fourteenth Amendment and ascribes to it the grandest and noblest of purposes—the elimination of caste structure. He insists that antidiscrimination, as the principle that controls the application of that amendment, be construed with this broad purpose in mind and if need be, that a new principle—the group-disadvantaging principle—be articulated in order to make this purpose even more explicit. He also insists that the various statutes that prohibit discrimination—the principal argumentative props of the process school—should be construed derivatively. These statutes, unlike the Fourteenth Amendment, may contain in so many words a specific ban on "discrimination based on race," but, so the effects theorist argues, these statutes should be seen as a legislative adoption of the prevailing constitutional principle. When that principle is interpreted to forbid the use of criteria that effectively disadvantage blacks, the statutes should be interpreted in a similar fashion.

The process school emphasizes not only the precise language in which the statutory norm is cast but also the traditional rule that conditions judicial intervention on a finding that the defendant is at fault. This fault exists when a white is given a job over a black even though the black scored higher on a test; the employer is said to be acting wrongfully because race is unrelated to any legitimate purpose and is a factor over which individuals have no control. But the requisite fault is said to be lacking when the selection is made on the basis of the individual's performance under some nonracial standard, such as a job-related test. On the other hand, those who subscribe to an effects test emphasize the prospective nature of the remedy typically sought in these cases (an injunction to forbid the use of the criterion in the future) and deny the need for a finding of fault. Such a finding may be necessary to justify damages or the criminal sanction, because these remedies require the defendant to pay for what he did in the past, and presumably such a burden can be placed only on someone who acted wrongfully. But an injunction simply directs that the defendant do what is just and does not presuppose that the defendant has acted wrongfully. Alternatively, the effects theorist might contend that if fault is necessary, it can be found in the defendant's willingness to persist in the use of the contested criterion with full knowledge of its consequences for the racial minority. Such persistence connotes a certain moral indifference.

The disadvantaging that the effects test seeks to avoid is usually defined in terms of the status of a group (for example, the criterion has a greater adverse impact on blacks than on whites and thus tends to perpetuate their subordinate position). Some see this group orientation as alien to our jurisprudence, and thus find a further reason for turning away from an effects test. Borrowing the Court's language in SHELLEY V. KRAEMER (1948), they insist that "[t]he rights created by the first section of the Fourteenth Amendment are, by its terms, guaranteed to the individual" and that "[t]he rights established are personal rights." But those who subscribe to the effects test see the well-being of individuals and of groups as inextricably linked: They believe that the status of an individual is determined in large part by the status of the group with which he is identified. Slavery itself was a group phenomenon, and any corrective strategy must be structured in group terms. Effects theorists also point to practices outside the racial context that display a concern for the welfare of groups such as religious minorities, women, the handicapped, labor, and consumers, and for that reason insist that a group orientation is thoroughly compatible with American legal principles.

In the late 1960s and early 1970s, the Supreme Court responded to these arguments and moved toward adopting an effects test in cases such as *Gaston County v. United States* (1969), GRIGGS V. DUKE POWER CO. (1971), and SWANN V. CHARLOTTE-MECKLENBURG BOARD OF EDUCATION (1971). There was, however, an element of ambiguity or hesitation in the Court's response. The Court prohibited the use of seemingly innocent criteria that disadvantaged blacks, even when their use served some legitimate interests, but the Court did not justify its decisions solely in terms of the adverse effects of the criteria. In addition, the Court characterized the adverse effect as a vestige of an earlier use of race. For example, a literacy test was disallowed as a qualification for voting not simply because it disqualified more blacks than whites but also because it perpetuated the disadvantages previously imposed on blacks in segregated schools. This insistence on analyzing the disadvantage as a vestige of past discrimination may have reflected a commitment to the process test insofar as the Court treated the earlier procedural imperfection (the assignment to schools on the basis of race) as the legally cognizable wrong and the present practice (the literacy test) as merely a device that perpetuates that wrong. But at the same time, the concern with past discrimination surely reflected some commitment to the effects test, for it resulted in the invalidation of facially innocent criteria that in fact served legitimate ends. Disallowing today's literacy test would avoid perpetuating yesterday's discrimination in the educational system, but only by compromising an interest the Court had previously deemed legitimate, namely, that of having a literate electorate. In fact, an interpretation of antidiscrimination law to forbid practices that perpetuate past discrimination could become functionally coextensive with an interpretation that makes effects decisive if some global practice such as slavery is taken as the relevant past discrimination, if the victims of past discrimination are identified in group terms, and if the remedial burden is placed on parties who had no direct role in the earlier discrimination. All disparate effects can be seen as a vestige of the special and unfortunate history of blacks in America.

By the mid-1970s, however, it became clear that the Court was not inclined to broaden its concern with past discrimination so as to make it the functional equivalent of the effects test. In fact, the Court turned in the opposite direction—away from effects and toward process. As Justice POTTER STEWART announced, "Reconstruction is over." The Court did not flatly repudiate its earlier decisions, but instead tried to limit them by confining the effects test to those antidiscrimination norms that were embodied in statutes. For constitutional claims of discrimination, the Court in cases such as WASHINGTON V. DAVIS (1976) and MOBILE V. BOLDEN (1980) required a showing that the process was flawed, or more precisely, that the defendant "intended to discriminate." The plaintiff had to show that the defendant's decision was based on race, or that he chose the seemingly innocent criterion not to further legitimate ends but to exclude or disadvantage blacks. The Court continued to honor claims of past discrimination, but by and large insisted that those claims be advanced by individually identifiable victims of the earlier discrimination, that past acts of discrimination be defined with a great deal of specificity, and that the causal links of those acts to the present racially disparate effects be manifest. No global claims of past discrimination have been allowed.

There is a certain irony in this distinction between statutory and constitutional claims, and in the Supreme Court's decision to confine the effects test to the statutory domain, for the statutes are couched in terms less congenial to such a test. The statutes speak specifically in terms of decisions based on race, while the Fourteenth Amendment speaks of equal protection. (Antidiscrimination is but the judicially constructed principle that is to guide the application of that provision.) Arguably, the distinction between statute and Constitution might reflect the Court's desire to find some way of limiting the practical impact of the effects test, for under the Fourteenth Amendment an effects test would have the widest scope and present the greatest possibilities of judicial intervention. The Fourteenth Amendment extends to all state practices and, because of its universality (it protects every "person"), could be used to protect even those groups that are not defined in racial terms. Indeed, in *Washington v. Davis* the Court expressed the fear that under the effects test the Fourteenth Amendment might even invalidate a sales tax because of its disproportionately adverse impact on the poor (never for a moment pausing to consider whether suitable limiting principles could be developed for avoiding such a result). The Court's distinction between statutory and constitutional claims might also stem from a desire to devise a means for sharing with other political institutions responsibility for the sacrifice of legitimate interests entailed in the application of an effects test. When attached to the statute, the effects test and its disruptive impact become the responsibility of both Court and Congress, since Congress remains free to repeal the statute or otherwise disavow the test.

In the mid-1970s, at the very moment the Court was struggling to identify the circumstances in which the use of a seemingly innocent criterion could be deemed a form of racial discrimination and was moving away from an effects test, it also had to confront the other major interpretive issue posed by antidiscrimination law, the issue of AFFIRMATIVE ACTION. The Court had to decide whether the norm against racial discrimination prohibits giving preference to blacks.

For much of our history, it was assumed that race-based action would be hostile to blacks and that therefore colorblindness would work to the advantage of blacks or at least shield them from hostile action. During the Second Reconstruction, however, as the drive for racial equality grew stronger, an assertedly "benign" use of race became more common. Many believed that even the honest application of legitimate criteria would not significantly alter the unequal distributional patterns that were produced among the races first under slavery and then under Jim Crow, and that it would be necessary, at least for the immediate or foreseeable future, to give blacks a preference in order to improve their status relative to other groups.

These affirmative action programs typically included other minorities, such as Hispanics, as beneficiaries, but were primarily seen as addressed to blacks and did not extend to all disadvantaged groups, such as the poor or white ethnic minorities. They had a distinctive racial cast and were sometimes described as a form of "reverse discrimination." These programs were also typically structured so as to require the decision maker to achieve a certain number of blacks or other minorities within the institution, say, as employees or students. Often that number equaled the percentage of blacks or other minorities in the general population, and was variously described as a goal or quota, depending on which side of the issue one was on. A "goal" was said to establish the minimum rather than the maximum and to be more flexible than a "quota." But more significantly, the term "goal" did not have the odious connotations of the term "quota," which had been used in the past to describe numerical limits on the admission of minorities, limits that were designed to preserve rather than eradicate the caste structure.

For the most part, these affirmative action programs were not treated as a constitutional or statutory requirement. Some of those who subscribed to an effects test argued that the failure to institute preferential programs would constitute a practice that perpetuated the subordinate position of blacks and thus would be itself a form of racial discrimination. But this argument equated inaction with action, and either for that reason or because the

effects test was having difficulties of its own, this argument never established a toehold in the law. Equally unsuccessful were the arguments that emphasized those antidiscrimination laws, such as the federal fair employment statute or the executive order governing government contractors, that not only prohibited discrimination but also commanded in so many terms "affirmative action"; the inclusion of these two words were deemed insufficient to alter or add to the basic obligations of the law. The issue posed by affirmative action programs was therefore one of permissibility, rather than obligation: Were these programs consistent with the prohibition against racial discrimination?

Sometimes the purported beneficiaries of the programs (or people speaking on their behalf) objected to them on the theory that the use of race was not wholly benign. Affirmative action was premised on the view that the racial minorities would not fare well under a colorblind policy, thus implying that these minorities are not as well equipped as whites to compete under traditional meritocratic criteria. They are being told, as they were under Jim Crow, that they are inferior—nothing "reverse" about this distinction. This complaint forced those who ran affirmative action programs to be secretive or discreet about what they were doing, but it did not bring those programs to an end or even present an especially formidable obstacle. The proponents of affirmative action explained that the race-based preference was premised on an assessment of the group's history in America, on the wrongs it suffered, not on a belief about innate ability, and as such could not justifiably be seen as giving rise to a slight. The use of race is benign, they insisted, because it improves the status of blacks and other racial minorities by giving them positions, jobs, or other concrete material advantages that they otherwise would not enjoy, at least not in the foreseeable future.

Affirmative action programs have also been attacked by whites, especially when there are discernible differences in the applicants under standard nonracial criteria and when scarce goods, such as highly desired jobs or places in professional schools, are being allocated. In such circumstances favoring a black because of his race necessarily means disfavoring a white because of his race; a job given to one is necessarily denied another. The rejected white applicant cannot truly claim that he is stigmatized even in these circumstances; no one is suggesting he is inferior. His exclusion comes as the by-product or consequence of a program founded on other principles—not to hurt him or the members of his group, but to help the disadvantaged. On the other hand, the rejected white applicant does not rest his complaint solely on the fortuity of the general, racially unspecific language of the antidiscrimination norm, the fact that discrimination based on *any* race is prohibited. The white applicant can also claim that he is being treated unfairly, since he is being judged on the basis of a criterion over which he has no control and which is unrelated to any conception of merit. The rejected white applicant might not be stigmatized, but he can insist that he is being treated unfairly.

This claim of individual unfairness finds support in the process theory of antidiscrimination: If the purpose of antidiscrimination law is to preserve the integrity of a process, to insure that individuals are treated fairly and to prevent them from being judged on the basis of irrelevant criteria, then it would not seem to matter whether the color used in the process were white or black. In either instance, the selection process would be unfair. The program may be well-intentioned, but the intention is of little solace to the rejected white applicants who, as Justice LEWIS F. POWELL put it, are being forced "to bear the burdens of redressing grievances not of their making."

Some of the proponents of affirmative action deny that there is any unfairness to the rejected white applicant. They argue that the claim of unfairness presupposes a special moral status for certain nonracial or meritocratic standards of evaluation, such as grades or performance on a standardized test, and that the requisite moral status is in fact lacking. The white has no "right" to be judged on the meritocratic standard. The more widely shared view among the proponents of affirmative action, however, acknowledges the unfairness caused to individual whites by the preference for blacks but treats it as a necessary, yet regrettable cost of eliminating caste structure. As Justice HARRY A. BLACKMUN put it, "In order to get beyond race, we must first take account of race. There is no other way." Those who take this position, like those who support an effects test, argue that the purpose of antidiscrimination law is to guard against those practices that would perpetuate or aggravate the subordinate position of blacks and other racial minorities and that it would be a perversion of history now to use that law to stop programs designed to improve the status of these groups.

The Supreme Court confronted the issue of affirmative action and weighed these arguments in two different settings. In one, affirmative action was undertaken at the behest of a court order. The theory underlying such orders is not that affirmative action is directly required by an antidiscrimination statute or by the Constitution but rather that it is needed to remedy a pattern or practice of discrimination. Affirmative action is part of the court's corrective plan. A court might, for example, require a company to grant a preference in the seniority system to blacks who were previously excluded from the company and thus unable to earn seniority rights equal to those of whites. The Supreme Court has accepted such remedial uses of race, although it has insisted that this kind of preference be limited to identifiable victims of past discrimination and that some regard be given to the interests of the innocent whites who might be adversely affected by the preferences. For example, blacks might be preferred for vacancies, but will not necessarily be allowed to force the layoff of whites.

The second setting consists of the so-called voluntary affirmative action programs, which are adopted not under orders from a court but out of a sense of moral duty or a belief that the eradication of caste structure is a desirable social policy. These voluntary affirmative action programs have proved more troublesome than the remedial ones, in part because they are not limited to individually identifiable victims of past discriminations (they are truly group oriented), but also because they are not preceded by a judicial finding that the institution has previously discriminated and they are not carried out under the close supervision of a court. The Supreme Court approved these affirmative action programs, but its approval has not been a blanket one. By the mid-1980s, it was established that under certain circumstances color consciousness is permissible, but the Court has been divided in its effort to define or limit these circumstances.

These divisions have been especially pronounced when the voluntary programs were used in higher education. In the first case, DEFUNIS V. ODEGAARD (1974), involving admissions to a state law school, the Court heard arguments and then dismissed the case on grounds of MOOTNESS because the rejected white applicant had graduated by the time the Court came to decide the case—a disposition that underscored the difficulty of the issue and the internal divisions on the Court. A few years later, the Court took up the issue again, in REGENTS OF UNIVERSITY OF CALIFORNIA V. BAKKE (1978), this time at the insistence of a rejected white applicant to a state medical school. In this case the Court reached the merits, but the divisions were even more apparent. No single opinion commanded a majority.

Four Justices thought the preferential program in *Bakke* unlawful. They stressed an antidiscrimination statute, which prohibited, in so many terms, discrimination based on race. These Justices reasoned that a preference for blacks is as much a discrimination based on race as one for whites. No discrimination means no discrimination. Another Justice thought preferential programs could be justified as a means of diversifying the student body, but he objected to the manner in which the particular program before the Court had been implemented. He would allow race to be considered in the admissions process, but would not permit separate tracks for applicants according to race. The remaining four Justices joined in an opinion that would sustain the program as it was in fact implemented, but two of these Justices also wrote separate opinions.

These deep-seated divisions did not resolve themselves substantially in the years following *Bakke*. One voluntary program received a slightly more resolute acceptance by the Court, however, in FULLILOVE V. KLUTZNICK (1980). This program was established by Congress and required a preference for minority-owned businesses in awarding contracts for federally funded public works projects. Although, once again, no single opinion commanded a majority of the Court, the vote of the Justices shifted from 1–4–4 to 6–3, and Chief Justice WARREN E. BURGER, who had objected (without qualification) to the preferential program in *Bakke*, voted to uphold this one. He also wrote one of three opinions that supported the constitutionality of the program. The Chief Justice studiously avoided choosing among "the formulas of analysis" articulated in *Bakke; that is, he refused to say whether the affirmative action program had to meet the "compelling" interest standard or whether it was sufficient if the corrective ends of the program were deemed "important" or just "legitimate" and the means substantially related to those ends. He simply said, whatever the standard, this program meets it. He did, however, specifically and repeatedly mention one factor that might be the key to the change in his position and the Court's attitude in general: "Here we pass, not on a choice made by a single judge or a school board, but on a considered decision of the Congress and the President."

With this emphasis on the role played by the coordinate branches of government in the affirmative action program, the Chief Justice returned to an idea that emerged in the analysis of the Court's treatment of facially innocent criteria, and that might well explain the Court's determination to confine the effects test to statutes: The Court is more prepared to accept the costs and dislocations that are entailed in the eradication of caste structure when it can share the responsibility for this project with the other branches of government. The Court does not want to go it alone. This suggests that the fate of equality will depend not only on the substantive commitments of the Justices, on their determination to bring the subordination of blacks and other racial minorities to an end, but also on their views about the role of the Court. The content of antidiscrimination law will in good measure depend on the willingness of the Justices to use their power to lead the nation, or if that impulse is lacking, on the willingness of the other branches of government to participate aggressively in the reconstruction of a society disfigured by one century of slavery and another of Jim Crow.

OWEN M. FISS
(1986)

Bibliography

BELL, DERRICK 1980 *Race, Racism and American Law*. Boston: Little, Brown.

BREST, PAUL 1976 In Defense of the Antidiscrimination Principle. *Harvard Law Review* 90:1–54.

COHEN, MARSHALL; NAGEL, THOMAS; and SCANLON, THOMAS 1977 *Equality and Preferential Treatment*. Princeton, N.J.: Princeton University Press.

EISENBERG, THEODORE 1981 *Civil Rights Legislation*. Charlottesville, Va.: Michie Co.

FISHKIN, JAMES 1983 *Justice, Equal Opportunity and the Family*. New Haven, Conn.: Yale University Press.

FISS, OWEN 1971 A Theory of Fair Employment Laws. *University of Chicago Law Review* 38:235–314.

—— 1976 Groups and the Equal Protection Clause. *Philosophy and Public Affairs* 5:107–177.

FREEMAN, ALAN 1978 Legitimizing Racial Discrimination through Antidiscrimination Law: A Critical Review of Supreme Court Doctrine. *Minnesota Law Review* 62:1049–1119.

GARET, RONALD 1983 Communality and Existence: The Rights of Groups. *Southern California Law Review* 56:1001–1075.

GUNTHER, GERALD 1972 In Search of Evolving Doctrine on a Changing Court: A Model for Newer Equal Protection. *Harvard Law Review* 86:1–48.

KARST, KENNETH and HOROWITZ, HAROLD 1974 Affirmative Action and Equal Protection. *Virginia Law Review* 60:955–974.

RAE, DOUGLAS 1981 *Equalities*. Cambridge, Mass.: Harvard University Press.

TUSSMAN, JOSEPH and TEN BROEK, JACOBUS 1949 The Equal Protection of the Laws. *California Law Review* 37:341–381.

RACIAL DISCRIMINATION
(Update 1)

In the mid-1980s, most observers would have said that the Supreme Court's view of racial discrimination was in equipoise. Some of the Justices seemed sympathetic to the aggressive purposeful use of racial criteria to end the legacy of racial subordination; others were skeptical of "benign discrimination" and looked instead to a constitutional principle of colorblindness as the cornerstone of a society free of discrimination. The last several terms have made plain the ascendancy of the latter view. It is now evident that a majority of the Justices are prepared to view with suspicion and hold to the highest standard of constitutional scrutiny governmental efforts to use racial classifications even to assist members of racial minorities. At the same time, governmental actions that disadvantage racial minorities will be sustained absent clear and unambiguous evidence of impermissible racial animus.

AFFIRMATIVE ACTION advocates are particularly concerned about the Court's recent willingness to view benign racial classifications with the same suspicion with which it has traditionally treated classifications intended to oppress. Where this leaves racially conscious programs is unclear, except that as before the stronger the showing that a RACIAL PREFERENCE is related to a bona fide remedial goal, the greater the likelihood the Court will sustain it.

Thus in WYGANT V. JACKSON BOARD OF EDUCATION (1986), the Justices overturned a plan under which a school board extended to minority teachers what a plurality of the Court called "preferential protection against layoffs." The plan was part of the collective-bargaining agreement between the board and the union representing school teachers and was defended before the Court as an effort to alleviate "social discrimination" by providing a diverse set of role models in public schoolrooms. A three-Justice plurality declared that the proper test was STRICT SCRUTINY and held the plan invalid because more specific findings of prior discrimination were necessary before the layoff protection could be said to serve a COMPELLING STATE INTEREST.

In contrast, in UNITED STATES V. PARADISE (1987), the Justices voted 5–4 to sustain a federal district court's imposition of a "one-for-one" hiring plan, pursuant to which the Alabama Department of Public Safety was obliged to remedy its past failure to hire black troopers by hiring one black trooper for each white trooper hired. The SOLICITOR GENERAL argued that even when a racially conscious remedial program was ordered by a court, strict scrutiny was the proper test, and the program could survive only on a showing of a compelling state interest. Four Justices, in an opinion by Justice WILLIAM J. BRENNAN, refused to decide this question, ruling that the program could meet any level of scrutiny because it was "justified by a compelling interest in remedying the discrimination that permeated entry-level practices and the promotional process alike." The plurality further noted that the district court had imposed the one-for-one plan only after the department had repeatedly failed to comply with earlier decrees.

Probably the most controversial benign discrimination decision—and the one with the most far-reaching implications—was RICHMOND (CITY OF) V. J. A. CROSON CO. (1989), in which the Justices struck down a program under which the City of Richmond required its prime contractors to subcontract thirty percent of the dollar amount of each contract to minority-owned firms. In Croson, a majority of the Justices ruled explicitly that strict scrutiny was the proper level of review for benign discrimination cases. Although there was no majority opinion on the point, six Justices repudiated as insufficiently narrow the city council's defense that the program was needed to eliminate the effects of societal discrimination.

Although it is true that the Justices have always taken the position that even benign classifications are subject to the highest level of constitutional scrutiny, they have not previously applied the rule with quite the strictness used in Croson. Indeed, FULLILOVE V. KLUTZNICK (1980), which sustained a federally mandated set-aside program for certain construction projects, is in one sense indistinguishable: in Fullilove and in Croson, the relevant body (in the first case the Congress, in the other the city council) had before it no record of past discrimination. This aspect of Fullilove can be preserved by reference to the special fact-finding competence of the Congress, although this reed is a thin one because the Congress found no facts; in any case, the Justices are noticeably less hospitable to Fullilove-style set-asides by state or local governments than they were to Congress's set-asides a decade ago. But at least six Justices seem prepared to pay strong deference to the power of Congress to adopt programs of affirmative action in enforcing the FOURTEENTH AMENDMENT.

At the same time, the Court has arguably shown increasing sensitivity to certain claims of racial discrimination in the CRIMINAL JUSTICE SYSTEM. Thus in Hunter v. Underwood (1985), a unanimous Court struck down a neutrally applied disenfranchisement of persons convicted of misdemeanors involving "moral turpitude" on the ground that it was originally enacted decades earlier for the purpose of discriminating against black citizens. The following term, in BATSON V. KENTUCKY (1986), the Justices eased the burden of a defendant seeking to prove that the prosecution had used its peremptory challenges to exclude jurors on the basis of race. On the same day, the Justices decided in Turner v. Murray that a defendant in a capital case has the right to examine prospective jurors about racial bias.

But the trend has gone only so far. In the following term, the Justices made plain their resistance to inferring impermissible discriminatory motivation from circumstantial evidence, especially statistical evidence. In MCCLESKEY V. KEMP (1987), a black convicted of murder argued that Georgia's decision to sentence him to death violated the Eighth and Fourteenth Amendments because statistics demonstrated that black defendants, especially black defendants whose victims were white, were far more likely than white defendants to receive CAPITAL PUNISHMENT. The statistics (generally referred to as the Baldus study, after the principal author of the underlying work) were stark indeed; they indicated, among other disparities, that capital juries in Georgia handed down death sentences to black defendants whose victims were white twenty-two times more frequently than they did to black defendants whose victims were black.

The McCleskey majority, however, was unimpressed, responding tersely, "We refuse to assume that what is unexplained is invidious." This answer in a sense eluded McCleskey's point, which was that the disparity was great enough to place the burden of explanation on the state. The Court replied that other explanations were plausible, adding that juror discretion should not be condemned or disturbed simply because of an "inherent lack of predictability." As long as forbidden racial animus was not the only possible explanation, the Court would not assume that animus was at work.

As the dissenters pointed out, the result in *McCleskey* seemed to stand as a departure from the BURGER COURT decision in *Arlington Heights v. Metropolitan Housing Development Corp.* (1977). In *Arlington Heights*, the Justices suggested that racial animus might be inferred from "a clear pattern" of official behavior, "unexplainable on grounds other than race." The *McCleskey* majority was correct that other explanations for the Baldus data are conceivable, and some critics have offered them. But in *McCleskey*, the Justices declined even to speculate.

Nevertheless, in important respects, *McCleskey* differed from other racial-discrimination cases. First, as several observers have noted, the Baldus study most strongly supports an argument that the murderers of black people are systematically treated with greater leniency than the murderers of white people. If one believes that the death penalty deters the crime of murder, then the implication is that the state is doing less to protect the lives of black people than to protect the lives of white people. Warren McCleskey, convicted of killing a police officer while committing another felony, was not a particularly attractive candidate to raise this issue. The better case (unfortunately for the Supreme Court's paradoxical ruling in *Linda R.S. v. Richard D.*, which denied standing to raise a claim that the law is inadequately enforced) would be one brought by law-abiding black citizens seeking to protect their lives and property.

A second distinction between *McCleskey* and other cases is that, had it gone the other way, *McCleskey* might have opened up a Pandora's box of claims that blacks in the criminal process—from arrests to sentencing—are treated more harshly than whites, claims that are supported by considerable empirical literature. Even if the literature is accurate (again, there are critics), it is difficult to imagine what practical relief might be fashioned in such cases. For those who are convicted, mandatory resentencing is one possibility, although the continued judicial monitoring of sentencing disparities could produce a procedural nightmare. The fear that this slippery slope lay ahead might well have been a part of the majority's calculus.

The Justices have also worked important changes in the interpretation of one of the keystones of the "Second Reconstruction," Title VII of the CIVIL RIGHTS ACT OF 1964. In *Ward's Cove v. Antonio* (1989), the Justices reexamined the burden of proof of a plaintiff relying on the Court's decision in GRIGGS V. DUKE POWER CO. (1971). *Griggs* had read Title VII to prohibit an employment practice with racially identifiable disparate impacts unless the employer was able to show a business necessity for the test. In *Ward's Cove*, the Court ruled 5–4 that the plaintiff must carry the burden of demonstrating the causal link to the composition of the market of people qualified to do the job in question. Critics of *Ward's Cove* argued that the decision had shifted the burden from the employer to the employees and would make employment-discrimination cases more difficult to prove; defenders responded that Title VII plaintiffs should be required to prove all elements of their claims.

Depending on one's point of view, then, the recent work of the Supreme Court in the area of racial-discrimination law has represented either a tragic abandonment of the judiciary's traditional role as protector of the racially oppressed or a return to the shining principles of color-blindness as the fundamental rule for government action. But not all significant changes in the area of racial discrimination require judicial action. In fact, one of the most important developments of recent years involved an attempted legislative correction of a judicial wrong. The WORLD WAR II decisions sustaining the internment of Japanese Americans are widely regarded as among the most horrific judicial decisions of the twentieth century (although it must be said that the programs could never have been approved had the President and Congress not imposed them in the first place). In the mid-1980s, federal courts vacated the convictions of Gordon Hirabayashi, Minoru Yasui, and Fred Korematsu for evading registration for internment. A DAMAGES claim by former detainees was rejected by the Federal Circuit in 1988 on statute of limitations grounds, but in August of that year, the Congress adopted legislation apologizing for the internment program and granting to each surviving internee compensation of roughly $20,000—not perhaps the same as justice, but at least an acknowledgment that justice was due.

STEPHEN L. CARTER
(1992)

(SEE ALSO: *Constitutional Remedies; Capital Punishment and Race; Japanese American Cases; Race-Consciousness; Sentencing.*)

Bibliography

AREEN, JUDITH et al. 1989 Constitutional Scholars' Statement on Affirmative Action After *City of Richmond v. J. A. Croson Co. Yale Law Journal* 98:1711–1716.
FRIED, CHARLES 1989 Affirmative Action After *City of Richmond v. J. A. Croson Co.*: A Response to the Scholars' Statement. *Yale Law Journal* 99:155–161.
KENNEDY, RANDALL L. 1988 *McCleskey v. Kemp*: Race, Capital Punishment, and the Supreme Court. *Harvard Law Review* 101:1388–1443.

RACIAL DISCRIMINATION
(Update 2)

Supreme Court decisions at the end of the 1980s heralded the ascendancy of colorblind constitutionalism. Decisions in the 1990s confirmed the preeminence of that vision.

In SHAW V. RENO (1993), the Court ruled in favor of a FOURTEENTH AMENDMENT challenge to North Carolina's enactment of a majority-black ELECTORAL DISTRICT, created pursuant to an agreement with the U.S. Department of Justice under the terms of the VOTING RIGHTS ACT OF 1965. MOBILE V. BOLDEN (1980) requires that one show both an intent to discriminate and discriminatory effect to prevail on an EQUAL PROTECTION challenge to electoral districting. The challengers of the North Carolina plan, which resulted in the election of the first African American member of Congress from that state since RECONSTRUCTION, alleged neither, claiming instead a violation of their right to "participate in a 'color-blind' electoral process." Despite the novelty of this claim, the Court held that they had stated an adequate claim for relief. Focusing on the "extreme irregularity" in the shape of the district, *Shaw* suggested that the districting legislation "was unexplainable on grounds other than race," and so, prohibited under the Fourteenth Amendment absent a showing of a COMPELLING STATE INTEREST. *Shaw* worked a substantial revision of equal protection doctrine in this area, although it did so on the highly context-specific basis of district shape.

Shaw says less about the majority's general concern for quashing racial discrimination than about its concern that government not consider race in efforts to remedy past discrimination. Consider ADARAND CONSTRUCTORS, INC. V. PEÑA (1995). At issue was the STANDARD OF REVIEW to apply when the federal government relies on a racial classification in an AFFIRMATIVE ACTION program: the STRICT SCRUTINY necessary where the government harms a racial group; or, in recognition of the benign purpose of the classification, a less onerous intermediate standard. Because strict scrutiny is nearly always fatal to the law under review, the answer to this question goes directly to the viability of government-sponsored affirmative action programs. A plurality in FULLILOVE V. KLUTZNICK (1980) upheld a federal program similar to the one at issue in *Adarand* along lines approximating an intermediate standard of review. The Court in RICHMOND (CITY OF) V. J. A. CROSON CO. (1989), however, ruled that where a municipality attempted a similar program, it would have to meet the higher level of justification. *Croson* distinguished the reach of the federal government in the area of race relations, stressing the power to remedy racism vested in Congress by the FOURTEENTH AMENDMENT, SECTION 5. Only the federal government would be allowed leeway in designing race-based remedies; other governmental actors would be held to a stricter standard regardless of whether they sought to harm or help minorities. Relying on *Fullilove* and *Croson*, the Court in METRO BROADCASTING, INC. V. FCC (1990) used an intermediate standard to uphold a federal affirmative action program. Nevertheless, *Adarand* sidestepped *Fullilove* and OVERRULED *Metro Broadcasting*, imposing a heightened level of justification on the federal government. Congress, like the states, now faces strict scrutiny in relying on racial classifications, irrespective of whether for harmful or remedial purposes. (Note, though, that *Adarand* held off on whether strict scrutiny means the same thing for Congress as for others, leaving open the future possibility of relatively more though still limited deference to the former.)

The MAJORITY OPINIONS in *Croson*, *Shaw*, and *Adarand*, all by Justice SANDRA DAY O'CONNOR, stop just short of announcing that government may never rely on race in the effort to remedy social inequality. Meanwhile, Justices ANTONIN SCALIA and CLARENCE THOMAS strongly urge the Court to move to full colorblindness. In his concurrence in *Adarand*, Scalia suggests that "government can never have a 'compelling interest' in discriminating on the basis of race in order to 'make up' for past racial discrimination in the opposite direction." Thomas expounds "a 'moral and constitutional equivalence' between laws designed to subjugate a race and those that distribute benefits on the basis of race in order to foster some current notion of equality." Whether the Court will complete or retreat from its attack on affirmative action remains to be seen. For now, however, the Court seems far more concerned with limiting race discrimination of the remedial than of the invidious sort. In this context, one cannot help but recall Charles L. Black, Jr.'s injunction, in responding to criticism of BROWN V. BOARD OF EDUCATION (1954), that we laugh when confronted with the argument that SEGREGATION amounted to "equal treatment." Such laughter might be appropriate here, too, in response to the suggestion that affirmative action and Jim Crow be morally and legally equated, were it not for the fact that it is a majority of Supreme Court Justices who insist on the equation.

IAN F. HANEY LÓPEZ
(2000)

Bibliography

FREEMAN, ALAN 1978 Legitimizing Racial Discrimination Through Antidiscrimination Law: A Critical Review of Supreme Court Doctrine. *Minnesota Law Review* 62:1049–1119.

GOTANDA, NEIL 1991 A Critique of "Our Constitution is Colorblind." *Stanford Law Review* 44:1–68.

SYMPOSIUM 1996 Race-Based Remedy. *California Law Review* 84:875–1232.

RACIAL PREFERENCE

Debate about racial-preference policies stirs particularly strong passions because it evokes one of the central animating concerns of liberal constitutionalism—its opposition to any system of hereditary castes. But there is little agreement today about what the constitutional principle of equality actually requires.

Some version of racial equality has always been insisted on, at least since the ratification of the FOURTEENTH AMENDMENT. Even in the 1890s, when the Supreme Court acquiesced to racial SEGREGATION in the South, it insisted that the separation of the races should not be understood to "imply the inferiority of either race" or be taken as a sign of governmental preference for one race over another. At the same time, however, the Court observed in PLESSY V. FERGUSON (1896) that "in the nature of things," the Fourteenth Amendment "could not have been intended to . . . enforce social as distinguished from political equality. . . ." The Court treated racial bias and inequality among private citizens as equivalent to class antagonisms between rich and poor or to sectarian tensions between rival religious faiths—facts of life that a constitutional government could not expect to suppress.

For a brief period following the modern Supreme Court's ruling against school separation in BROWN V. BOARD OF EDUCATION (1954), there seemed to be an emerging consensus that equality would, after all, be best served by dismantling all racial distinctions in public law. Thus, the historic CIVIL RIGHTS ACT OF 1964 prohibited, in general terms, "discrimination on the basis of race," rather than discrimination against blacks or other racial minorities in particular. But, among other things, the 1964 legislation sought for the first time to prohibit EMPLOYMENT DISCRIMINATION throughout the American economy. Was this done to enforce a new ideal of social indifference to race or to improve the economic condition of depressed minorities?

Legislative history might be cited to support either view, but the latter view largely prevailed in federal enforcement policy. By the early 1970s, federal officials had come to define RACIAL DISCRIMINATION as any employment standard that disproportionately excluded minority applicants, regardless of the employer's intent; in this and other ways, government policy, with approval from the courts, pressed employers to redefine their hiring and promotion policies to secure "appropriate" percentages of employees from specified minority groups, even if this required passing over better-qualified whites. (See, for example, GRIGGS V. DUKE POWER (1971) and UNITED STEELWORKERS OF AMERICA V. WEBER (1979).) With federal encouragement, state programs also offered preferences to minority students in admissions to professional schools (REGENTS OF UNIVERSITY OF CALIFORNIA V. BAKKE, 1978); other programs began to offer preferences to minority businessmen, as, for example, to minority-owned firms bidding for federal construction grants (FULLILOVE V. KLUTZNICK, 1980).

Court decisions upholding such practices generally invoked the need to "remedy" past discrimination, implying that localized preferences were acceptable only as temporary correctives to offset the effects of particular past abuses. In 1990, however, a five-Justice majority of the Supreme Court upheld a minority-preference policy in the award of broadcast licenses by the Federal Communications Commission (FCC). Noting the small number of minority-owned stations, the Court, in METRO BROADCASTING, INC. V. FCC (1990), endorsed an explicit preference policy as a permissible device for ensuring broadcasting "diversity," disclaiming any need to consider whether there had actually been a history of past discrimination in this particular field.

Critics of such preference policies—including dissenting Justices—have protested that they violate the spirit of constitutional guarantees and the letter of the CIVIL RIGHTS laws by prescribing different standards for whites and minorities. Worse, the critics argue, such policies treat minority individuals, not as actual individuals with their own personal merits, but as mere representatives of their racial groups. Defenders of preferential policies insist that civil-rights legislation and constitutional guarantees have been established to help minorities overcome the effects of discrimination and that such help should not be denied for the sake of an entirely abstract and unrealistic doctrine of equal treatment. They argue that guarantees of equality or nondiscrimination should be seen as bulwarks against policies that "stigmatize" or "subjugate" people because of their race, and no AFFIRMATIVE ACTION program, they say, can seriously be regarded as "stigmatizing" or "subjugating" whites as a whole. The critics of preference policies respond that, insofar as preference policies assume that whites would still exclude others without such mandatory preferences, the policies do stigmatize whites—as racist; insofar as preference policies assume that blacks and other minorities could not compete in American society without such governmental preferences, they stigmatize minorities as incapable.

Not surprisingly, critics of preference policies, emphasizing the potential for manipulation and abuse in governmental controls, would place more reliance on the working of private-market decision making; those who defend preference policies tend to take a much more sanguine view of governmental intervention and to regard racially unequal outcomes in the market as inherently suspect. But the debate about racial preference is not simply a special case of a larger argument about the proper scope of government. Neither liberals nor conservatives on the Supreme Court would be likely, for example, to tolerate a policy that sought to enhance broadcasting "diversity" by providing preference to non-Jewish or non-Protestant firms in the award of broadcasting licenses by the FCC.

In fact, the Court has repeatedly struck down governmental financial aid to religious schools, even though such programs might well be seen as efforts to equalize educational opportunity for religious minorities. Such programs, the Court insisted in LEMON V. KURTZMAN (1973), carry too much potential for political divisiveness, setting religious school constituencies against public school constituencies. Yet many of the same Justices and commentators who have most insistently opposed such aid to religious minorities have been quite sympathetic to government preference policies based on race. The difference is not plausibly explained on the grounds that religion is more divisive than race in contemporary American society. If anything, it seems to be the severity of racial divisions in American society that makes proponents of racial-preference policies regard them as necessary.

Recent studies suggest that despite two decades of racial preference policies the gap between whites and blacks in earnings and in educational attainments is scarcely diminished since the 1960s and in some areas is greater than it was. Some critics of racial preference see this as an additional reason for abandoning such programs. Many supporters of these programs regard this fact instead as an additional reason for redoubling the scale and intensity of preference. This may prove an area of constitutional dispute that is too large to be solved by mere judicial pronouncements.

JEREMY RABKIN
(1992)

Bibliography

ABRAM, MORRIS B.   1986   Affirmative Action: Fair Shakers and Social Engineers. *Harvard Law Review* 99:1312–1326.
STRAUSS, DAVID A.   1986   The Myth of Colorblindness. *Supreme Court Review* 1986:99–134.

RACIAL QUOTAS

Programs of AFFIRMATIVE ACTION, aimed at increasing opportunities for women and members of racial and ethnic minorities in employment and higher education, have sometimes taken the form of numerical quotas. In REGENTS OF UNIVERSITY OF CALIFORNIA V. BAKKE (1978) sixteen places in a state university medical school's entering class were reserved for minority applicants; in FULLILOVE V. KLUTZNICK (1980) ten percent of funds in a federal public works program were reserved for minority-owned businesses. Such quotas have been challenged as denials of the EQUAL PROTECTION OF THE LAWS, with mixed doctrinal results.

Opponents of racial quotas maintain that it is offensive to penalize or reward people on the basis of race—in short, that the Constitution is, or ought to be, colorblind. Opponents discern in quotas a subtle but pervasive racism, in the patronizing assumption that persons of particular colors or ethnic backgrounds cannot be expected to meet the standards that apply to others. This assumption, the opponents argue, is, in its own way, a BADGE OF SERVITUDE, stigmatizing the quotas' supposed beneficiaries. Some opponents see quotas as part of a general trend toward dehumanization, robbing individuals of both personal identity and human dignity, lumping them together in a collectivity based on other people's assumptions about racially defined traits.

Unfortunately for today's America, race has never been a neutral fact in this country. Those who defend affirmative action generally admit to some uneasiness about the potential abuse of racial distinctions. They argue, however, that there is no real neutrality in a system that first imposes on a racial group harsh disadvantages, readily transmitted through the generations, and then tells today's inheritors of disadvantages that from now on the rules prohibit playing favorites. If either compensation for past RACIAL DISCRIMINATION or the integration of American institutions is a legitimate social objective, the proponents argue, a government in pursuit of those objectives can hardly avoid taking race into account.

The recent attack on racial quotas draws fuel from an emotional reservoir filled two generations ago by universities that limited admission of racial and religious minorities—most notably Jews—to specified small quotas. This ugly form of discrimination was part of a systematic stigmatization and subordination of minority groups by the dominant majority. The recent quotas are designed to remedy the effects of past discrimination, and—when they serve the objective of compensation or integration—are not stigmatizing. They do, however, use race or ethnic status as a means of classifying persons, and thus come under fire for emphasizing group membership rather than "individual merit."

The right to equal protection is, indeed, an individual right. Yet the term "individual merit" misleads in two ways. The word "individual" misleads by obscuring the fact that every claim to equality is a claim made on behalf of the group of persons identified by some set of characteristics: race, for example, or high college grades and test scores. To argue against a racial preference is not to support individual merit as against a group claim, but to argue that some other group, defined by other attributes, is entitled to preference.

"Merit" misleads by conveying the idea of something wholly intrinsic to an individual, apart from some definition of community needs or purposes. When we reward achievement, we are not merely rewarding effort, but are also giving out prizes for native talents and environmental advantages. Mainly, we reward achievement because society wants the goods produced by the combination of talents, environment, and effort. But it is also reasonable to look to past harms and potential contributions to society in defining the characteristics that deserve reward. We admit college achievers to law schools not to reward winners but to serve society with good lawyers. If it be legitimate to seek to end a system of racial caste by integrating American society, nothing in the idea of individual merit stands in the way of treating race as one aspect of "merit."

Race-conscious remedies for past governmental discrimination were approved in decisions as early as SWANN V. CHARLOTTE-MECKLENBURG BOARD OF EDUCATION (1971). Affirmative action quotas pose another question: can government itself employ race-conscious remedies for the effects of past societal discrimination? In *Fullilove*, six Justices agreed on an affirmative answer to that question, at least when Congress prescribes the remedy. *Bakke* was complicated by a statutory claim; its result—and its practical effect in professional school admissions—was a distinction between racial or ethnic quotas, which are unlawful, and the use of racial or ethnic status as "one factor" in admission, which is lawful.

The distinction was a political success; it drew the fangs from a controversy that had turned venomous. But the distinction between a quota and a racial factor is more symbol than substance. If race is a factor, it will decide some cases. How many cases? The weight assigned to race surely will be determined by reference to the approximate number of minority admittees necessary to achieve the admitting university's goals of educational "diversity." The difference between saying "sixteen out of a hundred" and "around sixteen percent" is an exercise in constitutional cosmetics—but it seems to have saved affirmative action during a critical season.

KENNETH L. KARST
(1986)

Bibliography

KARST, KENNETH L. and HOROWITZ, HAROLD W.   1974   Affirmative Action and Equal Protection. *Virginia Law Review* 60:955–974.

VAN ALSTYNE, WILLIAM W.   1979   Rites of Passage: Race, the Supreme Court, and the Constitution. *University of Chicago Law Review* 46:775–810.

RACKETEER INFLUENCED AND CORRUPT ORGANIZATIONS ACT

The Racketeer Influenced and Corrupt Organizations Act (RICO) was enacted by Congress in 1970 to provide federal prosecutors with a powerful tool against organized crime. RICO has been used against the ruling commission of the Mafia in New York City, against corrupt politicians running local government agencies, against Croatian terrorists, against political demonstrators, against the Sicilian Mafia for importing billions of dollars of heroin into the United States in the pizza connection case (the longest criminal trial in federal history), in the largest criminal tax-fraud prosecution in history, and against massive insider-trading securities fraud.

RICO is a complex statute that creates both criminal sanctions and civil remedies, enforceable by the government or by injured private parties. The heart of the statute defines four crimes. First, it is illegal to establish, operate, or acquire an interest in any enterprise affecting either INTERSTATE COMMERCE or FOREIGN COMMERCE with income from a pattern of racketeering activity or collection of an unlawful debt. Second, the act prohibits acquiring or maintaining an interest in any such enterprise through a pattern of racketeering activity or collection of an unlawful debt. Third, it is a crime for any employee or associate of any such enterprise to participate in the enterprise through a pattern of racketeering activity or collection of an unlawful debt. And fourth, it is illegal to conspire to violate any of the first three provisions. A "pattern" of racketeering requires the commission of two or more "predicate offenses" within a ten-year period. These offenses include nine categories of state crimes and twenty-six federal crimes, including murder; drug trafficking; bribery; and mail, wire, and securities fraud. As discussed in *United States v. Turkette* (1981), an "enterprise" includes any individual, partnership, corporation, association, union, or group of individuals associated in fact, whether legitimate or illegitimate. Conviction under RICO carries severe criminal penalties and forfeiture of ill-gotten gains. A person may be liable for triple damages, costs, and attorneys' fees in a private civil RICO action. RICO is unique in its complexity among criminal statutes because of the sheer number of potential predicate offenses and because of the indefinite terms used in defining a violation.

In *H.J. Inc. v. Northwestern Bell Telephone Co.* (1989) the Supreme Court interpreted a "pattern of racketeering activity" to require both "continuity" and "relationship": two or more predicate offenses that are somehow related and that pose a threat of continued criminal activity must be committed within a ten-year period. Four of the more conservative Justices, although concurring in the JUDGMENT, suggested that the pattern requirement may be unconstitutionally void for vagueness in both criminal and civil cases. Because it is not clear what RICO requires beyond two predicate offenses, a potential defendant may not know whether his or her conduct is covered by RICO.

Jews for the Preservation of Firearms Ownership and the Women and Guns movement, for example, maintain that the Second Amendment should be read to protect an individual right to bear arms, because Jews and women will then be able to protect themselves against violent anti-Semitism and misogyny.

In other words, these constitutional interpreters are radical in two ways: first, they distrust politics as a means of resolving difference; and second, they are deeply sectarian advocates for their particular identity groups, not proponents of society as a whole. Those two features, however, are shared—to a reduced degree—by much of the American population. If these groups are radical, then, it is only because they are different in degree, not kind, from the rest of America. As a result, they squarely raise the question whether the American citizenry could plausibly develop a populist constitutional interpretation that is not radical; that is, that affirms political compromise and seeks the good of the whole. If such a thing is not possible, the Court may have good reason to claim to be the final arbiter of the meaning of the Constitution.

DAVID C. WILLIAMS
(2000)

(SEE ALSO: *Gun Control; Incorporation Doctrine; Nonjudicial Interpretation of the Constitution.*)

Bibliography
AHO, JAMES A. 1990 *The Politics of Righteousness: Idaho Christian Patriotism.* Seattle: University of Washington Press.

BROWN, RICHARD MAXWELL 1975 *Strain of Violence: Historical Studies of American Violence and Vigilantism.* New York: Oxford University Press.

EHRMAN, KEITH A. and HENNIGAN, DENNIS A. 1989 The Second Amendment in the Twentieth Century: Have You Seen Your Militia Lately? *University of Dayton Law Review* 15:5–58.

KATES, DON B. 1983 Handgun Prohibition and the Original Meaning of the Second Amendment. *Michigan Law Review* 82:204–273.

QUIGLEY, PAXTON 1989 *Armed & Female.* New York: E. P. Dutton.

SIMKIN, JAY; ZELMAN, AARON; and RICE, ALAN M. 1994 *Lethal Laws.* Milwaukee, Wisc.: Jews for the Preservation of Firearms Ownership.

STOCK, CATHERINE MCNICOL 1996 *Rural Radicals: Righteous Rage in the American Grain.* Ithaca, N.Y.: Cornell University Press.

WILLIAMS, DAVID C. 1996 The Militia Movement and Second Amendment Revolution: Conjuring with the People. *Cornell Law Review* 81:879–952.

RADIO

See: Broadcasting

RAILROAD COMMISSION OF TEXAS v. PULLMAN COMPANY

See: Abstention Doctrine

RAILROAD CONTROL ACT
40 Stat. 451 (1918)

Railroad service virtually ceased during the severe winter of 1917–1918. The extraordinary wartime volume of traffic and the railroads' fiscal and physical inability to meet its demands prompted President WOODROW WILSON to take control of all railway transport in the country on December 26, 1917. Congress ratified his proclamation in March 1918, by "emergency legislation enacted to meet conditions growing out of war."

The substance of the act concerned reimbursement of the owners for the use of their property while under government management. Congress set JUST COMPENSATION for this TAKING OF PROPERTY at the average operating income for the prior three years and also insured "adequate and appropriate [monies] for the maintenance, repair, renewals and depreciation of property." This legislation temporarily superseded much of the regulatory power of the Interstate Commerce Commission (ICC). It authorized the President to initiate "reasonable and just" rates which became effective without the ordinarily required wait and without ICC approval. That body could review the reasonableness of the rates but must give "due consideration" to the "unified and coordinated national control" and the stipulation that the roads "are not in competition." The constitutionality of the act as a whole was never challenged but separate sections were sustained under the WAR POWERS in a series of cases.

DAVID GORDON
(1986)

RAILROAD REGULATION

See: Economic Regulation

RAILROAD RETIREMENT ACT
48 Stat. 1283 (1934)

This act established a retirement and pension plan for railroad employees engaged in INTERSTATE COMMERCE. Congress specified "promoting efficiency and safety in interstate transportation" among the purposes of the act. Each employee, whose participation was mandatory, would be required to retire after thirty years service or at sixty-five, receiving thereafter an annuity based upon his length of service. Contributions from both employee and the carrier would finance these payments. A Railroad Retirement Board would adjust the contributions, initially set at two percent of a worker's salary and doubled by the carrier, and would administer the act. Congress further authorized the board to make actuarial surveys and keep pertinent records and data. The act vested district courts with JURISDICTION to enforce board orders and to review administrative questions.

A 5–4 Supreme Court voided the law in RAILROAD RETIREMENT BOARD V. ALTON (1935) as a violation of DUE PROCESS OF LAW and outside the commerce power, a decision effectively nullified in STEWARD MACHINE CO. V. DAVIS (1937).

DAVID GORDON
(1986)

RAILROAD RETIREMENT BOARD v. ALTON RAILWAY COMPANY
295 U.S. 330 (1935)

In the spring of 1935, as the FRANKLIN D. ROOSEVELT administration made plans for a general SOCIAL SECURITY ACT, the Supreme Court held unconstitutional the RAILROAD RETIREMENT ACT of 1934, which established a program of compulsory retirement and old age pensions for railroad workers engaged in INTERSTATE COMMERCE. Justice OWEN ROBERTS, for a five-member majority, found the act violative of DUE PROCESS OF LAW and unauthorized by the COMMERCE CLAUSE. By exacting a percentage of payrolls for a pension fund, the act, Roberts said, was a "naked appropriation of private property" for the benefit of workers. The act was also "bad" because no reasonable connection existed between the welfare of railroad workers and the efficiency or safety of interstate transportation.

Chief Justice CHARLES EVANS HUGHES, joined by Justice LOUIS D. BRANDEIS, BENJAMIN N. CARDOZO, and HARLAN FISKE STONE, dissented. The MAJORITY OPINION shocked Hughes because it went beyond the invalidation of this particular pension plan; the majority's "unwarranted limitation" on the commerce clause denied wholly and forever the power of Congress to enact any social welfare scheme. Relying on GIBBONS V. OGDEN (1824) for the scope of the commerce power, Hughes observed that its exercise had the widest range in dealing with interstate railroads. He accepted Congress's judgment that the plan enhanced efficiency and safety. Moreover, the precedents supported the constitutionality of the act, he argued; the act did not differ in principle from workmen's compensation acts for railroad employees, which the Court had sustained. It had also upheld a congressional enactment that empowered the Interstate Commerce Commission to take excess profits from some railroads for the benefit of others. (See DAYTON GOOSE CREEK RAILROAD CO. V. UNITED STATES.) The Court's opinion helped provoke the constitutional crisis of 1937.

LEONARD W. LEVY
(1986)

RAILWAY EXPRESS AGENCY v. NEW YORK
336 U.S. 106 (1949)

Railway Express is a leading modern example of the Supreme Court's deference to legislative judgments in the field of ECONOMIC REGULATION. The Court unanimously upheld a New York City "traffic safety" ordinance forbidding advertisements on vehicles but exempting delivery vehicles advertising their owners' businesses. No one mentioned the FIRST AMENDMENT. (See COMMERCIAL SPEECH.) Justice WILLIAM O. DOUGLAS, for the Court, first waved away a DUE PROCESS attack on the ordinance. Turning to the companion EQUAL PROTECTION attack, Douglas said that the city "may well have concluded" that advertising vehicles presented a greater traffic hazard than did trucks carrying their owners' messages. "We cannot say that that judgment is not an allowable one." The opinion typifies the Court's use of the most deferential RATIONAL BASIS review of economic regulation.

Justice ROBERT H. JACKSON expressed some doubt as to the Court's reasoning but concurred, referring to the law's historic distinctions between "doing in self-interest and doing for hire." Along the way he uttered the decision's most memorable words: "there is no more effective practical guarantee against arbitrary and unreasonable government than to require that the principles of law which officials would impose on a minority must be imposed generally."

KENNETH L. KARST
(1986)

RAINES v. BYRD

See: Congressional Standing

RANDOLPH, EDMUND
(1753–1813)

In 1776 Edmund Jenings Randolph, lawyer, mayor of Williamsburg, and aide to General GEORGE WASHINGTON, was the youngest delegate to the convention that adopted the

VIRGINIA DECLARATION OF RIGHTS AND CONSTITUTION. He became the state's first attorney general under the new constitution and was later a delegate to Congress, where he favored amending the ARTICLES OF CONFEDERATION to give Congress the power to levy import duties. He was a member of the Annapolis Convention of 1786 and later the same year defeated RICHARD HENRY LEE to become governor of Virginia.

Randolph led Virginia's delegation to the CONSTITUTIONAL CONVENTION OF 1787, where he introduced the VIRGINIA PLAN. He did not, however, sign the finished Constitution, which, he believed, gave too much power to the President and so tended toward monarchy. Nevertheless, in 1788 he argued and voted in the state convention for RATIFICATION OF THE CONSTITUTION. He argued that there was no alternative except disunion and that a second convention could be called to perfect the document.

President Washington appointed Randolph the first attorney general of the United States, making him a colleague of and mediator between THOMAS JEFFERSON and ALEXANDER HAMILTON. When Jefferson resigned in 1794, Randolph succeeded him as secretary of state, but he was himself forced to resign the next year when British publication of captured French dispatches led to charges of TREASON and bribery against Randolph. This disgrace ended his political career, but he remained an eminent lawyer. In 1807 he was chief defense counsel when AARON BURR was tried for and acquitted of treason.

DENNIS J. MAHONEY
(1986)

RANDOLPH, JOHN
(1773–1833)

John Randolph of Roanoke, Virginia, congressman and sometime senator, advocated the constitutional doctrines of STATES' RIGHTS and STRICT CONSTRUCTION that became identified with southern opposition to the federal government and that eventuated in SECESSION. Excepting his support for the LOUISIANA PURCHASE, Randolph consistently preferred the claim of state to federal SOVEREIGNTY. A bitter critic of the Federalist federal judiciary, he managed or mismanaged the IMPEACHMENT of Justice SAMUEL CHASE in 1804.

Breaking with THOMAS JEFFERSON in 1806, Randolph commenced a career of opposition to almost every sitting President and to most national policies. His principles were straightforward. He believed that the Constitution was a compact among sovereign states. Sovereignty did not inhere in the federal government, and the admission of new states was a device to weaken the original, com-

pacting states. He espoused the southern view that regarded every attempt to expand federal power as an attack on SLAVERY, and he regarded democracy and nationalism as leveling and centralizing invasions of ancient state privileges and mores. He viewed with especial bitterness the rulings of the MARSHALL COURT.

ROBERT DAWIDOFF
(1986)

Bibliography

DAWIDOFF, ROBERT 1979 *The Education of John Randolph.* New York: Norton.

RASMUSSEN v. UNITED STATES

See: Insular Cases

RATE REGULATION

See: Economic Regulation

RATIFICATION OF CONSTITUTIONAL AMENDMENTS

The delegates to the CONSTITUTIONAL CONVENTION of 1789 decided upon the outlines of the AMENDING PROCESS after only a few hours of debate. The requirement that any proposed amendment be ratified by three-fourths of the states was adopted unanimously, but was, like so much of the Constitution, the result of a compromise. Initially the convention seems to have assumed that amendments to the federal charter would require ratification by all the states; but five state delegations were willing to set the requirement as low as two-thirds of the states. No form of ratification other than by the states as entities was proposed or discussed in the convention.

JAMES MADISON, writing in THE FEDERALIST #39, described the method of ratifying amendments to the new Constitution as "partly federal, partly national." The method is [con]federal in that ratification is accomplished by the states as states, and not by a referendum of the people or a national majority. At the same time, the method is national in that it does not require the assent of all the constituent states to alter the terms of the federal union. A pure theory of FEDERALISM, as it was understood by the founding generation, would not have sanctioned imposition of an amended compact upon unconsenting parties.

Our first constitution, the ARTICLES OF CONFEDERATION, had required the unanimous consent of the states to any amendment. For that reason, during the "critical period" between 1781 and 1789 no amendments were adopted, even when decisive weaknesses in the confederal system were apparent. The requirement for unanimous ratification of amendments made the Constitutional Convention and the new Constitution necessary.

Article V in fact provides for state ratification of constitutional amendments in one or the other of two distinct modes, leaving the choice of mode to Congress. The first mode is ratification by state legislatures, the second is ratification by conventions. In two centuries of government under the Constitution Congress has proposed thirty-three constitutional amendments and in thirty-two cases has prescribed state legislatures as the agents of ratification. The single exception was ratification of the TWENTY-FIRST AMENDMENT, repealing PROHIBITION.

The constitutional provision relating to ratification is little more than an outline. The details have been filled in as the need has arisen. Although the state legislatures derive their authority to ratify amendments from the federal Constitution, the size of the majority required to effect ratification is determined by the constitution, statutes, or legislative rules of each state. Many, perhaps most, prescribe an extraordinary majority for that purpose.

An amendment automatically becomes part of the Constitution when it is ratified by the requisite number of states, but someone must be designated to receive the certificates of ratification, to count them, and to announce publicly that ratification is complete. Originally Congress delegated this task to the secretary of state, but it is now performed by a relatively minor official, the director of general services. Congress itself proclaimed the ratification of the FOURTEENTH AMENDMENT.

Article V sets no time limit within which the states must act on proposed amendments. The Framers supposed that the ratification process would occur at roughly the same time throughout the country. RATIFICATION OF THE CONSTITUTION itself took nine months; the BILL OF RIGHTS was ratified in just over two years. The convention provided no definite time period after which a proposal for amendment would lapse. Therefore, a recurring question has been how long the states have to ratify proposed amendments.

The principles of democracy and CONSTITUTIONALISM would be ill-served if ratification of constitutional amendments by the several states did not have to be accomplished roughly contemporaneously. This goal has been met in the case of every successful amendment. Although seven years has become the standard period for the states to consider ratification, no amendment has, in fact, required as long as four years for ratification. The TWENTY-SECOND AMENDMENT required the longest time, forty-seven

and one-half months; the TWENTY-SIXTH AMENDMENT required the shortest period, four months. The average time for ratification of a constitutional amendment has been eighteen months.

As a legal matter, ratification must be accomplished within a "reasonable" time, but no statute or court decision has defined just how long a period that is. The CHILD LABOR AMENDMENT, proposed in 1924, was ratified by three state legislatures as late as 1937, and the Supreme Court declined to hold that those ratifications were ineffective. The Supreme Court, in *Dillon v. Gloss* (1920), upheld the power of Congress to set a seven-year limit on the ratification period; but in *Coleman v. Miller* (1939) the Court refused to set such a limit on its own account where Congress failed to exercise the power.

The EIGHTEENTH, TWENTIETH, Twenty-First, and Twenty-Second AMENDMENTS comprise the ratification time limit within their texts. In several other cases, Congress has prescribed the time limit (invariably seven years) in the JOINT RESOLUTION proposing the amendment. Only once did Congress attempt to extend the prescribed time limit: when the seven years allotted for ratification of the so-called EQUAL RIGHTS AMENDMENT (ERA) expired in 1979, Congress—by less than the two-thirds majority required for the original proposal—voted to extend the ratification period for an extra three and one-half years. The failure of the proposed amendment's supporters to garner sufficient ratifications even in the extended time period averted a constitutional crisis over the issue of time limits.

A matter frequently debated but never definitively resolved is whether the states, during the period for consideration of a proposed amendment, may alter a decision once one is taken. The question arose with regard to the Fourteenth Amendment and was revived during the controversy over the ERA. Indeed, there seems to be no doubt that a state, having declined to ratify a proposed amendment, may, within the allotted time, alter that decision and ratify the amendment. It is less certain whether a state that has voted to ratify a proposed amendment may subsequently rescind such a ratification. In 1868 Congress and Secretary of State WILLIAM H. SEWARD declared the Fourteenth Amendment ratified, apparently counting the ratifications of two states (New Jersey and Ohio) that had voted to rescind their ratifications. On the date of the declaration a sufficient number of states had ratified to render the disputed votes irrelevant. Expiration in 1983 of the extended time limit for ratification of the ERA made the question of rescinded ratifications of that proposal moot.

The requirement of state ratification presupposes that the state legislatures are free to choose whether or not to ratify a proposed amendment. But this is not always true. Ratification of the Fourteenth Amendment was secured, in part, because Congress made such ratification a condition for readmission of the states of the former Confederacy. Clearly Congress, amidst the crisis of Civil War and Reconstruction, stretched the limits of its authority by imposing that condition.

Controversies concerning the ratification of constitutional amendments are almost prototypically POLITICAL QUESTIONS. Only rarely has the Supreme Court decided such controversies. In *Hawke v. Smith* (1920) and *Leser v. Garnett* (1922) the Court rejected attempts to submit the question of ratification to a popular vote or to condition ratification on approval in a REFERENDUM. In *United States v. Sprague* (1931) the Court refused to impose any limit on Congress's freedom to choose between the two constitutional modes of ratification. The effect of the few cases the Court has decided has been, as in *Dillon* and *Coleman,* to reserve the power of final determination to Congress.

DENNIS J. MAHONEY
(1986)

Bibliography

FREEDMAN, SAMUEL S. and NAUGHTON, PAMELA J. 1978 *ERA: May a State Change Its Vote?* Detroit, Mich.: Wayne State University Press.

ORFIELD, LESTER 1942 *The Amending of the Federal Constitution.* Ann Arbor: University of Michigan Press.

RATIFICATION OF THE CONSTITUTION

Plans for a convention to revise the ARTICLES OF CONFEDERATION were in fact a subterfuge, because the delegates in Philadelphia convened in May 1787 with no serious thought whatever of an attempt to keep that instrument in force. But a legal problem had to be resolved, for the Articles were a fact and their revision was to be made only by unanimous agreement of the Continental Congress which "the legislatures of every state" would later confirm. Delegates to the CONSTITUTIONAL CONVENTION OF 1787, including several lawyers who later became Supreme Court Justices, wasted little time in disposing of such restrictions, but they were wary of the manner in which the Constitution could be made acceptable to the people. The solution hit upon by JAMES MADISON in his VIRGINIA PLAN was to circumvent the state legislatures and ask Congress to send whatever plan they adopted in Philadelphia to "assemblies of Representatives . . . expressly chosen by the people, to consider decide thereon." Frankly fearful of local officeholders who would see the new Constitution as a threat to "the importance they now hold," the Virginia delegates were united on this point. "Nine States had been

required in all great cases under the Confederation that number was on that account preferable," GEORGE MASON suggested, and his logic prevailed.

After some maneuvering, the expiring Continental Congress by unanimous resolution forwarded the Constitution to the states for their approbation, thus placing an implicit seal of congressional approval on Article VII. The principle of a two-thirds majority rather than unanimity was crucial. Ominously, Rhode Island had sent no delegate to the convention. To avoid embarrassing obstructions, prudence dictated a fair trial for the Constitution, provided key state conventions ratified the document. Rarely in American history has such a sweeping change moved so rapidly through the cumbersome machinery of disparate state governments, and the phenomenon can be explained only in the adroit handling of GEORGE WASHINGTON's implied endorsement along with the urgency which supporters of the Constitution preached in pamphlets and newspapers or wherever influential citizens congregated.

Much of the credit for the Federalists' strategy must go to James Madison. As a central figure at the convention and in the Continental Congress he carefully brought forward the accompanying documents which gave an impression of unanimity by the framers and the forwarders. Using his franking privilege (as a congressman), Madison maintained a correspondence with colleagues in the principal state capitals and coordinated plans to hold conventions at the proper tactical time. Ratification by the conventions in Pennsylvania, Massachusetts, and Virginia was essential, for these three states contained most of the nation's people and much of its wealth. In New York a surly band controlled the state government and was in no hurry to surrender its profitable customs collecting to a national government, but these men could not withstand pressure from the commercial community if all the other large states ratified. Rhode Island was doubtful, and New Jersey and Georgia were unnecessary, owing to the smallness of their populations and their geographic positions.

The Federalists had powerful allies in the newspapers, some ninety-eight in number, most of which printed the Constitution *in toto* shortly after September 17. In Philadelphia, Boston, and New York the leading journals soon printed essays favoring the Constitution and denouncing the opposition Anti-Federalists as obstinate "placemen" (state officeholders) fearful of losing their jobs or "wrongheaded" on other grounds. Pennsylvania Federalists moved swiftly but could not outrace their friends in Delaware, who hurriedly called a three-county convention and became the first ratifying state on December 7 (30–0). In Philadelphia, the first stirrings of Anti-Federalist activity included publication of attacks on the Constitution's lack of a BILL OF RIGHTS, but as that argument was picked up elsewhere the high-handed legislature called a convention that was heavily weighted with delegates from eastern counties favorable to the Federalist cause. Before farming communities in western counties could organize, the Pennsylvania convention ratified on December 12 (46–23). New Jersey fell in line on December 18 (38–0). Then word came that Georgia had also unanimously ratified on January 2, 1788 (26–0). After perfunctory debate, Connecticut ratified on January 9 (128–40).

Before they could enjoy these triumphs, the Federalists learned that the failure to include a bill of rights, the fears of an overbearing (and tax-hungry) "consolidated" government, and a variety of local circumstances would slow ratification and might jeopardize the whole process. Massachusetts became the focal point of Federalist efforts, for rumblings from town meetings indicated that opposition was greater than anticipated. A phalanx of Harvard-trained lawyers, supported by commercial and shipping interests, accepted a set of recommendatory amendments to weaken the major Anti-Federalist positions, and on February 6 the Federalists won, 187–168.

New York Anti-Federalists began to counterattack. They urged friends in New Hampshire to reject the Constitution, and there is some murky evidence that a quick vote would have gone against ratification. Both sides finally settled on a postponement until June. Madison helped ALEXANDER HAMILTON write the essays of "Publius" (these became a classic treatise titled THE FEDERALIST) for the New York newspapers and continued to send his morale-building, organizing letters to friends in the South. An unexpected stumbling block to ratification came from Baptist ministers and congregations, who voiced concern that freedom of conscience was not safeguarded by the Constitution.

Meanwhile, Maryland Federalists lost patience with their long-winded opponents in the Annapolis convention and ratified on April 28 (63–11). The recommended amendments from Massachusetts Anti-Federalists were used as a talking point, but when the argument came to whether amendments could be part of a conditional ratification, the Federalists lost their tempers. Madison hurried back to Virginia, aware that PATRICK HENRY and Mason would form the most powerful Anti-Federal combination possible. New York seemed safely Anti-Federalist, for Governor George Clinton and his friends talked and printed venomous attacks on the Constitution and its Federalist drafters. Hamilton counted heads and asked Madison if a conditional ratification would suffice. No, Madison replied, a ratification with any strings attached would leave New York out of the Union. After slight Anti-Federal resistance, South Carolina ratified on May 23 (149–73). In Rhode Island, the people rejected ratification directly, 237 yeas to 2,708 nays.

Ratification by Virginia on June 25 was uncertain until a crucial ballot was won by Federalists, who captured the eight doubtful votes from western areas. Madison, JOHN MARSHALL, and EDMUND RANDOLPH led the charge against Henry and Mason, but they agreed to recommend amendments adding a bill of rights to preserve some good will on the final roll call (89–79). The ninth state, New Hampshire, had already ratified on June 21, 1788 (57–46). The news from Virginia, however, sent a thrill through the North. Diarist JOHN QUINCY ADAMS noted that jubilant Federalists fired muskets far into the night when the tidings from Richmond reached Boston. With ten states now committed, the Constitution was sure of a trial. Even so, a powerful, entrenched Anti-Federal faction prevented action by the North Carolina convention, which adjourned to await future developments and a possible second convention that diehard Anti-Federalists thought might patch up another version of the Constitution (with a bill of rights among the additions). A test vote on ratification lost, 184–84, but New York fooled everybody by ratifying on July 26 (30–27).

Within four months, all the states except North Carolina and Rhode Island had set in motion machinery to elect the new federal Congress and a President. The knowledge that Washington supported the Constitution and would be the first President tipped the balance in crucial situations. Washington's stature, the concession by Madison and others that amendments adding a bill of rights would be proposed forthwith, and the overwhelming support of the press were the chief reasons that ratification proceeded with relative speed. The new government was operating, and Madison had introduced a bill of rights by the time North Carolina ratified on November 21, 1789 (197–99). Rhode Island narrowly ratified on May 29, 1790 (34–32), to become a fully participating member of the Union. Few scars remained. The hastily drawn lines of the ratification battle soon faded, and the divergent political philosophies that emerged in the next decade had little to do with the intense struggle of 1787–1788.

ROBERT A. RUTLAND
(1986)

Bibliography

FARRAND, MAX, ed. (1911) 1966 *The Records of the Federal Convention of 1787*, 4 vols. New Haven, Conn.: Yale University Press.

MAIN, JACKSON TURNER 1961 *The Antifederalists: Critics of the Constitution, 1781–1788*. Chapel Hill: University of North Carolina Press.

RUTLAND, ROBERT A. 1966 *The Ordeal of the Constitution: The Antifederalists and the Ratification Struggle of 1787–1788*. Norman: University of Oklahoma Press.

WOOD, GORDON S. 1969 *The Creation of the American Republic, 1776–1787*. Pages 306–344. Chapel Hill: University of North Carolina Press.

RATIFIER INTENT

Ratifier intent is a form of ORIGINAL INTENT or ORIGINALISM that emphasizes the meanings and understandings of the Constitution possessed by those who ratified it. The ratifiers were the members of the state CONSTITUTIONAL CONVENTIONS that ratified the Constitution. The importance of ratifier intent derives from the widely held opinion that the consent of the governed, who alone were sovereign, legitimated the Constitution. The CONSTITUTIONAL CONVENTION OF 1787 had exceeded its instructions: to recommend revisions of the ARTICLES OF CONFEDERATION. Although the Confederation Congress transmitted the Constitution to the states for RATIFICATION, thereby implicitly agreeing to the scrapping of the Articles of Confederation, the fact remains that the Convention had violated its commission. Consequently, leading Framers of the Constitution insisted, as JAMES MADISON said, that "the legitimate meaning" of the Constitution should be sought "not in the opinions or intentions of the body which planned and proposed the Constitution, but in the sense attached to it by the people in their respective State Conventions, where it received all the authority which it possessed." Thus, as its ratification rather than its framing imbued the Constitution with its legitimacy, so ratifier intent rather than original intent (the understandings of the Framers) defined the text. This is the CONSTITUTIONAL THEORY of the matter as transmitted by the Framers.

One should not have to choose between the intent of the Framers and that of the ratifiers. All contemporary expositions should be considered if they illumine a constitutional issue. Moreover, from the broadest perspective, ratifier intent and original intent almost coincided: government by consent of the governed; majority rule under constitutional restraints that limit majorities; guarantees of rights that prevail against the legislative as well as executive branch; a federal system; three branches of government, including a single executive, a BICAMERAL legislature, and an independent judiciary; an elaborate system of CHECKS AND BALANCES; and representative government and elections at fixed intervals. The founding generation also believed in measuring the powers of government, rather than the rights of the people, and they assumed a NATURAL RIGHTS philosophy. They concurred on a great many fundamental matters. Without doubt, the Constitution reflects a coherent and principled POLITICAL PHILOSOPHY. All of this consensus bespeaks an enormously important and ascertainable set of original understandings shared by Framers and ratifiers, even by Federalists and ANTI-FEDERALISTS. But none of this history enables judges to reach decisions favoring one side of a constitutional issue rather than another in real cases that come before courts.

More perplexing still is the fact that ratifier intent with respect to the meanings of particular clauses of the Constitution is more often than not unascertainable. The main reason for this is that the historical record is too skimpy to sustain a constitutional JURISPRUDENCE of ratifier intent. In a 1954 report, the National Historical Publications Commission declared that the reporters of the ratification period took notes on the debates "and rephrased those notes for publication. The shorthand in use at that time was too slow to permit verbatim transcription of all speeches, with the result that a reporter, in preparing his copy for the press, frequently relied upon his memory as well as his notes and gave what seemed to him the substance, but not necessarily the actual phraseology, of speeches. Different reportings of the same speech exhibited at times only a general similarity, and details often recorded by one reporter were frequently omitted by another." Reporters used their notes to spur their memories, and their reports were no better than their understandings.

When Jonathan Elliot began publication of his *Debates* in 1827, he collected the previously published records of the state ratifying conventions. He misleadingly called his collection *The Debates in the Several State Conventions, on the Adoption of the Federal Constitution.* In fact, Elliot unreliably reported the proceedings of only five states plus some fragments of others. He acknowledged that the debates may have been "inaccurately taken down" and "too faintly sketched." ELBRIDGE GERRY, a member of the Constitutional Convention who became an Anti-Federalist leader, complained that the "debates of the State Conventions, as published by the short-hand writers, were generally partial and mutilated."

For Pennsylvania, Elliot published only the speeches of two advocates of ratification. The editor of the debates for Massachusetts apologized for his inaccuracies and omissions deriving from his inexperience. He also doctored some speeches and provided a few spurious ones. The reporter for New York made similar remarks and recorded only the debates for the first half of convention's proceedings, reverting to a skeletal journal of motions for the remainder. In Virginia, where the debates were most fully reported and by a reporter sympathetic to ratification, James Madison and JOHN MARSHALL expressed dissatisfaction with the results. Madison informed Elliot that he found passages that were "defective," "obscure," "unintelligible," and "more or less erroneous." Marshall complained that if he had not seen his name prefixed to his speeches he would not have recognized them as his own. He further declared that the speeches of PATRICK HENRY, the leader of the opposition, were reported worst of all. Similar criticisms apply to the proceedings of North Carolina, whose first convention rejected the Constitution and whose second was wholly unreported.

These are the five states (Pennsylvania, Massachusetts, New York, Virginia, and North Carolina) whose records provide a basis, however inadequate, for determining ratifier intent. We have only scraps of material for the other states, with the exception of Rhode Island, which ratified so late as to count for nearly nothing. Although the people acting through state ratifying conventions gave the Constitution its authority, the ratifiers' intent should not be confused or conflated with legitimacy. Ratification legitimated the text that the Constitutional Convention recommended; the Convention did not recommend its intention, only the text, and the ratifying conventions only ratified the text, without providing a basis for a constitutional jurisprudence based on ratifier intent or understanding.

Justice JOSEPH STORY made the definitive rejection of ratifier intent in his *Commentaries on the Constitution:* "In different states and in different conventions, different and very opposite objections are known to have prevailed. Opposite interpretations, and different explanations of different provisions, may well be presumed to have been presented in different bodies, to remove local objections, or to win local favor. And there can be no certainty, either that the different state conventions in ratifying the constitution, gave the same uniform interpretation to its language, or that even in a single state convention, the same reasoning prevailed with a majority" (1st ed. 1833, I, pp. 388–389).

Story continued by noting that the terms of the Constitution impressed different people differently. Some drew conclusions that others repudiated; some understood its provisions strictly, others broadly. Ratifiers in different conventions revealed a diversity of interpretations. To THOMAS JEFFERSON's demand that ratifier intent be honored as much as possible, Story retorted that it was not possible; he ridiculed "the utter looseness, and incoherence of this canon." No way existed to determine "what was thought of particular clauses" of the Constitution when it was ratified. "In many cases no printed debates give any account of any construction; and where any is given, different persons held different doctrines. Whose is to prevail?" Story concluded that determining ratifier intent is hopeless because "of all the state conventions, the debates of five only are preserved, and these very imperfectly. What is to be done, as to other eight states?" Ratifier intent, despite its present support by some constitutional scholars, including Robert Bork and Charles Lofgren, is as lacking in historical basis or practical application as it may be theoretically attractive.

LEONARD W. LEVY
(1992)

(SEE ALSO: *Bork Nomination; Constitutional Interpretation.*)

Bibliography

BORK, ROBERT H. 1989 *The Tempting of America: the Political Seduction of the Law.* New York: Free Press.
HUTSON, JAMES H. 1986 The Creation of the Constitution: The Integrity of the Documentary Record. *Texas Law Review* 65: 1–39.
LEVY, LEONARD W. 1988 *Original Intent and the Framers' Constitution.* New York: Macmillan.
LOFGREN, CHARLES A. 1988 The Original Understanding of Original Intent. *Constitutional Commentary* 5:77–113.

RATIO DECIDENDI

(Latin: "Reason for being decided.") A statement made in an OPINION OF THE COURT is either *ratio decidendi* or OBITER DICTUM. *Ratio decidendi* refers to a statement that is a necessary part of the chain of reasoning leading to the DECISION of the case, while obiter dictum ("said by the way") refers to any other statement in the opinion. The distinction is clear in theory but, in practice, may be difficult to apply to any given case.

No federal court may properly pass on a legal or constitutional question that is not brought before it in a CASE OR CONTROVERSY, and a court properly resolves only those questions necessary to decide a case before it. The resolution of a particular question is the court's HOLDING on that question, and the reasoning necessary to the resolution of a question properly before the court is *ratio decidendi.* The *ratio decidendi* is thereafter binding as a rule of law when the case is cited as precedent. Although a judge may have a clear idea of what arguments were necessary to reach the decision in a case and may attempt to convey that idea in his opinion, it is the courts that apply the case as precedent in future decisions that finally establish which statements were obiter dicta and which *ratio decidendi.*

DENNIS J. MAHONEY
(1986)

RATIONAL BASIS

The "rational basis" STANDARD OF REVIEW emerged in the late 1930s, as the Supreme Court retreated from its earlier activism in the defense of economic liberties. We owe the phrase to Justice HARLAN FISKE STONE, who used it in two 1938 opinions to signal a new judicial deference to legislative judgments. In UNITED STATES V. CAROLENE PRODUCTS CO. (1938), Stone said that an ECONOMIC REGULATION, challenged as a violation of SUBSTANTIVE DUE PROCESS or of EQUAL PROTECTION, would be upheld unless demonstrated facts should "preclude the assumption that it rests upon some rational basis within the knowledge and experience of the legislators." In *South Carolina State Highway Department v. Barnwell Brothers, Inc.* (1938), Stone proposed "rational basis" as the standard for reviewing STATE REGULATIONS OF COMMERCE. (Later, Stone would accept the necessity for more exacting judicial scrutiny of such laws.) To complete the process, the Court adopted the same deferential posture toward congressional judgments that local activities substantially affected INTERSTATE COMMERCE and thus might be regulated by Congress under the COMMERCE POWER. In all its uses, "rational basis" represents a strong presumption of the constitutionality of legislation.

Yet even so minimal a standard of JUDICIAL REVIEW does, in theory, call for some judicial scrutiny of the rationality of the relationship between legislative means and ends. And that scrutiny of means makes sense only if we assume that the ends themselves are constitutionally required to serve general, public aims; otherwise, every law would be self-justifying, as precisely apt for achieving the advantages and disadvantages it achieves. Although the Court has sometimes suggested in economic regulation cases that even a search for legislative rationality lies beyond the scope of the judicial function, some such judicial scrutiny is required if our courts are to give effect to generalized constitutional guarantees of liberty and equality. Today's assumption, therefore, is that a law depriving a person of liberty or of equal treatment is invalid unless, at a minimum, it is a rational means for achieving a legitimate legislative purpose.

Even so relaxed a standard of review appears to call for a judicial inquiry always beset by uncertainties and often dominated by fictitious assumptions. Hans Linde has demonstrated the unreality attendant on judicial efforts to identify the "purposes" served by a law adopted by legislators with diverse objectives, or objectives only tenuously connected to the public good. Lacking sure guidance as to those "purposes"—which may have changed in the years since the law was adopted—a court must rely on counsel's assertions and its own assumptions. But in its inception the rational basis standard was not so much a mode of inquiry as a formula for validating legislation. Thus, in MCGOWAN V. MARYLAND (1961), the Supreme Court said, "A statutory discrimination will not be set aside if any state of facts reasonably may be conceived to justify it." Part of the reason why the rational basis standard survives in federal constitutional law is that it is normally taken seriously only in its permissive feature (*United States Railroad Retirement Board v. Fritz*, 1980). A number of state courts, interpreting STATE CONSTITUTIONAL LAW, do take the rational basis standard to require a serious judicial examination of the reasonableness of legislation. And the Supreme Court itself, in its late-1960s forays into the reaches of equal protection doctrine lying beyond racial equality, sometimes labeled legislative classifications as "irrational" even as it insisted that state-imposed inequalities be justified against more exacting standards of review. (See HARPER V. VIRGINIA STATE BOARD OF ELECTIONS; LEVY V. LOUISIANA; SHAPIRO V. THOMPSON.) Since that time, the explicit recognition of different levels of judicial scrutiny of legislation has allowed the Court to reserve the rhetoric of rational basis for occasions thought appropriate for judicial modesty, in particular its review of "economic and social regulation." Some substantive interests call for heightened judicial scrutiny of legislative incursions into them; absent such considerations, the starting point for constitutional analysis remains the rational basis standard.

KENNETH L. KARST
(1986)

Bibliography
LINDE, HANS A. 1976 Due Process of Lawmaking. *Nebraska Law Review* 55:197–255.

RATIONAL BASIS
(Update)

For decades, the rational basis test seemed so deferential that no law could flunk it. In the 1980s, however, the Supreme Court began to give teeth to the standard. For example, in CLEBURNE V. CLEBURNE LIVING CENTER, INC. (1985), the Court used the rational basis test to strike down a Texas municipality's ZONING law that had been used to impede the creation of a group home for persons suffering from MENTAL ILLNESS.

By the 1990s, the rational basis test was no longer meek. It was explicitly used to invalidate state laws in two of the Court's most important CIVIL RIGHTS cases, HODGSON V. MINNESOTA (1990) and ROMER V. EVANS (1996). *Hodgson* was the first case in which Justice SANDRA DAY O'CONNOR voted to hold an ABORTION law unconstitutional. It dealt with a Minnesota law regulating the circumstances under which minors could obtain abortions; Minnesota required minors to get consent from both parents, rather than only from one. O'Connor joined an opinion by Justice JOHN PAUL STEVENS in which he concluded that Minnesota's two-parent consent was "not reasonably related to any legitimate state interest." Stevens reasoned that the two-parent consent requirement was likely to be important only in those cases where the two parents were not communicating with one another, and that requiring the minor to inform both parents under such circumstances was likely to do more harm than good.

Later, in PLANNED PARENTHOOD V. CASEY (1992), O'Connor co-authored an opinion that reaffirmed the existence of a constitutional right to get an abortion, but formulated that right in terms of the "undue burden" standard. That standard is a kind of "reasonableness" test. It is arguably more akin to a strong rational basis standard than to STRICT SCRUTINY.

In *Romer*, the Court reviewed an amendment to the Colorado state constitution that prohibited the state or its local jurisdictions from protecting gay rights. Writing for himself and five others, Justice ANTHONY M. KENNEDY announced that Colorado's law failed to survive scrutiny under the rational basis test. Kennedy explained that "the amendment seems inexplicable by anything but animus toward the class that it affects" and hence "lacks a rational relationship to legitimate state interests."

This revival of the rational basis test may reflect profound changes in attitudes toward JUDICIAL REVIEW. The deferential version of rational basis scrutiny emerged in the wake of the NEW DEAL, when the Court had damaged its reputation by obstructing economic reform. Justices and scholars felt compelled to defend the legitimacy of judicial review; Justice FELIX FRANKFURTER, in particular, was an eloquent advocate for judicial restraint. Over the last three decades, however, the Court has become more secure about its power. It seems fair to say, as Professor Louis Michael Seidman did in his comment on *Romer*, that "[t]oday, no sitting Justice is a consistent advocate of judicial restraint." Under these changed circumstances, it is perhaps unsurprising that several of the Justices once again feel comfortable making naked judgments about the reasonableness of LEGISLATION.

CHRISTOPHER L. EISGRUBER
(2000)

Bibliography

SEIDMAN, LOUIS MICHAEL　1996　*Romer's* Radicalism: The Unexpected Revival of Warren Court Activism. *Supreme Court Review* 1996:67–122.

R. A. V. v. CITY OF ST. PAUL
505 U.S. 377 (1992)

In *R. A. V. v. City of St. Paul*, the Supreme Court struck down a St. Paul, Minnesota ordinance that proscribed cross-burning and other actions "which one knows or has reasonable grounds to know" will cause "anger, alarm or resentment in others on the basis of race, color, creed, religion or gender." The Court was unanimous that the law was unconstitutional, but agreed about little else. Four members of the Court—Justices BYRON R. WHITE, HARRY A. BLACKMUN, JOHN PAUL STEVENS, and SANDRA DAY O'CONNOR—concurred in the judgment, but solely on the ground that the ordinance was overly broad, sweeping within its pro-

scription expression that should be protected. It is safe to assume that these Justices would have upheld a narrowly drawn statute that prohibited HATE CRIME. The other five members of the Court, in the MAJORITY OPINION of Justice ANTONIN SCALIA, reached further, characterizing the St. Paul ordinance—and presumably any content-discriminatory hate crime law—as an unconstitutional content-based regulation of speech in violation of the FIRST AMENDMENT.

In *R. A. V.*, the defendant Robert Viktora, then a minor, was accused of burning a cross on the lawn of Russell and Laura Jones and their children, an African American family that had recently moved into the neighborhood. In moving to dismiss the indictment, Viktora asserted both that the ordinance was overbroad and that it was an unconstitutional, content-based restriction on his FREEDOM OF SPEECH. The Minnesota Supreme Court rejected the OVERBREADTH challenge because that court construed the ordinance narrowly to apply only to FIGHTING WORDS, and therefore not to apply to any expression protected by the First Amendment. Although a minority of the U.S. Supreme Court concluded that this limiting construction by the Minnesota court did not save the ordinance from overbreadth, Scalia was prepared to accept that all of the expression reached by the ordinance was proscribable. He thus had to reach the content-based challenge.

Scalia's OPINION FOR THE COURT used a limited categorical approach to the First Amendment. Acknowledging that fighting words, along with other categories of expression such as OBSCENITY and defamation, are not entitled to full First Amendment protection, Scalia asserted that these forms of expression nevertheless enjoy some limited protection and are not "entirely invisible to the Constitution." Within any of these categories, expression may be proscribed only on the basis of its categorical nature and not on the basis of its content.

Scalia's approach to the content-neutrality DOCTRINE did not purport to require the state to proscribe either all forms of proscribable speech or none at all. Rather, he identified two exceptions to the general unacceptability of content-based restrictions on expression. First, choices may be made as to which forms of speech to proscribe so long as these choices do not address the content of the expression. For example, regulations restricting obscene communications when the medium of communication is the telephone, according to Scalia, permissibly regulate the medium but not the message. Second, Scalia would also exempt from the content-neutrality rule regulations that address content for the "very reason the entire class of speech at issue is proscribable" in the first place. For example, a regulation prohibiting only obscenity "which is the most patently offensive *in its prurience*" would be permissible.

Scalia concluded that the St. Paul ordinance fell within neither exception. Instead, when he applied his approach to the St. Paul ordinance, he concluded that the city had established a regulation aimed directly at racist speech and biased beliefs rather than at fighting words generally or at a subgroup of fighting words selected for reasons other than the content of those words. He thus held that the ordinance impermissibly chose sides in the debate over racial prejudice. In perhaps the most famous sentence in the Court's *R. A. V.* opinion, Scalia wrote: "St. Paul has no such authority to license one side of a debate to fight freestyle, while requiring the other to follow Marquis of Queensbury Rules."

The ultimate reach of *R. A. V.* was substantially limited by the Court's decision one year later in WISCONSIN V. MITCHELL (1993), which upheld a Wisconsin hate crime law providing enhanced penalties for crimes motivated by racial bias.

FREDERICK M. LAWRENCE
(2000)

Bibliography

LAWRENCE, FREDERICK M. 1993 Resolving the Hate Crimes/ Hate Speech Paradox: Punishing Bias Crimes and Protecting Racist Speech. *Notre Dame Law Review* 68:673–721.
SYMPOSIUM 1991 Free Speech and Religious, Racial and Sexual Harassment. *William and Mary Law Review* 32:207–351.

RAWLE, WILLIAM
(1759–1836)

A Philadelphia lawyer and Federalist, Rawle declined GEORGE WASHINGTON's offer to become the first attorney general of the United States. As United States attorney for Pennsylvania, he was the government prosecutor in the cases arising from the WHISKEY REBELLION (1794) and FRIES' REBELLION (1798). Rawle also advocated the existence of a FEDERAL COMMON LAW OF CRIMES. He is best remembered as one of the earliest COMMENTATORS ON THE CONSTITUTION. His *New View of the Constitution* (1825) was widely used as a textbook. Although he was a nationalist, he was the first to advocate the right of state SECESSION.

LEONARD W. LEVY
(1986)

RAYMOND MOTOR TRANSPORTATION COMPANY v. RICE
434 U.S. 429 (1978)

Continuing a line of decisions begun in SOUTHERN PACIFIC COMPANY V. ARIZONA (1945), an 8–0 Supreme Court struck down a state highway regulation as an unconstitutional burden on INTERSTATE COMMERCE. A Wisconsin statute barred trucks over fifty-five feet in length from state highways as a safety measure. Two trucking companies challenged the law under the COMMERCE CLAUSE. A strong demonstration that the law made, at best, a negligible contribution to highway safety combined with the state's failure to provide an adequate defense of the measure led the Court to override the strong presumption usually given such laws.

In *Kassel v. Consolidated Freightways Corp. of Delaware* (1981), Iowa made a "more serious effort to support the safety rationale of its [fifty-five foot limit] than did Wisconsin in *Raymond*," but a 6–3 Court, relying on *Raymond*, struck down the Iowa statute on the same grounds.

DAVID GORDON
(1986)

READ, GEORGE
(1733–1798)

George Read of Delaware was a signer of both the DECLARATION OF INDEPENDENCE and the Constitution. A frequent speaker at the CONSTITUTIONAL CONVENTION OF 1787, he favored a consolidated national government and proposed abolition of state boundaries. He was a leader of the ratification movement in Delaware, and later he served as state chief justice and as a United States senator.

DENNIS J. MAHONEY
(1986)

REAGAN, RONALD
(1911–)

Born in Tampico, Illinois, brought up in Dixon, Illinois, a graduate of Eureka College, Illinois, Ronald Reagan came from the American Midwest, while his adult life was largely spent in California, leading to a classic California combination of midwestern seriousness of purpose and California casualness of style. Coming to maturity in 1932, he was first a convinced follower of FRANKLIN D. ROOSEVELT, changing his political beliefs in response to his perceptions of communist infiltration in the late 1940s, and formally becoming a Republican only in 1962. A radio announcer as a young man, then an actor (playing in more than fifty motion pictures), then for three years an Army captain, then for five years president of the Screen Actors Guild, he became a spokesman for the General Electric Company, traveling nationally to speak to company employees and civic groups on domestic and patriotic themes. In 1966 he defeated five other candidates to win the Republican nomination for governor of California and was then elected over the incumbent Edmund Brown by a historic margin of nearly one million votes. He was easily reelected in 1970. His two terms as governor of the most populous state in the Union were marked by a dramatic reduction in the number of welfare recipients, a small increase in the number of state employees, and a large increase in the funding of higher education.

In 1976 he fell sixty votes short of defeating President GERALD R. FORD for the Republican nomination for the presidency. In 1980 he defeated five other candidates to capture the nomination, and he won the presidential election by a landslide of 489 electoral votes. In 1984 he was reelected, this time taking the votes of forty-nine of the fifty states and emerging in a position to put his stamp on the judiciary of the nation.

Three themes characterize President Reagan's approach to the Constitution. They are the necessity of moral virtue if American democracy is to work; the importance of FEDERALISM; and the guiding force of American practices approved by the Founding Fathers. These themes run through Reagan's public pronouncements on a variety of specific topics bearing on constitutional law. For example, he has seen the solution to the problem of curbing crime in America as first restoring a sense of moral seriousness to the criminal trial, so that it is not seen as a bureaucratized bargaining process. At the same time, he has criticized courts for taking on tasks for which they are unfitted and so slighting their essential role of determining guilt or innocence; and he has proposed legislation limiting the use of HABEAS CORPUS review of state courts by federal judges.

Traditional functions for the courts, less federal supervision, an infusion of moral purpose—these are remedies that Reagan sees as congruent with the Constitution even as interpreted by the Supreme Court. For another example, he has opposed the imposition of RACIAL QUOTAS in EDUCATION, hiring, or housing, even when the quotas are disguised as AFFIRMATIVE ACTION. Belief in equality under the law does not in his view require reverse discrimination. Nothing in a Constitution he sees as colorblind supports a contrary conclusion. In other areas his views require constitutional amendment.

Religion is the foundation of morality, and morality is inseparable from government—this note in American politics is as old as WASHINGTON'S FAREWELL ADDRESS, which Reagan has frequently invoked. In Reagan's own words, "We poison our society when we remove its theological underpinnings," and again, "Without God there is no virtue because there is no prompting of conscience."

From this perspective, the Court-compelled exclusion of religious exercises from the public schools is disastrous and is unwarranted by the Constitution, which, Reagan has repeatedly remarked, says nothing about public education or prayer. In Reagan's words, the FIRST AMENDMENT "was not meant to exclude religion from our schools." Reagan has affirmed his belief in a "wall of separation" between church and state. In an American tradition as old as ROGER WILLIAMS, he sees the primary function of that wall as protecting religion from governmental intrusion. The Supreme Court, in his view, has been guilty of such intrusion.

Federalism influences this approach. The Supreme Court, interpreting the Constitution, often conceives of itself as though it were a superior, benign, and neutral agency that is not part of the national government. Reagan has cut through this position and identified the Court as the champion of a particular ideology, imposing uniform requirements in disregard of local custom. Justified where there was a national mandate to eliminate RACIAL DISCRIMINATION, the Court has acted in this way even, he believes, where it has discovered no national mandate. Reagan's criticism of the Court on RELIGION IN THE PUBLIC SCHOOLS not only affirms earlier American traditions; it also reflects attachment to the local autonomy that federalism fosters.

The religion Reagan refers to is biblical religion, described by him as "our Judaeo-Christian heritage." He quotes both Old and New Testaments in his public addresses. The Ten Commandments, he has observed, have not been improved upon by the millions of laws enacted since their promulgation. He issued a proclamation of National Bible Week and rejoiced that twenty-five states followed suit. He sees no constitutional barrier to a believer, as President, acknowledging the God of the Bible, speaking of the moral values he derives from his belief in God, and taking seriously such slogans as "one nation under God" and "in God we trust."

Public testimony to moral values based on religion has been conjoined with insistent rejection of religious intolerance. Reagan has consistently denounced bigotry, but he contends that those who have excluded biblical religion from the schools are themselves "intolerant of religion." They have denied a freedom to exercise religion as old as the practice of prayers in legislatures, the employment of chaplains by the military, and the invocation of God before opening any court. Such American traditions are his guide to the meaning of the Constitution in an area crucial for him in the formation of morality.

Critical of the Supreme Court's individual decisions in a manner sanctioned by the example of THOMAS JEFFERSON, ABRAHAM LINCOLN, and FRANKLIN D. ROOSEVELT, Reagan has not denied the Court's authority. He has favored correction of the prayer decision by the adoption of a constitutional amendment permitting voluntary group prayer in the schools. The government in his view should tolerate and accommodate the religious beliefs, speech, and conduct of the people; it should not direct their religious beliefs, speech, or conduct. For that reason, Reagan's school prayer amendment expressly prohibits any governmental role in composing the words of prayers to be said in the public schools.

The constitutional right to abortion, announced by the Supreme Court in ROE V. WADE (1973), has been the object of repeated criticism by Reagan. He has taken the extraordinary step, for a sitting President, of publishing a book, *Abortion and the Conscience of a Nation* (1984), in which he declares that "there is no cause more important than affirming the transcendent right to life of all human beings, the right without which no other rights have any meaning." On January 22, 1985, the twelfth anniversary of *Roe v. Wade*, he addressed the prolife march in Washington as the marchers prepared once again to ask the Supreme Court to change its position, and told them that he was "proud to stand with you in the long march to protect life." No other constitutional decision of the Supreme Court has been so vigorously, persistently, and personally condemned by an American President.

Reagan has consciously used the presidency as "a bully pulpit" to proclaim that there is no proof that the child in the womb is *not* human; that the child in midterm and later abortion feels pain; and that over 4,000 such children are killed every day in America, 15,000,000 in the first decade since ROE V. WADE. Such facts alone, he believes, will make most people reconsider and seek reversal of *Roe*.

How the reversal is accomplished has not been a matter of great concern to Reagan. He endorsed reversal by amendment of the Constitution. He attempted to persuade the Senate to end a FILIBUSTER that killed the Helms Bill that would have used Congress's power under section 5 of the FOURTEENTH AMENDMENT to define life as including the unborn. Passage of the bill (itself without sanctions) would undoubtedly have led to state legislation on abortion that would have given the Supreme Court the opportunity of looking at abortion in the light of the congressional definition. It has been speculated that Reagan believes the most practical way of effecting the result he desires is by his appointments to the Supreme Court.

In the cases of abortion and of prayer, Reagan has sought amendments reversing Supreme Court decisions that upset traditional balances. In the case of the balanced BUDGET, he has asked for something new, a constitutional restraint that would prevent federal expenditures exceeding federal revenues. The desirability of such an amendment had, however, been voiced as early as 1798 by Thomas Jefferson. In Reagan's view, a balanced budget amendment could be a powerful tool for reducing the federal establishment and restoring economic power to the states. Federalism would be enhanced by its enactment. The traditional role of the states would very likely be increased. Reagan also perceives a moral element: habitual deficit spending by the federal government is an easy evasion of responsibility. In his second Inaugural Address, on January 21, 1985, Reagan called for passage of the Balanced Budget Amendment.

Citizens and Presidents must interpret the Constitution as well as lawyers and judges. President Reagan's approach to the Constitution is not dependent on the reasoning advanced by recent Justices of the Supreme Court to justify or rationalize their decisions. He has employed older and broader criteria. For him the Constitution does not mean the gloss put upon it by opinions of the Court but the original document illumined by tangible traditions and by reflection on its foundation in moral realities. He has evidenced a strong commitment to the essentials that the Constitution presupposes and at the same time preserves.

JOHN T. NOONAN, JR.
(1986)

Bibliography

REAGAN, RONALD 1984 *Abortion and the Conscience of a Nation*. New York: Thomas Nelson.
REAGAN, RONALD 1981–1985 *Presidential Papers*. Washington, D.C.: Government Printing Office.
SMITH, HEDRICK et al. 1980 *Reagan the Man, the President*. New York: Macmillan.
WHITE, F. CLIFTON 1980 *Why Reagan Won: A Narrative History of the Conservative Movement*. Chicago: Regnery Gateway.

REAGAN, RONALD
(1911–   )
(Update)

No President since FRANKLIN D. ROOSEVELT devoted as much of his administration's attention to the courts and the Constitution as did Ronald Reagan. After a career as an actor and spokesman for General Electric, Reagan was catapulted into politics by a famous televised speech on behalf of Barry Goldwater's presidential campaign. Twice elected governor of California, Reagan was hailed as the conservative standard-bearer in his unsuccessful race for the Republican presidential nomination in 1976. He came to office in 1980 pledging to reinvigorate the idea of LIMITED GOVERNMENT—to restore what he saw as the constitutional foundations of American politics. In part, this restoration would involve restricting the federal government's encroachments on individual freedom and on the prerogatives of state governments. But more important, it would require that the doctrines stimulating the federal government's inordinate growth be publicly discredited and supplanted.

Reagan won the 1980 presidential election by a large margin and set to work to lower federal tax rates and shore up America's defenses. These tasks absorbed most of his and his administration's attention even after his still more massive electoral victory in 1984; but Reagan wished always to make the "Reagan Revolution" something broader and deeper—what he called in his 1985 State of the Union Address "a Second American Revolution." The changes in economic and defense policy won in the great legislative battles of his first term had therefore to be parlayed into a general rethinking of the purposes of American politics and, especially, of the functions served by the courts.

Large changes in American electoral politics, particularly in the wake of so-called critical or realigning elections, do eventually register on the judiciary (as in 1937, with the "switch in time" that "saves nine") and sometimes on the Constitution itself (for example, the Civil War amendments). Indeed, in Reagan's view, the LIBERALISM that he attacked had always put a high premium on control of the judiciary, from FDR's COURT-PACKING PLAN to the activism of Chief Justice EARL WARREN to President JIMMY CARTER's efforts to apply strict AFFIRMATIVE ACTION standards to judicial appointments. But Reagan faced the novel circumstance of trying to undo a series of divisive liberal measures that the Supreme Court itself had directed—the legalization of ABORTION, the expulsion of prayer from the public schools, the promulgation of the EXCLUSIONARY RULE, and so forth.

These issues were particularly important to the social conservatives who had joined with traditional Republicans and anticommunists in the 1960s and 1970s to form the coalition that would eventually sweep Reagan into office. Although Reagan campaigned both in 1980 and 1984 for the overruling of such Supreme Court decisions, he himself did little to dislodge them, except to call for constitutional amendments to protect the life of the unborn and to allow voluntary SCHOOL PRAYER in public classrooms. To confront the Court more directly would have risked alienating the more libertarian members of his coalition, which was united more by its common enemies than by common principles. Instead, he concentrated his administration's energies on the selection of judges pledged to exercise "judicial restraint" and, therefore, more likely over time to modify or overturn their predecessors' activist decisions.

It is probably in this way that the Reagan administration will have its great effect on CONSTITUTIONAL INTERPRETATION. In the course of his presidency, Reagan appointed more than 400 federal judges, nearly half the federal bench, as well as three Supreme Court Justices; and he elevated WILLIAM H. REHNQUIST to CHIEF JUSTICE of the Supreme Court in 1986. All these appointments were vetted and approved by an elaborate machinery centered in the Justice Department's Office of Legal Policy and overseen by a newly created White House Judicial Selection Committee. Critics objected to the screening procedure, claiming that it politicized the judicial selection process by subjecting candidates to a "litmus test" on such issues as abortion and CRIMINAL PROCEDURE. But the Reagan administration denied the charge, arguing that the reviews focused not on specific issues, but on the candidates' general approach to legal and constitutional interpretation, which the President was entitled to consider, and that in any event the liberal critics were applying a double standard.

The issue was raised desultorily in some of Reagan's nominations to the Supreme Court—SANDRA DAY O'CONNOR in 1981, the first woman ever nominated (pursuant to a 1980 campaign promise by Reagan); ANTONIN SCALIA in 1986, who replaced Rehnquist when the latter was elevated to Chief Justice; and ANTHONY M. KENNEDY in 1988—but it was raised acutely in the confirmation hearings of Rehnquist and above all of Robert H. Bork. The latter was denied confirmation by the Senate after a long, bitter, and very public struggle over the meaning of "judicial restraint" and of what Attorney General Edwin Meese had called "a jurisprudence of original intention." After Bork's defeat, Reagan nominated Douglas H. Ginsburg, who was forced to withdraw on account of disclosures about his personal life and controversy over his conduct as Justice Department attorney. Shortly thereafter, Reagan nominated Kennedy, who finally assumed the seat vacated by Justice LEWIS F. POWELL half a year earlier.

The significant question concerned the meaning of "judicial restraint." Did it mean, as its liberal critics claimed, that judges would respect only those laws and PRECEDENTS approved by conservatives and restrain all the others? Or did it entail genuine respect for the language of the Constitution and a principled deference to the rights of legislative majorities, as its defenders maintained? The controversy over "restraint" therefore pointed to the larger question of the meaning of the Constitution itself. Did the Constitution embody an ORIGINAL INTENT that judges must regard as authoritative? Liberals such as Justice WILLIAM J. BRENNAN argued, somewhat contradictorily, that judges could not know what the Framers' intentions 200 years ago were; that even if they could, times have changed and interpretation of the Constitution could not be bound by the views of "a world that is dead and gone"; and that what the Framers actually intended was to leave the Constitution open-ended and alive, so that it might be adjusted to changing times and values. To this, conservatives such as Bork and Rehnquist replied that the Framers' intentions were either clearly spelled out in the Constitution or not, and if not, then it was up to Congress or the states to make law as they saw fit.

But this answer begged the question of whether in ascertaining the Framers' intentions a distinction did not have to be made between the spirit and the letter of the Constitution; or, to put it differently, whether precisely in order to understand the Constitution as the Framers understood it, one did not have to distinguish between its principles and the application (or compromise) of those principles, for example, in the so-called three-fifths compromise. The alternative to seeking such principles as a ground of the Constitution's authority was to accept the letter of the law as itself the highest authority, or more exactly, to accept as just and lawful whatever the sovereign majority decreed in the Constitution or in statute law, no matter how irrational or unjust. That is to say, the alternative was a form of legal POSITIVISM or formalism. That Bork's position came close to this became painfully clear in the debate over the RIGHT OF PRIVACY during his confirmation hearings. In short, although his JURISPRUDENCE emphatically rejected judicial tyranny, it did not seem to afford a principled defense against majority tyranny. To that extent, it fell short of the NATURAL LAW principles that justified limited government and that had informed the "original intention" of the Constitution's Framers.

As President, Reagan relied on his Justice Department and SOLICITOR GENERAL to encourage the narrowing of the liberal precedents left over from the Warren and Burger courts. The administration succeeded in persuading the Supreme Court to enlarge existing exceptions to the exclusionary rule, to create new ones, and to narrow the acceptable occasions for court-ordered affirmative-action remedies. But Reagan refused to issue an EXECUTIVE ORDER forbidding set-asides and other forms of reverse discrimination in executive-branch contracts and was saddled with an amended Voting Rights Act (1982) that went far toward establishing proportional representation (i.e., quotas) for selected minorities as the paramount goal of legislative redistricting. The Reagan administration's reluctance to face a public debate on CIVIL RIGHTS and affirmative action left it vulnerable to attack by the advocates of racial and ethnic entitlements who insisted that anyone who was against the "empowerment" of favored minorities through RACIAL QUOTAS (although the dread word was seldom used) was against civil rights.

Although his administration did much to remind the American people that a strong, purposeful President could initiate profound political change, Reagan was often frustrated by Congress. In a remarkable victory that, along with Reagan's landslide electoral win, seemed to promise a fundamental shift in American politics, the Republicans gained control of the SENATE in 1980—only to lose it six years later; they never came close to taking control of the HOUSE OF REPRESENTATIVES. The result was divided government and a long running battle over foreign and domestic policy in which the administration had the upper hand

only in its first two years. From these struggles arose at least two interesting lines of constitutional controversy.

The first concerned FOREIGN AFFAIRS, specifically, the scope of the President's discretion under statute law and the Constitution to order covert activities abroad. Stung by congressional opposition to its initial program of "covert" aid to the forces seeking to overthrow the Sandinista regime in Nicaragua, the administration turned to a more overt strategy of aid, appealing directly to the Congress and the people for support. Although sometimes endorsing Reagan's commitment to arm resistance fighters in communist-controlled countries (e.g., in Afghanistan), the Congress vacillated on aid to the Contras fighting in Nicaragua. During Reagan's presidency, at least two versions of the BOLAND AMENDMENT were passed, along with two or three later modifications of the amendment, each restricting Contra aid in different and conflicting ways.

Against the background of Reagan's desire to support the Nicaraguan resistance, and his need to exploit the ambiguities of the Boland Amendment in order to do so, arose the IRAN-CONTRA AFFAIR—a tangled enterprise run out of the National Security Council (NSC) and aimed at a deal involving the release of hostages held by pro-Iranian terrorists, arms sales to Iran, and the diversion of profits to the Contras in Nicaragua. Fearing another WATERGATE scandal, the administration discharged the accused parties, launched its own inside and outside investigations, called for an INDEPENDENT COUNSEL, and cooperated with two congressional committees appointed to investigate the affair. The larger legal questions turned on whether or not the NSC was covered by the Boland Amendment's ban on aiding the Contras; the constitutional question as to whether or not the President's authority as COMMANDER-IN-CHIEF (or his oath of office) enabled him to act, for the sake of *salus populi*, on the margins of or even against a congressional statute. In the event, the constitutional issue was quickly eclipsed by the debate over the statutory question and by the dramatic testimony and trial of Oliver North, a hitherto obscure NSC staffer.

In other foreign-policy matters, Reagan enjoyed a wide latitude. He committed U.S. forces to Lebanon, to the raid on Libya, to the liberation of Grenada, and to protection of Kuwaiti oil tankers in the Persian Gulf without invoking the War Powers Resolution and indeed with minimal congressional consultation.

The second interesting line of skirmishes between the Reagan administration and Congress concerned the executive's independence on the domestic front. Here, many administration officials were keen to reign in the authority of the SPECIAL PROSECUTORS created by the Ethics in Government Act for the specific purpose of investigating members of the executive branch, and to curtail the proliferating means of congressional influence over the executive agencies. On the former topic, the Reagan administration argued that the law establishing special prosecutors violated the SEPARATION OF POWERS by impinging on the executive's right to initiate, conduct, and terminate criminal prosecutions and led, in many cases, to the criminalizing of policy differences. But the Supreme Court upheld the law by a 7–1 vote in *Morrison v. Olson* (1988).

On the latter question—the extension of congressional power over the executive and independent agencies—Reagan faced even greater opposition. Although the administration convinced the Supreme Court of the unconstitutionality of the LEGISLATIVE VETO in IMMIGRATION AND NATURALIZATION SERVICE V. CHADHA (1983), Congress continued to pass (and Reagan continued to sign) laws containing such provisions, as well as the even more dubious "committee veto," whereby executive branch decisions may be disallowed by the vote of a single congressional committee.

But the legislative veto was only one of a multitude of ways by which the Congress and its swarm of subcommittees harassed the Reagan administration. In particular, Reagan's appointees complained of the "micromanagement" of the executive agencies by subcommittee chairs and individual members of Congress cajoling and threatening on behalf of their constituents and other friendly interest groups. By this tactic, members of Congress could pass broad, vaguely worded laws serving popular causes and then take credit for saving their constituents from the onerous consequences of the very same laws. The use of omnibus continuing resolutions in place of budget bills was yet another tactic to restrict the executive branch's freedom to veto specific budget bills and its right to decide how to execute the programs funded in the bills.

Reagan himself did not take a leading role in protesting what he regarded as these legislative encroachments on the executive, leaving his subordinates to do most of the disputing. He did vehemently object to being presented with the choice of either signing or vetoing at one stroke the entire BUDGET of the federal government, but nevertheless signed the mammoth Continuing Resolution and Fiscal Year 1988 Budget Reconciliation Act. Rather than precipitate a fiscal, political, and constitutional crisis, he chose to reemphasize his call for two constitutional amendments—one creating a LINE-ITEM VETO for the President and the other mandating a BALANCED BUDGET—to strengthen the hand of future Presidents.

For a conservative President, Reagan appealed for an unusual number of constitutional amendments. In part, this was a backhanded admission of his reluctance to engage in direct costly political combat over the budget, school prayer, abortion, and other controversial subjects.

This reluctance was not so much temperamental as it was a reflection of a strategic political decision he had made before entering office in 1980, a decision to try to control the national political agenda by concentrating on two critical issues: reducing taxes and strengthening America's defenses. Of course, Reagan's decision was also shaped by the internal weaknesses of his own coalition, which he was never sufficiently able to overcome to bring about a thoroughgoing political realignment like the NEW DEAL.

Perhaps his greatest constitutional achievement did not have to do with the institutions of government at all. Reagan strove mightily to restore Americans' confidence in themselves as a fundamental force for good in the world, and in his speeches he seldom failed to remind his fellow citizens of a connection with the heroes and statesmen of the American past. In this way, he helped revive their faith in the goodness of the Constitution itself, a faith that had been sorely tried in the dark decades of the 1960s and 1970s.

CHARLES R. KESLER
(1992)

(SEE ALSO: *Bork Nomination; Budget Process; Congress and Foreign Policy; Congressional War Powers; Conservatism; Presidential War Powers; Race-Consciousness; Racial Discrimination; Racial Preference; Rehnquist Court; Senate and Foreign Policy; War Powers.*)

Bibliography

JONES, CHARLES O., ed. 1988 *The Reagan Legacy: Promise and Performance.* Chatham, N.J.: Chatham House.

JONES, GORDON S. and MARINI, JOHN, eds. 1988 *The Imperial Congress: Crisis in the Separation of Powers.* New York: Pharos Books.

MAHONEY, DENNIS J. and SCHRAMM, PETER W., eds. 1987 *The 1984 Election and the Future of American Politics.* Durham, N.C.: Carolina Academic Press.

REAGAN, RONALD 1980–1989 *Presidential Papers.* Washington, D.C.: U.S. Government Printing Office.

REAGAN v. FARMERS' LOAN & TRUST CO.
154 U.S. 362 (1894)

In a grotesque opinion the Supreme Court unanimously held unconstitutional a rate schedule fixed by a state railroad commission. Justice DAVID BREWER for the Court had no doubt that the economic validity of rates was subject to JUDICIAL REVIEW, and he found that these rates were "unjust and unreasonable," meaning too low in the estimate of the Court. They resulted, he said with exaggeration, in "a practical destruction to rights of property." Four years later, in SMYTH V. AMES (1898), the Court finally

2130   REAL EVIDENCE

adopted SUBSTANTIVE DUE PROCESS as the basis for such a ruling, but in this case the Court seemed unready to embrace such an extravagant position, despite previous flirtations with it. Here the Court cast about for something more familiar and found it in the concepts of EQUAL PROTECTION and JUST COMPENSATION, which it united. The difficulty was that the just compensation clause of the Fifth Amendment bound only the national government, not the states, and it applied only in cases of EMINENT DOMAIN, when private property was taken for a PUBLIC PURPOSE. Nothing of that sort had happened here. Brewer, however, declared that the commission's rates denied "equal protection which is the constitutional right of all owners of other property," and then he ruled that the equal protection clause "forbids legislation . . . by which the property of one individual is, without compensation, wrested from him for the benefit of another, or of the public." Thus the Court incorporated the substance of the just compensation clause of the Fifth Amendment into the Fourteenth for the benefit of railroads, though the Court refused in other cases of this period to incorporate into the FOURTEENTH AMENDMENT the rights that protected accused persons or victims of RACIAL DISCRIMINATION. (See INCORPORATION DOCTRINE.) Moreover, this was not a case of eminent domain and the property of the railroad was not "wrested" without compensation. More rationally, Brewer sought to devise an economic test for determining the reasonableness of a rate schedule: whether the rate was equivalent to the market value of the use of the property. That economists found such a test to be unsound was not so significant as the Court's arrogating to itself the power to determine reasonableness by economic criteria that thrust it into judgments better suited to legislative and administrative agencies. (See ECONOMIC REGULATION AND THE CONSTITUTION.)

LEONARD W. LEVY
(1986)

REAL EVIDENCE

Real evidence is supplied by a thing that is inspected by the jury, or other trier of fact. (Statements by witnesses are called testimonial evidence.) The acquisition and use of real evidence in the criminal process intersects with constitutional doctrine in various ways. For example, the EXCLUSIONARY RULE may forbid the offering of evidence—such as a gun or a bag containing marijuana—that has been obtained in an unconstitutional SEARCH AND SEIZURE. Correspondingly, the probability that such real evidence will be found in a particular place may, under the doctrine

of PROBABLE CAUSE, justify the issuance of a SEARCH WARRANT.

KENNETH L. KARST
(1986)

REAPPORTIONMENT

Direct democracy is not possible in a nation as populous as the United States is now, or even as it was in 1787 when the Constitution of the United States was drafted. Accordingly, the objective was then, and is now, to devise and implement as fair and effective a plan of democratic REPRESENTATION as possible.

The idea of fair and effective representation at each level of government was not new in 1787. The search for such a formula lies at the center of Anglo-American political thought. In 1690 JOHN LOCKE sought to abolish England's rotten boroughs by urging that, "it being the interest as well as the intention of the people, to have a fair and equal representation, whoever brings it nearest to that is an undoubted friend to and establisher of the government, and cannot miss the consent and approbation of the community."

Although Britain did not put an end to its rotten boroughs until near the middle of the twentieth century, the issue of how best to structure a truly representative government was very much alive at the time the various proposals for the American Constitution were being debated. At last a compromise was struck in the CONSTITUTIONAL CONVENTION OF 1787, giving equal representation to each state in the Senate and representation based on population in the House of Representatives. Article I, section 2, of the Constitution provides that "Representatives . . . shall be apportioned among the several states . . . according to their respective numbers . . . ," with recomputation of the apportionment every ten years, and each state to have at least one representative regardless of population. But the task of fixing the formula for the apportioning process was left to Congress, and no directions at all were established to guide the states in the parallel function of allocating seats in the state legislature or in local governmental bodies. We are not, however, left entirely in doubt about what Congress thought appropriate for apportionment in the states. The NORTHWEST ORDINANCE of 1787 provided that representation in the territorial legislatures to be created in that area should be based on population. In general, the states accepted the principle of reasonably equal population among legislative districts, but the principle was often modified by assurances of at least one representative from each county or township or municipality. Departures from population equality may not have been egregious in this time of mostly rural dispersal; but by the late nineteenth and early twentieth centuries what had once been minor deviations became major divergences.

JOHN QUINCY ADAMS observed in 1839 that the division of sovereign powers between the states and the nation, as set out in the Constitution, gave us "the most complicated government on the face of the globe." The twentieth century has proved how right he was. The interaction between increasingly potent national and state governments, frequently aggravated by friction arising out of competition for power, has produced a delicately balanced division of power and a complexity of relationships probably unsurpassed in the history of governmental institutions.

Yet it is the proud boast of FEDERALISM in the United States that the governments of the fifty states and that of the nation can work together in common purpose rather than in a relationship of competition and mistrust. Moreover, it is a basic premise of representative democracy in the United States that the people are entitled to representation somewhat in proportion to their numbers, at every level of government. The tradition of majority rule cannot otherwise be attained. Neither the division of sovereign powers prescribed in the federal system nor the fairness of legislative representation formulas can long be left unattended. Vigilant superintendence by an informed electorate is essential.

Even the wisest political scientists have difficulty in defining the precise meaning of representative democracy. There is, however, general agreement that representative democracy in the United States includes something of liberty, equality, and majority rule. Even though these qualities are scarcely less abstract, it can surely be said that representative democracy relates to the processes by which citizens exert control over their leaders. From the time of the Constitutional Convention debate has centered on the extent to which, and the ways in which, majority control over leaders should be exercised. Congress has wrestled with the issue, with inconclusive results. In 1842, for example, Congress required each state to establish compact, contiguous, single-member congressional districts as nearly equal in population as possible. These criteria, however, lapsed in 1911. In any event, no enforcement method had been established, and the courts considered the issue none of their business.

Not until more than a hundred years after the RATIFICATION OF THE CONSTITUTION in 1789 did such states as California, Illinois, Michigan, New York, Ohio, and Pennsylvania, responding to new pressures, abandon the equal-population principle in one or both houses. So widespread had been the original acceptance of the equality concept that no fewer than thirty-six of the original state constitutions provided that representation in both houses of the state legislature would be based completely, or predominantly, on population. Between 1790 and 1889 no state was admitted to the Union in which its original constitution did not provide for representation principally based on population in both houses of the state legislature.

To speak of the equal-population principle as the basis for apportionment of those nineteenth-century legislatures is not to say that there was mathematically precise equality among the districts at that time. The western states, for example, commonly relied on county lines in drawing their apportionment formulas. The distortions that resulted from assuring each county at least one representative, for example, or from grouping whole counties to form election districts, were much less pronounced in agricultural and rural America than in present-day industrial and urban America. The population of the United States, outside the few great commercial centers in the East, was spread thinly across the face of the country.

The drift from relative equality to substantial inequality would have moved at about the same pace as the shift in population from rural to urban America; and that would have been bad enough. But some states accelerated the trend away from the equality principle by other devices as well. As state legislatures were enlarged, additional seats were granted to the areas of new growth without diminishing representation of the declining population areas. As the population of rural areas declined, state legislatures abandoned even the formal acceptance of equal population as a controlling principle, typically guaranteeing each county (or township) one representative. Some states, unable or unwilling to change the constitutional requirement for equality among districts, simply ignored the mandate for decennial change. (Tennessee is a good example; the state constitutional requirement of reapportionment every ten years was ignored between 1901 and 1961, giving rise in 1962 to BAKER V. CARR.)

The consequence of these factors, singly or in combination, was by the middle of the twentieth century a remarkable skewing of voter impact, ordinarily giving the less populated areas of a state a disproportionate influence in legislative representation. The impact was most marked at the state and local legislative levels, but not without considerable influence on congressional districting as well.

By the middle of the twentieth century the disparities in legislative representation were marked. Thus, in the then ninety-nine state legislative chambers (forty-nine bicameral legislatures plus the Nebraska unicameral legislature), thirty-two relied in large part on population; eight used population, but with weighted ratios; forty-five combined population and area considerations; eight granted representation to each unit; five had fixed constitutional apportionments; and one (the New Hampshire Senate) was based on state tax payments. These conclusions somewhat understate the actual disregard of population as the basis of representation because this summary is drawn exclusively from the state constitutional requirements, without adjustment for violation of those provisions.

The time has come to ask: what is (re)apportionment and what is (re)districting? The question is well put, for the terms are sometimes (confusingly) used interchangeably. But there is a difference. Apportionment is ordinarily described as the allocation of legislative seats by a legislative body to a subordinate unit of government, and districting as the process of drawing the final lines by which each legislative district is bounded. Thus, Congress apportions the number of congressional districts to which each state is entitled, based on population figures disclosed at each decennial census. Each state legislature then draws lines that divide the state into as many congressional districts as have been allocated to it by Congress.

State legislatures, on the other hand, both apportion the distribution of state legislative seats *and* draw the district lines that determine which voters will make each selection. Therein lies the problem, clearly rooted in the political ambition of each political group to overcome its opposition, before the voting begins, on the basis of the dispersion of voters eligible to vote for one candidate rather than another.

By the early 1960s the act and the impact of malapportionment were everywhere apparent, typically to the apparent disadvantage of individual voters in heavily populated districts and to the apparent advantage of voters in sparsely populated districts. Despite the fact that many state constitutions required reapportionment every ten years and included formulas requiring approximate population equality, no legislative chamber came closer to that goal than two to one, and the disparity between most populous to least populous district was in many states more than ten to one and in several more than one hundred to one. To put the matter another way, in twelve states fewer than twenty percent of the voters lived in districts that elected a majority of the state senators, and in seven states fewer than thirty percent of the voters lived in districts that elected a majority of the members of the lower house.

State courts occasionally acted to deal with the most egregious abuses, but the federal courts, until 1962, adamantly refused to intervene. Although the Supreme Court had long recognized the right of citizens to vote free of arbitrary impairment by STATE ACTION when such impairment resulted from dilution by false tally or by stuffing of the ballot box, the Court had declined to deal with apportionment and districting abuses on the grounds that the issue was not justiciable, that is, not appropriate for federal judicial intervention. As Justice FELIX FRANKFURTER said in COLEGROVE V. GREEN (1946), "Courts ought not to enter this political thicket."

Finally, the case of interference with the exercise of the franchise was made so clearly that a majority of the Court was persuaded that only federal judicial intervention could put an end to this denial of equality. The case that triggered this change in attitude provided a dramatic illustration of flagrant abuse of voter rights by a state legislature that had openly flouted its own state constitution for more than half a century.

The Tennessee Constitution had required, since 1870, that the number of senators and representatives in the general assembly "be apportioned among the several counties or districts, according to the number of qualified electors in each. . . ." Moreover, the state constitution required reapportionment in accordance with the equal-population standard every ten years. Between 1901 and 1961, however, the legislature had not acted on the matter. As a result, thirty-seven percent of the Tennessee voters lived in districts that elected twenty of the thirty-three senators, and forty percent of the voters lived in districts that elected sixty-three of the ninety-nine members of the lower house. The federal court challenge was brought by voters in urban areas of the state, who invoked the Constitution of the United States and claimed that they had been denied the EQUAL PROTECTION OF THE LAWS, "by virtue of the debasement of their votes."

The resulting Supreme Court decision, *Baker v. Carr*, did not rule on the substance of the equality claim, but did hold that the issue was properly within the JURISDICTION OF THE FEDERAL COURTS and was justiciable. Only Justices Frankfurter and JOHN MARSHALL HARLAN dissented.

Within two years the Supreme Court signaled how it would decide the equality issue. GRAY V. SANDERS (1963), while not strictly an apportionment case, involved the closely related issue of voter discrimination. The election practice there challenged was the Georgia "county-unit" system, as it applied to statewide primaries: a candidate for nomination who received the highest number of popular votes in a county was considered to have carried the county and to be entitled to two votes for each representative to which the county was entitled in the lower house of the general assembly. The majority of the county unit vote was required to nominate a candidate for United States senator or state governor, while a plurality was sufficient for nomination of candidates for other offices. Because the most populous county (Fulton, with a 1960 population of 556,326) had only six unit votes, while the least populous county (Echols, with a 1960 population of 1,876) had two unit votes, "one resident in Echols County had an influence in the nomination of candidates equivalent to 99 residents of Fulton County."

Georgia argued that, because the ELECTORAL COLLEGE

permitted substantial inequalities in voter representation in a "winner-take-all" system, parallel systems should be permitted to the states. Moreover, the state argued that because United States senators represent widely divergent numbers of voters, the same should be permitted in one house of a state legislature. But the Supreme Court rejected all such analogies as inapposite: "The inclusion of the electoral college in the Constitution, as the result of specific historical concerns, validated the collegiate principle despite its inherent numerical inequality, but implied nothing about the use of an analogous system by a State in a statewide election. No such specific accommodation of the latter was ever undertaken, and therefore no validation of its numerical equality ensued."

While conceding that states "can within limits specify the qualifications of voters both in state and federal elections," the Court denied that a state is entitled to weight the votes "once the geographical unit for which a representative is to be chosen is designated. . . ." Accordingly, the Court concluded: "The conception of political equality from the DECLARATION OF INDEPENDENCE, to Lincoln's Gettysburg Address to the FIFTEENTH, SEVENTEENTH, and NINETEENTH AMENDMENTS can mean only one thing—ONE PERSON, ONE VOTE." The fatal defect in the Georgia plan was that the votes were weighted on the basis of geography as an expression of legislative preference for rural over urban voters.

The next franchise case decided by the Supreme Court with full opinion, WESBERRY V. SANDERS (1964), was also not a state legislative apportionment case; it was a congressional districting case not very dissimilar from *Colegrove v. Green*—except in result. Plaintiffs were qualified voters of Fulton County, Georgia, entitled to vote in the state's fifth congressional district, which had a 1960 population of 823,680, as compared with the 272,154 residents of the ninth district.

After the decision in *Baker v. Carr*, the Court had little difficulty deciding that such issues were justiciable in federal courts. The substantive ruling, however, came as something of a surprise. Plaintiffs had argued principally that the gross population disparities violated the equal protection clause of the FOURTEENTH AMENDMENT. The Supreme Court, however, adopted what had been a subordinate contention, that the Georgia arrangement violated Article I, section 2, of the Constitution, which prescribed that representatives be chosen "by the People of the several States." Justice HUGO L. BLACK, writing for the majority of six, stated that this provision, when construed in its historical context, means "that as nearly as practicable one man's vote in a congressional election is to be worth as much as another's. . . . To say that a vote is worth more in one district than in another would not only run counter to our fundamental ideas of democratic government, it

would cast aside the principle of a House of Representatives elected "by the People,' a principle tenaciously fought for and established at the Constitutional Convention." That result, at first surprising in view of the non-specific constitutional text, was well supported in the Court's review of the relevant history. For example, at the Constitutional Convention JAMES WILSON of Pennsylvania had said that "equal numbers of people ought to have an equal number of representatives," and representatives "of different districts ought clearly to hold the same proportion to each other, as their respective constituents hold to each other."

Reliance on section 2 of Article I rather than on the equal protection clause has had significant consequences. From that date forward the Court has been less tolerant of population variations among congressional districts than of those in state legislative districts, as to which the population-equality principle has, since REYNOLDS V. SIMS (1964), been based on the equal protection clause of the Fourteenth Amendment.

Reynolds v. Sims and its five companion cases completed the original round of apportionment and districting cases and constituted the foundation on which all subsequent litigation has built. On June 15, 1964, the Court invalidated the state legislative apportionment and districting structure in Alabama (the *Reynolds* case), Colorado, Delaware, Maryland, New York, and Virginia. One week later the Court struck down the formulas in nine additional states, foretelling a complete reapportionment revolution.

Reynolds v. Sims was illustrative. The complaint in that case alleged that the last legislative reapportionment in the state had been based on the 1900 federal census despite a state constitutional requirement for decennial reapportionment. Accordingly, because the population growth had been uneven, urban counties were severely disadvantaged by the state legislature's failure to reapportion every ten years and by the state constitution's provision requiring each of the sixty-seven counties to have at least one representative in the lower house with a membership of 106. The Supreme Court of the United States ruled unequivocally in favor of the equal-population principle: "We hold that, as a basic constitutional standard, the Equal Protection Clause requires that the seats in both houses of a bicameral state legislature must be apportioned on a population basis. Simply stated, an individual's right to vote for state legislators is unconstitutionally impaired when its weight is in a substantial fashion diluted when compared with votes of citizens living in other parts of the state."

The decisions in *Wesberry* and *Reynolds* required adjustment of congressional districting practices in all states (except the few states with only one representative each) and of all state legislative districting practices. Despite considerable adverse reaction in the beginning and substantial litigation to determine the full significance of the decisions, by and large compliance was secured; and further adjustments were made after the results of the 1970 and 1980 censuses were determined.

Two principal types of questions remained to be worked out after the first decisions were announced: how equal is "equal" in congressional districting and in state legislative apportionment and districting? and to what extent does the equal-population principle apply to the thousands of local governmental units and the even larger number of special districts that serve multitudinous quasi-governmental purposes?

Despite criticism of the *Reynolds* decision based on an assumption that the Court had demanded mathematical exactness among election districts, the Court explicitly acknowledged the permissibility of some variation: "We realize that it is a practical impossibility to arrange legislative districts so that each one has an identical number of residents, or citizens, or voters. Mathematical exactness or precision is hardly a workable constitutional requirement." The important obligation is for each state to "make an honest and good faith effort to construct districts, in both houses of its legislature, as nearly of equal population as is practicable."

From the beginning the *Reynolds* Court acknowledged that states could continue to place some reliance on political subdivision lines, at least in drawing the lines for state legislative bodies. "Since almost invariably there is a significantly larger number of seats in state legislative bodies to be distributed within a state than congressional seats, it may be feasible to use political subdivision lines to a greater extent in establishing state legislative districts than in congressional districting while still affording adequate representation to all parts of the State." A further reason for at least limited adherence to local political subdivision lines is the highly pragmatic proposition that, to do otherwise, "[i]ndiscriminate districting, without any regard for political subdivisions, may be little more than an invitation to partisan gerrymandering."

Acknowledging the principle that population deviations are permissible in state districting implementation of rational state policy, the Supreme Court has recognized that de minimis numerical deviations are unavoidable. Maximum deviations in Connecticut of 7.83 percent among house districts and 1.81 percent among senate districts were upheld in *Gaffney v. Cummings* (1973). Texas deviations of 9.9 and 1.82 percent respectively among house and senate districts were similarly approved in *White v. Regester* (1973). In MAHAN V. HOWELL (1973) the Court upheld a Virginia plan despite a maximum deviation of 16.4 percent, on the grounds that the plan could "reasonably

be said to advance the rational state policy of respecting the boundaries of political subdivisions," but cautioned that "this percentage may well approach tolerable limits."

The requirement of population equality is far more exacting in the drawing of congressional district lines. In *Kirkpatrick v. Preisler* (1969) the Court struck down Missouri's 1967 Redistricting Act despite the fact that the most populous district was 3.13 percent larger and the least populous 2.84 percent smaller than the average district. In explanation the Court stated, "Since 'equal representation for equal numbers of people [is] the fundamental goal for the House of Representatives,' the 'as nearly as practicable' standard requires that the State make a good faith effort to achieve precise mathematical equality. Unless population variances among congressional districts are shown to have resulted despite such effort, the State must justify each variance, no matter how small." In *Karcher v. Daggett* (1983) the Supreme Court invalidated a deviation of less than one percent among New Jersey congressional districts because the state had failed to make "a good-faith effort to achieve precise mathematical equality" in population among its congressional districts. In sum, because local units of government are less important as factors in the representation of relatively large numbers of persons in the Congress than for smaller numbers of persons in the state legislature, population deviations among congressional districts are strictly scrutinized, while a more tolerant review is accorded state districting. But even in state districting the excesses of the past are no longer tolerable; above the *de minimis* level deviations must be held within narrow limits and must be justified in terms of preservation of political subdivisions, compactness and contiguity of districts, and respect for natural or historical boundaries.

No matter how close the judicial superintendence of population equality, one problem remains. In congressional and state legislative districting alike, even the most exact adherence to the equal-population principle does not assure protection against legislative line-drawers who seek partisan advantage out of the process. "GERRYMANDER" is the term used to describe such efforts to preserve partisan power or to extend such power through manipulative use of the process. The term originated in 1812 in Massachusetts, where political maneuvering had produced a salamander-shaped district which was named after ELBRIDGE GERRY, then governor. From that time forward the gerrymander has been an altogether too-common fact of American political life. Nevertheless, despite repeated attempts to persuade the Supreme Court to enter this new "political thicket," the Court has denied that there is any constitutional ground for superintending the apportionment and districting process other than the equal-population principle. Accordingly, the states remain free, so far as the United States Constitution is concerned, to construct congressional and state legislative districts that resemble salamanders or other equally peculiar creatures. And many state legislatures have done just that, particularly where one party is in secure control of the state legislative process. Where party control of the two houses of a bicameral legislature is divided, or where the governor is of a different party, the drawing of congressional and state legislative district lines is likely to be worked out by political compromise or, that failing, by the courts.

More seemly alternatives are possible, but they are not often adopted in the absence of JUDICIAL REVIEW over the process except as to population equality among districts. Congress has the authority to set standards of compactness and contiguity that would avoid the worst abuses and could be enforced in the courts. State legislatures could adopt similar standards to control the process within their own states, but few political leaders are willing to relinquish the prospect of present or future partisan advantage to be secured out of the districting process.

Like state legislative districting, the districting of counties, municipalities, or other local governmental units is constitutionally permitted to deviate to some extent from full equality if it can be demonstrated that the governmental unit has made "an honest and good faith effort" to construct districts "as nearly of equal population as practicable." Local governments may use MULTIMEMBER DISTRICTS if there is a history of such representation and if such plans are not part of a deliberate attempt to dilute or cancel the voting strength of racial or political elements in the governmental unit. Despite that limitation, local governments, like states, may use ethnic or minority population data in constructing districts designed to elect representatives of that minority or ethnic group. (See UNITED JEWISH ORGANIZATION V. CAREY.)

Supreme Court intervention in the apportionment and districting process has unquestionably restructured congressional and state legislative representation. Gross population disparities among election districts have been evened out so that the democratic promise of fair representation has been made possible of realization. But no court, even so powerful a body as the Supreme Court of the United States, can assure democratic representation. The ultimate test of the democratic process will depend upon the level of concern of the voters and their willingness to insist that their legislative representatives take whatever action is necessary to prevent excesses.

There are two principal types of gerrymandering, both of which should be controlled. The bipartisan or "incumbent survival" plan is designed to assure as far as possible the reelection of incumbents, sometimes regardless of party affiliation; the technique is to distribute party registration or proven party supporters to the legislators who

will benefit most. The partisan plan is designed to maintain or increase the number of seats held by the majority party; the technique is to "waste" votes of the opposition party either by concentrating the voters loyal to that party in as few districts as possible, or by dispersing the opposition voting strength among a number of districts in which it cannot command majorities. Control of these abuses is not likely to come from party leadership. Voters concerned with the integrity of the process must demand an end to such practices, calling for state constitutional amendments or statutes requiring that districts be compact and contiguous.

Redistricting should be a matter of special concern for ethnic and racial minorities, many of whom are concentrated in urban centers. Typically, minority spokesmen claim that fair representation requires districts that will elect members of their own groups. When legislatures act to meet such demands, other groups are likely to feel disadvantaged. That issue was litigated to the Supreme Court in *United Jewish Organization v. Carey*. In that case a New York redistricting plan had been modified to bring it into compliance with the VOTING RIGHTS ACT OF 1965. In the process the act divided a community of Hasidic Jews in order to establish several substantially nonwhite districts. The Court upheld the plan, ruling that such a use of racial criteria was justified in fulfillment of congressional legislative policy in the Voting Rights Act.

Somewhat related to the issue just discussed is the question whether municipalities and other local legislative bodies should be permitted to require at-large elections for all the seats in the legislative unit. Such a practice may make it impossible for a minority group in the community to secure representation, even though one or more members of that minority might be elected if single-member districts were used. The Supreme Court held, in MOBILE V. BOLDEN (1980), that multimember district elections would be tolerated, even where the impact on minority groups was demonstrated, unless it could be shown that the plan was adopted with racially discriminatory intent. However, the Voting Rights Act of 1982 overturned that ruling; under the act, invidious intent need not be shown if impact disadvantageous to identifiable minorities can be established.

In the era before the application of computer technology to politics, it was common for politicians and their staffs to spread out maps on office floors, using adding machines for their arithmetic, slowly building new districts from census tracts and precinct figures. Because most redistricting decisions must be made sequentially—one boundary change requires another, which requires yet another—the computer is perfectly designed to speed the process and allow for more sophisticated analysis. The computer not only makes available numerical population counts, voter history, and party registration, but also permits a graphic display of the areas represented.

These technical advances have resulted in what may be styled the second reapportionment revolution. They place in the hands of those responsible for redistricting a vast array of information for use in drawing district lines. It follows, for better or for worse, that the computer's twin features of speed and accuracy can advance the goal of "fair and effective representation" as well as engineer the nearly perfect gerrymander.

At the time of the reapportionment decisions of the early 1960s, commentators speculated about the decisions' likely impact on the representational process. The most common prediction was that the urban areas would dominate state legislatures, with a general tendency toward liberal legislative policies. It is by no means clear that this prediction has come true. Enlarged influence of the suburbs, often with a conservative representation and not infrequently allied with rural representatives, has been the more typical reality. The one thing that can be said with confidence is that adoption of the equal-population principle has ended the worst abuses and assured basic fairness in the most important features of the democratic process.

ROBERT B. MCKAY
(1986)

Bibliography

ADAMS, BRUCE   1977   A Model State Reapportionment Process: The Continuing Quest for "Fair and Effective Representation." *Harvard Journal on Legislation* 14:825–904.
COMMON CAUSE   1977   *Reapportionment: A Better Way.* Washington, D.C.: Common Cause.
DIXON, ROBERT G.   1968   *Democratic Representation: Reapportionment in Law and Politics.* New York: Oxford University Press.
GROFMAN, BERNARD et al., eds.   1981   *Representation and Redistricting Issues.* Lexington, Mass.: D. C. Heath.
MCKAY, ROBERT B.   1965   *Reapportionment: The Law and Politics of Equal Representation.* New York: Twentieth Century Fund.
POLSBY, NELSON, ed.   1971   *Reapportionment in the 1970s.* Berkeley: University of California Press.

REAPPORTIONMENT
(Update)

In 1991, reapportionment and redistricting were the most open, democratic, and racially egalitarian in American history. A series of Supreme Court decisions beginning with SHAW V. RENO in 1993, however, insured that the 2001 redistricting would be completely different.

The 1982 amendments to the VOTING RIGHTS ACT and the Court's interpretation of them guaranteed minority groups unprecedented influence over redistricting in the 1990s. When Congress in 1981–1982 considered requiring proof of only a racially discriminatory effect, rather than a racially discriminatory intent, to void state or local election laws, critics warned that this amendment would lead inexorably to racial GERRYMANDERING and drives for proportional representation for minority groups. Congress adopted it anyway, and in an authoritative 1982 U.S. SENATE report, it directed the U.S. Department of Justice not to allow states and localities in the Deep South and scattered areas throughout the country to put into force laws that had racially discriminatory effects. The Justice Department therefore became an active ally of minority voters during the 1990s redistricting.

In the most important VOTING RIGHTS decision of the 1980s, *Thornburg v. Gingles* (1986), Supreme Court Justice WILLIAM J. BRENNAN, JR., writing for the Court, sustained the new effect standard. Drawing on the 1982 Senate report and testimony from hearings on the Voting Rights Act, Brennan ruled that if a minority group was sufficiently large and geographically compact to dominate an electoral district, and if voting in the area was racially polarized, then states and localities had to draw districts that would enable minority voters to elect candidates of their choice. In 1991, however, redistricting planners largely disregarded the compactness requirement because "compactness" was notoriously difficult to define—Brennan had not even tried to define it, and Congress in 1989 had rejected a compactness standard for congressional districts.

To facilitate the 1991 redistricting, the U.S. Census Bureau rapidly made population and ethnic data, already keyed to voting precincts, widely available in machine-readable form. Ethnic and interest groups, as well as factions of the POLITICAL PARTIES, individual politicians, and members of the general public were given access to computers and software that made drawing districts for local, state, and congressional seats quick and easy. Many of them drafted competing redistricting plans and took vigorous parts in hearings and debates. Organizations representing African American and Latino voters, such as the National Association for the Advancement of Colored People, the Mexican American Legal Defense and Education Fund, and the AMERICAN CIVIL LIBERTIES UNION, were especially active.

Both Republicans and Democrats initially supported drawing more minority opportunity districts in 1991. Republicans sought to pack largely Democratic African Americans and Latinos into as few districts as possible, sacrificing those seats in order to maximize Republican seats. Democrats, who had to draw minority opportunity districts to satisfy their core constituents, aimed to minimize their party's losses of seats by extracting minorities from predominantly Republican districts, often producing jagged district boundaries. The result was the largest gain in minority representation since the 1870s, modest losses in overall Democratic representation in Congress, and, in reaction to both of these, a radical shift in Supreme Court DOCTRINE by a five-person conservative Republican majority on the Court.

The Court had ruled in a series of cases in the 1970s and 1980s that, in order to have STANDING to sue under the FOURTEENTH and FIFTEENTH AMENDMENTS, plaintiffs had to prove injury—namely, vote dilution. In any event, a state's intent to comply with the Voting Rights Act, the Court decided in UNITED JEWISH ORGANIZATIONS V. CAREY (1977), justified race-conscious redistricting. Therefore, when five white North Carolinians challenged two 57-percent black congressional districts that had elected the state's first African American members of Congress in the twentieth century on the grounds that planners had taken race into account in drawing the districts, the majority of a three-judge federal DISTRICT COURT panel dismissed the case. In a bitterly contested 5–4 decision, the Supreme Court overturned the lower court in *Shaw*, granting the white plaintiffs standing on the grounds that the sprawling districts conveyed a symbolic message of racial difference to voters and public officials. It did not matter that whites were not discriminated against—their votes were not diluted—nor did it matter whether the message that whites and blacks differed politically was true. The Fourteenth Amendment, Justice SANDRA DAY O'CONNOR said, prohibited any intentional governmental distinctions between people on racial grounds.

After the *Shaw* decision, losing congressional candidates, along with advocates of what they called "colorblind" policies, joined by southern state Republican parties that began to treat redistricting as an AFFIRMATIVE ACTION issue, challenged all but one black- or Latino-majority congressional district in the South that had initially been drawn in the 1990s, and several majority–minority districts outside the South, as well. When a district court invalidated two majority-black Georgia districts that were much more compact than those in North Carolina, the *Shaw* majority of the Supreme Court affirmed, condemning every district drawn for "predominantly racial" reasons or in which race had been used "as a proxy" for Democratic voting. After this decision, MILLER V. JOHNSON, no longer was a *Shaw*-type claim restricted to majority–minority districts or those whose shape annoyed some Justices. *Miller* and two 1996 decisions dismissed compliance with the Voting Rights Act and attempts to overcome past discrimination or current racial-bloc voting as justifications for race-conscious districting. Attempts to make it possible for "DISCRETE AND INSULAR MINORITIES" to elect candidates of their choice, the majority ruled, were much less important than adherence to what it termed "traditional districting principles." These newly discovered "traditional" principles included not only compactness and protecting incumbents, but also, for instance, the much-broken habit of drawing separate districts in Georgia's four corners and, according to one district judge, preserving the power of various white ethnic "communities of interest." By contrast, Justice ANTHONY M. KENNEDY dismissed as "offensive and demeaning" the notion that African Americans might form a community of interest. And strikingly unlike its treatment of pro-Democratic race-conscious districting plans, the Supreme Court in *Voinovich v. Quilter* (1993 and 1996) sustained the deliberate, openly admitted packing of African Americans into state legislative districts by Ohio Republicans. Why *Miller's* "predominant reason" or "race as a proxy" tests did not apply to Republicans, the Court did not explain.

In a biting dissent in *Bush v. Vera* (1996), Justice JOHN PAUL STEVENS accused the majority of using race as an indirect means of attacking political gerrymanders. After seeming to open the door to challenges to partisan gerrymanders by ruling them JUSTICIABLE in *Davis v. Bandemer* (1986), the Court had set the standard of proof so high as practically to foreclose such cases, and later it rejected without comment legal assaults on bipartisan gerrymanders and on the whole notion that legislators should influence the shape of their districts. It also allowed the Bush Administration to block efforts to use statistical sampling to insure that minority group members and other predominantly poor people were not undercounted by the CENSUS, a decision that skewed the allocation of congressional seats toward the predominantly white, Republican suburbs.

Thus, as always before in American history, party politics suffused the redistricting of the 1990s, but this time disguised behind the mask of race. Racial dividing lines, long the most deep and consistent in the country's politics, increasingly split Republicans from Democrats. Since any indication that race has been considered in the drawing of district lines can be used in the inevitable legal challenges to every major redistricting in 2001, there will be a strong incentive to conduct such discussions in secret or in coded language. Ironically, then, the REHNQUIST COURT has twisted the Fourteenth Amendment into a barrier to the equal participation of minorities in allocating political power, one which operates differentially against the political party to which they overwhelmingly adhere, and it has so judicialized the redistricting process as to hamper popular participation and open, frank deliberations concerning the key cleavage in American politics. This is an outcome that the WARREN COURT hardly could have foreseen when it strode self-confidently into the political thicket in BAKER V. CARR (1962).

J. MORGAN KOUSSER
(2000)

(SEE ALSO: *Electoral Districting.*)

Bibliography

CONGRESSIONAL QUARTERLY 1993 *Congressional Districts in the 1990s.* Washington, D.C.: Congressional Quarterly, Inc.

GROFMAN, BERNARD; HANDLEY, LISA; and NIEMI, RICHARD G. 1992 *Minority Representation and the Quest for Voting Equality.* New York: Cambridge University Press.

KOUSSER, J. MORGAN 1999 *Colorblind Injustice: Minority Voting Rights and the Undoing of the Second Reconstruction.* Chapel Hill, N.C.: University of North Carolina Press.

LUBLIN, DAVID 1997 *The Paradox of Representation: Racial Gerrymandering and Minority Interests in Congress.* Princeton, N.J.: Princeton University Press.

THERNSTROM, ABIGAIL M. and THERNSTROM, STEPHAN T. 1997 *America in Black and White: One Nation Indivisible.* New York: Simon & Schuster.

REASONABLE DOUBT

Proof beyond a reasonable doubt is the highest level of proof demanded in American courts. It is the usual standard for criminal cases, and in criminal litigation it has constitutional grounding in decisions of the United States Supreme Court. Although the reasonable doubt standard is not often used in noncriminal settings, there are exceptional situations, usually where liberty is placed in jeopardy, when a JURISDICTION will borrow the criminal standard of proof for a civil case.

Any standard of proof chosen by an American court recognizes that in all litigation there is the chance of a mistake. If opposing litigants agree on the various matters that constitute their case, usually the case is settled. There is little for a judge or a jury to do. Once a dispute arises, however, adversaries offer conflicting EVIDENCE and conflicting interpretations of evidence to decision makers. Rarely, if ever, is there a dispute in which every witness and every aspect of physical and scientific evidence presented by opposing parties point with perfect certainty to one specific conclusion. Witnesses may suffer from ordinary human frailties—they have memory problems; they sometimes confuse facts; they see events differently from each other; they have biases and prejudices that call into question their judgment; and they may be frightened and

have trouble communicating on the witness stand. Physical evidence might be damaged or destroyed and thus of minimal or no use at trial. Or, it might be difficult to connect physical evidence with the parties before the court. Even scientific tests often provide little more than probabilities concerning the relationship of evidence to the issues in a case.

Were judges and juries required to decide cases on the basis of absolute certainty about what occurred, it is doubtful that they ever would find the standard satisfied. Whoever was required to prove the case would always lose. Recognizing that absolute certainty is not reasonably possible, American courts have chosen to demand less. How much less determines the extent to which they are willing to accept the risk of error in the course of litigation.

In criminal cases the typical requirement is that the government must prove the essential elements of any offense it chooses to charge beyond a reasonable doubt. This means that, although the decision maker need not be certain that a defendant is guilty before convicting, any reasonable doubt requires that it find the defendant not guilty. Such a standard allocates most of the risk of error in criminal cases to the state. It cannot assure that no innocent person will ever be convicted, but the standard is demanding enough to make it most unlikely that someone who is actually innocent will be found guilty. It is more likely that truly guilty persons may go free, but that is the price American criminal justice pays to avoid mistakes that harm the innocent.

It is uncertain when this standard of proof was first used in criminal cases. In early England, whether or not a person would be convicted depended on his ability to produce compurgators or to avoid misfortune in an ordeal. Subsequently, success turned on whether or not a suspect could succeed in trial by combat. As trial by jury replaced other forms of proof, the jurors originally decided cases on the basis of their own knowledge, and even if they relied on informants, the jurors themselves were responsible for the accuracy of the facts. Not until the notion of an independent fact finder, typically a jury, developed was a standard of proof very meaningful. With the development of the independent and neutral fact finder, the "beyond a reasonable doubt" concept took on importance.

Although there is no mention of the proof beyond a reasonable doubt concept in the United States Constitution, trial by jury is in all but petty cases guaranteed by the Sixth Amendment, and with the Supreme Court's decision in DUNCAN V. LOUISIANA (1968), this right is now binding on the states. By the time the Sixth Amendment was adopted, proof beyond a reasonable doubt was closely associated with the right to an impartial jury guaranteed by the Constitution in criminal cases.

Thus, it is not surprising that the Supreme Court has found the proof beyond a reasonable doubt standard to be constitutionally required in criminal cases with respect to all essential elements of offenses charged, whether the criminal case is litigated in state or federal court (IN RE WINSHIP, 1970). The Court associated the high proof standard with the strong presumption of innocence in criminal cases and observed that before a defendant may be stigmatized by criminal conviction and punished for criminal wrongdoing, DUE PROCESS requires the state to prove guilt beyond a reasonable doubt. (See *Jackson v. Virginia*, 1979.)

There is little agreement on exactly what a reasonable doubt is. No single definition of reasonable doubt has ever gained acceptance in American courts. There does seem to be some consensus that a decision maker should understand that a reasonable doubt is one based in reason as applied to the proof offered in a case. This elaboration of the standard is consistent with the oath that judges administer to jurors who are called upon to decide a case. Beyond this, it is difficult to define the term. Any language that is used is likely to be challenged as being either too demanding or not demanding enough.

Judges and juries have come to know that the proof beyond a reasonable doubt standard represents American regard for liberty and the dignity of the individual who stands against the state and who seeks to preserve his freedom and independence. A reasonable doubt will protect him.

STEPHEN A. SALTZBURG
(1986)

(SEE ALSO: *Burden of Proof.*)

Bibliography

KALVEN, HARRY, JR. and ZEISEL, HANS   1966   *The American Jury.* Boston: Little, Brown.

TRIBE, LAURENCE H.   1971   Trial by Mathematics: Precision and Ritual in the Legal Process. *Harvard Law Review* 84:1329–1393.

REASONABLE EXPECTATION OF PRIVACY

An issue of extraordinary importance in determining the scope of the protection of the FOURTH AMENDMENT is the interpretation of the word "searches" in that amendment's proscription of "unreasonable searches and seizures." If certain conduct of state or federal officials is deemed not to constitute either a search or seizure, then Fourth Amendment requirements need not be met. On the other hand, if that activity is a search or seizure, then it is unconstitutional unless those requirements—that the conduct be undertaken only upon a certain quantum of evidence (PROBABLE CAUSE), and in many instances that it be undertaken only upon prior judicial approval—have been met. How this issue comes out is a matter of considerable practical significance in criminal prosecutions, for the Fourth Amendment's EXCLUSIONARY RULE usually dictates suppression of evidence if the amendment's limitations were exceeded in acquiring it.

The Supreme Court has had difficulty in developing a workable definition of the word "searches." At an earlier time, as in *Hale v. Henkel* (1906), the Court was inclined to say that "a search ordinarily implies a quest by an officer of the law," yet it soon became clear that not every instance of seeking evidence was a search. In OLMSTEAD V. UNITED STATES (1928), for example, the Court held that the placing of a tap on telephone wires and thereby eavesdropping on the defendant's conversations was no search. As the Court later explained in SILVERMAN V. UNITED STATES (1961), there was no Fourth Amendment search unless the police had physically intruded into "a constitutionally protected area." These areas were enumerated in the Fourth Amendment itself: "persons," including the bodies and clothing of individuals; "houses," including apartments, hotel rooms, garages, business offices, stores, and warehouses; "papers," such as letters; and "effects," such as automobiles. But then came the landmark decision of KATZ V. UNITED STATES (1967), which overruled the *Silverman* standard and gave birth to the "reasonable expectation of privacy" test.

Katz was convicted in federal court on a charge of transmitting wagering information by telephone in violation of federal law. At trial the government was permitted to introduce, over defendant's objection, evidence of his end of telephone conversations, overheard by FBI agents who had attached an electronic listening and recording device to the exterior of a public telephone booth from which Katz habitually placed long-distance calls. The court of appeals affirmed Katz's conviction, reasoning that the ELECTRONIC EAVESDROPPING did not amount to a Fourth Amendment search because the microphone had not penetrated the wall of the telephone booth. Before the Supreme Court, the parties disputed whether the booth was a "constitutionally protected area," but the Court declined to address that issue, noting that "the Fourth Amendment protects people, not places. What a person knowingly exposes to the public, even in his home or office, is not a subject of Fourth Amendment protection. . . . But what he seeks to preserve as private, even in an area accessible to the public, may be constitutionally protected." The Court then held, "The Government's activities in electronically listening to and recording the petitioner's words violated the privacy upon which he justifiably relied while using the telephone booth and thus constituted a "search and seizure' within the meaning of the Fourth Amendment."

In his concurring opinion in *Katz*, Justice JOHN M. HARLAN joined the opinion of the Court, but then explained what he took this opinion to mean. Lower courts and ultimately the Supreme Court itself came to rely upon the Harlan elaboration of the *Katz* test: "My understanding of the rule that has emerged from prior decisions is that there is a twofold requirement, first that a person have exhibited an actual (subjective) expectation of privacy and, second, that the expectation be one that society is prepared to recognize as "reasonable." Courts and commentators thereafter attempted to ascertain the meaning of each of these two requirements.

The first part of the Harlan formulation arguably finds support in that part of the *Katz* majority opinion which declared that the government conduct directed at Katz "violated the privacy upon which he justifiably relied." However, an actual, subjective expectation of privacy deserves no place in a statement of what the Fourth Amendment protects. By use of a subjective test, it would be possible for the government by edict or known systematic practice to condition the expectations of the populace in such a way that no one would have any real hope of privacy. Harlan later appreciated this point, observing in his dissent in UNITED STATES V. WHITE (1971) that analysis under *Katz* must "transcend the search for subjective expectations," for "our expectations, and the risks we assume, are in large part reflections of laws that translate into rules, the customs and values of the past and present."

Although a majority of the Court acknowledged in *Smith v. Maryland* (1979) that in some situations the subjective expectation of privacy test "would provide an inadequate index of Fourth Amendment protection," the Court sometimes appears to rely on it nevertheless. Illustrative is *California v. Ciraolo* (1986), holding that the Fourth Amendment was not violated by warrantless aerial observation of marijuana plants inside a fenced backyard of a home. Though the state conceded the defendant had a subjective privacy expectation, the Court offered the gratuitous observation that because "a 10-foot fence might not shield these plants from the eyes of a citizen or a policeman perched on the top of a truck or a 2-level bus," it was "not entirely clear" whether the defendant "therefore maintained a subjective expectation of privacy from *all* observations of his backyard, or whether instead he manifested merely a hope that no one would observe his unlawful gardening pursuits." The unfortunate implication of this comment is that a defendant cannot even get by

the first *Katz* hurdle unless he has taken steps to ensure against all conceivable efforts at scrutiny.

The second branch of the Harlan elaboration in *Katz*, apparently an attempt to give content to the word "justifiably" in the majority's formation, prompted the Court on later occasions, as in TERRY V. OHIO (1968), to refer to the *Katz* rule as the "reasonable 'expectation of privacy' test." This language is perhaps unfortunate, for it might be read to mean that police activity constitutes a search whenever it uncovers incriminating actions or objects which the law's hypothetical reasonable man would expect to be private— that is, which as a matter of statistical probability were not likely to be discovered. Though the Court has wisely rejected such an interpretation, as in OLIVER V. UNITED STATES (1984), it still leaves the question of precisely what makes a reliance on privacy "justified" in the *Katz* sense.

In his *White* dissent, Harlan asserted that this question must "be answered by assessing the nature of a particular practice and the likely extent of its impact on the individual's sense of security balanced against the utility of a conduct as a technique of law enforcement." Thus, he added, "those more extensive intrusions that significantly jeopardize the sense of security which is the paramount concern of Fourth Amendment liberties" are searches. Anthony Amsterdam has similarly asserted that the "ultimate question" posed by *Katz* "is whether, if the particular form of surveillance practiced by the police is permitted to go unregulated by constitutional restraints, the amount of privacy and freedom remaining to citizens would be diminished to a compass inconsistent with the aims of a free and open society."

But this is unfortunately not how the Court has subsequently interpreted *Katz*, as is apparent from a sampling of more recent cases. In *United States v. Miller* (1976) the Court held that a person has no justified expectation of privacy in the records of his banking transactions kept at financial institutions with which he has done business, because the documents "contain only information voluntarily conveyed to the banks and exposed to their employees in the ordinary course of business." This conclusion overlooks the fact that bank employees examine checks briefly and one at a time, and thus do not construct conclusions about the customer's lifestyle, while police who study the totality of one's banking records can acquire a virtual current biography. The Court's error in *Miller* was compounded in *Smith v. Maryland*, holding that one has no legitimate expectation of privacy in the numbers he dials on his telephone because those numbers are conveyed to the telephone company's switching equipment and, in the case of long-distance calls, end up on the customer's bill. Thus, the defendant in *Smith* could not object to police use of a pen register to determine all numbers he dialed, though once again the more focused police examination of the information revealed much more than the limited and episodic scrutiny that the phone company employees might give the same numbers.

In *United States v. Knotts* (1983) the Court similarly held that it was no search for police to keep track of a person's travels by using a "beeper" because "anyone who wanted to look" could have learned, without such assistance, of the defendant's 100-mile journey from Minneapolis into rural northern Wisconsin. But to learn what the beeper revealed—that the beeper-laden container of chemicals purchased in Minneapolis was now in a particular secluded cabin 100 miles away—would have taken an army of bystanders in ready and willing communication with one another. And then there is *Ciraolo*, holding that it is no search for police to look down from an airplane into one's solid-fenced backyard because "any member of the public flying over this airspace who glanced down could have seen everything that these officers observed." This ignores the fact, as the four dissenters put it, that "the actual risk to privacy from commercial or pleasure aircraft is virtually nonexistent."

In each of these cases, a majority of the Court failed to appreciate that "privacy is not a discrete commodity, possessed absolutely or not at all" (as Justice THURGOOD MARSHALL put it in his *Smith* dissent) and that there is a dramatic difference, in privacy terms, between the sporadic disclosure of bits and pieces of information to a small and often select group for a limited purpose and a focused police examination of the totality of that information regarding a particular individual. Such decisions leave the promise of *Katz* unrealized and ignore the teachings of the Supreme Court's germinal search and seizure decision, BOYD V. UNITED STATES (1886). There, Justice JOSEPH P. BRADLEY wrote that "constitutional provisions for the security of person and property should be liberally construed" in order to forestall even "the obnoxious thing in its mildest and least repulsive form," as "illegitimate and unconstitutional practices get their first footing in that way, namely, by silent approaches and slight deviations from legal modes of procedure."

Some hope—modest, given the outcome of the case—is to be found in *Florida v. Riley* (1989), holding that an officer's naked-eye observation into the defendant's residential greenhouse from a helicopter 400 feet off the ground was no search. Significant for present purposes is the observation of Justice HARRY A. BLACKMUN, dissenting, that a "majority of the Court" (the four dissenters and one concurring Justice) believe that the reasonableness of the defendant's expectations "depends, in large measure, on the frequency of nonpolice helicopter flights at an altitude of 400 feet." This means, Justice WILLIAM J. BRENNAN concluded in his dissent, that a majority of the Court does not accept "the plurality's exceedingly grudging Fourth Amendment theory, [whereunder] the expectation of privacy is defeated if a single member of the public could conceivably position herself to see into the area in question without doing anything illegal." *Riley* thus may signal a rejection of the all-or-nothing approach to privacy, thereby giving the *Katz* reasonable expectation of privacy test new meaning.

WAYNE R. LAFAVE
(1992)

(SEE ALSO: *Open Fields Doctrine; Plain View Doctrine; Right of Privacy; Search and Seizure; Unreasonable Search; Warrantless Searches; Wiretapping.*)

Bibliography

AMSTERDAM, ANTHONY G. 1974 Perspectives on the Fourth Amendment. *Minnesota Law Review* 58:349–477.

GUTTERMAN, MELVIN 1988 A Formulation of the Value and Means Models of the Fourth Amendment in the Age of Technologically Enhanced Surveillance. *Syracuse Law Review* 39: 647–735.

JUNKER, JOHN M. 1989 The Structure of the Fourth Amendment: The Scope of the Protection. *Journal of Criminal Law and Criminology* 79:1105–1184.

REASONABLE SEARCH

See: Unreasonable Search

RECALL

Among the reforms introduced during the Progressive era was the recall, a device by which the people, at an election, can remove an official from office before his term expires. Unlike IMPEACHMENT, recall does not involve an accusation of criminality or misconduct, and it is commonly used when the official decides or acts contrary to the opinion of a significant segment of his constituency.

Although recall is widely used at the state and local levels, there is no provision for recall of national officials. Moreover, because senators and representatives hold office under the United States Constitution, they are not subject to recall under state law.

DENNIS J. MAHONEY
(1986)

RECIPROCAL TAX IMMUNITIES

See: Intergovernmental Immunity

RECONSTRUCTION

The Framers of the Constitution did not anticipate a civil war or contemplate the constitutional problems in rebuilding the Union after such a conflict. From ABRAHAM LINCOLN's first proposal for restoring the Union in 1863 to the withdrawal of the last federal troops from the South in 1877, Reconstruction was at heart a series of constitutional questions involving the power of the federal government vis-à-vis the states and the relations among the various branches of the national government.

The key issue from the very beginning centered on the nature of the Union. The South claimed that as a compact of states, the Union could be dissolved by the single expedient of the sovereign states choosing to withdraw. The North saw the Union as indissoluble. As Chief Justice SALMON P. CHASE later wrote in TEXAS V. WHITE (1869), "The Constitution, in all its provisions, looks to an indestructible Union, composed of indestructible States." The northern view had prevailed by force of arms, and the Union had been preserved. But if the states had never left the Union, as Lincoln had claimed throughout the CIVIL WAR, then why would a reconstruction be necessary to put them back in a status they had never left?

Lincoln approached this question in the same commonsense manner he had approached the war. The Constitution did not specifically authorize the federal government to deal with a civil war, but it was inconceivable that the Framers had not intended for the government to have all the adequate powers to preserve and defend itself. Throughout the war, Lincoln relied on the "adequacy of the Constitution" theory to justify actions that could not be grounded on a specific constitutional clause.

Common sense told him that if theoretically the states could not leave the Union, in initiating the war they had at least left their proper role in that Union, and some actions would have to be taken to make theory and reality whole again. The Ten-Percent Plan, whereby one-tenth of a state's 1860 voters would swear support of the Constitution and "reestablish" state government in return for presidential recognition, must be seen not as Lincoln's final word on the subject but as a wartime measure designed to draw the southern states back with the promise of leniency. Moreover, Lincoln wanted to retain his flexibility; if the Ten-Percent Plan worked, well and good, but if not, then he would try something else. The President vetoed the WADE-DAVIS BILL not because he disagreed with its provisions but because it left him too little room for maneuver. The three state governments set up under Lincoln's plan proved failures, and there is evidence that the President and Congress were moving toward agreement on a new plan at the time of his assassination.

Where Lincoln had shown flexibility and open-mindedness in approaching the problem, his successor took a rigid and uncompromising position: the States had never left the Union, and therefore the federal government had no business telling them what they had to do in order to return to the Union. In ANDREW JOHNSON's mind, Reconstruction amounted to little more than a brief period of readjustment, with oversight over this readjustment completely a presidential function. Just as Lincoln, as COMMANDER-IN-CHIEF, had the constitutional authority for directing the war, so now he, as commander-in-chief, would have similar power in tidying up the last few problems of that war. In taking this view, Johnson completely misunderstood how Lincoln had worked closely with congressional leaders to have Congress support his policies.

Over the summer of 1865 the southern states, at Johnson's direction, held conventions to revise their constitutions (primarily to abolish SLAVERY) and to elect representatives to Congress. In the President's mind, when these representatives joined the Thirty-ninth Congress in December 1865, the Union would be whole and the readjustment process at an end. He did not believe then or later that Congress had any power to force the southern states to do anything they did not freely choose to do themselves. The former Tennessee senator, unlike many of his southern colleagues, had been a strong defender of the Union, but like them he shared a strong commitment to STATES' RIGHTS.

Congress obviously did not share Johnson's view and recognized that if it seated the southern representatives, Reconstruction would be at an end before the legislators could examine the situation or frame their own plan. Moreover, they believed that the people of the North wanted assurances that the fruits of their victory—the preservation of the Union and the abolition of slavery—would be protected in the peace to follow. With congressional refusal to seat the southerners, two conflicts began, one between the national government and the former Confederate states and the other between Congress and the President, both revolving around the question of what powers the national government had over the states.

Congress passed several bills in early 1866 to assist the newly freed blacks and to create legal protections for their rights. Supporters of these measures relied on what they considered the broad mandate of the THIRTEENTH AMENDMENT, ratified in December 1865, which included the first enforcement clause in any amendment. Some scholars have suggested that it is the Thirteenth, and not the Fourteenth, Amendment that recast relations between the states and the national government by giving Congress power over what had hitherto been an internal state matter.

When Congress discussed Reconstruction in early

1866, many Republicans believed that the Thirteenth Amendment by itself gave Congress sufficient power to carry out the broad aims of giving the former slaves full rights as citizens of the United States. Freedom, as they saw it, involved not just the formal abolition of slavery but also the eradication of any signs of inferior status. According to this view, Congress had all necessary power to enact whatever LEGISLATION it thought necessary and proper to secure these goals.

Andrew Johnson, however, claimed that the amendment did little more than formally abolish slavery, and although the evidence is strong that its framers meant more than that, the Republican leadership in Congress worried that the Supreme Court might adopt his view. One can therefore see the FOURTEENTH AMENDMENT as an effort to clarify the ORIGINAL INTENT of the Thirteenth and as Congress's Reconstruction plan. By making its goals explicit through a constitutional amendment, Congress intended to quiet all concerns about the legitimacy of its plan.

One should also note that aside from invalidation of the Confederate debt and restrictions on some leaders of the rebellion, the Fourteenth Amendment was not punitive. Congress, as well as Johnson, wanted to see the southern states back in their proper role as quickly as possible. This is clear in the June 1866 report of the JOINT COMMITTEE ON RECONSTRUCTION, which, while documenting southern intransigence and oppression of the freedom, is moderate in tone. Ratify the Fourteenth Amendment, the report implies, and welcome back. In fact, Tennessee, which had always had a large Unionist faction, promptly ratified and Congress admitted it back into the Union in 1866.

The committee report is also noteworthy for its discussion of the constitutional issues involved in Reconstruction. Aside from repudiating Johnson's view of Reconstruction as solely a presidential function, it examined the constitutional status of the former Confederate states. In talking about "forfeited rights," it struck a position halfway between those who claimed that the states had never left the Union and therefore had retained all their rights and the radical view of "state suicide," in which the states had ceased to exist as legal entities. Rather, the states had as a result of their rebellion forfeited basic political rights as members of the Union and, until restored fully to the Union, could enjoy only those rights granted to them by the Congress. The report relied on the fact that the Constitution assigned the power for creating new states to Congress, not the President; by implication the task of refixing the states in the Union also belonged to Congress.

The report is a commonsensical effort to deal with practical problems, but its theoretical basis is inconsistent. The states had forfeited all rights and existed as states only at the sufferance of Congress, yet they were being asked to exercise one of the most important political powers under the Constitution—changing the organic framework of government through amendment.

At Johnson's urging, the other southern states refused to follow Tennessee's example, and this refusal raised the question of whether ratification of the amendment required three-fourths of those states still in the Union or three-fourths of all the states—including the southern states now in a constitutional limbo. Here again one can only contrast Johnson's rigid adherence to a theoretical premise that flew in the face of the reality and Congress's efforts to reach a workable solution of a problem fraught with constitutional bombshells.

The election of 1866 ought to have made clear to Johnson that the North overwhelmingly favored the congressional Republican position, but he continued his efforts to thwart Congress. The events of 1867, with continuing tensions between President and legislature, led to a political impasse unforeseen by the Framers—a chief executive who, repudiated at the polls, refused to accept that judgment and who did his best, not to execute duly passed laws of Congress, but to thwart their implementation. There is an ongoing debate over what the Framers intended as grounds for IMPEACHMENT, but a number of scholars believe that the device serves as an instrument of last resort for resolving a political deadlock that would otherwise paralyze the government. Although the Senate failed to convict by a single vote, the impeachment proceeding had the desired effect: while Johnson still refused to cooperate with Congress, he no longer attempted to obstruct its will. By then, however, the damage had been done; the intransigence of the southern states, encouraged by Johnson, led to a prolonged Reconstruction and a legacy of bitterness.

Hovering in back of much of the congressional debate in 1866 and 1867 was a concern over what the Supreme Court would say in regard to the Reconstruction statutes. By then, no one questioned the power of the Court to declare acts of Congress unconstitutional, and if the Justices should adhere to the traditional view of limiting federal interference in state affairs, then the entire congressional program might be voided. The Court's decision in EX PARTE MILLIGAN (1866) and in two cases striking down LOYALTY OATHS alarmed Congress, which quickly passed a law narrowing the Court's jurisdiction in certain areas. But in the only case in which the Court directly addressed the constitutional question of Reconstruction, *Texas v. White* (1869), the Court confirmed the congressional view that whatever the theoretical relationship of the states to the Union, the war had at least temporarily suspended that relationship and its associated rights.

While Reconstruction was no doubt a political disaster for all concerned, constitutionally it has confirmed the approach taken initially by Lincoln and later by the Congress that in extreme situations one has to interpret the docu-

derstanding clauses, and other devices to achieve black disfranchisement.

                                    LEONARD W. LEVY
                                         (1986)

REFERENDUM

Among the political reforms introduced during the Progressive era was the referendum, by which acts of the legislature are referred to the people for their approval or rejection at an election. Referenda may be initiated by the legislature itself or by petition of the people. The referendum is a check on such abuses as corrupt legislation or blatantly partisan gerrymandering of legislative districts (see GERRYMANDER) but it also provides a way for politicians to avoid responsibility for controversial measures.

Reformers have frequently advocated a national referendum procedure. However, legislation authorizing a national referendum would probably be unconstitutional, and an amendment authorizing it would almost certainly fail to receive congressional approval.

                                    DENNIS J. MAHONEY
                                         (1986)

REGAN v. WALD
468 U.S. 222 (1984)

A 1982 Treasury Department regulation prohibited travel-related business transactions with Cuba. Persons who wished to travel to Cuba, but were inhibited from doing so by the regulation, sued to enjoin its enforcement. The Supreme Court, 5–4, followed ZEMEL V. RUSK (1965) and HAIG V. AGEE (1981) in rejecting claims based on the RIGHT TO TRAVEL protected by the Fifth Amendment's DUE PROCESS clause. The dissenters argued that Congress had not authorized the regulation.

                                    KENNETH L. KARST
                                         (1986)

REGENTS OF UNIVERSITY OF CALIFORNIA v. BAKKE
438 U.S. 265 (1978)

Perhaps the Supreme Court's majority in DEFUNIS V. ODEGAARD (1974) thought a delay in deciding on the constitutionality of racial preferences in state university admissions would give time for development of a political consensus on the issue. The result was just the opposite; by the time *Bakke* was decided, the question of RACIAL QUOTAS and preferences had become bitterly divisive.

Bakke, a nonminority applicant, had been denied admission to the university's medical school at Davis. His state court suit had challenged the school's program setting aside for minority applicants sixteen places in an entering class of 100. Bakke's test scores and grades exceeded those of most minority admittees. The California Supreme Court held that the racial preference denied Bakke the EQUAL PROTECTION OF THE LAWS guaranteed by the FOURTEENTH AMENDMENT.

A fragmented United States Supreme Court agreed, 5–4, that Bakke was entitled to admission, but concluded, in a different 5–4 alignment, that race could be taken into account in a state university's admissions. Four Justices thought the Davis quota violated Title VI of the CIVIL RIGHTS ACT OF 1964, which forbids the exclusion of anyone on account of race from any program aided by federal funds. This position was rejected, 5–4. Four other Justices argued that the Davis quota was constitutionally valid as a reasonable, nonstigmatizing remedy for past societal discrimination against racial and ethnic minorities. This view was rejected by Justice LEWIS F. POWELL, who concluded that the Davis quota was a denial of equal protection. His vote, along with the votes of the four Justices who found a Title VI violation, placed Bakke in Davis's 1978 entering class.

Justice Powell's opinion on the constitutional question began by rejecting the notion of a "BENIGN" RACIAL CLASSIFICATION. He concluded that the burden of remedying past societal discrimination could not constitutionally be placed on individuals who had no part in that discrimination—absent the sort of constitutional violation that had been found in school DESEGREGATION cases such as SWANN V. CHARLOTTE-MECKLENBURG BOARD OF EDUCATION (1971), where color-conscious remedies had been approved. While rejecting quotas, Justice Powell approved the use of race as one factor in a state university's admissions policy for the purpose of promoting diversity in its student body.

Race is relevant to "diversity," of course, mainly because past societal discrimination has made race relevant to a student's attitudes and experiences. And if one's membership in a racial group may be a factor in the admissions process, it may be the decisive factor in a particular case. The Powell opinion thus anticipates a preference for minority applicants; how much of a preference will depend, as he says, on "some attention to numbers"—that is, the number of minority students already admitted. The difference between such a system and a racial quota is mostly symbolic.

The press hailed Justice Powell's opinion as a judgment of Solomon. As a contribution to principled argument about equal protection doctrine, it failed. As a political solution, however, it was a triumph. The borders of preference became blurred, so that no future applicant could blame her rejection on the preference. At the same time, a university following a "diversity" approach to admissions was made safe from constitutional attack. AFFIRMATIVE ACTION was thus saved, even as Bakke was ushered into medical school and racial quotas ringingly denounced. Almost miraculously, the issue of racial preferences in higher education virtually disappeared from the political scene, and legislative proposals to abolish affirmative action were shelved. Solomon, it will be recalled, succeeded in saving the baby.

KENNETH L. KARST
(1986)

Bibliography

BLASI, VINCENT 1979 Bakke as Precedent: Does Mr. Justice Powell Have a Theory? *California Law Review* 67:21–68.

KARST, KENNETH L. and HOROWITZ, HAROLD W. 1979 The Bakke Opinions and Equal Protection Doctrine. *Harvard Civil Rights-Civil Liberties Law Review* 14:7–29.

WILKINSON, J. HARVIE, III 1979 *From Brown to Bakke*. New York: Oxford University Press.

REGULATORY AGENCIES

Regulatory agencies are governmental bodies created by legislatures to carry out specified state or national policies. Such an agency is typically responsible for regulating one particular area of social or economic life; it is staffed by specialists who develop the knowledge and experience necessary to enforce complex regulatory laws. Regulatory agencies normally combine the powers to make rules, to adjudicate controversies, and to provide ordinary administrative services, functions corresponding to the legislative, judicial, and executive powers of the separate branches of government. They fill in the gaps of general policy by bringing order, method, and uniformity to the process of modern government.

Although administrative agencies are as old as the federal government, the national regulatory process as we know it today began with the creation of the Interstate Commerce Commission in 1887. Granted extensive authority over the booming railroad industry, the commission received broad rule-making and adjudicatory powers, broader than those of any previous agency. It set the trend, and the goal, for future agencies by being the first governmental unit "whose single concern was the well-being," as James Landis said, "in a broad public sense, of a vital and national industry."

Since the NEW DEAL, regulatory agencies have become the most visible tool for the achievement of national policy. They provide a form of centralized supervision which

in earlier periods of American history was deemed neither necessary nor desirable. Their proliferation paralleled the development of national industries and the emergence of Congress as a policymaking body unable to supervise the details of administration. At the same time, a growing welfare state has recognized new interests such as welfare entitlements and equal employment opportunity. New regulatory agencies have been created to provide sympathetic administration of the new national policy goals, and to resolve conflicts by procedures less formalized and adversarial—and far less costly—than those prevailing in courts of law.

The character and origin of a regulatory agency depend on the nature of its tasks. Generally, such agencies fall into three main categories: independent regulatory commissions; executive agencies; and government corporations. The independent commissions, so called because of their relative freedom from executive control, are the most important, and include such agencies as the Interstate Commerce Commission (ICC), Securities and Exchange Commission (SEC), Federal Trade Commission (FTC), National Labor Relations Board (NLRB), and Nuclear Regulatory Commission (NRC). Each independent commission is headed by a multimember board appointed by the President with the ADVICE AND CONSENT of the Senate. Congress has sought to guarantee the commissions' independence by establishing their governing boards on a bipartisan basis, providing fixed terms of office for board members, and authorizing the President to remove them only for reasons specified by statute.

The executive agency, an example of which is the Environmental Protection Agency, is one whose administrator and top assistants are appointed by the President, to whom they report directly and who may remove them freely. The executive agency lies squarely within the executive branch; its position within the constitutional framework of SEPARATION OF POWERS is thus more clearly defined than that of the independent regulatory agencies. The government corporation, an example of which is the Tennessee Valley Authority, is created by statute for a stated purpose and is wholly owned by the government. This model has been used when a project, because of its duration or its required investment, cannot easily be achieved through private development.

Regulatory agencies differ significantly in the range of their powers and their modes of operation. For example, the work of the NLRB is almost exclusively judicial in character. Although it has broad authority under the WAGNER ACT and TAFT-HARTLEY ACT, the NLRB has chosen to exercise only adjudicatory powers. The Equal Employment Opportunity Commission, on the other hand, has no formal power to adjudicate claims or impose administrative sanctions. The sensitive and highly controversial character of its mission—to carry out the antidiscrimination provisions of Title VII of the CIVIL RIGHTS ACT OF 1964— prompted Congress to limit EEOC's authority to "informal methods of conference, conciliation, and persuasion." If these methods fail the alleged victim of discrimination may sue in federal court. Even though EEOC itself may not issue final orders, its guidelines for dealing with patterns of discrimination in employment, together with its field investigations in particular cases, often induce compliance. The result is a significant regulatory effect.

An immense body of administrative law, found in the voluminous *Code of Federal Regulations* and in a multitude of specialized publications, has been created by these and other administrative agencies.

The development and structure of regulatory agencies have strained the constitutional theory of separation of powers, for the agencies typically blend functions of all three branches of government. Yet the Supreme Court has sought to accommodate the constitutional theory with the needs of effective government, and thus to preserve the constitutional balance underscored by the principle of separation of powers. The constitutional basis for Congress's power to create regulatory agencies is derived from Article I. Section 1 grants "[a]ll legislative powers" to Congress; section 8 enumerates these powers and vests Congress with the additional power to make laws NECESSARY AND PROPER for carrying them into effect. Regulatory agencies have always been regarded as necessary and proper means of achieving the ends of national policy.

Implicit in the theory of separation of powers is the doctrine that delegated authority cannot be redelegated. Under this principle Congress cannot constitutionally invest the executive (or, for that matter, the judiciary) with the power of legislation. How then is it possible to justify the rule-making power conferred on agencies? The Supreme Court's answer is that such authority is permissible if the authorizing statute embodies a policy and provides guidelines to channel administrative action. Of course, within these guidelines agencies exercise considerable discretion. In theory, however, they are not legislating in a constitutional sense when exercising their discretion; they are simply carrying out legislative policies established by Congress.

Reality, however, had not easily converged with theory. Despite its reiteration of the doctrine forbidding delegation, the Supreme Court has consistently allowed "directionless" delegations of legislative authority. Not until the 1930s did the Court actually invalidate congressional statutes for excessive delegation of legislative power. But these precedents soon fell from favor as the Court proceeded to uphold subsequent legislative mandates as vague as those previously nullified. Some delegations have been disturbingly broad. For example, the Federal Com-

munications Commission is to use its licensing power in the "public convenience, interest, or necessity." The Court upheld this "supple instrument" of delegation as being "as concrete as the complicated factors for judgement in such a field" permit. Nevertheless, the doctrine forbidding delegation still lives in theory. As recently as 1974, in *National Cable Television v. United States*, the Supreme Court construed a federal statute narrowly so as to avoid the implication from a literal reading of the statute that taxing power—clearly a legislative function—had been conferred on the Federal Communications Commission.

The doctrine forbidding legislative delegation has had its corollary in challenges to the constitutionality of regulatory agencies' exercise of judicial functions. The contention is that these functions are inconsistent with Article III's grant of the JUDICIAL POWER to courts. Yet the Supreme Court has upheld the delegation of adjudicatory functions to regulatory agencies, so long as the courts retain power to determine whether the agencies have acted within their legislative mandates.

The obverse of the delegation issue concerns strategies by which Congress may take back authority it has granted. Despite congressional efforts to ensure their independence, regulatory agencies came under criticism of liberals who complained that, instead of regulating in the public interest, the agencies had become the clients of the special interest they were supposed to regulate. More recently, conservatives have attacked regulatory agencies for pervasive bureaucratization, for growing unaccountability, and for disregard of their legislative mandates. The congressional response to these criticisms has taken a number of forms, including attempts to deregulate certain industries and the effort to reserve a power of LEGISLATIVE VETO of agency actions.

The legislative veto, adopted by Congress with increasing frequency in the 1970s, when public criticism of regulatory agencies was at its zenith, poses serious constitutional issues. Congress required various executive agencies to report to it in advance of specified kinds of proposed action. Then, if Congress (or, in some cases, one house of Congress) should adopt a resolution of disapproval within a certain time, the proposed action was effectively "vetoed." The Supreme Court held this mechanism unconstitutional in IMMIGRATION AND NATURALIZATION SERVICE V. CHADHA (1983), as applied to the one-house veto of a deportation order. First, the Court held, the congressional veto was a legislative act requiring passage by both houses of Congress. Second, and more serious, the congressional veto offended Article II, which requires any legislative act to be presented to the President for his approval before it takes effect.

The President as chief executive is commanded by Article II of the Constitution to "take care that the Laws be faithfully executed." From an early time, Presidents claimed an inherent constitutional power to remove any executive official whom they or their predecessors had appointed. This claim was vindicated in MYERS V. UNITED STATES (1926). But in HUMPHREY'S EXECUTOR V. UNITED STATES (1935) the Supreme Court refused to apply this theory of inherent power to the removal of a member of an independent agency exercising quasi-legislative and quasi-judicial powers. Distinguishing between a "purely executive" officer and an officer of an independent agency, the Court sustained Congress's authority, when creating regulatory agencies, to fix the terms of commissioners and specify the exclusive grounds for their removal. In *Weiner v. United States* (1958) this principle was applied to the removal of a member of the War Claims Commission, whose organizing statute specified no grounds for removal. The Court noted the adjudicatory nature of the agency's work, and thus concluded that Congress had not made it part of the executive establishment under the political control of the President. The Supreme Court has recognized that independent agencies cannot exercise their statutory duties fairly or impartially, as Congress intended, unless they are free from executive control.

The combination of investigatory, prosecutorial, and adjudicatory functions within the same regulatory agency has also been the subject of constitutional litigation. In *Winthrop v. Larkin* (1975), however, the Supreme Court reaffirmed its long-standing view that the mixture of these functions within a single agency or person does not violate DUE PROCESS unless the presumption of honesty and integrity of officers exercising these functions is overcome by evidence of actual bias or prejudgment in a particular case. Even though the separation of these functions within the regulatory context is not constitutionally commanded, legislators have often concluded that the best mix of efficiency and impartiality is maintained when prosecutorial and judicial functions are performed by different officers within an agency.

All regulatory agencies are subject to the constitutional requirement of PROCEDURAL DUE PROCESS. The right to a hearing must be granted when an agency takes action directly affecting rights and obligations: those affected must be given NOTICE and an opportunity to present their case in a FAIR HEARING. The process due in any particular case depends on the nature of the liberty or property interest involved. If these interests are constitutionally recognized then notice and even a prior hearing may be required before agency action can be taken. Whether the RIGHT TO COUNSEL, cross-examination, and other trial-type procedures will be required depends on the importance of the private interest at stake when balanced against the government's interest and the risk of erroneous deprivation under an agency's normal operating procedures.

The extent to which agency determinations are subject to judicial review is governed by the Administrative Procedure Act. Generally, administrative action is unreviewable if committed by statute to agency discretion. Courts may, however, set aside even discretionary action when it is "arbitrary, capricious, an abuse of discretion, or otherwise not in accordance with law." Under the act, the courts are to sustain agency findings of fact if they are supported by substantial evidence. Although the definition of "substantial" may differ from court to court, the Supreme Court retains the final say on whether the rule has been properly applied in a given case.

DONALD P. KOMMERS
(1986)

Bibliography

DAVIS, KENNETH C. 1969 *Discretionary Justice.* Baton Rouge: Louisiana State University Press.
FREEDMAN, JAMES O. 1978 *Crisis and Legitimacy.* Cambridge: At the University Press.
KOHLMEIER, LOUIS M. 1969 *The Regulators.* New York: Harper & Row.
LANDIS, JAMES 1938 *The Administrative Process.* New Haven, Conn.: Yale University Press.
REDFORD, EMMETT S. 1969 *The Regulatory Process.* Austin: University of Texas Press.

REGULATORY TAKINGS

The central disputes of modern takings law revolve around the legal rules governing the dispossession and regulation of private PROPERTY under the takings clause of the Fifth Amendment, which states: "nor shall private property be taken for public use, without just compensation." The point of departure for this analysis is the Supreme Court's critical decision in LUCAS V. SOUTH CAROLINA COASTAL COUNCIL (1992).

The expression "regulatory taking" is a relatively recent addition to the Court's lexicon, having been formally introduced in the dissent of Justice WILLIAM J. BRENNAN, JR., in *San Diego Gas & Electric Co. v. City of San Diego* (1981). Even before the terminology took hold, however, the Court had struggled over the classification of various government actions that in some fashion denied or restricted the use that a private owner could make of his own land. The "easy" cases have long involved the physical TAKING OF PROPERTY; that is, cases in which the government has forced a private party to part with permanent possession of all or part (even a very small part) of private property, which is then occupied or used by the government itself or by some private individual under government authorization. In these cases, the Court has gravitated toward a rule of virtual per se compensability on the ground that the exclusive right to possession is the cardinal element of a system of private property. Denial of that FUNDAMENTAL RIGHT to JUST COMPENSATION is not justified or excused by any gain that the state realizes from the occupation or use of the property in question. The public benefit may justify the government taking, but it does not excuse government from its obligation to pay for damages. It is hard to see how the rule could be otherwise without gutting the just compensation requirement of the takings clause.

The hard question asks what, if anything, should be done with those government regulations that allow a landowner to retain exclusive possession of his land, but restrict the way in which he may use it. The types of restrictions in question include the traditional setbacks for building, or density requirements for planned-unit development. More recently, these restrictions have expanded to embrace total or partial moratoria on private development imposed for environmental objectives: lands are designated as wetlands, sensitive dunes, coastal lands, or habitat for an endangered species. The restrictions on use could be total or partial, and they could have a large or small impact on the value of the regulated land. The burning question is which, if any, of these restrictions require the state to compensate the owner of the property, and how much.

These questions have provoked a heated judicial debate, but the outlines of the current position have been clarified to some degree by Justice ANTONIN SCALIA's 1992 opinion in *Lucas*. That opinion uses two tests to determine whether the state owed compensation when it imposed land use restrictions. The first asks whether the property continues to have any viable economic use after the restrictions are imposed. The second asks whether, if no viable economic use survives, the state can advance some legitimate interest to justify the restriction in question. If, however, the land use restriction does not wholly destroy the land's entire economic value, then the state prevails without having to show the justifications demanded in cases of total economic loss. As applied to the *Lucas* case itself, the Court tests required the South Carolina Coastal Council to pay Lucas full value for two plots of land on which it prevented him from building any houses. The promotion of tourism within the region and the possible prevention of the further deterioration of public beachfront property did not fall within the nuisance-prevention rationales needed to justify the regulation.

The first question posed by *Lucas* asks why total and partial land use restrictions are treated differently. One explanation is that the test was designed to reaffirm the soundness of earlier cases that had held that government restrictions on new uses of currently productive property withstand taking challenges. For example, in PENN CEN-TRAL TRANSPORTATION CO. V. NEW YORK CITY (1978), the owner of the profitable Penn Central terminal did not receive compensation, solely because it was prohibited from building a new addition in the upper airspace. The test does not, however, answer the question of whether an owner is deprived of all economic use when the prohibition against further development is applied to buildings that cannot turn a profit under current use. Under current law, the owner is likely to face an uphill battle to gain further rights of development, except in the so-called exaction cases in which the state seeks to condition the grant of a building permit on the surrender of some possessory interest in land, such as a public easement across the property. In these cases the strict compensation requirement of the physical cases is applied, notwithstanding the owner's consent to the bundled transaction that contains both the permit approval and the surrender of the possessory interest.

The economic viability test poses greater problems in evaluating land use restrictions on vacant property slated for private development. *Lucas* was the easy case for compensation because the state's total prohibition rendered the property worthless. But state and local governments have learned that partial restrictions on land use can slow down and perhaps block development without running afoul of the takings clause. Determined local governments frequently shower individual landowners with boundless DUE PROCESS, which allows (and requires) repeated submissions of new development plans for detailed public examination. The chance that development will be approved allows the state to take advantage of the well-established Court rule that bars a landowner from court until a final adverse judgment has been made on its permit applications. But this tactic raises delicate factual disputes over whether the restrictions imposed are so severe that all economic value has been drained out of the project even if formal permission to build has been or may be granted. The upshot is that expert witnesses must often speculate as to whether any rational builder could turn a profit within established conditions.

Unfortunately, the Court has left it unclear how the cutoff line for viability should be determined. Suppose land costs $100 to acquire and new construction for the best project allowed by the government costs $200. If that project is worth only $150 on completion, then the landowner makes a compelling case that he has lost all economic viability of the land. The owner loses in both respects: the cost of the improvement exceeds its benefit, and nothing is recouped for the cost of the land. Next suppose that the best possible project is worth $250 on completion. Now economic viability is highly contested, because the allowable project permits the landowner to recover his variable costs but requires him to lose some portion of the initial investment in the land. Here it is better to classify the project as nonviable because its total costs exceed total benefits once the regulation is put into place. No one would purchase land unless the initial costs were protected against subsequent state regulation. But the sharp reduction in the capital value of land is a common feature of ZONING restrictions, and so it is still unclear as to how a landowner with undeveloped property would fare with this type of claim. It may well be that he has greater chances of success in attacking a denial of a specific permit than a general zoning ordinance, because the individualized determination in the permit case opens up greater avenues of abuse. But the outcome is unclear today.

Nonetheless, it appears that the project is economically viable if an especially advantageous new project—total cost $300—could generate $500 before regulation but only $400 after regulation. In this case, the losses from regulation reduce anticipated profits but do not impose out-of-pocket costs. In effect, the superior opportunities of the astute owner are put at risk under regulation. The same result appears to hold if raw land originally costs $100 but appreciates to $500 before regulation reduces its value back to $100. Now state regulation that reduces its value to its original cost will probably survive constitutional challenge. In effect, the takings clause is read to protect only the original cost, but not the value of property. That result introduces a troublesome asymmetry by allowing the state to capture land appreciation while saddling the owner with its depreciation. Thus if the land had been sold to a new owner for $500 before the regulation was imposed, then value has been converted into cost, increasing the likelihood that compensation must be paid. But why encourage individuals to make useless sales of property in order to insulate themselves from the adverse effects of regulation? In principle, the strongest line is to insist that any reduction in value attributable to land use restrictions be compensable unless it has been justified in light of some legitimate PUBLIC PURPOSE.

What purposes will justify the state's total destruction of the value in land? Scalia's answer turned to the state law of nuisance (as represented by the Restatement of Torts), which generally allows either the state or private owners to enjoin various forms of discharges (such as pollution) that enter either public lands and waters, or the land or water of other private individuals. This antinuisance limitation is held to be "inherent in the fee simple title," which means in effect that the state has done little more than enforce long-standing limitations on land use that private landowners could enforce in disputes with each other. The great advantage of this test is that it prevents neighbors from resorting to the political process to take interests in land that they (collectively) would have

to purchase if acting in their individual capacities. So understood, the legitimate public purpose test failed in *Lucas* because no one could claim that the construction of a single-family home in keeping with neighboring lots could rise to the level of a COMMON LAW nuisance.

A broad gap exists, however, between the ordinary single-family home and garden-variety nuisances. It is unclear in individual cases whether state restrictions could be justified on the belief that the public is entitled to a viewing easement over private land; or whether the federal and state governments may refuse to grant dredging and filling permits; or whether habitat preservation of endangered species falls under the Endangered Species Act. Classically, these cases involved government restrictions that provide unquestioned public benefits, many of which extend not only to local landowners, but (as with the preservation of endangered species) to the public at large. At present, some lower courts have shown an erratic willingness to hew to the narrower common law definition of nuisance in these regulatory takings cases. Substantial monetary judgments for individualized burdens have become more common in recent years.

Most recently, the Supreme Court affirmed, in *City of Monterey v. Del Monte Dunes* (1999), an award of substantial damages to a landowner who had received an endless run-around from local land use regulators about the possible development of its thirty-eight-acre beachfront property site. The case upheld the right of landowners to have jury trials on both key issues in a modern regulatory takings case—did the regulation deprive the landowner of all viable economic use, and was there a state justification for the restrictions it imposed. *Monterey* also held that the "substantial proportionality" test of DOLAN V. CITY OF TIGARD (1994) did not apply to ordinary land use cases. But overall it gave little guidance as to what principles governed or why. The full issue will doubtless return to the Supreme Court for further clarification.

The issue of takings has transmuted itself into the familiar question of what level of scrutiny should be applied to evaluate the state interest in imposing its land use restrictions. The traditional view since the court's decision in EUCLID V. AMBLER REALTY (1926) has used general deference to justify the low RATIONAL BASIS standard of review. The large battle in takings is whether the Court's renewed interest in the area will lead to movement away from deference and toward higher scrutiny of land use decisions.

RICHARD A. EPSTEIN
(2000)

Bibliography

COYLE, DENNIS 1993 *Property Rights and the Constitution: Shaping Society Through Land Use Regulation.* Albany: State of New York Press.

EPSTEIN, RICHARD A. 1993 *Lucas v. South Carolina Coastal Council:* A Tangled Web of Expectations. *Stanford Law Review* 45:1369–1392.

——— 1997 *Babbitt v. Sweet Home Chapters of Oregon:* The Law and Economics of Habitat Preservation. *Supreme Court Economic Review* 5:1–57.

FARBER, DANIEL A. 1992 Economic Analysis and Just Compensation: An Anti-Discrimination Theory of Takings. *International Review of Law and Economics* 12:125–138.

FISCHEL, WILLIAM A. 1995 *Regulatory Takings: Law, Economics, and Politics.* Cambridge, Mass.: Harvard University Press.

TREANOR, WILLIAM MICHAEL 1995 The Original Understanding of the Takings Clause and the Political Process. *Columbia Law Review* 95:782–887.

REHABILITATION ACT
87 Stat. 355 (1973)

In addition to providing funding and research incentives for various programs to aid the handicapped, Congress incorporated antidiscrimination provisions into the Rehabilitation Act. In federally assisted programs, the act prohibits discrimination solely by reason of handicap against an "otherwise qualified handicapped individual." In addition, the act requires federal executive agencies to take AFFIRMATIVE ACTION to employ handicapped individuals. In *Southeastern Community College v. Davis* (1979) the Supreme Court held that the Rehabilitation Act does not forbid a nursing school from imposing relevant physical qualifications upon participants in its training programs.

THEODORE EISENBERG
(1986)

(SEE ALSO: *Disabilities, Rights of Persons With; Disability Discrimination.*)

Bibliography

BURGDORF, ROBERT L., JR. 1980 *The Legal Rights of Handicapped Persons.* Baltimore: Paul H. Brookes Publishing Co.

REHEARING

A party who is dissatisfied with the court's decision or opinion in a case may request the court to reconsider. The term "rehearing" refers to such a reconsideration, usually by an appellate court.

By statute, the Supreme Court's APPELLATE JURISDICTION over cases coming from the state courts is limited to questions of federal law that have been properly drawn in question in the lower courts. This requirement normally is not satisfied by a litigant who raises a federal question for the first time in a petition for rehearing after a state supreme court has decided the case. However, if the state court entertains the petition and actually considers the federal question, the question can be brought to the Supreme Court.

The Supreme Court itself receives between 100 and 200 petitions for rehearing each year, seeking reconsideration of its own decisions or opinions. Fewer than one percent of these petitions are granted. By rule, the Court has provided that a petition for rehearing will be granted only by the vote of a majority of the Justices, including at least one Justice who concurred in the decision. By custom, a Justice who did not participate in that decision does not vote on the petition for rehearing.

One occasion for granting a petition for rehearing is the case in which the Supreme Court has affirmed the lower court's decision by a 4–4 vote. If the missing Justice was ill and has recovered, or if a ninth Justice has been appointed to fill a vacancy, it may seem likely that a majority will be mustered once the Court returns to full strength. Absent such a circumstance, the typical petition for rehearing achieves little but delay and the chance for a parting shot.

KENNETH L. KARST
(1986)

Bibliography

STERN, ROBERT L. and GRESSMAN, EUGENE 1978 *Supreme Court Practice,* 5th ed. Chap. 15. Washington, D.C.: Bureau of National Affairs.

REHNQUIST, WILLIAM H.
(1924–   )

William Rehnquist joined the Supreme Court in 1971 at age forty-seven. He had been a clerk to Justice ROBERT H. JACKSON and a practitioner in Arizona. At the time of his appointment, he was the assistant attorney general for legal counsel—as President RICHARD M. NIXON described the post on appointing him, "the President's lawyer's lawyer."

Brilliant, charming, and deeply conservative, he has become the intellectual leader of the court—a fact that is not obvious from the statistics. Many terms he has dissented more than any other Justice, often alone. Rehnquist's influence lies in setting the terms of the debate. His dissents mark the path for future developments. His MAJORITY OPINIONS have been unusually influential, in part because Chief Justice WARREN E. BURGER regularly assigns him the most difficult and interesting cases, and in part because the opinions articulate approaches that have substantial general importance.

Rehnquist follows a structural approach in which the original understanding and the text of the Constitution assume great importance. The states play a substantial role in this structure, and a vision of an allocation of functions between state and federal governments lies at the center of Rehnquist's thought. He takes seriously the proposition that the federal government has limited powers and that the states hold sway over substantial fields. The Justice also has a view of the allocation of powers within the federal government in which judges play only a limited role. Judges may enforce some explicit guarantees, such as the right to FREEDOM OF SPEECH, but Rehnquist sees their more important function as enforcing the decisions of the political branches rather than questioning them. Judges must patrol the allocation of powers among other contending claimants, but once a political branch acts within its capacity, the decision, no matter how unwise, binds the courts.

This highly deferential approach follows from a belief that the Framers of the Constitution settled little but governmental structure, leaving the rest to future generations. Judges have no authority to restrict the powers of the political branches. They cannot invoke a decision by the Framers or political branches allocating power to the courts, and they cannot point to any other source of authority. Rehnquist is a moral skeptic and so rejects arguments that the Constitution authorizes judges to insist that other branches keep up with evolving notions of decent conduct; he believes that only the political process can define decency.

Justice Rehnquist outlined his approach in a solitary dissent to TRIMBLE V. GORDON (1977). The majority held that a statute discriminating against illegitimate children violated the EQUAL PROTECTION clause of the FOURTEENTH AMENDMENT. Calling that clause a "classic paradox" that "makes sense only in the context of a recently fought Civil War," Rehnquist continued:

> In the case of equality and equal protection, the constitutional principle—the thing to be protected to a greater or lesser degree—is not even identifiable from within the four corners of the Constitution. For equal protection does not mean that all persons must be treated alike. Rather, its general principle is that persons similarly situated should be treated similarly. But that statement of the rule does little to determine whether or not a question of equality is even involved in a given case. For the crux of the problem is *whether persons are similarly situated* for purposes of the STATE ACTION in issue.

Rehnquist therefore finds the constitutional guarantee of equality empty and thus vulnerable to being made a mere vessel for the beliefs of modern judges about what things *should* count as the pertinent similarities and differences. In his view, however, the Constitution does not resolve that question, which is at root political, to be resolved by political processes. The equal protection clause is limited

to the CIVIL WAR concern, race. Within that field the prohibition is absolute, and race is a forbidden classification. Rehnquist has opposed governmental racial distinctions of all sorts, preferential "set-asides" for construction work, which the majority approved in FULLILOVE V. KLUTZNICK (1980), and preferences for private employment, which were sustained in UNITED STEELWORKERS V. WEBER (1979), as well as those stigmatizing blacks.

He applies the same approach to almost every other aspect of the Constitution. The FIRST AMENDMENT disables government from stopping speech—the subject debated by the Framers—but does not require government to facilitate speech, for example, by creating rights of access to information. Judicial expansion of the amendment's core meaning is unauthorized. A judge may not properly pursue the principles or values that underlie the document, because every principle has its limit, and the Constitution left adjustments to the political branches. As Rehnquist wrote in an article published in 1976: "Even in the face of a conceded social evil, a reasonably competent and reasonably representative legislature may decide to do nothing. It may decide that the evil is not of sufficient magnitude to warrant any governmental intervention. It may decide that the financial cost of eliminating the evil is not worth the benefit which would result from its elimination. It may decide that the evils which might ensue from the proposed solution are worse than the evils which the solution would eliminate." The judge must accept the political answers to these problems.

This limitation does not imply judicial passivity. The judge must rigorously enforce any actual constitutional decisions to remove issues from the political process. The BILL OF RIGHTS contains some of these decisions, but the most important are those concerning the structure of government. Rehnquist is perhaps best known for his enforcement of principles of FEDERALISM that cannot be found in the constitutional text. Writing for a bare majority in NATIONAL LEAGUE OF CITIES V. USERY (1976), he concluded that the structure of the Constitution withheld from Congress any power to regulate the operation of "states as states." As a result, the Court held, Congress could not require state and local governments to pay the minimum wages applicable to private parties. The Justice also has read into many statutes limits founded on a perceived need to maintain the role of states as coordinate centers of power.

But decisions based on the structure of the Constitution do not always favor the states. Often Rehnquist has joined holdings under the COMMERCE CLAUSE restricting the powers of states to levy discriminatory taxes or otherwise hinder INTERSTATE COMMERCE, even though neither legislation not any clear textual command prohibits this discrimination. He wrote the court's opinion in FITZPATRICK V. BITZER (1976), holding that in the exercise of its power under the Fourteenth Amendment, Congress may authorize suits against the states, even though the ELEVENTH AMENDMENT appears to deprive federal courts of JURISDICTION to entertain such suits.

The allocation of powers within the federal government also has been a theme of Rehnquist's work. He has attempted to revive the "antidelegation" doctrine, arguing that Congress may not grant uncertain decision-making powers to the executive branch. He joined the Court's opinion in BUCKLEY V. VALEO (1976), invalidating Congress's effort to appoint officers to administer the election laws, characterizing that effort as an intrusion on the executive power. And he supplied the theory and vote necessary to strike down in NORTHERN PIPELINE CONSTRUCTION CORP. V. MARATHON PIPE LINE CO. (1982) a grant of judicial power to BANKRUPTCY judges who lacked life tenure of office.

Part of Rehnquist's influence among the Justices comes from his distinctive style. Most judicial opinions come in shades of gray, following a dull formula notable only for turgid prose and abundant footnotes. Justice Rehnquist's opinions come closer to lavender than gray. They are relatively short and lively. One began with a limerick. Rehnquist often uses colorful (if strained) metaphors. The opinions are less copiously documented than those of his colleagues, but not because he does not know the references—they appear in the appropriate quantities in his articles. The Justice has simply chosen to write in an entertaining style. His opinions are read, and being read is the first step in being influential.

Some critics, including David L. Shapiro, have accused Rehnquist of intellectual dishonesty, because he is willing to distinguish a case on a marginally relevant basis, or to purport to honor PRECEDENT while disavowing the earlier case's rationale. Timid or weak Justices routinely treat precedents so, but Rehnquist is neither timid nor weak. That is why his nimble treatment of precedent is troubling. No one can attribute his conduct to inadvertence or to the work of a law clerk.

Justice Rehnquist is not always cavalier in distinguishing or narrowing unpleasant precedents. He will attack earlier cases openly in separate or DISSENTING OPINIONS, only to distinguish them in opinions for the Court. His opinion in *National League of Cities* purported to preserve some cases he had attacked, in solitary dissent, a year before, in *Fry v. United States* (1975). Part of his approach to precedent arises from his understanding that the author of a majority opinion speaks not for himself but for the Court as institution. He therefore tries to preserve precedents with which he does not agree, by flimsy distinctions if necessary. The result may seem contrived, but it is often essential to the functioning of the Court.

The ultimate test of honesty is whether a Justice faithfully distinguishes his constitutional views from his personal ones. Most Justices see little difference, leading to the conclusion that the Constitution follows the personal view rather than the reverse. Yet Rehnquist, who generally opposes governmental control of economic affairs, believes that the Constitution allows the political branches to establish and maintain a welfare state with extensive ECONOMIC REGULATION. He follows his jurisprudence to its logical conclusions. Though he supports property rights, he wrote an opinion in PRUNEYARD SHOPPING CENTER V. ROBINS (1980) sustaining the authority of a state to restrict those rights in the interest of fostering political speech with which the property owner disagreed.

In 1986 President RONALD REAGAN nominated Rehnquist to succeed Warren Burger as Chief Justice of the United States. One may expect Chief Justice Rehnquist to retain the same coherent picture of a government in which judges police structure rather than substance.

FRANK H. EASTERBROOK
(1986)

Bibliography

POWELL, JEFF 1982 The Compleat Jeffersonian: Justice Rehnquist and Federalism. *Yale Law Journal* 91:1317–1370.

REHNQUIST, WILLIAM H. 1976 The Notion of a Living Constitution. *Texas Law Review* 54:693–706.

SHAPIRO, DAVID L. 1976 Mr. Justice Rehnquist: A Preliminary View. *Harvard Law Review* 90:293–357.

REHNQUIST, WILLIAM H.
(1924–)
(Update 1)

William H. Rehnquist grew up in Milwaukee and was educated at Stanford, Harvard, and Stanford Law School. He served as a law clerk to Supreme Court Justice ROBERT H. JACKSON and then entered into private practice in Phoenix. In 1969, through his association with Deputy Attorney General Richard Kleindienst and work as a Republican party official in Phoenix, he went to Washington as Assistant Attorney General for the Office of Legal Counsel. On January 7, 1972, he, along with LEWIS F. POWELL, was sworn in as an Associate Justice of the Supreme Court. On September 26, 1986, he was sworn in as CHIEF JUSTICE of the United States, only the third sitting Justice to be so elevated. Despite widespread disagreement with Rehnquist's views among legal academics, there is little dispute that he is among the ablest Justices who have ever served on the Court.

Justice Rehnquist's vision of the nation's constitutional structure, emphasizing the words and history of that document, is expressed in three doctrines: STRICT CONSTRUCTION (of both the Constitution and of statutes), judicial restraint, and FEDERALISM. He summarized this vision in a 1976 speech at the University of Texas:

> It is almost impossible . . . to conclude that the [Founding Fathers] intended the Constitution itself to suggest answers to the manifold problems that they knew would confront succeeding generations. The Constitution that they drafted was intended to endure indefinitely, but the reason for this well-founded hope was the general language by which national authority was granted to Congress and the Presidency. These two branches were to furnish the motive power within the federal system, which was in turn to coexist with the state governments; the elements of government having a popular constituency were looked to for the solution of the numerous and varied problems that the future would bring.

In other words, as he stated, dissenting, in TRIMBLE V. GORDON (1977), neither the original Constitution nor the CIVIL WAR amendments made "this Court (or the federal courts generally) into a council of revision, and they did not confer on this Court any authority to nullify state laws which were merely felt to be inimical to the Court's notion of the public interest."

During his early years on the Court, despite the presence of three other Republican appointees, Justice Rehnquist was often in lone dissent, espousing a view of STATES' RIGHTS and limited federal judicial power that many regarded as anachronistic. For example, in *Weber v. Aetna Casualty and Surety Company* (1972), SUGARMAN V. DOUGALL (1973), and FRONTIERO V. RICHARDSON (1973), he resisted the view of the other eight members of the Court that the EQUAL PROTECTION clause of the FOURTEENTH AMENDMENT applied to, and required heightened scrutiny of, state-sponsored discrimination against illegitimate children, resident aliens, and women, respectively. Indeed, he insisted that the equal protection clause had only marginal application beyond cases of RACIAL DISCRIMINATION. In the area of CRIMINAL PROCEDURE Rehnquist urged that the Court overrule MAPP V. OHIO (1961), which applied the EXCLUSIONARY RULE to the states. Rehnquist also seemed hostile to MIRANDA V. ARIZONA (1966), though he never directly argued that it should be reversed. Still, even in his early years on the Court, Justice Rehnquist was less likely to be in dissent than the liberal Justices WILLIAM O. DOUGLAS, WILLIAM J. BRENNAN, and THURGOOD MARSHALL; and the ideas expressed in some of Rehnquist's early dissents, such as in CLEVELAND BOARD OF EDUCATION V. LAFLEUR (1974) and *Fry v. United States* (1975) were influential in majority opinions in the years to come.

The 1975 term saw Justice Rehnquist come into his own as the leader of the (ever-shifting) conservative wing of the Court. In that term he wrote for the Court in PAUL V. DAVIS (1976), holding that reputation, standing alone, was not a constitutionally protected "liberty" interest subject to vindication under the guarantee of PROCEDURAL DUE PROCESS OF LAW; in NATIONAL LEAGUE OF CITIES V. USERY (1976), holding that the TENTH AMENDMENT limited Congress's power under the COMMERCE CLAUSE to regulate the states; and in RIZZO V. GOODE (1976), holding that "principles of federalism" forbade federal courts from ordering a restructuring of a city police force in response to constitutional violations. In *National League of Cities*, Rehnquist used an expansive reading of the Tenth Amendment to strike down a federal statute that regulated the wages and hours of state government employees, although such regulation was otherwise concededly within Congress's commerce power. The opinion showed that when faced with a choice between judicial restraintstrict constructionism and states' rights, Justice Rehnquist was prepared to defend the latter aggressively. However, the potential significance of the first decision limiting Congress's use of the commerce power since 1936 was eroded by subsequent Court majorities, first refusing to follow, and then overruling, *National League of Cities* in GARCIA V. SAN ANTONIO METROPOLITAN TRANSIT AUTHORITY (1985). Despite Justice Rehnquist's prediction in dissent that this issue would return to haunt the Court, it seems unlikely that the Court will really disable Congress from establishing national control of virtually any area in which Congress chooses to assert itself. Whatever the political leanings of the other Justices, a majority generally seems to believe that the strong national-weak state governmental system is the proper direction for the country.

When dissenting, Rehnquist makes his most telling points in opposing the majority's efforts to enact "desirable" social policy with little support from the constitutional or statutory provisions that they purport to be interpreting. An example is UNITED STEEL WORKERS OF AMERICA V. WEBER (1979). In that case, Kaiser Aluminum Company and the United Steelworkers had devised a "voluntary" affirmative action plan under which half of available positions in an on-the-job training plan would be reserved for blacks. Weber, excluded solely because he was white, filed suit based on Title VII of the CIVIL RIGHTS ACT OF 1964. The statute provides that "it shall be unlawful for an employer . . . to fail or refuse to hire . . . any individual . . . because of such individual's race." The statute goes on to say that its provisions are not to be interpreted "to require any employer . . . to grant preferential treatment to any individual or group." Moreover, as a unanimous Court had recognized only three years before in *McDonald v. Santa Fe Trail Transportation Co.* (1976), the "uncontradicted legislative history" showed that Title VII "prohibited racial discrimination against the white petitioners . . . upon the same standards as would be applicable were they Negroes." Nevertheless, in *Weber*, a 5–2 majority, reversing the lower courts, found that discrimination against whites was not within the "spirit" of Title VII and consequently not prohibited. In a bitter dissent, Justice Rehnquist accused the majority of Orwellian "new-speak" and concluded that "close examination of what the Court proffers as the spirit of the Act reveals it as the spirit of the present majority, not the 88th Congress." Similarly in ROE V. WADE (1973), where the majority based a woman's right to an ABORTION on a constitutional RIGHT OF PRIVACY that arose not from the terms but from the "penumbras" of the BILL OF RIGHTS, Rehnquist wrote, "To reach its result, the Court necessarily has had to find within the scope of the Fourteenth Amendment a right that was apparently completely unknown to the drafters of the Amendment." Whatever the wisdom of the policies announced in these cases, it is difficult to disagree that Rehnquist's reading of the textual material in question was the more accurate one.

It is ironic that Rehnquist, often condemned as a right-wing ideologue was, in *Weber* and *Roe,* as in many other cases, advocating a view of the Court's role that had previously been vigorously advanced by the progressive members of the Court. In MOREHEAD V. NEW YORK EX REL. TIPALDO (1936), for example, the dissenting opinion of Justice HARLAN F. STONE, joined by Justices LOUIS BRANDEIS and BENJAMIN CARDOZO, declared: "It is not for the Court to resolve doubts whether the remedy by regulation is as efficacious as many believe, or better than some other, or is better even than blind operation of uncontrolled economic forces. The legislature must be free to choose unless government is rendered impotent. The Fourteenth Amendment has no more imbedded in the Constitution our preference for some particular set of economic beliefs, than it has adopted in the name of liberty the system of theology which we happen to approve."

In criminal procedure, Rehnquist's views are driven by the same narrow view of the role of courts in a tripartite federal system, and he frankly admits that his goal when he came on the Court was to "call a halt to a number of sweeping rulings of the Warren Court in this area." In this objective he generally was joined by the other appointees of RICHARD M. NIXON and by Justice BYRON WHITE. Consequently, the 1970s and 1980s saw a series of decisions aimed at making it easier for the police to investigate crimes and harder for defendants to upset their convictions because of police investigatory errors. For example, in *Rakas v. Illinois* (1978) the Court, per Rehnquist, made it more difficult for a defendant to establish STANDING to litigate SEARCH AND SEIZURE violations; in UNITED STATES V. ROBINSON (1973) the scope of police SEARCHES INCIDENT TO ARREST was expanded; and in *United States v. Leon* (1984) the Court, per Justice White, established a GOOD FAITH EXCEPTION to the exclusionary rule in search warrant cases. However, neither Rehnquist nor any of his fellow conser-

vatives sought to undercut the FUNDAMENTAL RIGHTS to counsel, appeal, and TRIAL BY JURY that had been applied to the states by the Warren Court. In a 1985 interview, despite the feeling of most Court watchers that the BURGER COURT had not dismantled the major criminal procedure protections of the Warren Court, including the MIRANDA RULES and the exclusionary rule, Justice Rehnquist pronounced himself satisfied that the law was "more even-handed now than when I came on the Court."

If Rehnquist has not been successful in exempting states from congressional control, he has frequently prevailed in his efforts to exempt state courts from federal court interference. To do this, he has taken the 1971 decision in YOUNGER V. HARRIS, which counseled restraint by federal courts in enjoining ongoing state criminal proceedings, and extended it greatly. In *Rizzo* and in *Real Estate Association v. McNary* (1981) he held that "principles of federalism" limited a federal court's ability to enjoin not just the judicial branch but the executive branch of state governments as well and that this comity limitation was not confined to criminal proceedings. Nor, as he held in *Doran v. Salem Inn, Inc.* (1975), was it necessary that a state criminal proceeding predate a federal action for the federal action to be barred by principles of comity.

Similarly, in the area of federal HABEAS CORPUS for state prisoners, Rehnquist and his conservative colleagues have advanced the dual goals of limiting federal court interference with state court adjudications and enhancing the finality of criminal convictions. The most significant holding in this line of cases is the decision in WAINWRIGHT V. SYKES (1977). In this case, Rehnquist, writing for a six-Justice majority, held that a defendant's failure to raise an issue at the appropriate stage of a state criminal proceeding barred the federal courts from considering that issue later under habeas corpus, absent a showing by the defendant of good cause for the failure and prejudice to his case. *Sykes* thus largely overruled FAY V. NOIA (1963), which had allowed new issues to be raised on federal habeas corpus unless they had been deliberately bypassed by the defendant in state proceedings. *Sykes* represented a significant diminution of the power of federal courts to interfere with state convictions. The trend continued in 1989 in the significant case of *Teague v. Lane,* authored by Justice SANDRA DAY O'CONNOR, where the Court held that "new" rules of criminal procedure generally should not apply retroactively on habeas corpus to defendants whose state convictions had become final before the new law was established. In *Butler v. McKellar* (1990), Justice Rehnquist defined "new" broadly so as to make it very difficult for state prisoners to obtain federal habeas relief.

Consistent with his stance on federalism and judicial restraint, Rehnquist is the Court's leading advocate of a restrictive interpretation of the ESTABLISHMENT CLAUSE of the FIRST AMENDMENT. He set forth his view in detail in a DISSENTING OPINION in WALLACE V. JAFFREE (1985), where the majority struck down Alabama's statutorily required moment of silence for "meditation or voluntary prayer" in public schools. Rehnquist rejected the "wall of separation between church and state" principle of EVERSON V. BOARD OF EDUCATION (1947), arguing that history did not support this rigid interpretation of the First Amendment. According to Rehnquist, JAMES MADISON viewed the purpose of the establishment clause as simply "to prohibit the establishment of a national religion, and perhaps to prevent discrimination among sects. He did not see it as requiring neutrality on the part of the government between religion and irreligion." Consequently, Rehnquist would have found no defect in a state statute that openly endorsed prayer, much less a "moment of silence."

In a similar vein, in FIRST NATIONAL BANK V. BELLOTTI (1978), Rehnquist, in a sole dissent, refused to recognize a First Amendment COMMERCIAL SPEECH right for corporations, and in VIRGINIA STATE BOARD OF PHARMACY V. VIRGINIA CONSUMER COUNCIL (1976) he refused to recognize a First Amendment right of consumers to receive commercial information. In short, in the First Amendment area, as in all others, he would generally give the legislative branch, whether state or federal, greater freedom to plot its own course than his colleagues would.

When, in June of 1986, WARREN BURGER announced his resignation as Chief Justice and President RONALD REAGAN nominated Rehnquist as his replacement, there was a firestorm of protest among liberals. Senator Edward Kennedy denounced Justice Rehnquist as having an "appalling record on race" and liberal columnists branded him a rightwing extremist. A concerted effort was undertaken to find something in his past that might provide a basis for defeating the nomination. Assorted allegations were raised concerning contacts with black voters when he was a Republican party official in Phoenix, the handling of a family trust, a memo he had written to Justice Jackson as a law clerk urging that the SEPARATE BUT EQUAL DOCTRINE not be overruled in BROWN V. BOARD OF EDUCATION OF TOPEKA (1954,1955), and a racially restrictive covenant in the deed to his Phoenix house. The Senate perceived that these allegations were either unproven or, if true, were "ancient history" and irrelevant to his fitness for the post of Chief Justice. Significantly, no serious charge of misconduct was shown as to Rehnquist's fourteen and a half years as an Associate Justice on the Supreme Court. In the end, after much sound and fury, he was confirmed by a vote of 65–13.

If the 1975 term saw Rehnquist "arrive" as a major force on the Court, it was the 1987 term, his second year in the post, that saw him mature as Chief Justice. In a speech given in 1976 he had discussed the role of Chief Justice, citing CHARLES EVANS HUGHES as his model: "Hughes believed that unanimity of decision contributed to public confidence in the Court. . . . Except in cases involving matters of high principle he willingly acquiesced in silence rather than expose his dissenting views. . . . Hughes was also willing to modify his own opinions to hold or increase his majority and if that meant he had to put in disconnected thoughts or sentences, in they went."

Following his own advice, in the 1987 term he achieved a high level of agreement with his fellow Justices (ranging from 57.6 percent with Justice Thurgood Marshall to 83.1 percent with Justice ANTHONY KENNEDY). His administrative abilities in the 1987 term won the praise of Justice HARRY BLACKMUN, who deemed him a "splendid administrator in conference." For the first time in years, the Court concluded its work prior to July 1. During that term, Rehnquist showed that he could be flexible, joining with the more liberal Justices to subject the dismissal of a homosexual CIA agent to judicial review and to support the First Amendment claims of *Hustler* magazine to direct off-color ridicule at a public figure. Most significantly, in *Morrison v. Olson* (1988) Rehnquist wrote for a 7–1 majority upholding the office of INDEPENDENT COUNSEL against a challenge by the Reagan administration. In a decision termed an "exercise in folly" by the lone dissenter, Justice ANTONIN SCALIA, Rehnquist held that the appointments clause was not violated by Congress's vesting the power to appoint a SPECIAL PROSECUTOR in a "Special Division" of three United States Court of Appeals judges. Nor did the act violate SEPARATION OF POWERS principles by impermissibly interfering with the functions of the executive branch. While the act can be shown to have theoretical flaws, Rehnquist could not be faulted if he perceived that a truly independent prosecutor was a necessary check on the many abuses of executive power, including criminal violations, that were occurring during the latter years of the Reagan administration and in upholding a check on those abuses in an opinion that gained the concurrence of a substantial majority of his colleagues. Rehnquist's performance during the 1988 term led the *New York Times*, which had vigorously opposed his elevation to Chief Justice, to praise him with faint damnation. "While he is certainly no liberal, or even a moderate, his positions are not always responsive to the tides of fashionable opinion among his fellow political conservatives."

Indeed, while Rehnquist's judicial philosophy is undoubtedly born of a staunch political conservatism, the principles of federalism and strict construction will frequently prevail even when they lead to a "liberal" result. For example, in PRUNEYARD SHOPPING CENTER V. ROBINS (1980) he wrote the opinion upholding state constitutional provisions that allowed political demonstrators to solicit signatures for a petition in a shopping center. He recognized "the authority of the state to exercise its POLICE POWER or its sovereign right to adopt in its own Constitution individual liberties more expansive than those conferred by the Federal Constitution." Similarly, in *Hughes v. Oklahoma* (1979) he dissented when the Court invalidated a state's attempt to preserve its wildlife. And, in *Pennell v. City of San Jose* (1988), he upheld the city's rent control ordinance in the face of a due process challenge by landlords. In numerous criminal cases, such as *United States v. Maze* (1974) and *Ball v. United States* (1985), he has voted to reverse criminal convictions on the ground that the government had failed to prove that the defendant's conduct had violated the terms of the (strictly construed) statute.

But if the 1987 term showed that Rehnquist could be flexible as Chief Justice, that term and the 1988 term also had him, in most cases, leading the Court in a conservative direction. In a series of close cases decided in the 1987 term, ranging across the landscape of the BILL OF RIGHTS, the Court denied an equal protection challenge to user fees for bus transportation to school, denied a claim by Indians that a Forest Service logging road through a national forest would interfere with their free exercise of religion, denied food stamps to striking workers, allowed censorship of a school newspaper, upheld federal tort immunity for defense contractors, and allowed illegally discovered evidence to be used against a criminal defendant under the "independent source" exception to the exclusionary rule.

The 1988 term demonstrated that Rehnquist was still prepared to be flexible. For example, in *City of Canton v. Harris* he joined an opinion by Justice White that held that a city could be liable for damages under SECTION 1983, TITLE 42, U.S. CODE for poor training of police officers and that a new trial was not barred; Justices O'Connor, Kennedy, and Scalia, on the other hand, wanted to dismiss the plaintiff's case because the plaintiff could not have met the "deliberate indifference" standard of proof. Such flexibility was rarely called for during the 1988 term, however, and the conservatives stayed together most of the time. The leading case of the term was WEBSTER V. REPRODUCTIVE HEALTH SERVICES (1988). Here Chief Justice Rehnquist and four others upheld a Missouri statute that forbade public funding and the use of public hospitals for abortions. The decision was consistent with Rehnquist's views of state's rights and strict construction of the federal Bill of Rights. Rehnquist observed that "our cases have recognized that the due process clauses generally confer no affirmative right to government aid, even where such aid may be necessary to some life, liberty or property interests of which the government itself may not deprive the individual." Because a state is under no constitutional obligation to provide public hospitals at all, it is free to condition their use

however it wishes. This notion, that beneficiaries of public largess must accept the "bitter [restrictions] with the sweet" has been a hallmark of Rehnquist's jurisprudence since he first expressed it in ARNETT V. KENNEDY in 1974. However, Rehnquist (at least temporarily) was unable to convince Justice O'Connor that it was time to abandon the "rigid" framework of *Roe v. Wade* that gave a woman an absolute right to an abortion during the first trimester of pregnancy. This failure resulted even though he had drafted a compromise that continued to recognize a limited constitutional right to abortion.

Despite the current national debate on abortion, it seems unlikely that the country in the foreseeable future will be confronted with a constitutional problem of the magnitude of the legal discrimination against blacks (and the closely related problem of police abuse of the rights of criminal suspects) that faced the Warren Court. Consequently, it is also unlikely that the judicial activism displayed by the Warren Court to deal with these problems will seem as morally necessary or politically desirable in the future. Thus, while Justice Rehnquist's vision of a vigorous Tenth Amendment checking Congress's power vis-à-vis the states seems unlikely to prevail in the long term, his view of a more limited role for the federal Constitution, and hence for the federal courts, probably will be the wave of the future. Having reached its highest point in the 1960s, the "Rights Revolution"—already dying during the Burger Court years—terminated with the appointment of William Rehnquist as Chief Justice of the United States; it probably will not recur after he steps down.

CRAIG M. BRADLEY
(1992)

(SEE ALSO: *Conservatism; Rehnquist Court*.)

Bibliography

BRADLEY, CRAIG M. 1987 Criminal Procedure in the Rehnquist Court: Has the Rehnquisition Begun? *Indiana Law Journal* 62:273–294.

DAVIS, SUE 1989 *Justice Rehnquist and the Constitution.* Princeton, N.J.: Princeton University Press.

POWELL, H. JEFFERSON 1982 The Compleat Jeffersonian: Justice Rehnquist and Federalism. *Yale Law Journal* 91: 1317–1370.

REHNQUIST, WILLIAM H. 1976 Chief Justices I Never Knew. *Hastings Constitutional Law Quarterly* 3:637.

——— 1976 The Notion of a Living Constitution. *Texas Law Review* 54:693–706.

——— 1987 *The Supreme Court: How It Was, How It Is.* New York: Morrow.

SHAPIRO, DAVID L. 1976 Mr. Justice Rehnquist: A Preliminary View. *Harvard Law Review* 90:293–357.

REHNQUIST, WILLIAM H.
(1924–)
(Update 2)

William Hobbes Rehnquist served as an Associate Justice of the Supreme Court and later ascended to the position of CHIEF JUSTICE of the United States. Rehnquist was born in 1924 outside of Milwaukee, Wisconsin. After initially attending Kenyon College and serving in the U.S. Army for three years during WORLD WAR II, he received his undergraduate degree from Stanford University in 1948. Prior to attending law school, Rehnquist then received an M.A. in political science from Stanford in 1949, followed by an M.A. in government from Harvard in 1950. In December, 1951, he was graduated first in his class from Stanford Law School. Rehnquist then served as a law clerk to Justice ROBERT H. JACKSON, thereafter entering private practice in Phoenix, Arizona. During his years in Phoenix, Rehnquist was an outspoken, politically active conservative, criticizing the WARREN COURT for "extreme solicitude for the claims of Communists and other criminal defendants" and at one point opposing OPEN HOUSING LAWS as an unjustifiable infringement on private PROPERTY RIGHTS. When RICHARD M. NIXON was elected President, he chose Rehnquist to head the Office of Legal Counsel in the U.S. Department of Justice. In that position, Rehnquist often served as the administration's spokesman on controversial legal issues.

After the resignation of the second JOHN MARSHALL HARLAN and HUGO L. BLACK in 1971, Nixon nominated Rehnquist and LEWIS F. POWELL to serve as Associate Justices. Rehnquist's nomination was by far the more controversial of the two; indeed, it set off a bitter struggle over confirmation in the U.S. SENATE. No one questioned Rehnquist's intellectual capacity; however, Senate liberals were disturbed by his record on CIVIL RIGHTS. In particular, they focused on two points. The first was a memorandum that Rehnquist had written for Justice Jackson in connection with BROWN V. BOARD OF EDUCATION (1954) which argued that PLESSY V. FERGUSON (1896) "was right and should be reaffirmed." The second was Rehnquist's participation in a Republican poll-watching project that challenged voting credentials in predominantly African American and Hispanic neighborhoods in Phoenix. Rehnquist responded that Jackson himself had requested a defense of *Plessy*, and that he had engaged in no wrongdoing during the poll-watching project. Ultimately, Rehnquist was confirmed on a 68–26 vote.

In personal terms, Rehnquist soon became known on the Court for his friendliness, informality, and irreverent sense of humor. From a jurisprudential perspective, it quickly became clear that he would vindicate the fears of his liberal detractors and the hopes of his conservative supporters. During the BURGER COURT era, Rehnquist was the most conservative Justice on the Court, and also the most able of the four Nixon appointees. His opinions reflect a technical mastery of the law, and are marked by a forceful writing style that at times employs colorful, emotionally charged imagery to underscore distaste for the positions of his more liberal colleagues.

Because of these qualities, Rehnquist was chosen by President RONALD REAGAN to succeed WARREN E. BURGER as Chief Justice in 1986. The CONFIRMATION PROCESS reprised the political struggle that had taken place in 1971. Once again, liberal senators opposed the nomination, harshly criticizing Rehnquist's record on civil rights; once again, their effort to derail the nomination was unsuccessful. Rehnquist was confirmed by a vote of 65–32, and assumed the office of Chief Justice on September 26, 1986.

Ironically, Rehnquist's elevation to the Chief Justiceship coincided with the appointment of Justice ANTONIN SCALIA, who displaced Rehnquist as the intellectual leader of the conservative wing of the Court. During his tenure as Chief Justice, Rehnquist has been as likely to vote with SANDRA DAY O'CONNOR and ANTHONY M. KENNEDY as with Scalia and CLARENCE THOMAS, both of whom were more firmly committed to conservative ideology. *Bush v. Vera* (1996) exemplifies this point. There, rather than joining Scalia and Thomas in arguing that all consideration of race in ELECTORAL DISTRICTING was unconstitutional, Rehnquist agreed with O'Connor and Kennedy in concluding that the Constitution requires only that "legitimate districting principles [not be] 'subordinated' to race."

The significance of cases such as *Vera* should not be overstated in evaluating Rehnquist's judicial philosophy. He remains a staunch conservative, fiercely opposed to the basic principles of liberal constitutionalism. For example, in PLANNED PARENTHOOD V. CASEY (1992), Rehnquist voted to overturn ROE V. WADE (1973) and deconstitutionalize the law of ABORTION, rather than simply to modify *Roe* and its progeny as successfully advocated by O'Connor and Kennedy.

Rehnquist's opposition to *Roe* reflects his basic approach to CONSTITUTIONAL INTERPRETATION, which in turn embodies the standard conservative political ideology of the late 1960s and early 1970s. Stung by the liberal activism of the Warren Court, conservatives had generally become vociferous advocates of the concept of judicial restraint generally, and a commitment to a jurisprudence based on the ORIGINAL INTENT of the Framers of the Constitution in particular. Not surprisingly, Rehnquist became the foremost defender of ORIGINALISM on the Court. He expressed this philosophy in "The Notion of a Living Constitution":

[T]o the extent that it makes possible an individual's persuading one or more appointed federal judges to impose on other individuals a rule of conduct that the popularly elected branches of government would not have enacted and the voters have not and would not have embodied in the Constitution, . . . [nonoriginalist review] is genuinely corrosive of the fundamental values of our democratic society.

Among the best-known examples of the application of these principles are Rehnquist's DISSENTING OPINIONS in cases such as SUGARMAN V. DOUGALL (1973) and TRIMBLE V. GORDON (1977), where he argued that enhanced scrutiny under the EQUAL PROTECTION clause should be limited to cases involving race-based classifications. The same jurisprudential philosophy has served Rehnquist well in cases where liberals have sought to deploy the Constitution in support of their values on issues ranging from school DESEGREGATION to CRIMINAL PROCEDURE, RELIGIOUS LIBERTY, and gay rights. In dealing with these cases, he was the most consistent and effective advocate of judicial restraint on the Burger Court. Rehnquist has been equally effective in articulating conservative positions on issues of STATUTORY INTERPRETATION involving matters such as HABEAS CORPUS, civil rights, and business regulation generally. As Chief Justice, he has continued to be a strong advocate for these positions.

By contrast, in cases where litigants have attempted to deploy the Constitution *against* liberal government programs, Rehnquist's voting pattern clearly reflects the tensions inherent in much of the conservative political–judicial theory of the late-twentieth century. Rehnquist was the Burger Court Justice who was most likely to uphold constitutional challenges raised by conservatives against liberal political programs, including cases involving FEDERALISM, property rights, and AFFIRMATIVE ACTION. He has continued to support conservative activism on a variety of issues during his Chief Justiceship. Moreover, in some of these cases, Rehnquist's positions are hard to explain in terms other than pure politics; for example, his categorical rejection of race-based affirmative action plans in cases such as FULLILOVE V. KLUTZNICK (1980) is inexplicable in any other terms. In other cases, however, Rehnquist has emphasized the principle of judicial restraint in rejecting constitutional challenges raised by conservatives. For example, following his general theory that CORPORATIONS are creatures of the state and thus constitutionally subject to whatever restraints the state government wishes to impose, Rehnquist voted to uphold restraints on corporate political activities in cases such as FIRST NATIONAL BANK OF BOSTON V. BELLOTTI (1978)—hardly a policy that most conservative politicians would embrace. In short, despite his obvious gifts, Rehnquist has never fully resolved the potential conflicts between "judicial conservatism"

and the political conservatism with which it has become associated. Nonetheless, he remains one of the most important and influential justices of the post-Warren era.

EARL M. MALTZ
(2000)

Bibliography

BOLES, DONALD E.   1987   *William Rehnquist: Judicial Activist.* Ames, Iowa: Iowa State University Press.
DAVIS, SUE   1988   *Justice Rehnquist and the Constitution.* Princeton, N.J.: Princeton University Press.
POWELL, JEFF   1982   The Compleat Jeffersonian: Justice Rehnquist and Federalism. *Yale Law Journal* 91:1317–1370.
REHNQUIST, WILLIAM H.   1976   The Notion of a Living Constitution. *Texas Law Review* 54:693–706.
SHAPIRO, DAVID L.   1976   Mr. Justice Rehnquist: A Preliminary View. *Harvard Law Review* 90:293–357.

REHNQUIST COURT

The Rehnquist Court began its reign in September of 1986 when President RONALD REAGAN appointed WILLIAM H. REHNQUIST Chief Justice to replace retiring Chief Justice WARREN E. BURGER. This article reviews the first four years of the Rehnquist Court. Before his appointment as Chief Justice, however, Rehnquist had served as an Associate Justice on the BURGER COURT for almost fifteen years. Like Burger, he was originally appointed by President RICHARD M. NIXON to redeem a specific campaign promise to promote law and order through Court appointments that would stem the tide of WARREN COURT decisions protecting the rights of the criminally accused and to pursue his more general philosophical commitment to appoint "strict constructionists . . . to interpret the law, not to make law."

The Burger Court itself made a fairly quick start in redeeming Mr. Nixon's law-and-order pledge, although the Rehnquist Court has continued and in some ways even accelerated this redemption. It seems highly likely that the elevation of Rehnquist, in conjunction with two subsequent appointments by President Reagan and one by President GEORGE BUSH, will complete the more general transformation of the Court contemplated by President Nixon's commitment to STRICT CONSTRUCTION.

This broader transformation has been steady but slow. It has been steady because Republican Presidents holding the conservative values associated with "strict construction" have controlled the White House continuously since Nixon's election, except for the four-year interlude of President JIMMY CARTER, who did not have the opportunity to appoint a single Justice. It has been slow partly because some of the appointees did not turn out as conservative as expected and partly because some of the conservatives replaced other conservatives rather than liberals. Of President Nixon's four appointments, only one, Chief Justice Burger, remained consistently faithful to the conservative cause, whereas Justice LEWIS F. POWELL proved to be a moderate and Justice HARRY A. BLACKMUN became increasingly liberal. Justice JOHN PAUL STEVENS, appointed by President GERALD FORD, has also proved to be a moderate; one of President Reagan's first two appointments replaced a moderate, Justice SANDRA DAY O'CONNOR replacing Justice POTTER J. STEWART, and the other, Justice ANTONIN SCALIA, replaced conservative Justice Burger.

The key appointment giving the conservatives on the Rehnquist Court a clear majority on most if not all issues did not come until President Reagan's 1988 appointment of Justice ANTHONY M. KENNEDY to replace retiring Justice Powell. Ironically, this appointment was made only after the Senate, following a historic controversy, had rejected Mr. Reagan's first candidate to replace Powell, Judge Robert Bork, on the ground that he was too conservative. Kennedy, during his first two terms in office, has proved to be as conservative as many expected Bork might have been, and the principal effect of the Senate's rejection of Bork appears to have been that President Bush in nominating his first Court appointee, DAVID H. SOUTER, to replace liberal stalwart WILLIAM J. BRENNAN searched for a conservative who, unlike Bork, had published nothing indicating his views on any important constitutional questions.

"Strict construction" is sometimes equated with a strategy of interpreting the Constitution according to the "plain meaning" of the text or the intention of its Framers. In fact, however, this interpretive strategy had not proved so far to be of great importance, except with regard to the methodology used by the Court to decide whether rights not expressly mentioned in the text are impliedly protected, where a variation of it has gained prominence. The form of strict construction, or CONSERVATISM, that has gradually come to dominate the Court, however, has been based more on institutional and political than on historical or textual commitments.

Institutionally, most of the Republican appointees have been inclined to resolve any doubts about how the Constitution should be interpreted by upholding actions of other agencies of government. This inclination probably rests mainly on three interconnected institutional commitments: a vision of democracy that pictures majoritarian-responsive institutions as its centerpiece and the life-tenured Court as antidemocratic; a vision of the management of society as a complex matter best delegated to various experts and professionals, like school boards and other ADMINISTRATIVE AGENCIES; and a vision of FEDERALISM that views with suspicion the intrusion of federal power including the JUDICIAL POWER, into areas of decision making traditionally left to state and local government.

Politically, most of the Republican appointees have

been guided or at least disciplined by the values associated with the constituency of the Republican party in late twentieth-century America. The Burger Court sat and the Rehnquist Court is sitting in an era when the historically dispossessed are actively seeking possession: blacks and other racial minorities; the poor and the homeless; women; gays; and other groups, like the handicapped, who have in different ways been marginalized in our society.

The Republican party has sought in a variety of ways to accommodate the interests of these groups, but it has been the party of mainstream America, not the party of the dispossessed. While Republicans and Democrats have vied for the "law and order" vote, the Republican party has been the more consistently and vocally anticriminal. The party has sought a moderate, compromising posture on the matters touching the protection of minority groups, women, and the handicapped. It has generally aligned itself at least rhetorically with traditional and to some extent religiously inspired moral views on controversial social questions such as ABORTION and homosexuality. While it has often conformed to the realities of interest-group politics, it has tended to resist governmental redistributive programs that would tax or otherwise interfere with property interests, preferring to rely instead on a relatively unregulated market to provide full employment and thus help the poor.

The behavior of the Rehnquist Court has been quite consistent with these political commitments, although at the same time, it is worthy of emphasis that a consistent and cohesive "Rehnquist Court" does not yet exist in one important sense. Even the conservative Justices sometimes disagree over outcomes and often, in important ways, over the rationale for decisions. As a result, the Court is often at least doctrinally splintered.

The Supreme Court, like the Republican party, has often sought what might be characterized as compromises; but on the whole, it is the Court of mainstream America, not the dispossessed. In a high percentage of important constitutional cases, its institutional and political commitments have pointed in the same direction. When these commitments have conflicted, it has to this point usually refrained from imposing its values, instead deferring to the governmental agencies whose decisions are challenged. There are some important exceptions, most notably in its resistance to AFFIRMATIVE ACTION programs, but these have been few and on the whole restrained. For example, although it has sometimes protected PROPERTY RIGHTS against governmental regulation, its rulings to this point do not remotely promise a return to pre-NEW DEAL ideology. Occasionally, chiefly in FREEDOM OF SPEECH cases, it has acted in ways that might be interpreted as neither institutionally nor politically conservative, as in upholding against regulation the speech rights of flag burners, but such cases are also rare. The Rehnquist Court has been, largely but not completely, a passively rather than an actively conservative court.

In one view the Court's overall performance shows only that the system is working as it is supposed to work: the presidential appointment power is the main effective check on these nine Justices who are accountable to no electorate, and twenty years of Republican Presidents has had an effect on the Supreme Court.

The Rehnquist Court has continued the Burger Court's contraction of the RIGHTS OF THE CRIMINALLY ACCUSED and convicted, in general subordinating these rights to law-and-order concerns, except in a subclass of cases in which the prosecution behaved outrageously in a way that might have tainted the guilt determination. Both courts have restricted the application of the FOURTH AMENDMENT's prohibition of unreasonable SEARCHES AND SEIZURES and the Fifth Amendment's prohibition of compulsory self-incrimination, limited the scope of the EXCLUSIONARY RULE, interpreted the Eighth Amendment so as to allow the states great discretion in reinstituting and administering CAPITAL PUNISHMENT, and virtually eliminated the possibility of HABEAS CORPUS and other postconviction challenges to final judgments of criminal conviction.

UNITED STATES V. SALERNO (1987), in which the Court upheld against Eighth Amendment attack the pretrial detention of dangerous defendants, exemplifies the Court's law-and-order commitment. *Maryland v. Buie* (1990) is an example of the priority the Court gives to law enforcement goals over Fourth Amendment rights claims. In this case, the Court sanctioned the use of evidence turned up after an arrest in a "protective sweep" of a house, on less than PROBABLE CAUSE, that someone dangerous might have been in the areas searched. The Court seems prepared in many contexts to abandon not only the probable cause requirement but any concept of individualized suspicion as a condition to search, as in *Michigan Department of State Police v. Sitz*, (1990) where it upheld highway-checkpoint sobriety testing. *Teague v. Lane* (1989) made it much more difficult for constitutional claims by prisoners to be heard in the federal courts, holding that federal habeas corpus is unavailable for the assertion of a right not clearly established by precedent unless the right would apply retroactively. For all practical purposes, this ruling requires a prisoner to show that fundamentally unfair governmental practices might have led to the conviction of someone innocent.

The seeds of the Rehnquist Court's more general conservative agenda, also sown during the Burger Court era, include both broad propositions of law that serve to eliminate whole categories of potential constitutional rights and smaller but continuous doctrinal innovations that cumulatively have made ever more difficult the establish-

ment of a violation of rights. The most important developments of the former have been the following: (1) the Court's unwillingness to interpret the Constitution to protect "implied" rights not explicitly mentioned in the text; (2) its limitation of the concept of constitutional rights to negative private rights against governmental interference, rejecting claims of rights to affirmative governmental assistance or subsidy; and (3) its understanding that the government's fundamental constitutional obligation is to refrain from targeting racial, gender, or religious groups for relatively disadvantageous treatment. It rejects any obligation of government to make accommodations in order to protect or benefit any such groups, and to some extent restricts government from making such accommodations for racial (although not for religious) groups.

Illustrative of the Rehnquist Court's narrow approach to defining the rights protected by the Constitution are *Michael H. v. Gerald D.* (1989) and *Burnham v. Superior Court of California* (1990). The former case raised the question as to how the term "liberty" in the due process clause of the FOURTEENTH AMENDMENT should be interpreted; and the latter raised the question as to how the term "DUE PROCESS OF LAW" should be interpreted.

In *Michael H.*, state law conclusively presumed that a child born to a married woman living with her husband was a child of the marriage. A genetic father argued that this law infringed on his "liberty" interest in establishing his paternity. In many prior cases, the Court had held that "liberty," in the due process clause, included implied FUNDAMENTAL RIGHTS not expressly mentioned in the Constitution when they were "implicit in the concept of ordered liberty" or "deeply rooted in this Nation's history and tradition." These formulations do not answer the questions of how and at what level of abstractness traditional values should be identified. The *Michael H.* plurality, following the Burger Court's lead in BOWERS V. HARDWICK (1986), chose to conceptualize this question very narrowly, asking not even whether our traditions recognize the rights of natural fathers, but rather whether they recognize those of adulterous natural fathers; on this basis the Court rejected the claim.

This historically concrete way of identifying constitutional rights does not necessarily eliminate implied constitutional rights, first, because the Court might (or might not) let stand previously announced implied rights, and second, because it is always possible that some small number of states might in the future restrict rights that have been traditionally and widely respected by all the other states. But it does very substantially limit the potential category of implied rights. Moreover, it does so in an odd way, given the traditional assumption that the main point of constitutional rights is to protect minorities: after *Bowers* and *Michael H.*, the stronger, more widespread, and more historically entrenched a rights-restrictive majoritarian imposition, the less likely the Court will find a constitutional violation.

The *Bowers* approach was applied by four Justices in *Burnham,* with the concurrence of enough others to constitute a majority, to reject a claim that subjecting an individual to a state's JURISDICTION on the basis of his fleeting presence within the state amounted to a denial of liberty "without due process of law." The opinion of the four by Justice Scalia found that fleeting physical presence, which would have been thought a sufficient predicate for jurisdiction when the Fourteenth Amendment was adopted, had been assumed to be sufficient since then in many state decisions. This "continuing tradition" was sufficient to validate the practice of founding jurisdiction on a fleeting presence, whether or not it might otherwise be thought unfair.

Cruzan v. Director of Missouri Department of Health (1990) suggests that the Court is not prepared to scuttle the implied-rights doctrine completely, but is also not disposed to use it aggressively. The Court found a sufficiently concrete tradition recognizing the right of individuals to refuse medical treatment to imply that this choice was a protected liberty that included the RIGHT TO DIE under at least some circumstances. Nonetheless, it held that the state's interest in insisting that the choice be shown by clear and convincing evidence was sufficiently strong in the case at hand to justify disallowing a patient's parents from making the decision, even though the patient herself could not make it because she was in a vegetative state.

The best known and most practically important of the pre-Rehnquist Court's decisions protecting implied constitutional rights is ROE V. WADE (1973), where the Court ruled that the Constitution impliedly protects a woman's right to have an abortion. The Rehnquist Court's general unreceptiveness to implied-rights claims does not bode well for the future of this right, and some of the sitting Justices have already announced their willingness to overrule *Roe.* Whether or not the right to abort will survive may depend on the vote of newly appointed Justice Souter, but even if the right survives, smaller but incrementally important shifts in doctrine by the Rehnquist Court have already weakened it significantly.

These shifts had their genesis in Burger Court decisions protecting the implied "privacy" right of individuals to decide their own family living arrangements, but only if the challenged regulation "substantially interfered" with the right. This substantial-interference concept has so far been important mainly in privacy right cases, although it is theoretically transplantable to other areas of constitutional law. Its patent importance at this point is in the abortion rights controversy where, in one or another formulation, it has appeared from time to time in majority and concurring opinions, including those of the Rehnquist Court, and it might prove important if five Justices are not able to agree that *Roe v. Wade* should be overruled. Use of the substantial-interference requirement, which has been endorsed most consistently by Justice O'Connor, would enable the majority even if it is unable to overrule *Roe,* to allow much greater state regulation of abortion than prior decisions have allowed.

For example, although it is not entirely clear what the criteria are for deciding when a regulation substantially interferes with the right to abort, some opinions suggest that only a regulation making abortions illegal qualifies. If so, waiting periods, mandatory antiabortion counseling, spousal and parental consent requirements, and other forms of regulation previously held unconstitutional would become permissible in the future. Even if the requirement were construed to have a lesser meaning, such as "making abortions very much more difficult to obtain," greater regulatory discretion would be available in the future than it has been in the past.

The ancestry of the Court's refusal to recognize positive constitutional rights to governmental assistance are decisions of the Burger Court that effectively terminated enlargement of the "fundamental interest" branch of EQUAL PROTECTION jurisprudence bequeathed to it by the Warren Court, along with decisions that rejected the claim that liberties protected against governmental interference are also entitled to affirmative governmental protection.

The Warren Court has held that individuals had an equality-based right to the subsidized provision of "fundamental" services or rights they were too poor to afford, such as counsel and other important defense services in criminal cases. Warren Court decisions had suggested that which rights were "fundamental" for these purposes would depend on the degree to which they were of practical importance to people. The Burger Court did not overturn the particular rulings of the Warren Court, but early in its tenure, did effectively undercut the equal-protection basis of the doctrine and consequently its future growth, ruling that henceforth rights would be regarded as fundamental only if they were constitutional rights, irrespective of their practical importance. These opinions, however, left open the possibility that such "real" constitutional rights might sometimes include subsidy rights.

Burger Court decisions eventually repudiated this suggestion in holding that the right to abort, although a constitutional right, did not include the right to governmental Medicaid payments for abortions for those too poor to afford them. According to these decisions, constitutional rights are negative entitlements available to individuals only to stop governmental interference with the use of private resources.

The Rehnquist Court has perpetuated this jurisprudence of negative rights, holding in the abortion context, for example, that the closing of state hospitals to abortions did not violate the right to abort because the state's action left women who wanted abortions exactly where they would have been had the state never operated public hospitals—that is, dependent on their private resources.

DESHANEY V. WINNEBAGO COUNTY DEPARTMENT OF SOCIAL SERVICES (1989) suggests, moreover, that the Rehnquist Court's commitment to the jurisprudence of negative rights is pervasive and extends beyond the abortion issue. In this case, the Court held that governmental social-service officials did not violate the rights of a boy by failing to remove him from a father whom they knew was continuously beating him and whose beatings eventually resulted in severe brain damage to the boy. The Court found no violation of the boy's right not to be deprived of liberty without due process. It ruled that due process protects individuals only against the government's interfering with their liberty and imposes no "affirmative obligation" on government to take action to protect that liberty. Just as the "culprit" in abortion-subsidy cases is not the government, but rather the pregnant woman's poverty, so (in this view) the boy's father, not the state, was the source of his problem.

The Rehnquist Court's pursuit of a "neutrality" concept of the government's basic constitutional obligation arguably has fairly deep roots in constitutional history, but is grounded most immediately in the Burger Court's WASHINGTON V. DAVIS (1976) decision, which held that unless the plaintiff is challenging a law that expressly classifies people on the basis of race, he or she can successfully challenge a governmental action as racially discriminatory only by proving that it was undertaken for a discriminatory purpose. The vision of racial justice that *Washington* has retrospectively been understood to endorse in subsequent Burger and Rehnquist Court decisions interpreting it is one of neutrality in a double sense: first because the Constitution requires governmental racial neutrality, *any* use by government of race as a classifying trait in law is suspect and likely to be struck down. And second, because the Constitution requires nothing more of government than racial neutrality, its actions are immune from attack so long as it does not act for a racially bad purpose.

This vision has substantially constrained attempts on behalf of minority groups to use law and legal institutions to better their lots in two distinct fashions, one by way of constitutional legitimation and the other by way of constitutional restriction. First, a governmental action that produces effects that disadvantage minority groups to a greater extent than other groups is constitutionally legitimate unless a plaintiff can meet the difficult burden of proving that this relative racial disadvantage was a purpose of the action. Second, voluntary attempts by government specifically and expressly to benefit racial minority groups—commonly called benign or reverse discrimination or affirmative action—are seriously vulnerable to constitutional invalidation.

The Rehnquist Court has vigorously confirmed and extended both the legitimation and restriction branches of the neutrality principle bequeathed to it. In MCCLESKEY V. KEMP (1987), for example, it rejected, on the ground of a failure of proof of discriminatory purpose, a claim by a black criminal defendant sentenced to death that the state's death penalty was administered in a racially discriminatory fashion. McCleskey's discrimination claim was based on a statistical study that, controlling for extraneous variables, found that a black defendant charged with killing a white in Georgia was four times more likely to be sentenced to death than someone charged with killing a black. The Court conceded, arguendo, the statistical reliability of the evidence, but found that even this statistical pattern would not prove that McCleskey himself was sentenced to death because of racial considerations. The case evidently shows the depth of the Rehnquist Court's commitment to its neutrality principle. Even conceding the correctness of the Court's criticism of the proof as to this individual defendant, the statistical evidence showed systematic RACIAL DISCRIMINATION and therefore proved that *some* (even if nonidentifiable) individual black murderers of whites were being sentenced to death for racial reasons. Even proof of a pattern of purposeful racial discrimination that might well have infected McCleskey's sentence was not sufficient to establish constitutional illegitimacy without evidence linking this nonneutrality to McCleskey himself.

The depth of the Rehnquist Court's commitment to its neutrality principle is also illustrated by its interpretation of the CIVIL RIGHTS ACT OF 1964, which prohibits among other things racial discrimination by employers. Burger Court decisions had held that proof that an employment practice disadvantaged minority group members to a greater extent than others, although insufficient to establish a presumptive constitutional violation by government, *was* sufficient to establish a presumptive violation of the statute by either governmental or private employers. On such a showing, the burden shifted to the employer to establish the business necessity of the challenged practice, failing which the practice would be found illegal.

In *Wards Cove Packing Co., Inc. v. Antonio* (1989), the Rehnquist Court changed this evidentiary framework in a way that requires the plaintiff to prove almost as much as he or she would need to establish intentional discrimination. After *Wards Cove*, the employer, in response to a showing that the challenged practice disproportionately disadvantages minority group members, need only come forward with some evidence of a business justification, after which the plaintiff must prove that the practice does not serve "in a significant way, the legitimate employment goals of the employer." A plaintiff who can meet this difficult burden will have come very close to proving that the discrimination was intentional because he or she would have shown that the putatively innocent purpose for the racial injury was a bogus explanation.

The restrictive branch of the neutrality principle arises in cases involving benign or reverse discrimination, a practice whose constitutionality was left extremely uncertain by a series of Burger Court decisions. The Rehnquist Court's decision in RICHMOND (CITY OF) V. J. A. CROSON CO. (1989) communicates at a minimum that a majority of the Justices (1) see governmental actions that allocate benefits to minority races on the express basis of race as equally or almost as constitutionally troublesome as actions that expressly disadvantage them on the basis of race; (2) believe that few goals are adequate to justify such actions; and (3) will insist that these goals be pursued through race-neutral means whenever possible.

The "degree of troublesomeness" issue is important because it directly affects the "level of scrutiny" or burden of justification that reverse discrimination cases trigger. Under basic principles of constitutional law that have largely been settled for some time, most laws are constitutional so long as they rationally promote legitimate goals of government. One major historical exception to this rule is laws that expressly classify people for burdens or benefits on the basis of race, which are unconstitutional unless the government establishes that they are necessary to serve goals of compelling importance, a justification burden that is very difficult to satisfy.

The special rule for race cases, however, developed in a line of cases involving governments' acting out of racial hostility or prejudice to the detriment of minority groups. Some have argued and some Justices have agreed that reverse discrimination, which does not share this characteristic, is not so constitutionally troublesome and therefore should be judged under a less demanding justification standard. *Croson* is the first reverse-discrimination case in which a majority of Justices were able to agree on the burden of justification applicable in reverse-discrimination cases. They found such cases sufficiently troublesome to invoke the demanding justification standard historically applied in hostile-discrimination cases, effectively adopting a broad rule requiring governmental neutrality with regard to race.

The remaining important question in *Croson* was under what conditions, if any, this demanding justification standard might be met. A variety of claims have been historically made in an attempt to justify governmental programs that expressly allocate benefits like admission to state medical or law schools or governmental contracts to minority racial groups. Some, for example, see such programs as justified by the goal of preventing the perpetuation of racial underclasses or castes, promoting racial integration in the professions or work force, or creating role models for minority youth. Although *Croson* is not the first and will not be the last Supreme Court decision to consider this question, a majority of the Court indicates that such goals will be treated skeptically. The majority apparently endorsed the view that only one goal was of sufficiently "compelling" importance to justify reverse discrimination, namely, remedying the effects of past discrimination. Although the decision is less than clear on this point, it seems to imply that state and local government must meet a quite demanding standard in proving that the minority beneficiaries of reverse discrimination are in fact suffering present disadvantages by reason of former discrimination either against the particular individual beneficiaries themselves or other members of their race.

A year after *Croson*, the Rehnquist Court upheld reverse discrimination authorized by Congress with respect to broadcast-media licensing in METRO BROADCASTING, INC. V. FEDERAL COMMUNICATIONS COMMISSION (1990), applying a less demanding standard of review. Five Justices apparently believed that the Court owes greater deference to Congress in such cases than to state and local legislative bodies, for Congress is a coequal branch of government with a variety of constitutional powers that confer on it some degree of discretion in matters of national racial-commercial policy. One of the five, Justice Brennan, has since been replaced by Justice Souter, and it is therefore difficult to predict whether the *Metro* distinction between state-local and federal reverse discrimination or a uniform application of *Croson* will ultimately prevail.

The neutrality principle that has played such an important role in the development of race law has been equally important in SEX DISCRIMINATION cases, where the same basic rule applies: laws that expressly discriminate on gender grounds are suspect (although subject to a less demanding justification than racial classifications), and in the absence of express gender classification, a plaintiff must prove that a challenged action was taken for a gender-discriminatory purpose. The Rehnquist Court has decided no equal protection cases involving gender discrimination, but has given no reason to suspect that it will depart from its neutrality principle. In fact, its recent assimilation of the free exercise of religion clause to the neutrality principle indicates that its commitment to that principle is quite robust.

This assimilation occurred in EMPLOYMENT DIVISION, DEPARTMENT OF HUMAN RESOURCES OF OREGON V. SMITH (1990), which presented the question as to whether Oregon's penalization of the religious use of peyote violated Smith's right to the free exercise of his religion. Before *Smith*, a law that had the effect of burdening a person's ability to follow a religion was unconstitutional unless shown necessary to the accomplishment of a goal of compelling importance. *Smith* holds that with certain very limited exceptions a "*neutral* law of general applicability" cannot be challenged as an interference with the free exercise of religion. The upshot is that, in the future, adjudication under the free exercise clause will parallel racial and gender equal protection adjudication. Laws that expressly require or prohibit religious practices are not religion neutral and will therefore trigger a heavy burden of justification. But laws that are of general applicability, like those prohibiting drug use, are religion neutral and are not subject to successful constitutional attack unless they were adopted or enforced for the purpose of discriminating against a religion, notwithstanding that their effect burdens certain religious practices. Thus, for example, a law prohibiting the serving of alcohol to minors could be enforced against the Catholic use of wine in communion, although the major religions probably have enough political influence to secure accommodating legislation, and the brunt of *Smith* will likely be borne, as in *Smith* itself, by minority religions.

To say that a principle of "neutrality" pervades the Rehnquist Court's jurisprudence of race, gender, and religion is not of course the same as saying that the Court is employing the only tenable, or the right, or even an internally consistent concept of neutrality, for neutrality is no more self-defining than "equality." With regard to race, for example, critics might argue that for the government to act in a truly neutral way its actions should not disproportionately disadvantage members of some racial groups relative to others, irrespective of its purpose, at least when the subject of the disadvantageous treatment is important. They might also say that even if purpose rather than effect is a proper measure of neutrality, the evidence system through which the Court determines purpose is nonneutral, for it rests implicitly on the assumption that government does not usually engage in racial discrimination, rather than the opposite assumption. Finally, these critics might say that the neutrality of current governmental actions cannot be fairly judged without regard to its past actions and, consequently, that what might appear to be a nonneutral conferral of governmental advantages to racial groups previously purposefully disadvantaged by government is better characterized as the pursuit of racial neutrality over time. The Rehnquist Court's neutrality concept might be seen as an attempt to compromise competing political interests, but the underlying questions of principle and policy certainly cannot be resolved by reference to the unadorned concept of neutrality.

No question in contemporary constitutional law better illustrates this proposition than what constitutes an unconstitutional ESTABLISHMENT OF RELIGION. The Rehnquist Court has addressed this question several times, but has not yet supplied a clear answer. All of the Justices who disagree with its answer appear to believe they are being religiously neutral, yet their answers differ significantly. Three answers have figured prominently: (1) the government may not take actions that in fact benefit religion (a major part of the pre-Rehnquist Court test and one favored by some current Justices); (2) it may not take actions that amount to active proselytizing for a religion (the test favored by four Justices); and (3) it may not take actions that create the appearance that it is endorsing religion (the test favored by two "swing" Justices and therefore likely in the short run to prove determinative of the outcome of many cases).

These competing visions of neutrality were all at work in COUNTY OF ALLEGHENY V. AMERICAN CIVIL LIBERTIES UNION (1989), where the Court was called on to decide whether either of two Christmas displays by the city of Pittsburgh violated the ESTABLISHMENT CLAUSE. One was a crèche in the county courthouse, and the other a side-by-side display of a Christmas tree and a menorah in front of a public building. A majority of the Court, apparently pursuing what appeared to five Justices a neutral principle that would simultaneously assure that government does not help or hurt religion too much, applied the "no appearance of endorsement" test, and held the crèche unconstitutional and the other display constitutional. The Court found that the factual context of the first display created the appearance of an endorsement of religion, whereas that of the second created the appearance of a celebration of a winter holiday season. Those Justices who applied the "no benefit in fact" test would have held both displays unconstitutional for their nonneutral favoring of the Christian and Jewish religions. Those who applied the "no proselytizing" test criticized the other opinions for their nonneutral hostility toward religion and would have upheld both because neither coerced anyone to support or participate in a religion.

The establishment clause cases illustrate not only the elusiveness of the "neutrality" concept but also, when read together with the free exercise cases, an asymmetry in Rehnquist Court jurisprudence between racial and religious neutrality apparently reflective of the Court's "mainstream America" predisposition.

With regard to its legitimation function, the neutrality concept operates similarly in race and religion cases: regulations are legitimate even if they produce nonneutral effects, so long as they are facially and purposively neutral. With regard to its restrictive function, however, Rehnquist Court neutrality presumptively prohibits regulations that specially benefit minority races, but permits those that specially benefit religious groups, so long as they do not appear to endorse a religion (or, perhaps, so long as they do not actually proselytize).

The Rehnquist Court has also pursued its conservative agenda through numerous smaller but cumulatively important doctrinal avenues. One example is the privacy rights doctrine that interferences must be "substantial" before they will be regarded as constitutionally troublesome. Many other examples might be given, but one will suffice: the Court's use in free-speech cases of the threshold PUBLIC FORUM concept effectively to foreclose speech rights on most kinds of public property and its related apparent willingness to accept without serious scrutiny governmentally proffered justifications for regulating speech activities in the few public places where individuals do have the right to engage in expressive activities.

In free speech cases, the Rehnquist Court has been reasonable if sporadically protective of traditional constitutional rights. It has struck down many regulations restricting speech, not only in well-publicized cases, such as those involving FLAG DESECRATION, but in more mundane settings, such as newsrack placements and handbilling. One area in which it has been less protective, however, concerns the right to engage in expressive activities in public places, a right that has historically been particularly important to the dispossessed who lack the resources to project their views through other media.

The Court's tolerance toward restrictions of speech in public places derives from the Burger Court's legacy, but again, it seems fairly clear that the Rehnquist Court enthusiastically subscribes to the intuitions that informed that legacy. The questions as to whether and to what extent the free speech clause entitles individuals to engage in expressive activity on public property has been implicit in constitutional law for along time, but for a variety of reasons went largely unaddressed in early cases. The Court was not forced to confront it directly until the mid-1960s, when civil rights demonstrators began to use unconventional sites such as libraries and jails as demonstration locations. The early decisions often rested on unclear reasoning, although for at least a time, the dominant trend was to protect the demonstrators' rights unless the government could prove that the demonstration actually interfered with the normal use of the property.

The Burger Court eventually decided on a tripartite classification of public places and hence speech rights. Streets and parks were labeled "public forums," and speech regulation in these places was "sharply circumscribed." In particular, even so-called content-neutral or "time, place, and manner" restrictions were unconstitutional unless, among other things, they were "narrowly tailored to serve a significant government interest." A second type of public forum consisted of places the government had voluntarily opened for speech purposes, and regulations here were subject to the same constitutional limits. All other kinds of public property were not public forums, and speech activity in such places could be prohibited unless, in substance, the government was simply trying to suppress views it opposed.

Because relatively few places were true public forums and therefore available for speech activities as a matter of right, one important question that remained concerned the circumstances in which the Court would find that property had been voluntarily opened for speech. Additionally, because content-neutral regulation of true public forums is far more common than content-based regulation, the practical effect of these rules on access even to streets and parks depended largely on the circumstances in which the Court would find that "time, place, and manner" regulations were adequately "narrowly tailored."

The current answers to these questions come largely from Rehnquist Court decisions and are not very speech protective. With regard to voluntarily opened forums, the main case is HAZELWOOD SCHOOL DISTRICT V. KUHLMEIER (1988), where the Court upheld the authority of public school officials to censor from a student newspaper articles about student pregnancy and the effect of divorce on students. Although the Court might have decided the case as it did on alternative grounds, its decision suggests that the category of voluntarily opened forums is a very small if not an empty one. It held that the newspaper was not such a forum because school officials had retained curricularly based editorial rights; therefore, even though the paper had always been open to the student body at large to submit opinions and articles, it had not been opened for general student speech purposes. The same theory would seem available for a wide variety of public property. Managers of public auditoriums, for example, might make their facilities broadly available, but retain the right to exclude certain subject matters (although perhaps not viewpoints). After *Hazelwood*, the Court, in this same vein, held in *United States v. Kokinda* (1990) that handbilling and fund solicitation on the sidewalk leading from a parking lot to a post office could be banned because the sidewalk was neither a true nor opened public forum, having been built for post office business purposes.

The most important case on the related question of when a content-neutral regulation is sufficiently "narrowly tailored" to survive constitutional attack is *Ward v. Rock Against Racism* (1989), where the Court appeared to hold that this requirement is met so long as the government can accomplish its goal better with the regulation at issue than without it. The Court did say that a regulation may not burden speech more than is necessary to accomplish the government's legitimate goal, but it simultaneously rejected the view that the government must use the means that would accomplish its goal with the least restriction of speech; it is unclear how these two propositions can co-exist. For example, a ban on all picketing on a certain side-walk would be more effective in accomplishing the goal of pedestrian free movement than no ban would. Thus, it would seem to be constitutional under *Ward*, unless it burdens speech more than is necessary; if it does so, it would seem that this is because pedestrian free movement could have been assured by means that are less restrictive of speech. How *Ward* will ultimately be interpreted is uncertain, but if one takes seriously the idea that any contribution toward a goal validates a content-neutral regulation—and related decisions of the Rehnquist Court suggest that it does take this idea seriously—the Court will have given speech rights so little weight in the balance that virtually all non-content-based restrictions on access, even to true public forums, will survive constitutional attack.

LARRY G. SIMON
(1992)

(SEE ALSO: *Capital Punishment and Race; Race-Consciousness; Religious Liberty; Right Against Self-Incrimination.*)

Bibliography

ABRAMS, J. MARC and GOODMAN, S. MARK 1988 End of an Era? The Decline of Student Press Rights in the Wake of *Hazelwood School District v. Kuhlmeier. Duke Law Journal* 1988: 706–732

Constitutional Scholars' Statement on Affirmative Action After *City of Richmond v. J. A. Croson Co.* 1988 *Yale Law Journal* 98:1711–1716.

ESTRICH, SUSAN R. and SULLIVAN, KATHLEEN M. 1989 Abortion Politics: Writing for an Audience of One. *University of Pennsylvania Law Review* 138:119–155.

FRIED, CHARLES 1989 Affirmative Action After *City of Richmond v. J. A. Croson Co.*: A Response to the Scholars' Statement. *Yale Law Journal* 99:155–161.

KARST, KENNETH L. 1989 Private Discrimination and Public Responsibility: *Patterson* in Context. *Supreme Court Review* 1989:1–51.

SOIFER, AVIAM 1989 Moral Ambition, Formalism, and the "Free World' of *DeShaney. George Washington Law Review* 57:1513–1532.

TUSHNET, MARK 1988 The Emerging Principle of Accommodation of Religion (Dubitante). *Georgetown Law Journal* 76: 1691–1714.

WERHAN, KEITH 1987 The O'Briening of Free Speech Methodology. *Arizona State Law Review* 19:635–679.

REHNQUIST COURT
(Update)

The Supreme Court moved in sharply conservative directions after WILLIAM H. REHNQUIST was elevated from asso-ciate to CHIEF JUSTICE, replacing retiring Chief Justice WARREN E. BURGER, and an even more conservative Justice, ANTONIN SCALIA, filled Rehnquist's seat in 1986. But its evolving DOCTRINES came in fits and spurts as the Court's center further shifted with subsequent changes in the composition of the high bench.

The balance on the Court changed dramatically in 1988 with President RONALD REAGAN's last appointee, Justice AN-THONY M. KENNEDY, replacing Justice LEWIS F. POWELL, JR. Powell had been the pivotal vote on major controversies over ABORTION, AFFIRMATIVE ACTION, and the rights of les-bian and gay citizens. The balance, then, again shifted in 1990 and 1991 with the arrival of President GEORGE H. W. BUSH's two appointees, Justices DAVID H. SOUTER and CLAR-ENCE THOMAS. They replaced the two most liberal justices, respectively, WILLIAM J. BRENNAN, JR., and THURGOOD MAR-SHALL. After his initial two terms, however, Souter broke ranks, and on the most divisive issues he now generally votes with Justice JOHN PAUL STEVENS and President WIL-LIAM J. CLINTON's two appointees, RUTH BADER GINSBURG and STEPHEN G. BREYER. As a result, in the 1990s the Rehnquist Court often split 5–4 on its most controversial rulings. Kennedy and Justice SANDRA DAY O'CONNOR cast the con-trolling votes, forcing more conservative Justices to accommodate their views of the Court's role and of CON-STITUTIONAL INTERPRETATION.

The changing course of the Rehnquist Court is regis-tered in its treatment of liberal PRECEDENTs laid down by the BURGER COURT and the WARREN COURT. Initially, a ma-jority agreed with the Chief Justice's long-standing view of precedent; namely, that prior rulings dealing with CIVIL RIGHTS and CIVIL LIBERTIES decided by bare majorities al-ways should be open for reconsideration and reversal. In the first four TERMS of the Rehnquist Court eleven pre-cedents were OVERRULED along with twelve more in the 1990 and 1991 terms. Yet, overturning so many precedents in such a short period of time created a controversy that came to a head when the Justices considered whether to overrule the watershed abortion decision, ROE V. WADE (1973), in PLANNED PARENTHOOD V. CASEY (1992). In a bit-terly divided 5–4 decision in *Casey*, the Court's plurality and joint opinion issued by Kennedy, O'Connor, and Sou-ter upheld "the essence of *Roe*" partly on the institutional ground that its reversal would hurt the Court's prestige and legitimacy. The battle over that decision apparently curbed the Court's appetite for reaching out to overturn liberal precedents. Since the 1993 term only one or two precedents have been annually overruled, which is in line with the historical average.

Rehnquist, nonetheless, commands a majority for many of the positions he staked out as a dissenting Justice during the years of the Burger Court. Notably, the Court has moved in more conservative directions on issues involving the RIGHTS OF THE CRIMINALLY ACCUSED, CAPITAL PUNISH-MENT, FEDERALISM, and affirmative action. Kennedy, O'Connor, Scalia, and Thomas also share the Chief Justice's reluctance to approve lower federal court orders to achieve school DESEGREGATION, to expand SUBSTANTIVE DUE PROCESS, or to recognize unenumerated FUNDAMENTAL RIGHTS.

The trend toward contracting the rights of the criminally accused that emerged during the Burger Court not merely continued but became more far-reaching, as the Rehnquist Court reversed decisions of the Burger Court deemed too cumbersome and unworkable for law enforcement. In *California v. Acevedo* (1991), for example, two precedents were overruled in holding that police may search any container in any part of an automobile stopped on PROBABLE CAUSE. In general, the scope of the FOURTH AMENDMENT prohibition of unreasonable SEARCHES AND SEIZURES has been sharply restricted. The doctrine that the Fourth Amendment protects "reasonable expectations of privacy," proclaimed in KATZ V. UNITED STATES (1967), became in the hands of the Rehnquist Court the touchstone for limiting the Fourth Amendment's application to WARRANTLESS SEARCHES and seizures, as well as for upholding random DRUG TESTING of students and employees. While the Warren Court's controversial ruling in MAPP V. OHIO (1961) extending the EXCLUSIONARY RULE to the states was not overruled, the "good faith" exception to it created by the Burger Court was extended to include police reliance on mistaken computer records of outstanding arrest warrants in *Arizona v. Evans* (1995). Likewise, the landmark ruling in MIRANDA V. ARIZONA (1966) on the Fifth Amendment prohibition of compulsory self-incrimination has not been overruled, but the Court has approved numerous exceptions to the application of *Miranda*. In addition, the Rehnquist Court made it easier both to impose capital punishment and to expedite the execution of those on death row.

For the first time since the 1937 constitutional crisis over the invalidation of NEW DEAL LEGISLATION, a bare majority of the Rehnquist Court limited Congress's power under the COMMERCE CLAUSE. In a series of rulings, including NEW YORK V. UNITED STATES (1992), UNITED STATES V. LÓPEZ (1995), *Seminole Tribe of Florida v. Florida* (1996), *Printz v. United States* (1997), and *Mack v. United States* (1997), Congress was held to have exceeded its inherent powers under the commerce clause and to infringe on principles of federalism. Nevertheless, the TENTH AMENDMENT has not been resurrected as the strong barrier to congressional legislation that it once was. The Court declined invitations to overrule GARCIA V. SAN ANTONIO METROPOLITAN TRANSIT AUTHORITY (1985), which reversed an opinion written by Rehnquist for a bare majority in NATIONAL LEAGUE OF CITIES V. USERY (1976) asserting the Tenth

Amendment was a limitation on Congress. However, in *Printz* and *New York,* the Court held that Congress violated the Tenth Amendment when it sought to "commandeer" state legislatures or administrative offices to carry out federal programs. In other respects, too, the Rehnquist Court's lack of deference to Congress is striking. In *City of Boerne v. Flores* (1997), the Court struck down the RELIGIOUS FREEDOM RESTORATION ACT as exceeding Congress's enforcement power under the FOURTEENTH AMENDMENT, SECTION 5. Congress had sought to reestablish the standard set forth in SHERBERT V. VERNER (1963), effectively creating exceptions for religious minorities from otherwise generally applicable laws, that was jettisoned by the Rehnquist Court in EMPLOYMENT DIVISION, DEPARTMENT OF HUMAN RESOURCES OF OREGON V. SMITH (1990). In *City of Boerne,* the Justices also stressed that the Court alone defines the scope of constitutional rights. Furthermore, in *Alden v. Maine* (1999), the Court held that the Constitution's federal "structure and history" not only shields states from being sued in federal courts but also makes them immune from lawsuits filed in state courts that seek to enforce federal rights against them.

Somewhat ironically, since a majority of the Rehnquist Court was appointed by Republican Presidents who embraced a strong view of PRESIDENTIAL POWERS, the Court has not been deferential to claims of presidential authority, except with respect to the executive's ability to reinterpret statutory authorizations as in RUST V. SULLIVAN (1991). *Morrison v. Olson* (1988) upheld the appointment of INDEPENDENT COUNSELs to investigate the President and his subordinates. CLINTON V. JONES (1997) unanimously held that Presidents may be subject to civil lawsuits while in office. *Clinton v. City of New York* (1998) struck down Congress's grant of the LINE-ITEM VETO to the President.

As indicated by its reversal of precedents and rejection of assertions of congressional and presidential power, the Rehnquist Court is conservative but not restrained. The Court's JUDICIAL ACTIVISM is evident as well in its rulings invalidating state, local, and federal affirmative action programs, from RICHMOND (CITY OF) V. J. A. CROSON CO. (1989) to ADARAND CONSTRUCTORS, INC. V. PEÑA (1995), which overturned METRO BROADCASTING, INC. V. FCC (1990). So too, in a line of 5–4 rulings following SHAW V. RENO (1993), the Court struck down the creation of majority-minority ELECTORAL DISTRICTS under the VOTING RIGHTS ACT OF 1965. In these and other areas, the Rehnquist Court thwarted the democratic process and the authority of elected representatives at the national, state, and local levels.

Another major jurisprudential theme of the Rehnquist Court is its embrace of the liberal principle of governmental neutrality toward race, gender, and political expression. That principle of governmental nondiscrimination and freedom of expression is interwoven in rulings on the

FIRST AMENDMENT guarantees of FREEDOM OF SPEECH and FREEDOM OF THE PRESS, on the one hand, and the FOURTEENTH AMENDMENT guarantee of EQUAL PROTECTION OF THE LAWS, on the other.

The Rehnquist Court's commitment to the principle of equal treatment and nondiscrimination in enforcing the First Amendment is underlined by its invalidation of numerous laws aimed at punishing particular forms of speech, ranging from those outlawing FLAG DESECRATION and HATE SPEECH, to bans on "patently offensive" sex-related communications on cable television and on the INTERNET. At the same time, greater protection for COMMERCIAL SPEECH was given in *44 Liquormart, Inc. v. Rhode Island* (1996).

In invalidating affirmative action programs, a bare majority of the Court emphasized the idea that "the Constitution is colorblind" and applied the strict scrutiny test to judge race-conscious government action. The Court, over Rehnquist's objections, not only repeatedly rejected the use of racially based PEREMPTORY CHALLENGES in jury selection but also extended the ruling of BATSON V. KENTUCKY (1986) to sex-based peremptory challenges in *J. E. B. v. Alabama* (1994). In addition, a majority of the Court appears to agree that STRICT SCRUTINY should be reserved solely for RACIAL DISCRIMINATION cases. The majority has no interest in expanding the categories of suspect and "quasi-suspect" nonracial classifications, or of fundamental rights and interests, to which the Burger Court suggested that the strict scrutiny test or an intermediate test of heightened scrutiny might apply. When finding impermissible SEX DISCRIMINATION in UNITED STATES V. VIRGINIA (1996), for example, a majority could not be mustered for explicitly declaring gender, like race, to be a suspect category subject to the strict scrutiny test. Besides reserving strict scrutiny for cases of racial discrimination, the Rehnquist Court invalidated some forms of nonracial discrimination simply on the basis of the RATIONAL BASIS test. Thus, the Court found no rational basis for laws discriminating against people with MENTAL ILLNESS in *Heller v. Doe* (1993) or against gays and lesbians in ROMER V. EVANS (1996).

In all these areas, the Rehnquist Court has been activist, not passive, in asserting its power. In two respects, however, the Court has exercised self-restraint. First, as noted, the Court is decidedly reluctant to recognize unenumerated fundamental rights, as with claims to a RIGHT TO DIE with the assistance of a physician. Second, the Court has become increasingly restrained in exercising its traditional supervisory role over lower federal and state courts, even when they render conflicting rulings. Fewer and fewer cases have been annually granted review and, consequently, the plenary docket has declined sharply. In the 1998 term, for instance, only about 80 cases were granted review out of more than 8,000 petitions for CER-

TIORARI on the docket. In historical perspective, the Court had not handed down so few cases in a term since 1953. By comparison, the Burger Court faced dockets of around 5,000 cases and annually decided between 170 and 180 cases, or about three percent, whereas the Rehnquist Court hears less than one percent of its much larger docket. In sum, the Rehnquist Court is conservative and activist, but also less concerned about correcting errors in the lower courts and about ensuring the certain and stable application of the law.

DAVID M. O'BRIEN
(2000)

Bibliography
O'BRIEN, DAVID M.   1996   Charting the Rehnquist Court's Course: The Center Folds, Holds, and Shifts. *New York Law Review* 60:981–998.
———   1997   The Rehnquist Court's Shrinking Plenary Docket. *Judicature* 81:58–65.
SAVAGE, DAVID G.   1992   *Turning Right: The Making of the Rehnquist Supreme Court.* New York: John Wiley & Sons.
SCHWARTZ, BERNARD   1996   *The Unpublished Opinions of the Rehnquist Court.* New York: Oxford University Press.
SIMON, JAMES F.   1995   *The Center Holds: The Power Struggle Inside the Rehnquist Court.* New York: Simon & Schuster.

REID v. COVERT
KINSELLA v. KRUEGER
354 U.S. 1 (1957)

In a 6–2 decision, the Supreme Court invalidated a provision making the Uniform Code of Military Justice applicable to civilians accompanying the armed forces abroad, and reversed the COURT-MARTIAL convictions of two women who had murdered their servicemen husbands on military bases overseas.

Justice HUGO L. BLACK, for a plurality, held that neither the power to make rules for governing the armed forces nor any international agreement could free the government from the procedural requirements of Article III, section 2, and the Fifth and Sixth Amendments.

DENNIS J. MAHONEY
(1986)

REITMAN v. MULKEY
387 U.S. 369 (1967)

By an overwhelming majority, California's voters adopted an INITIATIVE measure ("Proposition 14") adding to the state constitution a provision repealing existing OPEN HOUSING LAWS and forbidding the enactment of new ones. Following the lead of the state supreme court, the Supreme Court held, 5–4, that the circumstances of Proposition 14's adoption demonstrated state encouragement of private RACIAL DISCRIMINATION in the sale and rental of housing. Justice BYRON R. WHITE, for the majority, said this encouragement amounted to STATE ACTION in violation of the FOURTEENTH AMENDMENT. Justice JOHN MARSHALL HARLAN, for the dissenters, argued that Proposition 14 merely withdrew the state from regulation of private conduct; the state court determinations of "encouragement" were not fact findings, but mistaken readings of the Supreme Court's own precedents.

Taken seriously, the *Reitman* decision implies an affirmative state obligation to protect against private racial discrimination in housing. The Supreme Court, far from reading the decision in this manner, has consistently rejected litigants' efforts even to invoke the "encouragement" doctrine there announced. *Reitman* thus lies in isolation, awaiting resurrection. But the trumpet call announcing the end of the world of state action doctrine, seemingly so close in the final years of the WARREN COURT, now seems far away.

KENNETH L. KARST
(1986)

RELEASED TIME

Twice, in MCCOLLUM V. BOARD OF EDUCATION (1948) and again in ZORACH V. CLAUSEN (1952), the Supreme Court considered FIRST AMENDMENT challenges to the practice of releasing public school pupils from their regular studies so that they might participate in programs for religious instruction.

The first such program, in Gary, Indiana, in 1914, provided that, with parental consent and cooperation of church authorities, children could be released for one or more periods each week to go to churches of their own faith and there participate in religious instruction, returning to the public school at the end of the period, or if the period was the last of the day, going home.

The idea spread to other communities, but, for a variety of reasons, quite slowly. In rural and small urban communities, such as Champaign, Illinois, it was found more effective to have the religious instruction take place within the public schools rather than in the church schools.

In Champaign in 1940, an interfaith council with Protestant, Roman Catholic, and Jewish representatives was formed to offer religious instruction within the public schools during regular school hours. Instructors of religion were to be hired and paid by or through the interfaith council, subject to the approval and supervision of the public school superintendent. Each term the public school

teachers distributed to the children cards on which parents could indicate their consent to the enrollment of their children in the religion classes. Children who obtained such consent were released by the school authorities from the secular work for a period of thirty minutes weekly in the elementary schools and forty-five minutes in the junior high school. Only Protestant instruction was conducted within the regular classroom; children released for Roman Catholic or Jewish instruction left their classroom for other parts of the building. Nonparticipants were also relocated, sometimes accompanied by their regular teachers and sometimes not. At the end of each session, children who had participated in any religious instruction returned to the regular classroom, and regular class work was resumed.

McCollum v. Board of Education (1948) was a suit, brought in a state court by the mother of a fifth grader, challenging the constitutionality of Champaign's program. In the Supreme Court, counsel for the school authorities argued that the establishment clause did not apply to the states, and that the contrary HOLDING in EVERSON V. BOARD OF EDUCATION (1947) should be overruled. This the Court refused to do, reasserting *Everson's* conclusion about the scope of the establishment clause.

No more successful was the argument that historically the establishment clause had been intended to forbid only preferential treatment of one faith over others, whereas the Champaign program was open equally to Protestants, Roman Catholics, and Jews. Here, too, the Court found no reason to reconsider its statement in *Everson* that the clause barred aid not only to one religion but equally to all religions.

Where, the Court said, pupils compelled by law to go to school for secular education are released in part from their legal duty if they attend religious classes, the tax-supported public school system's use to aid religious groups to spread their faiths falls squarely under the ban of the First Amendment. Not only are the public school buildings used for the dissemination of religious doctrines, but the state also affords sectarian groups an invaluable aid, helping to provide pupils for their religious classes through the use of the state's compulsory public school machinery. This, the Court concluded, was not SEPARATION OF CHURCH AND STATE.

Although the Court's language appeared to encompass in its determination of unconstitutionality released time plans providing for off-school religious instruction (and Justice HUGO L. BLACK who wrote the opinion so interpreted it), the majority reached a contrary conclusion in *Zorach v. Clausen* (1952).

Zorach involved New York City's program, which restricted public school participation to releasing children whose parents had signed consent cards and specifically forbade comment by any principal or teacher on the attendance or nonattendance of any pupil upon religious instruction. This situation, said the Court speaking through Justice WILLIAM O. DOUGLAS, differed from that presented in the *McCollum* case. There, the classrooms had been used for religious instruction and the influence of the public school used to promote that instruction. Here, the public schools did no more than accommodate their schedules to allow children, who so wished, to go elsewhere for religious instruction completely independent of public school operations. The situation, Douglas said, was not different from that presented when a Roman Catholic student asks his teacher to be excused to attend a mass on a Holy Day of Obligation or a Jewish student to attend synagogue on Yom Kippur.

Government, Justice Douglas said further, may not finance religious groups nor undertake religious instruction nor blend secular and sectarian education nor use secular institutions to force one or some religion on any person. Government, however, must be neutral in respect to religion, not hostile. "We are," he said, "a religious people whose institutions presuppose a Supreme Being. When the state encourages religious instruction or cooperates with religious authorities, it follows the best of our traditions. For it then respects the religious nature of our people and accommodates the public service to their spiritual needs."

On the basis of *McCollum* and *Zorach,* the present law is that released time programs are constitutional so long as the religious instruction is given off the public school premises and the public school teachers and authorities are involved in it only by releasing uncoerced children who choose to participate in it.

LEO PFEFFER
(1986)

Bibliography

PFEFFER, LEO   (1953) 1967   *Church, State and Freedom.* Boston: Beacon Press.
Released Time for Religious Education in New York City Schools. 1949   Public Education Association.
STOKES, A. P. and PFEFFER, LEO   1964   *Church and State in the United States.* New York: Harper & Row.

RELIGION AND FRAUD

Few responsibilities are more sensitive and difficult to meet than drawing a line between punishable obtaining of property under false pretenses and constitutionally protected free exercise of religion. In the one major case to reach the Supreme Court, *United States v. Ballard* (1944), the Court split three ways in its decision.

Ballard involved the conviction of organizers of the "I Am" movement, indicted for using the mails to defraud because they falsely represented that they had supernatural powers to heal the incurably ill, and that as "Divine messengers" they had cured hundreds of afflicted persons through communication with Saint Germain, Jesus, and others. The trial court had instructed the jury that they should not decide whether these statements were literally true, but only whether the defendants honestly believed them to be true.

On appeal the majority of the Supreme Court agreed with the trial judge. Under the principles of SEPARATION OF CHURCH AND STATE and RELIGIOUS LIBERTY, it held, neither a jury nor any other organ of government had the competence to pass on whether certain religious experiences actually occurred. A jury could no more constitutionally decide that defendants had not shaken hands with Jesus, as they claimed, than they could determine that Jesus had not walked on the sea, as the Bible related. The limit of the jury's power was a determination whether defendants actually believed that what they recounted was true.

Chief Justice HARLAN FISKE STONE dissented on the ground that the prosecution should be allowed to prove that none of the alleged cures had been effected. On the other extreme Justice ROBERT H. JACKSON urged that the prosecution should not have been instituted in the first place, for few juries would find that the defendants honestly believed in something that was unbelievable. Nevertheless the majority decision remains the law, and is not likely to be OVERRULED after a half-century of acceptance.

LEO PFEFFER
(1986)

Bibliography

PFEFFER, LEO   (1953) 1967   *Church, State and Freedom.* Boston: Beacon Press.

RELIGION AND FREE SPEECH

Religious speech was at the heart of the historical development of FREEDOM OF SPEECH principles—as any student of JOHN MILTON or the Jehovah's Witnesses can attest. But in recent decades, concerns arising under the ESTABLISHMENT CLAUSE caused religious speech to receive significantly less protection than secular speech, whenever the speech occurred in a PUBLIC FORUM or involved public benefits. This disparity is now diminishing.

Under the separationist interpretation of the establishment clause that flourished roughly between WORLD WAR II and the 1980s, the FIRST AMENDMENT was thought to bar government "aid" to the propagation of religious ideas. At the same time, with the rejection of the right–privilege distinction, the free speech clause came to be understood as barring the government from discriminating on the basis of viewpoint, and sometimes content, in the distribution of government benefits. These two principles were obviously in conflict. The free speech clause was thought to require viewpoint neutrality; the establishment clause was thought to require viewpoint exclusion from government benefit programs in many circumstances.

The conflict first came to the fore in WIDMAR V. VINCENT (1981). A public university extended the benefit of free access to meeting rooms to all student organizations, but out of concern for the SEPARATION OF CHURCH AND STATE, denied this benefit to groups who were engaged in religious speech or activity. Although the appellate court ruled against the religious students, the Supreme Court reversed, and established the principle that when the government has created a forum for free speech, religious speakers are entitled to take equal advantage of it.

In two cases in 1995, these principles were extended to more difficult and controversial contexts. In CAPITOL SQUARE REVIEW & ADVISORY BOARD V. PINETTE (1995), the Court faced the issue of whether a group (which happened to be the Ku Klux Klan, although it was treated as an ordinary religious speaker) could display a large cross in a municipal square, in a space that had been opened for display of symbols by private speakers. Four Justices, led by ANTONIN SCALIA, advocated a categorical principle that the establishment clause does not bar private religious expression on government PROPERTY, if a forum has been opened to the public for speech and permission to speak, if any, was granted on the same terms as other private groups. Three Justices, led by SANDRA DAY O'CONNOR, maintained that each case should be evaluated on its facts to determine whether a reasonable observer would perceive governmental endorsement.

In ROSENBERGER V. RECTOR & VISITORS OF THE UNIVERSITY OF VIRGINIA (1995), the equal access principle was extended to the "metaphorical" forum of student activities funding. The Court held that a student publication that was otherwise eligible for funding could not be excluded on the basis of its religious orientation.

In these cases, therefore, the Court resolved the apparent conflict between free speech and establishment clause principles by extending the principle of viewpoint neutrality (originally a free speech DOCTRINE) to the ESTABLISHMENT OF RELIGION, in place of the prior emphasis on no-aid separationism.

MICHAEL W. MCCONNELL
(2000)

(SEE ALSO: *Accommodation of Religion; Government Aid to Religious Institutions; Religious Symbols in Public Places.*)

RELIGION AND SECULARISM IN CONSTITUTIONAL INTERPRETATION AND DEMOCRATIC DEBATE

Although the FIRST AMENDMENT forbids any law "respecting an establishment of religion, or prohibiting the free exercise thereof," the term "religion" is not defined. In its first efforts to define the term, the Supreme Court adopted a theistic approach: In DAVIS V. BEASON (1890), the Court described religion as "[having] reference to one's views of his relations to his Creator, and to the obligations they impose or reverence for his being and character, and of obedience to his will." Similarly, in 1931, Chief Justice CHARLES EVANS HUGHES wrote that "the essence of religion is belief in a relation to God involving duties superior to those arising from any human relation."

Theistic definitions of religion most likely reflect the majority view of those who drafted and adopted the Constitution. The nineteenth and twentieth centuries, however, brought increasing numbers of nontheistic and pantheistic religious adherents to the United States. Responding to both the rise of religious pluralism and modern developments in systematic theology, in the 1960s and 1970s the Court experimented with broader definitions of religious belief. In UNITED STATES V. SEEGER (1965), the Court considered the conscientious-objector provisions of the Military Training and Service Act. After canvassing the works of modern theologians including Paul Tillich, the Court interpreted the act's accommodation for "beliefs in relation to a Supreme Being" to include objections based on what Tillich called one's "ultimate concern." Under this definition, any strongly held belief would qualify as religious. Expanding on this theme, in *Welsh v. United States* (1970), the Court held that "religious beliefs" protected by the act included any belief analogous or "parallel" to those of a religious person. Applying this definition, the *Welsh* Court rejected the defendant's own assertion that his beliefs were not religious. According to the Court, "very few registrants are fully aware of the broad scope of the word 'religious' as used in [the Act]."

Although the Court was interpreting a statute in the SELECTIVE SERVICE cases, its broad definition of religion was motivated by a concern that any narrower approach would violate the ESTABLISHMENT CLAUSE. Such a broad definition of religious belief, however, creates a host of conundrums: If any belief is at least potentially religious, how is the term "religion" meaningful as a class of beliefs and activities receiving unique protection under the free exercise clause? Moreover, expansive definitions of religion presumably apply equally to the free exercise and establishment clauses. Thus, if it is true, as some Justices have suggested, that ethical systems like "secular humanism" are religions protected under the Constitution, then public school administrators arguably have "established religion" any time they attempt to inculcate secular values in their students.

In the decades following the selective service cases, in cases such as WISCONSIN V. YODER (1972) and THOMAS V. INDIANA REVIEW BOARD (1981), the Court occasionally suggested in dicta that the Constitution protects only religious belief, not secular philosophy. Nevertheless, the Court has never specifically defined the term "religion" under the Constitution, and has expressly stated that "religious beliefs need not be acceptable, logical, consistent, or comprehensible to others in order to merit First Amendment protection." In practice, it is extremely rare for a court to dispose a RELIGIOUS LIBERTY claim on the ground that the belief at issue is "secular" and not "religious." Most free exercise opinions focus not on the religious nature of the individual's beliefs, but on whether the government was justified in its refusal to accommodate those beliefs.

Despite these difficulties in defining what is religious and what is secular, two recurrent themes of constitutional commentary raise the issue of religion and secularism in democratic debate. First, to what extent does the Constitution protect or permit religious arguments in the public square? Second, to what extent is it morally appropriate to use or rely on religious arguments in favor of particular laws?

Under current interpretations of the speech and establishment clauses, not only is it permissible for a private individual to deploy either religious or secular arguments in democratic debate, CANTWELL V. CONNECTICUT (1940) makes clear that it is unconstitutional to prohibit such expression. Similarly, private individuals may rely on religious arguments in deciding whether or not to vote in favor of a particular public policy. Indeed, such reliance probably could not be prevented.

A more difficult question is posed when legislators use or rely on religious rationales in their decisions to vote on proposed laws. Under the LEMON TEST for establishment clause violations, all laws must have a secular purpose. This rule does not invalidate laws that coincide with religious principles; that would require invalidating much of the civil and criminal code, including laws against murder. The Court requires only that laws have some secular purpose, even if the law simultaneously advances some religious principle or belief. In theory, this leaves both legislators and private citizens free to use or rely on religious rationales, as long as some secular rationale suffices to justify the law.

In practice, however, the Court has not always deferred to the secular rationales offered in support of laws that were vigorously promoted by religious groups. For example, in *Edwards v. Aguillard* (1987), the Court invalidated a "balanced treatment" statute that required the teaching of both evolution and creation science, or neither, in the public schools for lack of a secular purpose. WALLACE V. JAFFREE (1985) invalidated a state "moment of silence in public schools" law in part on the basis of legislative statements supporting prayer in public schools. To the extent that religious adherents or organizations publicly advance religious grounds for the adoption of particular laws, they increase the risk that courts will discount secular justifications for regulation and hold that the law was solely motivated by a religious rationale.

During the 1970s and 1980s, there was an additional link between private religious advocacy and the constitutionality of particular government programs. At that time, the Court interpreted the "entanglement" prong of the three-pronged *Lemon* test as discouraging religious-based political discourse or, as some Justices put it, "political division along religious lines." These Justices believed that religiously motivated political discourse was such a danger to democratic debate that it justified—and most often required—exclusion of religious organizations from general government funding programs. No outcome in any case turned expressly on the "political entanglement" analysis, and, since the 1980s, the Court has downplayed the idea that religious political discourse is disfavored under the Constitution.

Even if religious arguments in the public square are constitutionally protected, there remains the question of whether such arguments are morally justifiable. Political theorists like John Rawls and Bruce Ackerman argue that participants in a liberal democracy should argue in terms that are accessible to all citizens, regardless of religious belief. Because religious-based arguments are inaccessible to nonbelievers, these arguments either should be voluntarily removed from public political debate or only presented in tandem with accessible secular arguments.

If people believe that both religious and secular arguments support their position, arguably they have a moral obligation to present the secular as well as the religious argument in public debate. Morally (and strategically) it seems better to use reasons that unite rather than divide. The more difficult issue, however, involves the obligations of religious believers who are not convinced that any secular rationale supports their preferred policy. In this situation, the believers face a difficult choice: They must present solely the religious argument (which is inaccessible to nonbelievers), advance secular rationales that they themselves find unconvincing, or say nothing at all. Under theories advanced by Rawls and Ackerman, the first option is off-limits; therefore, the religious believer must either dissemble or remain silent.

Such constraints are unacceptable to scholars like Michael Perry and David Smolin, both of whom argue that religious arguments are valuable additions to public debate. Perry argues that, since it is inevitable that some people will rely on religious rationales, it is better to welcome religious arguments to the public square where they can be debated and tested. Smolin rejects the idea that religious arguments are necessarily inaccessible to nonbelievers: Major religions like Judaism, Islam, and Christianity are premised on the belief in a very public and accessible revelation of God. Moreover, instead of being inherently divisive, religious arguments often may constitute a kind of common ground between individuals with otherwise polarized cultural or political perspectives.

Voluntary restraint theories, whatever their form, are efforts to combat what many view as the tendency of religious belief to polarize public debate. Ironically, however, some of the most important advances in CIVIL RIGHTS have been accompanied by impassioned—and polarizing—religious rhetoric. The most obvious examples are the historic speeches of the religious ABOLITIONISTS and activists in the CIVIL RIGHTS MOVEMENT of the 1960s. In the end, whatever might be gained by secularizing public debate might come at the cost of religiously inspired moral urgency.

KURT T. LASH
(2000)

Bibliography

ACKERMAN, BRUCE A. 1980 *Social Justice in the Liberal State.* New Haven, Conn.: Yale University Press.

LASH, KURT T. 1997 Civilizing Religion. *George Washington Law Review* 65:1100–1119.

PERRY, MICHAEL J. 1997 *Religion in Politics: Constitutional and Moral Perspectives.* New York: Oxford University Press.

RAWLS, JOHN 1993 *Political Liberalism.* New York: Columbia University Press.

SMOLIN, DAVID M. 1996 Cracks in the Mirrored Prison: An Evangelical Critique of Secularist Academic and Judicial Myths Regarding the Relationship of Religion and American Politics. *Loyola of Los Angeles Law Review* 29:1487–1512.

RELIGION CLAUSES IN INTERACTION

There has been a long-term tension between the FIRST AMENDMENT's two religion clauses, one forbidding government to promote or "establish" religion, the other forbidding government to abridge the "free exercise" of religion. On the one hand, under the much-criticized (but still formally governing) LEMON TEST, any government action whose purpose or primary effect is to aid religion violates the ESTABLISHMENT CLAUSE. On the other hand, under the *Sherbert–Yoder* test (the rule for a quarter century prior to 1990), the free exercise clause periodically required the state to accommodate religion.

Unfortunately, the Supreme Court's few direct confrontations with the problem before the mid-1980s had been unsatisfying. It was not until *Corporation of the Presiding Bishop of the Church of Jesus Christ of Latter-Day Saints v. Amos* (1987) that the Court addressed the issue at any length. In upholding Congress's exemption of religious groups from a general statutory ban on religious discrimination in employment, the Court simply announced that "under the *Lemon* analysis, it is a permissible legislative purpose to alleviate significant governmental interference with the ability of religious organizations to define and carry out their religious missions." This conclusory analysis prompted Justice SANDRA DAY O'CONNOR, who concurred separately, to accurately observe:

> On the one hand, a rigid application of the *Lemon* test would invalidate legislation exempting religious observers from generally applicable government obligations. By definition, such legislation has a religious purpose and effect in promoting the free exercise of religion. On the other hand, judicial deference to all legislation that purports to facilitate the free exercise of religion would completely vitiate the Establishment Clause. Any statute pertaining to religion can be viewed as an "accommodation" of free exercise rights.

Several major developments during the past decade have produced some thoughtful approaches to resolving the conflict between the clauses. First, the highly controversial ruling in EMPLOYMENT DIVISION, DEPARTMENT OF HUMAN RESOURCES OF OREGON V. SMITH (1990) held that the free exercise clause affords no right to a religious exemption from a neutral law (i.e., one of general applicability) even though it imposes a substantial burden on religious practice. Abandoning the *Sherbert–Yoder* test— which had required exemptions from generally applicable regulations that substantially burdened religious exercise, unless there was a "compelling interest" for not doing so and the law was the "least restrictive means" for accomplishing that interest—the free exercise clause was reduced to prohibiting only those government actions that single out one or all religions for adverse treatment. By no longer demanding special treatment for religion, the free exercise clause's incompatibility with the establishment clause's "no aid" edict was largely eliminated. Still, the question remains: If government voluntarily exempts religion from generally burdensome regulations does this violate the establishment clause?

The other important efforts have involved the Court's implicit renunciation of the *Lemon* test under the establishment clause in favor of competing approaches, all of which speak to the interaction between the religion

imical to their religious beliefs and therefore violates their right to free exercise of religion. The Supreme Court has not yet dealt with this issue, and its pronouncements elsewhere offer little guidance. The Court has often stated that a substantial burden of free exercise can be justified only by a COMPELLING STATE INTEREST pursued by the least restrictive means. Public schools have denied that their teaching burdens free exercise at all because their teaching is secular, not religious; children need not accept what is taught, and children are not compelled to attend public schools, but are free to attend private schools. Dissatisfied parents reply that free exercise is burdened if children are taught that their religion is wrong, although the children do not have to profess acceptance of the schools' teaching, and although others consider the issues in question secular. These parents stress that young impressionable children may not understand that they are free to reject the school's teaching or may be too intimidated to express their disagreement. They also argue that the option of attending private schools is too expensive to remove the burden on free exercise.

Even if the curriculum does burden free exercise, public schools claim a compelling state interest in giving all children this education. Most observers concede that states have an interest in teaching basic skills such as reading and writing. However, it is debatable how important the state's interest is in other areas, including moral values and sex education. If a public school does burden free exercise without compelling justification, some accommodation of the religious students may be necessary as a remedy. Many school systems excuse students from certain programs to which they have religious objections, and some schools provide students with alternative instruction. The latter approach can be expensive and administratively burdensome; the former may prevent the child from obtaining essential skills. Suggestions that children be given VOUCHERS to attend private schools, meanwhile, have been attacked as both violative of the establishment clause and destructive of the objectives of public education.

The legal need for accommodation may no longer be as pressing as it once was, however. The Supreme Court recently indicated in EMPLOYMENT DIVISION, DEPARTMENT OF HUMAN RESOURCES OF OREGON V. SMITH (1990) that it has abandoned the "compelling state interest" standard. If the Court adheres to this position, public schools would not be constitutionally required to show a compelling reason for subjecting children to teaching that is hostile to their religion.

In addition to controversies over school curriculum, disputes have also multiplied over the use of public school facilities by student religious groups. In WIDMAR V. VINCENT (1981), the Supreme Court insisted that public university facilities generally available to student groups and speakers also be open to student religious groups. In 1984, Congress tried to extend this principle to secondary schools by adopting the Equal Access Act, which forbids public secondary schools from discriminating on the basis of the content of speech when affording student groups access to school facilities outside school hours. However, the school may not sponsor, and school employees may not participate in, student religious groups.

Some critics believed that the act was unconstitutional because of the possibility that school employees would become involved and that students would perceive the provision of facilities to student religious groups as endorsing religion. The Court disagreed in BOARD OF EDUCATION OF WESTSIDE COMMUNITY SCHOOLS V. MERGENS (1990), holding that the act did not violate the establishment clause.

Although the Court has repeatedly struck down daily school prayers, many schools have included prayers or benedictions in special school events. The Supreme Court has upheld the opening of legislative sessions with prayers in MARSH V. CHAMBERS (1983), but the differences in the public school context have persuaded some lower courts that the practice cannot be permitted there.

The Supreme Court has said that public schools may study the Bible as literature and history, but not for devotional purposes. This has required lower courts to decide case by case whether particular programs meet this standard or improperly include religious indoctrination.

Public school teachers occasionally endorse or criticize religious beliefs in the classroom. Courts generally have tried to distinguish between teachers' statements of their own beliefs, which are permissible and protected by the rights of free speech and free exercise, and propagandizing, which infringes on both the students' right of free exercise and the establishment clause. Lower courts have also upheld regulations against teachers' regularly wearing distinctively religious garb.

GEORGE W. DENT
(1992)

(SEE ALSO: *Equal Access; Religious Fundamentalism; Religious Liberty; Separation of Church and State.*)

Bibliography

DENT, GEORGE W.   1988   Religious Children, Secular Schools. *Southern California Law Review* 61:863–941.

STROSSEN, NADINE   1986   "Secular Humanism" and "Scientific Creationism": Proposed Standards for Reviving Curricular Decisions Affecting Students' Religious Freedom. *Ohio State Law Journal* 47:333–407.

RELIGION IN PUBLIC SCHOOLS
(Update 2)

The place of religion in public schools has been the subject of significant controversy in America for well over a century. A number of different issues related to this general subject have come to the fore in recent years. First, the question of publicly sponsored worship exercises in public schools has remained prominent. In 1998, the U.S. HOUSE OF REPRESENTATIVES defeated a proposed constitutional amendment that, if enacted, would have legalized state-sponsored worship in public facilities, including schools. In LEE V. WEISMAN (1992), the Supreme Court ruled that the ESTABLISHMENT CLAUSE prohibited officially sponsored prayer at public middle school commencement ceremonies. Although the ruling in *Lee* clearly extended to all public schools through and including high school, many state universities have continued to have prayer at commencements. For those who believe that the primary focus of the establishment clause is to forbid state coercion on matters of religion, the age and maturity difference between university graduates and younger students may be sufficient reason to permit state universities to do what lower schools may not. A broader view of nonestablishment, focusing on the dangers of government sponsorship of religious exercise, would suggest that state university commencement prayers are no less unconstitutional than their counterparts at high school or below.

Another issue that followed in the wake of *Lee* is whether schools may arrange to have students decide whether to have student-led prayers at commencement. Although lower courts have divided on this question, most have held that school officials are responsible for the content of graduation ceremonies, and that official initiation of student-led prayers at commencement is also unconstitutional. Whether student speakers acting entirely on their own at commencement may engage in worship is a more difficult question, although words of personal spiritual commitment would be a constitutionally safer course than a student-led prayer involving the entire class or audience.

The issue of student-initiated prayers is connected to a larger question about student religious expression at school. Although student worship as an official part of the program at school-sponsored public events (athletic events and assemblies as well as commencements) is constitutionally questionable, much student religious expression in public schools is private rather than government speech and is therefore perfectly permissible. So long as religious speech by students is not school-sponsored, and does not constitute harassment of others, there are no grounds to suppress the speech simply because it occurs on school property. Of course, what constitutes school sponsorship, and what amounts to harassment, are frequently open to debate and controversy. School sponsorship implies active support, rather than a passive refusal by school officials to censor the speech. Harassment, too, requires more than trivial annoyance or an atmosphere of discomfort for some caused by the religious practices of others; for student religious speech to constitute harassment, ordinarily it must be personally hostile toward a particular individual or group.

Constitutional tolerance for private religious speech on school property extends beyond students in the years of compulsory education. In LAMB'S CHAPEL V. CENTER MORICHES UNION FREE SCHOOL DISTRICT (1993), a unanimous Supreme Court held that school officials could not exclude a community-based religious group from access to school property for evening meeting space permitted to other community groups. In a more controversial decision, a closely divided Court in ROSENBERGER V. RECTOR & VISITORS OF THE UNIVERSITY OF VIRGINIA (1995) held that the university could not exclude a student-written journal of religious opinion from a program, financed by student fees, designed to subsidize the printing costs of student journals generally. Justice DAVID H. SOUTER'S DISSENTING OPINION in *Rosenberger* argued strenuously that the subsidy involved taxation to finance the publication of proselytizing religious messages, which he deemed forbidden by the establishment clause. Both *Lamb's Chapel* and *Rosenberger* represent the Court's continued rejection of government reliance on the establishment clause as a reason for permitting discrimination against private religious expression on government property, including schools.

In a different twist on religion in the public schools, the Court's decision in BOARD OF EDUCATION OF KIRYAS JOEL VILLAGE SCHOOL DISTRICT V. GRUMET (1994) invalidated the New York legislature's attempt to create a public school district in a community populated entirely by a group of Satmar Hasidic Jews, who live according to traditional European Orthodox Jewish folkways. The legislature had created the district so as to permit public financing of a school for learning-disabled children in the village; all other children in the village attended private Hebrew academies. Despite the attractiveness of this objective, the Court treated the law that set up the district as a form of sectarian religious favoritism, which the Constitution forbids. The need for the special district evaporated with the Court's decision in AGOSTINI V. FELTON (1997), which OVERRULED a prior decision that had forbidden publicly financed remedial teaching of religious school students on religious school premises. As a result of *Agostini*, the village of Kiryas Joel no longer needs a public school district within its borders; it may now obtain state support for teaching learning disabled children at the sites of the religious academies in the village.

IRA C. LUPU
(2000)

(SEE ALSO: *Accommodation of Religion; Establishment of Religion; Government Aid to Religious Institutions; Religion and Free Speech; Religious Diversity and the Constitution; Religious Liberty; School Prayers.*)

Bibliography

LUPU, IRA C.   1996   Uncovering the Village of Kiryas Joel. *Columbia Law Review* 96:104–120.

PAULSEN, MICHAEL S.   1993   *Lemon* Is Dead. *Case Western Reserve Law Review* 43:795–863.

SHERRY, SUZANNA   1992   *Lee v. Weisman:* Paradox Redux. *Supreme Court Review* 1992:123–153.

RELIGIOUS DIVERSITY AND THE CONSTITUTION

In their 1993 book *One Nation Under God: Religion in Contemporary American Society,* sociologists Barry A. Kosmin and Seymour P. Lachman analyze the most extensive survey of American religion ever conducted. More than 113,000 Americans answered questions about their religious identity; nearly 90 percent identified themselves as religious, the overwhelming number (86 percent) as Christian. The remaining 3.3 percent, representing about six million Americans, included not only Jews, Muslims, Buddhists, and Hindus, but also approximately 23,000 Taoists, 18,000 Rastafarians, and 6,000 Shintoists, not to mention 8,000 Wiccans. One ought not, of course, believe that "Christians" represent any kind of monolithic community: 46,000,000 Catholics (26.2 percent of the American population) and 34,000,000 Baptists (19.4 percent), the two largest denominations, are joined in the category "Christian" by no fewer than 40 other groups, none of them containing more than 8 percent of the population. These range from such well-known groups as the Methodists (8 percent) and Presbyterians (2.8 percent) to Mormons (1.4 percent), Jehovah's Witnesses (0.8 percent), Christian Scientists (about 0.15 percent), and even smaller groups such as the Quakers and component groups within the broad category of Christian evangelical or pentacostalist churches. And, of course, one could easily point to dramatic differences within the approximately 2 percent of Americans who are Jews, as one places members of the Reform and Conservative wings of Judaism next not only to the Modern Orthodox, but also to the various Hassidic sects.

There are at least two inferences that one can draw from this list: First, it assumes that we know exactly what we are talking about when we identify persons as "religious" rather than, presumably, "irreligious." But what is it, precisely, that joins together the Evangelical Protestant, Reformed Jew, Buddhist, Scientologist, and Wiccan? It surely is not, for example, belief in a supernatural divinity who commands various behaviors at threat of divine punishment. Perhaps all that unites them is that they ask their adherents to think deeply about the purpose of life.

Why do we care what, if anything, all of these groups have in common? One answer is simple: The FIRST AMENDMENT guarantees in its text only the "free exercise of religion," as against, say, a general right to follow one's own moral precepts derived from Kantian moral theory or Benthamite utilitarianism. Several classic Supreme Court cases, particularly from the Vietnam era dealing with conscientious objection, attempted, with notable lack of success, to wrestle with the problem of defining religion. Many other first-rate minds have subsequently confronted the issue, though the various definitions presented have proved satisfying primarily to their authors and, alas, to few other scholars or judges.

Second, even if we are confident we can tell the difference between religious and nonreligious groups, we must confront the fact that the various groups that we call religious differ in far more than belief. There would be relatively little interest in "religious diversity and the Constitution" if all that differentiated religions were theology. The free speech provisions of the First Amendment, at least as interpreted by the modern Court, would be enough to protect the most outrageous theological (or antireligious) opinions. However, what triggers constitutional litigation under the free exercise clause is, not surprisingly, "exercise"; that is, action. The actions in question are, to be sure, predicated on beliefs—slaughtering animals or drinking wine or smoking peyote is a way of showing devotion to one's gods; one is commanded to refrain from participating in immoral wars or simply to refuse to engage in any kind of work on sabbatical days; and so on. But the nub of the matter is the activity believed to follow from such beliefs.

It is a settled tenet of constitutional analysis that belief and action are separable. Or so the Court has consistently claimed at least since the seminal case of REYNOLDS V. UNITED STATES (1879), where the Court had no compunctions about jailing a Mormon leader for the behavior of bigamous marriage, whatever its linkage to then-central Mormon doctrine. During the 1960s and 1970s, however, the Court seemed to modify the belief-action distinction when, for example, it required state unemployment compensation to be given to Seventh Day Adventists who refused, in violation of state law, to be available for jobs that required working on Saturday, SHERBERT V. VERNER (1963), or exempted the Old Order Amish in Wisconsin from having to comply with compulsory education laws that would have required Amish children to attend schools through age sixteen, WISCONSIN V. YODER (1972).

The belief-action distinction returned with a vengeance in EMPLOYMENT DIVISION, DEPARTMENT OF HUMAN RESOURCES OF OREGON V. SMITH (1990), where the Court overturned the Oregon Supreme Court's holding that the free exercise clause required an exemption from Oregon's law prohibiting the use of peyote for Native Americans who ingested the drug as part of religious ceremonies. Implausibly distinguishing the cases mentioned above, the Court held that otherwise neutral laws could be applied to bar religious practices, whatever their importance to the group in question. Whatever the free exercise clause meant, it was not, apparently, the right to engage in any behavior that offended general legal precepts.

The clause did prohibit the state from passing laws that were (or seemed) intended to limit only idiosyncratic religious practices. In CHURCH OF THE LUKUMI BABALU AYE, INC. V. HIALEAH (1993) the Court struck down an ordinance passed by Hialeah, Florida, that was clearly an effort to prohibit members of the Santería religion, a syncretic blend of traditional African and Roman Catholic views and practices, from slaughtering animals. Hialeah made no attempt to protect animals from being shot by hunters or slaughtered by butchers. A truly general protection of animal rights would have been a different case.

In *Smith*, the Court seemed to suggest that legislatures could in fact allow religious exemptions; such accommodations, however, were not constitutionally required. Congress accepted this apparent invitation in 1993, passing, almost unanimously, the RELIGIOUS FREEDOM RESTORATION ACT (RFRA), which would have put all governments, national, state, and local, to the test of demonstrating that a "compelling interest" justified "burden[ing]" one's religiously motivated behavior. (Congress claimed that this was the standard established in *Sherbert* and *Yoder*.) The Court, however, invalidated RFRA in 1997, holding that the law was beyond congressional power, at least when applied to state and local governments; it was deemed an unacceptable challenge to the Court's institutional monopoly over CONSTITUTIONAL INTERPRETATION. A number of states are passing their own quasi-RFRAs, however, and the general issues posed by the statute will certainly continue to be with us (and RFRA probably remains active as a limitation on the national government).

Even if there were only relatively few religious denominations, it might still be difficult to know in advance what sorts of accommodations a law like RFRA (or expansive reading of the free exercise clause, as in *Sherbert* and *Yoder*) might require. Can ZONING laws be applied to churches; do prisons have a duty to honor the dietary requirements of all (or any) religions; do Fundamentalist

parents have a constitutional right to have their children excused, during the school day, from classes that are teaching "satanic" material; can bankruptcy law be applied to recapture religious tithes made within four months of the declaration of bankruptcy? All of these, and more, were the subject of live lawsuits following the passage of RFRA, and they serve to test any theory of the practical impact of religious diversity on constitutional interpretation.

SANFORD LEVINSON
(2000)

(SEE ALSO: *Nonjudicial Interpretation of the Constitution; Religious Liberty.*)

Bibliography

CHOPER, JESSE H. 1995 *Securing Religious Liberty: Principles for Judicial Interpretation of the Religion Clauses.* Chicago: University of Chicago Press.

EISGRUBER, CHRISTOPHER L. and SAGER, LAWRENCE G. 1994 The Vulnerability of Conscience: The Constitutional Basis for Protecting Religious Conduct. *University of Chicago Law Review* 61:1245–1315.

McCONNELL, MICHAEL W. 1990 The Origins and Historical Understanding of Free Exercise of Religion. *Harvard Law Review* 103:1409–1517.

NOTE 1978 Toward a Constitutional Definition of Religion. *Harvard Law Review* 91:1056–1089.

SYMPOSIUM 1996 Religion and the Constitution. *Journal of Contemporary Legal Issues* 7:271–1516.

RELIGIOUS FREEDOM

See: Religious Liberty

RELIGIOUS FREEDOM RESTORATION ACT
107 Stat. 1488 (1993)

The FIRST AMENDMENT free exercise clause provides that "Congress shall make no law . . . prohibiting the free exercise" of religion, a limitation that today extends to all branches and levels of government, including states and localities. Until the 1960s, the clause had been narrowly interpreted: although religious belief was protected absolutely, religious conduct was protected only in limited circumstances, such as from intentionally discriminatory laws. Beginning with SHERBERT V. VERNER (1963), however, the Supreme Court broadened its interpretation, holding that the clause barred at least some unintentional, INCIDENTAL BURDENS resulting from the application of otherwise valid laws or policies. In WISCONSIN V. YODER (1972), for example, the Court held that the Old Order Amish could not be required by state law to send their children to school beyond the eighth grade, even though the law applied uniformly to all Wisconsin citizens and did not intentionally discriminate against or burden religion.

In 1990, the Court again narrowed the scope of the clause. In EMPLOYMENT DIVISION, DEPARTMENT OF HUMAN RESOURCES OF OREGON V. SMITH (1990) the Court confined the *Sherbert–Yoder* standard to cases involving similar factual or legal claims and held that the clause normally does not prohibit laws that incidentally burden religious practices, as long as they are "neutral" (i.e., not aimed at religion) and "generally applicable" (i.e., applicable to a broad range of persons or activities).

Smith ignited a firestorm of criticism, eventually prompting Congress to enact the Religious Freedom Restoration Act (RFRA) of 1993. Initially cosponsored by Senators Orrin Hatch and Edward Kennedy, and supported by a diverse coalition of religious and other organizations, RFRA overwhelmingly passed the U.S. SENATE and the U.S. HOUSE OF REPRESENTATIVES, and was signed into law by President WILLIAM J. CLINTON on November 16, 1993.

RFRA's principal purpose was "to restore the compelling interest test as set forth in [*Sherbert* and *Yoder*] and to guarantee its application in all cases where free exercise of religion is substantially burdened. . . ." Specifically, RFRA provided that the "Government shall not substantially burden a person's exercise of religion even if the burden results from a rule of general applicability" unless "it demonstrates that application of the burden to the person—(1) is in furtherance of a compelling governmental interest; and (2) is the least restrictive means of furthering that compelling governmental interest." RFRA applied to all laws—federal, state, and local—"whether statutory or otherwise, and whether adopted before or after [its enactment]."

By requiring a COMPELLING STATE INTEREST and the LEAST RESTRICTIVE MEANS—the so-called STRICT SCRUTINY of *Sherbert* and *Yoder*—RFRA displaced *Smith* in cases where religion was substantially burdened, but the law was neutral and generally applicable. This stricter scrutiny proved beneficial for some, though certainly not all, RFRA claimants. The government often had little difficulty identifying a "compelling interest," such as public health or prison security, but periodically failed to demonstrate that it employed the "least restrictive means" (i.e., that the compelling interest could not have been achieved without burdening religious practice to a lesser degree). Accordingly, it was this latter requirement on which successful RFRA claimants tended to prevail.

RFRA's application, particularly to prisoners, grew somewhat controversial with time, and the broad consensus favoring the abstract concept of religious freedom dissipated in the actuality of genuine legal disputes. RFRA's most serious problem, however, had little to do with RELIGIOUS LIBERTY as such; rather, critics asserted that Congress altogether lacked the power to enact the statute. In *City of Boerne v. Flores* (1997), the Court agreed with the critics and invalidated the statute, at least as it applies to state and local law.

RFRA had been defended under Congress's FOURTEENTH AMENDMENT enforcement power. Section 1 of that amendment imposes several limitations on the states—among them the guarantee of DUE PROCESS, which the Court had previously held to include the free exercise of religion—and it empowers Congress, in section 5, "to enforce, by appropriate legislation," these limitations. In the Court's view, however, RFRA was not a valid attempt by Congress to "enforce" the Fourteenth Amendment because it prohibited many laws that were constitutional under *Smith*, and because Congress had not made factual findings demonstrating "a congruence and proportionality" between such prohibitions and the prevention or remediation of actual constitutional violations.

Buttressing its holding that Congress exceeded its section 5 power, the Court noted concerns regarding both the SEPARATION OF POWERS and FEDERALISM. First, by displacing the Court's 1990 interpretation of the free exercise clause in *Smith*, RFRA appeared to be a congressional usurpation of the JUDICIAL POWER to render authoritative CONSTITUTIONAL INTERPRETATIONS. Second, RFRA's application to all state and local laws appeared to be a congressional intrusion into certain legal domains reserved to the states. Although noting RFRA's incongruence with both DOCTRINES, the Court gave no clear indication of the independent significance of either doctrine.

The Court left open the question of RFRA's validity as applied to federal law, and the lower courts are presently divided on that issue. Although no Fourteenth Amendment or federalism problems exist, the separation of powers issue remains. Additionally, RFRA may violate the First Amendment prohibition on the ESTABLISHMENT OF RELIGION because it protects only religious conduct and thus appears to favor religion over nonreligion. This was the position of Justice JOHN PAUL STEVENS concurring in *City of Boerne* and remains an issue even if RFRA is otherwise valid as applied to federal law.

SCOTT C. IDLEMAN
(2000)

Bibliography

BERG, THOMAS C. 1994 What Hath Congress Wrought? An Interpretive Guide to the Religious Freedom Restoration Act. *Villanova Law Review* 39:1–70.

CONKLE, DANIEL O. 1995 The Religious Freedom Restoration Act: The Constitutional Significance of an Unconstitutional Statute. *Montana Law Review* 56:39–93.

GRESSMAN, EUGENE and CARMELLA, ANGELA C. 1996 The RFRA Revision of the Free Exercise Clause. *Ohio State Law Journal* 57:65–143.

HAMILTON, MARCI A. 1994 The Religious Freedom Restoration Act: Letting the Fox into the Henhouse Under Cover of Section 5 of the Fourteenth Amendment. *Cardozo Law Review* 16:357–398.

LAYCOCK, DOUGLAS and THOMAS, OLIVER S. 1994 Interpreting the Religious Freedom Restoration Act. *Texas Law Review* 73:209–245.

VAN ALSTYNE, WILLIAM W. 1996 The Failure of the Religious Freedom Restoration Act Under Section 5 of the Fourteenth Amendment. *Duke Law Journal* 46:291–325.

RELIGIOUS FUNDAMENTALISM

Nathaniel Hawthorne perhaps best captured the paradox of religious fundamentalism in America in his stories about the Puritans. Repelled by the Puritans' intolerance, Hawthorne admired their realism and their unswerving devotion to principle. The latter trait he vividly depicted in his short story "The Gray Champion" (1835), where a first-generation Puritan mysteriously returns to Boston in 1689 to thwart the subjugation of the colonies by King James II. Like a fiery Old Testament prophet, the old Puritan—the "Gray Champion" of the story's title—denounces the usurpations of Royal Governor Sir Edmund Andros and urges the people to resistance.

The character of the Gray Champion symbolizes the Puritans' rigid idealism, an idealism that typifies religious fundamentalism in general. In Hawthorne's view, this idealism constituted both a threat and a promise to republican government. It constituted a threat because it fostered religious intolerance, which if enforced by the state, could destroy civil liberty. It represented a promise because it produced a firm commitment to moral principle, which if properly exercised, could help sustain republicanism. Hence the ultimate paradox of fundamentalism: Its intolerance may destroy republican government, but its rigorous attachment to moral principle may be needed to defend it.

One of the greatest achievements of American CONSTITUTIONALISM was the manner in which it resolved this paradox by harnessing the moral idealism of fundamentalism while restraining its potential for bigotry. The Founders harnessed fundamentalism's moral idealism by stressing the importance of morality in civic life and by acknowledging the crucial role churches played in fostering this morality. At the same time, the Founders sought to temper fundamentalism's intolerance by ensuring that government power would never be used to resolve theological differences.

The Founders' arrangement produced an institutional separation between church and state even while forging a practical tie between religion and politics on the basis of morality. Religious fundamentalists were discouraged by the nature of the regime from using the government to promote their theological beliefs; but the door was left open for them to enter the political arena as citizens in order to promote government policies in accord with both the principles of the Constitution and the "laws of nature and nature's God" on which those principles are premised.

The political activities of religious fundamentalists in the new nation (primarily evangelical Christians) reflected the Founders' understanding of the role of religion in society. Many evangelicals opposed state funding of churches because they thought it corrupted religion, and gradually even the congregationalists who supported ESTABLISHMENTS OF RELIGION changed their minds. Hence, when evangelicals became involved in politics in the early nation, they generally sought to do so on the basis of principles of civic morality that were held in common by both reason and revelation. in the years before the CIVIL WAR, they entered the political arena by the thousands to spearhead crusades against dueling, lotteries, war, poverty, prostitution, alcoholism, and SLAVERY. These political activities on behalf of secular concerns proved that religious fundamentalism could fulfill a vital political function by serving as the political conscience of the nation.

Nowhere can this be seen more clearly than in the controversy over Cherokee removal from Georgia. Federal treaties had guaranteed the Cherokees their lands on the condition that they become both peaceful and "civilized." In 1828 and 1829, the Georgia legislature tried to legislate the Cherokee Nation out of existence, extending its laws over Cherokee lands and demanding that the federal government remove the Indians. The evangelical missionaries who had been working among the Cherokees rose to the Indians' defense. They based their arguments against removal not simply on biblical morality but on the natural right of property, the inviolability of contracts, and the God-given equality of all men proclaimed in the DECLARATION OF INDEPENDENCE, which they argued applied to Indians as well as white men.

Unfortunately, both Congress and the President rebuffed the evangelicals' efforts on behalf of the Cherokees, and the government eventually relocated the Indians further west by force. The controversy nevertheless demonstrated that religious fundamentalists could fulfill the role that the Founders had created for them: they could put their idealism to constructive use by intervening in politics on the basis of principles of natural justice rather than doctrines of sectarian theology.

None of this is to suggest that religious fundamentalists completely forswore introducing sectarian theology into politics in the early nation. Before the Civil War, numerous evangelicals claimed that America had been founded as a "Christian nation," and many sought to introduce sectarian religion into public education. After the Civil War, some even wanted to amend the Constitution to recognize the authority of Jesus Christ and Christianity. In the twentieth century, widespread support persisted among evangelicals for state-sponsored prayer and Bible reading in the public schools. Nevertheless, these efforts were more the exception than the rule, and sometimes actions that seemed directed at obtaining state support for religion were actually much more complicated. For instance, evangelicals were vigorously criticized for trying to mix church and state in the early nineteenth century when they sought repeal of a law requiring many post offices to be open on Sunday. Yet one reason evangelicals found this law so offensive was that it compelled church members employed by the post office to break the sabbath in violation of their religious beliefs. Thus, evangelicals sought repeal of the law (at least in part) to protect a person's natural right to RELIGIOUS LIBERTY protected by the free exercise clause of the FIRST AMENDMENT.

The political significance of religious fundamentalism eventually diminished as the number of fundamentalists declined and as most remaining fundamentalists abandoned politics after the repeal of the EIGHTEENTH AMENDMENT. Yet the very forces of secularization that some had thought decimated religious fundamentalism may have spurred its resurgence in the late 1970s and 1980s. As social ills proliferated and many persons became disenchanted with both the political liberalism and the moral permissiveness of mainline Christian denominations, evangelicalism prospered and political action by evangelicals reemerged with a vengeance. Social issues such as ABORTION, PORNOGRAPHY, and EUTHANASIA attracted the new evangelicals' attention, much as dueling, slavery, and intemperance had sparked the actions of their forebears in the nineteenth century.

In one key respect, however, many of the new evangelical activists were different from those who came before. In the past, most conservative Christians had continued to lobby for at least a limited state power to sponsor religious exercises, such as devotional Bible reading and organized prayers in public schools. Although support for these activities did not disappear in the 1980s, it did become much less noticeable, as evangelicals focused more on eliminating the government's power to restrict individual religious expression than on promoting a state power to promote religion.

This new emphasis on individual religious freedom can be ascribed at least in part to the changing nature of church-state conflicts in the 1970s and 1980s. Whereas previous church-state battles had focused on how much the government could do to promote religion while staying within the confines of the ESTABLISHMENT CLAUSE, new controversies concerned how far the state could go in restricting individual religious expression. Public high school students were forbidden by school authorities from meeting on their own during lunch or before school for prayer and Bible study. Churches were prevented from utilizing public facilities readily available for use by other community groups, and zoning laws were invoked to curtail religious activities in private homes. In addition, many parents faced the choice of either removing their children from public schools or allowing their children to be taught the permissibility of behaviors they found morally unacceptable. Some religious parents who tried to teach their children at home were jailed. These new conflicts caused many evangelicals to see government as the problem rather than the solution, and they accordingly sought ways to curb what they regarded as state-sponsored persecution of their religious beliefs and practices.

One result was an attempt to apply the free exercise clause to curriculum objections in the public schools. In 1986, a group of fundamentalist parents in Tennessee petitioned to have their children exempted from a school reading program because they believed the content of the readers disparaged their religious beliefs. The Tennessee parents did not want to change school curriculum; they simply wanted to teach their children reading at home, while allowing the children to participate in the rest of the school's academic program. The district court granted this request, but a three-judge panel on the court of appeals unanimously reversed. However, the judges could not agree on the reasons for reversal. One judge argued that the reading program did not burden the children's free exercise rights because it did not tell them what to believe. A second judge maintained precisely the opposite, arguing that a broader purpose of the reading was to inculcate certain "values"; according to this judge, this purpose gave the school district a COMPELLING STATE INTEREST in not allowing exemptions to the program. The third judge, meanwhile, claimed that the reading program did burden free exercise, but he did not want to issue a new precedent in this area without express guidance from the Supreme Court. This the Supreme court declined to give, although it later made clear in EMPLOYMENT DIVISION, DEPARTMENT OF HUMAN RESOURCES OF OREGON V. SMITH (1990) that it had no intention of broadening free exercise rights. *Smith* suggests that further litigation using the free exercise approach is likely to fail.

In a related area, there have been efforts by evangelicals to have CREATIONISM taught in public schools. Unlike fundamentalists from an earlier era, the new creationists do not argue that evolution should not be taught; they only contend that whenever evolution is taught, "scientific creationism" must also be taught in order to protect the students' right to study different points of view. Hence, they argue their case in terms of ACADEMIC FREEDOM. In *Edwards v. Aguillard* (1987), however, the Supreme Court struck down a Louisiana law that adopted this approach as violative of the establishment clause.

One new rationale that has not been invalidated by the Court is EQUAL ACCESS, which calls for religious expression to be protected as speech under the First Amendment. The primary idea behind equal access is that religious individuals and groups should be accorded the same access to public facilities as nonreligious individuals and groups. For example, if a public library rents rooms to community groups for meetings, it should not be able to forbid religious groups from renting the rooms for religious meetings because this would be discriminating against certain groups on the basis of the content of their speech. Similarly, if high school students have the right to pass out political leaflets to their classmates on school grounds, then they must also have the right to pass out religious leaflets. The equal access rationale has been applied by evangelicals with particular success in the public high school setting, where many schools previously had denied religious student groups the same right to meet on school grounds routinely afforded to other student groups. The Supreme Court sustained federal legislation providing a limited statutory right to equal access in public secondary schools in BOARD OF EDUCATION OF WESTSIDE COMMUNITY SCHOOLS V. MERGENS (1990).

The development of equal access is yet another indication of how successful the Founders were in setting up a system where the political demands of religious fundamentalism would be framed in terms of generally applicable moral principles rather than petitions based on divine right. In America, religious fundamentalists have increasingly recognized that the same laws that protect other citizens also protect them and that they do not need special privileges conferred by the government to prosper.

JOHN G. WEST, JR.
(1992)

(SEE ALSO: *Bender v. Williamsport; Cherokee Indian Cases; Government Aid to Religious Institutions; Religion in Public Schools; Separation of Church and State; School Prayers; Sunday Closing Laws.*)

Bibliography

HAWTHORNE, NATHANIEL 1970 "The Gray Champion," "The Man of Adamant," and "The Maypole of Merrymount." In *Hawthorne: Selected Tales and Sketches*. New York: Holt, Rinehart, and Winston.
JAFFA, HARRY V. 1990 *The American Founding as the Best Regime: The Bonding of Civil and Religious Liberty*. Mont clair, Calif.: Claremont Institute for the Study of Political Philosophy and Statesmanship.
STOKES, ANSON PHELPS 1950 Church and State in the United States, 3 vols. New York: Harper and Brothers.
WEST, JOHN G., JR. 1991 The Changing Battle over Religion in the Public Schools. *Wake Forest Law Review* 26:361–401.

RELIGIOUS INSTITUTIONS AND GOVERNMENT AID

See: Government Aid to Religious Institutions

RELIGIOUS LIBERTY

Although the FIRST AMENDMENT's mandate that "Congress shall make no law respecting an ESTABLISHMENT OF RELIGION, or prohibiting the free exercise thereof" is expressed in unconditional language, religious liberty, insofar as it extends beyond belief, is not an absolute right. The First Amendment, the Supreme Court said in CANTWELL V. CONNECTICUT (1940), "embraces two concepts—freedom to believe and freedom to act. The first is absolute but, in the nature of things, the second cannot be. Conduct remains subject to regulation of society."

Although the Court has repeated this dualism many times, it does not explain what the free exercise clause means. There is no need for a constitutional guarantee protecting freedom to believe, for, as the COMMON LAW had it, "the devil himself knows not the thoughts of man." Even if freedom to believe encompasses freedom to express what one believes, the clause adds nothing, since FREEDOM OF SPEECH and FREEDOM OF THE PRESS are specifically guaranteed in the amendment. Indeed, before *Cantwell* was decided, the Court applied the free speech rather than free exercise guarantee to challenges against state laws allegedly impinging upon religious liberty. Moreover, the word "exercise" connotes action or conduct, thus indicating that the framers had in mind something beyond the mere expression of a belief even if uttered in missionary activities.

In America the roots of religious liberty can be traced to ROGER WILLIAMS, whose pamphlet, "The Bloudy Tenent of Persecution for cause of Conscience, discussed in a Conference between Truth and Peace," asserted that it was God's command that "a permission of the most Paganish, Jewish, Turkish, or Antichristian consciences and worships, be granted to all men in all Nations and Countries." Another source was THOMAS JEFFERSON'S VIRGINIA STATUTE OF RELIGIOUS LIBERTY, adopted in 1786, which declared that no person should be compelled to frequent or support any religious worship nor suffer on account of religious opinions and beliefs.

By the time the First Amendment became part of the Constitution in 1791, practically every state in the Union, to a greater or lesser degree, had enacted constitutional or statutory provisions securing the free exercise of religion. Indeed, it was the absence of a BILL OF RIGHTS whose proponents invariably called for a guarantee of religious freedom, that was the most frequently asserted objection to the Constitution presented to the states for approval. The necessary approval was obtained only because the Constitution's advocates promised that such a bill would be added by amendment after the Constitution was adopted.

Although the First Amendment was framed as a limitation of congressional powers, Supreme Court decisions have made it clear that executive and judicial action were likewise restricted by the amendment. Thus in *Anderson v. Laird* (1971) the Supreme Court refused to review a decision that the secretary of defense violated the First Amendment in requiring cadets in governmental military academies to attend chapel. As to the judiciary, unquestionably a federal court could not constitutionally disqualify a person from testifying as a witness because he was an atheist. (See TORCASO V. WATKINS.)

Since the Court's decision in *Cantwell* the states are subject to the restrictions of the free exercise clause no less than the federal government. Because our federal system leaves to the states what is generally called the POLICE POWER, there were few occasions, prior to *Cantwell*, when the Supreme Court was called upon to define the meaning of the clause. The few that did arise involved actions in the TERRITORIES, which were subject to federal laws and thus to the First Amendment. Most significant of these was REYNOLDS V. UNITED STATES (1879), wherein the Supreme Court upheld the constitutionality of an act of Congress criminalizing POLYGAMY in any American territory. In rejecting the defense that polygamy was mandated by doctrines of the Holy Church of Latter-Day Saints (Mormons) and thus was protected by the free exercise clause, the Court stated what was later echoed in *Cantwell*, that although laws "cannot interfere with mere religious belief, they may with practice." It could hardly be contended, the Court continued, that the free exercise clause barred prosecution of persons who engaged in human sacrifice as a necessary part of their religious worship.

Since Reynolds was charged with practicing polygamy, the Court's decision did not pass upon the question whether teaching it as a God-mandated duty was "mere religious belief" and therefore beyond governmental interference. In DAVIS V. BEASON (1890) the Court decided that such teaching was "practice," and therefore constitutionally subject to governmental restrictions.

Teaching or preaching, even if deemed action, is however not beyond all First Amendment protection, which encompasses freedom of speech as well as religion. In GITLOW V. NEW YORK (1925) the Supreme Court declared for

the first time that the free speech guarantee of the First Amendment was incorporated into the FOURTEENTH AMENDMENT by virtue of the DUE PROCESS clause in the latter and thus was applicable to the states. Accordingly, the Jehovah's Witnesses cases that first came to the Court in the 1930s were initially decided under the speech rather than the religion clause (LOVELL V. GRIFFIN, 1938; *Schneider v. Irvington,* 1939). It was, therefore, natural for the Court to decide the cases under the CLEAR AND PRESENT DANGER test that had first been announced in SCHENCK V. UNITED STATES (1919), a case involving prosecution for speaking against United States involvement in World War I.

In another sense, this too was quite natural since, like Schenck, the Witnesses were pacifists, at least in respect to wars in this world. (In *Sicurella v. United States,* the Court in 1955 ruled that a member of the sect was not disqualified from conscientious objector exemption because the sect's doctrines encompassed participation by believers in serving as soldiers in the Army of Christ Jesus at Armageddon.) Nevertheless, unlike Schenck and other opponents to American entry in World War I, the Witnesses (like the Friends) did not vocally oppose American entry into the war but limited themselves to claiming CONSCIENTIOUS OBJECTION status.

The Court did not apply the clear and present danger test in a case involving a member of the Jehovah's Witnesses whose child was expelled from public school for refusing to participate in the patriotic program of flag salute. In that case, *Minersville School District v. Gobitis* (1940), the Court, in an opinion by Justice FELIX FRANKFURTER, rejected the assertion as a defense of religious freedom. (See FLAG SALUTE CASES.) The antipolygamy law, he stated, was upheld in *Reynolds* not because it concerned action rather than belief, but because it was a valid general law, regulating the secular practice of marriage.

The majority of the Court, however, soon concluded that *Gobitis* had been incorrectly decided, and three years later the Court overruled it in *West Virginia State Board of Education v. Barnette* (1943). There the Court treated the Witnesses' refusal to salute the flag as a form of speech and therefore subject to the clear and present danger test. In later decisions, the Court returned to *Cantwell* and treated religious freedom cases under the free exercise rather than free speech clause, although it continued to apply the clear and present danger test.

Unsatisfied with that test, Justice Frankfurter prevailed upon his colleagues to accept a differently worded rule, that of BALANCING competing interests, also taken from Court decisions relating to other freedoms secured in the Bill of Rights. When a person complains that his constitutional rights have been infringed by some law or action of the state, it is the responsibility of the courts to weigh the importance of the particular right in issue as against the state's interest upon which its law or action is based. For example, the right of an objector not to violate his religious conscience by engaging in war must be weighed against the nation's interest in defending itself against foreign enemies, and, in such weighing, the latter interest may be adjudged the weightier.

The majority of the Court accepted this rule, but in recent years it has added an element that has almost turned it around. Justice Frankfurter believed that a citizen who challenged the constitutionality of state action had the burden of convincing the court that his interest was more important than the state's and should therefore be adjudged paramount. Establishing an individual's right superior to the state's interest was a particularly heavy burden to carry, but it was made even heavier by Justice Frankfurter's insistence that any doubt as to relative weights must be resolved in favor of the state, which would prevail unless its action were patently unreasonable. Recently, however, the Court has taken a more libertarian approach, requiring the state to persuade the courts that the values it seeks to protect are weightier. In the language of the decisions, the state must establish that there is a COMPELLING STATE INTEREST that justifies infringement of the citizen's right to the free exercise of his religion. If it fails to do so, its law or action will be adjudged unconstitutional. (See THOMAS V. REVIEW BOARD OF INDIANA; UNITED STATES V. LEE.)

In accord with this rule, the Court, in the 1972 case of WISCONSIN V. YODER, expressly rejected the belief-action test, holding that Amish parents could not be prosecuted for refusing to send their children to school after they had reached the age of fourteen. "Only those interests of the highest order," the Court said, "and those not otherwise served can overbalance the legitimate claim to the free exercise of religion."

Religious liberty is protected not only by the free exercise clause but also by the clause against ESTABLISHMENTS OF RELIGION. In EVERSON V. BOARD OF EDUCATION (1947) and later cases, the Court has stated that under the establishment clause, government cannot force a person to go to church or profess a belief in any religion. In later decisions, the Court has applied a three-pronged purpose-effect-entanglement test as a standard of constitutionality under the establishment clause. The Court has held, in *Committee for Public Education and Religious Liberty v. Nyquist* (1973), for example, that a challenged statute must have a primary effect that neither advances nor inhibits religion, and must avoid government entanglement with religion. (See SEPARATION OF CHURCH AND STATE.)

The Supreme Court's decisions in the arena of conflict between governmental concerns and individuals' claims to religious liberty can be considered in relation to the four categories suggested by the Preamble to the Constitution: national defense, domestic tranquillity, the establishment of justice, and GENERAL WELFARE. In resolving the issues before it in these decisions the Court has spoken in terms of clear and present danger, balancing of competing interests, or determination of compelling governmental interests, depending upon the date of the decision rendered.

Probably no interest of the government is deemed more important than defense against a foreign enemy. Individual liberties secured by the Constitution must yield when the nation's safety is in peril. As the Court ruled in the SELECTIVE DRAFT LAW CASES (1918), the prohibition by the THIRTEENTH AMENDMENT of involuntary servitude was not intended to override the nation's power to conscript an army of—if necessary—unwilling soldiers, without which even the most just and defensive war cannot be waged.

By the same token, exemption of Quakers and others whose religious conscience forbids them to engage in military service cannot be deemed a constitutional right but only a privilege accorded by Congress and thus subject to revocation at any time Congress deems that to be necessary for national defense. However, even in such a case, Congress must exercise its power within the limitations prescribed by the First Amendment's mandate of neutrality among religions and by the EQUAL PROTECTION component of the Fifth Amendment's due process clause. Hence, in exercising its discretion, Congress could not constitutionally prefer some long-standing pacifist religions over others more recently established.

Exemption of specific classes—the newly betrothed, the newly married, the fainthearted, and others—goes back as far as Mosaic times (Deuteronomy 20:1–8). Since all biblical wars were theocratic, there was no such thing as religious exemption. In England, Oliver Cromwell believed that those whose religious doctrine forbade participation in armed conflict should constitute an exempt class. So too did the legislatures in some of the American colonies, the Continental Congress, and a number of the members of the Congress established under the Constitution. Madison's original draft of what became the SECOND AMENDMENT included a provision exempting religious objectors from compulsory militia duty; but that provision was deleted before Congress proposed the amendment to the states. The first national measure exempting conscientious objectors was adopted by Congress during the Civil War; like its colonial and state precedents, it was limited to members of well-recognized religious denominations whose articles of faith forbade the bearing of arms.

The SELECTIVE SERVICE ACT of 1917 exempted members of recognized denominations or sects, such as the Friends, Mennonites, and Seventh-Day Adventists, whose doctrine and discipline declared military service sinful. The 1940 act liberalized the requirements for exemption to encompass anyone who by "reason of religious training and belief" possessed conscientious scruples against "participation in war in any form." In 1948, however, the 1940 act was further amended, first, to exclude those whose objection to war was based on "essentially political, sociological or philosophical views or a mere personal code," and second, to define religion as a belief in a "Supreme Being."

In view of the Court's holding in *Torcaso v. Watkins* (1961) that the Constitution did not sanction preferential treatment of theistic religions over other faiths, limitation of exemption to persons who believe in a "Supreme Being" raised establishment clause issues. In UNITED STATES V. SEEGER (1965) the Court avoided these issues by interpreting the statute to encompass a person who possessed a sincere belief occupying a place in the life of its possessor parallel to that filled by the orthodox belief in God of one who clearly qualified for the exemption. Applying this definition to the three cases before it, the Court held that Selective Service boards had erroneously denied exemption: to one who expressed a "belief in and devotion to goodness and virtues for their own sakes, and a religious faith in a purely ethical creed"; to another who rejected a relationship "vertically towards Godness directly," but was committed to relationship "horizontally towards Godness through Mankind and the World"; and to a third who defined religion as "the supreme expression of human nature," encompassing "man thinking his highest, feeling his deepest, and living his best."

Because exemption of conscientious exemption is of legislative rather than constitutional origin, Congress may condition exemption on possession of belief forbidding participation in all wars, excluding those whose objection is selective and forbids participation only in what they personally deem unjust wars, such as that in Vietnam. The Court sustained such an act of Congress in *Gillette v. United States* (1971). However, independent of any statutory exemption, the Court held in *Thomas* that, at least in peacetime, disqualification of a person from unemployment insurance benefits for conscientious refusal to accept an offered job in a plant that manufactured arms violated the free exercise clause.

Closely related to military service as an aspect of national defense is national unity, cultural as well as political. The relevant constitutional issues reached the Supreme Court in 1923 in three cases involving Lutheran and Reformed schools, and, two years later, in two cases involving a Roman Catholic parochial and a nonsectarian private school. The former cases, reflecting post-World War I hostility to German-speaking Americans, were decided by the Court in MEYER V. NEBRASKA (1923) and two companion cases. These involved the conviction of teachers of German who violated statutes forbidding the teaching of a foreign language to pupils before they had completed eight grades of elementary schooling. The Court, in reversing the convictions, relied not only on the constitutional right of German teachers to pursue a gainful occupation not inherently evil or dangerous to the welfare of the community, but also the right of parents to have their children taught "Martin Luther's language" so that they might better understand "Martin Luther's dogma." The cases were decided long before the Court held that the free exercise clause was incorporated in the Fourteenth Amendment's due process clause and therefore were technically based upon the teachers' due process right to earn a livelihood and the parents' due process right to govern the upbringing of their children.

In PIERCE V. SOCIETY OF SISTERS and its companion case, *Pierce v. Hill Military Academy* (1925), the Court invalidated a compulsory education act that required all children, with limited exceptions, to attend only public schools. A single opinion, governing both cases, relied upon *Meyer v. Nebraska* and based the decision invalidating the law on the due process clause as it related to the school owners' contractual rights and the parents' right to control their children's education, rather than to the free exercise rights of teachers, parents, or pupils. Nevertheless, since the Court's ruling in *Cantwell* that the free exercise clause was applicable to the states, *Pierce* has often been cited by lawyers, scholars, and courts as a free exercise case, and particularly one establishing the constitutional rights of churches to operate parochial schools. Had *Pierce* been decided after *Cantwell* it is probable that free exercise would have been invoked as an additional ground in respect to the Society of Sisters' claim; the opinion as written did note that the child was not the mere creature of the state and that those who nurtured him and directed his destiny had the right, coupled with the high duty, to recognize and prepare him for additional obligations.

Reference has already been made to the Supreme Court's decision in *West Virginia State Board of Education v. Barnette* upholding the First Amendment right of Jehovah's Witnesses public school pupils to refrain from participating in flag salute exercises, although there the Court predicated its decision on the free speech rather than the free exercise mandate of the Amendment.

Jehovah's Witnesses' creed and conduct affected not only national defense through pacifism and alleged failure to pay respect to the flag but also governmental concern with domestic tranquillity. What aggravated hostility to the sect beyond its supposed lack of patriotism were its militant proselytizing methods, encompassing verbal attacks on organized religion in general and Roman Catholicism in particular. In their 1931 convention the Witnesses declared their mission to be "to inform the rulers and the people of and concerning Satan's cruel and oppressive organization, and particularly with reference to Christiandom, which is the most visible part of that visible organization." God's purpose was to destroy Satan's organization and bring quickly "to the obedient peoples of the earth peace and prosperity, liberty and health, happiness and life."

This is hardly new or surprising. Practically every new religion, from Judaism through Christianity and Islam to the present, has been predicated upon attacks against existing faiths; indeed, this is implied in the very term "Protestant." Clearly, those who wrote the First Amendment intended it to encompass attacks upon existing religions. (In BURSTYN V. WILSON, 1952, the Court invalidated a statute banning "sacrilegious" films.) Attacks on existing religions are almost invariably met with counterattacks, physical as well as verbal, by defenders of the accepted faiths.

The assaults upon the Jehovah's Witnesses were particularly widespread and intense for a number of reasons. Their conduct enraged many who felt that their refusal to salute the flag was unpatriotic, if not treasonous. Their attacks upon the Christian religion infuriated many others. The evidence in *Taylor v. Mississippi* (1943), for example, included a pamphlet suggesting that the Roman Catholic Church was responsible for flag saluting. The book *Religion*, by the Witnesses' first leader, Charles T. Russell, described their operations: "God's faithful servants go from house to house to bring the message of the kingdom to those who reside there, omitting none, not even the houses of the Roman Catholic hierarchy, and there they give witness to the kingdom because they are commanded by the Most High to do so. . . . They do not loot nor break into the houses, but they set up their phonographs before the doors and windows and send the message of the kingdom right into the ears of those who might wish to hear; and while those desiring to hear are hearing, some of the "sourpusses' are compelled to hear."

The predictably resulting resort to violence and to law for the suppression of the Witnesses' activities gave rise to a host of Supreme Court decisions defining for the first time both the breadth and the limitations of the free exercise clause (and also, to some extent, the free speech clause). Most of the Jehovah's Witnesses cases were argued before the Supreme Court by Hayden Covington; his perseverance, as well as that of his client, was manifested by the fact that before *Minersville School District v. Gobitis* was decided, the Court had rejected his appeals in flag salute cases four times. The Court had accepted JURISDICTION in *Gobitis*, as well as its successor, *Barnette*, because, notwithstanding these previous rejections, the lower courts had decided both cases in the Witnesses' favor.

The Witnesses were not the only persons whose aggressive missionary endeavors and verbal attacks upon other faiths led to governmental actions that were challenged as a violation of the free exercise clause and were defended as necessary to secure domestic tranquillity. In KUNZ V. NEW YORK (1951), the Court held that a Baptist preacher could not be denied renewal of a permit for evangelical street meetings because his preachings, scurrilously attacking Roman Catholicism and Judaism, had led to disorder in the streets. The Court said that appropriate public remedies existed to protect the peace and order of the communities if the sermons should result in violence, but it held that these remedies did not include prior restraint under an ordinance that provided no standards for the licensing official.

Jehovah's Witnesses were the major claimants to religious liberty in the two decades between 1935 and 1955. During that period they brought to the Supreme Court a large number of cases challenging the application to them of a variety of laws forbidding disturbing the peace, peddling, the use of SOUNDTRUCKS, as well as traffic regulations, child labor laws, and revenue laws.

In *Cantwell v. Connecticut* (1940) the Court held that the First Amendment guaranteed the right to teach and preach religion in the public streets and parks and to solicit contributions or purchases of religious materials. Although a prior municipal permit might be required, its grant or denial might not be based upon the substance of what is taught, preached, or distributed but only upon the need to regulate, in the interests of traffic control, the time, place, and manner of public meetings. In COX V. NEW HAMPSHIRE (1940) the Court ruled that religious liberty encompassed the right to engage in religious processions, although a fee might be imposed to cover the expenses of administration and maintenance of public order. The Constitution, however, does not immunize from prosecution persons who in their missionary efforts use expressions that are lewd, obscene, libelous, insulting, or that contain "fighting" words which by their very utterance, the Court declared in CHAPLINSKY V. NEW HAMPSHIRE (1942), inflict injury or tend to incite an immediate breach of the peace. The Constitution also secures the right to distribute religious handbills in streets and at publicly owned railroad or bus terminals, according to the decision in *Jamison v. Texas* (1943), and, according to *Martin v. City of Struthers* (1943), to ring doorbells in order to offer house occupants religious literature although, of course, not to force oneself into the house for that purpose.

Related to the domestic tranquillity aspects of Jehovah's Witnesses claims to use public streets and parks are the claims of other feared or unpopular minority religious groups (often referred to as "sects" or, more recently, "CULTS") to free exercise in publicly owned areas. In HEF-

FRON V. INTERNATIONAL SOCIETY FOR KRISHNA CONSCIOUSNESS (ISKCON) (1981) the Court held that a state rule limiting to specific booths the sale or distribution of merchandise, including printed material, on public fair grounds did not violate the free exercise clause when applied to members of ISKCON whose ritual required its members to go into all public places to distribute or sell its religious literature and to solicit donations.

Discriminatory treatment, however, is not constitutionally permissible. Thus, in *Cruz v. Beto* (1972) the Supreme Court upheld the claim of a Buddhist prisoner in Texas that his constitutional rights were violated by denying him use of the prison chapel, punishing him for sharing his Buddhist religious materials with other prisoners, and denying him other privileges, such as receiving points for attendance at religious services, which enhanced a prisoner's eligibility for early parole consideration. While a prisoner obviously cannot enjoy the free exercise of religion to the same extent as nonprisoners, the Court said, he is protected by the free exercise clause subject only to the necessities of prison security and discipline, and he may not be discriminated against simply because his religious belief is unorthodox. This does not mean that every sect within a prison, no matter how few in number, must have identical facilities or personnel; but reasonable opportunities must be afforded to all persons to exercise their religion without penalty.

One of the most difficult problems facing a court arises when it is called upon to decide between free exercise and the state's interest in preventing fraud. The leading case on the subject is *United States v. Ballard* (1944), which involved a prosecution for mail fraud. The INDICTMENT charged that the defendants, organizers of the "I Am" cult, had mulcted money from elderly and ill people by falsely representing that they had supernatural powers to heal and that they themselves had communicated personally with Heaven and with Jesus Christ.

The Court held that the free exercise clause would be violated if the state were allowed to seek to prove to a jury that the defendants' representations were false. Neither a jury nor any other organ of government had power to decide whether asserted religious experiences actually occurred. Courts, however, could constitutionally determine whether the defendant himself believed that what he recounted was true, and if a jury determined that he did not, they could convict him of obtaining money under false pretenses. The difficulty with this test, as Justice ROBERT H. JACKSON noted in his dissenting opinion, is that prosecutions in cases such as *Ballard* could easily degenerate into religious persecution; juries would find it difficult to accept as believed that which, by reason of their own religious upbringing, they deemed unbelievable.

In providing for "affirmation" as an alternative to "oath" in Article II, section 1, and Article VI, section 3, the framers of the Constitution, recognizing that religious convictions might forbid some persons (specifically Quakers) to take oaths, manifested their intention that no person in the judicial system—judge, lawyer, court official, or juryman—should be disqualified from governmental service on the ground of religion. In *Torcaso v. Watkins* (1961) the Court reached the same conclusion under the First Amendment as to state officials (for example, notaries public), and in *In re Jenison* (1963), the Court refused to uphold a conviction for contempt of court of a woman who would not serve on a jury because of the biblical command "Judge not that ye not be judged."

Resort to secular courts for resolution of intrachurch disputes (generally involving ownership and control of church assets) raises free exercise as well as establishment problems. As early as 1872 the Court held in *Watson v. Jones* that judicial intervention in such controversies was narrowly limited: a court could do no more than determine and enforce the decision of that body within the church that was the highest judicatory body according to appropriate church law. If a religious group (such as Baptist and Jewish) were congregational in structure, that body would be the majority of the congregation; if it were hierarchical (such as Roman Catholic or Russian Orthodox), the authority would generally be the diocesan bishop.

That principle was applied by the Supreme Court consistently until *Jones v. Wolf* (1979). There the court held that "neutral principles of law developed for use in all property disputes" could constitutionally be applied in church schism litigation. This means that unless the corporate charter or deeds of title provide that the faction loyal to the hierarchical church will retain ownership of the property, such a controversy must be adjudicated in accordance with the laws applicable to corporations generally, so that if recorded title is in the name of the local church, the majority of that body is entitled to control its use and disposition. The Court rejected the assertion in the dissenting opinion that a rule of compulsory deference to the highest ecclesiastical tribunal is necessary in order to protect the free exercise of those who formed the association and submitted themselves to its authority.

Where a conflict exists between the health of the community and the religious conscience of an individual or group, there is little doubt that the free exercise clause does not mandate risk to the community. Thus, as the Court held in JACOBSON V. MASSACHUSETTS (1905), compulsory VACCINATION against communicable diseases is enforceable notwithstanding religious objections to the procedure. So, too, fluoridation of municipal water supplies to prevent tooth cavities cannot be enjoined because of objection by some that drinking fluoridated water is sinful.

Where the life, health, or safety of individuals, rather than communities at large, is involved the constitutional principles are also fairly clear. When the individuals are children, a court may authorize blood transfusions to save their lives notwithstanding objection by parents (such as Jehovah's Witnesses) who believe that the procedure violates the biblical command against the drinking of blood. The underlying principle was stated by the Court in PRINCE V. MASSACHUSETTS (1944) upholding the conviction of a Jehovah's Witness for violating the state's child labor law in allowing her nine-year-old niece to accompany and help her while she sold the sect's religious literature on the city's streets. "Parents," the Court said, "may be free to become martyrs themselves. But it does not follow that they are free, in identical circumstances, to make martyrs of their children before they have reached the age of full and legal discretion when they can make that choice for themselves." It follows from this that unless mental incompetence is proved, a court may not authorize a blood transfusion upon an unconsenting adult.

The Court also balances competing interests in determining the constitutionality of enforcing compulsory Sunday laws against those whom religious conscience forbids labor or trade on the seventh rather than the first day of the week. In MCGOWAN V. MARYLAND and *Two Guys from Harrison-Allentown v. McGinley* (1961) the Court upheld the general validity of such laws against an establishment clause attack. Although their origin may have been religious, the Court said, the laws' present purpose was secular: to assure a weekly day for rest, relaxation, and family companionship.

Two other cases, *Gallagher v. Crown Kosher Super Market* (1961) and *Braunfeld v. Brown* (1961), decided at the same time, involved Orthodox Jews who observed Saturday as their day of rest and refrained from business on that day. In these cases the Court rejected the argument that requiring a Sabbatarian either to abstain from engaging in his trade or business two days weekly or to sacrifice his religious conscience, while requiring his Sunday-observing competitors to abstain only one day, imposed upon the Sabbatarian a competitive disadvantage, thereby penalizing him for his religious beliefs in violation of the free exercise clause. Exempting Sabbatarians, the Court held, might be administratively difficult, might benefit non-Sabbatarians motivated only by a desire for a competitive advantage over merchants closing on Sundays, and might frustrate the legitimate legislative goal of assuring a uniform day of rest. Although state legislatures could constitutionally elect to grant an exemption to Sabbatarians, the free exercise clause does not require them to do so.

In SHERBERT V. VERNER (1963), however, the Court reached a conclusion difficult to reconcile with that in *Gal-* *lagher* and *Braunfeld*. Denial of unemployment insurance benefits to a Seventh-Day Adventist who refused to accept tendered employment that required working on Saturday, the Court held, imposed an impermissible burden on the free exercise of religion. The First Amendment, it said, forbids forcing an applicant to choose between following religious precepts and forfeiting government benefits on the one hand, or, on the other, abandoning the precepts by accepting Sabbath work. Governmental imposition of such a choice, the Court said, puts the same kind of burden upon the free exercise of religion as would a fine imposed for Saturday worship.

The Court upheld statutory tax exemptions for church-owned real estate used exclusively for religious purposes in WALZ V. TAX COMMISSION (1970), rejecting an establishment clause attack. In *Murdock v. Pennsylvania* (1943) and *Follett v. Town of McCormack* (1944), however, the Court ruled that under the free exercise clause a revenue-raising tax on the privilege of canvassing or soliciting orders for articles could not be applied to Jehovah's Witnesses who sold their religious literature from door to door; in the same cases, the Court stated that an income tax statute could constitutionally be applied to clergymen's salaries for performing their clerical duties.

In *United States v. Lee* (1982) the Court upheld the exaction of social security and unemployment insurance contributions from Amish employers. The employers argued that their free exercise rights had been violated, citing 1 Timothy 5:8: "But if any provide not . . . for those of his own house, he hath denied the faith, and is worse than an infidel." Compulsory contribution, the Court said, was nonetheless justified; it was essential to accomplish the overriding governmental interest in the effective operation of the social security system.

To sum up, the Supreme Court's decisions in the arena of religious liberty manifest a number of approaches toward defining its meaning, specifically clear and present danger, the balancing of competing interests, and the establishment of a compelling state interest justifying intrusion on free exercise. On the whole, the Court has been loyal to the original intent of the generation that wrote the First Amendment to accord the greatest degree of liberty feasible in our society.

LEO PFEFFER
(1986)

(SEE ALSO: *Widmar v. Vincent.*)

Bibliography

GIANELLA, DONALD 1968 Religious Liberty: Non-Establishment and Doctrinal Development: Part I, The Religious Liberty Guarantee. *Harvard Law Review* 80:1381–1431.

HOWE, MARK DEWOLFE 1965 *The Garden and the Wilderness:*

Religion and Government in American Constitutional History. Chicago: University of Chicago Press.

KAUPER, PAUL G.   1964   *Religion and the Constitution.* Baton Rouge: Louisiana State University Press.

MANWARING, DAVID R.   1962   *Render unto Caesar: The Flag Salute Controversy.* Chicago: University of Chicago Press.

PFEFFER, LEO   (1953)   1967 *Church, State and Freedom.* Boston: Beacon Press.

STOKES, AANSON P.   1950   *Church and State in the United States.* New York: Harper & Brothers.

—— and PFEFFER, LEO   1965   *Church and State in the United States.* New York: Harper & Row.

TRIBE, LAWRENCE H.   1978   *American Constitutional Law.* Mineola, N.Y.: Foundation Press.

RELIGIOUS LIBERTY
(Update 1)

Religious liberty finds its protection in three provisions of the Constitution: the prohibition of RELIGIOUS TESTS for office in Article IV and the FREE EXERCISE and ESTABLISHMENT CLAUSES of the FIRST AMENDMENT. Because the first is self-executing and the last is involved mostly with issues of government aid, endorsement, or sponsorship of religious activities, the bulk of constitutional litigation over religious liberty has taken place under the free-exercise clause.

In recent history, there have been two general conceptions of the protections afforded by the free-exercise clause. The broad conception, which prevailed in the Supreme Court from 1963 (and arguably earlier) until 1990, holds that no law or government practice can be allowed to burden the exercise of religion unless it is the least restrictive means of achieving a government purpose of the highest order—a "compelling" governmental purpose. The narrow conception, adopted by a 5–4 vote in 1990, holds that the free-exercise clause prohibits only those laws that are specifically directed to religious practice.

The classic statement of the broad conception is found in SHERBERT V. VERNER (1963). In this case, the Court required the state of South Carolina to pay unemployment compensation benefits to a Seventh-Day Adventist notwithstanding her refusal to accept available jobs that would have required her to work on Saturday, her Sabbath. According to the Court, denial of benefits was tantamount to a fine for following the tenets of her religion. Since *Sherbert,* the Court has required states to pay unemployment compensation to others whose religious tenets conflicted with the requirements of available employment: to a Jehovah's Witness who would not work on armaments, in THOMAS V. INDIANA REVIEW BOARD (1981); to a convert to the Seventh-Day Adventist Church, in

Hobbie v. Unemployment Appeals Commission (1987); and to a Christian who would not work on Sunday, in FRAZEE V. ILLINOIS DEPARTMENT OF EMPLOYMENT SECURITY (1989). In *Frazee,* the Court unanimously held that the claimant was entitled to benefits, even though his belief was not mandated by the particular religious denomination of which he was a member. The decision thus confirmed that the right of religious liberty extends to all sincerely held religious convictions and not just to those of established denominations.

In years immediately following *Sherbert,* the Court extended free-exercise protection to other conflicts between religious conscience and civil law, including compulsory education above the eighth grade, in WISCONSIN V. YODER (1972), and jury duty, in *In re Jennison* (1963). After 1972, however, the Court turned aside every claim for a free-exercise exemption from a facially neutral law, outside the narrow context of unemployment compensation. Particularly noteworthy examples included GOLDMAN V. WEINBERGER (1986), in which the Court upheld an Air Force uniform requirement that prevented an Orthodox Jew from wearing his skullcap (yarmulke) while on duty indoors; *Tony Susan Alamo Foundation v. Secretary of Labor* (1985), in which the Court upheld imposition of minimum-wage laws on a religious community in which the members worked for no pay; and LYNG V. NORTHWEST INDIAN CEMETERY PROTECTIVE ASSOCIATION (1988), in which the court allowed construction of a logging road through National Forest lands sacred to certain northern Californian Indian tribes, even though the road would "virtually destroy the Indians' ability to practice their religion."

In each of these cases, the Court either held that the "compelling interest" test of *Sherbert* had been satisfied or that there were special circumstances making that test inappropriate to the particular case. Thus, during this period, the formal legal doctrine sounded highly protective of the rights of religious conscience, but in practice, the government almost always prevailed.

In 1990, the Court abandoned the compelling-interest test in EMPLOYMENT DIVISION, DEPARTMENT OF HUMAN RESOURCES OF OREGON V. SMITH (1990), holding that "the right of free exercise does not relieve an individual of the obligation to comply with a "valid and neutral law of general applicability on the ground that the law proscribes (or prescribes) conduct that his religion prescribes (or proscribes)." The *Smith* case involved the sacramental use of peyote by members of the Native American Church. Although twenty-three states and the federal government specifically exempt Native American Church ceremonies from the drug laws, Oregon does not. The Supreme Court held that the free-exercise clause does not require an exemption.

After *Smith*, the only laws or governmental practices that can be challenged under the free-exercise clause are those in which this clause applies "in conjunction with other constitutional protections," such as cases involving free speech or childrearing, or those in which the law is "specifically directed at their religious practice." Thus, laws discriminating against religion as such would be subject to constitutional challenge. Such cases are unusual in the United States. The only example in recent decades was *McDaniel v. Paty* (1978), which involved a Tennessee law barring members of the clergy from service in the state legislature or a state CONSTITUTIONAL CONVENTION. Because Tennessee had singled out a religious class for a special civil disability, its statute was struck down. Another case of discrimination against religion was WIDMAR V. VINCENT (1981), in which a public university attempted to bar student religious groups from campus facilities. *Widmar*, however, was decided under the free-speech clause, not the free-exercise clause. Except for *McDaniel* and *Widmar*, almost every free-exercise case to come before the Supreme Court involved an ostensibly neutral law of general applicability, now resolved under *Smith* without inquiry into the strength of the governmental purpose.

The debate between the broad and narrow readings of the free-exercise clause goes back even before the proposal and ratification of the First Amendment from 1789 to 1791. JOHN LOCKE and THOMAS JEFFERSON both apparently opposed exemptions; JAMES MADISON favored them, at least in some circumstances. The same issue arose under several of the STATE CONSTITUTIONS, yielding conflicting results. The majority of the state constitutions adopted before the First Amendment contained language that suggests the broad reading. Georgia, for example, guaranteed that "[a]ll persons whatever shall have the free exercise of their religion; provided it be not repugnant to the peace and safety of the State" (Georgia Constitution of 1777, Article LVI). Although it is perilous to draw firm conclusions from abstract legal language, the "peace and safety" proviso would appear to be unnecessary unless the free-exercise guarantee were understood to entail some exceptions from otherwise valid laws. Moreover, in actual practice, conflicts between minority religious tenets and general law in colonial and preconstitutional America were not infrequently resolved by crafting exemptions. Examples included exemptions from oath requirements and from military conscription. The evidence, however, is thin because eighteenth-century America gave rise to few conflicts between religious and civil dictates.

If the narrow reading of the free-exercise clause announced in *Smith* remains in force, it will cause major changes in the constitutional rights both of religious individuals and of institutions. It is not uncommon for minority religious practices to conflict with "generally applicable" rules or regulations, and henceforth, any relief from such conflicts must come from the legislatures. Some religious groups—those more numerous or politically powerful—will be able to protect their interests in the political process; some will not. The Supreme Court commented in *Smith*, "It may fairly be said that leaving accommodation to the political process will place at a relative disadvantage those religious practices that are not widely engaged in; but that unavoidable consequence of democratic government must be preferred to a system in which each conscience is a law unto itself."

For many years, some Justices maintained that laws or government policies that exempted religious organizations or religiously motivated individuals from laws applied to others were themselves suspect under the establishment clause. For example, Justice JOHN MARSHALL HARLAN, in the CONSCIENTIOUS OBJECTION cases during the VIETNAM WAR, concluded, in *Welsh v. United States* (1970), that it would be unconstitutional to recognize religious objections to military service without also recognizing nonreligious conscientious objection. More recently, the Court, in WALLACE V. JAFFREE (1985), struck down state efforts to accommodate the religious need of some school children for voluntary prayer through an officially declared moment of silence, and in THORNTON V. CALDOR, INC. (1985), the Court invalidated a statute that required private employers to honor the needs of Sabbath observers in determining days off.

In *Corporation of Presiding Bishop v. Amos* (1987), however, the Court unanimously upheld a federal statute exempting religious organizations from the prohibition on discrimination on the basis of religion in employment. The Court reasoned that it is permissible for the government to remove government-imposed obstacles to the free exercise of religion, even if, in some sense, this gives preferential treatment to religious organizations. And in TEXAS MONTHLY, INC. V. BULLOCK (1989), when a fragmented Court struck down a Texas law exempting religious magazines from sales tax, the plurality was careful to note that benefits conferred exclusively on religious organizations are constitutionally permissible if they "would not impose substantial burdens on nonbeneficiaries" or if they "were designed to alleviate government intrusions that might significantly deter adherents of a particular faith from conduct protected by the Free Exercise Clause."

Thus, although individuals or religious bodies can no longer challenge generally applicable government action under the free-exercise clause, the courts have also become more likely to uphold legislation designed to accommodate religious exercise.

MICHAEL W. MCCONNELL
(1992)

(SEE ALSO: *Board of Education of Westside Community Schools v. Mergens; Equal Access; Lemon Test; Religion in Public Schools; Religious Fundamentalism; Separation of Church and State.*)

Bibliography

LAYCOCK, DOUGLAS 1986 A Survey of Religious Liberty in the United States. *Ohio State Law Journal* 47:409–451.

LUPU, IRA C. 1989 Where Rights Begin: The Problem of Burdens on the Free Exercise of Religion. *Harvard Law Review* 102:933–990.

MCCONNELL, MICHAEL W. 1990 The Origins and Historical Understanding of Free Exercise of Religion. *Harvard Law Review* 103:1409–1517.

RELIGIOUS LIBERTY
(Update 2)

Religious liberty in a broad sense—the liberty of persons to make decisions about religious matters—is central to both concepts in the FIRST AMENDMENT's religion provision, free exercise and nonestablishment. The ESTABLISHMENT CLAUSE secures a person's liberty to reject or refrain from religious activity. But religious liberty in a stricter, positive sense—the liberty to follow religion and engage in religious activity—is the particular concern of the free exercise clause and, where the religious activity involves expression, the FREEDOM OF SPEECH guarantee as well.

The Supreme Court has upheld strong free speech protection for citizens' religious expression. Several recent decisions forbid the government to exclude the speech of private individuals or groups from a public institution or PUBLIC FORUM solely because the speech is religious in content, including LAMB'S CHAPEL V. CENTER MORICHES SCHOOL DISTRICT (1993), CAPITOL SQUARE REVIEW AND ADVISORY BOARD V. PINETTE (1995), and ROSENBERGER V. RECTOR & VISITORS OF UNIVERSITY OF VIRGINIA (1995).

Sharp controversy continues, however, over the constitutional protection of religious activity that is primarily conduct rather than speech. One narrower view holds that government has power to punish or restrict religiously motivated conduct as long as it does not single it out; that is, the free exercise clause gives religious believers no protection from laws that apply generally to certain conduct. The Court adopted this view—with some potentially significant limits and exceptions—in EMPLOYMENT DIVISION, DEPARTMENT OF HUMAN RESOURCES OF OREGON V. SMITH (1990), holding that a state could apply its "generally applicable" criminal law against peyote use to Native American religious believers who used the drug in their worship services.

A broader view holds that the free exercise of religion requires government to have a strong reason for substantially restricting religious conduct, even when the restriction comes through a law that applies generally. This view, which held sway in the Court from 1963 into the late 1980s, would require the government to accommodate, or exempt, sincere religious practice unless the reason for restricting the practice was important or even "compelling" (the language of SHERBERT V. VERNER (1963) and WISCONSIN V. YODER (1972)).

According to the pro-accommodation view, the free exercise clause recognizes that religious believers claim a duty to a power outside (or above) the state—a belief prevalent at the time of the founding and enunciated, for example, in JAMES MADISON's *Memorial and Remonstrance Against Religious Assessments* (1785)—and such a competing allegiance is infringed as much by a general law as by one aimed at religion. Moreover, with today's increase in both government regulation and RELIGIOUS DIVERSITY, most instances of government suppression of religious exercise will result from general laws rather than deliberate discrimination.

Opponents answer that ACCOMMODATION OF RELIGION in the form of exemptions from general laws wrongly favors religious motives over other motives for acting. They add that religious practice cannot be entirely unregulated (consider, for example, ritual human sacrifice), and say that there is no principled line for distinguishing laws that are sufficiently important to override religious freedom from laws that are not. Some opponents go so far as to claim that religious exemptions are constitutionally prohibited; others simply say they are not constitutionally required. *Smith* took the latter view, suggesting that legislatures could exempt religion but did not have to do so.

Since *Smith*, religious liberty issues have fallen into two categories. The first is how much protection for religious conduct remains under the free exercise clause as interpreted narrowly in *Smith*. The Court's standard left open the question of when a law is "generally applicable" and thus immune from challenge. Nearly every law contains some exception (for example, small-business exemptions from commercial regulations, or medicinal-use exceptions to drug laws). Exempting religious conduct whenever any secular exception exists would vindicate religious exercise as a PREFERRED FREEDOM, but it would also mean that *Smith* had little effect in expanding government's discretion. In CHURCH OF LUKUMI BABALU AYE, INC. V. CITY OF HIALEAH (1993), the Court applied *Smith* to invalidate laws that prohibited almost nothing but religiously motivated conduct—in that case, laws against animal killing that exempted numerous forms of killing (hunting, fishing, even kosher slaughter) but covered the ritual sacrifices of the Santería sect. But when a law contains some exceptions but still applies widely, the result under *Smith* is uncertain.

A related source of protection might be found in *Smith*'s suggestion that when a highly discretionary standard, leading to differing results in particular cases, is applied to restrict religion, there must be a compelling reason for the result. Finally, *Smith* indicated that when religious conduct implicates another constitutionally recognized interest (such as free speech or parents' control over their children's upbringing), the "hybrid" of the two rights should trigger strict JUDICIAL REVIEW. The scope of this argument is uncertain; but at the least, courts should give careful attention when religious persons or groups assert other constitutional rights such as speech or the FREEDOM OF ASSOCIATION (as is common, for example, in cases involving the selection and discipline of clergy).

The second major religious liberty question after *Smith* has been the authority of other actors, especially legislatures, to protect religious conduct from generally applicable laws where the federal courts under *Smith* would not. Many such accommodations appear in particular federal and state statutes, such as exemptions of religious entities from some ANTIDISCRIMINATION LEGISLATION and exemptions of faith-healing practices from some child-endangerment laws. Such exemptions have been challenged as establishments because they give religious conduct special protection. It is one thing to say (as *Smith* does) that legislatures are not required to accommodate religion; it is quite another, and far more restrictive of religious liberty, to say that legislatures are not even permitted to accommodate.

The Court has upheld statutory accommodations in principle, but has disapproved them in some instances. *Smith*, with its emphasis on legislative discretion, expressly invited statutory exemptions; and decisions such as *Corporation of Presiding Bishop of the Church of Latter-Day Saints v. Amos* (1987) state that leaving religion unregulated does not necessarily advance religion to an unconstitutional degree. But other decisions have struck down religious exemptions as excessive favoritism for religion, especially where the measure shifted significant burdens to nonbelievers—for example, a tax exemption in *Texas Monthly v. Bullock* (1989) and a blanket exemption from Sabbath work in *Estate of Thornton v. Caldor* (1985). No explicit majority standard has emerged for this question. The most recent decision, BOARD OF EDUCATION OF KIRYAS JOEL SCHOOL DISTRICT V. GRUMET (1994), invalidated a New York school district created to accommodate the religious needs of children in one insular Hasidic Jewish sect, but it suggested again that accommodations that did not explicitly single out one faith would (at least sometimes) be permissible.

Meanwhile, Congress and state legislatures pursued another response to *Smith*: LEGISLATION not to protect religion from a particular law, but to restore the pre-*Smith*, religion-protective general standard for all claims. Under the RELIGIOUS FREEDOM RESTORATION ACT (RFRA), passed by Congress in 1993, all federal and state laws that "substantially burden" religious exercise once again had to be justified by a "compelling governmental interest." Some states have also passed their own statutes ("mini-RFRAs") protecting religious conduct against all but compelling interests.

Both the congressional RFRA and the state statutes will probably be challenged as excessively favoring and thus establishing religion—although more likely in particular applications than on their face. But RFRA also faced questions whether it fell within Congress's ENUMERATED POWERS. The Court in *City of Boerne v. Flores* (1997) held that insofar as RFRA overrode state and local laws, it exceeded the power of Congress to enforce the provisions of the FOURTEENTH AMENDMENT against states. Congress, the Court said, was limited to enforcing free exercise as the Court had interpreted it (the *Smith* rule), not the more religion-protective standard of RFRA.

After *Boerne*, RFRA's more religion-protective standard still may apply to federal laws, where the statute can be seen as simply an exercise of the power of Congress to amend each law it has enacted. Opponents claim in response that even as to federal laws, RFRA unconstitutionally invades the province of the judicial branch to declare general standards for religious liberty. The tension between Court and Congress over the proper general scope of religious liberty may continue for some time. Meanwhile, some state constitutions and mini-RFRA statutes reflect the more protective standard of religious liberty.

THOMAS C. BERG
(2000)

Bibliography

BERG, THOMAS C. 1995 Slouching Toward Secularism: A Comment on *Kiryas Joel School District v. Grumet. Emory Law Journal* 44:433–499.

EISGRUBER, CHRISTOPHER L. and SAGER, LAWRENCE G. 1997 Congressional Power and Religious Liberty After *City of Boerne v. Flores. Supreme Court Review* 1997:79–139.

HAMBURGER, PHILIP A. 1992 A Constitutional Right of Religious Exemption: An Historical Perspective. *George Washington Law Review* 60:915–948.

LAYCOCK, DOUGLAS 1990 The Remnants of Free Exercise. *Supreme Court Review* 1990:1–68.

LUPU, IRA C. 1992 The Trouble With Accommodation. *George Washington Law Review* 60:743–781.

MCCONNELL, MICHAEL W. 1990 The Origins and Historical Understanding of Free Exercise of Religion. *Harvard Law Review* 103:1409–1517.

RELIGIOUS SCHOOLS

See: Government Aid to Religious Institutions

RELIGIOUS SYMBOLS IN PUBLIC PLACES

In 1984 the Supreme Court, in LYNCH V. DONNELLY, rejected a constitutional challenge to the display of a publicly financed nativity scene—a crèche—in a private park in Pawtucket, Rhode Island. Chief Justice WARREN E. BURGER's decision for a 5–4 majority evoked deep resentment in many quarters, particularly among non-Christians who opposed the use of public funds to depict an event—the birth of Jesus to the Virgin Mary—that is a central tenet of Christianity. Moreover, the decision appeared to be a sharp departure from the Court's establishment clause precedents, particularly LEMON V. KURTZMAN (1971), in which the Court set forth the three "tests" that the ESTABLISHMENT CLAUSE imposes on government actions involving religion: "The statute must have a secular legislative purpose . . . its principal or primary effect must be one that neither advances nor inhibits religion . . . [and] the statute must not foster "an excessive government entanglement with religion."

Conceding that the crèche was a religious symbol, the majority opinion nevertheless perceived the Pawtucket display as essentially a secular recognition of the historical origins of the Christmas season and therefore a permissible accommodation to religion. The Chief Justice's opinion observed that the display contained a Santa Claus, sleigh, candy-striped poles, and some reindeer. Critics chided the Court for creating a "two-reindeer" rule and, more seriously, for demonstrating extreme insensitivity to non-Christians.

As lower courts and local governments addressed the questions that *Lynch v. Donnelly* left unanswered, they were guided in large part by Justice SANDRA DAY O'CONNOR's concurring opinion in which she reformulated the three-part LEMON TEST by emphasizing that the "purpose" and "effect" prongs of the test are designed to prevent government practices that endorse or disapprove of religion. "Endorsement," she wrote, "sends a message to adherents that they are outsiders, not full members of the political community." Based on this interpretation of *Lemon*, Justice O'Connor concluded that the purpose of the crèche was not to endorse Christianity but to celebrate a public holiday of secular significance, notwithstanding its religious aspect. As for the effect of the crèche, its "overall holiday setting . . . negates any message of endorsement" of the religious aspect of the display. Justice O'Connor's "endorsement" test provided a more focused approach than the open-ended emphasis on "accommodation" in Chief Justice Burger's opinion and has been widely followed in subsequent cases even by Justices who disagreed with her conclusion that the Pawtucket crèche was constitutional.

After five years of extensive litigation and public controversy, the Supreme Court revisited the religious-display issue in 1989 when, in COUNTY OF ALLEGHENY V. AMERICAN CIVIL LIBERTIES UNION, it ruled that (1) a privately financed crèche, without holiday trappings and embellished with a banner proclaiming "Gloria in Excelsis Deo," was unconstitutional as displayed in the main staircase of a county courthouse; and (2) an eighteen-foot menorah situated outside a county office building was constitutional as part of a display that featured the menorah alongside a forty-five-foot Christmas tree and a "Salute to Liberty" sign reminding viewers that "We are the keepers of the flame of liberty and our legacy of freedom." In light of the retirement of Justice WILLIAM J. BRENNAN in July of 1990, the division on the Court in the *Allegheny* case was significant. Four Justices (WILLIAM H. REHNQUIST, BYRON R. WHITE, ANTONIN SCALIA, and ANTHONY M. KENNEDY) would have upheld both displays because there was no governmental effort to coerce or proselytize, and three Justices (Brennan, THURGOOD MARSHALL, and JOHN PAUL STEVENS) found both displays unconstitutional. Thus, the votes of Justices HARRY A. BLACKMUN and O'Connor produced majorities upholding one display (the menorah) and invalidating the other (the crèche).

The Pawtucket crèche posed a risk of government endorsement because it was publicly financed. The Allegheny County displays, although privately financed, posed a similar danger because they were located in or near government buildings. By eschewing a clear test that would bar all government-financed displays with religious messages, or privately financed displays adjacent to government buildings, certain Justices on the Court were compelled in both cases to emphasize the design of the display as the key element of constitutionality. It was predictable, therefore, that governments would almost certainly invite litigation if they paid for holiday displays containing religious symbols or placed them in front of or in government buildings. Such displays require a fact-specific evaluation to determine whether the religious message has been sufficiently mixed with the secular holiday observance to avoid the overall impression of governmental endorsement of religion. A subject as intensely personal as religion is likely to evoke strong reactions if religious displays are constructed with public funds or if they are placed in locations that give them some type of official status.

These disputes, and the attendant divisiveness, can be minimized, however, if private groups, rather than the government, pay for holiday displays that contain religious symbols and if such displays are placed in traditional forums, like parks and plazas, that are normally used for speeches, displays, or other expressions of opinion. Indeed, the free-speech provisions of the FIRST AMENDMENT probably protect the right of a private group to display a crèche or menorah in a PUBLIC FORUM, even without holiday trappings, as the symbolic expression of the celebration of the holiday season.

Since the Supreme Court's decision in *Allegheny County*, there is evidence that local communities have indeed adopted policies that avoid the divisiveness that the establishment clause was intended to prevent. They have relied increasingly on private groups to sponsor religious holiday displays and have selected locations that are not adjacent to public buildings such as city halls and courthouses. This development has the salutary effect of compelling governments, private parties, and courts to consider the nature of the forum rather than the numbers of reindeer, the prominence of Santa Claus, or the relative sizes of a menorah and a Christmas tree.

If governments desire to participate more actively in celebrating the Christmas season, the traditional Christmas tree provides a constitutionally acceptable alternative. Christmas trees have acquired a sufficiently secular meaning as a symbol of the holiday season so that their display does not endorse Christianity regardless of who bears the cost or wherever the tree may be located. If communities display understanding and restraint, the Constitution need not prevent the Christmas holiday season from serving as an occasion for uniting Americans rather than dividing them along religious lines.

NORMAN REDLICH
(1992)

Bibliography

DORSEN, NORMAN and SIMS, CHARLES   1985   The Nativity Scene Case; An Error of Judgment. *University of Illinois Law Review* 1985:837–868.

REDLICH, NORMAN   1984   "Nativity Ruling Insults Jews." *New York Times*, March 26, 1984.

VAN ALSTYNE, WILLIAM   1984   Trends in the Supreme Court: Mr. Jefferson's Crumbling Wall—A Comment on *Lynch v. Donnelly. Duke University Law Journal* 1984:770–787.

RELIGIOUS TEST FOR PUBLIC OFFICE

As early as the seventeenth century ROGER WILLIAMS expressed his dissent from the common practice, inherited from England, of imposing a religious test for public office. However, by the beginning of the eighteenth century even Rhode Island had adopted the pattern prevailing among the other colonies and had enacted a law that limited CITIZENSHIP and eligibility for public office to Protestants.

Most liberal of these was Pennsylvania's law, which re-

quired a belief that God was "the rewarder of the good and punisher of the wicked." At the other extreme was that of North Carolina, which disqualified from office any one who denied "the being of God or the truth of the Protestant religion, or the divine authority of either the Old or New Testament."

After the Revolutionary War, however, the states began the process of disestablishment, including the elimination of religious tests. The 1786 VIRGINIA STATUTE OF RELIGIOUS LIBERTY, for example, asserted that "our CIVIL RIGHTS have no dependence on our religious opinions," and "the proscribing of any citizen as unworthy of being called to office of trust and emolument, unless he profess or renounce this or that religious opinion, is depriving him injuriously of those privileges and advantages to which in common with his fellow citizens he has a NATURAL RIGHT." The CONSTITUTIONAL CONVENTION OF 1787 unanimously adopted the clause of Article VI providing that "no religious Test shall ever be required as a qualification to any Office or public Trust under the United States."

The prohibition applies only to federal offices, and some states having religious tests in their constitutions or laws did not repeal them but contented themselves with limiting them to belief in the existence of God. One of these was Maryland, where an otherwise fully qualified appointee to the office of notary public was denied his commission for the office for refusing to sign the oath.

In TORCASO V. WATKINS (1961) the Supreme Court ruled the denial unconstitutional, relying upon both the no-establishment and the free exercise clauses of the FIRST AMENDMENT. As to the former, it asserted that the clause does not bar merely preferential treatment of one religion over others (although even such limited interpretation would require invalidation since the oath preferred theistic over nontheistic faiths such as "Buddhism, Taoism, Ethical Culture and Secular Humanism and others") but also preferential treatment of religion as against nonreligion. The opinion also invoked the free exercise clause in concluding that the provision invades "freedom of religion and belief."

The converse of religious tests for public office, reflecting a prevalent anticlericalism, was the disqualification of clergymen from serving in public office. A majority of the states had such provisions when the Constitution was written, but in *McDaniel v. Paty* (1978) the Supreme Court held such laws violative of the First Amendment's free exercise clause.

LEO PFEFFER
(1986)

Bibliography

PFEFFER, LEO   (1953) 1967   *Church, State and Freedom.* Boston: Beacon Press.

—— 1975 *God, Caesar and the Constitution.* Boston: Beacon Press.

RELIGIOUS USE OF STATE PROPERTY

In WIDMAR V. VINCENT (1981) the Supreme Court ruled that a state university's exclusionary policy in respect to students' use for prayer or religious instruction of premises generally available to students for nonreligious use violated the FIRST AMENDMENT's guarantee of FREEDOM OF SPEECH.

Earlier, relevant decisions, mostly involving Jehovah's Witnesses, were handed down before the Court ruled in CANTWELL V. CONNECTICUT (1940) that the free exercise of religion clause, like the free speech clause, was applicable to the states no less than to the federal government. Quite naturally, therefore, it applied to religious meetings and conversionary efforts the CLEAR AND PRESENT DANGER (later COMPELLING STATE INTEREST) test formulated in SCHENCK V. UNITED STATES (1919) in respect to political speech and meetings and continued to do so after *Cantwell.*

In *Jamison v. Texas* (1943) the Court rejected a contention that a city's power over streets and parks is not limited to making reasonable regulations for the control of traffic and maintenance of order, but encompasses power absolutely to prohibit use for communication of ideas, including religious ones. No doubt, it ruled in NIEMOTKO V. MARYLAND (1951), a municipality may require a permit to hold religious meetings or, as in *Cox v. New Hampshire* (1941), public parades or processions, in streets and parks, but only to regulate time and place, and it may not refuse a permit by reason of the meeting's content, even if it includes verbal attacks upon some religions. This is so, the Court ruled in KUNZ V. NEW YORK (1941), even where prior missionary meetings had resulted in disorder because of the minister's scurrilous attacks on Roman Catholicism and Judaism, because the added cost of providing police to prevent possible violence does not justify infringement upon First Amendment rights.

Nor, as the Court held in *Schneider v. Irvington* (1939), may a municipality prohibit distribution of leaflets, including religious ones, on public streets and parks in order to prevent littering; the constitutional way to avoid littering is by arresting litterers, rather than restricting rights secured by the amendment. For the same reason, it reversed the conviction of a Jehovah's Witness who rang door bells to distribute religious handbills, in violation of an ordinance (enacted in part to prevent criminal entry) prohibiting ringing of doorbells or knocking on doors to distribute handbills.

The Court, in *Widmar*, did not hold that a state university must provide premises for student prayer and religious instruction, but only that it may not exclude such use if premises are provided for other noncurricular purposes. It is hardly likely that it intended thereby to overrule MCCOLLUM V. BOARD OF EDUCATION (1948), wherein it outlawed religious instruction in public schools even where limited to pupils whose parents consent thereto. The distinction between the two situations lies in the fact that *McCollum* involved students of elementary and secondary school ages, whereas *Widmar* concerned students of college age who are generally less likely to be unduly influenced by on-premises prayer meetings.

In LYNCH V. DONNELLY (1984) the Court upheld the use of municipal funds to finance the cost of erecting and illuminating a life-size nativity scene in Pawtucket, Rhode Island, as part of an annual Christmas display. (Although the display was on private property, the Court made it clear that the result would have been the same had it been on town-owned property.) The Court based its decision on the recognition that Christmas had become a national secular holiday in American culture.

LEO PFEFFER
(1986)

Bibliography

PFEFFER, LEO 1985 *Religion, State and the Burger Court.* Buffalo, N.Y.: Prometheus.

REMAND

A remand is an appellate court's act in returning a case to a lower court, usually unnecessary when the appellate court affirms the lower court's judgment. When the Supreme Court reverses or vacates a state court judgment, it customarily remands for "proceedings not inconsistent" with the Court's decision.

KENNETH L. KARST
(1986)

REMEDIES

See: Constitutional Remedies; Exhaustion of Remedies

REMOVAL OF CASES

When a civil or criminal case within CONCURRENT federal and state JURISDICTION is filed in state court, Congress may choose to offer the parties the right to remove it from state to federal court. Indeed, removal is the only way to provide for ORIGINAL federal JURISDICTION in some cases, such as those in which a FEDERAL QUESTION appears for the first time in the defendant's answer to the complaint. Because federal removal jurisdiction is treated as derivative from state jurisdiction, a suit improperly filed in state court may not be removed.

Congress has employed removal ever since the JUDICIARY ACT OF 1789. The device serves two principal purposes. First, removal can equalize the position of plaintiffs and defendants with respect to choice of forum. For example, federal statutes allow defendants to remove most DIVERSITY JURISDICTION and federal question cases that the plaintiff could have brought initially in federal court. Second, removal can provide access to a more sympathetic federal forum for defendants who are asserting federal rights as defenses. For example, statutes permit federal officers and others acting under federal authority to remove suits brought against them for conduct within the scope of that authority. Another statute authorizes removal of suits by individuals whose rights under federal equal rights laws cannot be enforced in state court. (See CIVIL RIGHTS REMOVAL.)

Federal statutory law provides that if a removable claim is joined in the same suit with a nonremovable claim, the entire suit may be removed if the two claims are "separate and independent." If the nonremovable claim is sufficiently separate to satisfy the statutory requirement, however, it may not be within the federal court's PENDENT or ANCILLARY JURISDICTION. In such cases, the statute resolves the constitutional problem by granting the federal court discretion to remand the nonremovable claim to state court.

CAROLE E. GOLDBERG-AMBROSE
(1986)

Bibliography
COHEN, W.   1961   Problems in the Removal of a "Separate and Independent Claim or Cause of Action." *Minnesota Law Review* 46:1–41.

REMOVAL POWER, PRESIDENTIAL

See: Appointing and Removal Power, Presidential

RENDELL-BAKER v. KOHN

See: *Blum v. Yaretsky*

RENDITION

See: Fugitive from Justice; Fugitive Slavery

RENTON (CITY OF) v. PLAYTIME THEATRES
475 U.S. 41 (1986)

Renton, Washington, passed a ZONING ordinance that prohibited adult theaters from locating within 1,000 feet of any residence, church, park, or school. The owners of two adult theaters filed suit, claiming the ordinance violated the FIRST AMENDMENT. The Supreme Court disagreed, holding 7–2 that the ordinance was a constitutional response to the serious social problems created by adult theaters.

Writing for six members of the majority, Justice WILLIAM H. REHNQUIST argued that, even though the ordinance was clearly directed at theaters showing a certain kind of film, the law was properly analyzed as a "content neutral" regulation because it was "aimed not at the *content* of the films shown at 'adult motion picture theatres,' but rather at the *secondary effects* of such theatres on the surrounding community." According to Rehnquist, because the ordinance left 520 acres of land on which adult theaters could still locate, it represented a valid time, place, and manner regulation of the type upheld by the Court in many other "content neutral" cases. Rehnquist did not dispute that the zoning restriction might impose financial hardship on adult theaters, but said the First Amendment does not compel the state "to ensure that adult theaters, or any other kinds of speech-related businesses . . . will be able to obtain sites at bargain prices."

In dissent, Justice WILLIAM J. BRENNAN objected to the majority's classification of the ordinance as "content neutral." But even under that standard, the ordinance was still unconstitutional according to Brennan because it was not narrowly tailored to fit a significant governmental interest.

JOHN G. WEST, JR.
(1992)

(SEE ALSO: *Young v. American Mini Theatres, Inc.*)

REPEAL ACT

See: Civil Rights Repeal Act

REPORTER'S PRIVILEGE

The reporter's privilege issue posed in BRANZBURG V. HAYES (1972) is a microcosm of the difficulties of both journalism and law in accommodating traditional procedures and principles to the development of widespread disenchantment and disobedience in American society. For knowledge about dissident groups we must depend on the efforts of journalists, efforts that will be impeded if the subjects believe that reporters' information will become available to law enforcement agencies. Yet the legal system has important interests in prompt detection and prosecution of crimes. Anglo-American judges have long boasted that no person is too high to escape the obligation of testifying to a GRAND JURY. This obligation is an important guarantee of equality in the operation of criminal law. Thus, courts have historically been unsympathetic to claims that certain kinds of information should be privileged from disclosure before the grand jury. Only the RIGHT AGAINST SELF-INCRIMINATION and the attorney-client privilege have achieved general recognition from American courts.

In *Branzburg*, three cases joined for decision, three reporters had declined to provide requested information to a grand jury. The reporters argued for a special privilege, arguing that compulsory testimony would significantly diminish the flow of information from news sources.

The opinions of a closely divided Supreme Court spanned the spectrum of possible FIRST AMENDMENT responses. Justice BYRON R. WHITE's majority opinion rejected the notion of a journalist's claim of privilege, calling the journalists' fear speculative. Even assuming some constriction in the flow of news, White argued, the public interest in investigating and prosecuting crimes reported to the press outweighs that in the dissemination of news about those activities when the dissemination rests upon confidentiality.

After seemingly rejecting both the theoretical and the empirical arguments for a journalist's privilege, the majority opinion concluded with an enigmatic suggestion that the door to the privilege might not be completely closed. "Newsgathering," the majority noted obliquely, "is not without its First Amendment protection": "[G]rand jury investigations if instituted or conducted other than in good faith, would pose wholly different issues for resolution under the First Amendment. Official harassment of the press undertaken not for purposes of law enforcement but to disrupt a reporter's relationship with his news sources would have no justification."

Moreover, the majority opinion made clear that the subject of reporter's privilege is an appropriate one for legislative or executive consideration. It noted that several states already had passed SHIELD LAWS embodying a journalist's privilege of the kind sought.

In a brief but important concurring opinion, Justice LEWIS F. POWELL emphasized that "we do not hold that . . . state and federal authorities are free to 'annex' the news media as an investigative arm of government." No "harassment" of newsmen will be tolerated, Powell continued, if a reporter can show that the grand jury investigation is "not being conducted in good faith" or if

he is called upon for information "bearing only a remote and tenuous relationship to the subject of the investigation." Lower courts have generally followed the Powell approach to claims of reporter's privilege.

Four Justices dissented. For Justice WILLIAM O. DOUGLAS, the First Amendment offered immunity from appearing or testifying before a grand jury unless the reporter were implicated in a crime. Justice POTTER J. STEWART, for himself and Justices WILLIAM J. BRENNAN and THURGOOD MARSHALL, wrote a careful but impassioned dissent. From the right to publish Stewart deduced corollary right to gather news. This right, in turn, required protection of confidential sources. Stewart recognized that the interest of the government in investigating crime could properly outweigh the journalist's privilege if the government could show that the information sought were "clearly relevant to a precisely defined subject of governmental inquiry"; that the reporter probably had the relevant information; and that there were no other available source for the information.

Later decisions have uniformly rejected claims of special privilege for reporters in other factual settings. In ZURCHER V. STANFORD DAILY (1978) the Supreme Court denied that the First Amendment gave any special protection to newsrooms against police searches and seizures. And in HERBERT V. LANDO (1979) the Court rejected a claim that journalists should be privileged not to respond to questions about the editorial processes or their subjective state of mind concerning stories involved in libel actions. Thus the Court has left the question of reporter's privilege to legislative treatment through shield laws and to prosecutorial discretion.

BENNO C. SCHMIDT, JR.
(1986)

Bibliography

BLASI, VINCENT   1971   The Newsman's Privilege: An Empirical Study. *Michigan Law Review* 70:229.

REPORT OF THE CONFERENCE OF CHIEF JUSTICES ON FEDERAL-STATE RELATIONSHIPS
(August 23, 1958)

By the late 1950s resentment grew among many state officials over the Supreme Court's increasing monitoring of state policies and activities. The Conference of State Chief Justices, with Southerners among the prime movers, issued a long critique of the Supreme Court's rulings, condemning the body's activism, "policy making," and departures from STARE DECISIS. The report chiefly criticized the Court for: increasing national power at the expense of the states through the use of the GENERAL WELFARE CLAUSE, FEDERAL GRANTS-IN-AID, and the doctrine of PREEMPTION; and curtailing state authority in state LEGISLATIVE INVESTIGATIONS, public employment, admission to the bar, and administration of the criminal law. The report called for rebuilding a strong FEDERALISM; the Court's curtailment of its own policymaking; and restoration of the "great principle of distribution of powers among the various branches of government and between levels of government—the crucial base of our democracy." Court defenders responded by pointing to the need for uniform national constitutional standards, particularly in THE CIVIL RIGHTS area, maintaining the "democracy" of JUDICIAL REVIEW.

PAUL L. MURPHY
(1986)

Bibliography

PRITCHETT, C. HERMAN 1961 *Congress versus the Supreme Court, 1957–1961.* Minneapolis: University of Minnesota Press.

REPRESENTATION

Representation is standing or acting in the place of another, normally because a group is too large, dispersed, or uninformed for its members to act on their own. It is not necessarily democratic; nor is it necessarily connected to the idea of government by consent. Democratic representation, based on the concept that governmental legitimacy rests on the reasoned assent of individual citizens, dates from the seventeenth century.

This concept has long been taken seriously in the United States. Colonial assemblies won as much domestic legislative power in the fifty years before the AMERICAN REVOLUTION as Parliament had won in 500, with broader voting constituencies than Parliament's and more conviction that the representatives should speak for their local constituencies rather than for the nation at large. Both this "inner revolution" and the outward break with England asserted a NATURAL RIGHT to government by consent of the governed and treated consent as more than a legal fiction. "NO TAXATION WITHOUT REPRESENTATION" was the slogan asserting this right. A guarded commitment to majority rule has helped put the right into practice. As THOMAS JEFFERSON declared in his first inaugural address, "though the will of the majority is in all cases to prevail, that will to be rightful must be reasonable."

The Constitution put certain restraints on majority rule: it banned some acts outright; it divided its majorities by SEPARATION OF POWERS and FEDERALISM; and it permitted an electorate that was restricted mostly to white male landowners. Yet the Constitution was democratic for its day; it has since expanded both the number of elective offices and the franchise; and its very barriers to majority whim, requiring the creation of broad, stable coalitions to rule, have brought about a majority rule stronger and more reasonable than might have evolved from a less fettered regime. JAMES MADISON, explaining and defending the Constitution in THE FEDERALIST, extolled the principle of representation as the device that made majority rule compatible with good government. Representation made possible the extended republic, embracing a large enough territory and population to be safe from foreign aggression and a great enough diversity of economic and other interests to minimize the danger of majority faction. Indirect self-government through a limited number of representatives required coalition-building, with diverse factions compromising their antagonistic goals. Representation also facilitated deliberation: direct democracy (exemplified by the Athenian Assembly) smacked too much of mob rule.

But the Constitution left many questions of representation unsettled. Whom, exactly, do the representatives represent? Does the representative speak for his district, state, or nation? Does he speak only for his supporters and his party, or for opponents, nonvoters, and the unfranchised as well? Does he speak for the whole people or for a coalition of interests? Answers depend on what representation is expected to accomplish and how it is structured.

There has been little agreement in American history about the goals of representation. Some, such as Jefferson and ABRAHAM LINCOLN, have argued that the purpose of the regime is to protect individual rights of liberty and equality. Others, such as JOHN C. CALHOUN, with his doctrine of concurrent majorities, have argued that protection of STATES' RIGHTS or property rights is the basic goal. Still others, such as ALEXANDER HAMILTON and STEPHEN A. DOUGLAS, have emphasized institutional stability and regularity.

Structural variation can drastically affect the quality of representation. A representative can be a symbol, a sample, an agent, or a trustee, elected directly or through intermediaries, individually or jointly accountable to a territorial or an ideological constituency. The American system, with two-party competition for single-member districts, bicameral legislatures, and separate executive branch, has had accessible representatives who speak for their local constituencies (though they are more than agents and are not bound by detailed constituent "instruction") but may be hard to unite on national issues. The British system, combining legislative and executive powers, and with disciplined national parties, has produced representatives who speak for the nation and coalesce easily on national issues but are much less accessible and attentive to district interests than American representatives. Proportional representation, used by several European governments since WORLD WAR I, usually has MULTIMEMBER DISTRICTS, with seats divided by proportion of vote for each party. Proportional representation reflects public ideological variety, often with a small party for every view. By focusing on ideological issues, it tends to discourage compromise and produce weak, volatile coalitions, such as those of Weimar Germany and the Fourth French Republic.

American reformers have greatly extended the franchise without greatly changing the structure or working of government. In the Progressive era, 1880–1920, they also sought to cleanse elections of control by party and financial bosses with "good government" reforms: Australian ballot; PRIMARY ELECTIONS, INITIATIVE, REFERENDUM, and RECALL; nonpartisan civil service; nonpartisan local elections, corrupt practices acts, and weakening of the speaker's control over the HOUSE OF REPRESENTATIVES. These reforms reduced corruption but also undermined party discipline and lowered voter turnout.

Academic reformers responded to these changes in three different ways. Some called for less separation of powers and more disciplined national parties on the British model. Others wanted to make every office elective, including party, cabinet, and corporate leaders, and to make elections more "representative" with public funding, REAPPORTIONMENT, proportional representation, or quotas. Yet others called for councils of experts to take over problems that elected representatives had failed to solve.

These prescriptions have been partially fulfilled in the adoption of structural change but less so in the delivery of promised results. National power has been enlarged over state, public over private, expert over amateur, and judicial over legislative. Blacks have the right to political equality; legislative districts are equalized; public funding of presidential campaigns has been increased; presidential nomination has been made almost plebiscitary. But these reforms did not still complaints that the system was producing unrepresentative leadership. Reformers deplored most of the candidates in the reformed presidential elections of the 1970s and public turnout sank to new lows. The winning candidate in 1980 and 1984 argued that private consumer sovereignty was the truest form of democracy.

Over the years the Supreme Court, though once reluctant to take sides on POLITICAL QUESTIONS, has become an important player in the game of reform. Chief Justice JOHN MARSHALL first laid down the political question doctrine in OBITER DICTUM in MARBURY V. MADISON (1803), forbearing to "intermeddle with the prerogatives of the executive." "Questions, in their nature political," he wrote, "can never

be made in this court." Chief Justice ROGER B. TANEY, in LUTHER V. BORDEN (1849), declared that the republican or representative character of state domestic government was "political in its nature" and reserved by judicial prudence—and perhaps also by constitutional mandate under the GUARANTEE CLAUSE—for resolution by the "political branches, not the judiciary." The Dorr controversy in *Luther* involved many of the same issues as BAKER V. CARR (1962), but the Court lacked the political strength, the appearance of constitutional authority, and the enforcement technique to intervene effectively.

Against the disfranchisement of blacks, prohibited on paper after 1870 by the FIFTEENTH AMENDMENT, the Court provided no lasting protection until 1944, when it ended the white primary—although it had intervened against some administrative abuses and would later intervene aggressively against franchise restrictions under both the Fourteenth and Fifteenth Amendments. Almost all other state representation questions—validity of delegations of authority, of legislative enactments, of party nomination decisions, and of initiatives and referenda—the Court found nonjusticiable.

The Court's list of nonjusticiable political questions appeared to include unequal or "malapportioned" electoral districts, especially after COLEGROVE V. GREEN (1946). But in *Baker v. Carr*, over objections from Justices FELIX FRANKFURTER and JOHN MARSHALL HARLAN that the Court was entering a "quagmire" of insoluble questions, the majority held that apportionment was not a political question and was "within the reach of judicial protection under the FOURTEENTH AMENDMENT." In REYNOLDS V. SIMS (1964), the Court proclaimed that "ONE PERSON, ONE VOTE" is the "fundamental principle" of the Constitution, applicable to both houses of state legislatures and to local and special-purpose elections—even if most of the voters involved opposed it. The principle does not, however, apply to the United States SENATE, the ELECTORAL COLLEGE, or most aspects of party organization. Nor does it seem to apply to the manipulation of effective votes through gerrymandering (see Gerrymander) and multimember districting unless these are surgically exclusive of a protectable minority, as in GOMILLION V. LIGHTFOOT (1960). *Gomillion* invalidated a law excluding from the city limits of Tuskegee, Alabama, all but four or five black voters while keeping every white voter. In a series of cases beginning with *Wright v. Rockefeller* (1965) and highlighted by UNITED JEWISH ORGANIZATIONS V. CAREY (1977) and MOBILE V. BOLDEN (1980), the Court has repeatedly refused to interfere with nonsurgical districting to the obvious disadvantage of racial or religious minorities who as individuals would have been eminently protectable against franchise discrimination. The difference between districting discrimination against groups and franchise discrimination against individuals is that franchise discrimination is easy to remedy, but districting discrimination is not. Courts have equalized nominal votes by equal apportionment but not effective votes—votes that actually elect the voter's candidate—because there is no way short of proportional representation to equalize every group's effective vote.

Besides holding apportionment justiciable, the reapportionment cases did something more radical: they treated districting discrimination and franchise discrimination as if they were virtually interchangeable, and they invoked the EQUAL PROTECTION clause of the Fourteenth Amendment to protect a "right to vote" against "dilution" by unequal districts. But the framers of the Fourteenth Amendment had insisted that it left suffrage "exclusively under the control of the states"; construing it to grant a federal right to vote would seem to render at least five subsequent voting rights amendments, including section 2 of the Fourteenth Amendment, superfluous. This "parthenogenesis of a VOTING RIGHT," combined with an aggressive application of STRICT SCRUTINY, led to the judicial abolition of POLL TAX, property, and taxpayer qualifications on voting, and all but the shortest RESIDENCY REQUIREMENTS. It also cleared the way for the passage of the VOTING RIGHTS ACT OF 1965 and, paradoxically, gave a boost to the TWENTY-SIXTH AMENDMENT (eighteen-year-old vote)—and, possibly, to the proposed DISTRICT OF COLUMBIA REPRESENTATION AMENDMENT.

These voting rights decisions substantially aided the "inclusion process" in a formal sense. Some critics feel that this aid was a desirable end in itself; others argue that, by overriding the choices of elected representatives and creating constitutional authority *ex nihilo*, the Court has debased the vote in substance more than it has enlarged it in form. As the nation enters its third century under the Constitution, the inclusion process has been judicialized but hardly completed—and the same may be said of the ancient debate over political representation.

WARD E. Y. ELLIOTT
(1986)

Bibliography

ELLIOTT, WARD E. Y. 1975 *The Rise of Guardian Democracy: The Supreme Court's Role in Voting Rights Disputes, 1845–1969.* Cambridge, Mass.: Harvard University Press.

REPRODUCTION AND THE CONSTITUTION

See: Abortion and the Constitution; Race, Reproduction, and Constitutional Law

REPRODUCTIVE AUTONOMY

Commencing in 1942 in SKINNER V. OKLAHOMA, and most intrepidly in 1973 in ROE V. WADE, the Supreme Court has secured against unwarranted governmental intrusion a decision fundamental to the course of an individual's life—the decision whether to beget or bear a child. Government action in this area bears significantly on the ability of women, particularly, to plan and control their lives. Official policy on reproductive choice may effectively facilitate or retard women's opportunities to participate in full partnership with men in the nation's social, political, and economic life. Supreme Court decisions concerning BIRTH CONTROL, however, have not yet adverted to evolving sex equality-equal protection doctrine. Instead, high court opinions rest dominantly on SUBSTANTIVE DUE PROCESS analysis; they invoke basic liberty-autonomy values difficult to tie directly to the Constitution's text, history, or structure.

Skinner marked the first occasion on which the Court referred to an individual's procreative choice as "a basic liberty." The Court invalidated a state statute providing for compulsory STERILIZATION of habitual offenders. The statute applied after a third conviction for a FELONY "involving moral turpitude," defined to include grand larceny but exclude embezzlement. The decision ultimately rested on an EQUAL PROTECTION ground: "Sterilization of those who have thrice committed grand larceny, with immunity for those who are embezzlers, is a clear, pointed, unmistakable discrimination." Justice WILLIAM O. DOUGLAS's opinion for the Court, however, is infused with substantive due process tones: "We are dealing here with legislation which involves one of the basic CIVIL RIGHTS of man. Marriage and procreation are fundamental to the very existence and survival of the race." Gerald Gunther has noted that, in a period marked by a judicial hands-off approach to economic and social legislation, *Skinner* stood virtually alone in applying a stringent review standard favoring a "basic liberty" unconnected to a particular constitutional guarantee.

Over two decades later, in GRISWOLD V. CONNECTICUT (1965), the Court grappled with a state law banning the use of contraceptives. The Court condemned the statute's application to married persons. Justice Douglas's opinion for the Court located protected "zones of privacy" in the penumbras of several specific BILL OF RIGHTS guarantees. The law in question impermissibly intruded on the marriage relationship, a privacy zone "older than the Bill of Rights" and "intimate to the degree of being sacred."

In EISENSTADT V. BAIRD (1972) the Court confronted a Massachusetts law prohibiting the distribution of contraceptives, except by a registered pharmacist on a doctor's prescription to a married person. The Court avoided explicitly extending the right announced in *Griswold* beyond use to distribution. Writing for the majority, Justice WILLIAM J. BRENNAN rested the decision on an equal protection ground: "whatever the rights of the individual to access to contraceptives may be," the Court said, "the right must be the same for the unmarried and the married alike." *Eisenstadt* thus carried constitutional doctrine a considerable distance from "the sacred precincts of marital bedrooms" featured in *Griswold*.

The Court's reasoning in *Eisenstadt* did not imply that laws prohibiting fornication, because they treat married and unmarried persons dissimilarly, were in immediate jeopardy. Rather, Justice Brennan declined to attribute to Massachusetts the base purpose of "prescrib[ing] pregnancy and the birth of an unwanted child as punishment for fornication."

In 1977, in CAREY V. POPULATION SERVICES INTERNATIONAL, the Court invalidated a New York law prohibiting the sale of contraceptives to minors under age sixteen and forbidding commercial distribution of even nonprescription contraceptives by anyone other than a licensed pharmacist. Justice Brennan reinterpreted the pathmarking precedent. *Griswold*, he noted, addressed a "particularly "repulsive" intrusion, but "subsequent decisions have made clear that the constitutional protection of individual autonomy in matters of childbearing is not dependent on [the marital privacy] element." Accordingly, "*Griswold* may no longer be read as holding only that a State may not prohibit a married couple's use of contraceptives. Read in light of [*Eisenstadt* and *Roe v. Wade*], the teaching of *Griswold* is that the Constitution protects individual decisions in matters of childbearing from unjustified intrusion by the State."

Roe v. Wade declared that a woman, guided by the medical judgment of her physician, has a FUNDAMENTAL RIGHT to abort her pregnancy, a right subject to state interference only upon demonstration of a COMPELLING STATE INTEREST. The right so recognized, Justice HARRY L. BLACKMUN wrote for the Court, falls within the sphere of personal privacy recognized or suggested in prior decisions relating to marriage, procreation, contraception, family relationships, child-rearing and education. The "privacy" or individual autonomy right advanced in *Roe v. Wade* is not explicit in our fundamental instrument of government, Justice Blackmun acknowledged; however, the Court viewed it as "founded in the FOURTEENTH AMENDMENT's [and presumably the FIFTH AMENDMENT's] concept of personal liberty and restrictions upon state action." Justice Blackmun mentioned, too, the district court's view, derived from Justice ARTHUR J. GOLDBERG's concurring opinion in *Griswold*, that the liberty at stake could be located in the NINTH AMENDMENT's reservation of rights to the people.

The Texas criminal abortion law at issue in ROE V. WADE was severely restrictive; it excepted from criminality "only a *lifesaving* procedure on behalf of the mother, without regard to pregnancy stage and without recognition of the other interests involved." In the several years immediately preceding the *Roe v. Wade* decision, the Court noted, the trend in the states had been "toward liberalization of abortion statutes." Nonetheless, the Court's rulings in *Roe v. Wade* and in a companion case decided the same day, *Doe v. Bolton* (1973), called into question the validity of the criminal abortion statutes of every state, even those with the least restrictive provisions.

The sweeping impact of the 1973 rulings on state laws resulted from the precision with which Justice Blackmun defined the state interests that the Court would recognize as compelling. In the first two trimesters of a pregnancy, the state's interest was confined to protecting the woman's health: during the first trimester, "the abortion decision and its effectuation must be left to the medical judgment of the pregnant woman's attending physician"; in the next three-month stage, the state may, if it chooses, require other measures protective of the woman's health. During "the stage subsequent to viability" (roughly, the third trimester), the state may protect the "potentiality of human life"; at that stage, the state "may, if it chooses, regulate, and even proscribe, abortion except where it is necessary, in appropriate medical judgment, for the preservation of the life or health of the mother."

Sylvia Law has commented that no Supreme Court decision has meant more to women. Wendy Williams has noted that a society intent on holding women in their traditional role would attempt to deny them reproductive autonomy. Justice Blackmun's opinion indicates sensitivity to the severe burdens, mental and physical, immediately carried by a woman unable to terminate an unwanted pregnancy, and the distressful life she and others in her household may suffer when she lacks the physical or psychological ability or financial resources necessary for child-rearing. But *Roe v. Wade* bypassed the equal protection argument presented for the female plaintiffs. Instead, the Court anchored stringent review to the personal autonomy concept found in *Griswold*. Moreover, *Roe v. Wade* did not declare an individual right; in the Court's words, the decision stated a joint right of "the woman and her responsible physician . . . in consultation."

The 1973 abortion rulings have been called aberrational, extraordinarily activist interventions by a Court reputedly deferential to STATES' RIGHTS and legislative judgments. John Hart Ely criticized *Roe v. Wade* as a decision the Court had no business making because freedom to have an abortion "lacks connection with any value the Constitution marks as special."

Archibald Cox described his own view of *Roe v. Wade*

as "less rigid" then Ely's. He said in a 1975 lecture: "The Court's persistent resort to notions of substantive due process for almost a century attests the strength of our natural law inheritance in constitutional adjudication." Cox considered it "unwise as well as hopeless to resist" that strong tradition. *Roe v. Wade* nevertheless foundered, in his judgment, because the Court did not (and, he believed, could not) articulate an acceptable "precept of sufficient abstractness." The critical parts of the opinion, he commented, "read like a set of hospital rules and regulations."

Paul Freund expressed a similar concern in 1982. He thought *Roe v. Wade* epitomized a tendency of the modern Supreme Court (under Chief Justice WARREN E. BURGER as well as Chief Justice EARL WARREN) "to specify by a kind of legislative code the one alternative pattern which will satisfy the Constitution, foreclosing further experimentation by Congress or the states." In his view, "a law which absolutely made criminal all kinds and forms of abortion could not stand up; it is not a reasonable accommodation of interests." But the Court "adopted what could be called the medical point of view—making distinctions that turn on trimesters." The Court might have drawn other lines, Freund suggested; it might have adopted an ethical rather than a medical approach, for example, by immunizing abortions, in a manner resembling the American Law Institute proposal, "where the pregnancy was the result of rape or incest, where the fetus was severely abnormal, or where the mother's health, physical or mental, would be seriously impaired by bringing the fetus to term." (The Georgia statutes struck down in *Doe v. Bolton*, companion case to *Roe v. Wade*, were patterned on the American Law Institute's model.) If the Court had proceeded that way, Freund commented, perhaps "some of the bitter debate on the issue might . . . have been averted; at any rate the animus against the Court might have been diverted to the legislative halls."

Animus there has been, in the form of anti-abortion constitutional amendments introduced in Congress in 1973 and each session thereafter; proposals for "human life" legislation, in which Congress, upon the vote of a simple majority, would declare that the Fourteenth Amendment protects the life of "persons" from the moment of conception; and bills to strip the Supreme Court of JURISDICTION to decide abortion cases. State legislatures reacted as well, adopting measures aimed at minimizing the impact of the 1973 ruling, including notice and consent requirements, prescriptions for the protection of fetal life, and bans on public expenditures or access to public facilities for abortion.

Some speculated that the 7–2 judgments in the 1973 cases (Justices BYRON R. WHITE and WILLIAM H. REHNQUIST dissented) were motivated in part by population concerns and the specter of unwanted children born to women living in grinding poverty. But in 1977, the Court voted 6–3 against pleas to extend the 1973 rulings to require public assistance for an indigent woman's elective (not medically necessary) abortion. First, in *Beal v. Doe*, the Court held that the federally established Medicaid program did not require Pennsylvania, as a condition of participation, to fund elective abortions. Second, in MAHER V. ROE the Court ruled that the equal protection clause did not command Connecticut, which furnished Medicaid funds for childbirth, to pay as well for elective abortions. Finally, *Poelker v. Doe* held that the city of St. Louis did not violate the equal protection clause by providing publicly financed hospital services for childbirth but not for elective abortions.

The impoverished Connecticut women who sought Medicaid assistance in *Maher* maintained that, so long as their state subsidized childbirth, it could not withhold subsidy for abortion, a far less expensive and, at least in the first trimester, less risky procedure. Stringent equal protection review was required, they urged, because the state had intruded on the "fundamental right" declared in *Roe v. Wade*. Justice LEWIS F. POWELL, writing for the Court, responded that the right recognized in *Roe* did not require government neutrality as to the abortion decision; it was not a right to make a choice unchecked by substantive government control. Rather, it was a right restraining government from obstructing a woman's access to private sources to effectuate her decision. Because the right *Roe v. Wade* secured, as explained in *Maher*, was not impinged upon (and because disadvantageous treatment of needy persons does not alone identify SUSPECT CLASSIFICATION requiring close scrutiny), Connecticut's funding refusal could be sustained if it related "rationally" to a "constitutionally permissible" purpose. The policies to encourage childbirth in preference to abortion and to protect potential life supported the *Maher* regulation. There was, in the Court's view, no issue here, as there had been in *Roe v. Wade*, of an attempt "to impose [the state's] will by force of law."

Although criticized as irrational in the reproductive choice context, the distinction Justice Powell drew between government carrot and government stick had been made previously in other settings. But in *Maher*, unlike other cases in which the carrotstick distinction had figured, the state could not justify its funding bar as an attempt to conserve public funds. In comparison to the medical costs of childbirth and the subsequent costs of child-rearing borne by public welfare programs, the costs of elective abortions are insubstantial.

The *Maher* logic was carried further in HARRIS V. MCRAE (1980). The federal law at issue, known as the HYDE AMENDMENT, excluded even therapeutic (medically needed) abortions from the Medicaid program. In holding, 5–4, that the Hyde Amendment survived constitutional review, the Court reiterated the distinction drawn in *Maher*. Justice JOHN PAUL STEVENS, who had joined the majority in *Maher*, switched sides in *McRae* because he discerned a critical difference between elective and therapeutic abortions in the context of the Medicaid program. Congress had established two neutral criteria for Medicaid benefits—financial need and medical need. The pregnant women who challenged the Hyde Amendment met both criteria. By creating an exception to the medical need criterion for the sole purpose of deterring exercise of the right declared "fundamental" in *Roe v. Wade*, Justice Stevens reasoned, the sovereign had violated its "duty to govern impartially."

Following the bold step in the 1973 abortion rulings, the public funding rulings appear incongruous. The direct, practical effect of the funding rulings will not endure, however, if the legislative trend again turns in the direction discernible at the time of the *Roe v. Wade* decision. National and state legislators may come to question the wisdom of a childbirth-encouragement policy trained on Medicaid-eligible women, and to comprehend more completely the centrality of reproductive autonomy to a woman's control of her life's course.

May the state require spousal consent to the abortion decision of a woman and her physician when the state itself may not override that decision? In PLANNED PARENTHOOD V. DANFORTH (1976) the Court held unconstitutional Missouri's requirement of spousal consent to a first-trimester abortion. Justice Blackmun, for the six-member majority, declared that the state may not delegate authority to any person, even a spouse, to veto abortions which the state may not proscribe or regulate. A husband, of course, has a vital interest in his wife's pregnancy, Justice Blackmun acknowledged. But the woman's stake is more compelling; therefore the final decision must rest with her.

Although government may not remove the abortion decision from the woman and her physician unless its action demonstrably serves a compelling interest in the woman's health or in potential life, a state may act to ensure the quality of the decision. In *Danforth* the Court unanimously upheld Missouri's requirement that, prior to a first-trimester abortion, a woman certify that she has given her informed, uncoerced consent. The abortion decision is stressful, the Court observed; it should be made with "full knowledge of its nature and consequences." A state's authority in this regard, however, is limited. Regulations must be genuinely necessary to secure enlightened consent; they must be designed to inform rather than persuade; and they must not interfere with the physician's counseling discretion.

In *Akron v. Akron Center for Reproductive Health* (1983) the Court, 6–3, speaking through Justice Powell, struck down a series of regulations that exceeded these limits. One regulation required the physician to tell any woman contemplating an abortion that the unborn child is a human life from conception; to tell her the details of the anatomical characteristics of the fetus; and to enumerate the physical and psychological risks of abortion. The Court held this regulation invalid because it was designed to persuade women to forgo abortions, and because it encroached upon the physician's discretion to decide how best to advise the patient. The Court also invalidated as unnecessary to secure informed, uncoerced consent a twenty-four-hour waiting period between consent and abortion and a requirement that the physician personally convey information to the woman.

The Court has not yet had occasion to pass upon a regulation designed to render the birth-control-through-contraception decision an informed one. In *Bolger v. Youngs Drug Product Corporation* (1983), however, a majority held that government may not block dissemination of information relevant to that decision. At issue was a federal statute (the Comstock Act) prohibiting the mailing of contraceptive advertisements. All eight participating Justices held the statute unconstitutional as applied to the promotional and informational literature in question because the legislation impermissibly regulated COMMERCIAL SPEECH. (Earlier, in *Carey*, the Court had invalidated an analogous state regulation on the same ground.) Five Justices joined in a further ruling that the federal statute violated the right to reproductive autonomy because it denied adults truthful information relevant to informed contraception decisions.

The trimester scheme established in *Roe v. Wade* has guided the Court's ruling on state regulation of abortion procedures. Under that scheme, the state may not interfere with a physician's medical judgment concerning the place and manner of first-trimester abortions because abortions performed at that stage are less risky than childbirth. Thus in *Doe v. Bolton* (1973), the companion case to *Roe v. Wade*, the Court invalidated a Georgia requirement that even first-trimester abortions be performed in a full-service hospital. In *Connecticut v. Menillo* (1975), however, the Court, per curiam, explicitly relied upon one of the underpinnings of *Roe v. Wade*, the need for a physician's medical judgment, to uphold a state's conviction of a nonphysician for performing an abortion.

The ban on state regulation of a physician's performance of first-trimester abortions is not absolute; it does not exclude regulation serving an important state health interest without significantly affecting the abortion decision. A unanimous bench in *Danforth* so indicated in upholding a Missouri regulation requiring maintenance of records of all abortions, for disclosure only to public health officials, for seven years.

Roe v. Wade declared that after the first trimester, because an abortion entails greater risks, the state's interest in women's health could justify "place and manner" regulations even if the abortion decision itself might be affected. However, the Court has attentively scrutinized procedural regulations applicable after the first trimester to determine whether, in fact, they are reasonably related to the protection of the patient's health in light of current medical knowledge. Several regulations have failed to survive the court's scrutiny. In *Doe v. Bolton*, for example, the Court struck down Georgia's requirement that a hospital committee and two doctors, in addition to the woman's physician, concur in the abortion decision. And in *Danforth*, the Court struck down a Missouri ban on use, after the first trimester, of saline amniocentesis, then the most widely used second-trimester abortion procedure. Justice Blackmun, for the majority, observed that although safer procedures existed, they were not generally available. Consequently, the regulation in practice would either require the use of more dangerous techniques or compel women to forgo abortions.

The Court had three 1983 encounters with regulations alleged to connect sufficiently with a women's health: *Akron*, *Planned Parenthood Association v. Ashcroft*, and *Simopoulos v. Virginia*. In *Akron* and *Ashcroft*, the Court invalidated regulations requiring that abortions, after the first trimester, be performed in licensed acute-care hospitals. Justice Powell, for the majority, said that although current medical knowledge justified this requirement during much of the relevant period, it was unnecessary during the first four weeks of the second trimester; medical advances had rendered abortions safe at that stage even when performed in less elaborate facilities. The hospital requirement significantly burdened a woman's access to an abortion by raising costs substantially; therefore it must be tied more precisely to the period in which it was necessary. In *Simopoulos*, on the other hand, the Court upheld the limitation of second-trimester abortions to licensed facilities (including nonacute care facilities licensed to perform abortions during the first four to six weeks of the second trimester).

These three decisions indicate the Court's readiness to test specific second-trimester regulations that increase the cost of abortions against advances in medical technology. However, the majority in *Akron*, although aware that medical advances had rendered early second-trimester abortions safer than childbirth, explicitly refused to extend beyond the first trimester an across-the-board proscription of burdensome "place and manner" regulations.

Only in the last stage of pregnancy, after viability, does the state's interest in potential life become sufficiently compelling to allow the state to forbid all abortions except those necessary to preserve the woman's health. The point at which viability occurs is a medical judgment, the Court said in *Roe v. Wade, Danforth,* and *Colautti v. Franklin* (1979); the state may not establish a fixed measure of that point after which nontherapeutic abortions are illegal.

When postviability abortions occur, may the state impose manner requirements in the interest of preserving a viable fetus? The answer appears to be yes, if the regulations are not overbroad. In *Danforth* the Court invalidated a regulation requiring the physician to exercise due care to preserve the fetus; the regulation was not limited to postviability abortions. In *Ashcroft*, however, a 5–4 majority sustained a law requiring a second physician to attend a postviability abortion and attempt to preserve the life of the fetus. Even the dissenters agreed that such a regulation could stand if trimmed; they objected to Missouri's regulation because it required a second physician even at abortions using techniques that eliminated any possibility of fetal survival.

Dissenting in *Akron*, Justice SANDRA DAY O'CONNOR, joined by Justices White and Rehnquist, strongly criticized the Court's trimester approach to the regulation of abortion procedures. *Roe v. Wade's* medical model, she maintained, had been revealed as unworkable in subsequent cases. Advances in medical technology would continue to move forward the point during pregnancy when regulation could be justified as protective of a woman's health, and to move backward the point of viability, when the state could forbid abortions unless they were necessary to preserve the patient's life or health. The *Roe v. Wade* framework thus impelled legislatures to adjust their laws to changing medical practices, and called upon courts to examine legislative judgments, not as jurists applying "neutral principles" but as "science review boards."

More fundamentally, Justice O'Connor disapproved the interest balancing exhibited by the Court in the 1973 decisions. Throughout pregnancy, she said, the state has "compelling interests in the protection of potential human life and in maternal health." (In *Beal* the Court had said that the state does have an interest in potential life throughout a pregnancy, but that the interest becomes *compelling* only in the postviability stage.) Justice O'Connor's analysis, it appears, would permit from the beginning of pregnancy the regulation *Roe v. Wade* permits only in the final trimester: state proscription of abortion except to preserve a woman's health.

Vagueness doctrine has occasionally figured in the Court's review of state regulation of abortion procedures. In *Colautti*, the Court invalidated as too vague to supply adequate notice a statute attaching a criminal sanction to a physician's failure to exercise due care to preserve a fetus when there is "sufficient reason to believe that the fetus may be viable." And in *Akron*, a vagueness handle was employed to strike down a provision mandating the sanitary and "humane" disposal of aborted fetuses.

Minors have constitutional rights, but state authority over CHILDREN'S RIGHTS is greater than over adults'; the state may protect minors because of their immaturity and "peculiar vulnerability," and in recognition of "the importance of the parental role in child rearing." Justice Powell so observed in his plurality opinion in *Bellotti v. Baird* (1979), and no Justice has disagreed with these general statements. In concrete cases concerning the reproductive autonomy of minors, however, the Court has been splintered.

In *Danforth*, the Court invalidated, 5–4, a law requiring a parent's consent for most abortions performed on unmarried women under the age of eighteen. The majority did not foreclose a parental consent requirement for minors unable to make the abortion decision in an informed, mature manner.

The Court "continue[d] the inquiry" in *Bellotti*. Massachusetts required unmarried minors to obtain the consent of both parents or, failing that, the authorization of a state judge "for good cause shown." The Court voted 8–1 to invalidate the law, but split 4–4 on the rationale. Justice Stevens, writing for four Justices, thought the case governed by *Danforth*. Justice Powell, writing for four other Justices, attempted to provide guidance for state legislators. The abortion decision is unique among decisions facing a minor, he observed; it cannot be postponed until attainment of majority, and if the fetus is carried to term, the new mother will immediately face adult responsibilities. A blanket requirement of parental consent, using age as a proxy for maturity, was too sweeping. Yet the state's interest in ensuring the quality of a minor's abortion decision and in encouraging family participation in that decision would justify a law requiring either parental consent or the determination of an independent decision maker that abortion is in the minor's best interest, or that she is mature enough to decide for herself.

Justice Powell's *Bellotti* framework, although by 1983 only a two-member view, became, in *Akron* and *Ashcroft*, the de facto standard governing consent statutes. In *Ashcroft*, the Court upheld, 5–4, a statute conditioning a minor's abortion on either parental consent or a juvenile court order. Justice Powell and Chief Justice Burger voted to uphold the provision because, as indicated in *Bellotti*, the juvenile court must authorize an abortion upon finding that the abortion is in the minor's best interest or that the minor is mature enough to make her own decision. Three other Justices viewed the consent requirement as imposing "no undue burden on any right that a minor [arguably] may have to undergo an abortion." Four Justices dissented because the statute permitted an absolute veto, by parent or judge, "over the decision of the physician and his patient."

In *Akron*, however, the Court struck down, 6–3, an ordinance requiring all minors under age fifteen to have either parental or judicial consent. Because *Akron* failed to provide explicitly for a judicial determination of the minor's maturity, Justice Powell and the Chief Justice joined the four *Ashcroft* dissenters in condemning the consent provision.

With respect to contraception, no clear statement has emerged from the Court on the extent of state and parental authority over minors. In *Carey* the Court, 7–2, struck down a ban on the distribution of contraceptives to persons under age sixteen. The state sought to justify the measure as a means of deterring sexual activity by minors. There was no majority decision, but six Justices recognized that banning birth control would not in fact deter sexual activity.

May the state require parental consent to the minor's use of contraceptives? At least five Justices, it appears from the *Carey* decision, would state unequivocally that minors have no right to engage in sexual activity in face of disapproval of the state and of their parents. But it is hardly apparent that any minor-protective interest supports stopping the young from effectuating a decision to use nonhazardous contraceptives when, despite the views or commands of the state and their parents, they do engage in sexual activity.

Arguably, such a provision would serve to preserve parental authority over a decision many people consider a moral one. *Danforth* indicated that this end is insufficient to justify requiring parental consent for an abortion. Yet, as Justice Powell's *Bellotti* opinion illustrates, at least some Justices consider the abortion decision unique. Perhaps the issue will remain undecided. For practical reasons, lawmakers may be deterred from conditioning a minor's access to contraceptives on parental consent or notification. Many minors whose parents would wish them to use birth control if they engaged in sexual activity would nevertheless fail to seek parental consent for fear of disclosing their sexual activities. As five Justices indicated in *Carey*, deliberate state policy exposing minors to the risk of unwanted pregnancies is of questionable rationality.

In *Akron*, which came to the Court a decade after *Roe v. Wade*, Justice Powell acknowledged the continuing argument that the Court "erred in interpreting the Constitution." Nevertheless, *Akron* commenced with a reaffirmation of the 1973 precedent. As *Akron* itself illustrates, the Court typically has applied *Roe v. Wade* to restrict state efforts to impede privately financed access to contraceptives and abortions.

It appears safe to predict continued "adher[ence] to STARE DECISIS in applying the principles of *Roe v. Wade*." But other issues remain beyond the zone of secure prediction. Current opinions do not indicate whether the Court eventually will relate its reproductive autonomy decisions to evolving law on the equal status of men and women. Nor can one forecast reliably how science and population will influence the next decades' legislative and judicial decisions in this area.

The development of a safe, efficient, inexpensive morning-after pill, for example, may alter the reproductive autonomy debate by further blurring distinctions between contraceptives and abortifacients, and by sharply reducing occasions for resort to clinical procedures. A development of this order may diminish in incidence and detail both legislative activity and constitutional review of the kind sparked in the decade following *Roe v. Wade*. Moreover, it is at least possible that a different question will confront the Court by the turn of the century: If population size becomes a larger governmental concern, legislators may change course, and measures designed to limit childbirth may become the focus of constitutional controversy.

RUTH BADER GINSBURG
(1986)

Bibliography

BREST, PAUL 1981 The Fundamental Rights Controversy: The Essential Contradictions of Normative Constitutional Scholarship. *Yale Law Journal* 90:1063–1112.

BYRN, ROBERT 1973 An American Tragedy: The Supreme Court on Abortion. *Fordham Law Review* 41:807–862.

COX, ARCHIBALD 1976 *The Role of the Supreme Court in American Government.* New York: Oxford University Press.

DEMBITZ, NANETTE 1980 The Supreme Court and a Minor's Abortion Decision. *Columbia Law Review* 80:1251–1263.

DESTRO, ROBERT 1975 Abortion and the Constitution: The Need for a Life Protective Amendment. *California Law Review* 63:1250–1351.

ELY, JOHN HART 1973 The Wages of Crying Wolf: A Comment on *Roe v. Wade. Yale Law Journal* 82:920–949.

ESTREICHER, SAMUEL 1982 Congressional Power and Constitutional Rights: Reflections on Proposed "Human Life" Legislation. *Virginia Law Review* 68:333–458.

FREUND, PAUL 1983 Storms over the Supreme Court. *American Bar Association Journal* 69:1474–1480.

HEYMANN, PHILIP and BARZELAY, DOUGLAS 1973 The Forest and the Trees: *Roe v. Wade* and its Critics. *Boston University Law Review* 53:765–784.

LAW, SYLVIA 1984 Rethinking Sex and the Constitution. *University of Pennsylvania Law Review* 132:955–1040.

PERRY, MICHAEL 1976 Abortion, the Public Morals, and the Police Power: The Ethical Function of Substantive Due Process. *UCLA Law Review* 23:689–736.

—— 1978 The Abortion Funding Cases: A Comment on the Supreme Court's Role in American Government. *Georgetown Law Journal* 66:1191–1245.

REGAN, DONALD 1979 Rewriting *Roe v. Wade. Michigan Law Review* 77:1569–1646.

TRIBE, LAURENCE H. 1978 *American Constitutional Law* Pages 921–934. Mineola, N.Y.: Foundation Press.

REPUBLICAN FORM OF GOVERNMENT

The Constitution requires that "The United States shall guarantee to every State in this Union a Republican Form of Government" (Article IV, section 4). The ideal of republican government antedated the Constitution and supplied some substantive criteria for the guarantee. The concept of republican government has changed and expanded over time, but it has influenced constitutional development only indirectly.

THOMAS JEFFERSON'S 1776 draft constitution for Virginia, various Revolutionary-era state constitutions, and the NORTHWEST ORDINANCE (1787) mandated republican government in the states or TERRITORIES. When the GUARANTEE CLAUSE was adopted at the CONSTITUTIONAL CONVENTION OF 1787, the concept of republican government had identifiable connotations to the Revolutionary generation. In a negative sense, it excluded monarchical government and the creation of nobility. Because the Framers believed that internal disorder threatened republican institutions, they fused the guarantee clause with the clause in Article IV authorizing the federal government to suppress domestic violence. But in its positive connotations, republican government implied popular SOVEREIGNTY, a balance and SEPARATION OF POWERS, and LIMITED GOVERNMENT.

The contributions of ALEXANDER HAMILTON and JAMES MADISON in THE FEDERALIST reflected these negative and positive emphases. In numbers 6, 21, 22, 25, 34, and 84, Hamilton stressed the nonmonarchical character of republican governments and the need for a central authority powerful enough to suppress insurrections so as to forestall republican degeneration into absolutism. Madison, however, in numbers 10, 14, 39, and 43, emphasized the representative and majoritarian nature of republican government, contrasting it with direct democracies. SHAYS' REBELLION in central Massachusetts (1786–1787), rumors of monarchical plots and overtures late in the Confederation period, and federal response to the WHISKEY REBELLION (western Pennsylvania, 1794) lent weight to the emphasis that Hamilton reflected.

Conservative judges in the antebellum period insisted that statutes must conform to "certain vital principles in our free republican governments," in the words of Justice SAMUEL CHASE in CALDER V. BULL (1798) (SERIATIM OPINION.) He claimed that "the genius, the nature, and the spirit of our state governments" voided unconstitutional legislation even without specific constraints in the state constitutions. Thus the concept of republican government became a fecund source of authority for judges seeking to restrain legislative innovation that affected property in such matters as liquor PROHIBITION and the Married Women's Property Acts.

In Rhode Island's Dorr Rebellion (1842), frustrated suffrage reformers abandoned hope that the state's conservative political leadership (called the "Freeholders' Government") would rectify the severe malapportionment and disfranchisement that existed under the royal charter of 1662, which still served as the state's constitution. They therefore applied the DECLARATION OF INDEPENDENCE literally to write a new constitution at a convention elected by the votes of all adult males, including those not entitled by existing law to vote. They then elected a government under the new constitution, including the "People's Governor," Thomas Wilson Dorr. The Freeholders, relying on Hamilton's nonmonarchic conception of republican government, insisted that a government was republican if it enjoyed the support of the enfranchised voters. By imposing martial law, the Freeholders crushed the Dorrite government. They then instituted suffrage reforms under a new state constitution.

The Dorr Rebellion was the matrix for LUTHER V. BORDEN (1849), where Chief Justice ROGER B. TANEY provided the first significant judicial hints about the meaning of republican government. Though Taney rebuffed Dorrite efforts to have the Court declare the Freeholder and subsequent regimes illegitimate, he conceded that "according to the institutions of this country, the sovereignty in every State resides in the people of the State, and . . . they may alter and change their form of government at their own pleasure." But he nullified this concession by applying the POLITICAL QUESTION doctrine: whether the people have altered their government is a question to be decided by the political branches of the national government (Congress and the President), whose determination is binding on the courts.

The constitutional controversy over SLAVERY turned partly on the nature of republican forms of government. In the debates over the admission of Missouri in 1819–1821, antislavery congressmen asserted that slavery was inconsistent with republican government. ABOLITIONISTS later maintained that slavery violated natural law by depriving slaves of the right to their liberty, their persons, and their labor. Southern spokesmen after 1835 developed the position that slavery was not only compatible with republicanism, but actually conducive to it, creating a leisured master class freed for the disinterested pursuit of civic responsibilities.

The slavery controversy echoed in debates on Reconstruction between 1862 and 1875. Many Republicans supported policies that would have given blacks the vote, assured equal rights for all, and excluded southern states from representation in Congress until they had eradicated the vestiges of slavery and secessionist sentiment. They demanded that Congress force these improvements on the southern state governments. Democrats and other conservatives, on the other hand, identified the essence of republicanism with self-government—for whites only. Though adoption of the MILITARY RECONSTRUCTION ACTS (1867–1868) evidenced a Republican willingness to exact certain minima from the southern states, such as the program reflected in sections 1 through 4 of the FOURTEENTH AMENDMENT, the party soon fell back to a more compromising position. Senator JACOB HOWARD of Michigan reflected a Republican consensus late in Reconstruction when he defined a republican form of government as one "in which the laws of the community are made by their representatives, freely chosen by the people. . . . [I]t is popular government; it is the voice of the people expressed through their representatives." He was echoed by Chief Justice MELVILLE W. FULLER in *In re Duncan* (1891): the "distinguishing feature of [the republican] form is the right of the people to choose their own officers for governmental administration, and pass their own laws in virtue of the legislative power reposed in representative bodies."

However, the Supreme Court has otherwise consistently declined to specify substantive characteristics of a republican form of government, sometimes using the political-question doctrine to avoid doing so. Chief Justice MORRISON R. WAITE observed in MINOR V. HAPPERSETT (1875) that "no particular government is designated as republican, neither is the exact form to be guaranteed, in any manner especially designated." In *Pacific States Telephone and Telegraph Co. v. Oregon* (1912) Chief Justice EDWARD D. WHITE refused to declare that direct-democracy innovations such as the REFERENDUM or the INITIATIVE fell afoul of the constitutional guarantee. In the previous year, though, President WILLIAM HOWARD TAFT vetoed the Arizona/New Mexico admissions bill because it provided for judicial RECALL. Taft condemned the "possible tyranny of a popular majority." In BAKER V. CARR (1962) Justice WILLIAM J. BRENNAN refused to use the guarantee clause as a basis for requiring REAPPORTIONMENT, relying instead on the EQUAL PROTECTION clause. But he trimmed back the breadth of the political question DOCTRINE, leaving open the remote possibility that the Supreme Court might someday take on a more active role in delineating the substantive content of republican forms of government.

Unless it does so, however, the nature of republican government will be determined largely outside judicial forums, and the constitutional guarantee of republican government in the states will be enforced, as it has been consistently since before the Civil War, by Congress and, derivatively, the President.

WILLIAM M. WIECEK
(1986)

Bibliography

BONFIELD, ARTHUR   1962   *Baker v. Carr*: New Light on the Constitutional Guarantee of Republican Government. *California Law Review* 1962:245–263.

——— 1962   The Guarantee Clause of Article IV Section 4: A Study in Constitutional Desuetude. *Minnesota Law Review* 46:513–572.

WIECEK, WILLIAM M.   1972   *The Guarantee Clause of the U.S. Constitution.* Ithaca, N.Y.: Cornell University Press.

WOOD, GORDON S.   1969   *The Creation of the American Republic, 1776–1787.* Chapel Hill: University of North Carolina Press.

REPUBLICANISM

Republicanism was the ideology of the AMERICAN REVOLUTION, and as such, it still influences much of what Americans believe; in recent years it has had a renewed importance in American constitutional thought. It is difficult for us today to appreciate the revolutionary character of this republican ideology. We live in a world in which almost all nations purport to be republican; even those few countries that remain monarchies, such as Britain and Sweden, are more republican in fact than some others that claim to be republican in theory. But to the monarchy-dominated world of the eighteenth century, republicanism was a radical ideology; indeed, it was to the eighteenth century what Marxism was to be for the nineteenth century. Republicanism was a countercultural ideology of protest, an intellectual means by which dissatisfied people could criticize the luxury, selfishness, and corruption of eighteenth-century monarchical culture.

Yet it would be a mistake to think of republicanism, in the English-speaking world at least, as a distinct and coherent body of thought set in opposition to monarchy or to the English COMMON LAW tradition of rights and liberties. In the greater British world, republican thinking blended with monarchy to create the mixed and LIMITED GOVERNMENT of the English constitution that was celebrated everywhere by enlightened theorists like MONTESQUIEU. Britons regarded the republican part of their constitution, the House of Commons, as the principal bulwark protecting their individual rights and liberties from encroachment by monarchical power. Thus, the sharp distinction drawn by some historians and political theorists today between the civic tradition of republicanism, often identified with James Harrington, and the common law tradition of personal and property rights, often identified with JOHN LOCKE, would not have been clear to eighteenth-century Englishmen.

Republicanism, however, was more than a form of government; it was also a form of life—a set of beliefs that infused the cultures of the Atlantic world in the age of Enlightenment. Its deepest origins were in ancient Rome and the great era of the Roman republic. The enlightened world of the eighteenth century found most of what it wanted to know about the Roman republic from the writings of the golden age of Latin literature, between the breakdown of the republic in the middle of the first century B.C. to the establishment of the empire in the middle of the second century A.D. The celebrated Latin writers of this time—Cicero, Sallust, Tacitus, and Plutarch, among others—lived when the greatest days of the republic had passed, and thus, they contrasted the growing stratification, corruption, and disorder they saw around them with an imagined earlier world of rustic simplicity and pastoral virtue. Roman farmers had once been hardy soldiers devoted to their country. But they had become selfish, corrupted by luxury, torn by struggles between rich and poor, and devoid of their capacity to serve the public good. In their pessimistic explanations of the republic's decline, these Latin writers left a legacy of beliefs and ideals—about the good life, about citizenship, about political health, about social morality—that have had an enduring effect on Western culture.

This great body of classical literature was revived and updated during the Renaissance and blended into a tradition of what has been called "civic humanism." This classical republican tradition stressed the moral character of the independent citizen as the prerequisite of good politics and disinterested service to the country. To be good citizens, men had to be free of control by other men and free of the influence of selfish interests.

The classical republican tradition passed into the culture of northern Europe. In England it inspired the writings of the great seventeenth-century republicans JOHN MILTON, James Harrington, and Algernon Sidney. And it was carried into the eighteenth century by scores of popularizers and translators. By the late eighteenth century, being enlightened was nearly equivalent to believing in republican principles; many Englishmen even described the English monarchy as being a republic in fact. This republican tradition had a decisive effect on the thinking of the American revolutionary leaders.

Republicanism meant for the American revolutionaries in 1776 more than eliminating a king and instituting an elective system of government; it meant setting forth moral and social goals as well. Republics required a particular sort of independent, egalitarian, and virtuous people, a simple people who scorned luxury and superfluous private expenditure, who possessed sufficient property to be free from patronage and dependency on others, and who were willing to sacrifice many of their selfish interests for the res publica, the good of the whole community. Republican equality meant a society whose distinctions were based only on merit. No longer would one's position rest on whom one knew or married or on who one's father was.

Such dependence on a relatively equal, uncorrupted, and virtuous populace that had a single perceived public good made republics very fragile and often short-lived. Monarchies were long-lasting; they could maintain order from the top down over large, diverse, and even corrupt populations through their use of patronage, hereditary privilege, executive authority, standing armies, and an ES-TABLISHMENT OF RELIGION. But republics, such as the American states, had to be held together from below, from virtue, from the consent and sacrifice of the people themselves. Consequently, as Montesquieu and other theorists had warned, republics necessarily had to be small in territory and homogeneous and moral in character. The only republics existing in the eighteenth century—the Netherlands and the city-states of Italy and Switzerland—were small and compact. Large heterogeneous states that had tried to establish republics—as England had in the seventeenth century—were bound to end up in chaos, resulting in some sort of military dictatorship, like that of Oliver Cromwell. If it was too large and composed of too many diverse interests, a republic would fly apart.

It was little wonder, then, that the Americans in 1776 embarked on their experiment in republicanism in a spirit of great risk and high adventure. Nothing resembling their confederation of thirteen independent republican states had existed since the fall of Rome.

By 1787, however, American leaders had lost some of their earlier confidence in the American people's capacity for republicanism. Experience with popular government in the 1770s and 1780s, especially in the democratic state legislatures, had increasingly cast doubt on the people's virtue and disinterestedness. Selfish and local interests had captured majority control of the popularly elected legislatures and had used their lawmaking authority to promote their partial interests at the expense of the general good and minority rights. Such abuses of power by democratic state legislatures, wrote a concerned JAMES MADISON in 1787, had brought "into question the fundamental principle of republican government, that the majority who rule in such governments are the safest guardians both of public good and of private rights." Suddenly the people's civic liberty, their participation in government, which lay at the heart of republicanism, seemed incompatible with their personal rights and liberties.

Such a conflict between majoritarian republicanism and minority rights had not been anticipated by the revolutionaries. The Americans of 1776 had thought that the people's republican participation in government was the best guarantee of the people's personal rights. They had

assumed, said Madison in a series of 1780s letters, speeches, and working papers, culminating in his essays in THE FEDERALIST, that the people composing a republic "enjoy not only an equality of political rights, but that they have all precisely the same interests and the same feelings in every respect," which was why republics were supposed to be small in size. They had thought that in such small republics "the interest of the majority would be that of the minority also; the decisions could only turn on mere opinion concerning the good of the whole of which the major voice would be the safest criterion; and within a small sphere, this voice could be most easily collected and the public affairs most accurately managed."

Now, however, to Madison and other national leaders, with a decade's experience behind them, these assumptions about republicanism seemed "altogether fictitious." No society, no matter how small, "ever did or can consist of so homogeneous a mass of citizens." All "civilized societies" were made up of "various and unavoidable" economic distinctions and marketplace interests: rich and poor, creditors and debtors, farmers and manufacturers, merchants and bankers, and so on.

In a small republic, such as each of the thirteen states, it was sometimes possible for one of these competing factions or partial interests to exploit the popular electoral process and gain majority control of the legislature and pass laws oppressive of other groups and interests and contrary to the common interest of the community. This problem of tyrannical and factious legislative majorities, the contradiction between public and private liberty, was precisely what had troubled most of the states since 1776, and it was the principal cause of the crisis that had led to the formation of the new national Constitution. "To secure the public good and private rights against the danger of such a faction, and at the same time to preserve the spirit and the form of popular government," wrote Madison, was "the great object to which our inquiries are directed."

Madison and other Framers solved the problem in 1787 by standing the body of conventional assumptions about the size of the republics on its head. Instead of trying to keep the republic small and homogeneous, Madison seized on, and ingeniously developed, David Hume's radical suggestion that a republican government operated better in a large territory than in a small one. The republic, said Madison, had to be so enlarged, "without departing from the elective basis of it," that "the propensity in small republics to rash measures and the facility of forming and executing them" would be stifled. In a large republican society "the people are broken into so many interests and parties, that a common sentiment is less likely to be felt, and the requisite concert less likely to be formed, by a majority of the whole." Madison and the other Framers, in other words, accepted the reality of diverse competing partial interests in American society and were quite willing to allow them free play in the society.

But not, it was hoped, in the new national government. Madison was not a modern-day pluralist. He did not expect the new federal government to be neutralized into inactivity by the competition of these numerous diverse interests. Nor did he see public policy or the common good emerging naturally from the give-and-take of these clashing interests. He did not expect the new national government to be an integrator and harmonizer of the different interests in the society; instead, he expected it to be a "disinterested and dispassionate umpire in disputes between different passions and interests in the State." And it would be able to play that role because the men holding office in the new central government would by their fewness of number and the largeness of the electoral districts most likely be "men who possess the most attractive merit, and the most diffusive and established characters." Thus, the Founding Fathers hoped that the new extended national republic would be led by enlightened men who were free of local constituent pressures and selfish marketplace concerns and who would deliberate in a disinterested manner and promote the general good. To this extent, the Framers clung to the tenets of classical republicanism.

But they clung even more firmly to the tenets of their belief in personal rights and liberties, whether defined as common law protections like HABEAS CORPUS and TRIAL BY JURY or as natural rights like a free conscience in matters of religion. Indeed, protecting these personal rights, including the individual's right to pursue happiness and property, was increasingly regarded as the principal end of government, to which republicanism was only a means, and not a very adequate one at that. Hence, SEPARATION OF POWER, CHECKS AND BALANCES, BILLS OF RIGHTS, the independent judiciary, and JUDICIAL REVIEW all worked to limit the power of government and to undermine the classical republican reliance on the general will of a united people.

The democratic revolution of the decades following the creation of the Constitution further transformed the tradition of classical republicanism. In the North at least, it virtually destroyed the classical republican dream of an enlightened aristocracy acting as disinterested umpires over the economic and political struggles of the society. POLITICAL PARTIES emerged to reestablish patronage and to promote the partisan local interests of people, and countless individuals took off in pursuit of their private happiness. By the middle of the nineteenth century, America gave as free a rein to commercial activity and the self-interestedness of people as any society in history.

But much of the republican tradition has remained alive, even to this day. Republicanism tempers the scramble for private wealth and happiness, and accounts for many of the Americans' ideals and aspirations: for their belief in equality and their dislike of pretension and privilege; for their relentless yearning for individual autonomy and freedom from all ties of dependency; for their periodic hopes that some political leaders might rise above parties and become truly disinterested umpires and deliberative representatives, hopes expressed, for example, in the election of military heroes and in the mugwump and Progressive movements; for their long-held conviction that farming is morally healthier and freer of selfish marketplace concerns than other activities; for their preoccupation with the fragility of the Republic and its liability to corruption; and, finally, for their remarkable obsession with their own national virtue—an obsession that still bewilders the rest of the world.

GORDON S. WOOD
(1992)

(SEE ALSO: *Constitutional History Before 1776; Constitutional History, 1776–1789; Natural Rights and the Constitution; Political Philosophy of the Constitution; Republican Form of Government; Social Compact Theory.*)

Bibliography

POCOCK, J. G. A. 1975 *The Machiavellian Moment: Florentine Political Thought and the Atlantic Republican Tradition.* Princeton, N.J.: Princeton University Press.

WOOD, GORDON S. 1969 *The Creation of the American Republic, 1776–1787.* Chapel Hill: University of North Carolina Press.

REPUBLICANISM AND MODERN CONSTITUTIONAL THEORY

Recent historical scholarship has traced a linkage between the civic tradition of republicanism and the Constitution devised by the Framers. The histories have turned academic American constitutional thought toward a renewed interest in traditional republican ideas about politics. Neorepublican scholarship seeks to adapt such ideas to various contemporary issues of constitutional-legal doctrine and practice.

Characteristically figuring in this neorepublican "revival" is a cluster of normative notions. As construed by contemporary legal scholars, republicanism demands strong accountability of the government to "the people" considered as their own ultimate rulers. It promotes active citizenship—participation in politics—as partially constitutive of the good life for all. It aims at public regarding laws that define rights in accord with consensually accepted values and set policies in accord with the general good. It urges sincerely deliberative, multivocal, independent-minded political debate ("dialogue") as the way to identify such values, rights, policies, and goods. It demands unrestricted access to political debate and influence for people from all sectors of society regardless of private means; looks askance at social hierarchies, material deprivations, and conflicts of interests that may compromise independent-minded, energetic, or public-spirited citizenship and governance; and seeks protection of cultural diversity and personal self-formation against undue governmental and social encroachment.

In moments of detached contemplation, all these aims and impulses may perhaps cohere as aspects of one aspirational vision of CONSTITUTIONALISM or even as steps in an argument about how constitutionalism ought ideally to work. Set in the field of actual, contemporary American constitutional-legal disputation, however, republicanism figures not as a stock set of answers, but as an agenda of questions. In live contexts of dispute already framed by the past development of American constitutional-legal doctrine and practice, the various "republican" impulses have uncertain, controversial, and sometimes arguably inconsistent implications.

Consider how various "republican" aims have actually been invoked to generate positions in contemporary constitutional-legal debates. For example, republicanism insists strongly on the nonidentity of the sovereign people with the government and on the government's subservience to the people's will. From such insistence stems support for the idea judicially championed by Justice WILLIAM J. BRENNAN and credited by him to ALEXANDER MEIKLEJOHN: the "central meaning" of the FIRST AMENDMENT is to secure the public forum of debate among citizens against governmental machination and control. Another republican precept, however, is that opportunity for access to this forum and influence in it should be equal for all regardless of wealth and other forms of social power. These two republican antipathies—to government control over the public forum and to socially unequal access to the forum—have carried seemingly contradictory implications for constitutional-legal doctrine. In BUCKLEY V. VALEO, for example, the Supreme Court condemned legislative attempts to cap political campaign expenditures—professedly as a way of controlling domination of politics by the wealthy—as a departure from constitutionally required state neutrality.

Somewhat similarly, republican concern for the independent-minded public regarding quality of people's political motivations has produced diametrically opposed stances toward governmentally directed redistributions of wealth. From one side, it is argued that redistributions are required to assure the material prerequisites of political competence and independence to all who may participate, as voters or activists, in America's sweepingly democratic political system. From the other side, it is argued that by allowing governments to tamper with distribution we invite exactly the kind of self-serving political motivation that republicanism decries.

Out of regard for protecting cultural diversity and personal self-direction against potentially totalitarian control by the state, scholarship in the neorepublican vein has called for strong judicial enforcement of constitutional barriers (including UNENUMERATED RIGHTS) against governmental encroachments on conscience, privacy, and association. At the same time, however, republican-style regard for the polity's underlying sense of solidarity has been cited by scholars and judges as justification for government restraint of arguably self-formative expression or conduct—a Nazi street march, a sexually explicit publication, homosexual sex in private—when construed as offensive or destructive to an enveloping political "community" or "tradition."

Out of regard for the public directedness of laws and for the deliberative quality of law making, some neorepublican scholarship has drawn a broader defense of wide-ranging JUDICIAL ACTIVISM: Against partisan laws, such scholarship sets vigorous judicial scrutiny of the public justifications for statutes challenged under the equal protection and due process guaranties as "irrationally" discriminatory or injurious to liberty or property. Against narrowly strategic and self-serving legislative politics, such scholarship pictures appellate courts—actual or potential—as sites of open-minded deliberative dialogue. At the same time, however, republican encomia to active citizenship and popular self-government have put new energy into JAMES BRADLEY THAYER's old objection to the habitually court-privileging character of American constitutional practice: It saps the people's determination to govern themselves.

A number of difficulties confront transplantation of historical republican thought to the contemporary American constitutional scene. First, the normative elements in republican thought depend on descriptive ones that are not fully true to contemporary American experience. Second, republicanism's valorization of political activity for its own sake, as an aspect of the good life, does not match prevailing American understanding. Third, republican thought is not easily reconcilable with the fixture of JUDICIAL SUPREMACY in the American practice of constitutionalism.

When historians say the the Framers envisioned a constitutional scheme in which competent representatives deliberate and act in the common interest, this means that the Framers not only desired such a competent deliberative institution, but supposed they had successfully designed one in the Congress their charter constituted. But then, presumably, this supposition would have governed the Framer's conception of the judiciary's role, leaving little room for censorious JUDICIAL REVIEW of the "rationality" of congressional action. Today, however, few Americans believe that Congress will or can be relied on to perform consistently up to the standard of the Madisonian deliberative model. How, in these circumstances, do we go about redeeming the Framer's design?

One answer offered by neorepublican scholarship is that reviewing courts should aggressively engage in "after the fact" evaluations of both the public merits of congressional enactments and the deliberative quality of congressional processes. The aim is to prevent, by deterrence and nullification, partisan or ill-conceived legislation that presumably would not have issued from a Congress actually functioning in accordance with Madisonian expectations. Leaving aside the difficulties of execution of this judicial commission, it is questionable republican doctrine. It does not speak to republicanism's attribution of value to direct personal engagement in the political process.

In the republican tradition, realization of the putative common good is not the whole point of broad-based political activity. A person's engagement, as an equal, in joint pursuit with others of the common good is republicanly valued as a vital aspect of personal freedom. It is far from clear how this personally emancipatory value of civic participation can at all be realized at two removes: first, from the people to the Congress and, then, from the Congress to the Court. It may be true that a person's ulterior interests can be represented in a functional sense, more or less accurately, by delegates. The experience of citizenship as public freedom, however, is a different matter. Freedom is representable, if at all, only pictorially, not functionally. Representation of interests may conceivably, if things go well, succeed in effectuating people's interests fairly. But representations—dramatizations—of freedom do not realize people's freedom.

Here, historical republicanism may seem to offer assistance. Traditional republican thought articulates political activity into distinct and complementary roles—including those of electors as well as of officials—and professes to see the juice of political freedom flowing through all the circuits. This idea occurs not only in canonical republican writings, such as those of James Harrington; it is apparent as well in the thought of American Framers such as JAMES WILSON. The idea supposes that everyone can be politically active, in the freedom-conferring way, in public encounters by which we elect, instruct, and evaluate political representatives. It depends, however, on what today seems an unacceptably inegalitarian assignment of a good—"positive" (participatory) political freedom—that by republicanism's own account is humanly fundamental. Moreover, it attributes to electoral politics a liveliness, immediacy, and accessibility that contemporary American experience cannot easily credit.

In view of contemporary realities in the political life of the continental republic, some observers conclude that the best that can now be done on behalf of the republican strain in constitutional thought is to protect and nurture civic dialogic engagement not within the national constitutional setup, but beyond it. Such observers see local associations, both governmental and nongovernmental, as the realms that in modern life remain for the "positive" freedom of political action. With varying emphases, they accordingly suggest that constitutional law best serves this freedom through judicial specification and enforcement of supportive legal rights respecting municipal and associational autonomy, political expression, cultural and ideological diversity, personal self-formation through associations both intimate and civic, and personal independence construed as "liberty" and "property." In effect, the suggestion is to pump content from civic-republican wellsprings into the liberal doctrine of LIMITED GOVERNMENT; it is to direct a participatory-communitarian ideology of politics to the purposes of a judicially administered, libertarian HIGHER LAW.

This makes for a troubled, diluted republicanism. In quintessential republican thought, a right against the government is strictly a matter of here-and-now popular political will. Such a right can exert no force against the political resolutions that alone confer its existence. In quintessential republican thought, if there are constitutional rights, this is only because and insofar as the people politically engaged have so resolved. This is rather a far cry from the judge-led constitutionalism on which Americans have come to rely for assurance of their liberties. The republican premise that the polity, with good fortune, can lead itself by unconstrained political deliberation to a duly libertarian general will is one for which modern political wisdom does not easily allow. Political modernism not only denies the existence of any publicly demonstrable and compelling moral reality; it further doubts the possibility on which quintessential republican thought is grounded: that political conversation, unconstrained by an externally enforced higher law of rights, can itself sustain the social conditions of a true dialogic concourse of free persons.

FRANK I. MICHELMAN
(1992)

(SEE ALSO: *Republicanism.*)

Bibliography

EPSTEIN, RICHARD A.   1987   Beyond the Rule of Law: Civic Virtue and Constitutional Structure. *George Washington Law Review* 56:149–171.

FALLON, RICHARD H., JR.   1981   What Is Republicanism, and Is It Worth Reviving? *Harvard Law Review* 102:1695–1735.

MICHELMAN, FRANK I.   1986   The Supreme Court, 1985 Term—Foreward: Traces of Self-Government. *Harvard Law Review* 100:4–77.

———   1990   Tutelary Jurisprudence and Constitutional Property. In Ellen Paul and Howard Dickman, eds., *Liberty, Property, and the Future of Constitutional Development*, pages 127–171. Albany: State University of New York Press.

SYMPOSIUM   1987   Republicanism and Liberalism in American Constitutional Thought. *William and Mary Law Review* 29:57–112.

———   1989   The Civic Republican Tradition. *Yale Law Journal* 97:1493–1723.

REPUBLICAN PARTY

The Republican party was organized in response to the KANSAS-NEBRASKA ACT (1854), which allowed SLAVERY in the Kansas and Nebraska territories. This was a repudiation of the MISSOURI COMPROMISE (1820), which had prohibited all SLAVERY IN THE TERRITORIES west and north of Missouri and for a generation had served as the basis of all sectional accommodation on slavery and territorial settlement. This new political organization was initially known as the Anti-Nebraska party.

As a coalition of former Whigs, antislavery Democrats, former Know-Nothings, and abolitionists who had been in the Liberty and Free-Soil parties, Republicans differed among themselves on such issues as currency, banking, and tariffs. But they all agreed on the need to stop the extension of slavery in the territories. In his "House Divided" speech of 1858 ABRAHAM LINCOLN expressed this view, noting that he wanted to "arrest the further spread of it [slavery], and place it where the public mind shall rest in the belief that it is in the course of ultimate extinction." Republicans were also motivated by the fear that freedom was actually on the defensive and that a "slave-power conspiracy" threatened the liberty of all Americans.

Especially after the decision in DRED SCOTT V. SANDFORD (1857), Republicans feared a nationalization of slavery. Lincoln worried there might soon be "another Supreme Court decision, declaring that the Constitution of the United States does not permit a *state* to exclude slavery from its limits. . . . We shall lie down pleasantly dreaming that the people of Missouri are on the verge of making their State free; and we shall awake to the reality, instead, that the Supreme Court has made Illinois a slave state." The implications of *Dred Scott* were clear to Republican leaders. Lincoln argued that "the logical conclusion" from Chief Justice ROGER BROOKE TANEY's opinion was "that what Dred Scott's master might lawfully do with Dred Scott, in the free State of Illinois, every other master might lawfully do with any other one, or one thousand slaves, in Illinois, or in any other free State." In 1856, Senator Henry Wilson, a future vice-president, stated that the party's "object is to overthrow the Slave Power of the country."

This battle with the slave-power conspiracy did not mean an all-out assault on slavery wherever it existed. Most Republicans agreed, however reluctantly, that the Constitution did not permit the federal government to interfere with slavery in the states. Some Republicans, including Lincoln, even acknowledged the constitutional obligation to return fugitive slaves, although many other leading Republicans, including SALMON P. CHASE, WILLIAM SEWARD, and THADDEUS STEVENS, were active in defending fugitive slaves and their white allies.

Whatever their differences over the fugitive slave laws, Republicans agreed that the Constitution was fundamentally antislavery. This interpretation was at odds with both the southern view and the abolitionist view of WILLIAM LLOYD GARRISON that the Constitution was a proslavery compact and thus a "covenant with death." Republicans tied their CONSTITUTIONAL THEORY to the DECLARATION OF INDEPENDENCE to argue that the thrust of the Constitution—the intent of the Framers—was against slavery.

The constitutional principles of the antebellum Republican party can be organized around the party's election slogan—Free Soil, Free Labor, Free Speech, Free Men—and by the party's endorsement of the principles of the Declaration of Independence.

"Free Soil" had two meanings for the Republicans. First, it meant closing the territories to slave settlement. Until the CIVIL WAR mooted the issue, Republicans consistently opposed allowing any new slave states into the Union and fought against allowing masters to bring their slaves into any of the territories. They argued that Congress had full authority to prohibit all slavery in the territories. This left the party in a constitutional quandary after the ruling in *Dred Scott v. Sandford*. Republicans could not maintain their Free Soil position without opposing the Supreme Court. They tried to extricate themselves from this dilemma by asserting that Taney's rulings on the power of Congress over slavery in the territories and on the status of free blacks to sue in federal courts were OBITER DICTA that had no legitimate constitutional authority. The Republican editor Horace Greeley declared in the *New York Tribune* that Taney's opinion was "atrocious," "wicked," "abominable," and had no more constitutional authority than what might be heard in any "Washington bar-room."

Republicans also believed that "Free Soil" should dictate national policy on western lands. Thus, the party supported the HOMESTEAD ACT and the MORRILL ACT as ways of stimulating western settlement.

The Republican commitment to "Free Labor" centered on the dignity of labor, the importance of individual enterprise in nineteenth-century northern society, and a middle class culture of hard work. One Iowa Republican proclaimed that America's greatness was based on the fact that "even the poorest and humblest in the land, may, by industry and application, attain a position which will entitle him to the respect and confidence of his fellowmen." Free labor was also the opposite of slave labor. Free labor meant "Free Men" to Republicans. While the party opposed the extension of slavery, Republicans acknowledged that the national government had no power to end slavery in the states. But, wherever the national government had power over slavery, Republicans wanted to exercise that power.

Tied to the free-labor and free-men beliefs of Republicans was strong support, at least for the era, for black rights. Republicans were horrified by Chief Justice Taney's assertion in *Dred Scott* that blacks could not be citizens of the United States or sue in federal courts. In states like Massachusetts, where blacks could vote, Republicans worked for full integration. In states like Iowa, Wisconsin, and Connecticut, where blacks could not vote, Republicans worked to remove race as a criterion for suffrage. Not all Republicans were racial egalitarians, but most believed in minimal equality for blacks, even if they opposed full social and political equality. The connection between some racial fairness and free labor was articulated by Lincoln in his debate with STEPHEN A. DOUGLAS at Quincy, Illinois: "There is no reason in the world why the negro is not entitled to all the rights enumerated in the Declaration of Independence—the right of life, liberty and the pursuit of happiness. I hold that he is as much entitled to these as the white man. I agree with Judge Douglas that he is not my equal in many respects, certainly not in color—perhaps not in intellectual and moral endowments; but in the right to eat the bread without leave of anybody else which his own hand earns, he is my equal and the equal of Judge Douglas, and the equal of every other man."

The party was also committed to "Free Speech" and other basic CIVIL LIBERTIES. Republicans believed that the South had violated the BILL OF RIGHTS by suppressing freedom of expression and that the South and slavery stood for the suppression of FREEDOM OF SPEECH and violence against any who dared to oppose slavery. This belief was given credence by the banning of *Uncle Tom's Cabin* in most of the South and such incidents as the caning of Senator CHARLES SUMNER by Congressman Preston Brooks of South Carolina and the expulsion from South Carolina and

Louisiana of two Massachusetts commissioners who were attempting to negotiate an end to the arrest of free black sailors entering those states. Republicans believed that the Bill of Rights restricted the states, as well as the federal government, and that BARRON V. CITY OF BALTIMORE (1833), the leading precedent on this issue (which reached the opposite conclusion), had been wrongly decided.

The greatest test of Republican constitutional theory was SECESSION and the Civil War. Republicans firmly believed that the Union was "perpetual" and could not be broken by any state or group of states. Republicans rejected the radical Garrisonian view that there should be "no union with slaveholders." The Republicans rejected the southern notion that secession was permissable. Lincoln declared in his inaugural, "I hold that, in contemplation of universal law and the Constitution, the Union of the United States is perpetual."

In the Civil War era Republicans constitutionalized much of their thought and theory. The THIRTEENTH AMENDMENT ended slavery, the FOURTEENTH AMENDMENT overturned the doctrine of *Dred Scott* on black CITIZENSHIP, and the FIFTEENTH AMENDMENT enfranchised blacks on the same basis as whites. Through the PRIVILEGES AND IMMUNITIES and DUE PROCESS clauses of the Fourteenth Amendment, Republicans appeared to apply the Bill of Rights to the states, thus overturning *Barron v. Baltimore*. Finally, through the EQUAL PROTECTION and due process clauses of the Fourteenth Amendment, Republicans seemed to guarantee substantive equality to blacks all over the nation. Supreme Court decisions in the SLAUGHTERHOUSE CASES (1873), CIVIL RIGHTS CASES (1883), and PLESSY V. FERGUSON (1896) undermined the Republican goals of a nationalization of CIVIL RIGHTS and civil liberties. The late-nineteenth-century Supreme Court, although dominated by Republicans, failed to interpret the new amendments in light of the party's antebellum constitutional theory.

PAUL FINKELMAN
(1992)

Bibliography

FEHRENBACHER, DON E. 1978 *The Dred Scott Case.* New York: Oxford University Press.

FINKELMAN, PAUL 1981 *An Imperfect Union: Slavery, Federalism, and Comity.* Chapel Hill: University of North Carolina Press.

FONER, ERIC 1970 *Free Soil, Free Labor, Free Men: The Ideology of the Republican Party.* New York: Oxford University Press.

HYMAN, HAROLD M. and WIECEK, WILLIAM M. 1982 *Equal Justice Under Law: Constitutional Developments, 1837–1877.* New York: Harper & Row.

RESERVED POLICE POWER

If a state reserves a power to alter, amend, or repeal a charter of incorporation before or when granting that charter, the CONTRACT CLAUSE is not necessarily a bar to the exercise of the state police power. In HOME BUILDING AND LOAN ASSOCIATION V. BLAISDELL (1934), the Court ruled that a state may modify or abrogate contracts because existing laws, by becoming part of the contracts, limit their obligations and because "the reservation of essential attributes of sovereign power is also read into contracts." That principle had originated in the concurring opinion of Justice JOSEPH STORY in DARTMOUTH COLLEGE V. WOODWARD (1819), when he declared that a corporate charter could not be changed unless a power for that purpose were reserved in the charter itself. Thereafter the states began to reserve such a power not only in charters, but in general acts of incorporation and in state constitutions, which applied to all charters subsequently granted. In 1877, when the court sustained a rate-fixing statute enacted under the reserved police power, it declared that the power must be reasonably exercised, consistent with the objects of the charter, and must not violate VESTED RIGHTS. In a 1936 case in which the Court repeated that formulation, as it had many times before, it stated that the reserved power prevented reliance on the contract clause. Never has the Court clarified its standards to explain why it has struck down some regulations under the reserved power yet has sustained others.

The reserved power nevertheless weakened the contract clause's service as a bastion of inviolable corporate charters. In 1884, for example, the Court held that because a private water works company was a public utility, its rates could be fixed by government authority under a reservation clause enacted after the state granted a charter giving the company an equal voice in the fixing of rates. The rise of the DOCTRINE of the reserved police power and the related doctrine of the INALIENABLE POLICE POWER forced the defenders of property rights to seek a more secure constitutional base than the contract clause, thus contributing to the emergence of SUBSTANTIVE DUE PROCESS OF LAW in the 1890s. Dozens of cases involved the application of the reserved police power even after the FOURTEENTH AMENDMENT replaced the contract clause as the main basis for invalidating state regulations. These cases did not, however, produce consistent principles that fixed ascertainable limits on the reserved power. The Court reserved to itself the final power to decide when it will enforce constitutional limitations on the reserved police power. Today the Court speaks of "the reserved powers doctrine" without making the "formalistic distinction" between powers that are reserved and those that are inalienable. *Home Building and Loan Association v. Blaisdell*

(1934) obliterated a distinction between the reserved police power and the inalienable police power.

LEONARD W. LEVY
(1986)

Bibliography

WRIGHT, BENJAMIN F. 1938 *The Contract Clause of the Constitution.* Pages 195–213. Cambridge, Mass.: Harvard University Press.

RESERVED POWERS OF STATES AND PEOPLE

See: Tenth Amendment

RESIDENCE REQUIREMENTS

Most states limit some benefits, such as welfare payments or free medical care for indigents, to state residents; all states limit voting to residents. Legislative classifications based on nonresidence or out-of-state CITIZENSHIP are not subjected to heightened judicial scrutiny under the EQUAL PROTECTION clause, and these residence requirements consistently pass the relaxed RATIONAL BASIS test.

Because state citizenship and residence are "essentially interchangeable" for purposes of the PRIVILEGES AND IMMUNITIES clause of Article IV, however, discriminations against nonresidents are scrutinized more carefully under that provision. The state must justify such discriminations by showing that they are substantially related to dealing with some special problem or condition caused by nonresidents. A state might constitutionally charge out-of-staters more than residents for a license to cut timber, if the increased charge bore some fair relation to increased costs of enforcing conservation laws against nonresidents. Similarly, nonresidents might constitutionally be denied WELFARE BENEFITS or charged higher tuition for attending a state university, because residents have supported the welfare system and the university out of general tax revenues. The notion of a "political community" justifies limiting the vote to residents.

Discriminations not so justified, however, violate Article IV's privileges and immunities clause when they touch privileges that are deemed "fundamental" to interstate harmony. (See TOOMER V. WITSELL, 1948, commercial shrimping; HICKLIN V. ORBECK, 1978, employment; DOE V. BOLTON, 1973, abortion; NEW HAMPSHIRE SUPREME COURT V. PIPER, 1985, practice of law.)

Requirements of residence for a specified period raise an additional constitutional problem. The Court has invalidated a number of these durational residence requirements on EQUAL PROTECTION grounds, also invoking the RIGHT TO TRAVEL or migrate interstate. (See SHAPIRO V. THOMPSON, 1969, welfare benefits; DUNN V. BLUMSTEIN, 1972, one-year requirement for voting invalid; later decisions allow fifty-day residence qualification; *Memorial Hospital v. Maricopa County*, 1974, nonemergency medical care for indigents; *Zobel v. Williams*, 1982, payment of bonuses apportioned to length of residence in the state. But see SOSNA V. IOWA, 1975, one year's residence a valid requirement for access to divorce court.) William Cohen has argued persuasively that these decisions are consistent with a theory that validates a state's durational residence requirement only when the requirement is a reasonable test of a newcomer's intent to remain a resident of the state. The Supreme Court has not yet embraced this theory—or, indeed, any coherent theory explaining its decisions concerning durational residence requirements.

KENNETH L. KARST
(1986)

Bibliography

COHEN, WILLIAM 1984 Equal Treatment for Newcomers: The Core Meaning of National and State Citizenship. *Constitutional Commentary* 1:9–19.
VARAT, JONATHAN D. 1984 "Citizenship" and Interstate Equality. *University of Chicago Law Review* 48:487–572.

RESIDENTIAL SEGREGATION

Residential segregation refers to the physical or spatial separation of groups. While residential segregation along racial and ethnic lines affects various groups, its most persistent and pervasive manifestations primarily disadvantage African Americans. SEGREGATION is both a condition of life and a process of group differentiation and distinction. As condition and process, it is closely related to INVIDIOUS DISCRIMINATION. The condition of segregation is primarily that of social and territorial isolation and containment. Now, as in the past, the basis of segregation is the actual or perceived incompatibility of groups due to conflicts in values, interests, behavior, and associational preferences. As a legacy of SLAVERY, black-white racial segregation has served in significant part as a substitute for caste. Segregation continues today as a part of the ideology of the color line, implicitly defining the African American's place, role, and status.

Racial segregation in American cities and metropolitan areas is marked both by the large extent of racial separation of blacks from whites within and between given neighborhoods and by the pattern of blacks concentrated in central cities and whites dispersed throughout the suburbs. African Americans are now an urban people, with eighty percent of them residing in cities. The high degree of segregation tends to isolate African Americans—and, to a lesser degree, Hispanics and Asians—from amenities, opportunities, and resources that benefit social and economic well-being.

During the first half of this century, the "Great Migration" of the southern black population primarily to the urban North and Midwest was a significant factor in creating a national presence and elevating the so-called Negro problem into one of national dimensions. This change inspired blacks to press their unfulfilled claims not only on the nation's moral sense but also on its lawmaking institutions, including the courts. National principles, supported by constitutional law, became a principal means of attacking inequality of fact and opportunity.

Although the Supreme Court decision in BROWN V. BOARD OF EDUCATION (1954) is more celebrated, challenges to residential segregation preceded attacks on segregation in public schools. These residential segregation cases focused on two segregation props, racially zoned municipal areas and RESTRICTIVE COVENANTS related to transferring property. In BUCHANAN V. WARLEY (1917), fifty years after the FOURTEENTH AMENDMENT was ratified, the Supreme Court relied on the amendment's due process clause to invalidate a municipal ordinance that prohibited blacks from purchasing or occupying a dwelling located on any block where a majority of the dwellings were white-occupied. The Supreme Court struck down similar acts of de jure segregation in *Harmon v. Taylor* (1927) and in *City of Richmond v. Deans* (1930).

One white reaction to the *Buchanan* decision was the restrictive covenant, a contractual devise by which purchasers of real property assume an obligation not to dispose of the property to certain designated classes (i.e., blacks particularly and non-Caucasians generally). In 1948, as part of the black campaign against residential segregation, the Supreme Court held in SHELLEY V. KRAEMER (1948) that state court enforcement of the restrictive covenants was unconstitutional STATE ACTION that violated the Fourteenth Amendment's EQUAL PROTECTION clause.

During the 1950s the federal government began to take steps toward weakening the de jure basis of racial segregation. Simultaneously, however, across the land racial homogeneity was being established by white surburbanization. This movement solidified the de facto basis of racial segregation in housing and therefore in schools as well. As historian Richard Polenberg has observed, "Suburbanization encouraged the growth of a racially segmented society, offering a classic example of how demographic trends would work at cross purposes with constitutional, political, and social change." Suburbanization, however, was not simply a matter of demographics, family settlement, and economic opportunity. Political decisions at the state, local, and federal levels not only contributed heavily to suburbanization but also to its virtually all-white nature.

The city-suburbs segregation has become a subject of special importance because arguably the exclusion of blacks from the suburbs denies them access to newer, better-quality housing, less crime-ridden neighborhoods, public schools with higher-achieving students, new and viable job opportunities, and local governments with adequate tax bases to support appropriate municipal services delivery. For many blacks, however, there are certain drawbacks to suburban integration, because it may dilute central-city black voting strength and rob central-city black communities of potential leadership and representation. Moreover, stable integration that depends on relatively low numbers of blacks to avoid neighborhood tipping, white flight, and resegregation preempts the potential for social cohesiveness and the maintenance of black identity.

Although the legacy of racism directed toward African Americans had virtually frozen in the effects of past residential discrimination and segregation by the 1960s, the modern era of OPEN HOUSING LAWS did not begin until 1968. Four significant events occurred that year within months of each other: first, on March 1, the Kerner Commission released the *Report of the National Advisory Commission on Civil Disorders;* second, on April 4, MARTIN LUTHER KING, JR., was assassinated; third, on April 11, President LYNDON B. JOHNSON signed into law Title VIII of the CIVIL RIGHTS ACT OF 1968 (the Fair Housing Act); and fourth, on June 17, the Supreme Court revitalized the CIVIL RIGHTS ACT OF 1866 when it decided JONES V. ALFRED H. MAYER CO. (1968), making it clear that this statute, enforcing the THIRTEENTH AMENDMENT, prohibited both public and private acts of RACIAL DISCRIMINATION in the sale or leasing of housing.

The Kerner Commission report recognized that the nation was rapidly moving toward two separate Americas and that within two decades, "this division could be so deep that it would be almost impossible to unite." The societies described were blacks concentrated within large central cities and whites located in the suburbs, in smaller cities, and on the periphery of large central cities. The report also recognized that community enrichment had to be an important adjunct to integration, "for no matter how ambitious or energetic the program, few Negroes now living in central cities can be quickly integrated. In the meantime, large-scale improvement in the quality of ghetto life is essential." Many commentators see the Kerner Commission report and Dr. King's assassination as precipitating passage of the Fair Housing Act, similar legislation having failed to pass in 1966 and 1967.

Title VIII, the nation's primary open housing law, contains broad prohibitions against public and private housing discrimination, including lending and brokering practices. The act prohibits discrimination on the basis of race, national origin, religion, or sex. As amended in 1988, the law now also includes as protected classes the handicapped and families with children. The act provides for independent enforcement by private lawsuits or Justice Department lawsuits, as well as enforcement through the administrative channels of the Department of Housing and Urban Development (HUD). Prior to the 1988 amendments, federal administrative enforcement power was largely ineffective, restricted to conciliation.

In the late 1960s and early 1970s, fair housing advocates focused heavily on integrating suburbs. A primary target was economic-racial exclusionary land use practices. Although exclusionary ZONING was seen as the principal device for maintaining the race- and class-based segregation of inner-city residents, other local government exclusionary devices often worked in combination with zoning. Those devices included voter initiatives and referenda, as in JAMES V. VALTIERRA (1971), HUNTER V. ERICKSON (1969), and REITMAN V. MULKEY (1967); withdrawal from, or nonparticipation in, housing and community development programs designed to benefit the poor; tactics of delay and obstruction of private efforts to develop low-income housing; privately caused displacement; publicly supported urban revitalization or gentrification that displaced nonwhite residents; and HUD's sale of formerly subsidized properties acquired through foreclosure, without protecting the low-income character of those properties.

In the area of exclusionary zoning on the basis of race, two significant Supreme Court equal protection cases were decided in the 1970s, *Warth v. Seldin* (1975) and ARLINGTON HEIGHTS V. METROPOLITAN HOUSING DEVELOPMENT CORPORATION (1977). In *Warth* a 5–4 majority held that plaintiffs, who included low-income housing developers, prospective tenants, and local tax-paying residents, all lacked STANDING to challenge the town's zoning ordinance that prevented the construction of low- or moderate-income housing. According to the Court, plaintiffs' allegations were insufficient to demonstrate "an actionable causal relationship between Penfield's zoning practices and petitioners' asserted injury." The Court found, among other facts, that no specific project was ready for development and likely occupancy by the poor and nonwhite plaintiffs. Moreover, the townspeople's "right to live" in an integrated community was seen by the Court as an "indirect harm" that resulted from the exclusion of others and thus violated the prudential standing rule that prohibits the assertion of rights on behalf of third parties.

The *Arlington Heights* opinion reaffirmed the WASHINGTON V. DAVIS (1976) holding that violation of the equal protection clause required evidence of discriminatory purpose, and held that even evidence of such a purpose would not necessarily invalidate state action; it would merely shift to defendant the burden of showing that "the same decision would have resulted even had the impermissible purpose not been considered."

Title VIII claims, on the other hand, aside from applying to PRIVATE DISCRIMINATION, revealed two clear advantages to claimants over equal protection claims: (1) standing was broadly defined, as even rights of third parties could be asserted (*Trafficante v. Metropolitan Life Insurance Company*, 1972 and *Havens Realty Corporation v. Coleman*, 1982), and (2) discriminatory effects would establish a claim for relief.

The protracted institutional litigation associated with the *Gautreaux* case—begun in 1967 and producing thirty-four opinions, including one Supreme Court opinion, HILLS V. GAUTREAUX (1976)—successfully challenged the Chicago Housing Authority's site selection and tenant assignment as violations of the equal protection clause and the Fair Housing Act. The Supreme Court opinion in *Gautreaux* distinguished the case from MILLIKEN V. BRADLEY (1974), which had overturned a lower court decision ordering interdistrict busing of public school children in Detroit and its suburbs as a desegregation remedy. In *Gautreaux* the Court granted such metropolitan relief, obligating HUD to act beyond Chicago's boundaries in effectuating desegregation of the housing authority buildings. The Court distinguished *Gautreaux* from *Milliken* by emphasizing that the federal government had violated its constitutional equal protection obligations; the interdistrict remedy was commensurate with the constitutional violation. Although *Gautreaux* was hailed as a doctrinal success, its remedial results were, at best, mixed. For many years no public housing was produced in Chicago or in the metropolitan areas, and many intended beneficiaries chose not to avail themselves of the limited access to housing beyond Chicago.

During the 1980s the Supreme Court diluted the effectiveness of the 1866 Civil Rights Act. In MEMPHIS V. GREENE (1981) the Supreme Court upheld a white neighborhood's street closure that blocked black access to the city through the white neighborhood. The Court held that this closure did not sufficiently implicate black property rights and therefore the act was not violated. Moreover, the Court concluded that the facts indicated an inconvenience to blacks, but not a BADGE OF SERVITUDE that could violate the Thirteenth Amendment.

A year after *Greene*, in *General Building Contractors Association v. Pennsylvania* (1982), the Supreme Court found that a related provision of the 1866 act required intentional discrimination to constitute a violation. In light of *General Building Contractors* most lower federal courts are requiring intent as part of all fair-housing claims under the 1866 act. Thus, Title VIII now virtually stands alone as a viable basis for challenging private action that causes racially discriminatory effects. In *Huntington Branch NAACP v. Town of Huntington* (1988) the Supreme Court endorsed the discriminatory-effect theory for Title VIII claims in a limited per curiam affirmance.

Housing segregation is often closely related to de facto public school segregation. In the highly publicized case of *United States v. Yonkers Board of Education* (1987), a Second Circuit opinion affirmed the trial court's finding that the city had confined its subsidized housing to areas of concentrated nonwhite population and that this action had contributed to the segregation of the city's public schools. As a remedy the district court ordered the city to permit construction of subsidized housing in white, nonpoor residential areas and to implement a magnet-school program. When the city council refused to implement the housing plan, the court held both the city and the council members in contempt, levying substantial fines. The Supreme Court in *Spallone v. United States* (1990) upheld the fines against the city, but disapproved the fines against individual council members.

There is growing black skepticism and loss of faith in integration, particularly in light of the disproportionately high poverty rate of blacks and the continuously high rates of housing segregation for blacks of all socioeconomic classes. At the time of Title VIII's enactment, its sponsors thought that the statute's emphasis on antidiscrimination would lead to residential integration. Congress perceived antisegregation and antidiscrimination as complementary remedies. Often, however, in the name of integration or desegregation, racial discrimination against individuals has occurred and housing opportunities actually have been decreased. In the principal "integration maintenance" decision, *United States v. Starret City Associates* (1988), the Supreme Court denied certiorari, leaving intact a Second Circuit decision holding that Title VIII was violated by a RACIAL QUOTA limiting black access to an apartment complex in order to maintain integration. Interestingly, the NAACP supported the Justice Department's challenge to the integration maintenance scheme at issue.

Housing persists as one of black America's most intractable social issues. For most of white America, on the other hand, home ownership in a supportive neighborhood of choice represents the highest achievement in terms of status and material acquisition, while simultaneously serving to validate the incentives associated with equality of opportunity. This vision of the American dream, however, is sullied and distorted by racism and economic subjugation. Even accepting the moral imperative and the practical necessity of integrated housing for the national commonwealth, it is difficult to escape the conclusion of Derrick Bell: "Discrimination in housing, with its vices of segregated housing patterns and inadequate and overpriced housing for minorities, continues to be one of those areas where the law is unable or unwilling to keep up with conditions in the real world."

JOHN O. CALMORE
(1992)

Bibliography

CALMORE, JOHN O. 1989 To Make Wrong Right: The Necessary and Proper Aspirations of Fair Housing. Pages 77–110 in Janet Dewart, ed., *The State of Black America 1989.* New York: National Urban League.

GOERING, JOHN, ed. 1986 *Housing Desegregation and Federal Policy.* Chapel Hill: University of North Carolina Press.

KUSHNER, JAMES A. 1983 *Fair Housing: Discrimination in Real Estate, Community Development and Revitalization.* Colorado Springs, Colo.: ShepardsMcGraw-Hill.

SCHWEMM, ROBERT 1990 *Housing Discrimination Law and Litigation.* New York: Clark Boardman Company, Ltd.

RES JUDICATA

(Latin: "The thing has been adjudicated.") The term is used broadly to refer to two kinds of effect given to a court's judgment: extinguishing claims and thus barring future litigation ("claim preclusion"), or conclusively determining certain issues that might arise in future litigation ("issue preclusion").

KENNETH L. KARST
(1986)

RESOLUTIONS OF STAMP ACT CONGRESS

See: Stamp Act Congress, Resolutions of

RESTRAINT OF TRADE

See: Antitrust Law

RESTRICTIVE COVENANT

Until the Supreme Court ruled their judicial enforcement unconstitutional in SHELLEY V. KRAEMER (1948), restrictive covenants were widely employed to achieve the racial SEGREGATION of urban neighborhoods in America. A restrictive covenant is a contract among owners of land, mutually limiting the uses of land covered by the covenant. Many such covenants have benign purposes: all the owners on a residential block, for example, might agree that houses will be set back thirty feet from the street. Racial covenants, however, limited the occupancy of homes on the basis of the occupants' race. They rested on an ugly premise: excluding blacks or Asians would, as one Louisiana court put it, make a neighborhood "more attractive to white people."

Such covenants were commonly adopted by landowners, or written into deeds of newly developed land, beginning in the late nineteenth century. Under existing property law, they were enforceable not only against their signers, but against the signers' heirs, assignees, and purchasers—at least so long as "conditions" had not changed. The use of the covenants accelerated after the Supreme Court decided, in BUCHANAN V. WARLEY (1917), that municipal ZONING ordinances specifying where persons of one race or another might live were unconstitutional. The typical covenant ran for twenty-five years, but some ran for fifty years or even in perpetuity.

Restrictive covenants cannot be said to be the sole cause, or even the primary cause, of residential segregation before 1948. The poverty of most blacks was itself a severe restriction on the purchase of homes; and middle-class blacks who could afford to buy were steered to "colored sections" by real estate brokers and lenders. (The latter practices became violations of federal law only in 1968.) Yet the covenants surely played their part in the segregative process, a part they could play only because they were enforceable in court.

If an owner started to build a house too close to the street, in violation of a restrictive covenant, the neighbors would be entitled to an INJUNCTION ordering the owner to stop. They might also be entitled to damages, if they could demonstrate some loss. But, subject to the covenant's limitations, the owner would be entitled to occupy the property, or sell it to any purchaser. The owner of property subject to a racial covenant, however, could not—so long as the covenant was enforceable—sell it to blacks for their use as a residence. The racial covenants, then, not only restricted black would-be buyers but also restricted the owners' free alienation of property—an interest recognized in the COMMON LAW since the thirteenth century. Yet the state courts regularly enforced the covenants.

The Supreme Court lent its approval in 1926, in CORRIGAN V. BUCKLEY, holding that judicial enforcement of a racial covenant did not even raise a substantial federal question; any discrimination was private action, not STATE ACTION. (The case arose not in a state, covered by the FOURTEENTH AMENDMENT, but in the DISTRICT OF COLUMBIA. The Court correctly sensed, however, that a similar problem would arise if an EQUAL PROTECTION guarantee were found applicable to governmental action in the District.)

Over the next two decades, the NAACP searched for opportunities to bring to the Court new challenges to the judicial enforcement of racially restrictive covenants. They finally succeeded in *Shelley,* where the Court did find state action in a state court's injunctive relief to enforce a covenant against black buyers of a home. On the same day, in *Hurd v. Hodge* (1948), the Court reached a comparable result in an attack on judicial enforcement of a covenant in the District of Columbia. No constitutional issue was decided in *Hurd;* the Court based its decision on "the public policy of the United States."

Five years later, the Court took away the last remaining weapon of persons who would seek to use racial covenants as a way of keeping their neighborhoods white. In BARROWS V. JACKSON (1953) the Court held that a state court violated the Fourteenth Amendment by using a covenant as a basis for awarding damages against persons who sold their house to black buyers.

One of the worst features of the racial covenants was their contribution to the symbolism of black inferiority. The removal of that symbolism, wherever it may be found, is necessary if the Fourteenth Amendment's promise of equal CITIZENSHIP is to be fulfilled. But ending the judicial enforcement of racial covenants did not end residential segregation, a phenomenon that has declined only slightly since 1940.

KENNETH L. KARST
(1986)

Bibliography

HENKIN, LOUIS 1962 *Shelley v. Kraemer:* Notes for a Revised Opinion. *University of Pennsylvania Law Review* 110:473–505.

VOSE, CLEMENT E. 1959 *Caucasians Only.* Berkeley: University of California Press.

RETROACTIVITY OF JUDICIAL DECISIONS

LEGISLATION ordinarily does not apply retroactively to conduct occurring prior to its adoption but only to actions taking place after enactment. Indeed, the potential unfairness of some retroactive legislation is so great that certain forms of legislative retroactivity are specifically prohibited by the Constitution. The EX POST FACTO clauses of the Constitution prohibit retroactive criminal penalties, and the CONTRACT CLAUSE limits state legislation that would impair the obligation of pre-existing contracts. In addition, certain other fundamentally unfair forms of legislative retroactivity may violate constitutional due process guarantees.

Judicial decisions, on the other hand, ordinarily *are* retroactive in application. To some extent, such retroactivity is a consequence of the nature and function of the judicial decision-making process. Traditional lawsuits and criminal prosecutions concern the legal consequences of acts that have already taken place. If judicial decisions in such cases are to adjudicate the issues between the parties, those decisions necessarily must apply to prior events. The retroactive effect of judicial decisions, however, commonly extends beyond application to the particular parties involved in a case. To the extent that a judicial decision constitutes a new legal precedent, it will ordinarily be applied to all undecided cases that are subsequently litigated, regardless of whether the relevant events occurred before or after the new precedent was announced.

Although traditional judicial decisions are, in theory, completely retrospective in nature, two sets of legal doctrines place important practical limits on the actual breadth of decisional retroactivity. Statutes of limitations, which require suits to be brought within some specified period of time after the relevant events occur, limit the retrospective application of new precedents to the length of the prescribed limitations period; and the doctrines of RES JUDICATA and collateral estoppel prevent the relitigation of cases and issues that have been finally decided before the new precedent is announced. In addition, as in the case of retroactive legislation, there are some circumstances of fundamental unfairness in which constitutional principles may prevent the retroactive use of judicial decisions. By analogy to the constitutional prohibition of ex post facto laws, for example, the Supreme Court in *Bowie v. City of Columbia* (1964) held it unconstitutional to apply a new expansive judicial interpretation of a criminal statute to prior conduct.

The principal theoretical basis supporting the broad traditional retroactivity of judicial decisions is the abstract idea that courts (unlike legislatures) do not make, but merely find, the law. This theory in effect denies the existence of retroactivity; under the theory the events in question were always subject to the newly announced rule, although that rule had not been authoritatively articulated.

The theory that judicial decisions do not make law does not always reflect reality. Perhaps the clearest example of apparent judicial lawmaking is a court's overruling of an earlier judicial decision regarding the meaning of the COMMON LAW, a statute, or a constitutional provision. Even when no earlier decision is overruled, judicial decisions or interpretations may announce genuinely new principles. When judicial decisions thus create new law, it is plausible to argue that the new principles should not be given the retroactive effect normally accorded to judicial decisions, but should instead be treated more like new legislation and given prospective effect only. These arguments are strongest when individuals or governments have relied (perhaps irrevocably) upon earlier decisions in shaping their conduct. In such circumstances, retroactive application may cause unanticipated and harmful results.

In response to these and similar considerations, some courts have used the practice of PROSPECTIVE OVERRULING of prior decisions. Such a court, in overruling a precedent upon which substantial reliance may have been placed, may announce in OBITER DICTUM its intention to reject the old doctrine for the future, but nevertheless apply the old rule to the case at hand and to other conduct prior to the new decision. Alternatively, the court may apply the new rule to the parties before it, thus making the announcement of the new rule HOLDING rather than "dictum," but may otherwise reserve the rule for future application. In *Great Northern Railway Company v. Sunburst Oil and Refining Company* (1932) the Supreme Court held that the Constitution permits either of these forms of prospective overruling. The *Sunburst* decision gave constitutional approval to prospective judicial overruling of common law precedents and of decisions interpreting statutes. Such prospective overruling has primarily been used in two kinds of cases: new interpretations of statutes relating to property and contract rights, and the overruling of doctrines of municipal and charitable immunity from tort liability.

The most prominent and controversial recent issue concerning prospective overruling, however, has involved the retroactivity of new Supreme Court decisions enlarging the constitutional rights of defendents in criminal proceedings. During the 1950s and 1960s, the Court significantly broadened the rights of criminal defendants with respect to unconstitutional SEARCHES AND SEIZURES, POLICE INTERROGATION AND CONFESSIONS, the scope of the RIGHT AGAINST SELF-INCRIMINATION, and the inadmissibility of unconstitutionally obtained evidence. The Court has ruled that some of these new constitutional interpretations should not be given general retrospective application.

The extent of the possible retroactive application of new doctrines affecting the constitutionality of criminal convictions is greater than in most other areas of law because of the potential availability of post-conviction relief to prisoners whose convictions might be effectively challenged if the newly announced rules were applicable to prior convictions. Petitions for HABEAS CORPUS are not subject to statutes of limitations or to the ordinary operation of the doctrine of *res judicata*. Thus, in 1961, when the Supreme Court decided in MAPP V. OHIO that the Constitution prohibits states from basing criminal convictions upon EVIDENCE obtained in violation of the FOURTH and FOURTEENTH AMENDMENTS, full retroactivity of that decision would have permitted a great many prisoners to challenge their convictions, no matter when their trials had occurred. Because the *Mapp* decision was based upon the

interpretation of constitutional provisions dating from 1791 and 1868, the theoretical arguments for full retroactivity were strong. However, *Mapp* overruled the opinion of the Court in WOLF V. COLORADO (1949), which had held, directly contrary to *Mapp*, that the states were free to use unconstitutionally obtained evidence in most circumstances. Although police could hardly have legitimately relied upon *Wolf* in engaging in unconstitutional searches, state prosecutors and courts might have relied upon *Wolf* in using unconstitutionally obtained evidence. The primary reason given by the Court for the *Mapp* decision, moreover, was to deter police misconduct; the *Mapp* EXCLUSIONARY RULE is not a safeguard against conviction of the innocent. Retroactive application of *Mapp* to nullify pre-existing convictions would thus arguably contribute little to the main purpose of the *Mapp* rule while permitting guilty defendants to escape their just punishment. Similar issues have surrounded the potential retroactivity of other new Supreme Court decisions enlarging the constitutional rights of criminal defendants.

The Supreme Court has resolved these retroactivity issues by employing a test focusing on three main criteria: whether the purpose of the new rule would be furthered by its retroactive application; the extent of the reliance by law enforcement authorities and courts on prior decisions and understandings; and the likely effect of retroactive application on the administration of justice. Using this approach the Court held, in *Linkletter v. Walker* (1965), that the *Mapp* decision would be applied to trials and direct APPEALS pending at the time of the *Mapp* decision, but not to state court convictions where the appeal process had been completed prior to announcement of the *Mapp* opinion. The same rule of general nonretroactivity has been applied to new constitutional interpretations prohibiting comment on a defendant's failure to take the witness stand at trial; establishing the MIRANDA RULES for police warnings to persons interrogated; prohibiting WIRETAPPING without judicial SEARCH WARRANTS; and limiting the permissible scope of SEARCHES INCIDENT TO ARRESTS. On the other hand, full retroactivity has been accorded to new decisions requiring provision of free counsel for INDIGENTS in criminal trials; requiring proof beyond a REASONABLE DOUBT in state criminal proceedings; and broadening the definition of constitutionally prohibited DOUBLE JEOPARDY. In general, rules designed to protect innocent persons from conviction have been given full retroactive application, while rules primarily intended to correct police and prosecutorial abuses that do not implicate guilt have been given limited retroactivity. The practical significance of these retroactivity decisions has been diminished in recent years by Supreme Court decisions that limit the availability of post-conviction relief to incarcerated persons (for example, STONE V. POWELL, 1976) and by the current Supreme Court's general opposition to continued expansion of defendants' constitutional rights in criminal proceedings.

PAUL BENDER
(1986)

Bibliography

FIELD, OLIVER P. 1935 *The Effect of an Unconstitutional Statute.* Minneapolis: University of Minnesota Press.

RETROACTIVITY OF LEGISLATION

A characteristic of arbitrary government is that the state can alter retroactively the legal status of acts already done. Therefore, proposals to prohibit various types of retroactive LEGISLATION encountered the opposition of those delegates to the CONSTITUTIONAL CONVENTION OF 1787 who believed such laws were "void of themselves" and that a formal prohibition would "proclaim that we are ignorant of the first principles of legislation." There are, nevertheless, three such prohibitions in the Constitution: Congress may not pass EX POST FACTO laws and the states may not pass ex post facto laws or laws impairing the OBLIGATION OF CONTRACTS.

There are sound historical reasons for supposing that the Framers meant to proscribe both criminal and civil legislation with retrospective application. But JOHN DICKINSON had warned the convention that WILLIAM BLACKSTONE's commentaries treated "ex post facto" as a technical term applying only to criminal law. In CALDER V. BULL (1798), the Supreme Court relied on Blackstone's authority to confine the constitutional prohibition to criminal laws.

The CONTRACT CLAUSE ultimately proved a mere parchment barrier to retroactive legislation. It does not apply to the federal government and the courts have so interpreted it as to make it a weak defense against retroactive state laws.

DENNIS J. MAHONEY
(1986)

RETROACTIVITY OF LEGISLATION
(Update)

LEGISLATION is "retroactive" when it applies new legal consequences to conduct that occurred before the legislation took effect. Congress and state legislatures generally may enact legislation that has retroactive effects when their intent to do so is clear. In *Landgraf v. USI Film Products* (1993), the leading recent case on retroactivity of legisla-

tion, the Supreme Court held that the CIVIL RIGHTS ACT OF 1991, enacted to restore the scope of CIVIL RIGHTS laws the Court had narrowly interpreted in 1989, did not apply to claims arising before the act's effective date. The Court applied a presumption against statutory retroactivity and, the act's restorative purpose notwithstanding, held that Congress had not clearly indicated an intent that the provisions at issue apply retrospectively. (No similar clear-statement hurdle or presumption against retroactive application applies to judicial decisions, which are governed by a general rule in favor of retroactive application, except on HABEAS CORPUS review.)

There is no general constitutional prohibition against retroactive legislation; the Constitution does, however, prohibit certain types of retroactive legislation. The various constitutional anti-retroactivity provisions reflect fundamental considerations of fairness, including protection of reasonable reliance and settled expectations, and the RULE OF LAW principle that behavior should be governed by rules publicly fixed in advance. Retroactive laws can deprive persons of fair notice of the illegality of contemplated behavior, and create opportunities for legislative retribution or favoritism against identifiable groups.

Among the constitutional prohibitions on retroactive legislation are the EX POST FACTO clauses of the Constitution, which prohibit retroactive application of certain federal and state laws. The Supreme Court since CALDER V. BULL (1798) has construed those prohibitions to apply only to new penal laws that disadvantage the defendant. Laws violate the prohibition on ex post facto laws if they punish acts that were noncriminal when committed, increase the punishment for or aggravate an existing crime after it was committed, or deprive an individual of a defense that was available when the conduct occurred. Retroactive application of new SENTENCING guidelines or mandatory sentence provisions, and elimination of "good time" credits for time served in prison are examples of measures the Court has invalidated under the ex post facto clause, whereas the Court upheld a statute that decreased the frequency of routine parole suitability hearings to persons convicted before its enactment. Justice CLARENCE THOMAS in a recent CONCURRING OPINION suggested that *Calder* be reexamined and the ex post facto clauses be applied to civil legislation as well as criminal, but no other member of the Court joined in that suggestion.

With the ex post facto clause unavailable to address civil retroactive legislation, other constitutional provisions, including the guarantee of DUE PROCESS, the CONTRACT CLAUSE, and the TAKINGS clause, set the relevant limitations. The contract clause imposes constitutional constraints on the states' ability retroactively to impair "the Obligation of Contracts." The contract clause protects against state laws that impair governmental or private contracts; by its terms the clause does not apply to federal laws. Its principal purpose was to prevent debtor relief laws, thereby ensuring that new legislation could not vitiate obligations previously incurred.

Until the nineteenth century, the contract clause was the principal ground for judicial invalidation of state legislation infringing on private business and PROPERTY interests. The Court has traditionally been most skeptical of states' efforts to relieve themselves of their own contractual obligations. By the close of the nineteenth century, however, the contract clause largely lost its practical importance as an impediment to retroactive legislation. States increasingly framed their own contractual obligations so as to preserve their latitude to modify contractual provisions, thereby avoiding contract clause problems. During the Great Depression, the Supreme Court in HOME BUILDING & LOAN ASSOCIATION V. BLAISDELL (1934) upheld even a retroactive debtor relief law as an economic emergency measure, concluding that such a public purpose justified the law, and characterizing it as preserving the value of creditors' accrued rights. Following *Blaisdell*, invalidations of legislation under the contract clause have been rare.

Although the contract clause does not apply to federal legislation, the due process clause of the Fifth Amendment has been interpreted to place similar limitations on federal government power to legislate to impair private or governmental contracts, or to impose retroactive civil liability. Under the due process clause, the Court asks whether the law in question is rationally related to a legitimate governmental purpose. During the *Lochner* era, the Court skeptically reviewed ECONOMIC REGULATION, and repeatedly relied on SUBSTANTIVE DUE PROCESS to invalidate economic legislation that interfered with settled economic expectations of CORPORATIONS and private property owners. The Court in RAILROAD RETIREMENT BOARD V. ALTON RAILWAY CO. (1935), for example, voided as a substantive due process violation a federal law that required the railroad to establish a pension fund retrospectively covering even some employees who no longer worked for the railroad. Since the 1930s, however, the Court has not invalidated any law as retroactive in violation of substantive due process. In one leading case, *Usery v. Turner Elkhorn Mining Co.* (1976), the Court upheld legislation requiring employers to provide benefits to coal miners who contract black lung disease, including miners who had stopped working long before the legislation was enacted, as a rational way to spread the costs of the disease, even though the law admittedly upset the employers' settled expectations.

A fractured majority in *Eastern Enterprises v. Apfel* (1998) signaled that the current Court's tolerance of retroactive legislation has its bounds. A four-member plurality, in an opinion by Justice SANDRA DAY O'CONNOR, held that a federal law requiring companies that had engaged in mining, even if they no longer did so, to fund lifetime health benefits for former miners was a REGULATORY TAKING of the employers' property in violation of the takings clause of the Fifth Amendment. Although the law did not involve the physical invasion of property that has traditionally been the focus of takings clause jurisprudence, the plurality believed that the employers' economic interests sufficed to trigger a takings analysis, and that the law fell short of the clause's requirement of "justice and fairness." Under a three-part analysis looking to the law's economic impact on employers, the degree to which it interfered with employers' investment-backed expectations, and the nature of the governmental action in singling out certain classes of employers to bear an unanticipated burden based on conduct long past, the plurality concluded that the law amounted to a taking. It imposed "a severe retroactive liability on a limited class of parties that could not have anticipated the liability"—a liability that the plurality viewed as "substantially disproportionate to the parties' experience."

The remaining five members of the Court in *Eastern Enterprises* believed that the statute was properly analyzed under the due process rather than the takings clause. Justice ANTHONY M. KENNEDY concurred in the judgment in part on the ground that the law violated substantive due process. Noting that "[s]tatutes may be invalidated on due process grounds only under the most egregious of circumstances," Kennedy nonetheless concluded that the law at issue was "far outside the bounds of retroactivity permissible under our law." Kennedy dissented, however, from the plurality's takings analysis on the ground that the law implicated no identified property interest, but merely monetary liability. The four remaining Justices would have upheld the law as fundamentally fair and therefore consistent with due process.

Eastern Enterprises demonstrates that there is current vitality to the non-retroactivity principle in the context of civil legislation. Both the plurality and Kennedy, however, emphasized the exceptional nature of the legislation at issue in that case, suggesting that they contemplate that most legislation may still apply retroactively consistent with the Constitution, provided that the intent of Congress or the state legislature in that regard is clear.

CORNELIA T. L. PILLARD
(2000)

REVENUE SHARING

One consequence of the massive increase in the size and power of the federal government that began in the 1930s was the preemption by the federal government of the sources of revenue that had previously supported the state and local governments. The inability of such governments to find adequate stable sources of income seemed to pose grave problems for American FEDERALISM.

Funds appropriated by the federal government already flowed to state and local governments in the form of FEDERAL GRANTS-IN-AID, often with the effect of coopting those governments as administrators of federally mandated programs. The federal grants brought with them various restrictions as well as burdensome paperwork requirements.

One solution was to return to the state and local governments a share of the tax revenues collected by the federal government, not in support of particular federal programs but as general revenue to be spent for local purposes, with a minimum of restrictions. In the late 1960s, the idea of general revenue sharing was adopted by the Republican party as part of its proposal for a "new federalism." In 1972, Congress, at the urging of President RICHARD M. NIXON, enacted the State and Local Fiscal Assistance Act. The act authorized the distribution of $30 billion to state and local governments over a five-year period. Of that sum, one-third was allocated to the states and two-thirds to counties, cities, and other local governments to be distributed according to a flexible formula taking into account population, locally generated revenues, and other factors. The major restriction was a ban on RACIAL DISCRIMINATION in funded activities.

The program was extended in 1976; in 1980, a revised version was enacted that eliminated the states from the distribution scheme. Any revitalization of federalism as a result of revenue sharing has been less than apparent.

DENNIS J. MAHONEY
(1986)

Bibliography

SCHEFFER, WALTER F., ed. 1976 *General Revenue Sharing and Decentralization.* Norman: University of Oklahoma Press.

REVERSE DISCRIMINATION

See: Racial Preference; Racial Quotas

REVISED STATUTES OF THE UNITED STATES
18 Stat. 1 (1875)

In 1866, Congress authorized the President to appoint a commission "to revise, simplify, arrange, and consolidate all statutes of the United States." The revision, completed

in 1874 and modified in 1878, constituted the first official codification of the general and permanent laws of the United States. The revision supersedes the original public laws it consolidated. Except for those portions of the revision that have been repealed, amended, or superseded by subsequent compilations of federal statutes, the revision remains the authoritative statement of federal statutes enacted prior to 1874.

The revision was not supposed to work substantive changes in the code. But some relatively straightforward statutes became hopelessly confused as a result of the revision. Its most drastic effects may have been upon CIVIL RIGHTS statutes designed to enhance and protect constitutional rights. The revision's treatment of the JURISDICTION of the federal courts to hear civil rights cases brought under SECTION 1983, TITLE 42, UNITED STATES CODE, generated a century of confusion that was furthered by Justice HARLAN FISKE STONE's opinion in HAGUE V. CIO (1939) and that culminated in *Lynch v. Household Finance Corporation* (1972), *Chapman v. Houston Welfare Rights Organization* (1979), and a 1980 amendment providing for jurisdiction in all such cases. The revision's scattering of the CIVIL RIGHTS ACT OF 1866 throughout the Code contributed to that provision's century of near dormancy, to the Court's questionable reading of the 1866 act's intended scope in JONES V. ALFRED H. MAYER CO. (1968) and RUNYON V. MCCRARY (1976), to a confusing of CIVIL RIGHTS REMOVAL statutes that the Court only slightly illuminated in *Georgia v. Rachel* (1966) and *City of Greenwood v. Peacock* (1966), and to a misunderstanding, manifested in *Robertson v. Wegmann* (1978) and *Board of Regents v. Tomanio* (1980), of Congress's intent with respect to the role of state law in federal civil rights cases.

THEODORE EISENBERG
(1986)

Bibliography

SUNSTEIN, CASS 1982 Section 1983 and the Private Enforcement of Federal Law. *University of Chicago Law Review* 49: 401–409.

REYNOLDS v. SIMS
377 U.S. 533 (1964)

Once the Supreme Court declared in BAKER V. CARR (1962) that legislative districting presented a justiciable controversy, lawsuits were filed in more than thirty states challenging existing legislative apportionments. Six of these cases were decided by the Court on the same day, and the Court held all six states' apportionments unconstitutional. The main opinion was written in *Reynolds v. Sims*, the Alabama case; all six opinions of the Court were by Chief

Justice EARL WARREN, who believed until his death that *Reynolds* was the most important decision rendered by the Court during his tenure. The vote in four of the cases was 8–1, and in the other two, 6–3. Justice JOHN MARSHALL HARLAN dissented in all six cases, joined in two of them by Justices POTTER STEWART and TOM C. CLARK.

Baker v. Carr had been a response to decades of stalemate in the political process. Population shifts from rural areas to cities in the twentieth century had not been accompanied by changes in the electoral maps of most states. As a result, vast disparities in district populations permitted control of both houses of the typical state legislature to be dictated by rural voters. In Alabama, for example, Mobile County, with a population over 300,000, had three seats in the lower house, while Bullock County's two representatives served a population under 14,000. If JUDICIAL REVIEW normally defers to majoritarian democracy, here the premise for that deference was lacking; legislators favored by these apportionment inequalities were not apt to remedy them.

Baker had rested decision not on the GUARANTEE CLAUSE but on the EQUAL PROTECTION clause of the FOURTEENTH AMENDMENT. In the early 1960s, the Court had heightened the STANDARD OF REVIEW in equal protection cases only when RACIAL DISCRIMINATION was present; for other cases, the relaxed RATIONAL BASIS standard prevailed. Some Justices in the *Baker* majority had based their concurrence on the total arbitrariness of the Tennessee apportionment scheme there challenged. Justice WILLIAM O. DOUGLAS, concurring, had even said, "Universal equality is not the test; there is room for weighting." The *Baker* dissenters and academic critics had argued that the apportionment problem was unsuitable for judicial determination because courts would be unable to devise principled standards to test the reasonableness of the "weighting" Justice Douglas had anticipated; the problem belonged, they had said, in the category of POLITICAL QUESTIONS. The *Baker* majority had replied blandly: "Judicial standards under the Equal Protection Clause are well developed and familiar," and courts could determine that malapportionment represented "*no* policy, but simply arbitrary and capricious action." The suggestion was plain: departures from district population equality would be valid if they rested on legitimate policies.

Reynolds belied this suggestion. In a sweeping opinion that Archibald Cox called a *coup de main*, the Court discarded almost all possible justifications for departing from a strict principle of equal district populations and established for state legislative districts the ONE PERSON, ONE VOTE formula it had recently used in other electoral contexts. (See GRAY V. SANDERS; WESBERRY V. SANDERS.) The Court thus solved *Baker*'s problem of judicially manageable standards by resort to a mechanical test that

left no "room for weighting"—and, not incidentally, no room for legislative evasion. The companion cases to *Reynolds* demonstrated the strength of the majority's conviction. *Maryland Committee for Fair Representation v. Tawes* (1964) rejected the "federal analogy" and imposed the population equality principle on both houses of a bicameral legislature, and LUCAS V. FORTY-FOURTH GENERAL ASSEMBLY OF STATE OF COLORADO (1964) insisted on the principle in the face of a popular REFERENDUM approving an apportionment that departed from it. In *Reynolds* itself the Court made clear that the states must keep their legislative apportionments abreast of population shifts as reported in the nation's decennial census.

In short, numbers were in, and a political theory of interest representation was out: "Citizens, not history or economic interests, cast votes." Justice Stewart, dissenting in two of the cases, took another view: "Representative government is a process of accommodating group interests through democratic institutional arrangements." Fairness in apportionment thus requires effective representation of the various interests in a state, a concern that the principle of district population equality either ignored or defeated. But Justice Stewart's premise—that equal protection required only an apportionment scheme that was rationally based and did not systematically frustrate majority rule— was rejected by the Court. Because voting "is a fundamental matter in a free society," the Chief Justice said, the dilution of the strength of a citizen's vote "must be carefully and meticulously scrutinized." *Reynolds* was the crucial decision in the line of equal protection cases developing the doctrine that voting is a FUNDAMENTAL INTEREST, whose impairment calls for STRICT SCRUTINY. (See HARPER V. VIRGINIA BOARD OF ELECTIONS; KRAMER V. UNION FREE SCHOOL DISTRICT NO. 15.)

The Court's disposition of the six REAPPORTIONMENT cases, and its memorandum orders in other cases in succeeding months, left little doubt that the Justices had learned a lesson from their experience in BROWN V. BOARD OF EDUCATION (1954–1955). Here there would be no ALL DELIBERATE SPEED formula to extend the time for compliance with the decision. Lower courts were expected to move quickly—and did move quickly—to implement the doctrine announced in *Reynolds*. Even so, politicians had some time to mount a counterattack. Thirty-two state legislatures requested the calling of a CONSTITUTIONAL CONVENTION to overturn *Reynolds*. Senator Everett Dirksen gained substantial support when he introduced a proposed constitutional amendment to the same end. Bills were offered in both houses of Congress to withdraw the federal courts' JURISDICTION over reapportionment cases. But all these efforts came to nothing. The jurisdictional bills failed; the Dirksen proposal did not pass either house; the constitutional convention proposal, which had been carried forward with little publicity, withered in the remaining state legislatures when it was exposed to political sunlight.

The reason for the politicians' protest was obvious to all: many of them anticipated losing their own seats, and many others foresaw reduced influence for certain interests that rural representatives had favored. The public, however, overwhelmingly approved the principle of "one person, one vote" when the issue was tested in opinion polls; the politicians' counterattack failed because the people sided with the Court.

Academic criticism of the WARREN COURT has prominently featured *Reynolds* as a horrible example. The Court, the critics say, failed to write an opinion that reasoned from generally accepted premise to logically compelled conclusion. That is a telling criticism if, as HENRY HART was fond of saying, "reason is the life of the law." But reason is not the *life* of the law, or of anything else. It is a mental instrument to be used by judges and other humans along with their capacities for other ways of knowing: recognizing textures, patterns, analogies, relations that are not demonstrated by "if . . . then" syllogisms but grasped intuitively and at once. Perhaps the public was more ready to accept "one person, one vote" than were the Warren Court's critics because people who are not lawyers understand that the Supreme Court's most important product is justice. Surely they understood that the *Reynolds* formula, for all its inflexibility, more truly reflected our national sense of political justice than did the "cancer of malapportionment"—the term is Professor Cox's—that preceded it.

It is, by definition, hard to justify innovation by reference to the conventional wisdom. The beginnings of judicial DOCTRINE, like other beginnings, may be more easily felt than syllogized. Ultimately, if constitutional intuitions are to be translated into constitutional law, coherent explanation must come to replace the vague sense of doing the right thing; consolidation is an essential part of the Supreme Court's task. Yet to deny the legitimacy of a decision whose underlying value premises are clear, on the ground that the decision does not follow deductively from what has gone before, is to deny the legitimacy of judicial creativity—and it is our creative judges whom we honor most.

Reynolds v. Sims did not remake the political world; it mostly transferred power from rural areas to the conservative suburbs of large cities. But the decision touched a deep vein of American political egalitarianism and gave impetus to a doctrinal development as important as any in our time: recognition of the values of equal citizenship as the substantive core of the Fourteenth Amendment.

KENNETH L. KARST
(1986)

Bibliography

CASPER, GERHARD　1973　Apportionment and the Right to Vote: Standards of Judicial Scrutiny. *Supreme Court Review* 1973: 1–32.

DIXON, ROBERT G., JR.　1968　*Democratic Representation: Reapportionment in Law and Politics.* New York: Oxford University Press.

McKAY, ROBERT B.　1965　*Reapportionment: The Law and Politics of Equal Representation.* New York: Twentieth Century Fund.

REYNOLDS v. UNITED STATES
98 U.S. 145 (1879)

This case established the principle that under the guarantee of RELIGIOUS LIBERTY, government may not punish religious beliefs but may punish religiously motivated practices that injure the public interest. Reynolds violated a congressional prohibition on bigamy in the territories and appealed his conviction in Utah on FIRST AMENDMENT grounds, alleging that as a Mormon he had a religious duty to practice POLYGAMY. Chief Justice MORRISON R. WAITE for a unanimous Supreme Court ruled that although government might not reach opinions, it could constitutionally punish criminal activity. The question, Waite declared, was whether religious belief could be accepted as justification of an overt act made criminal by the law of the land. Every government, he answered, had the power to decide whether polygamy or monogamy should be the basis of social life. Those who made polygamy part of their religion could no more be exempt from the law than those who believe that human sacrifice was a necessary part of religious worship. Unless the law were superior to religious belief, Waite reasoned, every citizen might become a law unto himself and government would exist in name only. He did not explain why polygamy and human sacrifice were analogous, nor did he, in his simplified exposition, confront the problem whether an uncontrollable freedom of belief had much substance if the state could punish the dictates of conscience: belief without practice is an empty right. Moreover, Waite did not consider whether belief should be as absolutely free as he suggested; if polygamy was a crime, its advocacy had limits.

LEONARD W. LEVY
(1986)

RHODE ISLAND v. INNES
446 U.S. 291 (1980)

Innes explained the meaning of "interrogation" under MIRANDA V. ARIZONA (1966). *Miranda* declared, "If the individual states that he wants an attorney, the interrogation must cease until an attorney is present." Everyone agreed that the suspect in *Innes* had received his *Miranda* warnings and invoked his RIGHT TO COUNSEL, and that he was in custody. The question was whether he had been interrogated.

Police arrested a man suspected of a shotgun murder. Repeatedly they advised him of his *Miranda* rights, and a captain instructed officers about to transport him to the stationhouse not to question him in any way. During a brief automobile ride, one officer said to another, within the suspect's hearing, that they ought to try to find the shotgun because a child might discover it and kill herself. The suspect promptly volunteered to take the police to the shotgun. Again the police gave the *Miranda* warnings. The suspect replied that he understood his rights but wanted the gun removed from the reach of children. His statements and the gun were introduced in EVIDENCE at his trial, over his objection. The state supreme court reversed his conviction, finding a violation of *Miranda*.

A 6–3 Supreme Court decided that the police had not interrogated the suspect. Justice POTTER STEWART for the majority construed *Miranda* broadly to mean that interrogation includes questioning or a "functional equivalent"—any words or actions by the police reasonably likely to elicit any response from their suspect. Here there was no interrogation, only a spontaneous admission. The dissenters believed that an officer deliberately referred to the missing gun as a danger to innocent children in the hope of eliciting from the suspect an incriminating statement; whether that happened cannot be known. If the Court majority had believed that the officer making the remark had understood the suspect's psychological makeup and that an appeal to his conscience might have worked, that majority would have decided that the suspect had been interrogated. Contrary to the view of Justice JOHN PAUL STEVENS, dissenting, *Miranda* was not narrowed.

LEONARD W. LEVY
(1986)

(SEE ALSO: *Police Interrogations and Confessions.*)

RHODE ISLAND AND PROVIDENCE PLANTATIONS, CHARTER OF
(July 8, 1663)

ROGER WILLIAMS founded Providence in 1636 as a shelter for anyone "distressed in conscience." His covenant was the first anywhere to exclude the civil government from religious matters. From the beginning the towns that became Rhode Island practiced RELIGIOUS LIBERTY, welcoming Quakers and Jews, and enjoyed SEPARATION OF CHURCH AND STATE. John Clarke, a Baptist minister who was Williams's friend and co-worker, was influential in the framing of the code of laws of 1647 establishing a "democratical" government. The restoration of the Stuarts in 1660 forced Rhode Island to secure a charter; Clarke was Williams's emissary to Charles II, who granted the first American charter guaranteeing religious liberty. The MARYLAND ACT OF TOLERATION (1649) was a statute; the charter of Rhode Island, which remained its constitution until 1842, made the guarantee a part of FUNDAMENTAL LAW. The language of the charter on this key provision was Clarke's. It referred to the colony's "livlie experiment" to show that a civil state could best be maintained if the inhabitants were secured "in the free exercise and enjoyment of all theire civill and religious rights." All peaceable persons might "freelye and fullye hav and enjoye his and theire owne judgments."

LEONARD W. LEVY
(1986)

Bibliography

PERRY, RICHARD L., ed. 1959 *Sources of Our Liberties.* Pages 162–179. New York: American Bar Foundation.

RIBNIK v. MCBRIDE
277 U.S. 350 (1928)

Guided by TYSON AND BROTHER V. BANTON (1927), the Supreme Court voided a New Jersey statute regulating fees charged by employment agencies. The majority held that although widespread evils existed which were subject to regulation, the establishment of prices for a private business was outside legislative power. Justice HARLAN FISKE STONE's dissent, joined by Justices OLIVER WENDELL HOLMES and LOUIS D. BRANDEIS, denied any distinction between illegal price controls and other, acceptable regulations. (See ADAMS V. TANNER; OLSEN V. NEBRASKA EX REL. REFERENCE BOND ASSOCIATION.)

DAVID GORDON
(1986)

RICHMOND (CITY OF) v. J. A. CROSON CO.
488 U.S. 469 (1989)

In FULLILOVE V. KLUTZNICK (1980) the Supreme Court upheld an act of Congress requiring that ten percent of certain federal subsidies to local governments be set aside for contractors that were minority-owned business enterprises (MBE). In *Croson* the Court invalidated a similar AFFIRMATIVE ACTION ordinance adopted by a city. The ordinance, adopted for a five-year term, required a prime contractor to allocate thirty percent of the dollar amount of the contract to MBE subcontractors. A waiver was authorized in the event that MBE were not available. The Court held, 6–3, that this scheme denied nonminority businesses the EQUAL PROTECTION OF THE LAWS.

Justice SANDRA DAY O'CONNOR wrote an opinion that was in part the OPINION OF THE COURT and in part a PLURALITY OPINION. A majority concurred in the opinion's basic building blocks: that the appropriate standard of review for a state and local affirmative action program was STRICT SCRUTINY; that the city had not offered sufficient evidence of "identified discrimination" that could justify a race-conscious remedy; and that the city's program, even if it were remedial, was not sufficiently narrowly tailored to such discrimination. In addition, she spoke for a plurality in concluding that Congress's remedial powers, unlike those of the states, could extend to remedying past societal discrimination. (See FOURTEENTH AMENDMENT, SECTION 5 (JUDICIAL CONSTRUCTION).) Justice ANTHONY M. KENNEDY, concurring, dissociated himself from the latter position, and Justice ANTONIN SCALIA, also concurring, argued that the city had power to use race-conscious remedies only for its own discrimination. Justice JOHN PAUL STEVENS concurred only in the view that Richmond's plan was not justified by sufficient evidence of past discrimination and was not narrowly tailored.

Justice O'Connor concluded that Richmond could constitutionally provide a race-conscious remedy not only for its own past discrimination but also for past discrimination by private contractors or trade associations in the Richmond area. She also concluded that such discrimination might be proved by statistics showing a serious disparity between the percentage of qualified MBE in the area and the percentage of contracts awarded to MBE. Here, however, the city had shown only that the MBE contracts were extremely low in comparison with the percentage of minorities in Richmond's general population. To achieve a "narrowly tailored" program, she said, Richmond would have to show that race-neutral alternatives were unworkable, and to peg its MBE set-aside percentage at a figure that bore a clearly stated relation to the percentage of qualified MBE.

Justice THURGOOD MARSHALL wrote a sharply worded opinion for the three dissenters. He argued that strict scrutiny was inappropriate and that Richmond's ordinance served the important purposes of remedying the effects of a pattern of past discrimination and keeping the city from reinforcing that pattern. He found the Richmond council's conclusions about past discrimination, both by the city and by private contractors, to be soundly based. Justice HARRY A. BLACKMUN also dissented.

Although many civil rights advocates regarded *Croson*

as a serious setback for affirmative action, it may turn out, like REGENTS OF UNIVERSITY OF CALIFORNIA V. BAKKE (1978), to be a blessing in disguise for their cause. Certainly, *Croson*'s standards for affirmative action in state and local government contracting will, in some communities, prevent any effective affirmative action. One of the legacies of RACIAL DISCRIMINATION is the paucity of minority businesses in many of the fields in which governments offer contracts. However, Justice O'Connor's explicit approval of statistical proof of past discrimination offers considerable opportunity, particularly for states and for large cities, to satisfy the Court's requirements. More important, six Justices not only reaffirmed the *Fullilove* precedent, which had seemed vulnerable, but also issued to Congress a sweeping invitation to engage in broad-scale affirmative action of its own aimed at remedying the effects of past societal discrimination.

KENNETH L. KARST
(1992)

Bibliography

Constitutional Scholars' Statement on Affirmative Action After *City of Richmond v. J. A. Croson Co.* 1989   *Yale Law Journal* 98:1711–1716.

FRIED, CHARLES 1989   Affirmative Action After *City of Richmond v. J. A. Croson Co.*, A Response to the Scholars' Statement. *Yale Law Journal* 99:155–161.

Scholars' Reply to Professor Fried 1989   *Yale Law Journal* 99: 163–168.

RICHMOND NEWSPAPERS, INC. v. VIRGINIA
448 U.S. 555 (1980)

Richmond Newspapers recognized a constitutional right of access to criminal trials. It marked the first time a majority embraced any such FIRST AMENDMENT claim. Yet division and bitterness obviously remained from the splintered decision a year earlier in GANNETT V. DEPASQUALE, which had held that the Sixth Amendment did not preclude closing a pretrial suppression hearing to the press and public.

In *Richmond Newspapers*, a 7–1 majority distinguished *Gannett* and held that the press and public share a right of access to actual criminal trials, though the press may enjoy some preference. In the PLURALITY OPINION, Chief Justice WARREN E. BURGER found a right to attend criminal trials within "unarticulated rights" implicit in the First Amendment rights of speech, press, and assembly, as well as within other constitutional language and the uninterrupted Anglo-American tradition of open trials. This right to an open trial prevailed over efforts by Virginia courts to close a murder trial, premised on the defendant's request to do so. The trial judge had made no particularized finding that a FAIR TRIAL could not be guaranteed by means less drastic than total closure.

Justice WILLIAM H. REHNQUIST was alone in dissent, but only Justices BYRON R. WHITE and JOHN PAUL STEVENS concurred in Burger's opinion. Justice LEWIS F. POWELL took no part in the decision. Four Justices concurred separately in the JUDGMENT. They differed about whether *Gannett* actually was distinguishable, what weight to give history, and what particular constitutional basis mandated the result.

Richmond Newspapers decided only the UNCONSTITUTIONALITY of a total ban on public access to actual criminal trials when there is no demonstration that alternative means could not guarantee a fair trial. Yet the decision is significant for its recognition of a First Amendment right to gather newsworthy information; moreover, some Justices identified a broad right to receive information about government, including the activities of the judicial branch.

AVIAM SOIFER
(1986)

RIGHT . . .

See also: Freedom of . . .

RIGHT AGAINST SELF-INCRIMINATION

The Fifth Amendment is virtually synonymous with the right against self-incrimination. One who "pleads the Fifth" is not insisting on grand jury INDICTMENT, freedom from DOUBLE JEOPARDY, or JUST COMPENSATION for property taken by the government—all safeguarded in the same amendment. He is saying that he will not reply to an official query because his truthful answer might expose him to criminal jeopardy. He seems to be saying that he has something to hide, making the Fifth appear to be a protection of the guilty; it is, but probably no more so than other rights of the criminally accused. The right against self-incrimination is the most misunderstood, unrespected, and controversial of all constitutional rights.

Its very name is a problem. It is customarily referred to as "the privilege" against self-incrimination, following the usage of lawyers in discussing evidentiary privileges (for example, the husband-wife privilege, the attorney-client privilege). Popular usage, however, contrasts "privilege" with "rights," and the Fifth Amendment's clause on self-incrimination creates a constitutional right with the same status as other rights. Its "name" is unknown to the Constitution, whose words cover more than merely a right or privilege against self-incrimination: "no person . . . shall be compelled in any criminal case to be a witness against himself." What does the text mean?

The protection of the clause extends only to natural persons, not organizations like corporations or unions. A member of an organization cannot claim its benefits if the inquiry would incriminate the organization but not him personally. He can claim its benefits only for himself, not for others. The text also suggests that a prime purpose of the clause is to protect against government coercion; one may voluntarily answer any incriminating question or confess to any crime—subject to the requirements for WAIVER OF CONSTITUTIONAL RIGHTS. In some respects the text is broad, because a person can be a witness against himself in ways that do not incriminate him. He can, in a criminal case, injure his civil interests or disgrace himself in the public mind. Thus the Fifth can be construed on its face to protect against disclosures that expose one to either civil liability or INFAMY. The Fifth can also be construed to apply to an ordinary witness as well as the criminal defendant himself. In Virginia, where the right against self-incrimination first received constitutional status, it appeared in a paragraph relating to the accused only. The Fifth Amendment is not similarly restrictive, unlike the Sixth Amendment which explicitly refers to the accused, protecting him alone. The location of the clause in the Fifth, rather than in the Sixth, and its reference to "no person" makes it applicable to witnesses as well as to the accused.

On the other hand, the clause has a distinctively limiting factor: it is restricted on its face to criminal cases. The phrase "criminal case" seems to exclude civil cases. Some judges have argued that no criminal case exists until a formal charge has been made against the accused. Under such an interpretation the right would have no existence until the accused is put on trial; before that, when he is taken into custody, interrogated by the police, or examined by a GRAND JURY, he would not have the benefit of the right. Nor would he have its benefit in a nonjudicial proceeding such as a LEGISLATIVE INVESTIGATION or an administrative hearing. The Supreme Court has given the impression that the clause, if taken literally, would be so restricted; but the Court refuses to take the clause literally. Thus, in COUNSELMAN V. HITCHCOCK (1892), the Court held that the Fifth does protect ordinary witnesses, even in federal grand jury proceedings. Unanimously the Court declared, "It is impossible that the meaning of the constitutional provision can only be that a person shall not be compelled to be a witness against himself in a criminal prosecution against himself." Although the Court did not explain why it was "impossible," the Court was right. Had the framers of the Fifth intended the literal, restrictive meaning, their constitutional provision would have been a meaningless gesture. There was no need to protect the accused at his trial; he was not permitted to give testimony, whether for or against himself, at the time of the framing of the Fifth. Making the criminal defendant competent to be a witness in his own case was a reform of the later nineteenth century, beginning in the state courts with Maine in 1864, in the federal courts by an act of Congress in 1878.

Illumination from the face of a text that does not mean what it says is necessarily faint. Occasionally the Court will display its wretched knowledge of history in an effort to explain the right against self incrimination. Justice FELIX FRANKFURTER for the Court, in ULLMANN V. UNITED STATES (1956), drew lessons from the "name" of "the privilege against self-incrimination," but conceded that it is a provision of the Constitution "of which it is peculiarly true that "a page of history is worth a volume of logic." TWINING V. NEW JERSEY (1908), the most historically minded opinion ever delivered for the Court on the right, was misleading and shallow when it was not inaccurate on the question whether the right was "a fundamental principle of liberty and justice which inheres in the very idea of free government."

The American origins of the right derive largely from the inherited English COMMON LAW system of criminal justice. But the English origins, so much more complex, spill over legal boundaries and reflect the many-sided religious, political, and constitutional issues that racked England during the sixteenth and seventeenth centuries: the struggles between Anglicanism and Puritanism, between Parliament and king, between limited government and arbitrary rule, and between freedom of conscience and suppression of heresy and SEDITION. Even within the more immediate confines of law, the history of the right against self-incrimination is enmeshed in broad issues: the contests for supremacy between the accusatory and the inquisitional systems of procedure, the common law and the royal prerogative, and the common law and its canon and civil law rivals. Against this broad background the origins of the concept that "no man is bound to accuse himself" (*nemo tenetur seipsum accusare*) must be understood and the concept's legal development traced.

The right against self-incrimination originated as an indirect product of the common law's accusatory system and of its opposition to rival systems which employed inquisitorial procedures. Toward the close of the sixteenth century, just before the concept first appeared in England on a sustained basis, all courts of criminal jurisdiction habitually sought to exact self-incriminatory admissions from persons suspected of or charged with crime. Although defendants in crown cases suffered from this and many other harsh procedures, even in common law courts, the accu-

satory system afforded a degree of fair play not available under the inquisitional system. Moreover, torture was never sanctioned by the common law, although it was employed as an instrument of royal prerogative until 1641.

By contrast, torture for the purpose of detecting crime and inducing confession was regularly authorized by the Roman codes of the canon and civil law. "Abandon all hope, ye who enter here" well describes the chances of an accused person under inquisitorial procedures characterized by PRESENTMENT based on mere rumor or suspicion, indefiniteness of accusation, the oath *ex officio*, secrecy, lack of CONFRONTATION, coerced confessions, and magistrates acting as accusers and prosecutors as well as "judges." This system of procedure, by which heresy was most efficiently combated, was introduced into England by ecclesiastical courts.

The use of the oath *ex officio* by prerogative courts, particularly by the ecclesiastical Court of High Commission, which Elizabeth I reconstituted, resulted in the defensive claim that "no man is bound to accuse himself." The High Commission, an instrument of the Crown for maintaining religious uniformity under the Anglican establishment, used the canon law inquisitorial process, but made the oath *ex officio*, rather than torture, the crux of its procedure. Men suspected of "heretical opinions," "seditious books," or "conspiracies" were summoned before the High Commission without being informed of the accusation against them or the identity of their accusers. Denied DUE PROCESS OF LAW by common law standards, suspects were required to take an oath to answer truthfully to interrogatories which sought to establish guilt for crimes neither charged nor disclosed.

A nonconformist victim of the High Commission found himself thrust between hammer and anvil: refusal to take the oath or, having taken it, refusal to answer the interrogatories meant a sentence for contempt and invited Star Chamber proceedings; to take the oath and respond truthfully to questioning often meant to convict oneself of religious or political crimes and, moreover, to supply evidence against nonconformist accomplices; to take the oath and then lie meant to sin against the Scriptures and risk conviction for perjury. Common lawyers of the Puritan party developed the daring argument that the oath, although sanctioned by the Crown, was unconstitutional because it violated MAGNA CARTA, which limited even the royal prerogative.

The argument had myth-making qualities, for it was one of the earliest to exalt Magna Carta as the symbol and source of English constitutional liberty. As yet there was no contention that one need not answer incriminating questions after accusation by due process according to common law. But a later generation would use substantially the same argument—"that by the Statutes of Magna

Charta . . . for a man to accuse himself was and is utterlie inhibited"—on behalf of the contention that one need not involuntarily answer questions even after one had been properly accused.

Under Chief Justice EDWARD COKE the common law courts, with the sympathy of Commons, vindicated the Puritan tactic of litigious opposition to the High Commission. The deep hostility between the canon and common law systems expressed itself in a series of writs of prohibition issued by Coke and his colleagues, staying the Commission's proceedings. Coke, adept at creating legal fictions which he clothed with the authority of resurrected "precedents" and inferences from Magna Carta, grounded twenty of these prohibitions on the allegedly ancient common law rule that no man is bound to accuse himself criminally.

In the 1630s the High Commission and the Star Chamber, which employed similar procedures, reached the zenith of their powers. But in 1637 a flinty Puritan agitator, JOHN LILBURNE, refused the oath. His well-publicized opposition to incriminatory questioning focused England's attention upon the injustice and illegality of such practices. In 1641 the Long Parliament, dominated by the Puritan party and common lawyers, condemned the sentences against Lilburne and others, abolished the Star Chamber and the High Commission, and prohibited ecclesiastical authorities from administering any oath obliging one "to confess or to accuse himself or herself of any crime."

Common law courts, however, continued to ask incriminating questions and to bully witnesses into answering them. The rudimentary idea of a right against self-incrimination was nevertheless lodged in the imperishable opinions of Coke, publicized by Lilburne and the Levellers, and firmly associated with Magna Carta. The idea was beginning to take hold of men's minds. Lilburne was again the catalytic agent. At his various trials for his life, in his testimony before investigating committees of Parliament, and in his ceaseless tracts, he dramatically popularized the demand that a right against self-incrimination be accorded general legal recognition. His career illustrates how the right against self-incrimination developed not only in conjunction with a whole gamut of fair procedures associated with "due process of law" but also with demands for freedom of conscience and expression. After Lilburne's time the right became entrenched in English jurisprudence, even under the judicial tyrants of the Restoration. As the state became more secure and as fairer treatment of the criminally accused became possible, the old practice of bullying the prisoner for answers gradually died out. By the early eighteenth century the accused was no longer put on the stand at all; he could not give evidence in his own behalf even if he wished to, although he was permitted to tell his story, unsworn. The prisoner was regarded as incompetent to be a witness for himself.

After the first quarter of the eighteenth century, the English history of the right centered primarily upon the preliminary examination of the suspect and the legality of placing in evidence various types of involuntary confessions. Incriminating statements made by suspects at the preliminary examination could be used against them at their trials; a confession, even though not made under oath, sufficed to convict. Yet suspects could not be interrogated under oath. One might be ensnared into a confession by the sharp and intimidating tactics of the examining magistrate; but there was no legal obligation to answer an incriminating question—nor, until 1848, to notify the suspect or prisoner of his right to refuse answer. One's answers, given in ignorance of his right, might be used against him. However, the courts excluded confessions that had been made under duress. Only involuntary confessions were seen as a violation of the right. Lord Chief Baron Geoffrey Gilbert in his *Law of Evidence* (1756) declared that although a confession was the best evidence of guilt, "this Confession must be voluntary and without compulsion; for our Law . . . will not force any Man to accuse himself; and in this we do certainly follow that Law of Nature" that commands self-preservation.

Thus, opposition to the oath *ex officio* ended in the common law right to refuse to furnish incriminating evidence against oneself even when all formalities of common law accusation had first been fulfilled. The prisoner demanded that the state prove its case against him, and he confronted the witnesses who testified against him. The Levellers, led by Lilburne, even claimed a right not to answer any questions concerning themselves, if life, liberty, or property might be jeopardized, regardless of the tribunal or government agency directing the examination, be it judicial, legislative, or executive. The Leveller claim to a right against self-incrimination raised the generic problem of the nature of SOVEREIGNTY in England and spurred the transmutation of Magna Carta from a feudal relic of baronial reaction into a modern bulwark of the RULE OF LAW and regularized restraints upon government power.

The claim to this right also emerged in the context of a cluster of criminal procedures whose object was to ensure fair play for the criminally accused. It harmonized with the principles that the accused was innocent until proved guilty and that the BURDEN OF PROOF was on the prosecution. It was related to the idea that a man's home should not be promiscuously broken into and rifled for evidence of his reading and writing. It was intimately connected to the belief that torture or any cruelty in forcing a man to expose his guilt was unfair and illegal. It was indirectly associated with the RIGHT TO COUNSEL and the right to have witnesses on behalf of the defendant, so that his lips could remain sealed against the government's questions or accusations. It was at first a privilege of the guilty, given the nature of the substantive law of religious and political crimes. But the right became neither a privilege of the guilty nor a protection of the innocent. It became merely one of the ways of fairly determining guilt or innocence, like TRIAL BY JURY itself; it became part of due process of the law, a fundamental principle of the accusatorial system. It reflected the view that society benefited by seeking the defendant's conviction without the aid of his involuntary admissions. Forcing self-incrimination was thought to brutalize the system of criminal justice and to produce untrustworthy evidence.

Above all, the right was closely linked to FREEDOM OF SPEECH and RELIGIOUS LIBERTY. It was, in its origins, unquestionably the invention of those who were guilty of religious crimes such as heresy, schism, and nonconformity, and later, of political crimes such as TREASON, SEDITIOUS LIBEL, and breach of PARLIAMENTARY PRIVILEGE. More often than not, the offense was merely criticism of the government, its policies, or its officers. The right was associated, then, with guilt for crimes of conscience, of belief, and of association. In the broadest sense it was not so much a protection of the guilty, or even the innocent, but a protection of freedom of expression, of political liberty, and of the right to worship as one pleased. The symbolic importance and practical function of the right certainly settled matters, taken for granted, in the eighteenth century. And it was part of the heritage of liberty that the common law bequeathed to the English settlers in America.

Yet, the right had to be won in every colony, invariably under conditions similar to those that generated it in England. The first glimmer of the right in America was evident in the heresy case of John Wheelwright, tried in 1637 in Massachusetts. In colony after colony, people exposed to the inquisitorial tactics of the prerogative court of the governor and council refused to answer to incriminating interrogatories in cases heavy with political implications. By the end of the seventeenth century the right was unevenly recognized in the colonies. As the English common law increasingly became American law and the legal profession grew in size, competence, and influence, Americans developed a greater familiarity with the right. English law books and English criminal procedure provided a model. From Edmond Wingate's *Maxims of Reason* (1658), which included the earliest discussion of the maxim, *"Nemo tenetur accusare seipsum,"* to Gilbert's *Evidence*, law books praised the right. It grew so in popularity that in 1735 BENJAMIN FRANKLIN, hearing that a church wanted to examine the sermons of an unorthodox minister, could declare: "It was contrary to the common Rights of Mankind, no Man being obliged to furnish Matter of Ac-

cusation against himself." In 1754 a witness parried a Massachusetts legislative investigation into seditious libel by quoting the well-known Latin maxim, which he freely translated as "A Right of Silence as the Priviledge of every Englishman." In 1770 the attorney general of Pennsylvania ruled that an admiralty court could not oblige people to answer interrogatories "which may have a tendency to criminate themselves, or subject them to a penalty, it being contrary to any principle of Reason and the Laws of England." When, in 1770, New York's legislature jailed Alexander McDougall, a popular patriot leader who refused answer to incriminating queries about a seditious broadside, the public associated the right with the patriot cause, and the press printed the toast, "No Answer to Interrogatories, when tending to accuse the Person interrogated." Thereafter the New York legislature granted absolute immunity to recalcitrant malefactors whose testimony was required in trials or investigations.

In 1776 the VIRGINIA CONSTITUTION AND DECLARATION OF RIGHTS provided that in criminal prosecutions the accused party cannot "be compelled to give evidence against himself." Every state (eight including Vermont) that prefaced its constitution with a bill of rights imitated Virginia's phrasing, although two, by placing the clause in a section apart from the rights of the accused, extended the right to third parties or witnesses. Whether the right was constitutionally secured or was protected by common law made little difference, because the early decisions, even in states that constitutionally secured the right, followed the common law rather than the narrower phrasing of their constitutions. For example, the PENNSYLVANIA CONSTITUTION of 1776 had a self-incrimination clause that referred to "no man," which the 1790 constitution narrowed to "the accused." Nevertheless, in the first case on this clause the state supreme court applied it to the production of papers in civil cases and to questions involving exposure to "shame or reproach."

During the controversy over the RATIFICATION OF THE CONSTITUTION of 1787, only four states recommended that a comprehensive bill of rights should be added to the new document, but those four demanded a self-incrimination clause modeled on the conventional phrasing that no person should be compelled to give evidence against himself. JAMES MADISON, in framing what became the Fifth Amendment, urged in sweeping language that no person should be "compelled to be a witness against himself." That phrasing was amended to apply only to criminal cases, thereby permitting courts to compel a civil defendant to produce documents against himself, injuring his civil interest without infringing his traditional rights not to produce them if they could harm him criminally. Whether the framers of the clause in the Fifth meant it to be fully co-extensive with the still expanding common law principle is unknown. The language of the clause and its framers' understanding may not have been synonymous, especially because a criminal defendant could not testify under oath even in the absence of the self-incrimination clause. It was intended as a ban on torture, but it also represented the opinion of the framers that the right against self-incrimination was a legitimate defense possessed by every individual against government. The framers were tough-minded revolutionaries who risked everything in support of their belief that legitimate government exercises its powers in subordination to personal rights. The framers were not soft, naive, or disregardful of the claims of law and order. They were mindful that the enduring interests of the community required justice to be done as fairly as possible: that no one should have to be a witness against himself in a criminal case was a central feature of the accusatory system of criminal justice, which the framers identified with fairness. Deeply committed to a system of criminal justice that minimized the possibilities of convicting the innocent, they were not less concerned about the humanity that the law should show even to the offender. The Fifth Amendment reflected their judgment that in a society based on respect for the individual, the government shouldered the entire burden of proving guilt and the accused need make no unwilling contribution to his conviction.

What is the present scope of the right and how have the Supreme Court's interpretations compared with the history of the right? Generally the Court has construed the clause of the Fifth as if the letter killeth. Seeking the spirit and policies of the clause, the Court has tended to give it an ever widening meaning, on the principle that "it is as broad as the mischief against which it seeks to guard," as the Court said in *Counselman*. In effect the Court has taken the position that the Fifth embodied the still evolving common law of the matter rather than a rule of fixed meaning. Often the Court has had history on its side without knowing it, with the result that many apparent innovations could have rested on old practices and precedents.

History supported the decision in BOYD V. UNITED STATES (1886) connecting the Fifth and FOURTH AMENDMENTS and holding that the seizure of one's records for use as evidence against him compels him to be a witness against himself. Beginning in the early eighteenth century the English courts had widened the right against self-incrimination to include protection against the compulsory production of books and papers that might incriminate the accused. In a 1744 case a rule emerged that to compel a defendant to turn over the records of his corporation would be forcing him to "furnish evidence against himself." In the 1760s in WILKES'S CASES, the English courts extended the right to prevent the use of GENERAL WARRANTS to seize private papers in seditious libel cases. Thus the right against self-incrimination and FREEDOM OF THE PRESS, closely allied in their origins, were linked to freedom from unreasonable SEARCHES AND SEIZURES. In *Entick v. Carrington* (1765), Lord Camden (CHARLES PRATT) declared that the law obliged no one to give evidence against himself "because the necessary means of compelling self-accusation, falling upon the innocent as well as the guilty, would be both cruel and unjust; and it should seem that search for evidence is disallowed upon the same principle." American colonists made similar arguments against WRITS OF ASSISTANCE, linking the right against UNREASONABLE SEARCH to the right against self-incrimination. UNITED STATES V. WHITE (1944), which required the production of an organization's records even if they incriminated the witness who held them as custodian, was a departure from history.

That the right extends to witnesses as well as the accused is the command of the text of the Fifth. Protection of witnesses, which can be traced to English cases of the mid-seventeenth century, was invariably accepted in American manuals of practice as well as in leading English treatises throughout the eighteenth century. The Supreme Court's decision in *McCarthy v. Arndstein* (1924), extending the right to witnesses even in civil cases if a truthful answer might result in a forfeiture, penalty, or criminal prosecution, rested on dozens of English decisions going back to 1658 and to American precedents beginning in 1767. In a little known aspect of MARBURY V. MADISON (1803), Chief Justice JOHN MARSHALL asked Attorney General LEVI LINCOLN what he had done with Marbury's missing commission. Lincoln, who probably had burned the commission, refused to incriminate himself by answering, and Marshall conceded that he need not reply, though he was a witness in a civil suit.

Many early state decisions held that neither witnesses nor parties were required to answer against themselves if to do so would expose them to public disgrace or infamy. The origins of so broad a right of silence can be traced as far back as sixteenth-century claims by Protestant reformers such as William Tyndale and Thomas Cartwright in connection with their argument that no one should be compelled to accuse himself. The idea passed to the common lawyers and Coke, was completely accepted in English case law, and found expression in WILLIAM BLACKSTONE's *Commentaries* as well as American manuals of practice. Yet the Supreme Court in BROWN V. WALKER (1896) restricted the scope of the historical right when ruling that the Fifth did not protect against compulsory self-infamy. Its decision was oblivious to history as was its reaffirmation of that decision in *Ullmann v. United States* (1956).

From the standpoint of history that 1896 holding and its 1956 reaffirmation correctly decided the main question whether a grant of full immunity supersedes the witness's right to refuse answer on Fifth Amendment grounds. Colonial precedents support absolute or transactional immunity, as did the IMMUNITY GRANT decisions in 1896 and 1956. The Court departed from its own precedents and history when ruling in KASTIGAR V. UNITED STATES (1972) that limiting the right to use and derived-use immunity does not violate the right not to be a witness against oneself.

History supports the decisions made by the Court for the first time in *Quinn v. United States* (1955) and WATKINS V. UNITED STATES (1957) that the right extends to legislative investigations. As early as 1645 John Lilburne, relying on his own reading of Magna Carta and the PETITION OF RIGHT, claimed the right, unsuccessfully, before a parliamentary committee. In 1688 the Pennsylvania legislature recognized an uncooperative witness's right against self-incrimination. Other colonial assemblies followed suit though New York's did not do so until forced by public opinion after McDougall's case. That Parliament also altered its practice is clear from the debates in 1742 following the refusal of a witness to answer incriminatory questions before an investigating committee. The Commons immunized his testimony against prosecution, but the bill failed in the Lords in part because it violated one of the "first principles of English law," that no person is obliged to accuse himself or answer any questions that tend to reveal what the nature of his defense requires to be concealed. In 1778 the Continental Congress investigated the corrupt schemes of Silas Deane, who invoked his right against self-incrimination, and Congress, it seems, voted that it was lawful for him to do so.

History belies the TWO-SOVEREIGNTIES RULE, a stunting restriction upon the Fifth introduced by the Court in 1931 but abandoned in MURPHY V. WATERFRONT COMMISSION (1964). The rule was that a person could not refuse to testify on the grounds that his disclosures would expose him to prosecution in another jurisdiction. The Court mistakenly claimed that the rule had the support of historical precedents; history clearly contradicted that rule as the Court belatedly confessed in 1964.

History supports the rule of *Bram v. United States* (1897) that in criminal cases in the federal courts—this was extended by MALLOY V. HOGAN (1964) to the state courts, too—whenever a question arises whether a confession is incompetent because it is involuntary or coerced, the issue is controlled by the self-incrimination clause of the Fifth. Partly because of JOHN H. WIGMORE's intimidating influence and partly because of the rule of *Twining* denying that the FOURTEENTH AMENDMENT extended the Fifth to the states, the Court until 1964 held that the coercion of a confession by state or local authorities violated due process of law rather than the right

against self-incrimination. Wigmore, the master of evidence, claimed that the rule against coerced confessions and the right against self-incrimination had "no connection," the two being different in history, time or origin, principle, and practice.

Wigmore was wrong. From the fact that a separate rule against coerced confessions emerged in English decisions of the eighteenth century, nearly a century after the right against self-incrimination had become established, he concluded that the two rules had *no* connection. That the two operated differently in some respects and had differing rationales in other respects led him to the same conclusion. But he focused on their differences only and so exaggerated those differences that he fell into numerous errors and inconsistencies of statement. The relationship of the two rules is apparent from the fact that the shadow of the rack was part of the background from which each rule emerged. The disappearance of torture and the recognition of the right against compulsory self-incrimination were victories in the same political struggle. The connections among torture, *compulsory* self-incrimination, and *coerced* confessions was a historical fact as well as a physical and psychological one. In the sixteenth and seventeenth centuries, the argument against the three, resulting in the rules that Wigmore said had no connection, overlapped. Compulsory self-incrimination was always regarded by its opponents as a species of torture. An act of 1696 regulating treason trials required that confessions be made willingly, without violence, and in open court. The quotation above from Geoffrey Gilbert disproves Wigmore's position. When the separate rule against coerced confessions emerged, its rationale was that a coerced confession is untrustworthy evidence. There remained, however, an indissoluble and crucial nexus with the right against self-incrimination because both rules involved coercion or the involuntary acknowledgment of guilt. Significantly the few references to the right against self-incrimination, in the debates on the ratification of the Constitution, identified the right with a protection against torture and inquisition, that is, against coerced confessions. Wigmore fell into error by assuming that the right against self-incrimination had a single rationale and a static meaning. In fact it always had several rationales, was an expanding principle of law, and spun off into different directions. One spin-off was the development of a separate rule against coerced confessions. If there was "an historical blunder," it was made by the English courts of the eighteenth century when they divorced the confessions rule from the self-incrimination rule.

History is not clear on the Court's distinction between TESTIMONIAL COMPULSION, which the Fifth prohibits, and nontestimonial compulsion, which it does not prohibit. Blood samples, photographs, fingerprints, voice exemplars, and most other forms of nontestimonial compulsion are of modern origin. The fact that the Fifth refers to the right not to be a witness against oneself seems to imply the giving of testimony rather than keeping records or revealing body characteristics for identification purposes. The distinction made by the Court in SCHMERBER V. CALIFORNIA (1966) was reasonable. Yet, limiting the Fifth to prohibit only testimonial compulsion poses problems. The accused originally could not testify at all, and the history of the right does not suggest the *Schmerber* limitations. The common law decisions and the wording of the first state bills of rights explicitly protected against compelling anyone to give or furnish "evidence" against himself, not just testimony.

The fact that history does not support some of the modern decisions limiting the scope of the right hardly means that history always substantiates decisions expanding it. Decisions like *Slochower v. Board of Education* (1956) and GARRITY V. NEW JERSEY (1967), which protect against penalizing the invocation of the right or chilling its use, draw no clear support from the past. Indeed, the decision in GRIFFIN V. CALIFORNIA (1965) which prohibited comment on the failure of a criminal defendant to testify on ground that such comment "is a remnant of the inquisitorial system" is historically farfetched.

Finally, history is ambiguous on the controversial issue whether the right against self-incrimination extends to the police station. When justices of the peace performed police functions and conducted the preliminary examination of suspects, their interrogation was inquisitorial in character (as it is in the interrogation rooms of modern police stations) and it usually had as its object the incrimination of the suspect. Yet he could not be examined under oath, and he did have a right to withhold the answer to incriminating questions. On the other hand, he had no right to be told that he need not answer or be cautioned that his answers could be used against him. However, the right against self-incrimination grew out of a protest against incriminating interrogation *prior to* formal accusation. That is, the maxim *nemo tenetur seipsum prodere* originally meant that no one was obligated to supply the evidence that could be used to indict him. Thus, from the very inception of the right, a suspect could invoke it at the earliest stages of his interrogation.

In MIRANDA V. ARIZONA (1966) the Supreme Court expanded the right beyond all precedent, yet not beyond its historical spirit. *Miranda's* purpose was to eliminate the inherently coercive and inquisitional atmosphere of the interrogation room and to guarantee that any incriminating admissions are made voluntarily. That purpose was, historically, the heart of the Fifth, the basis of its policy. Even the guarantee of counsel to effectuate that purpose

has precedent in a historical analogy: the development of the right to counsel originally safeguarded the right against self-incrimination at the trial stage of prosecution. When the defendant lacked counsel, he had to conduct his own case, and although he was not put on the stand and did not have to answer incriminating questions, his failure to rebut accusations and insinuations by the prosecution prejudiced the jury, vitiating the right to silence. The right to counsel permitted the defendant's lips to remain sealed; his "mouthpiece" spoke for him. In *Miranda* the Court extended the protection of counsel to the earliest stage of a criminal action, when the need is the greatest because the suspect is most vulnerable.

Nevertheless, the *Miranda* warnings were an invention of the Court, devoid of historical support. Excepting rare occasions when judges intervened to protect a witness against incriminatory interrogatories, the right had to be claimed or invoked by the person seeking its protection. Historically it was a fighting right; unless invoked it offered no protection. It did not bar interrogation or taint an uncoerced confession as improper evidence. Incriminating statements made by a suspect could always be used at his trial. That a person might unwittingly incriminate himself when questioned in no way impaired his legal right to refuse answer. He lacked the right to be warned that he need not answer; he lacked the right to have a lawyer present at his interrogation; and he lacked the protection of the strict waiver requirements that now accompany the MIRANDA RULES. From a historical view, the decision in BREWER V. WILLIAMS (1977) and the limits on interrogation imposed by RHODE ISLAND V. INNES (1980) extraordinarily inflate the right. What was once a fighting right has become a pampered one. Law should encourage, not thwart, voluntary confessions. The Fifth should be liberally construed to serve as a check on modern versions of the "third degree" and the spirit of McCarthyism, but the Court should distinguish rapists and murderers from John Lilburne and realize that law enforcement agencies today are light years away from the behavior revealed in BROWN V. MISSISSIPPI (1936) and CHAMBERS V. FLORIDA (1940).

The Court said in PALKO V. CONNECTICUT (1937) that the right against compulsory self-incrimination was not a fundamental right; it might be lost, and justice might still be done if the accused "were subject to a duty to respond to orderly inquiry." Few would endorse that judgment today, but it is a yardstick for measuring how radically different the constitutional law of the Fifth became in half a century.

History surely exalts the right if precedence be our guide. It won acceptance earlier than did the freedoms of speech, press, and religion. It preceded a cluster of procedural rights such as benefit of counsel. It is older, too, than immunities against BILLS OF ATTAINDER, EX POST FACTO laws, and unreasonable searches and seizures. History also exalts the origins of the right against self-incrimination, for they are related to the development of the accusatorial system of criminal justice and the concept of FAIR TRIAL; to the principle that FUNDAMENTAL LAW limits government—the very foundation of CONSTITUTIONALISM; and to the heroic struggles for the freedoms of the FIRST AMENDMENT. History does not, however, exalt the right against the claims of justice.

LEONARD W. LEVY
(1986)

Bibliography

FRIENDLY, HENRY J.   1968   The Fifth Amendment Tomorrow: The Case for Constitutional Change. *University of Cincinnati Law Review* 37:671–726.

GRISWOLD, ERWIN   1955   *The 5th Amendment Today.* Cambridge, Mass.: Harvard University Press.

HOOK, SIDNEY   1957   *Common Sense and the Fifth Amendment.* New York: Criterion.

KAMISAR, YALE   1980   *Police Interrogation and Confessions: Essays in Law and Policy.* Ann Arbor: University of Michigan Press.

LEVY, LEONARD W.   1968   *Origins of the Fifth Amendment: The Right against Self-Incrimination.* New York: Oxford University Press.

MAYERS, LEWIS   1959   *Shall We Amend the Fifth Amendment?* New York: Harper & Row.

MORGAN, EDMUND M.   1949   The Privilege against Self-Incrimination. *Minnesota Law Review* 34:1–37.

WIGMORE, JOHN HENRY   1961   *Evidence in Trials at Common Law,* vol. 8, rev. by John T. McNaughton. Boston: Little, Brown.

RIGHT AGAINST SELF-INCRIMINATION
(Update)

In the original edition of this *Encyclopedia,* Leonard W. Levy characterized the right against self-incrimination as "the most misunderstood, unrespected, and controversial of all constitutional rights," yet stressed that the Supreme Court "has tended to give it an ever widening meaning" unconfined by textual literalism. Recent Fifth Amendment jurisprudence has brought an end to this expansion of scope without clarifying the theoretical underpinnings of the right. While scholars propose and criticize alternative conceptual foundations for this right, the Supreme Court has been content to point to a grab bag of motivations, including humaneness to suspects, commitment to "accusatorial" procedures and a fair state-individual balance, distrust of confessions, concern for privacy, and respect for the human personality. The Court has made little effort to assign different weights or distinct roles to these concerns or to link them explicitly to the outcomes of particular cases. Current law indeed suggests that the Court's primary aim is to prevent the right against self-incrimination from interfering unduly with the paramount truth-finding function of the CRIMINAL JUSTICE SYSTEM.

Achieving this aim is particularly difficult because the Fifth Amendment, unlike the FOURTH AMENDMENT, does not prohibit only "unreasonable" intrusions on the right that it protects; thus, the Court is at least officially reluctant to "balance" the Fifth Amendment right against competing government interests. Moreover, the Fifth Amendment appears on its face to forbid admission of EVIDENCE compelled from the defendant, leaving no room to argue—as with the Fourth Amendment—that exclusion of improperly obtained evidence is a judicially created remedy to which courts may freely create exceptions. The Fifth Amendment right must instead be limited by the manner in which it is defined and by the explanations given to the key terms in that definition.

The right against self-incrimination forbids the government to compel an individual to provide testimonial or communicative evidence that could be used to incriminate that individual. Only a natural person, not an organization, can claim this right, but with regard to items a person holds as custodian for an organization. However, it may be claimed in any forum in which government seeks to compel a response, whether by legal process or through the informal coercive pressures of police interrogation, and with regard to any item that could potentially furnish a link in a chain of incriminating evidence, even though not sufficient in itself to convict. In most contexts, this right is deemed waived unless actively claimed by the right holder, and it is inapplicable to evidence for whose disclosure the government grants the right holder IMMUNITY (against any use, direct or indirect, to convict the right holder of crime).

MIRANDA V. ARIZONA (1966), which extended the right against self-incrimination to the POLICE INTERROGATION context, established special rules for this setting, elaborated in subsequent opinions. Statements by a person interrogated while in custody are presumed compelled, and hence, are inadmissible at trial to prove guilt, unless the suspect is told before the interrogation that he or she has the right to remain silent, to consult a lawyer before any questioning, and to have the lawyer present during questioning; that a lawyer will be provided if the suspect wants but cannot afford one; and that anything the suspect says can be used against him or her in court. If the suspect requests a lawyer, no questioning is permitted until one is provided, unless the suspect initiates further discussion with the police. If the suspect consents to questioning but subsequently indicates a desire to remain silent, the interrogation must cease.

The principal recent developments have arisen in two quite different contexts. One is the police-interrogation setting—unique because (as will be discussed) the detailed rules of *Miranda* and its progeny are only tenuously related to the constitutional ban on compelled self-incrimination. The other development, which unequivocally implicates the constitutional right itself, comprises efforts by investigatory targets to resist official demands for the production of evidence that could potentially lead to criminal charges. Opinions in both areas exhibit the Court's efforts to minimize interference with the truth-finding process.

The recent police-interrogation decisions preserve the *Miranda* doctrine while restricting its scope. The Court's reluctance to overrule *Miranda* outright is surprising in light of opinions strikingly eroding the doctrine's legitimacy. These opinions, culminating in OREGON V. ELSTAD (1985), view the *Miranda* doctrine not as commanded or entailed by the Fifth Amendment, but as a set of "prophylactic rules" devised by the Court to forestall genuine constitutional violations. Breach of *Miranda*'s requirements need not, therefore, violate the constitutional right against self-incrimination. This view leaves the Court free (as in *Elstad*) to hold certain evidence derived from such a breach admissible in circumstances in which the fruits of a constitutional violation must be suppressed. But it also undermines the very foundation of *Miranda*: why may the Court require police to obey rules that the Court itself concedes are neither required by the Constitution nor imposed to remedy constitutional violations? Both friends and critics of *Miranda* suggested that the Court was preparing to discard the doctrine altogether.

This has not happened, however, nor have opinions since *Elstad* crucially exploited the nonconstitutional status of *Miranda*. Rather, the Court has simply narrowed *Miranda*'s reach in various ways. "Interrogation," which triggers the warning requirement, includes conduct the police should know is likely to prompt incriminating admissions. Yet *Arizona v. Mauro* (1987) held that allowing (and recording) a meeting between an arrestee and his wife was not "interrogation," despite police awareness that such admissions might occur. Telling an unsophisticated suspect that a lawyer would be appointed "if and when you go to court" could cast doubt on the required notice that the lawyer would be provided "before any questioning." Yet *Duckworth v. Eagan* (1989) found no ambiguity, analyzing the amended warnings from a legally knowledgeable standpoint.

Most notably, the Court has repudiated suggestions—arguably latent in *Miranda* itself—that the *Miranda* doctrine guarantees a "rational," "responsible," or "fully informed" choice between silence and speech. Instead, the Court treats the doctrine solely as forestalling coercion and has found WAIVERS OF THE CONSTITUTIONAL RIGHT to silence valid in a variety of situations where the suspect's decision was less than "rational" or "fully informed." In *Moran v. Burbine* (1986), the police did not tell the suspect that a lawyer hired by his sister was trying to reach him. In *Colorado v. Barrett* (1987) the suspect apparently thought only written statements could be used against him. In *Colorado v. Spring* (1987) a suspect arrested for a firearms violation agreed to talk without knowing he would be questioned about an earlier murder in a different jurisdiction. Most strikingly, COLORADO V. CONNELLY (1986) found voluntary a *Miranda* waiver by a MENTALLY ILL suspect in the grip of paranoid delusions, reasoning that only official coercion would render a waiver "involuntary."

In its *Miranda* jurisprudence the Court is dealing with what it views as a judge-made supplement to the right against self-incrimination. Its desire to keep the doctrine within narrow bounds may thus say little about the Court's commitment to the core concerns animating this right. The recent decisions concerning production of evidence, however, evince a readiness to limit the Fifth Amendment right itself.

In *Fisher v. United States* (1976) the Court distinguished the contents of items sought by the government and the act of producing those items. Each requires separate analysis, and the Fifth Amendment is violated only if either the contents or act of production is, by itself, compelled, testimonial, and incriminating. (In effect, as Peter Arenella has observed, a Fifth Amendment violation occurs only when the government's compulsion creates incriminating testimonial evidence that did not previously exist.) One result was to make the self-incrimination right harder to invoke; documents whose contents were created voluntarily are shielded only if the compelled act of producing them is itself both testimonial and incriminating. In contrast, by acknowledging that production itself could implicitly communicate incriminating information, *Fisher* opened a novel route for Fifth Amendment arguments. The REHNQUIST COURT's decisions in this area narrow that route in three ways.

First, the criterion for "testimonial" or "communicative" evidence was tightened in *Doe v. United States* (1988) to permit compelling a suspect to sign a directive authorizing foreign banks to release information about any accounts he might have. Although executing the directive would communicate directions to the banks, the Court insisted that only the communication of factual assertions or information counts as "testimonial." The Court left unexplained how informing a bank that it is authorized to make specified disclosures does not count as conveying "information."

More significantly, the "collective entity rule" precluding self-incrimination claims with respect to documents held as custodian for an organization was found applicable to the custodian's act of production, not merely the documents' contents. The collective-entity rule reflected the Court's view that the personal nature of the Fifth Amendment right was inconsistent with the impersonal representative capacity in which the custodian holds organizational records. After *Fisher*, the Court could have reinterpreted the rule as existing because the contents of such records were not created under compulsion—implying nothing about an act that was compelled. But BRASWELL V. UNITED STATES (1988) rejected this harmonization of the collective-entity and *Fisher* doctrines. The Court instead extended its pre-*Fisher* explanation of the collective entity rule by insisting that the representative capacity in which custodians hold documents makes even their individual acts of production not "personal." This strained "sleight of hand" insistence that a natural individual's overt behavior is somehow not that individual's "personal" act allowed the Court to escape an implication of its own act/content distinction that it feared would eviscerate the investigation of white-collar crimes.

Finally, in *Baltimore City Department of Social Services v. Bouknight* (1990), the Court combined *Braswell's* custodial rationale with an amorphous expansive exception to the self-incrimination right for noncriminal regulatory schemes to reject the self-incrimination claim of a suspected child abuser ordered to produce her son in court. Although the mother's act of production would testify to her control over the child and could thereby assist her prosecution, the Court appealed to cases rejecting Fifth Amendment challenges to civil regulatory requirements not confined to groups inherently suspect of criminal activities. Reliance on this exception is troubling, however, because of its extraordinary manipulability. (Why, for example, regard as "civil" and "regulatory" a state juvenile-protection scheme intimately related to criminal laws against child abuse?) Doubts are scarcely dispelled by the Court's additional argument that Bouknight's status as custodian for her son under a prior court order was analogous to that of a custodian of corporate records. The "custodian" argument had never before extended beyond agents of collective entities, and it entailed ignoring this "custodian's" prior and continuing status as mother.

OBITER DICTUM in *Bouknight* suggests that if the state should later seek to prosecute the mother, it may be prohibited from using the testimonial aspects of her act of production. Similarly, *Braswell* stated that although the government could compel a custodian to produce organizational records, it could not in a subsequent prosecution of the custodian divulge that he or she produced those records. There is a tension between these obiter dicta and the HOLDING in each case that compelled production does not violate the Fifth Amendment. This tension suggests that the Court may be uneasy with the extent to which its decisions have in fact cut into the core area of the right against self-incrimination. In an unacknowledged fashion, the Court may be balancing the individual's self-incrimination right and the social goal of truth finding in an effort to accommodate both concerns.

DAVID DOLINKO
(1992)

Bibliography

ARENELLA, PETER 1982 Schmerber and the Privilege Against Self-Incrimination: A Reappraisal. *American Criminal Law Review* 20:31–61.

DOLINKO, DAVID 1986 Is There a Rationale for the Privilege Against Self-Incrimination? *UCLA Law Review* 33:1063–1148.

SCHULHOFER, STEPHEN 1987 Reconsidering *Miranda*. *University of Chicago Law Review* 54:435–461.

SEIDMAN, LOUIS MICHAEL 1990 Rubashov's Question: Self-Incrimination and the Problem of Coerced Preferences. *Yale Journal of Law and the Humanities* 2:149–180.

STUNTZ, WILLIAM 1988 Self-Incrimination and Excuse. *Columbia Law Review* 88:1227–1296.

WHITE, WELSH 1986 Defending Miranda: A Reply to Professor Caplan. *Vanderbilt Law Review* 39:1–22.

RIGHT OF PRIVACY

Long before anyone spoke of privacy as a constitutional right, American law had developed a "right of privacy," invasion of which was a tort, justifying the award of money damages. One such invasion would be a newspaper's embarrassing publication of intimate facts about a person, or a statement placing someone in a "false light," when the story was not newsworthy. Other invasions of this right were found in various forms of physical intrusion, or surveillance, or interception of private communications. The Constitution, too, protected some interests in privacy: the FOURTH AMENDMENT forbade unreasonable SEARCHES AND SEIZURES; the Fifth Amendment offered a RIGHT AGAINST SELF-INCRIMINATION; the THIRD AMENDMENT, a relic of the Revolutionary War, forbade the government to quarter troops in a private house in peacetime without the owner's consent. Even so, despite Justice LOUIS D. BRANDEIS's famous statement in the WIRETAPPING case of OLMSTEAD V. UNITED STATES (1928), there was no general constitutional "right to be let alone." Nor does any such sweeping constitutional right exist today. Beginning with GRISWOLD V. CONNECTICUT (1965), the Supreme Court has recognized a constitutional right of privacy, but the potentially broad scope of that right remains constricted by the Court's current interpretations of it.

Griswold held invalid a Connecticut law forbidding the use of contraceptives, in application to the operators of a BIRTH CONTROL clinic who were aiding married couples to violate the law, offering them advice and contraceptive devices. Justice WILLIAM O. DOUGLAS, writing for the Court, disavowed any reliance on SUBSTANTIVE DUE PROCESS to support the decision. Although the statute did not violate the terms of any specific guarantee of the BILL OF RIGHTS, said Douglas, the Court's decisions had recognized that "specific guarantees in the Bill of Rights have penumbras, formed by emanations from those guarantees that help give them life and substance." The FREEDOM OF ASSOCIATION, although not mentioned in the FIRST AMENDMENT, had been protected against intrusions on the privacy of political association. The Third, Fourth, and Fifth Amendments also created "zones of privacy." The *Griswold* case concerned "a relationship lying within the zone of privacy created by several fundamental constitutional guarantees." Furthermore, the idea of allowing police to enforce a ban on contraceptives by searching the marital bedroom was "repulsive to the notions of privacy surrounding the marriage relationship."

Connecticut had not been enforcing its law even against drugstore sales of contraceptives; the governmental prying conjured up in the *Griswold* opinion was not really threatened. What *Griswold* was protecting was not so much the privacy of the marital bedroom as a married couple's control over the intimacies of their relationship. This point emerged clearly in EISENSTADT V. BAIRD (1972), which extended the right to practice contraception to unmarried persons, and in CAREY V. POPULATION SERVICES INTERNATIONAL (1977), which struck down three laws restricting the sale and advertisement of contraceptives.

In *Eisenstadt* the Court characterized the right of privacy as the right of an individual "to be free from unwarranted intrusion into matters so fundamentally affecting a person as the decision whether to bear or beget a child." The prophecy in those words came true the following year when the Court, in ROE V. WADE (1973), held that the constitutional right of privacy recognized in *Griswold* was "broad enough to encompass a woman's decision whether or not to terminate her pregnancy." This right to decide whether to have an abortion was qualified only in the later stages of pregnancy; during the first trimester of pregnancy it was absolute. Abandoning *Griswold*'s PENUMBRA THEORY, the Court placed the right of privacy within the liberty protected by the DUE PROCESS clause of the FOUR-TEENTH AMENDMENT. (See ABORTION AND THE CONSTITUTION.)

As the *Roe* dissenters pointed out, an abortion operation "is not 'private' in the ordinary usage of that word." Liberty, not privacy, was the chief constitutional value at stake in *Roe*. In later years various Justices have echoed the words of Justice POTTER STEWART, concurring in *Roe*, that "freedom of personal choice in matters of marriage and family life" is a due process liberty. Indeed, Justice Stewart's formulation was too narrow; the Court's decisions have gone well beyond formal marriage and the traditional family to protect a much broader FREEDOM OF INTIMATE ASSOCIATION. Yet that freedom is often defended in the name of the constitutional right of privacy.

From the time of the *Griswold* decision forward, privacy became the subject of a body of legal and philosophical literature notable for both analytical quality and rapid growth. The term "privacy" cried out for definition—not merely as a feature of constitutional law, where the Supreme Court had offered no more than doctrinal impressionism, but more fundamentally as a category of thought. Is privacy a situation, or a value, or a claim of right? Is privacy itself the subject of our moral and legal claims, or is it a code word that always stands for some other interest? However these initial questions be answered, what are the functions of privacy in our society? These are not merely philosophers' inquiries; in deciding "right of privacy" cases judges also answer them, even if the answers are buried in assumptions never articulated.

Not until 1977 did the Supreme Court begin to map out the territory occupied by the constitutional right of privacy. In WHALEN V. ROE the Court upheld a state law requiring the maintenance of computerized records of persons who obtained various drugs by medical prescription. "The cases sometimes characterized as protecting 'privacy,'" said the Court, "have in fact involved at least two different kinds of interests. One is the individual interest in avoiding disclosure of personal matters, and another is the interest in independence in making certain kinds of important decisions." This passage is noteworthy in two respects: first, its opening words suggest a new awareness that "privacy" may not be the most informative label for an interest in freedom of choice whether to marry, or procreate, or have an abortion, or send one's child to a private school. Second, the passage strongly hints that some interests in informational privacy—freedom from disclosure—are constitutionally protected not only by the First, Fourth, and Fifth Amendments but also by a more general right of privacy.

The *Whalen* opinion was written by Justice JOHN PAUL STEVENS, who has consistently urged an expansive reading of the "liberty" protected by the due process clauses. As if to emphasize that the right of privacy is merely one aspect of a broadly defined right of substantive due process, Justice Stevens cited, to support his reference to the interest in independence in making important decisions, ALLGEYER V. LOUISIANA (1897), which established the FREEDOM OF CONTRACT as a due process right. If the "important decisions" part of the right of privacy is to be absorbed back into the body of substantive due process, and if informational privacy is to become part of a redefined constitutional right of privacy, the contours of this new right will for the first time approach the meanings of "privacy" in common speech. Before *Whalen*, it was possible to say that the one interest most conspicuously left unprotected by the constitutional right of privacy was privacy itself. In any event, even after *Whalen*'s suggestive analysis, the Supreme Court has continued to speak of "the" constitutional right of privacy.

There is a sense in which personal decisions about sex and marriage and procreation are private decisions. Indeed, the word "private" serves better than "privacy" to indicate the interests in personal autonomy at stake in such cases. Both words can refer to such forms of privacy as seclusion and secrecy; to do something in private is to do it free from public or general observance, and private information consists of facts not publicly or generally known. But "private" has another meaning that lacks any similar analogue in the idea of privacy. Private property, for example, is property that is one's own, subject to one's control, from which one has the right to exclude others if one chooses to do so. It makes perfect sense to speak of a power of decision as private in this sense. From this perspective the line of "privacy" opinions from *Griswold* to *Roe* and beyond can be seen as seeking to identify the circumstances in which the decision "to bear or beget a child" is one that "belongs" to the individual, one from which the public—even the state—can be excluded. Calling such an interest "privacy," however, is a play on words; any freedom from governmental regulation might just as easily be called "privacy." Perhaps Justice Stevens was making this point in his *Whalen* opinion when he cited *Allgeyer*, a case in which the liberty at stake was freedom to buy insurance from an out-of-state company.

Much of what government does in the way of regulating behavior intrudes on privacy in its commonly understood senses of solitude and nondisclosure. Yet even when these forms of privacy are assimilated to the constitutional right of privacy, the result is not wholesale invalidation of governmental action. The *Whalen* decision itself is illustrative. Recognizing that the drug records law threatened some impairment of both the interest in nondisclosure and the interest in making personal decisions, the Court nonetheless concluded that the law's informational security safeguards minimized the chances of serious harm to those interests and that the law was a reasonable means of minimizing drug abuse. More serious threats of disclosure of accumulated personal information, the Court said, might exceed constitutional limitations. The clear implication is that future claims to a constitutional right of privacy in the form of nondisclosure will be evaluated through a process of judicial interest balancing.

Even a judge who regards privacy as a constitutional value in itself, something more than a label for other interests, will be pressed to consider why privacy is important, in order to place the proper weights in a given case's decisional balance. The commentary on privacy regularly identifies several overlapping values. If governmental "brainwashing" would be unconstitutional, as all observers assume, the reason surely lies in the widely shared sense that the essentials of due process "liberty" include a healthy measure of control over the development of one's own individuality. That control undoubtedly requires some amount of privacy in the form of nondisclosure and seclusion. To have the sense of being a person, an individual needs some degree of control over the roles she may play in various social settings; control over the disclosure of personal information contributes to this process. Similarly, both learning and creative activity require a measure of relaxation and refuge from the world's intrusions.

A closely related function of informational privacy is its value as a foundation for friendship and intimacy. Although a cynic might say that the most effective way for an individual to preserve the privacy of his thoughts and feelings would be never to disclose them, that course would sacrifice the sort of sharing that constitutes a central value of intimate association—which, in turn, is crucial to the development of individuality. It is here that we can see clearly the overlap between privacy as selective nondisclosure and "privacy" as autonomy in intimate personal decisions. Justice Douglas's *Griswold* opinion spoke to both concerns: he sought to defend the privacy of the marital bedroom against hypothetical government snooping and to defend a married couple's autonomy over the intimacies of their relationship. The special constitutional status of the home, recognized in decisions ranging from search and seizure doctrines to the "private" possession of OBSCENITY protected in STANLEY V. ILLINOIS (1969), draws not only on the notion of the home as a sanctuary and place of repose but also on the home's status as the main locus of intimate associations.

Finally, privacy in the sense of seclusion or nondisclosure serves to encourage freedom, both in the sense of political liberty and in the sense of moral autonomy. The political privacy cases from NAACP V. ALABAMA (1958) to GIBSON V. FLORIDA LEGISLATIVE INVESTIGATION COMMITTEE (1963) and beyond rest on the premise that disclosure of political associations is especially harmful to members of political groups that are unpopular or unorthodox. When the Army engaged in the domestic political surveillance that produced the Supreme Court's 5–4 nondecision in LAIRD V. TATUM (1972), its files were filled with the names of those who "were thought to have at least some potential for civil disorder," not with the names of Rotarians and Job's Daughters. A similar threat is posed by disclosure of one's homosexual associations or other intimate associations outside the mainstream of conventional morality. Such a case, like *Griswold*, implicates both privacy as nondisclosure or seclusion and "privacy" as associational autonomy.

On the other side of the constitutional balance, opposed to the interest in informational privacy, may be ranged any of the interests commonly advanced to support the free exchange of information. To further many of those interests, the common law of defamation erected an elaborate structure of "privileges," designed to protect from liability persons who made defamatory statements in the course of exchanging information for legitimate purposes: a former employer might give a servant a bad reference; a newspaper might criticize the town mayor. As these examples show, informational privacy is by no means the only constitutional interest that may be raised in such cases. Not only has the law of defamation been hedged in with First Amendment limitations; liability for the tort of invasion of privacy must also pass judicial scrutiny aimed at avoiding violations of the FREEDOM OF THE PRESS. Although the Supreme Court has not ruled on the matter, undoubtedly the First Amendment will be read to include a "newsworthiness" defense to an action for damages for invasion of privacy by publication of intimate facts. Even where the First Amendment is not involved directly as a constitutional limit on the award of damages or the imposition of punishment under state law, that amendment's values must be taken into account in evaluating any claim that a state has violated an individual's constitutional right of informational privacy. (See GOVERNMENT SPEECH.) Perhaps for this reason, most lower federal courts have been reluctant to find in Justice Stevens's *Whalen* opinion a general invitation to expand the constitutional right of privacy's protections against disclosure of information.

Nor has the Supreme Court been ready, in the years since ROE V. WADE, to extend either branch of the constitutional right of privacy. The Court's best-known opportunities for widening the scope of the right have come in "important decisions" cases involving nonmarital intimate relationships (including homosexual ones; see SEXUAL PREFERENCE AND THE CONSTITUTION) and the asserted right to control one's own personal appearance (including dress and hair length). In some of these cases the Court has avoided deciding cases on their constitutional merits; in no case has the Court validated the claim of a right of privacy. On principle, the intimate association cases seem

clearly enough to be governed by *Griswold* and its successor decisions. Yet the Court has temporized, displaying what ALEXANDER BICKEL once called "the passive virtues," evidently awaiting the formation of a sufficient political consensus before extending constitutional protection to unconventional intimate associations.

One factual context in which the Court seems likely to continue its hospitality to "privacy" claims touching intimate personal decisions is that of governmental intrusions into the body. The abortion decisions, of course, are the modern starting point. Compulsory smallpox VACCINATION, once upheld as a health measure, stands on shakier constitutional ground now that smallpox has been virtually eradicated. Compulsory STERILIZATION, too, is unconstitutional in the absence of justification by some COMPELLING STATE INTEREST. The Supreme Court has explicitly redescribed SKINNER V. OKLAHOMA (1942) as a "privacy" case. By analogy, the right of a competent adult to refuse medical treatment seems secure, even when that choice will probably lead to death. (See EUTHANASIA.)

If the Supreme Court comes to accept Justice Stevens's broad reading of due process "liberty," it makes little difference whether the bodily intrusion cases be seen as raising "privacy" issues. There are occasions, however, when governmental invasions of the body implicate not only the interest in autonomy over one's own body but also privacy in its true sense of nondisclosure and seclusion. An appalling case in point is *Bell v. Wolfish* (1979). Inmates of a federal detention center, held in custody before being tried on criminal charges, sued to challenge the constitutionality of various conditions of their confinement. One challenged practice was the systematic subjection of every inmate to visual inspection of his or her body cavities after every "contact visit" with a person from outside the center, whether or not anyone had any suspicion that contraband was being smuggled into the center. A 5–4 Supreme Court held that the searches were not unreasonable and thus presented no Fourth Amendment problem; the majority did not separately consider any constitutional right of privacy founded on due process. The two main dissenting opinions, emphasizing substantive due process, insisted that the government must offer substantial justification for such a degrading invasion of privacy. (See ROCHIN V. CALIFORNIA.) Justification was lacking: the lower court had found that the searches were ineffective in detecting smuggled goods, and the government's argument that the searches deterred smuggling was an obvious makeweight.

There was no significant physical invasion of the body in the *Wolfish* case. Yet the privacy interests of the individuals searched were not far removed from those involved in the abortion and sterilization cases. The detainees sought vindication of their right to be afforded the dignity of respect, not just for their bodies but for their persons. The very pointlessness of the searches in cases where suspicion was lacking heightened the humiliation, to the point that many inmates had given up visits by family members. The case illustrates perfectly the convergence of the interests in personal autonomy and informational privacy in an individual's control over his own personality. When government seriously invades that sphere, due process demands important justification.

Several states guarantee a right of privacy in their state constitutions. The various state supreme courts have relied on these provisions to hold unconstitutional not only invasions of informational privacy, such as police surveillance, but also invasions of personal autonomy, such as laws limiting the occupancy of a house to members of a family, or forbidding the possession of marijuana for personal use. If the Supreme Court were to follow the doctrinal leadership of these courts, it would not be the first time. (See INCORPORATION DOCTRINE.)

Both types of interests protected by the federal constitutional right of privacy are susceptible to either broad or narrow interpretation. A generalized "privacy" right to make important decisions, like a generalized right of informational privacy, resists clear-cut definition. Every extension of a constitutional right of personal autonomy detracts from the power of government to regulate behavior in the public interest (as government defines that interest); and every extension of a constitutional right of informational privacy detracts from the free flow of communication. The problem for the courts, here as in EQUAL PROTECTION and other areas of constitutional growth, is the stopping-place problem. It is no accident that most discussions of the newer constitutional right of privacy turn to questions about the proper role of the judiciary—a theme that has dominated discussion of substantive due process since it appeared on the constitutional scene a century ago. The problem of defining a constitutional right and the problem of establishing the courts' proper constitutional role are two faces of the same inquiry. A constitutional right that defies description not only fails to protect its intended beneficiaries but also undermines the position of the courts in the governmental system.

Justice Stevens's opinion in WHALEN V. ROE begins to point the way toward the resolution of the uncertainties that have surrounded the constitutional right of privacy ever since the *Griswold* decision. It does aid constitutional analysis to separate the right into the two strands of personal autonomy and informational privacy. Yet it remains useful to recognize, as Justice Stevens has continued to remind us, that both strands remain part of a single substantive due process principle: significant governmental invasions of individual liberty require justification, scaled in importance according to the severity of the invasions. The right of privacy, then, is no more susceptible to pre-

cise definition than are such rights as due process or equal protection. What can be identified are the substantive values that inform the right of privacy. These values, as the Supreme Court's decisions show, are centered in the respect owed by the organized society to each individual as a person and as a member of a community. When governmental officers invade a person's control over her own body, or development of individual identity, or intimate associations—either by restricting decisional autonomy or by intruding on privacy in the sense of nondisclosure or solitude—then the Constitution demands that they be called to account and made to justify their actions.

For the future, the fate of the right of privacy, like that of all constitutional rights, will depend on the courts only secondarily. In the long run, the crucial questions will be how much privacy and what kinds of privacy we value. Total privacy—that is, isolation from others—is not merely unattainable; hardly anyone could stand it for long. In some societies people neither have nor want much of what we call privacy. Yet even among Australian aborigines who eke out their precarious living in a desert that often fails to provide walls, there are rules of restraint and social distance, and, when all else fails, the magic of secret names. Our own constitutional right of privacy will grow or wither as our own society's rules of restraint and social distance form and dissolve.

KENNETH L. KARST
(1986)

Bibliography

BOSTWICK, GARY L. 1976 A Taxonomy of Privacy: Repose, Sanctuary, and Intimate Decision. *California Law Review* 64: 1447–83.
GAVISON, RUTH 1980 Privacy and the Limits of Law. *Yale Law Journal* 89:421–71.
GERETY, TOM 1977 Redefining Privacy. *Harvard Civil Rights-Civil Liberties Law Review* 12:233–96.
GREENAWALT, KENT 1974 Privacy and Its Legal Protections. *Hastings Center Studies* 2:45–68.
HENKIN, LOUIS 1974 Privacy and Autonomy. *Columbia Law Review* 74:1410–33.
Symposium on Privacy 1966 *Law and Contemporary Problems* 31:251–435.
TRIBE, LAURENCE H. 1978 *American Constitutional Law.* Chap. 15. Mineola, N.Y.: The Foundation Press.
WESTIN, ALAN F. 1967 *Privacy and Freedom.* New York: Atheneum.

RIGHT OF PRIVACY
(Update)

Despite extensive litigation and commentary, the right of privacy has remained uncertain in constitutional law since it was first established in GRISWOLD V. CONNECTICUT (1965). The ABORTION decision in ROE V. WADE (1973] raised the level of controversy about the right of privacy without clarifying the scope or nature of the rights understood under this concept. Sharp criticism of the vagueness of the concept of privacy and persistent doubts about its supporting constitutional text and traditions have not hampered the vitality of the right of privacy. In some areas, such as the RIGHT TO DIE, privacy and related concepts have made notable advances in constitutional law. Senate hearings on recent Supreme Court nominees, notably those leading to the rejection of Robert H. Bork and the confirmation of DAVID H. SOUTER seem to confirm these advances as political achievements. We cannot be sure, however, whether or not particular rights (such as the right to abortion) will survive changes in the personnel of the Court.

Recent majorities on the Supreme Court have generally identified the FOURTEENTH AMENDMENT's guarantee of "liberty" as the source of privacy rights. This is a notable shift for two reasons. First, it signals the willingness on the part of recent Justices to accept SUBSTANTIVE DUE PROCESS as a legitimate concept in constitutional law, so long as it does not touch on economic or labor matters. To Justices of the generation of WILLIAM O. DOUGLAS and HUGO L. BLACK, adjudication under such a general rubric was perilous. It encouraged judicial excess. Douglas went to great, perhaps absurd, lengths in *Griswold* to find textual sources for a right to privacy in the First, Third, Fourth, Fifth and Eighth Amendments. ARTHUR GOLDBERG sought to find privacy in the NINTH AMENDMENT. This is now widely understood as a fool's errand.

Second, the preference for a more general source of rights reflects continuing uncertainty about definition of the right of privacy together with an unwillingness to surrender its advantages. Whatever its source, Justice HARRY A. BLACKMUN wrote in *Roe v. Wade*, "[t]his right of privacy . . . is broad enough to encompass a woman's decision whether or not to terminate her pregnancy." Justices in more recent decisions have sometimes altogether avoided the term privacy, with conservatives often speaking of "liberty interests" and liberals of personal or "intimate" decisions. In *Cruzan v. Missouri Department of Health* (1990), the "right to die" case, Chief Justice WILLIAM H. REHNQUIST made this avoidance explicit: "Although many state courts have held that a right to refuse treatment is encompassed by a generalized constitutional right of privacy, we have never so held." The issue, he added, "is more properly analyzed in terms of a 14th Amendment liberty interest."

Outside of the law of SEARCH AND SEIZURE, privacy has proven extremely hard to define. Scholars have been unable to agree on the elements of ordinary usage, CONSTITUTIONAL HISTORY, or moral philosophy from which to construct a normative concept. The concept itself has been of little but rhetorical help in deciding particular cases in which, typically, regulation is seen to invade an individual's preference for seclusion or immunity. All this has made the precedents of *Griswold* and *Roe* hard to confine by ordinary arguments. The steps from privacy in marital sexuality to privacy in abortion and from heterosexuality to homosexuality have not been easy to resist when arguments are made in terms of a right to privacy possessed by all persons.

However disappointing to those awaiting clarification, the turn from privacy to liberty may nonetheless make good legal and political sense. Privacy as a term has no plain reference or meaning for most of us. "The right to be let alone," as EARL WARREN and LOUIS BRANDEIS called it, covered many situations and many abuses. In CRIMINAL PROCEDURE, the protection of "persons, papers, and effects" refers to those things (including one's own body) over which we normally exercise complete control. But the transportation from one context to another—search and seizure, for example, to sexuality—leaves much of the force of argument, as well as PRECEDENT and tradition, behind. We are left then with an argument for immunity unaided by the concept under which immunity is claimed. Obviously, private life—*la vie privée*—must shelter information, decisions, and behaviors of many different kinds. The question is, which ones are to be protected against regulation or governmental intrusion?

Liberty is not much more helpful in this regard than is privacy. Yet liberty offers a plainer inquiry with less confusion and less of a temptation to believe that we will find our rights by simply defining a concept. Moreover, liberty, unlike privacy, is a concept with a long constitutional history.

The inquiry that now seems to govern adjudication is whether or not fundamental liberties extend to certain aspects of private life, including sexuality, reproduction, and perhaps dying. Often, regulations have reached these matters in connection with medical treatment. Thus, the right to die is the right to refuse medical treatment where it might prolong life. The right to abortion is the right to choose whether or not to terminate a pregnancy before the fetus is viable outside the womb. We may generalize from these instances to a concept of privacy in intimate associations or intimate decisions, but the Supreme Court's response to this generalization remains equivocal: Sexuality between consenting adults of the opposite sexes seems at this point effectively protected. Although *Griswold* relied on the context of MARRIAGE for its extension of protection to information about the use of BIRTH CONTROL, EISENTADT V. BAIRD (1972) seemed to make clear that this context was unnecessary. We should note, however, that the effective protection for disapproved behavior lies in a conjunction of privacy decisions from the Supreme Court and, of equal or greater importance, regulatory reforms from the various state legislatures that permit a greater range of behaviors than heretofore. Sodomy statutes remain on the books in many states, and it is not yet clear that unmarried heterosexual sodomy would be held to be protected by the Supreme Court.

In BOWERS V. HARDWICK (1986) the Court upheld a Georgia statute that made sodomy a felony in a case in which charges had been filed and then withdrawn against two consenting adult males. The 5–4 decision sharply divided the Court. "The issue presented," wrote Justice BYRON R. WHITE, for the majority, "is whether the Federal constitution confers a fundamental right upon homosexuals to engage in sodomy. . . ." Justices Blackmun, WILLIAM J. BRENNAN, THURGOOD MARSHALL, and JOHN PAUL STEVENS dissented. "This case is no more about a fundamental right to engage in homosexual sodomy," Justice Blackmun wrote, "than STANLEY V. GEORGIA (1969) was about a fundamental right to watch obscene movies, or KATZ V. UNITED STATES (1967) was about a fundamental right to place interstate bets from a telephone booth." For the dissenters, Brandeis's dissent in OLMSTEAD V. UNITED STATES (1928) provided the applicable concept, "the right to be let alone," as Warren and Brandeis had described it (without any reference to sexuality) in their famous *Harvard Law Review* article on the "Right to Privacy." Thus, Blackmun insisted on a certain understanding of the concept of privacy: "I believe we must analyze respondent's claim in the light of the values that underlie the constitutional right to privacy. If that right means anything, it means that, before Georgia can prosecute its citizens for making choices about the most intimate aspects of their lives, it must do more than assert that the choice they have made is an "abominable crime not fit to be named among Christians."

The incommensurability of these points of view may be understood from at least three angles. First, and most obvious to students of the concepts of privacy and liberty, there is a difference over the level of abstraction at which the argument will be joined. The majority refused to accept the claim that adult homosexuals might shelter their consensual sexual practices under the same general liberty as adult heterosexuals. To the majority, the assertion is of an immunity to engage in a homosexual act consistently condemned in our tradition. The dissenters argue that this act must be understood in relation to other sexual intimacies protected by the Fourteenth Amendment. It is, after all, an expression of sexuality between consenting adults in the bedroom of a private apartment. (A houseguest had admitted the policeman into the apartment and directed him to Hardwick's bedroom.) Neither position is refutable as illogical or inconsistent. The choice of a level of abstraction will often decide a dispute over rights; yet

there seems to be no conclusive argument that one level of abstraction is the appropriate one for a given case. What makes one level preferable to another is the sense of coherence and completeness at that level of whatever issues are understood as pertinent. This is inevitably a circular process of reasoning. Intimacy and sexuality seem the relevant terms to the dissenters, but not to the majority, which focuses on homosexuality. A simpler way to understand this difference is to note that, as always, each side in legal argument denies the applicability of the other side's precedents. In this case, the majority will not accept the force and bearing of *Griswold, Eisenstadt,* and *Roe v. Wade.* For the dissenters, however, these are the relevant precedents, pointing the way to a different result.

Finally, there is an important line of argument, going back to the younger Justice JOHN MARSHALL HARLAN in *Poe v. Ullman* (1961), that tradition should inform our understanding of the concept of liberty. Constitutional traditions, like others, are notoriously inexact. Moreover, there are good traditions and bad ones. Yet it is undeniable that legal and institutional traditions give us a context in which to understand the terms and arrangements provided for in the Constitution. DUE PROCESS is one example, JUDICIAL REVIEW is another, and privacy may be a third.

Harlan, in *Poe* and *Griswold,* relied on a specific tradition, namely, marriage. The various measures of restriction and permission attached to it by law suggested to him that the concept of privacy had constitutional standing in protecting the uses of sexuality—including contraception—by husband and wife. He never went beyond this point, however, retiring from the Court in 1971, one year before the *Eisenstadt* decision and two years before *Roe v. Wade.*

Eisenstadt's majority opinions had relied on an EQUAL PROTECTION argument that left the factual question of the marital status of the recipient of a contraceptive unresolved. Justice Brennan's language, however, was unambiguous: "If the right of privacy means anything, it is the right of the *individual,* married or single, to be free from unwarranted governmental intrusion into matters so fundamentally affecting a person as the decision whether to bear or beget a child." This language may be said either to disregard tradition or to generalize it, raising it to a more abstract level. Only in MOORE V. CITY OF EAST CLEVELAND (1977) has the Court openly pursued Harlan's approach. In this case, the Court invalidated a ZONING ordiance disallowing residence in the same house of a grandmother and two grandchildren who were cousins rather than siblings. Justice LEWIS F. POWELL cited Harlan's reasoning in *Poe* in a plurality opinion insisting on "the sanctity of the family." "Ours is by means a tradition limited to respect for the bonds uniting the members of the nuclear family," he wrote.

Predictions about the future of the right to privacy must rely in part on assumptions about appointments to the Court. The Bork hearings seemed to suggest that a consensus now exists—in the Senate and in public opinion—on the importance of the right to privacy in constitutional law. This consensus does not mean, however, that the right to an abortion is secure. With the departure of Justice Brennan, *Roe v. Wade* is vulnerable to reversal. Justices ANTHONY M. KENNEDY, ANTONIN SCALIA, and Byron White, along with the Chief Justice, have all suggested an eagerness to reverse. Justice SANDRA DAY O'CONNOR has also indicated her preference for a new and less restrictive standard of review in abortion cases, although without clarifying its implications. Regulation that does not "unduly" burden abortion will survive judicial scrutiny, she wrote in HODGSON V. MINNESOTA (1990). This may well be the last decision to leave *Roe*'s holding in place. What seems unlikely is that *Griswold* or *Eisenstadt* will be reversed. Indeed, many would foresee the likelihood of an extension of privacy protections to homosexuals as inescapable, however conservative the Court. If so, cultural acceptance may ultimately prove more crucial in constitutional debate than the conclusions of scholarship or formal argument.

Similarly, the right to die as an aspect of privacy, liberty, or both, seems at this point to have secured its toehold in constitutional law. Like sexual privacy at the time of *Griswold,* this right remains uncertain in scope and definition, and the concept at work—once we move beyond a narrow statement of the right to refuse treatment—is both elastic and ambiguous. But these are not fatal intellectual flaws in constitutional law. Privacy, like many legal concepts, is not so much a philosophical conception as a practical one, more readily identified by its messy precedents than by its tidy definition.

TOM GERETY
(1992)

Bibliography

BAKER, RICHARD ALLAN   1989   The Senate of the United States: "Supreme Executive Council of the Nation," 1787–1800. *Prologue* 21:299–313.

BICKFORD, CHARLENE BANGS and BOWLING, KENNETH R.   1989 *Birth of the Nation: The First Federal Congress 1789–1791.* Madison, Wis.: Madison House.

BOWLING, KENNETH R.   1968   Politics in the First Congress 1789–1791. Ph.D. diss., University of Wisconsin.

SILBEY, JOEL H.   1987   "Our Successors Will Have an Easier Task": The First Congress Under the Constitution, 1789–1791. *This Constitution* 17:4–10.

SMOCK, RAYMOND W.   1989   The House of Representatives: First Branch of the New Government. *Prologue* 21:287–297.

RIGHT OF PROPERTY

See: Property Rights

RIGHT OF REVOLUTION

The right of revolution is not a right that is defined and protected by the Constitution but a NATURAL RIGHT. It would be absurd for a constitution to authorize revolutionary challenges to its authority. However, it would not have been absurd for the preamble to the Constitution to have acknowledged the right of revolution, as, for example, the preamble to the PENNSYLVANIA CONSTITUTION of 1776 had done. It was unnecessary to include such an acknowledgment in the Constitution of 1787, for the Constitution did not supplant the DECLARATION OF INDEPENDENCE of 1776, which remained the first organic law of the United States. The "people" who "ordain and establish this Constitution" are the same "people" who in 1776 "assume among the powers of the earth, the separate and equal station to which the Laws of Nature and of Nature's God entitle them." The Declaration, borrowing the reasoning of JOHN LOCKE, succinctly states the American doctrine of the right of revolution:

We hold these truths to be self-evident, that all men are created equal, that they are endowed by their Creator with certain unalienable Rights, that among these are Life, Liberty and the pursuit of Happiness. That to secure these rights, Governments are instituted among Men, deriving their just powers from the consent of the governed, That whenever any Form of Government becomes destructive of these ends, it is the Right of the People to alter or abolish it, and to institute new Government, laying its foundation on such principles and organizing its powers in such form, as to them shall seem most likely to effect their Safety and Happiness. Prudence, indeed, will dictate that Governments long established should not be changed for light and transient causes; and accordingly all experience hath shown, that mankind are more disposed to suffer, while evils are sufferable, than to right themselves by abolishing the forms to which they are accustomed. But when a long train of abuses and usurpations, pursuing invariably the same Object evinces a design to reduce them under absolute Despotism, it is their right, it is their duty, to throw off such Government, and to provide new Guards for their future security.

Recognition of the right of revolution is, in this view, implicit in the recognition of human equality. A people who recognize that they are equal members of the same species—that no human being is the natural ruler of another—accept that the inequalities necessarily involved in government are not natural but must be "instituted" and operated by "consent"; and that the primary end of government is not the promotion of the interests of one allegedly superior class of human beings but the security of all citizens' equal rights to "life, liberty, and the pursuit of happiness." It follows that it is the right and the duty of such a people to change their government when it persistently fails to effect this end. This right and duty, the Declaration says, belongs not to all peoples but only to those enlightened peoples who recognize human equality and natural rights, and who will therefore exercise their revolutionary right to establish right-securing government by consent.

Not only the revolutionaries of 1776 but also the Framers of the Constitution of 1787 justified their actions on this basis. In THE FEDERALIST #40 and #43 JAMES MADISON cites the Declaration's right of revolution to explain and to support the revolutionary proposals of the CONSTITUTIONAL CONVENTION. Madison argues that political leadership (by patriots like those assembled in Philadelphia) is needed in a revolution because "it is impossible for the people spontaneously and universally to move in concert towards their object." Thus, while the right of revolution is justly exercised when an enlightened people feel and judge that their government threatens to lead them back into an anarchical state of nature by failing to fulfill the duties they have entrusted to it, a revolution need neither wait for nor involve an anarchical disruption of society. However, exercise of the right of revolution (in contrast to mere CIVIL DISOBEDIENCE) can well necessitate and justify war. Those who exercise the right of revolution must prudently measure their forces.

ALEXANDER HAMILTON, in *The Federalist* #16, acknowledged that no constitution can guarantee that a widespread revolutionary opposition to the government will never occur; such opposition might well proceed "from weighty causes of discontent given by the government" itself. In contrast to Marxist doctrines of revolution, the American doctrine does not anticipate a future in which the right of revolution can safely disappear. It is therefore a cause for concern that today the right of revolution is obscured not only because it is a natural rather than a constitutional right but also because natural rights are no longer generally recognized by political theorists and jurists.

JOHN ZVESPER
(1986)

Bibliography

MANSFIELD, HARVEY C., JR. 1978 *The Spirit of Liberalism.* Cambridge, Mass.: Harvard University Press.
STOURZH, GERALD 1970 *Alexander Hamilton and the Idea of Republican Government.* Stanford, Calif.: Stanford University Press.

RIGHT OF REVOLUTION
(Update)

The original entry in this encyclopedia argues that, although the right of revolution may be a NATURAL RIGHT, it cannot be a constitutional right, because it would be illogical for a constitution to sanction a revolt against its own authority. This argument has been common in American history: among others, ABRAHAM LINCOLN (in his First Inaugural Address) and the Supreme Court, in DENNIS V. UNITED STATES (1951), both subscribed to it. Yet this argument rests on a quite narrow definition of revolution, as an insurrection against the fundamental legal order entrenched in the Constitution. A different, and perhaps more common, definition of revolution would refer to any armed uprising against a sitting government. So defined, a right of revolution could indeed be a constitutional right. Sitting governments sometimes defend the constitutional order, but sometimes they seek to subvert it. Under the latter circumstances, revolutionary movements may arise to conserve and protect the constitutional order against the assault of a lawless government. A constitution could—with perfect logical consistency— guarantee a right of revolution for such "conservative" movements. These revolutions seek to overthrow, not the Constitution, but a government that itself seeks to overthrow the constitutional order.

Throughout American history, revolutionary movements have sought to portray themselves as "conservative" constitutionalists. Many of the leaders of the American War for Independence maintained that they were merely protecting the ancient British constitution against parliamentary and monarchical innovation. In the late twentieth century, leaders of the MODERN MILITIA movement claim to be the intellectual heirs of PATRICK HENRY and THOMAS JEFFERSON, protecting the Constitution against a federal government run amok. Whatever their other weaknesses, these claims are not conceptually incoherent: the American constitution could guarantee a right of revolution without logical inconsistency.

Yet although the Constitution could protect such a right, it is a different, and very controversial, question whether it actually does so. The most obvious and popular possible location for a constitutional right of revolution is the SECOND AMENDMENT, which provides: "A well regulated Militia, being necessary to the security of a free State, the right of the people to keep and bear Arms, shall not be infringed." The meaning of this provision is today intensely contested. One school of thought, the individual rights view, holds that the amendment protects the right of individuals to own private arms so as to, inter alia, resist a tyrannical government. The other main school of thought, the STATES' RIGHTS view, maintains that the amendment protects the right of the states to arm their militias (currently, the state National Guards) as a check on federal power; for some in this school, this checking function apparently includes the ability to resist federal tyranny by force of arms. The principal disagreement between these two schools, then, concerns who possesses the constitutional right to arms to resist government— individuals or collective organizations under state control.

This commentator takes an intermediate position: The amendment protects the right of the American people as an organic whole to own arms so as to make a revolution against tyrannical government. The possessors of Second Amendment rights thus have both individual and collective aspects: They are neither state militias nor disconnected individuals but individual members of a highly unified, revolutionary people. If such a people does not exist, neither can the right to arms for revolutionary purposes; under such circumstances, armed insurrection would constitute not a revolution but vicious civil war. The drafters of the Second Amendment realized that revolutions work as a check on government only when the citizenry is highly unified and homogeneous. When it is not, revolutions tend to become either authoritarian and oppressive or anarchical and oppressive. Under such circumstances, the normal processes of electoral politics and JUDICIAL REVIEW are better checks against tyranny; revolutions eliminate one form of tyranny merely to install another. Even under conditions of disunity, individuals may possess a natural right to arms so as to resist oppression, but the drafters of the Second Amendment sought to protect a constitutional right to arms only for a united people. Because the American citizenry may have since ceased to be such a people, the Second Amendment's revolutionary aspects may also have since ceased to have real meaning.

In short, then, there is fairly broad agreement that originally, one purpose of the Second Amendment was to guarantee a right of someone (individuals, militias, a people) to own arms so as to resist some level (state, federal) of government if it should become tyrannous. (This agreement is, however, not unanimous: A very few would read the amendment as an essentially symbolic statement without any substantive impact). Yet that agreement demonstrates only that the Constitution protects a right to own arms, not that the Constitution directly protects a right of revolution. That distinction, although subtle, is meaningful, for the following reason. It would be possible to read the Constitution's approach to the right of revolution in either of two ways. First, the Constitution might guarantee

a right to arms for revolution, but might not protect the right of revolution itself, because once the revolution has commenced, the nation has been plunged into a state of nature and so the constitutional order has been suspended. In this view, although the right to arms may be constitutional, the right of revolution is only a natural right. Accordingly, once the revolution begins, it ceases to be governed by constitutional norms but instead must look to some extraconstitutional body of standards for its goals and methods. Even in this view, the Constitution indirectly or implicitly recognizes a right of revolution; it does not, however, supply the source of that right nor limit its goals or methods. Alternatively, the Constitution might protect both a right to arms and a right to revolution. Citizens own arms so that they might make a "conservative" revolution dedicated to preserving the fabric of the existing Constitution. Such revolutionary movements are therefore sharply limited by the Constitution itself: They must seek only to restore the Constitution, not some new system of government, and they must honor the Constitution's norms during the conduct of the revolution itself.

A constitutional revolution and a revolution based on natural right are therefore, conceptually, quite different. In practice, however, it is very difficult to determine which sort of revolution was contemplated by the drafters of the Second Amendment, because the drafters themselves failed to explore the distinction. In all likelihood, the reason for this failure lies in their immediate historical experience. The drafters of the amendment doubtless looked to the American Revolution as their paradigm of a legitimate revolution. The makers of the American Revolution themselves freely mixed constitutional and natural law defenses of resistance to Great Britain. Sometimes, especially early in the resistance, they claimed merely to be protecting the British constitution; at other times, as in the DECLARATION OF INDEPENDENCE itself, they claimed to be exercising their natural right of revolution to defend their other natural rights. In general, as time went on, the revolutionaries came to rely less on constitutional arguments and more on natural law arguments; over the years, their goals grew from the relatively modest desire of reinstating the ancient constitution as they understood it to completely remodeling their government according to principles of natural justice. Later American resistance movements have generally followed the same path of freely mixing constitutional and natural law defenses of the right of revolution.

In theory, then, the American Constitution could, without logical inconsistency, protect a right of revolution, but in practice, American revolutionaries have not sharply distinguished between constitutional and natural law rights of revolution. It is important to note that this failure to distinguish does not clearly indicate that there is no free-standing constitutional right of revolution (nor does it clearly indicate that there is one); rather, it suggests merely that Americans have tended to draw simultaneously on both the Constitution and natural law in justifying their revolutions. This simultaneous reliance grows naturally from the fact that Americans have often claimed that the primary content of their Constitution is natural law itself. In short, then, American constitutional argumentation has not clearly resolved or even seriously addressed whether the right of revolution is a constitutional right or only a natural right. Instead, American revolutionaries have defended their revolutions as rooted in both natural and constitutional law, and opponents of those revolutions have denounced them as rooted in neither.

DAVID C. WILLIAMS
(2000)

Bibliography

EHRMAN, KEITH A. and HENNIGAN, DENNIS A. 1989 The Second Amendment in the Twentieth Century: Have You Seen Your Militia Lately? *University of Dayton Law Review* 15:5–58.

LEVINSON, SANFORD 1989 The Embarrassing Second Amendment. *Yale Law Journal* 99:637–659.

MAIER, PAULINE 1972 *From Resistance to Revolution.* New York: Random House.

WILLIAMS, DAVID C. 1997 The Constitutional Right to "Conservative" Revolution. *Harvard Civil Rights-Civil Liberties Law Review* 32:415–447.

——— 1991 Civic Republicanism and the Citizen Militia: The Terrifying Second Amendment. *Yale Law Journal* 101:551–615.

WOOD, GORDON S. 1969 *The Creation of the American Republic, 1776–1787.* New York: W. W. Norton.

RIGHT–PRIVILEGE DISTINCTION

There are at least two ways of distinguishing between "privileges" and "rights" in the context of American constitutional law and history, and careful analysis does not confound the two. The text of the Constitution refers to both privileges and rights, and uses "privileges" as a term of art denoting a class of rights that may be invoked defensively, to excuse one from a legal restraint or obligation. In another usage, privileges have both an inferior status to and a less permanent existence than rights, being subject to revocation by the government or to the imposition of conditions on their exercise. There is no foundation in the Constitution for the latter distinction.

In the Constitution, a privilege is one kind of right. The word privilege appears four times. The first appearance is in the PRIVILEGE FROM ARREST in civil cases enjoyed by members of Congress during congressional sessions. The second appearance is the guarantee of the "privilege of

the writ of HABEAS CORPUS," yet that "privilege" has at least as great a degree of status and permanence as any right in the Constitution. The other appearances are in the PRIVILEGES AND IMMUNITIES clauses of Article IV and of the FOURTEENTH AMENDMENT: the citizens of each state are entitled to the privileges and immunities of citizens in the several states; and no state may abridge the privileges or immunities of citizens of the United States.

Privileges are associated with, but are distinct from, immunities. A privilege is an exemption from a legal restraint or duty (such as the duty to testify in court), while an immunity is an exemption from liability (usually civil liability). Thus members of Congress are privileged from arrest and immune from having to answer in another place for their SPEECH OR DEBATE. The way in which the word is used in the Constitution suggests that a privilege is a kind of right distinguished not by revocability or conditionability but by the fact that it cannot be asserted until some authority has taken action against one. One can exercise the right of RELIGIOUS LIBERTY or the right of peaceable assembly on one's own initiative; but one cannot demand that the state show cause for holding one in jail until one is actually held, and one cannot refuse to answer questions until questions are asked. A constitutional privilege is defensive, but it may be asserted as of right. Thus there is not necessarily a diminution of the RIGHT AGAINST SELF-INCRIMINATION when that right is called a privilege.

The word "right," standing alone, along with the word "freedom" and the phrase "right of the people," is used in the Constitution to designate a right that one may assert affirmatively and which the government is precluded from invading. Among these are NATURAL RIGHTS, which antedate the Constitution, such as the FREEDOM OF SPEECH, the right of the people to keep and bear arms, and the right of the people to be secure in their persons, houses, papers, and effects. Another category of constitutional rights comprises procedural rights, both civil and criminal.

Precise usage of constitutional terms is hampered by an unfortunate rhetorical use of the terms "right" and "privilege." Even JAMES MADISON seems, on occasion, to have used "privilege" to mean a special boon conferred by authority and subject to revocation at the pleasure of the grantor. Subsequently, because the power to revoke a right includes the power to impose conditions upon its exercise, "privilege" came, in certain rhetorical circumstances, to stand for rights that were conditionable.

This rhetorical use of "right" and "privilege" was introduced into American public law by OLIVER WENDELL HOLMES. Writing as a justice of the Massachusetts Supreme Judicial Court, Holmes commented in 1892 on the freedom of speech of PUBLIC EMPLOYEES: "The petitioner may have the constitutional right to talk politics, but he has no constitutional right to be a policeman." Public employ-

ment was, for Holmes, not a right but a privilege. In GOLD-
BERG V. KELLY (1970) the Supreme Court stated that it had
abandoned the right-privilege distinction. WELFARE BENE-
FITS might be a privilege, in the sense that the state could
constitutionally abolish a welfare program, but a particular
beneficiary's benefits could not be terminated except by
procedures that satisfied the requirements of PROCEDURAL
DUE PROCESS.

Similarly, the federal courts today interpret the FIRST
AMENDMENT to protect public employees against at least
some restrictions on their constitutional freedoms. Government, the Court has said, "may not deny a benefit to a
person because he exercises a Constitutional right." Yet
rights—even First Amendment rights—are defined more
narrowly for public employees than they are for others, as
the validation of the HATCH ACT demonstrated. (See UN-
CONSTITUTIONAL CONDITIONS.)

In recent years the Court has erected new barriers to
the invocation of the right to procedural due process, requiring that a claimant establish deprivation of a liberty
or property interest before due process even becomes an
issue and paying considerable deference to state law in
defining both types of interest. In refusing to characterize
some important interests as liberty or property, the Court
has relegated those interests to an inferior status. Thus
the Holmesian right-privilege distinction, once abandoned, has been welcomed home in new clothes.

DENNIS J. MAHONEY
KENNETH L. KARST
(1986)

Bibliography

HOHFELD, WESLEY N.   1923   *Fundamental Legal Conceptions.*
New Haven, Conn.: Yale University Press.

MONAGHAN, HENRY P.   1977   Of "Liberty" and "Property." *Cornell Law Review* 62:401–444.

VAN ALSTYNE, WILLIAM W.   1968   The Demise of the Right-Privilege Distinction in Constitutional Law. *Harvard Law Review*
81:1439–1464.

———   1977   Cracks in "The New Property." *Cornell Law Review* 62:445–493.

RIGHTS ISSUES IN
HISTORICAL PERSPECTIVE

Rights conflicts begin in legally constituted relationships
that produce roles or identities. Typical relationships include ruler–ruled, husband–wife, master–servant, property owner–government, employer–employee, parent–
child, and landlord–tenant. A claim to rights often requires a prior self-recognition of one's status, for example,
as a wife, servant, property owner, or parent. Throughout

American history, many rights claimants may simply have
meant to secure from courts or other legal institutions
what they were entitled to, within the received terms of
traditional COMMON LAW relationships. But by the middle
years of the nineteenth century, claimants also drew from
the Constitution a variety of rhetorical tools that allowed
them to claim "rights" to change or destroy established
relationships, to free themselves.

Traditional relational identities developed on the terrain of legal DOCTRINES that extended back before American history, often to medieval English law. In legal
relationships, rights were a resource over which combat-
ants struggled. Sometimes a right asserted by the one
meant the other possessed no right. If I owned land, you
either were on my land by permission or you were a tres-
passer. As often, or as likely, a right asserted meant someone else had a corresponding duty. If I owned land, the
government's agents, the police, had a duty to arrest trespassers. If I owned a factory, the government owed me an
INJUNCTION to prevent the union from achieving its aims
by interfering with what I regarded as my rights. A husband's rights, within a regime of common law coverture,
implied a wife's duty to obey. A wife's rights, within the
same regime, identified a husband's duty to support.

In order to assert a right, a claimant had to understand
herself as within a relationship. But often the claimant's
understanding of the relationship deviated from established legal identities. From the early years in the nineteenth century, for example, many mothers drew from the
wider culture a sense of themselves as rightful caretakers
of their children. But their understanding had no connection to the established law of child custody. Prior to the
middle of the nineteenth century, mothers had no right to
custody. Husband-fathers alone had that right, a right they
could lose only by misconduct. Married mothers, by contrast, were, in WILLIAM BLACKSTONE's phrase, entitled only
to "reverence and respect." And even when a father lost
his right, there was no legal reason why a mother would
necessarily gain it.

Litigants struggled over the terms of their relational
identities on doctrinal terrain filled with contradictory understandings and incoherencies. Different judges emphasized different aspects of the same rules, interpreted them
in widely differing ways, made the simple complex. Moreover, American history in all its cultural and economic and
political dimensions constantly pulled at received legal expectations. A country founded on a revolt of sons against
a parental nation would not look at parents and see absolute rights holders. Although the inherited law of MAR-
RIAGE included a duty on the part of wives to live within
their husband's household, no American court ever enforced a husband's right to "recapture" his wife. By the
1840s, mothers often triumphed over fathers in custody

disputes, even though mothers still had no legal "right" to custody.

Over a long period that began in the eighteenth century, contractually constituted identities replaced many received relational hierarchies founded in custom, established religion, common law, or statute. In nineteenth-century America, the diverse and manifold identities of servants, a few understood as "casual" laborers, far more as "domestic" servants located in household relationships, merged together into the new contractually constituted "worker" or "employee." In the late twentieth century, marital rights and identities that were once understood as fixed and noncontractual became contractualized and negotiable. The magic of contract law often re-created threatened hierarchies—famously so, in the workplace. But throughout American history, this shift from status to contract was usually understood by commentators and litigants alike as weakening established legal identities.

American FEDERALISM further weakened the capacity of law to enforce identities. Most identities were founded in laws and practices made in the states. But the states were part of a country where multiple jurisdictions made laws, but none of them had the capacity to compel loyalty and submission. Husbands may have owed a theoretically inescapable duty of support to their wives, but in America it was so very easy to leave and abandon, to go elsewhere. And the knowledge that exit was easy shaped the laws in the various states and shaped the conduct of many caught up in received identities. CORPORATIONS were always subject to the regulatory and POLICE POWER of the state. But in the real world of American capitalism, corporations could always leave, and take their wealth and jobs and taxes elsewhere.

By the middle years of the nineteenth century, many Americans imagined their core rights as rooted less in positive law and established relationships, and more in an identity freed from dyadic relationships. Freed slaves insisted on what one planter identified as their "wild notions of rights and freedom." The woman's rights activist ELIZABETH CADY STANTON wrote of "the inalienable right of all to be happy." Autonomy, the capacity of the free individual to imagine and realize a personal future not defined by prescriptive relationships, became a root value.

After the CIVIL WAR emancipatory visions of NATURAL RIGHTS came to be identified with a few phrases in the federal Constitution—primarily portions of the BILL OF RIGHTS and the RECONSTRUCTION amendments—and with the first two sentences of the DECLARATION OF INDEPENDENCE. Those phrases carried meanings that would have surprised their authors. Rights claimants read subversive and disruptive and utopian messages in the texts, drawing on diverse and contradictory sources, including English common law, liberal political thought, Enlightenment phi-

losophy, post-Reformation theology, the medieval peasant's vision of self-ownership and freedom, and, above all else, the emergent understanding that a legitimate political order had to be one that destroyed the BADGES OF SERVITUDE. The identification of constitutional language with emancipatory aspirations apparently resulted from the happenstance that a moral critique of SLAVERY and a celebration of the virtues of free LABOR developed contemporaneously with American constitutionalism. The exaltation of freedom required the antithesis of enslavement. Nearly all of the varying meanings derived from the phrase "EQUAL PROTECTION OF THE LAWS" were rooted in contending visions of what was overthrown with the end of American chattel slavery, understood as a long-standing and established legally constituted relationship.

Rights litigants transformed core phrases of the federal Constitution into critical tools, ways to challenge vested and received relational identities. Long-standing legal powers were recast as violating constitutional rights. The police power—the state's capacity to protect the "health" of the community—had long justified laws against MISCEGENATION and other restrictions on marital capacity. But through the lens of constitutional rights consciousness, such powers became suspect, even if supported by political majorities. One should not have to understand oneself as guilty of "illicit intercourse" when one knew oneself as married. Nor should one who engaged in homosexual sexual practices have to know himself as a criminal sodomite. Federal judicial authority, within the limits of the STATE ACTION requirement of the FOURTEENTH AMENDMENT, became, at least potentially, a continuing challenge to relationships founded in state law.

Because constitutional texts had to be reinterpreted to do the work of divesting relational identities, and because that work had to be done by judges and other legal actors with differing capacities and agendas, meanings of rights always remained ambiguous. Litigants may have wanted to destroy vested structures that imposed and reinforced subordination. But often even the language of victory was muffled and confused. The idea of a "colorblind" Constitution that the NAACP LEGAL & EDUCATIONAL DEFENSE FUND drew out of the first Justice JOHN MARSHALL HARLAN's DISSENTING OPINION in PLESSY V. FERGUSON (1896) and that triumphed in BROWN V. BOARD OF EDUCATION (1954) was intended as a constitutional challenge to racial subordination and white hegemony. Yet the demand for absolute government neutrality between the races became the foundation for "reverse discrimination" arguments made by white men who feared losses when African Americans and other persons of color gained from the destruction of previous hierarchies. Always there lurked a variety of rhetorical moves that allowed courts to re-create traditional relational identities. Homosexual sodomy remained subject to state proscription, not a constitutionally protected private right. Constitutional rights only occasionally triumphed over traditional state powers and practices; nor did they often destroy traditional VESTED RIGHTS and identities. There was always some plausibility to the claim that a commitment to change through constitutional rights assertions was a form of false consciousness, that faith in constitutional change was a diversion of human and moral capital away from serious political struggle.

The significance of rights disputes for American CONSTITUTIONAL HISTORY lay less in the victories than in the faith diverse Americans invested in constitutional language. For many, hopes became identified with constitutionalism: the hope of an end to ascribed identities, the hope of change to mere law and merely vested rights and to conventional practices, the hope for newly recognized rights. The power of the faith in emancipatory textual meanings sometimes survived a generation or several generations of contrary constitutional doctrine. Rights consciousness undercut and challenged the structures that created and reinforced vested rights and identities, including received constitutional doctrine. And out of faith and hope survived the promise of a democratic constitutionalism; of a society in which all participated as destroyers and creators of constitutional order.

HENDRIK HARTOG
(2000)

Bibliography

CLARK, ELIZABETH B. 1995 "The Sacred Rights of the Weak": Pain, Sympathy, and the Culture of Individual Rights in Antebellum America. *Journal of American History* 82:463–493.

SMITH, ROGERS M. 1997 *Civic Ideals: Conflicting Visions of Citizenship in U.S. History.* New Haven, Conn.: Yale University Press.

TEN BROEK, JACOBUS 1951 *The Antislavery Origins of the Fourteenth Amendment.* Berkeley: University of California Press.

THELEN, DAVID, ed. 1988 *The Constitution and American Life.* Ithaca, N.Y.: Cornell University Press.

TOMLINS, CHRISTOPHER L. 1993 *Law, Labor, and Ideology in the Early American Republic.* New York: Cambridge University Press.

RIGHTS OF THE CRIMINALLY ACCUSED

In criminal prosecutions, the state can bring its authority, organizational power, and resources to bear against individuals. History, particularly precolonial and early colonial English history, demonstrated to the American Revolutionaries that governments could and did use their prosecution powers abusively—to imprison or destroy political enemies, tyrannize or cow populations, and preserve or advance unpopular regimes or policies. For such reasons, the Constitution and BILL OF RIGHTS included provisions restricting governmental use of prosecution powers and granting the criminally accused procedural protection.

Among these are specific denials of governmental authority to take certain kinds of actions, such as constitutional proscriptions on EX POST FACTO LAWS, BILLS OF ATTAINDER, and suspension of HABEAS CORPUS. The Fifth, Sixth, and Eighth Amendments accord the criminally accused specific criminal process rights. In addition, there are criminal process rights and protections mentioned neither in the Constitution nor the Bill of Rights, such as the right of proof of guilt beyond a REASONABLE DOUBT, which the Supreme Court has concluded are necessarily implied from the Constitution, history, and American practice. Finally, the FOURTH AMENDMENT right against unreasonable SEARCHES AND SEIZURES, a right accorded to all persons in the United States, has particular significance and impact in criminal proceedings.

Of principal importance are the criminal defendant's inferred and specifically listed constitutional trial rights. Although not expressly mentioned in the Constitution, first and foremost among these is the right of trial under an *adversary* system of trial. Adversary trial, as opposed to inquisitional trial, was the established form of trial at COMMON LAW, and has always been the American practice—so much so that it has been deemed an essential feature of the Sixth Amendment right to a fair trial. In an inquisitional system of trial, judicial officials take an active role in advancing a prosecution and eliciting facts, and lawyers, or party representatives, play a rather passive role. In contrast, in the adversarial system, the parties to a prosecution, through their attorneys, control the presentation of EVIDENCE, and the judge plays the more passive role of umpire, attempting to insure both a fair contest between the parties and a fair fact determination. Party control of the presentation of evidence significantly enhances its ability to shape evidence to its advantage or to influence the fact finder, particularly in jury trials, where laypersons determine facts and decide questions of criminal responsibility.

Although criminal adversary trial is grounded in a rhetoric of a fair contest between equals as a way to accord both fairness to defendants and to discover truth, adversary trial actually has an asymmetric structure in which the prosecution has greater burdens and obligations than the defense. In particular, the prosecution has the burden of presenting a prima facie case against a defendant—the burden of proving guilt beyond a reasonable doubt—and an obligation to disclose to the defense evidence favorable to the defendant and material relevant to issues of guilt or punishment.

Although rarely considered to be a right of the accused,

the government's burden of first presentation of evidence does confer potential strategic or tactical advantages on the defense in a criminal case. Knowing the specific nature of the prosecution's case, the defense can shape its own proofs for greatest benefit. Similarly, the prosecution's burden of proving guilt beyond a reasonable doubt, which the Supreme Court held in *In re Winship* (1970) to be a constitutional requirement, is, in effect, a defendant's right to require the government to prove guilt to a substantial certainty. This high burden inhibits the government from bringing or winning prosecutions based on weak evidence, and precludes the use of evidentiary presumptions that might favor it.

The prosecution also has a duty to disclose evidence. This requirement, which is derived from DUE PROCESS fairness considerations, insures there is no miscarriage of justice through failure to disclose evidence bearing on guilt. There is, however, no reciprocal, counterpart defense duty to disclose evidence favorable to the prosecution. With narrow exception, the Court has interpreted the requirements of adversary trial and the Fifth Amendment RIGHT AGAINST SELF-INCRIMINATION to prohibit the government from requiring the defense to provide evidence to the prosecution or otherwise to assist it in its case.

Adversary trial, as now understood, also assumes attorney representatives for each party, and the Court has interpreted the Sixth Amendment RIGHT TO COUNSEL to guarantee criminal defendants the right to be represented by an attorney at all "critical stages" of a criminal proceeding. This right applies in any case, FELONY or MISDEMEANOR, in which an accused, if convicted, will suffer incarceration as a punishment. A "critical stage" is any occasion, once a criminal prosecution has been initiated, where the state takes action (usually in a proceeding where the defendant is present) that can be adverse to the defendant's interests in not being incarcerated or convicted. In addition, in the famous case of MIRANDA V. ARIZONA (1966), the Supreme Court held that criminal suspects in custody have a right to consult with counsel, if they wish, before speaking with police.

Criminal defendants have a right to representation by counsel of their choice if they can afford it or to appointed counsel if they cannot. The Sixth Amendment, however, also implies a right of self-representation, and the criminally accused may represent themselves if they knowingly and intelligently choose to do so.

The right to counsel when there is attorney representation also entails a right to "effective" assistance of counsel, that is, counsel generally competent to handle a criminal case, actually making decisions of a kind that competent criminal-trial attorneys would make, and not suffering from any conflict of interest that would impair or bias the representation. Finally, in the case of the INDIGENT, the right to effective assistance of counsel combined with the more general right to a FAIR TRIAL may also require some state financial assistance in investigating or presenting a case, for example, payment of expert-witness fees.

The Sixth Amendment also accords a criminally accused the right to an impartial jury. TRIAL BY JURY is of particular importance because jurors are laypersons from the community, not governmental functionaries, and independent jury decision making in criminal cases can provide further protection against possible governmental overreaching. The Court has interpreted the jury-trial right to apply in prosecutions for all crimes except petty offenses, the latter defined as those punishable by no more than six months in prison and a $500 fine. This right includes the right to a PETIT JURY selected from a larger group of persons, called the jury venire, which is cross-sectionally representative of the community.

Federal criminal juries must be composed of twelve persons and return unanimous verdicts. The Court has, however, interpreted the jury-trial requirement as applied to the states through FOURTEENTH AMENDMENT due process to permit state criminal trial juries with as few as six members, but no fewer, that number being thought sufficiently large to provide the benefits of representativeness and of group deliberation. Similarly, the Court has concluded that state criminal trial juries, at least where there is a twelve-person jury, require only a substantial majority, rather than unanimity, to convict.

Criminal defendants have Sixth Amendment rights to confront and cross-examine witnesses. The right to CONFRONTATION is essentially a right to have the witnesses against the accused to appear in open court to make a face-to-face accusation, a requirement thought to enhance the reliability of witness statements. The associated right of cross-examination is in effect the right to test both the witness and his or her testimony in open court before the fact finder. With few exceptions, these rights entail that where a witness against the defendant is available, the government must produce that witness in court, rather than use previously recorded statements of the witness. In addition, the state may not impose rules restricting the defense's relevant cross-examination of a testifying witness.

The Sixth Amendment also gives criminal defendants the right to COMPULSORY PROCESS to require the attendance at trial of witnesses in their behalf. This right is obviously important where a defendant has witnesses who could testify favorably, but are unwilling to appear in court. The right, however, is also read as a general right to present evidence in one's behalf and thus operates to prohibit states from restricting the defendant's presentation of relevant and generally reliable evidence. For example, when a state rule of HEARSAY evidence operates to exclude from a criminal trial trustworthy evidence that may be favorable to the defendant, the right to present evidence would override this rule.

Finally, the Sixth Amendment confers on criminal defendants rights to a SPEEDY TRIAL and a PUBLIC TRIAL. Defendants may desire speedy trials so they do not languish in jail or to quickly resolve the criminal accusation. Yet criminal defendants often seek to delay a criminal trial, either because they are not prepared or because they perceive some advantage in delay, such as the fading of witnesses' memories. For such reasons, the Court has held that delay in coming to trial does not of itself violate the speedy-trial right. Instead, the Court uses a multifactor BALANCING TEST to determine when the right was violated. This test considers the length of delay, the government's reasons for it, the defendant's assertion or waiver of his or her speedy-trial right, and the actual prejudice to the defendant. This test obviously gives little guidance, and it is apparent that even quite long delays of years may not trigger the right. In contrast, it is necessary to note that the government also has an interest in speedy trials and that both state and federal governments have statutes regulating trial delay. Because of such statutes, the speedy-trial right as a control over the timing of trials has receded far into the background.

The public-trial right protects defendants from unfair or abusive trials by ensuring that trials are open to public scrutiny. However, although defendants may demand that their trial be open to the public, they do not have a right to close their trial without a showing of real necessity. The Court has concluded that the FIRST AMENDMENT free-speech and free-press guarantees entail public and press access to criminal trials so that the public can remain informed regarding the administration of criminal justice. Because criminal trials are presumptively open and only a weighty justification can justify closure, a defendant's public-trial right no longer retains much practical importance.

The Fifth Amendment provides three additional rights for the criminally accused: the right to INDICTMENT by GRAND JURY, the right against self-incrimination, and the protection against DOUBLE JEOPARDY. In theory, the grand jury acts as a check on governmental prosecution by committing the decision to indict a person of a crime to a group of ordinary citizens rather than vesting it in state officials. In practice, however, grand juries rarely operate independently of the prosecutors' offices providing them with information and guidance. Consequently, grand juries do not in fact constitute any significant check on criminal charging. Furthermore, the Supreme Court has not required the states to indict by grand jury. Although many states nonetheless use grand juries, state prosecutors generally are also free to charge persons by information, that is, a charging paper issuing solely from the prosecutor's office rather than from the grand jury.

The right against self-incrimination, which is the right to refuse to give evidence against oneself, however, does play an important role in criminal justice. The right protects a criminal defendant from governmental compulsion to speak, an abusive practice common in England in pre-colonial and early colonial history. In a criminal trial it amounts to a defendant's right to remain silent and not to take the stand to testify. Because comment by the prosecution on a defendant's refusal to testify—by claiming the refusal evidences guilt—might bring pressure on a defendant to testify, the Court has also held that prosecution comment on a defendant's silence violates the privilege.

More important, the right against self-incrimination now plays a critical role in analyzing and resolving issues regarding POLICE INTERROGATIONS of suspects, which results in confessions or inculpatory statements. Originally, the Court viewed Fifth and Fourteenth Amendment due process as requiring the state accord a suspect "fundamental fairness." The Court found police coercion of confessions or incriminating statements inhumane and unfair, forbade such practices, and barred the prosecution's use of such material in criminal trials whenever the defendant's statements were deemed involuntary. For various reasons, the voluntariness test proved unsatisfactory and unworkable. Police forces continued to use questionable techniques in seeking confessions and resorted to deceptive or progressively more subtle, yet nonetheless manipulative or abusive, interrogation practices. Finally, the Court took a major step to solve the general police-interrogation problem, and in *Miranda v. Arizona* held the right against self-incrimination applicable outside the context of a trial. Specifically, the Court held that when police conduct a custodial interrogation of a suspect they must respect the suspect's right to remain silent and cannot interrogate him or her if he or she does not knowingly, intelligently, and voluntarily agree to the interrogation. In *Miranda* the Court also concluded that the right of a criminal suspect to consult with counsel before speaking to police was essential to protect the suspect's right to remain silent if he or she chose to exercise it. Consequently, *Miranda* also held that when a suspect asks to speak with an attorney, all interrogation must cease until the suspect has consulted with an attorney or appropriately waived his or her right to do so. To insure that suspects understood their rights and could invoke them, *Miranda* further required police to give suspects they arrest or hold a set of "*Miranda*" warnings. These advise suspects of their right to silence, that their statements may be used against them, and that they have a right to an attorney appointed free of charge if necessary.

The Fifth Amendment further protects criminal defendants from double jeopardy, that is, from multiple prosecutions for the same offense by the same jurisdiction or for reprosecutions for the same offense after acquittal or conviction. Disallowing multiple or successive prosecutions, this clause prevents the government from rehearsing its proofs to perfect them and from persecuting or exhausting individuals through repeated efforts to convict. The double-jeopardy clause applies once the state places the accused in "jeopardy," which occurs in a jury trial when the jury is empaneled and sworn and in a trial to a judge when the first witness is sworn. Before these events, although the state may be advancing a criminal case against an individual, jeopardy is not thought to "have attached," and dismissals during this period do not bar the refiling of charges or a subsequent prosecution. The clause also does not bar reprosecutions where a convicted person has had his or her conviction overturned on grounds other than the insufficiency of the evidence to convict.

The double-jeopardy clause does not prohibit different "sovereigns" from prosecuting for the same offense. As many criminal offenses violate both state and federal law—for example, bank robbery—multiple prosecutions for the same offense are possible. As a matter of policy, however, federal and state prosecutors usually decline to prosecute an individual for the same offense when the other sovereign has prosecuted.

The Fourth Amendment protects all persons, not just the criminally accused, from UNREASONABLE SEARCHES and seizures. As a practical matter, however, it has special application in criminal prosecutions because, when the government unlawfully searches or seizes from one whom it criminally charges, the remedy that the courts apply is the exclusion of the evidence unlawfully taken from that person's criminal trial.

In general, exclusion of evidence is the remedy courts apply to governmental violations of a defendant's Fourth, Fifth, or Sixth Amendment rights that result in evidence that the government seeks to use against the defendant at trial. This might occur when the government unlawfully searches and seizes, coerces a confession or statement from a person or obtains statements in violation of the MIRANDA RULES, or improperly obtains evidence through violation of a suspect's or accused's Sixth Amendment right to counsel. There has been considerable debate as to whether an accused in any of these situations has a *constitutional right* to have such evidence excluded or exclusion of evidence is simply a default remedy applied in the absence of any other effective sanction for the violation of constitutional rights. If there is no constitutional right to exclusion, the government could avoid the exclusion of evidence by providing other remedies for rights violations, at least where the remedies were thought to constitute sanctions as effective as exclusion. As a practical matter,

however, neither the federal nor state governments have provided equally effective remedies, and courts and commentators continue to speak of an accused's "right" to have unlawfully obtained evidence excluded.

The Eighth Amendment proscribes excessive BAIL and CRUEL AND UNUSUAL PUNISHMENT. Under Supreme Court decisions applying the bail clause, an accused does not necessarily have the right to be released on bail. The Court has held that the excessive-bail provision prohibits bails set at a figure higher than an amount reasonably calculated to insure that the accused will make his or her necessary appearances in criminal proceedings and will submit to sentence if found guilty. However, the Court has also upheld PREVENTIVE DETENTION statutes under which persons shown to be dangerous to others if released may be denied bail.

The Eighth Amendment's cruel and unusual punishment clause applies both to capital and noncapital punishments. Strictly speaking, the clause protects the convicted, not the accused, but its importance to an accused's prospects of punishment warrants its inclusion here. The Court has held CAPITAL PUNISHMENT cruel and unusual when it is applied arbitrarily, irrationally, or discriminatorily or when it is seriously disproportionate to the offense committed. With regard to noncapital punishments, the Court has held that the clause prohibits punishments that involve torture or the unjustifiable infliction of involuntary pain. It has also applied the clause to strike down confinements whose length or conditions are disproportionate to the crime or that involve serious deprivations of a prisoner's basic human needs (such as failure to provide medical care) and punishments involving loss of CITIZENSHIP for status.

GARY GOODPASTER
(1992)

Bibliography

DAMASKA, MIRJAN 1975 Presentation of Evidence and Fact-finding Precision. *University of Pennsylvania Law Review* 123:1038–1106.
———— 1983 The Adversary System. In Kadish, Sanford, ed. *Encyclopedia of Crime and Justice.* Vol. 1, pages 24–29. New York: Macmillan and Free Press.
LaFAVE, WAYNE R. and ISRAEL, JEROLD H. 1984 *Criminal Procedure.* 4 Vols. St. Paul, Minn.: West Publishing Co.

RIGHT TO BAIL

See: Bail

RIGHT TO BEAR ARMS

See: Second Amendment

RIGHT TO BE INFORMED OF ACCUSATION

The Sixth Amendment provides that "[i]n all criminal prosecutions, the accused shall enjoy the right . . . to be informed of the nature and cause of the accusation. . . ." The right was recognized in English law prior to adoption of the Constitution and exists today in every state, under state law and through judicial interpretation of the DUE PROCESS clause of the FOURTEENTH AMENDMENT. The notice of accusation contemplated by the Sixth Amendment is the formal charge of crime to which the accused must respond by pleading guilty or not guilty; it does not include the notice issues that may arise in the investigative phase of a criminal proceeding.

The "notice clause" makes no reference to the institution that must produce the charge, the instrument through which notice must be given, or the precise function of the notice. But these details are supplied by other provisions of the Constitution, by history, and by judicial opinions. Where the accused is charged with an infamous federal crime, usually a FELONY, the Fifth Amendment requires that the accusation must be made by the INDICTMENT of a GRAND JURY. For lesser federal crimes, an INFORMATION drafted by a prosecutor or even a complaint will suffice. In the states, any of these processes may be used because indictment by grand jury is not required by the Fourteenth Amendment.

Over the years, the charging instrument has been assigned several roles by the courts. It provides the notice required by the Sixth Amendment, and it assists in enforcing the provisions of the Fifth Amendment dealing with the grand jury, DOUBLE JEOPARDY, and due process. For example, indictments and informations must demonstrate that the offense charged is not the same as one for which the accused has already been placed in jeopardy. And indictments must reflect the decisions of the grand juries that returned them.

The unique function of the Sixth Amendment's notice clause—as distinct from the facilitative role it plays for the Fifth Amendment—is to require advice to the accused of the charge against him so that he may decide whether to concede his guilt or, if he does not, so that he may prepare to defend himself at trial. The notice must also contain enough detail to enable the court to determine whether the charge is sufficient in law to support a conviction. To perform these functions, the notice must state the basic facts regarding each element of the offense with "reasonable particularity of time, place and circumstances." Such notice is especially important in an adversary system that contemplates a trial as a climactic event. Without notice, defendants would find it difficult to proceed expeditiously, and frequent continuances might be necessary; trial judges would have no manageable criterion for determining the relevance of EVIDENCE or the instructions to be given to juries; and appellate courts would have inadequate standards for review.

Few cases have tested the limits of the notice clause, for both the federal government and the states now have statutes or rules of court that define what must appear in the charging instrument and these requirements usually reflect the constitutional standard. For example, Rule 7 of the FEDERAL RULES OF CRIMINAL PROCEDURE requires a "plain, concise and definite written statement of the essential facts constituting the offense charged." There are state decisions, however, that suggest how little might now be constitutionally required of the initial charge in a criminal case. In these cases, state laws authorized indictments that informed defendants only of the names or citations of the statutes they were accused of violating. In *People v. Bogdanoff* (1930) New York's high court upheld the constitutionality of such a "short form indictment." Although the New York statute involved in that case has not survived, the opinion called attention in dramatic fashion to changes that may have made the law of "notice" partially obsolete. The routine maintenance of trial records was said to provide a basis for determining whether a prior proceeding involved the same offense as the one charged in the indictment. And the availability of grand jury minutes made it possible to determine whether the offense charged at trial was the same as the one contemplated by the grand jury. The only interest of the accused remaining to be protected by the charging instrument itself, said the court, was an adequate opportunity to prepare for trial; that interest could be served by a bill of particulars, continuances, and other measures. In sum, the notice clause—stripped of its relation to the jeopardy and grand jury provisions—may be satisfied not only by a single charging document but also by a process of notice that enables the defendant to understand the charge and defend against it.

The logic of a flexible conception of notice, rooted less in form than in concern for the defendant's need to prepare for trial, led inevitably to the position that many defects in the indictment or information—which might have led to dismissal in an earlier, more formalistic period—were now regarded as merely technical. For example, the doctrine of "fatal variance" had prohibited any departure in the course of trial from the offense charged. Such variances are now held to be HARMLESS ERROR so long as the defendant has not been materially prejudiced in making his defense and, if an indictment is involved, the trial falls fairly within the scope of the grand jury's charge.

As the specificity demanded of indictments and informations declined, defendants lost one of the principal means for learning about the prosecution's case in advance of trial. Pleadings in criminal cases had been assimilated to an increasingly liberal law of civil procedure, but those changes had not been accompanied in CRIMINAL PROCEDURE by the pretrial DISCOVERY which had emerged to compensate for looser pleadings in civil cases. Beginning in the 1960s, however, pretrial disclosure of the prosecution's case has become more available to the defendant, some of it mandated by the due process clause. This expansion of the process of notice before and during trial has minimized the problems of law and policy which relatively spare charges might otherwise have presented under the notice clause of the Sixth Amendment.

ABRAHAM S. GOLDSTEIN
(1986)

Bibliography

GOLDSTEIN, ABRAHAM S.   1960   The State and the Accused: Balance of Advantage in Criminal Procedure. *Yale Law Journal* 69:1149, 1172–1180.
SCOTT, AUSTIN, JR.   1982   Fairness in Accusation of Crime. *Minnesota Law Review* 41:509–546.
WRIGHT, CHARLES ALAN   1982   *Federal Practice and Procedure, Criminal*, 2nd ed. Vol. 1, Sections 125–126. St. Paul, Minn.: West Publishing Co.

RIGHT TO CONFRONT WITNESSES

See: Confrontation, Right of

RIGHT TO COUNSEL

The constitutional right to counsel in American law encompasses two broad categories of rights: first, rights of persons to retain and employ counsel in official proceedings and, second, rights of persons who because of financial incapacity or other reasons are unable to procure the assistance of lawyers, to have counsel appointed in their behalf.

The modern rights to counsel are the product of a historical evolution extending over a half-millennium. English criminal procedure in the early modern era diverged sharply from today's institutions of adversary criminal justice. In the Tudor and Stuart regimes, legal proceedings in which the crown's interests were strongly implicated were heavily tilted in favor of the state and against the accused. Thus it was only in the least serious cases, those involving MISDEMEANORS, that the privilege of the accused to present his defense by counsel was recognized. Not until the end of the seventeenth century was a similar right granted defendants in TREASON trials (along with the right to have counsel appointed by the court when requested).

Over 140 years were to elapse before Parliament recognized the right of the accused to retain and employ counsel in FELONY trials. The earlier recognition of the right to counsel in treason cases reflects the fact that members of Parliament were themselves frequent targets of treason prosecutions launched by the crown. Throughout the eighteenth century the incongruity of a system that recognized counsel rights in misdemeanor and treason cases but withheld them in felony cases at a time when as many as 150 felonies were punishable by death was widely perceived and sometimes protested.

In the American colonies there was great variation in practices and statutory provisions relating to rights of counsel in criminal cases. By 1776, however, the right of attorneys retained by the accused to perform defense functions in courts appears to have been widely conceded, and in several of the colonies practices were considerably in advance of those then prevailing in England. In Pennsylvania, for example, the appointment of counsel for impoverished defendants in capital cases was mandated by statute; and in Connecticut even more liberal practices of appointment were established in the quarter-century before the American revolution.

Rights to counsel entered American constitutional law through provisions included in the early state constitutions and with the ratification of the Sixth Amendment to the federal Constitution in 1791. Seven of the original states and Vermont adopted constitutional provisions relating to the rights to counsel, and the right so protected was that to retain and employ lawyers in criminal trials. By the beginning of the nineteenth century only two states, Connecticut and New Jersey, appear clearly to have recognized a right in the accused to request appointment of counsel in all serious cases; and in neither was the privilege created by a constitutional provision.

Included in the Sixth Amendment, upon which most of the modern law of counsel rights depends, is the following clause: "In all criminal prosecutions, the accused shall enjoy the right . . . to have the Assistance of Counsel for his defense." There is no direct evidence of the framers' intentions in drafting the language or of the understanding of those who ratified the amendment. Yet the general assumption until well into the present century was that the right constitutionally protected was one to employ counsel, not to have counsel assigned.

One of the most remarkable features of Sixth Amendment history is the paucity of judicial authority on the counsel clause for nearly a century and a half after the amendment's ratification. There was no comprehensive exegesis in the Supreme Court, and only a scattering of holdings in the lower federal courts. The relative absence of authoritative interpretation may be explained in part by the long delay in establishing a system of federal criminal

APPEALS and the strict limitations applied to the HABEAS CORPUS remedy in the federal courts. The landmark decision in JOHNSON V. ZERBST was not handed down until 1938, six years after the Court had begun its delineation of the rights to counsel protected by the DUE PROCESS clause of the FOURTEENTH AMENDMENT in state criminal prosecutions. (See POWELL V. ALABAMA.) *Johnson* was comprehensive and far-reaching. The Court, through Justice HUGO L. BLACK, without pausing to canvass the historical understanding of the counsel clause, held that a federal trial court lacked power "to deprive an accused of his life and liberty unless he has or waives the assistance of counsel." Second, the assistance of counsel "is an essential jurisdictional prerequisite" to a federal court's power to try and sentence a criminal defendant. Hence the habeas corpus remedy may be invoked by a prisoner to set aside his conviction if the Sixth Amendment right to counsel was withheld at his trial. Third, although the right to have counsel assigned may be waived, allegations of waiver will be closely scrutinized. WAIVER OF CONSTITUTIONAL RIGHTS involves "an intentional relinquishment of a known right or privilege." The trial judge has a "protecting duty" to see that the accused understands his rights to legal assistance, and if the judge determines that the defendant has waived his rights, the record of the trial should clearly reveal the judge's determination and the basis for it.

In holding that the counsel clause not only creates a right to make use of a retained lawyer in federal criminal proceedings but also mandates the assignment of counsel for an accused otherwise unable to procure legal assistance, *Johnson v. Zerbst* upset the long-prevailing understanding to the contrary. Yet the decision did not immediately produce a major alteration in the actual practices of federal criminal justice. Many federal district courts before 1938, with the active encouragement of the Department of Justice, had been assigning counsel to indigent defendants in felony cases. The lawyers so appointed typically received no compensation for their services and were hampered in having no resources for pretrial investigations of their cases or for many other incidents of trial. *Johnson v. Zerbst* did little to improve this situation. It was not until a quarter-century later that Congress enacted the Criminal Justice Act of 1964 and for the first time provided, however inadequately, a system of compensated legal assistance in the federal courts.

In the celebrated case of *Powell v. Alabama*, decided in 1932, the Supreme Court made its first significant contribution to the constitutional law of counsel rights in Fourteenth Amendment cases. *Powell*, in addition, was one of the great seminal decisions in the Court's history and strongly influenced the development of the entire modern constitutional law of CRIMINAL PROCEDURE. The decision arose out of one of the most famous of twentieth-century criminal prosecutions, that of the Scottsboro defendants. Seven illiterate young blacks were arrested on the charge of raping two white women. After INDICTMENT the accused were divided into groups and tried in three separate trials. No lawyer having come forward to represent the defendants, the trial judge appointed "all the members of the bar" to assist in the arraignment, an act later described by the Supreme Court as merely "an expansive gesture." At the trial no lawyer was designated to assume personal responsibility for protecting the defendants' interests. Each trial was completed in a single day, and in each the jury convicted the accused and sentenced them to death. The convictions were affirmed in the Alabama Supreme Court, the chief justice vigorously dissenting.

At the time of the *Powell* decision, the Supreme Court had rarely employed the federal judicial power to upset state criminal prosecutions. (See MOORE V. DEMPSEY.) The determination of the Court that the procedures in the Alabama trial had violated the accused's rights to due process of law protected by the Fourteenth Amendment was, therefore, an event of portentous significance. The Court held that both the right of the defendants to retain counsel and the right to have counsel assigned in their behalf had been nullified. The speed with which the Scottsboro defendants had been rushed to trial and conviction deprived them of an opportunity to secure legal assistance, and the arrival of lawyers eager to provide representation for the defendants shortly thereafter indicated that the haste was seriously prejudicial. Beyond this, the Court found that the failure to make an effective appointment of counsel in behalf of the accused, given the circumstances of the case, constituted a denial of due process.

The constitutional theory of Justice GEORGE SUTHERLAND's opinion for the court is important, for it dominated thought about the rights of counsel for the next three decades. Whatever else the protean phrase "due process of law" contemplates, argued the Court, it encompasses the requirement of NOTICE and hearing in criminal cases. A FAIR HEARING, in turn, encompasses the right to counsel. In one of the Court's best-known OBITER DICTA, Justice Sutherland wrote: "The right to be heard would be, in many cases, of little avail if it did not comprehend the right to be heard by counsel. [Even the intelligent and educated layman] requires the guiding hand of counsel at every step of the proceedings against him. Without it, though he be not guilty, he faces the danger of conviction because he does not know how to establish his innocence."

Although the *Powell* decision was placed on a broad constitutional base, one susceptible of future doctrinal development, the actual HOLDING of the case was narrowly drawn. Thus the right of the accused to receive an assignment of counsel in *Powell* was made to rest on such considerations as that the charge was a capital offense, that the defendants were young, inexperienced, illiterate, and the like. The question that immediately became pressing was how far the *Powell* precedent would be extended when one or more of the circumstances in that case were absent. It was widely assumed that the Fourteenth Amendment might require the state to appoint counsel for an INDIGENT defendant in any capital case, even though a considerable interval elapsed before the proposition was authoritatively stated in *Bute v. Illinois* (1948). The more important question, however, was whether a "flat requirement" of counsel similar to the Sixth Amendment rule imposed on the federal courts in *Johnson v. Zerbst* would also be found applicable to state prosecutions by reason of the Fourteenth Amendment. A definitive negative answer came in BETTS V. BRADY (1942).

In *Betts* the defendant was convicted of robbery, a noncapital felony. At his trial in the state court, the accused, an unemployed farm hand said by the Supreme Court to be "of ordinary intelligence," requested the appointment of counsel to assist in his defense. The request was denied by the trial judge, and the accused participated in the defense by examining his own witnesses and cross-examining those of the prosecution. When, after conviction, defendant was denied *habeas corpus* relief in the state courts, he took his case to the Supreme Court alleging that the denial of counsel at his trial violated due process of law. Justice OWEN ROBERTS for the Court denied that due process required the assignment of counsel for indigent defendants in every state felony case. There was, in the view of the Court's majority, nothing in historical or contemporary practice to validate the claim. Rather, the question in each case was whether in the totality of circumstances presented, appointment of counsel was required to insure the accused a fair hearing. In the present case, the Court said, there was no such necessity. The issue upon which the defense rested, that of alibi, was simple and straightforward. There were no special circumstances of mental incapacity or inexperience that placed defendant at a serious disadvantage in maintaining his defense.

Criticism of the *Betts* decision began with Justice Black's vigorous dissent in that case and was promptly amplified in the press and the writings of legal commentators. Two principal reasons for the reluctance of the Court's majority to impose the obligation of assigning counsel in all state felony prosecutions can be identified. First, the prevailing opinion in *Betts* reflected the Court's deference to state autonomy, a deference widely believed at the time to be mandated by the nature of American FEDERALISM. The administration of criminal justice was an area in which state powers of self-determination were thought to be particularly broad. Second, there was the related concern that the states were poorly prepared suddenly to assume the

obligation of providing legal aid for unrepresented defendants in all state felony cases. The problem was not only that lawyers and resources would have to be supplied in pending and future cases, but also that hundreds of state prisoners had been convicted in trials in which no assistance of counsel was received. The concern was freely articulated by Justice FELIX FRANKFURTER when in *Foster v. Illinois* (1947) he wrote: "Such an abrupt innovation . . . would furnish opportunities hitherto uncontemplated for opening wide the prison doors of the land."

Nevertheless, with the passage of time opinion increasingly supported the overturning of *Betts* and recognition of a "flat requirement" of counsel in state as well as federal prosecutions. The *Betts* rule, far from strengthening federalism, exacerbated the relations of state and federal courts. Because under *Betts* the requirement of appointing counsel depended on the unique circumstances of the particular case, the resulting decision often provided little guidance to state judges dealing with cases in which the facts were significantly different. Many state judges came to favor the broader rule of *Johnson v. Zerbst* because of its greater certainty. It became apparent to many state officials that ultimately *Betts v. Brady* would be overruled, and in anticipation of the event they created systems of legal aid on their own initiative, supplying counsel for unrepresented defendants in all serious state cases. Meanwhile it had become increasingly difficult for the states to protect convictions in the Supreme Court when defendants argued that "special circumstances" had required appointment of counsel at the trial. In the thirteen years before *Betts* was overruled in GIDEON V. WAINWRIGHT (1963), no state conviction was upheld by the Court against a claim of special circumstances. It is significant also that when the *Gideon* case was pending before the Court, the attorneys general of twenty-two states filed AMICUS CURIAE briefs asking that *Betts* be overruled and the broader rule of appointment recognized.

Although the opinion of Justice Black for the court is unprepossessing, *Gideon v. Wainwright* marked a new era in the constitutional law of counsel rights. Portions of the opinion appear to pay deference to the older theories of fair hearing, and others seem to suggest that counsel must be assigned to unrepresented defendants on grounds of equality. Ultimately, however, *Gideon's* constitutional basis is the Sixth Amendment: the Sixth Amendment is "subsumed" in the provisions of the Fourteenth Amendment, and hence the same obligations relating to assignment of counsel for the indigent accused in federal courts are also owed in state prosecutions. Since the *Gideon* case there has been a flowering of constitutional doctrine relating to counsel rights in many important areas of the criminal process.

Although the prevailing opinion in the *Gideon* case did

not specifically limit its holding to felony trials, most observers believed that the right to counsel for indigent defendants would not apply in all misdemeanor cases. Following *Gideon*, state and lower federal courts devised various formulas for dealing with counsel rights in small-crime prosecutions. The state of Florida, borrowing from cases involving the constitutional right to jury trial, provided that counsel rights should not attach in prosecutions for "petty offenses," i.e., crimes punishable by not more than six months' imprisonment. (Cf. BALDWIN V. NEW YORK, 1970.) In ARGERSINGER V. HAMLIN (1972), nine years after *Gideon*, the Supreme Court rejected Florida's use of the petty-offense concept. In effect, the Court ruled that any deprivation of liberty, even for a few days, is a sanction of significant gravity. Accordingly, no unrepresented defendant may be jailed for any term unless he has waived counsel at the trial. The *Argersinger* holding dramatically expanded the legal aid obligations of state systems of criminal justice. Adequate practical implementation of counsel rights in small-crimes courts is yet to be fully attained in many jurisdictions.

The right recognized in *Argersinger* was defined further in *Scott v. Illinois* (1979). In the latter case an unrepresented defendant was sentenced for an offense which under state law was punishable by both fines and imprisonment. The sentence actually imposed, however, was a monetary fine. The Court, through Justice WILLIAM H. REHNQUIST, ruled that because the unrepresented accused was not actually sentenced to jail, his constitutional rights had not been denied. Ironically, Scott's rights were given less protection than he would have received if the Court had adopted the petty-offense formula in *Argersinger;* that formula would have looked to the penalties authorized by a statute, not solely to those actually imposed.

Because of the comparative modernity of criminal appeals in Anglo-American legal history, the Supreme Court's consideration of constitutional rights of representation in appellate proceedings was not preceded by extensive COMMON LAW experience. The first substantial discussion of constitutional rights to counsel on appeal occurred in DOUGLAS V. CALIFORNIA (1963) decided on the same day as the *Gideon* case. A California rule of court authorized the state intermediate appellate court to scrutinize the record in a pauper's appeal "to determine whether it would be of advantage to the defendant or helpful to the appellate court to have counsel appointed." Pursuant to this authority the court denied counsel to defendant, adjudicated his appeal, and affirmed his criminal conviction. In the Supreme Court the defendant successfully asserted that the California procedures violated his Fourteenth Amendment rights.

In reaching its result the Court relied primarily on an obligation in the state to accord equal treatment to rich and poor appellants and revived an earlier dictum of

Justice Black in GRIFFIN V. ILLINOIS (1956): "There can be no equal justice where the kind of trial a man gets depends on the amount of money he has." Here the obligation of equal treatment was not met. Had defendant been able to retain his own lawyer, his appeal, regardless of its merits, would have been presented by counsel. Because of his poverty and the decision of the appellate court not to assign a lawyer to him, he was unrepresented on appeal. Whatever the implications of the Court's theory, the obligation of the state to provide "equal treatment" to the poor does not necessarily mean that the treatment must be identical to that meted out to appellants able to hire their own lawyers. Thus, the opinion asserts, "absolute equality is not required." In illustrating this possibility, the Court strongly implied that the constitutional obligation to assign counsel involved in *Douglas* may apply only to the first appeal. If an indigent represented by an assigned counsel is unsuccessful in the intermediate appellate court and decides to seek further review in the state's highest court, he may submit to the latter the brief prepared by counsel in the intermediate court, but the highest court may not be under obligation to assign a lawyer to conduct the second appeal. A decade later the Court made explicit what had been suggested in the *Douglas* case. In ROSS V. MOFFITT (1974) the Court sustained the validity of North Carolina procedures that provided the indigent with counsel in the first appeal but denied his requests for representation when he sought a discretionary review in the state supreme court and later, when seeking a WRIT OF CERTIORARI in the United States Supreme Court.

The limitations recognized by the Court, however, do not appear to have seriously inhibited the availability of appellate remedies to indigent defendants. Arguably, this may be true in part because the Court was essentially correct in concluding that the decencies of fair hearing and reasonable equality of treatment can be accorded such appellants without offering counsel in all stages of the appellate procedure. Also, many jurisdictions have gone beyond the constitutional minima and supply counsel throughout the review process. Perhaps of equal importance is a series of cases that have overcome many of the difficulties that earlier confronted impoverished criminal litigants in the appellate courts. As early as 1956, the Court in *Griffin v. Illinois* held that a convicted defendant may not be denied access to an appellate remedy because of his poverty. Under state law the appellant could perfect his appeal only by use of a stenographic transcript of the trial proceedings, the latter being unavailable to him because he had no funds to purchase it. Under these circumstances, the Court ruled, the state must furnish the prisoner with a transcript. In the years following, the *Griffin* principle was broadly applied. (For example, *Burns v. Ohio*, 1950; see WEALTH DISCRIMINATION.)

Recognition of counsel rights and the removal of obstacles to review for indigent prisoners have greatly widened opportunities for appellate regulation of the trial process. They have, at the same time, created substantial problems for the administration of justice in the appellate courts. Economic constraints may operate on appellants "paying their own way" so as to deter the filing of frivolous appeals. No such constraints influence the indigent prisoner. The resulting problems go beyond the swelling of the dockets of appellate courts and also include certain difficulties for lawyers assigned by the courts to represent indigent appellants. Many such attorneys believe, often rightly, that the appeals of their clients cannot be supported on any substantial legal grounds. Yet efforts by the lawyers to withdraw from representation may, on occasion, prejudice the interests of their clients and, in some instances, may be motivated by the lawyers' design to escape onerous and unprofitable obligations. Efforts to balance such considerations have not as yet resulted in a satisfactory resolution. The rule announced by the Supreme Court requires the appointed lawyer seeking to be relieved of the case to allege that it is "wholly frivolous." The motion must be accompanied by a brief referring to anything in the record that might arguably support the appeal. How matters may be both "arguable" and "wholly frivolous" is not explained, and the effect of the rule must be to induce the lawyer to remain in the case regardless of his professional judgment of frivolity. The Massachusetts Supreme Judicial Court, in *Commonwealth v. Moffett* (1981) recognizing this effect, simply refused to permit counsel to withdraw solely on grounds of absence of merit in the appeal.

Other questions relating to counsel rights have arisen in the postconviction criminal process. As early as *Mempa v. Ray* (1967) a unanimous Court held that an indigent defendant, who had been placed on probation after conviction and given a deferred sentence, was entitled to be represented by counsel when his probation was revoked and he was sentenced to imprisonment. In *Gagnon v. Scarpelli* (1973), however, the Court ruled that although due process requires a hearing whenever a probation or parole is revoked, counsel need not be appointed unless special circumstances dictate the need for legal representation. This dubious resurrection of the *Betts v. Brady* doctrine, long since rejected at the criminal trial, was justified in part by the need to preserve "flexibility" in procedures leading to revocation. The American Bar Association in its *Standards of Criminal Justice* repudiated the *Gagnon* rule and called for appointment of counsel in such cases.

One of the most striking characteristics of the WARREN COURT was its allegiance to the adversarial system of criminal justice. This dedication inevitably resulted in the expansion of constitutional rights to counsel. Thus, the adversary system was strengthened in areas where it already existed, such as the criminal trial, and also extended to other areas where it had had little or no operation, such as pretrial police interrogations. Clearly the Court's attitudes toward a rejuvenated adversarial process reflected some of its deepest convictions about the proper containment of state power in the administration of criminal justice. Introducing lawyers into the interrogation rooms of police stations, for example, was intended to achieve values going beyond those ordinarily associated with counsel rights. In addition to advising his client, the lawyer could serve as a witness to police interrogatory activity and a deterrent to police abuse. His presence might often be indispensable to the preservation of the suspect's RIGHT AGAINST SELF-INCRIMINATION and other constitutional rights.

Concern with proper representation of defendants' interests in the pretrial phases of the criminal process was expressed by the Supreme Court in its earliest cases involving rights to counsel. Even in *Powell v. Alabama* (1932) the Court had referred to the pretrial preparation of the defense as "the most critical" period in the criminal proceedings. Before the decision of *Gideon v. Wainwright* (1963) the Court had begun mandating the appointment of counsel for unrepresented accused persons at various "critical stages of the proceedings." Thus in *Hamilton v. Alabama* (1961) the murder conviction of the indigent accused was reversed because of the absence of defense counsel at the pretrial arraignment.

The more difficult problems, however, were those of the accused's rights after ARREST but before formal commencement of the judicial proceedings by bringing the accused into court for preliminary hearing or arraignment. The issues were squarely drawn in the companion cases of *Crooker v. California* and *Cicenia v. La Gay* (1958). In the former, petitioner, who was under sentence of death, complained that the confession introduced against him at his trial had been obtained in a period of incommunicado questioning during which time he was denied the opportunity to confer with his own attorney. A narrowly divided Court affirmed the conviction, Justice TOM C. CLARK emphasizing the "devastating effect" of the presence of counsel in the interrogation room on criminal law enforcement.

Crooker and *Cicenia* were overruled in ESCOBEDO V. ILLINOIS (1964) which represented the high-water mark of judicial protection of Sixth Amendment counsel rights in the pretrial interrogatory process. In a 5–4 decision the Court ruled that at the point in questioning when suspicions of the police have "focused" on the party being interrogated, even if this occurs before defendant is indicted for a criminal offense, the right of the party to consult with an attorney cannot constitutionally be denied. Two years later the Court decided the famous case of MIRANDA V. ARIZONA (1966), holding that whenever a suspect has been taken into custody he may not be interrogated until he has been given the "fourfold" warning: the arrested party must be advised that he has a right to remain silent, that he is entitled to consult with a lawyer, that the lawyer may be present at the interrogation, and that if he is unable to hire an attorney, counsel will be supplied. (See MIRANDA RULES.)

Although the prevailing opinion in *Miranda* reaffirmed the holding of the *Escobedo* case, the impact of the latter was considerably modified. Thus, use of the "focus" concept, while not expressly rejected, was for practical purposes abandoned. Again, although the *Miranda* opinion reaffirmed the existence of Sixth Amendment counsel rights in pretrial interrogation, the emphasis of the opinion is significantly different. The dominant view regarded the right to counsel in the interrogation situation as an incident to and a necessary means for protection of the Fifth Amendment's right against self-incrimination. The emphasis on that right is so dominant that the rights to representation recognized in *Miranda* have sometimes been referred to as Fifth Amendment rights to counsel.

The *Miranda* case did not bring lawyers into interrogation rooms so frequently as was hoped or feared at the time the decision was handed down. One principal weakness of the prevailing opinion was its failure to insist that a suspect's decision to waive the presence of counsel must itself be made only with the advice of a lawyer. In consequence, rights to counsel are frequently waived by persons in police custody. One study published shortly after the *Miranda* ruling revealed as few as seven percent of the suspects requesting stationhouse counsel. The tendency toward widespread waiver of *Miranda* rights appears to have continued in the intervening years.

Even before *Escobedo*, the Court had contributed another important strand to counsel doctrine in MASSIAH V. UNITED STATES (1964). After the defendant in that case had been indicted for a narcotics offense, government agents induced an accomplice of Massiah to draw him into conversation in an electronically "bugged" automobile. Incriminating admissions made by the defendant were overheard by the agents and introduced against him at the trial. In reversing Massiah's conviction, the Court ruled that the ELECTRONIC EAVESDROPPING violated defendant's rights to counsel, which rights had "attached" when the INDICTMENT against him was returned. Contemporary reaction to the *Massiah* decision was generally critical. Many commentators believed that if a wrong had been done to Massiah it consisted not of a denial of counsel rights, but rather an invasion of his Fourth Amendment RIGHT TO PRIVACY, or perhaps of the introduction of an "involuntary" confession against him. Again, to conceive of the rights to counsel attaching only at the return of the indictment leaves open to police officials an opportunity of frustrating the rule by simply delaying the indictment or INFORMATION.

After the decision of *Escobedo* it was widely assumed that the *Massiah* precedent had been drained of vitality. Yet in the widely noted case of BREWER V. WILLIAMS (1977) *Massiah* was invested with renewed significance. Although *Brewer* might readily have been decided by an application of the *Miranda* rule, the Court chose instead to reverse the conviction on the grounds of denial of counsel, reliance being placed on the *Massiah* precedent. Later decisions, building on *Massiah*, appear to assert a right in the defendant not to be approached by the government for evidence of his own guilt in the absence of counsel, once judicial proceedings are initiated by return of an indictment or other in-court proceedings (*United States v. Henry*, 1980). In New York the state courts have transcended the *Massiah* precedent by interpreting state law to mean that whenever a lawyer enters a case in behalf of the defendant, even when this occurs before indictment, the accused in custody may not waive his right to counsel in the absence of his lawyer (*People v. Hobson*, 1976). Although the New York rule alleviates the restrictions imposed by the Supreme Court on the *Massiah* doctrine, it is of limited value to indigent defendants, who ordinarily do not acquire counsel before the commencement of judicial proceedings.

A final area of pretrial counsel rights involves LINEUPS. Misidentification of the accused by prosecution witnesses constitutes perhaps the most prolific source of erroneous convictions; police lineups and other identification procedures often spawn such errors. In UNITED STATES V. WADE (1967) the Court responded to these problems by designating the pretrial identification confrontation between witnesses and the accused as a "critical stage" of the proceedings and hence one requiring the presence of the accused's attorney. An identification made at a lineup in which the suspect's right to counsel was not honored may not be introduced at the criminal trial. An in-court identification is not summarily barred, but before it can be employed as evidence, the prosecution must establish by "clear and convincing evidence" that it was based on observations other than those made at the flawed lineup. After this promising beginning the Court backed away, and the view appears established that unless the identification evidence was obtained by methods so defective as to deny due process of law, an identification obtained in the absence of counsel may be introduced in court if the lineup occurred before return of an indictment. (See KIRBY V. ILLINOIS.) Limiting rights of counsel to the postindictment period is especially devastating in these areas because identification efforts are typically undertaken before formal charges are made. In UNITED STATES V. ASH (1973) the Court has also refused to supervise other identification procedures, such as those involving the use of photographic files. The problems of convicting the innocent through misidentification persist, and the Court has relegated their solutions largely to administrative and legislative action.

Basic to the rights of counsel is the quality of the legal representation supplied the criminal accused. Yet growth of the law in this area is inhibited by the fear that close judicial scrutiny of the competency of such representation will provide numerous and unwarranted opportunities for disappointed criminal litigants to attack their convictions. Such administrative concerns resulted in the once widely recognized rule that convictions were not to be reversed on incompetency grounds unless the performance of defense counsel constituted a "mockery of justice." The formula employed in the Supreme Court today is considerably more demanding: counsel's advice must not fall "outside the range of competence demanded of attorneys in criminal cases" (*Tollet v. Henderson*, 1953). The application of the "ordinary competence" test, however, results in the reversal of comparatively few criminal convictions. Thus in *United States v. Decoster* (1979) the District of Columbia Court of Appeals refused to upset a conviction in which a court-appointed lawyer failed to interview his client's co-defendants or any other witnesses before trial. Failures to achieve the objective of adequate defense in criminal cases are often not the product of the professional incompetence of lawyers. In many cases the court-appointed lawyer is on the staff of an inadequately funded legal aid agency that must impose wholly unrealistic case loads on its attorneys. Similar problems also often affect the privately retained lawyer who because of the economics of criminal law practice may be under pressure to accept more cases than he can adequately handle. The courts alone cannot be expected to solve problems of this sort, but it is doubtful that instances of inadequate defense will be significantly abated until the courts articulate and apply specific minimum standards of counsel performance.

The right of an indigent litigant to demand appointment of counsel from the state in noncriminal proceedings has received comparatively little judicial consideration or development. In the famous case of IN RE GAULT (1967) the Court recognized a right to counsel in a state juvenile court delinquency proceeding. Some courts have held that, where necessary to a fair hearing, a similar right is possessed by an indigent petitioner in an habeas corpus action. Since juvenile court and habeas corpus proceedings, although "civil" in form, are analogous or intimately related to the criminal process, the precedents in neither category represent a significant expansion of counsel rights into noncriminal areas.

In *Lassiter v. Department of Social Services* (1981) the question was whether counsel must be appointed to represent an indigent mother in a proceeding brought by the state to terminate her parental rights. In such a proceeding the defendant faces a sanction often considered more severe than a sentence of imprisonment, and, given the nature of the issues, the defendant's need for professional assistance is at least as great as that of the accused in many criminal cases. Although recognizing these considerations, the Court's majority limited the right to counsel to the situation in which all the circumstances in a particular case make legal representation necessary for a fair hearing, and it concluded that such considerations were not shown to be present in the *Lassiter* case. This latter-day revival of the *Betts v. Brady* precedent is regrettable in view of the needs for counsel in these proceedings and the comparatively small social costs involved in making counsel available routinely in all such cases. Like *Betts*, however, the *Lassiter* holding may represent a step toward a more satisfactory ultimate result.

In the development of the modern constitutional law of criminal procedure, questions of the rights of counsel have held a central position. This centrality is not surprising; counsel rights are integral to an adversarial system of justice, and the expansion and refurbishing of that system have been a dominant objective of constitutional procedural law from the decision of *Powell v. Alabama* in 1932 to the present. In the intervening years, issues of counsel rights have continued to emerge in a variety of contexts. It may be anticipated that this course of constitutional events will continue so long as the Supreme Court places significant reliance on the adversarial system as the principal mechanism to control and order the applications of state power in the criminal process.

FRANCIS A. ALLEN
(1986)

(SEE ALSO: *Nix v. Williams.*)

Bibliography

ALLEN, FRANCIS A. 1975 The Judicial Quest for Penal Justice: The Warren Court and the Criminal Cases. *Illinois Law Forum* 1975:518–542.

ATTORNEY GENERAL'S COMMITTEE 1963 *Poverty and the Administration of Federal Criminal Justice.* Washington: Government Printing Office.

BEANEY, WILLIAM A. 1955 *The Right to Counsel in American Courts.* Ann Arbor: University of Michigan Press.

HOLTZOFF, A. 1944 Right to Counsel under the Sixth Amendment. *New York University Law Review* 20:1–22.

KAMISAR, YALE 1962 Betts v. Brady Twenty Years Later. *Michigan Law Review* 61:219–282.

——— 1978 Brewer v. Williams, Massiah and Miranda: What Is Interrogation? When Does It Matter? *Georgetown Law Journal* 67:1–101.

LEVINE, F. and TAPP, J. 1973 The Psychology of Criminal Identification: The Gap from Wade to Korley. *University of Pennsylvania Law Review* 121:1079–1131.

RIGHT TO DIE

The "right to die" is an ambiguous, and therefore expansive, phrase. It can encompass the right to refuse life-sustaining medical treatment, the right to commit suicide, the right to have a doctor assist a person in suicide, and the right of third parties to kill legally incompetent patients by administering lethal doses of drugs or by removing food, water, respirators andor other medical care.

The constitutional arguments for the right to die are premised on either the RIGHT OF PRIVACY or on the right to liberty guaranteed by the DUE PROCESS clause of the FOURTEENTH AMENDMENT. Several lower federal courts, as well as state supreme courts, have held that the right of privacy includes at least a limited right to die. In *Cruzan v. Director, Missouri Department of Health* (1990), however, the Supreme Court suggested that right-to-die cases fit more appropriately within the due process framework.

Cruzan involved the tragic plight of Nancy Cruzan, who sustained severe head injuries in a car accident in 1983. After three weeks in a coma, she improved sufficiently that she could chew and swallow food. A feeding tube was nevertheless inserted into her stomach in order to make long-term care easier. Subsequent efforts to rehabilitate her failed.

In 1987 Nancy's parents sought to stop the food and hydration provided through the tube, arguing that their daughter was in a "persistent vegetative state," manifesting no awareness of herself or her environment. They further said that previous to her accident Nancy had indicated that she would not want to be kept alive in such a condition. The trial court granted the Cruzans' request, but the Missouri state supreme court reversed, ruling that not enough evidence had been presented to demonstrate that Ms. Cruzan would in fact choose to forgo food and liquids if she were competent to make the choice. The U.S. Supreme Court narrowly upheld the constitutionality of this determination by a vote of 5–4.

Writing for the majority, Chief Justice WILLIAM H. REHNQUIST said that according to previous decisions of the Court, "a competent person has a constitutionally protected liberty interest in refusing unwanted medical treatment" based on the due process clause. This liberty interest is not inviolable, however. It must be weighed against various state interests, including the state's commitment to the preservation of human life. According to Rehnquist, this commitment justifies prohibitions against both homicide and assistance to commit suicide. It also justifies state measures to prevent suicide. In Rehnquist's words, "we do not think a State is required to remain neutral in the face of an informed and voluntary decision by a physically-able adult to starve to death."

Nancy Cruzan, of course, was not physically able; and for the purpose of this case, Rehnquist assumed that while competent able persons may not have the constitutional right to starve themselves to death, competent persons requiring artificially administered food and fluids do. The question was how this right could be applied to an incompetent individual like Nancy Cruzan. Concerned about the possible abuse of the power to remove life-sustaining treatment from others, Missouri had stipulated that food and hydration can be removed from an incompetent patient only when there is clear and convincing evidence that this is what the patient would have wanted under the circumstances. In the case of Nancy Cruzan, the Missouri supreme court held that insufficient evidence had been presented to make this determination. Rehnquist and the majority concluded that in this particular case this was a permissible way to safeguard the state's interest in protecting human life.

However, the Court also hinted that a different result might be required in a situation where a person had duly appointed a third party to make decisions in the case of the person's incompetency. In other words, had Nancy Cruzan made clear prior to her accident that she wanted her parents to make medical decisions for her if she ever became incompetent, the Court might have compelled the state to carry out the parents' wishes. Justice SANDRA DAY O'CONNOR emphasized this point in her concurring opinion.

Dissenting, Justice WILLIAM J.BRENNAN claimed that more than enough evidence existed to show that Nancy Cruzan did not want to be kept alive in her present condition. Even if there had not been sufficient evidence to determine Cruzan's wishes, however, the state still had no right to maintain her life according to Brennan. Instead, it was obligated by the due process clause to leave the decision over whether or not to remove medical treatment to "the person whom the patient himself would most likely have chosen as proxy or . . . to the patient's family."

Justice JOHN PAUL STEVENS, in a separate dissent, adopted a different approach. He articulated an objective "best interests" test whereby the courts would determine if it is in the best interests of the patient to continue to receive life support. Reviewing Nancy Cruzan's tragic condition, Stevens concluded that her "best interests" unquestionably dictated that food and fluids be shut off. Some might find chilling Stevens's expansive definition of "best interests," however, for it apparently included a patient's interest in not being a burden to others. At the end of his opinion, Stevens spoke of Nancy's "interest in minimizing the burden that her own illness imposes on others . . . [and] in having their memories of her filled predominantly with thoughts about her past vitality rather than her current condition."

Several aspects of the right to die raise difficult questions. Many oppose physician-assisted suicide, for example, because suicide wishes are often fleeting and irrational. They add that if society makes suicide too easy, efforts to prevent suicide may be undermined. Advocates for persons with disability claim this is already happening, pointing to a case in California where a court sanctioned the request of a disabled woman to starve herself to death in a hospital—despite clear evidence that the woman was severely depressed because of recent personal tragedies.

The power of third parties to deny life-sustaining measures to incompetent patients is equally problematic. Underlying much of the discussion over incompetent patients is the assumption that these persons are not fully human. This came out with force in the dissents in *Cruzan*, where Justices Brennan and Stevens both claimed that Nancy existed in a state "devoid of thought, emotion and sensation." This contention was fundamental to their arguments, because it allowed them to claim that the state could have no legitimate interest in preserving Nancy's life, because no human life in fact existed for the state to protect.

There are serious problems, however, with premising the right to die on judgments about someone else's humanity. Such judgments are not nearly so clear or so objective as many presume. Nancy Cruzan, for example, was supposed to be oblivious to her environment. Yet the trial court heard testimony from nurses who testified that Nancy tracked with her eyes, smiled after being told stories, and cried after family visits. Even in cases where a patient cannot respond at all, one may question whether this alone is a sufficient indicator of a person's loss of cognitive faculties. Research on coma victims who have recovered shows that the mere fact that they could not respond outwardly while comatose did not mean they had lost their humanity. They could hear what others said about them in their hospital room. They experienced emotions. They dreamt. But if persons in a persistent vegetative state retain their humanity in some fundamental sense, the assumption that the state has *no* interest in protecting their lives becomes much less persuasive.

The application of the right to die to incompetent patients other than those in persistent vegetative states is even more problematic. The right to die has been used to justify withholding food, fluids, and basic medical treatment from a wide array of incompetent individuals, from conscious stroke victims to infants with Down's Syndrome or treatable physical disabilities such as spina bifida. Disability groups complain that in these cases the right to die is nothing more that the right to discriminate against the physically and mentally hadicapped. They argue that not only is such discrimination not constitutionally protected, it is constitutionally proscribed by guarantees of due process and EQUAL PROTECTION.

Like ABORTION, the right to die implicates some of the most fundamental beliefs humans hold about the nature of human life. Right-to-die cases often require judges to be physicians and philosophers as well as jurists, and few would pretend that a judge's role in such cases is either enviable or easy.

JOHN G. WEST, JR.
(1992)

(SEE ALSO: *Euthanasia; Patient's Rights.*)

Bibliography

ARKES, HADLEY 1987 "Autonomy" and the "Quality of Life": The Dismantling of Moral Terms. *Issues in Law and Medicine* 2:421–433.

BARRY, ROBERT 1988 *Protecting the Medically Dependent: Social Challenge and Ethical Imperative.* Stafford, Va.: Castello Institute.

BOPP, JAMES JR. 1987 Is Assisted Suicide Constitutionally Protected? *Issues in Law and Medicine* 3:113–140.

LONGMORE, PAUL K. 1987 Elizabeth Bouvia, Assisted Suicide and Social Prejudice. *Issues in Law and Medicine* 3:141–168.

RIGHT TO DIE
(Update)

The question posed by claims for a "right to die" is whether states may prohibit people from hastening their own death or obtaining the assistance of others for that purpose. Since the 1970s, many courts have recognized the existence of a constitutional right to refuse medical treatment even though this refusal would hasten death. These rulings do not, however, constitute a generalized "right to die" for individuals who do not need medical interventions to prolong life. In 1997, the U.S. Supreme Court directly addressed this issue regarding the constitutionality of state laws prohibiting physician-assisted suicide, and held that no such right existed.

State laws against homicide have traditionally been applied to forbid people from hastening either their own or others' deaths. Under English COMMON LAW, suicide was prohibited, though the state sanctions were necessarily indirect—through property inheritance forfeitures and burial degradations for the act of suicide and the imposition of criminal penalties for unsuccessful suicide attempts. During the course of the nineteenth century, American state legislatures abandoned these measures but at the same time enacted civil commitment laws phrased broadly enough to authorize psychiatric custodial confinement for suicide attempts. The abolition of English common law penalties thus did not clearly indicate that American legislators viewed suicide as a "right."

American law has also traditionally held that physicians

are obliged to obtain consent from mentally competent patients before embarking on any medical treatment. On its face, this requirement would imply that a mentally competent person had a right to refuse life-prolonging medical treatment notwithstanding that hastened death would result from this refusal. It was not until the 1970s, however, that American courts drew out this implication. The landmark ruling, *In re Quinlan* (1976), was rendered by the New Jersey Supreme Court in a case involving Karen Ann Quinlan, a twenty-one-year-old woman in a persistent vegetative state whose parents sought judicial approval to remove the mechanical ventilator that assisted her breathing. The court held that if Quinlan had been mentally competent, she would have had a right to discontinue this medical treatment. In reaching this conclusion the court relied not only on the common law rule requiring a patient's consent for medical treatment generally but also on the recent decision of the U.S. Supreme Court in ROE V. WADE (1973). The state court reasoned that if the constitutional RIGHT OF PRIVACY protected a woman's control over her bodily integrity regarding the choice to abort, it followed that all individuals had a constitutional right to control medical interventions into their bodies. The state court further concluded that although Quinlan was not mentally competent, she should not thereby lose this constitutional protection of her bodily integrity but that the right should be available to her through the exercise of "substituted judgment"; that is, through someone such as her parent or court-appointed guardian speaking for her.

Strictly speaking, the *Quinlan* case did not establish a "right to die." The state court's formulation of Quinlan's constitutional right was to protect her bodily integrity; from this perspective, the question whether these interventions were necessary for her continued life was incidental to her basic claim against any unconsented medical treatment. Nonetheless, the context of the case and the court's discussion of that context gave clear prominence to the proposition, as the court itself put it, that mechanical prolongation of her life "only to vegetate a few measurable months with no realistic possibility of returning to any semblance of cognitive or sapient life [would] compel Karen to endure the unendurable." Changes in medical technology and in population demographics during the preceding several decades, moreover, gave a new sense of urgency to this concern about "unendurable" prolongation of life. Advances in public health and individual medical treatments had led to increasing numbers of people surviving into old age but burdened with substantial, chronic disabilities. The intense media attention to Karen Ann Quinlan's case suggested that her plight symbolized a widespread public concern about excessive and inhu-

mane applications of life-prolonging medical technologies.

Judicial decisions following *Quinlan*, however, highlighted opposite concerns—that withholding life-prolonging medical care could be excessive and inhumane. The New Jersey Supreme Court had assumed that, although Karen Ann was incompetent, her father could appropriately speak on her behalf; subsequent court cases that authorized withholding treatment from incompetent patients raised questions about the role of family or other substituted decisionmakers. In *Superintendent of Belchertown State School v. Saikewicz* (1977), decided immediately after *Quinlan*, the Supreme Judicial Court of Massachusetts ruled that medical treatment for leukemia, which most likely would have prolonged life for less than a year but with considerable physical discomfort, could be withheld from a profoundly retarded sixty-six-year-old man who had lived most of his life in a state retardation institution. The court came to this conclusion even though it conceded that the overwhelming majority of mentally "normal" people would have opted for the treatment; and critics charged accordingly that this ruling reflected an invidious discrimination against people with mental disabilities. In 1982, the Indiana Supreme Court affirmed that parents of a Down syndrome newborn could refuse life-saving surgery to correct an esophageal obstruction. This ruling reflected devaluation of retarded people even more than in *Saikewicz*, for the surgery was entirely curative and universally performed for other newborns with this condition. Following considerable media coverage of this case, known only as *Baby Doe*, Congress adopted the Child Abuse Amendments of 1984, withholding federal funds from states unless they enacted laws requiring medical treatment for infants with virtually any likelihood of extended life. Within five years, such laws were adopted in every state, thus effectively repudiating the *Baby Doe* ruling.

The first case to come to the U.S. Supreme Court regarding refusal of life-prolonging medical treatment also involved a person who could not speak for herself. In *Cruzan v. Director, Missouri Department of Health* (1990), parents sought judicial permission to remove a feeding tube from their adult daughter who was in a persistent vegetative state from brain injury in a car accident seven years earlier. The Missouri Supreme Court had ruled that there was no "clear and convincing evidence," as required under state law, that the daughter herself, when mentally competent, had expressed unwillingness to accept medical treatment in these circumstances. The U.S. Supreme Court, by a 5–4 vote, held that this ruling did not violate the Constitution. Chief Justice WILLIAM H. REHNQUIST, writing for the Court, stated that "the principle that a competent person has a constitutionally protected liberty interest in refusing unwanted medical treatment may be inferred from our prior decisions." Nonetheless, Rehnquist held, states have constitutional authority to impose high evidentiary standards in determining the wishes of an incompetent person. In a CONCURRING OPINION, Justice SANDRA DAY O'CONNOR observed that the Court's ruling should encourage individuals to complete advance directives or appoint health-care proxies to implement their wishes if they subsequently became incompetent; she also suggested that states would be constitutionally obligated to give effect to these instruments. In 1990, Congress enacted the Patient Self-Determination Act requiring that medical institutions receiving federal funds inform all entering patients about their rights under state law to make advance directives or appoint health-care proxies. Subsequent studies have shown, however, that relatively few people—between 5 percent and 29 percent of the population—have in fact completed such instruments.

Controversy about discriminatory implications of a right to refuse medical treatment was, moreover, not restricted to its application to incompetent people. There were also concerns that some disabled people would devalue themselves, or act on the basis of social devaluation of them, in deciding to forego life-prolonging treatment. These concerns were exemplified for some critics in a ruling by a California appellate court in *Bouvia v. Superior Court* (1986) regarding a quadriplegic woman with severe cerebral palsy who sought a court order directing hospital authorities to remove a feeding tube. The court ruled that Elizabeth Bouvia had a constitutionally based privacy right to refuse this treatment. In describing Bouvia's circumstances, the court appeared to base its sympathy for her claim on the seeming "uselessness, unenjoyability and frustration" of her disabled state. Critics responded, however, that the court ignored aspects of Bouvia's life—such as her recent miscarriage and divorce, her brother's death, her job loss and homelessness— which might have been more powerful motivations for her wish to end her life and, if she had been able-bodied, would have led judges to question her mental competency rather than to insist on acquiescence to that wish. These critics alleged confirmation in their concerns about devaluation of disabled people in Rehnquist's dictum in *Cruzan*, "We do not think that a State is required to remain neutral in the face of an informed and voluntary decision by a physically-able adult to starve to death"—thus appearing to imply that a constitutional right to refuse feeding by medical means could be restricted to physically disabled adults.

Claims for a constitutional "right to die" thus implicate conflicting concerns. On one side, the principle demanding respect for autonomous personal choice (whether understood in constitutional terms as a privacy right or a liberty interest) clearly militates against any forced medical treatment. On the other, invidious social attitudes toward disabled people not only implies that others, even including family members, may not be trustworthy guardians for the interests of mentally incompetent people; these attitudes also suggest the existence of societal coercions toward mentally competent adults with physical disabilities that could lead them to devalue themselves and construe a "right to die" as an obligation to die.

These conflicting concerns were powerfully presented in constitutional challenges to state laws in Washington and New York imposing criminal penalties for assisting suicide. Plaintiffs alleged that states were constitutionally obliged to exempt from these laws physicians who assisted mentally competent, terminally ill patients requesting hastened death. In the Washington case, the U.S. Court of Appeals for the Ninth Circuit held that there was a FUNDAMENTAL RIGHT to control over one's bodily integrity, based on the privacy right or liberty interest established by *Roe*, that extended to individual control over the timing and manner of one's death and that, for mentally competent people who were already imminently dying of some terminal illness, the state had no adequately compelling interest in prohibiting physicians from assisting them toward hastened death. The U.S. Court of Appeals for the Second Circuit rejected this finding of a fundamental right but nevertheless held that New York's law drew irrational distinctions by obliging physicians to respect patients' refusals of life-prolonging treatment, thus hastening their deaths by acts such as removal of feeding tubes, while prohibiting physicians from respecting patients' requests for other physician actions to hasten death, such as prescriptions for lethal medications. The Second Circuit ruled that this irrational treatment violated the EQUAL PROTECTION guarantee of the FOURTEENTH AMENDMENT.

In *Washington v. Glucksberg* and *Vacco v. Quill* (1997), the U.S. Supreme Court unanimously reversed both appeals court rulings. In opinions joined by five Justices, Rehnquist held in the Washington case that neither the text of the Constitution nor the extensive historical existence of state law prohibitions supported the claim for a fundamental right to physician-assisted suicide; in the New York case, he held that the distinction between circumstances where physicians acted to hasten death, on the one hand, and withheld treatment but the patient's disease itself was the "active" cause of death, on the other hand, was well-accepted and plausible enough as to satisfy the constitutional standard of scrutiny for legislative rationality. Four Justices, though concurring in the result, were not so definitive in rejecting the constitutional claims against the assisted suicide prohibitions.

Justice JOHN PAUL STEVENS was most clearly inclined toward finding a constitutional right; he concurred only on the ground that the statutes were challenged facially rather than as applied and that, though he was unwilling to strike down the prohibitions in all circumstances, there were some limited circumstances where an adequate case could be made regarding terminally ill, mentally competent patients. In footnotes to his majority opinions, Rehnquist accepted Stevens's position that the Court's ruling did not "absolutely foreclose" such future constitutional claims, though his opinions read as a whole appeared strongly inhospitable to any such claims.

Justice DAVID H. SOUTER wrote an extensive concurring opinion that also appeared favorably disposed toward finding a constitutional right to assisted suicide for terminally ill patients. He expressed reluctance to endorse this conclusion, however, because of the concerns raised by states about whether this right could not be adequately confined to true volunteers and would instead have coercive force on vulnerable people such as the elderly, the poor, minority group members, or the chronically disabled. Because there was no practical experience in the implementation of this right in any U.S. jurisdiction and the empirical data from the Netherlands—the only country where physician-assisted suicide had been legally recognized—was limited and subject to conflicting interpretations, Souter found that state legislatures were better suited than courts to assess the gravity of these practical concerns. He stated, however, that if there were "legislative foot-dragging in ascertaining the facts" he would re-examine his position and seemed to imply that he would then be prepared to proceed toward an independent judicial finding of some constitutional protection for assisted suicide.

Justice STEPHEN G. BREYER also wrote a concurring opinion indicating his favorable disposition toward a constitutional right for terminally ill patients who requested hastened death to avoid intractable physical pain. Breyer observed, however, that the litigative record indicated that physical pain could already be adequately palliated by various means, including sedation that might itself hasten death, and that such effective palliation was not prohibited by state law. However, he continued, if "state law . . . prevent[ed] the provision of palliative care, including the administration of drugs as needed to avoid pain at the end of life," then the Court "might have to revisit its conclusion" rejecting a constitutional right to assisted suicide.

O'Connor made a similar observation in her separate opinion but she joined Rehnquist's opinions, thus providing the fifth vote to make them opinions for the Court. Accordingly, O'Connor's position was itself more favorably disposed toward a possible future judicial finding of a constitutional right than was explicitly acknowledged in the Rehnquist opinions whose majority status depended on

O'Connor's concurrence. (Justice RUTH BADER GINSBURG also wrote a very brief concurrence, endorsing O'Connor's separate opinion but refusing to join the Court's opinions.)

Taken together, the separate opinions in the assisted suicide cases thus undermine the apparent force of the Court's unanimous rejection of a constitutional right. In fact, five of the Justices spoke with varying degrees of approbation about the prospect that some future litigation would present sufficiently compelling facts for judicial finding of such a right. For O'Connor, Breyer, and Ginsburg, the existence of a right to assisted suicide would depend on whether a terminally ill person could avert physical pain by any other state-sanctioned means. For Stevens, the existence of this right would be justified by claims for autonomous choice generally, not necessarily restricted to palliation of physical pain specifically; but the claim must be presented in a more narrowly focused context than a facial challenge to the prohibitory state laws. Souter similarly did not restrict his attention to claims for relief of physical pain, but he was not prepared to find a constitutional right to assisted suicide until state legislatures had sufficient time "to experiment" and engage in fact-finding about the possibility of confining the practice of assisted suicide to truly voluntary, mentally competent, terminally ill people.

If the U.S. Supreme Court were ultimately to hold that individuals had a constitutional right to a physician's assistance in hastening their death, this would clearly constitute a "right to die." This would be a much clearer acceptance of such a right than the numerous state rulings—implicitly endorsed by the Court's dicta in *Cruzan*—which have already found a constitutional right to refuse life-prolonging treatment because of the direct bodily intrusion represented by nonconsensual medical interventions. The Court's 1997 decisions in *Glucksberg* and *Vacco* do not definitively dispose of this more generalized claim, though it does seem unlikely that the Court would be prepared to revisit this question soon.

Deliberation about the legality of physician-assisted suicide is, however, likely to go forward in the immediate future in state legislatures and popular ballot INITIATIVES. In 1994, Oregon voters (by a 51 percent margin) approved legalization of physician prescriptions of lethal medication requested by mentally competent patients who were diagnosed with illnesses likely to be fatal within six months. The constitutionality of this law was challenged on equal protection grounds but this challenge was rejected by the Ninth Circuit Court of Appeals and CERTIORARI was denied by the U.S. Supreme Court in *Lee v. Oregon* (1997). States are thus free to authorize this practice; the Oregon voters reaffirmed their approval by a wider margin in 1996, making this state the first U.S. jurisdiction to endorse a "right to die," limited to mentally competent people already suffering from a fatal illness. Whether other states will follow; whether this right will be extended to mentally incompetent people (as the constitutional right to refuse treatment has been applied); whether this right will be extended beyond terminally ill people to others whose physical or psychological suffering leads them to request assisted suicide (as the Netherlands Supreme Court has endorsed); whether the U.S. Supreme Court will ultimately re-examine its refusal to proclaim a generalized constitutional "right to die"—these are all questions that remain open and vexing.

ROBERT A. BURT
(2000)

Bibliography

COMMITTEE ON CARE AT THE END OF LIFE, INSTITUTE OF MEDICINE 1997 *Approaching Death: Improving Care at the End of Life.* Washington, D.C.: National Academy Press.

GERRY, MARTIN H. and NIMZ, MARY 1987 The Federal Role in Protecting Babies Doe. *Issues in Law and Medicine* 2:339–355.

LONGMORE, PAUL K. 1987 Elizabeth Bouvia, Assisted Suicide and Social Prejudice. *Issues in Law and Medicine* 3:141–168.

NEW YORK STATE TASK FORCE ON LIFE AND THE LAW 1994 *When Death Is Sought: Assisted Suicide and Euthanasia in the Medical Context.* New York: New York State Task Force on Life and the Law.

SYMPOSIUM 1998 Physician-Assisted Suicide: Facing Death after *Glucksberg* and *Quill. Minnesota Law Review* 82:885–1101.

WEIR, ROBERT F., ed. 1997 *Physician-Assisted Suicide.* Bloomington: Indiana University Press.

RIGHT TO JURY TRIAL

See: Trial by Jury

RIGHT TO KNOW

The phrase "right to know" does not appear in the text of the FIRST AMENDMENT, nor has it been used as an organizing category in Supreme Court opinions. Nonetheless, the phrase captures several major themes in First Amendment law, and its frequent appearance in editorials concerning FREEDOM OF THE PRESS attests to its rhetorical appeal. The phrase conjures up the citizen critic responsible for democratic decision making and a vigilant press acting as public trustee in gathering and disseminating vital information. It recalls the companion ideas of LISTENERS' RIGHTS and the MARKETPLACE OF IDEAS.

The "right to know" is a slogan, but it is not empty and its content is not exhausted by conceptions of self-government, the marketplace of ideas, or listeners' rights.

To be sure, such conceptions provide rationales for a right to know. Most court decisions preventing government from interfering with speakers' liberty have the effect of protecting the right to know. Some decisions are explicitly founded upon theories of listeners' rights, and, indeed, listeners have occasionally been the plaintiffs challenging the offending government action. Not every decision protecting a speaker's liberty, however, is appropriately characterized as protecting a right to know. For example, opinions in which the court has used the OVERBREADTH DOCTRINE to invalidate convictions for using fighting words find little support in any claim of a right to know. A police officer may learn something by being exposed to insulting language, but protection of speech in such decisions rests on a defense of speaker liberty for its own sake, wholly apart from anything the audience may learn.

If decisions protecting speaker's liberty are not always premised upon a right to know, neither are claims of the right to know limited to assertions of speaker's liberty. Indeed, the most intriguing question begged by the expression "right to know" is the scope of such a right. Does the public have a constitutional right to know anything that speakers themselves are unwilling to provide? To date, there is no judicial authority for the proposition that the public or the press has any First Amendment right to information voluntarily withheld by private actors. Indeed, even though the press is sometimes said to act as trustee for the public in getting information, the public has no constitutional right to compel the press to disclose any information it may choose to withhold.

The fighting issue is the extent to which the public or press has a constitutional right to know information that government officials wish to withhold. For a long time it appeared there was no such right. By 1978, no Supreme Court holding contradicted Chief Justice WARREN E. BURGER's contention in *Houchins v. KOED* that "neither the First not Fourteenth Amendment mandates a right of access to government information or sources of information within the government's control." Or, as Justice POTTER STEWART put it in an often-quoted statement, "[T]he First Amendment is neither a Freedom of Information Act nor an Official Secrets Act."

RICHMOND NEWSPAPERS, INC. V. VIRGINIA (1980) constituted the Court's first break with its past denials of constitutional rights of access to information within government control. The Court held that in the absence of some overriding consideration requiring closure, the public possessed a First Amendment right to be present at a criminal trial. Some of the Justices in *Richmond Newspapers* would have opted for a general right of access to governmental information subject to a degree of restraint dictated by the nature of the information and the strength of the government's interests in nondisclosure. Other

Justices would have confined the right of access to places traditionally open to the public. What *Richmond Newspapers* makes clear, however, is that the First Amendment is a sword as well as a shield and that the right to know promises to be a developing area of First Amendment law.

STEVEN SHIFFRIN
(1986)

Bibliography

BEVIER, LILLIAN 1980 An Informed Public, an Informing Press: The Search for a Constitutional Principle. *Stanford Law Review* 68:482–517.

EMERSON, THOMAS I. 1976 Legal Foundations of the Right to Know. *Washington University Law Quarterly* 1976:1–24.

RIGHT TO PETITION

The petition clause of the FIRST AMENDMENT is understood by the courts today to protect a broad range of communications with governmental bodies and governmental officials, including both legislators and members of the executive branch. It has also been held to protect activity related to creating the petition and obtaining signatures. In spite of this broad contemporary understanding, the petition clause receives little attention, in large measure because other clauses of the First Amendment, notably those guaranteeing FREEDOM OF SPEECH and FREEDOM OF THE PRESS, have been expanded so greatly that their protections have largely subsumed those protecting petitions. Protection of petitionary rights has not expanded in step with the protection accorded speech and press.

The modern jurisprudence inverts historical practice. Petitions were once the core mode of what we now call political speech. Moreover, the power accorded to such speech was, in many respects, effectively greater than political speech today. It embodied not just the persuasive and didactic elements of speech, but also a form of political practice, more akin to voting than to expression. Petitioning was born in and became a part of a political culture in many ways vastly different from that of a modern liberal polity. More organically conceived, more explicitly hierarchical, its organicism and hierarchy were reflected in mutual social and political obligations. It is telling that petitions not only embodied, but were sometimes even styled, prayers. By definition, then, they were a request from the subject to the sovereign, from the less powerful to the more. Both in style and substance, therefore, they legitimated the extant political hierarchy. Legitimation came at a price, however, paid by the powerful. In return for hierarchical deference subjects could insist that their prayers be heard and considered.

Both the English and American colonial practice bear out petition's role in such a political culture. While petitioning originated before MAGNA CARTA, it is in the Great Charter that reciprocity and hierarchy are first most clearly stated. In return for the allegiance of the barons the king pledged to respect certain of their rights. Were the king's officers to transgress those rights, the barons were to name four of their number who were to notify the sovereign and ask that the offense be redressed—in other words, they were to petition. Petition thus was understood as a communication that required consideration. Over the ensuing centuries the spectrum of English society that could take advantage of petitioning expanded beyond the barons to subjects more generally, becoming part of English constitutionalism. Moreover, those prayers also came to embody the legislative agenda as Parliament used petitions as the vehicle to express the LEGISLATIVE POWER to withhold taxes until the prayers of petitioners were considered.

English settlers brought petitioning to the colonies as part of the trans-Atlantic migration of political culture. In the many charters and similar constitutional documents of the colonies, the right to petition was protected, in increasingly explicit terms. Colonial practice reflected the expansion of the exercise of petitioning England had seen; indeed, the colonies picked up the pace. As petitioners in England had done, colonial petitioners expanded the notion of what the meaning of a grievance was, so that a petition seeking a redress of a grievance often became more than a request for an individual remedy or plea for assistance. They became, as they were in the nascent form envisioned by Magna Carta, vehicles for the expression— often the collective expression—of concern or outrage over matters of policy and administration. Not only did the subject matter expand, those seeking redress constituted a growing spectrum of colonial society, regularly including nonvoting and unpropertied white men and ultimately even including the occasional petition from women, free blacks, Native Americans, and slaves.

That petitions were not just speech, or the written evidence of speech, is evident not just from their powerful place in an older political culture. They could mandate attention, but they had to do so in a manner both formal and deferential. As the *Trial of the Seven Bishops* (1688) made explicit, not just any communication, nor even any written communication, created a petition. Rather, to be accorded the protection of petitions from, for example, a prosecution for SEDITION, the communication had to contain "petitionary parts." At a bare minimum, a petition had to be addressed to an authority such as the king. It had to state a grievance. It had to pray for relief. And the term "prayer" had meaning. Even a radical request had to be decorously stated or it could be rejected. This requirement was more than a formalism, more than an insistence on civility in political discourse. Petitions were legitimate only insofar as they acknowledged constitutional authority and deferred to that authority.

As a matter of symbolic politics, therefore, when the rebellious colonies declared their independence, they did so only after listing in the DECLARATION OF INDEPENDENCE their many "Oppressions" for which they sought "Redress" in petitions stated "in the most humble terms." These petitions were "answered only by repeated injury." Thus, the sovereign had severed the bonds of mutual obligation, not they, and had become "unfit to be the ruler of a free people."

In the Confederation era, the expectation both of legislative supremacy and the congruency of the legislative and popular interests meant that explicit statements protecting the right to petition were largely absent from the ARTICLES OF CONFEDERATION, but were part of the newly minted state constitutions. The Revolution, however, wrought a theoretical difficulty for petitioning. If the people were sovereign, then petitions could not really be prayers. Instead, they became statements and the controversy became not whether they should embody deference, but whether they could embody commands, that is, instructions, to representatives. To be sure, in some colonies during the eighteenth century a practice of instruction had existed. The Revolution, however, with its theme of POPULAR SOVEREIGNTY, rendered what had previously been merely practical problems of enforcement of instructions into first-rank theoretical problems of REPRESENTATION and SOVEREIGNTY.

The FIRST CONGRESS evaded those problems in drafting what became the First Amendment. It deliberately retreated from suggestions that the right to petition be transformed into the power to instruct, believing no legislator would forego the wise counsel of the citizenry but refusing to turn the representatives into reflecting machines. Furthermore, while the members of Congress believed that citizens would show respect for elected officers, it was clear that deference was no longer required. Indeed, at least at the state level, "remonstrance" was sometimes constitutionally sanctioned.

If deference no longer defined petitionary power, what of the bonds of mutual obligation when the citizenry was sovereign? Despite the evasion embodied in the First Amendment, masked by a rhetoric that seemed merely to continue a protected right, much had changed. In place of allegiance exchanged for protection had come a democratic power, one which underlay the REPUBLICAN FORM OF GOVERNMENT created in the Constitution. Granted, democratic power was restrained by certain processes of election and contained by restrictions on the use of governmental power. Nonetheless, ultimate authority was popular. The most immediate expression of that power was

the vote, which, unlike petition, depended for its power on being massed in numbers sufficient to win elections. Winners of elections owed their power to that mass of the electorate that created their victory. Although winning numbers might be built on ever-shifting bases, those bases consisted solely of voters. Thus, if nonvoters were not represented by those who voted, they had no theoretical way to compel attention toward their grievances. Bonds of reciprocity characteristic of a more organic society were minimized; electoral power was elevated. Thus, as the polity became ever more democratic, those without electoral power saw their most important vehicle for political expression and participation—petition—lose much of its value.

What became of petition in the United States? The answer comes in two forms, one federal and the other state. The fears expressed in the debate in the First Congress in which those who sought instruction, not petitioning, feared that Congress would ignore the wise counsel of the citizenry were soon apparently realized. At the federal level Congress at first attempted to deal with petitions as had colonial assemblies. Congress received petitions, engaged in readings, referrals, and committee consideration.

The procedures became ever more bureaucratic and perfunctory, however, as other means of influencing the federal legislature came to the fore. Some historians have suggested that Congress was overwhelmed by the number of petitions it received, others have suggested that petitions against SLAVERY brought forth a topic that was finally too controversial for actual consideration. Both factors came together in the famous antislavery petition drive that precipitated the congressional gag rule of the 1830s and 1840s, which barred reception of antislavery petitions. Closer examination of the evidence, however, reveals something quite different.

Despite growing importance of other methods of influencing Congress, petition continued to be a relatively effective vehicle for redress of what we today call private grievances, such as veterans' and widows' benefits, whether in the form of private bills or general legislative relief. While it is certainly true that the style of petitions and the quality of their reception changed for more public grievances, such as antislavery, the flow of petitions continued. Both the nineteenth and twentieth centuries have witnessed large-scale petition campaigns, such as those dealing with the WOMAN SUFFRAGE MOVEMENT, POLYGAMY and the admission of Utah to statehood, PROHIBITION, and calls to impeach Supreme Court Justices. None reached the size or sustained their energies for so long as antislavery, but they were significant nonetheless. The statements embodied in the petitions are also generally briefer, blunter, and more charged than in pre-Constitutional days. This change is not surprising. As petitions ceased to be vehicles that actually required detailed consideration, neither comprehensiveness nor civility was necessary. Petitioners adapted petitions to mass democracy, making them vehicles of political drama in electoral politics. Brevity, blunt statement, and electricity were useful in that role. The petitioners also used petitions to bootstrap themselves, at least eventually, into power in the electorate. Women's involvement in mass politics, for example, had its origins in women's involvement in the antislavery campaign.

The states saw similar adaptation. Petition continued to be a vehicle to obtain private benefits, such as charters of incorporation. Political petitions continued at the state level, too, ultimately culminating in the movements embodied in such phenomena as ballot INITIATIVES, REFERENDA, and electoral recall, features of democratic mass electoral politics.

The protections for prosecution necessary for petitioners in the pre-Constitutional era have become less necessary as electoral politics itself makes it possible to remove oppressive legislators. More importantly, speech and press protections have expanded so greatly that they cover much of what was once protected by the right to petition—and they do so for a much wider range of communicative activities. Thus, the jurisprudence of petition is now somewhat obscure, relegated to interstices of the law and embodied in such specialized DOCTRINES as the Noerr-Pennington doctrine in ANTITRUST. Petition and its protections have not disappeared; they have adapted and become less important as the political culture that gave rise to them has itself been replaced.

GREGORY A. MARK
(2000)

Bibliography

BAILEY, RAYMOND C. 1979 *Popular Influence Upon Public Policy: Petitioning in Eighteenth-Century Virginia.* Westport, Conn.: Greenwood Press.

HIGGINSON, STEPHEN A. 1986 Note: A Short History of the Right to Petition Government for the Redress of Grievances. *Yale Law Journal* 96:142–166.

MARK, GREGORY A. 1998 The Vestigial Constitution: The History and Significance of the Right to Petition. *Fordham Law Review* 66: 2153–2231.

MILLER, WILLIAM LEE 1996 *Arguing About Slavery: The Great Battle in the United States Congress.* New York: Alfred A. Knopf.

SMITH, DON L. 1971 The Right to Petition for Redress of Grievances: Constitutional Development and Interpretations. Unpublished Ph.D. Dissertation: Texas Tech University.

RIGHT TO REMAIN SILENT

See: Right Against Self-Incrimination

RIGHT TO TRAVEL

The right to travel is a doctrinal orphan grown to vigorous adulthood. As the ARTICLES OF CONFEDERATION (1781) recognized expressly, the freedom of interstate movement follows logically from the recognition of our nationhood. The Constitution contains no similarly explicit guarantee, but the logic of nationhood remains, reinforced by two centuries of nationlizing experience. The modern right to travel may still be searching for its doctrinal sources, but its historical base is secure.

Personal mobility is a value Americans have always prized. FRANKLIN D. ROOSEVELT brushed the edges of this idea when he greeted the Daughters of the American Revolution as fellow "immigrants." The nineteenth century, the formative era for our constitutional law, was also the century of the frontier. The twentieth century brought the automobile—and the moving van; each year nearly one family in five changes residence.

The power of Congress to protect the freedom of interstate movement is a theme both old and new. The great decision in GIBBONS V. OGDEN (1824) recognized that the COMMERCE CLAUSE authorized congressional regulation of the interstate transportation of persons as well as goods. The modern reach of congressional power is illustrated by the holding in *Griffin v. Breckinridge* (1971) that Congress can protect CIVIL RIGHTS by prohibiting private interferences with the right of black persons or civil rights workers to travel interstate.

The commerce power of Congress has long been held to imply limits on STATE REGULATION OF COMMERCE. When a state interferes with the interstate movement of persons, it must provide weighty justification for so burdening commerce. EDWARDS V. CALIFORNIA (1941) shows how difficult it is for a state to justify this sort of regulation.

The *Edwards* majority, resting decision on the commerce clause, said nothing about the right to travel. Four Justices, while not disputing the commerce ground, preferred to base decision on the PRIVILEGES AND IMMUNITIES clause of Article IV. This clause, which superseded the Articles of Confederation provision guaranteeing "free ingress and egress" from one state to another, had been interpreted early in the nineteenth century (in CORFIELD V. CORYELL, 1823) to include the "fundamental" right of a citizen of one state to travel through or migrate to another.

The Constitution's other privileges and immunities clause—that of the Fourteenth Amendment—is yet another potential source for a right of interstate travel. The concurring Justices in *Edwards* echoed the words of Chief Justice ROGER B. TANEY, dissenting in the PASSENGER CASES (1849), when they said that the freedom of interstate travel was one of the privileges of national citizenship. (See *Crandall v. Nevada,*1868; SLAUGHTERHOUSE CASES, 1873.)

This doctrinal untidiness has the blessing of the Supreme Court. Speaking for the Court in UNITED STATES V. GUEST (1966), Justice POTTER STEWART, who yielded to no one in expressing his affection for the right to travel, said: "The constitutional right to travel from one State to another ... occupies a position so fundamental to the concept of our Federal Union. It is a right that has been firmly established and repeatedly recognized. ... Although there have been recurring differences in emphasis within the Court as to the source of the constitutional right to travel, there is no need to canvas those differences further. All have agreed that the right exists. ... We reaffirm it now."

Guest involved the power of Congress to protect interstate travel, a power easily inferable from the commerce clause. When the WARREN COURT expanded the reach of the right to travel as a limit on the states, the Court selected still another constitutional weapon: the EQUAL PROTECTION clause. SHAPIRO V. THOMPSON (1969) established the modern pattern. The Court invalidated state laws limiting WELFARE BENEFITS to persons who had been residents for a year. Such a durational RESIDENCE REQUIREMENT impaired the right to travel, which was a FUNDAMENTAL INTEREST; accordingly, the states must justify the impairment by showing its necessity as a means for achieving a COMPELLING STATE INTEREST. The justifications offered in *Shapiro* failed this STRICT SCRUTINY standard of review.

In two decisions following *Shapiro,* the Court refined its analytical style for cases implicating the right to travel interstate. Both opinions were written by Justice THURGOOD MARSHALL. DUNN V. BLUMSTEIN (1972) held unconstitutional a state law limiting voting to persons with one year of residence in the state and three months in the county. Justice Marshall elaborated on *Shapiro:* That opinion had emphasized the illegitimacy of a state's purpose to deter interstate migration, but had not insisted on a showing that any welfare applicants had, in fact, been deterred from migrating. Strict judicial scrutiny was required, irrespective of any such showing, whenever a state law penalized interstate migration, and here the durational residence qualifications for voting amounted to a penalty. Failing the test of strict scrutiny, they must be invalidated. A year later, in *Marston v. Lewis* (1973) and *Burns v. Fortson* (1973), the Court upheld fifty-day residence qualifications for voting, remarking that "the 50-day registration period approaches the outer constitutional limits in this area."

The "penalty" analysis was fully developed in *Memorial Hospital v. Maricopa County* (1974), when the Court struck down a one-year county residence qualification for an indigent to receive free nonemergency hospital or health care. Denial to new residents of "a basic necessity of life" amounted to a "penalty" on interstate migration and medical care was as much a necessity as welfare subsistence. This analysis allowed Justice Marshall to distinguish *Starns v. Malkerson* (1971), in which the Court had summarily affirmed a lower court's decision upholding a one-year durational requirement for receiving state higher education at reduced tuition rates.

Beyond elucidating the sort of penalty on interstate travel that would require strict judicial scrutiny, the *Dunn* and *Memorial Hospital* opinions also emphasized the right to migrate to another state for the purpose of settling there, as differentiated from the right merely to travel. Commentators have made much of this distinction, but little turns on it in practice, and any serious effort to reduce the right to travel to a right of migration would turn away from the right's historical sources in national citizenship.

By 1975, the right to travel's doctrinal state was cluttered with furniture. The stage direction for the next event might read: "Enter Justice WILLIAM H. REHNQUIST, bearing an axe." SOSNA V. IOWA (1975) confronted the Court with a one-year residence qualification for access to the state's divorce court. Writing for the majority, Justice Rehnquist (the only dissenter in *Memorial Hospital*) not only concluded that the limitation was valid; he reached that conclusion without discussing "penalties" or even the equal protection clause. Indeed, the only doctrinal reference in his whole treatment of the merits of the case was a summary rejection of a marginal argument addressed to the short-lived doctrine of IRREBUTTABLE PRESUMPTIONS.

Doctrinal demolition seems to have been Justice Rehnquist's aim; throughout his opinion he referred abstractly to "the constitutional issue," without saying what the issue was, and he concluded by saying that the one-year qualification was "consistent with the provisions of the United States Constitution." Distinguishing *Shapiro* and the other recent precedents, he remarked that the states' interests in those cases had touched nothing more than budgetary or record-keeping considerations. In *Sosna,* the state was concerned to protect the interests of defendant spouses and possible minor children, and also to make its divorce decrees safe from COLLATERAL ATTACK. Thus the state might "quite reasonably" choose not to be a divorce mill. Predictably, the *Sosna* dissenters were led by Justice Marshall, who expressed his dismay over the dismantling of the only theory yet constructed to explain the modern right to travel decisions. What had happened to strict scrutiny, to the notion of penalties on interstate travel, to the link between the right to travel and the equal protection clause? The majority's silence on all these questions persisted for seven years.

In ZOBEL V. WILLIAMS (1982) an 8–1 Supreme Court struck down an Alaska law that would have distributed much of the state's vast oil revenues to its adult residents, apportioning distributions on the basis of length of residence in the state. For the Court, Chief Justice WARREN E. BURGER rested decision on the equal protection clause, remarking that "right to travel analysis" was "little more than a particular application of equal protection analysis." The state's purpose to reward citizens for past contributions was ruled out by SHAPIRO V. THOMPSON; to uphold Alaska's law would invite apportionment of all manner of taxes and benefits according to length of residence, a result that was "clearly impermissible." Concurring, Justice SANDRA DAY O'CONNOR rejected the equal protection ground, but argued that requiring nonresidents settling in the state "to accept a status inferior to that of old-timers" would impose one of the "disabilities of alienage" prohibited by the privileges and immunities clause of Article IV. In a separate concurrence, Justice WILLIAM J. BRENNAN returned to the origins of the right to travel; even if no specific provision of the Constitution were available, he found that right's "unmistakable essence in that document that transformed a loose confederation of States into one Nation."

William Cohen has suggested a sensible rule of thumb for the durational residence decisions: Equality of treatment for newcomers is required, but durational residence requirements are permitted as tests for residents' intention to remain in the state, that is, tests for state citizenship. Until the Court accepts this view, constitutional doctrine concerning the right to interstate travel remains where it was in the mid-1960s: "All are agreed that the right exists," but it has itself become a rootless wanderer.

The right to international travel is quite another matter. Its doctrinal location is clear: the Fifth Amendment's due process clause. Congressional power to regulate this liberty is wide-ranging. ZEMEL V. RUSK (1966) sustained the government's refusal to issue a passport valid for travel to Cuba, and CALIFANO V. AZNAVORIAN (1978) upheld the withholding of social security benefits during months when beneficiaries are out of the country. In the latter case, the Court remarked that "indirect" congressional burdens on the right of international travel should not be tested by the strictness attending penalties on interstate travel, but were valid unless they were "wholly irrational." Direct restrictions on travel, such as the denial of a passport, are undoubtedly to be tested against a somewhat higher—but as yet unspecified—level of judicial scrutiny. And when Congress regulates foreign travel in a way that discriminates against the exercise of FIRST AMENDMENT freedoms, strict scrutiny is called for. Thus APTHEKER V. SECRETARY OF STATE (1964) held unconstitutional the denial of passports to members of the Communist party.

The decisions recognizing a right to travel abroad have been concerned with travel itself, and not with a more limited right to migrate. The reasoning of those decisions is readily extended to congressional regulation of interstate travel. The commerce clause unquestionably em-

powers Congress to control the interstate movement of persons, but, like all the powers of Congress, that clause is subject to the provisions of the BILL OF RIGHTS. Congress obviously could not constitutionally forbid members of the Communist party to travel interstate. First Amendment considerations aside, the liberty protected by the Fifth Amendment's due process clause bars Congress from any arbitrary restrictions on interstate travel. The point has practical importance, for the broad sweep of the commerce power has made the prohibition of interstate movement one of the favorite regulatory techniques of Congress. Almost certainly the extremely permissive standard of the *Aznavorian* decision (upholding restrictions unless they are "wholly irrational") would apply to "indirect" congressional regulations of interstate travel. A direct prohibition, however, very likely would encounter a judiciary ready to insist on a more substantial justification.

The notion that the freedom to travel is a liberty protected by the guarantee of due process need not be limited to congressional restrictions on travel. The Fourteenth Amendment's due process clause surely is equally capable of absorbing the right to travel as a limitation on the states. The main barrier to recognizing the right to travel as an aspect of SUBSTANTIVE DUE PROCESS, no doubt, is the Supreme Court's reluctance to contribute further to the development of substantive due process as a vehicle for active judicial intervention in legislative policymaking.

For a season, then, the right of interstate travel is left without certain doctrinal underpinnings. Its capacity to survive on its own, cut off from the usual doctrinal supports, indicates that it draws nourishment from something else. The something else is our strong sense that we are not only a collection of states but a nation.

KENNETH L. KARST
(1986)

Bibliography

BAKER, STEWART A.   1975   A Strict Scrutiny of the Right to Travel. *UCLA Law Review* 22:1129–1160.

BARRETT, EDWARD L., JR.   1976   Judicial Supervision of Legislative Classification—A More Modest Role for Equal Protection? *Brigham Young University Law Review* 1976:89–130.

BLACK, CHARLES L., JR.   1969   *Structure and Relationship in Constitutional Law.* Pages 27–30. Baton Rouge: Louisiana State University Press.

COHEN, WILLIAM   1984   Equal Treatment for Newcomers: The Core Meaning of National and State Citizenship. *Constitutional Commentary* 1:9–19.

RIGHT TO TRAVEL
(Update)

The Supreme Court has invalidated, often by the narrowest of margins, laws that deny to new state citizens benefits extended to long-term citizens. Until recently, the Court has applied puzzling and conflicting rationales for doing so.

Two cases dealt with veterans' preferences. *Hooper v. Bernalillo County Assessor* (1985) struck down a New Mexico law that granted a tax exemption to veterans of the VIETNAM WAR only if they resided in the state before May 8, 1976. Chief Justice WARREN E. BURGER's opinion followed the same path as his opinion in *Zobel v. Williams* (1982), concluding that the distinction between eligible and noneligible veterans violated EQUAL PROTECTION OF THE LAWS because "the statutory scheme cannot pass even the minimum rationality test." The dissent by Justice JOHN PAUL STEVENS argued that the state's need to budget for the future provided sufficient justification to pass the RATIONAL BASIS test. The same 6–3 division split the Justices in the other veterans' benefit case one year later, but ATTORNEY GENERAL OF NEW YORK V. SOTO-LÓPEZ (1986) produced different doctrinal arguments. The Court struck down a New York law that limited a veterans' civil service preference to veterans who resided in New York when they entered military service. Burger and Justice BYRON R. WHITE followed *Hooper*, arguing that the denial of the veterans' preference to new residents failed the equal protection rational basis standard. The PLURALITY OPINION of Justice WILLIAM J. BRENNAN, JR., however, relied on a "penalty" rationale, concluding that "even temporary deprivations of very important benefits and rights can operate to penalize migration."

Another case dealing with discrimination against new citizens involved a complicated Vermont statute providing an exemption from payment of use taxes for automobiles purchased in other states. The exemption was available only for persons who were Vermont residents when they purchased the automobiles. White's OPINION FOR THE COURT in WILLIAMS V. VERMONT (1985) held that the different treatment of new and old Vermont residents failed the rational basis standard.

The doctrinal confusion was tested, and resolved, in a case involving state limits on WELFARE BENEFITS awarded to new state citizens. SHAPIRO V. THOMPSON (1969) had established that states cannot deny all welfare benefits to recent arrivals. Instead, a number of states limited new citizens to the welfare benefits they would have received in their states of origin. The Court in SAENZ V. ROE (1999) rejected the argument that these limitations, unlike the total denial of welfare benefits, were reasonable and neither deterred nor penalized the right of interstate migration. Section 1 of the FOURTEENTH AMENDMENT provides that United States citizens become citizens of a state the moment they establish residence there. Whether travel was actually deterred was "beside the point" because the right to "travel" involved in this case was "the right of the newly arrived citizen to the same privileges and immunities enjoyed by other citizens of the same State." Giving new citizens lesser benefits treated them as less than full state citizens.

In some cases, state laws imposing a waiting period might be justified as a reasonable test of bona fide residence. In SOSNA V. IOWA (1975), the Court sustained a requirement of one year's residence before filing for divorce. In VLANDIS V. KLINE (1973), the Court upheld a requirement that new residents pay out-of-state tuition in public universities during their first year. In *Saenz*, however, new arrivals were not awarded smaller benefits because there was doubt that they were bona fide residents.

The equal citizenship rationale of the *Saenz* case is new, but it is consistent with the outcome in all of the previous cases. It invalidates all laws giving new arrivals smaller state benefits, except those laws reasonably designed to assure bona fide state residence.

WILLIAM COHEN
(2000)

Bibliography

COHEN, WILLIAM 1994 Discrimination Against New State Citizens: An Update. *Constitutional Commentary* 11:73–79.

RIGHT TO VOTE

See: Voting Rights

RIGHT-TO-WORK LAWS

Union security provisions in LABOR contracts have required membership in, or financial support of, the signatory union by employees, as a condition of employment by the signatory employer. Concern that such provisions could be used to restrict employment unduly, to penalize dissent, and to infringe on employees' associational interests, stimulated the enactment of state right-to-work laws. Such laws, now operative in approximately twenty states, prohibit conditioning of employment on union membership or, generally, on financial support of a union.

The TAFT-HARTLEY ACT (1947) amended the National Labor Relations Act (NLRA) (1935) and imposed new restrictions on union security provisions, barring requirements of full-fledged union membership before or after employment and limiting compulsory membership to payment of uniform dues and initiation fees. Congress's approach appeared responsive to the argument that unions should be permitted, through collective bargaining, to secure financial support from all members of a bargaining unit, including those not members of the union, because the union's duty of fair representation encompasses all of them. Nonetheless, section 14(b), enacted by the Taft-

Hartley Act, permitted states to prohibit union security provisions otherwise legal under the NLRA. This extraordinary deference to state labor law contrasts sharply with the preemption of more restrictive state laws by the 1951 Railway Labor Act amendments (now applicable to both airline and railway employees).

The Supreme Court, in *Lincoln Federal Labor Union v. Northwestern Iron Metal Co.* (1949) and a companion case, *American Federation of Labor v. American Sash Co.,* upheld state right-to-work laws against challenges based on the CONTRACT CLAUSE and constitutional guarantees of FREEDOM OF SPEECH, FREEDOM OF PETITION and assembly, EQUAL PROTECTION, and DUE PROCESS OF LAW. The Court, moreover, negated any equal protection requirement that state remedies for discrimination against union members and nonmembers, respectively, be coextensive. The Court wryly observed that the unions' due process contentions were a reversion to the doctrines of LOCHNER V. NEW YORK (1905), ADAIR V. UNITED STATES (1908), and COPPAGE V. KANSAS (1915), which the Court had discarded—after having used them to invalidate prohibitions of YELLOW DOG CONTRACTS and other measures designed to protect workers' associational interests.

In *Retail Clerks v. Schermerhorn* (1963) the Supreme Court upheld state power "to enforce their laws restricting the execution and enforcement of union-security agreements." The Court, however, significantly limited state authority, stating that "[it] begins only with the actual negotiation and execution of the type of agreement described by §14(b)." Consequently, under section 14(b), a state could not properly enjoin PICKETING for an agreement proscribed by state law. The Court did not explain the reasoning behind the apparent anomaly of permitting a state to prohibit a completed agreement but not economic pressure to secure it. The Court may, however, have feared that state authority over such antecedent pressures would too often be used to restrict activity protected by the NLRA, such as peaceful picketing that publicizes substandard working conditions.

Otherwise valid union security agreements raise questions under the FIRST AMENDMENT when dissidents object to the use of compulsory financial exactions for political and other purposes not central to collective bargaining.

BERNARD D. MELTZER
(1986)

Bibliography

HAGGARD, T. 1977 Compulsory Unionism, the NLRB and the Courts: A Legal Analysis of Union Security Agreements. Philadelphia: Industrial Research Unit, Wharton School, University of Pennsylvania.

RIPENESS

People who anticipate harm occasionally attack a law's constitutionality before it is applied to them, or even before the law takes effect. A federal court may decline to decide such a case for lack of ripeness if it is unclear that adjudication is needed to protect the challengers, or if information sufficient to permit intelligent resolution is not yet available. A matter of timing and degree, ripeness is grounded both in Article III's CASE OR CONTROVERSY requirement and the federal courts' reluctance to issue constitutional decisions needlessly or prematurely. Delaying decision may cause interim hardship and allow unconstitutional harm to occur, but further developments may narrow the issues, or produce important information, or even establish that no decision is needed.

The Supreme Court's ripeness decisions display varying sensitivity to these sometimes conflicting factors. Normally, a court is more likely to defer resolution of fact-dependent issues, like those based on a particular application of a law, than it is to defer adjudication of strictly legal issues. A single case may present some issues ripe for adjudication, but others not ripe. Ripeness decisions mainly respond, however, to the degree of contingency or uncertainty of the law's expected effect on the challenger.

Where leeway exists, the court may be influenced by determining whose interests a quicker decision would serve. Thus, when federal civil servants fearing dismissal for violation of the HATCH ACT asked that the political activities they were contemplating be declared constitutionally protected in *United Public Workers v. Mitchell* (1947), the Court found the case unripe absent enforcement of the act against some particular employee behavior. Similarly, a challenge to IMMIGRATION policy was held unripe in *International Longshoremen's Union v. Boyd* (1954) despite a strong indication that, without a ruling, resident ALIENS risked jeopardizing their right to return to the United States. With little doubt that the laws would be applied, the challengers nonetheless were forced to act at their peril. By contrast, when a delay in decision has threatened to frustrate government policy, the Court has resolved anticipatory challenges to laws whose future application appeared inevitable, including legislation restructuring some of the nation's railroads in the *Regional Rail Reorganization Act Cases* (1974) and the FEDERAL ELECTION CAMPAIGN ACTS in BUCKLEY V. VALEO (1976).

Sensitivity to the government's interest in quick resolution even led the Court to uphold a federal statute limiting aggregate operator liability for nuclear power plant explosions in *Duke Power Co. v. Carolina Environmental Study Group, Inc.* (1978), despite evidence that explosions are unlikely and serious doubt that this statute would ever be applied. Because injury to the asserted right of unlimited recovery for nuclear disaster was unlikely to occur soon, if at all, the constitutional issues did not seem ripe; yet the Court concluded that the case was ripe, because the normal operation of nearby nuclear plants (whose development the statute had facilitated) threatened imminent pollution—even though the suit had not questioned the pollution's legality.

As the *Duke Power* case illustrates, the inherent policy choice in ripeness decisions—between finding constitutional adjudication premature and finding prevention of harm or validation of government policy timely—embodies important perceptions of judicial role in a regime characterized by the SEPARATION OF POWERS.

JONATHAN D. VARAT
(1986)

Bibliography

WRIGHT, CHARLES A.; MILLER, ARTHUR R.; and COOPER, EDWARD H. 1984 *Federal Practice and Procedure.* Vol. 13A:112–214. St. Paul, Minn.: West Publishing Co.

RIPENESS
(Update)

Like the STANDING and MOOTNESS DOCTRINES, the ripeness doctrine has been used to regulate the timing of federal courts' adjudication of challenges to government action. The principal purpose of all three doctrines is to verify that the plaintiff presently suffers the kind of concrete injury that has traditionally been the business of Anglo-American courts to remedy. In a moot case, the plaintiff has sued too late; in an unripe case, the plaintiff has sued too early.

Ripeness questions arise in at least three types of cases. In one group of cases, the plaintiff challenges the validity of ADMINISTRATIVE AGENCY regulations. In a second group, the plaintiff challenges the constitutionality of LEGISLATION. The third category consists of cases in which the plaintiff alleges a pattern and practice of unconstitutional law enforcement.

Frequently the plaintiff sues to have an administrative regulation declared invalid even before the administrative agency seeks to have it enforced. The agency typically argues that the case is unripe for adjudication. In *Abbott Laboratories v. Gardner* (1967), the Supreme Court set forth a two-part test to determine whether such cases are ripe. First, the court must determine whether the issues presented are "fit" for judicial resolution. That is, are the facts and procedural posture of the case sufficiently de-

veloped at this time to support a wise decision? Second, the court must consider how much hardship the parties would suffer if adjudication were deferred. In practice, the *Abbott Laboratories* test has contributed to the routine adjudication of regulations even before they are administratively enforced. The abundance of preenforcement review, in turn, may have impaired the quality and effectiveness of administrative rulemaking and adjudication.

The *Abbott Laboratories* test has sometimes been applied to cases posing constitutional challenges to legislation. The Court's record in this area is not a model of consistency. In general, however, the Court has tended to find such cases ripe when the plaintiff must either forgo what he believes is constitutionally protected conduct or engage in it and risk punishment. *Steffel v. Thompson* (1974) exemplifies the cruel dilemma. The plaintiff wished to distribute antiwar handbills at a private SHOPPING CENTER. He believed the activity was protected by the FIRST AMENDMENT. However, his handbilling companion had already been arrested and charged with criminal trespass. Unless the court were to resolve his claim for DECLARATORY JUDGMENT, he would be left with a choice between forgoing what he believed was protected conduct and the real possibility of punishment. The Court found the case ripe.

In a number of cases, plaintiffs have sought injunctions against police departments, prosecutors, or even judges who were allegedly engaged in patterns of racially discriminatory law enforcement. The Court has generally found such cases unripe. Individuals must wait until the allegedly discriminatory acts occur, then seek damages or criminal prosecution of the wrongdoers. These opinions manifest the protean quality of the ripeness doctrine. The Court's ripeness analysis in these cases relies heavily on conceptually unrelated notions about the proper relationship between federal courts and state SOVEREIGNTY. It remains to be seen whether the marriage of these unrelated ideas will form an important part of the genius of American constitutional government or whether it will subvert the very foundations of individual liberty under the RULE OF LAW.

EVAN TSEN LEE
(2000)

Bibliography

FALLON, RICHARD H., JR. 1984 Of Justiciability, Remedies, and Public Law Litigation: Notes on the Jurisprudence of *Lyons. New York University Law Review* 59:1–75.
MASHAW, JERRY 1994 Improving the Environment of Agency Rulemaking: An Essay on Management, Games, and Accountability. *Law and Contemporary Problems* 57:185–257.

NICHOL, GENE 1987 Ripeness and the Constitution. *University of Chicago Law Review* 54:153–183.

RIZZO v. GOODE
423 U.S. 362 (1978)

Rizzo exemplifies the BURGER COURT's inhospitability to INSTITUTIONAL LITIGATION aimed at broad structural reform. Philadelphia citizens sued the mayor and other officials in federal court, alleging condonation of a pattern of police mistreatment of minority residents and others. The district court held long hearings, validated the plaintiffs' charges, and ordered the defendants to submit a comprehensive plan to improve complaint procedures and police discipline.

The Supreme Court, 5–3, held this order improper. The Court implied that the controversy lacked RIPENESS, and suggested that YOUNGER V. HARRIS (1971) might protect the action of state executives as well as state courts. The decision, however, rested on the ground that police supervisors had been insufficiently involved in the proved misconduct to justify the court's systemwide order.

KENNETH L. KASRT
(1986)

ROANE, SPENCER
(1762–1822)

Spencer Roane, a Virginian, was the foremost judicial exponent of STATES' RIGHTS in the era of the MARSHALL COURT, and President THOMAS JEFFERSON would have made him Chief Justice of the United States had the opportunity arisen. Roane served for twenty-eight years (1794–1822) on Virginia's highest court. Before then he was a state legislator. He opposed RATIFICATION OF THE CONSTITUTION and never abandoned his belief that the national government possessed powers dangerous to the states.

Roane supported the authority of his court to hold unconstitutional a state act and even a congressional act, but he denied the authority of the Supreme Court to hold a state act unconstitutional. As leader of the nation's most influential state court he regarded the Supreme Court as a rival, and his words carried extrajudicial influence. He founded the Richmond *Enquirer* and ran Virginia politics. By the close of his life he headed an organization that controlled Virginia's press, its banks, its congressional delegation, and all three branches of its state government. He was JOHN MARSHALL's most formidable foe and outspoken opponent.

In the controversy leading to MARTIN V. HUNTER'S LESSEE (1816), Roane's court held unconstitutional section 25 of the JUDICIARY ACT OF 1789. In 1815 he described the United States as "a confederation of distinct sovereignties." His constitutional decisions differed from the Marshall Court's even on matters not involving the nature of the Union. He sustained the act later held void in TERRETT V. TAYLOR (1815) and supported the state in a case similar to DARTMOUTH COLLEGE V. WOODWARD (1819).

His vehement opposition to the nationalist doctrines of MCCULLOCH V. MARYLAND (1819) and COHENS V. VIRGINIA (1821) led him to denounce the Marshall Court in a series of essays in the Richmond *Enquirer*, which Jefferson warmly acclaimed and even JAMES MADISON tentatively endorsed. Roane's views on the Union were probably closer to those of 1787 than Marshall's. Doubtlessly Roane loved the "federal union" as he understood it, although Marshall called him "the champion of dismemberment." Roane was an able, orthodox judge who died a sectional advocate.

LEONARD W. LEVY
(1986)

Bibliography
MAYS, DAVID J. 1928 Judge Spencer Roane. *Proceedings of the Thirty-Ninth Annual Meeting of The Virginia State Bar Association* 39:446–464.

ROBBINS v. CALIFORNIA

See: *Ross, United States v.*

ROBEL v. UNITED STATES
389 U.S. 258 (1967)

Over two dissents, the WARREN COURT struck down on FIRST AMENDMENT grounds a section of the SUBVERSIVE ACTIVITIES CONTROL ACT of 1950 that prohibited the employment of members of the Communist party in "defense facilities" designated by the secretary of defense. Because the statute failed to distinguish between those who supported the unlawful goals of the party and those who did not, wrote Chief Justice EARL WARREN, its OVERBREADTH violated the right of association protected by the FIRST AMENDMENT. Warren rejected government arguments seeking to justify the provision by the WAR POWER and national security interests. "It would indeed be ironic if, in the name of national defense, we would sanction the subversion of one of those liberties—the freedom of association—which makes the defense of the Nation worthwhile." Justices BYRON R. WHITE and JOHN MARSHALL HARLAN dissented, observing that the majority "arrogates to itself an independent judgement of the requirements of national security."

MICHAEL E. PARRISH
(1986)

ROBERTS, OWEN J.
(1875–1955)

Best known as an Associate Justice of the United States Supreme Court, Owen Josephus Roberts had a varied preliminary career—law practice and teaching, administration, and public service. In 1930, after the Senate Judiciary Committee rejected the nomination of Circuit Judge John J. Parker, President HERBERT C. HOOVER appointed Roberts, a Philadelphia Republican, who was approved without a dissenting vote. That same year, CHARLES EVANS HUGHES returned to the Court as Chief Justice of the United States.

Roberts and Hughes came to the Court in a period of sharp disagreement concerning not only the role of government in economic and social affairs but also the nature and scope of the judicial function itself. Both men were destined to play significant roles. Examples abound, and Hughes and Roberts were often joined. They agreed, for example, in sustaining Minnesota's moratorium on mortgage foreclosures in HOME BUILDING AND LOAN ASSOCIATION V. BLAISDELL (1934).

In NEBBIA V. NEW YORK (1934) Roberts, without using the word "emergency," upheld a New York statute regulating the price of milk. In WOLFF PACKING COMPANY V. COURT OF INDUSTRIAL RELATIONS (1923) Chief Justice WILLIAM HOWARD TAFT had invoked the concept of business AFFECTED WITH A PUBLIC INTEREST as a test of legitimate government power. Rejecting this test, Roberts observed: "The phrase can mean no more than that an industry for adequate reason is subject to control for the public good." Roberts also opposed the judicial notion that prices and wages were constitutionally immune from regulation. Thus the constitutional barriers Justice GEORGE H. SUTHERLAND had erected in ADKINS V. CHILDREN'S HOSPITAL (1923) against the District of Columbia minimum wage for women as the "heart of a contract" were weakened. Citing *Munn v. Illinois* (1877), Roberts recalled: "The DUE PROCESS clause makes no mention of sales or prices. . . . The thought seems, nevertheless, to have persisted that there is something peculiarly sacrosanct about prices and wages."

Roberts's *Nebbia* opinion also disavowed a broad scope of judicial power. Here, as in UNITED STATES V. BUTLER (1936), the judicial function involved "only one duty, to lay the article of the Constitution which is involved beside the statute which is challenged and to decide whether the latter squares with the former." The *Nebbia* opinion was thus hailed as indicating fair weather for FRANKLIN D. ROOSEVELT's NEW DEAL legislation. Without specifying any particular level of government, Roberts declared: "This Court from the early days affirmed that the power to promote the general welfare is inherent in government." Yet, speaking for the Court in RAILROAD RETIREMENT BOARD V. ALTON RAILWAY COMPANY (1935), Roberts argued that Congress lacked power under the COMMERCE CLAUSE to pass any compulsory pension act for railroad workers. Hughes, LOUIS D. BRANDEIS, BENJAMIN N. CARDOZO, and HARLAN F. STONE dissented, the last rating this decision "the worst performance of the Court in my time."

UNITED STATES V. BUTLER apparently put the New Deal's legislative program beyond the scope of the TAXING AND SPENDING POWER. Roberts, invoking the TENTH AMENDMENT, argued that judicial endorsement of the AGRICULTURAL ADJUSTMENT ACT would "sanction legislative power without restriction or limitation" and convert Congress into a "parliament of the whole people, subject to no restrictions save such as are self-imposed." Roberts also voted with the conservatives in CARTER V. CARTER COAL COMPANY (1936), which set aside the Coal Conservation Act. Again the stumbling block was the Tenth Amendment. Coal mining, like agriculture, was local and therefore beyond the reach of national authority.

Meanwhile, overwhelming popular approval of the New Deal in the 1936 presidential election and the continuing high level of unemployment made it apparent that reliance on the states to cope with the economic emergency was misplaced. Blocking national action were four Supreme Court Justices, sometimes joined by Hughes and Roberts.

Roberts's judicial record appears inconsistent. Although the cases involved different issues, the shift between *Nebbia* on the one hand and *Alton* and *Butler* on the other is a clear instance of change. Some observers charged that Roberts, alarmed by Roosevelt's court-packing proposal of February 1937, shifted from a vote against the minimum wage in MOREHEAD V. NEW YORK EX REL. TIPALDO (1936) to one in favor of it in WEST COAST HOTEL COMPANY V. PARRISH (1937). Thus Roberts became famous as "a man of many minds."

In the personal rights area Roberts was, on occasion, conspicuously on the liberal side. Joined by Brandeis, Sutherland, and Butler, he dissented in *Snyder v. Massachusetts* (1934), insisting that when a jury visits the scene of a crime, the defendant and counsel must be present. In *Schneider v. Irvington* (1939) he voted to set aside a city ordinance restricting FREEDOM OF THE PRESS and distribution of nonadvertising circulars and pamphlets.

In HERNDON V. LOWRY (1937) Roberts wrote for the Court, which reversed the conviction of Angelo Herndon, a black organizer for the Communist party, who had been found guilty of inciting insurrection by trying to enlist other blacks in that organization. The Georgia courts sentenced Herndon to eighteen years in prison. Said Roberts of the state act that penalized any attempt to incite an insurrection against the state: "The statute, as construed and applied, amounts merely to a dragnet which may enmesh anyone who agitates for a change of government if a jury can be persuaded that he ought to have foreseen his words would have some effect in the future conduct of others. No reasonably ascertainable standard of guilt is prescribed. So vague and indeterminate are the boundaries thus set to the FREEDOM OF SPEECH and assembly that the law necessarily violates the guarantees of liberty embodied in the FOURTEENTH AMENDMENT." In BETTS V. BRADY (1942), however, Roberts for the Court held that the right to be represented by counsel in a noncapital felony case was not essential to due process of law (overruled in GIDEON V. WAINRIGHT, 1961).

During WORLD WAR II, when the Court, speaking through Justice HUGO L. BLACK in *Korematsu v. United States* (1944), upheld the compulsory transfer of Japanese American citizens to relocation centers, Roberts wrote an eloquent dissent. Joined by FRANK MURPHY and ROBERT H. JACKSON, he challenged Black's majority opinion, then the prevailing public view. He wrote: "[This] is the case of convicting a citizen as a punishment for not submitting to imprisonment in a concentration camp, based on his ancestry, and solely because of his ancestry, without evidence or inquiry concerning his loyalty and good disposition towards the United States. . . . I need hardly labor the conclusion that constitutional rights have been violated."

Roberts and all his colleagues, including Stone, had held in GROVEY V. TOWNSEND (1935) that voting in PRIMARY ELECTIONS was not a constitutional prerogative but a privilege of party membership. In the famous case of UNITED STATES V. CLASSIC (1941) the Court, again speaking through Stone, without mentioning *Grovey*, ruled that participation in primaries was a right secured by the Constitution. Thus, with the adherence of Roberts, but without discussing *Grovey*, Stone brought traditional southern election customs to the brink of destruction. More alert than Roberts, commentators knew that another precedent had been broken. In 1944, when the Court overruled *Grovey*, Roberts exploded. "Not a fact differentiates that case (*Grovey*) from this, except the names of the parties. . . . If this Court's opinion in the *Classic* case discloses its method of overruling earlier decisions, I can protest that in "fairness,' it should rather have adopted the open and frank way of saying what it was doing. . . ." "The instant decision," Roberts fumed in SMITH V. ALLWRIGHT (1944), "tends to bring the adjudication of this tribunal into the same class as a restricted railroad ticket, good for this day and train only."

New trends and new judicial personnel in a rapidly changing world disturbed Roberts. He asserted that law had become not a chart to govern but a game of chance. By 1941 the cordial relations he had previously enjoyed with his colleagues became strained. When Roberts retired in 1945, Chief Justice Stone drafted the customary letter to a departing colleague commenting: "You have made fidelity to principle your guide to decision." Black and WILLIAM O. DOUGLAS strongly objected, contending that this was precisely the quality Roberts lacked. Consequently no farewell letter was sent.

Roberts was a modest man, sensitive to his shortcomings. On leaving the bench he commented: "I have no illusion about my judicial career. . . . Who am I to revile the good God that did not make me a Marshall, a Taney, a Bradley, a Holmes, a Brandeis, or a Cardozo?"

ALPHEUS THOMAS MASON
(1986)

Bibliography

LEONARD, CHARLES A. 1971 *A Search for Judicial Philosophy: Mr. Justice Roberts.* Port Washington, N.Y.: Kennikat Press.

MASON, ALPHEUS T. 1956 *Harlan Fiske Stone: Pillar of the Law.* New York: Viking.

NOTE 1955 Owen J. Roberts—In Memoriam. *University of Pennsylvania Law Review* 104:311–317.

ROBERTS v. CITY OF BOSTON
5 Cush. (Mass.) 198 (1850)

In BROWN V. BOARD OF EDUCATION (1954) the Court observed that the SEPARATE BUT EQUAL DOCTRINE "apparently originated in *Roberts v. City of Boston.*" Chief Justice LEMUEL SHAW's opinion in that case had an extraordinary influence. The courts of at least ten states relied on it as a precedent for upholding segregated education. In HALL V. DECUIR (1878) the Supreme Court cited it as an authority for the rule that "equality does not mean identity." In PLESSY V. FERGUSON (1896) the Court relied on it as the leading precedent for the validity of state legislation requiring racial SEGREGATION in places where whites and blacks "are liable to be brought in to contact," and in GONG LUM V. RICE (1927) the Court explained *Roberts* as having sustained "the separation of colored and white schools under a state constitutional injunction of EQUAL PROTECTION, the same as the FOURTEENTH AMENDMENT. . . ."

Roberts arose as a TEST CASE to determine the validity of Boston's requirement that black children attend segregated schools. CHARLES SUMNER, attacking that requirement, denied that a racially separate school could be equal, because it imposed a stigma of caste and fostered prejudice.

Shaw, for a unanimous Supreme Judicial Court, agreed that the case presented the question whether the separate schools for blacks violated their constitutional right to equality. But he reasoned that all rights must depend on laws adapted to the "respective relations and conditions" of individuals. He believed that the school committee had exercised "a discriminating and honest judgment" in deciding that the good of both races was best promoted by the separate education of their children. The law, Shaw said in reply to Sumner, did not create prejudice, probably could not change it, and might only foster it by "compelling" both races to attend "the same schools." Thus, by a singular absence of considered judgment, the court found no constitutional violation of equal protection in compulsory racial segregation as long as blacks had an equal right to attend public schools.

LEONARD W. LEVY
(1986)

ROBERTS v. LOUISIANA

See: Capital Punishment Cases of 1976

ROBERTS v. UNITED STATES JAYCEES

See: Freedom of Association

ROBINSON, UNITED STATES v.
414 U.S. 218 (1973)

The Supreme Court here resolved the question whether the FOURTH AMENDMENT permits a full search of the person INCIDENT TO ARREST for a minor offense. This question is particularly acute in cases of traffic offenses, where police commonly make arrests in order to search drivers and their automobiles.

In *Robinson* the police stopped an automobile and arrested its driver for operating the vehicle without a license. A search of his clothing uncovered heroin. Because searches incident to arrest are allowed for the purpose of discovering concealed weapons and evidence, Robinson's counsel argued that such searches are unjustified in connection with routine traffic arrests: they will seldom yield evidence related to the traffic offense itself, and the chances of the driver's being armed are usually minimal.

The Supreme Court ruled, however, that a search incident to a custodial arrest requires no justification beyond the arrest; it is not an exception to the warrant requirement, but rather is itself a reasonable search. It was "speculative" to believe that those arrested for driving without

a license "are less likely to be armed than those arrested for other crimes." Any lawful arrest justifies "a full search of the person."

JACOB W. LANDYNSKI
(1986)

ROBINSON-PATMAN ACT
49 Stat. 1526 (1936)

The rapid growth of chain stores during the Depression effectively bypassed the price discrimination prohibitions of the CLAYTON ACT by altering the basic lines of competition which that act addressed. Shortly after the Supreme Court invalidated the NATIONAL INDUSTRIAL RECOVERY ACT'S codes of fair competition (beginning in SCHECHTER POULTRY CORPORATION V. UNITED STATES, 1935), Representative Wright Patman introduced a corrective bill into the House designed to regulate chain stores' use of economies of scale. As finally passed, the act amended section 2 of the Clayton Act. Although one section of the new act allowed price discrimination made "in good faith" to match a competitor's price, the act generally outlawed discrimination that "substantially lessened" competition or tended to create a monopoly. Other provisions prohibited the taking or making of allowances or commissions to buyers if not made proportionally. Buyers were also forbidden from "knowingly receiving" or inducing any discrimination. Although the act provided for suits by the Department of Justice and private individuals, the burden of enforcement fell on the FEDERAL TRADE COMMISSION. By tightening and narrowing section 2 of the Clayton Act, this legislation protected smaller firms by reducing the competitive advantages of large chains.

DAVID GORDON
(1986)

Bibliography
HANSEN, HUGH C. 1983 Robinson Patman Law: A Review and Analysis. *Fordham Law Review* 51:1113.

ROCHIN v. CALIFORNIA
342 U.S. 165 (1952)

To dispose of evidence, Rochin swallowed drug capsules. Officers pummeled his stomach and jumped on him in an effort to make him throw up the evidence. That failing, they rushed him to a hospital where a doctor, on police instructions, pumped an emetic solution through a tube into Rochin's stomach, forcing him to vomit the capsules. With that evidence the state convicted Rochin as a drug pusher. The Supreme Court unanimously reversed his conviction. Justice FELIX FRANKFURTER, for the Court, held that the state had violated Rochin's right to DUE PROCESS OF LAW. Due process, said Frankfurter, however "indefinite and vague," outlawed "conduct that shocks the conscience." State prosecutions must not, at the risk of violating due process, offend the "sense of justice" or of "fair play." Due process enjoined a respect for the "decencies of civilized conduct."

Justices HUGO L. BLACK and WILLIAM O. DOUGLAS, concurring separately, repudiated Frankfurter's reasoning as excessively subjective. His "nebulous" standard of due process, they believed, allowed the Court to draw upon undefinable notions of justice or decency or fairness. They would have ruled that the state violated Rochin's Fifth Amendment RIGHT AGAINST SELF-INCRIMINATION, which the FOURTEENTH AMENDMENT incorporated.

LEONARD W. LEVY
(1986)

ROCK ROYAL CO-OP, INC., UNITED STATES v.

See: *Wrightwood Dairy Co., United States v.*

RODNEY, CAESAR A.
(1772–1824)

Elected to the HOUSE OF REPRESENTATIVES in 1802, Jeffersonian Congressman Caesar Augustus Rodney became one of the managers of the IMPEACHMENT of Justice SAMUEL CHASE. In that capacity he argued that any deviation from GOOD BEHAVIOR on the part of a judge constituted a MISDEMEANOR in the constitutional sense and was, therefore, an impeachable offense even if not an indictable crime.

As attorney general of the United States (1807–1811), Rodney asserted President THOMAS JEFFERSON's right to overrule a federal court decision on enforcement of the EMBARGO ACTS and defended, in EX PARTE BOLLMAN AND SWARTWOUT (1807), prosecutions for constructive TREASON.

DENNIS J. MAHONEY
(1986)

ROE v. WADE
410 U.S. 113 (1973)
DOE v. BOLTON
410 U.S. 179 (1973)

In these cases the Supreme Court confronted the emotionally charged issue of abortion. The decisions invalidated two states' ABORTION laws—and, by inference, similar laws in a majority of states. As a result, the Court was plunged into prolonged and intense controversy, ranging from questions about the bearing of morality on constitutional law to questions about the proper role of the judiciary in the American system of government. The Court held unconstitutional a Texas law forbidding abortion except to save the pregnant woman's life and also invalidated several features of a Georgia law regulating abortion procedures and limiting abortion to Georgia residents.

The two women whose fictitious names grace the cases' titles were pregnant when they filed their actions in 1970, but not at the time of the Supreme Court's decision. The Court nonetheless held that their cases were not moot; rigid application of the MOOTNESS doctrine would prevent appellate review of an important issue that was capable of repetition. Nine doctors were also held to have STANDING to challenge the Georgia law; the intervention of a doctor under prosecution in Texas was held improper under the equitable ABSTENTION principle of YOUNGER V. HARRIS (1971); and a Texas married couple was denied standing because the woman had not been pregnant. The Court thus proceeded to the constitutional merits.

The *Roe* opinion, by Justice HARRY A. BLACKMUN, reviewed the history of abortion laws and the recent positions on abortion taken by medical groups and the American Bar Association, but the Court grounded its decision on neither history nor current professional opinion. Instead, the Court relied on a constitutional right of PRIVACY previously recognized in GRISWOLD V. CONNECTICUT (1965) and now relocated in the "liberty" protected by the DUE PROCESS clause of the FOURTEENTH AMENDMENT. This right included "a woman's decision whether or not to terminate her pregnancy," which decision was a FUNDAMENTAL INTEREST that could be restricted only on a showing of a COMPELLING STATE INTEREST.

The Court identified two state interests that would qualify as "compelling" at different stages in pregnancy: protection of maternal health and protection of potential life. Before discussing these interests, however, the Court dealt with a preliminary question: whether a fetus was a PERSON within the meaning of the Fourteenth Amendment. In an abortion, of course, it is not the state that denies life to a fetus; presumably the point of the Court's question was that if a fetus were a "person," the amendment should not be read to bar a state from protecting it against being aborted. The Court concluded, however, that a fetus was not a "person" in the amendment's contemplation. In reaching this conclusion, Justice Blackmun said: "We need not resolve the difficult question of when life begins." Absent a consensus among doctors, philosophers, or theologians on the issue, "the judiciary, at this point in the development of man's knowledge, is not in a position to speculate as to the answer." In any event, the law had never recognized the unborn "as persons in the whole sense." That conclusion alone, however, could not dispose of the question of the state's power. A state can constitutionally protect beings (or even things) that are not persons—including fetuses, which surely can be protected by law against certain kinds of experimentation or disposal, even though the law may be motivated by a feeling that fetuses share our common humanity.

The Court did recognize the state's interests in protecting maternal health and potential life; each would become "compelling" at successive stages of pregnancy. During the first trimester of pregnancy, neither interest is compelling; the abortion decision and its implementation must be left to the woman and her doctor. During the second trimester, the interest in maternal health becomes sufficiently compelling to justify some state regulations of the abortion procedure. When the fetus becomes "viable"—capable of life outside the womb, around the beginning of the third trimester of pregnancy—the state's interest in potential life becomes sufficiently compelling to justify prohibiting abortion except to preserve the "life or health" of the mother.

This scheme of constitutional rights has the look of a statute and evidently was influenced by New York's liberal law and the American Bar Association's model abortion law. Investigative reporters tell us that the three-part scheme resulted from negotiation among the Justices, and it is hard to see it as anything but a compromise between banning abortion altogether and turning over the entire abortion decision to the pregnant woman.

Justice BYRON R. WHITE, dissenting, complained that the Court had permitted abortion to satisfy "the convenience, whim or caprice of the putative mother." Chief Justice WARREN E. BURGER, concurring, responded that the Court had rejected "any claim that the Constitution requires abortion on demand" in favor of a scheme relying on doctors' "medical judgments relating to life and health." The Court's opinion deals ambiguously with the doctor's decisional role. At one point it states that the abortion decision "must be left to the medical judgment of the pregnant woman's attending physician." Yet the Court's decision rests on the constitutional right to privacy, which includes "a woman's decision whether or not to terminate her pregnancy." Very likely Justice Blackmun, a former general counsel of the Mayo Clinic, was influenced by the medical authorities he cited. Indeed, the Blackmun and Burger opinions both convey an inclination to convert abortion issues into medical questions. Linking the state's power to forbid abortions with "viability" is one example—although it is unclear how the Court will respond when medical technology permits the preservation of very young fetuses outside the womb. Similarly, a supposed lack of medical

consensus made the Court reluctant to decide when life begins.

The issues in *Roe*, however, were not medical issues. First, there is no medically correct decision concerning an abortion when the pregnant woman's health is not endangered. Second, there is no lack of medical consensus about what happens in the normal process of reproduction from insemination to birth. In some sense "life" begins at conception; to say otherwise is not to make a medical judgment but to decide a question of law or morality. The problem before the Court in *Roe* was to determine whether (or when) a state could constitutionally protect a fetus. The state's interest in potential life surely begins at the time of conception, and arguably before. Yet if *Griswold* and EISENSTADT V. BAIRD (1972) remained good law, the state could not constitutionally protect that interest by forbidding contraception. Most people do not equate the use of "morning after" pills or intrauterine devices with murder, although these forms of "contraception" are really ways of effecting abortion after conception. In 1973 no state was enforcing its abortion laws against such practices. Yet the argument that "life" begins at conception, for purposes of defining legal or moral rights, embraced the claims of both the newest embryo and the eight-month fetus. There was evident artificiality in the Court's selection of "viability" as the time when the state's concerns for potential life became "compelling," but there would have been artificiality in any resolution of the issue of state power other than an all-or-nothing decision.

In *Roe*'s companion case, *Doe v. Bolton*, the Court held invalid four provisions of Georgia law, requiring that abortions be: (1) performed in hospitals accredited by the Joint Commission on Accreditation of Hospitals; (2) approved by hospital staff committees; (3) approved in each case by two physicians other than the pregnant woman's doctor; and (4) limited to Georgia residents. The latter requirement was an obvious violation of Article IV's PRIVILEGES AND IMMUNITIES clause, and the other three were held to impose unreasonable restrictions on the constitutional right recognized in *Roe*.

The *Roe* opinion has found few defenders; even the decision's supporters are inclined to offer substitute justifications. *Roe*'s critics divide roughly into two groups: those who regard abortion as murder, and those who think the Supreme Court exceeded its proper institutional bounds, failing to ground its decision in the Constitution and merely substituting its own policy judgment for that of the people's elected representatives.

The latter criticism touched off an impressive succession of essays on JUDICIAL REVIEW. It was the former group of critics, however, who dominated the politics of abortion. The "right to life" movement was, for a time, one of the nation's most effective "single issue" groups, achieving enough respect from legislators to permit the adoption of laws withdrawing governmental financial aid to poor women who seek abortions. (See MAHER V. ROE, 1977; HARRIS V. MCRAE, 1980.) Various constitutional amendments to overturn *Roe* were proposed in Congress, but none was submitted to the states for ratification. In the early 1980s Congress considered, but did not adopt, a bill declaring that "human life begins from the moment of conception." Congress also heard proposals to withdraw federal court jurisdiction over abortion cases. (See JUDICIAL SYSTEM.) Yet the *Roe* decision has weathered all these political storms.

Roe's stability as a precedent is founded on the same social and political base that initially supported the decision. It was no accident that *Roe* was decided in the 1970s, when the movement against SEX DISCRIMINATION was winning its most important constitutional and political victories. The abortion question was not merely an issue between pregnant women and their unwanted fetuses; it was also a feminist issue, going to women's position in society in relation to men. Even today American society imposes a greater stigma on unmarried women who become pregnant than on the men who father their children, and society still expects women to take the major responsibility for contraception and child care. The implications of an unwanted pregnancy or parenthood for a woman's opportunities in education, employment, and personal association—indeed, for the woman's definition of self—are enormous. Justice White's dissenting remark, that abortion regulation is an issue about which "reasonable men may easily and heatedly differ," perhaps said more than he intended to say.

KENNETH L. KARST
(1986)

(SEE ALSO: *Reproductive Autonomy.*)

Bibliography

ELY, JOHN HART   1973   The Wages of Crying Wolf: A Comment on *Roe v. Wade. Yale Law Journal* 82:920–949.
HENKIN, LOUIS   1974   Privacy and Autonomy. *Columbia Law Review* 74:1410–1433.
Symposium on the Law and Politics of Abortion.   1979   *Michigan Law Review* 77:1569–1646.
TRIBE, LAURENCE H.   1978   *American Constitutional Law.* Pages 923–934. Mineola, N.Y.: Foundation Press.
WOODWARD, BOB and ARMSTRONG, SCOTT   1979   *The Brethren: Inside the Supreme Court.* Pages 165–189, 229–240. New York: Simon & Schuster.

ROGERS v. LODGE
458 U.S. 613 (1982)

Rogers v. Lodge involved a successful challenge to an at-large electoral scheme for county commissioners in Burke County, Georgia. The Supreme Court noted that at-large systems are not unconstitutional per se and that a challenge could succeed only upon a showing that the system was established or maintained for a discriminatory purpose. All sides conceded that blacks in Burke County had free access to registration, voting, and candidacy for office. The issue was not, therefore, equal participation in the electoral process but "effective" participation. The Court held that where there was evidence of the lingering effects of past RACIAL DISCRIMINATION that had limited "the ability of blacks to participate effectively in the political process," the district court was justified in finding that an electoral scheme that did not hold at least the potential of electing minority members to office in proportion to their numbers was maintained for discriminatory purposes in violation of the EQUAL PROTECTION clause. Thus the Court, while not requiring proportional representation, nevertheless permitted it to be used as the test in determining whether an electoral system worked to "diminish or dilute the political efficacy" of minorities.

EDWARD J. ERLER
(1986)

ROGERS v. RICHMOND
365 U.S. 534 (1961)

This is one of numerous cases prior to MALLOY V. HOGAN (1964) dealing with the question whether a confession was voluntary under a DUE PROCESS standard or coercive in violation of that standard. *Rogers* is significant because it was the first case in which the Court repudiated the test of trustworthiness as an element of the due process standard. Justice FELIX FRANKFURTER, for a 7–2 Court, declared that even if a confession were true or reliable, it should be excluded from admission in evidence if involuntary. Our system is accusatorial, not inquisitorial, Frankfurter said, and therefore the state must establish guilt by evidence not coerced from the accused.

LEONARD W. LEVY
(1986)

ROMER v. EVANS
517 U.S. 620 (1996)

Adopted by REFERENDUM in 1992, Amendment 2 to the Colorado Constitution provided that no state entity could provide any protection against discrimination based on homosexuality. The scope of Amendment 2 was unclear. Certainly it partially repealed several gay-rights ordinances, invalidating their protections for homosexuals but not their protections for heterosexuals. Likely it also barred state entities from telling their employees not to deny services to gay citizens. It could be repealed only by another amendment to the Colorado Constitution. In *Romer v. Evans* (1996), the Supreme Court invalidated Amendment 2 as a violation of the federal EQUAL PROTECTION clause.

Romer did not say that Amendment 2 unconstitutionally imposed electoral-process handicaps on a voting minority; or that SEXUAL ORIENTATION is a SUSPECT CLASSIFICATION; or that BOWERS V. HARDWICK (1986) is bad law.

Instead, the six-Justice majority held that Amendment 2 violated the Constitution's guarantee of equal protection of the laws "in the most literal sense" because it denied a designated group equality in seeking aid from the government. Furthermore, Amendment 2 failed RATIONAL BASIS review because it was so sweeping and yet so ill-fitted to the single trait it identified that the Court refused to credit its asserted justifications (FREEDOM OF ASSOCIATION and conservation of ANTIDISCRIMINATION resources). Amendment 2 showed "animus," a "bare . . . desire to harm an unpopular political group"—legislative purposes already ruled invalid in cases such as *Department of Agriculture v. Moreno* (1973) and CLEBURNE V. CLEBURNE LIVING CENTER, INC. (1985).

Justice ANTONIN SCALIA (with Chief Justice WILLIAM H. REHNQUIST and Justice CLARENCE THOMAS) vehemently disagreed. Far from denying equal protection of the laws, Scalia said, Amendment 2 only barred state subdivisions from giving special rights to an insistent minority. *Hardwick* had held that a popular majority rationally expresses its disapproval of homosexuality by criminalizing homosexual sodomy; surely voters can elect instead the more tolerant terms of Amendment 2. Indeed, the majority's silence about *Hardwick*, and the complete lack of PRECEDENT supporting its theory of "literal" violation, show indifference to the RULE OF LAW, judicial will to usurp democratic processes, and elite contempt for popular moral views.

Romer raises more questions than it answers. Is *Hardwick* OVERRULED? How far can government go in discriminating against homosexuals on the grounds of popular disapproval of them? When is antidiscrimination a "special right"? Does Amendment 2 exemplify the virtues or the dangers of DIRECT DEMOCRACY? Who decides on controversial social control measures promoting the good life: localities, state legislatures, state plebescites, or federal courts enforcing the Constitution?

JANET E. HALLEY
(2000)

Bibliography

FORD, RICHARD 1999 Law's Territory: A History of Jurisdiction. *Wisconsin Law Review* 97:843–930.

KARLAN, PAMELA S. 1997 Just Politics?: Five Not So Easy Pieces of the 1995 Term. *Houston Law Review* 34:289–313.

KEEN, LISA and GOLDBERG, SUZANNE 1998 *Strangers to the Law: Gay People on Trial.* Ann Arbor: University of Michigan Press.

SEIDMAN, LOUIS MICHAEL 1996 *Romer's* Radicalism: The Unexpected Revival of Warren Court Activism. *Supreme Court Review* 1996:67–121.

SUNSTEIN, CASS R. 1996 Foreword: Leaving Things Undecided. *Harvard Law Review* 110:4–101.

SYMPOSIUM 1997 Gay Rights and the Courts: The Amendment 2 Controversy. *University of Colorado Law Review* 68:285–452.

ROOSEVELT, FRANKLIN D.
(1882–1945)

Franklin Delano Roosevelt, four-time President of the United States, received his formal instruction in the constitutional system at Harvard College (1900–1904) and Columbia Law School (1904–1907). The mood of the Progressive period, however, was more potent than academic doctrine in shaping his understanding of the constitutional process.

His kinsman THEODORE ROOSEVELT, for whom he cast his first presidential vote in 1904, saw the Constitution "not as a straitjacket . . . but as an instrument designed for the life and healthy growth of the Nation." T. R. further saw the courts as "agents of reaction" and the President as the "steward of the people." If necessary, the President must be prepared to act as the savior of the Constitution against the courts, a role in which T. R. cast himself when he proposed the recall of judicial decisions in 1912. Service under WOODROW WILSON confirmed the young Franklin Roosevelt's belief in a spacious reading of executive authority, and experience as assistant secretary of the navy in wartime Washington showed him how emergency expanded presidential initiative.

After the Wilson administration, Roosevelt's return to legal practice was interrupted when he was crippled in 1921 by poliomyelitis. Elected governor of New York in 1928, he soon confronted the consequences of the Wall Street crash of 1929. He foresaw no constitutional objections to his state programs of unemployment relief, public power development, and land planning. "The United States Constitution," he said in a 1930 speech, "has proved itself the most marvelously elastic compilation of rules of government ever written." Though Roosevelt's purpose in that speech was to vindicate STATES' RIGHTS, he proved marvelously elastic himself when elected President in 1932. Favoring the concentration of power at whatever level of government he happened to be serving, he became thereafter a resolute champion of federal authority.

"Our Constitution," he said in his first inaugural address, "is so simple and practical that it is possible always to meet extraordinary needs by changes in emphasis and arrangement without loss of essential form." He hoped, he continued, to preserve the normal balance between executive and legislative authority. However, if the national emergency remained critical, "I shall ask the Congress for the one remaining instrument to meet the crisis—broad Executive power to wage a war against the emergency." He thus combined optimism about the essential elasticity of the Constitution with an understanding that extraordinary executive initiative must rest, not on inherent presidential power, but on the delegation to the President of powers possessed by Congress. To this he added a certain pessimism about the federal courts, assuming, as he had said during the 1932 campaign, that the Republican party had been in "complete control of all branches of the Federal Government . . . the Supreme Court as well."

For this last reason he was in no hurry to send NEW DEAL legislation through the gantlet of the Supreme Court. The first major test came in February 1935 over the constitutionality of the congressional JOINT RESOLUTION of June 1933 abrogating the so-called gold clause in public and private contracts. If the Court invalidated the resolution, the result would increase the country's total debt by nearly $70 billion. Roosevelt prepared a radio speech attacking an adverse decision and planned to invoke EMERGENCY POWERS to mitigate the effects. But while the Court, in PERRY V. UNITED STATES (1935), held the repudiation of the gold clause unconstitutional with regard to government bonds (though not to private obligations), it also held that, because the plaintiff had suffered no losses, he was not entitled to compensation. The administration's monetary policy remained precariously intact. (See GOLD CLAUSE CASES.)

But three months later in a 5–4 decision the Court nullified the Railroad Retirement Act as an invalid use of the commerce power. Then on May 27, in SCHECHTER POULTRY CORP. V. UNITED STATES it struck down the NATIONAL INDUSTRIAL RECOVERY ACT on two grounds: that the act involved excessive DELEGATION OF POWER by Congress, and that it exceeded the reach of congressional power under the COMMERCE CLAUSE. The vote against the National Recovery Administration was unanimous, as were two other decisions the same day—"Black Monday" in the eyes of New Dealers—one holding the FRAZIER-LEMKE FARM BANKRUPTCY ACT unconstitutional, the other denying the President the power to remove a member of a regulatory commission without congressional consent. If the Court was warning Roosevelt not to go to extremes, Roosevelt responded by warning the Court not to go to extremes either. Calling the SCHECHTER decision "more important probably than any decision since [DRED SCOTT V. SANDFORD

(1857)]," he said that it carried the Constitution back to "the horse-and-buggy definition of INTERSTATE COMMERCE."

Undeterred, the Court majority prosecuted its attack. In January 1936 six Justices in UNITED STATES V. BUTLER pronounced agriculture a "local" subject, beyond Congress's power, and set aside the AGRICULTURAL ADJUSTMENT ACT. Justice HARLAN F. STONE protested a "tortured construction of the Constitution" in an eloquent dissent. The Court majority, however, proceeded to strike down the Guffey Bituminous Coal Conservation Act, the Municipal Bankruptcy Act, and, finally, in MOREHEAD V. NEW YORK EX REL. TIPALDO (1936), a New York minimum wage law. The Court, Roosevelt now said, had thereby created a "no-man's-land' where no Government—State or Federal—can function." Between 1789 and 1865 the Court had declared only two acts of Congress unconstitutional; now, between 1934 and 1936, it invalidated thirteen. Doctrines propounded by the Court majority held out small hope for the SOCIAL SECURITY ACT, the WAGNER NATIONAL LABOR RELATIONS ACT, and other New Deal laws awaiting the judicial test. Roosevelt concluded that "[JOHN] MARSHALL's conception of our Constitution as a flexible instrument—adequate for all times, and, therefore, able to adjust itself as the new needs of new generations arose—had been repudiated."

By 1936 apprehension was spreading about the destruction of the New Deal by the unelected "Nine Old Men." Congress and the law schools were astir with proposals to rein in the Court. Roosevelt outlined three possibilities to his cabinet: limiting the power of the Court to invalidate congressional legislation; making an explicit grant to Congress of powers now in dispute; or ("a distasteful idea") packing the Court by appointing new judges. The first two courses required constitutional amendments. Roosevelt soon decided that an amendment would be difficult to frame, even more difficult to ratify, and in any event subject to judicial interpretation. The problem lay not in the Constitution but in the Court. In early 1936 he instructed Attorney General HOMER CUMMINGS to prepare in utmost secrecy a plan, short of amendment, that would overcome the Court's resistance.

Roosevelt did not make the Court an issue in the 1936 campaign. But his smashing victory in November convinced him that the moment had arrived. Cummings proposed legislation providing for the appointment of new Justices when sitting Justices failed to retire at the age of seventy. Roosevelt sprang the plan in a message to Congress on February 5, 1937. Claiming overcrowded dockets and overworked and overage judges, Roosevelt requested legislation that would enable him to appoint as many as six new Justices.

Postelection euphoria had evidently marred Roosevelt's

usually astute political judgment. Wider consultation might at least have persuaded him to make his case as an honest confrontation of power. The pretense that he was seeking merely to ease the burdens of the Court relied on arguments that Chief Justice CHARLES EVANS HUGHES soon demolished in a letter to the Senate Judiciary Committee. By the time Roosevelt began to present the true issue— "We must take action to save the Constitution from the Court and the Court from itself"—his initial trickiness had lost the court plan valuable momentum.

The Chief Justice had further resources. On March 29, in WEST COAST HOTEL V. PARRISH, a 5–4 Court upheld a Washington minimum wage law, thereby in effect over-ruling the *Tipaldo* decision taken the preceding term. The "switch in time" that "saved nine" was provided by Justice OWEN J. ROBERTS; because *Parrish* had been argued in December, Roberts's second thoughts, if affected by external circumstances, responded to the election, not to the Court plan. In March, the Court also upheld a slightly modified version of the Farm Bankruptcy Act rejected two years earlier. In April, in *National Labor Relations Board v. Jones Laughlin Steel Corporation*, the Court approved the National Labor Relations Act in a 5–4 decision in which, as Roberts later conceded, both he and Hughes reversed the position they had taken in condemning the Guffey Act the year before. In May the Court upheld the Social Security Act.

In two months, the Court, under the pressure of the election and the Roosevelt plan, wrought a constitutional revolution, recognizing in both federal and state governments powers it had solemnly denied them in the two previous years as contrary to the Constitution. It greatly enlarged the federal commerce power and the TAXING AND SPENDING POWER, gave new force to the GENERAL WELFARE CLAUSE, altered the application of the DUE PROCESS clause to the states, and abandoned the doctrine of excessive delegation as a means of invalidating federal legislation.

The Court's revisionism, by lessening the felt need for reform, strengthened opposition, already vehement, to the President's plan for the Court. Democrats joined Republicans in denouncing "court-packing." In May the decision of Justice WILLIS VAN DEVANTER to resign, opening the way for Roosevelt's first Supreme Court appointment, further weakened pressure for the plan. In the interests of Senate passage, Roosevelt promised the vacancy to the majority leader Senator Joseph T. Robinson. As Robinson was both old and conservative, he was an anomalous reform choice. By summer Roosevelt was belatedly ready to entertain compromise. But Robinson's death in July brought the bitter struggle to an end.

The insouciance with which Roosevelt presented the Court plan exacted heavy costs in the future of his domestic program, the unity of his party, the confidence of

the electorate, and his own self-confidence. Still, the plan attained its objective. As ROBERT H. JACKSON summed it up, "The President's enemies defeated the court reform bill— the President achieved court reform." The plan forced the Court to abandon rigid and restrictive constitutional views; at the same time, the plan's rejection eliminated COURT PACKING as a precedent for the future. History may well conclude both that Roosevelt was right to propose the plan and that the opposition was right to beat it.

In the next half dozen years Roosevelt made the Court his own, appointing HUGO L. BLACK (1937), STANLEY F. REED (1938), FELIX FRANKFURTER (1939), WILLIAM O. DOUGLAS (1939), FRANK MURPHY (1940), JAMES F. BYRNES (1941), Robert H. Jackson (1941), and WILEY B. RUTLEDGE (1943) as Associate Justices and Harlan F. Stone as Chief Justice (1941). In time the Roosevelt Court itself split between the apostles of judicial restraint, who had objected to the methods of the "Nine Old Men," and the activists, who had objected only to their results. But the new Court was united in affirming the reach of the national government's constitutional power to meet the social and economic problems created by the Great Depression.

With the status of New Deal legislation thus assured, Roosevelt's next tangle with constitutional issues took place in FOREIGN AFFAIRS. The Court in UNITED STATES V. CURTISS-WRIGHT EXPORT CORPORATION (1936) had unanimously endorsed the propositions that "the powers of external SOVEREIGNTY did not depend upon the affirmative grants of the Constitution" and that the President had in foreign affairs "a degree of discretion and freedom from statutory restriction which would not be admissible were domestic affairs alone involved." But Congress still had statutory control over vital areas of foreign policy. Neutrality, for example, had been a congressional prerogative since 1794. While Roosevelt requested discretionary neutrality legislation, he saw no practical choice but to accept mandatory laws passed by a stubbornly isolationist Congress. These laws placed the administration in a foreign policy straitjacket from which it sought to wriggle free to the very eve of Pearl Harbor.

Congress, too, retained the constitutional power to declare war. As Roosevelt reminded the French prime minister during the fall of France in 1940, assurance of aid did not imply military commitments; "only the Congress can make such commitments." And legislative power extended to a variety of defense questions. When Winston S. Churchill asked for the loan of old American destroyers, Roosevelt initially responded that "a step of that kind could not be taken except with the specific authorization of the Congress." Later Roosevelt was persuaded that he could make the transfer through executive action. Attorney General Robert H. Jackson's official opinion to this effect rested not on claims of inherent power as President or COMMANDER-IN-CHIEF but on the construction of laws passed by Congress. Critics found the argument strained, but public opinion supported the action.

The decisive step marking the end of American neutrality was the Lend-Lease Act, passed after full and vigorous debate in March 1941. Once Congress had authorized the lending and leasing of goods to keep Britain in the war, did this authority not imply an effort to make sure that the goods arrived? So Roosevelt evidently assumed, trusting that a murky proclamation of "unlimited national emergency" in May 1941 and the impact of Nazi aggression on public opinion would justify his policy. When Grenville Clark urged a joint resolution by which Congress would explicitly approve measures necessary to assure the delivery of supplies, Roosevelt replied in July that the time was not "quite right." The renewal of the draft the next month by a single-vote majority in the House of Representatives showed the fragility of congressional support. By autumn the navy, on presidential orders and without congressional authorization (until Neutrality Act revision in November), was fighting an undeclared war against Germany to protect convoys in the North Atlantic.

Roosevelt's actions in the latter part of 1941, like ABRAHAM LINCOLN's after the fall of Fort Sumter, were arguably unconstitutional, though not without historical precedent. He did not seek to justify the commitment of American forces to combat by pleas of inherent power as President or as Commander in Chief, and thereby proposed no constitutional novelties. If pressed, he perhaps would have associated himself with JOHN LOCKE, THOMAS JEFFERSON, and Abraham Lincoln in asserting not continuing presidential power but emergency prerogative to be exercised only when the life of the nation was at stake.

Entry into war, as always, increased unilateral presidential authority. When under the New Deal Roosevelt had acted most of the time on the basis of specific statutes, as a war President he acted very often on the basis of general powers claimed as "Commander in Chief in wartime" and on emergency powers activated by proclamation and conferred on an all-purpose agency, the Office of Emergency Management. Of the agencies established in 1940–1943 to control the war economy, only one, the Office of Price Administration, rested on a specific statute.

This statute ironically provoked Roosevelt's most notorious assertion of unilateral authority. The Price Control Act contained a farm parity provision deemed threatening to the anti-inflation program. Roosevelt told Congress in September 1942 that, if it did not repeal the provision within three weeks, he would refuse to execute it. "The President has the powers, under the Constitution and under Congressional Acts," he declared, "to take measures necessary to avert a disaster which would interfere with the winning of the war." He added, "When the war is won,

the powers under which I act automatically revert to the people—to whom they belong."

The international threat, as always, increased pressure on CIVIL LIBERTIES. In 1940, while protesting his sympathy with OLIVER WENDELL HOLMES's condemnation of wiretapping in OLMSTEAD V. UNITED STATES (1928), Roosevelt granted his attorney general qualified permission to wiretap "persons suspected of SUBVERSIVE ACTIVITIES against the United States." Given the conviction Roosevelt shared with most Americans that a Nazi victory in Europe would have endangered the United States, he would have been delinquent in his duty had he not taken precautionary measures. Though we know now that the internal menace was exaggerated, no one could be sure of that at the time.

Roosevelt, however, extended his concern to include Americans honestly opposed to intervention, directing the Federal Bureau of Investigation to investigate isolationists and their organizations. There was so little government follow-up of Roosevelt's prodding, however, that the prods were evidently taken by his subordinates as expressions of passing irritation rather than constant purpose. In 1941 Roosevelt appointed FRANCIS BIDDLE, a distinguished civil libertarian, as attorney general and kept him on the job throughout the war despite Biddle's repeated resistance to presidential requests that threatened the BILL OF RIGHTS.

Roosevelt's preoccupation with pro-Nazi agitation increased after Pearl Harbor. "He was not much interested in the theory of SEDITION," Biddle later recalled, "or in the constitutional right to criticize the government in wartime. He wanted this anti-war talk stopped." In time, his prods forced a reluctant Biddle to approve the indictment of twenty-six pro-Fascist Americans under a dubious application of the law of CRIMINAL CONSPIRACY. A chaotic trial ended with the death of the judge, and the case was dropped.

Biddle also resisted the most shameful abuse of power within the United States during the war—the relocation of Americans of Japanese descent. Here Roosevelt responded both to local pressure, including that of Attorney General EARL WARREN of California, and to the War Department, where such respected lawyers as Henry L. Stimson and John J. McCloy demanded action. Congress ratified Roosevelt's EXECUTIVE ORDER before it was put into effect, so the relocation did not represent a unilateral exercise of presidential power. The Supreme Court upheld the program in the JAPANESE AMERICAN CASES (1943–1944).

Still, despite Roosevelt's moments of impatience and exasperation, his administration's civil liberties record during WORLD WAR II was conspicuously better than that of the Lincoln administration during the CIVIL WAR or of the Wilson administration during WORLD WAR I. In 1944 the AMERICAN CIVIL LIBERTIES UNION saluted "the extraordinary and unexpected record . . . in freedom of debate and dissent on all public issues and in the comparatively slight resort to war-time measures of control or repression of opinion."

Roosevelt's presidency vindicated his conviction that social reform and military victory could be achieved without breaching the Constitution. A believer in a strong presidency, he was himself a strong President within, on the whole, constitutional bounds. His deviations from strict constitutional propriety were mostly under impressions, sometimes mistaken, of clear and present international danger. Those of his successors who claimed inherent presidential WAR POWERS went further than he ever did.

Roosevelt was a political leader, not a constitutional lawyer, and he correctly saw that in its major phase constitutional law is often a question of political and economic philosophy. No doubt his understanding of the practical necessity of consent was more important than technical appreciation of constitutional limitations in keeping his actions within the frame of the basic charter. But his presidency justified his inaugural assertion that the Constitution could meet extraordinary needs by changes in emphasis and arrangement without loss of essential form. His legacy was a revivified faith in the adequacy of the Constitution as a progressive document, equal to domestic and foreign emergency and "capable of meeting evolution and change."

ARTHUR M. SCHLESINGER, JR.
(1986)

Bibliography

ALSOP, JOSPEH and CATLEDGE, TURNER 1938 *The 168 Days.* Garden City, N.Y.: Doubleday.

BIDDLE, FRANCIS 1962 *In Brief Authority.* Garden City, N.Y.: Doubleday.

FREEDMAN, MAX, ed. 1967 *Roosevelt and Frankfurter: Their Correspondence, 1928–1945.* Boston: Little, Brown.

JACKSON, ROBERT H. 1941 *The Struggle for Judicial Supremacy: A Study of a Crisis in American Power Politics.* New York: Knopf.

MASON, A. T. 1956 *Harlan Fiske Stone: Pillar of the Law.* New York: Viking.

SCHLESINGER, ARTHUR M., JR. 1957–1960 *The Age of Roosevelt,* vols. I-III. Boston: Houghton Mifflin.

ROOSEVELT, THEODORE
(1858–1919)

The son of a New York City merchant and philanthropist and a descendant of the original Dutch settlers of New Amsterdam, Theodore Roosevelt was graduated magna cum laude from Harvard College in 1879. He studied law for one year at Columbia University, but never completed law school or practiced law. When he was twenty-three years old he published his first book (the influential *Naval War of 1812*) and was elected to the New York state legislature on the Republican ticket. In his second term, having successfully campaigned for a LEGISLATIVE INVESTIGATION of statewide corruption, he was chosen minority leader of the state Assembly, and from that position he engineered passage of the state civil service reform measures proposed by Democratic Governor GROVER CLEVELAND.

In 1886, after two years of ranching in the Dakota badlands, Roosevelt returned to New York City and attempted to resume his political career, but he was defeated in his race for mayor. He held no political office until 1889, when President BENJAMIN HARRISON appointed him to the United States Civil Service Commission, a post in which he was retained when Cleveland returned to the presidency. In 1895, Roosevelt became president of the New York City Police Commission; for more than two years he did public battle with police corruption and demon rum.

When WILLIAM MCKINLEY was elected President, Roosevelt went back to Washington as the vigorous assistant secretary of the Navy. At the beginning of the Spanish American War in 1898, Roosevelt resigned his office in the Navy Department and raised a regiment of volunteer cavalry, which he subsequently led in combat in Cuba. Riding the crest of fame from his wartime exploits, Roosevelt was elected governor of New York in 1898 and vice-president of the United States in 1900.

Roosevelt succeeded to the presidency when McKinley was assassinated in September 1901. He immediately pledged that his aim was "to continue, absolutely unbroken, the policy of President McKinley." But neither his love of fame nor his reformist impulses would permit him to redeem that pledge. Having reached the highest office in the land at a younger age than anyone before or since, he displayed a degree of vigor and impatience far greater than his predecessors had done. He also had a more expansive view of the powers and duties of the President than any of his predecessors since ABRAHAM LINCOLN. Not only did he think of the presidency as a "bully pulpit" from which one might lead, rather than follow, public opinion, but he also conceived of the office as having a roving commission to do anything the public weal might require so long as the Constitution did not by its terms prohibit the proposed course of action.

In FOREIGN AFFAIRS, Roosevelt acted with particular energy. On his own initiative he imposed a form of government in the Philippines (a commission headed by WILLIAM HOWARD TAFT) that Congress subsequently confirmed in the Philippine Organic Act (1902). He arranged by treaty for America to take over the British interest in construction of a canal across the Isthmus of Panama and subsequently fomented a revolt of Panamanians against the government of Colombia so that a favorable PANAMA CANAL TREATY could be negotiated (1903) and work on the canal begun. When the Latin American countries of Venezuela and Santo Domingo (now the Dominican Republic) defaulted on loans from European banks, Roosevelt put those countries under American occupation and receivership rather than risk military intervention by Europeans in the Western Hemisphere. This policy he called his "corollary" to the MONROE DOCTRINE. When an American citizen was kidnapped in 1904 by a band of Moroccan brigands, Roosevelt ordered a force of sailors and marines to invade a neutral and sovereign state to secure the citizen's release. Roosevelt also personally mediated the settlement of the Russo-Japanese War in 1905 (thereby earning the Nobel Peace Prize), and his administration was instrumental in achieving agreements to guarantee the independence of Morocco (1906) and to settle disputes among the Central American republics (1907). When Congress refused to appropriate funds so that the United States fleet could make a round-the-world show-the-flag cruise, Roosevelt used his power as COMMANDER-IN-CHIEF to order the ships to go as far as they could, confident that Congress would appropriate the funds to bring them home.

In domestic policy, Roosevelt's administration was both nationalist and interventionist. Roosevelt resumed prosecutions under the SHERMAN ANTITRUST ACT (albeit not so vigorously as his later critics would have liked) and proposed what became the HEPBURN ACT (1906), giving the Interstate Commerce Commission authority to set railroad rates nationwide. He put the federal government into the business of conserving America's wild places and natural resources, creating the Inland Waterways Commission (1907) and the National Conservation Commission (1908).

Roosevelt was generally critical of the constitutional jurisprudence of his day, and especially of the Supreme Court's protection of SUBSTANTIVE DUE PROCESS OF LAW in cases relating to ECONOMIC REGULATION. He emphatically rejected the contention that criticism of the judiciary weakens respect for law and undermines the independence of the judiciary. In his sixth state-of-the-Union message, he said: "The judge has a power over which no review can be exercised; he himself sits in review upon the acts of both the executive and legislative branches of the government; save in the most extraordinary cases he is amenable only at the bar of public opinion; and it is unwise to maintain that public opinion in reference to a man with such power shall neither be exprest nor led." Influenced by some of the more radical strains of PROGRESSIVE CONSTITUTIONAL THOUGHT, he favored a right of popular "recall" of state judicial decisions, that is, of al-

lowing decisions to be overturned by a vote of the people. His first appointee to the Supreme Court, OLIVER WENDELL HOLMES of Massachusetts, initially so disappointed Roosevelt that the President remarked that he could "carve a judge with more backbone from a banana." Roosevelt's two other appointees, WILLIAM R. DAY and WILLIAM MOODY, both generally provided judicial support for state and federal regulation of business enterprise.

In 1908, Roosevelt did not seek reelection, but handpicked as his successor William Howard Taft. He then retired from politics to a life of writing and adventuring. But Roosevelt disapproved of the conservative tone assumed by the Taft administration and attempted to wrest the 1912 Republican nomination for himself. When Taft was renominated, Roosevelt formed his own party, the Progressive party, and ran for President anyway. Roosevelt's candidacy split the Republican vote and permitted the election of WOODROW WILSON.

Roosevelt was later reconciled to the Republican party and in 1916 campaigned for the Republican presidential candidate, CHARLES EVANS HUGHES. When the United States entered WORLD WAR I, Roosevelt asked President Wilson to authorize him to raise and command a volunteer division to serve in the expeditionary force; Wilson refused. After the war, Roosevelt opposed Wilson's plan for a League of Nations, preferring that the postwar world be dominated by an Anglo-American alliance. When he died, in 1919, Roosevelt was beginning to plan for yet another attempt at reelection to the presidency.

DENNIS J. MAHONEY
(1986)

Bibliography

BLUM, JOHN MORTON 1954 *The Republican Roosevelt.* Cambridge, Mass.: Harvard University Press.

MORRIS, EDMUND 1979 *The Rise of Theodore Roosevelt.* New York: Coward, McCann & Geohegan.

MOWRY, GEORGE E. 1958 *The Era of Theodore Roosevelt: 1900–1912.* New York: Harper & Brothers.

ROOSEVELT COURT

Following the constitutional crisis of 1937, President FRANKLIN D. ROOSEVELT, who had made no appointments to the Supreme Court in his first term, eventually named eight men to the bench between 1937 and 1943: HUGO L. BLACK, STANLEY F. REED, FELIX FRANKFURTER, WILLIAM O. DOUGLAS, FRANK MURPHY, JAMES F. BYRNES, ROBERT H. JACKSON, and WILEY B. RUTLEDGE as associate justices, and he elevated HARLAN FISKE STONE to be CHIEF JUSTICE—more appointments than any President other than GEORGE WASHINGTON.

It was assumed that Roosevelt's appointees would share his philosophy of government and would interpret the Constitution broadly to give the President and Congress adequate power to meet the nation's needs. In this the President and his followers were not disappointed. The so-called Roosevelt Court took a very liberal approach in its interpretation of the commerce power, giving near *carte blanche* to the federal government in any matters affecting business and labor. It abandoned SUBSTANTIVE DUE PROCESS and FREEDOM OF CONTRACT, which had been the main bulwarks of conservative jurists against NEW DEAL reform LEGISLATION, and it set about revising the traditional relationships among the government, the private sector, and the individual.

Perhaps the best example of the Roosevelt Court's broad view of the commerce power is its sustaining part of the Second Agricultural Administration Act (1938). In his Court opinion upholding the wheat quota provisions of the law in WICKARD V. FILBURN (1942), Jackson abandoned the old distinction between production (essentially a local activity) and commerce, and gave the federal government the power to regulate even the wheat grown on a farm for the farmer's own use.

After having been stymied for so long by freedom of contract arguments, reformers could now look to a Court that agreed that the federal government had power to regulate the labor market, and the Roosevelt Court sustained the New Deal labor policy enunciated in the 1935 WAGNER (NATIONAL LABOR RELATIONS) ACT. By treating labor as one of the important factors affecting INTERSTATE COMMERCE, the Court in several cases involving the National Labor Relations Board upheld its power to impose collective bargaining and union recognition, even on plants operating within just one state. The Court also upheld the wages and hours provisions of the 1938 FAIR LABOR STANDARDS ACT in UNITED STATES V. DARBY LUMBER COMPANY (1941).

But critics who charged that Roosevelt had replaced an autonomous judiciary with a rubber-stamp court misunderstood the fiercely independent nature of men like Black, Douglas, and Frankfurter. While they shared the New Deal perspective on commerce and labor, the Court's agenda was already changing. During the first part of the century the Court had confronted primarily economic issues; starting in the late 1930s, more and more cases involving individual CIVIL LIBERTIES and CIVIL RIGHTS appeared on the docket. While in general the Roosevelt appointees favored such rights, they differed significantly over how the BILL OF RIGHTS should be interpreted, which provisions should be applied to the states, and how far the Court should be involved in the emerging civil rights struggle.

In 1938, in his famous footnote four in UNITED STATES V. CAROLENE PRODUCTS CO., Stone had suggested that the courts should defer to legislatures in economic matters,

but that it should impose higher STANDARDS OF REVIEW in cases involving individual civil liberties and civil rights. The Court began to move in that direction during WORLD WAR II, when (with the exception of the JAPANESE AMERICAN CASES), it paid more attention to individual rights than had any other Court in history. But it got bogged down over the question of whether and how the DUE PROCESS clause of the FOURTEENTH AMENDMENT applied to the states.

Frankfurter, following the line set out by Justice BENJAMIN N. CARDOZO in PALKO V. CONNECTICUT (1937), argued that there should be only "selective" incorporation of the Bill of Rights, involving only those rights that could be ranked as "fundamental." Although Black had originally agreed with this view, during the war he came to espouse the notion of "total" incorporation of all the Bill of Rights in applying to the states. The clearest exposition of this division, which would occupy the Court through most of the 1940s and 1950s, can be found in the respective opinions of Black and Frankfurter in ADAMSON V. CALIFORNIA (1947). Although a majority of the Court adhered to Frankfurter's rationale, in the end they adopted Black's goal with a near total incorporation of all the Bill of Rights.

Although the four Justices appointed by HARRY S. TRUMAN diluted the "Roosevelt Court," it is important to keep in mind how long many of Roosevelt's appointees served on the bench. In 1954, the Court that handed down BROWN V. BOARD OF EDUCATION still had Black, Reed, Frankfurter, Douglas, and Jackson on it. Frankfurter served until 1962, Black until 1971, and Douglas until 1975. For more than three decades, all of the great decisions on REAPPORTIONMENT, civil rights, FREEDOM OF SPEECH, PROCEDURAL DUE PROCESS, and FEDERALISM bore the imprint of one or more members of the Roosevelt Court.

MELVIN I. UROFSKY
(2000)

(SEE ALSO: *Constitutional History, 1933–1945; Constitutional History, 1945–1961; Incorporation Doctrine.*)

Bibliography

CURRIE, DAVID P. 1990 *The Constitution in the Supreme Court: The Second Century, 1888–1986.* Chicago: University of Chicago Press.

CURTIS, MICHAEL KENT 1986 *No State Shall Abridge: The Fourteenth Amendment and the Bill of Rights.* Durham, N.C.: Duke University Press.

CUSHMAN, BARRY 1998 *Rethinking the New Deal Court: The Structure of a Constitutional Revolution.* New York: Oxford University Press.

LEUCHTENBURG, WILLIAM E. 1995 *The Supreme Court Reborn.* New York: Oxford University Press.

PRITCHETT, C. HERMAN 1954 *The Roosevelt Court: A Study in Judicial Politics and Values, 1937–1947.* New York: Macmillan.

UROFSKY, MELVIN I. 1997 *Division and Discord: The Supreme Court Under Stone and Vinson, 1941–1953.* Columbia: University of South Carolina Press.

ROSENBERG v. UNITED STATES
346 U.S. 273 (1953)

Over the vehement protests of three of its members (HUGO BLACK, FELIX FRANKFURTER, and WILLIAM O. DOUGLAS), the VINSON COURT vacated a STAY OF EXECUTION issued by Douglas that had halted the scheduled electrocution of Julius and Ethel Rosenberg. The Rosenbergs had been convicted and sentenced to death in 1951 for allegedly violating the 1917 ESPIONAGE ACT by passing secret information about the atomic bomb to the Soviet Union. Douglas had refused to join Black, Frankfurter, and HAROLD BURTON in earlier efforts to review the case by means of CERTIORARI and HABEAS CORPUS, but on June 17, 1953, after the Court had recessed for the term, he stayed the Rosenbergs' execution on the ground that their lawyers had raised a new argument deserving judicial scrutiny— the couple should have been tried under the Atomic Energy Act of 1946 rather than the earlier statute.

Responding to intense pressure from the Eisenhower administration, Chief Justice FRED VINSON recalled the Justices to Washington for special session. On June 19, a 6–3 majority overturned the stay and rejected Douglas's interpretation of the Atomic Energy Act. The Rosenbergs were executed that same evening. Frankfurter, who, with Black, had urged a full review of the case since the earliest appeals, later wrote that this last act of the Vinson Court was "the most disturbing single experience I have had during my term of service on the Court."

MICHAEL E. PARRISH
(1986)

Bibliography

RADOSH, RONALD and MILTON, JOYCE 1983 *The Rosenberg File: A Search for the Truth.* New York: Holt, Rinehart & Winston.

ROSENBERGER v. RECTOR & VISITORS OF THE UNIVERSITY OF VIRGINIA
515 U.S. 819 (1995)

Does the FIRST AMENDMENT ban on ESTABLISHMENT OF RELIGION mean that when a public university provides money for printing expenses for extracurricular student political, cultural, and ideological groups, that a nondenominational Christian student group must be excluded? The Supreme Court said "no" in *Rosenberger v. Rector & Visitors of the University of Virginia,* decided in 1995. The Christian group was not seeking special treatment: subsidies were going to a wide variety of student groups without regard to the opinions they were putting forth. By a 5–4 margin, the Court held that subsidizing the Christian newspaper along with all the others does not establish religion, and that it would violate the FREEDOM OF SPEECH for the university to discriminate against the Christians because of their religious message.

The case represents a clash between a "neutrality" view of the ESTABLISHMENT CLAUSE and a "separationist" view. Neutrality means that the government must not discriminate in favor of religion, but may provide benefits that are equally available to others. According to the separationist view—which first appeared in Supreme Court decisions in the late 1940s—government should be forbidden to give any "direct" support to religion, even on a nondiscriminatory basis.

Separationists try to distinguish between direct and indirect support in order to justify government services like police and fire protection for churches. But is nonprofit tax exemption direct or indirect aid? What about allowing a religious student group to meet on campus at the state university? Is there a relevant difference between providing the students a room and providing them a subsidy for printing costs?

The *Rosenberger* decision clearly leans toward the neutrality view of the First Amendment: that government programs should not discriminate for or against religion. But even the majority opinion was not unequivocal on this principle, and the four dissenters would have prohibited the printing subsidy as a violation of the establishment clause. *Rosenberger* is surely a step away from the idea that religious groups and institutions should be specially targeted for exclusion from public programs. But the argument for neutrality under the First Amendment has not— at least yet—conclusively been won.

MAIMON SCHWARZSCHILD
(2000)

(SEE ALSO: *Government Aid to Religious Institutions; Religious Liberty; Separation of Church and State.*)

ROSS, UNITED STATES v.
456 U.S. 798 (1982)

Ross altered the constitutional law of AUTOMOBILE SEARCHES. A UNITED STATES COURT OF APPEALS, following Supreme Court PRECEDENTS, had held that although police had PROBABLE CAUSE to stop an automobile and make a WARRANTLESS SEARCH of its interior, including its closed areas, they should have had a SEARCH WARRANT before opening closed containers that they had searched for evidence. And in *Robbins v. California* (1981) the Court had declared that unless a closed container, by its shape or transparency, revealed contraband, it might not be opened without a warrant. The rationale of requiring a warrant for such a search turned on the reasonable expectation of privacy protected by the FOURTH AMENDMENT. *Ross*, however, substantially expanded the automobile exception to the warrant requirement.

Justice JOHN PAUL STEVENS for a 6–3 Court declared that the question for decision was whether the police, making a warrantless search with probable cause, had a right to open containers found in a vehicle. A lawful search of any premises extended to the whole area where the object of the search might be found. Thus a warrant to search a vehicle authorizes the search of all closed areas within it, including containers. "The scope of a warrantless search based on probable cause," Stevens said, "is no narrower—and no broader—than the scope of a search authorized by a warrant supported by probable cause." Accordingly, the scope of the search depended on the EVIDENCE sought for, not on the objects containing that evidence. Having so reasoned, the Court necessarily overruled the *Robbins* holding.

Justices THURGOOD MARSHALL, WILLIAM J. BRENNAN, and BYRON R. WHITE, dissenting, lamented that "the majority today not only repeals all realistic limits on warrantless automobile searches, it repeals the Fourth Amendment warrant requirement itself"—patently an exaggeration. *Ross* did make a shambles of the reasoning in earlier cases on searching closed containers in automobiles, but the Court finally delivered an unambiguous opinion for the guidance of law enforcement officers. Whether or not the Court based the new rule on expediency for the purpose of assisting prosecutorial forces, it will likely have serious implications for the privacy of Americans using their vehicles.

LEONARD W. LEVY
(1986)

ROSS v. MOFFITT
417 U.S. 600 (1974)

Ross sharply limited the requirement of DOUGLAS V. CALIFORNIA (1963) that counsel be provided, free of charge, to INDIGENTS seeking to appeal from state convictions. The *Douglas* opinion had referred only to the "first appeal as of right," and here the Supreme Court's 6–3 majority drew the line defining the state's constitutional responsibility at precisely that point. There was no obligation to furnish counsel to pursue discretionary appeals or applications for Supreme Court review. Justice WILLIAM H. REHNQUIST's ma-

jority opinion did distinguish *Douglas*, but its reasoning drew heavily on the *Douglas* dissent of Justice JOHN MARSHALL HARLAN.

KENNETH L. KARST
(1986)

ROSSITER, CLINTON
(1917–1970)

Clinton Lawrence Rossiter III was a political scientist, constitutional scholar, and historian. His fascination with the response of constitutional government to the exigencies of crisis and war led to his first two books, *Constitutional Dictatorship* (1948) and *The Supreme Court and the Commander in Chief* (1951). His most widely read work, *The American Presidency* (1956, rev. ed. 1960), a deft and approving account of the Presidency's growth in power, influence, and responsibility, was perhaps the most influential study of that institution before Watergate. *Seedtime of the Republic*, a monumental intellectual history of the AMERICAN REVOLUTION, traced the roots of the Revolutionary generation's political ideas to seventeenth-century English republican thought. Rossiter's other works include *Parties and Politics in America* (1960), *Conservatism in America* (1955, rev. ed. 1962), *Alexander Hamilton and the Constitution* (1964), *1787: The Grand Convention* (1966), and the posthumously published *The American Quest, 1790–1860* (1971).

RICHARD B. BERNSTEIN
(1986)

ROSTKER v. GOLDBERG
453 U.S. 57 (1981)

Men subject to registration for possible military CONSCRIPTION challenged the exclusion of women from the registration requirement as a denial of EQUAL PROTECTION. The Supreme Court, 6–3, rejected this claim. Justice WILLIAM H. REHNQUIST, for the majority, paid great deference to Congress's authority over military affairs; with the most minimal judicial second-guessing of the congressional judgment, he concluded that men and women were "not similarly situated," because any draft would be designed to produce combat troops, and women were ineligible for combat. SEX DISCRIMINATION, in other words, was its own justification.

As the dissenters demonstrated, the exclusion of women from draft registration had resulted from no military judgment at all; the President and the Joint Chiefs of Staff had urged that women be registered. Rather, Congress had heard the voice of public opinion. It is not impossible that the Court itself heard that voice. Thus do sex-role stereotypes perpetuate themselves.

KENNETH L. KARST
(1986)

ROTH v. UNITED STATES
354 U.S. 476 (1957)

ALBERTS v. CALIFORNIA
354 U.S. 476 (1957)

Until *Roth* and *Alberts*, argued and decided on the same days, the Supreme Court had assumed that the FIRST AMENDMENT did not protect OBSCENITY. Squarely confronted with the issue by appeals from convictions under the federal obscenity statute (in *Roth*) and a California law outlawing the sale and advertising of obscene books (in *Alberts*), the Court held that obscenity was not constitutionally protected speech.

Justice WILLIAM J. BRENNAN, for the majority, relied on historical evidence that the Framers of the First Amendment had not intended to protect all speech, but only speech with some redeeming social value. Thus, the First Amendment protected even hateful ideas that contributed toward the unfettered exchange of information that might result in desired political and social change. Obscenity, however, was utterly without redeeming social importance, and was not constitutionally protected.

Neither statute before the Court defined obscenity; nor did the Court examine the materials to determine whether they were obscene. The Court nevertheless rejected the appellants' due process objections on the grounds that the statutes had given sufficient warning as to the proscribed conduct and the trial courts had applied the proper standard for judging obscenity.

The Court rejected the widely used test based on *Queen v. Hicklin* (1868) which judged a work's obscenity by the effect of an isolated excerpt upon particularly susceptible persons. The proper standard was "whether to the average person, applying contemporary community standards, the dominant theme taken as a whole appeals to prurient interest," that is, has a tendency to excite lustful thoughts. Because the obscenity of the materials involved in *Roth* was not at issue, the Court escaped the task of applying its definition. Ironically, the definition of obscenity was to preoccupy the Court for the next sixteen years. The Court, having designated a category of speech that could be criminally proscribed, now confronted the critical task of delineating that category.

Chief Justice EARL WARREN and Justice JOHN MARSHALL HARLAN, separately concurring, sought to limit the scope of the majority opinion. Warren, concurring in the result,

agreed that the defendants' conduct in commercially exploiting material for its appeal to prurient interest was constitutionally punishable. Harlan, concurring in *Alberts* and dissenting in *Roth*, believed the Court was required to examine each work individually to determine its obscene character, and argued that the Constitution restricted the federal government in this field more severely than it restricted the states. Justices WILLIAM O. DOUGLAS and HUGO L. BLACK, dissenting in both cases, enunciated the positions they were to take in the wave of obscenity cases soon to overwhelm the Court: obscenity, like every other form of speech, is absolutely protected by the First Amendment.

KIM MCLANE WARDLAW
(1986)

RULE OF FOUR

Even before Congress expanded the Supreme Court's discretionary CERTIORARI jurisdiction in 1925, the Court had adopted the practice of granting certiorari whenever four of the nine Justices agreed that a case should be heard. This "rule of four" was first made public in testimony concerning the bill that became the 1925 act. Some commentators have seen the adoption of that act as a congressional ratification of the practice; in any case, the rule is well established. In *Rogers v. Missouri Pacific R.R.* (1957) a majority agreed that the rule required the Court to hear a petition granted on the vote of four Justices, even though the other five might still think the case unworthy of review, unless new considerations had come to light in the meanwhile. As *New York v. Uplinger* (1984) makes clear, however, the vote of four Justices to *hear* a case does not require the Court to *decide* it if the other five Judges think a decision inappropriate.

The Court follows a similar practice in APPEAL cases coming from the state courts. The Court has even dismissed such an appeal "for want of a substantial FEDERAL QUESTION" over the expressed dissent of three Justices. When three members of the Court argue that a question is a substantial one, it probably is. The dismissal of an appeal under these circumstances reinforces the view that appeal, despite its theoretically obligatory nature as defined by Congress, has taken on much of the discretionary quality of the Court's certiorari policy.

KENNETH L. KARST
(1986)

Bibliography

LEIMAN, JOAN MEISEL   1957   The Rule of Four. *Columbia Law Review* 57:975–992.

RULE OF LAW

The rule of law is the general principle that government and the governed alike are subject to law, as regularly adopted and applied. The principle is nowhere express in the United States Constitution, but it is a concept of basic importance in Anglo-American constitutional law. In that context, it is not merely a positivist doctrine of legality, requiring obedience to any duly adopted doctrine, but a means to assure that the actions of all branches of government are measured against the fundamental values enshrined in the COMMON LAW and the Constitution.

The rule of law has its roots in classical antiquity, in the *Politics* of Aristotle and the works of Cicero. As an Anglo-American legal principle, the concept may be traced to MAGNA CARTA (1215). In the thirty-ninth clause of that instrument, King John promised the barons that "No free man shall be taken, imprisoned, disseized, outlawed, or banished, or in any way destroyed, nor will we proceed against or prosecute him, except by the lawful judgment of his peers and the LAW OF THE LAND." Four centuries later, with the principle well entrenched in the theory and practice of the English common law, EDWARD COKE challenged James I's assertion of the right to exercise an independent judicial power with the words of Henry Bracton: "Quod Rex non debet esse sub homine, sed sub Deo et lege" [The King ought not to be under man, but under God and the law.] After the chaos of revolution, commonwealth, and restoration, the Glorious Revolution of 1688 established the permanent subjection of the king to the law, both of the common law courts and of Parliament.

Coke's *Reports* and *Institutes*, JOHN LOCKE's *Second Treatise of Government* (1691), and the flood of English radical political writing that accompanied the events of the seventeenth and eighteenth centuries carried these ideas to the American colonies. They became a key element in the ideology of the American Revolution. THOMAS PAINE's *Common Sense* (1776) proclaimed, "that in America, *the law is king.* For as in absolute governments, the king is law, so in free countries the law ought to be king; and there ought to be no other." As the unprecedented era of constitution making that succeeded the American Revolution provoked more sophisticated analysis of the structure of government, it became clear that not only the executive but also the legislature must be subject to law. Thus, JOHN ADAMS more temperately but more tellingly expressed the principle of the rule of law in drafting the MASSACHUSETTS CONSTITUTION of 1780. The Declaration of Rights in that instrument called for the SEPARATION OF POWERS, "to the end it may be a government of laws and not of men." Chief Justice JOHN MARSHALL gave practical effect to Adams's words in the actual application of the new federal Consti-tution, using them in MARBURY V. MADISON (1803) to bolster his argument that William Marbury had a judicial remedy for the withholding of his commission by the secretary of state.

The principle was elaborated and definitively labeled "the Rule of Law" by the leading nineteenth-century English constitutional theorist Albert Venn Dicey (1835–1922). In his influential work, *Introduction to the Study of Law of the Constitution* (1885), Dicey ranked the rule of law with parliamentary SOVEREIGNTY and constitutional conventions as one of the three fundamental elements of the unwritten British constitution. He gave the term "rule of law" three meanings: a requirement that government act against the citizen only in accordance with "regular law" enforced in the "ordinary courts" and not arbitrarily or in the exercise of "wide discretionary authority"; a requirement that the government and all citizens be equal before the law and equally subject to the ordinary courts; and a formulation reflecting the fact that constitutional rights were grounded not in abstract principles but in "the ordinary law of the land" as enforced in the courts.

Dicey's views of the rule of law have been rigorously elaborated by later political theorists, notably Friedrich Hayek in his *Constitution of Liberty* (1960) and other works. The fundamental nature of the rule of law as the basis of a moral and just social order has been recognized in more general terms in works such as Lon Fuller's *The Morality of Law* (1964) and John Rawls's *A Theory of Justice* (1971). It is also seen in the efforts of internationalists in the 1960s to establish international doctrines of world peace and human rights through a "world rule of law." More recently, critics have challenged the legitimacy of the rule of law, characterizing it as simply a cover for the maintenance of power by privileged social classes. Roberto Unger, in *Law and Modern Society* (1976), questioned the viability of the rule of law in the modern welfarecorporate state as the liberal premises upon which it is based decline.

Dicey's elaboration of the rule of law has also been forcefully criticized in England and the United States because its prohibition of discretionary action is inconsistent with the widespread use of the administrative process that has become characteristic of modern democratic government. Kenneth Culp Davis, a leading American critic, attributed the virtual nonuse of the phrase in American judicial opinions to the unreality of Dicey's "extravagant version" of the doctrine. Its occasional appearance to highlight a discussion of fairness or legality reflects, according to Davis, only the tendency of some judges "to add the touch of poetry" to their work.

Nevertheless, the concept of the rule of law remains fundamental to Anglo-American constitutional jurisprudence. In Britain, it remains a device for calling upon the protections of the common law against legislative and executive intrusion. In the United States, at the most general level, the rule of law is invoked by judges as they seek to assure compliance by the federal and state governments with the guarantees of the BILL OF RIGHTS. Those guarantees, as interpreted by the courts, are binding upon the governments and individuals to whom they are addressed. The Supreme Court made this point clear in COOPER V. AARON (1958), rejecting the position of defiance toward a federal court's school desegregation order taken by the governor and legislature of Arkansas.

More specifically, the concept of the rule of law embodies what Laurence H. Tribe has characterized as "the Model of Governmental Regularity." This model describes requirements of generality and prospectivity of legislation and procedural regularity in administration and adjudication that are articulated in and enforced through the EX POST FACTO and BILL OF ATTAINDER clauses of the Constitution and the DUE PROCESS clauses of the Fifth and FOURTEENTH AMENDMENTS. Finally, the element of equality in Dicey's rule of law has received fundamental expression in the development of the EQUAL PROTECTION clause of the Fourteenth Amendment. That clause, as interpreted and applied by the Supreme Court in the second half of the twentieth century, has provided constitutional support for the most profound changes that our society has seen, short of revolution or civil war.

L. KINVIN WROTH
(1986)

Bibliography

ALLAN, T. R. S. 1985 Legislative Supremacy and the Rule of Law. *Cambridge Law Journal* 44:111–143.
DICEY, ALBERT VENN 1885 *Introduction to the Study of the Law of the Constitution.* London: Macmillan.
TRIBE, LAURENCE H. 1978 *American Constitutional Law.* Mineola, N.Y.: Foundation Press.

RULE OF REASON

The rule of reason was a statutory construction of the SHERMAN ANTITRUST ACT by the Supreme Court. Nothing better illustrated JUDICIAL POLICYMAKING than the rule of reason, which held that the Sherman Act excepted from its scope "good trusts" or "reasonable restraints of trade." The statute expressly declared illegal "every" contract, combination, and conspiracy in restraint of trade, and as a result the Court in several early cases rejected the argument that "every" did not mean what it said. The Court also denied that the statute should be construed in the light of the COMMON LAW, which had recognized the legal-

ity of certain ancillary restraints of trade on the ground that they were reasonable. For example, in UNITED STATES V. TRANS-MISSOURI FREIGHT ASSOCIATION (1897) the Court rejected the proposition that "Congress, notwithstanding the language of the [Sherman] act, could not have intended to embrace all contracts, but only such contracts as were in unreasonable restraint of trade." Said Justice RUFUS PECKHAM for the Court: "[w]e are, therefore, asked to hold that the act of Congress excepts contracts which are not in unreasonable restraint of trade." To read that rule of reason into the statute, Peckham answered, would be an exercise of JUDICIAL LEGISLATION.

That remained the Court's view until 1911, when it ignored its PRECEDENTS, the text of the statute, and the views of the Senate and the President. In 1909 the Senate had rejected a bill that proposed to amend the Sherman Act by incorporating the rule of reason. "To amend the antitrust act, as suggested by this bill," declared a subcommittee of the Senate Judiciary Committee, "would be to entirely emasculate it, and for all practical purposes render it nugatory as a remedial statute." In 1910 President WILLIAM HOWARD TAFT in a message to Congress had argued that no need existed to amend the scope of the Sherman Act. Yet in 1911, in two major antitrust cases, UNITED STATES V. STANDARD OIL COMPANY OF NEW JERSEY and *United States v. American Tobacco Co.*, Chief Justice EDWARD D. WHITE, who had dissented from earlier opinions repudiating the rule of reason, explicitly adopted it for an 8–1 Court. The sole dissenter, Justice JOHN MARSHALL HARLAN, echoing the *Trans-Missouri Freight* case, assaulted "judicial legislation"—the usurpation by the Court of a congressional function. The Sherman Act, Harlan insisted, included "every" restraint of trade, even a reasonable one. But Congress, in its 1914 antitrust legislation of the CLAYTON ACT and the FEDERAL TRADE COMMISSION ACT, by failing to attack the rule of reason acquiesced in it.

As a result of its rule of reason, the Supreme Court prevented effective use of the Sherman Act to prevent industrial consolidations of a monopolistic character. Thus, in *United States v. United Shoe Machinery Company* (1918), the Court held that the antitrust act did not apply to the company even though its dominating position in the industry approached that of an absolute monopoly which had restrained trade by its use of exclusive PATENT rights. In UNITED STATES V. UNITED STATES STEEL CORPORATION (1920) the Court held that the nation's largest industrial enterprise had reasonably restrained trade despite its "attempt to monopolize" in violation of the act. Similarly, in *United States v. International Harvester Company* (1927) the rule of reason defeated the government's case once again even though the company controlled a big proportion of the market and used exclusive dealer contracts to eliminate competition. Although the Court ruled that trade union activities came within the scope of the antitrust act, no union ever benefited from a Court finding that its restraint of trade was reasonable. The rule of reason, in short, proved to be of considerable importance in the history of JUDICIAL REVIEW, of the economy, and of government efforts to regulate monopolistic practices.

LEONARD W. LEVY
(1986)

(SEE ALSO: *Antitrust Law.*)

Bibliography

NEALE, A. D.   1970   *The Antitrust Laws of the United States of America.* Cambridge: At the University Press.

RUMMEL v. ESTELLE
445 U.S. 263 (1980)

OLIVER WENDELL HOLMES once said that the Supreme Court sits to expound law, not do justice. This case is proof. On the premise that the length of a sentence is "purely a matter of legislative judgment," Justice WILLIAM H. REHNQUIST for a 5–4 Court found no CRUEL AND UNUSUAL PUNISHMENT in Rummel's mandatory life sentence after his third felony conviction for obtaining $120.75 by false pretenses. Rummel argued that his sentence was disproportionate to his crime. Rehnquist replied that the possibility of a parole in twelve years and the right of a state legislature to fix penalties against recidivists overcame Rummel's argument. Rehnquist declared that the state legislature was acting within its competence in prescribing punishment and that the state has a legitimate interest in requiring extended incarceration of habitual criminals. The Court would not substitute its judgment for the legislature's and overturn a sentence which was neither inherently barbarous nor grossly disproportionate to the offense.

Justice LEWIS F. POWELL for the dissenters believed that Rummel's life sentence "would be viewed as grossly unjust by virtually every layman and lawyer." The cruel and unusual punishment clause of the Eighth Amendment, extended by the FOURTEENTH AMENDMENT to the states, Powell argued, prohibited grossly disproportionate punishments as well as barbarous ones. Rummel's three felonies netted him about $230 in frauds. He never used violence, threatened anyone, or endangered the peace of society. Texas treated his crimes as no different from those of a three-time murderer. The Court's decision weakened the use of the cruel and unusual punishment clause in noncapital cases.

LEONARD W. LEVY
(1986)

RUNYON v. MCCRARY
427 U.S. 160 (1976)

The CIVIL RIGHTS ACT OF 1866 gives all persons "the same right . . . to make and enforce contracts . . . as is enjoyed by white persons." In the *Runyon* case the Supreme Court, following its 1968 decision in JONES V. ALFRED H. MAYER CO., relied on the THIRTEENTH AMENDMENT as a source of congressional power and upheld the application of this provision to two private schools' exclusion of qualified black applicants.

Justice POTTER STEWART, writing for the Court, made clear that several issues concerning the act's coverage were being left open. The Court was not deciding whether the act forbade a private social organization to impose a racial limitation on its membership; nor was it deciding whether a private school might limit its students to boys or girls, or to members of some religious faith. *Runyon* itself involved "private, commercially operated, non-sectarian schools."

Although Congress is empowered to enforce the Thirteenth Amendment, the provisions of the BILL OF RIGHTS limit congressional power here as elsewhere. The school operators argued unsuccessfully that the application of the 1866 act to their admissions practices violated rights of association, parental rights, and the RIGHT OF PRIVACY.

In responding to the associational freedom claim, Justice Stewart came close to saying that the freedom to practice racial discrimination in the choice of one's associates is not entitled to constitutional protection—a view that surely would not survive in the context of marriage or other intimate association. Concurring specially, Justice LEWIS F. POWELL remarked on the strength of the associational freedoms that would be involved if the 1866 Act were applied to a racially discriminatory selection of a home tutor or babysitter.

The Court dismissed the parental rights claim with the comment that parents and school operators retained the right to use the schools to inculcate the values of their choice. The privacy claim was similarly rejected; parents had a right to send their children to private schools, but the schools remained subject to reasonable government regulation.

Justices BYRON R. WHITE and WILLIAM H. REHNQUIST dissented, arguing that *Jones* was wrongly decided and that the 1866 act had not been intended to forbid a private, racially motivated refusal to contract. Justice JOHN PAUL STEVENS, in a special concurrence, agreed with the dissenters' view of the 1866 act's purposes. However, he concluded, "for the Court now to overrule *Jones* would be a significant step backwards" in the process of eliminating RACIAL DISCRIMINATION; thus he joined the Court's opinion.

It was ever so; today's history almost always prevails in a contest with yesterday's.

KENNETH L. KARST
(1986)

RUST v. SULLIVAN
500 U.S. 173 (1991)

Congress, by means of Title X of the Public Health Service Act, provides for federal funding for family planning services. In 1988, the U.S. Department of Health and Human Services (HHS) issued new regulations that required subsidized clinics to refrain from advising their patients with respect to ABORTION. Private clinics and doctors employed at these clinics brought actions claiming that this limitation to concededly important speech violated the FIRST AMENDMENT. To resolve a split among the federal appeals courts, the Supreme Court granted CERTIORARI. In a 5–4 decision, the Court held that the "no abortion counseling" condition did not violate the FREEDOM OF SPEECH.

The no-abortion-speech limitation was first challenged on grounds of STATUTORY INTERPRETATION. The plaintiffs, on the basis of considerable authority, argued that given the importance of the First Amendment an ADMINISTRATIVE AGENCY, such as HHS, could not be vested with a power to limit speech except by clear and explicit authorization by Congress and that no such "clear statement" had been made for HHS. A majority of the Court, however, applied a different rule of construction, that of a deference to an agency's own interpretation of its enabling act. While agreeing that the necessary statutory authorization was "ambiguous," the MAJORITY OPINION in *Rust v. Sullivan*, authored by Chief Justice WILLIAM H. REHNQUIST, nonetheless concluded that HHS's interpretation (that it had been delegated the power) was a "plausible" and thus "permissible" construction of the act.

The next issue was whether the statute so construed—as authorizing HHS to condition its subsidies on the recipients refraining from speech about abortion—was constitutional. The majority held that it was, for at least two reasons. One reason centered on choice. The clinics were not forced to refrain from speaking; they might simply refuse the federal funds and then speak of abortion as they wished. Therefore, the right of the clinics to speak had not been taken; rather, they had of their own free choice given it up.

Otherwise, the Court emphasized the restricted scope of the no-abortion-counseling provision. The provision applied only to the clinic (and to that part of it financed by Title X funds); it did not apply to individuals in their speech outside the Title X project. As said by the majority, "[clinic] employees remain free to pursue abortion-related

activities when they are not acting under the auspices of the Title X project." Yet, for a number of women, the subsidized, low-cost Title X projects were likely the only viable and accessible forum for counseling with respect to their pregnancy. Therefore, any availability of clinic doctors outside these clinics was, to these people, not an effective source of information about abortion.

WILLIAM T. MAYTON
(2000)

RUTAN v. REPUBLICAN PARTY OF ILLINOIS
497 U.S. 62 (1990)

The governor of Illinois prohibited state entities under his control from hiring any employees without his express consent. Because more than 5,000 state positions become vacant in Illinois each year, this policy allowed the governor to make several thousand additional appointments. Evidence suggested that the governor's hiring policy operated as a PATRONAGE system, with the governor restricting appointments to people who belonged to his political party. Persons alleging that they had been denied jobs, promotions, transfers, or recall after layoffs because of their party affiliation filed suit, claiming that these employment practices violated their rights of speech and association guaranteed by the FIRST AMENDMENT. The challenge was based on previous cases such as *Elrod v. Burns* (1976), where the Court had held that the First Amendment barred political affiliation from being used as a reason for dismissal from most governmental jobs. In *Rutan*, the Court ruled 5–4 to extend the doctrine of *Elrod v. Burns* to promotions, transfers, recall from layoffs, and hiring decisions.

Writing for the majority, Justice WILLIAM J. BRENNAN applied the COMPELLING STATE INTEREST test used by the Court in many other types of cases, arguing that patronage clearly violates the First Amendment unless it is "narrowly tailored to further vital government interests." In Brennan's view, a general patronage system manifestly fails this test because it is not necessary to maintain either strong political parties or employee loyalty; these goals can be achieved by other means, such as having a handful of senior positions filled by political appointees.

Justice ANTONIN SCALIA, writing for the dissenters, argued that the compelling-interest standard was inappropriate for this case because the government was acting in the role of employer. Numerous decisions have upheld the idea that the government has more leeway in regulating the conduct of its employees than it does in regulating the behavior of ordinary citizens. According to Scalia, as long as the benefits of an employment practice can "reasonably be deemed to outweigh its 'coercive' effects," the practice should pass constitutional muster. In this case, Scalia believed that the perceived benefits clearly outweighed the coercive effects, because patronage has long been regarded as a cornerstone of our party system, "promoting political stability and facilitating the social and political integration of previously powerless groups." Scalia disputed the majority's contention that "parties have already survived" the demise of patronage. Saying the Court's assessment had "a positively whistling-in-thegraveyard character to it," Scalia noted recent evidence of party decline, including the substantial decrease in party competition for congressional seats. Reasonable men and women can differ about the appropriateness of patronage in various contexts, said Scalia; but this is precisely why the Court should respect the federal system and not impose its own will in the matter.

JOHN G. WEST, JR.
(1992)

RUTGERS v. WADDINGTON
(New York Mayor's Court, 1784)

Decided in 1784 by the Mayor's Court of New York City, this was an early state precedent for JUDICIAL REVIEW and the first reported case in which the constitutionality of a state act was attacked on the ground that it violated a treaty of the United States. The state's Trespass Act allowed Rutgers, who had fled New York when the British occupied the city, to sue for the value of rents lost while her property was held by British merchants under military authority. The statute barred defendants from pleading that military authority justified the "trespass" under acts of war and the law of nations. The Treaty of Peace, however, canceled claims for injuries to property during the war. ALEXANDER HAMILTON, representing the defendants, expressly argued that the court should hold the Trespass Act unconstitutional.

Chief Judge JAMES DUANE, for the court, declared that the state constitution embodied the COMMON LAW and that the common law recognized the law of nations. Duane also declared that the union of the states under the ARTICLES OF CONFEDERATION constituted "a FUNDAMENTAL LAW," according to which Congress had exclusive powers of making war and peace: "no state in this union can alter or abridge, in a single point, the federal articles or the treaty." His logic having led him to the brink of holding the Trespass Act void, Duane abruptly endorsed the prevailing Blackstonian theory of legislative supremacy. When the legislature enacted a law, "there is no power which can controul them . . . the Judges are not at liberty, altho' it appear to them to be unreasonable, to reject it: for this were to set the judicial above the legislative, which would be subversive of all government."

Duane then declared that the legislature had not intended to revoke the law of nations and that the court had to expound the statute to give the legislature's intention its effect, whereupon the court emasculated the statute. The judgment was that for the time the property was held under military order, acts done according to the law of nations and "buried in oblivion" by the treaty could not be redressed by the statute; Rutgers could not recover for trespass.

Technically the court had construed the act to conform to the treaty and the law of nations, but the legislature angrily resolved that the adjudication was "subversive of all law and good order" and that if a court could "dispense with" state law, "Legislatures become useless." Although a motion to remove the judges failed, a public protest meeting adopted "An Address to the People," angrily accusing the court of having "assumed and exercised a power to set aside an Act of the State." The "Address," severely condemning judicial review, was widely circulated, as was the pamphlet report of the case.

LEONARD W. LEVY
(1986)

RUTLEDGE, JOHN
(1739–1800)

John Rutledge, a wealthy lawyer, represented South Carolina in the STAMP ACT Congress (1765) and chaired that state's delegations to the First and Second Continental Congresses. He was a member of the committee that drafted the South Carolina Constitution (1776) and was elected the state's first president (1776–1778) and second governor (1779). He led his state's delegation to the CONSTITUTIONAL CONVENTION OF 1787, where he used his oratorical skill to advance a moderate STATES' RIGHTS position and to defend the interests of the southern slaveholding aristocracy. He opposed creation of a separate federal judiciary, but favored a provision making the federal Constitution and laws binding on state courts. After signing the Constitution, he served as a member of the South Carolina ratifying convention.

In 1789, President GEORGE WASHINGTON appointed Rutledge one of the original associate justices of the Supreme Court, but he resigned in 1791—having done only circuit duty—to become Chief Justice of South Carolina. In 1795, Washington appointed him Chief Justice of the United States, and he presided over the August 1795 term of the Court; but an intemperate speech against JAY'S TREATY alienated the Federalists, and the Senate refused to confirm his nomination. (See SUPREME COURT, 1789–1801.)

DENNIS J. MAHONEY
(1986)

RUTLEDGE, WILEY B.
(1894–1949)

When Wiley B. Rutledge joined the Supreme Court in January 1943, succeeding JAMES F. BYRNES, he helped to forge a liberal coalition that substantially redirected constitutional developments for the next six years. His sudden death in the summer of 1949, two months after the passing of Justice FRANK MURPHY, ended a brief era of liberal activism and ushered in the bleakest period for CIVIL LIBERTIES in the Court's history. President FRANKLIN D. ROOSEVELT's eighth and last appointment to the high bench, Rutledge remained, with the exception of Murphy, the most consistently liberal member of the STONE and VINSON COURTS.

When dean of the law school of the University of Iowa, Rutledge's support for FDR's NEW DEAL, including the "court-packing" proposal, earned him an appointment to the Circuit Court of Appeals for the District of Columbia in 1939. There he consistently endorsed the social and economic reforms of the Roosevelt administration and also compiled a strong record on civil liberties. In one opinion Rutledge dissented on FIRST AMENDMENT grounds when the judges upheld a local license tax levied against itinerant religious preachers.

A year later, as the newest member of the Stone Court, Rutledge provided the fifth and crucial vote in a coalition including HUGO L. BLACK, WILLIAM O. DOUGLAS, Murphy, and Chief Justice HARLAN FISKE STONE that overturned the Supreme Court's own ruling in a similar case decided six months earlier (*Jones v. Opelika*, 1943; MURDOCK V. PENN-SYLVANIA, 1943). He also joined Justice ROBERT H. JACKSON's opinion in *West Virginia State Board of Education v. Barnette* (1943). (See FLAG SALUTE CASES.)

Rutledge's jurisprudence blended economic nationalism with compassion for the economically disadvantaged and extreme sensitivity to individual rights. He endorsed, for example, interpretation of the WAGNER ACT to cover local newspaper carriers and believed that the minimum wage provisions of the FAIR LABOR STANDARDS ACT benefited all employees "throughout the farthest reaches of the channels of INTERSTATE COMMERCE."

To protect workers from exploitation, Rutledge believed, the federal government could prohibit entirely homework in the embroidery industry. To protect consumers from abuses, the federal government could prosecute insurance companies under the SHERMAN ANTITRUST ACT, despite more than a half century of precedent to the contrary. (See UNITED STATES V. SOUTH-EASTERN UNDERWRITERS ASSOCIATION.) He consistently supported the constitutional and statutory rights of working-class Americans, even when the legislative history of the particular law un-

der discussion appeared in doubt (UNITED STATES V. UNITED MINE WORKERS, 1947).

At the same time, Rutledge's concern for individual rights extended even to corporations and capitalists, two groups which often lay beyond the constitutional protection offered by other New Deal liberals on the Court. Unlike Justice FELIX FRANKFURTER, for example, he did not believe that Congress had intended in the pure FOOD AND DRUG LAWS to impose criminal liability upon corporate executives without a finding of personal culpability or negligence. Nor did he believe that Congress could punish violators of wartime price regulations without jury trials and without opportunity to contest the regulations' legality in enforcement proceedings. (See YAKUS V. UNITED STATES; JUDICIAL SYSTEM.)

Rutledge endorsed without hesitation the concept of PREFERRED FREEDOMS articulated by Justice Stone in UNITED STATES V. CAROLENE PRODUCTS CO. (1938). FREEDOM OF SPEECH and PRESS, RELIGIOUS LIBERTY, the right to vote, and judicial protection for "discrete and insular minorities" served as the cornerstones of his philosophy. Like Stone, he, too, failed to implement these ideals in the infamous JAPANESE AMERICAN CASES, but, those apart, his civil liberties record remained impeccable. His most memorable CIVIL LIBERTIES opinions came in *Thomas v. Collins* (1944), where he wrote for a five-man majority that reversed the conviction of a labor organizer who had been convicted of contempt for speaking at a union rally without a permit; in EVERSON V. BOARD OF EDUCATION (1947), where he dissented against an opinion that sustained the constitutionality of state aid to the parents of children in parochical schools for bus transportation; and IN RE YA-MASHITA (1946), where he and Murphy alone dissented against the drumhead trial of a vanquished Japanese general before an American military commission. With eloquence, heat, and sarcasm, Rutledge denounced the proceedings as "the most flagrant . . . departure . . . from the whole British American tradition of the COMMON LAW and the Constitution."

He subscribed as well to Justice Black's notion that the DUE PROCESS clause of the FOURTEENTH AMENDMENT "incorporated" the specific protections of the BILL OF RIGHTS, but in the case of ADAMSON V. CALIFORNIA (1947), Rutledge and Murphy were also prepared to go far beyond Black's reasoning to hold that "occasions may arise where a proceeding falls so far short of conforming to fundamental standards of procedure as to warrant constitutional condemnation in terms of a lack of due process despite the absence of a specific provision in the Bill of Rights." (See INCORPORATION DOCTRINE.)

Had Rutledge and Murphy lived, the course of constitutional development in the McCarthy era of the early

1950s might have been healthier for both the Court and the country.

MICHAEL E. PARRISH
(1986)

Bibliography

HARPER, FOWLER 1965 *Justice Rutledge and the Bright Constellation.* Indianapolis: Bobbs-Merrill.

MANN, W. HOWARD 1950 Rutledge and Civil Liberties. *Indiana Law Journal* 25:532–558.

RUTLEDGE COURT

See: Supreme Court, 1789–1801

SABLE COMMUNICATIONS OF CALIFORNIA v. FCC

See: Dial-a-Porn

SACCO AND VANZETTI CASE

See: *Commonwealth v. Sacco and Vanzetti*

SAENZ v. ROE
526 U.S. 489 (1999)

In *Saenz v. Roe*, the Supreme Court reinvigorated the constitutional RIGHT TO TRAVEL. California, concerned about becoming a "welfare magnet" because its generous WELFARE BENEFITS might entice indigent persons to immigrate from less-generous states, limited the maximum payment to a recipient during his or her first twelve months of residency to the amount he or she would have received in the prior state of residency. Congress expressly authorized states to discriminate between older and newer residents in this manner. The Court held 7–2, however, that the state statute violated the right to travel and that Congress could not authorize such a violation.

The Court had previously invalidated several state statutes discriminating between older and newer residents, but had failed to articulate a consistent constitutional theory or level of judicial scrutiny. In SHAPIRO V. THOMPSON (1969), the Court invalidated a state statute withholding all welfare from immigrants during their first year of state residency. The Court held that this welfare denial consti-

tuted a "penalty" on immigrants' right to travel to the state, and the statute could not survive STRICT SCRUTINY. The Court employed the same analysis to invalidate statutes withholding for one year the franchise in DUNN V. BLUMSTEIN (1972) and free medical care in *Memorial Hospital v. Maricopa County* (1974). More recent cases, however, such as *Zobel v. Williams* (1982) and ATTORNEY GENERAL OF NEW YORK V. SOTO-LÓPEZ (1986), produced no majority agreement on the level of scrutiny, with controlling factions subjecting residency distinctions merely to RATIONAL BASIS review under the EQUAL PROTECTION clause.

While many observers predicted that the Court in *Saenz* would retreat even further from *Shapiro*, the Court did precisely the opposite. The Court proclaimed that the "right to travel" embraces three different components: (1) the right of a citizen of one state to enter and to leave a second state, (2) the right to be treated as a welcome visitor rather than an unfriendly alien when temporarily visiting a second state, and (3) for those travelers who elect to become permanent residents of the second state, the right to be treated the same as other citizens of that state. This third component is grounded in both the CITIZENSHIP clause and the PRIVILEGES OR IMMUNITIES clause of the FOURTEENTH AMENDMENT, which together mean that "a citizen of the United States can, of his own volition, become a citizen of any State of the Union by a *bona fide* residence therein, with the same rights as other citizens of that State" (quoting the SLAUGHTERHOUSE CASES (1873)). The Court's partial reliance on the privileges or immunities clause is intriguing, both because it has essentially lain dormant since its parsimonious interpretation in *Slaughterhouse*, and because it seems superfluous in this case, given the Court's reading of the citizenship clause. Perhaps the Court means to signal some willingness to revisit the clause's historically cramped interpretation.

The Court declared that statutes violating this third component are subject to a STANDARD OF REVIEW that "may be more categorical than that articulated in *Shapiro*, but it is surely no less strict." The Court quickly dismissed the state's magnet-avoidance and fiscal justifications as insufficient to satisfy strict scrutiny's requirement of a COMPELLING STATE INTEREST. And the Court just as quickly, if somewhat mechanically, dismissed the relevance of Congress's authorization: the citizenship clause limits Congress as well as the states, and Congress cannot invoke its enforcement power under the FOURTEENTH AMENDMENT, SECTION 5 to restrict (as opposed to protect) individual rights.

Future battles over durational residency requirements will be fought over a new issue: whether the requirements are properly characterized as a test for bona fide citizenship, which requires an intention to settle in-state. The Court reaffirmed prior PRECEDENTS upholding one-year residency requirements for obtaining a divorce or college tuition subsidies. These cases were distinguishable, both because California did not dispute the bona fides of the welfare recipients' claim to state citizenship, and because welfare is not an easily portable benefit that can be taken back to the prior state. The portability distinction raises an interesting question: If a state may treat an immigrant college student as a noncitizen for a year with regard to tuition subsidies, may the state treat that same student as a noncitizen for all other purposes, including welfare? It is unclear why the intention to establish residency should be determined on a benefit-specific basis.

More than any of its doctrinal predecessors, *Saenz* issues an expressive proclamation about the nature of political identity in this country. Previous right to travel cases applied conventional SUBSTANTIVE DUE PROCESS and equal protection doctrinal constructs. In contrast, *Saenz* makes a statement about what belonging to America means. People enjoy both a state political affiliation, which does not admit of "degrees of citizenship"; and a national affiliation, which empowers people to choose a state affiliation for themselves. Durational residency requirements that discriminate among state citizens, even those that place no actual burdens on interstate migration, are incompatible with these axioms. Perhaps this determination best explains the Court's hint that this right to travel component might be "categorical" rather than "merely" requiring strict scrutiny; the right is not really centered in individual liberty (a concern generally subject to BALANCING against strong governmental interests), but rather expresses a commitment to a peculiarly American form of political identity, one that simply cannot be compromised.

EVAN H. CAMINKER

(2000)

SALERNO, UNITED STATES v.
481 U.S. 739 (1987)

In many nations of the world, governments imprison people believed to be dangerous because of their opinions. This does not happen in a free society. However, since the Bail Reform Act, passed by Congress in 1984, persons arrested for a specific category of serious offenses, those violating the RACKETEER INFLUENCES AND CORRUPT ORGANIZATIONS ACT (RICO), may be imprisoned while awaiting trial. This is PREVENTIVE DETENTION, which is based on the supposition that the prisoner will likely commit other crimes if let out on BAIL. When the Court sustained the constitutionality of the 1984 statute, Justice THURGOOD MARSHALL, dissenting, joined only by Justice WILLIAM J. BRENNAN, made the following remarkable statement:

This case brings before the Court for the first time a statute in which Congress declares that a person innocent of any crime may be jailed indefinitely, pending the trial of allegations which are legally presumed to be untrue, if the Government shows to the satisfaction of a judge that the accused is likely to commit crimes, unrelated to the pending charges, at any time in the future. Such statutes, consistent with the usages of tyranny and the excesses of what bitter experience teaches us to call the police state, have long been thought incompatible with the fundamental human rights protected by our Constitution. Today a majority of this Court holds otherwise. Its decision disregards basic principles of justice established centuries ago and enshrined beyond the reach of governmental interference in the Bill of Rights.

Justice JOHN PAUL STEVENS, dissenting separately, agreed with Marshall that the statute violated both the presumption of innocence and the Eighth Amendment's excessive-bail clause.

Chief Justice WILLIAM H. REHNQUIST, for the majority, first rejected the contention that the statute conflicted with the Fifth Amendment's DUE PROCESS clause. No conflict existed, he held, because Congress's purpose in authorizing pretrial detention was not penal, but merely regulatory. So construed, the statute did not authorize impermissible punishment without trial; it merely employed pretrial detention to protect the community against danger. Not only was SUBSTANTIVE DUE PROCESS not violated; the statute conformed with PROCEDURAL DUE PROCESS as well, because it provided for a full adversary hearing before a judge. The government had the burden of proving that to offer bail to the prisoner endangered society and that the prisoner had the RIGHT TO COUNSEL and all other trial rights.

Rehnquist also rejected the argument based on the Eighth Amendment's excessive-bail clause. It did not guarantee a right to bail, only that, when available, bail should not be excessive. In murder cases, bail can be denied. Moreover, in SCHALL V. MARTIN (1984), the Court had permitted pretrial detention of juveniles following a showing before a judge that the person might commit crimes if bailed. Finally, the bail clause bound courts, not Congress. Given the Court's extraordinary deference to Congress on an important Bill of Rights issue, *Salerno* may deserve a good part of Justice Marshall's denunciation and show the risks of judicial faineance. However, the risk comes from Congress, not an acquiescent Court, and Congress is controllable by the people.

LEONARD W. LEVY
(1992)

SAME-SEX MARRIAGE, I

In the American legal order, religious institutions do not define MARRIAGE. Civil marriage is a contractually based legal status recognized by national, state, and local governments for many purposes, to which countless privileges attach. While this status has long been defined and restricted primarily at the state level, the Constitution limits state power over marriage and should invalidate one of the most obdurate of eligibility criteria: that a marriage must be mixed-sex.

With the possible exceptions of certain marriages in which one spouse has transitioned to another sex, every state requires that couples who would marry must be male–female. This materially and symbolically potent exclusion of lesbians and gay men and some bisexual persons from civil marriage violates established constitutional principles in multiple ways.

The refusal to allow same-sex couples to marry violates the DUE PROCESS clauses of the Fifth Amendment and the FOURTEENTH AMENDMENT, under which the Supreme Court has recognized that the right to marry may not be significantly burdened absent extraordinary justification. In LOVING V. VIRGINIA (1967) the Court held that the right to marry is a FUNDAMENTAL RIGHT, and ZABLOCKI V. REDHAIL (1978) made clear that it embraces both negative rights to freedom from government prosecution for cohabiting as married and affirmative rights to enter government-sanctioned civil marriage. The prohibition on two men or two women marrying thus should trigger STRICT SCRUTINY, provided the right is defined at a sufficiently high level of generality.

Defenders of the heterosexual status quo argue that civil marriage has always involved the union of one man with one woman, and thus that there is no SUBSTANTIVE DUE PROCESS right to same-sex marriage "deeply rooted" in American history or "essential" to our scheme of ordered liberty. Yet it is inappropriate to take enduring characteristics of a person claiming a right into account in defining the contours of that right. The Court rejected such an effort in *Loving*, where Virginia argued that its MISCEGENATION law prohibiting marriages between white and black persons violated no fundamental right because mixed-race marriages had long been prohibited by law. Despite the long history of monoracial statutory marriage definitions, the Court held that Virginia's law infringed the fundamental right to marry.

Similarly, the right to marry should not by fiat and history be deemed to exclude same-sex marriages a priori. Rather, the two-sex requirement should have to survive strict scrutiny to be consistent with the due process clauses. However, in the RIGHT TO DIE case *Washington v. Glucksberg* (1997), a majority of the Court took a restrictive view of the proper formulation of substantive rights claimed to be protected under the due process clause, and it is conceivable that the Court would do so in this context and find no fundamental right to same-sex marriage.

Nonetheless, excluding same-sex couples from civil marriage also violates the constitutional guarantee of EQUAL PROTECTION OF THE LAWS, which demands that governmental classifications must withstand the appropriate level of scrutiny. Under cases such as UNITED STATES V. VIRGINIA (1996), governmental SEX DISCRIMINATION must survive at least intermediate scrutiny.

Defenders of the mixed-sex requirement contend that it does not classify on the basis of sex, for it equally forbids men and women to marry a person of the same sex. Somewhat surprisingly, lower courts have generally accepted this argument—with the notable exception of the Hawai'i Supreme Court in BAEHR V. LEWIN (1993), a decision under the equal protection clause of the Hawai'i state constitution. *Baehr* correctly observed that the U.S. Supreme Court had faced a logically equivalent argument in *Loving*, rejecting Virginia's fallacious contention that its miscegenation law did not violate the Fourteenth Amendment because it applied equally to white and black people. In fact, under Virginia law, a *black* woman, for example, was not allowed to marry a white man—the very facts of *Loving*, where Mildred Jeter could not marry Richard Loving—even though a *white* woman could marry a white man.

Mixed-sex marriage requirements similarly grant men and women different rights. Under current marriage laws, no woman would have the right to marry Mildred Jeter, even though most adult men would. It begs the question to insist that marriage is by nature a mixed-sex institution. Our laws embody political choices, not Platonic essences, and the point of equal protection analysis is to determine whether certain political choices are constitutionally forbidden. Hence, mixed-sex marriage laws must survive at least intermediate scrutiny. (Because nonrecognition of same-sex marriages also constitutes SEXUAL ORIENTATION discrimination—since it is designed to keep marriage heterosexual or to prevent "gay marriage," and since its overwhelming immediate effect is to prevent lesbians and gay men from marrying—the mixed-sex requirement should also be subject to strict scrutiny as a sexual orientation classification.)

Government refusal to recognize same-sex marriages is therefore unconstitutional, for it can survive neither strict nor intermediate scrutiny. The interests commonly invoked to defend the legal privileging of heterosexuality are procreation and child-rearing. Today, however, encouraging procreation ought not count as a "compelling" or even "important" governmental interest, for there is no evidence that the U.S. population is in any danger of harmful reduction. Moreover, the mixed-sex marriage requirement is neither "narrowly tailored" nor "substantially related" to promoting procreation or healthy child-rearing. Marriage law has not traditionally required that either potential spouse be capable of procreation—post-menopausal women and sterile persons are allowed to marry everywhere in the United States—and failure to "consummate" a marriage has rendered a marriage at most voidable but not necessarily void. There is no reliable social science evidence that most or all mixed-sex marriages provide a healthier child-rearing environment than same-sex marriages, and the Court has insisted in the racial context in PALMORE V. SIDOTI (1984) that government cannot shield children from the harms that may flow from being raised in a racially stigmatized family environment where parents' fundamental rights are at issue.

At base, the nationwide refusal to recognize same-sex marriages, the federal Defense of Marriage Act, its state-level copycat statutes, and arguments that recognizing same-sex marriages would somehow "undermine" the institution of marriage all reflect both a profound anxiety that heterosexual privilege may be eroding and an attempt to use the law to perpetuate the subordinate status of lesbian, gay, and bisexual persons. The Constitution, however, prohibits majorities from using the power of government to shore up such status hierarchies. As the first Justice JOHN MARSHALL HARLAN argued in his DISSENTING OPINION in PLESSY V. FERGUSON (1896), and as reaffirmed in the sexual orientation context in ROMER V. EVANS (1996), the Constitution "neither knows nor tolerates classes among citizens." It will be up to the courts and electorates throughout the nation to determine whether this noble principle will remain simply aspirational for gay, lesbian, and bisexual persons, or whether the nation will live up to its ideals of liberty and equality by eliminating the sex and sexual orientation discrimination of the current refusal to recognize civil same-sex marriages.

DAVID B. CRUZ
(2000)

Bibliography

BALKIN, J. M.　1997　The Constitution of Status. *Yale Law Journal* 106:2313–2374.

ESKRIDGE, WILLIAM N., JR.　1996　*The Case for Same-Sex Marriage: From Sexual Liberty to Civilized Commitment.* New York: Free Press.

KOPPELMAN, ANDREW　1994　Why Discrimination Against Lesbians and Gay Men Is Sex Discrimination. *New York University Law Review* 69:197–287.

SHERMAN, SUZANNE, ed.　1992　*Lesbian and Gay Marriage: Private Commitments, Public Ceremonies.* Philadelphia: Temple University Press.

STRASSER, MARK　1997　*Legally Wed: Same-Sex Marriage and the Constitution.* Ithaca, N.Y.: Cornell University Press.

SULLIVAN, ANDREW and LANDAU, JOSEPH, eds.　1997　*Same-Sex Marriage: Pro and Con, A Reader.* New York: Vintage Books.

SAME-SEX MARRIAGE, II

Constitutional claims in support of same-sex MARRIAGE involve two dominant themes: (1) that the Constitution protects as a FUNDAMENTAL RIGHT the choice to marry another consenting adult of the same sex and (2) that refusal to permit same-sex couples to marry denies them the EQUAL PROTECTION OF THE LAWS. Both claims fail existing standards of federal constitutional analysis, but state constitutional provisions may be interpreted differently.

The fundamental right argument for same-sex marriage posits the existence of unwritten constitutional rights such as the RIGHT OF PRIVACY, or of FREEDOM OF ASSOCIATION, or a right to marry. Laws that impinge upon fundamental rights are subject to heightened judicial scrutiny, and may only be sustained if necessary and narrowly tailored to effectuate a COMPELLING STATE INTEREST. If same-sex marriage is not a fundamental right, the LEGISLATION will be reviewed (and presumably sustained) under a lower standard of analysis that is more deferential to legislative discretion. The test for whether a practice or relationship not specifically identified in the Constitution is protected as "fundamental" is whether it is "deeply rooted in this Nation's history and tradition," or "implicit in the concept of ordered liberty." Clearly, same-sex relations are not so rooted or so essential. Thus, same-sex marriage is not a fundamental right.

Although many decisions have recognized that the right to marry is a fundamental constitutional interest, all of them have involved traditional male–female marriage, which is deeply rooted in the traditions and history of our people. In BOWERS V. HARDWICK (1986), the Supreme Court emphasized that there is "[n]o connection between family, marriage, or procreation on the one hand and homosexual activity on the other. . . ." Marriage receives special protection because according to MEYER V. NEBRASKA (1923), it is the foundation of the traditional home and family, and because marriage is linked to procreation. Same-sex marriage is distinguishable in both respects.

From the perspective of the basic social purposes of legal marriage recognition, traditional male–female unions and same-sex unions are not equivalent. In terms of promoting safe sexual relations, procreation, child rearing, cross-gender integration, complementarity, and fostering public virtue, for example, same-sex unions do not contribute to the public interest in ways comparable to the tremendous contributions of male–female marriages. The union of two persons of different genders creates a unique relationship of unmatched potential strengths and inimitable potential value to society. The integration of the universe of gender differences associated with sexual identity constitutes the core and essence of marriage. The heterosexual dimensions of the relationship are at the very core of what makes "marriage" what it is, and why it is so valuable to individuals and to society.

The equality arguments for same-sex marriage are based on the Court's decision in LOVING V. VIRGINIA (1967), where the Court ruled that laws prohibiting MISCEGENATION were unconstitutional. However, laws forbidding same-sex marriage are not comparable to laws forbidding interracial marriage; race has nothing to do with any legitimate purpose of regulating marriage, but sexual relations go to the very heart of the compelling state interest in defining the marital relationship. Likewise, eradicating RACIAL DISCRIMINATION is the core concern of the FOURTEENTH AMENDMENT, but no constitutional provision purports to forbid discrimination on the basis of SEXUAL PREFERENCE or relations.

Denial of same-sex marriage is not improper SEX DISCRIMINATION. Heterosexual marriage is the oldest gender-equality institution in the law. The requirement that marriage consist of both a man and a woman emphasizes the absolute equality and equal necessity of both sexes for the most fundamental unit of society, and the indispensable, equal contribution of both genders to the basic institution of our society. Nor are same-sex unions functionally equivalent to heterosexual marriages any more than other prohibited relations, such as incest.

The Court has never addressed any constitutional claim for same-sex marriage. Lower federal courts and state appellate courts have unanimously rejected claims that the federal Constitution mandates the extension of marital status or benefits to same-sex couples, and most have rejected state constitutional claims also. However, by 1998, courts in two states had indicated that claims for same-sex marriage might be asserted under state constitutional provisions. In BAEHR V. LEWIN (1993) and *Baehr v. Miike* (1996), Hawaiian courts had ruled that the state's refusal to permit same-sex marriage violates equality guarantees in the state constitution of Hawai'i. And a trial court in Alaska ruled that denial of marriage licenses to same-sex couples violated state constitutional guarantees of privacy and equality. However, in November 1998, the people of

both Hawai'i and Alaska ratified amendments to their state constitutions (2:1) to reject same-sex marriage. The equality argument seems to ignore the fact that heterosexual marriage laws treat men and women equally, requiring cross-gender marriage for both sexes. The privacy claim seems to confuse public toleration of private choices with private claims to public preferences; the right to privacy protects certain private conduct from public penalty, but does not compel the state to confer public benefits, privileges, and preferences on private choices. Nevertheless, these cases illustrate that state constitutions increasingly are the basis for constitutional claims for same-sex marriage.

LYNN D. WARDLE
(2000)

Bibliography

COOLIDGE, DAVID ORGON 1997 Same-Sex Marriage? *Baehr v. Miike* and the Meaning of Marriage. *South Texas Law Review* 38:1–119.
ESKRIDGE, WILLIAM 1995 *The Case for Same-Sex Marriage.* New York: Free Press.
WARDLE, LYNN D. 1996 A Critical Analysis of Constitutional Claims for Same-Sex Marriage. *Brigham Young University Law Review* 1996:1–101.

SAN ANTONIO INDEPENDENT SCHOOL DISTRICT v. RODRIGUEZ
411 U.S. 1 (1973)

Rodriguez was the BURGER COURT's definitive statement on the subject of EQUAL PROTECTION guarantees against WEALTH DISCRIMINATION—and the statement was that the Court wanted the subject to go away.

Under Texas law, the financing of local school districts relies heavily on local property taxes. Thus a district rich in taxable property can levy taxes at low rates and still spend almost twice as much per pupil as a poor district can spend, even when the poor district taxes its property at high rates. A federal district court, relying on WARREN COURT precedents, concluded that wealth was a SUSPECT CLASSIFICATION, that education was a FUNDAMENTAL INTEREST, and thus that strict judicial scrutiny of the state-imposed inequalities was required. The trial court also concluded that, even if the permissive RATIONAL BASIS standard of review were appropriate, the Texas school finance system lacked any reasonable basis. The Supreme Court reversed, 5–4, in an opinion by Justice LEWIS F. POWELL that was plainly designed as a comprehensive pronouncement about equal protection doctrine.

The opinion was definitive, as a coffin is definitive. Despite what the Court had said in BROWN V. BOARD OF EDU-

CATION (1954) about education as the key to effective citizenship, here it said that education was not a fundamental interest in the sense that triggered STRICT SCRUTINY—at least not when some minimal level of education was being provided. Indeed, said the majority, the courts lacked power to create new substantive rights by defining interests as "fundamental," unless those interests were already guaranteed elsewhere in the Constitution. Here was formal recognition of the Burger Court's zero-population-growth policy for fundamental interests.

Nor was wealth a suspect classification. Decisions such as GRIFFIN V. ILLINOIS (1956) and DOUGLAS V. CALIFORNIA (1963) had involved INDIGENTS "completely unable to pay" for the benefits at stake, who "sustained an absolute deprivation" of the benefits. Here, the deprivation was only relative; pupils in poor districts were receiving some education. Furthermore, although the trial court had found a significant correlation between district wealth and family wealth, the Supreme Court held the proof of that correlation insufficient; poor children, after all, might live in the shadows of a rich district's factories. In any case, Justice Powell concluded, the evidence was mixed on the question whether school spending affected the quality of education.

Because there was no occasion for strict scrutiny, the Court employed the rational basis standard of review. Contrary to the district court's conclusion, the Texas financing scheme was rationally designed to maintain local control over school spending and educational policy. Justice BYRON R. WHITE, dissenting, attacked this asserted rationality. If "local control" flowed from control over the spending of money, then Texas, by relying heavily on the property tax and by drawing its district lines, had parceled out that choice in an irrationally selective way, to rich districts and not to poor ones.

Justice THURGOOD MARSHALL's dissent was the most powerful equal protection opinion of the Burger Court era. He elaborated on his DANDRIDGE V. WILLIAMS (1970) dissent, rejecting a two-tier system of standards of review in favor of a "sliding-scale" approach tying the level of judicial scrutiny to the importance of the interests at stake and the degree to which the state's classification bore on the powerless. Here, on both counts, judicial scrutiny should be heightened well above the level of requiring only minimal rationality. In any case, the Court had not, in the *Griffin/Douglas* line of cases, insisted on a showing of absolute deprivation as a condition of strict scrutiny of wealth discrimination; the problem in those cases was the *adequacy* of an appeal, as affected by a discrimination between rich and poor. The Texas scheme could not survive any heightened judicial scrutiny—as the majority itself had virtually conceded.

Justice Powell, a former school board president, surely feared judicial intrusion into the decisions of local school officials. Beyond that narrow concern, the majority undoubtedly worried about judicial intrusion into the allocation of state resources. These are legitimate concerns. The question was, and remains, what kinds of economic inequality, *imposed by the state itself,* can be tolerated in the face of a constitutional guarantee of the equal protection of the laws.

KENNETH L. KARST
(1986)

(SEE ALSO: *Education and the Constitution; Plyler v. Doe.*)

Bibliography

MICHELMAN, FRANK I. 1969 The Supreme Court, 1968 Term—Foreword: On Protecting the Poor Through the Fourteenth Amendment. *Harvard Law Review* 83:7–59.

SANFORD, EDWARD T.
(1865–1930)

Edward Terry Sanford was the last of WARREN HARDING's four Supreme Court appointments. He had served fifteen years as a federal judge in Tennessee and, as with many of Harding's judicial appointments, he was chosen in large part because of Chief Justice WILLIAM HOWARD TAFT's lobbying activities.

For nearly seven years, Sanford loyally followed and served Taft. He began his tenure by joining a rare Taft dissent when the Court invalidated the DISTRICT OF COLUMBIA MINIMUM WAGE LAW in ADKINS V. CHILDREN'S HOSPITAL (1923). He was a regular member of the Chief Justice's Sunday afternoon extracurricular conferences, which excluded the Court's more liberal members such as OLIVER WENDELL HOLMES, LOUIS D. BRANDEIS, and HARLAN F. STONE. In a final coincidence, Sanford died on March 8, 1930, the same day as Taft.

Sanford's most important contribution to constitutional law during his brief tenure came in the area of CIVIL LIBERTIES. In GITLOW V. NEW YORK (1925) he led the Court in sustaining New York's criminal anarchy statute. Sanford's opinion largely reiterated the Court's BAD TENDENCY TEST regarding FREEDOM OF SPEECH, arguing that the state had a right to protect itself against speech that called for the overthrow of government. The state could not, he said, "reasonably be required to measure the danger from every such utterance in the nice balance of a jeweler's scale." But Sanford also acknowledged that the FOURTEENTH AMENDMENT incorporated the FIRST AMENDMENT's guarantees of free speech and FREEDOM OF THE PRESS against STATE ACTION. That INCORPORATION DOCTRINE had momentous consequences for the Court's later views of CIVIL RIGHTS and LIBERTIES.

In WHITNEY V. CALIFORNIA (1927) Sanford again sustained a criminal anarchy conviction. But the same day, in *Fiske v. Kansas*, he spoke for the Court when for the first time the Justices overturned a state conviction on the ground that a criminal anarchy statute had been applied to deny the defendant his freedom of speech, as guaranteed by the First and Fourteenth Amendments. Sanford found that the state had failed to provide evidence of the organization's criminal or violent purposes. Shortly after Sanford's death, the Court nullified a state criminal anarchy statute and a state law sanctioning the suppression of certain newspapers, with both decisions (STROMBERG V. CALIFORNIA, 1931; NEAR V. MINNESOTA, 1931) implementing Sanford's *Gitlow* incorporation doctrine.

Sanford generally concurred with the Court's decisions involving national and state ECONOMIC REGULATION. For example, he joined in approving ZONING laws in EUCLID V. AMBLER REALTY CO. (1926), and he agreed that a Pennsylvania statute requiring drugstore owners to be registered pharmacists was unconstitutional in *Lambert v. Yellowley* (1926). But in *Maple Floor Association v. United States* (1925) Sanford joined Taft's dissent protesting the Court's holding that trade associations did not violate the SHERMAN ANTITRUST ACT. In *Tyson v. Banton* (1927) Sanford, dissenting from a ruling that invalidated regulations of theater ticket brokers, invoked the STATE POLICE POWER doctrine of the GRANGER CASES (1877); he argued that because the brokers' business was AFFECTED WITH A PUBLIC INTEREST, the legislature could protect "the public from extortion and exorbitant rates."

Sanford's Supreme Court tenure was, on the whole, unremarkable. There is irony in that his *Gitlow* opinion, despite its antilibertarian result, laid the foundation for the mid-twentieth-century libertarian revolution and the nationalization of American CIVIL RIGHTS and CIVIL LIBERTIES.

STANLEY I. KUTLER
(1986)

Bibliography

RAGAN, ALLEN E. 1943 Mr. Justice Sanford. *East Tennessee Historical Society Publications* 15:74–88.

SAN MATEO COUNTY v. SOUTHERN PACIFIC RAILROAD

See: Person

SANTA CLARA COUNTY v. SOUTHERN PACIFIC RAILROAD

See: Person

SAWYER, LORENZO
(1820–1891)

In 1870 ULYSSES S. GRANT commissioned Lorenzo Sawyer of California judge of the Ninth Circuit Court, a position he filled until his death. Throughout these years, Sawyer shared circuit court duties with Supreme Court Justice STEPHEN J. FIELD.

Sawyer formulated a narrow interpretation of the PUBLIC PURPOSE DOCTRINE and STATE POLICE POWERS. He declared that a state could not, consistently with the FOURTEENTH AMENDMENT, define the public purpose to permit mining companies to cause flooding of private lands. Sawyer also resisted local efforts to discriminate against the Chinese under the guise of the POLICE POWER. In 1890 he struck down a San Francisco ordinance, which required Chinese to live and work in a designated area of the city, as an "arbitrary confiscation of property without DUE PROCESS or any process of law." Sawyer also invalidated other suspect uses of the police power that sought to harass the Chinese by outlawing the operation of laundries and opium parlors. Such measures, he ruled, placed "an unlawful inhibition upon the inalienable rights and liberties of [all] citizens. . . ."

Sawyer subscribed to the doctrine of DUAL FEDERALISM, but in *In Re Neagle* he forcefully recited the supremacy of the federal government. David Neagle, a United States marshal and bodyguard for Justice Field, had killed a man to protect Field. Sawyer issued a writ of HABEAS CORPUS releasing Neagle from custody by California officials on charges of murder. He held that the marshal had acted in pursuance of the laws of the United States and that "a state law, which contravenes a valid law of the United States, is, in the nature of things, necessarily void—a nullity."

Justice Field cast a large shadow over jurisprudence of the Ninth Circuit, but Sawyer also significantly shaped American constitutional law. His opinions were a major source of authority on the police powers of the states, the public purpose doctrine, and the Fourteenth Amendment.

KERMIT L. HALL
(1986)

Bibliography

SWISHER, CARL BRENT 1930 *Stephen J. Field, Craftsman of the Law.* Pages 325–326, 332, 337, 342, 352, 353, 355, 358–359. Washington, D.C.: Brookings Institution.

SCALES v. UNITED STATES
367 U.S. 203 (1961)

The Supreme Court, always careful to avoid declaring the Smith Act unconstitutional, instead employed statutory interpretation to emasculate its provisions. Here the Court held that the act's clause banning "membership" in certain organizations applied only to members active in the organization's affairs, knowing that its purpose was to bring about the overthrow of the government by force and violence as speedily as circumstances would permit, and with the specific purpose to bring about that overthrow. In the *Scales* case itself, the Court affirmed a conviction under the membership clause. Since that time, however, the act's forbidding BURDEN OF PROOF has discouraged further prosecutions.

MARTIN SHAPIRO
(1986)

SCALIA, ANTONIN
(1936–   )

Associate Justice Antonin "Nino" Scalia became the 103rd Justice of the United States Supreme Court on September 27, 1986. Justice Scalia came to the Court after a distinguished career in law, teaching, government, and as a federal appellate judge. He is the first Italian American to be appointed to the Court and was second of three conservative Supreme Court Justices appointed by President RONALD REAGAN. Scalia has established himself as an outspoken proponent of a jurisprudence that is profoundly at odds with the jurisprudence of later twentieth century LIBERALISM (i.e., the liberalism of the WARREN COURT) and differs in significant detail from current judicial conservatism of the role it assigns the judiciary. Before analyzing this jurisprudence, it is important to place it in the context of Scalia's life and professional career, both of which had revealed him as an articulate exponent of political CONSERVATIVE opinions.

Scalia was born in Trenton, New Jersey, on March 11, 1936, the only child of Italian immigrant parents. The family moved later to Queens, New York, where Scalia's father, S. Eugene Scalia, was a college professor, and his mother, Catherine Louise Panaro Scalia, was an elementary school teacher. S. Eugene Scalia was a scholar of romance language and literature who wrote several monographs on Italian literary history and criticism and translated Italian works into English. Antonin Scalia was a brilliant student. He graduated first in his class at a Manhattan Jesuit military academy, Xavier High School, and then repeated that accomplishment at Georgetown University, from which he graduated in 1957. He attended Harvard Law School, where he again excelled scholastically and was elected Note Editor of the *Harvard Law Review*. After graduation he entered practice with Jones, Day, Cockley & Reavis in Cleveland. He practiced corporate law with the firm until 1967, when he declined a partnership offer. Instead, he accepted a position on the faculty of the University of Virginia Law School.

At Virginia, Scalia began, both through his teaching and research, to develop a specialty in ADMINISTRATIVE LAW. He published several articles critical of procedural aspects of federal agencies before leaving Virginia to work in Washington, D.C. Scalia's conservative political orientation, which friends and colleagues identify as having been held by him consistently since college, led him to leave teaching to accept several positions in the administration of President RICHARD M. NIXON. He first served as general counsel in the executive office of telecommunications policy and then was appointed chairman of the Administrative Conference of the United States. The conference is responsible for studying common legal and management issues affecting federal executive branch agencies and for recommending improvements in administrative procedures. Scalia next became embroiled in the political battles of WATERGATE when he moved to the Department of Justice in the summer of 1974 as assistant attorney general in charge of the Office of Legal Counsel, the office that provides legal advice to the President. Among Scalia's first duties was drafting a defense of the President's claim that the tapes and records that Congress sought were his property, not the government's, and that they were protected from congressional subpoena by EXECUTIVE PRIVILEGE. After Nixon's resignation, following the Supreme Court's rejection of his argument, Scalia remained at the Justice Department until January 1977 when President GERALD R. FORD left office. He subsequently spent six months at the American Enterprise Institute, a conservative research organization, and then accepted a position as a professor at the University of Chicago School of Law.

Scalia taught at Chicago until his appointment to the federal appellate court bench in 1982. (He served one year as a visiting professor at Stanford Law School.) During his time at Chicago, Scalia established himself as a leading voice among conservative academics. He continued to write and teach in the area of administrative law, and he edited the American Enterprise Institute's journal *Regulation*, which was largely devoted to attacking regulatory excesses and advocating deregulation. Scalia also attacked judicial inattention to the provisions of the Administrative Procedure Act—most notably, the U.S. Court of Appeals for the District of Columbia's review of the work of the Nuclear Regulatory Commission in the *Vermont Yankee Nuclear Power Corp.* case (1978). From 1981 to 1982 Scalia served as chair of the administrative law section of the American Bar Association, and he used his office to call for lawyers to become involved in reforming administrative procedure to make it fit the new environment of deregulation.

Scalia's writings addressed other items on the conservative political agenda as well. He attacked AFFIRMATIVE ACTION in a 1979 article in the *Washington University Law Quarterly* both on principle and because he believed that it could not effectively overcome discrimination. He ridiculed white Anglo-Saxon judges such as Justice LEWIS F. POWELL and Judge JOHN MINOR WISDOM for justifying affirmative action as "restorative justice" when the members of white ethnic groups—such as Scalia's own Italian family—most often bore the cost of compensating blacks for the WASPs' prior treatment of blacks. Scalia further denounced the FREEDOM OF INFORMATION ACT for imposing prohibitive costs on the government and promoting openness at the cost of law enforcement, privacy, and national security, and at an American Enterprise Institute conference in 1978, he blasted the Supreme Court's 1973 ruling in ROE V. WADE for being an illegitimate exercise in judicial lawmaking.

Hence, by the early 1980s, when President Reagan was showing propensity to fill federal court positions with conservative legal academics, Nino Scalia was a prime candidate. He was first offered a position on the United States Court of Appeals for the Seventh Circuit in Chicago, but he turned it down, preferring instead the Court of Appeals for the District of Columbia. A vacancy on that court occurred in 1982, and he resigned his professorship at the University of Chicago to move his wife Maureen and their nine children to Washington, D.C.

Judge Scalia's tenure on the federal appellate bench was marked by the political conservatism of his opinions and by his ability to maintain strong personal working relationships on a court that had been politically and socially divided for many years. Among Scalia's notable opinions on the D.C. Circuit were those that supported the executive branch over both the legislative branch and independent federal agencies. For example, Scalia wrote an opinion striking down the GRAMM-RUDMAN-HOLLINGS ACT, on SEPARATION OF POWERS grounds. According to Scalia, the act impermissibly delegated executive branch functions to an official who was subject to removal by Congress. Scalia further gained attention by narrowing press protection from LIBEL suits in two opinions: one against the *Washington Post* and one in which his dissent would have allowed a suit against two political columnists. He also narrowly read Title VII contending in a dissent that sexual harassment on the job did not violate the provisions of the act.

Judge Scalia's conservative politics and his performance as a judge made him the choice of the Reagan administration in 1986 for the Supreme Court seat of Associate Justice WILLIAM H. REHNQUIST when the President elevated Rehnquist to the position of Chief Justice. The American Bar Association endorsed Scalia without qualification, and only a few feminist and civil rights groups opposed him at his confirmation hearings. He was subjected to far less criticism and hostile questioning than Rehnquist, and he avoided the political battle his fellow circuit judge, Robert Bork, experienced two years later when he was nominated to the court. The Senate approved Justice Scalia's nomination unanimously on September 16, 1986.

As a Supreme Court Justice, Scalia has received attention for the intellectual tenacity of his positions and for his jurisprudential methodology. Not unexpectedly, he voted most often with the Court's conservatives: Chief Justice Rehnquist, Justice ANTHONY M. KENNEDY, Justice SANDRA DAY O'CONNOR, and Justice BYRON R. WHITE. Over the years he has been on the Court, Scalia and the Chief Justice have agreed in about eighty-five percent of the Court's cases, which is similar to his rate of agreement with Justice Kennedy and only slightly higher than the rate with Justice O'Connor. He has agreed with Justice White at a slightly lower rate (seventy-five percent), whereas his agreement rates with Justices WILLIAM J. BRENNAN, THURGOOD MARSHALL, HARRY A. BLACKMUN, and JOHN PAUL STEVENS have been closer to fifty percent. That he has voted in support of conservative policies is not surprising. For example, Justice Scalia's dissent in WEBSTER V. REPRODUCTIVE HEALTH SERVICES (1989) argued that ROE V. WADE should be overturned. He joined the majority in striking down affirmative action plans in RICHMOND (CITY OF) V. J. A. CROSON CO. (1989), and he has rejected challenges to the constitutionality of CAPITAL PUNISHMENT.

What has been noted by commentators, however, is the jurisprudential vision that Justice Scalia has forcefully constructed through his opinions. The cornerstone of his jurisprudence is the limited role of the judge and the judiciary in the American constitutional system. In Scalia's understanding of American democracy, the Constitution granted the legislature and (by delegation) the executive the power to define rights and to determine the wisdom of specific policies designed or executed within their respective constitutional spheres. This may sound similar to the familiar criticism judicial conservatives have made to "judicial legislation" engaged in by liberal justices since the Warren Court. However, Scalia has taken the position further by advancing the argument for judicial restraint across all areas of judging, building on the critiques of JUDICIAL ACTIVISM offered by liberals such as Justices LOUIS D. BRANDEIS and FELIX FRANKFURTER and later elaborated by professors such as Harvard's HENRY HART and Herbert Wechsler. This position must be contrasted to the post-New Deal liberals as well as to many twentieth-century conservatives. Both have had at the core of their jurisprudence an active role for the judiciary as the balancers of society's interests. The liberals have envisioned the judge as the protector of individuals against majoritarian legislatures and thus have used concepts such as DUE PROCESS and EQUAL PROTECTION to create rights and strike down both federal and state legislation. Conservatives, typified by Chief Justice WILLIAM HOWARD TAFT, have believed that judges should ensure that the majority's legislative actions (which generally have taken the form of increased regulation of social and economic activities) are gradual and that property interests are protected.

Justice Scalia's differences with such conservatives can be illustrated through both his writings and his opinions. Perhaps the most striking comparison that can be made is between his article "The Rule of Law as a Law of Rules" and the writings of Chief Justice Taft. Taft celebrated the creation of "the rule of reasonableness" in determining violations of the provisions of the SHERMAN ANTITRUST ACT precisely because it left the federal judiciary as the arbiter of which monopolies were unlawful. Also, for Taft the glory of the COMMON LAW process was that judges made law incrementally and directed change through their opinions by the elaboration of rules and the application of facts to those rules. Scalia's article directly challenges both these points. He argues that judges should attempt to formulate general rules rather than gradually developing standards through common law case-by-case determinations. He maintains that cases decided by such standards are determined by the weight individual judges place on particular facts, thus allowing the individual to decide outcomes by his or her individual preferences. An example of what Justice Scalia means, as well as how his approach differs from both liberals and conservatives on the Supreme Court, can be found in a recent PUNITIVE DAMAGES case decided by the Court, *Pacific Mutual Life Insurance Co. v. Haslip* (1991). In this opinion, the majority (Justices Blackmun, Rehnquist, White, Marshall, and Stevens) considered the constitutionality of an award of punitive damages by an Alabama jury. The Court held in an opinion by Blackmun that punitive damages were not per se unconstitutional but that due process considerations required that both the process for instructing the jury as well as the amount awarded must be "reasonable" in order to be constitutional. The majority then discussed the factors that should be considered in testing the reasonableness of the award. Justice O'Connor in dissent argued that the Alabama punitive-damages scheme did not meet due process standards as it was impermissibly vague. Justice Scalia concurred in the result reached by the majority, but rejected both its reasoning and that of Justice O'Connor. He rejected the inquiry into the reasonableness or fairness of the procedures because "this jury-like verdict provides no guidance as to whether any *other* procedures are sufficiently "reasonable,' and thus perpetuates the uncertainty that . . . this case was intended to resolve." Justice Scalia instead derived a per se rule that these damages were constitutional by broadly canvassing this history of their use

and concluding that, since they had been "a part of our living tradition that dates back prior to 1868, I would end the suspense and categorically affirm their validity." He stated that "it is not for the Members of this Court to decide from time to time whether a process approved by the legal traditions of our people is "due' process, nor do I believe such a rootless analysis to be dictated by our precedents."

As this example reveals, Justice Scalia's attempt to implement judicial restraint requires an interpretive methodology that can derive categorical rules that are founded on something other than the judges' individual sense of what is right. He does not totally embrace ORIGINALISM as do other conservatives such as Robert Bork, although he acknowledges that the intent of the Framers is where analysis must begin. Instead, Justice Scalia has adopted a literalistic approach in which the plain and ordinary meaning of the language of texts—whether they be the U.S. Constitution, statutes, or regulations—must govern the judge's decision. For example, in *Morrison v. Olson* (1989), Justice Scalia issued the only dissent in the case that upheld the federal law governing the appointment of SPECIAL PROSECUTORS. His strongly worded attack on the majority's opinion centered on the wording of Article I. All EXECUTIVE POWER was vested in the President by the wording of Article I, and this law removed some of this power and thus was unconstitutional. He rejected any idea that the Court could balance the interests of the two branches to decide the reasonableness of this statutory scheme. Similarly, in *Cruzan v. Missouri Department of Health* (1990), Scalia concurred in the majority's decision to refuse to create a constitutional RIGHT TO DIE. He differed from the majority in that he would have forthrightly declared that no such right existed because to do so would be "to create out of nothing (for it exists neither in text nor tradition)."

This methodology requires several subsidiary rules. Because the ordinary meaning of the words are to govern, the intent of the drafters of legislation have no place in judicial analysis. Thus, Justice Scalia refused to resort to an inquiry into the legislative history of statutes. If the plain meaning of a law creates a hardship that was unintended or if enforcement of a law as written is unworkable, it is for the legislative branch to redraft the act rather than for judges to amend it through their interpretations. Scalia outlined this position in his first term on the Court in a concurrence in *Immigration & Naturalization Service v. Cardoza Fonseca* (1987). He stated that the Court's result was correct, but that it could reach the result through the plain meaning of the statute. Not only was the majority's inquiry into the legislative history unnecessary, it was also irrelevant. He thus rejected a technique not only used consistently by the Warren Court but also accepted by conservative Justices. Second, when the ordinary meaning of a text is not determinative, the judge should look to "objective" standards, such as the history and tradition of a particular practice. These would require consultation of historical sources and monographs, as well as judicial PRECEDENTS. An example of this approach was *Pacific Mutual*, where Justice Scalia relied on American common law history of punitive damages to determine what due process meant in this context. Similarly, in STANFORD V. KENTUCKY (1989) Justice Scalia determined that executing a juvenile was not "cruel and unusual" under the Eighth Amendment because, in part, a canvass of state laws showed that a majority allowed execution of sixteen-year-olds. Thus, he reasoned, the practice could not be considered unusual.

Two points should be made in concluding a review of Justice Scalia's strikingly innovative jurisprudential methodology. As most of the examples reveal, his approach is most often made in concurrences or individual dissents. At the Supreme Court he has not played the role of a consensus builder, and in fact, his sharp attacks on other Justices in dissent (most notably against Justice O'Connor in *Webster*) have received critical comment. Although there is some evidence that the Court has moved toward him on some issues, such as ignoring legislative history, he has yet to emerge as the intellectual leader of the Court, as opposed to a single highly intelligent voice. Second, his jurisprudence has been developed at a time when political conservatives have enjoyed considerable success in both legislative and executive branches on the state and federal levels. Although there is certainly some evidence that he has followed his methodology even when it has surprisingly resulted in liberal outcomes (he voted to strike down the FLAG DESECRATION statute in *Johnson v. Texas* and has reached prodefendant positions in several CRIMINAL PROCEDURE cases, it remains to be seen what might happen if the future were to bring a strongly liberal executive and legislature intent on expanding federal social and economic reform.

RAYMAN L. SOLOMON
(1992)

(SEE ALSO: *Coy v. Iowa; Johnson v. Transportation Agency; Lemon Test; Rutan v. Republican Party of Illinois.*)

Bibliography
COMMENT 1987 The Appellate Jurisprudence of Justice Antonin Scalia. *University of Chicago Law Review* 54:705–739.
ESKRIDGE, WILLIAM N., JR. 1990 The New Textualism. *University of California at Los Angeles Law Review* 37:621–691.
KANNAR, GEORGE 1990 The Constitutional Catechism of Antonin Scalia. *The Yale Law Journal* 99:849–865.
SCALIA, ANTONIN 1989 Originalism; The Lesser Evil. *University of Cincinnati Law Review* 57:849–865.
——— 1989 The Rule of Law as a Law of Rules. *University of Chicago Law Review* 56:1175–1188.

SCALIA, ANTONIN
(1936–)
(Update)

Antonin Scalia is an Associate Justice on the United States Supreme Court. A graduate of Harvard Law School, he taught law at the University of Virginia and at the University of Chicago. Between these academic appointments, Scalia held several legal positions, including head of the Justice Department's Office of Legal Counsel. In 1982, President RONALD REAGAN appointed Scalia to the United States Court of Appeals for the District of Columbia Circuit. In 1986, Reagan appointed Scalia the 103rd Justice of the United States Supreme Court.

Scalia is often viewed as a leader of the conservative backlash against the WARREN COURT. Notwithstanding his conservatism, his judicial philosophy is much more complex. Scalia differs in important respects from the other two Reagan appointees—SANDRA DAY O'CONNOR and ANTHONY M. KENNEDY—and even from WILLIAM H. REHNQUIST, whom Reagan elevated to Chief Justice. Of the conservative appointees, only CLARENCE THOMAS, appointed by President GEORGE H. W. BUSH, seems to share Scalia's philosophy (although Rehnquist may come close). That philosophy has been described by various labels, but TEXTUALISM or ORIGINALISM probably is most fitting.

Textualism is often confused with the philosophy of ORIGINAL INTENT. Thus, it is frequently said that courts should give effect to the intention of the legislators who enacted a law. But Scalia believes what the legislature actually enacted should control, rather than what it subjectively intended. Of course, the two may concur, but when they do not, courts must look to what the legislature promulgated, not what it intended to promulgate.

Scalia believes that a democratic society is bound by validly passed laws, not by the unexpressed intent of the lawgiver. Besides, judges are likely to conclude that the legislature intended what a reasonable and intelligent person ought to have intended, which means they are likely to decide the statute means what they think it should mean. Thus, we would have government by the unelected and politically unaccountable federal judiciary rather than by the politically responsible legislature.

Scalia distinguishes textualism from STRICT CONSTRUCTIONISM. A statute should not be construed strictly or leniently, he says; rather, it should be construed reasonably to stand for all that it fairly means. In *Smith v. United States* (1993), for example, the statute provided for an enhanced sentence if a person "uses" a gun in relation to a drug crime. Scalia dissented from the Court's holding that a person who sought to exchange an unloaded gun for cocaine had used a firearm in relation to a drug crime. To "use" a gun, Scalia argued, fairly connotes using the gun as a weapon, not as an item of exchange.

Scalia's view that the objective indication of the statutory words, rather than the LEGISLATIVE INTENT, should control has led him to reject legislative history—statements made in floor debates, committee testimony, and committee reports—in STATUTORY INTERPRETATION. The majority of legislators voted for the language in the law, not for the legislative history. Moreover, knowing that courts rely on legislative history, statements are made deliberately to influence expected litigation. Besides, the Constitution requires both Houses of Congress to pass a law and the President to have a chance to veto it. Committee reports do not satisfy these requirements.

Scalia applies the same principles to CONSTITUTIONAL INTERPRETATION. That is, he looks for the original meaning of the text, not what the Framers intended. He will consult THE FEDERALIST papers, because these show how the original document was understood by intelligent people at the time. He does not look to them as evidence of the intent of the Framers.

As Scalia has observed, however, the great debate today is between those few who think the Constitution's meaning does not change (whether they are textualists or adherents to the intent of the Framers) and the many who want to keep the Constitution current with the times. But the Constitution is a democratically adopted text (like statutes are), designed to make change difficult. Only the people, through the AMENDING PROCESS, have the authority to change it. Politically unaccountable judges do not have the authority to do so.

Scalia is critical of judges who argue that CAPITAL PUNISHMENT is CRUEL AND UNUSUAL PUNISHMENT in violation of the Eighth Amendment, even though the Constitution refers to the death penalty in three clauses. Under the notion of a LIVING CONSTITUTION, he says, each judge is free to decide if and when the death penalty became unconstitutional, with no guidance from the text. Harvard Law School Professor Laurence Tribe, however, says Scalia is not being faithful to his textualist approach. Scalia's position is sound, Tribe argues, only if the unexpressed intentions of the Framers control, but Scalia has argued against being bound by the intent of the Framers. Scalia would respond that the language of the Eighth Amendment, read in context, does not support finding the death penalty to be cruel and unusual.

Scalia has been most outspoken regarding the Court's interpretation of the Constitution's DUE PROCESS clauses, which prohibit any person from being deprived of life, liberty, or PROPERTY without due process of law. By their terms, these clauses are limited to process (the state can take life, liberty, or property if it provides due procedures), but departing from the text, the Court has used these clauses to protect certain substantive liberties, such as ABORTION and the right to terminate life support. Scalia has not attacked the very notion of SUBSTANTIVE DUE PROCESS but has said that due process only protects those liberties rooted in history and tradition, *Michael H. v. Gerald D.* (1989). In an abortion case, he also said that it does not follow that the Constitution does not protect childbirth simply because it does not protect abortion, PLANNED PARENTHOOD V. CASEY (1992). Scalia has also written that he would vote to strike down public flogging even if it could be demonstrated that such flogging was not cruel and unusual in 1791, when the Eighth Amendment was adopted. Each of the positions is a departure from pure textualism (or originalism).

MARYLAND V. CRAIG (1990) provides an example of how textualism differs from strict constructionism, and how it can produce results that are not conservative. The majority upheld a procedure that allowed a young sex-abuse victim to testify with the defendant being made to watch over closed-circuit television. Perhaps this was a reasonable procedure to save the victim psychic trauma, but Scalia nonetheless thought it violated the RIGHT OF CONFRONTATION guaranteed by the confrontation clause. When the Constitution was enacted, he argued in dissent, confrontation meant the right to meet face-to-face those who testify at trial. Judges do not have authority to balance a right the text explicitly provides against their view of the public interest.

JOSEPH D. GRANO
(2000)

Bibliography

DWORKIN, RONALD   1997   Fidelity as Integrity: The Arduous Virtue of Fidelity: Originalism, Scalia, Tribe, and Nerve. *Fordham Law Review* 65:1249–1268.

FOX, AUTUMN and MCALLISTER, STEPHEN R.   1997   An Eagle Soaring: The Jurisprudence of Justice Antonin Scalia. *Campbell Law Review* 19:223–309.

GERHARDT, MICHAEL J.   1994   A Tale of Two Textualists: A Critical Comparison of Justices Black and Scalia. *Boston University Law Review* 74:25–66.

LIESS, ELIZABETH A.   1993   Comment: Censoring Legislative History: Justice Scalia on the Use of Legislative History in Statutory Interpretation. *Nebraska Law Review* 72:568–585.

SCALIA, ANTONIN   1989   Originalism: The Lesser Evil. *Cincinnati Law Review* 56:849–865.

———   1997   *A Matter of Interpretation.* Princeton, N.J.: Princeton University Press.

SHATTUCK, TIMOTHY L. RASCHKE   1992   Justice Scalia's Due Process Methodology: Examining Specific Traditions. *Southern California Law Review* 65:2743–2791.

SCHAD v. MOUNT EPHRAIM
452 U.S. 61 (1981)

The Supreme Court, 7–2, reversed the conviction of the operators of an "adult" bookstore for violating a ZONING ordinance of a residential town by presenting live entertainment in the form of nude dancing. The state courts had construed the ordinance to forbid all live entertainment; so read, it fell afoul of the FIRST AMENDMENT doctrine of OVERBREADTH. The Court concluded that the state's asserted justifications (limiting commerce to residents' "immediate needs," and avoiding problems with parking, trash, and the like) were unsupported by the record, which showed that live entertainment was offered in three other establishments. The dissenters argued that, although banning other entertainment might present First Amendment problems, banning nude dancing did not.

KENNETH L. KARST
(1986)

SCHALL v. MARTIN
467 U.S. 253 (1984)

This is one of several cases showing that legal fictions infect JUVENILE PROCEEDINGS involving criminal conduct. *Schall* reflected the fictions that juveniles, unlike adults, "are always in some form of custody" and that PREVENTIVE DETENTION is not punitive and is designed to protect the youthful offender as well as society from the consequences of his uncommitted crimes. New York, without distinguishing first offenders from recidivists and without distinguishing trivial offenses from major crimes of violence, allowed juveniles, aged seven to sixteen, to be jailed for up to seventeen days pending adjudication of guilt. Justice WILLIAM H. REHNQUIST, for a 6–3 Supreme Court, ruled that preventive detention in the case of juveniles is compatible with the FUNDAMENTAL FAIRNESS required by the FOURTEENTH AMENDMENT's guarantee of DUE PROCESS OF LAW. Rehnquist found adequate procedural safeguards in the New York statute, noted that every state permitted preventive detention of juveniles accused of crime, and declared that the juveniles' best interests were served because preventive detention disabled them from committing other crimes prior to the date of court appearance. Justices THURGOOD MARSHALL, WILLIAM J. BRENNAN, and JOHN PAUL STEVENS, dissenting, insisted that the majority's factual argument did not survive critical scrutiny any more than did the statute provide due process.

LEONARD W. LEVY
(1986)

SCHECHTER POULTRY CORP. v. UNITED STATES
295 U.S. 495 (1935)

After the decision in this case, striking down the NATIONAL INDUSTRIAL RECOVERY ACT, a conservative gave thanks that the Constitution still stood, while a liberal wondered whether it stood still. The Supreme Court's "horse and buggy" interpretation, as President FRANKLIN D. ROOSEVELT called it, imperiled the power of the United States to control any part of the economy that the Court regarded as subject to the exclusive control of the states. Chief Justice CHARLES EVANS HUGHES, for the Court, first held the statute void because it improperly delegated legislative powers. Private business groups might frame codes governing their industries as long as NRA officials approved and the president promulgated them. Hughes said the president's discretion was "unfettered," and even Justice BENJAMIN N. CARDOZO, who had dissented in PANAMA REFINING CO. V. RYAN (1935), separately concurred and spoke of "delegation running riot." Improper DELEGATION [of power] could have been rectified by new legislation, but the Court also held the act unauthorized by the COMMERCE CLAUSE, leaving the impression that labor matters and trade practices were beyond the scope of congressional power unless in INTERSTATE COMMERCE or directly affecting it.

The government argued that although Schechter sold only in the local market, its business was in the STREAM OF COMMERCE. Ninety-six percent of the poultry sold in New York City came from out of state. Hughes rejected that argument by ruling that the flow of interstate commerce had ceased, because the poultry had come to a permanent rest in the city: it was sold locally and did not again leave the state. The government also invoked the SHREVEPORT DOCTRINE, arguing that even if the commerce here were local, it had so close and substantial a relationship to interstate commerce that its federal regulation was necessary to protect interstate commerce. Schechter's preferential trade practices, low wages, and long hours, in violation of the poultry code, enabled it to undersell competitors, diverting the interstate flow of poultry to its own market, injuring interstate competitors, and triggering a cycle of wage and price cutting that threatened to extend beyond the confines of the local market. This entire line of reasoning, Hughes said, proved too much. It laid the basis for national regulation of the entire economy, overriding state authority. It also ignored the fundamental distinction between direct and indirect effects upon interstate commerce. What that distinction was Hughes did not explain, but he asserted that Schechter's violations of the code only indirectly affected interstate commerce and therefore stood beyond national reach. Even Cardozo, joined by Justice HARLAN FISKE STONE, declared that "to find immediacy or directness here is to find it almost everywhere."

Schechter temporarily ended national regulation of industry and allowed Roosevelt to blame the Court, even though the NRA's code programs were cumbersome, unpopular, and scheduled for political extinction. The Court's views of the commerce clause made no substitute constitutionally feasible.

LEONARD W. LEVY
(1986)

SCHENCK v. UNITED STATES
249 U.S. 47 (1919)

The FREEDOM OF SPEECH provisions of the FIRST AMENDMENT played a singularly retiring role in American constitutional law until the time of WORLD WAR I or, more precisely, until the Russian Revolution and the Red Scare that it generated in the United States. The Sedition Act of 1798 (see ALIEN AND SEDITION ACTS) obviously posed serious First Amendment questions but was not tested in the Supreme Court and was soon repealed. A scattering of free speech claims and oblique pronouncements by the federal courts occurred after 1900, but speech issues, even when they did arise, typically appeared in state courts in the contexts of OBSCENITY prosecutions and labor disputes. The Court did not declare the First Amendment applicable to the states through the due process clause of the FOURTEENTH AMENDMENT (see INCORPORATION DOCTRINE) until GITLOW V. NEW YORK (1925). Furthermore, in its most direct pronouncement on the freedom of speech provision of the First Amendment, *Patterson v. Colorado* (1907), the Court, speaking through Justice OLIVER WENDELL HOLMES, had suggested that the provision barred only prior restraints, a position that Holmes abandoned in *Schenck*.

In 1917 Congress passed an ESPIONAGE ACT making it a crime to cause or attempt to cause insubordination in the armed forces, obstruct recruitment or enlistment, and otherwise urge, incite, or advocate obstruction or resistance to the war effort. Although there had been much bitter debate about U. S. entry into World War I, the speakers whose prosecutions raised First Amendment issues that ultimately reached the Supreme Court were not German sympathizers. They were left-wing sympathizers with the Russian Revolution who were provoked by the dispatch of Allied expeditionary forces to Russia. If the American war machine was to be turned on the Revolution, it must be stopped.

Prosecutions of such revolutionary sympathizers triggered three important federal court decisions that initiated the jurisprudence of the First Amendment: MASSES PUBLISHING COMPANY V. PATTEN (1917), *Schenck v. United States*, and ABRAMS V. UNITED STATES (1919). *Schenck* was the first major Supreme Court pronouncement on freedom of speech.

Schenck was general secretary of the Socialist Party which distributed to prospective draftees a leaflet denouncing CONSCRIPTION and urging recipients to assert their opposition to it. He was convicted of conspiracy to violate the Espionage Act by attempting to obstruct recruiting. Following his own earlier writing on attempts, Holmes, writing for a unanimous Court, said: It seems to be admitted that if an actual obstruction of the recruiting service were proved, liability for words that produced that effect might be enforced. The statute of 1917 . . . punishes conspiracies to obstruct as well as actual obstruction. If the act (speaking, or circulating a paper), its tendency and the intent with which it is done are the same, we perceive no ground for saying that success alone warrants making the act a crime. In response to Schenck's First Amendment claims, Holmes said:

> We admit that in many places and in ordinary times the defendants in saying all that was said in the circular would have been within their constitutional rights. But the character of every act depends upon the circumstances in which it is done. The most stringent protection of free speech would not protect a man in falsely shouting fire in a theatre and causing a panic. . . . The question in every case is whether the words used are used in such circumstances and are of such a nature as to create a CLEAR AND PRESENT DANGER that they will bring about the substantive evils that Congress has a right to prevent. It is a question of proximity and degree.

That the clear and present danger test was first announced in a context in which speech was treated as an attempt to commit an illegal act rather than in a situation in which the statute declared certain speech itself criminal was important for several reasons. First, the attempts context necessarily drew the judicial focus to the nexus between speech and criminal action and thus to the circumstances in which the speech was uttered rather than to the content of the speech itself. Questions of intent and circumstances, crucial to the law of attempts, thus became crucial to the danger test. Second, if the link between speech and illegal act was necessarily a question of degree, then much discretion was necessarily left to the judge. The clear and present danger test has often been criticized for leaving speakers at the mercy of judicial discretion. Having invoked the danger test, the Court affirmed Schenck's conviction. Third, supporters of judicial self-restraint subsequently sought to narrow the scope of the danger test by insisting that it was to be employed only in situations where the government sought to prosecute speech under a statute proscribing only action. In this view, the test was inapplicable when the legislature itself had proscribed speech, having made its own independent, prior judgment that a certain class of speech created a danger warranting suppression.

Although Holmes wrote in Schenck for a unanimous court, he and Justice LOUIS D. BRANDEIS were the danger test's sole supporters in the other leading cases of the 1920s: *Abrams, Gitlow,* and WHITNEY V. CALIFORNIA (1927). A comparison of these cases indicates that Holmes's "tough guy" pose was deeply implicated in his clear and present danger decisions. In the later cases, Holmes seemed to be saying that a self-confident democracy ought not to descend to the prosecution of fringe-group rantings about socialist revolution. In *Schenck*, however, where the speech was concretely pointed at obstructing war time recruitment, Holmes said: "When a nation is at war, many things that might be said in time of peace are such a hindrance to its effort that their utterance will not be endured so long as men fight and that no Court could regard them as protected by any constitutional right."

MARTIN SHAPIRO
(1986)

Bibliography

CHAFEE, ZECHARIAH 1941 *Free Speech in the United States.* Cambridge, Mass.: Harvard University Press.

SCHEUER v. RHODES
416 U.S. 236 (1974)

This decision established that high state officers are not absolutely immune from suit for constitutional violations. Ohio National Guard troops shot and killed four students demonstrating against the VIETNAM WAR. The deceased students' representatives sued Governor James Rhodes and other state officials, alleging reckless deployment of the Guard and unlawful orders to the Guard which led to the shootings. The Supreme Court held Rhodes not to be absolutely immune from suit. The Court did indicate that officials with substantial discretionary responsibilities are to be given greater deference than officials with more limited tasks. *Rhodes* connects the first SECTION 1983 case on EXECUTIVE IMMUNITY, PIERSON V. RAY, (1967), with later decisions such as WOOD V. STRICKLAND (1975) and *Procunier v. Navarette* (1978).

THEODORE EISENBERG
(1986)

SCHICK v. REED
419 U.S. 256 (1974)

In a 5–4 decision, the Supreme Court upheld the President's right to grant conditional clemency. Maurice

Schick, convicted of murder in 1954 by a court-martial, was sentenced to death. In 1960, under Article II, section 2, clause 1, of the Constitution, President DWIGHT D. EISENHOWER commuted the sentence to life imprisonment without parole. Citing FURMAN V. GEORGIA (1972), Schick asked the Court to hold the no-parole condition unconstitutional. But the court held that the PARDONING POWER flows from the Constitution alone and may not be limited except by the Constitution itself.

DENNIS J. MAHONEY
(1986)

SCHMERBER v. CALIFORNIA
384 U.S. 757 (1966)

Justice WILLIAM J. BRENNAN, for a 6–3 majority of the Supreme Court, ruled that the taking of a blood sample from the petitioner over his objections, to prove his guilt for driving under the influence of alcohol, did not constitute TESTIMONINAL COMPULSION and therefore did not violate the RIGHT AGAINST SELF-INCRIMINATION, nor did it constitute an invalid WARRANTLESS SEARCH under the EXIGENT CIRCUMSTANCES.

LEONARD W. LEVY
(1986)

SCHNECKLOTH v. BUSTAMONTE
412 U.S. 218 (1973)

The police may conduct a search without a warrant when consent is freely given. Before *Schneckloth*, some lower courts had taken the position that consent was not voluntary unless the prosecution could demonstrate that the person was aware of his right to refuse consent. Others held that knowledge of the right to refuse was merely one element to be considered, and that consent was established by the totality of the circumstances. In *Schneckloth* the Supreme Court adopted the latter position.

The Court distinguished the FOURTH AMENDMENT from other constitutional guarantees (for example, the RIGHT TO COUNSEL) for which the Court had required an intentional relinquishment of the right. The other guarantees intend to promote the ascertainment of truth in a trial; the Fourth Amendment, on the other hand, does not promote pursuit of truth but secures PRIVACY. The requirement of MIRANDA RULE warnings prior to POLICE INTERROGATION was also an inapposite analogy, for the coercion inherent in a custodial environment is unlikely to be duplicated "on a person's own familiar territory."

Justice LEWIS POWELL, concurring, set forth views later adopted by the Court in STONE V. POWELL (1976), proposing radical restrictions on the use of HABEAS CORPUS to review Fourth Amendment violations by state officers. Three dissenting Justices took the position that mere absence of coercion is not the equivalent of a meaningful choice; that "a decision made without actual knowledge of available alternatives" is not "a choice at all."

JACOB W. LANDYNSKI
(1986)

SCHNELL v. DAVIS
336 U.S. 933 (1949)

In a PER CURIAM opinion, the Supreme Court affirmed a district court JUDGMENT. Davis had brought a CLASS ACTION, arguing that enforcement of Alabama's "Boswell Amendment" violated the VOTING RIGHTS of blacks. The amendment, adopted in 1946 to circumvent the decision in SMITH V. ALLWRIGHT (1944), made the ability to "understand and explain" the Constitution a requirement for voter registration. The record showed that this "understanding clause" was used exclusively to deny registration to blacks. The Court held that the requirement violated the FIFTEENTH AMENDMENT because it was used to deny the right to vote on account of race or color.

DENNIS J. MAHONEY
(1986)

SCHOOL BUSING

Before BROWN V. BOARD OF EDUCATION (1954–1955) was decided, many a southern child rode the bus to school, passing on the way a bus headed in the other direction, loaded with children of another race. The busing of children was "one tool" used to maintain a system of school SEGREGATION. As late as 1970, before the Supreme Court had approved a single busing order, about forty percent of the nation's children rode buses to school. The school bus had permitted the replacement of rural one-room schoolhouses with consolidated schools; in the city, riding the bus had been thought safer than walking. School busing did not become the object of majoritarian anger until the 1970s, when the Supreme Court described it as "one tool" for dismantling a segregated system and affirmed its use not only in the South but also in the cities of the North and West.

In a rural southern county, the simplest form of DESEGREGATION might drastically reduce school busing; racial living patterns would permit integration of the schools through the discontinuation of racial assignments and assignment of children to the schools nearest their homes. In the cities, however, residential segregation had been so thorough that the abandonment of racial assignments and the substitution of a neighborhood school policy would not end the separation of school children by race. The question was asked: Would the Supreme Court insist on more than the end of racial assignments—on the actual mixing of black and white children in the schools—by way of dismantling segregation produced by deliberate official policy? In SWANN V. CHARLOTTE-MECKLENBURG BOARD OF EDUCATION (1971), the Court answered that question affirmatively. Then, in KEYES V. SCHOOL DISTRICT NO. 1 (1973) and COLUMBUS BOARD OF EDUCATION V. PENICK (1979), the Court extended *Swann*'s commands to the North and West, in ways that blurred the DE FACTO/DE JURE distinction. Once a constitutional violation is found, even in remote acts of deliberate segregation by a school board, then as a practical matter the district court's remedial goal becomes "the greatest possible degree of actual desegregation"—and that, in a large city, means the busing of massive numbers of children for the purpose of achieving the maximum practicable RACIAL BALANCE.

Apart from the busing ordered by courts, some busing for integration purposes has resulted from voluntary programs, mostly involving the busing of minority children to schools formerly populated by non-Hispanic whites. Political resistance has been directed not to those programs but to busing ordered by a court over the opposition of the school board and of large numbers of parents and children. The most outspoken protest has come from white parents. The responses of school board majorities have varied, from political warfare in Boston and Los Angeles to the "let's-make-it-work" attitude in Columbus.

President RICHARD M. NIXON, whose first electoral campaign adopted a "Southern strategy" and whose campaign for reelection included an attack on school busing, proposed congressional legislation to restrict busing. In 1974 Congress purported to forbid a federal court to order a student's transportation to a school "other than the school closest or next closest to his place of residence." This statute's constitutionality would have been dubious but for a proviso that canceled its effect: the law was not to diminish the authority of federal courts to enforce the Constitution.

The school busing issue has forced a reevaluation of the goals of desegregation. In *Brown* the chief harm of school segregation imposed by law was said to be the stigma of inferiority, which impaired black children's motivation to learn. The fact of separation of the races in urban schools may or may not have the same stigmatic effect—even though deliberately segregative governmental actions have contributed to residential segregation in cities throughout the nation. Stigma aside, it is far from clear that racial isolation alone impairs minority children's learning. In communities with substantial Hispanic or Asian American populations, concerns about the maintenance of cultural identity are apt to be expressed in opposition to taking children out of neighborhood schools and away from bilingual education programs. The call for "community control" of schools is heard less frequently in black communities today than it was around 1970, but some prominent black CIVIL RIGHTS leaders have placed increasing emphasis on improvement of the schools and decreasing emphasis on the busing of children.

Part of the reason for this shift in emphasis surely is a sense of despair over the prospects of busing as an effective means of achieving integration. Social scientists disagree on the amount of "white flight" that has resulted from court-ordered busing. Some demographic changes are merely extensions of a long-established pattern of middle-class migration to the suburbs. The Supreme Court in MILLIKEN V. BRADLEY (1974) made clear that metropolitan relief, combining city and suburban districts for purposes of school integration, was allowable only in rare circumstances. "White flight" can also take the form of withdrawal of children from public schools; recent estimates suggest that about one-fifth of the students in the nation's private schools have fled from desegregation orders. In this perspective, the neighborhood school is seen not only as a focus for community but also, less appetizingly, as a means for controlling children's associations and passing social advantage from one generation to the next. Either strategy of "white flight" costs money. It is no accident that the hottest opposition to court-ordered school busing has come from working-class neighborhoods, where people feel that they have been singled out to bear a burden in order to validate an ideal they have come to doubt.

School busing for integration purposes has come under strong political attack. Neither Congress nor a state can constitutionally prohibit busing designed to remedy *de jure* segregation. However, state measures limiting busing designed to remedy *de facto* segregation may or may not be upheld, depending on the legislation's purposes and effects. (See *Washington v. Seattle School District No. 1,* 1982; CRAWFORD V. LOS ANGELES BOARD OF EDUCATION, 1982.)

Sadly, it is realistic to assume the continuation of urban residential segregation, which has diminished only slightly since 1940, despite nearly half a century of civil rights litigation and legislation. (Even the migration of increasing numbers of middle-class black families to the suburbs has not significantly diminished residential segregation.) Given that assumption, the nation must choose between accepting racially separate schools and using school busing to achieve integration. The first choice will seem to many citizens a betrayal of the promise of *Brown.* The second choice faces opposition strong enough to threaten not only the nation's historic commitment to public education but

also its commitment to obedience to law. The resolution of this dilemma is a challenge not only to courts but also to school board members and citizens, demanding imagination, patience, and good will in quantities far beyond their recent supply.

KENNETH L. KARST
(1986)

Bibliography

BELL, DERRICK A., JR. 1976 Serving Two Masters: Integration Ideals and Client Interests in School Desegregation Litigation. *Yale Law Journal* 85:470–516.

DIMOND, PAUL R. 1985 *Beyond Busing: Inside the Challenge to Urban Segregation.* Ann Arbor: University of Michigan Press.

FISS, OWEN M. 1975 The Jurisprudence of Busing. *Law and Contemporary Problems* 39:194–216.

WILKINSON, J. HARVIE, III 1979 *From Brown to Bakke.* New York: Oxford University Press.

SCHOOL CHOICE

"School choice" programs offer parents the opportunity to apply government funds toward their child's tuition at a school of the parents' choice. Although some school choice programs involve only public educational institutions (giving parents, for example, a choice of magnet or charter schools), others offer to pay some or all of the child's tuition at a private religious or secular school. Although the Supreme Court in PIERCE V. SOCIETY OF SISTERS (1925) held that the Constitution protects the right of parents to choose to send their children to private schools, whether public funds may pay for the choice of a religious education has been the subject of a number of ESTABLISHMENT CLAUSE cases since the 1970s.

In LEMON V. KURTZMAN (1971), the Court struck down a program subsidizing the salaries of teachers of secular subjects in religious and secular schools. In holding that the program violated the FIRST AMENDMENT establishment clause, the Court articulated a three-part test in which GOVERNMENT AID TO RELIGIOUS INSTITUTIONS must: (1) have a secular purpose; (2) not have a primary effect of advancing or inhibiting religion; and (3) not result in undue entanglement of church and state. In COMMITTEE FOR PUBLIC EDUCATION AND RELIGIOUS LIBERTY V. NYQUIST (1973), the Court applied the LEMON TEST to invalidate a tuition reimbursement and tax deduction program for parents who sent their children to private schools, including private religious schools. According to the *Nyquist* Court, direct funding of any aspect of a sectarian institution has the impermissible effect of advancing the institution's religious mission.

In the 1980s and 1990s, however, the Court moved

away from the "no aid" approach of *Lemon* and toward a private-choice model that occasionally permits religious institutions to participate in school choice programs. In MUELLER V. ALLEN (1983), the Court upheld a state law providing parents a tax deduction for expenses incurred in educating their children at either public or private schools. Even if the program had the incidental effect of aiding sectarian education, the aid arrived at the school by way of private choice, not government direction. Thus, it could not be said that the government had advanced religion in violation of the establishment clause. Applying the same "private choice" approach in WITTERS V. WASHINGTON DEPARTMENT OF SERVICES FOR THE BLIND (1986), the Supreme Court upheld a particular student's use of a general college tuition assistance program to pay tuition at a religious college.

The Court has not yet directly considered whether a state may include religious schools in government-funded school voucher programs. However, the private-choice model appears to permit such a program as long as the aid is granted on a religiously neutral basis, includes both public and private schools, and arrives at the school by way of private choice. Should the Court uphold such a program, it will then have to decide whether states may exclude religious schools from such programs if such exclusion is no longer required by the establishment clause. Permitting nonmandatory exclusion of religious schools from government funding programs seems in tension with the Court's holdings under the FREEDOM OF SPEECH clause that government funding of private expressive activity cannot be denied on the basis of religious viewpoint, such as ROSENBERGER V. RECTORS & VISITORS OF THE UNIVERSITY OF VIRGINIA (1995). Nonmandatory denial of equal funding for religious schools also arguably violates the free exercise clause's prohibition of intentional discrimination on the basis of religious belief under EMPLOYMENT DIVISION, DEPARTMENT OF HUMAN RESOURCES OF OREGON V. SMITH (1990).

KURT T. LASH
(2000)

(SEE ALSO: *Establishment of Religion; Religion in Public Schools; Religious Liberty; Separation of Church and State.*)

SCHOOL DESEGREGATION

See: Desegregation; *Missouri v. Jenkins*; School Busing

SCHOOL PRAYERS

Few constitutional issues have generated as much public controversy, and as much confusion, as the question of prayer in public schools. The Supreme Court's 1962 decision in ENGEL V. VITALE concerned an official prayer that had been composed by a group of politically appointed officials, the New York State Board of Regents. The defendant school district required every school principal to direct that the Regents' prayer be recited in unison in every classroom at the beginning of each school day. The Court held that even though individual students were permitted to abstain from participating in the recitation, the program violated the ESTABLISHMENT CLAUSE because it "officially establishe[d] the religious beliefs embodied in the Regents' prayer."

One year later the Court applied the principle of *Engel* to religious readings selected by public officials. Laws in Pennsylvania and Baltimore required every public school to begin each day with the reading of verses from the Holy Bible and group recital of the Lord's Prayer. Students were permitted to be excused from participation upon written request of a parent or guardian. In ABINGTON TOWNSHIP SCHOOL DISTRICT V. SCHEMPP, the Court held that these programs also violated the establishment clause, which the Court interpreted to preclude actions by state or federal governments that had the purpose or primary effect of either advancing or inhibiting religion. The Court noted that while the FIRST AMENDMENT permitted the study of the Bible or religion as part of its program of education, it did not permit government to organize devotional religious exercises. The fact that the particular devotionals had been selected by government officials, rather than composed by them as in *Engel*, was not a difference of constitutional import.

The school prayer and Bible reading decisions sparked a substantial public outcry, and repeated, unsuccessful efforts were made to overturn the decisions by amending the Constitution. The decisions were misinterpreted by some to mean that even the utterance of a private prayer by an individual student while at school was unconstitutional. What the establishment clause actually prohibited was action by government officials that endorsed or inhibited religion, and not religious activity initiated by students and not encouraged or promoted by school officials.

As subsequent decisions would make clear, the Court had never held that prayer itself was necessarily precluded in public schools or other public buildings, as long as the prayer resulted wholly from the private choice of individual citizens. Although the Court in WALLACE V. JAFFREE (1985) invalidated an Alabama law providing for a moment of silence "for meditation or voluntary prayer," a majority of the Court strongly suggested that some laws providing for a moment of silence would be constitutional. Alabama had previously enacted a statute, sustained by the lower court and not challenged before the Supreme Court, which authorized a one-minute period of silence for meditation. The new statute before the Court in *Jaffree* added "prayer" as an expressly approved activity. Because students were provided an opportunity to pray under the earlier moment-of-silence statute, the new law's only additional purpose appeared to be "the State's endorsement and promotion of religion and a particular religious practice." This, the Court held, crossed the line into impermissible endorsement by the government. A majority of the Justices indicated, however, that they would sustain moment-of-silence laws that did not expressly single out prayer as one of the officially preferred activities.

When a statute creates an open, undesignated silent time, government itself has not undertaken to favor or disfavor religion. The seemingly trivial addition of the words "for prayer" to a moment-of-silence law crosses the line of constitutionality precisely because it is unnecessary to the goal of creating an opportunity for students to choose to pray. If a simple moment of silence is created at school, parents and religious leaders may, if they wish, suggest to their children or parishioners that they use the moment of silence for prayer. Expressly providing in the state's code of laws that "prayer" is a designated activity unnecessarily takes the state itself into the improper business of official endorsement and promotion of a religious exercise.

Ideally, a simple moment of silence is functionally a one-minute open forum which each student can fill as she chooses. Implementation of such a policy in a truly neutral fashion is, however, difficult in practice. The facts of some lower court cases suggest that teachers and school officials in some districts have encouraged or coerced students to pray during the silent moment. Teachers may appropriately ask students to remain quiet for the moment of silence; if teachers suggest or insist that students pray or adopt a prayerful attitude, they have invoked the authority of the state for an impermissible end.

The Court has also used the concept of the open forum to permit students at school to engage in spoken, group prayers as long as the religious activities are not encouraged, endorsed, or promoted by government or school officials. In WIDMAR V. VINCENT (1981), the Court held that a state university that allowed a wide range of voluntary student activity groups to meet in university facilities was not required by the establishment clause to deny access to student-initiated religious clubs whose meetings on school property included prayer and other devotionals. Indeed, such clubs had a free speech right of EQUAL ACCESS to the school's facilities on the same basis as volunteer student groups engaged in other speech activities. In BOARD OF EDUCATION OF WESTSIDE COMMUNITY SCHOOLS V. MERGENS (1990) the Court sustained the federal Equal Access Act that extended this principle to public secondary schools. The act provides that when a public school creates a "limited open forum" by allowing student-initiated, noncurri-

culum groups to meet at the school, it may not deny access to the school for meetings of other student-initiated groups on the basis of the "religious, political, philosophical, or other content of the speech at such meetings." One effect of the act is to give student religious clubs (whose meetings may include prayer) the same right to meet on campus as other noncurricular, student-initiated organizations like the chess club or the Young Democrats.

Even though many in the public remain unreconciled to the original school prayer and Bible reading decisions, and even though some recent decisions suggest that the Supreme Court is becoming more tolerant of some governmental promotion of religion, it seems unlikely that the Court's original decisions will soon be overturned either by the Court or by constitutional amendment. The constitutional principle remains for now, as it was when Justice HUGO BLACK wrote for the Court in *Engel*: "it is no part of the business of government to compose official prayers for any group of the American people to recite as part of a religious program carried on by government."

WALTER DELLINGER
(1992)

(SEE ALSO: *Bender v. Williamsport; Lemon Test; Religion in Public Schools; Separation of Church and State.*)

Bibliography

DELLINGER, WALTER 1986 The Sound of Silence: An Epistle on Prayer and the Constitution. *Yale Law Journal* 95:1631–1646.

LAYCOCK, DOUGLAS 1986 Equal Access and Moments of Silence: The Equal Status of Religious Speech by Private Speakers. *Northwestern University Law Review* 81:1–67.

SCHOOL PRAYERS
(Update)

Since the Supreme Court's decision in ENGEL V. VITALE (1962), the law has forbidden school officials from sponsoring worship exercises in public schools. Courts have given several reasons for this principle. First, pressure on students to conform to what is expected will lead some to engage in prayers in conflict with their own beliefs. Second, such exercises may be very divisive within a community; different religious groups may disagree concerning what prayers are appropriate, and they may engage in bitter disputes on the subject. At least one purpose of the ESTABLISHMENT CLAUSE was to minimize public conflict over matters of worship in public life. The Supreme Court applied the principle of *Engel* in WALLACE V. JAFFREE (1985) to an Alabama law requiring a moment of silence for meditation or prayer in public schools.

In recent years, the *Engel* principle has remained in active controversy. In 1998, the U.S. HOUSE OF REPRESENTATIVES defeated a proposed constitutional amendment which, if enacted, would have legalized state-sponsored worship in public facilities, including schools. Earlier in LEE V. WEISMAN (1992), the Court further extended the principle of *Engel* to prayers recited at a public middle school graduation ceremony by a member of the clergy invited to participate by school officials. The 5–4 majority Justices rested their judgment on a variety of grounds. The majority opinion, authored by Justice ANTHONY M. KENNEDY, asserted that attendance at graduation was, though not required by law, nevertheless obligatory as a matter of custom and community expectation. Moreover, he reasoned that peer pressure might well lead some students to acquiesce silently in graduation prayer, despite their disagreement with the content of the prayer. Thus, he concluded that graduation prayer was coercive and forbidden by the Constitution. Others in the Court majority agreed with that assessment, and went further to conclude that commencement prayer involved government endorsement and sponsorship of religion, both of which are independently forbidden by the establishment clause. The dissenters in *Lee,* led by Justice ANTONIN SCALIA, argued that commencement prayer was justified by a long-standing American tradition of using nondenominational prayer to mark public ceremonies. Although that historical assertion was correct, it was not responsive to the *Lee* majority's concern that public school commencement prayer involved both government sponsorship of religious exercise and coercive pressure on young people and their families.

After *Lee,* three kinds of questions have arisen. First, lower courts have held that state university commencements may include nondenominational, ceremonial benedictions. Because university graduates are adults, the coercive pressures on them are thought to be sufficiently less to justify the different outcome. This result rests on questionable reasoning; if government sponsorship of religious exercise is an independent vice, the age of the students should make no difference.

Second, some school districts responded to *Lee* by arranging commencements in ways that permitted the graduating seniors to choose student speakers and direct them to lead others in prayer at the ceremony. Although a few courts have upheld this practice, others have ruled that the school officials remain responsible for the content of commencement exercises; accordingly, school-sponsored, student-led prayer at commencement has been treated by most courts as equally unconstitutional as prayer led by officials or invited clergy.

Third, many school officials, teachers, and students have erroneously come to believe that purely private prayer by students on school PROPERTY is illegal. This is simply mistaken; so long as private prayers uttered by students—for example, saying Grace over lunch in the cafeteria—are neither sponsored by the school nor expressed in a way that harasses fellow students, such religious speech on school property is entirely within the students' rights of FREEDOM OF SPEECH and RELIGIOUS LIBERTY.

IRA C. LUPU
(2000)

(SEE ALSO: *Establishment of Religion; Religion and Free Speech; Religion in Public Schools.*)

Bibliography

PAULSEN, MICHAEL S. 1993 *Lemon* is Dead. *Case Western Reserve Law Review* 43:795–863.
SHERRY, SUZANNA 1992 *Lee v. Weisman:* Paradox Redux. *Supreme Court Review* 1992:123–153.

SCHOULER, JAMES
(1839–1920)

Massachusetts-born James Schouler, while a Union officer in the CIVIL WAR, contracted a fever that left him nearly deaf. He nevertheless rose to national prominence as an attorney and historian. Although his law practice was successful—his first Supreme Court victory was *Hosmer v. United States,* 1872)—he gave it up (because of his disability) in favor of teaching. His main historical work was the nationalistic *History of the United States under the Constitution* (7 volumes, 1880–1913), which he conceived as the first comprehensive account of American political and legal history. He also wrote *Constitutional Studies: State and Federal* (1897) and biographies of THOMAS JEFFERSON and ALEXANDER HAMILTON.

DENNIS J. MAHONEY
(1986)

SCHROEDER, THEODORE
(1864–1953)

Before WORLD WAR I, Theodore Schroeder, as FELIX FRANKFURTER said, was the foremost authority in the field of FIRST AMENDMENT rights. A prosperous lawyer, he could afford to be a full-time publicist in the cause of opposing all censorship and prosecutions for seditious, blasphemous, and obscene libels. In 1902 he founded the Free Speech League, the mainstay of CIVIL LIBERTIES until the founding of the American Civil Liberties Union. Roger Baldwin, one of the many civil libertarians whom Schroeder influenced, declared that Schroeder "was the Free Speech League." Schroeder was an uncompromising First

Amendment absolutist who defended anarchists, free-thinkers, and pornographers. He also advocated equal rights for women and defended Emma Goldman and Margaret Sanger. His major works include *"Obscene" Literature and Constitutional Law* (1911), *Free Speech for Radicals* (1916), *Constitutional Free Speech Defined and Defended* (1919), and *Free Speech Bibliography* (1922).

LEONARD W. LEVY
(1986)

Bibliography

AUERBACH, JEROLD 1972 (1911) Introduction to Schroeder, Theodore, *"Obscene" Literature and Constitutional Law.* New York: Da Capo Press.

SCHWABE v. NEW MEXICO BOARD OF BAR EXAMINERS
353 U.S. 232 (1957)

Schware was one of the early cases in which state bar examiners refused bar admission to persons suspected of communism. The Court overturned the refusal on DUE PROCESS grounds, holding that a finding that the applicant was a Communist party member before 1940 was constitutionally insufficient to overcome evidence of his later good moral character.

MARTIN SHAPIRO
(1986)

SCHWARTZ, BERNARD
(1923–1997)

Bernard Schwartz, described by *New York Times* commentator Anthony Lewis as "the most committed, productive legal scholar of our times," was born in New York City. After being graduated Phi Beta Kappa from New York's City College, he received his law degree from New York University (NYU) with the highest grades in the school's history and later received doctorates in laws and letters from Cambridge University and the University of Paris.

Schwartz started his fifty-year law-teaching career at NYU and then assumed the Chapman Chair at the University of Tulsa in 1992. He wrote more than sixty-five books and hundreds of articles, but was most recognized for his scholarship on administrative and constitutional law; he co-authored casebooks and textbooks, and wrote annual summaries of decisions on these topics.

Schwartz saw his major role as a reporter, explaining and critiquing the Supreme Court, not just for colleagues but also for the general educated public. Unlike the au-

thors of *The Brethren* (1979) and *Closed Chambers* (1998), he did not get into personality conflicts and clerk recollections, but instead focused on the process of decision-making in books such as *The Unpublished Opinions of the Warren Court* (1985), *The Unpublished Opinions of the Burger Court* (1985), *A History of the Supreme Court* (1993), and the popular American Bar Association award-winning book, *Decision: How the Supreme Court Decides Cases* (1996). He also explored individual cases and selected issues in numerous opinion articles for dozens of newspapers and organized conferences of scholars, practitioners, journalists, and political leaders on the jurisprudence of the WARREN COURT, the BURGER COURT, and the REHNQUIST COURT. Finally, he tried to involve the public in enjoying the criticism process by listing the best and worst Justices, best and worst decisions, and even the best and worst law-related movies in his *A Book of Legal Lists: The Best and Worst in American Law with 100 Court and Judge Trivia Questions* (1997).

Through intensive research of unpublished drafts, personal notes, internal memoranda, and other historical records, he sought "to tell what happened and not to shield the Court's inner processes from public view." Because of his candor backed up by scholarship, and obvious affection for the Court and all its members past and present, he received the continuing respect and recognition of even those he criticized. He was honored just prior to his death by being asked to present a talk, "Earl Warren: Super-Chief in Action," in the Chambers of the Supreme Court.

At the time of his death, Schwartz had indicated his annoyance with recent trends in the Court, such as hidden JUDICIAL ACTIVISM, where the Rehnquist Court majority was, in his opinion, dramatically changing constitutional principles "without acknowledging that they had done so." He also was concerned about the dramatic decrease in the number of cases the Court heard and about the possibility that the new highly political CONFIRMATION PROCESS might lead to mediocrity. An OLIVER WENDELL HOLMES, JR., a LOUIS D. BRANDEIS, or even a WILLIAM J. BRENNAN, JR., he thought, could not get through the White House review process or the U.S. SENATE confirmation process. He hoped to document these and other trends in a follow-up to his *Main Currents in American Legal Thought* (1993), which he had almost completed and had tentatively titled "A History of American Law and Legal Thought in the 20th Century."

MARTIN H. BELSKY
(2000)

SCHWIMMER, UNITED STATES v.
279 U.S. 644 (1929)

When Rosiki Schwimmer applied for NATURALIZATION, officials questioned whether she could take the oath to "uphold and defend the Constitution against all enemies" without reservation. She opposed war in all forms.

The question before the Supreme Court was whether Congress had intended to require willingness to perform combatant military service as a condition of naturalization. Justice PIERCE BUTLER spoke for the Court and held that Congress had. Justice OLIVER WENDELL HOLMES dissented, joined by Justice LOUIS D. BRANDEIS. Holmes noted that Schwimmer, a woman of almost sixty years, would never actually be called upon to serve. Furthermore, taking a position against resort to armed forces was simply a reform objective no different from favoring a unicameral legislature. Justice EDWARD T. SANFORD also dissented.

Schwimmer was overruled by GIROUARD V. UNITED STATES (1946).

RICHARD E. MORGAN
(1986)

SCIENCE, TECHNOLOGY, AND THE CONSTITUTION

The Constitution's only reference to science occurs in Article I, section 8, which grants, among other congresional powers, the authority to "promote Science and useful Arts" by establishing nationwide protection of PATENTS and COPYRIGHTS. Despite the document's otherwise silence on the subject, a constitutional law of science may be evolving—and inevitable and, to some extent, auspicious developement in our technological age. Indeed, cases involving some aspect of the constitutional status of science form a burgeoning part of constitutional law, principally, but not exclusively, under the FIRST AMENDMENT.

Perhaps the most obvious question about the status of science is whether scientific speech falls within the First Amendment's protection of FREEDOM OF SPEECH. Some critics, notably Robert Bork, have challenged the idea that scientific speech is fully protected, and no court has reached the question explicitly. The most likely answer, should a case arise, is that scientific communication is entitled to the same degree of First Amendment protection as other speech. A number of decided cases, including the Supreme Court's opinion in GRISWOLD V. CONNECTICUT (1965), contain OBITER DICTA referring to scientific speech as though it were in no way different from other First Amendment activity. If one sees the First Amendment's protection of speech as a means of enabling self-actualization or of discovering truth through the free interplay of ideas, the case for including scientific speech is straightforward. But even if one considers political debate as the core of the constitutional guarantee, in our society the use and regulation of technology form a central part of governmental activity. Debate concerning the scope and efficacy of these efforts will necessarily include a scientific component.

Scientific researchers insist that absolute freedom to communicate their ideas is neccessary to the scientific enterprise. Constitutional protection, however, is rarely absolute, and to say that scientific speech is protected is only a part of the answer. Like other speech, scientific speech may be subjected to regulation in certain circumstances. In particular, the federal government has increasingly sough to regulate the flow of scientific information in the name of NATIONAL SECURITY.

National security regulations on scientific speech fall into two broad categories. First, there are restrictions through which the government seeks ownership of the information in question. For example, under the "'born classified" provisions of the ATOMIC ENERGY ACT, inventions or discoveries that are "useful solely in the utilization of special nuclear material or atomic energy in an atomic weapon" are not patentable and, in many cases, are from their inception property of the federal government. The constitutionality of this restriction apparently has never been challenged, but given the plenary nature of congressional authority over the patent system, it is difficult to imagine that it would be struck down.

Second, there are restrictions through which the government, without regard to ownership, seeks to regulate the transmittal of the information in question. For example, a number of federal regulations seek to treat certain scientific information, especially information on "military critical technologies," as a commodity, subject to export restrictions. Another example is the consistent effort by the National Security Agency to discourage American researchers from publicly revealing (even in the United States) the fruits of any work with important implications for the field of encryption.

What the government must show to sustain its regulation is unclear because the constitutionality of national security restrictions on the communication of scientific information has been rarely tested. An exception is *United States v. The Progressive* (1979), in which the federal government sought to enjoin the publication of a magazine article that purportedly revealed how to construct a hydrogen bomb. A federal district court granted the INJUNCTION, holding that the publication of the article might do infinite damage to the nation's (and the world's) security, and therefore, the test of NEAR V. MINNESOTA EX. REL. OLSON (1931) and NEW YORK TIMES V. UNITED STATES (1971) was easily met. Before an APPEAL could be decided, however, the article was published elsewhere and the trial court's judgment was vacated as moot.

Critics mocked the court's reasoning, arguing that it would enable government to enjoin publication of many scientific ideas; all the court required was a showing of a minuscule possibility of infinite harm. As has subsequently become clear, moreover, the article involved in *The Progressive*, although setting out some of the theory behind the hydrogen bomb, did not actually reveal the critical model necessary to make the bomb explode. The trial judge undertook no close scrutiny of the article, however, resting his decision on the government's affidavits. In so doing, the judge showed far greater deference to the government's assertion of harm to the nation's national security than have courts confronted with similar claims when the speech in question has lacked a scientific component. The one lesson of *The Progressive* is that courts may view an argument that scientific speech will harm the nation's security with considerably greater sympathy than they have displayed for the same argument concerning other kinds of speech.

Not all attempted restrictions on scientific speech rest on a national security foundation. Perhaps the most controversial attempt has been the effort by some believers in the Genesis account of creation to prohibit or limit the teaching of the theory of evolution in public school classrooms. *Scopes v. State* (1927), in which Clarence Darrow battled eloquently, but in vain to prevent the conviction of a teacher for violating a ban on teaching the Darwinian theory of evolution in the public schools, is a part of our popular legal mythology, but the *Scopes* case was the zenith of judicial deference to creationism. In recent decades, the federal courts have been unwavering in their refusal to allow restrictions on the teaching of evolution in public schools. Thus in EPPERSON V. ARKANSAS (1968), the Supreme Court struck down a state prohibition on teaching evolution. In *Daniel v. Waters* (1975), a federal appeals court overturned a state law requiring that students be told that evolution is a theory, not a fact. In *Edwards v. Aguillard* (1987) the Supreme Court held UNCONSTITUTIONAL "balanced treatment" legislation that mandated the teaching of CREATIONISM alongside the theory of evolution.

A chorus of critics has suggested that by striking down balanced-treatment statutes the courts are in effect granting science itself a special constitutional status. Justice ANTONIN SCALIA, in his dissent in *Edwards*, did not embrace this broad-scale criticism, but he did raise a related objection to the Court's decision. He argued that the Louisiana legislature had determined, on the advice of people they considered scientists, that creation science was not just religious dogma but a scientific theory founded on evidence and subjected to testing. As yet, the Court had before it no interpretation by the Louisiana Supreme Court of the law's meaning and no evidence of its actual application in the schools. Thus, he argued, it was premature for the Court to conclude that the legislature's purpose was merely to promote a religious belief.

The more far-reaching criticism, that the courts are giving science a special status under the Constitution, is met head on by some critics who assert that the courts should do precisely that. Proponents of this view typically point to the views of the Founders, many of whom accepted a contemporaneous, philosophical, commonplace holding of scientific progress to be an essential component of human happiness. A few scholars, perhaps stretching an otherwise interesting historical point, have even tried to demonstrate that the Founders intended to write this doctrine into the Constitution itself.

This is an argumentative turn that matters because the more important problem for scientific researchers may not be potential restrictions on communication, but the possibility of limits on experiments. In this situation, the difficulty is not religious belief but public fear and skepticism. The use of bona fide health and safety arguments to justify the regulation of the use of technology is nothing new and raises no significant constitutional questions. Scientific experiment, however, lies somewhere between pure scientific speech and pure application of technology, and recent efforts at its regulation have led to constitutional controversy.

A particular focus of debate is the effort in recent years to restrict experimentation on recombinant deoxyribonucleic acid (rDNA) techniques and other aspects of the "new biology" because of popular concern over the results and the implications. Several years ago, for example, Cambridge, Massachusetts, the home of two of the nation's leading research universities, was urged to adopt an ordinance banning rDNA experiments. Cambridge finally settled for requiring compliance with certain federal guidelines, but for a time, the matter seemed to hang in the balance. Experts argued that the techniques were relatively safe, but many members of the public simply disbelieved the experts' claims.

In response to the wave of public fear in the 1970s and 1980s, several commentators urged a form of First Amendment protection for scientific experiment. The difficulty these theorists have faced is overcoming the distinction between speech and conduct that has long governed First Amendment jurisprudence; scientific experiment would seem to fall plainly on the conduct side of the divide. But theorists have challenged the application of this neat dichotomy to the distinction between scientific speech and scientific experiment. Some supporters of protection for experiment have claimed to find support in the original understanding of free speech, others have contended that experiment is as important as communication for self-actualization, and still others have argued that experimentation is protected because it is a prerequisite to the protected activity of scientific speech. Critics have responded that the First Amendment argument for protection of experiments is clever, but far-fetched. As the critics note, the Supreme court rejected an analogous claim, in *Houchins v. KQED* (1978), that the activity of news gathering is protected as a prerequisite to the protected activity of news reporting. No court has yet accepted the claim of a constitutional right to experiment; on the contrary, courts have occasionally granted injunctions against controversial scientific experiments.

Although freedom of scientific speech has been a central part of the scholarly debate on the constitutional status of science, most Americans are more directly concerned with the technologies that scientific research makes possible, not science itself. This concern has generated arguments for two quite different rights: the right to use technology without governmental interference and the right to be free of governmental use of technology. As a practical matter, courts have dealt with claims of both these kinds in much the same way as they have treated the arguments of scientific creationists: they have tried to follow the experts.

The claim of a right to use technology has been most prominent in debates over medical treatment. For example, in *Andrews v. Ballard* (1980), a federal district court upheld a claim to a constitutional right to choose acupuncture therapy. To reach this result, the court was forced to reconceptualize the Supreme Court's decisions in *Griswold v. Connecticut* and ROE V. WADE (1973) as involving not the RIGHT OF PRIVACY *simpliciter*, but rather the right to make a private choice whether to use medically approved BIRTH CONTROL technologies. The requirement of medical approval enabled the court to distinguish acupuncture, which a considerable number of researchers believe to hold genuine benefits, from such exotic drugs as laetrile, which the medical profession generally rejects as a cancer treatment. (The courts have rejected arguments for a constitutional right to use laetrile.)

The idea of a constitutional right to be free from governmental use of technology was rejected at the turn of the century in JACOBSON V. MASSACHUSETTS (1904). In this case, the Supreme Court rejected a constitutional challenge to a mandatory vaccination against smallpox. The Court cited the right of the state to protect itself, and faced with the argument that vaccination was unnecessary or dangerous, or both, responded that it was the responsibility of the legislature, not the Court, to choose among competing medical theories. More recently, courts have employed similarly deferential reasoning to sustain such regulations as forced medical care for children whose parents raise religious objections and mandatory AIDS testing of some federal employees.

Perhaps the most controversial among recent governmental uses of technology, however, is mandatory DRUG TESTING of employees. In NATIONAL TREASURY EMPLOYEES UNION V. VON RAAB (1989) and SKINNER V. RAILWAY LABOR EXECUTIVES ASSOCIATION, (1989) the Supreme Court rejected FOURTH AMENDMENT privacy challenges to two very different programs of drug testing. In *Skinner*, the Justices voted 7–2 to sustain federal regulations allowing railroads to require breath and urine tests to determine whether employees committing safety infractions had used alcohol or drugs. In *National Treasury Employees Union*, the Court voted 5–4 to uphold a program mandating urine tests for employees seeking transfer or promotion to positions in drug-interdiction programs.

Both cases were decided on technical Fourth Amendment arguments not relevant to this discussion. In each case, however, the majority found it necessary to make reference to the accuracy of the tests. Thus in *Skinner*, the Court stated that the breath and urine tests, "if properly conducted, identify the presence of alcohol and drugs in the biological samples tested with great accuracy." In *National Treasury Employees Union*, the Court took care to note that the test "is highly accurate, assuming proper storage, handling, and measurement techniques." In neither opinion did the Justices explicitly hold that the accuracy of the tests was a factor in their decision. Nevertheless, the fact that they mentioned the point at all and with such confidence raises the possibility that they might have reached a different result had serious expert challenges to the tests been available.

None of this suggests that expert agreement on a sufficiently accurate result is itself a decisive argument in favor of constitutionality. But these and other opinions plainly raise the possibility that the Supreme Court will defer to scientific expertise in answering constitutional questions. This judicial deference, if it exists, might reflect a recognition by the courts of their limited capacity to decide scientific questions. The difficulties that courts and legislatures alike have with science have led a number of commentators, notably Arthur Kantrowitz, to suggest the creation of a special science Court to decide the scientific components of complex policy and legal questions. Critics of the Science Court proposal call it undemocratic. Defenders argue that democracy would be better served if courts and other decisionmakers made no pretense of scientific expertise.

STEVEN L. CARTER
(1992)

Bibliography

CARTER, STEPHEN L. 1987 Evolutionism, Creationism, and Treating Religion as a Hobby. *Duke Law Journal* 1987:977.
CARTER, STEPHEN L. 1985 The Bellman, the Snark, and the Biohazard Debate. *Yale Law and Policy Review* 3:358.
DELGADO, RICHARD 1978 God, Galileo, & Government: To-

ward Constitutional Protection for Scientific Inquiry. *Washington Law Review* 53:349–404.

FERGUSON, JAMES R. 1979 Scientific Inquiry and the First Amendment. *Cornell Law Review* 64:639–665.

GOLDBERG, STEVEN 1979 The Constitutional Status of American Science. *University of Illinois Law Forum* 1979:1–33.

REDISH, MARTIN H. 1985 Limits on Scientific Expression and the Scope of First Amendment Analysis. *William and Mary Law Review* 26:863–907.

ROBERTSON, JOHN A. 1978 The Scientist's Right to Research: A Constitutional Analysis. *Southern California Law Review* 51: 1203–1279.

SCIENTIFIC CREATIONISM

See: Creationism

SCOPES v. TENNESSEE

See: *Tennessee v. Scopes*

SCOTT v. ILLINOIS

See: Right to Counsel

SCOTTSBORO CASES

See: *Norris v. Alabama*; *Powell v. Alabama*

SCREWS v. UNITED STATES
325 U.S. 91 (1945)

Southern law enforcement officers were prosecuted under section 242 of Title 18, United States Code, a federal CIVIL RIGHTS statute, for beating to death a black arrestee. Because section 242 proscribes only action "under COLOR OF LAW," and because congressional power to enforce the FOURTEENTH AMENDMENT was assumed to be limited to reaching STATE ACTION, the question arose whether behavior not authorized by state law could be either state action or action under color of law. The Court's affirmative answer, which relied in part on UNITED STATES V. CLASSIC (1941), both established section 242 as a weapon against police misconduct and nourished the post-1960 expansion of noncriminal civil rights litigation. MONROE V. PAPE (1961), relying on *Screws* and *Classic*, similarly interpreted the "under color of" law requirement for noncriminal civil rights actions brought under SECTION 1983, TITLE 42, UNITED STATES CODE. Exclusive reliance on state law to remedy police misconduct, a position advocated in dissent in *Screws* by Justices OWEN ROBERTS, FELIX FRANK-FURTER, and ROBERT H. JACKSON, would never again be the rule.

Screws also raised the question whether federal criminal civil rights statutes are unconstitutionally vague. Section 242 outlaws willful deprivations of rights secured by the Constitution. Because constitutional standards change constantly, there was doubt that section 242 provided potential defendants with adequate warning of proscribed behavior. In *Screws*, the Court sought to avoid this difficulty by holding that the word "willfully" in section 242 connotes "a purpose to deprive a person of a specific constitutional right." The Court's remand of the case to reinstruct the jury on the meaning of "willful" prompted Justice FRANK MURPHY to dissent, pointing out that the officers had contrived to beat their victim for fifteen minutes after he lost consciousness and arguing that the right to "life" protected by the Fourteenth Amendment surely included a right not to be murdered by state officials. The specific intent requirement has generated confusion in subsequent interpretations of the criminal civil rights statutes.

THEODORE EISENBERG
(1986)

SEARCH, UNREASONABLE

See: Unreasonable Search

SEARCH AND SEIZURE

The FOURTH AMENDMENT has the virtue of brevity and the vice of ambiguity. It does not define the PROBABLE CAUSE required for warrants or indicate whether a WARRANTLESS SEARCH or seizure is inevitably "unreasonable" if made without probable cause, so that the factual basis required for a constitutional search or seizure is unclear. The amendment does not define the relationship of the word "unreasonable" to the clause setting forth the conditions under which warrants may issue; it is thus unclear when a judicial officer's approval must be obtained before an ARREST or search is made. There is also uncertainty as to what official conduct is subject to the amendment's restraints, that is, just what actions amount to "searches and seizures" and threaten the "right of the people to be secure." Finally, there is ambiguity concerning how that right is to be enforced; unlike the Fifth Amendment RIGHT AGAINST SELF-INCRIMINATION, no mention is made of barring from EVIDENCE the fruits of a violation of the amendment. The Supreme Court has had to respond to each of these four fundamental questions. (See RIGHT-PRIVILEGE DISTINCTION.)

The warrant clause of the Fourth Amendment makes

it apparent that a valid ARREST WARRANT or SEARCH WARRANT may issue only upon a showing of probable cause to the issuing authority. This requirement is intended to prohibit resort to GENERAL WARRANTS and arrest and search on suspicion. As the Court noted in BRINEGAR V. UNITED STATES (1949), it is also intended "to give fair leeway for enforcing the law in the community's protection," and thus is best perceived as "a practical, nontechnical conception affording the best compromise that has been found for accommodating these often opposing interests" of individual privacy and collective security.

Though a literal reading of the Fourth Amendment does not compel this result, the prohibition upon "UNREASONABLE" SEARCHES and seizures has been construed to mean that even searches and seizures conducted without a warrant require probable cause. As explained in WONG SUN V. UNITED STATES (1963), "the requirements of reliability and particularity of the information on which an officer may act . . . surely cannot be less stringent [when an arrest is made without a warrant] than where an arrest warrant is obtained. Otherwise, a principal incentive now existing for the procurement of arrest warrants would be destroyed." But the amount of probable cause required for with-warrant and without-warrant searches is not exactly the same; the Court stated in *United States v. Ventresca* (1965) that because of the preference accorded to warrants, "in a doubtful or marginal case a search under a warrant may be sustainable where without one it would fail."

The same quantum of evidence is required whether one is concerned with probable cause to arrest or to search. Thus in SPINELLI V. UNITED STATES (1969), concerning probable cause for a search warrant, the Court found its earlier decision in DRAPER V. UNITED STATES (1959), concerning probable cause to arrest, to be a "suitable benchmark." But the arrest and search situations differ in important respects. For arrest, it must be sufficiently probable that an offense has been committed and that the particular individual to be arrested has committed it; for a search, it must be sufficiently probable that specified items are evidence of criminal activity and are to be found in the specified place. On a given set of facts one type of probable cause may be present but not the other.

The probable cause test is an objective rather than a subjective one. "If subjective good faith alone were the test," the Supreme Court said in *Beck v. Ohio* (1964), "the protections of the Fourth Amendment would evaporate, and the people would be 'secure in their houses, papers, and effects,' only in the discretion of the police." The question, therefore, is not what the arresting or searching officer thought but rather what a reasonable person with the experience and expertise of the officer would have thought. That assessment is to be made on all available

information regardless of its admissibility in a criminal trial because, as the Court said in *Brinegar*, the probable cause test is "not technical" and involves "the factual and practical considerations of everyday life on which reasonable and prudent men, not legal technicians, act." Thus credible HEARSAY may be considered, but a person's reputation, at least when stated in terms of unsubstantiated conclusions, cannot.

Although *Brinegar* declares that probable cause requires "less than evidence which would justify . . . conviction" but yet "more than bare suspicion" and also that the question is one of "probabilities," it gives no indication as to what degree of probability is required. Some of the Court's decisions—for example, *Johnson v. United States* (1948), holding that the smell of burning opium from within a hotel room did not amount to probable cause to arrest a particular occupant because until the subsequent entry she was not known to be the sole occupant of the room—suggest a more-probable-than-not standard. But the Supreme Court has never explicitly held that the Fourth Amendment requires this standard, and the lower courts have understandably found such an interpretation too stringent in at least some circumstances. Thus, it is not uncommon to find an appellate decision holding that an arrest near a crime scene was lawful even though the victim's description was not exact or detailed enough to single the arrested person out from all other persons in the vicinity, or that a search of a number of different places under a suspect's control is permissible even though no one of them is the more-probable-than-not location of the evidence sought.

Most of the Supreme Court's probable cause cases involve information from police informants, denizens of the criminal milieu who provide information in exchange for money or informal immunity regarding their own criminal conduct. In AGUILAR V. TEXAS (1964), where the search warrant affidavit merely recited that the affiants had "received reliable information from a credible person" that "narcotics and narcotics paraphernalia are being kept at the above described premises," the Court adopted a two-pronged test. This affidavit was held insufficient because, first, it did not disclose how the informant knew what he claimed to know concerning what was in the house; and second, it did not disclose how the affiants concluded that their informer was reliable. The first prong of this test has usually been met with details about how the informant acquired his knowledge (for instance, that he had just been inside the house and saw there a cache of narcotics from which the occupant made a sale), though it can be indirectly satisfied by self-verifying detail. As explained in *Spinelli*, if the informant gives a great many details about the criminal scheme (the precise amount of narcotics in the house, how it is wrapped, exactly where it is stored), then it may be inferred "that the informant had gained his information in a reliable way."

The second or "veracity" prong of *Aguilar* has typically been met on the basis of past performance, that is, by a recitation that this same informant previously has given information that turned out to be correct. Alternatively, it has sufficed to show, as in UNITED STATES V. HARRIS (1971), that the informant's statement included an admission against penal interest ("I bought some narcotics while I was in that house"), as people "do not lightly admit a crime and place critical evidence in the hands of the police in the form of their own admissions." The Supreme Court sometimes stressed that the informer's tale was partly corroborated, but there was considerable uncertainty as to just what deficiencies under the *Aguilar* twopronged test this corroboration overcomes. (Because the use of informants raises special concerns not present in other situations, no comparable showing of veracity is needed when the information has been obtained from a police officer or a cooperative citizen.)

The *Aguilar* test was abandoned in ILLINOIS V. GATES (1983) in favor of a more general "totality of the circumstances" approach. The *Aguilar* factors of veracity and basis of knowledge remain as "relevant considerations," but are no longer two independent requirements; "a deficiency in one may be compensated for . . . by a strong showing as to the other." This is an unfortunate development, for the *Aguilar* rule provided a necessary structure and more precise guidance to police and judges. Moreover, the *Gates* approach is unsound, for surely—as the Court has often held—a conclusory allegation ("there are narcotics in that house") is insufficient even when it comes from a source of unquestioned reliability. *Gates* will doubtless make it easier to establish probable cause than it has been previously; the Court deemed it sufficient that the police had received an anonymous letter with a conclusory assertion of drug trafficking and then had corroborated the letter with certain predicted behavior that was not otherwise suspicious.

One extremely important question regarding the Fourth Amendment probable cause test is whether it is fixed or variable, that is, whether it always requires the same quantum of evidence or whether this compromise between privacy and law enforcement interests may be struck differently on a case-by-case basis. For example, may it be concluded that the solution of an unsolved murder is of greater public concern than the solution of an unsolved shoplifting, so that an arrest or search concerning the former would require less evidence than one respecting the latter offense? When confronted with that question in *Dunaway v. New York* (1979), the Court answered in the negative, saying such a variable standard would be impracticable: "A single, familiar standard is essential to guide police officers, who have only limited time and expertise to reflect on and balance the social and individual interests involved in the specific circumstances they confront."

Another supposed variable in *Dunaway* was that the police action at issue was a brief detention of the suspect at the police station, not recorded as an arrest. Though the Court there found the detention "indistinguishable from a traditional arrest" and thus subject to the usual probable cause requirement, on other occasions the Supreme Court has used a BALANCING TEST: when the police action is significantly less intrusive than the usual arrest or search, there is a corresponding reduction in the required factual basis justifying that action. The leading decision is the STOP AND FRISK case, TERRY V. OHIO (1968), which with later decisions may be taken to mean, first, that a brief on-the-street detention of a suspect, a distinct police practice significantly less intrusive than a full-fledged arrest, is lawful upon a reasonable suspicion of criminality falling short of that needed to arrest; and second, that a frisk of that suspect for purposes of self-protection, a distinct police practice significantly less intrusive than a complete search of the person, is lawful upon a reasonable suspicion that the suspect is armed falling short of the probable cause required for a full search.

Although this balancing in *Terry* upheld a limited seizure and search on a watered-down version of probable cause, in other situations the Supreme Court has permitted very limited routine seizures or searches even absent any case-by-case showing of suspicion. Thus CAMARA V. MUNICIPAL COURT (1967) allowed a safety inspection of a dwelling, without any showing of the likelihood of code violations in that particular dwelling, where the inspection followed "reasonable legislative or administrative standards," such as those authorizing periodic inspection. And in *Delaware v. Prouse* (1979) the Court indicated its approval of stopping a vehicle for a driver's license and vehicle registration check, even absent suspicion that the driver was unlicensed or the car unregistered, as part of a roadblock conducted under standardized procedures.

Still another line of cases requires no factual basis for a particular seizure or search provided it is conducted in connection with some other search or seizure for which there is a sufficient basis. Where such relationships exist, the law would be very complex and difficult to apply if multiple factual bases were required, and thus sophistication has been rejected in favor of certain "bright lines" clearly marking the boundaries of permissible police conduct. Illustrative is UNITED STATES V. ROBINSON (1973), holding that a search of a person is permissible whenever that individual has just been subjected to a lawful custodial arrest. Though the Court in *Robinson* understood that search of the arrestee's person serves only to ensure that he does not have a weapon by which to make an escape or evidence of the crime which he might try to destroy or dispose of, it was not thought realistic to require separate police determinations whether there were grounds for arrest and whether the arrestee might be armed or in possession of evidence. Rather, the right to search was "piggybacked" onto the authority to arrest. By like reasoning, the Court held in *New York v. Belton* (1981) that the search of an automobile's passenger compartment can be piggybacked onto the contemporaneous arrest of an occupant, and in MICHIGAN V. SUMMERS (1981) that the brief detention of an occupant of a house can be piggybacked onto the contemporaneous execution of a search warrant for contraband there.

The Supreme Court has often expressed a preference for searches and seizures made pursuant to a warrant, reasoning that the warrant process protects Fourth Amendment rights by ensuring that critical decisions are made by "a neutral and detached magistrate." Thus the warrant-issuing authority may not be given to a prosecutor (COOLIDGE V. NEW HAMPSHIRE, 1971), or to a justice of the peace who receives a fee for warrants issued (*Connally v. Georgia*, 1977), but at least as to minor offenses may be granted to a clerk of the court acting under the supervision of a judge (*Shadwick v. City of Tampa*, 1972). The magistrate's responsibility is to make the critical probable cause decision which otherwise would be left to the police, and to ensure, as the Fourth Amendment requires, that the warrant describes the place to be searched and the person or things to be seized with such specificity that an officer can, as the Court put it in *Steele v. United States* (1925), "with reasonable effort ascertain and identify" the place, person, or thing intended.

Despite this preference for warrants, in many circumstances a search or seizure may constitutionally be made without a warrant. For one thing, no warrant need be obtained when EXIGENT CIRCUMSTANCES make a detour to a magistrate impracticable. Illustrative is the seminal AUTOMOBILE SEARCH case of CARROLL V. UNITED STATES (1925), where it was stressed that "it is not practicable to secure a warrant because the vehicle can be quickly moved out of the locality or jurisdiction in which the warrant must be sought." However, the Court has not always dealt with the exigent circumstances issue in a consistent fashion. In CHAMBERS V. MARONEY (1970) the Court extended the *Carroll* rule to a vehicle that was in police custody and inaccessible to anyone else. On the other hand, in *Vale v. Louisiana* (1970) the Court chastised the police for not having obtained a search warrant a day earlier, though the probable cause needed for its issuance had unexpectedly come to the attention of the officer for the first time just minutes before the warrantless search of the arrestee's dwelling.

These different attitudes suggest that considerations other than "exigent circumstances" are at play. For example, the Court is less willing to recognize exceptions to the warrant requirement for dwelling searches than for vehicle searches. Apparently perceiving that its expanded vehicle search rule could not be explained in terms of exigent circumstances, the Court in *United States v. Chadwick* (1977) offered another explanation: vehicles have a "diminished expectation of privacy" which makes them unworthy of the usual Fourth Amendment warrant requirement. Yet in *Arkansas v. Sanders* (1979) the Court found no such diminished expectation in a suitcase, even when placed in a vehicle. It is not immediately apparent why placing one's personal items in the trunk of a car manifests less of a privacy expectation than placing those same items in some other type of container. Perhaps that is why the Court responded in *United States v. Ross* (1982) with this curious rule for the container-in-a-car cases: the *Chambers* no-warrant rule applies if there is probable cause to search the entire vehicle, but the *Sanders* warrant rule applies if there is probable cause to search only the container in the vehicle.

Some decisions reflect the Court's belief that certain police intrusions are more serious than others and that the warrant process is necessary only for the more serious ones. Intrusions upon a possessory interest are generally viewed as less serious than intrusions into a privacy interest; the former alone do not require warrants. *Coolidge v. New Hampshire* teaches that if the police are lawfully present in a place executing a search warrant and find items they believe are subject to seizure but which are not named in the warrant, they usually may make a warrantless seizure of them and need not return to the magistrate for another warrant. By contrast, when the police come into lawful possession of a closed container, for example, one which was turned over to them because misdelivered, as in *Walter v. United States* (1980), further intrusion into the privacy of the container ordinarily requires a warrant.

Similar analysis partly explains the rule of *United States v. Watson* (1976) that an arrest in a public place may be made without a warrant even if there was ample opportunity to obtain one. The Court did not consider such a siezure as great a threat to Fourth Amendment values as, say, the search of a dwelling. Thus the situation changes if the arrest can be made only by entering private premises; the Court held in PAYTON V. NEW YORK (1980) that a warrant is then required absent true exigent circumstances. The situation also changes if the seizure of the person becomes more intrusive. As the Court explained in *Gerstein v. Pugh* (1975), no warrant is needed merely for "a brief period of detention to take the administrative steps incident to arrest," but if the arrestee is not promptly released then "the Fourth Amendment requires a judicial determination of probable cause as a prerequisite to extended restraint on liberty following arrest."

Yet another theme runs through the Court's decisions: no warrant is necessary when there is little for the magistrate to decide. The most obvious illustration is the rule that no search warrant is required for an inventory of an impounded vehicle because there are no special facts for the magistrate to evaluate. The point is also illustrated by comparing *Payton* with STEAGALD V. UNITED STATES (1981). Together the two cases stand for the proposition that an arrest warrant alone justifies entry into the intended arrestee's home to arrest him but not entry into a third party's home, which usually requires a search warrant. In the former situation, unlike the latter, there is no substantial need for a magistrate to determine on a case-by-case basis whether the suspect will probably be found in his own home. Sometimes, as in *Camara v. Municipal Court*, requiring warrants for housing inspections but permitting their issuance without a case-by-case probable cause showing, the Court has been sharply divided on the question of whether resort to the warrant process would be meaningful.

Still another consideration in the warrant cases of the Court is the need for "bright lines," the notion that case-by-case assessments simply are not feasible as to certain matters, so that a general rule applicable to all cases of a certain type is necessary. An example is *United States v. Watson*, holding that no warrant is required to arrest in a public place; a contrary holding, the Court said, would "encumber criminal prosecutions with endless litigation with respect to the existence of exigent circumstances, whether it was practicable to get a warrant, whether the suspect was about to flee, and the like." But in CHIMEL V. CALIFORNIA (1969) the Court overruled cases permitting a warrantless search of premises contemporaneous with a lawful arrest therein, rejecting the dissenters' claim that the earlier "bright line" rule was necessary because there often is "a strong possibility that confederates of the arrested man will in the meanwhile remove the items for which the police have probable cause to search."

The probable cause and warrant requirements of the Fourth Amendment limit the government only. They have no application to private illegal searches and seizures, as where a private person breaks into premises, seizes evidence of crime found therein, and turns that evidence over to the authorities. But if a government official should instigate or participate in such an activity, that involvement would make the private person an agent of the government. Though most Fourth Amendment cases involve the actions of police officers, the amendment unquestionably applies to other government officials as well.

The limitations of the Fourth Amendment extend only to "searches" and "seizures." The term "seizure" is considerably broader than "arrest"; thus the fact that a particular detention is not called an arrest or is less intrusive than an arrest does not mean the amendment is inapplicable. As the Court put it in *Terry v. Ohio*, "whenever a police officer accosts an individual and restrains his freedom to walk away, he has "seized' that person." That formulation leaves unresolved an issue of perspective: is the question whether the officer intended to restrain, or whether the suspect believed he was restrained? Either of these subjective states of mind would be difficult to prove apart from the self-serving statements of the officer and suspect, respectively, and thus an objective test is preferable. The courts, including the Supreme Court, have given insufficient attention to this matter. In *Florida v. Royer* (1983) a majority of the Court expressed the view "that a person has been "seized' within the meaning of the Fourth Amendment only if, in view of all of the circumstances surrounding the incident, a reasonable person would have believed that he was not free to leave." But few people feel free to walk away during a police-citizen encounter, and thus a workable test may require consideration whether the officer added to the inherent pressures by engaging in menacing conduct significantly beyond that accepted in social intercourse. Some governmental pressure causing a person to be in a certain place at a certain time, such as the GRAND JURY subpoena upheld in UNITED STATES V. DIONISIO (1973), does not amount to a Fourth Amendment seizure.

More difficult is the definition of a "search" within the meaning of the Fourth Amendment. The view requiring a physical intrusion into "a constitutionally protected area" was finally abandoned in *Katz v. United States* (1967), which involved ELECTRONIC EAVESDROPPING upon one end of a telephone conversation with a device attached to the outside of a public telephone booth. The Court held that this conduct was a search because the government "violated the privacy upon which [Katz] justifiably relied while using the telephone booth." Justice JOHN MARSHALL HARLAN, concurring in *Katz* in an opinion often relied upon by lower courts, enunciated "a twofold requirement, first that a person have exhibited an actual (subjective) expectation of privacy and, second, that the expectation be one that society is prepared to recognize as "reasonable."

The first of these two requirements clearly deserves no place in a theory of what the Fourth Amendment protects. Were it otherwise, as Anthony Amsterdam aptly put it, "the government could diminish each person's subjective expectation of privacy merely by announcing half-hourly on television . . . that we were all forthwith being placed under comprehensive electronic surveillance." Justice Harlan later came around to this position, counseling in his dissenting opinion in UNITED STATES V. WHITE (1971) that analysis under *Katz* must "transcend the search for subjective ecpectations," because our ecpectations "are in large part reflections of laws that translate into rules that customs and values of the past and present." A majority of the Court continues to use the "actual (subjective) expectation of privacy" formulatin, but cautioned in *Smith v. Maryland* (1979) that in some situations it "would provide an inadequate index of Fourth Amendment protection."

The Court has sometimes referred to the second *Katz* requirement simply as the "reasonable "expectation of privacy" test. From this, it might be assumed that investigative activity constitutes a search whenever it uncovers incriminating actions or objects which the law's hypothetical reasonable man would have expected to remain private, that is, those which as a matter of statistical probability were not likely to be discovered. But such an approach is unsound. Rather, as Justice Harlan later explained in his *United States v. White* dissent, the question here must "be answered by assessing the nature of a particular practice and the likely extent of its impact on the individual's sense of security balanced against the utility of the conduct as a technique of law enforcement." In Amsterdam's words, at the heart of the matter is "a value judgment": "whether, if the particular form of surveillance practiced by the police is permitted to go unregulated by constitutional restraints, the amount of privacy and freedom remaining to citizens would be diminished to a compass inconsistent with the aims of a free and open society."

Although *Katz*, so viewed, offers a useful approach to the question of what the Fourth Amendment protects, the Court's application of the test has been neither consistent nor cautious, as can be seen by comparing MARSHALL V. BARLOW'S INC. (1978) with *Smith v. Maryland* (1979). In *Marshall*, holding unconstitutional the warrantless inspection of business premises, the Court expressly rejected the government's claim that a businessman lacked any privacy expectation vis-à-vis the government when there was no such expectation as to others (in this instance, his employees). Rather, the Court reached the sensible conclusion that an unconsented entry would be a Fourth Amendment search even though the area entered was regularly used by the company's employees. But a year later, in *Smith*, rejecting the claim that there was a "legitimate expectation of privacy" in the numbers one dials on his telephone, the Court, though asserting that "our lodestar is *Katz*," concluded there was no such privacy expectation vis-à-vis the government because the telephone company's switching equipment had the capacity to record that information for certain limited business purposes. This unfortunate all-or-nothing view of privacy, as Justice THURGOOD MARSHALL noted in dissent, means that "unless a person is prepared to forego use of what for many has become a personal or professional necessity, he cannot help but accept the risk of surveillance."

In still another situation the Fourth Amendment's probable cause and warrant requirements are not applicable. This situation is most commonly called a CONSENT SEARCH, although when the facilitating party is active rather than passive it may be characterized as involving no search at all. At one time the consent doctrine was assumed to be grounded on the concept of waiver, but in SCHNECKLOTH V. BUSTAMONTE (1973) the Court, saying such an approach "would be thoroughly inconsistent with our decisions," held that the underlying issue was whether the person's consent was "voluntary." One reason the concept of waiver is inappropriate here is because it has long been recognized that sometimes one party may give a consent that will be effective against another. As the Court put it in *United States v. Matlock* (1974), where two or more persons have joint access to or control of premises "it is reasonable to recognize that any of the coinhabitants has the right to permit the inspection in his own right and that the others have assumed the risk that one of their number might permit the common area to be searched." The Court in *Matlock* found it unnecessary to pass upon the correctness of a position taken by several lower courts, namely, that the Fourth Amendment's reasonableness requirement is met if the police reasonably but mistakenly conclude that the consenting person has such authority.

The Fourth Amendment was a largely unexplored territory until BOYD V. UNITED STATES (1886), where the Supreme Court, weaving together the Fourth and Fifth Amendments, concluded that "the seizure of a man's private books and papers to be used in evidence against him" was not "substantially different from compelling him to be a witness against himself" and thus held that physical evidence the defendant was required to produce was inadmissible. *Boyd* was later confined by *Adams v. New York* (1904) to the situation in which a positive act was required of the defendant, but in WEEKS V. UNITED STATES (1914) the Court ruled that the "effect of the 4th Amendment" is to forbid federal courts to admit into evidence the fruits of Fourth Amendment violations. The same could not be said of the state courts, the Supreme Court decided in WOLF V. COLORADO (1949); whether exclusion of evidence was the best way to enforce the Fourth Amendment was "an issue as to which men with complete devotion to the protection of the RIGHT OF PRIVACY might give different answers." *Wolf* was overruled in MAPP V. OHIO (1961), where the majority concluded that other remedies for Fourth Amendment violations had proven worthless. Without an EXCLUSIONARY RULE operative at both the state and the federal level, the Constitution's assurance against unreasonable searches and seizures "would be "a form of words,' valueless and undeserving of mention in a perpetual charter of inestimable human liberties.""

Over the years the Court has given various explanations of the rationale for this exclusionary rule. In ELKINS V. UNITED STATES (1960) the Court emphasized "the imperative of judicial integrity"—that the courts not become "accomplices in the willful disobedience of a Constitution they are sworn to uphold." A second purpose, articulated by Justice WILLIAM J. BRENNAN, dissenting in UNITED STATES V. CALANDRA (1974), is that "of assuring the people—all potential victims of unlawful government conduct—that the government would not profit from its lawless behavior, thus minimizing the risk of seriously undermining popular trust in government." This second purpose is reflected in opinions as early as *Weeks*. Yet a third purpose, not explicitly mentioned in the earlier cases, is that of deterring unreasonable searches and seizures. Thus, in *Elkins* the Court emphasized: "The rule is calculated to prevent, not to repair. Its purpose is to deter—to compel respect for the constitutional guaranty in the only effectively available way—by removing the incentive to disregard it." In recent years the Court has relied almost exclusively upon this deterrence rationale.

Over the years the deterrence issue has occasioned intense debate; some claim the exclusionary rule does not deter and should be abandoned, and others claim that it does and should be retained. Hard evidence supporting either claim is unavailable, but some argue that a deterrent effect may be assumed because of such post-exclusionary-rule phenomena as the dramatic increase in the use of warrants and stepped-up efforts to educate the police on the law of search and seizure. The debate has recently centered on a proposed "good faith" exception to the Fourth Amendment exclusionary rule, allowing admission of illegally obtained evidence if the searching or seizing officer acted in a reasonable belief that his conduct was constitutionally permissible. A limited version of the exception was adopted by the Court in UNITED STATES V. LEON (1984), where the exclusionary rule was "modified so as not to bar the use in the prosecution's case-in-chief of evidence obtained by officers acting in reasonable reliance on a search warrant issued by a detached and neutral magistrate but ultimately found to be unsupported by probable cause." The majority reasoned that exclusion for purposes of deterrence was unnecessary in such circumstances, as exclusion would have no significant deterrent effect on the magistrate who issued the warrant, and there is no need to deter the policeman who justifiably relied upon the prior judgment of the magistrate. Whether *Leon* will be a stepping-stone to adoption of a broader (and, it would seem, less justifiable and more difficult to apply)

"good faith" exception, applicable also in without-warrant cases, remains to be seen.

The current dimensions of the Fourth Amendment exclusionary rule are mostly tailored to the deterrence rationale. The rule is not used in certain settings on the assumption that the incremental gain in deterrence is not worth the cost. Illustrative are *United States v. Calandra*, refusing to compel exclusion at the behest of a grand jury witness because it "would achieve a speculative and undoubtedly minimal advance in the deterrence of police misconduct at the expense of substantially impending the role of the grand jury"; and *United States v. Janis* (1976), declining to require exclusion in federal tax litigation of evidence uncovered in a state criminal investigation of gambling because "common sense dictates that the deterrent effect of the exclusion of relevant evidence is highly attenuated when the "punishment' imposed upon the offending criminal enforcement officer is the removal of that evidence from a civil suit by or against a different sovereign." Even in the context of a criminal trial the deterrent objective of the exclusionary rule is sometimes perceived as outweighed by competing considerations. This explains the rule in *Walder v. United States* (1954) that the government may use illegally obtained evidence to impeach the defendant's testimony, so that the defendant cannot "turn the illegal method by which evidence in the Government's possession was obtained to his own advantage, and provide himself with a shield against contradiction of his untruths."

Who may invoke the exclusionary rule? The rule of STANDING generally is that a constitutional challenge may be raised only by those who have an interest in the outcome of the controversy, and who are objecting to a violation of their own rights. A defendant in a criminal case against whom illegally obtained evidence is being offered certainly meets the first requirement, but he does not necessarily meet the second. As to the latter, the fundamental question is whether the challenged conduct intruded upon his freedom or expectation of privacy or only that of someone else, as *Rakas v. Illinois* (1978) illustrates. The Court held that passengers in a car did not have standing to object to a search under the seats and in the glove compartment of that vehicle. Essential to the holding were the conclusions that these passengers were not claiming that the car had been illegally stopped, that they "asserted neither a property nor a possessory interest in the automobile, nor an interest in the property seized," and that the areas searched were ones "in which a passenger *qua* passenger simply would not have a legitimate expectation of privacy." The Supreme Court refused in ALDERMAN V. UNITED STATES (1969) to adopt a rule of "target standing" allowing a defendant to object to any Fourth Amendment violation committed for the purpose of acquiring evidence for use against him. This refusal limits to some extent the deterrent effect of the exclusionary rule, for police sometimes deliberately direct an illegal search at one person because they are seeking evidence to use against another person they know will not be able to question their conduct.

What evidence is subject to challenge under the exclusionary rule? Under the FRUIT OF THE POISONOUS TREE doctrine, the exclusionary rule applies not only to the immediate and direct fruits of a Fourth Amendment violation (the physical evidence found in a search), but also to secondary or derivative evidence (a confession acquired by confronting a person with that physical evidence). Of course, in a criminal investigation the discovery of one fact often plays some part in the discovery of many others, and they in turn contribute to the uncovering of still others, and so on, but the fruits doctrine is not pushed this far. Even the fact first discovered by an illegal act does not become forever "inaccessible" for court use: it may still be proved "if knowledge of [the fact] is [also] gained from an independent source," as in SILVERTHORNE LUMBER CO. V. UNITED STATES (1920). The "inevitable discovery" doctrine accepted in *Nix v. Williams* (1984), whereunder illegally obtained evidence is admissible if "the prosecution can establish by a preponderance of the evidence that the information ultimately or inevitably would have been discovered by lawful means," likewise serves to put the police in no worse position than they would have been if their misconduct had not occurred. Another limitation is provided by the test in *Wong Sun v. United States*: "whether, granting establishment of the primary illegality, the evidence to which instant objection is made has been come at by exploitation of that illegality or instead by means sufficiently distinguishable to be purged of the primary taint." In that case the taint of one defendant's illegal arrest was deemed dissipated by his release on his own recognizance, so that the taint did not reach a subsequently given confession. Considerations close to the deterrent function of the exclusionary rule also come into play here. Thus, suppression of derivative evidence is much more likely if it appears that the primary illegality was a clearly unconstitutional act or that it was undertaken for the purpose of acquiring that derivative evidence. For example, a confession will be deemed the fruit of an obviously illegal arrest made in the hope of acquiring a confession.

It cannot be denied that there is ample room for reasonable disagreement regarding the rationales and results of a number of the Supreme Court's Fourth Amendment decisions. In the main, however, the Court's response to the four fundamental questions just discussed has been indisputably appropriate and sound. The decisions on the requisite factual basis for a seizure or search have generally struck a fair balance between privacy and law enforcement interests. The Court's rulings regarding the warrant requirement have prevented the warrant process from becoming so overburdened as to become a mechanical and meaningless routine, yet have provided added protection to those Fourth Amendment interests that are valued most. The decisions defining the activities to which the amendment applies—especially *Katz* and its justified expectation of privacy test—provide an approach that should enable the Court to protect against new threats to the individual's right to be free of intrusive government surveillance. Finally, it is the Court's insistence upon an exclusionary rule as an enforcement mechanism that has kept the Fourth Amendment from being reduced to "a form of words."

WAYNE R. LaFAVE
(1986)

Bibliography

AMSTERDAM, ANTHONY G.   1974   Perspectives on the Fourth Amendment. *Minnesota Law Review* 58:349–477.
GRANO, JOSEPH D.   1978   Perplexing Questions about Three Basic Fourth Amendment Issues: Fourth Amendment Activity, Probable Cause, and the Warrant Requirement. *Journal of Criminal Law and Criminology* 69:425–463.
KAMISAR, YALE   1983   Does (Did) (Should) the Exclusionary Rule Rest on a "Principled Basis" Rather Than an "Empirical Proposition"? *Creighton Law Review* 16:565–667.
LaFAVE, WAYNE R.   1978   *Search and Seizure: A Treatise on the Fourth Amendment,* 3 vols. St. Paul, Minn.: West Publishing Co.
LANDYNSKI, JACOB W.   1966   *Search and Seizure and the Supreme Court.* Baltimore, Md.: Johns Hopkins University Press.
OAKS, DALLIN H.   1970   Studying the Exclusionary Rule. *University of Chicago Law Review* 37:665–757.
UNITED STATES, CONGRESS, SENATE COMMITTEE ON THE JUDICIARY, SUBCOMMITTEE ON CRIMINAL LAW   1982   *The Exclusionary Rule Bills,* 97th Cong., 1st & 2d sess.

SEARCH AND SEIZURE
(Update 1)

Since 1985 the Supreme Court has refined and expanded upon previously articulated exceptions to the SEARCH WARRANT requirement, the PROBABLE CAUSE requirement, and the EXCLUSIONARY RULE. Few decisions have addressed novel issues or fashioned new approaches to the FOURTH AMENDMENT.

Earlier cases, beginning with CAMARA V. MUNICIPAL COURT, (1967) and TERRY V. OHIO (1968), established that a warrant and probable cause may not be needed when a search is undertaken primarily for noncriminal purposes or is limited in scope. Rather, the essential criterion of the Fourth Amendment is "reasonableness," which requires balancing the intrusiveness of a particular category of search against the special law enforcement needs served by the search. In recent years, the Court has increasingly applied a BALANCING TEST to permit the government to conduct WARRANTLESS SEARCHES and searches with less than probable cause, in pursuit of special law enforcement interests aimed at particular groups, including government employees, schoolchildren, probationers, prisoners, and automobile owners.

Two recent decisions upholding government employee DRUG TESTING programs illustrate both the advantages and the difficulties of a balancing approach to the Fourth Amendment. Balancing is attractive because it permits the Court to give a full account of competing interests and to adjust constitutional limitations accordingly. In SKINNER V. RAILWAY LABOR EXECUTIVES ASSOCIATION (1989), which upheld mandatory blood and urine testing of all railroad workers involved in train accidents or certain safety violations, the Court engaged in a two-stage analysis. First, the pervasively regulated nature of the railroad industry and railroad employees' awareness of the testing regime lessened the employees' REASONABLE EXPECTATION OF PRIVACY concerning their bodily fluids. Second, the government's interest in deterrence and detection of drug use by railroad workers, in order to ensure safety on the railroads, was sufficiently compelling to outweigh any residue of legitimate privacy expectations with respect to testing of bodily fluids.

The limitations of balancing analysis become apparent in a companion case, NATIONAL TREASURY EMPLOYEES V. VON RAAB (1989). At issue in *Von Raab* was a more sweeping program that required drug testing of all Customs Service employees hired or promoted into positions in which they would carry guns or come into contact with drugs. Yet *Skinner*—which, like all balancing opinions, was inherently fact-specific and conclusory—shed little light on how *Von Raab* should be resolved. Ultimately, a bare majority upheld the Customs Service program, concluding that the government's special need for honest "frontline offices" in the midst of a national illicit drug crisis outweighed any individual Customs Service employee's expectation of privacy. For Justice ANTONIN SCALIA, in dissent, the balance came out differently in *Von Raab* because there was no record of a history of substance abuse in the Customs Service, as there had been in the railroad industry of *Skinner*. Yet others might strike the opposite balance, upholding the program in *Von Raab* but not that in *Skinner*, on the ground that the Customs Service program contained a significant internal limitation not present in the railroad program: that the government could not use drug test results in criminal prosecutions.

The Customs Service program is almost unique in actually prohibiting introduction of acquired evidence in criminal trials, but in several other recent search cases the Court has invoked government interests other than criminal prosecution. Noncriminal motivation was critical in the school search case NEW JERSEY V. T.L.O. (1984). In the Court's view, the special interest of school authorities in maintaining order permits them to search a student when there are "reasonable" grounds for believing the search will yield evidence of a violation of a law or a school rule and the search is not especially intrusive. *T.L.O.* expressly withheld judgment as to whether the police, as opposed to school officials, could likewise conduct school searches without a warrant and on less than probable cause. Yet, in *New York v. Burger* (1987), the Court permitted evidence seized from automobile junkyards in warrantless ADMINISTRATIVE SEARCHES conducted by police officers to be used for penal, as well as administrative, purposes because the two purposes were sufficiently related.

The government's interest in effective supervision of particular groups was also determinative in *Griffin v. Wisconsin* (1987), which held that probation officers may search probationers' homes if there are "reasonable grounds" to suspect a probation violation, and in *O'Connor v. Ortega* (1987), which held that government supervisors may search employee offices for "work-related purposes" (in this case, to investigate alleged misconduct). The Court has declined to establish an explicit middle-tier cause standard somewhere between probable cause and the *Terry* "reasonable suspicion" standard. Nevertheless, the "reasonable scope" test of *T.L.O.* may implicitly create such an intermediate standard governing focused searches for primarily noncriminal purposes.

In several other recent cases, the Court has refused to impose Fourth Amendment limitations on particular categories of investigative activity on the basis that the activities at issue were not "searches" at all under the Fourth Amendment. In *California v. Ciraolo* (1985) and *Florida v. Riley* (1989), the Court concluded that there are no Fourth Amendment restrictions on aerial surveillance from publicly navigable airspace (by plane and by helicopter, respectively). In CALIFORNIA V. GREENWOOD (1988) the Court agreed with the great majority of lower courts in holding that police need neither particularized suspicion nor a warrant to seize trash placed for roadside pickup. In each of these cases, the Court applied the two-pronged test set forth in KATZ V. UNITED STATES (1967) for determining when government action invades privacy protected by the Fourth Amendment: first, whether the individual has an actual expectation of privacy and, second, whether any such expectation of privacy is reasonable or legitimate. The majority in each case concluded that any expectation of privacy was not one "the society" at large was prepared to accept as reasonable. The Court made clear that state law is not controlling either as to the creation of privacy expectations or as to their reasonableness, although FAA regulations apparently are highly relevant to both prongs of the test. Despite the invocation of *Katz*, each decision is more persuasive by analogy to the pre-*Katz* test for determining what constitutes a search under the Fourth Amendment: whether there has been a trespass upon traditionally recognized property interests.

The Supreme Court has continued to cast an unfavorable eye on the exclusionary rule, which precludes admission at trial of evidence obtained through an illegal search or seizure. Previously, in NIX V. WILLIAMS (1984), the Court had ruled that illegally seized evidence is admissible if it would have been "inevitably discovered" through an "independent source." In *Murray v. United States* (1988), a four-Justice majority (Justices WILLIAM J. BRENNAN and ANTHONY KENNEDY not participating) applied the logic of the INEVITABLE DISCOVERY and "independent source" exceptions to permit admission of evidence first viewed in an illegal search as long as the evidence was subsequently seized pursuant to an independently valid search warrant. The moral hazard of these two exceptions to the exclusionary rule is especially apparent in *Murray,* which may be read to provide an incentive to make an illegal search to determine whether obtaining a search warrant later would be worthwhile. Yet the Court is intent upon reminding us that there is also hazard—to society at large and to the integrity of criminal trials—in suppressing probative evidence, especially where probable cause existed apart from any illegal search.

The Court has also expanded the exclusionary rule's GOOD FAITH EXCEPTION, first developed in *United States v. Leon* (1984), to include warrantless administrative searches authorized by statutes later held to be unconstitutional; *Illinois v. Krull* (1987) held that the exception applies whenever the police officer acts "in good-faith reliance on an apparently valid statute." *Krull* thus signals a departure from *Leon,* which had given much weight to institutional considerations justifying reliance on search warrants issued by neutral, independent judicial officers. As Justice SANDRA DAY O'CONNOR indicated in dissent for herself and three others, legislative schemes authorizing warrantless searches do not invite such reliance, because legislators are not expected to operate as independent, politically detached interpreters of the Constitution.

Some recent cases have articulated the new Fourth Amendment standards. In *Winston v Lee* (1984) the Court recognized that the Fourth Amendment may prohibit as unreasonable certain forms of search and seizure (in this case extracting a bullet from the body) even when there is probable cause. Similarly, TENNESSEE V. GARNER (1984) held that the shooting death of a fleeing felon is an un-

reasonable form of seizure, even though there was probable cause to believe that the burglary invloved violence or that the felon otherwise presented a threat to someone's physical safety.

It was unclear after *Garner* whether successful termination of freedom of movement is a sine qua non for a "seizure" under the Fourth Amendment. The majority in *Michigan v. Chesternut* (1988) rejected both the state's argument that no seizure occurs "until an individual stops in response" to a show of authority and the defendant's contention that a seizure occurs as soon as the police "pursue" an individual; rather, the Court appeared to reaffirm the test of *Florida v. Royer* (1983) and *Immigration and Naturalization Service v. Delgado* (1984): there is a seizure when the police's actions would cause a reasonable person to believe she is not free to leave. During the term after *Chesternut,* however, in *Brower v. County of Inyo* (1989), a bare majority of the Court concluded that a seizure under the Fourth Amendment does not occur until there is an actual "termination of freedom through intentionally applied means."

In other cases, the Court has refused to develop new Fourth Amendment principles. *United States v. Sokolow* (1989) declined to hold a stop unconstitutional merely because it was based on a drug-courier profile; as long as there is *Terry*'s "reasonable suspicion" in the particular case, the police may stop the suspect. In *United States v. Verdugo-Urquidez* (1990), the Court refused to apply Fourth Amendment limitations to U.S. law enforcement agents operating against aliens in foreign jurisdictions.

KATE STITH
(1992)

(SEE ALSO: *Fourth Amendment.*)

Bibliography

GOLDSTEIN, ABRAHAM S. 1987 The Search Warrant, the Magistrate, and Judicial Review. *New York University Law Review* 62:1173–1217.

GRANO, JOSEPH 1984 Probable Cause and Common Sense: A Reply to the Critics of *Illinois v. Gates. University of Michigan Journal of Law Reform* 17:465–521.

KAMISAR, YALE 1987 Comparative Reprehensibility and the Fourth Amendment Exclusionary Rule. *University of Michigan Law Review* 86:1–50.

SEARCH AND SEIZURE
(Update 2)

The most important development in contemporary search and seizure law has been a fundamental change in the jurisprudential theories used to interpret this area of constitutional law. For most of the twentieth century, rules adopted during the "formalist" *Lochner* era dominated search and seizure theory. During the past three decades, however, these formalist ideas have gradually been supplanted by PRAGMATIST theories that are consistent with views about the nature of law and its uses now widely held in our legal culture. This change in theory has had profound practical consequences. It has altered the definition of individual privacy, property, and liberty rights, has expanded the scope of government power, and has tended to shift power from the judicial branch to the executive branch of government. To understand the significance of this recent transformation, it is necessary to examine the theories that governed search and seizure law for most of the century.

At the turn of the twentieth century, the Supreme Court frequently employed formalist theories to define the constitutional limitations upon searches and seizures. The first of these opinions, BOYD V. UNITED STATES (1886) is the classic example of FOURTH AMENDMENT formalism. The *Boyd* Court ruled that the enforcement of a SUBPOENA ordering the production of private business records violated the Fourth and Fifth Amendments separately, and also adopted an expansive, structural theory in which the two amendments were linked by principles of privacy, property, and liberty. The two amendments ran together to create a zone of privacy into which the government could not intrude to compel production of some forms of private property for use against citizens in criminal or quasicriminal proceedings. These were indefeasible rights strong enough to defeat the government's policy arguments that subpoenas should be permitted because they were valuable tools for achieving important social interests, like effective law enforcement and the collection of import duties.

The *Boyd* opinion utilized the formalist legal theories dominant at that time. It identified NATURAL RIGHTS embodied in the Constitution and the COMMON LAW, then deduced rules governing searches and seizures from those foundational principles. It treated property rights as FUNDAMENTAL RIGHTS and defined some as essential attributes of liberty, striking down a statute authorizing the government to invade the realm of private rights, including rights based on property law.

A Fourth Amendment EXCLUSIONARY RULE was implicit in *Boyd*, which held that the government could only seize items in which it had an interest recognized under property law. In WEEKS V. UNITED STATES (1914), the Court deployed this same formalist reasoning to justify the adoption of an explicit exclusionary rule. The Court held that private papers seized in a WARRANTLESS SEARCH of Weeks's home could not be used to convict him of a crime because the government had failed to satisfy the proce-

dural requirements set out in the warrant clause, and had violated the substantive restrictions that limited the government's power to seize private property. As it had in *Boyd*, the Court held that the seizure of private papers was unconstitutional.

At the beginning of the 1920s, the Court calcified its property-based theories by adopting the mere evidence rule, in which it reiterated its earlier decisions holding that the government could seize property only if it could demonstrate some legally cognizable property interest in the items. In *Gouled v. United States* (1921), OVERRULED by WARDEN V. HAYDEN (1967), the Court decreed that even a valid SEARCH WARRANT could not justify the search of a home or office unless the government or some private citizen had a recognized property interest in the item sought. Government actors could seize stolen or forfeited property, property concealed to avoid payment of duties, required records, counterfeit currency, and various criminal instrumentalities. Property was not seizable, however, if the government merely wanted to use it as evidence. The mere evidence rule survived for almost half a century despite its two fundamental defects. It obliterated the distinction between papers—property that can contain the expression of thoughts, ideas, and emotions— and all other forms of property, and it imposed excessive restrictions upon law enforcers.

Boyd's interpretive linkage of the Fourth Amendment with the Fifth Amendment privilege against self-incrimination suggested that papers could be treated differently from other tangible personal property. Papers, after all, possess inherent testimonial attributes. Most property does not. *Gouled* rejected this distinction, declaring that for Fourth Amendment purposes papers possess "no special sanctity" when compared to other forms of property. This conclusion confirmed the power of government agents to seize private papers that could be classified as contraband or criminal instrumentalities. On the other hand, the rule imposed unjustifiable constraints on law enforcers by prohibiting the search for and seizure of *any property*, regardless of its probative value, which the government wanted for use solely as evidence.

In other opinions issued during the 1920s, including *Marron v. United States* (1927), the Court reaffirmed that even if the government could establish a property interest in the property it had seized, compliance with the requirements of the warrant clause was the procedural prerequisite of a constitutional search or seizure. Even when the Court upheld WARRANTLESS SEARCHES and seizures, it still required that the government possess PROBABLE CAUSE. For example, the warrantless search of an automobile traveling on an open highway for illegal liquor was permitted if the officers possessed probable cause, because the vehicle's inherent mobility created an exigency: the criminals might escape along with their contraband, CARROLL V. UNITED STATES (1925).

In OLMSTEAD V. UNITED STATES (1928), overruled by KATZ V. UNITED STATES (1967), the Court employed a restrictive version of property-based formalism. The majority paid lip service to the linkage between private property and constitutional rights established in *Boyd, Weeks,* and *Gouled,* but abandoned the expansive vision of individual liberty that energized those earlier decisions. Although it was not the only opinion in which the Court employed formalist theories to uphold government searches and seizures, *Olmstead* sounded the deathknell for a critical part of the formalist construct—the integration of property law with an expansive interpretation of constitutional provisions designed to protect individual liberty. The Court held that the Fourth Amendment only regulated physical trespasses into constitutionally protected places, like homes and offices, and searches and seizures of people and tangible physical property. This property-based literalism led the Court to conclude that the installation and use of wiretaps on telephone poles did not constitute a search because there was no physical trespass into constitutionally protected areas, and no seizure occurred, because conversations were not tangible property protected by the Fourth Amendment.

During the forty years following *Olmstead, Lochner*-era theories continued to dominate the debate about the constitutional limitations upon searches and seizures. But in recent decades the Supreme Court has abandoned Fourth Amendment formalism. The emergence of pragmatist ideas in Fourth Amendment theory parallels changes in the broader legal culture. Pragmatism emerged as a coherent philosophy during the *Lochner* era, and it provided the theoretical foundations for the attack on legal formalism waged by scholars, judges, and lawyers during the early decades of the twentieth century. The pragmatist attack on legal formalism initially was energized by broader progressive social, political, economic, and intellectual movements.

The contemporary version of Fourth Amendment pragmatism rejects the formalist conception of strong individual rights, its linkage of liberty, privacy, and property rights, its value-based theory of CONSTITUTIONAL INTERPRETATION, and its emphasis upon formal reasoning. In their place the Justices have substituted pragmatist theories that do not treat privacy, liberty, and property as indefeasible rights, but rather as interests to be considered along with an expansive array of factors potentially relevant to deciding each case. Judges do not act as neutral interpreters of preexisting legal principles and rules, but instead act as social engineers utilizing various tools, including the SOCIAL SCIENCES, to help advance society's

present goals. As a result, judicial analysis typically relies upon nonformal reasoning that emphasizes social goals and policies as reasons for decision, and that applies legal rules only to advance those purposes. Rules need not be followed if they conflict with "better" social policies.

The Court's reasoning in *United States v. Leon* (1984) exemplifies how pragmatist methods diminish the power of rules. The Fourth Amendment's most definite rule is that "no warrants shall issue, but upon probable cause." In *Leon,* searches and seizures that produced incriminating evidence were conducted pursuant to a warrant that had been issued despite the absence of probable cause. The exclusionary rule supplies the standard remedy for such unconstitutional searches and seizures. Had the Court's majority engaged in rule-based decisionmaking, it likely would have concluded that although the suppression of evidence produces unfortunate social costs, they are an unavoidable byproduct of judicial application of relevant legal rules.

Instead, the Court based its decision upon pragmatist reasoning. It examined a variety of nonlegal sources of information relevant to the dispute, including statistical analyses of the impact of the exclusionary rule on the prosecution and conviction of suspected criminals. The Court concluded that on the case's facts, the costs to society of suppressing evidence probative of the defendant's guilt outweighed any countervailing benefits. Rather than accept a suboptimal outcome dictated by application of the amendment's text and the exclusionary rule, the majority established a "good faith" exception to the exclusionary rule designed to achieve a socially desirable outcome.

Although pragmatist reasoning has come to dominate search and seizure law under the "conservative" BURGER and REHNQUIST COURTS, the "liberal" WARREN COURT introduced the most important of these methods to Fourth Amendment theory. Cases in which judges engage in interest balancing exemplify this transformation.

The emergence of interest balancing as a central method for resolving Fourth Amendment disputes can be traced to a series of opinions issued by the Warren Court in the years 1966 to 1968. In the first, SCHMERBER V. CALIFORNIA (1966), the Court approved a blood test used as evidence supporting criminal charges of driving under the influence of alcohol. This intrusion into Schmerber's body was a warrantless search, but it did not violate the Fourth Amendment. The majority emphasized that the police possessed probable cause; that obtaining a warrant was impracticable because the inevitable diminishing of Schmerber's blood alcohol level as time passed created an exigency; and that the physical intrusion was relatively minor. The opinion employed an analytical process the Court later would label the "*Schmerber* balancing test," and concluded that the means used to obtain the blood sample satisfied the Fourth Amendment's standard of reasonableness.

The next significant Fourth Amendment balancing decision came a year later in CAMARA V. MUNICIPAL COURT (1967), which involved a resident's challenge to an ordinance that permitted housing inspectors to examine the interior of his home. The Court concluded that these inspections were searches, but authorized the issuance of warrants on the basis of information insufficient to provide probable cause to believe that any particular dwelling violated health and safety regulations. This weakening of the probable cause standard was coupled with an explicit turn to balancing. Although ostensibly adhering to the commands of the warrant clause, the Court stressed that "our holding emphasizes the controlling standard of reasonableness." The Court then made a critical assertion that ignored existing PRECEDENTS and laid the foundation for future balancing: "there can be no ready test for determining reasonableness other than by balancing the need to search against the invasion which the search entails."

The theoretical innovations adopted in *Camara* have provided the authority for many of the Court's subsequent opinions. None is more important than TERRY V. OHIO (1968), where the Court for the first time directly applied the Fourth Amendment to a common police activity, the "STOP AND FRISK" of a person whom the police suspect of criminal activity, but lack probable cause to arrest. Chief Justice EARL WARREN's opinion established for the first time that probable cause was not required to justify all searches and seizures.

The Court held that "stops and frisks" constituted an intermediate category of searches and seizures lying somewhere between consensual encounters ungoverned by the Fourth Amendment and intrusions amounting to arrests and full-blown searches. Because they were less intrusive than full-blown arrests and searches, the Court decided that stops and frisks could be justified by a degree of knowledge or certainty less than that required for greater intrusions. The opinion established an intermediate category of knowledge, labeled "reasonable suspicion," which was sufficient to justify these searches and seizures.

The reasonable suspicion standard requires that to justify "the particular intrusion the police officer must be able to point to specific and articulable facts which, taken together with rational inferences from those facts, reasonably warrant that intrusion." This definition describes a quantum of information less than probable cause and more than a mere hunch, but it also incorporates a balancing methodology. The Court not only examined the nature and quality of the information possessed by the police—as it would in deciding whether probable cause existed—but also balanced the quality of that information against the nature and extent of the government intrusion upon privacy and liberty interests. Citing *Camara* as its only authority, the Court reasserted the debatable principle that balancing supplied the only "ready test" for measuring the reasonableness of the intrusion. When it balanced, the Court found that the search and seizure of Terry was reasonable because the government's interest in effective crime detection and in protecting the safety of the public and the investigating officer outweighed the individual's interest in "personal security."

Since 1980 the Supreme Court has employed both *Terry*'s three-tiered model of police–citizen encounters and interest balancing to determine whether a wide variety of government activities are reasonable within the meaning of the Fourth Amendment. Even a small sample of these decisions reveals the impact of balancing on search and seizure law. In cases involving investigations of suspected drug trafficking and other criminal behavior, the Court has upheld investigative detentions of travelers in airports, the seizure of air travelers' luggage, and the detention of automobile travelers. In other cases employing balancing methods, the Court has approved limited suspicionless seizures of all motorists at sobriety checkpoints, approved suspicionless DRUG TESTS of high school athletes and adult employees, and applied a "balancing test" to determine whether suspects in criminal cases can be forced to submit to surgery that may reveal evidence of their guilt.

The cumulative weight of these decisions has led the Court to a startling rejection of the rule-based model that once dominated Fourth Amendment theory. The warrant rule no longer is the central conceptual tool for determining whether government conduct is reasonable for Fourth Amendment purposes, but is now the exception, limited to *some* criminal investigations. Nonformal interest balancing has replaced the warrant model as the basic method for determining whether searches and seizures are unreasonable.

The implementation of nonformal decisionmaking has been facilitated by a related change in how the Court interprets the relationship between the Fourth Amendment's two clauses. For most of the twentieth century, the Supreme Court used a "conjunctive" theory of the amendment that referred to the specific requirements set forth in the amendment's warrant clause to define what conduct constituted the "unreasonable searches and seizures" prohibited by its opening clause. Until recently, the Court attempted to enforce the basic principle that searches and seizures were unreasonable unless conducted pursuant either to a valid warrant or one of a few "jealously and carefully drawn" judicially created exceptions to the warrant requirement. Whether authorized by a warrant or an exception, most searches and seizures had to be justified by the probable cause standard articulated in the warrant clause.

This warrant-based model tended to allocate power to the judicial branch by requiring prior judicial approval of searches and seizures. Even in the majority of cases, where searches and seizures are conducted without warrants, the requirements of probable cause and a warrant or exception provided objective tests against which judges could measure the police conduct in subsequent proceedings. As a result, the conjunctive theory augmented judicial authority to review police conduct.

For decades this conjunctive interpretive model served as a central part of Fourth Amendment theory. In the past decade it has been replaced by a "disjunctive" theory that treats the warrant requirement as nothing more than an example of balancing relevant to some—but not all—criminal cases. The rules found in the warrant clause—including the requirement of probable cause—are no longer benchmarks against which the constitutionality of all searches and seizures are judged. Instead, decisionmakers must decide only if government satisfies some malleable standard of reasonableness, frequently applied by judges in an ad hoc manner. This approach is consistent with pragmatism's antiformalism and with its emphasis upon consequences.

Balancing is the quintessential pragmatist method. When the Court balances, the government usually wins. This results in part from the way it defines competing interests. Typically the Court places the individual criminal defendant's privacy, property, or liberty interests on one side of its metaphorical scales, and balances those discrete and isolated interests against the government's broad interest in protecting all of society from the transgressions of individual lawbreakers. With the issues so characterized, it is hardly surprising that judges usually "discover" that the balance favors the government. The interest all members of society share in being protected from crimes easily outweighs any interest an individual or small class of individuals may have in engaging in illegal behaviors. Social interests usually prevail, as well, when the Court decides what privacy expectations are reasonable.

Until the 1960s the Court generally relied upon the residue of the formalist linkage between property and privacy rights to determine whether government conduct constituted a search regulated by the fourth amendment. After *Olmstead*, a search was an intrusion entailing a physical trespass upon a constitutionally protected area. This formulation's failure to regulate the use of new technologies allowing the government to achieve nontrespassory seizures of intangible evidence, including conver-

sations, eventually drove the Warren Court to replace it with one grounded in legal pragmatism.

In *Katz v. United States* the Court held that FBI agents acting without a warrant violated the Fourth Amendment by attaching an electronic listening and recording device to the outside of a public telephone booth and monitoring Katz's conversations without first getting a search warrant. The Court explicitly overruled *Olmstead*'s property-based requirements of a trespass into a constitutionally protected area and the search and seizure of tangible property. Instead, the Court shifted the focus of the basic inquiry, concluding that the Fourth Amendment protects people and not places. As a result: "What a person knowingly exposes to the public, even in his own home or office, is not a subject of Fourth Amendment protection. But what he seeks to preserve as private, even in an area accessible to the public, may be constitutionally protected." Perhaps because the standard described in this passage is so amorphous, the Court quickly came to rely upon a two-part test taken from the second Justice JOHN MARSHALL HARLAN'S CONCURRING OPINION. Under this test, a protected Fourth Amendment interest exists when a person exhibits a subjective expectation of privacy and the expectation is one that society recognizes as "reasonable."

This two-part "expectations" formula has become the linchpin of Fourth Amendment privacy analysis, and the Court's decisions applying it rest upon the kinds of legal pragmatist ideas discussed above. By asking whether the expectation in dispute is one society is willing to recognize as reasonable, the test's second prong implicitly encourages decisionmakers to define fundamental constitutional values by referring to contemporary social values, goals, and attitudes. The ultimate goal of this analysis is not to obey existing legal authorities, even if those rules represent value choices made by the Framers that are embodied in the Constitution's text. The language of the test instead emphasizes present realities, found in the existing social context. By making the ultimate standard "reasonableness" from a social perspective, the test implements the pragmatist rejection of fixed truths and adopts a flexible standard that can be manipulated to achieve present instrumental goals.

The pragmatist foundations of contemporary expectations analysis are illustrated by the Court's leading opinion involving aerial surveillance of private property. In *California v. Ciraolo* (1986), police officers lacking probable cause conducted a warrantless inspection of Ciraolo's backyard from a private airplane flying at an altitude of 1,000 feet. They identified marijuana growing in the fenced yard, photographed it, and used this information to obtain a search warrant. Police officers executing the warrant seized the marijuana plants.

The Court acknowledged that the backyard lay within

the curtilage of the home, a conclusion that seemingly required suppression of the fruits of the warrantless aerial surveillance because the Court had only recently confirmed, in *Oliver v. United States* (1984), that the heightened Fourth Amendment protections associated with the home applied within its curtilage. Instead, a bare majority applied the *Katz* expectations test, and determined that this surveillance was not a search. The Justices recognized that Ciraolo had manifested a subjective expectation of privacy (his yard was concealed by two fences), but held that Ciraolo had no reasonable expectation of privacy because the warrantless observations "took place within public navigable airspace in a physically nonintrusive manner." *Katz* had expressly overruled the trespass doctrine, but the majority did not base its decision on constitutional rules; indeed it gave only a cursory nod to its own precedents. Instead, it looked to other sources. Because Federal Aviation Administration regulations permitted airplanes to fly at this altitude, someone *could* be up there, therefore we cannot reasonably expect privacy from eyes spying from above.

The majority's reasoning confirms the pragmatist bases of the Court's analysis. It was not the law as a system of rules that the Court cited to justify its reasoning. The decision ultimately seems to rest upon the Justices' idiosyncratic views about the relevant social context, including the nature of contemporary social realities and goals, rather than upon any reasoning from relevant constitutional authorities.

Once again, the introduction of pragmatist ideas into Fourth Amendment theory has overwhelmed the rule-based warrant model. In a remarkably diverse array of settings, the Court has concluded that intrusive government conduct did not constitute a search because the people affected had no reasonable expectation of privacy. For example, the Fourth Amendment does not regulate nontrespassory surveillance of buildings within a home's curtilage from a helicopter, and a person has no reasonable expectation of privacy in the contents of closed, opaque garbage bags deposited on the curb outside his home. Extensive attempts to exclude trespassers, including erecting fences and posting "no trespassing" signs, do not create a reasonable expectation of privacy in open fields or buildings lying within them. Installing an electronic beeper to monitor a person's travels in public does not invade a reasonable privacy expectation, but tracking the beeper in a private home may. Utilizing trained drug detection dogs to sniff travelers' luggage is not a search. In other cases, the Court has approved warrantless intrusions because people have a lessened expectation of privacy in their automobiles and containers located in them.

This kind of judicial behavior is not an anomaly in contemporary legal culture. It represents not an aberration from the norm, but rather is consistent with the pragmatist concept of legal decisionmaking now dominant in our legal culture. The Court's efforts at balancing to determine whether government conduct is reasonable and its efforts to define what expectations are reasonable exemplify pragmatist decisionmaking based upon subjective ideas about social realities and goals that is relatively unconstrained by antecedent rules. Because many of those rules have protected individual privacy, property, and liberty rights, Fourth Amendment pragmatism has produced a body of case law that tends to expand government power, particularly as exercised by law enforcers and others working in the executive branches of state, local, and federal governments.

MORGAN CLOUD
(2000)

Bibliography

ALEINIKOFF, T. ALEXANDER 1991 Constitutional Law in an Age of Balancing. *Yale Law Journal* 96:943–1005.

CLOUD, MORGAN 1996 The Fourth Amendment During the Lochner Era: Privacy, Property and Liberty in Constitutional Theory. *Stanford Law Review* 48:555–631.

CLOUD, MORGAN 1993 Pragmatism, Positivism, and Principles in Fourth Amendment Theory. *UCLA Law Review* 41:199–302.

HOFSTADTER, RICHARD 1955 *The Age of Reform.* New York: Random House.

HOLMES, OLIVER WENDELL, JR. 1881 *The Common Law.* Boston: Little, Brown.

JAMES, WILLIAM 1963 *Pragmatism and Other Essays.* New York: Washington Square Press.

SUMMERS, ROBERT S. 1982 *Instrumentalism and American Legal Theory.* Ithaca, N.Y.: Cornell University Press.

WHITE, MORTON G. 1949 *Social Thought in America: The Revolt Against Formalism.* New York: Viking Press.

SEARCH INCIDENT TO ARREST

WEEKS V. UNITED STATES (1914) recognized, as an exception to the FOURTH AMENDMENT's requirement of a SEARCH WARRANT, the authority of police to search a person incident to his arrest in order to discover concealed weapons or evidence. This principle has remained essentially unchallenged, although its application to a person arrested for a minor offense, such as a traffic violation, involving small likelihood of danger to the officer, was severely criticized by some Justices in UNITED STATES V. ROBINSON (1973). Extension of the allowable search from the person of the arrestee to include the area "in his control," in AGNELLO V. UNITED STATES (1925), planted the seed of conflict between those Justices who would allow a complete search of the premises and those who would limit the search to the area from which the arrestee could conceivably reach for weapons to wield or evidence to destroy.

Marron v. United States (1927) allowed the search to cover "all parts of the premises," but in *Go Bart v. United States* (1931) and *United States v. Lefkowitz* (1932) the Court condemned wholesale "rummaging of the place." Again, *Harris v. United States* (1947) upheld the search of an entire apartment, but *Trupiano v. United States* (1948) forebade even the seizure of contraband in PLAIN VIEW of the arresting officers. The pendulum again swung in *United States v. Rabinowitz* (1950), which authorized search of the whole place. By now the field was "a quagmire," as Justice TOM C. CLARK exclaimed, dissenting in *Chapman v. United States* (1961). One group of Justices took the position, essentially, that once officers are legitimately on premises to make an arrest, the accompanying search, no matter how extensive, is only a minor additional invasion of privacy and therefore reasonable. They conceded that the arrest must not serve as a pretext for the search, and that the search must be limited to objects for which the arrest was made, but these limitations are easily evaded. Justice FELIX FRANKFURTER provided intellectual leadership for the opposing view, arguing that when a search incident to arrest is allowed to extend beyond the need that gave rise to it, the exception swallows up the rule that a warrant must be obtained save in EXIGENT CIRCUMSTANCES. Moreover, because a warrant often will strictly limit the area to be searched, to authorize search of the entire premises has the novel effect of allowing searches incident to arrest a broader scope than searches under warrant.

So the matter stood until CHIMEL V. CALIFORNIA (1969). There the Court restored the balance between theory and practice by overruling *Harris* and *Rabinowitz* and limiting the scope of incident searches to the person of the arrestee and his immediate environs. Still, the *Chimel* limitation may not always apply. Where the police have strong reason to believe that confederates of the arrestee are hidden on the premises, they are presumably entitled, under the "hot pursuit" doctrine of WARDEN V. HAYDEN (1967), to make a "sweep" of the place in order to minimize the danger. The reverse would also seem to follow: once the arrestee has been subdued (assuming there is no reason to suspect the presence of confederates), the police no longer have authority to search even a limited area.

An important legal difference between search of the person's clothing and search of property within the area of his reach should be noted. Property under the arrestee's control, which might have been searched without a warrant immediately following the arrest, may not be searched later; to be lawful under *United States v. Chadwick* (1977) the search must be substantially contemporaneous with the arrest. However, in a radical departure

from the spirit, if not the letter, of the *Chimel* rule, the Court held in *United States v. Edwards* (1974) that authority to search the arrestee's clothing is not lost by the passage of time and may be exercised hours later, following his incarceration. The rationale for this difference appears to be that the arrestee's expectation of privacy in property not associated with his person remains undiminished. Absent a warrant, the property search must therefore be carried out promptly, as an exigency measure, or not at all.

Under *Illinois v. Lafayette* (1983), an arrestee's possessions may be inventoried in the police station prior to his incarceration so as to safeguard them against theft and protect the officers against spurious claims. Because it is considered a reasonable administrative procedure, "the inventory search constitutes a well-defined exception to the warrant requirement."

JACOB W. LANDYNSKI
(1986)

Bibliography

LaFAVE, WAYNE R.   1978   *Search and Seizure: A Treatise on the Fourth Amendment*. Vol. 2:406–466. St. Paul, Minn.: West Publishing Co.

LANDYNSKI, JACOB W.   1966   *Search and Seizure and the Supreme Court*. Pages 87, 98–117. Baltimore: Johns Hopkins University Press.

——— 1971   The Supreme Court's Search for Fourth Amendment Standards. *Connecticut Bar Journal* 45:2–30.

SEARCH WARRANT

The FOURTH AMENDMENT to the Constitution prohibits unreasonable SEARCHES AND SEIZURES and provides that "No Warrants shall issue, but upon PROBABLE CAUSE, supported by Oath or Affirmation, and particularly describing the place to be searched, and the persons or things to be seized." The Framers adopted the warrant clause in response to the use by British customs officers of GENERAL WARRANTS, known as WRITS OF ASSISTANCE, to enforce British trade laws.

A writ of assistance conveyed virtually unbridled discretion to search under the authority of the Crown. The writ was not required to be based on any facts giving reason to believe that a crime had been committed. Nor did it contain an inventory of things to be taken, the names of alleged offenders, or any limitation on the places to be searched. Once issued, a writ remained valid during the lifetime of the reigning sovereign.

Judicial interpretations of the warrant clause have expressed a strong preference for the use of a neutral and detached magistrate over the "hurried action" of a police officer engaged in the often competitive enterprise of ferreting out crime. Since COOLIDGE V. NEW HAMPSHIRE (1971) searches conducted outside the judicial process have been considered by the Supreme Court to be unreasonable per se unless they fall within one of the exceptions to the warrant requirement.

A magistrate who issues a search warrant may not occupy a dual role, both reviewing the facts presented to justify the warrant and actively participating in the criminal investigation or prosecution. Such a dual role creates a conflict of interest that is inimical to the objectives of the warrant clause. As the Supreme Court observed in UNITED STATES V. UNITED STATES DISTRICT COURT (1972), the Fourth Amendment protections cannot be properly guaranteed if searches "may be conducted solely within the discretion of the Executive Branch."

An important part of the Fourth Amendment's proscription against general warrants is that a warrant may be issued only upon probable cause. This requirement necessarily limits each warrant to a particular set of circumstances relating to a suspected criminal offense. The alleged facts must establish a reasonable basis to believe that the offense was committed and that contraband or EVIDENCE of the offense is located at the place to be searched. Although a finding of probable cause may rest upon HEARSAY or other evidence that would not be admissible at trial, the issuing magistrate must nonetheless carefully consider the reliability of such evidence, According to ILLINOIS V. GATES (1983), in assessing probable cause, a magistrate must make a "practical, commonsense" decision in view of all the circumstances set forth in the affidavit, including the "veracity" and "basis of knowledge" of the persons supplying the information.

The information that forms the basis for the search warrant must be sworn to by "oath and affirmation" at the time the warrant is issued. To ensure an independent review by the magistrate, the oath must attest to facts and circumstances, not merely to the affiant's conclusion that he believes he has probable cause for the search. Moreover, an insufficient affidavit cannot be rehabilitated later by testimony concerning facts known by the affiant or otherwise available, but not disclosed to the magistrate at the time of issuance of the warrant. A contrary rule, of course, would render the warrant requirement meaningless.

An important issue that remained unresolved until *Franks v. Delaware* (1978) was whether the accuracy of the information relied on to justify a search warrant may be challenged. In *Franks* the Supreme Court held that if it can be shown that the affiant intentionally or recklessly gave false or misleading information to the magistrate, a reviewing court may invalidate the warrant if the magistrate's finding of probable cause was based on the misinformation.

The warrant clause also precludes the issuance of general search warrants, for it commands that the warrant describe with particularity the place to be searched and the objects to be seized. In *Gouled v. United States* (1921) the Supreme Court held that law enforcement officers could not seize property, even though particularly described in a search warrant, when the property was merely of evidentiary value in a criminal proceeding. This MERE EVIDENCE RULE, which attempted to distinguish between mere evidence and contraband or other property that was a fruit or instrumentality of a crime, was both unsound and lacking in reason and historical support. The Court abandoned the rule in WARDEN V. HAYDEN (1967).

The purpose of the particularity requirement is to limit implicitly the scope of what the officer executing the warrant may do. As the Court stated in *Marron v. United States* (1927): "The requirement that warrants shall particularly describe the things to be seized makes general searches under them impossible and prevents the seizure of one thing under a warrant describing another. As to what is to be taken, nothing is left to the discretion of the officer executing the warrant." With respect to the place to be searched, the description must be such that the officer executing the warrant can, with reasonable effort, ascertain and identify the place intended.

As a practical matter, of course, law enforcement officers may not be completely divested of all discretion in executing search warrants. Moreover, notwithstanding the language in *Marron*, the Court has held that incriminating evidence not listed in a search warrant may be seized when observed in plain view by officers executing the warrant, provided that the officers inadvertently come upon the evidence. The particularity requirement, however, greatly circumscribes the officer's discretion and therefore plays an important role in minimizing the likelihood of police abuse.

JAMES R. ASPERGER
(1986)

Bibliography

LaFAVE, WAYNE R. 1978 *Search and Seizure: A Treatise on the Fourth Amendment.* Vol. 2:1–213. St. Paul, Minn.: West Publishing Co.
LASSON, NELSON B. 1937 *The History and Development of the Fourth Amendment to the United States Constitution.* Baltimore: Johns Hopkins University Press.

SECESSION

Secession, the withdrawal of a state from the American Union, first appeared as an impulse rather than an articulated constitutional doctrine. Inchoate secessionist movements agitated the southwestern frontier after the signing of JAY'S TREATY (1794). AARON BURR's alleged conspiracy was linked to them. Massachusetts Federalists who were disgruntled about the rising political power of the South and the western territories between 1803 and 1814 contemplated secession in correspondence among themselves. Before the CIVIL WAR, Garrisonian abolitionists developed doctrines of disunion, calling for both individual disallegiance and the withdrawal of the free states from a union with the slave states. Southern political leaders, uneasy about the spread of abolitionist and Free Soil sentiment in the north, occasionally voiced threats of secession.

JOHN C. CALHOUN developed the theoretical framework for secession, though ironically, he did so in order to avoid secession through the alternatives of INTERPOSITION and NULLIFICATION. Drawing on the thought of earlier STATES' RIGHTS ideologues such as JOHN TAYLOR of Caroline, JOHN RANDOLPH, and THOMAS COOPER, as well as the concepts of state sovereignty and the Union broached in the VIRGINIA AND KENTUCKY RESOLUTIONS of 1798–1799, Calhoun insisted that SOVEREIGNTY in America resided not in the nation but severally in the people of each of the states. The states created the national government, giving it only limited, specific, and delegated powers. The national government was thus the agent or the trustee for the people of the states, and the federal Constitution was merely a "compact" among sovereign states. If the national government abused its delegated powers by unconstitutional legislation or executive acts, the states could interpose their authority between the federal government and their people and could nullify federal legislation within their territory. But if enough other states ratified an amendment to the federal Constitution that authorized the nullified act, then the states had only the option of submitting to or withdrawing from the Union.

After the election of ABRAHAM LINCOLN in 1860, South Carolina radicals induced the legislature to call a convention to consider secession. The convention voted unanimously for secession, and in the "Declaration of the Immediate Causes [of] Secession" (1860) they asserted that the free states had violated the constitutional compact by failing to enforce the Fugitive Slave Acts vigorously and by enacting PERSONAL LIBERTY LAWS that impeded the recapture of fugitive slaves. The free states also had denied slaveholders' right of transit through their territory with their slaves, agitated against slavery, tolerated abolitionist societies, and permitted dissemination of abolitionist propaganda. They had permitted blacks to vote and had elected a sectional presidential candidate determined to effect the eventual abolition of slavery. Thus South Carolina, in order to protect its people and its peculiar institution, severed the union binding it to the other states and reassumed its status as "a separate and independent state."

Though all slave states were deeply divided over the wisdom and constitutionality of secession, Mississippi, Florida, Alabama, Georgia, Louisiana, and Texas also seceded by February 1, 1861. These seven states formed the Confederate States of America in February. After the firing on Fort Sumter, Virginia, North Carolina, Tennessee, and Arkansas seceded. A proslavery rump session of the Missouri legislature and a convention of Kentucky Confederate soldiers declared their states seceded, but both states, as well as the other border slave states, remained in the Union. After the defeat of southern forces in 1865, most of the Confederate states repudiated secession, but diehards in South Carolina merely repealed their secession ordinance instead of nullifying it. Nonetheless, secession as a constitutional remedy was dead, and the United States was thenceforth "one nation, indivisible."

WILLIAM M. WIECEK
(1986)

SECOND AMENDMENT

However controversial the meaning of the Second Amendment is today, it was clear enough to the generation of 1789. The amendment assured to the people "their private arms," said an article which received JAMES MADISON's approval and was the only analysis available to Congress when it voted. Subsequent contemporaneous analysis is epitomized by the first American commentary on the writings of WILLIAM BLACKSTONE. Where Blackstone described arms for personal defense as among the "absolute rights of individuals" at COMMON LAW, his eighteenth-century American editor commented that this right had been constitutionalized by the Second Amendment. Early constitutional commentators, including JOSEPH STORY, William Rawle, and THOMAS M. COOLEY, described the amendment in terms of a republican philosophical tradition stemming from Aristotle's observation that basic to tyrants is a "mistrust of the people; hence they deprive them of arms." Political theorists from Cicero to JOHN LOCKE and Jean-Jacques Rousseau also held arms possession to be symbolic of personal freedom and vital to the virtuous, self-reliant citizenry (defending itself from encroachment by outlaws, tyrants, and foreign invaders alike) that they deemed indispensable to popular government.

These assumptions informed both sides of the debate over RATIFICATION OF THE CONSTITUTION. While Madison, in THE FEDERALIST #46 assured Americans that they need never fear the federal government because of "the advantage of being armed, which you possess over the people of almost every other nation," opponents of ratification such as PATRICK HENRY declaimed: "The great principle is that every man be armed. Everyone who is able may have a gun." SAMUEL ADAMS proposed that "the Constitution never be construed . . . to prevent the people of the United States who are peaceable citizens from keeping their own arms." As much of this debate used the word "militia," it is necessary to remember that in the eighteenth century the militia was coextensive with the adult male citizenry. By colonial law every household was required to possess arms and every male of military age was required to muster during military emergencies, bearing his own arms. The amendment, in guaranteeing the arms of each citizen, simultaneously guaranteed arms for the militia.

In contrast to the original interpretation of the amendment as a personal right to arms is the twentieth-century view that it protects only the states' right to arm their own military forces, including their national guard units. This view stresses the Anti-Federalists' bitter opposition to the provisions of Article I, section 8, authorizing a standing army and granting the federal government various powers over state militias. Both textual and historical difficulties preclude acceptance of this exclusively STATES' RIGHTS view. For instance, Madison's proposed organization for the provisions of the BILL OF RIGHTS was not to append them, but to interpolate each amendment into the Constitution following the provision to which it pertained. Had he viewed the amendment as modifying the military-militia clauses of the Constitution (which he strongly defended against Anti-Federalist criticism), he would have appended it to those clauses in section 8. Instead, he planned to place what are now the First and Second Amendments in Article I, section 9, along with the original Constitution's guarantees against BILLS OF ATTAINDER and EX POST FACTO LAWS and against suspension of HABEAS CORPUS.

The states' rights interpretation simply cannot be squared with the amendment's words: "right of the people." It is impossible to believe that the First Congress used "right of the people" in the FIRST AMENDMENT to describe an individual right (FREEDOM OF ASSEMBLY,) but sixteen words later in the Second Amendment to describe a right vested exclusively in the states. Moreover, "right of the people" is used again to refer to personal rights in the FOURTH AMENDMENT and the NINTH AMENDMENT, and the TENTH AMENDMENT expressly distinguishes "the people" from "the states."

Interpreting the Second Amendment as a guarantee of an individual right does not foreclose all GUN CONTROLS. The ownership of firearms by minors, felons, and the mentally impaired—and the carrying of them outside the home by anyone—may be limited or banned. Moreover, the government may limit the types of arms that may be kept; there is no right, for example, to own artillery or automatic weapons, or the weapons of the footpad and gangster, such as sawed-off shotguns and blackjacks. Gun controls in the form of registration and licensing requirements are also permissible so long as the ordinary citizen's right to possess arms for home protection is respected.

DON B. KATES, JR.
(1986)

Bibliography

HALBROOK, STEVEN 1984 *That Every Man Be Armed: The Evolution of a Constitutional Right.* Albuquerque: University of New Mexico Press.

KATES, DON B., JR. 1983 Handgun Prohibition and the Original Meaning of the Second Amendment. *Michigan Law Review* 82:204–273.

MALCOLM, JOYCE 1983 The Right of the People to Keep and Bear Arms: The Common Law Tradition. *Hastings Constitutional Law Quarterly* 10:285–314.

SHALHOPE, ROBERT E. 1982 The Ideological Origins of the Second Amendment. *Journal of American History* 69:599–614.

SECOND AMENDMENT
(Update)

The Second Amendment provides: "A well regulated Militia, being necessary to the security of a free State, the right of the people to keep and bear Arms, shall not be infringed." Like the Roman god Janus, the Second Amendment appears to have two faces, each casting its gaze in a different direction. For others, it may call up the different image of an Escher print. What one sees in the Second Amendment seems to change before one's eyes. Nor has anything the Supreme Court yet said about the Second Amendment resolved its uncertainty. After two centuries of judicial opportunity for the Court to speak, to say something reasonably definitive, virtually nothing significant has been settled or laid to rest.

The right to keep and bear arms, confirmed in the amendment, was confirmed as a general right. That is, the Second Amendment declares the right to keep and bear arms belongs to "the people," and not to some more limited class. Early authorities expressed no confusion or disagreement on this point. As the leading nineteenth-century treatise writer on the Constitution, THOMAS M. COOLEY, observed in 1880:

The [Second] [A]mendment, like most other provisions in the Constitution, has a history. It was adopted with some modification and enlargement from the English Bill of Rights of 1688. *The Right is General* [i.e., shared by all, rather than some particular class]. The meaning of the provision undoubtedly is, that the people, from whom the militia must be taken, shall have the right to keep and bear arms; and they need no permission or regulation of law for the purpose.

And as recently as 1994, after reviewing an even wider assortment of materials, historian Joyce Malcolm summarized her conclusions in agreement with Cooley's observations, further explaining the context and the manner in which the Second Amendment was framed:

> The Second Amendment was meant to accomplish two distinct goals, each perceived as crucial to the maintenance of liberty. First, it was meant to guarantee the individual's right to have arms for self-defence and self-preservation. Such an individual right was a legacy of the English Bill of Rights. The clause concerning the militia was not intended to limit ownership of arms to militia members, or return control of the militia to the states, but rather to express the preference for a militia over a standing army.

These views, shared by a majority of scholars, also accord with the views of Justice JOSEPH STORY. Indeed, in one respect, Story, who had been appointed to the Court by JAMES MADISON in 1811 and published his *Commentaries on the Constitution* in 1833, went further in emphasizing the foundational nature of the Second Amendment, with respect to the right of the people to have personal arms beyond reach of control by government, going so far as to declare:

> The right of the citizens to keep, and bear arms has justly been considered, as the palladium of the liberties of a republic; since it offers a strong check against the usurpation and arbitrary power of rulers; and will generally, even if these are successful in the first instance, enable the people to resist, and triumph over them.

The Second Amendment, in Story's view, was thus not a mere restatement of the desirability of a well-regulated militia, followed by an uncertain vague reference. The Second Amendment, rather, while strongly endorsing a well-regulated militia (in preference to the maintenance of a standing army), was also emphatically a restraint on the reach of government, even as Story observed was true of other clauses in the BILL OF RIGHTS. Nor was there any suggestion, from any source, at the time the amendment was under discussion or review, of some more strained or compromised view. It was only in subsequent decades that a vastly more restricted version of the Second Amendment came to be advanced.

In *United States v. Miller* (1939), in the course of upholding a federal statute forbidding interstate transportation of an unregistered short barrel ("sawed-off") shotgun, the Court construed the Second Amendment as inapplicable to the case, declaring that there was no evidence in the record that this type of arm was "any part of ordinary military equipment" that could "contribute to the common defense."

To be sure, the Court has gone no further since that time, nor did it, in *Miller*, attempt to define, or otherwise construe, the substantive right protected by the Second Amendment. It did, nevertheless, thus suggest that whatever the protection provided by the Second Amendment, it may apply only to such arms as could count as "ordinary military equipment," and, since *Miller*, it is widely assumed that this is so. Yet, it has been argued that there is no reason why the citizen's right to keep and bear arms should necessarily encompass all arms that might today be seen as a part of "ordinary military equipment," or why, in turn, the limited usefulness of a particular arm as part of ordinary military equipment should on that account strip it of all Second Amendment protection from government forfeiture or ban. But the subject has not been critically reexamined in the courts, and this holding in *Miller* currently stands.

Lower federal courts, however, have since 1939 gone far beyond anything suggested by the Court in *Miller*. They have seized upon the *Miller* case to reduce the amendment's scope nearly to the vanishing point. Indeed, an opinion as recent as July, 1997 from the United States Court of Appeals for the Eleventh Circuit illustrates the near collapse. In the view of the prevailing lower court judges, the Second Amendment is solely a restraint on Congress insofar as it might seek to forbid even those (few) persons in active training and service of an active state-regulated militia, to possess such military-style arms they are authorized to have as part of that training and service, but nothing more. These courts thus very narrowly construe the Second Amendment purely as a limited STATES' RIGHT amendment, claimable only by persons in active, controlled state guard or militia units, which units in fact are already under nearly complete federal control anyway, pursuant to powers vested in Congress in Article I, section 8 (clause 16 grants power to Congress to provide for "organizing, arming, and disciplining the Militia," and such "training" the states are authorized to provide, shall itself take place "according to the discipline prescribed by Congress").

The "reasoning" imputed to the Second Amendment by these courts is labored, but essentially this: That, without this amendment, Congress might have sought to justify the establishment of a permanent, large standing army, by prohibiting members of well-regulated state militias from possessing arms—albeit state militias already themselves heavily subject to national regulation and control. This is, of course, a possible "reading" of the Second Amendment, albeit a reading leaving it rather empty of substance, and giving it virtually no useful work to do. Still, it is a reading and source of real encouragement to growing numbers of citizens appalled by the high incidence of gun-related deaths in the United States. Whether it will be sustained by the Supreme Court remains to be seen.

WILLIAM W. VAN ALSTYNE
(2000)

SECONDARY BOYCOTT

See: Boycott

SECOND EMPLOYERS' LIABILITY CASES

See: Employers' Liability Cases

SECOND WORLD WAR

See: World War II

SECTION 1983, TITLE 42, UNITED STATES CODE
(Judicial Interpretation)

Few statutes have fluctuated in importance as wildly as section 1983. From near total disuse—twenty-one reported cases from 1871 to 1920—it became one of the most litigated provisions of federal law. This drastic change is attributable both to developments in constitutional law and to developments peculiar to section 1983.

Section 1983's ascension matches the twentieth-century expansion of constitutional rights. As originally enacted in the Civil Rights Act of 1871, section 1983 at most provided a cause of action for deprivations, under color of state law, of constitutional rights. Until relatively recently, citizens had few constitutional rights enforceable against the states. In section 1983's early years, the modern expansions of the EQUAL PROTECTION and DUE PROCESS clauses had not occurred, the STATE ACTION doctrine immunized a broad range of activity from constitutional scrutiny, and the FOURTH AMENDMENT was in the infancy of its constitutional development.

An ill-considered dichotomy between classes of constitutional rights also hindered section 1983's growth. In an influential separate opinion in HAGUE V. CIO (1939), Justice HARLAN FISKE STONE argued that section 1983's jurisdictional counterpart, section 1343(3), should be interpreted to authorize federal courts to hear cases involving personal rights but not to hear cases involving mere property rights. This view influenced many courts' interpretations of section 1983 itself, again with limiting effect. In *Lynch v. Household Finance Corporation* (1972) the Court rejected the personal rightsproperty rights distinction. Paradoxically, a similar dichotomy between personal interests and economic interests continues to shape, indeed govern, interpretation of the equal protection clause.

Section 1983's text generated interpretive problems

that might have hindered its widespread use even if the Constitution had enjoyed a broader scope. As enacted, section 1983 protected "rights, privileges or immunities" secured by the Constitution. Its scope therefore depended upon what were viewed as rights, privileges, or immunities secured by the Constitution. Until the SLAUGHTERHOUSE CASES (1873), one might have thought the rights, privileges, or immunities so secured simply to be all constitutional rights. But the *Slaughterhouse Cases* narrowly interpreted the FOURTEENTH AMENDMENT's privileges or immunities clause to protect only a small subclass of constitutional rights. Some courts adopted a similar interpretation of section 1983. In addition, section 1983 reaches only deprivations "under color of" state law. Not until well into the twentieth century was it clearly recognized that behavior not authorized by state law might constitute action under COLOR OF LAW. A narrowly construed Constitution, the shadow cast by the *Slaughterhouse Cases*, the state action doctrine, and section 1983's text combined to minimize section 1983's importance.

In the 1920s, section 1983 provided actions for some deprivations of VOTING RIGHTS. Perhaps the Court relied on the section when, in NIXON V. HERNDON (1927), it allowed a damage action to go forward against state officials. In *Lane v. Wilson* (1939), another voting rights case, the Court expressly referred to section 1983 in approving a damage action. But these cases did not erode the important limitations on section 1983.

The erosion process commenced with early twentieth-century cases that construed state action to include some actions taken in violation of state law, and with EX PARTE YOUNG (1908), which held that the ELEVENTH AMENDMENT does not bar injunctive actions against state officials. In the 1940s, criminal CIVIL RIGHTS decisions also interpreted the phrase "under color of" law to include some unauthorized action. MONROE V. PAPE (1961) capped the process by interpreting section 1983 to protect at least all constitutional rights embodied in the Fourteenth Amendment and by holding the color of law requirement in section 1983 to be satisfied by the unauthorized action of police officers. *Monroe*, together with the wide expansion of constitutional rights of the 1950s and 1960s, assured section 1983's importance.

But section 1983's growth triggered a reaction, one that began with *Monroe* itself. If every constitutional violation generated a cause of action for damages there must be limits as to when defendants actually would be held liable. In *Monroe*, the Court, giving a questionable reading to section 1983's history, held that the section was not meant to render cities liable for constitutional violations. This limitation survived until MONELL V. DEPARTMENT OF SOCIAL SERVICES (1978), when the Court held that cities may be liable under section 1983 but that, in yet another questionable reading of the section's history, Congress did not intend cities to be liable for acts of city officials unless the acts constituted "official policy," a phrase destined to be the subject of much litigation. The reaction also includes some sentiment to impose an EXHAUSTION OF REMEDIES requirement in one or more classes of section 1983 cases.

With respect to individual defendants, the Court in a series of cases read into section 1983 an array of LEGISLATIVE, JUDICIAL, prosecutorial and EXECUTIVE IMMUNITIES. And in QUERN V. JORDAN (1979) the Court held that section 1983 was not meant to abrogate the Eleventh Amendment immunity of states. In OWEN V. CITY OF INDEPENDENCE (1980), however, the Court declined to extend to municipalities the good faith defense available to executive officials. The reaction to section 1983's expansion may also encompass a series of cases, including *Parratt v. Taylor* (1981), PAUL V. DAVIS (1976), INGRAHAM V. WRIGHT (1977), and *Estelle v. Gamble* (1976), narrowly interpreting constitutional rights. If a private cause of action accompanies every constitutional right, the Court may be hesitant to "constitutionalize" many rights. Finally, the Court held in *Carey v. Piphus* (1978) that a violation of PROCEDURAL DUE PROCESS, standing alone, will not support a substantial recovery of damages; to recover more than nominal damages a plaintiff in such a case must show actual harm. The Court left open the question whether this rule would apply to other types of constitutional violation.

For many years, courts disagreed over whether section 1983 provided a cause of action for violations of federal statutes by state officials. The REVISED STATUTES of 1874, which were not supposed to make substantive changes in the law, expanded section 1983's wording to include "laws." Over a century later, in *Maine v. Thiboutot* (1980), the Court interpreted section 1983 to provide a cause of action for at least some federal statutory claims.

THEODORE EISENBERG
(1986)

Bibliography

EISENBERG, THEODORE   1981   *Civil Rights Legislation.* Charlottesville, Va.: Michie Co.
———   1982   Section 1983: Doctrinal Foundations and an Empirical Study. *Cornell Law Review* 67:482–556.
FRIENDLY, HENRY J.   1973   *Federal Jurisdiction: A General View* Pp. 87–107. New York: Columbia University Press.
NAMHOD, SHELDON H.   1979   *Civil Rights & Civil Liberties Litigation.* Colorado Springs, Colo.: Shepard's.
NOTE   1977   Developments in the Law: Section 1983 and Federalism. *Harvard Law Review* 90:1133–1361.

SECURITIES LAW
AND THE CONSTITUTION

Following the 1929 stockmarket crash and the ensuing economic depression, Congress enacted the Securities Act of 1933 and the Securities Exchange Act of 1934 to restore investor confidence and provide for more efficient securities markets. Although both disclosure and regulatory provisions of the two statutes were challenged during the 1930s on constitutional grounds, the lower federal courts consistently held that both statutes were within Congress's power to regulate INTERSTATE COMMERCE and did not violate any other constitutional guarantees. In *Electric Bond & Share Co. v. Securities and Exchange Commission* (1937) the Supreme Court rejected constitutional attacks on certain provisions of the PUBLIC UTILITY HOLDING COMPANY ACT similar to the disclosure and registration requirements of the 1933 and 1934 acts, although the Court did not discuss the general validity of federal securities regulation.

Because both the states and the federal government regulate the securities markets, the Supreme Court has periodically undertaken to define the relationship between federal and state regulatory schemes by interpreting federal securities statutes. The first such case to raise constitutional questions of FEDERALISM grew out of the dramatic increase in hostile corporate takeover attempts in the late 1960s. In 1968 and 1970 Congress amended the 1934 act by adding certain provisions, known as the Williams Act, to regulate tender offers. A number of states immediately adopted takeover statutes of their own, presumably in order to protect local businesses from hostile takeovers. Because the state statutes gave more protection to target companies than did the Williams Act, tender offerors immediately challenged the state statutes as either invalid under the COMMERCE CLAUSE or preempted by the Williams Act.

In *Edgar v. Mite Corporation* (1982) the Supreme Court held that the Illinois takeover statute impermissibly burdened interstate commerce because the statute's nationwide reach significantly interfered with the economic benefits of tender offers while providing few benefits to Illinois. The Court's opinion was limited to the commerce clause holding, although three Justices also argued that the Williams Act preempted the Illinois regulatory scheme. A number of similar state takeover laws have subsequently been invalidated by lower federal courts on either commerce clause or PREEMPTION grounds.

Recent constitutional developments have suggested the possibility of FIRST AMENDMENT restraints on the disclosure aspects of securities regulation. Both the 1933 and 1934 acts regulate extensively the speech of corporate issuers and securities professionals by mandating some disclosures, prohibiting others, and by policing the content of various disclosure documents, all in the interest of preventing securities fraud, facilitating corporate suffrage, and providing investors with full and accurate information about securities and the securities markets. In VIRGINIA STATE BOARD OF PHARMACY V. VIRGINIA CITIZENS CONSUMER

COUNCIL (1976) the Court extended First Amendment protection to COMMERCIAL SPEECH, and in FIRST NATIONAL BANK OF BOSTON V. BELLOTTI (1978) the Court confirmed that corporate speakers could claim the benefits of the First Amendment. In CENTRAL HUDSON GAS & ELECTRIC CORP. V. PUBLIC SERVICE COMMISSION (1980) the Court indicated that while misleading commercial speech may be regulated, remedies must be "no broader than reasonably necessary to prevent the deception."

In 1985, the Supreme Court confronted the question of First Amendment constraints on federal securities regulation. In *Lowe v. Securities and Exchange Commission* the petitioner argued that First Amendment notions of prior restraint barred the SEC from enjoining publication of petitioner's securities newsletter under the Investment Advisers Act of 1940 after petitioner's investment adviser registration was revoked because of his illegal conduct. The Court avoided the First Amendment issue by holding that the petitioner was the publisher of a "bona fide newspaper" and thus statutorily exempt from regulation under the 1940 act. Justices BYRON R. WHITE and WILLIAM H. REHNQUIST and Chief Justice WARREN E. BURGER concurred in the result but argued that the First Amendment question should have been reached and decided. They indicated that the total bar on publication required by the 1940 act was too drastic a remedy for possibly deceptive speech, whether that speech was fully protected or merely commercial speech.

Although many of the disclosure provisions of the 1933 and 1934 acts presumably satisfy the *Central Hudson* tests, those aspects of both statutes requiring prepublication clearance of disclosure by the SEC or limiting informational activities by securities professionals may be regarded as sweeping too broadly to meet First Amendment requirements. In some areas, moreover, as in the application of the proxy rules to corporate and shareholder speech concerning issues of social and political significance, corporate speech may be entitled to full First Amendment protection. All these issues remain to be raised in the courts.

ALISON GREY ANDERSON
(1986)

SEDITION

Sedition is a comprehensive term for offenses against the authority of the government not amounting to TREASON. Such offenses might include the spreading of disaffection or disloyalty, conspiracy to commit insurrection, or any SUBVERSIVE ACTIVITY. Sedition tends toward treason, but does not reach the constitutionally defined offense of "levying war against the United States or adhering to their enemies, giving them aid and comfort."

Historically, the broad category of "sedition" has comprised several kinds of activity, although there has not always been consistency about which constituted criminal offenses. SEDITIOUS LIBEL, the uttering of words bringing the government or its officers into ridicule or disrepute, was an offense at COMMON LAW and under the ALIEN AND SEDITION ACTS of 1798. Seditious membership, that is, active, knowing, and purposeful membership in an organization committed to the overthrow of the government by unlawful means, is an offense under the Smith Act. Seditious advocacy, the public promotion of insurrection or rebellion, and seditious conspiracy, combining with others to subvert the government, violate several statutory provisions; but those offenses must be very carefully defined lest the statutes exert a CHILLING EFFECT on legitimate criticism of government.

The possibility of sedition poses a particular problem for constitutional democracy. Democratic governments, no less than any other kind, need to protect themselves against seditious activity. But measures taken in self-defense must not be so broad in their scope as themselves to become a threat to individual liberty. In the United States, the FIRST AMENDMENT to the Constitution protects FREEDOM OF THE PRESS, and FREEDOM OF ASSEMBLY AND ASSOCIATION; these specific constitutional guarantees limit the power of Congress and of the states to legislate against sedition.

For most of American history, the national and state governments exercised a CONCURRENT POWER to define and punish sedition. The power of Congress to legislate against sedition does not derive from any of the specific ENUMERATED POWERS, but is NECESSARY AND PROPER for the carrying out of several of them. In PENNSYLVANIA V. NELSON (1956) the Supreme Court held that Congress, by enacting a pervasive scheme of regulation, had preempted the field of legislation concerning sedition against the United States.

DENNIS J. MAHONEY
(1986)

SEDITION ACT
40 Stat. 553 (1918)

As WORLD WAR I progressed, enthusiastic war supporters argued more and more that the ESPIONAGE ACT OF 1917 did not adequately restrict domestic critics of the war effort. Advocates of additional restriction argued that weakness of the existing loyalty legislation forced citizens to take the law into their own hands. If firmer federal policies could be established, such distasteful forms of repression might be averted. Thus a more restrictive amendment to the Espionage Act was proposed and, despite strong congressional protest that the measure virtually terminated freedom of expression, was signed into law on May 16,

1918. The amendment, called the Sedition Act, defined eight offenses punishable by $10,000 fine or more than twenty years in prison, or both. The new offenses included: uttering, printing, writing, or publishing any disloyal, profane, scurrilous, or abusive language intended to cause contempt, scorn, contumely or disrepute as regards the form of government of the United States, or the Constitution, or the flag, or the uniform or the Army or Navy, or any language intended to incite resistance to the United States or to promote the cause of its enemies; urging any curtailment of production or anything necessary to the prosecution of the war with intent to hinder its prosecution; advocating, teaching, defending, or suggesting the doing of any of these acts; and words or acts supporting or favoring the cause of any country at war with the United States, or opposing the cause of the United States therein.

The 1918 act also enlarged the censorship functions of the postmaster general, empowering him to refuse to deliver mail to any individual or business employing the mails in violation of the statute. He was to order a letter that he deemed undeliverable to be returned to the sender with the phrase "Mail to this address undeliverable under the Espionage Act" stamped on the envelope. Thus the postmaster general was empowered to damage or destroy the business or reputation of any American citizen.

Enforced extensively in the period from May to November 1918, the measure virtually terminated wartime criticism until the Armistice. While efforts were made to reenact its provisions in a peace-time sedition statute during the A. MITCHELL PALMER "red scare" period, Congress balked and ultimately took the act off the books in March 1921.

The extremely broad language of the act would today make it vulnerable to attack on the grounds of OVERBREADTH. In 1919, however, the Supreme Court upheld the conviction of five anarchists for circulating a leaflet urging curtailment of war production and encouraging resistance to the participation of U.S. forces in opposition to the Russian revolution. Justice OLIVER WENDELL HOLMES wrote a famous dissent, joined by Justice LOUIS D. BRANDEIS, in ABRAMS V. UNITED STATES (1919). (See CLEAR AND PRESENT DANGER.)

PAUL L. MURPHY
(1986)

Bibliography

MURPHY, PAUL L. 1979 *World War I and the Origin of Civil Liberties in the United States.* New York: Norton.

SEDITIOUS LIBEL

Though its scope has varied greatly with time and place, the heart of the doctrine of seditious libel is the proposition that government may punish its critics for words it perceives as a threat to its survival. The offending words may be criticism of the government itself, or, more often, of its leaders. What constitutes seditious libel tends to be whatever the government fears most at the time. In fifteenth-century England, where reverence for the crown was considered essential to the safety of the realm, it was a crime to call the king a fool or to predict his death. In colonial America the most frequent offense was criticizing local representatives of the crown. In 1798, the Federalist party feared that Jeffersonian attacks would so undermine public confidence that the fledgling Republic would fall— or at least that the Federalists would lose the election of 1800. They therefore made it a crime to publish any false, scandalous, and malicious writing about either house of Congress or the President of the United States.

In England, seditious libels were once prosecuted as treason, punishable by death. Thus in 1663 William Twyn, who printed a book endorsing the right of revolution, was hanged, emasculated, disemboweled, quartered, and beheaded. Not until the eighteenth century did the law clearly distinguish seditious libel from treason; the latter then was confined to cases in which the seditious words were accompanied by some overt act. Seditious libel became a misdemeanor, punishable by fines, imprisonment, and the pillory. Prosecutions were common in England until the mid-nineteenth century.

Seditious libel was part of the received law in the American colonies, but it was received unenthusiastically. There probably were no more than a dozen seditious libel prosecutions in the entire colonial period, and few were successful. Although no one seems to have doubted that government should have some power to protect itself from verbal attacks, many complained that the doctrine as it had evolved in England allowed legitimate criticism to be swept within the ambit of the seditious libel proscription. The law allowed no defense of truth; the objective was to preserve respect for government, to which truthful criticism was an even greater threat than falsehood. And because the interests to be protected were the government's, it would hardly do to let a jury decide whether the words were actionable. The judges therefore kept for themselves the power to determine whether the speaker's intent was seditious; the jury was only allowed to decide whether he had uttered the words charged.

As ideas of POPULAR SOVEREIGNTY grew, critics on both sides of the Atlantic attacked these rules. In America the issue jelled in the 1735 trial of John Peter Zenger, a New York printer who had criticized the royal governor. Zenger's lawyer, Andrew Hamilton, argued that he should be allowed to defend Zenger by proving the truth of the publication, and that the jury should be allowed to decide whether the words were libelous. The judge rejected both arguments, but the jury acquitted Zenger anyway, even though he had admitted publishing the words. (See ZENGER'S CASE.)

The case made popular heroes of Zenger and Hamilton and destroyed the effectiveness of seditious libel law as a tool for English control of American dissent. There were few, if any, successful common law prosecutions in the colonies after *Zenger*. Colonial legislatures sometimes punished their critics for breaches of "parliamentary privilege," but public resentment eventually made this device ineffective, too.

The intended effect of the FIRST AMENDMENT on the law of seditious libel is still in dispute. It is clear that seditious libel was still the law in 1789, and that the Framers expressed no intent to preclude prosecutions for seditious libel. They certainly did not intend to prevent the states from prosecuting seditious libels; all agreed that the First Amendment was a limitation on federal power only. And within a decade, Congress passed the Sedition Act of 1798, under which the Federalists prosecuted a number of prominent Republican editors. Several Justices of the Supreme Court, sitting as circuit judges, enforced the act. This evidence has persuaded some modern scholars that the Framers had no intention of abolishing seditious libel.

Others have argued that the Framers had at least a nascent understanding that some freedom to criticize government was a prerequisite to self-government, and that England's rigorous concept of seditious libel was inconsistent with that need. Their failure explicitly to condemn it might be explained by the fact that seditious libel prosecutions had not been a serious threat in their lifetimes. The Sedition Act may have been an unprincipled effort by desperate Federalist partisans to keep control of the government, rather than a considered affirmation of the constitutionality of seditious libel.

The Supreme Court has never squarely held that the First Amendment forbids punishment of seditious libels. From WORLD WAR I through the McCarthy era, state and federal governments prosecuted numerous anarchists, socialists, and communists for advocating draft resistance, mass strikes, or overthrow of the government. Although the statutes authorizing these prosecutions were not called seditious libel acts, they had much the same effect. The Court generally upheld these convictions (usually over the dissents of the more libertarian Justices) until the 1960s, when in BRANDENBURG V. OHIO (1969) it adopted the view that punishment of mere advocacy is unconstitutional unless it is intended to produce imminent lawless action and is likely to do so.

Garrison v. Louisiana (1964) closely resembled a traditional seditious libel prosecution. A district attorney had been convicted of criminal libel for accusing local judges of laziness and corruption. The Court reversed his conviction, but implied that the prosecution might have been permissible if the state had proved that the defendant spoke with reckless disregard of the truth or falsity of his statements.

Nevertheless, the judgment of history is that seditious libel laws are inconsistent with FREEDOM OF SPEECH and FREEDOM OF THE PRESS. JAMES MADISON and THOMAS JEFFERSON argued in 1799 that the Sedition Act was unconstitutional. Justice OLIVER WENDELL HOLMES, dissenting in ABRAMS V. UNITED STATES (1919), wrote, "I wholly disagree with the argument of the Government that the First Amendment left the common law as to seditious libel in force. . . . I had conceived that the United States through many years had shown its repentance for the Sedition Act . . . by repaying the fines that it imposed." And in NEW YORK TIMES V. SULLIVAN (1964) the Court said, "Although the Sedition Act was never tested in this Court, the attack upon its validity has carried the day in the court of history."

DAVID A. ANDERSON
(1986)

(SEE ALSO: *Alien and Sedition Acts.*)

Bibliography
ANDERSON, DAVID A. 1983 The Origins of the Press Clause. *UCLA Law Review* 30:455–537.
LEVY, LEONARD W. 1984 *Emergence of a Free Press.* New York: Oxford University Press.
NELSON, HAROLD L. 1959 Seditious Libel in Colonial America. *American Journal of Legal History* 3:160–172.

SEEGER, UNITED STATES v.
380 U.S. 163 (1965)

At issue in the *Seeger* case was Section 6(j) of the Universal Military Training and Service Act. Originally enacted in 1940, the act exempted those who, as a matter of "religious training and belief," were opposed to participation in a war. In 1948, Congress amended this provision and defined religious belief as "an individual's belief in a relation to a supreme being involving duties superior to those arising from any human relation, but [not including] essentially political, sociological, or philosophical views. . . ."

Despite the textual evidence of a congressional intent to condition exemption on the theistic belief, Justice TOM C. CLARK, for the Supreme Court, interpreted the provision as requiring only a sincere and meaningful belief occupying in the life of its possessor a place parallel to that filled by the belief in God of those admittedly qualified for the exemption. Seeger had argued that if section 6(j) granted exemptions only on the basis of conventional theistic belief, it amounted to an ESTABLISHMENT OF RELIGION. Facing the unattractive alternatives of finding section 6(j) unconstitutional or reading it in a sufficiently broad fashion so as to secularize the exemption, the majority chose the latter.

RICHARD E. MORGAN
(1986)

(SEE ALSO: *Conscientious Objection.*)

SEGREGATION

From the beginning, RACIAL DISCRIMINATION in America has been a national phenomenon. Jim Crow was a southern name for the segregation of the races as part of a system of caste. But segregation antedated Jim Crow, and it began in the North and the West. The leading judicial decision upholding school segregation before the CIVIL WAR bears a name Northerners prefer to forget: ROBERTS V. BOSTON (1850). Blacks were either excluded entirely from PUBLIC ACCOMMODATIONS such as hotels, railroads, and theaters, or given separate accommodations. They were segregated in prisons and in churches. Several northern and western states even sought to bar the immigration of blacks; such a legal provision was adopted by Oregon voters by an eight-to-one margin.

Nor has this country's segregation been limited to blacks. As late as 1947, a federal court of appeals held that the segregation of Chicano children in a school district in California was invalid. The decision's ground was itself depressing: the state's statute authorized only the segregation of children whose ancestry was Indian, Chinese, Japanese, and Mongolian.

Still, it was the postabolition South that carried the segregation of the races to its fullest development, and blacks were the chief victims of the practice. Before slavery was abolished, of course, the dominance of whites was assured without any call for segregation. After abolition, the southern states adopted severe legal restrictions on blacks, which served to maintain white supremacy. (See BLACK CODES.) When the CIVIL RIGHTS ACT OF 1866 and the FOURTEENTH AMENDMENT not only ended these legal restrictions but also positively declared the CITIZENSHIP of the freed slaves, segregation was the southern response. By 1870, Tennessee had forbidden interracial marriages (see MISCEGENATION) and later came the "Jim Crow car" laws segregating railroad passenger seating.

Segregation was not, however, merely a creature of state legislation. It also resulted from private action: a hotel would refuse to take black guests; homeowners in a neighborhood would agree not to sell to black buyers. In such cases law played a role that was less obvious on the surface of events but was vital nonetheless. A black who sought the aid of the state courts in overcoming private discrimination would simply be turned away; state laws would deny any remedy.

Late in the nineteenth century, the Supreme Court gave its support to this system of interlocking discriminations. In the CIVIL RIGHTS CASES (1883), the Court held invalid a congressional statute forbidding racial discrimination by railroads, hotels, theaters, and restaurants. (See STATE ACTION.) And in PLESSY V. FERGUSON (1896) the Court upheld a Jim Crow car law against an EQUAL PROTECTION attack. (See SEPARATE BUT EQUAL DOCTRINE.) By the early twentieth century, the South was racially segregated to extremes that were at once tragic and ludicrous: separate telephone booths for blacks in Oklahoma; separate storage for textbooks used by black children in North Carolina and Florida schools; separate elevators for blacks in Atlanta; separate Bibles for swearing black witnesses in Georgia courts. The point of all this was nothing less than the denial to blacks of membership in a white-dominated society—the denial of citizenship itself, in defiance of the Fourteenth Amendment.

Some of the harms caused by racial segregation are harms to material interests: a black is denied accommodation at a hotel, or admission to a state university medical school (and thus to the medical profession), or the chance to live in a particular neighborhood or be a factory foreman. These material harms are serious, but the worst harms of segregation are psychic harms. The primary reason for segregating railroad passengers, of course, is to symbolize a caste system. The stigma of inferiority is a denial of a person's humanity, and the result is anguish and humiliation. The more the races are separated, the more natural it is for members of the dominant white race to see each black person not as an individual but simply as a black. Ralph Ellison, in his novel *Invisible Man* (1952), makes the point: "I am invisible, understand, simply because people refuse to see me. . . . When they approach me they see only my surroundings, themselves, or figments of their imagination—indeed, everything and anything except me. . . . You ache with the need to convince yourself that you do exist in the real world." To be a citizen, on the other hand, is to be respected as a person and recognized as a participating member in the society.

Jim Crow was a complex living system, and its dismantling would be no simple task. The field of segregation in housing exemplifies the difficulties. The NAACP's first major victory against segregation came in BUCHANAN V. WARLEY (1917), when the Supreme Court struck down a local ZONING ordinance aimed at maintaining segregated residential neighborhoods. But the decision by no means ended housing segregation, which continued as a result of private conduct. When the private discrimination was sufficiently connected with state action, as in the case of racially RESTRICTIVE COVENANTS enforced by state courts, the Fourteenth Amendment was an effective weapon against residential segregation. (See SHELLEY V. KRAEMER.) But in the absence of such state support, a landowner might simply refuse to rent or sell to blacks, and the would-be buyers would be without remedy. Two events in 1968 altered this portion of the doctrinal landscape. In JONES V. ALFRED H. MAYER CO. the Supreme Court concluded that the Civil Rights Act of 1866 forbade private discrimination in the sale of property. In the same year, Congress adopted a comprehensive fair housing law as part of the CIVIL RIGHTS ACT OF 1968. The new law forbade various forms of racial discrimination by lenders and brokers as well as private landlords and sellers. The combination of constitutional litigation and legislation aimed at ending housing segregation had achieved a radical restructuring of the law.

The restructuring of racial patterns in the neighborhoods where people live, however, has proved to be quite another matter. Middle-class blacks have largely left the core cities to live in suburbs, but the degree of racial segregation in residences has changed only slightly since 1940. The term "white flight," coined in the context of school desegregation, seems even more clearly applicable to residential patterns. It is hard to find stable interracial neighborhoods in any large city in the country, at any income level. (For discussion of related questions concerning the public schools—where continued patterns of segregation are related directly to residential segregation—see DESEGREGATION.)

In contrast, racial segregation in transportation and other public accommodations has come to an end. (See SIT-IN; CIVIL RIGHTS ACT OF 1964.) And laws forbidding interracial marriage collapsed under the double weight of equal protection and DUE PROCESS in LOVING V. VIRGINIA (1967). (See FREEDOM OF INTIMATE ASSOCIATION.) Employment discrimination, too, is in retreat—including the segregation of job categories by race—as a result of enforcement of the fair employment portions of the 1964 Act.

The segregation that remains in American society, then, is chiefly residential segregation—with its concomitant, a substantial extent of separation of the races in the public schools. There is irony here: the decision in the school segregation case, BROWN V. BOARD OF EDUCATION (1954), was the critical event in the demise of Jim Crow, but our big city schools are the one set of public institutions in which the races remain largely separated. Yet *Brown*'s impact on American life was important. The decision began more than a doctrinal movement; its implicit affirmation of the equal citizenship of all our people accelerated forces that have markedly changed not only race relations but also a wide range of other relationships formerly characterized by dominance and dependency.

It is easy now to see the social and economic changes in the country that permitted the success of the movement to end officially sponsored segregation. WORLD WAR II was the great watershed. By the time the war began, there was a critical mass of educated blacks, enough to provide a national movement not only with its great chiefs but with local leadership as well—and with a trained cadre of lawyers. The war produced waves of migration of blacks out of the rural South and into the cities of the North and West, where they very soon found a political voice. In part, too, the war had been billed as a war against Nazi racism—whatever we might be doing on the home front. (See JAPANESE AMERICAN CASES.) The expected postwar depression failed to appear, and the 1950s and 1960s were a time of economic expansion, conducive to a sympathetic reception for egalitarian claims. All this is familiar learning. Yet in the early 1950s there was no sense of inevitability surrounding the assault on segregation. If the sudden collapse of Jim Crow now seems inevitable, that in itself is a measure of the distance we have come. And if the end of segregation did not end a system of racial caste, that is a measure of the distance we have yet to travel.

KENNETH L. KARST
(1986)

Bibliography

BELL, DERRICK 1980 *Brown v. Board of Education* and the Interest-Convergence Dilemma. *Harvard Law Review* 93: 518–533.

LEVY, LEONARD W. and JONES, DOUGLAS 1972 Jim Crow Education: Origins of the "Separate but Equal" Doctrine. In Leonard W. Levy, *Judgments: Essays on American Constitutional History.* Chicago: Quadrangle Books.

LITWACK, LEON F. 1961 *North of Slavery.* Chicago: University of Chicago Press.

MYRDAL, GUNNAR 1944 *An American Dilemma.* New York: Harper & Brothers.

WOODWARD, C. VANN 1966 *The Strange Career of Jim Crow,* 2nd rev. ed. New York: Oxford University Press.

SEIZURE

See: Fourth Amendment; Search and Seizure

SELDEN, JOHN
(1584–1654)

A jurist, antiquary, and occasional member of Parliament, John Selden wrote extensively on the history of English law. With Sir EDWARD COKE he championed individual liberties and helped frame the PETITION OF RIGHT. He contended that Parliament's rights were secured by COMMON LAW and not enjoyed at the Crown's discretion.

DAVID GORDON
(1986)

SELECTIVE CONSCIENTIOUS OBJECTION

See: Conscientious Objection

SELECTIVE DRAFT LAW CASES
Arver v. United States
245 U.S. 366 (1918)

In 1917, Congress authorized CONSCRIPTION as a means of rapidly increasing the strength of the armed forces. All males between twenty-one and thirty were to register for the draft, and up to one million were selectively to be called up. The six petitioners were all convicted of failure to register.

A unanimous Supreme Court, speaking through Chief Justice EDWARD D. WHITE, rejected each of several constitutional arguments against the draft law. Since the power to raise armies is specifically granted, the Court held that Congress might adopt any means necessary to call the required number of men into service. Compulsion might be used since "a governmental power which has no sanction to it . . . is in no substantial sense a power." A number of ingenious arguments based on the historic nature and uses of the militia were rejected because the power to raise armies is distinct from the militia clause.

For the argument that conscription violated the THIRTEENTH AMENDMENT, White had only eloquent scorn: "We are unable to conceive upon what theory the exaction by the government from the citizen of his supreme and noble duty of contributing to the defense of the rights and honor of the nation . . . can be said to be the imposition of involuntary servitude."

DENNIS J. MAHONEY
(1986)

SELECTIVE EXCLUSIVENESS

Selective exclusiveness, or the *Cooley* doctrine, derives from the opinion of Justice BENJAMIN R. CURTIS for the Supreme Court in COOLEY V. BOARD OF PORT WARDENS (1852). Before that case, conflict and confusion characterized the Court's decisions in COMMERCE CLAUSE cases. Some

Justices believed that Congress's power to regulate interstate and FOREIGN COMMERCE was an EXCLUSIVE POWER and others that the states shared CONCURRENT POWER over commerce. Some believed that a distinction existed between the national power over commerce and the STATE POLICE POWER.

Cooley provided a compromise doctrine that transformed judicial thinking. The Court recognized that commerce embraces a vast field of diverse subjects, some demanding a single uniform rule that only Congress might make, and others best served by state regulations based on local needs and differences. Thus the doctrine treated congressional power as exclusive on a selective basis—in only those cases requiring uniform legislation; and the states shared a concurrent power in other cases. In cases of conflict, of course, congressional action would prevail.

The *Cooley* formulation necessarily failed to provide a means by which the Court could discern which subjects were national and which local. Accordingly the Justices were able to manipulate the doctrine to sustain or invalidate state legislation as they wished. In time, judicial analysis focused on the purposes of the legislation and the degree to which it adversely affected the flow of commerce, rather than on the nature of the subject regulated. No formulation could diminish the free play of judicial discretion.

LEONARD W. LEVY
(1986)

Bibliography

FRANKFURTER, FELIX   1937   *The Commerce Clause under Marshall, Taney, and Waite.* Chapel Hill: University of North Carolina Press.

SELECTIVE INCORPORATION

See: Incorporation Doctrine

SELECTIVE PROSECUTION

See: Prosecutorial Discretion and
Its Constitutional Limits

SELECTIVE SERVICE ACT
40 Stat. 76 (1917)

In the National Defense Act of 1916, the General Staff prepared a blueprint for increasing the military, but it failed to recruit adequate personnel through a voluntary system. With war declared, President WOODROW WILSON in April 1917 sent to Congress a bill to "Authorize the President to Increase Temporarily the Military Establishment." After a six-week debate, the Selective Service Act of 1917 was enacted. The measure vested the President with the power to raise an army by CONSCRIPTION. Enrollment and selection were to be carried out by 4,000 local civilian boards, appointed by the President and organized under federally appointed state directors. Although these boards operated under uniform federal regulations, they were given considerable discretion in meeting quotas and handling deferment applications. The manpower requirements for the war period were developed by the army General Staff and apportioned to the states. The order of induction was determined by lottery. Over twenty-four million American males were registered under the law. Nearly three million were selected and inducted.

The constitutionality of the law was early challenged by its opponents on the grounds of illegal DELEGATION OF POWER and a violation of the THIRTEENTH, Fifth, TENTH, and FIRST AMENDMENTS. The Supreme Court brushed aside such challenges in the SELECTIVE DRAFT LAW CASES (1918), determining that the powers of the central government to make war and support armies encompass the authority to impose compulsory military service.

PAUL M. MURPHY
(1986)

Bibliography

DUGGAN, JOSEPH S. 1946 *Legislative and Statutory Development of the Federal Concept of Conscription for Military Service.* Washington: Catholic University Press.

SELECTIVE SERVICE ACTS
Conscription Act
12 Stat. 731 (1863)
Burke-Wadsworth Selective Training and
Service Act
54 Stat. 885 (1940)
Universal Military Training and Service Act
62 Stat. 604 (1948)

The Constitution gives Congress the power to "raise and support armies" and to "provide and maintain a navy." The traditions of the American people have dictated that throughout most of our history peacetime military service has been voluntary and emergencies have been met, in the first instance, by activating the organized state militias. Conscription, drafting men for compulsory military duty, is available for the gravest emergencies. During the War of 1812, Congress considered, but did not adopt, a Draft Bill.

The first federal military draft in American history was

authorized by the Conscription Act of 1863. That act required registration of all able-bodied male citizens eighteen to forty-five years old, and provided that whenever a congressional district failed to provide its quota of volunteers the deficiency should be made up by drawing from the pool of registrants. The act further provided that the draftee could avoid service by providing a substitute or by paying $300. The first draft under the act, in July 1863, was the occasion of a week-long riot in New York City, in which over one thousand people were killed and over one-and-a-half million dollars worth of property was destroyed.

The first peacetime selective service law was the Burke-Wadsworth Act of 1940, requiring registration in anticipation of American entry into WORLD WAR II. The act, also known as the Selective Training and Service Act, was patterned after the SELECTIVE SERVICE ACT OF 1917: universal registration and classification administered by local boards. The 1940 act expired in 1947 and was replaced by the Universal Military Training and Service Act of 1948, which continued the basic scheme of the 1917 and 1940 statutes. The first draft under this act was in 1950, and conscription for the KOREAN WAR and VIETNAM WAR was done under provisions of that act. Registration under the act (renamed the Military Selective Service Act in 1967) ceased in 1975.

President JIMMY CARTER in 1980 sought and received congressional authorization to reimplement peacetime draft registration, but the 1980 measure provided for registration only, not for classification or conscription. (See ROSTKER V. GOLDBERG.)

DENNIS J. MAHONEY
(1986)

SELF-INCRIMINATION

See: Right Against Self-Incrimination

SEMINOLE TRIBE v. FLORIDA

See: Eleventh Amendment; Federalism;
Sovereign Immunity

SENATE

The United States Senate resulted from the decision of the CONSTITUTIONAL CONVENTION OF 1787 to replace the unicameral legislature that had functioned under the ARTICLES OF CONFEDERATION with a bicameral Congress. BICAMERALISM reflected the existing structure of the British Parliament and most of the state legislatures. The VIRGINIA PLAN originally proposed that the larger, popularly elected

HOUSE OF REPRESENTATIVES elect the smaller "second house," but the convention ultimately assigned the election of senators to the state legislatures. On the issue of representation, the Convention reached an impasse between delegates from larger states, who wanted both houses of Congress apportioned according to population, and those from smaller states, who demanded equal status. The GREAT COMPROMISE satisfied these conflicting demands by giving each state two seats in the Senate and assigning seats in the House by population. Equality was so essential for the smaller states that the Constitution further specified that "no State without its Consent, shall be deprived of its equal Suffrage in the Senate" (Article V).

The Senate (from the Latin *senatus*, council of elders) was expected to provide a check on the popularly elected House. Envisioning an American House of Lords, some delegates to the Constitutional Convention proposed that senators serve for life, at no salary. The convention rejected these strictures, but the Constitution assigns senators six-year terms and requires them to be at least thirty years of age and citizens for nine years (compared with two-year terms, a twenty-five-year age minimum, and seven years of citizenship for representatives). Although the federal Constitution sets no property-holding qualifications for senators, delegates depicted a Senate that would represent landed and commercial interests. "This checking branch must have great personal property," GOUVERNEUR MORRIS, insisted, "it must have the aristocratic spirit; it must love to lord it through pride." "A good Senate," said EDMUND RANDOLPH, would serve as a cure for the "turbulence and follies of democracy" under which the Congress of the Articles of Confederation had labored. JAMES MADISON observed that while the House might err out of fickleness and passion, the Senate would provide "a necessary fence against this danger."

The delegates first considered assigning appointment of judges and making of treaties to the Senate, but eventually divided these powers between the chief executive and the Senate. The Senate would advise and consent— or withhold consent—on presidential nominations and treaties negotiated by the executive branch. The Senate would share all powers of Congress and participate in all legislative functions. Senators could introduce and amend bills and resolutions without restriction, except that revenue bills must originate in the House, because "the people should hold the purse strings."

Despite their shared legislative powers, the Senate and House from the beginning have acted independently. The Senate sets its own rules, elects its own officers, judges the credentials of its members, and decides any contested elections (first by state legislatures and later by direct election after ratification of the SEVENTEENTH AMENDMENT in 1913). The Senate may also discipline its members through censure and expulsion. During its first two centuries the Senate censured eight senators for conduct ranging from violating Senate secrecy to financial misconduct. Most notably, in 1954 the Senate censured Senator Joseph R. McCarthy of Wisconsin for conduct "contrary to senatorial traditions," relating to his treatment of committee witnesses and other senators. Censure has not led to expulsion, except by the voters in the next election. The Senate has expelled only WILLIAM BLOUNT, charged with treasonous conspiracy in 1797, and fourteen senators who supported the Confederacy during the CIVIL WAR. Every other expulsion proceeding has ended either with the senator's vindication or with his resignation to avoid an expulsion vote.

Unlike the House, whose membership stands for election every two years, senators are divided into three classes elected at two-year intervals. Because at least two-thirds of the Senate continues in office from one Congress to the next, the Senate has defined itself as a continuing body that does not need to reestablish its rules at the start of each Congress. Although the House elects its own presiding officer, the vice-president of the United States serves as the president of the Senate. To preside in the vice-president's absence, the Senate elects a president pro tempore, generally the most senior member of the majority party. As the presiding officer, the vice-president has to play an essentially neutral role, voting only to break ties, speaking only with the permission of the Senate, and having his rulings subject to reversal by vote of the Senate.

The Constitution requires each house of Congress to publish a journal of its proceedings. Since 1789, the Senate has produced legislative and executive journals, which consist of short minutes of official actions taken on all bills, resolutions, treaties, and nominations. Separately from these journals, the *Congressional Record* evolved from stenographic notes published in private newspapers. Prior to the *Congressional Record*, these notes were compiled in the *Annals of Congress* (1789–1824), the *Register of Debates in Congress* (1824–1837), and the *Congressional Globe* (1833–1873).

For its first years the Senate met entirely in secret session, while the House immediately opened its doors. Seeing their role as a council to revise LEGISLATION drafted in the House and to advise the President on nominations and treaties, and having no need to appeal to their constituents, senators believed they could debate more freely and productively without a public gallery. In 1795, after much criticism in the press, the Senate regularly admitted the public to view legislative sessions, but continued to conduct most executive business—treaties and nominations—in closed session until 1929. Persistent leaks of executive sessions to the press steadily diminished their "secret" nature, and the Senate abandoned closed sessions, except for rare instances concerning highly classified information. Even after opening its doors, the Senate received minimal public attention. "Henceforth you will read little of me in the Gazettes," one representative notified his wife after his election to the Senate in 1804. "Senators are less exposed to public view than Representatives." House leadership in national affairs predominated through the War of 1812; but subsequently legislators of the stature of HENRY CLAY, DANIEL WEBSTER, and JOHN C. CALHOUN found the Senate a better forum for their sectional appeals and national aspirations. While Senate debate flourished, the House in 1847 established a "five-minute rule" for members' speeches. The smaller Senate clung to the tradition of unlimited debate, which took its most extreme form in the FILIBUSTER. This stalling devise gave the minority the opportunity to stop objectionable measures by occupying the floor with lengthy speeches and procedural delays. Not until 1917 did the Senate establish the first cloture rule, to provide a mechanism for cutting off debate.

Filibusters proved especially potent during the short second sessions of Congress. The Constitution originally set the opening date of Congress on the first Monday in December, more than a year after the elections. These first sessions generally met through the following spring. The second session again convened on the first Monday in December in the even-numbered years, but automatically expired on March 4. With the Senate facing an absolute deadline and with many of its members having retired or been defeated in the intervening election but not yet out of office, filibusters more easily prevailed. In 1933 the TWENTIETH AMENDMENT moved the opening of each session to January 3, which eliminated the long interregnum after elections and reduced the lame-duck filibusters. However, individual senators, no matter how junior, retain great capacity to defeat or delay legislation through amendments, objections to unanimous-consent requests, filibusters, and other parliamentary maneuvers generally not available to rank-and-file members of the House.

The Constitution grants members immunity from prosecution for their remarks in Congress. Judicial interpretations have extended the SPEECH OR DEBATE CLAUSE (Article I, Section 6) to cover a variety of congressional activity. In GRAVEL V. UNITED STATES (1972), the Supreme Court declared Senator Mike Gravel of Alaska and his staff immune from prosecution for making public classified portions of the *Pentagon Papers*. By contrast, the Court ruled in HUTCHINSON V. PROXMIRE (1979) that Senator William Proxmire of Wisconsin had immunity for statements made on the floor but not for information in his press releases and newsletters.

Exercising its ADVICE AND CONSENT power, the Senate in 1789 rejected President GEORGE WASHINGTON's nomination of Benjamin Fishbourn as naval officer of the port of Savannah, because of opposition from the senators from Georgia. Fishbourn's rejection was the first instance of "senatorial courtesy," by which the Senate deferred to the objections of senators from a nominee's home state. This practice has given senators great influence over the nominations of federal judges and attorneys from their states. In 1795 the Senate rejected Washington's nomination of JOHN RUTLEDGE as CHIEF JUSTICE of the United States, citing Rutledge's intemperate speeches on political issues. Over the next two centuries, the Senate rejected nearly twenty percent of all Supreme Court nominees, while it turned down only three percent of all Cabinet nominees. The disparity reflected senatorial attitudes that cabinet members should reflect the President's choices, but the Supreme Court is an independent branch not responsible to the President. The Senate has also tended to reject judicial appointments made during the President's last months in office.

Similarly, the Senate asserted its authority to advise and consent on the ratification of treaties. In 1789, at the urging of members, President Washington personally appeared in the Senate chamber to receive the Senate's advice on questions relating to the negotiation of treaties with several Indian nations. When the Senate deferred debate until the questions had been studied in committee, Washington determined not to repeat the experiment. Succeeding Presidents have generally limited themselves to seeking the Senate's consent rather than its advice.

In offering consent, the Senate has revised treaties through amendments, reservations, and understandings. In 1795 the Senate approved JAY'S TREATY with Great Britain only with the understanding that certain trade provisions would be renegotiated. In 1824 advocates of SLAVERY deliberately amended a treaty regarding suppression of the slave trade to cause Great Britain to reject the agreement. The following year, the Senate defeated a similar treaty with Colombia, marking its first formal rejection of a treaty. The Supreme Court consistently upheld the Senate's right to alter treaties, noting in *Haver v. Yaker* (1869) that "a treaty is more than a contract, for the Federal Constitution declares it to be the law of the land. If so, before it can become law, the Senate in whom rests authority to ratify it, must agree to it. But the Senate are not required to adopt or reject it as a whole, but may modify or amend it." Such revisions often provide the basis for consensus needed to achieve the constitutional two-thirds vote in favor of ratification. Most notably, the Senate's failure to agree on reservations to the Treaty of Versailles in 1919 and 1920 caused the treaty to fall short of a two-thirds vote of approval.

The division of power on foreign policy has been "an

invitation to struggle" between the President and Congress. Through its influence over treaties and diplomatic nominations, the Senate Foreign Relations Committee exerted considerable influence over foreign policy. By contrast, only through the passage of appropriations bills, largely dealing with foreign aid, has the House exerted comparable authority. Influential chairs of the Foreign Relations Committee, from CHARLES SUMNER and HENRY CABOT LODGE, SR., to J. William Fulbright, have strongly opposed and frustrated presidential policy. During the 1930s the Senate took the lead in enacting neutrality legislation. After American entry into World War II and particularly during the cold war that followed, the Senate adopted a generally bipartisan approach to foreign policy and accepted presidential leadership. Neither the KOREAN WAR nor the VIETNAM WAR was launched with a congressional DECLARATION OF WAR. Between 1955 and 1964, Congress enacted a series of resolutions to support presidential initiatives in Formosa (Taiwan), the Middle East, Berlin, Cuba, and the Tonkin Gulf. While often compared to blank checks, these resolutions were enacted to demonstrate national unity. Congressional consensus collapsed during the Vietnam War, with increasing numbers of senators protesting unilateral presidential actions. In 1973, Congress overturned a presidential veto and enacted the War Powers Resolution, requiring the President to report the use of American troops in combat and to withdraw troops unless authorized by Congress.

Exercising quasi-judicial powers, the Senate also sits as a court of IMPEACHMENT whenever the House of Representatives votes to impeach a federal official. Two-thirds of the senators must vote to convict. "Where else, than in the Senate should have been found a tribunal sufficiently dignified, or sufficiently independent?" asked ALEXANDER HAMILTON in *The Federalist* #65. Between 1789 and 1989 the House impeached sixteen federal officers—among them, a President, a senator, a cabinet member, and thirteen federal judges—on charges ranging from treason to intoxication. Three resigned voluntarily. The Senate found seven guilty and removed them from office. In 1868, by a single vote, the Senate declined to remove President ANDREW JOHNSON.

The Senate elects its own officers, sets its own rules, and appoints it own committees. Since 1789 the Senate has elected a secretary of the Senate, a sergeant at arms (originally called the doorkeeper), and a chaplain. Within its first week of business, a special committee proposed nineteen rules, which the Senate adopted with a single addition. There have been few general revisions of these rules. At first, the Senate operated chiefly as a committee of the whole, electing an array of ad hoc committees to deal with specific bills. In 1816, concerned with improving

continuity and permitting more specialization, the Senate established sixteen standing committees. After the creation of standing committees, senators no longer needed to give a day's notice or receive permission from a majority of members to introduce bills and resolutions. They have since introduced legislation at will, to be referred to the appropriate committee for initial consideration. For a time, the presiding officer appointed committee membership. Throughout the nineteenth century senators could be appointed to chair committees on which they had never served, based upon their seniority in the Senate as a whole. After reforms established in 1921, members advanced solely on the basis of seniority within a committee.

The committee system came to dominate the legislative process. By 1885, WOODROW WILSON described the federal system as "a government by chairmen of the Standing Committees of Congress." From time to time, the proliferation of committees has stimulated reforms leading to reductions in the number of committees and subcommittees. Most significant among these was the Legislative Reorganization Act of 1946, which revised committee jurisdiction and permitted the hiring of professional staffs. A series of reforms in the 1970s opened executive sessions of the committees to public view, provided for hiring minority staff members, and gave senators staff on each of their committees.

Committees have been the prime shapers of legislation and the vehicles for senatorial oversight and investigation. In the twentieth century the Senate increasingly played the role of investigator. Beginning with the 1924 Teapot Dome investigation of corruption in the WARREN G. HARDING administration and continuing through the investigation of banking and stock exchange practices after the 1929 stock market crash, the investigation of the national defense program during World War II, the crime investigations and the anticommunist hearings of the 1950s, and the WATERGATE hearings of 1973, Senate investigations have focused national attention on malfeasance and laid the groundwork for reform legislation. In a few investigations—those on the conduct of the Civil War, the attack on Pearl Harbor, and the IRAN-CONTRA AFFAIR—joint Senate and House committees conducted the proceedings. Senate committees also maintain regular oversight of the executive agencies. Although witnesses have raised objections regarding their rights while testifying, the Supreme Court in MCGRAIN V. DAUGHERTY (1927) and *Sinclair v. United States* (1929) has upheld the Senate's ability to subpoena private citizens and to hold recalcitrant witnesses in CONTEMPT OF CONGRESS, citing investigations as legitimate means to remedy social, political, and economic defects or to expose corruption and waste.

An important twentieth-century innovation has been

the emergence of the majority and minority leaders and whips as party leaders, legislative floor managers, and presidential spokesmen. During the nineteenth century, Senate leadership divided among the chairmen of the party caucuses and influential committees. Not until the 1920s did the parties designate official floor leaders and station them prominently in the chamber, giving them responsibility to manage their party's agenda and the legislative schedule. Rarely able to rely on party discipline in voting, Senate leaders gained influence through their ability to make committee appointments and schedule floor business and through the "power to recognition," by which the presiding officer calls first upon the majority and minority leaders before recognizing other senators. The post of Senate majority leader evolved to equal stature with the Speaker of the House. "The minority leader speaks for his party," Senator Robert C. Byrd noted. "But the majority leader, whether he be a Democrat or Republican, is the leader of the Senate."

Just as the United States Senate has preserved the polite parliamentary language, snuffboxes, and spittoons from centuries past, it has retained its original constitutional shape and functions. Yet the Senate has grown from a small council meeting in secret to a powerful legislative body, with more authority, independence, and media attention than the upper house of any other national legislature. Senators have jealously guarded and exercised the powers that the Constitution assigned to them, while developing the modern leadership, staff support, and rule changes necessary to meet vastly expanded legislative demands.

DONALD A. RITCHIE
(1992)

(SEE ALSO: *Appointment of Supreme Court Justices; Appointments Clause; Congressional Membership; Congressional Powers; Congressional Privileges and Immunities; Gulf of Tonkin Resolution; Legislative Investigations; McCarthyism; Senate and Foreign Policy; Senate Judiciary Committee; Senate Subcommittee on Constitutional Rights; Treaty Power.*)

Bibliography

BAKER, RICHARD A. 1988 *The Senate of the United States: A Bicentennial History.* Malabar, Fla.: Robert E. Krieger.

BYRD, ROBERT C. 1989 *The Senate, 1789–1989: Addresses on the History of the United States Senate.* Washington, D.C.: Government Printing Office.

HAYNES, GEORGE H. 1938 *The Senate of the United States: Its History and Practice,* 2 vols. Boston: Houghton Mifflin.

ROTHMAN, DAVID J. 1966 *Politics and Power: The United States Senate, 1869–1901.* Cambridge, Mass.: Harvard University Press.

SWANSTROM, ROY 1988 *The United States Senate, 1787–1801: A Dissertation upon the First Fourteen Years of the Upper Legislative Body,* Senate Document 100–31. Washington, D.C.: Government Printing Office.

SENATE AND FOREIGN POLICY

The text of the Constitution creates a special role for the United States SENATE in two key aspects of foreign policymaking, the approval of treaties and appointments. Article II, section 2, clause 2, provides that the President "shall have power, by and with the advice and consent of the Senate, to make treaties, provided two-thirds of the Senators present concur; and he shall nominate, and by and with the advice and consent of the Senate, shall appoint ambassadors and other public ministers and consuls." In addition to these explicitly conferred powers, the Senate, by practice and tradition, participates in JOINT RESOLUTIONS dealing with foreign policy; it takes part informally in other foreign policy activities as well.

Although the Senate in early years exercised an "advice" role in connection with treaty-making, that function has atrophied. The Senate can, and occasionally does, express its opinion concerning the desirability of concluding a certain treaty or concerning what outcome negotiations should produce. But it is the President who determines whether to commence negotiations and what topics those negotiations comprise. The President's responsibility for the conduct of international negotiations is plenary, and he may decline to transmit to the Senate a treaty he has signed.

Strictly speaking, the Senate does not "ratify" a treaty: the President does so after the Senate gives its advice and consent by a two-thirds majority of Senators present. This may seem like a steep requirement, but the Senate from the outset has rejected only about a dozen treaties. More frequently it approves a treaty subject to conditions that the President opposes, in which case he may decline to proceed with ratification. These conditions have been called "amendments," "reservations," "understandings," "statements," "declarations," and a variety of other terms, but the terminology is secondary to their substance. All are conditions to the Senate's approval, and if the Senate does condition its consent, the President, in bringing the treaty into effect, is required to honor the Senate's intent and modify the treaty accordingly.

The role of the Senate ends after the treaty takes effect. The President is responsible for its implementation and interpretation. A treaty is a law, and under the Constitution the President is charged with its faithful execution. During a well-publicized dispute between the Senate and the administration of RONALD REAGAN over the proper construction of the ABM Treaty, executive officials accused the Senate of meddling in the process of interpretation, while certain Senators charged that putative United States action based on the President's interpretation would have departed from the meaning of the treaty to the point of breaching the constitutional requirement that the law be faithfully executed.

The text of the Constitution makes no reference to the making of other international agreements on behalf of the United States, but Presidents have long concluded EXECUTIVE AGREEMENTS. These agreements have been concluded by Presidents with and without statutory authority. Either route obviates the requirement of two-thirds approval of the Senate—which explains both their popularity with Presidents and their unpopularity with some senators. The courts have provided no conclusive guidance as to when the treaty instrument is constitutionally required.

It has been argued that Senate participation also is required in ending a treaty. In GOLDWATER V. CARTER (1979), however, the Supreme Court declined to decide a challenge to the validity of the termination of the mutual security treaty with the Republic of China on Taiwan by President JIMMY CARTER. In light of the President's determinative role in initiating treaty relations and given past Senate acquiescence to presidential termination of several treaties in accordance with their terms, it is hard to see how a claim of Senate authority over treaty termination can be sustained. Treaty abrogation, however, is another matter. A president who ends a treaty in violation of its terms seemingly violates the presidential duty of faithful execution. Whether the Senate and President, acting together, can approve treaty abrogation and thereby end the treaty's status as the LAW OF THE LAND is an open question.

These constitutional matters are almost entirely a function of what the Senate Foreign Relations Committee has called "customary constitutional law"—practice acquiesced in by both political branches over many decades that has taken on the weight of a constitutional norm. Custom assumes particular significance in foreign affairs because so few judicial opinions mark the constitutional terrain. No court, for example, has upheld the power of the Senate to condition its consent to a treaty, but the practice has been unchallenged since the earliest days of the Republic and is now widely accepted as constitutionally permissible.

By contrast the Senate has not conditioned its consent to appointments, and it would be clearly impermissible today for the Senate to approve the appointment of a certain ambassador on the condition, say, that he resign and be reconfirmed after two years. Custom surrounding the APPOINTMENTS CLAUSE is different from that pertinent to the treaty clause.

In sheer numbers, the Senate's appointments work load is far heavier than its treaty work load. During the 96th Congress, for example, 2,728 nominations were referred to the Committee on Foreign Relations. By contrast, in a typical year no more than a dozen or so treaties are transmitted to the Senate for approval.

Many of these nominations are ambassadors, consuls, or other public ministers whose confirmation by the Senate is required by the Constitution. Others, however, are Foreign Service officers, whose appointment and promotion must be confirmed by the Senate under the Foreign Service Act of 1980. Other statutes require Senate confirmation of various United States representatives to international organizations and of executive-branch officials dealing with foreign affairs. These officials include the secretary of state and twenty-five other officials of the Department of State, as well as top appointees in the Arms Control and Disarmament Agency, the Peace Corps, and the United States Information Agency.

One notable exception to the requirement of Senate confirmation is the President's assistant for national security affairs, who heads the National Security Council. This exception has caused Senate critics concerned about "two secretaries of state" to argue for the enactment of a statute requiring Senate confirmation for this office. Executive officials have responded that such a requirement would impinge upon the President's constitutional foreign relations powers.

In fact, a variety of foreign affairs appointments have been made without Senate advice and consent. Delegates to international conferences and representatives in international negotiations often do not receive Senate approval. Presidents have on occasion given such persons the "personal rank" of ambassador or minister. But as the Foreign Relations Committee's onetime chairman Senator J. William Fulbright has pointed out, such designations are not appointments in the Article II sense and thus cannot confer additional legal powers or compensation upon the recipient.

On occasion, members of the Senate have themselves served as representatives to international negotiations. Some have not been appointed with the Senate's advice and consent; others have. The practice is in any event long-standing. In 1813, for example, Senator James A. Bayard of Delaware served as envoy extraordinary and minister plenipotentiary in negotiating and signing a commerce treaty with Russia. Bayard's appointment was accorded Senate advice and consent. Without Senate confirmation Senators Arthur Vandenberg and THOMAS T. CONNALLY served as members of the United States delegation to the San Francisco conference that drafted the UNITED NATIONS CHARTER. The United Nations Participation Act, enacted after the conference, expressly provides for the participation of members of Congress in the United States delegation to the United Nations. They are subject to Senate confirmation, but Vandenberg himself expressed reservations about the constitutionality of the arrangement. "I am increasingly impressed," he said, "with the difficulties confronted by "congressional' representatives because of their dual nature . . . it will always be true that a man cannot serve two masters. Yet that is precisely what I attempt to do . . . when I, as a Senator, sit in the United Nations as a delegate."

The mingling of executive and senatorial functions also occurs at less formal levels. During visits to the United States, foreign dignitaries often are invited for "tea" with the Foreign Relations Committee. The meetings are not open to the public, and although some time is consumed by social chitchat, it would be naive to think that substantive policy matters are not also reviewed. Ambassadors from foreign countries also meet on occasion with members of the Foreign Relations Committee and Senate leaders on legislative matters, as occurred in the 1970s during the normalization of relations with the People's Republic of China. And indirect contacts often occur during the consideration of treaties because the approval of conditions by the other signatory is required under international law and because Senate sponsors may not wish to render the treaty unacceptable by adding conditions that are unpalatable.

There is thus no airtight division between the foreign policy roles of the Senate and the executive. The Constitution, as reflected in custom deriving from two centuries of conflict and cooperation between Presidents and senators, reflects political accommodations reached by many different individuals representing many different philosophies over many different eras. It is not reducible to tidy "black-letter" formulas by which functions might be assigned neatly to one branch or the other. Yet it is perhaps the Constitution's very rejection of mechanical construction techniques that has given it the "play at the joints" necessary to adapt and survive.

MICHAEL J. GLENNON
(1992)

(SEE ALSO: *Congress and Foreign Policy; Congressional War Powers; Foreign Affairs; President and the Treaty Power; Presidential War Powers; Treaty Power; War Powers; War Powers Acts.*)

Bibliography

American Journal of International Law   October 1989   Volume 83, Number 4.

FRANK, THOMAS M. and GLENNON, MICHAEL J.   1987   *Foreign Relations and National Security Law*. St. Paul, Minn.: West Publishing Co.

GLENNON, MICHAEL J.   1990   *Constitutional Diplomacy*. Princeton, N.J.: Princeton University Press.

SENATE AND JUDICIAL APPOINTMENTS

The President nominates federal judges, but no person becomes a judge of a full-fledged federal court without first having been confirmed by the U.S. SENATE. Article II, section 2 of the Constitution stipulates that the President "shall nominate, and by and with the Advice and Consent of the Senate, shall appoint . . . Judges of the supreme Court, and all other Officers of the United States, whose Appointments are not herein otherwise provided for, and which shall be established by Law."

This provision expressly mentions only the Supreme Court because the Constitution, in Article III, gives Congress discretion to "ordain and establish" inferior federal courts. The most important inferior courts created by Congress are the United States DISTRICT COURTS and the United States Courts of Appeals. Judges of these "Article III courts," which possess the JUDICIAL POWER of the United States described in Article III of the Constitution, are nominated by the President and take office when the Senate votes to confirm the nomination. There are a few federal courts that are not Article III courts. Judges of these specialized courts (e.g., Bankruptcy Courts) are considered "inferior officers" of the United States and may be appointed, as Congress directs, by "the President alone, . . . the Courts of Law, or . . . the Heads of Departments." The more important federal judges are, however, nominated by the President and confirmed by the Senate.

The Constitution does not prescribe any particular method by which the President shall decide upon nominations, nor does the Constitution prescribe any particular method by which the Senate's ADVICE AND CONSENT is to be delivered. In practice, District Court nominees are selected by senators who share the President's political affiliation and who represent the state in which the District Court is located. Of course, the President actually makes the nomination. Nominees for the Courts of Appeals or the Supreme Court are usually considered more carefully and personally by the President. The SENATE JUDICIARY COMMITTEE evaluates each nominee and holds public hearings to assess the nominee's suitability. The committee may reject a nominee by refusing to forward the nomination to the full Senate; may recommend confirmation; or may recommend rejection by the Senate. Though the Constitution does not so specify, when the entire Senate votes, a nominee who receives a favorable vote by a majority of senators present and voting is confirmed. Once confirmed, judges hold office "during good Behavior," which means until they die, resign, or are removed by IMPEACHMENT and conviction.

There are no constitutional limits on the factors that

the Senate may consider in rendering its advice and consent on judicial appointments. In practice, the Senate attempts to insure that judicial nominees are professionally and temperamentally qualified people of integrity but, as with any political process, questions of political ideology are often considered relevant. About one of every four nominees to the Supreme Court has failed to be confirmed. The most recent unsuccessful nominees were Robert Bork and Douglas Ginsburg, in 1987.

When the Senate is not in session the President may make a "recess appointment" to a judicial office. Such appointments, authorized under Article II, section 2 of the Constitution, expire at the end of the next session of the Senate unless the Senate confirms the nominee. The most recent recess appointee to the Supreme Court was WILLIAM J. BRENNAN, JR.; appointed in 1956 and confirmed during the Senate's next session. JOHN RUTLEDGE, who served as CHIEF JUSTICE in 1795 as a recess appointee by GEORGE WASHINGTON, was never confirmed and holds the dubious distinction of being the only member of the Supreme Court who served as an unconfirmed recess appointee.

CALVIN R. MASSEY
(2000)

(SEE ALSO: *Bork Nomination.*)

Bibliography

BLAUSTEIN, ALBERT P. and MERSKY, ROY M. 1978 *The First One Hundred Justices.* Hamden, Conn.: Archon Books.
MASSEY, CALVIN R. 1991 Getting There: A Brief History of the Politics of Supreme Court Appointments. *Hastings Constitutional Law Quarterly* 19:1–21.
TRIBE, LAURENCE H. 1985 *God Save This Honorable Court.* New York: Random House.

SENATE JUDICIARY COMMITTEE

The Senate Judiciary Committee, created as a standing committee in 1816, is responsible for a vast array of constitutional and legislative issues. The subcommittee structure reveals the broad substantive areas covered by the committee.

The Subcommittee on Immigration and Refugee Affairs responds to illegal immigration, the admission and resettlement of refugees, NATURALIZATION, private relief bills, and international migration. The Simpson-Mazzoli Act in 1986 represented the first comprehensive overhaul of immigration laws since the McCarren-Walter Act of 1952. The Subcommittee on Antitrust, Monopolies, and Business Rights is responsible for such statutes as the SHERMAN ANTITRUST ACT of 1890 and the CLAYTON ACT, of 1914. The Subcommittee on Patents, Copyrights, and Trademarks monitors traditional statutes in its area and such emerging issues as home video recording and intellectual property rights. The Subcommittee on Technology and the Law oversees all laws relating to information policy, electronic privacy, and security of computer information. These issues frequently involve complex interpretations of SEARCH AND SEIZURE law.

The Subcommittee on Courts and Administrative Practice reports legislation dealing with new courts and judgeships, bankruptcy, court administration and management, judicial rules and procedures, administrative practices and procedures, tort reform and liability issues, and private relief bills other than immigration. One of the controversial bills to emerge from this subcommittee was the Judicial Councils Reform and Judicial Conduct and Disability Act of 1980, which created a procedure for disciplining federal judges in addition to the impeachment process. The constitutionality of this statute has been upheld by a number of appellate courts.

The Subcommittee on the Constitution has jurisdiction over all constitutional amendments. Amendments examined in recent years have dealt with ABORTION, a BALANCED BUDGET, EQUAL RIGHTS for women, SCHOOL BUSING, and SCHOOL PRAYER. The subcommittee is also responsible for legislation needed for CIVIL RIGHTS enforcement, including the VOTING RIGHTS ACT OF 1965, AFFIRMATIVE ACTION, and fair housing. Other duties involve CIVIL LIBERTIES, INTERSTATE COMPACTS, and criminal legislation related to constitutional issues, such as HABEAS CORPUS, CAPITAL PUNISHMENT, and the EXCLUSIONARY RULE.

The Senate Judiciary Committee reviews nominations for the Supreme Court, appellate courts, UNITED STATES DISTRICT COURTS, the ATTORNEY GENERAL, the SOLICITOR GENERAL, U.S. attorneys, marshals, and many other federal officials with duties to the courts. Some of the major controversies over Supreme Court appointments in recent years include the refusal in 1968 to advance Justice ABE FORTAS to the position of CHIEF JUSTICE, the rejection of Clement F. Haynsworth, Jr., and G. Harrold Carswell in 1969 and 1970, and the rejection of ROBERT H. BORK in 1987.

Hearings by the committee have helped clarify the boundaries of presidential powers in a number of areas, including the impoundment of appropriated funds, the use of EXECUTIVE PRIVILEGE to deny information to Congress, reliance on EXECUTIVE AGREEMENTS as a substitute for the treaty process, POCKET VETOES, and ELECTRONIC EAVESDROPPING conducted by administration officials without judicial warrant.

The committee has been tested under fire many times. A variety of court-stripping bills come before it for analysis, including such emotional subjects as abortion, school prayer, and school busing. Perhaps the committee's most enduring contribution to an independent judiciary came in 1937, when it voted against the Court-packing bill submitted by President FRANKLIN D. ROOSEVELT. In a report that contained probably the most stinging repudiation ever of a presidential proposal, the committee shredded the bill's premises, structure, content, and motivation. The authors of the report, using language scathing in tone, hoped that their emphatic rejection would help guarantee that "its parallel will never again be presented to the free representatives of the free people of America."

Until 1981 the Senate Judiciary Committee consistently selected only lawyers to serve as members. That practice ceased in 1981 when the committee added two nonlawyers, Jeremiah Denton of Alabama and Charles E. Grassley of Iowa. Another nonlawyer, Paul Simon of Illinois, joined the committee in 1985.

LOUIS FISHER
(1992)

Bibliography

SCHUCK, PETER H. 1975 *The Judiciary Committees: A Study of the House and Senate Committees.* New York: Grossman.

UNITED STATES SENATE 1982 *History of the Committee on the Judiciary, United States Senate, 1816–1981.* 97th Cong., 1st Sess., Senate Document No. 97–18.

SENATE SUBCOMMITTEE ON CONSTITUTIONAL RIGHTS

In 1955 the Civil Rights Subcommittee of the SENATE JUDICIARY COMMITTEE became the Subcommittee on Constitutional Rights. Subcommittee chair Thomas Hennings, a Missouri Democrat, urged the change because of the exclusive identification of CIVIL RIGHTS with race relations. He wanted the subcommittee to assert jurisdiction over a wider range of issues, particularly in response to the anticommunist assault on CIVIL LIBERTIES.

The subcommittee's first hearings explored the denial of DUE PROCESS in the loyalty-security programs of the DWIGHT D. EISENHOWER administration. Members also investigated passport suspensions, WIRETAPPING, ELECTRONIC EAVESDROPPING, government secrecy, and EXECUTIVE PRIVILEGE. Senator Hennings sponsored the first "freedom of information act" in 1958, but otherwise the subcommittee produced little legislation during the 1950s. Its main contribution was the obstruction of bills threatening to infringe on civil liberties or restrict the Supreme Court.

The SENATE regularly referred civil rights bills to the subcommittee, which held hearings on the civil rights bill of 1957. When the southern-dominated Judiciary Committee, chaired by Mississippi Democrat James O. Eastland, refused to report the subcommittee's bill to the floor, the Senate bypassed the committee entirely and debated the House of Representatives' bill instead.

Following Hennings's death in 1960, North Carolina Democrat SAMUEL J. ERVIN became subcommittee chair.

Because Ervin viewed civil rights legislation as an erosion of civil liberties, the subcommittee played no role in the enactment of the CIVIL RIGHTS ACT OF 1964 and helped to derail the omnibus civil rights bill of 1967. Yet under Ervin the subcommittee remained committed to civil liberties and reported out a "bill of rights" for mental patients in 1965, the Bail Reform Act of 1966, the Military Justice Act of 1968, and the Indian Bill of Rights in 1968. Over the chair's objections, the Senate ordered the subcommittee to report bills to extend the VOTING RIGHTS ACT in 1970 and the CIVIL RIGHTS COMMISSION in 1972.

Having consistently addressed matters of PROCEDURAL DUE PROCESS, privacy, FREEDOM OF SPEECH, FREEDOM OF THE PRESS, and SEARCH AND SEIZURE, subcommittee members became alarmed over alleged intrusions upon those rights by the administration of RICHARD M. NIXON. In 1971 the subcommittee focused attention on the violation of the RIGHT OF PRIVACY through government data banks and military spying. Senator Ervin strongly opposed administration proposals for PREVENTIVE DETENTION and fought for repeal of laws allowing NO-KNOCK ENTRY. The subcommittee proposed granting reporters protection against compulsory disclosure of sources, heard testimony relating to FBI surveillance of journalists, and conducted what Ervin called "a thorough and unprecedented series of hearings on the free press of America."

Given the conservatism of its parent committee, the subcommittee operated under considerable limitations. Not until Ervin became chair of the Government Operations Committee could he successfully guide to the floor the PRIVACY ACT of 1974. In part because of his long association with the subcommittee, Ervin became chair of the Select Committee on Presidential Campaign Activities that investigated the WATERGATE scandal.

Lacking Ervin's influence after his retirement, the Subcommittee of Constitutional Rights was abolished during a committee reorganization in 1977. For two decades, however, it had established a creditable record in defense of American rights and liberties.

DONALD A. RITCHIE
(1992)

(SEE ALSO: *Bail; Mental Illness and the Constitution; Military Justice.*)

Bibliography

KEMPER, DONALD J. 1965 *Decade of Fear: Senator Hennings and Civil Liberties.* Columbia: University of Missouri Press.

SENECA FALLS CONVENTION

On July 19 and 20, 1848, in Seneca Falls, New York, the first public meeting on behalf of women's rights was convened, thus inaugurating a movement that three-quarters of a century later resulted in the constitutional enfranchisement of women. The chief organizer was ELIZABETH CADY STANTON, then a mother of four living in this upstate industrial village. She was aided by Lucretia Mott, dean of American women abolitionists. The two had met in 1840 in London, and from then on Mott served as Stanton's mentor, sharing her radical Quaker convictions about the equality of the sexes with her apt pupil.

Around the world, 1848 was a year of international political upheaval and revolutionary inspiration. In Seneca Falls, Stanton, Mott, and three other women prepared a Declaration of Sentiments, Grievances and Resolutions. The preamble was modeled on the DECLARATION OF INDEPENDENCE, so as to endow women's discontent with political legitimacy. It claimed, "We hold these truths to be self-evident: that all men and women are created equal." A list of grievances indicted the long "history of repeated injuries and usurpations on the part of man toward woman," chief of which was the denial to women of "the inalienable right to the elective franchise." The Declaration also concentrated on the disabilities that law and custom imposed on wives by regarding them as the PROPERTY of their husbands. Women's exclusion from higher education, trades and professions, from church authority and moral responsibility, and from all that would build "faith in [their] own powers" was also protested.

The Declaration concluded with thirteen resolutions for future action, of which only the ninth, declaring that it is "the duty of the women of this country to secure to themselves their sacred right of the franchise," was controversial. Stanton's defense of the franchise demand was supported by Frederick Douglass, the only disfranchised man attending, and after debate the convention passed it. Two weeks later a second session of the convention was held in Rochester, which session focused on the grievances of working women. Newspaper coverage was widespread and uniformly disrespectful, but Stanton thought the former was well worth the latter. Beginning in 1850, national women's rights conventions were held annually, and a generation of female reformers began the complex task of undoing the deep legal bias against women's autonomy and establishing sexual equality.

ELLEN CAROL DuBOIS
(2000)

(SEE ALSO: *Woman Suffrage Movement.*)

Bibliography

DuBOIS, ELLEN CAROL 1978 *Feminism and Suffrage: The Emergence of an Independent Women's Movement in the U.S., 1848–1869.* Ithaca, N.Y.: Cornell University Press.
GORDON, ANN D., ed. 1997 *The Selected Papers of Elizabeth Cady Stanton and Susan B. Anthony.* Vol. 1. New Brunswick, N.J.: Rutgers University Press.
WELLMAN, JUDITH 1991 Seneca Falls Women's Rights Convention: A Study of Social Networks. *Journal of Women's History* 3:9–37.

SENTENCING

Anomalously, the constitutional law of criminal sentencing is a thinly developed field. Detailed procedural protections and an elaborate body of constitutional doctrine govern the investigation and adjudication of guilt in the pretrial and trial phases of a criminal case. The sentencing phase is just as important; indeed, for most defendants (who plead guilty without trial), the sentencing phase is even more important. Yet, outside the area of CAPITAL PUNISHMENT, sentencing is characterized by the almost complete absence of governing standards of substantive law, an extreme informality in prevailing procedures, and few constitutional restraints.

Although we ordinarily think of sentencing as a decision made by the judge after trial, the judge in reality shares sentencing authority with the legislature, the prosecutor, the jury, and the parole board or correctional agency. The division of authority varies widely from one jurisdiction to another and can have great impact upon the questions of constitutionality and fairness that arise.

The most important alternatives for the organization of sentencing authority are the mandatory, discretionary, and indeterminate systems. In a mandatory sentencing system, the sentence to be served upon conviction for a given crime is specified in the penal statute as a fixed term of years. Although the legislature ostensibly controls the sentence by defining it in advance, sentencing authority in a mandatory system tends in practice to become centered in the hands of the prosecutor, who decides which charges to file and, in effect, which mandatory sentences to seek. This prosecutorial decision is regarded as a discretionary one and is made without any hearing or other procedural formalities, without any governing standards, and without any opportunities for independent judicial review.

In the indeterminate sentencing system, neither the statute nor the judge limits the term to be served. The offender is sent to prison, potentially for life, and the time actually served is determined by the parole board. Usually that decision is based primarily on a judgment about whether an offender's progress toward rehabilitation makes him a good prospect for release. The parole board's decision is subject to few constitutional restraints. *Connecticut Board of Pardons v. Dumschat* (1981) holds that when a state's statutory regime treats parole as a privilege and creates no expectation of a right to early release, PROCEDURAL DUE PROCESS requirements do not apply at all.

When statutes do create an expectation of release, procedural due process requirements apply, but in *Greenholtz v. Inmates* (1979) the Supreme Court held that DUE PROCESS was satisfied by an opportunity to be heard and some indication of the reasons for denying parole. There is no RIGHT TO COUNSEL or right to confront or cross-examine witnesses in this context.

In a discretionary sentencing system, the penal statute sets only the boundaries within which the sentence must fall—a maximum sentence and sometimes a minimum sentence. These legislative boundaries typically leave a broad range of choice to the judge, who can choose the time to be served (or the fine or terms of probation) within the applicable limits. In some jurisdictions the judge's discretionary sentencing authority is qualified by legislative or administrative guidelines that require the sentence to fall within a narrow range unless the judge identifies unusual aggravating or mitigating circumstances. But many jurisdictions permit the judge to select any sentence within the broad legislatively authorized range without giving reasons and without facing appellate review.

In both mandatory and discretionary systems, sentencing authority is qualified by PLEA BARGAINING. The prosecutor may agree either to recommend a sentence or to fix a sentence that the judge must impose if the plea is accepted. The Constitution places few limits on the boundaries of plea negotiation. For example, the Supreme Court held in *Brady v. United States* (1970) that a guilty plea remains valid even if induced by the defendant's fear of facing the death penalty if he stands trial. On the other hand, the Constitution requires that plea agreements be respected by the government and by the courts. The Supreme Court held in *Santobello v. New York* (1971) that if a plea agreement is not honored, then the defendant has a constitutional right to withdraw the plea. In many jurisdictions, plea bargaining (with few constitutional restrictions) is in practice the principal mechanism for the determination of sentence.

In noncapital cases the Eighth Amendment's prohibition against CRUEL AND UNUSUAL PUNISHMENT has not been vigorously enforced. A punishment must be proportionate to the severity of the offense, but normally courts hold that any sentence within statutory limits satisfies this requirement. In SOLEM V. HELM (1983) the Court held that a sentence of life imprisonment without possibility of parole was cruelly disproportionate to an offense of issuing a bad $100 check, committeed by an offender with a record of six prior nonviolent felonies. The Court said that disproportionality should be determined by considering the gravity of the offense and the harshness of the penalty, sentences imposed for other crimes within the same jurisdiction, and sentences imposed for the same crime in other jurisdictions. Although this analysis could cast doubt on the severity of many sentences imposed on nonviolent offenders, in practice courts seldom strike down sentences that are less severe than life without possibility of parole.

Procedural due process requirements in noncapital cases are also slender. Under *Mempa v. Rhay* (1976) the defendant must be afforded the right to be heard at sentencing and the assistance of counsel. But there are only limited contexts in which the courts will recognize other trial-type safeguards.

The starting point for analysis of the procedural due process questions is *Williams v. New York* (1949). In *Williams* the Court upheld a death sentence imposed by a judge who had relied on a confidential presentence report. Emphasizing that "most of the information now relied upon by judges to guide them in the intelligent imposition of sentences would be unavailable if information were restricted to that given in open court by witnesses subject to cross-examination," the *Williams* Court held that the defendant had no right even to disclosure of the report.

Although courts continue to rely on *Williams* for the broad proposition that trial-type guarantees are inapplicable at the sentencing stage, subsequent decisions have qualified *Williams*. The case of *Garner v. Florida* (1977) makes clear that nondisclosure is impermissible in the capital sentencing context and suggests, though in general terms, a greater sensitivity to due process concerns even for noncapital sentencing. More important, *United States v. Tucker* (1972) invalidated a sentence based in part on prior convictions obtained without the assistance of counsel. The premise of *Tucker*, quite inconsistent with that of *Williams*, is that procedural due process is violated when a sentence is imposed on the basis of unreliable information.

Courts continue to have difficulty identifying the proper sphere of the *Tucker* principle. If given its full scope, it would swallow *Williams* and imply full rights to disclosure, confrontation, and cross-examination. Instead, most courts have limited *Tucker* narrowly. There is still no right to full disclosure of the presentence report, though the defense is normally made aware, at least in general terms, of its content. With respect to contested facts, there is no general right to cross-examination or to a formal evidentiary hearing. Instead, cases like *United States v. Weston* (1971) and *United States v. Fatico* (1978) hold that when factual claims are based on hearsay or other evidence that is difficult to challenge, reliability must be established either by cross-examination or by some form of sufficient corroboration. And there is no requirement that facts relevant to sentencing be proved beyond a REASONABLE DOUBT, even when such facts require that a substantially more severe punishment be imposed. Under *McMillan v. Pennsylvania* (1986) facts relied upon to support an aggravated sentence need be proved only by a preponderance of the evidence.

In capital cases, sentencing is governed by elaborate constitutional doctrines based primarily on the Eighth Amendment's prohibition against "cruel and unusual punishments." This prohibition has been held to embody both substantive and procedural requirements. In addition both the Eighth Amendment and the FOURTEENTH AMENDMENT EQUAL PROTECTION clause require evenhandedness in capital sentencing.

Sentencing proceedure in capital cases typicaly involves a TRIAL BY JURY on the question of guilt, followed by a seperate hearing (usually before the same jury) to determine sentence. The Supreme Court has not explicitly held that such a bifurcated trial is constitutionally mandated, but it has implied that bifurcation is neccessary when the death penalty is set by a jury. In some states, the jury's role is merely advisory and the judge may impose a death sentence, despite the jury's contrary recommendation.

Furman v. Georgia (1972), the first decision in the modern era of capital punishment precedent, held unconstitutional the then-common procedure of leaving the death penalty decision to the unguided discretion of the sentencing jury. The crucial opinions stressed that the pattern of death sentences imposed under such a system was so wanton and freakish as to violate the Eighth Amendment. *Furman* and its sequel, *Gregg v. Georgia* (1976), require guidance to the jury about aggravating and mitigating factors so that choice between life and death will not be made on a wholly arbitrary basis. Critics continue to wonder, however, whether jury instructions specifying standards in "boilerplate" terms will effect any real change in the rationality of the sentencing process.

Under *Furman* and *Gregg* the legislature must provide guidelines identifying relevant aggravating and mitigating circumstances. The guidelines may not be too rigid, however. The Court held in *Sumner v. Shuman* (1987) that the legislature may never make the death penalty mandatory, even for a narrowly specified class of offenses, such as murder by a prisoner already serving a life sentence without possibility of parole. Similarly, the Court held in *Lockett v. Ohio* (1976) and *Skipper v. South Carolina* (1986) that the states may not preclude the sentencing authority from considering as a mitigating factor any arguably extenuating aspect of the defendant's character or the offense.

There is a basic tension beneath these lines of authority. *Furman* requires guidelines to ensure that the death penalty is imposed predictably and uniformly, but *Sumner, Lockett,* and *Skipper* require that the sentencer retain discretion to respond to the circumstances of the individual case. In effect, the Supreme Court has interpreted the Eighth Amendment to require both evenhandedness through rules and individualization through case-by-case discretion. Recent emphasis on the latter consideration can leave the sentencing process open to the disparities and irrationalities that *Furman* intended to eliminate.

The dilemma may be inescapable so long as capital punishment is retained. The dramatic severity and finality of the ultimate penalty demand especially high degrees of both consistency and humanity. But human institutions are fallible. The conflicting dimensions of fairness are thus inherently difficult to realize in capital sentencing procedure.

The demand for evenhandedness should be heightened against the background of concern about racial bias in death penalty decisions. Many studies suggest that black defendants are more likely to suffer the death penalty than white defendants similarly situated and that the death penalty is more likely to be exacted for white than for black victims. For example, MCCLESKEY V. KEMP (1987) involved an empirical study showing that the death penalty is four times more likely in the case of defendants charged with killing whites than in the case of defendants charged with killing blacks. But the Court held that such a study, even if statistically valid, did not render the death penalty unconstitutional, in the absence of evidence that the jury in the particular case had been racially motivated. *McCleskey* is especially important to concerns about race bias because the evidence seemed to meet the usual burden of persuasion: the statistics showed that racial motivation was more likely than not. Yet, somewhat inconsistently with precedent in related areas, the Court held such a likelihood insufficient to "prove" RACIAL DISCRIMINATION.

In its substantive dimension the Eighth Amendment requires that the death penalty be proportional to culpability. Culpability has at least two aspects, one concerned with the nature of the crime and another concerned with the character of the offender. With respect to the former, the Supreme Court held in COKER V. GEORGIA (1977) that the death penalty may not be inflicted on a rapist who has neither taken nor endangered human life. Similarly, *Enmund v. Florida* (1982) and *Tison v. Arizona* (1987) held that an accomplice in murder may not be executed if he neither intended to kill nor acted with reckless indifference to life.

The Supreme Court has not yet decided whether the death penalty is permissible in the case of a person who kills unintentionally. In most states, a person who accidentally kills in the course of a robbery, burglary, or rape is guilty of first-degree murder, and in some states, such a person would be eligible for the death penalty. The Court's recent emphasis on the harm one causes suggests that the Court might view death as a proportionate penalty, despite the lack of intent to kill. Yet, viewed as a matter of culpability, *Enmund* teaches that it is "fundamental that causing harm intentionally must be [punished] more severely than causing the same harm unintentionally."

The second dimension of culpability concerns the character of the offender. The Court held in THOMPSON V. OKLAHOMA (1988) that to execute an offender who was under the age of sixteen at the time of the offense is impermissible. But STANFORD V. KENTUCKY (1989) upheld the constitutionality of executing a minor who had turned sixteen at the time of the offense, so long as the jury was permitted to consider the offender's youth as a mitigating factor. Similarly, PENRY V. LYNAUGH (1989) holds that a retarded offender may be executed, even if his "mental age" is equivalent to that of a seven-year-old child, provided that the jury is permitted to consider the mental impairment as a mitigating factor.

As a corollary of the principle that capital punishment must be proportionate to culpability, the sentencer must not give weight to facts that are irrelevant to blameworthiness. For example, BOOTH V. MARYLAND (1987) holds that the sentencing jury may not consider a "victim impact statement" that details unforeseeable harms suffered by the family of a murder victim.

The *Booth* principle, which requires that culpability be assessed in terms of acts and circumstances within the offender's knowledge or control, has recently come under criticism from members of the Court who believe that criminal justice responds inadequately to the interests of the victims. *South Carolina v. Gathers* (1989) indicates that a substantial minority of the Justices is prepared to overrule *Booth.* That step would not only permit the use of victim impact statements in capital sentencing but would also cut the proportionality requirement loose from its anchor in moral culpability. In effect, it would hold the defendant "responsible" for unforeseeable harms and events over which he had no control.

STEPHEN J. SCHULHOFER
(1992)

(SEE ALSO: *Capital Punishment and Race; Capital Punishment Cases of 1972; Capital Punishment Cases of 1976.*)

Bibliography

AMERICAN BAR ASSOCIATION 1980 *Standards for Criminal Justice 18–5.1 et seq.*, 2nd ed. Boston: Little, Brown.

KADISH, SANFORD H. 1962 Legal Norm and Discretion in the Police and Sentencing Process. *Harvard Law Review* 75:904–931.

NOTE 1968 Procedural Due Process at Judicial Sentencing for Felony. *Harvard Law Review* 81:821–846.

——— 1978 A Hidden Issue of Sentencing: Burdens of Proof for Disputed Allegations in Presentence Reports. *Georgetown Law Journal* 66:1515–1535.

SCHULHOFER, STEPHEN J. 1980 Due Process of Sentencing. *University of Pennsylvania Law Review* 128:733–828.

WHITE, WELSH S. 1987 *The Death Penalty in the Eighties.* Ann Arbor: University of Michigan Press.

SEPARATE BUT EQUAL DOCTRINE

The first type of racial SEGREGATION law to spread over the South was the "Jim Crow car" law, requiring blacks and whites to be seated separately in railroad passenger cars. When the Supreme Court held such a law valid in PLESSY V. FERGUSON (1896), the majority concluded that, so long as the facilities for each race were equal, the enforced separation of the races did not itself impose any inequality on black persons. In support of this separate but equal DOCTRINE, the Court drew on a pre-CIVIL WAR decision in Massachusetts, upholding racial segregation in the public schools. (See ROBERTS V. BOSTON.)

Although the doctrine originated in the context of state regulation of private conduct, it was soon extended to validate segregation in state-operated facilities. The races were separated by the law's command in courtrooms; in the public schools (see GONG LUM V. RICE); in state offices; in public parks, beaches, swimming pools, and golf courses; in prisons and jails. Some state institutions, such as universities, simply excluded blacks altogether; in most southern states there were separate state colleges for blacks. Throughout this system of segregation, the formal assumption was that facilities for blacks and whites might be separate, but they were equal.

Given the undoubted fact that segregation was imposed for the purpose of maintaining blacks in a condition of inferiority, the very term separate but equal is internally inconsistent. But the *Plessy* opinion had rejected the claim that racial separation itself imposed on blacks an inequality in the form of inferiority. (See BADGES OF SERVITUDE.) Yet *Plessy* set the terms of judicial inquiry in a way that ultimately undermined the separate but equal principle. The question of *justifications* for inequality was largely neglected; the Court focused on the question whether inequality *existed.*

In railroad cars, it was easy to achieve a rough equality of physical facilities. Similarly, a public swimming pool might be reserved for whites three days a week, reserved for blacks three days, and closed the other day. In education, however, inequalities of enormous proportion persisted up to the decision in BROWN V. BOARD OF EDUCATION (1954) and beyond. Black colleges lacked professional schools; black high schools emphasized vocational training and minimized preparation for college. In physical plants, teachers' salaries, levels of teacher training, counseling services, curricula—in every measurable aspect—the separate education offered blacks was anything but the equal of the education offered whites.

One strategy devised by the NAACP for ending school segregation was thus the filing of lawsuits aimed at forcing school boards to equalize spending for black education—at crushing expense. At the same time, a direct assault was made on segregation in higher education, and especially graduate education, where it was easiest to prove the inequality of facilities. (See MISSOURI EX REL. GAINES V. CANADA; SWEATT V. PAINTER.) These decisions, following *Plessy's* lead, focused on the bare question of inequality. Inevitably, these cases came to touch the question whether segregation itself implied unequal education. The *Brown* opinion pursued that inquiry, found educational inequality in the fact of enforced separation, and—without discussing any purported justifications for segregation—held school segregation unconstitutional.

Separate but equal thus ended its doctrinal sway in the field of education. Within a few years the Supreme Court, in a series of PER CURIAM opinions consisting entirely of citations to *Brown*, had invalidated all state-sponsored segregation. The separate but equal doctrine was laid to rest.

KENNETH L. KARST
(1986)

Bibliography

LEVY, LEONARD W. and JONES, DOUGLAS   1972   Jim Crow Education: Origins of the "Separate but Equal" Doctrine. In Levy, Leonard W., *Judgments: Essays on American Constitutional History.* Chicago: Quadrangle Books.

OBERST, PAUL   1973   The Strange Career of *Plessy v. Ferguson. Arizona Law Review* 15:389–418.

WOODWARD, C. VANN   1966   *The Strange Career of Jim Crow,* 2nd rev. ed. New York: Oxford University Press.

SEPARATION OF CHURCH AND STATE

The first provision of the BILL OF RIGHTS—known as the establishment clause—states that "Congress shall make no law respecting an ESTABLISHMENT OF RELIGION. . . ." This constitutional mandate seeks to assure the separation of church and state in a nation characterized by religious pluralism.

Justice WILEY B. RUTLEDGE observed in EVERSON V. BOARD OF EDUCATION (1947) that "no provision of the Constitution is more closely tied to or given content by its generating history than the religious clause of the FIRST AMENDMENT." Justice HUGO L. BLACK recounted in *Everson* that in the old world, "with the power of government supporting them, at various times and places, Catholics had persecuted

Protestants, Protestants had persecuted Baptists, Protestant sects had persecuted other Protestant sects, Catholics of one shade of belief had persecuted Catholics of another shade of belief, and all of these had from time to time persecuted Jews." And, he added, "these practices of the old world were transplanted to and began to thrive in the soil of the new America." For example, in Massachusetts, Quakers, Baptists, and other religious minorities suffered harshly and were taxed for the established Congregational Church. In 1776, the Maryland "Declaration of Rights" stated that "only persons professing the Christian religion" were entitled to religious freedom, and not until 1826 were Jews permitted to hold public office. The South Carolina Constitution of 1778 stated that "the Christian Protestant religion shall be deemed . . . the established religion of this state."

The specific historical record, rather than disclosing a coherent "intent of the Framers," suggests that those who influenced the framing of the First Amendment were animated by several distinct and sometimes conflicting goals. Thus, THOMAS JEFFERSON believed that the integrity of government could be preserved only by erecting "a wall of separation" between church and state. A sharp division of authority was essential, in his view, to insulate the democratic process from ecclesiastical depradations and excursions. JAMES MADISON shared this view, but also perceived church-state separation as benefiting religious institutions. Even more strongly, ROGER WILLIAMS, one of the earliest colonial proponents of religious freedom, posited an evangelical theory of separation, believing it vital to protect the sanctity of the church's "garden" from the "wilderness" of the state. Finally, there is evidence that one purpose of the establishment clause was to protect the existing state-established churches from the newly ordained national government. (Indeed, although disestablishment was then well under way, the epoch of state-sponsored churches did not close until 1833 when Massachusetts separated church and state.)

Even if the Framers' intent were unanimous and unambiguous, it still could not provide ready answers for many contemporary problems. First, a number of present-day church-state issues were not foreseen by the founders. For example, public education was virtually unknown in the eighteenth century; the Framers could have no position on the matter of RELIGION IN PUBLIC SCHOOLS—one of the most frequently adjudicated modern establishment clause questions. Second, implementing the Framers' precise thinking, even if discernible, might jeopardize values now considered secured by the establishment clause. As Justice WILLIAM J. BRENNAN speculated in ABINGTON TOWNSHIP SCHOOL DISTRICT V. SCHEMPP (1963), perhaps because the nation has become more religiously heterogeneous, "practices which may have been objectionable to no one in the time of Jefferson and Madison may today be highly offensive to . . . the deeply devout and the non-believers alike."

The varied ideologies that prompted the founders do, however, disclose a dominant theme: according constitutional status to RELIGIOUS LIBERTY and the integrity of individual conscience. Moreover, one of the main practices seen by many Framers as anathema to religious freedom was forcing the people to support religion through compulsory taxation. Jefferson viewed this as "sinful and tyrannical," and Madison found it abhorrent to compel "a citizen to contribute three pence only of his property" to a religious cause. The founders recognized that although government subsidy of religion may not directly influence people's beliefs, it coerces citizens either to contribute to their own religions or, worse, to support sectarian doctrines antithetical to their convictions.

By its terms, the ESTABLISHMENT CLAUSE applies only to the federal government ("*Congress* shall make no law. . . ."), but in *Everson* (1947) the Court ruled that the FOURTEENTH AMENDMENT made the clause applicable to the states. Before then, only two Supreme Court decisions had produced any significant consideration of the establishment clause. *Bradfield v. Roberts* (1899) had upheld federal appropriations to a Roman Catholic hospital for care of indigent patients. *Quick Bear v. Leupp* (1908) had sustained federal disbursement of funds, held in trust for the Sioux Indians, to Roman Catholic schools designated by the Sioux for payment of tuition. Neither opinion, however, attempted any comprehensive definition of the nonestablishment precept, an effort first undertaken in *Everson* where the Court stated:

> The "establishment of religion" clause of the First Amendment means at least this: Neither a state nor the Federal government can set up a church. Neither can pass laws which aid one religion, aid all religions, or prefer one religion over another. Neither can force nor influence a person to go to or to remain away from church against his will or force him to profess a belief or disbelief in any religion. No person can be punished for entertaining or professing religious beliefs or disbeliefs, for church attendance or nonattendance. No tax in any amount, large or small, can be levied to support any religious activities or institutions, whatever they may be called, or whatever form they may adopt to teach or practice religion. Neither a state nor the Federal Government can, openly or secretly, participate in the affairs of any religious organization or groups and *vice versa*. In the words of Jefferson, the clause against establishment of religion by law was intended to erect "a wall of separation between church and state."

Since then, there has been little agreement among the Justices, lower courts, and scholars as to what constitutes impermissible "aid" to, or "support" of, religion.

Beginning in the early 1960s and culminating in LEMON V. KURTZMAN (1971), the Court developed a three-part test for reviewing establishment clause challenges: "First, the statute must have a secular legislative purpose; second, its principal or primary effect must be one that neither advances nor inhibits religion . . . ; finally, the statute must not foster "an excessive government entanglement with religion." The *Lemon* test, despite its consistent invocation by the Court, has not been a model of coherence. Indeed, in an unusually candid OBITER DICTUM in COMMITTEE FOR PUBLIC EDUCATION V. REGAN (1980) the Court conceded that its approach "sacrifices clarity and predictability for flexibility," a state of affairs that "promises to be the case until the continuing interaction between the courts and the states . . . produces a single, more encompassing construction of the Establishment Clause." A better approach would read the establishment clause to forbid government action when its purpose is religious *and* it is likely to impair religious freedom by coercing, compromising, or influencing religious beliefs.

One of the nation's most politically divisive issues has been the proper place of religion in public schools. Decisions in the early 1960s, holding that prayer and Bible reading violate the establishment clause, precipitated serious efforts to reverse the Court by constitutional amendment. Later legislative proposals have sought to strip the federal courts of JURISDICTION over cases challenging voluntary school prayer.

The first cases concerning religion in public schools involved RELEASED TIME. In MCCOLLUM V. BOARD OF EDUCATION (1948) the Court invalidated an Illinois program of voluntary religious instruction in public school classrooms during school hours by privately employed teachers. Students whose parents signed "request cards" attended weekly classes in religion; others pursued secular studies elsewhere in the school during this period. The Court's opinion emphasized use of "the state's tax-supported public school buildings" and "the state's compulsory public school machinery." Four years later, in ZORACH V. CLAUSEN (1952), the Court upheld a New York City "off-premises" released time program. Released students attended classes at their respective religious centers; neither public funds nor public classrooms directly supported religion. In a much quoted and controversial passage, the Court observed: "We are a religious people whose institutions presuppose a Supreme Being. We guarantee the freedom to worship as one chooses. We make room for as wide a variety of beliefs and creeds as the spiritual needs of man deem necessary. . . . When the state encourages religious instruction or cooperates with religious authorities by adjusting the schedule of public events to sectarian needs, it follows the best of our traditions."

Neither *McCollum* nor *Zorach* propounded any specific

STANDARD OF REVIEW. A decade later, in ENGEL V. VITALE (1962), the Court invalidated a New York law providing for recitation of a state-composed prayer at the beginning of each public school day. Although the prayer was denominationally "neutral," and students could remain silent or leave the room, the Court declared that this "breaches the constitutional wall of separation between Church and State," because "it is no part of the business of government to compose official prayers."

The Court's approach soon underwent a dramatic revision. In *Abington Township v. Schempp* the Court held it unconstitutional for public schools to conduct daily exercises of reading student-selected passages from either the Old or New Testaments (without teacher comment) and recitation of the Lord's Prayer. Drawing on its rationale in the SUNDAY CLOSING CASES (1961), the Court articulated a "test" for government action challenged under the establishment clause: "[W]hat are the purpose and the primary effect of the enactment? If either is the advancement or inhibition of religion then the enactment exceeds the scope of legislative power as circumscribed by the Constitution. That is to say that to withstand the strictures of the Establishment Clause there must be a secular legislative purpose and a primary effect that neither advances nor inhibits religion." The Court ruled that the "opening exercise is a religious ceremony," emphasizing, however, that "objective" study of the Bible (presumably for its literary and historical value) was constitutionally permissible.

There are two difficulties with the Court's declared willingness—reaffirmed regularly since *Schempp*—to invalidate government action solely on the basis of a non-secular "purpose." First, although *Schempp* emphasized the establishment clause's requirement of a "wholesome neutrality" by the state toward religion, the Court has also made clear that the Constitution does not mandate an "untutored devotion" to this precept. Indeed, it has sometimes held that the free exercise clause *obliges* government to act with a nonsecular purpose—actually, to give a preference to religion—when the action is necessary to permit the unburdened exercise of religion.

Second, despite the *Schempp* test's condemnation of laws whose purpose is to "advance religion," the Court in *Zorach* had previously conceded that the released time program upheld had a nonsecular purpose: facilitation of religious instruction. *Zorach* has been specifically reaffirmed since *Schempp* was decided. Thus, the Court itself is not fully committed to its articulated doctrine that a religious purpose alone is sufficient to invalidate government action.

Although both *Engel* and *Schempp* declared that religious coercion was irrelevant under the establishment clause, the Court has nevertheless often carefully analyzed the elements of coercion and influence in programs it has considered. For example, in *Engel* the Court remarked on "the indirect coercive pressure upon religious minorities to conform to the prevailing officially approved religion." In *Zorach*, the Court emphasized its questionable conclusion that there was no "coercion to get public school students into religious classrooms." And in WIDMAR V. VINCENT (1981), in requiring a state university to provide student religious groups equal access to its facilities, the Court noted: "University students are . . . less impressionable than younger students and should be able to appreciate that the university's policy is one of neutrality towards religion."

The Court's sensitivity to religious coercion and influence in establishment clause challenges, its doctrinal pronouncements to the contrary notwithstanding, comports with an approach that recognizes that in accommodating the values underlying both the establishment and free exercise clauses, a nonsecular purpose cannot always be avoided, and that the primary offense to the establishment clause is some meaningful intrusion upon religious liberty.

Nearly two decades elapsed between *Schempp* and the BURGER COURT's first major decision on religion in public schools. In *Stone v. Graham* (1980) a Kentucky statute required posting a copy of the Ten Commandments (purchased with private funds) in all public school classrooms, with the notation: "The secular application of the Ten Commandments is clearly seen in its adoption as the fundamental legal code of Western Civilization and the COMMON LAW of the United States." Although the state court found that the legislature's purpose was not religious and sustained the law, the Supreme Court reversed.

The *Stone* opinion is significant for several reasons. First, it sheds further light on how the Court decides whether a legislative purpose is secular or religious. In *Schempp*, when the school board contended that the Bible reading program was not instituted for religious reasons (but rather to promote moral values, teach literature, and inspire student discipline), the Court brusquely replied that "surely, the place of the Bible as an instrument of religion cannot be gainsaid." In *Stone*, the Court stated that the Ten Commandments were not confined to "arguably secular matters" such as prohibition of murder and adultery but also prescribed religious duties such as observing the Sabbath and avoiding idolatry—adding that the law did not integrate the Bible or the commandments into an ethics, history, or comparative religion course. It quite peremptorily concluded that the program "serves no . . . educational function" and that "the Ten Commandments is undeniably a sacred text in the Jewish and Christian faiths, and no legislative recitation of a supposed secular purpose can blind us to that fact." *Stone* also reaffirms that a nonsecular purpose is itself enough to condemn a law under the establishment clause. Although the Court briefly considered the state program's potential for coercing or influencing children—observing that "if the posted copies of the Ten Commandments are to have any effect at all, it will be to induce the school children to read, meditate upon, perhaps to venerate and obey, the Commandments"—it nevertheless held that the law lacked a secular purpose and was invalid on that basis alone. This doctrine was vigorously reinforced in WALLACE V. JAFFREE (1985), which invalidated an Alabama statute authorizing a period of silence in public schools "for meditation or voluntary prayer," because the law was "entirely motivated by a purpose to advance religion." (The Justices plainly indicated that only a slightly different statutory formulation "protecting every student's right to engage in voluntary prayer during an appropriate moment of silence during the school day" would pass constitutional muster.)

Although regulatory laws allegedly enacted to aid religion have generated only a few Supreme Court decisions, they have significantly affected establishment clause jurisprudence. In MCGOWAN V. MARYLAND (1961) the Court upheld prohibition of the sale of most merchandise on Sundays. The Court conceded that the original purpose of Sunday closing laws was to encourage observance of the Christian Sabbath. But it found that, as presently written and administered, most such laws "are of a secular rather than of a religious character," seeking "to set one day apart from all others as a day of rest, repose, recreation and tranquility." The choice of Sunday, "a day of particular significance for the dominant Christian sects," did not "bar the state from achieving its secular goals."

McGowan emphasized that a Sunday closing law might violate the establishment clause if its purpose were "to use the State's coercive power to aid religion." This warning was fulfilled in EPPERSON V. ARKANSAS (1968), when the Court invalidated a law that excised the theory of human biological evolution from public school curricula. Reviewing the circumstances of its adoption in 1928, the Court found that "fundamentalist sectarian conviction was and still is the law's reason for existence."

Although Arkansas probably exceeded what the free exercise clause required for "accommodation" of fundamentalist religious doctrine, there was no indication that its anti-evolution statute coerced, compromised, or influenced school children to embrace fundamentalist doctrine. The Arkansas statute thus satisfied religious needs with no meaningful threat to religious liberty—the chief danger the establishment clause was intended to avoid. Yet, as in the Ten Commandments and moment-of-silence cases, a religious purpose alone proved fatal.

The Court first gave plenary consideration to the problem of public aid to church-related schools in *Everson v. Board of Education* (1947). A New Jersey township reimbursed parents for the cost of sending their children on public buses to and from schools, including Roman Catholic parochial schools. Although the Court asserted that "no tax . . . can be levied to support any religious activity or institution," it upheld the New Jersey program by a 5–4 vote. The majority conceded that without the program's subsidy some children might not be sent to church schools. But it reasoned that funding bus transportation for all pupils in both public and sectarian schools accomplished the "public purpose" of aiding parents in getting their children "safely and expeditiously to and from accredited schools." In this respect, New Jersey's aid program was similar to providing all schools with basic municipal services, such as fire and police protection. Furthermore, the state could not constitutionally exclude persons from its aid "because of their faith, or lack of it." (The *Everson* majority indicated that bus transportation might be the limit of permissible assistance.) The dissenters protested that the program aided children "in a substantial way to get the very thing which they are sent to [parochial schools] to secure, namely, religious training and teaching."

The Court did not again confront the issue of aid to church-related schools until BOARD OF EDUCATION V. ALLEN (1968). During the intervening two decades, the Court had developed the "secular purpose-secular effect" standard. *Allen* held that New York's lending secular textbooks, approved by local school boards, to all secondary school students, including those in church-related schools, had the secular purpose of furthering education and a primary effect that benefited students and parents, not religious schools.

The "excessive entanglement" prong of the Court's establishment clause test emerged two years later. WALZ V. TAX COMMISSION (1970) rejected the claim that New York's tax exemption for "real or personal property used exclusively for religious, educational or charitable purposes" supported religion in violation of the establishment clause. After finding that the exemption had the nonreligious purpose of avoiding inhibition on the activities of charities and other community institutions, the Court continued: "We must also be sure that the end result—the effect—is not an excessive government entanglement with religion. The test is inescapably one of degree. Either course, taxation of churches or exemptions, occasions some degree of involvement with religion. . . . [The question is] whether it is a continuing one calling for official and continuing surveillance leading to an impermissible degree of entanglement." The Court conceded that tax exemption accorded an indirect economic benefit to religion, but concluded that it gave rise to less government involvement than nonexemption. Taxing the churches would occasion "tax valuation of church property, tax liens, tax foreclosures, and the direct confrontations and conflicts that follow in the train of those legal processes."

In LEMON V. KURTZMAN (1971) the Court returned to the problem of church-related schools. Rhode Island subsidized public and private school teachers of secular subjects (not to exceed fifteen percent of their salaries); parochial school teachers agreed not to teach religion during the subsidy. The legislature had found that "the quality of education available in nonpublic elementary schools has been jeopardized [by] rapidly rising salaries." Pennsylvania reimbursed nonpublic schools for the salaries of teachers of "secular" subjects such as mathematics, physical science, physical education, and foreign languages. Church-related schools maintained accounts, subject to state audit, that segregated the costs of "secular educational service." Reimbursement for religiously oriented courses was prohibited.

The Court held that both programs violated the establishment clause. It acknowledged a secular purpose, but reasoned that the states' efforts to avoid a primary effect that advanced religion produced "excessive entanglement between government and religion." In the Court's view, church-related elementary and secondary schools had as their mission the inculcation of religious doctrine, especially among "impressionable" primary school pupils. Continuing state evaluation of school records "to establish the cost of secular as distinguished from religious instruction," and the state "surveillance necessary to ensure that teachers play a strictly nonideological role" were "pregnant with dangers of excessive government direction of Church schools and hence of Churches." Although this "administrative" entanglement was fatal, both laws risked another sort of entanglement: their "divisive political potential" along religious lines, given the likely demand for continuing and ever increasing annual appropriations.

The excessive entanglement criterion has been prominent in establishment clause adjudication since 1970; but it does not represent a value that either can or should be judicially secured by the establishment clause. The major fear of administrative entanglement between government and religion is that state regulation impairs the ability of religious groups to pursue their mission. This concern, however, is unfounded both doctrinally and empirically. At least since PIERCE V. SOCIETY OF SISTERS (1925) it has been understood that the Constitution permits the state to regulate church-related institutions whether or not it provides them financial assistance. Parochial school curricula, for example, have long been regulated without significant evidence of infringement of religious values. And if there were, the regulation would be invalid whether or not tied to monetary aid.

Another form of administrative entanglement regularly occurs when the state seeks to distinguish religion from nonreligion in order to grant an exemption from civil regulations. Although government scrutiny of religious beliefs is a sensitive task, the need for that scrutiny springs from the Constitution's explicit definition of religion as a subject for special treatment.

Similar objections can be raised to using "avoidance of political strife along religious lines" as a criterion for establishment clause adjudication. Indeed, if government were to ban religious conflict in the legislative process, serious questions of First Amendment political liberty would arise. But practical considerations, more than doctrinal ones, demonstrate the futility of making "political divisiveness" a constitutional determinant. Legislation does not violate the establishment clause simply because religious organizations support or oppose it. Religious groups have frequently differed on secular political issues—gambling, OBSCENITY, drug and GUN CONTROL, PROHIBITION, abolition of SLAVERY, racial integration, prostitution, sterilization, ABORTION, BIRTH CONTROL, divorce, the VIETNAM WAR, the EQUAL RIGHTS AMENDMENT, and CAPITAL PUNISHMENT, to name but a few. Churches and other religious groups have markedly influenced resolution of some of these matters. In the early 1980s, they actively debated the question of the nation's nuclear arms policy. Although a law may in fact promote a religious purpose, if the law serves genuinely secular ends—and impairs no one's religious liberty by coercing, compromising, or influencing religious beliefs—it should not be unconstitutional simply because its proponents and antagonists were divided along religious lines.

Moreover, even if government could or should eliminate religious fragmentation in the political arena, the establishment clause is an ineffective tool for the task. For example, forbidding aid to parochial schools does not effect a truce, but only moves the battleground; if children in parochial schools are excluded from school aid, their parents will tend to oppose increased funding of public schools.

The Court has viewed aid to church-related higher education more favorably than it has viewed aid to elementary and secondary schools. *Tilton v. Richardson* (1971), a companion case to *Lemon*, upheld federal construction grants to colleges for buildings and facilities that applicants agreed not to use for religious instruction. The government enforced this promise by on-site inspections. The Court easily found a secular purpose in the expansion of higher education opportunities. In reasoning that the subsidy's primary effect did not advance religion, it stated that, unlike elementary and secondary schools, church-related colleges were not "permeated" by religion. Their dominant motive is secular education; they normally afford a high degree of ACADEMIC FREEDOM for faculty and students; and their students are less susceptible to religious indoctrination than are school children. In sharp contrast to its generalized appraisal of parochial schools, the Court rejected a "composite profile" of a "typical sectarian" college. Instead, the Court found, on the record before it, that courses at the four recipient Roman Catholic institutions were taught according to professional academic standards. Moreover, the aid took the form of a one-time, single-purpose construction grant. Thus no appreciable governmental surveillance was required. Finally, the Court found the potential for "religious fragmentation in the political arena" lessened by the religious colleges' geographically diverse student bodies and the absence of religious affiliation of a majority of recipient colleges.

Decisions since *Tilton* have continued to sustain aid to religiously affiliated colleges. In *Hunt v. McNair* (1973) the Court upheld the use of South Carolina tax-exempt bonds to finance facilities for all colleges, so long as the facilities were limited to nonsectarian purposes. The Court placed the burden on those challenging the aid to establish that recipient colleges are "permeated" with religion. And in *Roemer v. Board of Public Works* (1976) the Court upheld Maryland grants of fifteen percent of the student cost in the state college system to all private colleges, if they certified that they used the funds for nonreligious purposes.

Subsequent decisions on aid to elementary and secondary schools have generally, but not unexceptionally, followed the path of *Lemon*. *Meek v. Pittenger* (1975) involved a program under which Pennsylvania lent instructional materials (such as maps, films, projectors, and laboratory equipment) to private schools, seventy-five percent of which were church-related. The Court agreed that the aid was ideologically neutral, but held that "when it flows to an institution in which religion is so pervasive that a substantial portion of its functions are subsumed in the religious mission," it has the primary effect of advancing religion. The Court also invalidated "auxiliary services" (such as standardized testing, speech therapy, and psychological counseling) by public employees for private school children on their schools' premises: "To be certain that auxiliary teachers remain religiously neutral . . . the State would have to impose limitations . . . and then engage in some form of continuing surveillance to ensure that those restrictions were being followed." In addition to this "administrative entanglement," the Court observed that the program promised to generate "political entanglement" in the form of "continuing political strife." (The Court reaffirmed this holding as to auxiliary services in 1985 in the COMPANION CASES of *Grand Rapids School District v. Ball* and AGUILAR V. FELTON.)

Two years after *Meek*, *Wolman v. Walter* (1977) illustrated how constitutionality may turn on slight changes in form. The Court upheld Ohio's provision of (1) speech, hearing, and psychological diagnostic services by public employees on private school premises; (2) therapeutic and remedial services by public employees at a "neutral site off the premises" of the private school (even if in an adjacent mobile unit); and (3) payment for standardized tests used in private schools (the dispositive factor being that the tests were drafted and scored by public employees). The Court distinguished *Meek* on paperthin grounds relating to the closeness of the connection between the services provided and the religious school's educational mission and to the likelihood that public employees would "transmit ideological views" to children.

Wolman invalidated state payment for field trips of private school pupils, distinguishing *Everson* on the basis of the school's control over the expenditure of the funds and the close relation of the expenditure to the school's curriculum. The Court also invalidated a program for lending instructional materials to students, but, as in *Meek*, reaffirmed *Allen* and upheld lending students secular textbooks.

COMMITTEE FOR PUBLIC EDUCATION V. REGAN (1980) upheld New York's reimbursing private schools for performing testing and reporting services mandated by state law. The tests were prepared by the state, but, unlike those in *Wolman*, some were administered and scored by private school personnel. Nevertheless, because the tests were mostly objective, the Court concluded that there was little risk of their religious use. The Court distinguished *Levitt v. Committee for Public Education* (1973), which had invalidated a similar New York statute because it did not provide for state audits to ensure that the public funds did not exceed the nonpublic school's actual cost. In *Regan*, the occasional audits were found adequate to prevent a religious effect but not so intrusive as to produce excessive entanglement.

As of the mid-1980s, the most effective way for government to assist elementary and secondary parochial schools is through the tax system. In COMMITTEE FOR PUBLIC EDUCATION V. NYQUIST (1973) the Court invalidated a New York program, which the Court agreed had a "secular purpose," that gave tuition grants to low-income parents and tax relief to middle-income parents of children in private schools. The Court held that this had the effect of aiding the religious functions of sectarian schools. The Court distinguished *Walz* on several grounds. First, unlike the *Nyquist* programs, tax exemptions for church property had ample historical precedent, being "widespread during colonial days" and currently "in force in all 50 states." Second, although property tax exemption tended to lessen involvement between church and state, the programs in *Nyquist* tended to increase it. Finally, the tax exemption in *Walz* went to a broad class of charitable, religious, and educational institutions, but the record in *Nyquist* showed that eighty-five percent of the children benefited attended sectarian schools, practically all run by the Roman Catholic Church.

A decade later, in MUELLER V. ALLEN (1983), the Court upheld a Minnesota program granting a state income tax deduction for parents with children in *any* nonprofit school, public or private. This deduction could be used for expenditures for tuition and transportation, as well as for textbooks and instructional materials and equipment (so long as they were not used to teach religion). The Court conceded that the "economic consequences" of the Minnesota program were "difficult to distinguish" from the New York program in *Nyquist*. But that it was difficult did not make it impossible. One difference the Court found was that *Mueller* involved "a genuine tax deduction," whereas the *Nyquist* tax credit was more like a direct grant than a tax benefit. The Court found most significant that the *Mueller* plan was available to all parents, not just those with children in private schools. Thus, the plan was "facially neutral" and its "primary effect" did not advance religion. The Court reached this conclusion even though ninety-six percent of the Minnesota deductions were taken by parents who sent their children to parochial schools—mainly Roman Catholic and Lutheran. As for the other four percent, there were only seventy-nine public school students who deducted tuition, which they paid because they attended public schools outside their districts for special reasons. Of course, children who attended public schools in their districts did get some deductions—for the cost of pencils, notebooks, and other incidentals not customarily provided.

The lesson to be drawn from all the elementary and secondary school decisions is that states wishing to provide significant financial assistance may do so simply by adopting the proper form. For example, New York could successfully revive its program invalidated in *Nyquist* by providing a tax benefit to all parents, including those whose children attend public schools, knowing that this would not appreciably increase the cost of the plan. But New York might be required to use the form of a tax deduction (rather than a tax credit or direct grant as in *Nyquist*), a difference of vital importance to parents with low incomes, who would obtain little benefit from a tax deduction.

Application of the Court's three-part test to the problem of GOVERNMENT AID TO RELIGIOUS INSTITUTIONS has generated ad hoc judgments incapable of being reconciled on a principled basis. The Court has assumed that the entire program of parochial schools is "permeated" with religion. But there is much dispute as to the facts. Some "secular" subjects in some parochial schools are unquestionably courses of religious indoctrination; other courses are truly secular; many probably fall between these polar charac-

terizations. Thus, public aid incidentally benefits religion. But virtually all government services to church-related facilities—whether bus transportation, police and fire protection, sewage connections, sidewalks, tuition grants, or textbooks—incidentally benefit their sectarian functions by releasing church funds for religious purposes.

The critical inquiry should be whether direct or indirect government assistance to parochial schools exceeds the value of the secular educational service the schools render. If it does not, there is no use of tax-raised funds to aid religion, and thus no danger to religious liberty. This inquiry differs from the Court's approach, which has often invalidated laws with secular purposes because of their effects in advancing religion. A state program with both a secular purpose and a secular effect does not threaten values underlying the establishment clause. Furthermore, when the Court invalidates such a law simply because it incidentally furthers religious interests, the Justices assert the power to assess the multiple impacts of legislation, to separate religious from secular effects, and then to determine which are paramount. Ultimately the Justices must then rely on their own subjective notions of predominance.

In the mid-1980s, the Court was twice confronted with the problem of government practices that specifically acknowledge religion. MARSH V. CHAMBERS (1983) upheld Nebraska's paying a chaplain to open each legislative session with a prayer. Proceeding unusually, the Court did not apply its three-part test. Rather, it relied first on history and tradition—pointing out that paid legislative chaplains and opening prayers existed in the Continental Congress, the First Congress, and every Congress thereafter, as well as in most states today and in colonies such as Virginia and Rhode Island, both of which were bastions of religious liberty. Second, the Court rested on the intent of the Framers, noting that just three days after the First Congress had authorized paid chaplains it approved the Bill of Rights; this made it difficult to believe that the Framers could conceive of the establishment clause as prohibiting legislative chaplains. Thus, the practice survived challenge even though Nebraska's purpose was unquestionably religious and the Court's doctrine is that such purpose alone produces an establishment clause violation.

A year later, in LYNCH V. DONNELLY (1984), the Court sustained Pawtucket, Rhode Island's inclusion of a nativity scene in the city's annual Christmas season display. The cost was nominal, unlike the $320 expended monthly for Nebraska's chaplain in *Marsh*. The Court reasoned that the purpose and effect were not exclusively religious but, rather, that "the creche in the display depicts the historical origins of this traditional event long recognized as a National Holiday." The opinion also emphasized that our history was replete with government recognition of religion's role in American life and with government expressions of religious belief. As examples, it pointed to presidential proclamations of national days of prayer and of Thanksgiving and Christmas as national holidays, public funding of a chapel in the Capitol and of chaplains in the legislature and in the military, "In God We Trust" as our statutorily prescribed national motto, the language "One Nation under God" as part of the Pledge of Allegiance, and the plethora of religious paintings in publicly supported galleries and in public buildings. Stating that "this history may help explain why the Court consistently has declined to take a rigid, absolutist view of the Establishment Clause," the Court strongly suggested that all these deeply ingrained practices were constitutional.

The final important church-state separation issue concerns the tension between the First Amendment's two religion clauses, one forbidding government to promote or "establish" religion, the other forbidding government to abridge the "free exercise" of religion. As observed in *Walz,* both "are cast in absolute terms, and either . . . if expanded to a logical extreme, would tend to clash with the other." Charting a course that offends neither provision presents a continual challenge for the Court; yet its few direct confrontations with the problem have been unsatisfying.

The two most celebrated free exercise clause decisions illustrate the inherent conflict. In SHERBERT V. VERNER (1962) a Seventh-Day Adventist was discharged by her employer because she would not work on Saturday, her Sabbath. South Carolina denied her unemployment compensation for refusing "suitable work," that is, a job requiring Saturday labor. The Court held that this denial violated the free exercise clause by conditioning benefits on a violation of her religious faith. Although the Court's decision implements the free exercise clause, the purpose of its ruling—like the purpose of the released time program in *McCollum*—is clearly to facilitate religious practice. Thus, the exemption required by the Court in the name of the free exercise clause appears to violate the Court's establishment clause doctrine, which renders invalid any government action with a nonsecular purpose. The Court's conclusory response was that "plainly we are not fostering the "establishment' of the Seventh-day Adventist religion" but rather governmental "neutrality in the face of religious differences."

In WISCONSIN V. YODER (1971) the Court held that application of school attendance requirements to the Old Order Amish violated the free exercise clause. In characterizing this as an "accommodation" for the Amish, the Court rejected the contention that this religious exemption violated the establishment clause: "The purpose and effect of such an exemption are not to support, favor, advance or assist the Amish, but to allow their centuries-old

religious society . . . to survive free from the heavy impediment compliance with the Wisconsin compulsory-education law would impose."

In THORNTON V. CALDOR, INC. (1985), however, the Court ruled that a state had gone too far in "accommodating" religion. It held that a Connecticut law that required employers to give a day off to employees on their Sabbath, "no matter what burden or inconvenience this imposes on the employer or fellow workers," had the "primary effect" of advancing "a particular religious practice" and thus violated the establishment clause. The Court emphasized the "absolute and unqualified right not to work" afforded the employees, although this appeared to be little different from the exemption that the Court itself had ordered in *Sherbert.*

Although there is considerable overlap in the purposes of the establishment and free exercise clauses—their central function being to secure religious liberty—the decisions disclose that each has an identifiable emphasis. In the main, the free exercise clause protects adherents of religious faiths from secularly motivated laws whose effect burdens them because of their particular beliefs. When the Court finds a violation of the free exercise clause, the law is normally held invalid as applied; all that is required is an exemption for the claimant from the law's otherwise proper operation. In contrast, the principal thrust of the establishment clause concerns religiously motivated laws that pose the danger to believers and nonbelievers of being required to support their own religious observance or that of others. When the Court finds a violation of the establishment clause, ordinarily the offensive provision is entirely invalid and may not be enforced at all.

A better approach would reconcile the conflict between the clauses by interpreting the establishment clause to forbid only those laws whose purpose is to favor religion, and then only if such laws tend to coerce, compromise, or influence religious beliefs. Under this standard, the religious exemption that the Court required in *Sherbert* would itself be unconstitutional because it impairs religious liberty by supporting religion with funds raised by taxation. Although the core value of religious liberty may forbid government to interfere with Sherbert's practice of Seventh-Day Adventism, it similarly forbids forcing other citizens to subsidize a religious practice. On the other hand, the proposed alternative approach probably would not change the result in *Yoder;* it is doubtful that exempting the Amish from the compulsory education law (or giving employees a day off on their Sabbath, as in *Thornton*) would tend to coerce, compromise, or influence religious choice. Finally, the alternative approach would distinguish *Yoder* from those decisions—such as *McCollum, Engel,* and *Schempp*—that have invalidated religious practices in public schools. Neither these programs nor the exemption in *Yoder* had a "secular" purpose. But, unlike *Yoder* and *Thornton*, the public school programs threatened religious liberty and were thus properly held to abridge the constitutional separation of church and state.

JESSE H. CHOPER
(1986)

Bibliography

ANTINEAU, CHESTER J.; DOWNEY, ARTHUR T.; and ROBERTS, EDWARD C. 1964 *Freedom from Federal Establishment*. Milwaukee, Wisc.: Bruce Publishing Co.

CHOPER, JESSE H. 1963 Religion in the Public Schools: A Proposed Constitutional Standard. *University of Minnesota Law Review* 47:329–416.

——— 1968 The Establishment Clause and Aid to Parochial Schools. *California Law Review* 56:260–341.

——— 1980 The Religion Clauses of the First Amendment: Reconciling the Conflict. *University of Pittsburgh Law Review* 41:673–701.

CURRY, THOMAS 1986 *The First Freedoms*. New York: Oxford University Press.

HOWE, MARK D. 1965 *The Garden and the Wilderness*. Chicago: University of Chicago Press.

KURLAND, PHILLP B. 1962 *Religion and the Law*. Chicago: Aldine Publishing Co.

LEVY, LEONARD W. 1986 *An Establishment of Religion*. New York: Macmillan.

MURRAY, JOHN C. 1960 *We Hold These Truths*. Chap. 2. New York: Sheed & Ward.

NOWAK, JOHN E.; ROTUNDA, RONALD D.; and YOUNG, J. NELSON 1983 *Handbook on Constitutional Law*, 2nd ed. Pages 1229–1281. St. Paul, Minn.: West Publishing Co.

PFEFFER, LEO 1984 *Religion, State, and the Burger Court*. Buffalo, N.Y.: Prometheus Books.

SCHWARTZ, ALAN 1968 No Imposition of Religion: The Establishment Clause Value. *Yale Law Journal* 77:692–737.

STOKES, ANSON PHELPS 1950 *Church & State in the United States*. 3 Vols. New York: Harper.

TRIBE, LAURENCE H. 1978 *American Constitutional Law*. Chap. 14. Mineola, N.Y.: Foundation Press.

SEPARATION OF CHURCH AND STATE
(Update)

In the law concerning religion and the Constitution, the period from the end of WORLD WAR II until the mid-1980s can be best characterized as the separationist period. Since 1985, however, two major developments have altered the face of the constitutional landscape. The first concerns interpretation of the ESTABLISHMENT CLAUSE of the FIRST AMENDMENT, upon which much separationist history and law is based. Although some establishment clause principles have been reaffirmed, others have been strongly questioned and several are in flux. Second, the free exercise clause of the First Amendment has become a significant springboard for litigation. Although the number of free exercise precedents has dramatically increased, the direction in which that body of law is heading remains difficult to discern.

Establishment clause problems generally fall into three categories—GOVERNMENT AID TO RELIGIOUS INSTITUTIONS, the role of RELIGION IN PUBLIC SCHOOLS, and government support of RELIGIOUS SYMBOLS IN PUBLIC PLACES or activities. In all three categories, a crucial and overarching question is whether the clause demands maximum separation of government and religious institutions (separationism) or, alternatively, whether government support of religion is acceptable so long as sectarian discrimination is avoided (accommodationism).

These competing themes remained submerged when an important principle related to the provision of aid to religious institutions was reinforced in the Supreme Court decision in WITTERS V. WASHINGTON DEPARTMENT OF SERVICES FOR THE BLIND (1986). In *Witters* the Court built upon MUELLER V. ALLEN (1983) in ruling that the establishment clause did not require a state to deny aid to a blind applicant who would use the grant to pay tuition in a program of preparation for the Christian ministry. Though the Justices differed among themselves on the rationale, all seemed to agree that the individual, not the state, was responsible for selecting the program in which the funds would be spent. Such a private choice creates no risk of forbidden church-state interaction and, when viewed in the aggregate with other individual choices of how to spend such grants, creates quantitatively little religious consequences.

This distinction between grants to individuals, which may be "spent" in religious institutions, and grants to the institutions themselves, which the state may not make, may be in danger of collapsing. Only a narrow and shaky majority on the Court reaffirmed the legal principles governing financial aid to religious institutions in the 1985 cases of *Grand Rapids School District v. Ball* and *Aguilar v. Felton*. Each case produced another in the line of dissents complaining of the "catch-22" of school aid law: categorical grants of benefits to parochial schools are impermissible aid to religion unless the benefits are monitored to eliminate the possibility of their use to promote religion, but the acts required to monitor restrictions on benefits produce forbidden interaction between church and state.

By 1988 these dissents had ripened into what may well signal a major change in the law governing aid programs. In BOWEN V. KENDRICK (1988) a 5–4 majority upheld portions of the Adolescent Family Life Act, which provides federal funds to religious as well as secular institutions for counseling teenagers on matters of sexuality and pregnancy. Despite the obvious dangers of religious indoctrination built into any program that enlists religiously affiliated institutions in counseling on such theologically charged matters, the Court shifted the basic focus of establishment clause analysis by asking whether such indoctrination had occurred in fact. Under its prior cases, the risk of such indoctrination would have been enough to doom the program. Although it is possible that litigants can prove in an individual case that government money is subsidizing religious counsel, the process of judicial decision making in aid to religion cases will be profoundly altered if the *Bowen* approach is extended to aid to schools and other kinds of church-supported programs. Such proof may be difficult to obtain, and the consequences of such proof will be to condemn isolated instances of abuse rather than to invalidate entire programs of state assistance.

The establishment clause principle that has changed least and seems strongest is that which prohibits the introduction of religious worship or sectarian theology into the public schools. Such an effort was handed a ringing defeat in *Edwards v. Aguillard* (1987), which invalidated a Louisiana statute requiring public schools to teach "creation science" whenever they teach biological theories of evolution. Despite the state's defense of the requirement as a protection of the ACADEMIC FREEDOM of those interested in pursuing CREATIONISM, the Court found this scheme to be a deliberate attempt to introduce sectarian religious teachings (in particular, the teaching of the Book of Genesis that God created the universe and all its life forms in six days) into the public schools. As such, the law ran afoul of the principle enunciated in the various school prayer cases that the public school must remain free of efforts at religious indoctrination. While teaching about religion may be permissible, teaching designed to inculcate or reinforce religious beliefs is not.

A third context for establishment clause litigation—government involvement with the display or production of religious symbols—has been the most volatile over the past several years. LYNCH V. DONNELLY (1984), discussed briefly in the original Encyclopedia entry for this topic, upheld the validity of a city's sponsorship of a Christmastime display that included a Nativity scene at its center. The uncertain scope of *Lynch* as authority for government support of displays with some religious significance led to a flurry of litigation in the lower courts involving both Christmas displays and other symbols with religious origins. One lower court, for example, found an establishment clause violation in the adornment of San Bernardino, California, police cars with a shield bearing a Latin cross and Spanish words translating to "With This We Conquer."

In 1989 the Supreme Court tried again to draw lines concerning government sponsorship of such symbols and displays. In COUNTY OF ALLEGHENY V. ACLU (1989), a case arising from the celebration of winter holidays in Pittsburgh, Pennsylvania, the Court reached mixed results: a Nativity scene displayed on the grand staircase of the Allegheny County Courthouse was held to constitute a violation of the establishment clause, while an eighteen-foot Hanukkah menorah displayed near a larger Christmas tree outside the city-county building was held not to violate the Constitution. This pair of results is explicable only by reference to the three main groupings on the Court that the *County of Allegheny* case produced. One group of four Justices—ANTHONY M. KENNEDY, WILLIAM H. REHNQUIST, ANTONIN SCALIA, and BYRON R. WHITE—would have upheld both displays on the ground that they were temporary and noncoercive, and therefore did not threaten to establish Christianity or Judaism or any combination of the two. Another group of three Justices—WILLIAM J. BRENNAN, THURGOOD MARSHALL, and JOHN PAUL STEVENS—would have invalidated both displays on the grounds that they included objects "which retain a specifically (religious) meaning" and therefore may not be supported by the government. The deciding votes in the cases were cast by Justices HARRY A. BLACKMUN and SANDRA DAY O'CONNOR, who adopted the view that government may display, but may not endorse, symbols that have religious meaning for some. Viewing both displays in their seasonal context, these two Justices found that the county had endorsed Christianity with its crèche display but was simply recognizing the secular aspects of the season's holidays with its Christmas tree and menorah combination.

These cases are troubling, and the problems they represent are difficult to solve. Atheists feel offended by any government acknowledgment of the existence of God; many religious people are deeply disturbed by the state's embrace or exploitation of religious symbols; and a line of cases that permits government to display menorahs and crèches next to Christmas trees, but not crèches standing alone, does not inspire confidence in the Court's judgment about law or religion. Solutions at the extreme—eliminating practices such as imprinting "In God We Trust" on coins and currency, on the one hand, or tolerating blatant endorsement by government of sectarian religious symbols, on the other—appear inconsistent with America's national traditions and values. A principled middle ground is hard to articulate and defend, however, as the *Allegheny County* case reveals.

The symbols cases may reflect a movement away from separationism and toward accommodationism. Though the latter takes many forms, the narrowest and most defensible version involves exemptions for religious activity from legislative burdens otherwise imposed on comparable activity. In *Corporation of Presiding Bishop v. Amos* (1987), for example, the Supreme Court upheld as an accommodation the exemption for religious institutions from the federal statutory ban on religious discrimination in employment.

Yet not all legislative efforts at accommodation survive establishment clause attack. In TEXAS MONTHLY, INC. V. BULLOCK (1989) a closely divided Court held it impermissible for a state to exempt only religious publications from the state's sales tax. Such an exemption involves the state in distinguishing religious from nonreligious activity and preferring the former. Accommodationism permits such a preference; separationism does not.

The provision protecting the "free exercise of religion" provoked substantial litigation after 1985, but dominant themes are yet to emerge from this body of law. The 1980s were a time of revival among fundamentalist religions in the United States and a time of decline for mainstream religions. One consequence of this was an increase in constitutional attacks under the free exercise clause upon laws that were not intentionally hostile to religion but nevertheless interfered with its practice.

The recent free exercise cases have produced mixed results. The Court's earlier holdings that conditions on unemployment compensation benefits must not, absent an unusually strong reason, interfere with religious practice were reaffirmed and extended in *Hobbie v. Florida Unemployment Appeals Commission* (1987) and FRAZEE V. ILLINOIS DIVISION OF EMPLOYMENT SECURITY (1989). But in a number of other cases, the Supreme Court rejected free exercise claims. Some of these were relatively uncontroversial; for example, in *Hernandez v. Commissioner of Internal Revenue* and *Graham v. Commissioner of Internal Revenue* (1989) the Court ruled against a claim by members of the Church of Scientology that they were constitutionally entitled to income tax deductions, as charitable contributions, for payment they had made to the church in direct exchange for "auditing" or "training" sessions. Suspicion about whether Scientology was a bona fide religion or an elaborate money-making scheme for its founder may have influenced the outcome of those cases. In *Tony and Susan Alamo Foundation v. United States* (1985) a unanimous Court—perhaps operating on similar suspicions—rejected a religious foundation's claim to be constitutionally exempt from the wage and hour restrictions of the federal FAIR LABOR STANDARDS ACT with respect to employees engaged in commercial activities. And in JIMMY SWAGGART MINISTRIES V. BOARD OF EQUALIZATION OF CALIFORNIA (1990) the Court built logically upon *Texas Monthly* by holding that the free exercise clause did not compel what the establishment clause forbade—an exemption for the distribution of religious material from the state's generally applicable sales and use tax.

In other free exercise cases, however, claims that appeared meritorious under the Court's announced standards fared equally poorly. In GOLDMAN V. WEINBERGER (1986) the Court held that the air force need not accommodate the religious concern of an Orthodox Jewish captain to wear a skullcap while on duty. Deferring to what seemed decidedly trivial objectives on the part of the military to preserve uniformity of appearance, the Court's majority treated the free exercise claim as deserving little respect. O'LONE V. ESTATE OF SHABAZZ (1987) extended this approach by granting wide authority to prison officials to refuse to accommodate the religious concerns of prison inmates through any prison regulations that are "reasonably related to legitimate penological interests." And, in what may be the most disturbing of this trio of cases about government enclaves, LYNG V. NORTHWEST INDIAN CEMETERY, (1988), a 5–4 majority concluded that the free exercise clause was not even implicated, much less violated, when the United States government proposed to build in a national forest a road that would disturb, by sight and sound, places of religious significance to several Native American tribes. Despite the use of open lands by the tribes for spiritual purposes over many centuries, the *Lyng* result effectively forecloses any and all free exercise litigation by Indian tribes against government land-use decisions that may despoil Indian holy places. Earlier, in *Bowen v. Roy* (1986), the Court had also rejected a free exercise claim by a Native American concerning the use of SOCIAL SECURITY numbers on government files pertaining to his family.

Fundamentalist Christians have fared little better in free exercise cases than have the Native American tribes. State courts have been unreceptive to attempts by parents to educate their children at home without state approval. And in a celebrated 1987 case that reached the United States Court of Appeals for the Sixth Circuit, *Mozert v. Hawkins County School Board*, a group of fundamentalist parents unsuccessfully sought to have their children exempted from a reading program in the public schools that they found objectionable to their religious beliefs. In the battle over education generally, and the public schools in particular, the separationists continue to prevail.

Characterized most generally, the trend in the Supreme Court has been toward easing some of the restrictions imposed on government by the establishment clause while maintaining or increasing the hurdles for free exercise claims. In such a world of deference to legislative judgment, accommodation is far more likely to emerge from the legislative branch than from the judicial branch. Accommodationism, so practiced, presents a substantial risk of favoritism for majority religions—that is, of replicating the evils that the religion clauses of the First Amendment were intended to combat.

IRA C. LUPU
(1992)

Bibliography

LEVY, LEONARD W. 1986 *The Establishment Clause: Religion and the First Amendment.* New York: Macmillan.

LUPU, I. C. 1989 Where Rights Begin: The Problem of Burdens on the Free Exercise of Religion. *Harvard Law Review* 102:933–989.

MCCONNELL, MICHAEL W. 1985 Accommodation of Religion. *Supreme Court Review* 1985:1–59.

SEPARATION OF POWERS

Any system of constitutional government must have as one of its central principles some degree of separation of powers. A system of government in which all legal power and authority is exercised by one person or group of people must depend entirely upon their self-restraint in the exercise of that power. The history of government does not suggest that such self-restraint is likely this side of heaven or utopia, and efforts to prevent the abuse of the powers of government have therefore focused on constitutional arrangements that divide and limit the powers of government.

The doctrine of the separation of powers consists of a number of elements: the idea of three separate branches of government, the legislature, the executive, and the judiciary; the belief that there are unique functions appropriate to each branch; and the assertion that the personnel of the branches of government should be kept distinct, no one person being able to be a member of more than one branch of government at the same time. The more pure or extreme the form of the doctrine, the greater the extent to which all three of these elements are insisted upon without reservation or modification. In past centuries political writers have proposed such extreme solutions in France, Britain, and America, and attempts have been made, unsuccessfully, to approximate as closely as possible to this extreme in practice. The spirit of the doctrine was expressed clearly in the Constitution of Virginia in 1776: "The legislature, executive and judiciary departments shall be separate and distinct, so that neither exercise the powers properly belonging to the other: nor shall any person exercise the powers of more than one of them at the same time. . . ."

A further aspect of the doctrine is the concern with the method by which the members of the executive and judicial branches are selected, for this will have implications for the extent to which the members of one branch may be able to influence the behavior of members of another. The more extreme versions of the doctrine therefore demand the direct election of members of all three branches of government in order that they should be responsible directly to the people, and not dependent upon each other. In the words of Samuel Williams, historian of Vermont, in 1794, "the security of the people is derived not from the nice ideal application of checks, balances, and mechanical powers, among the different parts of the government, but from the responsibility, and dependence of each part of the government, on the people."

The doctrine of the separation of powers, standing alone, however, has never been able to provide the kind of safeguards against the abuse of governmental power which it claims to provide. In practice we find that CHECKS AND BALANCES are required to prevent one or another branch of government from becoming too dominant. The idea of internal checks, exercised by one branch of government over the others, is drawn from the ancient theory of mixed government, and from the eighteenth-century "mixed and balanced constitution" of Great Britain. Thus JAMES MADISON, in THE FEDERALIST #48, undertook to show that unless the branches of government "be so far connected and blended as to give each a constitutional control over the others, the degree of separation which the maxim requires, as essential to a free government, can never in practice be duly maintained." All constitutional systems of government are therefore an amalgam of the separation of powers and checks and balances. The exact composition of this mixture was a central problem for the Framers of the federal Constitution, and their solution distinguished presidential-congressional government from parliamentary systems.

The emergence of a full-blown doctrine of the separation of powers was the result of a long process of development, involving the refinement of a set of concepts, including the idea of law itself, which today we largely take for granted. In early times the idea of law was very different from the modern concept of legislation or statute law. The latter view of law, consciously drafted and adopted by human rather than divine will, did not emerge clearly until the battle between king and parliament in seventeenth-century England sharpened the perception of law, lawyers, and politicians. The more radical opponents of royal power conceived of a parliament that was representative of the people, making laws which the king, or some other executive power, should put into effect. In the turmoil of civil war, this doctrine of the separation of powers was fashioned by a number of writers until it reached a recognizably modern form.

As the British constitutional crisis deepened, the doctrine was refined by those who, like JOHN MILTON, pointed to the arbitrary character of the Long Parliament, Henry Ireton in the Whitehall debates of 1649, and JOHN LILBURNE in *The Picture of the Councel of State* asserting that "the House itself was never (neither now, nor in any age before) betrusted with a Law executing power, but only with a Law making power." John Sadler in his *The Rights of the Kingdom* of 1649 asserted the basis of the separation of powers very clearly. The three powers of government, legislative, judicial, and executive, "should be in Distinct

Subjects; by the Law of Nature, for if Lawmakers be judges, of those that break their Laws; they seem to be judges in their own cause: which our Law, and Nature itself, so much avoideth and abhorreth, so it seemeth also to forbid, both the Lawmaker, and the Judge to Execute."

The execution of Charles I and the establishment of republican government stripped away the remaining vestiges of mixed government and left the separation of powers as the sole constitutional principle for the organization of the government of Great Britain. The Commonwealth produced the first written constitution of modern times, the Instrument of Government of 1653, and the doctrine of the separation of powers clearly inspired its authors. This document vested the supreme legislative authority in the lord protector and the people assembled in Parliament, but in effect the role of the protector in legislation was to be limited to a suspensive veto of twenty days. The Instrument also provided that "the exercise of the Chief Magistracy and the administration of the Government . . . shall be in the Lord Protector, assisted with a Council." Although the Instrument of Government was never an effective basis for government, from that time on the theory of the separation of powers emerged and reemerged whenever demands were made to limit the power of governments. The official defense of the Instrument, *A True State of the Case of the Commonwealth*, published in 1654, and probably written by Marchamont Nedham, expressed the theory behind the constitution when it criticized earlier institutional arrangements "which placing the legislative and executive powers in the same persons is a marvellous in-let of corruption and tyranny." At this point the idea of a judicial power distinct from the executive was still relatively undeveloped, to emerge more fully at the end of the seventeenth century, and then to blossom in the work of MONTESQUIEU and WILLIAM BLACKSTONE, and to be embodied in the Constitution of the United States.

With the restoration of Charles II in 1660 the basis of a new theory of the constitution was required. The principle of the separation of powers must be reasserted, as it was by JOHN LOCKE, but in the context of a "mixed and balanced" constitution, incorporating a role for the monarch and for the House of Lords. This amalgam of the separation of powers and checks and balances, the constitution of the Augustan Age of British politics, was lauded as the model of "a constitution of liberty." Montesquieu is popularly credited with a major role in the development of the separation of powers, but the theory was developed a hundred years before the publication of *The Spirit of the Laws* (1748). Indeed it is the influence of his work, particularly in the American colonies, rather than any intellectual contribution to the separation of powers, that gives such significance to the work of Montesquieu. Montesquieu's contribution to the separation of powers was es-

sentially his modern emphasis upon the three powers of government and the clear recognition of the importance of the power to judge, a point driven home by Blackstone in his *Commentaries on the Laws of England* (1765–1769). Blackstone, whose work was known to every lawyer in the American colonies, took Montesquieu's rather feeble notion of the judicial power and clothed it with the majesty of the English judges.

From the time of the first English settlements in America there was a continual interplay between ideas and events in the home country and the developing politics of the colonies. Mixed government and the separation of powers were common subjects of discussion in Massachusetts in the seventeenth century, and the constitutional debates over the role of king and parliament in England had their repercussions in America. In 1644, the elders of the church described the government of Massachusetts Bay as not a "pure aristocracy, but mixt of an aristocracy and democracy" and defended the "negative voice" which the governor and assistants exercised over decisions of the legislature. In 1679 the elders affirmed that the government of Massachusetts consisted in the "distribution of differing interest of power and privilege between the magistrates and freemen, and the distinct exercise of legislative and executive power." This statement preceded by eleven years the publication of Locke's *Second Treatise*. In the eighteenth century American thought fell into the same mold as that of other eulogists of the English constitution, adapting the terminology where necessary to fit the circumstances of colonial governments, until the increasing conflict between the English Parliament and the colonists brought to the foreground those aspects of the English system that were attracting criticism both at home and abroad, the cabinet system and the corrupt and unrepresentative House of Commons. In the colonies, Americans saw the mixing of legislative, executive, and judicial functions in the governors' councils and in the abuse of power by royal governors. With the upsurge of revolutionary fervor the doctrine of the separation of powers lay ready to hand, both as a stick with which to beat the British and as the basis for a truly American system of government.

The American achievement was to transform the theory of the mixed constitution, in which the powers of government were distributed among monarchy, aristocracy, and democracy, into a functionally divided system in which king and peers had no part, turning a class-based structure into one in which all the different branches of government drew their authority from the people. The first step in this process was taken when the revolutionary state constitutions were established in 1776 and succeeding years. These constitutions contained broad affirmations of the separation of powers, but the checks and balances of the

British model were out of favor. Consequently, popularly elected legislatures became the dominant branch of government.

The state legislatures soon began to act in ways that raised fears that the separation of powers, if not buttressed in some other way, meant that in practice, in THOMAS JEFFERSON's words, "All the powers of government, legislative, executive, and judiciary, result to the legislative body." The need for positive checks to the exercise of power was increasingly apparent. The *Essex Result* of 1778, recommending the form which the new constitution for Massachusetts should take, noted that "Each branch is to be independent, and further, to be so balanced, and able to exert such checks upon the others, as will preserve it from dependance on, or a union with them." Madison summed up the situation in *The Federalist* #48: "The conclusion that I am warranted in drawing from these observations is, that a mere demarcation on parchment of the constitutional limits of the several departments is not a sufficient guard against those encroachments which lead to a tyrannical concentration of all the powers of government in the same hands."

It was necessary therefore that the departments of government should "be so far connected and blended as to give to each a constitutional control over the others": the President to have a qualified VETO POWER and the PARDONING POWER, the Senate to play a part in appointments and in the ratification of treaties, and the Supreme Court, by implication at least, to have the power to declare legislative acts to be unconstitutional. As Madison observed in *The Federalist* #48, the three branches of government, although separate, must be "connected and blended" to ensure that each has some "constitutional control over the others."

Thus the separation of powers was not destroyed but rather reinforced by the adoption in the Constitution of a number of checks and balances. Although in some degree this represented a reversion to the pattern of the English Constitution, there was one vital respect in which no one wished to see the English model adopted. The popular denigration of George III as a tyrant in the revolutionary situation was understandable, but the members of the CONSTITUTIONAL CONVENTION had a much deeper understanding of the British political system. They understood the nature of the *"Cabinet Council* composed entirely of the principal officers of the great departments," they understood the role of the king's ministers in the legislature, and they knew well the system of crown influence and the role of unqualified members of the House of Commons. Their rejection of the whole basis of linking the executive and legislative branches of government in this way was complete, and Article I, section 6, of the Constitution, which provided that "no Person holding any Office under the United States, shall be a Member of either House during his Continuence in Office," was adopted without hesitation.

What then have been the practical effects of the separation of powers on the legal and political system of the United States? These effects can be seen in two broad, related areas: the decisions of the Supreme Court relating to "the powers of government," and the political articulation of the American system.

The Supreme Court has faced a number of difficulties which arise from the confusions inherent in the way the "separation of powers" evolved. The term "separation of powers" is sometimes used, as here, to refer to the doctrine that the major branches of government should be kept separate and limited to their own functions, but quite often the term is also used to include the checks and balances in the Constitution, which derive their rationale from a different source. Second, the word "power" is used ambiguously to mean both "branch" and "function." Finally, most of the Court's problems arise from the need to define the functions of government when it is argued that a particular branch has engaged in an activity outside its "proper" function. When the Constitution itself makes what the Court in BAKER V. CARR (1962) called "a textually demonstrable commitment" of an issue to a coordinate branch of government, then the Court has only to determine that to be the case, but what does the text demonstrate when it refers to "the legislative power" or "the executive power"? Such terms are vague indeed. The nub of the problem is that the functions of government can be defined only in the broadest conceptual terms—making rules, carrying rules into effect, and settling disputes arising out of the application of rules—but few activities of government fall unambiguously into such categories. The difficulty is particularly acute in any effort to categorize the exercise of the discretionary powers of government which the traditional doctrine of the separation of powers did not encompass. Indeed, the doctrine had been developed largely to render ineffective the exercise of such discretion in the form of the prerogatives of the Crown in England, or in the exercise of the powers of the governors in the American colonies.

As a consequence of these difficulties the Court has generally followed a pragmatic course in its decisions on the separation of powers. In practice the Court has generally accepted that no precise "watertight definition of government powers is possible." The first major issue facing the Supreme Court was to define its own role in the system of separation of powers and checks and balances. The Anti-Federalist and Jeffersonian interpretations of the Constitution looked back to the strict view that each branch of government not only should be separate from the others but also should not be dependent upon them, and therefore not subject to their control. Such an interpretation would rule out JUDICIAL REVIEW as it has come to be exercised in the United States, and faint echoes of this attempt to escape the JURISDICTION of the Court have been heard as recently as President RICHARD M. NIXON's claim to an absolute EXECUTIVE PRIVILEGE for tape recordings of his conversations with his aides. However, in MARBURY V. MADISON (1803) Chief Justice JOHN MARSHALL emphatically asserted that it was "the province and duty of the judicial department to say what the law is"—and, in the course of doing so, to rule upon the extent of the power and functions of the other branches of government. Respect is due to the interpretations put on the Constitution by other branches, but in the end, as the Court said in UNITED STATES V. NIXON (1974), "the 'JUDICIAL POWER OF THE UNITED STATES' vested in the federal courts by Art. III Sec. 1, of the Constitution can no more be shared with the Executive Branch than the Chief Executive, for example, can share with the Judiciary the power to override a Presidential veto. Any other conclusion would be contrary to the basic concept of separation of powers and checks and balances that flow from the scheme of a tripartite government." The Court has, of course, accepted that interference in the activities of the other branches of government, in particular the Congress, is a delicate and sensitive matter. The POLITICAL QUESTIONS doctrine protects the Court against becoming embroiled in matters that could drag it down into the morass of day-to-day politics, but the Court itself retains the right to determine what is, and what is not, a political question.

The Supreme Court has set limits to the exercise of the legislative powers of Congress either to interfere directly in litigation, to interpret earlier legislation, or to set aside decisions of courts already made. It has also ruled that, as in HAYBURN'S CASE (1792) and *United States v. Ferreira* (1853), Congress cannot impose upon the courts duties not considered to be judicial in character. In two major decisions the Supreme Court announced that the houses of Congress could not properly appropriate to themselves a judicial function. In KILBOURN V. THOMPSON (1881) the Court concluded that in committing a witness to prison for refusing to testify before a committee the House of Representatives had "not only exceeded the limit of its own authority, but assumed power which could only be properly exercised by another branch of the government, because the power was in its nature clearly judicial." And OBITER DICTUM in WATKINS V. UNITED STATES (1957), the Court said, "Nor is the Congress a law enforcement or trial agency. These are functions of the executive and judicial departments of government."

The Supreme Court has also prevented Congress from trenching upon the powers of the executive branch. In MYERS V. UNITED STATES (1926) the Court held that Congress could not limit by statute the President's power to remove executive officers, although in HUMPHREY'S EXECUTOR V. UNITED STATES (1935) it upheld congressional restrictions on the President's power to dismiss officers of independent regulatory agencies; and in BUCKLEY V. VALEO (1976) the Court invalidated the attempt by Congress itself to make appointments to the Federal Elections Commission. The Court quoted with approval the decision in *Springer v. Philippine Islands* (1928): "Legislative power, as distinguished from executive power, is the authority to make laws, but not to enforce them or appoint the agents charged with the duty of such enforcement. The latter are executive functions."

In general the Supreme Court has been generous in its interpretation of the powers of the President. However, in two important instances the Court has checked presidential power. In YOUNGSTOWN SHEET AND TUBE COMPANY V. SAWYER (1951) the Court held unconstitutional President Harry S. Truman's attempt to take over steel mills by EXECUTIVE ORDER, on the ground that "the President's power to see that the laws are faithfully executed refutes the idea that he is to be a lawmaker. The Constitution limits his functions in the lawmaking process to the recommending of laws he thinks wise and the vetoing of laws he thinks bad." And in *United States v. Nixon* (1974) the Court rejected the President's claim of executive privilege against a court order to produce tapes and documents relating to the Watergate investigations.

The area in which the Supreme Court has been subjected to the greatest degree of criticism for failing to maintain the spirit and practice of the separation of powers has been the way in which it has handled the question of the DELEGATION OF POWER by Congress to the executive branch and to independent regulatory commissions. In the modern administrative state, complex regulatory activities on the part of government necessitate agencies that will make rules (subordinate to statute law), apply those rules, and decide disputes arising out of their actions. The United States Congress, in establishing a large number of such agencies, has created a "headless fourth branch" of government. These agencies, in the words of Justice ROBERT H. JACKSON in *Federal Trade Commission v. Ruberoid Company* (1952), "have been called quasi-legislative, quasi-executive or quasi-judicial, as the occasion required, in order to validate their function within the separation of powers scheme of the Constitution. The mere retreat to the qualifying 'quasi' is implicit with confession that all recognized classifications have broken down, and 'quasi' is a smooth cover which we draw over our confusion as we might use a counterpane to conceal a disordered bed." Although the Court has said "that the legislative power of Congress cannot be delegated," in practice it has allowed very broad and ill-defined delegations of power to administrative agencies. In two instances such delegation of power has been disallowed: PANAMA REFINING CO. V. RYAN (1935) and SCHECHTER POULTRY CORP. V. UNITED STATES (1935). In the latter case the Court asserted that the proper delegation of power required Congress to establish "standards of legal obligation, thus performing its essential legislative function." Failure to enact such standards for the administrative agency to follow would be an attempt to transfer the legislative function of Congress to others. However, in numerous cases the Court has allowed delegation with little in the way of effective standards set by Congress, and giving to the administrative agency, as in the *Permian Basin Area Rate Cases* (1968), a wide and uncontrolled discretion. In the field of FOREIGN AFFAIRS the delegation of legislative power to the President and his ability to negotiate with foreign powers and make EXECUTIVE AGREEMENTS with them, are very wide indeed, as the Court recognized in UNITED STATES V. CURTISS-WRIGHT EXPORT CORP. (1936).

In all these areas of tension between the branches of government, therefore, the Supreme Court, despite the broad generalizations which appear from time to time in its opinions, has followed a pragmatic approach to the separation of power. However, in IMMIGRATION AND NATURALIZATION SERVICE V. CHADHA (1983) the Court, in the opinion of some, adopted a more theoretical and formal line of argument. In *Chadha* the Court invalidated the use of the LEGISLATIVE VETO, the device by which Congress reserved to itself the right to review administrative regulations and decisions taken under some 200 different statutes. The opinion, written by Chief Justice WARREN E. BURGER, concentrated on the narrow constitutional issues of "presentment" of legislation and BICAMERALISM, but referred to the theory of the separation of powers in the Constitution as dividing the powers of government into "three defined categories, legislative, executive and judicial" which are "functionally identifiable." An alternative approach was put by Justice LEWIS F. POWELL in a CONCURRING OPINION. His objection to the use of the legislative veto in this particular instance was that the House of Representatives had improperly exercised a judicial power by ruling on the case of a particular individual rather than making a general rule. In taking this position Justice Powell was appealing to an element of the separation of powers of long standing and of great importance: the generality of law, restricting the legislative power to the general rather than the particular.

Some critics of the Supreme Court argue with PHILIP KURLAND that as a consequence of its decisions "the ancient concept of the separation of powers and checks and balances has been reduced to a slogan, to be trotted out by the Supreme Court from time to time as a substitute for reasoned judgment." Whether or not this assessment

of the judicial history of the separation should be considered too harsh, the impact of the concept upon the day-to-day working of the American political system has undoubtedly been enormous in terms of the relationship between the administration and the Congress. The prohibition on simultaneous membership of the legislative and executive branches in Article I, section 6, of the Constitution distinguishes the American system from the vast majority of genuinely democratic regimes in the world, most of which follow the parliamentary model. The fact that the President and his administration must operate from outside the legislature, rather than from within it, makes a vast difference to the techniques that must be employed to gain the acquiescence of the legislature to policies proposed by the executive. Much more important than the distinction between legislative and executive functions is the fact of two distinct branches of government with no overlapping of personnel (the Vice-President of the United States excepted). This strict separation of the personnel of government is certainly not the only reason why American political parties are so decentralized, diffuse, and undisciplined, but it is certainly a very important factor. The consequences for the way in which government policies are formulated, evolved, enacted, and implemented are immeasurable.

M. J. C. VILE
(1986)

Bibliography

BARBER, SOTIRIOS A. 1975 *The Constitution and the Delegation of Congressional Power*. Chicago: University of Chicago Press.

ELLIOTT, E. DONALD 1984 *INS v. Chadha*: The Administrative Constitution, the Constitution, and the Legislative Veto. *Supreme Court Review* 1983:125–176.

GWYN, W. B. 1965 *The Meaning of the Separation of Powers*. New Orleans: Tulane University Press.

KURLAND, PHILLIP B. 1978 *Watergate and the Constitution*. Chicago: University of Chicago Press.

SCHWARTZ, BERNARD 1963 *A Commentary on the Constitution of the United States*. New York: Macmillan.

VILE, M. J. C. 1967 *Constitutionalism and the Separation of Powers*. Oxford: Oxford University Press.

SEPARATION OF POWERS
(Update)

During the 1990s, the Supreme Court attempted, in an unusual number of separation of powers cases, to give concrete meaning to that time-honored but abstract DOCTRINE, only to retreat to other, more specific and definable constitutional provisions to resolve those cases.

The Court attempted a comprehensive definition of the

doctrine in *Morrison v. Olson* (1988), in which it upheld the law establishing the INDEPENDENT COUNSEL. A statute violates the doctrine, the Court said, in three circumstances: (1) if the statute involves an effort by Congress to increase its own powers at the expense of those of the executive branch, (2) if the law impermissibly undermines the EXECUTIVE POWER, and (3) if the law "disrupts the proper balance between the coordinate branches [by] prevent[ing] the Executive Branch from accomplishing its constitutionally assigned functions." Applying this standard, the Court found that the independent counsel law worked no impermissible interference with the President's authority in violation of the principle of separation of powers.

In MISTRETTA V. UNITED STATES (1989), the Court returned to the three principles in upholding the validity of the U.S. Sentencing Commission. In subsequent separation cases, the Court reiterated this three-part test but notably declined to use it as a basis for resolving the disputes at hand, looking instead to the Constitution's APPOINTMENTS CLAUSE.

Thus, in 1991 the Court held, in *Freytag v. Commissioner of Internal Revenue*, that the appointment of special trial judges by the chief judge of the Tax Court did not violate the appointments clause. In 1994 the Court held, similarly, in *Weiss v. United States*, that the clause was not violated by the appointment of military judges by the Judge Advocate General to serve on special and general courts martial. Finally, in *Edmond v. United States* (1997), the Court upheld the authority of the U.S. Secretary of Transportation to appoint civilian members of the U.S. Coast Guard Court of Appeals, again in the face of an appointments clause challenge.

Dissatisfaction with the independent counsel law resurfaced during the second term of President WILLIAM J. CLINTON, when Kenneth Starr, an independent counsel appointed to investigate various alleged improprieties on the part of the President, recommended Clinton's IMPEACHMENT. His report was referred under the law to the Committee on the Judiciary of the U.S. HOUSE OF REPRESENTATIVES. The document triggered substantial debate over the scope, expense, and politics of Independent Counsel Starr's investigation and, for only the third time in American history, presidential impeachment hearings.

One of the grounds claimed by Starr to represent an impeachable offense was that the President had allegedly committed perjury during a deposition in a civil sexual harassment case when he testified about his sexual conduct with White House intern Monica Lewinsky. In 1997, the President argued to the Supreme Court that the Constitution required that federal courts defer civil litigation arising out of pretenure conduct against a President until

the end of his term. The ruling in CLINTON V. JONES (1997) went against the President. The Court reviewed other instances in which "[s]itting Presidents have responded to court orders to provide testimony or other information" and concluded that "such interactions between the Judicial and Executive Branches can scarcely be thought a novelty." Like "every other citizen who properly invokes" a federal court's JURISDICTION, the Court held that the sexual harassment plaintiff, Paula Jones, had a "right to an orderly disposition of her claims." Ultimately, after Jones continued to press the suit, the President settled out of court for $850,000. The Court in 1998 also rejected appeals by the Clinton administration directed at blocking the GRAND JURY testimony of U.S. Secret Service agents and lawyers in the White House Counsel's office in proceedings involving the Starr investigation.

The extent to which separation of powers principles control the activities of administrative officials caused the Court to revisit IMMIGRATION AND NATURALIZATION SERVICE V. CHADHA (1983) in 1991. In *Metropolitan Washington Airports Authority v. Citizens for the Abatement of Aircraft Noise* (1991), the Court held unconstitutional a law that gave power to a "Board of Review" (consisting of members of Congress) to veto decisions of the Washington, D.C., airport authority, an entity created by the laws of Virginia and the District of Columbia. Whether the Board of Review exercised executive or LEGISLATIVE POWER was irrelevant, the Court found; if the power was executive, the Constitution "does not permit Congress to exercise it," and if the power was legislative, the BICAMERALISM and PRESENTMENT requirements explained in *Chadha* were breached by the law.

The *Chadha* Court had insisted that the power to enact statutes may be exercised only "in accord with a single, finely wrought and exhaustively considered, procedure." This observation was recalled in perhaps the most important separation of powers case to be decided in recent years, *Clinton v. City of New York* (1998), which involved the constitutionality of the LINE-ITEM VETO. In the Line Item Veto Act of 1996, Congress enacted a provision that gave the President the power to "cancel in whole" any items of new spending or any "limited tax benefit" in newly enacted LEGISLATION. The President was required to notify Congress in a special message of each cancellation; if Congress, by a majority vote of each house (subject to possible presidential veto) disapproved the cancellation, the cancellation was rendered void.

This scheme, the Court held, ran contrary to the "finely wrought" procedure commanded by the Constitution in Article I, section 7, the same provision relied on by the Court in *Chadha* in invalidating the LEGISLATIVE VETO. Whether the law in question "impermissibly disrupts the balance of powers among the three branches of government," the Court concluded, it was unnecessary to decide. A DISSENTING OPINION by Justice STEPHEN G. BREYER, joined in part by Justices SANDRA DAY O'CONNOR and ANTONIN SCALIA, argued that "there is not a dime's worth of difference between Congress's authorizing the President to cancel a spending item, and Congress's authorizing money to be spent at the President's discretion. And the latter has been done since the founding of the nation."

As part of the litigation concerning the line-item veto, the Court had occasion to resolve a related separation of powers controversy that had divided lower courts since the 1970s—the issue of CONGRESSIONAL STANDING. *Raynes v. Baird* (1997) held that members of Congress did not have a sufficiently personal stake in the validity of the hitherto unused line-item veto to establish STANDING to challenge its constitutionality.

MICHAEL J. GLENNON
(2000)

Bibliography

CHEMERINSKY, ERWIN   1997   *Constitutional Law: Principles and Policies.* New York: Aspen Law and Business.
GLENNON, MICHAEL   1990   *Constitutional Diplomacy.* Princeton, N.J.: Princeton University Press.
RAVEN-HANSEN, PETER and BANKS, WILLIAM   1995   From Vietnam to Desert Shield: The Commander in Chief's Spending Power. *Iowa Law Review* 18:79–147.
SCHOENBROD, DAVID   1993   *Power Without Responsibility.* New Haven, Conn.: Yale University Press.
STONE, GEOFFREY R.; SEIDMAN, LOUIS M.; SUNSTEIN, CASS R.; and TUSHNET, MARK V.   1996   *Constitutional Law,* 3rd ed. New York: Aspen Law and Business.

SERIATIM

(Latin: "Severally" or "in series.") Members of multijudge courts sometimes deliver individual opinions seriatim rather than joining in a single "OPINION OF THE COURT." Before JOHN MARSHALL became Chief Justice, the Supreme Court followed this practice, requiring each Justice to explain his DECISION. Opinions delivered seriatim are necessarily less authoritative than those that carry the weight of the full Court or a majority of the Justices. For that reason Marshall abandoned the established practice in favor of giving an opinion of the court. THOMAS JEFFERSON, both in 1787 and later as President, favored a constitutional requirement that Supreme Court opinions be rendered seriatim.

DENNIS J. MAHONEY
(1986)

SERRANO v. PRIEST
5 Cal. 3d 584, 487 P.2d 1241, 96 Cal. Rptr 601 (1971)

This decision of the California Supreme Court produced a flurry of hope that the disgraceful inequalities in the financing of public schools might fall to an EQUAL PROTECTION attack. Two years after the *Serrano* decision, the Supreme Court of the United States dashed that hope in SAN ANTONIO INDEPENDENT SCHOOL DISTRICT V. RODRIGUEZ (1973).

Public schools throughout the nation are financed in major part through reliance on the local property tax. School districts that are property-wealthy thus can levy relatively low taxes and support their schools at high levels of spending per pupil. Poor districts, however, must levy taxes at much higher rates in order to spend at much lower levels per pupil. The California court in *Serrano* held this system unconstitutional, 6–1, both under the equal protection clause of the FOURTEENTH AMENDMENT and under parallel provisions of the state constitution. Because the decision merely reversed a trial court's determination that the complaint had not stated a valid constitutional claim, and remanded the case for trial, it was not a FINAL JUDGMENT and was not reviewable by the United States Supreme Court. Similarly, the ruling on state constitutional law was an ADEQUATE STATE GROUND, insulating the case from Supreme Court review.

The California court's opinion was devoted mainly to a discussion of the equal protection clause. Two grounds were found for subjecting the school finance scheme to STRICT SCRUTINY: the interest in education was held to be a FUNDAMENTAL INTEREST, and WEALTH DISCRIMINATION was held to be a SUSPECT CLASSIFICATION. Absent a showing of a COMPELLING STATE INTEREST justifying the inequalities in the state's statutory scheme, that scheme must fall.

The Supreme Court's *Rodriguez* decision, rejecting both the California court's bases for strict scrutiny, ended *Serrano*'s brief influence on the course of federal constitutional DOCTRINE. But other state courts reached similar results on the basis of their own state constitutions, and in California itself *Serrano* produced significant efforts to restructure public school finance.

KENNETH L. KARST
(1986)

SEVENTEENTH AMENDMENT

Proposed by Congress on May 16, 1912, the Seventeenth Amendment went into effect on May 31, 1913. The amendment provided for DIRECT ELECTION of United

States senators by the people of the states. Previously, under the first clause of Article I, section 3, senators had been chosen by the state legislatures.

Selection of United States senators by state legislatures had been an object of criticism for many years. Direct election of senators was first proposed in 1826; and after 1893 a constitutional amendment to establish direct election was proposed in Congress every year. Even without a constitutional amendment, popular choice of senators was becoming the rule. By 1912, twenty-nine of the forty-eight states had provided either for nomination by party primaries, with the individual legislators bound to vote for their party's nominee, or for a statewide general election, the result of which was binding on the legislature.

The objectives of direct election included reducing corruption in selection of senators, elimination of national-party domination of state legislatures, and immediate representation of the people in the SENATE. But there was actually little change in the characteristics of persons elected to the Senate or in the proceedings and activities either of the Senate or of the state legislatures as a result of the Seventeenth Amendment.

The amendment has not occasioned much litigation. In 1915, the Supreme Court held that the right to vote for United States senators was a privilege of United States CITIZENSHIP, protected by the PRIVILEGES AND IMMUNITIES clause; and in 1946 it held that that right could not be denied on account of race. The Court has also held that the Seventeenth Amendment does not require that a candidate receive a majority of the votes cast in order to be elected.

DENNIS J. MAHONEY
(1986)

SEVENTH AMENDMENT

An unexpectedly controversial provision of the document that emerged from the CONSTITUTIONAL CONVENTION OF 1787 was that giving the Supreme Court APPELLATE JURISDICTION "both as to law and fact." Anti-Federalists argued that the provision worked to abridge or deny the COMMON LAW right of TRIAL BY JURY in civil cases. Some, including PATRICK HENRY, went so far as to contend that it introduced the continental European civil law into the American court system. Although the convention had considered a clause protecting the right to a jury trial in civil cases, the clause was omitted; because the jury system varied somewhat from state to state, the meaning of the clause would not be certain. In the course of the RATIFICATION OF THE CONSTITUTION, five state conventions recommended an amendment to give the right explicit constitutional status.

The Seventh Amendment was proposed by Congress in

1789 and was ratified in 1791, as part of the BILL OF RIGHTS. As originally introduced by JAMES MADISON, the restriction on review of a jury's findings would have been inserted in Article III immediately after the definition of the Supreme Court's appellate jurisdiction. When the Bill of Rights was reorganized into a series of new articles, the restriction was joined to the general guarantee of a jury trial in federal civil cases.

The purpose of the amendment was not to extend the right to a jury trial but to preserve it as it then existed. The phrase "common law" did not purport to exclude cases arising under federal statutes but rather those cognizable in EQUITY or under ADMIRALTY AND MARITIME JURISDICTION. The word "jury" originally meant the common law jury of twelve men; but the Supreme Court held in *Colegrove v. Battin* (1973) that a jury of six members satisfied the general intent of the amendment. The Seventh Amendment is one of the very few provisions of the Bill of Rights not made applicable to the states under the INCORPORATION DOCTRINE. State courts would thus be free, under federal constitutional law, to dispense with juries altogether in civil cases.

Since the FEDERAL RULES OF CIVIL PROCEDURE in 1934 united the formerly discrete procedures of law and equity, new questions have emerged under the Seventh Amendment. In BEACON THEATRES INC. V. WESTOVER (1959) and DAIRY QUEEN, INC. V. WOOD (1962) the Supreme Court held that the right to jury trial attached to all issues of law of the type formerly triable to a jury at common law, even when those issues were "incidental" to equitable issues. In *Ross v. Bernhard* (1970) this principle was extended to STOCKHOLDER'S SUITS, which previously had been heard only under the rules of equity.

DENNIS J. MAHONEY
(1986)

SEVERABILITY

A court determines whether a statute is severable (or separable) in order to decide one of two different questions: When part of the law is unconstitutional, should the court hold the entire statute invalid, or merely the offending part? When the law can be applied validly to the litigant in court, should the court nonetheless hold the law invalid because it is capable of being applied unconstitutionally to others?

The first question was presented in CARTER V. CARTER COAL CO. (1936). Congress had regulated coal prices and the wages and hours of coal miners. After holding the wage and hour regulations invalid, the Supreme Court posed the severability issue in the usual way, as a question of LEGISLATIVE INTENT: if Congress had known the wage and hour provisions would be held invalid, would it still have regulated prices? Congress had stated plainly that if any part of the coal act were held invalid, the rest of the law remained effective. Nonetheless, the Court said, the price controls were so closely related to the labor provisions that Congress would not have enacted them alone. The price controls were thus invalid, whether or not they would have been valid if considered by themselves. The issue of severability calls into play the same kind of judgment employed in JUDICIAL REVIEW of the constitutionality of LEGISLATION.

Carter involved a federal statute. When a state law presents a similar question of severability, the Supreme Court ordinarily leaves that question to the state courts. However, a state statute may present the Court with the second type of severability issue. When a state law is IN-VALID ON ITS FACE—for example, under the FIRST AMEND-MENT doctrine of OVERBREADTH—the Court refuses to enforce the law because of its potential unconstitutional application to persons not in court. This practice moderates the effect of the rule denying a litigant STANDING to raise other persons' legal rights.

KENNETH L. KARST
(1986)

Bibliography
MONAGHAN, HENRY P. 1982 Overbreadth. *Supreme Court Review* 1982:1–39.
NOTE 1984 Severability of Legislative Veto Provisions: A Policy Analysis. *Harvard Law Review* 97:1182–1197.
STERN, ROBERT L. 1937 Separability and Separability Clauses in the Supreme Court. *Harvard Law Review* 51:76–128.

SEWARD, WILLIAM H.
(1801–1872)

William Henry Seward was a New York lawyer, governor (1838–1842), United States senator (1849–1861), and secretary of state (1861–1869). As governor he prevented the extradition to Virginia of three men accused of helping a slave escape, and thus set off a minor interstate squabble. In *Jones v. Van Zandt* (1847) Seward, as cocounsel with SALMON P. CHASE, unsuccessfully appealed the conviction of an Ohio Quaker accused of aiding fugitive slaves. In the Senate, Seward opposed the COMPROMISE OF 1850, asserting that on the issue of slavery there was "HIGHER LAW than the Constitution." He supported the admission of Kansas as a free state, attacked the Supreme Court's decision in DRED SCOTT V. SANDFORD (1857), and in 1858 declared that slavery had created "an irrepressible conflict" for the Union. During the SECESSION crisis Seward served on the Committee of Thirteen, and proposed that Congress guar-

antee to protect slavery wherever it existed. Seward thought secession was illegal, but he urged Lincoln to evacuate Fort Sumter and negotiate with Confederate officials. Seward initially opposed the EMANCIPATION PROCLAMATION and successfully urged Lincoln to delay it until after a Union military victory. In FOREIGN AFFAIRS he deftly negotiated to keep Britain and France out of the war, and avoided a conflict with Britain over the *Trent* affair. He also laid out the legal argument that led to a successful damage claim against Britain over the *Alabama*. During Reconstruction, Seward supported ANDREW JOHNSON's policies, and drafted many of his veto messages. He also negotiated the acquisition of Alaska (1867) from Russia.

PAUL FINKELMAN
(1986)

Bibliography
VAN DEUSON, GLYNDON G. 1967 *William Henry Seward.* New York: Oxford University Press.

SEX AND ANTIDISCRIMINATION LEGISLATION

See: Race and Sex in Antidiscrimination Law

SEX DISCRIMINATION

The application of constitutional principle to government action that distinguishes on the basis of sex is a late-twentieth-century development. From the 1860s until 1971, the record remained unbroken: the Supreme Court rejected every effort to overturn sex lines in the law. Equalizing the rights, responsibilities, and opportunities of men and women was not considered a judicial task; without offense to the Constitution, women could be kept off juries and barred from occupations ranging from law to bartending. Women could also be "protected" from long hours, night work, and hazardous jobs, as in MULLER V. OREGON (1908), but protection of this order limited women's opportunities and relied upon the notion that a woman "looks to her brother and depends upon him."

The Court explained its position in *Fay v. New York* (1947). The NINETEENTH AMENDMENT's ratification in 1920 gave women the vote, but only that; in other respects, the Constitution remained an empty cupboard for sex equality claims. Nearly a decade and a half later, in *Hoyt v. Florida* (1961), a unanimous bench reaffirmed the traditional view. The Court held that a volunteers-only system for females serving on juries encountered no constitutional shoal; it was rational to spare women from the obligation to serve in recognition of their place at the "center of home and family life."

Pervasive social changes following WORLD WAR II undermined the *Hoyt* assumptions. That period saw unprecedented growth in women's employment outside the home, a revived feminist movement, changing marriage patterns, and a decline in necessary home-centered activity. Expansion of the economy's service sector opened places for women in traditional as well as new occupations. Curtailed population goals, facilitated by more effective means of controlling reproduction, and extended lifespans counted as well among important ingredients in this social dynamic. These last two developments created a setting in which the typical woman, for the first time, was experiencing most of her adult years in a household not dominated by child care requirements. Columbia economics professor Eli Ginzberg appraised the sum of these changes as "the single most outstanding phenomenon of our century." The BURGER COURT, not noted for its activism in other areas, responded.

Through the 1960s, the Supreme Court had explained its EQUAL PROTECTION rulings in terms of a two-tier model. Generally, challenged legislation was ranked at the lower tier and survived judicial inspection if rationally related to a permissible government objective. Exceptional cases, ranged on the upper tier, involved FUNDAMENTAL RIGHTS (voting is a prime example) or SUSPECT CLASSIFICATIONS (race is a paradigm). Review in these exceptional cases was rigorous. To survive inspection, the legislative objective had to be compelling, and the classification, necessary to its accomplishment. (See STRICT SCRUTINY; COMPELLING STATE INTEREST.)

Equal protection adjudication in gender discrimination cases prompted "in between" standards. As the 1970s wore on, the STANDARD OF REVIEW for sex-based classification inched up toward the higher tier. The process commenced with *Reed v. Reed* (1971). A unanimous Court held that an Idaho estate administration statute, giving men preference over similarly situated women, denied would-be administrator Sally Reed the equal protection of the laws. *Reed* attracted headlines; it marked the first solid break from the Supreme Court's consistent affirmation of government authority to classify by sex. The terse *Reed* opinion acknowledged no departure from precedent, but Court-watchers recognized something new was in the wind.

Less than a year and a half after the laconic *Reed* decision, the Court came within one vote of declaring sex a "suspect" category. In FRONTIERO V. RICHARDSON (1973) the Justices held 8–1 that married women in the uniformed services were entitled to the same fringe benefits as married men. Under the laws declared unconstitutional, men received a housing allowance and health care for their ci-

vilian wives automatically; women received these family benefits only if they supplied over three-fourths of the couple's support.

Four of the Justices ranked sex a suspect classification. Justice LEWIS F. POWELL, concurring, articulated a prime reservation of the remaining five Justices: our eighteenth- and nineteenth-century Constitution-makers had evidenced no concern at all about the equality of men and women before the law. The Court must tread lightly, Justice Powell cautioned, when it enters the gray zone between CONSTITUTIONAL INTERPRETATION, a proper judicial task, and constitutional amendment, a job for the people's elected representatives.

No fifth vote has emerged for explicit placement of sex at the top tier of equal protection analysis, although the Court has repeatedly acknowledged that it applies a standard considerably more exacting than the lower tier RATIONAL BASIS test. If a classification based upon gender is to withstand constitutional challenge, the defender of the sex criterion must establish what the Court in *Kirchberg v. Feenstra* (1981) called "exceedingly persuasive justification"; the sex-based distinction will be condemned unless it "substantially furthers an important government interest." In MISSISSIPPI UNIVERSITY FOR WOMEN V. HOGAN (1982) the Court noted that it was unnecessary to "decide whether classifications based upon gender are inherently suspect," for the classification challenged there could not survive even intermediate tier scrutiny. If the Court continues to review categorization by gender with the rigor displayed in many of its 1973–1982 decisions, however, the "suspect" seal may eventually be placed on accumulated precedent.

Despite the absence of a majority opinion, the 8–1 *Frontiero* JUDGMENT was a notable way-paver for challenges to statutes that openly disadvantage or denigrate women. First, the Court did not invalidate the flawed legislation; it repaired it. Congress provided benefits for the military man's family; the Court, in effect, extended the same benefits to families in which the service member was female. Second, in contrast to the statute that figured in *Reed*—a nineteenth-century hangover repealed prospectively months before the Court heard Sally Reed's appeal—post-World War II legislation was at issue in *Frontiero*. Most significantly, *Frontiero* invalidated the type of gender line found most frequently in federal and state legislation. Wives were deemed dependent regardless of their own economic circumstances. Husbands were ranked independent unless they contributed less than one-fourth of the couple's support. In disallowing resort to this particular stereotype the Court set the stage for its subsequent disallowance of similar stereotypes in other settings.

Since *Frontiero*, with few exceptions, the Court has

regularly overturned legislation explicitly invoking a male/female criterion and perceived by the Justices as denigrating women. A Utah statute that required a parent to support a son until age twenty-one but a daughter only until eighteen was struck down in *Stanton v. Stanton* (1975). Using DUE PROCESS analysis, the Court invalidated laws excluding all women from jury duty save those who volunteered (TAYLOR V. LOUISIANA, 1975) or chose not to opt out (*Duren v. Missouri*, 1979). In *Kirchberg v. Feenstra* (1981) a unanimous bench condemned Louisiana's "head and master" law, which gave the husband alone a unilateral right to dispose of property jointly owned with his wife.

Even a noncontributory welfare program—the type of governmental largess generally left untouched by the judiciary—has been revised by Court decree to eliminate the law's discrimination against women. Congress had provided for public assistance benefits to families where dependent children had been deprived of parental support because of the father's unemployment; no benefits were allowed when mother, rather than father, qualified as the unemployed parent. "Congress may not legislate "one step at a time' when that step is drawn along the line of gender, and the consequence is to exclude one group of families [those in which the female spouse is a wage earner] altogether from badly needed subsistence benefits," Justice HARRY BLACKMUN concluded for a Court unanimous on the constitutional issue in CALIFANO V. WESTCOTT (1979). Although the Justices divided 5–4 on the appropriate remedy (the majority extending the benefit to families of unemployed mothers, the dissenters preferring to invalidate the entire program), all subscribed solidly to the equal protection ruling.

In 1837 Sarah Grimke made this plea: "I ask no favors for my sex, I surrender not our claim to equality. All I ask of our brethren, is that they . . . take their feet . . . off our necks. . . ." Does the equal protection principle operate with the same bite when men rather than women are the victims of explicit gender-based discrimination? Constitutional doctrine after *Reed* has evolved, with some insecurity, through three stages. In the first, statutes ostensibly favoring women were upheld if they were seen as "compensatory," even if that rationalization was entirely post hoc. Then the Court recognized more consistently that gender-based classifications rooted in "romantic paternalism" reinforce stereotypes and perpetuate anachronistic social assumptions that confine women's opportunities. In the third stage, the Court attempted a reconciliation of these two strands of doctrine: a classification that favors women can survive an equal protection attack, but only if it reflects a conscious legislative choice to compensate for past, gender-based inequities.

In two first-stage decisions the Court upheld laws that appeared to favor women. *Kahn v. Shevin* (1974) involved a $15-per-year state property tax saving for widows (along with the blind and the totally disabled) but not widowers. The classification, as the Court appraised it, was genuinely "benign"—it helped some women and harmed none. Following on the heels of *Kahn*, the Court ruled, in *Schlesinger v. Ballard* (1975), that it was not a denial of equal protection to hold a male naval officer to a strict "up or out" (promotion or discharge) system, while guaranteeing a female officer thirteen years of duty before mandatory discharge for lack of promotion.

Kahn and *Ballard* were greeted by some in a Panglossian manner. The decisions could be viewed as offering women the best of both worlds—a High Court ready to strike down classifications that discriminate against females, yet vigilant to preserve laws that prefer or favor them. But this analysis was uncritically optimistic. The classification attacked in *Kahn* was barely distinguishable from other products of paternalistic legislators who had regarded the husband more as his wife's guardian than as her peer. And in *Ballard*, neither contender challenged the anterior discrimination that accounted, in large measure, for the navy's promoting men more rapidly than women—the drastically curtailed opportunities and assignments available to navy women.

Sex as a proxy for need, or as an indicator of past discrimination in the marital unit, is a criterion too gross to survive vigorous equal protection scrutiny. The Court eventually demonstrated its appreciation that discrimination by gender generally cuts with two edges, and is seldom, if ever, a pure favor to women. A young widower whose wage-earning wife had died giving birth to the couple's son brought suit in *Weinberger v. Wiesenfeld* (1975). The unanimous Court declared unconstitutional the SOCIAL SECURITY ACT's provision of a mother's benefit for the caretaker of a deceased wage-earner's child. As in *Frontiero*, the remedy was extension of the benefit in question to the entire class of similarly situated individuals, males as well as females. In effect, the *Wiesenfeld* judgment substitutes functional description (sole surviving parent) for the gender classification (widowed mother) employed in the statute.

The government had urged that the sex differential in *Wiesenfeld* operated "to offset the adverse economic situation of women." But the Court read the legislative history closely and rejected "the mere recitation of a benign, compensatory purpose" as a hindsight apology for laws in fact based on twin assumptions: that man's primary place is at work, woman's at home; and that a gainfully employed woman is a secondary breadwinner whose employment is less crucial to her family than her husband's.

Wiesenfeld's focus on actual legislative purpose set a penetrating standard for sex classifications defended as "benign" or "compensatory." Gender classifications superficially favoring women and affecting interests ranging from the purchase of beer to attendance at a nursing school have accordingly been struck down.

CRAIG V. BOREN (1976) held unconstitutional an Oklahoma law allowing young women to purchase 3.2 percent beer at age eighteen, but requiring young men to wait until age twenty-one. *Orr v. Orr* (1979) declared violative of equal protection a statute that required husbands, but never wives, to pay alimony. CALIFANO V. GOLDFARB (1977) rejected social security classifications qualifying a widow for survivor's benefits automatically, a widower only upon proof that his wife supplied three-fourths of the couple's support.

The 4–1–4 judgment in *Goldfarb*, in contrast to the *Wiesenfeld* decision on which *Goldfarb* built, was a cliffhanger. The PLURALITY OPINION concentrated on discrimination against women as breadwinners. Justice JOHN PAUL STEVENS, who cast the swing vote in favor of widower Goldfarb, focused on the discrimination against the surviving male spouse. Why this discrimination against a class of men? Like the plurality, Justice Stevens refused to accept the government's hindsight compensatory justification for the scheme. Congress, the record suggested, had ordered different treatment for widows and widowers out of longstanding "habit"; the discrimination encountered by widower Goldfarb was "merely the accidental by-product of [the legislators'] traditional way of thinking about females." Four members of the Court, in dissent, repeated a long rehearsed argument: the sex-based classification accurately reflects the station in life of most women, it operates benignly in women's favor, and it is administratively convenient. In 1980, however, the Court adhered to *Goldfarb* with a clearer (8–1) majority, in WENGLER V. DRUGGISTS MUTUAL INSURANCE CO.

The most emphatic reaffirmation of *Wiesenfeld's* skeptical view of benign gender-based classification came in 1982, one day after expiration of the extended deadline for ratification of the proposed EQUAL RIGHTS AMENDMENT. The Court decided, 5–4, in *Mississippi University for Women v. Hogan*, that Mississippi's single-sex admissions policy for a nursing school failed to meet the heightened standard of review. Justice SANDRA DAY O'CONNOR, who, a century earlier under BRADWELL V. ILLINOIS (1873), could have been barred from practicing law without offense to the Constitution, wrote the majority opinion.

Challengers in most of the cases just surveyed contended against gross assumptions that females are (and should be) concerned primarily with "the home and the rearing of the family," males with "the marketplace and the world of ideas" (*Stanton v. Stanton*, 1975). The complainants did not assail the accuracy of these assumptions as generalizations. Rather, they questioned each law's er-

roneous treatment of men and women who did not fit the stereotype, and the fairness of gender pigeonholing in lieu of neutral, functional description. The traditional legislative slotting, they argued, amounted to self-fulfilling prophecy. A Court that in 1948, in GOESAERT V. CLEARY, had declared "beyond question" the constitutionality of legislation "drawing a sharp line between the sexes," was receptive in the 1970s to argument to which it would not "give ear" a generation earlier.

The Court has left a narrow passage open, however, for compensatory legislation that does not rest on traditional role-typing. In *Califano v. Webster* (1977) the Court distinguished from habitual categorization by sex a law designed, at least in part, to ameliorate disadvantages women experienced. A social security benefit calculation, effective from 1956 to 1972, established a more favorable formula for retired female workers than for retired male workers. The legislative history indicated that this scheme, unlike those in *Wiesenfeld* and *Goldfarb*, had been conceived in light of the discrimination commonly encountered by gainfully employed women, specifically, depressed wages for "women's work" and the early retirement that employers routinely forced on women but not on men. While tilting toward a general rule of equal treatment, the *Webster* PER CURIAM opinion approves genuinely compensatory classifications that are adopted for remedial reasons rather than out of prejudice about "the way women are," and are trimly tailored in scope and time to match the remedial end.

Neutrally phrased laws that disproportionately affect one sex have not attracted the heightened scrutiny generally accorded explicit gender-based classifications that serve as a proxy for a characteristic or condition susceptible of individual testing. Citing RACIAL DISCRIMINATION precedent, the Court has held that facially neutral classifications that disproportionately affect members of one sex are not necessarily sex-based. The Court has not yet considered in a constitutional setting whether official lines may be drawn based on actuarial differences, but statutory precedent indicates the answer will be "no."

"[G]ood intent or absence of discriminatory intent" does not immunize an employment practice from the equal opportunity requirement of Title VII of the CIVIL RIGHTS ACT OF 1964, which now covers both public and private employment. GRIGGS V. DUKE POWER CO., a notable 1971 Title VII race discrimination decision, so held. But in WASHINGTON V. DAVIS (1976) the Court held the *Griggs* principle inapplicable to race discrimination claims invoking the Constitution rather than Title VII. PERSONNEL ADMINISTRATOR OF MASSACHUSETTS V. FEENEY (1979) expanded the *Washington v. Davis* reasoning. *Feeney* involved an assault on exorbitant veterans' preferences in civil service as impermissibly gender-biased. Helen Feeney challenged the nation's most extreme veterans' preference—an absolute lifetime preference Massachusetts accorded veterans in a range of civil service positions. The preference had "a devastating impact upon the employment opportunities of women"; it operated to reserve top jobs for a class almost exclusively male. The purpose? Purely to aid veterans, surely not to harm women, Massachusetts (and the United States, AMICUS CURIAE) maintained. Of course, to become a veteran one must be allowed to serve her country, and the military had maintained highly restrictive quotas and more exacting qualification standards for females. When litigation in *Feeney* commenced, over ninety-eight percent of Massachusetts veterans were male.

Feeney sought accommodation of the conflicting interests—aiding veterans and opening to women civil service employment beyond the "pink-collar" ghetto. The typical "points-added" preference, she said, was not at issue, only the extreme arrangement Massachusetts had legislated, which placed a veteran with a minimum passing grade ahead of a woman with a perfect score, and did so for each promotion as well as for initial hiring. A preference so large, she argued, took too much from Pauline to pay Paul.

The Court rejected the proffered distinction between moderate and exorbitant preferences. The "discriminatory purpose" hurdle could not be surmounted absent proof that the Massachusetts preference "was originally devised or subsequently re-enacted because it would accomplish the collateral goal of keeping women in a stereotypic and predefined place in the Massachusetts Civil Service." The lawmaker must *want*, not merely anticipate, the consequences. Alone, disparate impact on one sex, however "devastating" and "inevitable," does not violate equal protection.

The discriminatory purpose requirement, as elaborated in *Feeney*, leaves a slack rein for legislative choices with foreseeable but undesigned adverse effects on one of the sexes. Suppose, for example, that the social security payments at issue in *Wiesenfeld* or *Goldfarb* had turned not on sex but on the deceased wage-earner's status as the family's principal breadwinner. In most families, husbands would fit that neutrally phrased description, wives would not. May Congress, without violating equal protection, resort to a "principal breadwinner" standard in social welfare legislation in the interest of fiscal economy? Would use of a "principal breadwinner" criterion survive constitutional review as a measure enacted "in spite of," rather than "because of" its practical effect—its reduction of the value to the family of the wife's earnings? The only, uncertain, guide is an obiter dictum from *Feeney*, in which the Court accepted that "covert" sex classifications, ostensibly neutral but in fact a pretext for sex-based discrimination, are vulnerable to equal protection attack.

Can actuarial differences, for example, in life expectancies, health records, or accident experiences, provide constitutionally valid grounds in any context for gender-based categorizations? Sex averaging has not fared well in post-1970 constitutional litigation. Thus, *Reed v. Reed* and *Frontiero v. Richardson* rejected as a basis for government action the generalization that "men [are] as a rule more conversant with business affairs than women"; *Craig v. Boren*, the fact that more 18–20-year-old males than females drink and drive; *Orr v. Orr* (1979), the reality that wives far more often than husbands "need" alimony. Legislation resting on characteristics, attributes, habits, or proclivities of the "typical man" or "typical woman" have been rejected for two reasons: they reinforce traditional restrictive conceptions of the social roles of men and women; and they burden members of one sex by employing gender as a proxy for a characteristic susceptible to individual testing or at least capable of sex-neutral description. But actuarial tables, their defenders point out, are used in situations in which individual testing is not feasible. The Court has not yet explicitly confronted actuarial tables in a constitutional context, but a Title VII decision may indicate the position the Court will take in an equal protection challenge to government action.

Los Angeles Department of Water and Power v. Manhart (1978) raised the question whether women could be required to pay more currently in order to receive monthly benefits on retirement equal to those received by men. The majority held the two-tier charges inconsistent with Title VII's prohibition of sex-based classification. All recognized in *Manhart* that the statement, "on the average, women live longer than men," is accurate, and that an individual's lifespan generally cannot be forecast with precision. But the majority refused to countenance a break from the general Title VII rule against sex averaging. Unquestionably, for pension purposes, women destined to die young are burdened by placement in an all-female class, and men destined to live long are benefited by placement in an all-male class. Moreover, Justice Stevens suggested for the majority, the group insurance context may not be an ideal setting for urging a distinction other than age: "To insure the flabby and the fit as though they were equivalent risks may be more common than treating men and women alike; but nothing more than habit makes one 'subsidy' seem less fair than the other." The Court adhered to *Manhart*, when invited to reconsider, or contain the holding, in *Arizona Governing Committee v. Norris* (1983).

Are women to have the opportunity to participate in full partnership with men in the nation's social, political, and economic life? Kenneth L. Karst has identified this overarching question, in its constitutional dimension, as one ripe for synthesis in the final quarter of the twentieth century. The synthesis envisioned would place within an encompassing sex equality framework cases involving explicit male/female classification as well as cases on REPRODUCTIVE AUTONOMY and pregnancy-linked regulation. That synthesis, however, may well depend on the clarity of directions from the political arena. The Court has treated reproductive choice cases under a "personal autonomy," not a "sex equality" rubric, and it has resisted argument that separate classification of pregnant women is sex-based.

In a bold 1973 ruling, ROE V. WADE, the Court struck down an anti-abortion law as unwarranted state intrusion into the decision of a woman and her doctor to terminate a pregnancy. *Roe v. Wade* has been typed aberrational— an extraordinarily activist decision issued from a bench reputedly deferential to legislative judgments. It bears emphasis, however, that the Court bypassed an equal protection argument presented for the female plaintiffs. Rather, the Court anchored stringent review to a concept of personal autonomy derived from the due process guarantee. Two decisions, particularly, had paved the way: GRISWOLD V. CONNECTICUT (1965), which held inconsistent with due process Connecticut's ban on use of contraceptives even by married couples, and EISENSTADT V. BAIRD (1972), which extended *Griswold* to strike down Massachusetts' prohibition on sales of contraceptives except to married persons by prescription.

Some speculated that *Roe v. Wade* and a companion 1973 decision, *Doe v. Bolton,* were motivated, at least in part, by concerns about unwanted children born into impoverished families. But in MAHER V. ROE (1977) the Court indicated that such speculations had been mistaken. The Court declined to extend the 1973 rulings to require state support for an indigent woman's elective abortion.

The impoverished women, on whose behalf constitutional claims to public assistance for abortion were pursued, relied primarily on the equal protection principle. They maintained that, so long as government subsidized childbirth, it could not withhold subsidy for abortion, a far less expensive, and, at least in the first trimester, less risky procedure. If government pays for childbirth but not abortion, then, the *Maher* plaintiffs argued, government intrudes upon a choice *Roe v. Wade* said the state must leave to doctor and patient. The Court, however, distinguished government prohibition from government support. Though the state could not bar access to a woman able to pay for an abortion, it was not required to buy an admission ticket for the poor woman. Rather, government could pursue a policy of encouraging childbirth (even if that policy would affect only the poor) by refusing Medicaid reimbursement for nontherapeutic abortions and by banning such abortions in public hospitals. Though widely criticized in the reproductive-choice context, the distinction between government stick and government carrot had

been made in other settings to which the Court referred in its 1977 ruling.

The *Maher* logic was carried further in HARRIS V. MCRAE (1980). The federal law at issue excluded even medically needed abortions from a medical benefits program. In holding, 5–4, that this exclusion violated neither the due process nor the equal protection clause, the Court reiterated the distinction drawn in *Maher:* though the government may not proscribe abortion, it need not act affirmatively to assure a poor woman's access to the procedure.

Following after the intrepid 1973 abortion decisions, the later public-funding-of-abortion rulings appear incongruous. The *Roe v. Wade* decision was not easy to reach or explain. Social and economic conditions that seem irreversible, however, suggest that the ruling made by the Court in 1973 will remain with us in the long run, while the later dispositions may eventually succumb to a different legislative view of state and national policy, and of the centrality of choice with respect to childbearing to a woman's control of her life's course.

When does disadvantageous treatment of pregnant workers operate to discriminate on the basis of sex? High Court decisions on that question display less than perfect logic and consistency.

School teachers may not be dismissed or placed on forced leave arbitrarily at a fixed stage in pregnancy well in advance of term. Such a rule conflicts with due process, the Court ruled in CLEVELAND BOARD OF EDUCATION V. LAFLEUR (1974). Similarly invoking due process, the Court held in *Turner v. Department of Employment Security* (1975) that pregnant women willing and able to work may not be denied unemployment compensation when jobs are closed to them. It is unlawful under Title VII, as interpreted by the Court in *Nashville Gas Co. v. Satty* (1977), for an employer to deprive women disabled by pregnancy of accumulated job-bidding seniority when they return to work.

But *Geduldig v. Aiello* (1974) held that a state-operated disability income protection plan could exclude pregnancy without offense to the equal protection principle. And in an analogous Title VII case, *General Electric Company v. Gilbert* (1976), the Court held that a private employer's exclusion of pregnant women from disability coverage did not discriminate on the basis of sex because all "nonpregnant persons," women along with men, were treated alike.

Lawyers may attempt to square the apparently contradictory constitutional decisions by referring to the different principles employed in the Court's analyses—equal protection in *Aiello*, due process in both *LaFleur* and *Turner.* But the particular due process theory of IRREBUTTABLE PRESUMPTIONS the Court pressed into service in *LaFleur* has lost favor with the Justices in other contexts.

A factor not fully acknowledged in the written opinions, and based more on the Justices' experience than on legal analysis, may account for the divergent responses. Perhaps the able pregnant woman seeking only to do a day's work for a day's pay, or the woman seeking to return to her job relatively soon after childbirth, is a credible figure to the Court, while the woman who asserts she is disabled by pregnancy is viewed with suspicion. Is she really incapacitated physically or is she malingering so that she may stay "where she belongs"—at home tending baby?

With respect to Title VII, Congress in 1978 simplified the judicial task by prospectively overruling *General Electric.* It amended the statute to say explicitly that classification on the basis of sex includes classification on the basis of pregnancy. The Court gave the amended statute a cordial reception in *Newport News Shipbuilding of Drydock Co. v. EEOC* (1983). The congressional definition placed in Title VII is not controlling in constitutional adjudication, but the Court may be stimulated by the legislature's action to revise its view, expressed in *Aiello* and *General Electric,* that singling out "pregnant persons" is not a sex-based action. Coming full circle, there will be pressure on the Court not simply to check regulation disadvantageous to pregnant women but to uphold new-style protective legislation—for example, laws requiring employers to grant to pregnant women a voluntary leave period not accorded others with temporarily disabling physical conditions.

In what areas does the Constitution allow explicit male/female classification? A few idiosyncratic problems survive.

According to current doctrine, the Constitution affords some leeway for discrimination with respect to parental rights and relationships, at least when children are born out of wedlock. A unanimous Court held in *Quilloin v. Walcott* (1978) that an unwed father who "has never exercised actual or legal custody over his child" has no constitutional right to block adoption approved by the mother. (In contrast, the Court held in *Caban v. Mohammed* [1979] that a state statute discriminated on the basis of sex in violation of equal protection when it permitted adoption of a child born out of wedlock solely on the mother's consent, even when the father's parental relationship with the child was substantial.) And according to *Parham v. Hughes* (1979) a state may condition an unwed father's (but not an unwed mother's) right to recover for wrongful death upon his legitimation of his child by court order. The main theme of the *Parham* opinion had been sounded earlier: women and men were not similarly situated for the purpose at hand—maternity is rarely in doubt, but proof of paternity is often difficult. Hence, as the Court held in LALLI V. LALLI (1978), the state may erect safeguards against spurious filiation claims. Those safeguards may be applied even when, as in *Parham,* father and child had a close and constant relationship.

MICHAEL M. V. SUPERIOR COURT (1981) upheld, 5–4, California's "statutory rape" law, under which a male who engages in sexual intercourse with an underage female commits a crime; a female who engages in sexual intercourse with an underage male does not. Both participants in the act that precipitated the prosecution in *Michael M.* were underage.

There was no majority opinion in *Michael M.* Justice WILLIAM H. REHNQUIST wrote for the Court's plurality. He postulated as the statute's purpose, as California had argued, the prevention of teenage pregnancy, and reasoned that males and females were not similarly situated in this setting. Nature inhibited the female, for she would suffer the consequences. The law could legitimately take into account this fact of life by punishing the male, who lacked a biological deterrent. Moreover, the plurality found persuasive California's further contention that sparing the female from criminal liability might encourage her to report the unlawful activity.

Given the ancient roots of the California law, Justice WILLIAM J. BRENNAN pointed out in dissent, it was plain that the sex classification "was initially designed to further . . . outmoded sexual stereotypes" (young women are not capable of consenting to an act of sexual intercourse, young men can make such decisions for themselves). For Justice Stevens, who dissented separately, the critical question in *Michael M.* was whether "the sovereign . . . govern[s] impartially" under a statute that authorizes punishment of the male, but not the female, even "when they are equally responsible" for the disfavored conduct, indeed even "when the female is the more responsible of the two." The answer, it seemed to Justice Stevens, was clearly "no."

Although by 1980 many states had amended all of their sex crime laws to render them equally applicable to males and females, *Michael M.* touched a sensitive nerve. In view of the 4–1–4 division, the decision may well remain an isolated instance.

ROSTKER V. GOLDBERG (1981) presented the politically loaded question whether Congress could confine draft registration to males. Congress had thought about the matter and decided it in 1980. It considered, on the administration's recommendation, authorizing the President to require registration by both sexes. But it decided on registration for males only. The Court's 6–3 decision upheld the sex classification. The opinion, written by Justice Rehnquist, underlined the special deference due congressional judgments in the areas of national defense and military affairs.

The *Rostker* opinion asserted that men and women were not similarly situated for the purpose at hand because women were excluded from combat service, an exclusion

"Congress specifically recognized and endorsed . . . in exempting women from registration." Reminiscent of *Schlesinger v. Ballard*, where no party challenged the dissimilar promotion opportunities for male and female naval officers, no party challenged the combat exclusion in *Rostker*. Even so, the executive branch had estimated that in the event of a major mobilization there would be a substantial number of noncombat positions in the armed services that conscripted women could fill. Against this backdrop *Rostker* may be explained as a WAR POWERS case, unlikely to have a significant influence in future sex discrimination cases.

Constitutional doctrine relating to gender discrimination, although still evolving, and variously interpreted, is nonetheless a remarkable judicial development. In contrast to race discrimination, an area in which constitutional interpretation is tied to amendments drawn with a view to the eradication of the legacy of black slavery, gender discrimination was not a concern to which the Reconstruction Congress (or the Founding Fathers) adverted. Nonetheless, the Court, since 1970, has creatively interpreted clauses of the Constitution (equal protection and, less securely, due process) to accommodate a modern vision of sexual equality in employment, in access to social benefits, in most civic duties, in reproductive autonomy. Such interpretation has limits, but sensibly approached, it is consistent with the grand design of the Constitution-makers to write a charter that would endure as the nation's fundamental instrument of government.

RUTH BADER GINSBERG
(1986)

(SEE ALSO: *Gender Rights*.)

Bibliography

BABCOCK, BARBARA A.; FREEDMAN, ANN E.; NORTON, ELEANOR H.; and ROSS, SUSAN C. 1974 *Sex Discrimination: Causes and Remedies* (Wendy Williams, Supplement 1978). Boston: Little, Brown.

GINSBURG, RUTH BADER 1978 Sex Equality and the Constitution. *Tulane Law Review* 52:451–475.

——— 1979 Sexual Equality under the Fourteenth and the Equal Rights Amendments. *Washington University Law Quarterly* 1979:161–178.

——— 1983 The Burger Court's Grapplings with Sex Discrimination. In V. Blasi, ed. *The Burger Court: The Counter-Revolution That Wasn't*. Pages 132–156. New Haven, Conn.: Yale University Press.

GUNTHER, GERALD 1972 Foreword: In Search of Evolving Doctrine on a Changing Court: A Model for a Newer Equal Protection. *Harvard Law Review* 86:1–48.

KANOWITZ, LEO 1969 *Women and the Law*. Albuquerque: University of New Mexico Press.

——— 1981 *Equal Rights: The Male Stake*. Albuquerque: University of New Mexico Press.

KARST, KENNETH L. 1976 Book Review. *Harvard Law Review* 89:1028–1036.

——— 1977 Foreword, Equal Citizenship under the Fourteenth Amendment. *Harvard Law Review* 91:1–68.

——— 1984 Woman's Constitution. *Duke Law Journal* 1984:447–508.

KAY, HERMA H. (1974) 1981 *Sex-Based Discrimination*, 2nd ed. St. Paul: West Publishing Co.

——— 1985 Models of Equality. *University of Illinois Law Review* 1985:39–88.

LAW, SYLVIA 1984 Rethinking Sex and the Constitution. *University of Pennsylvania Law Review* 132:955–1040.

TRIBE, LAURENCE H. 1978 *American Constitutional Law*. Pages 1060–1077. Mineola, N.Y.: Foundation Press.

WASSERSTROM, RICHARD A. 1977 Racism, Sexism, and Preferential Treatment: An Approach to the Topics. *UCLA Law Review* 24:581–622.

SEX DISCRIMINATION
(Update 1)

During the 1980s and early 1990s intense disagreement has arisen over the appropriate strategy for eliminating sex discrimination. Some courts and commentators argue for gender-neutral rules that define categories in purely functional terms. Others, who point out that gender-neutral rules promise equality only for women who can meet a "male standard," think that legal distinctions between the sexes are not only appropriate but necessary, at least in cases involving perceived biological differences. Still others refuse to think in terms of sameness and difference. They analyze each issue by asking whether the disputed rule furthers the domination of men and the subordination of women.

Those who favor gender-neutral rules argue that the equality and liberty of women is best furthered by treating women, like men, as autonomous individuals capable of exercising free choice. Their opponents believe that legal rules ought to acknowledge the degree to which many women are actually constrained in ways men are not—by direct and indirect pressures to engage in intercourse, to become pregnant, and to assume parenting and nurturing responsibilities. The disagreement is most painfully joined over laws, such as those granting unique benefits to pregnant women or mothers, that seem intended to help women but resemble earlier, unconstitutional "protective" legislation in assuming difference and dependency between men and women.

In the latter half of the 1980s, the Supreme Court was not asked to resolve this dispute in constitutional terms. No case presented an EQUAL PROTECTION challenge to a governmental distinction based on sex. The basic structure of intermediate review of gender-based rules was reaffirmed in passing in nongender cases such as CITY OF CLEBURNE V. CLEBURNE LIVING CENTER (1985) and *Kadrmas v. Dickinson Public Schools* (1988). In OBITER DICTA in a race case, MCCLESKEY V. KEMP (1987), the Court reaffirmed its earlier ruling that unconstitutional discrimination could not be established by unexplained statistical disparities that correlate with sex. This latter principle effectively eliminated use of the Constitution in suits such as those arguing theories of COMPARABLE WORTH, which challenged structural and economic disparities between the sexes.

The equal protection cases that touched on family relationships and gender roles did not involve classifications between men and women and thus did not call for "heightened scrutiny." For example, in *Bowen v. Owens* (1986) the Court ruled on an equal protection challenge to a distinction drawn by the SOCIAL SECURITY ACT. For a four-year period widowed spouses of deceased wage earners who remarried after the age of sixty continued to receive survivor's benefits, while divorced widowed spouses who remarried were not so treated. In this context, where the distinction was drawn within, rather than between, gender groups, the Court held that Congress could make presumptions about dependence: "Because divorced widowed spouses did not enter into marriage with the same level of dependency on the wage earner's account as widows or widowers, it was rational for Congress to treat these groups differently after remarriage."

Although no case directly raised the constitutional question, several Title VII cases gave the Court an opportunity to respond to the debate among advocates of Women's rights. The question was posed most starkly by *California Federal Savings and Loan v. Guerra* (1987), a challenge to a California statutory requirement that employers provide unpaid pregnancy disability leave. As amended by the Pregnancy Disability Act, Title VII of the CIVIL RIGHTS ACT OF 1964 specifies that discrimination on the basis of pregnancy is sex discrimination. Opponents of the California law argued that it was preempted by federal law because it required benefits for pregnant women that were not required for temporarily disabled men. The Court, in an opinion by Justice THURGOOD MARSHALL, found no conflict with the Title VII. Earlier protective legislation that had been held invalid under equal protection clause and Title VII was distinguished on the ground that it "reflected archaic or stereotypical notions about pregnancy and the abilities of pregnant workers." Justice Marshall found that Title VII and the state law shared a common goal of equal employment opportunity for women: "By taking pregnancy into account, California's . . . statue allows women, as well as men, to have families without losing their jobs."

Because the Court has not modified its holding in *Geduldig v. Aiello* (1974) that discrimination on the basis of pregnancy is not unconstitutional because it is not gender-based, *Guerra* raised no equal protection questions. But the decision indicates that the Court is willing to permit governmental distinctions between men and women when those distinctions appear to benefit women without perpetuating pernicious sex-role stereotypes. The decision leaves ambiguous exactly how the Court will determine whether such stereotyping exists. Justice Marshall described the statute as "narrowly drawn to cover only the period of *actual physical disability*." Yet "disability" seems an odd description for a common human condition like reproduction. The term suggests that mandatory pregnancy leave is necessary only because of real biological differences between men and women, and not as a remedy for the problem of inequality caused by the allocation of child-rearing responsibilities to women. Some commentators fear that in the long run mandatory pregnancy leave, like earlier forms of protective legislation, will decrease the actual employment opportunities of women by increasing the cost of hiring them.

A related question is whether the law ought to recognize a practice as discriminatory when it is said to harm women though it presents no threat to men who seem, at least superficially, to be similarly situated. Just as it has been difficult for the court to see pregnancy discrimination as sex discrimination, some lower courts refused to characterize sexual harassment claims as sex discrimination claims, especially when both men and women worked in an environment that only women perceived as hostile. In another Title VII case, MERITOR SAVINGS BANK V. VINSON (1986), the Supreme Court emphatically affirmed that claims of a hostile work environment are actionable under the statute as sex discrimination. Again, the Court was willing to look beyond formal equality of treatment to determine whether practices have different social meanings for, and thus different impacts on, men and women.

Many of the earliest constitutional sex discrimination cases decided by the Court involved challenges by men to "benign" gender distinctions that could be eliminated by simply extending the challenged benefit to men as well as women. In this respect, sex discrimination law differed from cases involving race; few racial classifications benefited blacks at the expense of whites. However, in challenges brought by men to AFFIRMATIVE ACTION programs, the claim is the same as in race cases: the preference ought to be eliminated, not simply be available without reference to gender or race. This similarity may explain why the Court's approach to gender-based affirmative action has tended to merge with its approach to race-based affirmative action, even though racial classifications are theoretically subject to a stricter level of scrutiny. In JOHNSON V. TRANSPORTATION AGENCY (1987) the Court found no violation of Title VII in a public employer's voluntary affirmative action plan that permitted the sex of an employee to be considered as one factor in promotion decisions for jobs in which women historically had been underrepresented. The Court approved the plan as a "moderate, flexible, case-by-case approach to effecting a gradual improvement in the representation of minorities and women in the Agency's work force." Title VII imposes identical restrictions on gender-based and race-based affirmative action plans, but the Court also cited WYGANT V. JACKSON BOARD OF EDUCATION (1986), a racial affirmative action case decided under the equal protection clause, as if it would provide the standards for evaluating a constitutional challenge to the *Johnson* plan. Thus, the Court, although reserving the question, suggested that the constitutional approach, like the Title VII approach, may be identical for both kinds of affirmative action.

Two years later, in RICHMOND V. J. A. CROSON CO. (1989), a constitutional case in which STRICT SCRUTINY, was applied to overturn a municipal set-aside plan for racial minorities, the Court signaled a new reluctance to approve government affirmative action plans that could not be justified by evidence of identified past discrimination. Whether the constitutional approach in *Richmond* will be applied to gender-based governmental affirmative action plans depends on whether gender classifications will be distinguished as calling for less searching scrutiny. Since intermediate review has been the standard in other gender-preference cases, governmental affirmative action designed to benefit women may, if the suggestion in *Johnson* is not followed, be found to raise no constitutional problems, even where identical plans benefiting racial minorities are unconstitutional.

Some efforts by LOCAL GOVERNMENTS to further sex equality have been challenged as unconstitutional under the FIRST AMENDMENT. Those that further women's claims for equal access to all-male institutions have proved most resistant to constitutional attack. In *Board of Directors of Rotary International v. Rotary Club* (1987) and NEW YORK STATE CLUB ASSOCIATION V. NEW YORK CITY (1988), the Supreme Court upheld state and local requirements that women not be excluded from membership in certain private organizations, despite the claim that the local laws infringed upon male members' First Amendment right to FREEDOM OF ASSEMBLY AND ASSOCIATION. The effort to impose local restrictions on PORNOGRAPHY as a step toward the elimination of the subordinate status of women has proved more vulnerable to constitutional challenge. In *Hudnut v. American Booksellers Association* (1986), a divided Supreme Court summarily affirmed a lower federal court's conclusion that a municipally created CIVIL RIGHTS action for women injured by pornography impermissibly burdened protected speech.

CHRISTINA BROOKS WHITMAN
(1992)

(SEE ALSO: *Feminist Theory and Constitutional Law; Gender Rights.*)

Bibliography

BECKER, MARY 1987 Prince Charming: Abstract Equality. *Supreme Court Review* 1987:201–247.
FINLEY, LUCINDA M. 1986 Transcending Equality Theory: A Way Out of the Maternity and the Workplace Debate. *Columbia Law Review* 86:1118–1182.
MACKINNON, CATHARINE A. 1987 *Feminism Unmodified: Discourses on Life and Law.* Cambridge, Mass.: Harvard University Press.
———— 1989 *Toward a Feminist Theory of the State.* Cambridge, Mass.: Harvard University Press.
OLSEN, FRANCES 1986 Statutory Rape: A Feminist Critique of Rights Analysis. *Texas Law Review* 63:387–432.
RHODE, DEBORAH 1989 *Justice and Gender.* Cambridge, Mass.: Harvard University Press.
WEST, ROBIN 1988 Jurisprudence and Gender. *University of Chicago Law Review* 55:1–72.
WILLIAMS, JOAN C. 1989 Deconstructing Gender. *Michigan Law Review* 1989:797–845.

SEX DISCRIMINATION
(Update 2)

While the NINETEENTH AMENDMENT gave women the right to vote, no provision of the Constitution explicitly prohibits sex discrimination. The Supreme Court has held, however, that EQUAL PROTECTION and DUE PROCESS protections of the Fifth Amendment and the FOURTEENTH AMENDMENT prohibit the federal and state governments from discriminating against either men or women because of sex.

In 1996, Justice RUTH BADER GINSBURG, the second woman ever appointed to the Court, wrote the majority opinion in UNITED STATES V. VIRGINIA, holding that Virginia could not exclude women from the Virginia Military Institute (VMI), the only single-sex state school in Virginia. That opinion departs substantially from sex discrimination cases decided before 1971 and appears to consolidate disparate decisions from 1971 until 1996. Before 1971, the Court had dismissed women's claims of unequal treatment on the ground that women are different from men. In *United States v. Virginia,* the Court explicitly disapproved one of those early opinions, GOESAERT V. CLEARY (1948), which had said that although the discrimination challenge was "beguiling," differences between men and women justified a state statute passed after WORLD WAR II prohibiting most women from working as bartenders.

In 1971, a legal sea change in gender equal-protection cases occurred. In *Reed v. Reed* (1971), with little explanation, a unanimous Supreme Court held that an Idaho statute preferring men over women in the administration of decedents' estates violated the Fourteenth Amendment, choosing not to follow PRECEDENT or the Idaho Supreme Court's reasoning that men were more likely than women to have business experience. By 1976 the Court had articulated a mid-tier analysis, requiring that a state's use of gender classifications be substantially related to the achievement of important governmental objectives. The mid-tier analysis is stricter than RATIONAL BASIS analysis, and less so than STRICT SCRUTINY analysis. The first upholds classifications that rationally relate to a legitimate governmental purpose. The second, applied in race and FUNDAMENTAL RIGHTS cases, requires the government to show that the classification is necessary to achieve a compelling purpose, or, stated differently, that no less discriminatory means are available to achieve that purpose.

Starting in 1976, the Court used the mid-tier analysis to invalidate many state and federal policies that treated men and women differently, including the age for drinking beer, CRAIG V. BOREN (1976); eligibility for SOCIAL SECURITY benefits, CALIFANO V. GOLDFARB (1977); spousal property management rights, *Kirchberg v. Feenstra* (1981); a state nursing degree only for women, MISSISSIPPI UNIVERSITY FOR WOMEN V. HOGAN (1982); and a prosecutor's use of PEREMPTORY CHALLENGES, *J. E. B. v. Alabama* (1994). The Court occasionally upheld differential treatment to remedy past discrimination, but decisions involving physical differences between men and women continued to resemble the decisions before 1971. For example, the Court upheld a male-only draft registration system because men and women were not similarly situated, ROSTKER V. GOLDBERG (1981); a statutory rape law applicable to men because only women become pregnant, MICHAEL M. V. SUPERIOR COURT (1981); and differential adoption rules for unmarried mothers and fathers, *Lear v. Robertson* (1983).

In the VMI case the trial court had rejected the equal protection challenge to VMI's all-male admissions policy because the school offered diversity to Virginia's educational system. The Supreme Court held, however, that the provision of diversity only for Virginia's sons and not its daughters violated the Fourteenth Amendment. The trial court had also based its ruling on its finding that admission of women would alter VMI's strenuous, punishing, and privacy-free "adversative method." Instead of holding that VMI complied with the Constitution because women and men are not similarly situated, the Supreme Court held that exclusion of women "ready, willing and able to benefit from [VMI's] opportunities" violated the Constitution, and that Virginia's establishment of an inferior women's leadership program in a private women's college was an insufficient remedy. Applying the methodology from some prior mid-tier cases, but also articulating a "skeptical scrutiny" standard and reiterating that official discrimination requires an "exceedingly persuasive justification"—hallmarks of strict scrutiny—the Court held that Virginia had not met its burden of proving, without reliance on stereo-

types, that no women could benefit from the program or that its interest in diversity was in fact the reason for the exclusion of women.

Rather than simply ordering women's admission to VMI, the Court required VMI to make "adjustments" and "alterations" in housing and skills training to "accommodate" the privacy and strength differences of female cadets. This remedy departed from remedies in past gender equal-protection cases, which merely eliminated gender requirements. This departure may signal an implicit raising of the level of scrutiny in gender equality cases from mid-tier to strict scrutiny. By ordering a remedy only for "capable" women, the Court apparently is using a "least-restrictive-means" analysis, holding that VMI can achieve its purpose in a manner less restrictive than excluding all women. By requiring VMI to alter housing and skill requirements, the Court apparently is saying that institutional alterations are less restrictive than exclusion of women. The Court relied on two RACIAL DISCRIMINATION cases, including MILLIKEN V. BRADLEY (1977), which had ordered institutional changes as part of a DESEGREGATION remedy.

By requiring VMI to admit only capable women, but also to make changes, Ginsburg apparently balanced two debated feminist viewpoints for achieving gender equality: whether governmental policies should provide equal treatment or, instead, equal results for men and women. In emphasizing that inherent differences between men and women are "cause for celebration, but not for denigration" of women, Ginsburg avoided the rationale of MULLER V. OREGON (1908) that women needed to be paternalistically protected.

Ginsburg cited two cases as examples of permissible sex classifications: *Califano v. Webster* (1977), which upheld computations of Social Security benefits to compensate women's economic disabilities; and *California Federal Savings & Loan Association v. Guerra* (1987), decided under Title VII of the CIVIL RIGHTS ACT OF 1964, an employment antidiscrimination statute. *Guerra* held that a state law requiring employers to provide pregnancy leaves did not violate Title VII. Because a prior constitutional pregnancy case, *Geduldig v. Aiello* (1974), had held that pregnancy discrimination is not sex discrimination, the citation of a Title VII pregnancy discrimination case in a constitutional sex discrimination opinion may cast doubt on the continuing validity of *Geduldig*, despite its citation in dicta in BRAY V. ALEXANDRIA WOMEN'S HEALTH CLINIC (1993), which held that a federal conspiracy statute cannot be used against people who obstruct access to abortion clinics. Because *Guerra* had described pregnancy leaves as allowing "women, as well as men, to have families without losing their jobs," its citation in a gender equality case requiring institutional alterations may imply that pregnancy leaves are constitutionally required for governmental employers. Consistent with this implication is the purpose section of the Family and Medical Leave Act of 1993, which identifies one of its purposes as promotion of equal employment opportunity pursuant to the Fourteenth Amendment.

There was no majority opinion in the Court's next constitutional sex discrimination case, *Miller v. Albright* (1998), upholding CITIZENSHIP laws that classified children of unmarried parents differently according to the sex of the citizen parent, despite the agreement of five Justices that gender classifications based on stereotypes are unlikely to withstand heightened scrutiny. Two of them upheld the statute saying that the plaintiff daughter could not raise her father's claims. Two Justices said only Congress can remedy citizenship claims. Only two found the statute constitutional.

Sexual assault or harassment claims raise constitutional issues when brought under federal statutes that impose criminal or civil liability upon persons who, under COLOR OF LAW, deprive others of rights protected by the Constitution. Sexual assault may be a due process violation; sexual harassment, a sex discrimination equal protection violation.

In *United States v. Lanier* (1997) the Court affirmed the federal conviction of a state judge who sexually assaulted several women in his judicial chambers, holding that freedom from sexual abuse is a protected due process liberty interest. The trial judge had instructed the jury that 18 U.S.C. § 242, which prohibits someone acting under color of state law from depriving another of constitutional rights, forbids serious and substantial misconduct, but not every unjustified grabbing by a state official. This is similar to the Supreme Court's definition, summarized in *Faragher v. City of Boca Raton* (1998), of WORKPLACE HARASSMENT actionable under Title VII. The conduct must be objectively and subjectively serious or pervasive to alter employment conditions. It must be more than merely offensive but, as stated in *Harris v. Forklift Systems, Inc.* (1993), need not cause psychological injury. *Oncale v. Sundowner Offshore Services, Inc.* (1998) held that it may include same-sex harassment.

Faragher, above, and *Burlington Industries, Inc. v. Ellerth* (1998) held that employers would be liable to employees who suffered severe, tangible, employment retaliation by harassing supervisors but not liable if there were no retaliation and if the employers had a plan, unreasonably unused by the employee, to prevent or correct supervisory harassment. The Supreme Court articulated a different standard for vicarious liability under Title IX of the Education Amendments of 1972, which prohibits sex discrimination by educational institutions receiving federal funds. *Gebser v. Lago Vista Independent School District* (1998) and *Davis v. Board of Education* (1999) held that school districts would be liable for teacher or peer sexual harassment of students only if the districts were knowingly and deliberately indifferent to the harassment.

CANDACE SAARI KOVACIC-FLEISCHER
(2000)

Bibliography

BABCOCK, BARBARA ALLEN et al. 1996 *Sex Discrimination and the Law: History Practice and Theory*, 2nd ed. Boston: Little, Brown and Company.

BARTLETT, KATHARINE and HARRIS, ANGELA 1998 *Gender and Law: Theory, Doctrine, Commentary*, 2nd ed. New York: Aspen Law and Business.

BERRY, MARY FRANCES 1993 *The Politics of Parenthood.* New York: Viking Penguin.

GREENBERG, JUDITH F.; MINOW, MARTHA L.; and ROBERTS, DOROTHY E. 1998 *Mary Jo Frug's Women in the Law*, 2nd ed. New York: Foundation Press.

KAY, HERMA HILL and WEST, MARTHA 1996 *Sex-Based Discrimination: Text, Cases and Materials*, 4th ed. (with 1999 Supplement). St. Paul, Minn.: West Group.

KOVACIC-FLEISCHER, CANDACE SAARI 1986 Remedying Underinclusive Statutes. *Wayne State University Law Review* 33: 39–95.

——— 1997 *United States v. Virginia*'s New Gender Equal Protection Analysis with Ramifications for Pregnancy, Parenting, and Title VII. *Vanderbilt Law Review* 50:845–915.

RHODE, DEBORAH 1997 *Speaking of Sex: The Denial of Gender Inequality.* Cambridge, Mass.: Harvard University Press.

UDELL, COLLIN O'CONNER 1996 Note: Signaling a New Direction in Gender Classification Scrutiny: *United States v. Virginia. Connecticut Law Review* 29:521–560.

SEX OFFENDER NOTIFICATION LAWS

"Megan's Law" is the name commonly used to refer to statutes that require the registration of those convicted of certain sexual offenses, and in some cases require the notification to the public of the release of a sexual offender into the community. These statutes were enacted primarily to address the particular dangers of recidivism posed by offenders who commit predatory acts against children, but by their terms usually embrace all forms of sexual predation. By 1999, each of the fifty states had enacted some form of registration and community notification provision, and federal law now requires, as a condition of federal funding, that each state engage in some form of community notification when "necessary to protect the public concerning a specific person required to register."

New Jersey's law, which was enacted in 1994 in reaction to the public outcry over the murder of six-year-old Megan Kanka by a convicted sex offender living in the neighborhood, is typical. It requires those convicted of serious sex-related offenses to register with state authorities, and classifies those registrants into three tiers representing low, moderate, or high risk of reoffense. Notification of low-risk registrants is made only to local law enforcement authorities, while notification of moderate-risk registrants is made to schools, women's shelters, or other institutions having custodial care of potential victims. High-risk registrants are the subject of widespread community notification of individual information, including photograph, place of residence, place of work or school, vehicle license plate number, and a general description of the victim of the registrant's prior sexual offense.

Various constitutional challenges have been brought against different aspects of Megan's Law. The most significant are challenges to the community notification provisions based on (1) DUE PROCESS OF LAW, where the tier classification process has not been subject to some form of judicial review; (2) the EX POST FACTO, DOUBLE JEOPARDY, and BILL OF ATTAINDER clauses, where community notification has been imposed upon those whose offenses predated the LEGISLATION; and (3) the RIGHT OF PRIVACY against government disclosure of individual information. Due process challenges have been the most successful, and most courts now require that some form of judicial review of the offender's classification in "moderate risk" or "high risk" categories be available before notification is made. At least one federal appellate court has also required that the state prove the elements necessary for notification by "clear and convincing evidence."

Challenges under the ex post facto and related clauses had some initial success in lower courts, based on the tentative conclusion that community notification constituted a form of "punishment." Absent a clear test for ascertaining what constitutes "punishment," those courts usually focused on the stigmatic and ostracizing effects of community notification, as well as the historical understanding of public humiliation as a punitive measure. Subsequent decisions, however, have upheld retroactive application of community notification provisions as remedial measures rather than punitive ones, and the Supreme Court recently suggested in *Hudson v. United States* (1997) that the test for punishment lies more in the subjective intent of the legislature than in the objective effects of the measure in question. As a practical matter, the doctrinal shift probably forecasts a limited likelihood of success for challenges to Megan's Law should the issue ever reach the Supreme Court, because legislatures will be able to shield laws that have harsh or punitive effects through outward manifestation of a subjective nonpunitive intent.

RONALD K. CHEN
(2000)

SEXUAL HARASSMENT

See: Sex Discrimination; Workplace Harassment and the First Amendment

SEXUAL ORIENTATION

Today government officially and systematically stigmatizes persons of homosexual orientation in two principal ways. The first is embodied in the sodomy laws that remain in about half of the states, and the second is embodied in laws and regulations restricting government employment to persons who are heterosexual. Most prominent among the employment restrictions are the federal government's regulations barring gay men and lesbians from serving in the ARMED FORCES.

In BOWERS V. HARDWICK (1986) the Supreme Court, 5–4, upheld the application to homosexual sex of a Georgia law making sodomy a crime punishable by imprisonment up to twenty years. The majority rejected a claim that the law violated the RIGHT OF PRIVACY that had been recognized within the doctrine of SUBSTANTIVE DUE PROCESS. Justice LEWIS F. POWELL, who provided the crucial fifth vote for the majority, originally voted with the dissenters, but after the Court's CONFERENCE switched his vote to uphold the law. In a CONCURRING OPINION, however, he noted that the case would be different for him if the state actually enforced the law by putting someone in prison.

Justice Powell's effort at accommodation leaves wholly untouched the most serious harm caused to gay and lesbian Americans by the sodomy laws. Although such a law played a role in the harassment of Michael Hardwick, the sodomy laws are rarely enforced by prosecution. Their mission today is to symbolize society's disapproval of persons who are gay or lesbian, legitimizing the identification of homosexuals as outsiders and thus encouraging not only police harassment but privately inflicted harm, from insults to trashing to violence. Stigma, in other words, is not just a by-product of the sodomy laws; it is their main function.

The *Hardwick* majority not only failed to deal with this problem of stigmatic harm but evaded the whole question of inequality. The Court noted that the Georgia law, despite its general language, was never applied to heterosexual sodomy; accordingly, the Court would not pronounce on the constitutionality of any such application. Having thus raised a serious issue of discrimination, the majority ignored the question whether the discrimination violated the guarantee of EQUAL PROTECTION OF THE LAWS.

A similar equal protection issue has been presented to a number of lower courts in the years since *Hardwick*, most frequently in contexts involving exclusion of persons identified as lesbians and gay men from government employment, notably service in the armed forces. Some judges have been sympathetic to these equal protection claims; but to date the prevailing view has rejected them, and thus far the Supreme Court has declined to review these decisions. The military exclusion policy, which seems likely to confront the Court with the equality issues in antigay discrimination, illustrates those issues as they may arise in other contexts as well.

The judges who conclude that heightened judicial scrutiny is appropriate for discriminations based on the status of homosexual orientation make a number of persuasive arguments. Gay men and lesbians have historically suffered from pervasive discrimination, both governmental and private. Despite some recent improvement in the lot of persons of homosexual orientation, this historic pattern continues today, seriously impairing the ability of lesbians and gay men to end discrimination through the political process. Sexual orientation bears little relation to the capacity to perform military tasks or any other tasks. Although a person's behavior and self-identification are subject to his or her control, the sexual orientation of persons who are exclusively homosexual is immutable. The usual indicia of SUSPECT CLASSIFICATIONS, in other words, are present in these cases.

Furthermore, discriminations against lesbians and gay men reinforce traditional stereotypes of gender; indeed, this reinforcement appears to be the main point of the military services' policy of exclusion. Putting the preservation of military secrets to one side, the main arguments of the Department of Defense are that ending the policy of exclusion would harm discipline, morale, and mutual trust; would invade the privacy of servicemembers; and would prejudice recruiting and "the public acceptability of military service." These arguments rest on the assumption that the existence of discrimination justifies government's imposition of further discrimination—an argument soundly rejected by the Supreme Court in the context of RACIAL DISCRIMINATION, as PALMORE V. SIDOTI (1984) made clear. If the services' arguments supporting the exclusion policy seem familiar, the reason is that during WORLD WAR II the leaders of the armed forces offered the same arguments—all of them—as reasons why racial integration of the services would impede the military mission.

The proposition that gay orientation increases security risk has no factual support. The concern expressed by the military services rests on the idea that homosexual orientation implies susceptibility to blackmail. In considerable measure, any such risk to security would be created by the policy of exclusion itself, which punishes disclosure of homosexuality with discharge. In any case, the risk disappears in the case of servicemembers known to be homosexual—who are the only ones excluded by these policy directives. The circularity of reasoning here is so obvious that even the Department of Defense has stopped barring civilians who are openly homosexual from receiving security clearances.

During World War II the military induction system examined eighteen million men and women and routinely (but perfunctorily) inquired into their sexual orientation.

Eventually, sixteen million of the examinees served in the armed forces. The number of gay and lesbian servicemembers during the war is estimated between 650,000 and 1,600,000; the induction examiners excluded between 4,000 and 5,000 persons on grounds of homosexual orientation, and the services discharged another 10,000 on these grounds. Today, too, scores, and perhaps hundreds, of thousands of gay and lesbian servicemembers are performing their jobs without incident. Despite several well-publicized group investigations of lesbians (called "witchhunts" by proponents and victims alike), the services generally deal with the exclusion policy in a reactive way, taking action in individual cases when they are directly confronted with the issue.

It was the military exclusion that introduced the American public, during World War II, to the idea that one's personal identity could focus on sexual orientation. Today, the service regulations require dismissal of a member who acknowledges being "a homosexual," provided that the relevant decision makers believe that statement. In such a case no conduct need be proved; the status of "homosexual" requires discharge even if the member is celibate. The regulations also require dismissal for a "homosexual act" (a category that includes not only sodomy but also touching and kissing), but make an exception for the case in which such an act is found to be out of line with the servicemember's general sexual behavior in the past and his or her desires or intentions for the future. If the decision makers conclude that the act is unlikely to recur, and the member declares his or her heterosexuality, then the member can be retained if his or her retention is for the good of the service. Thus, it is the member's public identity as "a homosexual" that requires discharge. The perceived harm in this situation is not that the member is unqualified to perform his or her assigned tasks—the records in these cases are replete with praise from commanders and other work associates—but that the image of the services will be tarnished. The focus of concern is the gender line, the maintenance of what a Marine general once called "the manliness of war."

The crucial question for the services in determining whether to exclude a member on this ground is the member's sexual identity. Although the regulations require a yes-or-no answer to the question of whether the member is "a homosexual," the question of identity is far more complex than can be comprehended in so simple a categorization. Humans are distributed over a considerable range of modes of sexual behavior and over an even greater range of thoughts and feelings about their sexual orientations. The result is that the exclusion regulations are a powerful inducement for servicemembers to resolve private ambivalence by suppressing the parts of themselves that are homosexual, or, even if they privately consider themselves to be gay, to adopt public identities that are unambiguously heterosexual. Whatever degree of self-betrayal one might find in either of these responses, undeniably both kinds of behavior serve the regulations' main purpose of maintaining the armed forces' public image.

The centrality of questions about public identity—for individual servicemembers and for the services themselves—naturally suggests a role for the FIRST AMENDMENT in challenges to the military's exclusion policy. One of the values protected by the FREEDOM OF INTIMATE ASSOCIATION is the power to shape one's own public identity by reference to one's intimate associations. The experience of the "gay liberation" movement shows that an individual's public avowal of homosexual orientation is not merely a self-defining statement; it is also a political act. Several recently litigated cases have involved discharges of servicemembers with sterling records in direct response to their "coming out," that is, publicly expressing their homosexual identity. Although some judges have found merit in First Amendment attacks on these discharges, most lower courts have rejected these claims. Ultimately, First Amendment doctrine in this context will surely follow the Supreme Court's disposition of parallel equal protection claims. Just as *Bowers v. Hardwick* is this generation's version of PLESSY V. FERGUSON (1896), a generous protection of the freedom to express one's gay or lesbian identity probably must await another generation's version of BROWN V. BOARD OF EDUCATION (1954).

KENNETH L. KARST
(1992)

(SEE ALSO: *Sexual Preference and the Constitution; Sexual Orientation and the Armed Forces.*)

Bibliography

BENECKE, MICHELLE M. and DODGE, KIRSTIN S.   1990   Recent Developments—Military Women in Nontraditional Job Fields: Casualties of the Armed Forces' War on Homosexuals. *Harvard Women's Law Journal* 13:215–250.

BÉRUBÉ, ALLAN   1990   *Coming Out Under Fire: The History of Gay Men and Women in World War Two.* New York: Free Press/Macmillan.

DEVELOPMENTS IN THE LAW—SEXUAL ORIENTATION AND THE LAW. 1989   *Harvard Law Review* 102:1508–1671.

HALLEY, JANET E.   1989   The Politics of the Closet: Towards Equal Protection for Gay, Lesbian, and Bisexual Identity. *UCLA Law Review* 36:915–976.

HARRIS, SETH   1989–1990   Permitting Prejudice to Govern: Equal Protection, Military Deference, and the Exclusion of Lesbians and Gay Men from the Military. *New York University Review of Law and Social Change* 17:171–223.

LAW, SYLVIA A.   1988   Homosexuality and the Social Meaning of Gender. *Wisconsin Law Review* 1988:187–235.

MOHR, RICHARD D.   1988   *Gays & Justice: A Study of Ethics, Society, and Law.* New York: Columbia University Press.

SUNSTEIN, CASS R.   1988   Sexual Orientation and the Constitution: A Note on the Relationship Between Due Process and Equal Protection. *University of Chicago Law Review* 55: 1161–1179.

SEXUAL ORIENTATION
(Update)

Despite significant legal and social advances in the last half of the twentieth century, lesbian, gay, and bisexual people in the United States still suffer rampant discrimination on the basis of sexual orientation. Discrimination at the hands of private individuals and organizations because of sexual orientation ranges from refusals to employ to violent attacks. But government itself officially commits much sexual orientation discrimination. Lesbian, gay, and bisexual people have been fired from teaching positions, discriminated against in custody and adoption decisions, excluded from government employment, and denied the right to marry the persons they love—all because of their sexual orientation. This direct governmental participation in the maintenance of a symbolic yet tangible second-class status, an official stigma, calls into question the depth of our national commitment to the egalitarian ideal reflected in the DECLARATION OF INDEPENDENCE and in the Constitution's guarantee of EQUAL PROTECTION OF THE LAWS.

Perhaps the most commonly invoked legal justification for anti-homosexual discrimination and stigmatization are sodomy laws and the Supreme Court's decision in BOWERS V. HARDWICK (1986). In *Bowers*, a 5–4 Court upheld, insofar as two persons of the same sex were concerned, a Georgia law making oral and anal intercourse a FELONY punishable by imprisonment for up to twenty years. The MAJORITY OPINION cursorily dismissed the argument that the law violated the RIGHT OF PRIVACY that had been recognized within the doctrine of SUBSTANTIVE DUE PROCESS.

Despite the overwhelmingly negative academic evaluation of *Bowers* as a constitutional decision, lower courts in the years since have relied on it frequently to reject equal protection challenges to governmental discrimination based on sexual orientation, especially challenges to the exclusion from the ARMED FORCES. *Bowers*, however, explicitly addressed a substantive due process issue, and the majority opinion had expressly disclaimed considering whether Georgia's practice of applying its sodomy law (which, in terms, applied to people regardless of the parties' sexes) solely to same-sex couples, violated the equal protection clause. Numerous courts—although not all—have nonetheless concluded that *Bowers* all but forecloses successful equal protection challenges to governmental antigay discrimination because it upheld criminal penalties for "the conduct" that is said to "define" the class of persons subject to discrimination.

Of course, oral and anal intercourse are just two of a myriad of ways in which two persons might express mutual affection or attraction, and heterosexual as well as lesbian, gay, and bisexual persons engage in such intercourse. Moreover, many commentators have argued that the history of criminal laws on which the *Bowers* majority relied for its DUE PROCESS HOLDING does not conclude all equal protection questions concerning sexual orientation discrimination. In particular, *Bowers* does not determine what level of scrutiny is warranted by governmental action on the basis of sexual orientation.

The Supreme Court has issued only one decision on the merits of a sexual orientation equal protection claim, and ROMER V. EVANS (1996) does not resolve the appropriate level of scrutiny. In concluding that a Colorado state constitutional amendment that made it more difficult for lesbian, gay, and bisexual persons to seek statutory protection from discrimination violated the equal protection clause, the Court held that the amendment did not even satisfy RATIONAL BASIS review, the lowest level of equal protection scrutiny. The Court thus had no need to determine whether discrimination on the basis of sexual orientation is properly subject to intermediate or STRICT SCRUTINY.

Even though they have not generally prevailed in the lower courts, judges and scholars who believe that governmental discrimination on the basis of sexual orientation warrants heightened judicial scrutiny make a number of persuasive arguments. Gay, lesbian, and bisexual individuals have historically suffered and still do suffer from pervasive discrimination, and thus the very costs of "coming out" seriously impair the prospects of achieving equality solely through the political process. People's sexual orientation is irrelevant to virtually any constitutionally significant capacities, such as the ability to be a loving parent or to follow a commander's orders. Moreover, to the extent that, however misguidedly, Supreme Court case law treats immutability of a personal characteristic as a relevant criterion in equal protection analysis, sexual orientation should count as immutable. Even if there are some people who might be able to change the direction of their emotions and attractions, a great many lesbian, gay, and bisexual persons experience their sexual orientation as beyond their control (some despite expensive and often painful efforts to become heterosexual). There is also both no way to know whether a given person might be that rare individual who could conceivably change orientations, and little or no justification for demanding that people try to so reconfigure their psyches. In short, the usual indicia of SUSPECT CLASSIFICATIONS are present in these cases.

In addition, some scholars and lower courts in state law cases have concluded that discrimination against lesbian, gay, and bisexual persons may constitute SEX DISCRIMINATION, subject to heightened equal protection scrutiny. The formal argument notes that sexual orientation is defined by the sex of the parties involved; the critical difference between, for example, a gay man and a heterosexual woman is their sex—for both are attracted to men. Thus, in this case, the same attractions and desires that are permissible or even celebrated when expressed by a woman become a basis for discrimination when expressed by a man. This is formal sex discrimination requiring "an exceedingly persuasive justification" under precedents such as UNITED STATES V. VIRGINIA (1996). A more functional argument contends that discrimination based on sexual orientation reinforces a patriarchal ideology in which women are deemed the only fit objects of sexual penetration, inferior to men and incomplete without them, and that such discrimination serves outmoded gender roles and hence is presumptively unconstitutional.

Despite the forceful equal protection arguments in favor of heightened scrutiny for sexual orientation classifications and governmental recognition of SAME-SEX MARRIAGE, it seems unlikely that courts will rush to insist that lesbian, gay, and bisexual people not be denied the full measure of equality. In time, however, it may well be, as one lower federal court confidently predicted in *Nabozny v. Podlesny* (1996), that "*Bowers* will soon be eclipsed in the area of equal protection by the Supreme Court's holding in *Romer v. Evans*" and that our governments will get out of the business of stigmatizing their citizens on the basis of sexual orientation.

DAVID B. CRUZ
(2000)

(SEE ALSO: *Marriage and the Constitution; Same-Sex Marriage; Sexual Orientation and the Armed Forces.*)

Bibliography
CRUZ, DAVID B. 1999 Controlling Desires: Sexual Orientation Conversion and the Limits of Knowledge and Law. *Southern California Law Review* 72:1297–1400.

HALLEY, JANET E. 1989 The Politics of the Closet: Towards Equal Protection for Gay, Lesbian, and Bisexual Identity. *UCLA Law Review* 36:915–976.

—— 1994 The Politics of Biology: A Critique of the Argument from Immutability. *Stanford Law Review* 46: 503–568.

KARST, KENNETH L. 1995 Myths of Identity: Individual and Group Portraits of Race and Sexual Orientation. *UCLA Law Review* 43:263–369.

KOPPELMAN, ANDREW 1994 Why Discrimination Against Lesbians and Gay Men Is Sex Discrimination. *New York University Law Review* 69:197–287.

LAW, SYLVIA A.   1988   Homosexuality and the Social Meaning of Gender. *Wisconsin Law Review* 1988:187–235.

RICHARDS, DAVID A. J.   1998   *Women, Gays, and the Constitution: The Grounds for Feminism and Gay Rights in Culture and Law.* Chicago: University of Chicago Press.

RUBENSTEIN, WILLIAM B.   1997   *Cases and Materials on Sexual Orientation and the Law,* 2nd ed. St. Paul, Minn.: West Publishing Co.

SUNSTEIN, CASS R.   1988   Sexual Orientation and the Constitution: A Note on the Relationship Between Due Process and Equal Protection. *University of Chicago Law Review* 55: 1161–1179.

SEXUAL ORIENTATION AND THE ARMED FORCES

In 1993, the antigay policy of the ARMED FORCES became the subject of LEGISLATION. Dubbed "Don't Ask, Don't Tell," these revised rules are widely understood to require military officials to refrain from asking about, and gay servicemembers to refrain from disclosing, their SEXUAL ORIENTATION. The statute includes "don't tell" but lacks "don't ask," however, and U.S. Department of Defense regulations, though they do include some limits on asking, expressly decline to provide servicemembers with any means of enforcing them. The statute's chief innovation is to require the discharge of any servicemember who engages in any physical contact that would manifest to a reasonable person that he or she has the intent or propensity to engage in homosexual acts. Department of Defense regulations go further, requiring discharge if the servicemember has engaged in any conduct that manifests an intent or propensity. Servicemembers can fend off discharge only by showing that they in fact have no propensity to engage in homosexual acts.

The most important idea of the 1993 statute is to put military antigay policy under the protection of the Supreme Court's holding in BOWERS V. HARDWICK (1986). *Hardwick* held that states could prohibit homosexual sodomy without violating the constitutional RIGHT OF PRIVACY. The military has a sodomy statute, and one federal court has held that the military has a compelling reason to enforce that statute selectively against homosexual (as opposed to heterosexual) acts of sodomy. But critics of the policy do not claim that servicemembers have a constitutional privacy right to come out, or to engage in conduct that indicates that they are gay; conversely, defenders of the policy do not claim that *all* gay servicemembers have engaged or will engage in sodomy. How could *Hardwick* matter?

The doctrinal logic works differently in the EQUAL PROTECTION and the FIRST AMENDMENT contexts. In equal protection, the key legal step is provided by the U.S. Court of Appeals for the District of Columbia Circuit's decision in *Padula v. Webster* (1987), which held that *Hardwick* forecloses heightened judicial scrutiny of state antigay discrimination because government can criminalize the "behavior that defines the class." The key factual step involves the propensity concept: On this theory, servicemembers who have shown that they are more likely than their peers to engage in same-sex sodomy are discharged on the basis of predicted bad conduct, and not discrimination against them or their social group. Similarly, the many First Amendment cases distinguishing speech from conduct, and permitting government to punish conduct the evidence for which is the perpetrator's speech about it, negate any First Amendment challenge to the discharge of a servicemember who has merely said "I'm gay." Courts construe that statement as an admission that the speaker has a propensity to commit same-sex sodomy, to which the First Amendment simply does not apply. Moreover, the rebuttable presumption device gives every servicemember being discharged a chance to demonstrate that he or she lacks a propensity. If the servicemember fails to do so, the law of evidence forces a formal conclusion that the servicemember does have a propensity, and that is not speech.

All of those steps are optional, however. Courts could say that *Hardwick* is bad law, or that it has been overturned sub silentio by the Supreme Court's decision in ROMER V. EVANS (1996), or that *Hardwick* is still good law but that sodomy is not a "behavior that defines the class." Courts could say that the words "I'm gay" are speech and warrant First Amendment protection. Courts could reject propensity as a proxy for conduct and find that Congress, when it refused every conduct-based idea proposed by President WILLIAM J. CLINTON (for instance, to require even-handed enforcement of the sodomy statute and to discharge, without regard to their sexual orientation, all servicemembers who engage in same-sex sex), showed an intent to disadvantage a social group (not its conduct) and to regulate speech (not conduct). They could say that the policy lends governmental support to private antigay prejudice and thus runs afoul of the decisions, from CLEBURNE V. CLEBURNE LIVING CENTER, INC. (1985) to *Romer,* holding that to be an illegal purpose. Finally, they could say that, by infiltrating the military with closeted homosexuals, the policy pursues its goals of unit cohesion, protection of troop privacy, and recruitment among youth who do not wish to associate with gay men and lesbians, irrationally.

One argument has consistently failed: The claim that the policy discriminates against servicemembers on the basis of their status and not their conduct. Every appellate court faced with a constitutional challenge has rejected that argument and upheld the statute. A Supreme Court decision about the constitutionality of the policy seems unlikely; instead, we are more likely to see litigation on regulatory questions, and executive or legislative changes in the rules and patterns of enforcement.

JANET E. HALLEY
(2000)

Bibliography

BENECKE, MICHELLE M. and OSBURNE, C. DIXON Annual *Conduct Unbecoming: The Annual Report on "Don't Ask, Don't Tell, Don't Pursue" Violations.* Washington, D.C.: Servicemembers Legal Defense Network.

HALLEY, JANET E. 1999 *Don't: A Reader's Guide to the Military's Anti-Gay Policy.* Durham, N.C.: Duke University Press.

LEONARD, ARTHUR S., ed. 1997 *Homosexuality and the Constitution, Volume II: Homosexuals and the Military.* New York: Garland Publishing.

SYMPOSIUM 1995 "Don't Ask, Don't Tell": Gays in the Military. *UMKC Law Review* 64:1–236.

SEXUAL PREDATOR LAWS

Perhaps the most vilified criminal in American society is the sex offender who preys on young children. To prevent convicted sex offenders from striking again, states have constructed a mosaic of laws. These laws include the registration of offenders, the notification of communities (together called "Megan's Laws," after a victim of a sex predator in New Jersey), and the newest state weapon, special involuntary commitment of sex offenders.

All fifty states now have some form of registration and notification laws, and a substantial number of states—among them, Washington, Kansas, Florida, and Wisconsin—have adopted and are considering special involuntary commitment statutes. The laws authorize the indefinite detention, possibly for life, of persons who have been previously convicted of a sex offense and are dangerous to society as a result of a mental abnormality or personality disorder. The mental abnormality or personality disorder requirement is lower than the general involuntary commitment statutes, which usually require a full-blown MENTAL ILLNESS, such as schizophrenia or bipolar (manic-depressive) disorder, coupled with dangerousness. Further, some laws, such as the one enacted in Kansas, appear to provide only minimal psychiatric treatment to those who are committed.

The Supreme Court considered the constitutionality of sexual predator involuntary commitment laws in *Kansas v. Hendricks* (1997). *Hendricks* involved a challenge to the Kansas sex predator involuntary commitment statute based on DUE PROCESS OF LAW, DOUBLE JEOPARDY, and the EX POST FACTO clause. All three constitutional claims were grounded on the premise that the involuntary commit-

ment really constituted an unlawful extension of the previous conviction because it was effectively criminal punishment without the required proof beyond a reasonable doubt.

In a 5–4 decision, the Court upheld the Kansas statute. Justice CLARENCE THOMAS, writing for the majority, concluded that the law did not violate any provision of the Constitution because it was civil in nature and did not impose a second criminal punishment. Thomas offered several reasons for this conclusion, including that the Kansas legislature had placed the commitment law within a larger civil statute, called the law civil, and enacted the law to protect the public, not to further punish criminals.

Thomas was not troubled by the apparent lack of psychiatric treatment provided by the law. He noted that the law was new and, under certain circumstances, mere detention could be an appropriate goal of the state. In essence, Thomas took a very deferential posture towards the legislature's power to safeguard society from heinous individuals.

Thomas's conclusion, and even his rationale, are at first glance appealing. It is easy to observe that Leroy Hendricks, who had a long history of sexually abusing children and had admitted to being unable to control his urge to molest children at times, deserved to spend the rest of his life isolated from society because of what he had done.

Despite these considerations, however, the Kansas legislature's sexual offender commitment law is constitutionally infirm and economically shortsighted. The detention of offenders such as Leroy Hendricks is criminal in nature and unconstitutional for several reasons. The first and perhaps foremost reason is the state's hidden intent to punish. Many experts in the psychiatric community agree that sex offenders are not treatable and will not benefit from involuntary hospitalization. They will be kept there, nonetheless, perhaps for life. Also, treatment is not afforded in jail, only after the incarceration period has run its course, indicating a less-than wholehearted concern by the legislature for "healing the sick." This form of indefinite warehousing of people without the provision of realistic treatment opportunities—and without the narrow tailoring that would promote as much liberty as possible—had never before been approved by the Court and appears to be a fancy substitute for imprisonment.

The Court's reduction in standards for involuntary commitment of sex predators also abuses the mental health system. The laws ignore the plain purpose of hospitalization, which is to treat and heal. As the 1996 *American Psychiatric Association Task Force's Report on Sexually Dangerous Offenders* noted, "The sexual predator statutes aim to achieve preventive detention of offenders who have completed their criminal sentences. The medical model of long-term civil commitment is used as a pretext for extended confinement that would otherwise be constitutionally impermissible." Instead of psychiatrists and psychologists using their expertise to treat people who can be helped by their services, the law permits hospitals to be clogged with untreatable sex offenders.

In addition, the mental "abnormality" test is so lacking in definitional coherence that it cannot be administered properly in a court of law. The term "abnormal" is vague and devoid of a concrete definition—indeed, even the psychiatrists and psychologists do not agree on what it means—to the extent that the standard is simply not workable.

Perhaps the greatest danger of legitimizing such a law, however, is the possibility that other "dangerous" mentally abnormal recidivist groups, such as drug addicts, spouse abusers, and people who drive under the influence of alcohol or drugs, could be the next subjects of involuntary commitment laws. This slippery slope would be a powerful regulatory tool for the legislature.

While preventing sex offender recidivism is extremely important, constitutional shortcuts will not work in the long run. Using the civil system to do the work of the CRIMINAL JUSTICE SYSTEM is neither laudatory nor efficient—taxpayers will be paying a substantial and increased amount for wasted psychological care for "patients" housed in expensive psychiatric institutions, many if not all of whom are untreatable and taking the space of more deserving, innocent mentally ill persons. If the legislature deems it appropriate to protect society from sex predators, it ought to enact criminal laws with lengthy criminal sentences or civil laws with cognizable standards, safeguards promoting freedom, and real treatment opportunities. While a "round-them-up" statute may have valid ends, it must be written using valid means as well. Without those constitutional means, involuntary commitment statutes should fall.

STEVEN I. FRIEDLAND
(2000)

SEXUAL PREFERENCE AND THE CONSTITUTION

Since the 1960s both legislation and judicial decisions have moved toward decriminalization of homosexual conduct and toward increased acceptance of homosexuals as parents, professionals, and public employees. A number of legal restrictions remain, however, mostly concerning employment and other material benefits. The Supreme Court has not fully considered the constitutional issues raised by these restrictions. In *Doe v. Commonwealth's Attorney* (1976) the Court summarily affirmed, 6–3 and

without opinion, a federal district court's dismissal of a constitutional challenge to Virginia's sodomy law, brought by two adult males who lived in a stable homosexual relationship. The absence of any serious threat of prosecution suggests that the Court's decision may have rested on a RIPENESS ground. In any case, *Doe* surely is not the Court's last word on the subject—although it provides an object lesson for anyone who would ignore the influence of conventional morality on the development of coherent constitutional principle.

Doe had been argued on the theory of a RIGHT OF PRIVACY, by analogy to the Court's decisions on BIRTH CONTROL and ABORTION. But "privacy," in its ordinary usage, fails to capture the essence of the constitutional claim. A middle-class homosexual couple need fear no prosecution if they keep their relationship private. It is precisely the public expression of homosexuality that produces sanctions; the interest at stake is in some sense the opposite of privacy, more akin to a FIRST AMENDMENT freedom of expression. Similarly, the issue of homosexual marriage, which has been addressed by some commentators as an issue of SEX DISCRIMINATION, seems better approached as a problem in symbolic expression of a homosexual couple's identity.

Recognition of homosexual relationships within a FREEDOM OF INTIMATE ASSOCIATION would place on government the burden of justifying its interference with those relationships. If a state had to prove that homosexuality alone disqualified a person from child custody or employment as a school teacher, its efforts to do so would demonstrate that the operative factor in the law's disqualifications was not risk of harm but stigma. Commentators have suggested that homosexuality be added to the list of SUSPECT CLASSIFICATIONS calling for STRICT SCRUTINY under the EQUAL PROTECTION clause, and there is force to the argument. Whether the problem be seen as one of equality or as an aspect of SUBSTANTIVE DUE PROCESS, most laws regulating homosexual conduct seem unlikely to survive serious constitutional scrutiny. What remains in question is the willingness of a majority of Justices for the Supreme Court to engage in that scrutiny.

KENNETH L. KARST
(1986)

Bibliography

PROJECT 1966 The Consenting Adult Homosexual and the Law: Empirical Study of Enforcement and Administration in Los Angeles County. *UCLA Law Review* 13:643–832.

RIVERA, RHONDA R. 1979 Our Straight-Laced Judges: The Legal Position of Homosexual Persons in the United States. *Hastings Law Journal* 30:799–955.

SYMPOSIUM 1985 The Legal System and Homosexuality—Approbation, Accommodation, or Reprobation? *University of Dayton Law Review* 10:445–813.

SHAPIRO v. THOMPSON
394 U.S. 618 (1969)

Two states and the DISTRICT OF COLUMBIA denied WELFARE BENEFITS to new residents during a one-year waiting period. The Supreme Court, 6–3, held that the state schemes denied the EQUAL PROTECTION OF THE LAWS and that the District's law violated the Fifth Amendment's equal protection component, as recognized in BOLLING V. SHARPE (1954).

Justice WILLIAM J. BRENNAN wrote for the Court. The RIGHT TO TRAVEL from one state to settle in another was a FUNDAMENTAL INTEREST, whose impairment was justified only on a showing of a COMPELLING STATE INTEREST. These statutes served to deter the entry of INDIGENTS and to discourage interstate travel for the purpose of obtaining increased welfare benefits, but those objectives were constitutionally illegitimate efforts to restrict the RIGHT TO TRAVEL. Equal protection considerations forbade a state to apportion its benefits and services on the basis of past tax contributions. The saving of welfare costs similarly could not "justify an otherwise invidious classification." Various arguments addressed to administrative convenience were also insufficiently compelling.

The Court also hinted that WEALTH DISCRIMINATION against the indigent might constitute a SUSPECT CLASSIFICATION, or, alternatively, that minimum subsistence might be a fundamental interest. Both these suggestions were sidetracked in later decisions such as SAN ANTONIO INDEPENDENT SCHOOL DISTRICT V. RODRIGUEZ (1973).

Chief Justice EARL WARREN dissented, joined by Justice HUGO L. BLACK. Warren argued that Congress had approved the one-year waiting periods in the SOCIAL SECURITY ACT. The majority rejected this statutory interpretation but added that in any event "Congress may not authorize the States to violate the Equal Protection Clause."

Justice JOHN MARSHALL HARLAN, in a long dissent, mounted a frontal attack on the WARREN COURT's expansion of the judicial role in equal protection cases through its heightening of the STANDARDS OF REVIEW in cases involving fundamental interests and suspect classifications. Here, as in other decisions of the same period, the Harlan dissent illuminates the Court's doctrinal path more effectively than does the majority opinion. It has always been possible for a Justice to combine clarity of vision with the wrong conclusion.

KENNETH L. KARST
(1986)

(SEE ALSO: *Invidious Discrimination.*)

SHAUGHNESSY v. UNITED STATES EX REL. MEZEI
345 U.S. 206 (1953)

Over the dissent of four Justices, the VINSON COURT upheld the authority of the ATTORNEY GENERAL to exclude and detain indefinitely an ALIEN without a hearing at Ellis Island solely on the basis of confidential information, "the disclosure of which would be prejudicial to the public interest." Justice ROBERT H. JACKSON, dissenting, wrote that he could not imagine how a hearing "would menace the security of this country."

MICHAEL E. PARRISH
(1986)

SHAW, LEMUEL
(1781–1861)

Lemuel Shaw was chief justice of Massachusetts from 1830 to 1860, during which time he wrote a record number of opinions, over 2,200, only one in dissent. He dominated his court as no other judge has. His opinions were often comprehensive, ponderous, analytical treatises. He often explained guiding principles in terms of policy or social advantage, placing his decisions on the broadest grounds. Justice OLIVER WENDELL HOLMES, attributing Shaw's influence to his "accurate appreciation of the requirements of the community," declared that "few have lived who were his equals in their understanding of the grounds of public policy to which all laws must be ultimately referred. It was this which made him . . . the greatest magistrate which this country has produced."

Before his appointment to the Supreme Judicial Court, Shaw had been a Federalist lawyer, a member of both branches of the state legislature, and a bank director. Shaw did not, however, fit the stereotype of the conservative Whig judge seeking DOCTRINES of VESTED RIGHTS to ward off legislative controls over business enterprise. He was the foremost champion of the power of government to promote and regulate the economy in the public interest. To call the POLICE POWER Shaw's invention would be an exaggeration, but not a great one. Unlike JOHN MARSHALL and ROGER B. TANEY, who viewed the police power as the residual powers of the state, Shaw defined it as the power of government "to trench somewhat largely on the profitable use of individual property" for the public good, and he distinguished the police power from other state powers. Shaw laid the foundations for the legal character of power companies, railroads, and water suppliers as public utilities, privately owned but subject to regulation for the public benefit. He would even have included manufacturers and banks. He was the first to hold that the power of

EMINENT DOMAIN cannot be restrained by or contracted away under the CONTRACT CLAUSE. At a time when that clause had become a bulwark of vested rights, making it a link between capitalism and constitutionalism, Shaw voided legislative alterations of chartered rights in only three cases, and in each the essential regulatory powers of the state were undiminished. Shaw was profoundly committed to JUDICIAL RESTRAINT. He held statutes unconstitutional in only nine reported cases, most often to protect the rights of the criminally accused. In as many cases Shaw repudiated the doctrine of SUBSTANTIVE DUE PROCESS drawn from WYNEHAMER V. NEW YORK (1856). Community rights rather than vested ones were Shaw's foremost concern.

In his COMMERCE CLAUSE opinions, too, Shaw sustained state powers. The Supreme Court agreed with him in the LICENSE CASES (1847) but reversed him in the PASSENGER CASES (1849), despite the sagacity of his empirical test to determine whether state and federal laws actually conflicted in their operation. In the absence of a federal law, Shaw would have sustained state legislation. He handed down the leading opinion on the constitutionality of the Fugitive Slave Act of 1850 in SIMS' CASE (1851), though he freed every sojourner slave (not a runaway) who reached Massachusetts. (See COMMONWEALTH V. AVES.) He originated the SEPARATE BUT EQUAL DOCTRINE that became the legal linchpin of racial SEGREGATION, and he upheld a conviction for BLASPHEMY in an opinion that abridged RELIGIOUS LIBERTY. In such cases he carried his doctrine of judicial restraint too far, but he towered over class and party, and his name became a synonym for judicial integrity and impartiality.

LEONARD W. LEVY
(1986)

Bibliography

ADLOW, ELIJAH 1962 *The Genius of Lemuel Shaw.* Boston: Court Square Press.

LEVY, LEONARD W. 1957 *The Law of the Commonwealth and Chief Justice Shaw.* Cambridge, Mass.: Harvard University Press.

SHAW v. RENO (1993) AND ITS PROGENY

North Carolina is subject to the preclearance provisions of section 5 of the VOTING RIGHT ACT OF 1965. The Voting Rights Section of the Civil Rights Division of the U.S. Department of Justice (DOJ) rejected a North Carolina congressional plan that provided for only a single black-majority congressional district, insisting that two such districts be drawn and suggesting several hypothetical configurations. A resubmitted plan with two majority–minority districts was given DOJ preclearance, but the new district in that plan looked nothing like any of the DOJ suggestions. The proposed North Carolina Twelfth Congressional District stretched 200 miles, included parts of numerous cities, and achieved contiguity of some of its parts only via connection along a single road, Interstate 85.

Because a majority of Supreme Court Justices, including SANDRA DAY O'CONNOR, had previously seemed willing to assent to race-conscious ELECTORAL DISTRICTING to safeguard the fundamental right to vote, the Court's 5–4 decision invalidating North Carolina's districting plan in *Shaw v. Reno* (*Shaw I*) came as a surprise to many experts. In a MAJORITY OPINION authored by O'Connor, and joined by WILLIAM H. REHNQUIST, ANTONIN SCALIA, ANTHONY M. KENNEDY, and CLARENCE THOMAS, the Court explained that it was troubled by the peculiar configuration of the Twelfth Congressional District, the least compact in the nation, and by the history that led to its creation, in which race appeared to play a major role. The majority also enunciated a new legal standard for legislative action on REPRESENTATION, in which an excessive reliance on race as a criterion in drawing electoral district was unconstitutional. In plans in which race was implicated, states were now required to prove that there was a COMPELLING STATE INTEREST in establishing the plan and that the districts were "narrowly tailored" to serve that interest.

While *Shaw I* merely remanded the North Carolina congressional plan to the district court for consideration under the new legal standard, *Shaw v. Hunt* (*Shaw II*) (1996), also decided 5–4 with the same lineup of Justices, declared North Carolina's congressional plan to be unconstitutional, rejecting claims that aspects of its peculiar configurations could better be assigned to political than to racial considerations. Even before *Shaw II*, however, *Shaw I* inspired similar challenges to race-based districting in other jurisdictions.

Most *Shaw*-type challenges came in jurisdictions that fell under the section 5 preclearance provisions (affecting sixteen states in whole or in part, including all states in the deep South). In covered jurisdictions, the failure to create as many majority–minority districts as the DOJ viewed as required by the act risked a preclearance denial and time-consuming litigation that was unattractive to politicians. By 1998, lower courts in states such as Louisiana, Georgia, South Carolina, and Texas had rejected plans precleared by DOJ; and when these cases were appealed to the Supreme Court the lower court decision was left standing, as in MILLER V. JOHNSON (1995). In these decisions the courts refused to excuse the majority– minority districts created to secure section 5 preclearance, and some of the opinions chastised the DOJ for its excessive zeal in pursuing race-conscious districting. Only in California were plans sustained against a *Shaw*-type challenge, by a PER CURIAM decision upholding a lower court. But, in that state, the plans under challenge were drawn by former state judges and plausibly defended as fully meeting traditional districting criteria.

Shaw I and subsequent decisions met a mixed reaction among legal scholars. The most important legal criticisms of the opinions concerned the logic underlying the court's broadening of STANDING to sue to include voters outside the challenged district; the Court's failure to specify the exact nature of the constitutional harm to white voters whose votes were not diluted; the murkiness and inherent judicial unmanageability of discerning when race is a "predominant factor"; and the use of a sledgehammer (a new constitutional standard) to solve a problem that could have been dealt with merely by tightening the criteria for enforcement of the Voting Rights Act. Ironically, the black-majority districts in question were actually more racially integrated than the white-majority districts in their states. Reaction to *Shaw* in the CIVIL RIGHTS community was more visceral, as some saw the *Shaw* line of cases as a further retreat from the Second Civil Rights Reconstruction (that of the 1960s), paralleling the betrayal of the First Reconstruction in the COMPROMISE OF 1877.

BERNARD GROFMAN
(2000)

Bibliography

DAVIDSON, CHANDLER and GROFMAN, BERNARD 1994 *The Quiet Revolution in the South: The Impact of the Voting Right Act, 1965–1990.* Princeton, N.J.: Princeton University Press.

GROFMAN, BERNARD, ed. 1998 *Race and Redistricting in the 1990s.* New York: Agathon Press.

GROFMAN, BERNARD and DAVIDSON, CHANDLER 1992 *Controversies in Minority Voting: The Voting Right Act of 1965 in Perspective.* Washington, D.C.: The Brookings Institution.

ISSACHAROFF, SAMUEL and KARLAN, PAMELA S. 1998 Commentary: Standing and Misunderstanding in Voting Rights Law. *Harvard Law Review* 111:2276–2292.

LOWENSTEIN, DANIEL HAYS 1998 You Don't Have to Be Liberal to Hate the Racial Gerrymandering Cases. *Stanford Law Review* 50:779–835.

PILDES, RICHARD and NIEMI, RICHARD 1993 Expressive Harms, 'Bizarre Districts,' and Voting Rights: Evaluating Election-District Appearance After *Shaw v. Reno. Michigan Law Review* 92:483–587.

SHAYS' REBELLION
(1786–1787)

The economic depression following the Revolutionary War fell especially harshly upon small farmers who relied on borrowed money to finance their crops. Falling prices led to default and foreclosure. Seven states resorted to deliberate inflation (through large issues of unsecured paper currency), stay laws, and other forms of DEBTOR'S RELIEF LEGISLATION.

The Massachusetts legislature, however, defeated all such proposals. Beginning in August 1786, mobs of impoverished farmers in central and western Massachusetts prevented the courts from functioning and ordering foreclosures. In September an armed force assembled at Springfield under Daniel Shays, a farmer and one-time Revolutionary army captain. On January 25, 1787, Shays attempted to seize the federal arsenal at Springfield, but his men were repulsed by artillery. On February 4, the rebels were routed and the leaders captured by the state militia.

Meanwhile, Massachusetts had applied to Congress for assistance. Although Congress authorized raising a small force to protect the arsenal, no aid was actually sent.

The effect of the rebellion was to raise the specter of disintegration of civil government and so to hasten the process of constitutional reform. Less than three weeks after the collapse of Shays Rebellion, Congress passed a resolution giving official sanction to the Annapolis Convention's call for the CONSTITUTIONAL CONVENTION OF 1787.

DENNIS J. MAHONEY
(1986)

Bibliography

SZATMARY, DAVID P. 1980 *Shays' Rebellion: The Making of an Agrarian Insurrection.* Amherst: University of Massachusetts Press.

SHELLEY v. KRAEMER
334 U.S. 1 (1948)

HURD v. HODGE
334 U.S. 24 (1948)

In 1926, in CORRIGAN V. BUCKLEY, the Supreme Court rejected a constitutional attack on judicial enforcement of racially RESTRICTIVE COVENANTS—contractual agreements between neighboring residential landowners limiting the occupancy of their houses to white persons. From that time forward, the NAACP sought to persuade the Court to reconsider and find the covenants' enforcement to constitute STATE ACTION in violation of the FOURTEENTH AMENDMENT. Finally, in *Shelley,* the Court granted review in two such cases, one from Missouri and one from Michigan. In both, white neighbors obtained INJUNCTIONS forbidding black buyers to occupy houses subject to racial covenants. The decision was widely anticipated to be important, both doctrinally and practically. Eighteen AMICUS CURIAE briefs supported the NAACP's position, and on the other side three white "protective associations" filed briefs, as did the National Association of Real Estate Boards. Counsel for the NAACP included CHARLES HOUSTON and THURGOOD MARSHALL.

The time was ripe for an overruling of *Corrigan*'s casual acceptance of racially restrictive covenants as a "private" means of imposing residential segregation. The armed forces had integrated at the end of the WORLD WAR II; in 1947 the President's Committee on Civil Rights had published a report calling attention to the importance of judicial enforcement to the effectiveness of the covenants; and President HARRY S. TRUMAN, a strong CIVIL RIGHTS advocate, had placed the weight of the executive branch on the NAACP's side by authorizing the SOLICITOR GENERAL to file an AMICUS CURIAE brief. The Supreme Court held, 6–0, that state courts could not constitutionally enjoin the sale to black buyers of property covered by restrictive covenants.

Shelley's result seems inescapable. Yet hardly anyone has a kind word for the *Shelley* opinion, written by Chief Justice FRED VINSON. *Corrigan* was not overruled but was characterized as a case involving only the validity of restrictive covenants and not their enforcement in courts. Standing alone, said Vinson, the racial covenants violated no rights; their enforcement by state court injunctions, however, constituted state action in violation of the Fourteenth Amendment. Taken for all it is worth, this reasoning would spell the end of the state action limitation—a loss many could cheerfully bear. But it is plain the Court had no such heroics in mind. The Justices were not ready to find state action in any private conduct the state might fail to prohibit. Yet the opinion never quite explained why, given the *Shelley* result, those larger doctrinal consequences do not follow. The opinion's elusive quality led PHILIP KURLAND to call it "constitutional law's *Finnegans Wake*."

Two decades later, in EVANS V. ABNEY (1970), the Court picked up the first shoe. *Shelley* was limited severely, and the power of a private owner to call on the courts to enforce his or her control over property was largely freed from constitutional limitations.

A companion case to *Shelley, Hurd v. Hodge* (1948), involved a racial covenant covering land in the DISTRICT OF COLUMBIA. Without reaching the question whether the Fifth Amendment guaranteed EQUAL PROTECTION (see BOLLING V. SHARPE), the Court held the judicial enforcement of the covenant to violate "the public policy of the United States."

KENNETH L. KARST
(1986)

Bibliography

HENKIN, LOUIS 1962 *Shelley v. Kraemer*: Notes for a Revised Opinion. *University of Pennsylvania Law Review* 110:473–505.

HOROWITZ, HAROLD W. 1957 The Misleading Search for "State Action." *Southern California Law Review* 30:208–221.

SHELTON v. TUCKER

See: Least Restrictive Means Test

SHEPPARD-TOWNER MATERNITY ACT
42 Stat. 224 (1921)

FEDERAL GRANTS-IN-AID to the states began in the mid-nineteenth century. As the federal government, in its new capacity as a welfare state, funded important social services, some congressmen and senators considered this form of federal spending socialistic and questioned its constitutionality.

In 1921, Congress passed the Maternity Act, a measure recommended by President WARREN G. HARDING, allocating funds to the states for health service for mothers and children, particularly in rural communities. This welfare measure sought to reduce maternal and infant mortality. Critics argued that federal funds could lawfully be spent only in connection with the ENUMERATED POWERS of Congress, and they asserted that the grant-in-aid was a subtle method of extending federal power and usurping functions properly belonging to the states. Further, since the formal acceptance of such grants by state legislatures brought federal supervision and approval of the funded state activities, the measure placed too much potentially coercive power in the hands of federal bureaucracies.

The Supreme Court was asked to rule on the act's constitutionality in separate suits brought by a taxpayer and the Commonwealth of Massachusetts. The Court did not rule on the merits in either case, holding that the state presented no justiciable controversy and that the taxpayer lacked STANDING to sue. (See TAXPAYER'S SUITS; FROTHINGHAM V. MELLON.) Still, many states refused to avail themselves of the provisions of the act, and Congress failed to renew it in 1929. Nonetheless, the projects of this period were a political precedent for much of the modern system of federally dispensed welfare.

PAUL L. MURPHY
(1986)

Bibliography

LEMONS, J. STANLEY 1960 The Sheppard-Towner Act: Progressivism in the 1920's. *Journal of American History* 55:776–786.

SHERBERT v. VERNER
374 U.S. 398 (1963)

Sherbert, a Seventh-Day Adventist, lost her job after the mill at which she had been working went on a six-day work week and she refused Saturday work. She filed for unemployment compensation, was referred to a job, but declined it because it would have required Saturday work. By declining proffered employment she was no longer "available for work" under South Carolina's rules and hence no longer eligible for unemployment benefits.

Justice WILLIAM J. BRENNAN, speaking for the Supreme Court, concluded that the disqualification imposed a burden on Mrs. Sherbert's free exercise of religion. The FIRST AMENDMENT, he declared, protected not only belief but observance. Even an incidental burdening of religion could be justified only if the state could show a COMPELLING STATE INTEREST in not granting an exemption.

This decision was a significant departure from the secular regulation approach to free exercise claims which had been affirmed by the Court as recently as *Braunfeld v. Brown* (1961). Brennan made little attempt to distinguish *Sherbert* from *Braunfeld*. Justice WILLIAM O. DOUGLAS, concurring, rejected the secular regulation approach.

Justice POTTER STEWART concurred in the result, disassociating himself from Brennan's reasoning. Stewart saw tension developing between the Court's interpretation of the free exercise and establishment clauses. To grant free exercise exemptions from otherwise valid secular regulations preferred religious over nonreligious people. In establishment clause cases, however, any governmental action that had the effect of advancing religion was forbidden. Stewart would have relieved the tension by relaxing the establishment clause rule.

Justice JOHN MARSHALL HARLAN, joined by Justice BYRON R. WHITE, dissented. For Harlan, the notion of a constitutional compulsion to "carve out an exception" based on religious conviction was a singularly dangerous one.

RICHARD E. MORGAN
(1986)

SHERMAN, ROGER
(1721–1793)

Roger Sherman was one of the leading members of the founding generation. For more than two decades he was simultaneously mayor of New Haven, Connecticut, a member of the state legislature, and a judge of the Superior Court. He was a delegate to the Continental Congress almost continuously from 1774 to 1784. He signed the DECLARATION OF INDEPENDENCE, the ARTICLES OF CON-FEDERATION, and the Constitution, the only person to sign all these founding documents.

At the CONSTITUTIONAL CONVENTION OF 1787, Sherman was a respected elder statesman. He distrusted a large and ill-informed populace and wanted all elections to national office mediated by the state legislatures. He formally introduced the GREAT COMPROMISE and argued strongly for its passage. He wrote the contingency provision prescribing election of the President by the HOUSE OF REPRESENTATIVES if there was no majority in the ELECTORAL COLLEGE. He opposed giving the President an absolute VETO POWER and erecting a system of federal courts inferior to the Supreme Court. He originally favored, but later gave up, a unicameral national legislature chosen by the state legislatures. He strongly supported the prohibitions on export duties and BILLS OF CREDIT

After the Convention, Sherman worked hard for RATIFICATION OF THE CONSTITUTION, writing newspaper articles (as "A Countryman") and attending the state ratifying convention. He was a member of the first House of Representatives (1789–1791) and of the United States Senate (1791–1793). In Congress, as in the Convention, Sherman opposed as unnecessary and unwise the enactment of a federal BILL OF RIGHTS.

DENNIS J. MAHONEY
(1986)

BOARDMAN, ROGER SHERMAN 1938 (1971) *Roger Sherman: Signer and Statesman.* Philadelphia: University of Pennsylvania Press. (Reprint, New York: Da Capo).

SHERMAN ANTITRUST ACT
26 Stat. 209 (1890)

This concisely worded law represented the first congressional attempt at ANTITRUST legislation. Neither the reasons for its approval nor its framers' intent are clear, but several circumstances ordained its passage. Individual state attempts to regulate monopoly were often unsuccessful; a federal statute would satisfy the need for uniform national policy as well as consistent practice. In addition, a heritage of antimonopoly sentiment and an economic depression combined to inflame public opinion against the industrial giants. Consequently, the platforms of both major parties contained antimonopoly planks in 1888, and, following his election, President BENJAMIN HARRISON asked Congress to redeem this pledge. Of sixteen bills introduced into the next Congress, one, sponsored by Senator John Sherman (Republican, Ohio), was briefly debated and then referred to the Judiciary Committee. Six days later the committee reported out a completely rewritten bill which received only cursory debate and passed 52–1 in the SENATE and 242–0 in the HOUSE. The lack of debate, particularly over such a potentially controversial bill, has never been satisfactorily explained. Often-cited possibilities include fierce interparty competition for support from the vigorously antimonopoly West and an underestimation of the act's importance. Contemporaries paid it little attention—the trusts and their congressional allies did not even bother to oppose the bill. Its proponents conceded that the act was an experimental entry into a new field of ECONOMIC REGULATION. In fact, it contained nothing new.

Although Senator Sherman was the moving force behind the bill, Senator George Edmunds (Republican, Vermont), chairman of the Senate Judiciary Committee, wrote most of it. Despite Edmunds's claim that it was "clear in its terms . . . [and] definite in its definitions," the act failed to define the two most important concepts in it: monopoly and restraint of trade. Although there is a debate over the (Anglo-American) COMMON LAW underpinnings of the act, most scholars agree that the common law forbade agreements in restraint of trade and CRIMINAL CONSPIRACY to monopolize. The controversy arises over these doctrines' application in America and the extent of their incorporation into the Sherman Act. The final bill also omitted any specific exemption for labor or farm organizations. Congress either meant to leave the issue to the courts (see LOEWE V. LAWLOR) or, more likely, believed an exemption was self-evident from the text.

The first section of the act outlawed "every contract, combination . . . or conspiracy, in restraint of trade" or INTERSTATE COMMERCE and was directed against joint action. Section 2—equally applicable to individuals—outlawed any means of achieving monopoly. Broader than section 1, this clause declared void any attempt, combination, or conspiracy to monopolize. It did not outlaw monopoly per se. Among the remaining provisions were those granting JURISDICTION to the CIRCUIT COURTS, providing for EQUITY proceedings, and authorizing treble damage suits.

Even with public support, the Sherman Act proved ineffective initially. The economic depression of the 1890s adversely affected business, and the general terms of the act required interpretation which could only come with time. The Court hamstrung the act in UNITED STATES V. E. C. KNIGHT (1895), holding that it did not apply to manufacturing. Even though a bare majority of the Court resuscitated the act against pooling arrangements in UNITED STATES V. TRANS-MISSOURI FREIGHT ASSOCIATION (1897), the government would not achieve any notable success until PHILANDER C. KNOX became ATTORNEY GENERAL under THEODORE ROOSEVELT. Then, in quick succession, the government won major victories in NORTHERN SECURITIES CO. V. UNITED STATES (1904) and SWIFT & CO. V. UNITED STATES

(1905). The next decade saw a limitation on antitrust policy as the Court formulated the RULE OF REASON and additional implementation by Congress which passed the CLAYTON and FEDERAL TRADE COMMISSION ACTS.

DAVID GORDON
(1986)

Bibliography

NEALE, A. D. and GOYDER, D. G. 1980 *The Antitrust Laws of the United States of America,* 3rd ed. Cambridge: At the University Press.

THORELLI, HANS B. 1955 *The Federal Antitrust Policy.* Baltimore: Johns Hopkins University Press.

SHIELD LAWS

In BRANZBURG V. HAYES (1972) and later decisions relating to an asserted REPORTER'S PRIVILEGE, the Supreme Court rejected the claim that the FIRST AMENDMENT should privilege reporters from having to respond to proper inquiries incident to legal proceedings. However, before and after *Branzburg,* more than half the states have passed legislation, called shield laws, that give reporters such a privilege. These laws vary considerably, as has their reception in the state courts. Some laws privilege reporters as to all information gathered in the course of their journalistic activities. Others privilege reporters only as to information gathered from confidential informants. Some laws make an exception to the privilege if a reporter has witnessed the commission of a crime.

A number of state courts have found state constitutional grounds for cutting back on shield laws. Thus one California decision held that a shield law could not immunize a reporter from having to answer a judge's questions about who had violated a judicial GAG ORDER against informing the press about evidence in a notorious criminal trial. And New Jersey's supreme court held that the state's law could not shield a reporter from inquiries by a defendant in a criminal case concerning information relevant to his defense.

BENNO C. SCHMIDT, JR.
(1986)

SHIRAS, GEORGE, JR.
(1832–1924)

George Shiras, Jr., was appointed to the Supreme Court by BENJAMIN HARRISON in 1892 and served for slightly more than a decade. A native of Pittsburgh and a Yale graduate, Shiras had maintained an independent, yet prosperous and varied law practice for nearly forty years before his appointment. He came to the Court without previous experience in public life and charted an independent course. His voting record suggests that he remained aloof from the era's policy debates yet maintained a fundamental distrust of institutional change. His unadorned and cool style and his emphasis on precedent and conventional rules of interpretation reflected his personality as well as his conception of the judicial function.

The 1890s were a transitional period in American public life, and the questions that crowded the Court's docket indicated the increasing scope and intensity of governmental interventions in economy and society. Three major classes of constitutional issues came up during Shiras's tenure. The first involved petitioners who sought enlarged judicial protection under the FOURTEENTH AMENDMENT for FREEDOM OF CONTRACT in the face of state laws regulating labor relations and the price of essential services. They got no encouragement from Shiras. In *Brass v. North Dakota* (1894), a grain elevator case, he refused to restrict the range of "businesses AFFECTED WITH A PUBLIC INTEREST" to those with a "virtual monopoly" at a particular location; he also spoke for the Court in *Knoxville v. Harbison* (1901), sustaining a Tennessee statute that required employers to pay their workers in cash or company-store scrip redeemable in cash. Justices DAVID J. BREWER and RUFUS PECKHAM, the FULLER COURT's leading apostles of laissez-faire, dissented in each instance. Yet Shiras was consistently aligned with Brewer and Peckham in the second class of cases, including UNITED STATES V. E. C. KNIGHT CO. (1895) and CHAMPION V. AMES (1903), involving federal authority under the COMMERCE CLAUSE in policy domains traditionally reserved to the states. Congressional regulation of manufacturing CORPORATIONS and public morals, like federal JUDICIAL REVIEW of STATE POLICE POWER regulations under the Fourteenth Amendment, necessitated new and, in Shiras's view, illegitimate departures in the organization of constitutional power.

Shiras wrote his most powerful opinions in the third class of cases, involving petitioners whose liberty or property was jeopardized by intensified federal activity in areas of acknowledged federal competence. He complained repeatedly about the majority's penchant for narrow construction of the Fifth Amendment's JUST COMPENSATION clause when riparian land was damaged by federal construction of dams and other river improvements. He also dissented sharply in BROWN V. WALKER (1896), contending that a federal immunity statute for persons required to testify before the Interstate Commerce Commission was an inadequate substitute for the Fifth Amendment RIGHT AGAINST SELF-INCRIMINATION. And in *Wong Wing v. United States* (1896) Shiras spoke for a unanimous Court that finally curbed Congress's draconian anti-Chinese program at the point where immigration officials were authorized to sentence illegal aliens to as much as one year of hard labor prior to deportation. The sentence of hard labor was an "infamous" one, Shiras explained. Consequently it could be invoked only after the Fifth and Sixth Amendment requirements of due process and TRIAL BY JURY had been met.

Shiras had determined at the time of his appointment to retire at seventy to avoid burdening his brethren because of age. He underscored his habitual divergence from conventional norms by carrying through his resolve. His retirement in 1903 attracted little notice, and his death more than twenty years later even less. Shiras's constitutional jurisprudence was simply too idiosyncratic to generate a significant following at the bar, in the law schools, or among the general public.

CHARLES W. McCURDY
(1986)

Bibliography

PAUL, ARNOLD 1969 George Shiras, Jr. Pages 1577–1591 in Leon Friedman and Fred L. Israel, eds., *The Justices of the United States Supreme Court, 1789–1969: Their Lives and Major Opinions.* New York: Chelsea House.

SHIRAS, WINFIELD 1953 *Justice George Shiras, Jr. of Pittsburgh.* Pittsburgh: University of Pittsburgh Press.

SHOPPING CENTERS

By the 1960s, shopping centers accounted for more than one-third of the nation's retail sales. Crowds of shoppers made the centers attractive places for the exercise of FIRST AMENDMENT rights such as PICKETING, leafleting, and the circulation of petitions. Two decades earlier, in MARSH V. ALABAMA (1946), the Supreme Court had assimilated the "company town" to the First Amendment DOCTRINE governing the use of an ordinary city street as a PUBLIC FORUM. When shopping center owners sought to prevent the use of their property for communications they had not approved, the question arose whether the centers, too, would be assimilated to the public forum doctrine.

The problem first came to the Supreme Court near the zenith of WARREN COURT activism in the defense of CIVIL LIBERTIES. In *Amalgamated Food Employees Union v. Logan Valley Plaza, Inc.* (1968), a bare majority held that union picketing of a store in a shopping center was protected by the First Amendment. Justice THURGOOD MARSHALL, for the Court, described the shopping center as the functional equivalent of the business district of the company town in *Marsh*. The author of the *Marsh* opinion, Justice HUGO L. BLACK, led the four dissenters.

When the issue returned to the Court, President

RICHARD M. NIXON's four appointees were sitting. A new 5–4 majority now held, in *Lloyd Corp v. Tanner* (1972), that the distribution of leaflets opposing the VIETNAM WAR could be forbidden by a shopping center's private owner. Justice LEWIS F. POWELL, for the majority, distinguished *Logan Valley:* the leafleting here had no relation to the center's activities, and here alternative means of communication were reasonably available on nearby streets. Justice Marshall led the dissenters.

The circle closed four years later, when a 7–2 majority, speaking through Justice POTTER STEWART (a *Lloyd Corp.* dissenter), said that *Lloyd Corp.* really had overruled *Logan Valley.* HUDGENS V. NLRB (1976), like *Logan Valley,* was a union picketing case. Justice Stewart pointed out that *Lloyd Corp.* had drawn an untenable distinction based on the content of messages being conveyed; because that distinction failed, it was necessary to make a yes-or-no decision on the assimilation of shopping centers to the doctrine governing company towns—and the majority's answer was "no."

Some passages in the *Lloyd Corp.* opinion had suggested that a shopping center owner had a constitutionally protected property right to exclude leafleters. That argument was flatly rejected by the Court in PRUNEYARD SHOPPING CENTER V. ROBBINS (1980). California's supreme court had ruled that the state constitution protected the right to collect signatures for a petition in a shopping center. The U.S. Supreme Court unanimously held that this principle of state constitutional law did not violate any federal constitutional rights.

KENNETH L. KARST
(1986)

Bibliography

TRIBE, LAURENCE H. 1978 *American Constitutional Law.* Pages 693–696, 1163–1167. Mineola, N.Y.: Foundation Press.

SHREVEPORT DOCTRINE

In the early twentieth century, the Supreme Court employed several DOCTRINES to sustain federal regulation of INTRASTATE COMMERCE. Among these, the Shreveport doctrine enjoyed a long tenure in the service of the COMMERCE CLAUSE. Since its elaboration, the Court has approved its use as a means of reaching a variety of activities, including professional football, minimum wages, crop control, and RACIAL DISCRIMINATION.

First announced in HOUSTON, EAST WEST TEXAS RAILWAY V. UNITED STATES—the Shreveport Rate Case—(1914), the doctrine permitted congressional regulation of purely local freight rates when, unmodified, they would have im-

peded INTERSTATE COMMERCE. The doctrine drew sustenance from the Court's distinction between direct and indirect EFFECTS ON COMMERCE in UNITED STATES V. E. C. KNIGHT COMPANY (1895) but reflected a new economic pragmatism. The Court recognized the integrated nature of the railroad system before it in the Shreveport Rate Case. It asserted that the commerce power "necessarily embraces the right to control . . . [intrastate] operations in all matters having such a close and substantial relation to interstate traffic that the control is essential or appropriate" to maintain a free flow of interstate commerce. The Court applied the doctrine throughout the 1920s in railroad cases such as DAYTON-GOOSE CREEK RAILWAY V. UNITED STATES (1924).

The judicial "revolution" of 1937 enhanced the use of the Shreveport doctrine. Earlier, the Court had struck down federal regulation in CARTER V. CARTER COAL COMPANY (1936) as an attempt to control activities only indirectly affecting interstate commerce, but it soon held that the WAGNER (NATIONAL LABOR RELATIONS) ACT legitimately regulated PRODUCTION (heretofore considered local), reiterating the "close and substantial relation" test of the Shreveport doctrine. (See NLRB V. JONES & LAUGHLIN STEEL CORP., 1937.)

The doctrine continued to grow in the 1940s. After several predictable decisions allowing federal regulation of intrastate milk prices (UNITED STATES V. WRIGHTWOOD DAIRY, 1942) by subjecting to federal control a local wheat crop "where no part of the product is intended for interstate commerce or intermingled with the subjects thereof." The Court declared that even local activity that "may not be regarded as commerce . . . may still . . . be reached by Congress if it exerts a substantial economic effect on interstate commerce . . . irrespective of whether such effect is what might at some earlier time have been defined as 'direct' or 'indirect'." This interpretation invited increasing use of the doctrine in antitrust cases, particularly under the SHERMAN ANTITRUST ACT, where, along with the STREAM OF COMMERCE DOCTRINE, it became a test of the law's applicability.

Congress and the Supreme Court continued this expansion in the 1960s. The CIVIL RIGHTS ACT OF 1964, based on the commerce clause, prohibits racial discrimination in PUBLIC ACCOMMODATIONS. The Court sustained application of the act to a local restaurant because "the absence of direct evidence connecting discriminatory restaurant service with the flow of interstate food . . . is not . . . a crucial matter." (See KATZENBACH V. MCCLUNG, 1964; *Daniel v. Paul,* 1969.) Criminal activity, too, fell within the doctrine's scope when the Court found ties between local loan-sharking and interstate commerce in PEREZ V. UNITED STATES (1971). The Court also included firearms in the doctrine's reach, sustaining a conviction under the OMNI-BUS CRIME CONTROL AND SAFE STREETS ACT for illegal possession, despite a minimal demonstration of the requisite connection with commerce (*Scarborough v. United States*, 1977).

The Shreveport doctrine helped bring about the demise of DUAL FEDERALISM. Because of the Justices' willingness to accede to congressional determinations, the Court's application of the doctrine has consistently followed its statement in *Board of Trade v. Olsen* (1923) that "this court will certainly not substitute its judgment for that of Congress in such a matter unless the relation of the subject to interstate commerce, and its effect upon it, are clearly nonexistent."

DAVID GORDON
(1986)

SIBRON v. NEW YORK

See: *Terry v. Ohio*

SIERRA CLUB v. MORTON
405 U.S. 727 (1972)

Acting as a public defender of the environment, the Sierra Club sued the secretary of the interior to enjoin approval of a ski resort development at Mineral King Valley in Sequoia National Forest. The Supreme Court, 4–3, denied the Club's right to JUDICIAL REVIEW of claimed statutory violations, for failure to allege harm to its members in their personal use of Mineral King. Significantly, however, the Court declared aesthetic and environmental interests, though widely shared, to be as deserving of judicial protection as economic interests. Thus, persons whose individual enjoyment of the environment is impaired by government action have STANDING to contest the action's legality.

JOHNATHON D. VARAT
(1986)

SILVERMAN v. UNITED STATES
365 U.S. 505 (1961)

To investigate gambling, DISTRICT OF COLUMBIA police officers inserted a microphone into a wall. The device touched a heating duct, enabling the police to overhear conversations throughout the house.

In *Goldman v. United States* (1942) the Court had afforded no constitutional protection against a microphone placed *against* a wall. By 1961 the Court, concerned about new methods of electronic surveillance, ruled that be-cause there was a physical penetration, albeit only a few inches, the overhearing was subject to the FOURTH AMENDMENT with no need to reconsider *Goldman* or earlier cases; that reconsideration occurred in KATZ V. UNITED STATES (1967).

HERMAN SCHWARTZ
(1986)

(SEE ALSO: *Electronic Eavesdropping.*)

SILVER PLATTER DOCTRINE

WEEKS V. UNITED STATES (1914), which formulated the EXCLUSIONARY RULE for federal prosecutions, made an exception for EVIDENCE seized by state officers in searches that did not meet FOURTH AMENDMENT standards. The evidence was usable in a federal trial when it was handed by the state to federal officers on "a silver platter" (Justice FELIX FRANKFURTER's phrase in *Lustig v. United States*, 1949). Participation by federal officers in the state search, no matter how minor, rendered the evidence inadmissible in federal cases under *Byars v. United States* (1927), as did even a search conducted by state officers alone if its purpose was the gathering of evidence for the federal government under *Gambino v. United States* (1927).

A combination of several factors led to the overruling of the silver platter doctrine in ELKINS V. UNITED STATES (1960). First, in WOLF V. COLORADO (1949), the Supreme Court had applied "the core" of the Fourth Amendment's standard (which did not, however, include the exclusionary rule) to the states. It therefore became incongruous to admit in federal court evidence which state officials had seized in violation of the Constitution. In addition, about half the states had adopted an exclusionary rule for unlawfully seized evidence; to allow federal authorities to use evidence which would have been excluded in the state courts served to frustrate the exclusionary policies of those states and to undermine the principle of FEDERALISM on which the silver platter doctrine was itself premised. The expansion of federal criminal law also undermined the vitality of the doctrine: a growing catalogue of crimes punishable by both federal and state governments evidently alerted the Court to the attendant possibilities of abuse by cooperative law enforcement.

Thus far the *Elkins* principle applies only to evidence in criminal cases. In *Janis v. United States* (1976), the Court held that evidence unlawfully seized by state officers can be used by the federal government (and vice versa) in civil proceedings (for instance, in a tax assessment case). The Court reasoned that the main purpose of the exclusionary rule is to deter unlawful searches, and that application of the rule should be tailored to this end.

When the officer is prevented from using the seized evidence to further a criminal prosecution, the principle of deterrence is amply served; exclusion of the evidence in a civil case would provide no significant reinforcement for Fourth Amendment values.

JACOB W. LANDYNSKI
(1986)

(SEE ALSO: *Two Sovereignties Rule.*)

Bibliography

LANDYNSKI, JACOB W. 1966 *Search and Seizure and the Supreme Court.* Pages 70–73, 149–158. Baltimore: Johns Hopkins University Press.

SILVERTHORNE LUMBER CO. v. UNITED STATES
251 U.S. 385 (1920)

Silverthorne was the first case to test the scope of the EXCLUSIONARY RULE, formulated in WEEKS V. UNITED STATES (1914), requiring exclusion from a federal trial of EVIDENCE obtained in an unconstitutional search.

Federal officers searched the Silverthorne Company's office; "without a shadow of authority," in Justice OLIVER WENDELL HOLMES's words, they "made a clean sweep of all the books, papers, and documents found there." Compounding the "outrage," the records were copied and photographed, and an INDICTMENT was framed on the basis of the information uncovered. The district court ordered the return of the originals but allowed the copies to be retained by the government, which then subpoenaed the originals. The Supreme Court reversed.

Holmes asserted that to allow the government to use the derivatively acquired evidence would mean that "only two steps are required [to render the evidence admissible] instead of one. In our opinion such is not the law. It reduces the 4th Amendment to form of words." Holmes added: "The essence of a provision forbidding the acquisition of evidence in a certain way is that not merely evidence so acquired shall not be used, but that it shall not be used at all." On this principle, an admission made by a suspect while he is under illegal arrest, as in WONG SUN V. UNITED STATES (1963), like a lead furnished by an illegally placed wiretap, as in NARDONE V. UNITED STATES (1939), may not be introduced into evidence because it is directly derived from an unlawful act. In *Nardone,* Justice FELIX FRANKFURTER dubbed the doctrine of the *Silverthorne* case as the FRUIT OF THE POISONOUS TREE.

JACOB W. LANDYNSKI
(1986)

SIMON v. EASTERN KENTUCKY WELFARE RIGHTS ORGANIZATION
426 U.S. 26 (1976)

In 1969 the Internal Revenue Service (IRS) amended its regulations governing nonprofit hospitals' obligations to provide care for INDIGENTS. A number of individuals and service organizations sued to set aside the modifications, claiming they would cause the denial of services to indigents. Following WARTH V. SELDIN (1975), the Supreme Court held that the plaintiffs lacked standing. Justice LEWIS F. POWELL, for the Court, declared that it was "purely speculative" whether any denials of hospital service to the plaintiffs could be traced to the IRS changes, or whether judicial relief against the IRS would increase the availability of such services to them. The plaintiffs thus could not meet Article III's requirement of CASES OR CONTROVERSIES. Justice WILLIAM J. BRENNAN, joined by Justice THURGOOD MARSHALL, argued that the plaintiffs had alleged a cognizable injury, but concurred in the result on grounds of RIPENESS.

DAVID GORDON
(1986)

SIMOPOULOS v. VIRGINIA

See: Reproductive Autonomy

SIMS' CASE
7 Cushing (Mass.) 285 (1851)

Chief Justice LEMUEL SHAW of Massachusetts, denying a writ of HABEAS CORPUS for a fugitive slave, delivered the first and most influential opinion sustaining the constitutionality of the Fugitive Slave Act of 1850. The case, which riveted national attention, had political and moral as well as constitutional significance; it reproduced hateful scenes of slavery in the North. The capture and rendition of a black man provoked denunciations of the COMPROMISE OF 1850. Without military force to execute the rendition, Shaw's decision would have been a dead letter in Massachusetts.

LEONARD W. LEVY
(1986)

(SEE ALSO: *Fugitive Slavery.*)

SINGLE-SEX EDUCATION

How does law construct distinctions based on gender? How does gender construct legal categories? The question of whether state-funded (or subsidized) schools may constitutionally have single-sex admissions policies provides one template for considering the role of law in making gender and the role of gender in making law.

Historically, law has barred women from an array of educational, legal, and professional opportunities. Until well into the second half of the twentieth century, such barriers were justified as appropriate in light of women's distinctive nature, temperament, and role in society. Law thus ascribed certain traits to women and found, because of those ascriptions, women unsuitable for diverse roles in civil, economic, and political life.

But, in a series of opinions beginning in 1971, constitutional jurisprudence shifted from approval to skepticism of gender-based classifications. Through cases addressing gender-based rules about who can serve as an executor of an estate or as a juror and who can consume alcohol, claim dependents, or confer dependency benefits, the Supreme Court developed what it termed a "heightened scrutiny" test of gender-based classifications and invalidated many (but not all) as impermissible.

Some institutions have, however, been conceived to be specially situated vis-à-vis the EQUAL PROTECTION clause. The ARMED FORCES offer one such example; in ROSTKER V. GOLDBERG (1981), the Supreme Court upheld a male-only military draft because women and men were assumed not equal for combat and because of the special place of the military in United States legal life. Age-based rules of sexuality provide a second example. In MICHAEL M. V. SUPERIOR COURT (1981), the Court upheld the constitutionality of a California statutory rape statute that punished men engaging in sex with women under the age of eighteen but imposed no such penalty on women. Women's ability to become pregnant was used as a justification for special protections, while dissenters argued that such laws situated women as actors without agency, as victims beset upon by men.

Education is a third context sometimes conceived as requiring distinctive jurisprudential rules. During the 1970s, lower courts were faced with challenges to all-boy schools, and in 1982, Joe Hogan's objection to the women-only admissions policy of a state nursing school reached the Supreme Court. The state defended the policy as appropriate AFFIRMATIVE ACTION for women. The majority in MISSISSIPPI UNIVERSITY FOR WOMEN V. HOGAN (1982), disagreed; Justice SANDRA DAY O'CONNOR explained for the Court that nursing has not been a career closed to women and the options provided to Mr. Hogan were not equal to those available to women. Two Justices, WILLIAM H. REHNQUIST and LEWIS F. POWELL, JR., proposed in dissent that the diversity provided by colleges ranging from co-ed to single-sex provided distinctive benefits and served legitimate state policies. The Court expressly left open the question of whether "SEPARATE BUT EQUAL" undergraduate institutions could be single-sex institutions.

More than a decade later, the Court returned to the question. Women challenged the all-male admissions policy of the Virginia Military Institute (VMI), self-described as teaching its students to become "citizen-soldiers." VMI defended by arguing that, because women and men had different styles of learning, the "adversative" environment of VMI was not suitable for women, who were sent instead to a program in a neighboring all-women's school, Mary Baldwin College. In UNITED STATES V. VIRGINIA (1996), the Court (in an opinion written by the Court's second woman Justice, RUTH BADER GINSBURG) held that Virginia had failed to afford equal benefits to members of both genders; the Court thus required women's admission to VMI. That ruling also resulted in the admission of women to South Carolina's all-male military school, The Citadel, about which challenges were pending in the lower courts.

The words used and the meaning of the standard by which the Court has assessed gender-based classifications have varied over the decades. In the VMI case, the Court required defenders of "gender-based government action" to shoulder the complete burden of demonstrating that an "exceedingly persuasive justification" exists for that action. Judges receiving such justifications were instructed to adopt an attitude of skepticism, founded in decades of state-sanctioned discrimination against women, and to insist upon a substantial link between the government's objectives and the classification adopted.

Such heightened scrutiny does not, however, render all gender classifications "impermissible." Rather, "[p]hysical differences between men and women" permit some classifications, but those classifications cannot be used "to create or perpetuate the legal, social, and economic inferiority of women."

Again, questions remain. What if VMI had created a separate set of facilities within its own boundaries, called it "VMI" and yet segregated women from men? What about all-women's colleges, created during the decades when women were barred from men's institutions and dedicated to enabling women full participatory rights? What about lower schools for adolescents, who are described by some researchers as specially susceptible to conforming to social expectations of stereotypically gendered behavior? What about all-girl classes in mathematics or science, fields particularly identified as inhospitable to women as students and professionals? What about the intersections of gender, race, and class? In New York City in the 1990s, special funding enabled the creation of an "all girls" junior high school to which public school students had access; in Detroit, Michigan, in the 1980s, a school created an all-male African American academy described as attentive to the distinct issues facing that set of children. And what about state subsidies, federal funds, and tax exemptions to private institutions? Should federal and state statutes maintain exceptions for single-sex organizations (like scouts), athletic programs, schools, any military programs, and prisons?

For some, the answer is that law should not sanction any gender distinctions unless absolutely necessary (and for some, virtually no distinctions are sustainable) and that to sanction such distinctions is to maintain and perpetuate them. For others, law must respond to the historically engendered understandings of the meaning of gender, race, SEXUAL ORIENTATION, and class and therefore can—selectively and self-consciously—provide remedial responses to those who are members of historically disfavored groups. For example, girls and women may be able to have all-female institutions not because they learn differently than do boys and men but because boys and men create hostile environments for females or because teachers may shift their attention away from females to males. For still others, law should not work to eradicate gender-based distinctions and, as long as diverse opportunities are provided, law should permit as much public and private choice as possible to let a variety of expressions of the meaning of gender co-exist.

While the VMI decision could be seen as ensconcing an exacting constitutional test for all gender-based classifications, a decision two years later in *Miller v. Albright* (1998) provides an apt reminder that many judges and commentators remain comfortable with gender-based distinctions, especially when traceable to either biological or parental roles. Federal law provided that CITIZENSHIP of children of citizen mothers was established at birth; confirmation of that citizenship, subject to proof of the mother's residence, was available at any time. A child of an alien mother and a citizen father, however, did not receive citizenship absent affirmative actions, within eighteen years of the birth, by the father or child to confirm their relationship. Justice JOHN PAUL STEVENS, announcing the Court's judgment and joined by Chief Justice Rehnquist, found that the classification was "supported by valid government interests" in fostering ties between the foreign-born child and the United States and that "biological differences between single men and single women provide a relevant basis for differing rules governing their ability to confer citizenship on children born in foreign lands." Justices O'Connor and ANTHONY M. KENNEDY recorded their concern about the gendered distinction but found the petitioner lacked STANDING to press a claim for her father, the citizen, and therefore upheld the statute. Justice ANTONIN SCALIA (who had dissented in the VMI case) and Justice CLARENCE THOMAS (who had not participated in the VMI case) joined the judgment on the ground that only Congress has the power to decide citizenship rules.

Justices Ginsburg, DAVID H. SOUTER, and STEPHEN G. BREYER objected on the merits to the classification and returned to the language of heightened scrutiny for gender-based classifications, the requirement of exceedingly persuasive justifications, and the insistence on a substantial relationship between the classification and the objectives stated.

In sum, biology remains—for Justices, judges, and commentators—a basis for line-drawing. Yet disagreements abound about when biology is relevant, when classifications create or perpetuate the legal, social, and economic inferiority of women, and when such categories are either appropriately compensatory, founded in "real differences," or creatively expressive of the richness of human life.

JUDITH RESNIK
(2000)

Bibliography

ALLEN BABCOCK, BARBARA; FREEDMAN, ANN E.; DELLER ROSS, SUSAN; WEBSTER WILLIAMS, WENDY; COPELON, RHONDA; RHODE, DEBORAH L.; and TAUB, NADINE 1996 *Sex Discrimination and the Law.* Boston: Little Brown.

BARTLETT, KATHARINE T. 1993 *Gender and Law: Theory, Doctrine, and Commentary.* Boston: Little Brown.

BECKER, MARY; GRANT BOWMAN, CYNTHIA; and TORREY, MORRISON 1994 *Cases and Materials on Feminist Jurisprudence: Taking Women Seriously.* St. Paul, Minn.: West Publishing Co.

ESKRIDGE, WILLIAM H., JR. and HUNTER, NAN D. 1997 *Sexuality, Gender and the Law.* Westbury, N.Y.: Foundation Press.

FRUG, MARY JOE 1992 *Women and the Law.* Westbury, N.Y.: Foundation Press.

HILL KAY, HERMA and WEST, MARTHA S. 1996 *Text, Cases, and Materials on Sex-Based Discrimination,* 4th ed. St. Paul, Minn.: West Publishing Co.

KARST, KENNETH L. 1991 The Pursuit of Manhood and the Desegregation of the Armed Forces. *UCLA Law Review* 38: 499–581.

THORNE, BARRIE 1993 *Gender Play: Girls and Boys in School.* New Brunswick, N.J.: Rutgers University Press.

SINKING FUND CASES
Union Pacific Railroad Co. v. United States
99 U.S. 700 (1879)
Central Pacific Railroad Co. v. Gallatin
99 U.S. 727 (1879)

Congress authorized the construction of transcontinental railroads and made massive grants and loans to them. Following the exposure of enormous corruption in the management of the roads, Congress enacted a statute requiring that twenty-five percent of the annual net earnings of the CORPORATIONS be paid into a sinking fund to guarantee payment of the debts owed to the federal treasury. The Supreme Court sustained the second statute on ground that Congress had reserved the power to alter or amend its original grant. However, Chief Justice MORRISON R. WAITE, for a 6–3 Court, said in an OBITER DICTUM that the United States binds itself by its contracts and that, although the CONTRACT CLAUSE applied only to the states, the Fifth Amendment's DUE PROCESS clause effectuated the binding by preventing the deprivation of property. Three Justices, WILLIAM STRONG, JOSEPH P. BRADLEY, and STEPHEN J. FIELD, wrote dissenting opinions based on Waite's dictum; they believed that the sinking-fund statute violated the Fifth Amendment. The decision is significant, therefore, because of the strong boost it gave to the emerging concept of SUBSTANTIVE DUE PROCESS. In effect, too, the Court incorporated contract clause reasoning into the due process clause as a means of protecting property when Congress "improperly interferes with VESTED RIGHTS." This strange doctrine operated, though infrequently, as late as 1936. (See LOUISVILLE JOINT STOCK LAND BANK V. RADFORD.)

LEONARD W. LEVY
(1986)

SIPUEL v. OKLAHOMA STATE BOARD OF REGENTS
332 U.S. 631 (1948)

PER CURIAM, reaffirming MISSOURI EX REL. GAINES V. CANADA (1938), the Supreme Court ordered Oklahoma to provide a black applicant with legal education in a state law school. Rather than admit her to the state university, the state roped off part of the state capitol, called it a law school for blacks, and provided three instructors. The Supreme Court avoided ruling on this mockery, saying the case had not presented the issue whether separate law schools satisfied the Constitution.

KENNETH L. KARST
(1986)

(SEE ALSO: *Sweatt v. Painter.*)

SIT-IN

The CIVIL RIGHTS MOVEMENT of the 1960s embraced more than lawsuits aimed at ending racial SEGREGATION in southern public institutions. It also included several forms of direct action, such as "freedom rides," in which blacks would ride on buses and trains, refusing to confine themselves to places set aside for black passengers. The quintessential form of direct action was the sit-in demonstration. The practice began in Greensboro, North Carolina, in 1960. Four black college freshmen went to a dime store lunch counter and ordered coffee. When they were told they would not be served, they sat at the counter, waiting, in silent protest against the indignity of RACIAL DISCRIMINATION. The next week they returned, joined by increasing numbers of students, white and black. Soon the sit-in technique spread to lunch counters throughout the South.

The impact of the sit-ins was enormous. Many stores and restaurants abandoned their discriminatory policies within a matter of weeks. Most, however, held out, and called the police. Sit-in demonstrators by the hundreds were arrested and charged with criminal TRESPASS. From 1960 to 1964, the problem of the sit-ins came to the Supreme Court over and over again.

When the segregating restaurant was a state operation (for example, a lunch counter in a courthouse), the Court could reverse the conviction by analogy to BROWN V. BOARD OF EDUCATION (1954). Even when the lunch counter was privately owned, the Court would reverse the conviction if it could find some public policy in the background, requiring or encouraging segregation. During the early 1960s the Court was pressed to abandon, or drastically alter, the STATE ACTION limitation, so as to create an equivalent FOURTEENTH AMENDMENT right to be free from racial discrimination in all privately owned PUBLIC ACCOMMODATIONS, irrespective of any state participation. The issue reached a climax—but not a resolution—in BELL V. MARYLAND (1964), when the Court again struck down a conviction on a narrow ground, without deciding the larger constitutional issue.

The Court was relieved of the need to face that issue when Congress adopted the CIVIL RIGHTS ACT OF 1964, which included a broad prohibition against racial discrimination in public accommodations. The Supreme Court quickly upheld the law's constitutionality in HEART OF ATLANTA MOTEL V. UNITED STATES (1964). Further, the Court held that the 1964 act applied with retroactive force, invalidating trespass convictions for sit-ins at public accommodations before the law's effective date (*Hamm v. City of Rock Hill*, 1964).

KENNETH L. KARST
(1986)

Bibliography

LEWIS, THOMAS P. 1963 The Sit-In Cases: Great Expectations. *Supreme Court Review* 1963:101–151.
PAULSEN, MONRAD G. 1964 The Sit-In Cases of 1964: But Answer Came There None. *Supreme Court Review* 1964:137–170.

SIXTEENTH AMENDMENT

The Sixteenth Amendment was designed to circumvent POLLOCK V. FARMERS' LOAN AND TRUST CO. (1895), in which the Supreme Court had held that a federal tax on income from property was a DIRECT TAX on that property and therefore invalid for want of apportionment among the states on the basis of population (Article I, sections 2 and 9). Following *Pollock*, powerful political forces continued to press for an income tax to replace the regressive consumption taxes then employed to finance the federal government. Indeed, an amendment might have been unnecessary, given the Supreme Court's philosophical shift in *Flint v. Stone Tracy Co.* (1911), upholding a corporate income tax as an excise on doing business in corporate form, not a tax on property.

Although there was sentiment for challenging *Pollock* by reenacting a personal income tax, President WILLIAM HOWARD TAFT urged a constitutional amendment. The Sixteenth Amendment was speedily passed and ratified in 1913. It provides: "The Congress shall have power to lay and collect taxes on incomes, from whatever source derived, without apportionment among the several States, and without regard to any census or enumeration."

Since the enactment of a new income tax statute in 1913, only a single Supreme Court decision has held an income tax provision unconstitutional. EISNER V. MACOMBER (1920) ruled that a stock dividend of common stock on common stock was not "income" because the element of "realization" was lacking. *Macomber* has been greatly undermined by subsequent cases, such as *Helvering v. Bruun* (1940) which treated the return of a lessor's property to him at the termination of a lease as a realization of income. Indeed, the current Court would probably dispense entirely with any constitutional requirement of a realization (or alternatively view a stock dividend as a realization). In *Helvering v. Griffiths* (1943) three dissenters would have overruled *Macomber* but the majority held that the constitutional issue had not been presented by the statute.

Eisner v. Macomber also purported to define "income" for constitutional purposes as "the gain derived from capital, from labor, or from both combined." This definition proved far too narrow; in *Commissioner v. Glenshaw Glass Co.* (1955), the Court rejected all considerations of source, holding a windfall constitutionally taxable as income.

Unlike *Macomber*, modern decisions go to considerable lengths to uphold the constitutionality of income tax provisions. For example, the lower courts upheld an income tax provision that taxed mutual insurance companies on their gross receipts in *Penn Mutual Indemnity Co. v. Commissioner* (1976). Because no deductions were allowed, the tax might have been levied even though the taxpayer had no gain. Similarly, lower courts have upheld a Code section that values property received for services by ignoring value-depressing restrictions on the property (*Sakol v. Commissioner*, 1978). Although the Supreme Court has not had occasion to confirm these broad holdings, the modern approach to claims of constitutional invalidity of tax statutes is to uphold them as indirect taxes or alternatively to define "income" with sufficient breadth to accommodate the provision in issue within the Sixteenth Amendment.

MICHAEL ASIMOW
(1986)

Bibliography

PAUL, RANDOLPH 1954 *Taxation in the United States.* Boston: Little, Brown.

SIXTH AMENDMENT

See: Compulsory Process, Right to;
Confrontation, Right of; Right to Counsel;
Speedy Trial; Trial by Jury

SKINNER v. OKLAHOMA
315 U.S. 535 (1942)

In *Skinner* the Supreme Court laid a doctrinal foundation for two of the most important constitutional developments of the twentieth century: the expansion of the reach of the EQUAL PROTECTION clause and the reemergence of SUBSTANTIVE DUE PROCESS as a guarantee of personal freedoms. The case arose out of an Oklahoma law authorizing STERILIZATION of a person convicted three times of "felonies involving moral turpitude." Skinner, convicted first of chicken stealing and then twice of armed robbery, was ordered sterilized by the state courts. The Supreme Court unanimously reversed, holding the sterilization law unconstitutional. Surely the decision seemed easy; no doubt the only serious question was the appropriate ground for decision.

The opinion of the Court, by Justice WILLIAM O. DOUGLAS, rested on equal protection grounds. The sterilization law contained an exception for violations of "prohibitory [liquor] laws, revenue acts, embezzlement, or political offenses." Although the state might constitutionally impose different penalties on embezzlement and other forms of stealing, it could not use so artificial a distinction as the basis for depriving someone of the right of procreation, "one of the basic civil rights of man." Because sterilization permanently deprived a person of a "basic liberty," said

Justice Douglas, the judiciary must subject it to "STRICT SCRUTINY." Here the state had offered no justification for the belief that inheritability of criminal traits followed the line between embezzlement and chicken stealing.

Surely the Court also recognized that the sterilization law's exceptions were white collar crimes. Justice Douglas said, "In evil or reckless hands" sterilization could "cause races or types which [were] inimical to the dominant group to wither and disappear." (The year was 1942; the Nazi theory of a "master race" was a major ideological target in WORLD WAR II.) Sterilization of some but not all who commit "intrinsically the same quality of offense" was "INVIDIOUS" DISCRIMINATION in the same way that RACIAL DISCRIMINATION was.

Chief Justice HARLAN FISKE STONE, concurring, found the Court's equal protection rationale unpersuasive, but found a denial of PROCEDURAL DUE PROCESS in the sterilization law's failure to give a three-time felon like Skinner an opportunity to show that his criminal tendencies were not inheritable. Given the prevailing scientific opinion that criminal traits were not generally inheritable, an individual should have a chance to contest the law's assumption. (This style of reasoning was in vogue briefly during the 1970s under the name of IRREBUTTABLE PRESUMPTIONS.) Justice ROBERT H. JACKSON agreed with both the Douglas and the Stone approaches.

Close to the surface of both the Douglas and the Stone opinions was a strong skepticism that any criminal traits were inheritable. Such an objection would seem fatal to Oklahoma's law on substantive due process grounds. But the Court had very recently abandoned substantive due process as a limit on ECONOMIC REGULATION, and in doing so had used language suggesting the complete demise of substantive due process. Both Douglas and Stone seemed to be avoiding the obvious ground that the law arbitrarily deprived Skinner of liberty. But *Skinner* can be seen today as not only a forerunner of a later Court's strict scrutiny analysis of equal protection cases involving FUNDAMENTAL INTERESTS and SUSPECT CLASSIFICATIONS but also a major early precedent for the development of a constitutional RIGHT OF PRIVACY as a branch of substantive due process.

KENNETH L. KARST
(1986)

(SEE ALSO: *Freedom of Intimate Association; Reproductive Autonomy.*)

Bibliography

KARST, KENNETH L.   1969 Invidious Discrimination: Justice Douglas and the Return of the "Natural-Law-Due-Process Formula." *UCLA Law Review* 16:716–750.

SKINNER v. RAILWAY LABOR EXECUTIVES ASSOCIATION
489 U.S. 602 (1989)

In this case, the Supreme Court significantly restricted the protections of the FOURTH AMENDMENT. The Court had never before sustained a BODY SEARCH apart from ARREST and without suspicion of individual wrongdoing, except with respect to prison inmates. In *Skinner* the Court sustained the constitutionality of government regulations requiring blood and urine tests by railroad employees involved in train accidents and by those who violated certain safety rules.

Employee abuse of alcohol and drugs resulting in jeopardy to the public explains the regulations and the decision. Drunken employees had caused accidents from the beginning of railroad history, and employees drugged by use of other substances were responsible for dozens of accidents killing and maiming passengers and inflicting damages amounting to millions of dollars.

A 7–2 Court, speaking through Justice ANTHONY M. KENNEDY, upheld both the compulsory and discretionary DRUG TESTING as well as the alcohol testing. Kennedy recognized that the urine and blood tests were searches within the meaning of the Fourth Amendment, but held that PROBABLE CAUSE was an irrelevant consideration. Searches had to be reasonable, but did not have to satisfy the SEARCH WARRANT requirement. Accordingly, the mandatory searches of employees involved in an accident did not violate the amendment because specificity individualized suspicion was not necessary. (Reasonable suspicion based on individual conduct was necessary, according to the federal regulations, when an employee had violated safety requirements but had not been involved in an accident.) Kennedy asserted, rather than explained, that the warrant requirement was irrelevant because it might stymie governmental objectives of promoting safety.

Similarly, he asserted that privacy interests implicated in the blood and urine testing were "minimal." Blood and breath tests were commonplace, safe, and painless. Urine testing, by contrast, was intrusive, but the expectations of privacy on the part of employees were diminished by their knowledge that their industry was severely regulated to promote safety and that their fitness was related to safety. The government interest in requiring the tests was simply compelling, overriding any privacy or Fourth Amendment rights that might prevail in a criminal case.

Justice THURGOOD MARSHALL, joined by Justice WILLIAM J. BRENNAN, shrilly dissented. The tests, which the majority thought to be minor invasions of privacy, were "draconian," exacted from employees who had personally given no basis for belief that they were guilty of working under the influence of drugs or alcohol. "The majority's acceptance of dragnet blood and urine testing ensures that the first, and worst, casualty of war on drugs will be the precious liberties of our citizens." All PRECEDENTS required individualized suspicion before warrantless blood testing could be sustained. Privacy interests offended by compulsory and supervised urine testing could not be dismissed as "minimal." The chemical analysis of blood and urine specimens also conflicted with privacy interests. Such analysis could reveal a variety of medical disorders that were none of the government's business. Marshall believed that railroad workers did not relinquish their constitutional rights by taking employment in a regulated industry; furthering the public safety had to be subordinated to constitutional rights.

If the entire public, not just airline employees, must submit to WARRANTLESS SEARCH without probable cause or individual suspicion to enter passenger areas in airports, promoting public safety in railroads seem an adequate reason for the testing of railroad employees who break safety rules or are involved in an accident. A consideration of that sort did not, however, obtain in the companion case of NATIONAL TREASURY EMPLOYEES UNION V. VON RAAB (1989).

LEONARD W. LEVY
(1992)

SLANDER

See: Libel and the First Amendment

SLAPPS

See: Strategic Lawsuits Against Public Participation in Government

SLAUGHTERHOUSE CASES
16 Wallace 36 (1873)

Most histories of the Constitution begin consideration of the judicial interpretation of the THIRTEENTH and FOURTEENTH AMENDMENTS with the *Slaughterhouse* decision of 1873. The decision is, to be sure, of vast significance. Justices JOSEPH P. BRADLEY and STEPHEN J. FIELD, dissenting, expressed embryonic DOCTRINES of FREEDOM OF CONTRACT and SUBSTANTIVE DUE PROCESS that were to dominate American jurisprudence for two generations.

In 1869, Louisiana, ostensibly as a public health measure, incorporated the Crescent City Stock Landing and Slaughterhouse Company and granted it a monopoly of licensed butchering in New Orleans. Butchers not parties

to the lucrative arrangement, after failing to crack the monopoly in the state courts, employed as counsel, in an appeal to the federal courts, former Supreme Court Justice JOHN A. CAMPBELL, who more recently had been a Confederate assistant secretary of war. Campbell argued before the Supreme Court that the excluded butchers had been deprived of their livelihoods by the state's deliberate discrimination, although Louisiana had disguised the corrupt monopoly as a health measure. Therefore the disputed statute violated the Thirteenth Amendment's ban on involuntary servitude, the 1866 CIVIL RIGHTS ACT's enforcements of that ban, and the Fourteenth Amendment's guarantees of EQUAL PROTECTION OF THE LAWS, and due process.

Among prominent counsel for the state, Senator MATTHEW HALE CARPENTER responded to Campbell's innovative brief. Carpenter easily assembled case law that sustained state restrictions on private economic relationships. He insisted that the STATE POLICE POWER amply undergirded the Louisiana statute. No federal constitutional question existed, Carpenter asserted. Both the Thirteenth and the Fourteenth Amendments were irrelevant to the litigants' rights and remedies. And, he prophesied, the federal system would be virtually revolutionized if the Court accepted Campbell's notions and legitimized a federal interest in individuals' claims to be exempt from state regulation.

Speaking through Justice SAMUEL F. MILLER, a majority of the Court was unready to accept Campbell's view that federal guarantees to individuals extended to trades (although, in the TEST OATH CASES, 1867, the Court had extended other federal guarantees to lawyers, ministers, and teachers). Instead, having accepted Carpenter's arguments, Miller reviewed the tradition of judicial support for state determination of ways to meet POLICE POWER responsibilities. Miller denied that exclusion from butchering deprived the appellants of federally protected rights to freedom, privileges and immunities, equal protection, or due process; the "one pervading purpose" of the postwar amendments, he said, was to liberate black slaves, not to enlarge whites' rights. The monopoly created by the state law could not be perceived as imposing servitude; the Thirteenth Amendment was irrelevant as a protection for livelihoods.

Turning to the Fourteenth Amendment, Miller separated federal from state privileges and immunities. He assigned to the states the definition of ordinary marketplace relationships essential to the vast majority of people. More important, he assigned to state privileges and immunities all basic CIVIL LIBERTIES and rights, excluding them from federal protection. Miller's sweeping interpretation relegated everyone, including Negroes, who had assumed that the Fourteenth Amendment had assigned the federal government the role of "guardian democracy" over state-defined CIVIL RIGHTS, to the state governments for effective protection. The national government could protect only the few privileges and immunities of national citizenship: the RIGHT TO TRAVEL, access to Washington, D.C., FREEDOM OF ASSEMBLY and PETITION, and HABEAS CORPUS. Miller and the majority ignored contemporary evidence that many of the framers of both amendments and of the 1866 Civil Rights Act did perceive federally protectable privileges and immunities in broad terms; did assign to federal courts the duty to protect those rights; did envision national civil rights as the essential bridge connecting individuals and states to the nation in a more perfect union. And the majority overlooked earlier contrary case law that spoke directly to the point of the amendments as requirements for federal protection against both state and private discriminations: *In re Turner* (1867) and BLYEW V. UNITED STATES (1872).

Ignoring also prewar uses of due process in DRED SCOTT V. SANDFORD (1857) and in LAW OF THE LAND clauses in state constitutions, and shrugging off the equal protection argument Campbell had advanced for the appellants, Miller reiterated his position that the postwar amendments protected only blacks against STATE ACTION. The federal protection the Court allowed was minimal and virtually irrelevant to the needs of freedmen, and, for all Americans, left the protection of rights fundamentally unchanged from the prewar condition.

Dissenting, Justices Joseph P. Bradley and Stephen J. Field dredged up Justice SAMUEL CHASE's 1798 opinion in CALDER V. BULL and that of Justice BUSHROD WASHINGTON in his much-quoted 1823 circuit opinion in CORFIELD V. CORYELL, plus the augmented emphases on judicial discretion in a long line of decisions. Bradley emphasized the Fourteenth Amendment's due process clause. Advancing beyond the views of Chief Justice ROGER B. TANEY in *Dred Scott*, he justified judicial intervention to defend substantive due process rights and insisted that a right to choose a calling is a property, a FUNDAMENTAL RIGHT that no state might demean casually. That right was the base for all liberty. The federal courts must repel any state attack on that right, even though the attack might be disguised as a health measure under police powers.

Field argued that the butchering monopoly created servitudes forbidden by the Thirteenth Amendment, but he concentrated on the Fourteenth's privileges and immunities clause. It embraced all the fundamental rights belonging to free men. The national Constitution and laws affirmed those rights. Arbitrary state inhibitions on access to a trade or professions demeaned national rights. Field conceded that states were free to exercise their police powers, even to regulate occupations. But state regulations must apply equally to all citizens who met the standards of the state regulations.

Later, jurists less respectful than Field of state-based FEDERALISM were to cut his *Slaughterhouse* dissent free of its privileges and immunities moorings. Combining his views with Bradley's emphases on the broad effect of the Fourteenth Amendment, later jurists and legal commentators were to transform them into doctrines of freedom of contract and substantive due process. Those doctrines, which were to reign until the twentieth century was well advanced, constrained needful state actions in numerous areas of life and labor.

HAROLD M. HYMAN
(1986)

Bibliography

BETH, LOREN P. 1963 The Slaughter-House Cases—Revisited, *Louisiana Law Review* 23:487–505.
FAIRMAN, CHARLES 1971 Reconstruction and Reunion, 1864–1868. Chap. 21 in Vol. VI, part 1, of the *Oliver Wendell Holmes Devise History of the Supreme Court of the United States.* New York: Macmillan.
HAMILTON, WALTON H. 1938 The Path of Due Process of Law. Pages 167–179 in Conyers Read, ed., *The Constitution Reconsidered.* New York: Columbia University Press.
HYMAN, HAROLD M. and WIECEK, WILLIAM M. 1982 *Equal Justice under Law: Constitutional Development 1835–1875.* Pages 472–483. New York: Harper & Row.

SLAVERY AND CIVIL LIBERTIES

In 1796 ST. GEORGE TUCKER, of Virginia, the law professor and judge, wrote *A Dissertation on Slavery.* Tucker noted that Americans had fought a revolution for liberty, swearing to "live free or die." At the same time, he said, "we were imposing upon our fellow men, who differ in complexion from us, a slavery, ten thousand times more cruel than the utmost extremity of those grievances and oppressions, of which we complained." Tucker lamented that a people who had declared "That *all men* are by nature *equally free* and *independent*" had "in defiance of so sacred a truth" tolerated SLAVERY. In the years that followed, it became clear that slavery would also threaten CIVIL LIBERTIES of white citizens, in the North as well as the South.

Slavery, Tucker said, totally abolished the slave's right to liberty and PROPERTY. After a "melancholy review" of brutal slave laws, Tucker concluded that the right to personal security had "at times been wholly annihilated or reduced to a shadow."

Slave codes typically denied slaves most basic rights: Slaves were required to obey their masters and to submit to whipping for actual or imagined infractions. They could not own property; travel without a pass; bear arms without special permission; assemble in groups of more than five; preach except under the supervision of their masters; or be taught to read. Husbands and wives and parents and children might be separated by sale. State laws often punished slaves much more harshly than whites for the same offense. Blacks, slave or free, were not permitted to testify in cases where whites were a party. Of course, some masters allowed slaves greater freedom than the letter of the law provided, including having limited property and even being taught to read.

Southern laws denied slaves all but the most basic protection of the law. Murder of a slave and (by the late antebellum period) torture were prohibited; but since slaves could not testify against whites, these protections were often unenforceable. In 1829 in *State v. Mann,* a woman held as a slave had committed "some small offense" for which the man who had rented her for a year "had attempted to chastise her." When the woman fled and refused to stop, he shot her. The North Carolina Supreme Court said that the renter enjoyed the rights of the master, and announced "we cannot allow the right of the master to be brought into discussion in the Courts of Justice. The slave, to remain a slave, must be made sensible, that there is no appeal from his master. . . ."

Basic constitutional protections of liberty and equality did not extend to slaves. For example, Virginia's highest court held that the guarantees of the state's Bill of Rights did not protect them.

The Fugitive Slave Act of 1850 denied blacks claimed as slaves a right to testify or to a TRIAL BY JURY before being delivered to a state where their color gave rise to a legal presumption that they were slaves. Opponents of slavery unsuccessfully invoked the right to a civil jury trial under the SEVENTH AMENDMENT and other rights of DUE PROCESS under the federal BILL OF RIGHTS.

Nor were denials of basic rights limited to slaves. In DRED SCOTT V. SANDFORD (1857), Chief Justice ROGER B. TANEY said that all blacks, free as well as slave, including those who were recognized as citizens by Northern states, were entitled to no rights or privileges under the federal Constitution. They had, as far as the Constitution was concerned, no rights a white man was bound to respect.

Many states and territories denied free blacks basic rights. For example, the Oregon territory denied them the right to testify in cases in which a white man was a party; to own property; or to enter the state. JOHN A. BINGHAM was an antislavery congressman from Ohio who later drafted the basic guarantees in section 1 of the FOURTEENTH AMENDMENT. Bingham insisted that free blacks were American citizens and that the ban on their testimony where whites were parties to the litigation denied these

citizens of the United States the national privilege not to be deprived of life, liberty, or property without due process of law.

Some abolitionists went further and insisted that the very institution of slavery, even in the states where it existed, violated the federal Bill of Rights—by denying people their liberty without due process of law. Since no legal process justified the denial of liberty to the slave and their descendants, slaves had, the argument insisted, been denied liberty without due process. While this view was not widely shared as to slaves in the Southern states, the REPUBLICAN PARTY platforms of 1856 and 1860 did announce that SLAVERY IN THE TERRITORIES violated the due process clause of the Fifth Amendment.

The denials of civil liberties discussed so far affected slaves and free blacks. But slavery had a more pervasive effect on liberty. In defense of slavery the South became a closed society in which discussion of one of the basic political and human rights issues of the day was forbidden.

With the rise of abolitionism in the 1830s, the Southern slave–owning elite began to demand that liberty in the North and South be restricted in order to protect the institution of slavery. Southern states demanded that abolition speech and press be silenced and abolition associations be prohibited.

The U.S. HOUSE OF REPRESENTATIVES passed a gag rule prohibiting reading or discussing antislavery petitions in Congress. Southern states passed laws making it criminal to publish items tending to cause slaves or free blacks to become discontent, a category that included most criticism of slavery. The Kansas Territory passed similar laws. What was not accomplished by law was enforced by mobs. As abolitionist evangelists attempted to convert Northern states to abolition in the mid-1830s, and after abolitionists sent their pamphlets to the Southern elite, Southerners exploded. A group of men seized sacks of mail from the Charleston post office and burned abolitionist publications. Southern slave holders and their allies demanded action against abolitionists, and many Northerners responded affirmatively.

Federal postmasters refused to mail abolitionist publications destined for the South. Northern mobs broke up abolition meetings and destroyed abolition presses. Elite Northerners, including prominent political leaders and "men of property and standing," cheered, justified, and often led the mobs. But these attacks on the FREEDOM OF SPEECH produced a backlash in the North.

By 1856 the newly formed Republican Party opposed expansion of slavery into new federal territories. Its slogan was "free speech, free soil, free territory, free men and Fremont." But the Southern quarantine against antislavery expression meant Republican candidates for President were unable to campaign in most of the South. The Constitution apparently provided no protection. In 1833, in BARRON V. CITY OF BALTIMORE, the Supreme Court had ruled that the guarantees of the federal Bill of Rights did not bind the states. In 1860 the North Carolina Supreme Court upheld the conviction of a minister for circulating an antislavery book used as a campaign document by Republicans in the North.

In response to suppression of antislavery speech in the South and attempts to suppress it in the North, many Americans including leading Republicans began to insist that FREEDOM OF THE PRESS, free speech, and RELIGIOUS LIBERTY were basic rights or privileges belonging to all individuals throughout the nation and which the states should obey.

This ideal contributed to the ratification of the Fourteenth Amendment in 1868. The amendment provided that all persons born in the nation and subject to its jurisdiction were citizens and that no state could abridge the PRIVILEGES OR IMMUNITIES of citizens of the United States or deny to any person EQUAL PROTECTION OF THE LAWS or due process. Many read it as guaranteeing basic national liberties to all Americans against state denial and as a direct response to the suppression of civil liberty in the interest of slavery in the thirty years before the CIVIL WAR. But in the 1873 SLAUGHTERHOUSE CASES the Supreme Court emptied the privileges or immunities clause of any significant meaning. And for many years the Court continued to hold guarantees of the federal Bill of Rights inapplicable to the states. Only in 1925 did the Court suggest that freedom of speech was protected against state denial by the INCORPORATION DOCTRINE.

The legacy of slavery lingered long after the passage of the RECONSTRUCTION amendments. Americans of African descent were segregated in their housing, educated in segregated schools starved of funds, and in much of the South denied the VOTING RIGHTS they had been guaranteed by the FIFTEENTH AMENDMENT. During the CIVIL RIGHTS revolution of the 1960s the nation began to protect Americans of African descent from SEGREGATION and from denial of their right to vote. The nation also protected them in their FIRST AMENDMENT and Fourteenth Amendment right to protest. By this time the Court had held most of the guarantees of the federal Bill of Rights applicable to the states.

The institution of slavery denied basic rights to slaves and to free American citizens. The struggle to abolish slavery produced constitutional guarantees of liberty that promised protection for basic liberties to all Americans.

MICHAEL KENT CURTIS
(2000)

(SEE ALSO: *Abolitionist Constitutional Theory; Constitutional History, 1829–1848; Constitutional History, 1848–1861; Constitutional History, 1861–1865; Constitutional History, 1865–1871; Fugitive Slavery; Right of Petition.*)

Bibliography

BARNES, GILBERT H.   1933   *The Antislavery Impulse, 1830–1844.* New York: D. Appleton-Century Co.

CURTIS, MICHAEL KENT   1993   The 1859 Crisis Over Hinton Helper's Book. The Impending Crisis: Free Speech, Slavery, and Some Light on the Meaning of the First Section of the Fourteenth Amendment. *Chicago-Kent Law Review* 68: 1113–1177.

———   1995   The Curious History of Attempts to Suppress Anti-Slavery Speech, Press, and Petition in 1835–37. *Northwestern University Law Review* 89:785–870.

———   1997   The 1835 Killing of Elijah Lovejoy by an Anti-Abolition Mob: Free Speech, Mobs, Republican Government, and the Privileges of American Citizens. *UCLA Law Review* 44:1109–1184.

DICKERSON, DONNA L.   1990   *The Course of Tolerance: Freedom of Press in Nineteenth-Century America.* New York: Greenwood Press.

EATON, CLEMENT   1964   *The Freedom-of-Thought Struggle in the Old South.* New York: Harper & Row.

MILLER, WILLIAM LEE   1996   *Arguing About Slavery: The Great Battle in the United States Congress.* New York: Knopf.

RICHARDS, LEONARD L.   1970   *Gentlemen of Property and Standing: Anti-Abolition Mobs in Jacksonian America.* New York: Oxford University Press.

SLAVERY AND PROPERTY

Slaves were people who were PROPERTY. In 1860, the aggregate value of the nearly four million slaves was more than $3 billion—the equivalent of roughly $58 billion in 1998. Slaves constituted 44 percent of all the South's wealth, with real estate—land and buildings—amounting to only 25 percent. A single slave represented a tremendous capital investment; during the 1850s, a young male slave in his late teens or early twenties might sell for well over $1,000.

As the antebellum Southern economy's most important assets, slaves were enmeshed in varying legal forms of credit and property relationships. The property interests in slaves could be divided in many ways. In his will, a husband might bequeath a slave to his widow for her use during the remainder of her lifetime; on her death, someone else—perhaps one of their children—might become the slave's owner. Likewise, unborn children could be the objects of property interests. A slave woman might be owned by one owner while her children, as they were born, could become the property of a different owner. As well, slaves were often leased, which gave the lessor and the lessee different interests regarding how well to treat the slave. A slave purchaser might also buy slaves on credit or might borrow using slaves as collateral. If the borrower failed to repay the debt, the sheriff might seize and sell the slaves on the courthouse steps. The creation and ownership of the different types of property interests spread quite widely Southerner's economic stake in SLAVERY as an institution.

When a slave succeeded in running away, whoever held a property interest in the escapee lost wealth. For anyone with even a fragment of a property interest in a runaway slave, the runaway's capture raised constitutional issues of financial importance. The original Constitution guaranteed the return of runaway slave property in Article IV, section 2, and Congress enacted a Fugitive Slave Law in 1793. With the passage of another law on FUGITIVE SLAVERY in 1850, Congress greatly strengthened the protection that Southerners enjoyed concerning the return of their runaway property. Among other things, the 1850 law obliged Northern officials *and* citizens to participate in the recapture of runaway slaves.

Slavery raised other property-related constitutional law issues. Slave owners who traveled could not take their slaves into free states or free territory. As the United States expanded westward, the question of whether new territory and newly admitted states would allow slavery became a divisive national political issue. The MISSOURI COMPROMISE in 1820 settled the issue for a time, designating certain areas as slave and others as free. With time, slaveowners wanted to expand into areas the Compromise had reserved for freedom. For slaveowners, the issue was their right to use their property as they chose. Opponents of slavery focused on the personal issue of the slave's freedom. The KANSAS–NEBRASKA ACT in 1854 let the voters decide whether a new state should permit slavery, which led to armed conflict in Kansas. In DRED SCOTT V. SANDFORD (1857), Scott claimed freedom because a former owner had taken him into free territory. The Supreme Court, with its infamous decision, declared the Missouri Compromise to have been an unconstitutional limitation of the PROPERTY RIGHTS of slave owners.

The constitutional issue of slave property was not settled until after the conclusion of the CIVIL WAR. During the course of the war, President ABRAHAM LINCOLN turned the conflict into a war against slavery with the EMANCIPATION PROCLAMATION. The ratification of the THIRTEENTH AMENDMENT in 1865 transformed those persons who were slave property into free people.

THOMAS D. RUSSELL
(2000)

Bibliography

FINKELMAN, PAUL 1981 *An Imperfect Union: Slavery, Federalism, and Comity.* Chapel Hill: University of North Carolina Press.

RANSOM, ROGER and SUTCH, RICHARD 1988 *Capitalists Without Capital: The Burden of Slavery and the Impact of Emancipation. Agricultural History* 62:133–160.

RUSSELL, THOMAS D. 1996 A New Image of the Slave Auction: An Empirical Look at the Role of Law in Slave Sales and a Conceptual Reevaluation of Slave Property. *Cardozo Law Review* 18:473–523.

SLAVERY AND THE CONSTITUTION

Long before the CONSTITUTIONAL CONVENTION OF 1787 the question of slavery had become the prime concern of many Americans. In the first and second Continental Congresses, the matter arose when several groups of slaves petitioned for their manumission. Nothing came of their pleas, of course. In THOMAS JEFFERSON's draft of the DECLARATION OF INDEPENDENCE, he accused the king of waging cruel war against human nature itself, "violating its most sacred rights of life and liberty in the persons of a distant people . . . captivating and carrying them into slavery in another hemisphere. . . ." Although slavery existed throughout the English colonies in 1776, the southern slaveholders in Congress forced rejection of this indictment of the king. If they won their independence on the basis of such an argument, they feared that there would no longer be any justification for slavery.

In some colonies the sentiment against slavery grew during the war for Independence; and the eventual use of slaves as soldiers in the war contributed to the feeling that they should be free. As the states gained their independence some prohibited the slave trade. Some went beyond that enacting legislation looking to the abolition of slavery altogether. Pennsylvania and Massachusetts passed such laws in 1780, followed by Connecticut and Rhode Island in 1784, New York in 1785, and New Jersey in 1786. While no states south of Pennsylvania abolished slavery during this period, several enacted laws facilitating manumission by slaveholders.

Meanwhile, the CONTINENTAL CONGRESS began to look at the question of slavery as it undertook to develop a national land policy. When Thomas Jefferson framed the ORDINANCE OF 1784 for the organization of government in the western territory, he included a provision that after the year 1800 there should be no slavery or involuntary servitude in any of the states to be organized. That provision was rejected. The idea persisted, however, that slavery should not be extended indefinitely. In the NORTHWEST ORDINANCE of 1787 Jefferson's language of 1784 was adopted with the caveat that fugitive slaves escaping into the Northwest Territory from one of the original states "may be lawfully reclaimed and conveyed to the person claiming his or her labor or service. . . ." The Ordinance did not apply south of the Ohio River, where slaveholders were more likely to settle than in the Northwest Territory.

It was inevitable that slavery should have been an important consideration at the Constitutional Convention. At a time when slavery was waning in the North, the southern states saw in slavery an increasing source of wealth both in the market value of slaves and in what slaves could produce. An economic interest so important could not be ignored by a convention one of whose major concerns was to protect property and to advance the economic interests of those who were to live within the new frame of government. Although there were numerous points at which the emerging document affected the institution of slavery, four were of prime significance to the future of slavery and, indeed, the fate of the Constitution.

One point had to do with the TAXING POWER of Congress. Southern delegates generally feared that in levying taxes, especially POLL TAXES, the federal government might discriminate against the South in the way it counted slaves. Closely connected with this was the perception that in apportioning representation, the South would suffer from any arrangement that did not recognize and count slaves as people. After considerable debate, some of it acrimonious, a compromise was reached. Direct taxes were to be apportioned among the several states according to population, thus making it impossible to raise a major portion of federal revenue by taxing property that existed only in one section of the country. In determining the basis of taxation *and* representation, five slaves were to be counted as equal to three free persons. The cryptic language in Article I, section 2, reads: "Representatives and direct Taxes shall be apportioned among the several States which may be included within this Union, according to their respective Numbers, which shall be determined by adding to the whole Number of free Persons, including those bound to Service for a Term of Years, and excluding Indians not taxed, three fifths of all other persons."

The other two points regarding slavery were handled with some dispatch, not because they were unimportant but because they did not come up until late in the session, when the weary delegates were eager to return to their homes. On the slave trade, several southern delegates were uncompromising. While those from Virginia and Maryland appeared to favor a prohibition of the trade, those from South Carolina and Georgia were unalterably opposed to the prohibition. To avoid a rupture between the delegates of the upper South and the North, who favored prohibition, and those of the lower South, the compromise was reached that the slave trade could not be ended before twenty years had elapsed. This language was added in Article II, Section 9: "The Migration or Importation of such Persons as any of the States now shall think proper to admit, shall not be prohibited by the Congress

prior to the Year one thousand eight hundred and eight, but a Tax or duty may be imposed on such Importation, not exceeding ten dollars for each Person."

Significantly, there was almost no opposition to the proposal that fugitive slaves be returned to their masters. The public obligation to return slaves, which had already been provided for in several Indian treaties between 1781 and 1786, was established in the Northwest Territory in 1787 along with the prohibition of slavery in that region. When the provision came before the Convention in late August, the delegates were in no mood for a protracted debate. The slaveholders had already won such sweeping constitutional recognition of slavery, moreover, that the question of fugitive slaves was something of an anticlimax. Without serious challenge, the provision was inserted in Article IV, Section 2: "No person, held to Service or Labour in one State, under the Laws thereof, escaping into another, shall, in Consequence of any Law or Regulation therein, be discharged from such Service or Labour, but shall be delivered up on Claim of the party to whom such Service or Labour may be due."

In dealing with slavery the delegates to the Convention made certain, as if out of a sense of guilt or shame, never to use the word "slave" or any of its variations in the Constitution itself. "Three fifths of all other persons," "Persons held to Service or Labour," and "Migration or Importation of Such Persons," were all mere euphemisms. Everyone knew what they meant. They were meant to shield the consciences of the delegates just as the clauses themselves were meant to protect the institution of slavery. In none of the deliberations did the delegates give serious consideration to abolishing slavery, even though slavery made a mockery of freedom, equality, and the rights of man. It did not make a mockery, however, of the rights of property. American independence and the new Constitution had the effect of giving slavery a longer life than it was to have in the British Empire.

It was the business of the Congress to enact legislation to carry out the objectives set forth in the Constitution. As far as slaves were concerned, this meant the enactment of legislation to facilitate the recovery of runaway slaves by their masters. The impetus for legislation came, however, not from concerns about fugitive slaves but in the call for a statute to facilitate the surrender of FUGITIVES FROM JUSTICE. When the governor of Pennsylvania was unable to persuade the governor of Virginia to give up three white men accused of kidnapping a Pennsylvania free Negro, he presented the facts in the case to President GEORGE WASHINGTON. When the President transmitted the matter to Congress, it responded by passing the Fugitive Slave Act of 1793. After dealing with the matter of the surrender of fugitives from justice in the first two sections, the law turned to the rendition of fugitive slaves.

Under the law a slaveholder could apply to a federal district or circuit judge for a certificate authorizing him to return his slave to the state from which he had fled. This certificate was to be granted after the master had captured his slave, and there were few federal judges at the time; therefore, the master was compelled to go to considerable expense and travel before enjoying the protection of the federal courts. The law did not authorize judges to issue warrants for the arrest of slaves and it did not compel federal authorities to aid in the pursuit of fugitive slaves. The lack of such provisions generated criticism by slaveholders for years to come.

Although under the law of 1793 many fugitives were recaptured and returned to the places from which they had fled, masters continued to complain about the difficulties of reclaiming their human property. Meanwhile, as antislavery sentiment gained momentum in the first decade of the century, opponents of slavery placed additional obstacles in the way of slaveholders seeking the return of their runaways. They began actively to aid fugitives, to urge federal judges not to issue certificates for the return of runaways, and to persuade local officers not to cooperate in their rendition. Slavemasters soon called for a more effective law, and in 1818, a stronger bill was introduced in the HOUSE OF REPRESENTATIVES. As it made its way through Congress, it was burdened with amendments introduced by antislavery legislators requiring proof of ownership before a court of record and making masters criminally liable for false claims. Although a version of the proposed law passed both houses, it was tabled when the conference committee was unable to resolve the problem of amendments.

As the new century began, many Americans turned their thoughts to the provision of the Constitution prohibiting Congress from closing the slave trade before 1808. The slave trade was flourishing, and the slave interests faced a curious dilemma. If the trade continued they risked increasing the chances of violence as unruly blacks from Africa or revolutionary and resourceful blacks from the Caribbean were imported. On the other hand, they required a larger number of slaves to tend their burgeoning plantations. Hoping that the national and state governments would provide safeguards against uprisings and insurrections, they were tempted to favor the continued importation of slaves. At least, they wished to keep their options open.

Ending the slave trade under the provision set forth in the Constitution was not a foregone conclusion, and the antislavery forces knew it. All through the decade they pressed for stringent federal legislation to end the trade. In January 1800, a group of free Negroes in Philadelphia called on Congress to revise its laws on the slave trade and on fugitives. When South Carolina reopened its ports to the trade in 1803, antislavery groups began to press Congress to act. Several resolutions were introduced in Congress condemning the slave trade, but that body took no conclusive steps. The question was brought dramatically before the country in December 1805, when Senator Stephen R. Bradley of Vermont introduced a bill to prohibit the slave trade after January 1, 1808, but the bill was indefinitely tabled. This measure set the stage for President Jefferson to address the issue in his annual message to Congress in December 1806. He called attention to the approaching date when Congress could constitutionally prohibit "all further participation in those violations of human rights which have been so long continued on the unoffending inhabitants of Africa, and which the morality, the reputation, and the best interests of our country have long been eager to proscribe."

Pursuant to the President's eloquent call, which was reminiscent of his draft of the Declaration of Independence, Congress proceeded to consider legislation outlawing the trade. Every provision of the proposed law was debated vigorously. Slaveholders, fearing that Africans smuggled into the United States would not be under the control of the law, wanted them seized and sold into slavery. The antislavery members of Congress strongly objected. The PROHIBITION OF THE SLAVE TRADE ACT (1807) was a compromise. It directed federal officers to be "governed by the provisions of the laws, now existing, of the several states prohibiting the admission or importation . . . of any Negro, mulatto, or other person of color."

In 1818 in the first supplementary act to the law of 1807, Congress sought to make the trade less attractive by increasing the penalty for anyone engaged in it. For example, a fine of $20,000 was replaced by a lowered fine and imprisonment for three to seven years. There were stiffer penalties for persons who knowingly purchased illegally imported Negroes; one-half of all forfeitures and fines were to go to informers. In 1819 Congress directed the President to use armed cruisers on the coasts of the United States and Africa to suppress the trade. Half the proceeds of a condemned ship would go to the captor as bounty, and the captured slaver was to be returned to the port from which it sailed. In the following year Congress provided that direct participation in the slave trade was an act of piracy, punishable by death.

The slave trade was profitable, and it continued despite federal legislation. State laws on the disposition of illegally imported Africans varied. North Carolina directed that such Africans "be sold and disposed of for the state." Georgia directed that the Africans either be sold or given to the Colonization Society for transportation to Africa, with the Society bearing all expenses. Despite these laws, most imported slaves seem to have escaped capture. There were so few captures and the federal officials did so little to enforce the statute of 1807 that it was nearly a dead letter. Slavers introduced their cargo into the United States from Galveston, then a part of Mexico, from Amelia Island in Florida, until 1819 a part of the Spanish Empire, and at various ports on the eastern and southern coasts of the United States. Secretary of the Treasury William H. Crawford confessed that the United States had failed to enforce the law.

Estimates regarding the numbers involved in the illicit slave trade varied. In the decades following passage of the supplementary acts, slavers easily evaded federal authorities, and enforcement received no more than lip service in Washington. In 1839 President MARTIN VAN BUREN called for revision of the laws covering the slave trade in order that "the integrity and honor of our flag may be carefully preserved." A decade later President Zachary Taylor invited the attention of Congress "to an amendment of our existing laws relating to the African slave trade, with a view to the effectual suppression of that barbarous traffic." Nothing happened, and the trade continued down through the Civil War. Because of its clandestine nature, precise figures are impossible; a recent student of the trade estimates that some 51,000 slaves were illegally imported by 1860.

Shortly after the United States purchased Louisiana in 1803, inhabitants from the older states began to settle in the newly acquired territory. When Louisiana entered the Union in 1812 as a slave state, eastern and northern interests began to appreciate the political and economic consequences of slave states entering the Union. They believed that under the Constitution the federal government could prevent the creation of slave states in the territories. They were determined, therefore, to prevent slave states from entering the Union, or, failing that, to limit the number of new slave states. When Missouri sought admission in 1818, northern members of Congress said that they would agree only on condition that the Missouri constitution forbid slavery. Southerners claimed that the restriction was discriminatory; some threatened disunion. After bitter debate, the impasse was resolved when Maine sought admission. Congress admitted Maine as a free state and Missouri as a slave state and declared that in the Louisiana territory slavery should not exist north of the southern boundary of Missouri.

The MISSOURI COMPROMISE stimulated the rivalry between the slave and free states, with each side searching for ways to enhance its advantage. While southern spokesmen insisted that the problems of slavery were local, they relied on the federal Constitution and laws to protect slavery in defiance of the FIRST AMENDMENT; they demanded that antislavery petitions to Congress be laid on the table without receiving notice. At the same time they demanded that Congress act to facilitate the return of fugitive slaves.

As antislavery sentiment in the North increased and abolitionists became more active in obstructing the return of fugitives, the Southerners' demands for protection became more shrill. There were numerous dramatic moments between 1830 and 1860, when abolitionists seized fugitive slaves from their captors or interrupted court proceedings to give accused fugitives the opportunity to flee.

In some northern states residents feared that the Fugitive Slave Law of 1793 would operate to the disadvantage of kidnapped whites and free Negroes accused of being runaway slaves. Consequently, state legislatures empowered state courts to rule in matters arising out of the 1793 law. The Pennsylvania statute of 1826 required the master to present to a magistrate proof of his claim to the alleged fugitive. If the magistrate was convinced the claim was well founded, he was to issue a certificate authorizing the removal of the runaway from the state. If, on the other hand, anyone had seized a person suspected of being a runaway and wrongfully removed him, he would, upon conviction, be deemed guilty of a felony and suffer fine and imprisonment. In due course and by amicable arrangement the Supreme Court ruled on the constitutionality of the Pennsylvania statute in PRIGG V. PENNSYLVANIA (1842), thereby significantly affecting the slavery question for the next two decades.

Edward Prigg, a slave catcher, seized a Negro woman and her children in Pennsylvania with the intention of returning them to their alleged owner in Maryland. When Prigg sought a certificate authorizing their removal, the magistrate, dissatisfied with the proof of ownership, declined to issue the certificate. Prigg took them anyway and was subsequently convicted for violating the 1826 law. The Supreme Court reversed the state court in a decision that had far greater significance than merely exonerating Prigg. Speaking for the Court, Associate Justice JOSEPH STORY declared the Pennsylvania PERSONAL LIBERTY LAW unconstitutional, because it invaded a field placed within the exclusive domain of the federal government by the Fugitive Slave Act of 1793 and by the Constitution itself. "Under the Constitution," said Story, the right to seize a runaway and the duty to deliver him pervaded "the whole Union with an equal and supreme force, uncontrolled and uncontrollable by State SOVEREIGNTY or State legislation." States could enforce the law of 1793, if they wished; but they could not be required to do so, Story added. Further, if an owner recaptured his fugitive slave he did not need a state magistrate's permission to return him to his place of abode.

By placing the fugitive slave question within the exclusive JURISDICTION of the federal government, Justice Story implicitly encouraged northern states that did not wish to cooperate in the enforcement of federal legislation on the subject. The decision promoted the belief, moreover, that antislavery forces could work through sympathetic state and local officials to prevent the recovery of fugitive slaves. Accordingly ten free states enacted personal liberty laws.

When slaveholders felt the impact of *Prigg* in relieving states of responsibility in enforcing the Fugitive Slave Law, they agitated for a more stringent federal law that neither abolitionists nor hostile state laws could nullify. Because the annual pecuniary loss in fugitive slaves was in the hundreds of thousands of dollars, slaveholders increased their pressure on Congress to act. Despite its validation in *Prigg*, the Act of 1793 was inadequate. State courts seemed to vie with abolitionists in their disregard for federal authority. What was needed was a new act of Congress providing effective federal machinery for its successful enforcement. Early in 1850, Senator James Mason of Virginia introduced a bill to that end. Thus began the long and tortuous route by which a new fugitive slave law made its way through Congress.

The debate on the bill was extensive and, at times, acrimonious, connected as it was with other matters that were to constitute the COMPROMISE OF 1850. In the Senate, WILLIAM H. SEWARD of New York wanted to guarantee to every alleged fugitive slave the right to TRIAL BY JURY. HENRY CLAY of Kentucky, on the other hand, wished to emphasize the right of the aggrieved master to recover his property from any place, including a free state, where the slave had fled. DANIEL WEBSTER of Massachusetts, to the surprise of many Northerners and Southerners, agreed with Clay and declared that "in regard to the return of persons bound to service, who have escaped into the free States . . . it is my judgment that the South is right, and the North is wrong." After the bill passed both houses, President Millard Filmore signed it on September 18, 1850.

The new fugitive slave law undertook to establish adequate federal machinery for its enforcement. Circuit courts were to appoint commissioners who, concurrently with circuit and district judges, had authority to grant certificates for the return of fugitive slaves. United States marshals were to execute warrants issued under the act, and a failure of diligent execution was punishable by a $1,000 fine. If a fugitive should escape from a marshal's custody, the marshal was liable for the slave's full value. When the marshal or claimant brought the slave before the court to request a certificate for his return, the alleged fugitive was not permitted to testify in his own behalf. Court disturbances, aiding or abetting fugitives, and harboring or concealing fugitives were punishable by a $1,000 fine and six months imprisonment.

Abolitionists and others attacked the Fugitive Slave Law as unconstitutional. Horace Mann said that it made war on the fundamental principles of human liberty. CHARLES SUMNER called it a "flagrant violation of the Constitution, and of the most cherished rights—shocking to

Christian sentiments, insulting to humanity, and impudent in all its pretensions." Others argued that the fugitive slave clause of the Constitution did not confer on Congress any power to enact laws for the recovery of fugitive slaves. They questioned the power of Congress, moreover, to give commissioners authority to render judgments that only United States judges could properly render under the Constitution. The denial to fugitives by the law of 1850 of the right to trial by jury and to CONFRONT and cross-examine witnesses was itself an unconstitutional denial of DUE PROCESS, its opponents argued. The fact that commissioners received fees instead of fixed salaries meant that they were themselves interested parties in fugitive slave cases. If the commissioner turned over the fugitive to his claimant, he received a ten dollar fee. If he freed the fugitive, the commissioner received only five dollars. What commissioner could be trusted to render impartial justice when his income depended on the kind of decision that he rendered?

The flight into Canada from northern cities of numerous free Negroes and fugitive slaves dramatized for many Northerners the new role of the federal government in obstructing the efforts of those who sought freedom. Many Northerners vowed to prevent enforcement of the new fugitive slave law. Fugitive slave cases increased, but so did rescues, accompanied by denunciations of federal officials. Friends of fugitives resorted to desperate measures such as kidnapping slave hunters and poisoning their bloodhounds. They organized vigilance committees not only to engage in action but also to express their moral revulsion to every effort to enforce the new law. In 1852 the Boston committee unsuccessfully attempted to prevent the rendition of Thomas Sims, an alleged fugitive from Georgia. Composed of such men as Theodore Parker, Wendell Phillips, Horace Mann, and Charles Sumner, the committee, on April 13 at 3 a.m., watched as the United States marshal walked Sims down State Street, past the spot where Crispus Attucks fell and to the wharf where the ship was waiting to take him back to Savannah. Six days later Sims was publicly whipped in Savannah, the first slave Massachusetts had returned.

Opponents of the Fugitive Slave Law of 1850 challenged it in the same way that opponents had challenged its predecessor. The Supreme Court ruling in STRADER V. GRAHAM (1851) could well have controlled the problem for years to come. After Jacob Strader, a citizen of Kentucky, helped several Negroes leave Kentucky, their alleged master sued Strader for damages. Strader claimed that the blacks were not slaves and that they made regular visits to Ohio where they worked as entertainers. These visits, Strader claimed, had caused them to become free even if they had previously been slaves because the Ordinance of 1787 forbade slavery in the Northwest Territory of which

Ohio had been a part. When the case reached the Supreme Court, Chief Justice ROGER B. TANEY, speaking for the entire bench, declared that whatever the status of the blacks while outside Kentucky, they were subject to Kentucky laws upon their return. Nothing in the Constitution, he insisted, could control the law of Kentucky on this subject.

Meanwhile, opposing forces in Kansas were attempting to settle the issue in their own way. The bill to organize Kansas and Nebraska as territories had repealed the Missouri Compromise and left to the inhabitants of the respective territories the decision whether the states-to-be would be slave or free. Abolitionists, believing there should be no more slave states under any circumstances, were determined to make Kansas as well as Nebraska free states. To that end, they undertook first to settle Kansas with persons who would vote for a free constitution and thus to discourage slaveholders from settling in Nebraska, which they were certain would become a free state. Proslavery forces were determined at least to make Kansas a slave state. Both sides were certain they had the Constitution on their side. After bitter arguments and bloody battles, Kansas voted for a free constitution. The South felt that its ambitions had been frustrated and its rights under the Constitution violated as well.

The antislavery forces would not let the decision in *Strader* stand without challenge. They hoped it might be modified, or even overruled, in another decision offering some protection to slaves who had been in free states. Soon another case, DRED SCOTT V. SANDFORD (1857), presented an ideal opportunity, they thought, to secure an unequivocal statement on the status of slaves in the free states and in the territories. Dred Scott, a Missouri slave, traveled with his master to the free state of Illinois, where they lived for a time, then to Minnesota, a free territory under the provisions of the Missouri Compromise. Upon their return to Missouri, his master sold Scott to a New York resident in a vain attempt to establish federal DIVERSITY JURISDICTION when Scott subsequently sued for his freedom. When the Supreme Court announced its decision on March 6, 1857, Chief Justice Taney was again the spokesman.

Taney declared that because Negroes had been viewed as belonging to an inferior order at the time that the Constitution was ratified, they were not citizens within the meaning of the Constitution's provision defining the permissible JURISDICTION of federal courts in cases between citizens of different states. Moreover Scott had not become free by virtue of the Missouri Compromise, because the Compromise was unconstitutional; Congress had no authority to prohibit slavery in the territories. In any case, Taney concluded, once Scott returned to Missouri his status was determined by Missouri law. In Missouri he was still a slave, and thus not a citizen of any state. The case was dismissed for want of jurisdiction.

The decision gave the proslavery forces more support than they could possibly have expected. Slavery's opponents called the decision wicked, atrocious, and abominable. Others hoped the decision would settle once and for all the grievous sectional issues that were about to destroy the Union. But the decision remained controversial. Its impact on events of the next few years is unclear. Perhaps it did not contribute significantly to the critical disputes and eventual divisions in the Democratic party. Perhaps the decision did not greatly stimulate the growth of the Republican party. Yet, as Don E. Fehrenbacher, the leading historian of the decision, has said, "it was a conspicuous and perhaps an integral part of a configuration of events and conditions that did produce enough changes of allegiance to make a political revolution and enough intensity of feeling to make that revolution violent."

The abolitionists, although embittered by the decision, did not relent in their effort to secure judicial support for their position. In a Wisconsin case, which came to the Supreme Court as ABLEMAN V. BOOTH (1859), they attempted once again to have the Fugitive Slave Law of 1850 declared unconstitutional. Sherman M. Booth, an abolitionist editor in Milwaukee, had been arrested for helping a Negro escape from a United States deputy marshal. The state courts pronounced the law unconstitutional and ordered Booth released. When the case reached the Supreme Court in 1859, Chief Justice Taney reversed the state courts, censured them for presuming to pass judgment on federal laws, and held that the Fugitive Slave Law was fully authorized by the Constitution.

Booth was the last opportunity the abolitionists would have to take their cause to the Supreme Court. They would win local victories, such as the denial of the right of transit by slaves through a free state, but the Fugitive Slave Law remained intact until the CIVIL WAR. It would take much more than court challenges or even local disturbances to dislodge the institution of slavery. The fact remained that slavery was so deeply imbedded in the Constitution itself and so firmly protected by it that both violent action and a constitutional amendment would be required to effect far-reaching and lasting change.

The violent action was not long in coming, but the outbreak of the Civil War did not put an end to slavery. President ABRAHAM LINCOLN insisted that the Confederate states were still in the Union and continued to enjoy the constitutional protection of slave property. Once the war began in earnest, however, there was no enforcement of the fugitive slave laws, and as slaves escaped to the Union lines, their emancipation became increasingly a part of the war's objectives. Congress early took steps to free certain slaves. The CONFISCATION ACT of August 6, 1861, declared that owners forfeited slaves engaged in hostile military service. In July 1862 Congress took additional steps in the Second Confiscation Act by granting freedom to slaves of traitors. Furthermore, the slaves of all persons supporting the rebellion were "forever free of their servitude. . . ." Although Lincoln had serious doubts about the constitutionality of the act, he signed it.

Meanwhile, Congress was moving speedily to emancipate the slaves whom it constitutionally could. It could not pass a universal emancipation bill, but it could and did abolish slavery in the DISTRICT OF COLUMBIA and the TERRITORIES. The emancipation bill for the District of Columbia precipitated a lengthy debate, during which President Lincoln persuaded the lawmakers to include an appropriation of $1,000,000 for compensation to owners not exceeding $300 for each slave and for the removal and colonization of the freedmen. Even so, Lincoln was reluctant to sign the bill. He signed it after Senator CHARLES SUMNER of Massachusetts and Bishop Daniel A. Payne of the African Methodist Episcopal Church pleaded with him to approve it. On June 19, 1862, Congress passed and sent to the President a bill abolishing slavery in the territories, with no provision for the compensation of owners, and Lincoln signed it.

The President continued to argue that the federal government could not emancipate the slaves unless it also compensated the owners and colonized the freedmen. Unfortunately for him, his arguments convinced neither the representatives of the border slave states nor the Negro delegations that visited him. Consequently, he was compelled to face the mounting pressures to free the slaves without any apparent constitutional means of doing so. Even as he moved toward an emancipation policy, Lincoln kept his own counsel. He listened patiently to the constant stream of delegations, some urging him to free the slaves, others insisting that he do nothing. The only thing he revealed was that the matter was on his mind, day and night, "more than any other."

In the late spring of 1862 Lincoln decided that he would emancipate the slaves by proclamation. The bleak military outlook pressed the decision on Lincoln. In July he read to the Cabinet a recently completed draft and solicited suggestions regarding language and timing. The members confined their remarks to possible political and military consequences. Lincoln agreed that a propitious moment to issue it would be in the wake of a Union victory, lest some view it as an act of desperation.

Although the battle of Antietam, September 17, 1862, was not the clear-cut victory for which Lincoln had been waiting, he decided to act anyway. On September 22, 1862, he issued the Preliminary EMANCIPATION PROCLAMATION, to take effect on January 1, 1863. Abandoning the notion of colonization, the President, in the final Proclamation, declared free those slaves in states or parts of states under Confederate control. He further declared that the freedmen would be received into the armed service of the United States "to garrison forts, positions, stations, and other places, and to man vessels in said service." Even without a comprehensive emancipation policy, Lincoln is reported to have said as he signed the document, "I never, in my life, felt more certain that I was doing right than I do in signing this paper."

Lincoln realized, of course, that his proclamation, primarily a war measure, did not actually free the slaves. Although military action set many of them free, either state or federal action or both were needed to achieve real and permanent freedom in law and practice. By early 1865, Tennessee, West Virginia, Maryland, and Missouri had taken steps to free their slaves. Delaware and Kentucky, like the Confederate states, had taken no such action by the end of the war.

It early became clear that only national action, preferably through a constitutional amendment, could provide a uniform emancipation policy. Yet some doubted the wisdom or even the prudence of using the Constitution to reform a domestic institution such as slavery. Others questioned the legality of amending the Constitution while eleven states remained outside the Union. The latter circumstance was a major reason why the proposed amendment to forbid slavery throughout the nation initially failed to get the necessary two-thirds approval of the House after it had passed the SENATE in the spring of 1864. After the election of 1864 and with the war winding down, the House finally approved the amendment on January 31, 1865. The following day, Lincoln was pleased to sign the resolution submitting the amendment to the states for ratification.

By December 18, 1865, twenty-seven states, including eight former Confederate states, had ratified the THIRTEENTH AMENDMENT, and it became part of the Constitution. One of the ironies was that the amendment could not have been ratified without the concurrence of the slave states whose governments Congress did not recognize in 1865. This seemed an appropriate way to end slavery, which was itself the most remarkable anomaly in the history of the country.

JOHN HOPE FRANKLIN
(1986)

(SEE ALSO: *Fugitive Slavery*.)

Bibliography

BECKER, CARL (1942) 1953 *The Declaration of Independence: A Study in the History of Political Ideas.* New York: Knopf.
BOWEN, CATHERINE DRINKER 1966 *Miracle at Philadelphia: The*

Story of the Constitutional Convention May to September 1787. Boston: Little, Brown.

CURTIN, PHILLIP   1969   *The Atlantic Slave Trade: A Census.* Madison: University of Wisconsin Press.

DuBois, W. E. BURGHARDT   (1896) 1954   *The Suppression of the African Slave Trade to the United States of America.* New York: Social Science Press.

FEHRENBACHER, DON E.   1978   *The Dred Scott Case: Its Significance in American Law and Politics.* New York: Oxford University Press.

FINKELMAN, PAUL   1981   *An Imperfect Union: Slavery, Federalism, and Comity.* Chapel Hill: University of North Carolina Press.

FRANKLIN, JOHN HOPE   1963   *The Emancipation Proclamation.* Garden City, N.Y.: Doubleday.

LEVY, LEONARD W.   1950   Sims' Case: The Fugitive Slave Law in Boston in 1851. *Journal of Negro History* 35:39–74.

ZILBERSMIT, ARTHUR   1967   *The First Emancipation: The Abolition of Slavery in the North.* Chicago: University of Chicago Press.

SLAVERY IN THE TERRITORIES

Slavery was confirmed by statute or royal decree in all the English, Spanish, and French colonies of North America. After American Independence, slavery therefore enjoyed a legal existence in all the states. In the NORTHWEST ORDINANCE of 1787, the Confederation Congress prohibited slavery in the Northwest Territory, although it also provided for the recapture of slaves escaping there. The First Congress reenacted this ban, but in legislation for the area southwest of the Ohio River it omitted the exclusion of slavery, so that slavery was free to penetrate into the TERRITORIES ceded by Virginia, New York, North Carolina, South Carolina, and Georgia. Slavery also existed in the French settlements that were to become Louisiana, Missouri, Illinois, and Indiana. The treaty of cession with France (1803), by which the United States acquired the LOUISIANA PURCHASE, guaranteed extant property rights, thus assuring slavery's perpetuation in those territories.

Despite the ban of the Northwest Ordinance, settlers in Ohio (particularly in the Virginia Military Reserve in the southwest quadrant of the territory), Indiana, and Illinois tried to introduce slavery, with the connivance of Indiana territorial governor William Henry Harrison in the case of Ohio, and at least the tacit consent of President THOMAS JEFFERSON. They failed in Ohio and Indiana, but in Illinois slavery continued in subterfuge forms in the lead mines of Galena and the salt mines of Shawneetown, and only a vigorous abolitionist effort prevented its legalization throughout the state in 1822.

The Constitution contained no direct allusion to slavery in the territories; the new states and territories clauses did not refer to it, although the fugitive slave clause permitted recapture of fugitives only from the states, not the territories. Consequently, when Missouri sought admission as a slave state in 1819, Congress had no textual guidance, and for the first time it had to extrapolate from what it could determine of the Framers' intent concerning the territories. The result was a long and bitter debate in which restrictionists argued that slavery was hostile to the spirit of republican government and should not be extended to the new lands, while slavery's supporters insisted that Congress lacked power to exclude slavery from any territory. Jefferson at the time joined the antirestrictionists, arguing that as slavery spread it would diffuse to the point where the black population, relative to the white, would dwindle in both the old states and the new territories. The Missouri controversy was settled by admitting Missouri as a slave state and Maine as a free state, while prohibiting slavery in all the Louisiana Purchase territory north of Missouri's southern boundary (3630). (See MISSOURI COMPROMISE.) Jefferson likened the Missouri debates to a "firebell in the night," the "knell of the union."

As the confrontation over slavery intensified in the 1830s, abolitionists and defenders of slavery amplified their constitutional and policy arguments about slavery's future in the territories. Abolitionists found two sources of congressional power to exclude slavery. They saw the territories clause (Article IV, section 3) as a plenary grant of power to the national government to regulate all matters of property and personal status in the territories. Further, the new states clause (Article IV, section 3) implicitly permitted restriction because it gave Congress power to prohibit a state's admission if it recognized slavery. Abolitionists also maintained that slavery was contrary to the principles of a republican form of government, which the United States must guarantee to each of the states.

Alarmed by such doctrines, JOHN C. CALHOUN in the period 1837–1847 elaborated doctrines that denied any exclusionary power to Congress. He insisted that the territories were the common property of all the states, and that it would be unjust to the slave states to exclude one form of property and its owners (slaves) when all other forms of property were not similarly restricted. Calhoun regarded Congress as the agent of the states (they being the principals) or as their trustee (they being the beneficiaries). By either legal metaphor, Congress lacked power to exclude slavery because that would discriminate against one group of states. He maintained that slavery was not only a positive good but also an essential element in the domestic and political structure of the slave states. Efforts to impede its spread were therefore not only insulting but threatening to the security of the states themselves.

This debate remained academic until 1845. Arkansas had been admitted as a slave state in 1836, the unorganized Indian Territory (modern Oklahoma) was not then targeted for white settlement, and many still considered the remainder of the Louisiana Purchase uninhabitable. But Texas's independence, followed by its request for admission, thrust the territorial debates to center stage, and for over a decade after the outbreak of the Mexican War the territorial issue eclipsed all other topics of the slavery controversy except the problem of fugitive slaves. Texas, a slaveholding Republic that had struck for Independence partly because the Mexican constitution had abolished slavery, presented the potential for more than one slave state; the JOINT RESOLUTION admitting it to statehood recognized its potential subdivision into five states.

When war with Mexico broke out in 1846, the future of the territories to be acquired from that country became a more urgent issue. A few persons suggested that the United States acquire no new territories, but that idea was lost in the tide of Manifest Destiny flooding the country in the 1840s. In 1846, Representative David Wilmot, a Pennsylvania Democrat, offered a proviso to an appropriations bill that used the language of the Northwest Ordinance to exclude slavery from all territories acquired as a result of the Mexican War. Democrats and other defenders of slavery were alarmed by the WILMOT PROVISO's popularity in the North (nearly all free state legislatures endorsed it), and especially by the Proviso's appeal to Northern Democrats, who resented Southern dictation of party policy on slavery-related subjects and wanted to preserve the new territories for free white settlement.

The Proviso's opponents introduced four alternative proposals. Many Southerners at first found the idea of extending the Missouri Compromise line attractive. The Polk administration, Justice JOHN CATRON of Tennessee, the NASHVILLE CONVENTION of 1850, and Senator JOHN J. CRITTENDEN of Kentucky in 1860 all suggested extrapolating the 3630 line as a simple and arbitrary solution to the Gordian knot of slavery in the territories. Despite its simplicity, the idea repeatedly failed. One of the reasons for its failure was that other Southern leaders, more determined to protect the South than to compromise the territorial issue, revised their 1820 position and insisted that any exclusion of slavery from the territories was unconstitutional. Their theories for a time were subsumed under the shorthand term "non-intervention," a name for a cluster of doctrines that adopted Calhoun's premises and went on to demand that the federal government protect slavery in all the territories and even establish it there by a federal territorial slave code if necessary.

Northern Democrats rejected this position, but they did not want to split the party by endorsing the Wilmot Proviso. Under the leadership of Lewis Cass of Michigan and STEPHEN A. DOUGLAS of Illinois, they proposed a third alternative: the doctrine of territorial sovereignty, more often but less accurately referred to as POPULAR SOVER-EIGNTY or squatter sovereignty. Cass and Douglas insisted that the future of slavery in the territories be decided by the settlers of the territories themselves, not by Congress. After 1850, they also began to adopt the Southern position that slavery's exclusion was not only unnecessary and gratuitously offensive to the South but also unconstitutional. Territorial sovereignty contained a central ambiguity: when were the settlers to decide? If, as Southern spokesmen demanded, territorial settlers could not exercise this prerogative until the eve of statehood, then slavery would establish a foothold, as it had in Missouri, and be impossible to dislodge. Northern proponents of territorial sovereignty, on the other hand, insisted that the settlers had a right to exclude slavery at any point after the organization of the territory. This view, in turn, forced Southerners to another doctrinal redoubt, when they claimed that just as Congress could not exclude slavery, neither could its creature, the territorial legislature. In this view, slavery could establish itself anywhere in American territories.

The Free Soil coalition of 1848, made up of New York Democrats, antislavery Whigs, and former political abolitionists, adopted the Wilmot Proviso as a principal plank in their program. But the COMPROMISE OF 1850 decisively rejected the Wilmot Proviso. In admitting California as a free state and organizing New Mexico and Utah Territories without restrictions as to slavery, Congress also rejected the Missouri Compromise line. But it also adopted the fourth alternative to the Wilmot Proviso, the "Clayton Compromise." Senator John Clayton of Delaware had proposed that all questions arising in TERRITORIAL COURTS concerning title to slaves or a black's claim to freedom be appealable directly to the United States Supreme Court, in effect inviting the Justices of the high court to try their hand at resolving the seemingly insoluble territorial issue. By adopting the Clayton Compromise, Congress admitted its inability to deal with the most exigent political issue of the day. Its desperate grasp at nonpolitical solutions not only confessed its impotence but also assumed the finality of an unpredictable resolution of a question that was ultimately metajudicial.

The KANSAS-NEBRASKA ACT of 1854 adopted the principle of territorial sovereignty, along with some vague and ambiguous allusions to nonintervention. It declared the Missouri Compromise defunct and implied that it was unconstitutional, thus representing a victory for both northern Democrats and Southerners. But this accommodation did not last long, as Kansas filled with authentic settlers and Missouri sojourners. Because most of the former hoped to see Kansas free and because all the latter were determined to make it a slave state, political controversy erupted into guerrilla warfare in the period known as "Bleeding Kansas." President JAMES BUCHANAN tried to force the proslavery LECOMPTON CONSTITUTION on the territory, over the wishes of a large majority of bona fide settlers, and thereby split the Democratic party into Southern-dominated and Douglas wings.

Meanwhile, Chief Justice ROGER B. TANEY and his colleagues took up the invitation tendered by Congress in DRED SCOTT V. SANDFORD (1857). Taney held, in the latter part of his opinion, that the Missouri Compromise was unconstitutional, and that Congress could not exclude slavery from a territory. He adopted three Calhounite positions in OBITER DICTA: the federal government had to protect slavery in the territories; territorial legislatures could not exclude slavery at any time before statehood; and the federal government was the trustee of the states or the territories. In passing, Taney suggested that congressional exclusion would deprive a slaveowner of rights to property protected by the DUE PROCESS clause of the Fifth Amendment. This adumbration of SUBSTANTIVE DUE PROCESS was merely a passing allusion, however, the emphasis of Taney's opinion lying instead in his interpretation of the new states clause.

In the LINCOLN-DOUGLAS DEBATES of 1858, ABRAHAM LINCOLN challenged Douglas to explain what was left of territorial sovereignty after *Dred Scott*. Douglas suggested the FREEPORT DOCTRINE: that Congress could for all practical purposes exclude slavery from a territory simply by not enacting a territorial slave code or extending any other protection for it there. Under one interpretation of SOMERSET V. STEWART (1772), there being no positive law to keep a person enslaved, slavery effectively could not establish itself. This led Mississippi Senator JEFFERSON DAVIS to demand that the federal courts protect slavery in the territories somehow, and, if this proved unavailing, that Congress enact a territorial slave code.

The Constitution of the Confederate States of America extended full federal protection to slavery in any territories the Confederacy might acquire. The Congress of the United States abolished slavery in all federal territories in 1862 (Act of June 19, 1862).

WILLIAM M. WIECEK
(1986)

(SEE ALSO: *Constitutional History, 1829–1848.*)

Bibliography

BESTOR, ARTHUR   1961   State Sovereignty and Slavery: A Reinterpretation of Proslavery Constitutional Doctrine, 1846–1860. *Journal of the Illinois State Historical Society* 54:117–180.

QUAIFE, MILO M.   1910   *The Doctrine of Non-Intervention with Slavery in the Territories.* Chicago: Chamberlin.

RUSSEL, ROBERT R.   1966   Constitutional Doctrines with Regard to Slavery in the Territories. *Journal of Southern History* 32:466–486.

SLOAN v. LEMON

See: *Committee for Public Education and Religious Liberty v. Nyquist*

SMITH, J. ALLEN
(1860–1924)

Lawyer, economist, and political scientist James Allen Smith was an influential spokesman for PROGRESSIVE CONSTITUTIONAL THOUGHT. His most important book was *The Spirit of American Government* (1901), subtitled "A Study of the Constitution: Its Origins, Influence and Relation to Democracy." Smith contended that the Constitution represented a reactionary and undemocratic retreat from the revolutionary principles of the DECLARATION OF INDEPENDENCE. He proposed to make the Constitution more democratic by eliminating CHECKS AND BALANCES, curbing the SUPREME COURT, and introducing DIRECT ELECTIONS for the President and SENATE along with REFERENDUM, and RECALL.

DENNIS J. MAHONEY
(1986)

SMITH v. ALLWRIGHT
321 U.S. 649 (1944)

In 1935 the Supreme Court had held in GROVEY V. TOWNSEND that the Texas Democratic party convention's rule excluding black voters from PRIMARY ELECTIONS was not STATE ACTION and thus violated no constitutional rights. *Allwright* involved the same question, raised in the same manner; Smith alleged that he was excluded from the Texas Democratic primary because of his race and sought damages from election officials under federal CIVIL RIGHTS laws. The case had become a plausible candidate for Supreme Court review because in UNITED STATES V. CLASSIC (1941) the Court had reconsidered the nature of a primary election by way of upholding Congress's power to forbid fraud in primary elections of nominees for federal offices. In *Classic*, the Court had concluded that Louisiana primary elections were, by law, an integral part of the machinery for electing officers.

Applying the *Classic* reasoning in *Allwright*, the Court overruled *Grovey v. Townsend* and held that the state's provision of machinery for primary elections was sufficiently connected with the party's conduct of those elections to satisfy the state action limitation of the FIFTEENTH AMENDMENT. Because that amendment forbade a state to deny or abridge the right to vote on account of race, Smith was entitled to damages if he could prove his allegations. Justice STANLEY F. REED wrote for the Court.

Justice OWEN ROBERTS, who had written for a unanimous Court in *Grovey*, dissented, complaining that the OVER-RULING of a DECISION after only nine years tended "to bring adjudications of this tribunal into the same class as a restricted railroad ticket, good on this day and train only." The obvious question was: why had Roberts joined in the *Classic* decision? Contemporary accounts suggest that at least some of the other Justices thought Roberts had been "duped" into concurring in *Classic*, and that Roberts knew they thought so. In the years between *Grovey* and *Allwright*, President FRANKLIN D. ROOSEVELT had made seven appointments to the Court. Justice Roberts's lone companion from the earlier days was Chief Justice HARLAN FISKE STONE, who had written the *Classic* opinion.

KENNETH L. KARST
(1986)

SMITH ACT

See: Alien Registration Act

SMYTH v. AMES
169 U.S. 466 (1898)

A unanimous Supreme Court, in this arrogation of power, proclaimed its acceptance of SUBSTANTIVE DUE PROCESS in rate regulation. The Court refused to "shrink from the duty" of exercising its judgment in a highly technical area of ECONOMIC REGULATION best left to experts. For the next forty years, the Court would review the rate schedules of REGULATORY COMMISSIONS seeking to accommodate shifting and illusory judicial standards of fairness.

In 1893 a Nebraska statute prescribed maximum rail rates for intrastate transportation. William Jennings Bryan defended the state legislature's power to fix reasonable rates for intrastate commerce; James Coolidge Carter urged that the Court limit the power when unreasonable rates effectively divested a railroad of its property. The question presented by the three cases consolidated here was whether those rates amounted to a TAKING OF PROPERTY without JUST COMPENSATION, thereby depriving the railroads of their property without DUE PROCESS OF LAW. Justice DAVID J. BREWER, sitting as a circuit judge in one of the cases, invented a "FAIR RETURN ON FAIR VALUE" test. He struck down the rates because they failed to provide a fair return on a fair valuation of the railroad property and thereby they effectively destroyed property.

Accepting Brewer's opinion, Justice JOHN MARSHALL HARLAN, for the Court, asserted that REAGAN V. FARMERS'

LOAN & TRUST COMPANY (1894) demonstrated the appropriateness of a judicial determination of the question. Courts, he said, must be free to inquire into the sufficiency of the rates set by the state legislature, even though the Nebraska constitution only granted the legislature the power to prescribe "reasonable' maximum rates." Admitting that the question could be "more easily determined by a commission" of experts, Harlan pursued the "considerations" which, "given such weight as may be just and right in each case," would allow a determination of reasonable rate. He declared that the "basis of all calculations . . . must be the fair value of the property being used." Then he listed a number of various aids to determine fair value: original construction costs, replacement or reproduction costs, stock values, the cost of permanent improvements, earning power under the prescribed rate structure, operating expenses, and other unspecified matters. The company, he concluded, was justified in asking a "fair return upon the value of that which it employs for the public convenience." The Nebraska statute had failed to provide that fair return and so deprived the railroad of its property without just compensation, thereby depriving it of due process of law under the FOURTEENTH AMENDMENT.

In *Smyth* the Court readily substituted its judgment on a question of policy for other branches of government. Regulatory commissions of all sorts would spend four decades attempting to second-guess the courts' efforts to determine what constituted a "fair return" on "fair value." Over those decades, the Court manipulated the fair value standards to the benefit of corporations. The Court relied primarily on two of Harlan's factors in assessing fair value. Until about 1918, high original costs governed the Court's determination of fair value. When the war ended and both costs and prices rose, the Court turned to replacement costs as a means of deciding fair value, again keeping rates high. The Court consistently avoided using earnings—perhaps the best economic measure—as a guide. Justices LOUIS D. BRANDEIS and OLIVER WENDELL HOLMES denounced the fair return rule throughout the 1920s and 1930s; their views gained adherents by the early 1940s. In *Federal Power Commission v. Natural Gas Company* (1942) the Court asserted that property value was not an essential factor in calculating a fair return, and the Supreme Court finally disavowed a judicial control of the question in FEDERAL POWER COMMISSION V. HOPE NATURAL GAS COMPANY (1944).

DAVID GORDON
(1986)

Bibliography

HALE, ROBERT LEE 1952 *Freedom through Law: Public Control of Private Governing Power*. Pages 461–500. New York: Columbia University Press.

SNEPP v. UNITED STATES
444 U.S. 507 (1980)

A former Central Intelligence Agency (CIA) employee, Frank W. Snepp III, published a book containing unclassified information about CIA activities in South Vietnam. Snepp did not submit the book to the CIA for prepublication review, in breach of his express employment agreement not to publish any information without the agency's prior approval or to disclose any *classified* information. In a decision remarkable for its procedural setting and for its failure to meet head-on the FIRST AMENDMENT issues implicated by the prior restraint, the Supreme Court, PER CURIAM, sanctioned the imposition of a constructive trust on all proceeds from the book's sales.

The Court recognized, as the government conceded, that Snepp had a First Amendment right to publish unclassified information. The Court found, however, that by virtue of his employment as a CIA agent, Snepp had entered a fiduciary relationship with the agency. Snepp breached the special trust reposed in him by failing to submit *all* material, whether classified or not, for prepublication review. That breach posed irreparable harm to the CIA's relationships with foreign governments and its ability to perform its statutory duties. The constructive trust remedy was thereby warranted.

Justice JOHN PAUL STEVENS, joined by Justices WILLIAM J. BRENNAN and THURGOOD MARSHALL, dissented, arguing that the remedy was unsupported by statute, the contract, or case law. He urged that the contract be treated as an ordinary employment covenant. On this theory, its enforcement would be governed by a rule of reason that would require a balancing of interests, including Snepp's First Amendment rights, and might justify an equity court's refusal to enforce the prepublication review covenant. Further, the alleged harm suffered by the government did not warrant the Court's "draconian" remedy, especially because the government had never shown that other remedies were inadequate. Stevens noted that the Court seemed unaware that it had fashioned a drastic new remedy to enforce a species of prior restraint on a citizen's right to criticize the government.

KIM McLANE WARDLAW
(1986)

(SEE ALSO: *Prior Restraint and Censorship.*)

SOBELOFF, SIMON E.
(1894–1973)

Born in Baltimore, Maryland, to immigrant parents, Simon Sobeloff began his long and distinguished public career at the age of fourteen as a congressional page. After graduation from the University of Maryland School of Law in 1915, Sobeloff alternated private practice with public service, including a term as United States attorney for the District of Maryland, until 1952. In that year, he was appointed chief judge of the Maryland Court of Appeals, and in 1954 President DWIGHT D. EISENHOWER named him SOLICITOR GENERAL of the United States.

While solicitor general, Sobeloff argued the government's case in the implementation phase of BROWN V. BOARD OF EDUCATION (1955) and also declined as a matter of conscience to sign the government's BRIEF in *Peters v. Hobby* (1955), a LOYALTY OATH case.

In 1955, President Eisenhower nominated Sobeloff to the United States Court of Appeals for the Fourth Circuit, but his confirmation was delayed for a year by southern Democrats who distrusted his views on school DESEGREGATION. Sobeloff served on the Fourth Circuit from 1956 until his death and was chief judge from 1958 to 1964.

As chief judge, Sobeloff wrote numerous majority opinions affirming school board attempts to comply with *Brown v. Board of Education*. He grew increasingly impatient with school board progress, however, and after retiring as chief judge, he dissented frequently in the numerous school desegregation cases heard EN BANC by the Fourth Circuit. Several of his dissents led to Supreme Court review and reversal of Fourth Circuit HOLDINGS that approved school board actions, as Sobeloff consistently argued for the complete dismantling of the desegregated school systems in the face of continued school board recalcitrance and delay.

Other Sobeloff dissents led to Supreme Court majority opinions, including *Davis v. North Carolina* (1966), which invalidated a confession given in coercive circumstances. In other cases, Sobeloff went further than the Supreme Court was prepared to go, holding, for example, that a harsher sentence on retrial following reversal of a conviction unconstitutionally conditioned the right to a FAIR TRIAL.

Frequently described by Maryland Governor Theodore R. McKeldin as a "champion of the underdog," Sobeloff reflected in his judicial opinions a consistent concern both for meticulous DUE PROCESS and for the rights of minorities, the underprivileged, the dissenter, and the prisoner.

ALISON GREY ANDERSON
(1992)

Bibliography

TRIBUTE ISSUE   1974   *Maryland Law Review* 34, no. 4:483–540.

SOCIAL COMPACT THEORY

An invention of political philosophers, the social contract or social compact theory was not meant as a historical account of the origin of government, but the theory was taken literally in America where governments were actually founded upon contract. The words "compact" and "contract" are synonymous and signify a voluntary agreement of the people to unite as a political community and to establish a government. The theory purports to explain why individuals should obey the law: each person, in a government that exists with the consent of the governed, freely and, in effect, continuously gives consent to the constitution of his community.

The theory hypothesizes a prepolitical state of nature in which people were governed only by the law of nature, free of human restraints. From the premise that man was born free, the deduction followed that he came into the world with God-given or NATURAL RIGHTS. Born without the restraint of human laws, he had a right to possess liberty and to work for his own property. Born naked and stationless, he had a right to equality. Born with certain instincts and needs, he had a right to satisfy them—a right to the pursuit of happiness. These natural rights, as JOHN DICKINSON declared in 1766, "are created in us by the decrees of Providence, which establish the laws of our nature. They are born with us; exist with us; and cannot be taken from us by any human power without taking our lives."

When people left the state of nature and compacted for government, the need to make their rights secure motivated them. ALEXANDER HAMILTON observed that "Civil liberty is only natural liberty modified and secured by the sanctions of civil society. . . . The origin of all civil government, justly established, must be a voluntary compact between the rulers and the ruled, and must be liable to such limitations as are necessary for the security of the absolute rights of the latter." The most detailed exposition of this theory was by JOHN LOCKE, the most brief and eloquent by THOMAS JEFFERSON in the preamble of the DECLARATION OF INDEPENDENCE. One of the self-evident truths in the latter is "That to secure these rights, Governments are instituted among Men, deriving their just powers from the consent of the governed. . . ."

The compact theory of government colored the thought and action of Americans during the colonial period and through the period of constitution making. The new world actually seemed like a state of nature, and Americans did in fact compact with each other; the theory seemed to fit the circumstances under which American political and constitutional institutions grew. Our system developed as a self-conscious working out of some of the implications of the compact theory.

The related but distinct idea, so important in Puritan thought, that people covenant with each other to make a church for their ecclesiastical polity, was extended to their secular polity. Even before the founding of Virginia a Separatist leader asked, "What agreement must there be of men? For church governors there must be an agreement

of the people or commonwealth." A half century before Locke's *Second Treatise*, THOMAS HOOKER, a founder of Connecticut, explained that in any relationship that involved authority there must be free agreement or consent. "This," he said, "appears in all covenants betwixt Prince and People, Husband and Wife, Master and Servant, and most palpable is the expression of this in all confederations and corporations . . . They should first freely engage themselves in such covenants. . . ." The first concrete application of the covenant theory to civil government was the Mayflower Compact (1620). The Pilgrims, putting theory into practice, solemnly did "covenant and combine . . . into a civil body politick," an experience multiplied over and again with the founding of numerous settlements in New England. (See FUNDAMENTAL ORDERS OF CONNECTICUT.)

The colonists also regarded their charters as compacts. As Hamilton said later, George III was "King of America, by virtue of a compact between us and the Kings of Great Britain." These colonies, Hamilton explained, were settled under charters granted by kings who "entered into covenants with us. . . ." Over a period of a century and a half, Americans became accustomed to the idea that government existed by consent of the governed, that the people created government, that they did it by written compact, and that the compact constituted their FUNDAMENTAL LAW. From practical experience as well as from revolutionary propaganda, Americans believed in the compact theory and they acted it out.

It was a useful tool, immediately at hand and lending historical and philosophical credibility, for destroying the old order and creating a new one. William Drayton, the chief justice of South Carolina, echoed a commonplace idea when he said that George III had "unkinged" himself by subverting the "constitution of this country, by breaking the original contract. . . ." The compact theory legitimated the right of revolution, as the Declaration of Independence made clear. Even before that declaration, colonial radicals contended that the Coercive Acts (see FIRST CONTINENTAL CONGRESS) "have thrown us into a state of nature," and justified contracting for a new government. After Independence a town orator in Boston declared that the people had reclaimed the rights "attendant upon the original state of nature, with the opportunity of establishing a government for ourselves. . . ." The colonies became states by a practice that mirrored the theory; they drew up written constitutions, often phrased as compacts, and purposefully put formal statements of the compact theory into those documents. The MASSACHUSETTS CONSTITUTION OF 1780 (still operative) declares: "The body politic is formed by a voluntary association of individuals; it is a social compact by which the whole people covenants with each citizen and each citizen with the whole people. . . ." A minister, Jonas Clark, said in a sermon that just government is founded in compact "and in compact alone." The new state constitution, he declared, was "a most sacred covenant or contract. . . ." The state CONSTITUTIONAL CONVENTION that framed that constitution was devised to institutionalize the compact theory.

Although the ARTICLES OF CONFEDERATION do not formally state that theory, letters of the members of the Continental Congress that framed the Articles show that they regarded themselves as making a compact for the union of states, and THE FEDERALIST #21 refers to "the social compact between the States. . . ." Similarly, at the Philadelphia CONSTITUTIONAL CONVENTION OF 1787, JAMES MADISON, declared that the delegates had assembled to frame "a compact by which an authority was created paramount to the parties, and making laws for the government of them." GEORGE WASHINGTON, on behalf of the "Federal Convention," when sending the new Constitution to the Congress of the Confederation for submission to the states, drew an analogy from compact theory: individuals left a state of nature by yielding up some liberty to preserve the rest, and the states surrendered some of their SOVEREIGNTY to consolidate the union. Some of the states, when formally ratifying the new Constitution, considered themselves to be "entering into an explicit and solemn compact," as New Hampshire declared. Chief Justice JOHN JAY observed, in CHISHOLM V. GEORGIA (1793), that every state constitution "is a compact . . . and the Constitution of the United States is likewise a compact made by the people of the United States to govern themselves."

The compact theory answers one of the most profound questions of political philosophy: why do people submit to the compulsions of government? The answer is that when they established government they consented to its exercise of power and agreed to obey it if it secured their rights. The compact theory has been remarkably fecund. From government by consent it led to political democracy. It also led to CONSTITUTIONALISM as LIMITED GOVERNMENT, to a concept of a constitution as fundamental law, to constitutions as written documents, to the constitutional convention as a way of writing the document, to the right of revolution when the government is destructive of the ends of the compact, and to concepts of civil liberty and written BILLS OF RIGHTS.

LEONARD W. LEVY
(1986)

Bibliography

MCLAUGHLIN, ANDREW C. 1932 *The Foundations of American Constitutionalism.* New York: New York University Press.
ROSSITER, CLINTON 1953 *Seedtime of the Republic: The Origin of the American Tradition of Political Liberty.* New York: Harcourt, Brace.
TATE, THAD W. 1965 The Social Contract in America, 1774–1787: Revolutionary Theory as a Conservative Instrument. *William and Mary Quarterly* 22:375–391.
WOOD, GORDON S. 1969 *The Creation of the American Republic, 1776–1787.* Chapel Hill: University of North Carolina Press.

SOCIAL PROGRAMS

See: Entitlement

SOCIAL SCIENCE IN CONSTITUTIONAL LITIGATION

All litigation, including constitutional litigation, resolves issues of law and fact. SOCIAL SCIENCE RESEARCH can help to clarify the facts on which a case may turn; and it can help the resolution of legal issues by laying before the courts data and analyses that bear on the choice of an appropriate legal rule.

Legal lore has it that the rise of social science in the law began with the BRANDEIS BRIEF, in which LOUIS D. BRANDEIS, special counsel for the state of Oregon, successfully bolstered the state's claim in MULLER V. OREGON (1908) that its statute limiting the working hours for women was constitutional. Although in theory the state merely had to show that such a regulation was not unreasonable, previous decisions had struck down laws regulating working hours of other employees as unreasonable invasions of the liberty of contract. The brief supported the reasonableness of the law in part by showing that a great many American states and even more countries abroad had similar statutes. It was an effective if modest social science effort.

More sophisticated techniques are to be found in contemporary constitutional litigation. Sampling, the most powerful tool of social science research, is now firmly established as an appropriate means of gathering EVIDENCE. If the survey was conducted without bias and if the technical requirements are met, a sample may be accepted as a reasonably accurate representation of the sampled universe. For instance, in support of a motion for change of VENUE in a criminal case, a sample survey measures the extent and depth of pretrial prejudice in the community. If a voluminous body of communications is at issue, sampling may be combined with a technique called content analysis. Thus, when the constitutionality of the work of the House Committee on Un-American Activities was litigated, a sample of the committee's public hearings was examined. This approach yielded a numerical statement of the frequency with which the committee asked its witnesses questions that transcended its constitutional authority. Similar content analysis has sometimes been used in support of a motion for change of venue, documenting the charge that a substantial part of the pretrial publicity originated in the prosecutor's office.

Proof of racial or other discrimination in jury selection, employment, and other contexts frequently employs sampling and subsequent statistical analysis. Such proof involves an analysis of the differences between the actual outcome of the selection process and the outcome that would have been expected if discrimination had no role in the process.

In *United States v. Hazelwood School District* (1977), for instance, the Supreme Court made its own probability computations to determine whether excluding the metropolitan area from the labor market in which a suburban school district hired its teachers would substantially weaken the government's statistical proof that the district had engaged in discrimination. Although the Court's statistical performance in *Hazelwood* was flawed in certain respects, similar methods in proving discrimination have become accepted in both federal and state courts.

Of particular interest are the cases in which the judicial system itself is charged with discrimination. The two main targets here are the administration of the death penalty and the selection of jurors. Evidence has been mounting, and finally has drawn the attention of the Supreme Court, that the death penalty is administered with bias, discriminating against black offenders who killed white victims. The major technical problem in distilling this evidence is to assure comparability of the homicides under analysis.

In the jury selection area, the statistical analysis of discrimination has had more impact. Despite substantial efforts in this direction, the lower courts have rejected these efforts. In *Castandeda v. Partida* (1977), for instance, the Court used a standard statistical formula to compute the probability that the disparity between the proportion of Mexican Americans serving on GRAND JURIES and their proportion in the county population could have arisen if grand jurors had been selected at random. The majority found the probability to be so minute (about one in a number with 140 zeros) that the discrepancy was sufficient to establish discrimination even though there were problems with the data used to estimate these proportions and even though the majority of jury commissioners were themselves Mexican Americans.

In the trial of Dr. Benjamin Spock and others accused of conspiring to obstruct the draft, the alleged discrimination involved female jurors. The allegation of bias in that case was directed not against the system but against the particular judge who consistently selected juries with significantly fewer women than those of his colleagues, although all drew from the same pool of potential jurors.

At times experimental social science research is offered to aid a court in assessing the consequences of its legal options or in ascertaining facts relevant to the choice of

these options. When the Supreme Court in BROWN V. BOARD OF EDUCATION (1954) held that segregated education was inherently unequal, the Court quoted with approval a lower court's finding that school segregation with the sanction of law produced feelings of inferiority among black children, affecting their motivation to learn. The Court remarked that its conclusion was "amply supported by modern authority." That authority, cited in a footnote, consisted of seven items. Five, such as Gunnar Myrdal's *American Dilemma*, dealt generally with problems of black education. Two bore more directly on the issue: a statement by thirty-two leading social scientists and an experiment conducted by the psychologist Kenneth Clark. Clark had given sixteen black children in a South Carolina elementary school a sheet of paper on which two dolls were drawn, identical in every respect except that the one was black, the other white. The children were asked, "Which doll would you like to play with?" "Which is the nice and which the bad doll?" "Which doll looks like you yourself?" Ten of the children liked the white doll best; eleven called the black doll the "bad" one; seven of the black children, when asked which doll was like themselves, picked the white one. From these answers and earlier research, Clark concluded "that these children . . . like other human beings who are subjected to an obviously inferior status in the society in which they live, have been definitely harmed in the development of their personalities. . . ."

Later, scholars disputed both the evidentiary power of that study and the weight the Justices had attached to it. The study, obviously limited in size and structure, today would hardly survive cross-examination. Most likely its major function was to buttress a position the Justices had reached on their own.

Social science research has provided more solid evidence in litigation over the constitutionality of juries with fewer than twelve members. In the two decisions that affirmed the legality of such juries, the Court cited a number of empirical studies purporting to show that these modifications did not affect the quality of the verdicts rendered by the smaller juries. Subsequently these studies were severely criticized, and five years later BALLEW V. GEORGIA held five-member criminal juries unconstitutional. Justice HARRY A. BLACKMUN's opinion repeatedly cited these critical views.

Most social science operations suffer from some imperfection, partly because their subject matter is so complex, and partly because of methodological flaws. Even if such imperfections are minor, courts may hesitate to accept social science findings that threaten to dislodge established rules. One type of effort to compensate for imperfection is "triangulation"—the confluence of evidence from independent studies that approach the same problem from different angles. An example is the series of studies of "death qualified" juries.

At one time, a New York statute allowed New York City to try murder and other crimes of public notoriety before specially selected BLUE RIBBON JURIES, whose members, among other qualifications, were required to have no objection to the death penalty. When the Court was asked to declare these juries unconstitutional because of alleged bias in favor of the prosecution, it declined by a bare majority on the ground that there was no proof of such bias. Speculation as to how such proof might be established led to the first study which found that jurors who were in favor of the death penalty were indeed more likely to convict, not only in capital trials, but generally. Six other studies followed, with different approaches; each replicated the result.

Witherspoon v. Illinois (1968), decided halfway through these studies, did not reach the issue. Although the Court agreed that merely having scruples about the death penalty was not sufficient cause for eliminating jurors, it dismissed the first few research findings, indicating that the exclusion of jurors with scruples against the death penalty would bias the jury in favor of conviction, as "too tentative and fragmentary." Subsequent efforts to convince other courts that the post-*Witherspoon* juries, too, were biased in favor of convicting defendants failed until 1983 and 1984 when two federal district courts in HABEAS CORPUS proceedings accepted the evidence provided in these studies and invalidated the convictions. Although the federal Courts of Appeals have divided on this issue and the Supreme Court has agreed to review one of these cases, these two decisions mark a preliminary acceptance of proof by triangulation.

The role of social science research in litigation is bound to grow in spite of deep-seated hesitancy on the part of the courts to look at statistical evidence. It is difficult to predict how fast and where the use of social science techniques will increase in constitutional litigation. Much will depend on the resourcefulness of social scientists in developing new research and the initiative of attorneys in presenting evidence that can sharpen the perception of litigated facts and aid courts in judging the consequences of their legal options.

HANS ZEISEL
DAVID KAYE
(1986)

Bibliography

BALDUS, D. and COLE, J. 1980 *Statistical Proof of Discrimination.* Colorado Springs, Colo.: Shepard's.

CAHN, EDMOND 1962 A Dangerous Myth in the School Segregation Cases. In Kenneth Clark, ed., *Confronting Injustice.* Pages 329–345. Boston: Little, Brown.

KAYE, DAVID 1980 And Then There Were Twelve: Statistical Reasoning, the Supreme Court, and the Size of the Jury. *California Law Review* 68:1004–1043.

——— 1982 Statistical Evidence of Discrimination. *Journal of the American Statistical Association* 77:773–783.

LEMPERT, RICHARD O. 1975 Uncovering "Nondiscernible" Differences: Empirical Research and the Jury-Size Cases. *Michigan Law Review* 73:643–708.

LOH, WALLACE D. 1984 *Social Research in the Judicial Process: Cases, Readings and Text.* New York: Russell Sage Foundation.

SAKS, MICHAEL J. 1974 Ignorance of Science Is No Excuse. *Trial* 10:18–20.

WALBERT, DAVID 1971 The Effect of Jury Size on the Probability of Conviction: An Evaluation of *Williams v. Florida. Case Western Law Review* 22:529–554.

ZEISEL, HANS 1968 *Some Data on Juror Attitudes Towards Capital Punishment.* Chicago: University of Chicago Center for Studies in Criminal Justice.

——— 1971 And Then There Were None: The Diminution of the Federal Jury. *University of Chicago Law Review* 38: 710–724.

——— 1980 Reflections on Experimental Techniques in the Law. *Journal of Legal Studies* 2:107–124.

——— 1985 *Say It with Figures*, 6th ed. Chap. 14. New York: Harper & Row.

——— and DIAMOND, SHARI 1974 "Convincing Empirical Evidence" on the Six-Member Jury. *University of Chicago Law Review* 41:281–295.

SOCIAL SCIENCE RESEARCH AND CONSTITUTIONAL LAW

"Let us," ROSCOE POUND urged in 1910, "look the facts of human conduct in the face. Let us look to economics and sociology and philosophy, and cease to assume that jurisprudence is self-sufficient. It is the work of lawyers," he continued, "to make the law in action conform to the law in the books, not by futile thunderings against popular lawlessness, nor eloquent exhortations to obedience to the written law, but by making law in the books such that law in action can conform to it." Pound's exhortation is an early expression of the Legal Realist view of the role of social science in law, including constitutional law, a view that is still significant today.

LEGAL REALISM attacked the classical conception of law with its assumptions about the independent and objective movement from preexisting rights to decisions in specific cases. In so doing, Realists opened the way for a vision of law, including constitutional law, as policy informed by facts about the world. They saw the twentieth century as a period of knowledge explosion and in the emerging social sciences the triumph of rationality over tradition, inquiry over faith, and the human mind over its environment. By using the questions and methods of science to provide factual material and to assess the consequences of legal decisions, Realists such as KARL LLEWELLYN claimed that an understanding of what law could do would help in establishing what law should do. Legal Realism thus initiated a dialogue between law and social science by staking a claim for the importance of phenomenon beyond legal categories and by attacking what Realists saw as the self-centered arrogance of legal decision makers.

Yet the origins of SOCIAL SCIENCE IN CONSTITUTIONAL LITIGATION are often traced back, before the Realists, to the BRANDEIS BRIEF, submitted in 1907 as part of the litigation of MULLER V. OREGON (1908), a case involving the constitutionality of maximum-hours laws for women. LOUIS D. BRANDEIS provided factual evidence, culled from already existing materials, that women workers had special health needs such that legislating special protection might be deemed reasonable. Judged by today's standards his brief hardly qualifies as social science evidence. However, the Supreme Court's explicit citation of it suggested that there might be a receptive audience for systematic fact-gathering efforts in subsequent cases.

A close second to the Brandeis Brief as the best known example of the role of social science in constitutional law is the famous doll study by psychologist Kenneth Clark. Clark did an experiment with young black children in the South, giving them a drawing of two otherwise identical dolls, except that one of the dolls was white, the other black. The children were asked which dolls they would like to play with, which looked like themselves, and which were nice and which were bad. Most of the children liked the white doll best and called the black doll bad. This study, along with several others, was cited by the Court in BROWN V. BOARD OF EDUCATION (1954) in support of the proposition that " '[s]egregation of white and colored children in public schools has a detrimental effect upon colored children.' " The Court further observed that "whatever may have been the extent of psychological knowledge at the time of PLESSY V. FERGUSON [(1896), this finding is amply supported by modern authority."

Over the last several decades, research based on such techniques as experiments, public opinion surveys, and quantitative analysis of archival data has multiplied, such that today it is common to see citations to social science research decorating the footnotes of court opinions dealing with a wide variety of constitutional issues including those having to do with the FOURTEENTH AMENDMENT guarantee of EQUAL PROTECTION OF THE LAWS, *Morgan v. Kerrigan* (1976); the constitutionality of regulations of OBSCENITY, *Paris Adult Theatre I v. Slaton* (1973); whether the Sixth Amendment mandates JURY SIZE, *Williams v. Florida* (1970); and whether CAPITAL PUNISHMENT violates the Eighth Amendment prohibition of CRUEL AND UNUSUAL

PUNISHMENT, *Gregg v. Georgia* (1976). While the increasingly prevalent citation of social science seems to be fulfilling the Realist aspiration to tether law more completely to the world through the work of social scientists, social science seldom compels particular factual conclusions or legal results. At best, social science identifies contingencies, establishes probabilities, or points out tendencies.

Moreover, courts rarely commission their own research. The work presented to them is sometimes sponsored directly by parties to constitutional litigation and, where it is not directly sponsored, it is always mobilized in the service of advocacy. For nearly every social science study establishing some probability or tendency, there are others qualifying, disputing, or contradicting its conclusions. The persuasiveness of social science research ultimately depends on the persuasiveness of the narratives in which they are embedded and their reception in the prevailing political climate. As a result, courts can easily quarrel with or ignore research with which they disagree.

A particularly powerful demonstration of the ability of courts to sidestep the results of even the best social science research is provided by the case of MCCLESKEY V. KEMP (1987). There the Court was presented with the Baldus study, a scientifically rigorous analysis based on advanced multiple regression techniques showing that, in death penalty cases, the best predictor of whether a murderer would receive a death rather than a life sentence was the race of his victim. This research showed that when all other factors were taken into account, murderers of white victims were four times more likely to receive a death sentence than murderers of black victims. The plaintiff contended that this finding raised serious equal protection and Eighth Amendment issues.

The Baldus study, while carried out with the encouragement of the NAACP LEGAL DEFENSE AND EDUCATION FUND, was directly responsive to the concerns of Justices in earlier death penalty cases who complained, as Chief Justice WARREN BURGER did in *Furman v. Georgia* (1972), that there was "no empirical basis for concluding that juries have generally failed to discharge the responsibilities . . . of choosing between life and death in individual cases according to the dictates of community values." In addition, the study was designed to address critiques made by Justices of earlier studies of racial disparities in death penalty cases involving rape, critiques calling them "interesting and provocative" but insufficiently comprehensive to serve as proof of RACIAL DISCRIMINATION. Yet even after these efforts the Baldus research did not persuade the Court. The Court assumed the validity of the Baldus research; nonetheless, it found that the study did not show that racial considerations "actually" enter into any particular sentencing decisions and that "At most, the Baldus study indicates a discrepancy that appears to correlate with race. Apparent discrepancies in sentencing are an inevitable part of our criminal justice system."

Despite the Baldus study's fate, it marked the high point of one part of the Realist project of using social science to produce factual predicates for constitutional decisions. But there was, and remains, a second part of the Realist mandate for social science; namely, to measure or assess the impact of constitutional decisions once they are made in the hope of producing results that can be used to reassess or revise those decisions where necessary. Here social science identifies gaps, of the kind that Pound foresaw, between the law on the books and the law in action. There are now literally hundreds of social science studies that focus on Court decisions like *Brown* or MIRANDA V. ARIZONA (1966) and seek, in the words of Abraham Blumberg, "to ascertain the validity and viability of . . . (those) decisions which may rest on wholly erroneous assumptions about the contextual realities of social structure." Occasionally, though not very often, that work finds its way into cases in which courts are asked to expand, amend, revise, or reverse earlier decisions.

At the end of the twentieth century, the Realist vision of the roles of social science in constitutional law is as controversial as it has ever been. For some it continues to mark the path of an enlightened engagement between academic knowledge and legal policy. As Judge Richard Posner recently said, echoing the Legal Realist exhortation of more than a half-century ago, "I would like to see the legal professoriat redirect its research and teaching efforts toward fuller participation in the enterprise of social science, and by doing this make social science a better aid to judges' understanding of the social problems that get thrust at them in the form of constitutional issues." Others reject the hope of the Realists. They claim that it is wedded to an unduly positivist and narrow view of social science and that it limits social science to a politically reformist role. Additionally, what counts as social science knowledge is itself "up for grabs," with positivism under attack and with new epistemologies pressing themselves forward.

Many now seek a broader role for social knowledge. They believe that social research should be directed less toward charting the vicissitudes of particular constitutional decisions and more toward understanding the pervasive role of constitutional and other bodies of law in legitimating political power, maintaining social inequality, and constituting the taken-for-granted world. For them social science should do more than provide data for, or study the fate of, constitutional decisions by courts assumed to stand outside society. It should instead help us understand constitutional law not, as the Realists did, as something removed from social life, occasionally intervening to try to correct injustices, but as inseparable from and fused with all social relations and practices.

AUSTIN SARAT
(2000)

Bibliography

BALDUS, DAVID; WOODWORTH, GEORGE; and PULASKI, CHARLES 1989 Equal Justice and the Death Penalty: A Legal and Empirical Analysis. Boston, Mass.: Northeastern University Press.

BLUMBERG, ABRAHAM 1967 The Practice of Law as a Confidence Game. *Law and Society Review* 1:15–38.

CLARK, KENNETH and CLARK, MAMIE 1947 Racial Identification and Preference in Negro Children. Pages 169–178 in Theodore Newcomb and Eugene Hartley, eds., *Readings in Social Psychology.* New York: Henry Holt.

GORDON, ROBERT 1984 Critical Legal Histories. *Stanford Law Review* 36:57–126.

LLEWELLYN, KARL 1931 Some Realism About Realism. *Harvard Law Review* 44:1222–1264.

MONAHAN, JOHN and WALKER, LAURENS 1994 *Social Science in Law: Cases and Materials*, 3rd ed. Westbury, N.Y.: The Foundation Press.

POSNER, RICHARD 1998 Against Constitutional Theory. *New York University Law Review* 73:1–22.

POUND, ROSCOE 1910 Law In Books and Law In Action. *American Law Review* 44:12–38.

SARAT, AUSTIN 1990 Off to Meet the Wizard: Beyond Validity and Reliability in the Search for a Post-empiricist Sociology of Law. *Law and Social Inquiry* 15:155–170.

SARAT, AUSTIN and SILBEY, SUSAN 1988 The Pull of the Policy Audience. *Law and Policy* 10:98–166.

SARAT, AUSTIN and KEARNS, THOMAS R. 1993 Beyond the Great Divide: Forms of Legal Scholarship and Everyday Life. Pages 21–62 in Austin Sarat and Thomas R. Kearns, eds., *Law in Everyday Life.* Ann Arbor: University of Michigan Press.

SCHLEGEL, JOHN 1980 American Legal Realism and Empirical Social Science–II. *Buffalo Law Review* 29:195–323.

SOCIAL SECURITY ACT
49 Stat. 620 (1935)

The Social Security Act of 1935, as subsequently amended, is the primary source of federal and federal-state cooperative social welfare programs. In addition to the program popularly denominated "social security," which now includes old age, survivors, and disability insurance, and the fiscally related medical assistance program for the aged (Medicare), the current Social Security Act also provides grants to states for many federally regulated programs, such as unemployment compensation, services to poor families with children (Aid to Families with Dependent Children), services to the aged, blind, and disabled (Supplementary Security Income), health care for the poor (Medicaid), and maternal and child welfare services.

The act has been a fertile source of constitutional litigation. The cooperative federal-state unemployment compensation scheme was narrowly sustained as a legitimate congressional exercise of the power "to lay and collect taxes . . . to . . . provide . . . for the GENERAL WELFARE of the United States" in STEWARD MACHINE CO. V. DAVIS (1937). In a companion case, HELVERING V. DAVIS (1937), seven Justices agreed that the federal social security old age retirement benefits program was well within the purview of Congress's TAXING AND SPENDING POWER.

The act has generated a number of important PROCEDURAL DUE PROCESS cases. GOLDBERG V. KELLY (1970) held that due process requires an evidentiary hearing *prior* to the termination of WELFARE BENEFITS. Justice WILLIAM J. BRENNAN, writing for a majority of six, reasoned that a subsequent hearing would be inadequate to protect the interests of the eligible recipient deprived of basic subsistence while she awaited her opportunity to challenge termination of benefits. *Goldberg v. Kelly* was narrowly construed in MATHEWS V. ELDRIDGE (1976), which held that due process does not require a prior evidentiary hearing when social security disability benefits are terminated after a Social Security Administration determination that the worker is no longer disabled. The Court distinguished *Goldberg* on two grounds: *Goldberg* involved public assistance for the INDIGENT while social security disability benefits are not based on financial need; and the opportunity for a prior hearing is less valuable to the recipient when the administrative conclusion is based on expert medical testimony, as in a disability termination case, rather than on a wide variety of facts and witness credibility, as in a public assistance case.

The social security program embodied a number of gender-based assumptions about economic dependence that were challenged as violative of the EQUAL PROTECTION guarantee in *Weinberger v. Wiesenfeld* (1975) and CALIFANO V. GOLDFARB (1977). In *Wiesenfeld,* the Court required that "mother's benefits," payable to an insured worker's widow who cares for the worker's child, be extended equally to similarly situated widowers. In *Goldfarb,* the Court held invalid a requirement that widowers but not widows prove actual dependency on the deceased insured worker.

In another group of cases prospective social welfare beneficiaries have constitutionally challenged the substantive conditions of individual grants. In *Flemming v. Nestor* (1960), *Weinberger v. Salfi* (1975), and *Mathews v. DeCastro* (1976), the Supreme Court rejected such challenges.

GRACE GANZ BLUMBERG
(1986)

Bibliography

ALTMEYER, ARTHUR 1968 *The Formative Years of Social Security.* Madison: University of Wisconsin Press.
DEPARTMENT OF HEALTH, EDUCATION AND WELFARE 1960 *Basic Readings in Social Security: The 25th Anniversary of the Social Security Act.* Washington, D.C.: Government Printing Office.
WITTE, EDWIN 1962 *The Development of the Social Security Act.* Madison: University of Wisconsin Press.

SOCIOLOGICAL JURISPRUDENCE

Sociological JURISPRUDENCE is one of the most important schools of legal thought in the twentieth century. Its major proponent in the United States was ROSCOE POUND (1870–1964), a prolific writer who was dean of the Harvard Law School from 1916 to 1936. A number of other legal educators and judges also contributed in varying degrees to the theory or practice of sociological jurisprudence. They included five former members of the Supreme Court—OLIVER WENDELL HOLMES, LOUIS D. BRANDEIS, Harlan Fiske Stone, BENJAMIN N. CARDOZO, and FELIX FRANKFURTER. Even though the doctrines of these jurists were anything but uniform, they shared a number of important attitudes and ideas.

The movement for a sociological jurisprudence emerged during the Progressive era. Pound interpreted it as the "movement for pragmatism as a philosophy of law," the purpose of which was to facilitate legal reform and social progress. Although legal change should take place under the leadership of lawyers, the agenda of sociological jurisprudence did not focus on changes in legal institutions. Rather, it stressed reform of prevailing conceptions of the study, interpretation, and application of law.

This emphasis reflected a particular diagnosis of the ills of the American legal system at the outset of the twentieth century. These problems included judicial hostility to laws designed to protect workers, which courts often construed narrowly or held unconstitutional. Decisions of the Supreme Court applying the doctrine of SUBSTANTIVE DUE PROCESS are a classic example of the tendency. The advocates of sociological jurisprudence assailed this judicial response to social legislation, which they attributed to several factors. One was the isolation of the study of law from the social sciences. This condition allegedly fostered an ignorance of social realities and needs that contributed to unjust decisions. "Unless we know the facts on which legislators may have acted," Justice Brandeis pointed out in BURNS BAKING CO. V. BRYAN (1924), "we cannot properly decide whether they were . . . unreasonable, arbitrary, or capricious. Knowledge is essential to understanding; and understanding should precede judging."

Pound maintained that another factor contributing to

judicial decisions that obstructed social progress was ME-CHANICAL JURISPRUDENCE, or the rigid deduction of decisions from established principles without regard to their practical effects. He argued that this kind of syllogistic reasoning not only obscured judges' wide range of choice in selecting premises but also contributed to their intolerance of laws limiting FREEDOM OF CONTRACT. The very different attitude of Justice Holmes was one reason why advocates of sociological jurisprudence held him in such high esteem.

These criticisms were the basis of the characteristic reform objectives of sociological jurisprudence. A fundamental goal was the development of a better factual understanding of the practical effects of legal precepts and institutions. Cardozo proposed a Ministry of Justice which would study and observe the "law in action." In "The Living Law" Brandeis recommended "broader education . . . continued by lawyer and judge throughout life: study of economics and sociology and politics which embody the facts and present the problems of today." This idea strongly conditioned the unorthodox BRANDEIS BRIEF in MULLER V. OREGON (1908), an approach that Brandeis and other lawyers such as Felix Frankfurter used in a number of subsequent cases. Only two of the 113 pages of this brief presented the traditional kind of legal argument, while the rest consisted largely of factual evidence of the bad effects on women of excessive hours of work. Brandeis argued that these data showed that the Oregon law, which limited women's working hours to ten per day, was a reasonable limitation of freedom of contract. His argument favorably impressed the Justices, who unanimously upheld the law.

The prescription for abandoning "mechanical jurisprudence" was a more pragmatic approach to judicial decision making. No one expressed this idea better than Cardozo, who insisted that law is a means to the end of "social welfare" or "social justice." He argued that judges should interpret general constitutional limitations to serve this end. The changing meaning of the word "liberty" in the due process clauses of the Fifth and FOURTEENTH AMENDMENTS is an example. (See INCORPORATION DOCTRINE.) Similar beliefs conditioned Frankfurter's suggestion that constitutional law "in its relation to social legislation, is . . . but applied politics, using the word in its noble sense."

These ideas reflected a justifiable dissatisfaction with the content of American constitutional law earlier in this century. The adequacy of the sociological jurists' diagnosis of and reforms for these evils is another matter. To begin with, they tended to exaggerate the causal significance of "mechanical jurisprudence" and judicial ignorance of social needs. Neither of these factors ordinarily influence the actual decisions of the Justices or their choice of premises as much as their policy preferences or attitudes. Furthermore, conservative Justices might (and did) use Cardozo's

"method of sociology" for their own purposes. "Social welfare" and "social justice" are subject, after all, to a multitude of interpretations. In some cases a majority of the Justices invalidated laws defended by a "Brandeis brief." The extent to which that technique influenced them to uphold other laws is uncertain, but its impact may have been corroborative rather than decisive. The use of social science evidence in BROWN V. BOARD OF EDUCATION (1954) illustrates this tendency. Finally, social scientists often disagree about the interpretation of the facts or their implications for public policy.

To say this is not to imply that the value of sociological jurisprudence was negligible. Its greatest contribution to constitutional law was that it served as a positive force for upholding social legislation. If its efficacy in this regard was limited, at least it provided support for judges inclined to hold such legislation constitutional. Moreover, knowledge of the actual effects of legal precepts and institutions is essential for informed evaluations of them. The call of sociological jurisprudence for studies of these effects was, thus, a step in the right direction.

WILFRID E. RUMBLE
(1986)

Bibliography

BRANDEIS, LOUIS D.   1916   The Living Law. Address before the Chicago Bar Association, January 3, 1916.
CAHILL, FRED V.   1952   *Judicial Legislation.* New York: Ronald Press.
ROSEN, PAUL L.   1972   *The Supreme Court and Social Science.* Urbana: University of Illinois Press.
RUMBLE, WILFRID E.   1968   *American Legal Realism.* Ithaca, N.Y.: Cornell University Press.
WHITE, G. EDWARD   1978   *Patterns of American Legal Thought.* Indianapolis: Bobbs-Merrill.

SODOMY

See: *Bowers v. Hardwick*; Sexual Orientation; Sexual Preference and the Constitution

SOLEM v. HELM
463 U.S. 277 (1983)

Expanding the coverage of the Eighth Amendment's CRUEL AND UNUSUAL PUNISHMENT clause, the Supreme Court held that in addition to barbaric sentences it prohibits criminal sentences that are disproportionate to the crime for which a defendant is convicted. Jerry Helm, a habitual offender, passed a bad check and received the most severe punishment—life imprisonment without possibility of parole—that South Dakota could impose for any crime. A 5–4 Court decided that because Helm's six prior FELONY convictions were for relatively minor nonviolent crimes against property and because he was treated more severely than other criminals who had committed more serious crimes, his sentence was significantly disproportionate to his crime. The dissenting Justices saw "judicial usurpation" of state sentencing discretion, especially in cases of incorrigible recidivists.

LEONARD W. LEVY
(1986)

SOLICITOR GENERAL

The solicitor general is a senior officer of the United States Department of Justice with special responsibilities in the representation of the United States and its officers and agencies before the Supreme Court, and in the administration of justice in the federal appellate courts.

The title—solicitor general—like that of ATTORNEY GENERAL is derived from English usage, but the functions of the offices are quite different in the United States. In England, both offices are political in the sense that they are filled by members of Parliament. In the United States, neither the attorney general nor the solicitor general is a member of Congress. The attorney general is a member of the Cabinet. He advises the President, works with members of Congress on legislative matters and judicial appointments, holds press conferences and is otherwise responsible for governmental and public relations. He is also charged with administering a large department which includes the FEDERAL BUREAU OF INVESTIGATION, the Bureau of Prisons, the Immigration and Naturalization Service, and other important agencies. Though he has policy and administrative responsibilities of great importance, he has virtually no time to be a lawyer in the traditional sense.

Until 1870, the attorney general functioned alone with only a small staff, and in association with the United States attorneys in the various states, over whom he had little authority. In 1870, apparently as an economy device (to eliminate the cost of retaining private lawyers in the increasing number of cases), Congress established the Department of Justice, with the attorney general as its head. The statute provided that there should be in the Department "an officer learned in the law, to assist the Attorney-General in the performance of his duties, to be called the solicitor-general." Under the statute the solicitor general was authorized in the attorney general's discretion to argue "any case in which the government is interested" before the Supreme Court, or in any federal or state court." These statutory provisions remain to the present day, essentially unchanged.

In the years since 1870, the duties of the Department of Justice have greatly increased. Until 1953 the solicitor general was the second officer in the Department of Justice and served as acting attorney general in the attorney general's absence. The responsibilities of the attorney general have made it necessary to add a deputy attorney general and an associate attorney general, so that the solicitor general is now the fourth ranking officer in the department. But the solicitor general's responsibilities have remained essentially unchanged in substance—though greatly increased in volume—over the past sixty years. He remains the leading officer in the department functioning primarily as a lawyer.

As the pattern has developed, the solicitor general is not a politician, and he has only a minimum of political responsibility. His function is to be the government's top lawyer in the courts, particularly the Supreme Court, and by well-established tradition he is allowed considerable independence in carrying out this role. Bent and Schloss, describing the office as "the bridge between the Executive and the Judiciary," have said that "[t]he Solicitor General must often choose between incongruous roles and differing loyalties. He is still the government's lawyer, and he most frequently acts as an advocate. On the other hand, he also functions as a reviewer of government policies, an officer of the Court, and . . . a protector of the public interest."

In more specific terms, the organization of the Department of Justice assigns to the solicitor general four areas of responsibility. Two of these are of primary importance. First, the solicitor general is responsible for the representation of the United States and its officers and agencies in all cases before the Supreme Court of the United States. The BRIEFS which are filed on behalf of the government in the Supreme Court are prepared by him or under his direction. He argues the most important cases himself, and assigns the argument in other cases to members of his staff, to other lawyers in the Department of Justice or to lawyers for the agencies which may be involved in the cases before the Court. Second, the Solicitor General decides whether the United States will APPEAL in any case which it loses in any court, state or federal, or indeed in foreign courts. This function is not widely known, even in the legal profession. It is, however, a very important means of coordinating and controlling the government's litigation, so that cases of little importance are not taken to the appellate courts. It also serves to minimize the taking of inconsistent positions before the various appellate courts.

This function includes determining whether any case will be taken by the government to the Supreme Court. This is probably the most important responsibility assigned to the solicitor general. With few exceptions, no case can now be taken to the Supreme Court except on application for review—called a petition for a WRIT OF CER-TIORARI. In recent years, some four thousand such applications are made to the Court by all parties each year. Yet the Court can hear on the merits only about a hundred and fifty cases a year. This means that it is of great importance for the solicitor general to select with care the relatively small number of cases in which the government will file petitions. A high proportion of the solicitor general's petitions are in fact granted by the Court, which means that he has, as part of his responsibility, carried out an important part of the selection process necessarily confronting the Court.

In addition to the two functions just outlined, the solicitor general has two other responsibilities. These assist him in carrying out his role as overall controller of Government APPELLATE JURISDICTION. First his authorization must be obtained before the United States or one of its officers or agencies files a brief as friend of the court—AMICUS CURIAE—in any appellate court. Second his authorization must be obtained before a petition for REHEARING *en banc*—before the whole court—is filed in any UNITED STATES COURT OF APPEALS. The courts of appeals are overburdened, and hearings EN BANC present serious logistical problems. Requiring authority from the solicitor general means that such petitions are rarely filed, and only in the most important cases.

The solicitor general's office is a relatively small one, though it has grown slowly in recent years. At the present time it numbers about twenty lawyers in addition to the solicitor general himself; and, including secretaries and aides, the total number of personnel in the office is about fifty. Thus it can operate in much the same way as a moderate-sized law firm. There is considerable pressure in the office as the cases keep coming in, from all parts of the country, and almost all of them are subject to relatively short deadlines.

In the nature of things, the solicitor general cannot be a specialist. The cases coming to his desk involve every field of law—constitutional law, ADMINISTRATIVE LAW, criminal law, tax law, antitrust law, labor law, international law, ENVIRONMENTAL PROTECTION, energy, and every other field with which the government is concerned. Inevitably, the staff in the office specialize to some extent, and there are four deputy solicitors general, each of whom has special responsibilities for particular areas. But there are no rigid lines, and all lawyers in the office are available to handle the various types of cases as they come in.

The solicitor general's role in the Supreme Court is limited to the representation of the United States, its officers, and its agencies. Other cases which may be of great importance involve private parties, or states or their subsidiaries. Thus, the cases involving BIRTH CONTROL (GRISWOLD V. CONNECTICUT, 1965) and abortion (ROE V. WADE, 1973)

were not handled by the solicitor general. But more than half of the cases before the Supreme Court (particularly those heard by the Court on the merits) are "government cases," that is, cases in which the United States, or its officers or agents, are parties. It is important to the Court to have these cases handled in competent fashion, and the research and ideas, and policy decisions, lying behind the solicitor general's advocacy before the Supreme Court can influence the decisions reached by the Court.

Much of the government's litigation before the Supreme Court, though important, does not attract wide public attention. From time to time, though, cases coming before the Court are rather spectacular in terms of public interest. Reference may be made, for example, to YOUNGSTOWN SHEET & TUBE CO. V. SAWYER (1952), where the Court invalidated the action of President HARRY S. TRUMAN in seizing the steel industry during the KOREAN WAR, the Pentagon Papers case (NEW YORK TIMES CO. V. UNITED STATES, 1971), and UNITED STATES V. NIXON (1974), where the Court held that the White House tapes made under the direction of President RICHARD M. NIXON must be turned over in response to a SUBPOENA from a GRAND JURY. For the most part, though, the work of the solicitor general and his staff is rather straightforward professional work.

It is important to recognize that in all cases the solicitor general is an advocate and not a judge. However, he is a very special sort of advocate. There are some positions which he will not support because he thinks the government's position is clearly wrong in law. On rare occasions, in such cases, he "confesses error" before the Court. The Court is not bound by such a confession, but it usually accepts the solicitor general's conclusion. There are other cases where the solicitor general will not himself defend the government's position, but he thinks a "respectable" defense can be made, and he assigns another government lawyer who is willing to do so to present that defense. Illustration of this may be found in *Peters v. Hobby* (1955), involving the LOYALTY-SECURITY PROGRAM during the 1950s, and in *Gutknecht v. United States* (1970), involving "delinquency reclassification" under the SELECTIVE SERVICE ACT. But the solicitor general will frequently advocate a position which he believes to be worthy of presentation to the Court even though he might not decide in favor of that position if he were a judge. Laymen sometimes have difficulty in accepting this, but, within limits, it is inherent in the role of a lawyer, and it is inherent in the position of the solicitor general. For he is the government's chief advocate. The function of deciding cases is assigned to others.

In this situation, the solicitor general's role is sometimes a difficult one. Whenever he decides not to take a case before the Supreme Court, he is in effect depriving the Court of the opportunity to decide it. This is, indeed, an important part of his function, in view of the fact that many more applications come to the Court than it can possibly accept. The solicitor general's judgment that the chances of success in a particular case are slim is obviously a relevant consideration. Yet there are cases of such importance that he should take the case to the Court, in order to obtain a definitive decision, even though he has little faith in the government's position.

An illustration is found in *United States v. United States District Court* (1972). This involved the validity of so-called national security WIRETAPS, made on executive authority (the President or the attorney general) alone, without a judicial warrant. As the cases before the Supreme Court developed, it seemed unlikely that the Court would uphold such wiretaps, at least in cases of domestic security. Yet the attorney general needed to know. If he had such authority, cases might develop where he would need to use it. If he did not have the authority, he should have the definitive decision of the Supreme Court, by which he would, of course, abide. A petition was filed with the Court in order that the question might be definitively settled, and the Court granted the petition. In due course, the Court held that domestic "national security" wiretaps are illegal under the FOURTH AMENDMENT, when made without a court warrant. Thus the solicitor general, though himself dubious about the government's case, played his appropriate role in obtaining a definitive decision on an important public question.

In the daily routine of his office the solicitor general has many decisions to make. In making these decisions, he may be subject to various pressures. These pressures may be wholly legitimate professional pressures from other lawyers in the government seeking to persuade him to accept their view. He frequently gives hearings, too, to opposing lawyers. There may also be various forms of political pressure—rarely presented as such—from Capitol Hill, or from other officers of the government. The solicitor general should be able to receive such representations and come to his own conclusions. Attorneys general have usually been firm in their support of the solicitor general. And, indeed, the fact that the decision is assigned to the solicitor general may serve to protect the attorney general from such pressures. But the attorney general and the President are the solicitor general's superiors, and if he receives an order from above he must decide whether the matter is one of principle for him; if it is, he must resign. As far as is known, no solicitor general has ever resigned for such a reason. But this is what happened to Attorney General Elliott Richardson and Deputy Attorney General William Ruckelshaus, when they refused to comply with President Nixon's order to discharge Archibald Cox as Special Prosecutor in 1973.

Special problems arise when officers or agencies differ from the position of the solicitor general, and especially when two or more agencies have different interests or points of view which they present vigorously to the solicitor general or his staff. A situation of this sort arose in the case of *Fortnightly Corp. v. United Artists Television, Inc.* (1968), involving cable television. The Copyright Office in the Library of Congress had one view about the case. The Federal Communications Commission had another. And the Antitrust Division in the Department of Justice had still a third. All views were strongly advocated. The solicitor general negotiated separately with the lawyers for each office concerned. None would yield. Then he held a meeting at which all interested lawyers were present, hoping that some sort of a consensus would emerge. Unfortunately, none did, and the solicitor general concluded that he had no alternative but to formulate his own view, which he submitted to the Court.

This case exemplifies one of the important roles of the solicitor general, in resolving differences within the government, so that a single position may be presented to the Court. When these differences arise within the Justice Department, or between the several executive departments, the solicitor general seeks to persuade but eventually may have to make his own decision. The situation is somewhat more difficult when the difference is with one of the "independent agencies," such as the Federal Trade Commission or the Securities and Exchange Commission.

For historical reasons, it has long been settled that the Interstate Commerce Commission and the Maritime Commission can appear before the Supreme Court through their own lawyers. With respect to the other agencies, however, the statutory provisions are not explicit. Though there is occasionally some tension, the solicitor general has been able to maintain effective control over agency cases in the Supreme Court. In this process, various devices are used. He sometimes advises the Court that the agency has a different view. He sometimes authorizes the agency to file a brief stating its view. By and large, the agencies believe that the solicitor general's support is important and helpful, and this belief is reinforced by the standing of the solicitor general before the Court. Cases of this sort are carefully considered in the solicitor general's office, and full hearings are given to the lawyers from the agencies involved. In this way problems of real difficulty have been resolved with substantial satisfaction on the part of all concerned.

There is a final role of the solicitor general which, though long an important one, has been of increasing significance in recent years. This is the preparation and filing of briefs in the Supreme Court as a friend of the Court— amicus curiae. Under the Rules of the Supreme Court, the solicitor general is authorized to file such a brief without consent of the parties or special leave of the Court.

Frequently a case between private parties, or a state criminal prosecution, may raise a question of great interest to the federal government, though the latter is not a party. An example is TERRY V. OHIO (1968), involving the validity of a STOP AND FRISK by local police. The solicitor general filed an amicus brief in that case because of the great interest of the federal government in law enforcement. Through such briefs, the solicitor general protects the interests of the federal government, aids the Court by furnishing information and relevant legal materials, facilitates the handling of difficult questions with the "independent agencies" of the government, and, on occasion, presents his own views on novel constitutional questions.

In this way, the solicitor general has participated in cases involving SCHOOL DESEGREGATION, legislative CIVIL RIGHTS, and many other important questions of developing constitutional and statutory law. Within wide limits, the solicitor general has freedom to develop his own position in such briefs. The solicitor general and his staff have great experience in Supreme Court cases, and well-considered and carefully prepared briefs can be of considerable assistance to the Court through impartial and informed analysis of novel questions.

Indeed, a high proportion of briefs amicus filed by the solicitor general are prepared because of direct invitation from the Court. Such invitations are always treated as commands, and great care is taken in determining the position to be taken and in developing the materials to be included in the brief. In many ways, such briefs are the purest expression of the relation of trust and confidence which has long been established between the solicitor general and the Court.

It is this trust and confidence on which the position of the solicitor general before the Court, and his effective representation of the United States, in the long run depend.

ERWIN N. GRISWOLD
(1986)

Bibliography

NOTE 1969 Government Litigation in the Supreme Court. *Yale Law Journal* 78:1442–1481.

SOLICITOR GENERAL
(Update)

The solicitor general is the chief advocate in the Supreme Court for the United States government, its officers, and its agencies, but he is also known as the Tenth Justice. By tradition rather than constitutional mandate, the solicitor has a "dual responsibility" to the judicial and the executive branches, as Justice LEWIS F. POWELL observed. For gen-

erations (the solicitor's post was established in 1870), Supreme Court Justices have counted on the solicitor to look beyond the government's narrow interests and help guide them to the "right" result in the case at hand; they also expect him to pay close attention to the case's impact on the law. The solicitor's reach extends to the lower federal courts, as well: although the executive branch is usually represented there by other lawyers from the Justice Department, the solicitor approves all appeals taken by the government. After the Supreme Court issued its landmark ONE PERSON, ONE VOTE ruling in BAKER V. CARR (1962), which Chief Justice EARL WARREN called the most important decision of his tenure, an AMICUS CURIAE brief filed by Solicitor General Archibald Cox was credited with having persuaded at least two members of the Court's majority to treat REAPPORTIONMENT of electoral districts as a justiciable issue. Without those votes, the Court would have reaffirmed a lower court decision to leave the issue to the legislature as a POLITICAL QUESTION.

The Court's explicit reliance on the solicitor in its interpretation of the Constitution and development of a new legal doctrine in the *Baker* case fits larger patterns. The solicitor general plays a major role in determining which cases the government will contest in the Supreme Court. As a result of this screening, in recent years the Supreme Court has granted approximately eighty percent of the petitions for a writ of CERTIORARI submitted by the solicitor, as opposed to only three percent of those submitted by other lawyers across the country. Furthermore, the solicitor has won approximately eighty percent of his cases. In cases dealing with the Constitution in particular, the Court has shown special interest in the views of the SG, as he is informally called. The Justices have regularly invited him to file amicus briefs even in cases to which the United States is not a party.

In 1977 an executive-branch controversy about the solicitor general's amicus filings led to the first official statement about the solicitor's role in the century-old history of the office. Offering then-conventional wisdom among constitutional lawyers, a Justice Department memorandum stated that the solicitor general should be relatively "independent" within the department and the executive branch. The memorandum gave four reasons for this view: "The Solicitor General must coordinate conflicting views within the Executive Branch; he must protect the Court by presenting meritorious claims in a straightforward and professional manner and by screening out unmeritorious ones; he must assist in the orderly development of decisional law; and he must 'do justice'—that is, he must discharge his office in accordance with law and ensure that improper concerns do not influence the presentation of the Government's case in the Supreme Court."

The transformation of the Supreme Court's docket during the years of both the WARREN COURT and the BURGER COURT led to a serious reconsideration of the solicitor general's role, however, and to a basic disagreement about the propriety of such "independence." The discussion was prompted by actions within, affecting, and officially taken by the solicitor's office during the administration of RONALD REAGAN, as the administration sought to enact a vision of the Constitution largely at odds with views that had evolved in the legal mainstream since midcentury. Within the solicitor's office, for the first time, a deputy was hired to ensure that the government's filings conformed to the ideological views of the administration. The administration tolerated scant dissent from those views, and during a period of turmoil, it drove away a notable share of the office's nonpartisan career lawyers: the office suffered a fifty percent turnover in one year, or twice the normal rate. The first Reagan solicitor general, REX E. LEE, a conservative whose advocacy was not aggressive enough to satisfy more influential administration officials, was forced out with this group. After leaving office, he said, "There has been this notion that my job is to press the Administration's policies at every turn and announce true conservative principles through the pages of my briefs. It is not. I'm the Solicitor General, not the Pamphleteer General."

In the Justice Department, in key cases like THORNBURGH V. AMERICAN COLLEGE OF OBSTETRICIANS AND GYNECOLOGISTS (1986), dealing with the right to ABORTION, the solicitor general played only an academic role in determining whether the government would file a brief; the decision was essentially made by other officials in the department and the White House. Monitored by a Justice Department official who amounted to a "shadow solicitor" (William Bradford Reynolds, the assistant attorney general for civil rights as well as counselor to Attorney General Edwin Meese), the SG was changed from the legal conscience of the government into a partisan spokesman for the President.

At the height of this period, during the 1985 term of the Supreme Court, the solicitor general's advocacy drew explicit criticism in opinions written by Justices from across the legal spectrum on the moderately conservative Burger Court. In at least a dozen and a half cases, the Supreme Court cited instances of overstatements or inaccurate representations in SG briefs about legislative history, court holdings, and other basic tools of legal reasoning. In a televised interview not long after, Justice THURGOOD MARSHALL commented, "They can't separate the political from the legal. They write political speeches and put the word 'brief' on them." He added, "The solicitor general is the government's spokesman in this Court. It's always been true until the past decade or so. Now it seems as though he speaks only for the President, and not for the rest of the government."

The Reagan administration's explanation of these shifts was that its approach to the solicitor general's role and his aggressive conservative advocacy were required in order to persuade the Court to overturn a range of flawed liberal precedents. Eventually it seemed that forces at large in the rest of the legal culture, which were later especially apparent on the REHNQUIST COURT at the close of the divisive 1988 term, had also affected the solicitor's approach.

In particular, a breakdown in consensus about constitutional law, represented by the high percentage of Supreme Court cases decided by a bare one-vote majority (in the 1988 term, twenty-four percent of the total cases decided), seemed to some to challenge the notion that any expert could have a "clear vision of what the law requires," as the 1977 Justice Department memorandum claimed for the solicitor. This breakdown seemed to reemphasize the solicitor's primary duty of advocacy for the executive branch and of carrying to the Court the positions of the administration he serves.

To observers of the solicitor general's office who hold to the belief that the law can have a reassuring sense of continuity despite its contradictions, a measure of stability that contributes to social order, and an integrity provided by, among other things, the careful practice of legal reasoning, a significant way to work toward maintaining those qualities is by preserving an appropriate measure of independence for the solicitor general. Such independence represents an expression of faith in the idealized political neutrality of his office.

Still, as controversy about the nature of law has played out most dramatically in disagreements over how to interpret the Constitution, even to scholars the solicitor general's role has recently become heavily layered with political choices.

LINCOLN CAPLAN
(1992)

(SEE ALSO: *Attorney General and Department of Justice.*)

Bibliography

CAPLAN, LINCOLN 1988 *The Tenth Justice: The Solicitor General and the Rule of Law.* New York: Vintage Books.
SYMPOSIUM 1988 The Role and Function of the United States Solicitor General. *Loyola Law Review* 21:1047–1271.

SOMERSET'S CASE
98 Eng. Rep. 499 (K.B., 1772)

The case of *Somerset v. Stewart*, decided by King's Bench (the highest COMMON LAW court in England) in 1772, profoundly affected the constitutional status of slavery in England and in the United States after independence (because the precedent had become part of American common law). In a brief opinion, Lord Mansfield, Chief Justice, held that slavery "must be recognized by the law of the country where it is used." He further declared that "the state of slavery is of such a nature, that it is incapable of being introduced on any reasons, moral or political; but only [by] positive law." *Somerset's Case* did not abolish slavery in England or America, but until the 1850s it was interpreted to mean that slavery did not exist where it was not established by positive law (which, according to Chief Justice JOHN MARSHALL in *The Antelope* [1825], might include custom as well as statutory law). Abolitionists construed Mansfield's words to mean either that slavery was universally illegitimate or that it had a legal existence only where affirmatively established by a slave code. They denied that the federal government had power to establish slavery in any territory or district, or to protect it anywhere. (See ABOLITIONIST CONSTITUTIONAL THEORY.) This argument became the basis of the Republican "Freedom national, slavery local" slogan of the 1850s and was reflected in STEPHEN A. DOUGLAS'S FREEPORT DOCTRINE of 1858. *Somerset's Case* also complicated interstate relations in the matter of fugitive and sojourning slaves; some free states in the 1850s refused to recognize the continuation of an individual's slave status in a free JURISDICTION. (See FUGITIVE SLAVERY.) Southern jurists responded by repudiating the liberating potential of the *Somerset* doctrine after 1851, dismissing Mansfield's words as OBITER DICTA or error.

WILLIAM M. WIECEK
(1986)

SONZINSKY v. UNITED STATES
300 U.S. 506 (1937)

The unanimous OPINION in this case indicated that the spirit animating the DECISION in BAILEY V. DREXEL FURNITURE CO. (1922) was dead: the Supreme Court would no longer inquire into Congress's motives in enacting a tax measure. The National Firearms Act of 1934 imposed an annual EXCISE TAX on manufacturers and dealers of firearms, excepting handguns. The Court refused to consider that the tax was not imposed to raise a revenue and was a penalty to suppress traffic in a commodity normally subject only to state regulation. Compulsory registration provisions of such statutes, however, were later held unconstitutional in MARCHETTI V. UNITED STATES (1968).

LEONARD W. LEVY
(1986)

SOSNA v. IOWA
419 U.S. 393 (1975)

Iowa limited access to its DIVORCE court to persons who had resided in the state for one year. Sosna, denied a divorce under this law, brought suit in a federal court challenging the one-year limitation's constitutionality. By the time her case reached the Supreme Court, the year had passed. Because the case had been properly certified as a CLASS ACTION, however, the Court rejected the state's invitation to dismiss the action for MOOTNESS. On the merits, a six-Justice majority, speaking through Justice WILLIAM H. REHNQUIST, upheld the statute.

Justice Rehnquist breathed no word concerning "penalties" on the exercise of the RIGHT TO TRAVEL interstate. Instead, he merely noted that previous decisions had struck down durational RESIDENCE REQUIREMENTS only when they were justified entirely on the basis of budgetary or record-keeping considerations. Here, he said, the state had an interest in protecting the rights of defendant spouses and of any minor children. Further, the state might wish to avoid "officious intermeddling" in another state's primary concerns and to protect its own divorce decrees against COLLATERAL ATTACK. "A state such as Iowa may quite reasonably decide that it does not wish to become a divorce mill." In any event, an Iowa plaintiff was merely delayed in getting a divorce, not denied one altogether.

Justice BYRON R. WHITE dissented, arguing that the case was moot. Justice THURGOOD MARSHALL dissented on the merits, joined by Justice WILLIAM J. BRENNAN. The Court's analysis did not subject this penalty on exercise of the right to travel to the STRICT SCRUTINY it deserved but improperly employed a functional equivalent of the RATIONAL BASIS standard of review. Iowa's most important interest, protecting the integrity of its decrees, could be achieved by the less restrictive means of merely requiring a divorce plaintiff to be domiciled in the state. And the delay-denial distinction was false; a plaintiff would be denied marital freedom (and the freedom to remarry) during an entire year.

KENNETH L. KARST
(1986)

SOUNDTRUCKS AND AMPLIFIERS

When the Framers of the FIRST AMENDMENT wrote a ban on laws "abridging" FREEDOM OF SPEECH into the Constitution, the range of the human voice was relatively limited. The invention of electronic sound amplification equipment in the twentieth century potentially extended that range even into distant buildings and behind locked doors. Loudspeakers and bullhorns, whether stationary or mobile, present a particular problem of speech regulation: to what extent does the right to speak override the expectation of peace and privacy enjoyed by members of the public? Especially troubling are soundtrucks, amplifier-equipped motor vehicles that blare political slogans or advertising messages while roving the streets of residential neighborhoods.

The problem of soundtrucks and amplifiers was addressed by the Supreme Court in two famous cases. In *Saia v. New York* (1948) a 5–4 Court struck down a city ordinance requiring permission of the chief of police before a soundtruck could be used within the city limits. The ordinance provided no standard for the police chief to apply in granting or withholding permission. Eight months later, in KOVACS V. COOPER (1949), a five-Justice majority (including the *Saia* dissenters) upheld an ordinance prohibiting the operation within a city of soundtrucks that emitted "loud or raucous noises." The plurality thought the "loud and raucous" test an adequate standard of regulation, while two concurring Justices understood the ordinance as a ban on all soundtrucks.

The danger of public regulation of amplified speech is that restrictions ostensibly directed to the time, place, and manner of speaking will be used as a pretext for controlling the content of speech. But, as technology makes the outside world ever more intrusive into the realm of individual privacy, the right of the people to provide themselves freedom from loud and raucous utterance, whatever its content, can only become more valuable.

DENNIS J. MAHONEY
(1986)

SOUTER, DAVID H.
(1939–   )

David Hackett Souter, who became Associate Justice of the Supreme Court of the United States in 1990, was born on September 17, 1939, in Melrose, Massachusetts. He was graduated from Harvard College in 1961 and was awarded a Rhodes Scholarship. From 1961 to 1963 he studied at Oxford University. He then returned to Harvard for his legal education and graduated from Harvard Law School in 1966.

Following law school, Justice Souter practiced law at a private firm in Concord, New Hampshire, for two years. This is the only time that Justice Souter spent in the private sector. In 1968, he accepted a position as assistant attorney general for the State of New Hampshire. During the next ten years he rose to the top of the state attorney general's office, becoming deputy attorney general in 1971 and attorney general in 1976.

In 1978, Justice Souter was appointed to the Superior Court of New Hampshire. Five years later, he was elevated to the New Hampshire Supreme Court, where he served until 1990. In early 1990 he was appointed by president GEORGE BUSH to the United States Court of Appeals for the First Circuit. He served on that court for only five months, participating in only one week of oral arguments and writing no opinions.

On July 20, 1990, Justice WILLIAM J. BRENNAN, JR., resigned from the Supreme Court of the United States after thirty-four years of service. Five days later, President Bush nominated Justice Souter to be Associate Justice of the Supreme Court. Justice Souter's nomination was perceived by both supporters and opponents to be historically significant. This was true for several reasons, few of them related to Justice Souter himself.

First, during Justice Brennan's long and distinguished tenure, Brennan became the leading symbol of the "liberal" approach identified with the Supreme Court under Chief Justice EARL WARREN—an approach concerned with promoting equality and protecting individual rights against the government. Supporters of that approach viewed with alarm the prospect that Justice Brennan would be replaced by the appointee of a Republican President who had made a campaign issue of Supreme Court decisions supported by the liberal wing of the Court.

Second, Justice Souter was the ninth consecutive Justice to have been appointed by a Republican President; no Democratic President had made an appointment to the Supreme Court for twenty-three years, since President LYNDON B. JOHNSON appointed Justice THURGOOD MARSHALL in 1967. While there had been comparable periods in history—Democratic Presidents FRANKLIN D. ROOSEVELT and HARRY S. TRUMAN, for example, appointed thirteen consecutive Justices—those were periods in which one party thoroughly dominated national politics. By contrast, Justice Souter was appointed at a time when Democrats held a majority in the Senate, as they had for all but six of the previous thirty-two years. This long-standing division of power in Washington, combined with the perception among Democratic senators that President Bush and President RONALD REAGAN consciously sought to make judicial appointments that would change the political orientation of the federal courts, made partisan controversy over Justice Brennan's replacement almost inevitable no matter who the replacement was.

Third, both supporters and opponents perceived Justice Souter to be a crucial appointment in determining the direction of the Court. Senate Judiciary Committee Chair Joseph Biden, for example, asserted that no nomination had been so significant to the future of the Court since the 1930s. In particular, both supporters and opponents of the nomination expected that Justice Souter would cast the decisive vote on whether the Constitution permits the states to outlaw ABORTION. After the Supreme Court's 1989 decision in WEBSTER V. REPRODUCTIVE HEALTH SERVICES, which upheld significant state restrictions on abortion, supporters of the right to an abortion believed that four Justices were prepared to overrule ROE V. WADE (1973), the decision that first established that right. Partly in response to *Webster*, abortion was an important issue in several closely watched political campaigns in 1989. Justice Souter had made few significant public statements about *Roe v. Wade* or the constitutional right to an abortion, and his views on abortion were the subject of intense investigation, and speculation, in the period between his nomination and his eventual confirmation by the Senate in October 1990.

Finally, Souter's nomination to the Court occurred in the shadow of the rejection of President Ronald Reagan's nomination of Judge Robert Bork to the Supreme Court, in 1987. The nationally televised hearings on the BORK NOMINATION were the longest confirmation hearings on any Supreme Court nomination in history, and during the confirmation battle Bork's fate became a major national political issue. Bork had made extensive public statements on many issues of constitutional law and philosophy and was a nationally known, highly controversial figure in legal circles. Justice Souter, by contrast, had made virtually no public statements on broad issues of constitutional law and was unknown outside of New Hampshire. Those inclined to be suspicious of Justice Souter suggested that President Bush had deliberately sought out an unknown candidate who would pursue the President's agenda but who did not have the record that made Bork vulnerable. Others, including supporters of Bork, argued that the Souter nomination confirmed their fears that the treatment of Bork made it impossible for anyone except an undistinguished anonymity to be confirmed to the Supreme Court.

Souter's record was revealing in certain respects. Even among his opponents, few criticized the overall quality of the more than 100 opinions he wrote while a justice of the New Hampshire Supreme Court. Few questioned his general intellectual ability. His opinions as a state supreme court justice showed a tendency to favor the interests of the government over those of criminal suspects. Apart from that, however, his New Hampshire opinions revealed few clear patterns. Accordingly, reporters and investigators for concerned interest groups made extraordinary efforts to uncover information that might shed light on Souter's views, particularly on the abortion issue. Ultimately little such material was uncovered.

Souter's confirmation hearings were the third longest in history (after those of Bork and Justice LOUIS D. BRANDEIS). Justice Souter himself testified for almost twenty hours, the second longest time for any Supreme Court nominee (after Bork). The hearings were notable in several respects.

Perhaps most significant, senators asked, and Souter answered, numerous substantive questions about the nominee's views on specific issues of constitutional law. Justice Souter made specific statements about his views on RACIAL DISCRIMINATION; AFFIRMATIVE ACTION to aid racial minorities; SEX DISCRIMINATION; legislative REAPPORTIONMENT and the principle of ONE PERSON, ONE VOTE; congressional power to enforce the FOURTEENTH AMENDMENT's guarantees of DUE PROCESS and EQUAL PROTECTION against the states; the enforcement of the BILL OF RIGHTS against the states through the Fourteenth Amendment's due process clause; the free speech clause, free exercise clause, and ESTABLISHMENT CLAUSE of the FIRST AMENDMENT; and the decision in MIRANDA V. ARIZONA (1966), which required police officers to warn suspects in custody before interrogating them. Souter commented specifically on several Supreme Court decisions—endorsing, for example, the landmark expansions of free speech rights in NEW YORK TIMES V. SULLIVAN (1964) and BRANDENBURG V. OHIO (1969), but criticizing the standard for judging establishment clause issues specified in the LEMON TEST and the approach that Justice ANTONIN SCALIA took to the role of tradition in determining the rights protected by the due process clause. Justice Souter also engaged in broad-ranging discussions with members of the SENATE JUDICIARY COMMITTEE on the significance of the intentions of the Framers of the Constitution and on a Supreme Court Justice's obligation to follow precedent.

Souter's extensive substantive answers were significant principally because, before the Senate hearings, there had been considerable controversy over whether it was proper for Senators to ask Supreme Court nominees their views on specific issues, and whether it was obligatory, or even appropriate, for the nominee to answer. Some recent nominees (notably Justice Scalia) had refused to answer substantive questions about constitutional issues, and many thought that Bork's uninhibited willingness to answer contributed to his downfall. Souter's extensive answers buttressed the position of those who maintained that nominees should be expected to give their views on constitutional issues in detail to the Senate committee.

Souter's hearings were also significant for what he did not disclose. Despite repeated questioning, he declined to state his views on whether the Constitution protected the right to an abortion and on whether *Roe v. Wade* should be overruled. Ultimately, many senators who believed that this issue was of the first importance, and that a Supreme Court nominee was obligated to disclose his views on it, voted to confirm Justice Souter despite his reticence.

Another conspicuous aspect of Souter's confirmation process was the role of groups of private citizens interested in specific issues. Those groups had played a significant role in mobilizing public opinion against the Bork nomination, and many—especially groups concerned about the possible overruling of *Roe v. Wade*—testified against Justice Souter and attempted, unsuccessfully, to rally public opinion against him. In this respect as well, the Souter nomination confirmed the trend toward the increased politicization of the Supreme Court nomination process.

Finally, Souter's confirmation hearings were significant because of the extraordinary degree of preparation that preceded them and the increasing tendency of confirmation hearings to take on the aspect of choreographed productions. The Bush administration assigned several officials to help Souter prepare for the Senate hearings, and Souter spent most of the period between his nomination and the hearings studying intensely and practicing his responses to anticipated questions from the senators. His preparation was manifestly successful: most observers considered his testimony at the hearings to be a virtuoso performance in which he demonstrated careful thought on a wide range of constitutional issues to which he had not been greatly exposed while on the New Hampshire Supreme Court. Justice Souter was confirmed by an overwhelming vote in the Senate despite the salience of the abortion issue and his refusal to indicate his views on that issue. This emphasis on careful preparation to defuse political difficulties is another respect in which it seems likely that Justice Souter's confirmation process established a lasting pattern.

The cases decided through April 1991 of Justice Souter's first Term on the Supreme Court revealed little about his orientation, and what they did reveal was not surprising. The most important cases during that period dealt with CRIMINAL PROCEDURE, and in each of them Justice Souter voted in favor of the government. Perhaps the most significant single vote was in *Arizona v. Fulminante* (1991), where a 5–4 majority of the Court (in an opinion by Chief Justice WILLIAM H. REHNQUIST) ruled that the admission of a coerced confession in a criminal trial can be harmless error. Observers speculated, plausibly, that Justice Brennan would have reached the opposite conclusion and that Justice Souter's appointment determined the result on this issue. In *McClesky v. Zant* (1991), Justice Souter joined a six-Justice majority (in an opinion by Justice Kennedy) in adopting a rule that sharply limited the ability of prisoners to bring successive federal habeas corpus petitions. The

ruling was issued in a capital case, and its most marked effect will be to cut off the avenues of federal judicial review available to defendants who have been sentenced to death. Finally, in *California v. Hodari D.* (1991), Justice Souter, with six of his colleagues, joined an opinion (written by Justice Scalia) that adopted a narrow construction of the term "seizure" in the Fourth Amendment: The Court ruled that a suspect who ran away when a police officer ordered him to stop was seized not at the time the order was given but only when he was finally restrained. In all of these cases, Justice Souter's votes confirmed the strong tendency he had shown in his opinions on the New Hampshire Supreme Court to favor the government in criminal cases.

DAVID A. STRAUSS
(1992)

Bibliography

Nomination of David H. Souter to Be an Associate Justice of the United States Supreme Court, Senate Executive Report No. 101–32, 101st Cong., 2d Sess. (October 1, 1990).

SOUTER, DAVID H.
(1939–)
(Update)

David Hackett Souter was nominated by President GEORGE H. W. BUSH and confirmed as the 105th Justice of the Supreme Court in 1990. At the time, he was portrayed as the "stealth candidate" because, even though previously serving on the New Hampshire Supreme Court, he was not widely known and did not have a record of publications like that of the 1987 unsuccessful nominee, Judge Robert H. Bork. At his confirmation hearings, though, he expressed respect for PRECEDENT, dissociated himself from a jurisprudence of ORIGINAL INTENT, and acknowledged the "majestic generality" of guarantees like the DUE PROCESS clause.

Although more conservative than the Justice he replaced on the bench, WILLIAM J. BRENNAN, JR., Souter does not share the conservative judicial philosophy of Bush's other appointee, Justice CLARENCE THOMAS. To be sure, in his first couple of years on the Court he voted with conservatives on the REHNQUIST COURT, casting the pivotal vote in controversial rulings like RUST V. SULLIVAN (1991), which upheld the government's denial of funding for family planning organizations that perform ABORTIONS. More recently, he has established a record of voting most frequently (over 80 percent of the time) with Justices JOHN PAUL STEVENS, RUTH BADER GINSBURG, and STEPHEN G. BREYER. Together, they are most often in dissent in 5–4 decisions. He votes next most often with Justices SANDRA DAY O'CONNOR and ANTHONY M. KENNEDY, and least often with Chief Justice WILLIAM H. REHNQUIST and Justices ANTONIN SCALIA and Thomas.

Souter is a conservative jurist but a conservative in the tradition of the second Justice JOHN MARSHALL HARLAN. Indeed, he frequently cites that Justice's celebrated DISSENTING OPINION from the dismissal of an APPEAL for lack of JUSTICIABILITY in POE V. ULLMAN (1961), urging the Court's recognition of a constitutional RIGHT OF PRIVACY and embracing the concept of SUBSTANTIVE DUE PROCESS. Souter thus joined Kennedy and O'Connor in a PLURALITY OPINION in PLANNED PARENTHOOD V. CASEY (1992) upholding "the core meaning" of the landmark ruling in ROE V. WADE (1973), and he wrote the portion of that opinion dealing with the DOCTRINE of STARE DECISIS. He also embraced Harlan's understanding of the protection of the due process clause in his CONCURRING OPINIONS in the 1997 RIGHT TO DIE cases, as well as in writing for the Court in *County of Sacramento v. Lewis* (1998).

Although Souter joined the majority in NEW YORK V. UNITED STATES (1992), he has otherwise dissented from the Rehnquist Court's bare majority rulings on FEDERALISM, limiting the LEGISLATIVE POWER of Congress, and defending STATES' RIGHTS in UNITED STATES V. LÓPEZ (1995), *Seminole Tribe of Florida v. Florida* (1996), *Printz v. United States* (1997), and *Mack v. United States* (1997). He also wrote for the dissenters from the Court's ruling in *City of Boerne v. Flores* (1997), striking down the RELIGIOUS FREEDOM RESTORATION ACT (1993).

Souter likewise joined Stevens, Ginsburg, and Breyer in ADARAND CONSTRUCTORS, INC. V. PEÑA (1995), dissenting from the Court's invalidation of a federal AFFIRMATIVE ACTION program and overturning of METRO BROADCASTING, INC. V. FCC (1990). So too, he dissented in SHAW V. RENO (1993) AND ITS PROGENY, which struck down the creation of majority-minority ELECTORAL DISTRICTS.

At the same time, Souter sided with majorities in extending the scope of the FOURTEENTH AMENDMENT EQUAL PROTECTION clause in the area of nonracial discrimination. He joined, for example, Ginsburg's OPINION FOR THE COURT in UNITED STATES V. VIRGINIA (1996) holding that a public, all-male military college ran afoul of the Fourteenth Amendment in refusing to admit females. He also joined Kennedy's opinion in ROMER V. EVANS (1996), striking down a state constitutional amendment that forbid localities from enacting ordinances outlawing SEXUAL ORIENTATION discrimination.

On the rights of the accused and matters of CRIMINAL PROCEDURE, however, Souter generally sides with conservatives. Still, he wrote an important opinion for a bare majority in *Withrow v. Williams* (1993), upholding inmates' right to HABEAS CORPUS on grounds that police violated

their rights under MIRANDA V. ARIZONA (1966) and distinguishing STONE V. POWELL (1976). He also dissented from the Court's rejection of a FOURTH AMENDMENT challenge to random DRUG TESTING of student athletes in *Vernonia School District 47J v. Acton* (1995).

Besides championing the concept of substantive due process against criticisms advanced by Scalia and Thomas, Souter has written notable opinions staunchly defending RELIGIOUS LIBERTY on the one hand, and, on the other, a strict SEPARATION OF CHURCH AND STATE under the FIRST AMENDMENT. Besides joining the majority in striking down an ordinance banning "ritual animal sacrifice" in CHURCH OF THE LUKUMI BABALU AYE, INC. V. CITY OF HIALEAH (1993), his concurring opinion sharply disagreed with the Court's analysis of the free exercise clause in EMPLOYMENT DIVISION, DEPARTMENT OF HUMAN RESOURCES OF OREGON V. SMITH (1990). With respect to the ESTABLISHMENT CLAUSE, he vigorously defends the theory of a "high wall of separation." Writing for the majority in BOARD OF EDUCATION OF KIRYAS JOEL VILLAGE SCHOOL DISTRICT V. GRUMET (1994), he struck down the creation of a special school district for a religious community. By contrast, he dissented from rulings permitting GOVERNMENT AID TO RELIGIOUS INSTITUTIONS in, for example, *Zobrest v. Catalina Foothills School District* (1993), ROSENBERGER V. RECTOR & VISITORS OF THE UNIVERSITY OF VIRGINIA (1995), and AGOSTINI V. FELTON (1997).

Souter has established a reputation for thoughtful, well-written opinions that often reexamine the historical basis for and development of constitutional guarantees. Actively engaging in oral arguments from the bench, he possesses the charm and wit of a New Englander. He considers himself "a conservative, from a conservative state" and yet jokes "that he makes his living writing liberal dissents."

DAVID M. O'BRIEN
(2000)

Bibliography

GARROW, DAVID J.   1994   Justice Souter Emerges. *The New York Times Magazine*, Sept. 25, pp. 36–43, 52–55, 64.

SOUTH CAROLINA v. KATZENBACH
383 U.S. 301 (1966)

The decision upheld the constitutionality of portions of the VOTING RIGHTS ACT OF 1965. Southern states attacked, as an intrusion upon state SOVEREIGNTY and on other grounds, portions of the act suspending tests or devices used to measure voter qualifications, barring new voter qualifications pending approval by federal authorities, providing for the appointment of federal voting examiners to register voters, and determining which states and political subdivisions were subject to the act's coverage.

In sustaining the legislation under the FIFTEENTH AMENDMENT, the Supreme Court, in an opinion by Chief Justice EARL WARREN, rejected the argument that Congress could do no more than forbid violations of the Fifteenth Amendment and must leave the fashioning of remedies for violations to the courts. Congressional findings that case-by-case litigation was inaduquate to vindicate VOTING RIGHTS justified the decision "to shift the advantage of time and inerta from the perpetrators of the evil to its victims."

THEODORE EISENBERG
(1986)

SOUTH CAROLINA EXPOSITION AND PROTEST

See: Exposition and Protest

SOUTH CAROLINA ORDINANCE OF NULLIFICATION
(1832)

South Carolinians' objections to the expansion of federal authority focused on protective tariffs enacted in 1828 and 1832. They were most concerned, however, about potential external threats to the security of slavery, including threats from the federal government. Inspired by constitutional theories of JOHN C. CALHOUN, the South Carolina legislature called a convention to nullify the tariff.

On November 24, 1832, the convention adopted the Ordinance of Nullification, which declared that Congress lacked power to adopt a protective tariff. The tariff measures were therefore "null, void, and no law, nor binding upon this State, its officers or citizens." The ordinance voided all contracts and judicial proceedings designed to collect the tariff, prohibited state officials from enforcing it, required the state legislature to enact legislation that would "prevent the enforcement and arrest the operation" of the tariffs, prohibited appeals of tariff-related cases to the Supreme Court, required all public officials and jurors to take an oath to support the ordinance and supportive legislation, and warned that any coercive federal act would trigger the state's SECESSION. South Carolina also subsequently nullified the federal FORCE ACT that empowered President ANDREW JACKSON to collect the tariff. Though the Nullification Ordinance produced a major constitutional crisis in 1832, it was a short-term failure. President Jackson and all the Southern states denounced it, and South Carolina never found occasion to put its requirements to the test. But the Ordinance was a major step in implementing the theory of NULLIFICATION and, as such, pointed to secession.

WILLIAM M. WIECEK
(1986)

Bibliography
CURRENT, RICHARD N.　1963　*John C. Calhoun.* New York: Washington Square Press.

SOUTH CAROLINA ORDINANCE OF SECESSION
(1860)

JOHN C. CALHOUN, the foremost theorist of SECESSION, had argued that the United States Constitution was a compact among sovereign states. When one of the parties to the compact (federal government or other state) had violated its terms by enacting or condoning unconstitutional acts, and other remedies such as INTERPOSITION and NULLIFICATION proved futile, an aggrieved party could withdraw from the compact and resume the independent status it enjoyed previously.

In response to ABRAHAM LINCOLN's election, the South Carolina legislature called a convention to consider secession. On December 20, 1860, the convention, meeting at Charleston, unanimously adopted the Ordinance of Secession, a brief statement declaring that "the union now subsisting . . . is hereby dissolved." Four days later, the Convention approved the "Declaration of the Causes of Secession," a brief exposition of secessionist and compact theory. In it, the Carolinians accused the free states of violation or half-hearted enforcement of the Fugitive Slave Acts, tolerating abolitionist agitation, and electing a presidential candidate pledged to the eventual abolition of slavery. Therefore South Carolina declared itself an "independent state, with full power to levy war, conclude peace, contract alliances, establish commerce, and to do all other acts and things which independent States may of right do."

WILLIAM M. WIECEK
(1986)

Bibliography
POTTER, DAVID M.　1976　*The Impending Crisis, 1848–1861.* New York: Harper & Row.

SOUTH DAKOTA v. DOLE

See: Conditional Spending

SOUTH DAKOTA v. NEVILLE
459 U.S. 553 (1983)

In this case the Supreme Court answered a question left unresolved by earlier decisions: can a state use as evidence the fact that a person arrested for drunk driving refused to take a blood-alcohol test? GRIFFIN V. CALIFORNIA (1965) had held that adverse comment on a defendant's refusal to testify impermissibly burdened the RIGHT AGAINST SELF-INCRIMINATION, and SCHMERBER V. CALIFORNIA (1966) had held that a state could compel the taking of a blood-alcohol test without violating that right, which protected against testimonial compulsion only, not compulsion of physical evidence drawn from the body. In *Neville* the Court ruled that a state that authorized a driver to refuse a blood-alcohol test could introduce that refusal as evidence against him. The Court relied not on the earlier distinction between TESTIMONIAL AND NONTESTIMONIAL COMPULSION but on the fact that the element of compulsion was altogether absent here because the state did not require the test.

LEONARD W. LEVY
(1986)

SOUTH-EASTERN UNDERWRITERS ASSOCIATION v. UNITED STATES
322 U.S. 533 (1944)

The statement in PAUL V. VIRGINIA (1869) that insurance did not constitute INTERSTATE COMMERCE underlay seventy-five years of acquiescence and spawned an intricate network of state regulation. The question of federal regulation did not come before the Court until this indictment of an underwriters' association for violating the SHERMAN ANTITRUST ACT. A 4–3 Court, led by Justice HUGO L. BLACK, declared that insurance was commerce subject to federal regulation. Moreover, the Sherman Act applied, and the underwriters could properly be convicted for its violation. Justice ROBERT H. JACKSON, dissenting in part, conceded the fact of interstate commerce but felt obliged to follow the well-established legal fiction to the contrary until Congress acted to regulate. Chief Justice HARLAN FISKE STONE dissented, predicting chaos when state regulation was discontinued because federal controls did not exist. Justice FELIX FRANKFURTER joined Stone, admitting the reach of federal power but denying that the Sherman Act was intended to extend to insurance.

DAVID GORDON
(1986)

(SEE ALSO: *Prudential Insurance Company v. Benjamin.*)

SOUTHERN MANIFESTO
(March 11, 1956)

Southern politicians generally opposed the Supreme Court's ruling in BROWN V. BOARD OF EDUCATION (1954). Virginia and other states resurrected the doctrine of INTERPOSITION, and Georgia threatened NULLIFICATION. The most considered statement of segregationist constitutional theory was the declaration against INTEGRATION made by ninety-six southern congressmen and senators, in March 1956, led by Senator Harry F. Byrd of Virginia. The manifesto argued: *Brown* represented a clear abuse of judicial power; the FOURTEENTH AMENDMENT, which did not mention education, was not intended to affect state educational systems; PLESSY V. FERGUSON (1896) was still good law; DESEGREGATION would cause chaos and confusion in the states affected. The manifesto called upon the people of the states to "resist forced integration by any lawful means" and concluded with a pledge "to use all lawful means to bring about a reversal of this decision which is contrary to the Constitution, and to prevent the use of force in its implementation." Federal response to such abstract defiance was notably lacking, although a group of distinguished leaders of the American bar denounced attacks on the Supreme Court as "reckless in their abuse, . . . heedless of the value of JUDICIAL REVIEW and . . . dangerous in fomenting disrespect for our highest law."

PAUL MURPHY
(1986)

Bibliography

MUSE, BENJAMIN 1964 *Ten Years of Prelude: The Story of Integration Since the Supreme Court's 1954 Decision.* New York: Viking.

SOUTHERN PACIFIC CO. v. ARIZONA
325 U.S. 761 (1945)

Arizona prohibited operation of a railroad train more than fourteen passenger cars or seventy freight cars long. The Supreme Court, 7–2, held the law an unconstitutional burden on INTERSTATE COMMERCE. Chief Justice HARLAN FISKE STONE, for the Court, emphasized the magnitude of that burden; the law forced the railroad to operate thirty percent more trains in the state, and to break up and remake trains; its total yearly cost to both railroads operating in the state was a million dollars. Stone also noted that requiring more trains would produce more accidents; the state's safety argument was weak. This interest-balancing analysis was far more demanding than the "RATIONAL BA-

SIS" STANDARD OF REVIEW Stone had employed in *South Carolina State Highway Department v. Barnwell Bros., Inc.* (1938), upholding limits on truck widths and weights. *Southern Pacific* set the standard for future challenges to STATE REGULATIONS OF COMMERCE in the transportation field.

KENNETH L. KARST
(1986)

SOVEREIGN IMMUNITY

At COMMON LAW the sovereign, although subject to the law, was immune from the JURISDICTION of its own courts. The English doctrine of sovereign immunity was established at an early time, probably in the thirteenth century; but long before the American Revolution the jurisdictional exemption of the sovereign, though remaining theoretically absolute, was riddled with exceptions. Judicial process against the sovereign was available through petition of right and other procedures resting upon waiver of immunity, and subordinate officers could be sued for damages attributable to official acts and were subject to process by prerogative writ.

Because sovereign immunity was part of the common law heritage existing when the Constitution was adopted, the courts later embraced the doctrine as an implicit limitation upon their jurisdiction. Hence, some provisions of Article III of the Constitution were interpreted as subject to this qualification. The immunity of the United States, first acknowledged by the Supreme Court in *United States v. McLemore* (1846), became a complete exemption, protecting the federal government and its agencies from unconsented suit in any court by any plaintiff. State immunity was initially rejected by the Court in CHISHOLM V. GEORGIA (1793), but that unpopular HOLDING was quickly reversed by the ELEVENTH AMENDMENT. The amendment, in juxtaposition with Article III, was subsequently construed to immunize the states from unconsented suits by private plaintiffs and by foreign governments in federal court.

The states, however, are not immune from suit by either the United States or other states. As a matter of state law, states commonly have claimed immunity from suit by private plaintiffs in state court. The power of Congress to lift the states' common law immunity seems restricted only by the limitations of the JUDICIAL POWER of the United States as defined in Article III, the general limitations of congressional power, and—arguably—some core notion of state sovereignty. (See NATIONAL LEAGUE OF CITIES V. USERY.)

The immunity doctrine is in tension with the RULE OF LAW, and pragmatic justifications for its perpetuation are unpersuasive. By means of statutes waiving immunity and

through judicial interpretation, the ambit of the exemption has been drastically reduced. Congressional legislation creating the COURT OF CLAIMS in 1855 and later enactments, such as the Tucker Act (1887) and the FEDERAL TORT CLAIMS ACT (1946), subject the United States to suit on many kinds of claims. The states, by state constitutional provision or statute, have abolished completely or restricted their own immunity—often in state judicial proceedings only, less commonly in federal court actions. Moreover, as a practical matter, the impact of the doctrine is significantly restricted by differentiating suits against public officers for official acts done or threatened pursuant to unconstitutional or legally deficient authorization from suits against the government itself. Although the courts permit state and federal officers to assert sovereign immunity where the suit against them is adjudged to be substantially against the government itself, such cases are generally limited to suits seeking damages or restitution for past acts where judgment will expend itself upon the public treasury, those seeking to dispossess the government of property, and some suits seeking specific performance. As a consequence of these developments, sovereign immunity has become a narrow and ill-defined jurisdictional bar, whose contemporary legitimacy and utility are doubtful.

CLYDE E. JACOBS
(1986)

Bibliography

DAVIS, KENNETH C. 1970 Supp. *Administrative Law Treatise.* Pages 895–940. St. Paul, Minn.: West Publishing Co.
HOLDSWORTH, SIR WILLIAM S. 1944 *A History of English Law.* Vol. 9 of 15. London: Methuen.

SOVEREIGN IMMUNITY
(Update)

The DOCTRINE of sovereign immunity holds that a sovereign cannot be sued without its consent. Although the Constitution nowhere refers to the sovereign immunity either of the states or the United States, the doctrine is well-entrenched for both levels of government and has even been applied to territories. For states sued in federal courts, the doctrine of sovereign immunity is treated as embodied in the ELEVENTH AMENDMENT, even though by terms that section speaks only of the scope of the judicial power. The Court has recently held, in *Alden v. Maine* (1999), that a state's constitutional immunity from suit exists not only in federal courts but also in the state's own courts. The sovereign immunity of the federal government has been established by judicial inference. The two lines of cases (state and federal sovereign immunity) frequently borrow from one another, particularly on the question of whether a suit against a governmental officer should be treated as one against the sovereign.

Who is a "sovereign," what counts as consent, and whether the immunity applies in the courts of another sovereign, are issues that affect how broadly the doctrine prevents JUDICIAL REVIEW of (and remedies for) government wrongdoing. In the last century, the federal government has by LEGISLATION waived its sovereign immunity for contract and TAKINGS claims, for some COMMON LAW tort claims against the United States, and for most forms of injunctive or other nonmonetary relief against federal employees. Although a statutory clause giving an agency authority to "sue and be sued" is generally treated as waiving immunity, the Supreme Court has generally applied the "consent" requirement with rigor, construing claimed waivers of immunity narrowly. For example, interest on damage awards against the United States is not permitted unless explicitly authorized. Eleventh Amendment immunity for states sued in federal courts has also been broadly interpreted.

Apart from statutory waivers of immunity, a key to determining the effect of sovereign immunity is the availability or unavailability of other remedies to uphold the RULE OF LAW and provide individual justice. Generally a simple INJUNCTION against a government officer to refrain from future action that violates federal law will not be treated as barred by sovereign immunity. Sometimes referred to as the EX PARTE YOUNG principle, the availability of such relief against government officers mitigates the effects of sovereign immunity, and is of fundamental importance. An illustration of the importance of this principle is suggested by cases such as YOUNGSTOWN SHEET & TUBE V. SAWYER (1952), in which the Court, without referring to sovereign immunity, upheld a court order enjoining the U.S. Secretary of Commerce from carrying out the President's order to seize steel plants. Claims against officers that could result in government liability for accrued damages in contract or tort, and claims involving title to PROPERTY held by the sovereign, are more likely to result in rulings that the suits are "really" against the sovereign. Sovereign immunity is less likely to bar an action against an officer for a trespassory wrong, and does not bar either damage awards against officers individually or defenses in a government enforcement action.

Although some have attempted to ground sovereign immunity doctrine in SEPARATION OF POWERS concerns, it is as much history as logic that explains differences between those claims against officers that do not require the sovereign's consent and those that are treated as actions against the government requiring consent. In UNITED STATES V. LEE (1880), the Court, in a 5–4 decision, upheld federal JURISDICTION over a suit against federal officials to recover land wrongly held by U.S. Army officers. The majority questioned whether the sovereign immunity doctrine could be justified in the United States, given its origin with the personal immunity of the hereditary monarch; nonetheless, the Court did not regard itself as free simply to disavow the doctrine. The *Lee* dissenters invoked sovereign immunity as an "axio[m] of public law," not limited to monarchies, and made separation of powers arguments against permitting courts to enter judgments against officers that might interfere with important government functions by, for example, dispossessing the U.S. Army from occupying forts necessary for defense. While *Lee* permitted the suit against the officers notwithstanding the immunity of the United States, a similar effort was denied in *Malone v. Bowdoin* (1962), which followed the more restrictive view set forth in *Larson v. Domestic & Foreign Commerce* (1949) concerning when the government's consent is required for suit brought nominally against an officer. While a 1976 statute authorizing suits for nonmonetary relief against federal officers diminished the importance of *Larson* for review of federal action, *Larson* has continued to influence the scope of states' immunities in federal courts.

MARBURY V. MADISON (1803), which contemplated that MANDAMUS could issue to the U.S. Secretary of State, established for U.S. constitutionalism the importance of the principle that government itself be constrained by law, and further established a presumption that for every right, there be a remedy. Notwithstanding its long roots in U.S. constitutional cases (as well as in state law), sovereign immunity is in tension with both of these aspirations.

VICKI C. JACKSON
(2000)

Bibliography

CURRIE, DAVID P.   1984   State Sovereign Immunity and Suits Against Government Officers. *Supreme Court Review* 1984: 149–168.

ENGDAHL, DAVID E.   1972   Immunity and Accountability for Positive Government Wrongs. *University of Colorado Law Review* 44:1–79.

JAFFE, LOUIS L.   1963   Suits Against Governments and Officers: Sovereign Immunity. *Harvard Law Review* 77:1–39.

PFANDER, JAMES   1997   Sovereign Immunity and the Right to Petition: Toward a First Amendment Right to Pursue Judicial Claims Against the Government. *Northwestern University Law Review* 91:899–1014.

WOOLHANDLER, ANN   1997   The Common Law Origins of Constitutionally Compelled Remedies. *Yale Law Journal* 107:77–164.

SOVEREIGNTY

The single term "sovereignty" is used to denote two distinct (although related) concepts of constitutional significance. It refers both to the autonomy of a state with respect to its legislative JURISDICTION and to the supreme authority within the state. There are historical reasons why the same term is used for both, but to confound them is a serious and all-too-common error. The term itself comes from the Latin *superans* (meaning "rising above" or "overcoming") through the French *souverain*.

Sovereignty, in the first sense, is a concept derived from international law. A state is sovereign if it is independent of other states and possesses the authority to determine its relationship to other states and to regulate its own internal affairs. Sovereignty, in this sense, is the essential condition required for membership in the family of nations. Sovereign states do not ordinarily make treaties or wage formal war except with other states recognized as sovereign. International law also recognizes some communities as semisovereign, that is, as possessing certain, but not all, of the attributes of sovereignty. The member states of a federal union are in this category.

Internally the several states of the United States are legally sovereign in this sense insofar as they possess jurisdiction, the legitimate authority to declare the law within their territory. But this sovereignty is not unlimited. As the Supreme Court said in PARKER V. BROWN (1943), "The governments of the states are sovereign within their territory save only as they are subject to the prohibitions of the Constitution or as their action in some measure conflicts with powers delegated to the National Government, or with Congressional legislation enacted in the exercise of those powers." The jurisdiction of the states is constitutionally limited by subject as well as by territory, but within their sphere the state governments are as supreme as the national government is within its sphere. This is the meaning of what JAMES MADISON in THE FEDERALIST #39 called the "compound republic."

The states enjoy some other attributes of sovereignty: they may not without their consent be sued in their own courts or in the courts of the United States (see SOVEREIGN IMMUNITY; ELEVENTH AMENDMENT) and they possess independent and plenary authority to lay and collect taxes on persons, things, or transactions within their jurisdiction. Among themselves, also, the states are sovereign. The jurisdiction of a state is exclusive of the other states. Disputes between or among states in cases not governed by the Constitution, an INTERSTATE COMPACT, or a federal statute are resolved according to the principles of international law. But the sovereignty of the states does not limit or diminish the sovereignty of the Union. In all international affairs and in domestic affairs properly subject to it, the government of the United States is sovereign. Without its consent, the United States may not be sued in the courts either of the United States or of the several states.

In political theory sovereignty is generally held to be indivisible; careful writers thus distinguish between the indivisible sovereignty of the people and the powers or attributes of sovereignty that are divided between the national and state governments. Hence ALEXANDER HAMILTON, in *The Federalist* #32, wrote of "the division of the sovereign power." But not all political actors are so careful; it is not uncommon for politicians, judges, or commentators to refer to a "division of sovereignty" in the federal system.

The second meaning of sovereignty as the single, supreme authority within a state, above the law and uncontrollable except by its own will, was introduced into political theory by Jean Bodin in his *Six Bookes of the Commonwealth* (1576). Its most extreme expression was given by Thomas Hobbes who, in *Leviathan* (1651), asserted that opposition to tyranny was identical with opposition to sovereignty, or, in other words, that there is no standard except its own will against which the actions of the sovereign can be judged. A democratic, but no less radical, form was given to this concept of sovereignty by Jean-Jacques Rousseau in *The Social Contract* (1762).

Originally an analytical or explanatory formulation, the notion of a single, indivisible power in the state became a prescriptive article of the Tory political creed. WILLIAM BLACKSTONE identified the King-in-Parliament as the sovereign in England. Governor THOMAS HUTCHINSON, in his famous dispute with the Massachusetts Assembly in 1773, ascribed that same status to Parliament within the British Empire—denying that the provincial legislatures of America had any power or authority except by Parliament's grace. To the Whigs of America the Hobbesian idea of sovereignty, as it was stated by Hutchinson, represented a threat to the liberty they had inherited and the self-government they had established. As an empirical assertion the indivisibility of sovereignty seemed to be disproved by the federal systems of Germany, Switzerland, and the Netherlands, as well as by the British imperial system as it existed in the mid-eighteenth century; and as a prescriptive formula it was all too clearly intended to subvert American home rule.

The social contract theory expressed in the DECLARATION OF INDEPENDENCE and the first state constitutions was a rejection of the Tory doctrine of sovereignty. Neither the government nor any branch or officer of the government justly exercises any power except by the consent of the governed. The doctrine of equality of rights means that no person or body of persons is above the law. The claim of the Declaration, our most fundamental constitutional document, is that there can be no sovereign but the people. This doctrine of POPULAR SOVEREIGNTY was identified by ALEXIS DE TOCQUEVILLE as the defining characteristic of American constitutionalism. Both the national and state governments derive their powers from the people through the Constitution. Each exercises jurisdiction, but neither possesses sovereignty in the absolute, Hobbesian sense.

The Hobbesian notion of sovereignty was translated from a political to a legal concept in the nineteenth century by the British jurist John Austin, who argued that there was no HIGHER LAW against which the decrees of the state could be measured, and so the power of the legislature was absolute. In this revived form it was brought to America as part of the intellectual baggage of legal positivism.

Throughout American history a favorite rhetorical device has been to identify one level of government—usually the state—as sovereign. The success of this device depends upon the ambiguity of the term. That a political body exercises jurisdiction, is supreme within its sphere, and is autonomous in its internal affairs does not mean that it, its government, or its legislature is immune to the sanctions of the law or is free of the constraints of higher law. To speak of the "sovereign states" is not entirely inaccurate if the speaker refers to their autonomy within their own sphere, but it derives its force by evoking the notion of indivisibility and illimitability drawn from the other sense of the term. The rhetoric seemingly denies that the sovereign states are comprised within a sovereign Union.

Within the American regime the ultimate power and authority to alter or abolish the constitutions of government of state and Union resides only and inalienably with the people. If it be necessary or useful to use the term "sovereignty" in the sense of ultimate political power, then there is no sovereign in America but the people.

DENNIS J. MAHONEY
(1986)

Bibliography

DIAMOND, MARTIN (1970) 1981 *The Founding of the Democratic Republic.* Itasca, Ill.: F. E. Peacock.
JAFFA, HARRY V. 1965 *Equality and Liberty: Theory and Practice in American Politics.* New York: Oxford University Press.
LASKI, HAROLD J. 1921 The Foundations of Sovereignty. Pages 1–29 in *The Foundations of Sovereignty and Other Essays.* New Haven, Conn.: Yale University Press.

SPAIGHT, RICHARD DOBBS
(1758–1802)

Richard Dobbs Spaight represented North Carolina at the CONSTITUTIONAL CONVENTION OF 1787 and signed the Constitution. An infrequent speaker, Spaight favored strong national government. He was a leader of the RATIFICATION movement in North Carolina and was later elected governor and congressman. In a controversy with JAMES IRE-DELL over BAYARD V. SINGLETON (1787), he denounced JUDICIAL REVIEW as undemocratic.

DENNIS J. MAHONEY
(1986)

SPECIAL INTEREST GROUPS

See: Interest Group Litigation; Interest Groups

SPECIAL MASTER

A special master is an officer appointed by a court to assist it in a particular proceeding. When the Supreme Court exercises its ORIGINAL JURISDICTION, normally it appoints a special master to take EVIDENCE, make findings of fact, and submit a draft decree. The master's recommendations are advisory; decision rests with the Court. Many of the Supreme Court's special masters are former federal judges.

KENNETH L. KARST
(1986)

SPECIAL PROSECUTOR

Special prosecutors, also known as INDEPENDENT COUNSEL, are private attorneys appointed to investigate and, if need be, to prosecute government officials accused of criminal wrongdoing. In 1978 Congress enacted a law providing for the appointment of special prosecutors investigating executive branch officials as part of the Ethics in Government Act. The law was revised and reenacted in 1983 and 1987. It has come under heavy attack by some as violative of the SEPARATION OF POWERS, but the Supreme Court sustained the law in *Morrison v. Olson* in 1988.

As currently codified in 28 U.S.C. §§ 591–599, the independent counsel statute provides that a majority of members of Congress of either party sitting on the judiciary committee of either house may request an independent counsel to investigate allegations against a wide array of executive branch officials. Once the members have requested a special prosecutor under the law, the ATTORNEY GENERAL must initiate a preliminary investigation into the allegations, and unless the attorney general can certify that "there are no reasonable grounds to believe that further investigation is warranted . . ." he or she must subsequently apply to a special panel of federal judges for appointment of a special prosecutor. The panel, rather than the attorney general, chooses the special prosecutor and determines the scope of the counsel's investigation. Once appointed, the counsel may be fired by the attorney general only for "good cause, physical disability, mental incapacity, or any other condition that substantially impairs the performance of such independent counsel's duties"— determinations that are all subject to review by the federal courts.

Defenders of the law cite the WATERGATE scandal and argue that the law is necessary to curtail executive branch corruption in cases that the executive branch would rather not prosecute. Critics, however, claim that the statute violates the principle of equality because its provisions apply solely to the executive branch and not to Congress or the judiciary. They also charge that it places an unfair burden on those being investigated. The "no reasonable grounds" standard practically assures that the attorney general will appoint an independent counsel once requested by Congress; and unlike ordinary prosecutors, independent counsels command virtually unlimited financial resources and may extend their investigations for years.

Most important critics contend that the law undermines the separation of powers established by the Constitution. It does this most explicitly by appearing to violate the Constitution's appointments clause, which grants the President alone the power to nominate all executive branch officials except "inferior officers." More subtly, the law seems to shift the balance of power in political battles between the executive and legislative branches. According to the Constitution, the proper congressional remedy for executive branch wrongdoing is IMPEACHMENT by the House and trial by the Senate. This process safeguards the executive branch from unwarranted attacks by the legislature because it requires Congress to lay its own prestige on the line whenever it prosecutes executive officials. Congress is less likely to impeach executive officials on purely partisan grounds because in so doing it risks losing public support. The independent counsel law, however, insulates Congress from these political costs. Because an independent counsel is ostensibly separate from Congress, it allows members of Congress to cloak partisan attacks behind a façade of impartiality. In short, critics allege, the independent-counsel law almost invites use as a political weapon.

The law's potential for abuse is well illustrated by the case of Theodore Olson, an attorney who served in the Office of Legal Counsel in the Reagan Justice Department. Olson provided legal advice to the administration during its dispute with Congress over the release of documents held by the Environmental Protection Agency (EPA). The administration invoked EXECUTIVE PRIVILEGE and refused to hand over some of the documents requested by Congress; a rancorous political battle ensued. After it was over, Democratic staff members to the House Judiciary Committee produced a 3,000-page report critical of the Justice Department's role in advising the administration in the controversy. Republicans on the committee strenuously objected to the report as an exercise in partisanship, noting among other facts that no committee or subcommittee meetings were ever held to authorize the report. Nevertheless, House Democrats used the report as the basis for requesting an independent counsel investigation of Justice Department officials.

An independent counsel was subsequently appointed to determine whether Olson gave false and misleading testimony to Congress with regard to the executive privilege controversy. After a six-month investigation, independent counsel Alexia Morrison acknowledged that Olson's testimony "probably d[id] not constitute a prosecutable violation of any federal law." But instead of ending the investigation, Morrison sought permission to expand it. When both the attorney general and the judicial panel that appointed her rebuffed this request, Morrison nevertheless continued the inquiry. All told, Morrison investigated Olson for nearly three years, spending about a million dollars in the process—and forcing Olson to spend roughly the same amount of money defending himself. While still under investigation, Olson challenged the constitutionality of the independent counsel law, and in *Morrison v. Olson*, a federal appeals court struck down the statute, holding that it violated not only the appointments clause but also Article III of the Constitution and the principle of the separation of powers. The Supreme Court reversed by a vote of 7–1.

Writing for the majority, Chief Justice WILLIAM H. REHNQUIST maintained that the independent counsel law does not violate the appointments clause because the independent counsel is an "inferior officer" under the clause and hence requires no presidential nomination. Neither does the law violate Article III of the Constitution by giving the judiciary executive powers because the power to appoint the independent counsel derives from the appointments clause rather than Article III. Finally, the law does not violate the separation of powers because (according to Rehnquist) it does not compel the attorney general to ask for an independent counsel and because the executive branch retains some power to remove an independent counsel from office. Moreover, the law "does not involve an attempt by Congress to increase its own powers at the expense of the Executive Branch."

The lone dissenter, Justice ANTONIN SCALIA, scoffed at this last statement, accusing the majority of ignoring the political realities that clearly underlay the case. He further criticized the majority for its circumscribed reading of the separation of powers. According to Scalia, the question before the Court was simple and unambiguous. The Court had to determine whether the prosecutorial function is a purely executive power. If it is, then the independent counsel law had to be struck down unless it granted the executive branch complete control over the independent counsel. Because no one disputed the fact that the pros-

brought against him. In *United States v. Lovasco* (1977) the Supreme Court indicated that, in unusual cases, an accused may be able to establish a violation of the due process clause as a result of oppressive pretrial delay where actual prejudice can be demonstrated and inadequate justification exists. Government "bad faith," as when a charge is delayed, or dismissed and subsequently asserted at a later time in order to "forum shop," stockpile charges, or achieve some other tactical advantage, might also constitute a denial of due process. But the degree of protection afforded to an accused against unreasonable delay between commission of an offense and formal charges will depend on the applicable statute of limitations in most cases.

Statutory provisions implement the constitutional provision in many states and in federal prosecution. Encouraged by the *American Bar Association Standards for Criminal Justice, Speedy Trial* (1968), many jurisdictions have set specific legislative time limits within which a defendant must be brought to trial. Perhaps the most important of these statutes is the federal Speedy Trial Act of 1974, defining in detail permissible time periods in different types of cases and setting forth grounds for dismissal of charges with and without prejudice. Assertion of rights under these statutes is more likely to provide effective protection to an accused than reliance on the Constitution except in extraordinary cases.

A. KENNETH PYE
(1986)

Bibliography

AMSTERDAM, ANTHONY G. 1975 Speedy Criminal Trial: Rights and Remedies. *Stanford Law Review* 27:525–543.
GODBOLD, JOHN C. 1972 Speedy Trial—Major Surgery for a National Ill. *Alabama Law Review* 24:265–294.
LAFAVE, WAYNE R. and ISRAEL, JEROLD H. 1985 *Criminal Procedure.* St. Paul, Minn.: West Publishing Co.
WHITEBREAD, CHARLES H. 1980 *Criminal Procedure.* Mineola, N.Y.: Foundation Press.

SPEEDY TRIAL
(Update 1)

Since the original publication of this *Encyclopedia*, the Supreme Court has decided only one case of note regarding the constitutional right to a speedy trial. In *United States v. Loud Hawk* (1986) the Court concluded that a delay of ninety months did not entitle the defendant to relief. The Court analyzed the case under the four-factor analysis of BARKER V. WINGO (1972)—length of delay, reason for delay, defendant's assertion of the right, and prejudice to the defendant. The Court concentrated on the

first two of these factors in concluding that the right to a speedy trial had not been violated.

Beginning with the length of delay, the Court concluded that a substantial period during which the INDICTMENT was dismissed should be excluded when considering the speedy trial claim. It followed the reasoning used in UNITED STATES V. MACDONALD (1982) that once an indictment has been dismissed the defendant is no longer subject to public accusation; thus, a major concern of the speedy trial right is eliminated. The government's publicly expressed desire to prosecute Loud Hawk if successful on its appeal of the dismissal did not constitute public accusation for purposes of triggering the protection of the right to a speedy trial. Additionally, Loud Hawk had been unconditionally released, and during the ninety-month period, he was without any restraint on his liberty.

The Court concluded that the reason for most of the delay—an interlocutory appeal by the government—contributed little weight to the defendant's claim. Given the important public interest in appellate review, delay for this purpose is generally justified. Moreover, both the strength of the government's legal position and the importance of the issue further justified the delay. Finally, the Court concluded that the portion of the delay caused by the defendant's own interlocutory appeals did not count toward substantiating a violation of the speedy trial right. Typically, the defense would be required to show either unreasonable or unjustifiable delay by the prosecution or appellate courts before delays occasioned by its own appeals would count in the balance. No reason existed to count such delay in Loud Hawk's case because his appeals were frivolous.

The scarcity of constitutional decisions on the right to speedy trial reflects the fact that the federal Speedy Trial Act of 1974 and similar legislation in many states provide far more protection than does the Constitution. Dismissals for violation of the Sixth Amendment right to a speedy trial are also rare. *Loud Hawk* illustrates the major reasons for this result. The test fashioned by the Supreme Court is entirely too indeterminate and manipulable. The four *Barker* factors will rarely cut in the same direction. Often the defendant cannot show that he sought a speedy trial; defendants, especially those at liberty pending trial, usually have an interest in delay. When the factors are mixed, the courts generally avoid the draconian result of dismissal of the prosecution with prejudice, which is the only permissible remedy under the Sixth Amendment. Probably for the same reason, courts have resolved many of the subsidiary issues under the four-part test in favor of the government, as the Court did in *Loud Hawk*, by concluding that lengthy delay during appellate review should not be given any effective weight.

Occasionally a case is dismissed where a defendant has

suffered substantial prejudice because of delay or where the government has acted in bad faith. However, for the vast bulk of the cases, the speedy trial statutes, despite their weaknesses, remain the primary guardians of the defendant's and the public's right to speedy justice.

ROBERT P. MOSTELLER
(1992)

(SEE ALSO: *Criminal Justice System; Criminal Procedure.*)

Bibliography

LAFAVE, WAYNE R. and ISRAEL, JEROLD H. 1985 *Criminal Procedure.* St. Paul, Minn.: West Publishing Co.
MISNER, ROBERT L. 1983 *Speedy Trial: Federal and State Practice.* Charlottesville, Va.: Michie.

SPEEDY TRIAL
(Update 2)

The Sixth Amendment right to a speedy trial continues not to be a subject of extensive litigation. Constitutional claims in most cases have been eclipsed by the Federal Speedy Trial Act and its state counterparts, which provide more detailed and demanding rules for prompt prosecution than the constitutional floor the Supreme Court has set in its interpretations of the Sixth Amendment right.

The four factors identified by the Court in BARKER V. WINGO (1972)—whether delay before trial was uncommonly long; whether the government or defendant is more to blame for the delay; whether defendant, in due course, asserted his right to a speedy trial; and whether defendant suffered prejudice—still govern analysis of constitutional speedy trial claims. The case of *Doggett v. United States* (1992) provided a rare but instructive Court application of this test. Doggett was indicted for his alleged role in a drug conspiracy in 1980 and an arrest warrant was issued. When agents went to arrest him, however, they learned that he had left the country, possibly unaware of the fact that he had been indicted. The government took some measures to apprehend Doggett—sending word of the arrest warrant to customs officials and entering his name, temporarily, in an international computer system—but did not take other measures that they might easily have employed if they had been anxious to catch him. Two years later, Doggett reentered the country under his own name, unhindered by customs officials, and resettled. It was not until 1988 that the U.S. Marshal's Service conducted a simple credit check on persons with outstanding arrest warrants and, in a few minutes, found Doggett's address. Doggett was arrested and, not surprisingly, raised a speedy trial challenge to his prosecution, brought eight and one-half years after his indictment.

Applying the *Barker v. Wingo* test, the Court ruled in his favor, holding that the extraordinarily long delay was due to the government's negligence, and that since the government stipulated that Doggett might have been unaware of the indictment, he could not be faulted for having failed to invoke his right to be tried promptly. The weakness in Doggett's case was that he could not show precisely how his ability to defend himself might have been prejudiced. The Court, however, held that so lengthy a delay was "presumptively prejudicial," an expansive approach that dismayed four dissenting Justices. This generosity was warranted for, as the majority pointed out, it may be virtually impossible in some cases for a defendant to establish, years after the relevant events, that the delay has caused any particular form of evidence to disappear.

Although prejudice is only one of four factors considered under the constitutional test, the Court in dicta in another case, *Reed v. Farley* (1994), made a surprising comment on this factor in the course of discussing whether speedy trial provisions of the Interstate Agreement on Detainers "effectuated" the constitutional right: "A showing of prejudice is required to establish a violation of the Sixth Amendment Speedy Trial Clause, and that necessary ingredient is missing here." Although this comment was in dicta and therefore does not change the previous law that a showing of prejudice would not necessarily be required if the defendant had a particularly strong case on the other factors, if a majority of the Court now believes that prejudice should be a threshold showing for a constitutional claim, future cases may call the long-settled law of *Barker v. Wingo* and even the newer presumptive prejudice holding of *Doggett* into question.

SUSAN N. HERMAN
(2000)

Bibliography

GUIDELINES FOR APPLICATION OF FEDERAL SPEEDY TRIAL ACT 1985 *Federal Rules Decisions* 106:271.

SPEISER v. RANDALL
357 U.S. 513 (1958)

The Supreme Court invalidated on DUE PROCESS grounds a noncommunist oath required for a California property tax exemption. *Speiser* is a leading early case in the series breaking down the RIGHT-PRIVILEGE DISTINCTION and establishing that due process must be strictly observed where FUNDAMENTAL RIGHTS are infringed.

MARTIN SHAPIRO
(1986)

SPENDING POWER

The power to spend public funds is so much a sine qua non of government that ordinarily it needs no express authorization in constitutions, including those of the several states. However, because the U.S. Constitution was designed to give the federal government specified powers, particularly the fiscal power lacking under the ARTICLES OF CONFEDERATION, Article I, section 8, begins its enumeration of powers of Congress with the power to "lay and collect taxes, duties, IMPOSTS, and excises, to pay the debts and provide for the common defense and general welfare of the United States." The list continues with specified objects of lawmaking, such as commerce, bankruptcy, coinage, war and military and naval forces, and (in Article IV, section 3) the territory or other property of the United States. From the start, there was controversy whether the implicit power to spend revenues for the "general welfare of the United States" extended beyond the enumerated objects of congressional law-making powers.

JAMES MADISON, in THE FEDERALIST #41 and later as President, maintained the restrictive view of the spending power. ALEXANDER HAMILTON, in his influential Report on Manufactures, argued for broad national power to appropriate funds in pursuit of whatever Congress determines to be in the "general welfare," such as subsidies for chosen forms of economic activity; and as President, GEORGE WASHINGTON took Hamilton's view. But the appropriation of national funds for purposes not otherwise within Congress's law-making powers, particularly for construction of INTERNAL IMPROVEMENTS, remained debatable; President JAMES MONROE, for instance, first maintained Madison's view, but later changed his position.

Congress, however, early induced the construction of state agricultural colleges and private railroads by subsidies other than tax revenues, such as grants of public lands, followed in 1900 by supplemental appropriations from general funds. In the 1923 cases of *Massachusetts v. Mellon* and FROTHINGHAM V. MELLON, the Supreme Court declined to review the constitutionality of federal funds for state maternity programs in suits by a state and a taxpayer. But in UNITED STATES V. BUTLER (1935), the Court adopted Hamilton's broad reading of the GENERAL WELFARE CLAUSE even while striking down a program that tied agricultural subsidies to crop reduction on grounds that it invaded regulatory powers reserved to the states.

A broader understanding of Congress's regulatory powers soon undermined concerns about state powers as a limitation on the spending power, and this understanding has persisted to this day. Thus, the Supreme Court has let Congress condition federal funds for state highways on a state's restructuring its highway commission (*Oklahoma v. Civil Service Commission*) or on raising the minimum age

for purchasing alcoholic beverages, as long as such conditions are not unrelated to the federal interest in the funded program (*South Dakota v. Dole*). STATE CONSTITUTIONS, in contrast, commonly dedicate some tax revenues to specified purposes, such as roads, and entirely forbid spending for certain purposes, for instance, to invest in private enterprises. State constitutions also forbid deficit spending, and some have adopted spending ceilings. The FIRST AMENDMENT and many state constitutions forbid public spending for support of religion, with different results; purchasing secular textbooks for parochial school students, for instance, has been permitted under the First Amendment (BOARD OF EDUCATION V. ALLEN, 1968), but forbidden under some state constitutions.

The national and state executive and legislative branches often contend over control of spending. Article I, section 9, prohibits spending without a congressional appropriation and mandates an accounting to the public. Unlike many governors, the President cannot veto individual items in an appropriation bill, but some Presidents have asserted power not to spend—to "impound"—unwanted appropriations; Congress in turn has countered by steps such as creating enforceable contract claims to carry out its programs.

Difficult issues arise mainly in applying constitutional guarantees of individual rights to state and federal spending programs. For instance, a person facing potential loss of essential government benefits, such as welfare payments, is entitled to procedures satisfying DUE PROCESS OF LAW (GOLDBERG V. KELLY, 1971), but may have to submit to home visits for which officers otherwise would have to meet FOURTH AMENDMENT standards (WYMAN V. JAMES, 1971). The Supreme Court has found denials of EQUAL PROTECTION when states deny benefits to resident aliens (GRAHAM V. RICHARDSON, 1971) or to recent residents (SHAPIRO V. THOMPSON, 1969), but not when Congress does so (*Mathews v. Diaz*, 1976). As of 1989, the Court remained fragmented as to the effects of the equal-protection clause in limiting preferences in public contracting for members of racial or ethnic minorities (RICHMOND (CITY OF) V. J. A. CROSON CO., 1989). The Court's formula that Article IV's PRIVILEGES AND IMMUNITIES clause requires any state preference in favor of its own residents against those of other states to rest on nonresidency as a "peculiar source of [the] evil" may not govern most direct spending of state funds, but the Court has applied it to public contracting (*United Building & Construction Trades Council v. Camden*, 1984).

The First Amendment and its state equivalents are crucial but complex constraints on government programs pursued with public funds rather than regulatory sanctions. A national controversy in 1990 concerned standards for denying grants by the National Endowment for the Arts on grounds of OBSCENITY, provisions ultimately repealed by Congress. In principle, government may not require otherwise qualified beneficiaries of spending programs to abandon constitutionally privileged views or conduct; the problem is what may legitimately constitute a qualification. The Court held in SHERBERT V. VERNER (1963) that a state could not constitutionally deny unemployment compensation to one who had religious scruples against working on Saturdays. However, in the central arena of political expression, which government may not restrict directly, the Court in BUCKLEY V. VALEO (1976) held not only that Congress could offer widely supported candidates public-election campaign funds and exclude others with less preexisting support but also that this public funding could be conditioned on limiting campaign expenditures from private funds. In *Federal Communications Commission v. League of Women Voters* (1984) a statutory ban on editorializing by noncommercial broadcasters receiving federal funds was found to exceed First Amendment bounds. Yet public libraries, public theaters, public museums, and public broadcasters necessarily must select on what to spend public funds, and selection is not always easily distinguishable from disqualification.

Denying the use of the spending power to "coerce" or to "penalize" what government could not directly command or forbid does not clearly distinguish UNCONSTITUTIONAL CONDITIONS from required performance or from valid preconditions and limits of a governmental program. A distinction between an impermissible sanction and a permissible refusal to subsidize depends on the choice of the assumed baseline, as does a distinction between denying support by public funds and by tax exemptions. Analysis also is colored by whether a constitutional claim starts from a vocabulary of rights, which focuses attention on the impact on individuals, or from a vocabulary of constitutional limitations, which focuses on forbidden governmental choices of ends or of means. In cases of the latter type, inquiry into the policy goals and motivations of governmental actors may be unavoidable.

HANS A. LINDE
(1992)

(SEE ALSO: *Taxing and Spending Powers.*)

Bibliography

ADVISORY COMMISSION ON INTERGOVERNMENTAL RELATIONS 1987 *Fiscal Discipline in the Federal System: National Reform and the Experience of the States.* Washington, D.C.: U.S. Government Printing Office.

CORWIN, EDWARD S. 1923 The Spending Power of Congress Apropos the Maternity Act. *Harvard Law Review* 36:548–582.

KREIMER, SETH 1984 Allocational Sanctions: The Problem of Negative Rights in a Positive State. *University of Pennsylvania Law Review* 132:1293–1397.

LINDE, HANS A. 1965 Constitutional Rights in the Public Sector: Justice Douglas on Liberty in the Welfare State. *Washington Law Review* 39:4–46.

McGUIRE, O. M. 1935 The New Deal and the Public Money. *Georgetown University Law Review* 23:155–195.

ROSENTHAL, ALBERT J. 1987 Conditional Federal Spending and the Constitution. *Stanford Law Review* 39:1103–1164.

SPINELLI v. UNITED STATES
393 U.S. 410 (1969)

In *Spinelli* the Supreme Court explicated and expanded the PROBABLE CAUSE standards for SEARCH WARRANTS set forth in AGUILAR V. TEXAS (1964).

Spinelli was convicted under federal law of crossing state lines to conduct gambling operations. A detailed FBI affidavit, on which the search warrant was based, stated in part that Spinelli was "known" to law enforcement officers as a bookmaker, and that a confidential informant had established that Spinelli was operating as a bookmaker.

The Court ruled that the INFORMANT's testimony could not count toward the establishment of probable cause, because the affidavit failed to establish the informant's reliability or to clarify his relationship to Spinelli. The Court rejected the government's claim that the tip gave "suspicious color" to Spinelli's activities, and that, conversely, the surveillance helped corroborate the informant's tip (he had, for example, provided the correct numbers of two telephones listed in someone else's name in an apartment frequented by Spinelli). Such a "totality of the circumstances" approach, said the Court, painted "with too broad a brush." The *Spinelli* approach was abandoned in ILLINOIS V. GATES (1983).

JACOB W. LANDYNSKI
(1986)

SPOT RESOLUTIONS
(1847)

Congressman ABRAHAM LINCOLN (Whig, Illinois) introduced a series of eight resolutions in the House of Representatives on December 22, 1847. Intended to show the illegality of the Mexican War, the resolutions were in the form of interrogatories, challenging President JAMES K. POLK to name the exact spot upon which American blood was first shed in the war and to concede that that spot was on soil rightfully claimed by Mexico. The contention of the northern Whigs, including Lincoln, was that Polk had used his power as COMMANDER-IN-CHIEF of the Army to provoke the Mexicans into war in order to seize new territory into which SLAVERY could be extended.

In a brilliant speech in January 1848 Lincoln explained that accurate answers to his interrogatories would demonstrate that "the War with Mexico was unnecessarily and unconstitutionally commenced by the President." He claimed that the President had usurped Congress's constitutional power to declare war and disputed Polk's claim that Congress, by appropriating money for the conduct of the war, had sanctioned its commencement.

The Spot Resolutions, like the WILMOT PROVISO, were meant to embarrass the administration by linking the Mexican War with the slave power in the public mind. The House tabled Lincoln's resolutions but passed another resolution condemning Polk's conduct.

DENNIS J. MAHONEY
(1986)

Bibliography

JOSEPHY, ALVIN M., JR. 1975 *History of the Congress of the United States.* Pages 188–193. New York: American Heritage Publishing Co.

SPRINGER v. UNITED STATES
102 U.S. 586 (1881)

Springer contested the constitutionality of a federal income tax statute on ground that it was a DIRECT TAX not apportioned on the basis of state population. The Supreme Court unanimously upheld the tax on ground that the only direct taxes are taxes on land and CAPITATION TAXES.

LEONARD W. LEVY
(1986)

(SEE ALSO: *Pollock v. Farmers' Loan & Trust Co.*)

STAFFORD v. WALLACE
358 U.S. 495 (1922)

Seventeen years after SWIFT & COMPANY V. UNITED STATES (1905), the Supreme Court again approved the extension of federal authority to local activities. A nationalistic exposition of the COMMERCE CLAUSE ran through the opinion in which the Court not only reaffirmed but also extended the STREAM OF COMMERCE DOCTRINE. Commission men, who sold animals on consignment, sued to enjoin enforcement of the PACKERS & STOCKYARDS ACT. They asserted that because they provided only "personal services" and were not engaged in INTERSTATE COMMERCE, they were not subject to the act. For a 7–1 Court, Chief Justice WILLIAM HOWARD TAFT followed Justice OLIVER WENDELL HOLMES's

opinion in *Swift* and sustained the act. Congress had acted reasonably in securing an "unburdened flow" of interstate commerce. Moreover, the stockyards were "not a place of rest or final destination . . . but a throat through which the current [of commerce] flows." Because the commission men were essential to maintaining this flow, their activities were properly part of interstate commerce and subject to the act. Justice JAMES C. MCREYNOLDS dissented without opinion. By reviving and reapplying the stream of commerce DOCTRINE, the Court built a foundation on which the NEW DEAL would later support its ECONOMIC REGULATIONS.

DAVID GORDON
(1986)

STAMP ACT CONGRESS, RESOLUTIONS OF
(October 19, 1765)

These resolutions, adopted by the delegates of nine American colonies meeting in an intercolonial congress, expressed the basis of the American constitutional position in the quarrel with Great Britain leading to the AMERICAN REVOLUTION. The mother country, financially exhausted by a great war from which the American colonies stood to gain the most, decided to retain an army in America and to require the colonists to pay a small fraction of the cost of their defense. Parliamentary legislation aimed at raising a revenue in America was, however, unprecedented before the Sugar Act of 1764. That act provoked the first constitutional protests from the colonies. In form the 1764 legislation had regulated their ocean trade, thus imposing an "external" tax. The Stamp Act of 1765 imposed "internal" taxes on every sort of legal document and most business documents; on college diplomas, liquor licences, and appointments to offices; and on playing cards, newspapers, advertisements, almanacs, books, and pamphlets. Admiralty courts, which operated without juries and used inquisitional procedures, had JURISDICTION over offenses against the act. American opposition was so vehement and widespread that the act proved to be unenforceable.

The Stamp Act Congress addressed itself to two constitutional issues raised by the act of Parliament. After asserting that the colonists were entitled to all the rights and liberties of Englishmen, the congress resolved that Parliament, a body in which the colonists were not represented and which could not represent them, had no constitutional authority to tax them. Several resolutions condemned TAXATION WITHOUT REPRESENTATION and endorsed the principle that only their own assemblies could constitutionally tax the American colonists. The congress also endorsed the right to TRIAL BY JURY and condemned the unprecedented extension of admiralty court jurisdiction as subversive of colonial liberties.

The Stamp Act was in force for only four months before Parliament repealed it, not because of the American constitutional protests but because of the protests of British merchants who suffered from a boycott of their goods by American importers. To save face, Parliament accompanied its repealer with the Declaratory Act of 1766, which insisted that Great Britain had full power to make laws for America "in all cases whatsoever." The American position, that "no taxes . . . can be constitutionally imposed . . . but by their respective legislatures," was founded on a different view of the British constitution, even a different understanding of the meaning of a CONSTITUTION and of the word "unconstitutional." A local court in Virginia gratuitously condemned the Stamp Act as unconstitutional and therefore not binding.

LEONARD W. LEVY
(1986)

Bibliography

MORGAN, EDMUND S. and HELEN M.   1953   *The Stamp Act Congress*. Chapel Hill: University of North Carolina Press.

STANBERY, HENRY S.
(1803–1881)

An Ohio lawyer and United States attorney general (1866–1868), Henry Stanbery opposed congressional reconstruction and prepared many of President ANDREW JOHNSON's veto messages. Nevertheless, in MISSISSIPPI V. JOHNSON (1867) Stanbery successfully defended executive enforcement of congressional statutes by arguing that the SEPARATION OF POWERS barred the Supreme Court from issuing an INJUNCTION against the President. Similarly, in *Georgia v. Stanton* (1868) he successfully argued that the case involved POLITICAL QUESTIONS beyond the Court's JURISDICTION. In 1868 Stanbery resigned his office to defend Johnson at his IMPEACHMENT trial. Stanbery's insistence on DUE PROCESS slowed the trial and helped achieve Johnson's acquittal.

PAUL FINKELMAN
(1986)

Bibliography

MENEELY, A. HOWARD   1935   Henry Stanbery. In *Dictionary of American Biography*, Vol. 27:498–499. New York: Scribner's.

STANDARD OF REVIEW

Some constitutional limitations on government are readily susceptible to "interpretation," in the sense of definition and categorization. Once a court categorizes a law as a BILL OF ATTAINDER, for example, it holds the law invalid. Other limitations, however, are expressed in terms that make this sort of interpretation awkward: the FREEDOM OF SPEECH, the EQUAL PROTECTION OF THE LAWS, DUE PROCESS OF LAW. The judicial task in enforcing these open-ended limitations implies an inquiry into the justifications asserted by government for restricting liberty or denying equal treatment. The term "standards of review," in common use since the late 1960s, denotes various degrees of judicial deference to legislative judgments concerning these justifications.

The idea that there might be more than one standard of review was explicitly suggested in Justice HARLAN FISKE STONE's opinion for the Supreme Court in UNITED STATES V. CAROLENE PRODUCTS CO. (1938). Confirming a retreat from the JUDICIAL ACTIVISM that had invalidated a significant number of ECONOMIC REGULATIONS over the preceding four decades, Stone concluded that such a law would be valid if the legislature's purpose were legitimate and if the law could rationally be seen as related to that purpose. Stone added, however, that this permissive RATIONAL BASIS standard might not be appropriate for reviewing laws challenged under certain specific prohibitions of the BILL OF RIGHTS, or laws restricting the political process, or laws directed at DISCRETE AND INSULAR MINORITIES. Such cases, Stone suggested, might call for a diminished presumption of constitutionality, a "more exacting judicial scrutiny."

The WARREN COURT embraced this double standard in several doctrinal areas, most notably in equal protection cases. The permissive rational basis standard continued to govern review of economic regulations, but STRICT SCRUTINY was given to laws discriminating against the exercise of FUNDAMENTAL INTERESTS such as voting or marriage and to laws employing SUSPECT CLASSIFICATIONS such as race. The strict scrutiny standard amounts to an inversion of the presumption of constitutionality: the state must justify its imposition of a racial inequality, for example, by showing that the law is necessary to achieve a COMPELLING STATE INTEREST. Today active judicial review of both the importance of legislative purposes and the necessity of legislative means is employed not only in some types of equal protection cases but also in fields such as the freedom of speech and RELIGIOUS LIBERTY. It has even attended the rebirth of SUBSTANTIVE DUE PROCESS.

Inevitably, however, cracks appeared in this two-tier system of standards of review. The Court used the language of "rational basis" to strike down some laws, and in cases involving SEX DISCRIMINATION it explicitly adopted an intermediate standard for reviewing both legislative ends and means: discrimination based on sex is invalid unless it serves an "important" governmental purpose and is "substantially related" to that purpose. A similar intermediate standard is now part of the required analysis of governmental regulations of COMMERCIAL SPEECH. In practical effect, the Court has created a "sliding scale" of review, varying the intensity of judicial scrutiny of legislation in proportion to the importance of the interests invaded and the likelihood of legislative prejudice against the persons disadvantaged. The process, in other words, is interest-balancing, pure and simple. Justice WILLIAM H. REHNQUIST, writing for the Court in ROSTKER V. GOLDBERG (1981), remarked accurately that the Court's various levels of scrutiny "may all too readily become facile abstractions used to justify a result"—a proposition well illustrated by the *Rostker* opinion itself.

KENNETH L. KARST
(1986)

Bibliography

GUNTHER, GERALD 1972 The Supreme Court, 1971 Term—Foreword: In Search of Evolving Doctrine on a Changing Court: A Model for a Newer Equal Protection. *Harvard Law Review* 86:1–48.

STANDARD OIL COMPANY v. UNITED STATES
221 U.S. 1 (1911)

UNITED STATES v. AMERICAN TOBACCO COMPANY
211 U.S. 106 (1911)

John D. Rockefeller, owner of the nation's first, largest, and richest trust and controller of the nation's oil business, scorned his competitors and contemned the law. His disregard for the SHERMAN ANTITRUST ACT helped earn him, in 1909, a dissolution order which the trust appealed to the Supreme Court. Rockefeller thereby provided Chief Justice EDWARD D. WHITE with the occasion to celebrate the conversion of a majority of the Court to his viewpoint, enabling him to write the RULE OF REASON into antitrust law. After nearly fifteen years of effort, White had managed to enlarge judicial discretion in antitrust cases, even though the oil trust did not urge the doctrine upon the Court; indeed, it was unnecessary to the case's disposition.

Chief Justice White, leading an 8–1 Court, ruled that only an "unreasonable" contract or combination in restraint of trade would violate the law. White had effectively amended the law to insert his test: section 1 of the Sherman Act would henceforth be interpreted as if it said, "Every unreasonable contract, combination . . . or conspiracy in restraint of trade . . . is hereby declared to be illegal."

Standard Oil, however, lost the case. The record, said

White, showed clearly and convincingly that this trust was unreasonable. Systematic attempts to exclude or crush rivals and the trust's astounding success demonstrated the violation beyond any doubt.

Justice JOHN MARSHALL HARLAN concurred in the result but dissented from the Court's announcement of the rule of reason. Harlan observed that Congress had refused to amend the act to incorporate the rule of reason, and he lashed out at the majority's "judicial legislation," predicting that the new policy would produce chaos. His call echoed in Congress where Democratic pressure grew to write the rule of reason out of the Sherman Act. That pressure would eventually find partial release in supplementary antitrust legislation, passage of the CLAYTON ACT in 1914. The rule of reason prevailed, however, although the Court applied a double standard. When massive business combinations such as United States Steel Corporation, United Shoe Machinery Company, and International Harvester came before the Court, they were found to have acted reasonably, restraints of trade notwithstanding. In antitrust action against labor unions, however, the Court ignored that rule.

In the companion *American Tobacco* case, Chief Justice White attempted to mitigate a too vigorous federal antitrust policy by ordering reorganization, not dissolution, of the Tobacco Trust. He thereby heartened business interests by showing solicitousness for property rights and a stable economy.

DAVID GORDON
(1986)

Bibliography

BRINGHURST, BRUCE 1979 *Antitrust and the Oil Monopoly: The Standard Oil Cases, 1890–1914.* Westport, Conn.: Greenwood Press.

STANDING

In the United States, unelected, life-tenured federal judges may decide legal issues only when they are asked to do so by appropriate litigants. Such litigants are said to have standing to raise certain legal claims, including constitutional claims, in the federal courts.

A litigant's standing depends on two sets of criteria, one constitutionally required and one not, each ostensibly having three parts. The constitutional criteria derive from Article III's job description for federal judges, which permits them to declare law only when such a declaration is necessary to decide CASES AND CONTROVERSIES. These criteria center on the notion of an injured person's asking a court for a remedy against the responsible party, and each criterion corresponds to one of the three participants—to the plaintiff, the defendant, and the court, respectively. The plaintiff must assert that he suffered a cognizable personal injury; that the defendant's conduct caused the injury; and that the court's judgment is substantially likely to relieve it. The three nonconstitutional criteria for standing are "prudential" rules, self-imposed by the courts for their own governance, rules which Congress can eliminate if it chooses. These criteria, too, serve to diminish the frequency of substantive pronouncements by federal judges, but they focus on the legal basis of the suit, not on the plaintiff's actual injury. The first nonconstitutional criterion concerns representation: to secure judicial relief, injured litigants normally must assert that the injurious conduct violated their own legal rights, not the rights of third parties. The second assumes that government violations of everyone's undifferentiated legal rights are best left to political, not judicial, response: no one has standing if his or her legal position asserts "only the generalized interest of all citizens in constitutional governance." The third "prudential" criterion for standing seeks assurance that the law invoked plausibly protects the legal interest allegedly invaded: whatever interest is asserted must be "arguably within the zone of interests to be protected or regulated by the statute or constitutional guarantee in question."

Standing issues rarely surface in traditional suits, but federal courts applying these guidelines frequently deny standing to "public interest" plaintiffs anxious to challenge the legality of government behavior. The aim is not only to prevent federal judges from proclaiming law unless such declarations are needed to resolve concrete disputes, but also to promote proper conditions for intelligent adjudication (including adversary presentation of the facts and legal arguments) and to foster adequate representation of affected interests. When litigants ask federal courts to restrict the constitutional authority of politically accountable public officials, moreover, apprehension about unwise or excessive judicial intervention heightens, and the standing limitations may be applied with particular force.

Collectively, the Supreme Court's standing criteria often overlap; they are applied flexibly—sometimes inconsistently—to give the Supreme Court considerable discretion to exercise or withhold its power to declare law. The way that discretion is exercised reflects any particular Court's ideology of JUDICIAL ACTIVISM AND RESTRAINT and the substantive, constitutional rights it is either eager or reluctant to enforce.

The refinements of standing doctrine illustrate this flexibility and discretion. The core requirement of cognizable personal injury, for example, demands that the plaintiff have suffered injury to an interest deemed deserving of judicial protection. Over time, the Court has expanded the category of judicially acknowledged injuries beyond economic harm to include reputational, environmental, aesthetic, associational, informational, organizational, and voter harms, among others. Because of its vision of constrained judicial power in a representative democracy, however, the Court steadfastly forbids TAXPAYERS' SUITS and citizens' suits asserting purely ideological harm, particularly the harms of frustration, distress, or apprehension born of unlawful government conduct. Resting on lack of cognizable injury, the ban on citizen standing thus appears constitutionally compelled, although it effectively duplicates the nonconstitutional barrier to asserting generalized grievances, which appears to rest on the absence of a cognizable legal interest. Less diffuse, but in ALLEN V. WRIGHT (1984) nonetheless held an insufficiently personal injury, is the feeling of stigma arising from discrimination directed, not personally, but against other members of the plaintiff's race. If the type of injury is judicially approved and the plaintiff personally suffered it, however, the fact that many others have suffered it will not negate standing. For example, in UNITED STATES V. SCRAP (1973) a student activist group was deemed to have standing based on widespread environmental injury.

Flexibility also characterizes the Court's degree of insistence on the remaining constitutional criteria. The closeness of the causal link between defendant's conduct and plaintiff's injury has varied from *United States v. SCRAP*, which accepted a loose connection between the Interstate Commerce Commission's approval of freight rate increases for scrap materials and increased trash problems in national parks, to *Allen v. Wright* (1984), which found too attenuated a seemingly closer link between the Internal Revenue Service's allegedly inadequate enforcement of the law requiring denial of tax exemptions to racially discriminatory private schools and "white flight" in public school districts undergoing DESEGREGATION. Similarly, insistence that judicial relief be substantially likely to redress plaintiff's injury has varied from *Linda R. S. v. Richard D.* (1973), where mothers of illegitimate children seeking to force prosecution of the fathers for nonsupport were denied standing because a court order supposedly would result only in jailing the fathers, not in increased support, to *Duke Power Co. v. Carolina Environmental Study Group* (1978), where neighbors of nuclear power plants, seeking relief from present injury caused by normal plant operation, were granted standing to contest (unsuccessfully) the constitutional validity of a federal statute limiting recovery of DAMAGES for potential nuclear disasters, despite considerable uncertainty that a legal victory for the plaintiffs would stop the plants' normal operations.

Of the nonconstitutional criteria, only the usual prohibition against representing third-party rights needs elaboration, primarily because of its different forms and its significant exceptions. When a personally injured plaintiff seeks to argue that the injurious conduct violated the legal rights of others, the prohibition, beyond serving the usual objectives of standing, serves also to protect nonlitigants who may not wish to assert their own rights or would do so differently (and perhaps more effectively) if they became litigants. Major exceptions to that prohibition respond to this policy by allowing representation, even of constitutional rights, when the Court concludes that the absent third parties would benefit rather than suffer from a substantive decision. One important example of this exception is the case in which third parties would have difficulty asserting their own rights, as in NAACP V. ALABAMA (1958), where the CIVIL RIGHTS group was permitted to assert its members' right to remain anonymous. Another example is the case in which the disputed conduct affects special plaintiff-third party relationships in ways suggesting that the plaintiff and third-party interests coincide. Under this exception doctors can represent patient rights to abortion, private schools can represent parent rights to choose private education, and sellers can represent the rights of young consumers to buy beer or contraceptives.

The Court generally denies standing when persons constitutionally subject to regulation urge that the regulation would be unconstitutional in application to others. This rule preserves legislative policy in cases where the law is applied constitutionally. Again, however, there is an exception, invoked most often in FIRST AMENDMENT challenges of VAGUENESS and OVERBREADTH, when the law's very existence would significantly inhibit others from exercising important constitutional rights and thus deter them from mounting their own challenge.

A final example is the case in which uninjured representatives seek to champion the legal rights of injured persons they represent outside of litigation. Thus, associations, not injured themselves, may sue on behalf of their members' injuries, provided that the members would have standing, the associations seek to protect interests germane to their purposes, and the claims and requested relief do not require individual member participation. And a state, which normally lacks standing as *parens patriae* to represent the claims of individual citizens, or even of all its citizens in opposition to the federal government, may represent its citizens when the injury alleged substantially affects the state's general population, especially if suit by individual citizens seems unlikely.

Like other JUSTICIABILITY doctrines, standing rules often thwart attempts to induce federal courts to make or reform constitutional or other law. How often the rules have that result will depend not only on the articulated criteria of standing but also on the Supreme Court's receptivity to the substance of the underlying claims and its judgment of the desirability and likelihood of political solutions.

JOHNATAN D. VARAT
(1986)

Bibliography

NICHOL, GENE R., JR. 1984 Rethinking Standing. *California Law Review* 72:68–102.
SCOTT, KENNETH E. 1973 Standing in the Supreme Court: A Functional Analysis. *Harvard Law Review* 86:645–692.
VINING, JOSEPH 1978 *Legal Identity: The Coming of Age of Public Law.* New Haven, Conn.: Yale University Press.

STANDING
(Update)

Standing law defines those who may obtain judicial redress in federal court. In suits between private individuals, there is usually little analytical difficulty in determining what constitutes judicial cognizable injury and thus who has standing to sue. But in suits by private individuals against the government, there can be considerable difficulty. In such cases, plaintiffs are sometimes not injured in a conventional sense, not suffering, for example, physical harm or monetary loss. Rather, plaintiffs sometimes sue as "private attorneys general," seeking judicial redress against allegedly illegal governmental conduct affecting the general population.

There are both constitutional and subconstitutional standing requirements. The constitutional requirement derives from Article III, which limits federal courts to deciding "cases" and "controversies." Under current law, a plaintiff may satisfy Article III by showing, first, that she has suffered "injury in fact," defined as a concrete and particularized invasion of a legally protected interest; second, that the injury is fairly traceable to defendant's conduct; and third, that the injury will likely be redressed by a favorable judicial decision.

A plaintiff may satisfy the subconstitutional standing requirement by showing that she has a cause of action under a statute, a COMMON LAW rule, or a constitutional provision. In borderline cases, the Supreme Court has developed two approaches. First, in a series of administrative law cases that includes *Association of Data Processing Service Organizations v. Camp* (1970) and *National Credit Union Administration v. First National Bank & Trust* (1998), the Court has required a plaintiff to be "arguably within the zone of interests" of a relevant statute or constitutional guarantee. This test is essentially an instruction to construe statutes generously in favor of standing. Second, in another series of cases that includes *Warth v.*

Seldin (1975), the Court has asked whether there is "prudential standing." A grant of prudential standing means that the Court, in the exercise of "prudence," has found a sufficiently clear indication of congressional intent to create a cause of action for plaintiff. In most prudential standing cases, the Court has declined to find standing.

Despite the Court's persistent efforts to fit standing decisions into the framework just described, the considerations involved are often too varied to be captured by general formulations. Cases applying the "injury in fact" criterion have been particularly unruly, producing decisions that are extremely difficult to reconcile. For example, in UNITED STATES V. STUDENTS CHALLENGING REGULATORY AGENCY PROCEDURE (SCRAP) (1973), the Court found injury in fact for a group of law students seeking to compel the preparation of an Environmental Impact Statement analyzing possible environmental effects of a minuscule increase in railroad rates. The students alleged that the rate increase could cause environmental damage as a result of increased recycling costs. Further, in *Havens Realty Corp. v. Coleman* (1982), the Court found injury in fact for a professional black "tester" who had been told, falsely, that an apartment was not for rent, even though the tester had no actual desire to occupy the apartment. Yet, in LUJAN V. DEFENDERS OF WILDLIFE (1992), the Court refused to find injury in fact for wildlife enthusiasts who sought to compel agency consultation concerning federally funded projects that might adversely affect habitats for endangered species. The plaintiffs had previously visited the areas where the species lived but had no specific plans and no airplane tickets for return visits.

Among the many considerations involved in standing cases, perhaps the most important is SEPARATION OF POWERS. In most cases, standing restrictions confine the role of the judiciary by reducing and sometimes even eliminating certain kinds of litigation. But in some cases, standing restrictions expand the role of the judiciary, because a judicial decision that plaintiff lacks Article III standing means that Congress may not grant standing. This phenomenon may be seen in two recent cases. In *Lujan* Congress had granted standing to "any person" to enforce the Endangered Species Act. The Court held that plaintiffs satisfied the statute but lacked Article III standing because they had suffered no injury in fact. In *Raines v. Byrd* (1997), Congress had granted standing to "any Member of Congress" to challenge the constitutionality of the federal law providing the President with a limited LINE-ITEM VETO. The Court held that members of Congress lacked Article III standing because they had not suffered "sufficiently concrete injury" from the law's operation.

At this point in its development, standing doctrine frequently does not correspond to the Court's actual decisions. As the second Justice JOHN MARSHALL HARLAN complained more than thirty years ago in FLAST V. COHEN (1968), standing is a "word game played by secret rules." But given the importance of standing decisions, it is perhaps better for now to have the right results than the right DOCTRINE. One may hope that eventually, in the great tradition of common law courts, the Court will decide enough standing cases to understand what it has done, and from those cases to construct a coherent legal doctrine.

WILLIAM A. FLETCHER
(2000)

Bibliography

FLETCHER, WILLIAM A. 1988 The Structure of Standing. *Yale Law Journal* 98:221–291.
PUSHAW, ROBERT J. 1996 Justiciability and Separation of Powers: A Neo-Federalist Approach. *Cornell Law Review* 81: 394–512.
SUNSTEIN, CASS R. 1988 Standing and the Privatization of Public Law. *Columbia Law Review* 88:1432–1481.

STANFORD v. KENTUCKY
492 U.S. 361 (1989)

By a 5–4 vote, the Court held that the infliction of CAPITAL PUNISHMENT on juveniles who committed their crimes at sixteen or seventeen years of age did not violate the CRUEL AND UNUSUAL PUNISHMENT clause of the Eighth Amendment, applied to the states by the FOURTEENTH AMENDMENT.

Justice ANTONIN SCALIA, for the majority, acknowledged that whether a punishment conflicts with evolving standards of decency depends on public opinion. But in examining the laws of the country, Scalia found that a majority of the states permit the execution of juvenile offenders. He refused to consider indicia of society's opinion other than by examination of jury verdicts and statutory law. Public opinion polls and the views of professional associations seemed to invite constitutional law to rest on "uncertain foundations." The Court also ruled that the imposition of death on juvenile offenders did not conflict with the legitimate goals of penology.

The four dissenters, led by Justice WILLIAM J. BRENNAN, argued that the Eighth Amendment prohibits the punishment of death for a person who committed a crime when under eighteen years of age. The dissenters relied on a far wider range of indicia of public opinion than did the majority to reach their conclusion that evolving standards of decency required a different holding. They argued too that the death penalty is disproportionate when applied to

STANLEY v. GEORGIA
394 U.S. 557 (1969)

Authorized by a SEARCH WARRANT, federal and state agents entered and searched Stanley's home for evidence of bookmaking activities. Instead they found film, which was used to convict him for possession of obscene material. The Supreme Court reversed, holding that mere possession of obscenity in one's home cannot constitutionally be made a crime.

Prior OBSCENITY decisions had recognized a legitimate state interest in regulating public dissemination of obscene materials. In *Stanley*, however, the Court recognized two fundamental constitutional rights that outweighed the state interest in regulating obscenity in a citizen's home: the FIRST AMENDMENT right to receive information and ideas, regardless of their social worth, and the constitutional right to be free from unwanted government intrusion into one's privacy.

As justification for interfering with these important individual rights, the state asserted the right to protect individuals from obscenity's effects. The Court rejected that argument, viewing such "protection" as an attempt to "control . . . a person's thoughts," a goal "wholly inconsistent with the philosophy of the First Amendment."

Justices POTTER J. STEWART, WILLIAM J. BRENNAN, and BYRON R. WHITE concurred in the result, on the ground that the SEARCH AND SEIZURE were outside the lawful scope of the officers' warrant, and thus violated Stanley's FOURTH AMENDMENT rights.

KIM MCLANE WARDLAW
(1986)

STANTON, EDWIN M.
(1814–1869)

A prominent antebellum attorney, Edwin McMasters Stanton was an active member of the Supreme Court bar and was the chief government investigator and counsel in the California land claims cases. In 1859 he successfully defended Congressman Daniel Sickles in a murder trial with the then novel defense of temporary insanity.

In 1860 Stanton became JAMES BUCHANAN's lame duck ATTORNEY GENERAL. An ardent Unionist, Stanton urged support for the garrison at Fort Sumter and the arrest for TREASON of the South Carolina commissioners. During the interregnum Stanton secretly met with Republican senators informing them of the administration's complicity with secessionists. He also worked secretly with General Winfield Scott to move troops to protect Washington while preventing the shipment of arms to the South.

As secretary of war (1862–1868) Stanton vastly reduced corruption and political influence on promotions, while building a highly efficient military. Stanton was an early advocate of emancipation and the use of black troops. Zealous in supporting the Union, Stanton used the War Department to arrest civilians suspected of treason, disloyalty, or disrupting recruitment and rigorously enforced internal security. During the 1863 and 1864 elections Stanton furloughed troops so they could return home to vote, used the army to intimidate opponents, and allowed officers to campaign.

After ABRAHAM LINCOLN's assassination Stanton was ruthless in finding and prosecuting anyone connected with John Wilkes Booth's plot. Despite President ANDREW JOHNSON's opposition, Stanton supported the CIVIL RIGHTS ACT OF 1866 and the FREEDMAN'S BUREAU, while working closely with Congress to support MILITARY RECONSTRUCTION. Stanton's backing of generals sympathetic to congressional goals prevented Johnson from implementing his reconstruction program. Fear that Johnson would fire Stanton led to the TENURE OF OFFICE ACT and then to IMPEACHMENT proceedings when Johnson tried to replace Stanton. Stanton aided the impeachment managers by giving them war department documents and information, lobbying wavering senators, and writing "anonymous" editorials denouncing Johnson. After Johnson's acquittal Stanton resigned. In 1869 President ULYSSES S. GRANT nominated Stanton to the Supreme Court, but he died before confirmation.

PAUL FINKELMAN
(1986)

Bibliography

THOMAS, BENJAMIN P. and HYMAN, HAROLD M. 1962 *Stanton: The Life and Times of Lincoln's Secretary of War.* New York: Knopf.

STANTON, ELIZABETH CADY
(1815–1902)

Elizabeth Cady was born in Johnstown, New York, to Daniel Cady, influential legal reformer, and Margaret Livingston Cady, from one of the state's oldest landed families. She received the best education available to young women, at Emma Willard's Troy Academy, but resented the fact that only men could attend college. At the age of twenty-five, she married Henry Brewster Stanton, noted abolitionist orator and organizer. Honeymooning with him in

---

young offenders and significantly fails to serve the goals of capital punishment.

LEONARD W. LEVY
(1992)

London to attend an international antislavery convention, she met Lucretia Mott, dean of American female abolition, who served as her mentor in the ideas of women's rights.

Eight years later, in 1848, Stanton and Mott called the first American women's rights convention. Held in Stanton's home town in New York, the SENECA FALLS CONVENTION demanded a whole list of reforms, at the head of which was political rights. Three years later, Stanton met SUSAN B. ANTHONY, a temperance advocate from nearby Rochester, and they began a lifelong collaboration. Together they petitioned, lobbied, and addressed the New York legislature to pass a comprehensive Married Women's Property Act, which it did in 1860. During the CIVIL WAR, they agitated for constitutional abolition and emancipation, black and woman suffrage.

In the RECONSTRUCTION years, Stanton's woman suffrage leadership became highly contentious. She and Anthony pushed first to have the invidious references to a "male" electorate removed from the FOURTEENTH AMENDMENT and then to have "sex" included in the list of prohibited disfranchisements in the FIFTEENTH AMENDMENT. Once these amendments were ratified without including women's demands, they shifted their argument to an innovative constitutional construction in which woman suffrage was permitted by the Constitution as amended. In 1874, the Supreme Court struck down their argument, but for the rest of her life, Stanton insisted on the link between woman suffrage and the sovereignty and dignity of national CITIZENSHIP.

Stanton was identified with other reforms and aspects of women's emancipation. She called for reform in the laws and customs of MARRIAGE, to make it an egalitarian and more easily dissolvable pact. From there, she undertook a campaign for what she called "self-sovereignty," the establishment of an ethic of female sexual and reproductive self-determination. In this, she was closely allied with the free-love radical Victoria Woodhull in the early 1870s. The reform passion of Stanton's final years was freethought. She argued that notions of women's inferiority were, at their root, the product of a patriarchal Christianity, a belief that alienated her from the growing ranks of organized middle-class womanhood at century's end.

Stanton had seven children, of whom two, her daughter Harriot and her son Theodore, became important women's rights figures in their own right. She died in 1902.

ELLEN CAROL DuBOIS
(2000)

(SEE ALSO: *Woman Suffrage Movement.*)

Bibliography

BANNER, LOIS 1980 *Elizabeth Cady Stanton: A Radical for Women's Rights.* Boston: Little, Brown.
DuBOIS, ELLEN, ed. 1991 *Elizabeth Cady Stanton, Susan B. Anthony: A Reader.* Boston: Northeastern University Press.
GRIFFITH, ELISABETH 1984 *In Her Own Right: The Life of Elizabeth Cady Stanton.* New York: Oxford University Press.
STANTON, ELIZABETH 1898 *Eighty Years and More: Reminiscences, 1815–1897* (1991 reprint). Boston: Northeastern University Press.

STARE DECISIS

(Latin: "to stand by decided [cases].") The DOCTRINE of *stare decisis*, one of the key elements of Anglo-American COMMON LAW, embodies the principle that PRECEDENTS are to be followed in the adjudication of cases. The substance of the law is revealed through the decisions of courts in cases between individuals or between an individual and the government, and adherence to precedent transforms the decisions in those cases into a settled body of public law. Once an issue of law has been resolved in a case by a court of competent JURISDICTION, the HOLDING in the case is determinative of the issue for that court and subordinate courts; and it offers guidance, as well, to courts of coordinate jurisdiction. Courts proceed, as a general rule, by following and applying precedents or else by distinguishing them (that is, by showing how the facts of the instant case render the precedent inapposite). Most frequently a court faces the question of which of two or more lines of precedent to follow. The doctrine of *stare decisis* lends stability and predictability to the legal order, but it is not absolute: courts may dispose of precedents that are outdated, or that have undesirable consequences, by OVERRULING them. The federal courts, and especially the Supreme Court, have tended in recent years to diminish the force of *stare decisis* in constitutional cases.

DENNIS J. MAHONEY
(1986)

STARE DECISIS
(Update)

Stare decisis, or the principle of following PRECEDENT, is uncertain as to both its scope and its strength. With respect to its scope, there are three basic models of what it means to follow precedent.

Under the first model of stare decisis, a court follows precedent if it merely takes into account the present traces of what prior courts have done. Thus, under this model, a court is always free to decide the case before it as it believes best in terms of moral and policy considerations. To the extent that earlier decisions have induced reliance and created specific expectations, or to the extent that earlier decisions have created a claim of equal treatment of present and past litigants, to that extent the present court's judgment about what is the right decision to reach may differ from what its judgment would have been in the absence of the earlier decisions. But the present court is never required by past decisions to depart from its judgment about what is morally optimal in the present.

Under the second model of stare decisis, the present court is more constrained by earlier decisions than it would be under the first model. Under this model, the present court must construct a principle that would produce the results (not necessarily the opinions) of the earlier decisions and then decide the present case under that principle. If the earlier decisions were, in the present court's view, incorrect, then the covering principle may require the present court to reach what it believes is a morally incorrect or suboptimal decision in the case before it. For this reason, the second model is more constraining than the first.

Under the third model of stare decisis, the constraint that earlier decisions exercise over present decisions is the product of the rules laid down by the earlier courts in their opinions. In other words, under this model, the earlier courts are like legislatures. In deciding cases, they lay down rules for later courts to follow.

Normally, when courts are required to interpret a text such as a statute or a constitution, they translate the vague textual rule into a clearer one. In a subsequent case involving the same provision, the principle of stare decisis requires the court to apply the earlier court's rule reformulation of the provision as if it were the correct meaning of the provision. Thus, in cases involving interpretation of nonjudicial texts, the third model is usually the model employed, even if it is not the model employed in purely COMMON LAW contexts. Sometimes, however, the courts do not translate a vague textual standard into a clear(er) rule but instead engage in common law decisionmaking under that textual standard. The Supreme Court has treated many of the individual rights provisions of the Constitution this way, a case in point being its elaboration of the term "liberty" under the DUE PROCESS clauses. Whenever the Court is elaborating the constitutional text in this common law manner, then the scope of precedential constraint on its decisions depends on which of the three models of stare decisis the Court adopts.

The second controversy over the principle of stare decisis concerns not its scope but its strength. When may a precedent case or cases be overruled? If the answer is that precedents may be overruled whenever the present court disagrees with them, then the second and third models of stare decisis collapse and we are left with only the first model, under which precedents need never be overruled because only their present effects must be taken into account. If, on the other hand, precedents may never be overruled, then the strength of the principle of stare decisis is infinite.

In constitutional law, proposals regarding the strength of the principle vary, from according the principle very little strength (so that the Court can always overrule its earlier decisions with which it now disagrees, and other courts and government officials may depart from Court precedents in anticipation of Court OVERRULINGS), to according the principle considerable strength, so the Court can overrule its precedents only if it believes them both wrong as interpretations and unjust or mischievous in application. On this latter view, other courts and officials cannot anticipate overrulings by the Court.

There are some proponents of the position that stare decisis should not apply at all to constitutional decisions, so that no one is bound by the Court's CONSTITUTIONAL INTERPRETATIONS except in the actual cases in which the interpretations are rendered. No one advocates the opposite extreme; namely, that not even the Court can overrule its precedents—though this position would settle constitutional controversies more than the other positions regarding the strength of precedent.

LARRY ALEXANDER
(2000)

(SEE ALSO: *Planned Parenthood v. Casey.*)

STATE

The DECLARATION OF INDEPENDENCE declares that the "united colonies" are, as they ought MK MM to be, "free and independent states." The term "states" was chosen to indicate their status as autonomous political communities. The state was the result of the SOCIAL COMPACT, binding man to man and subjecting all to rule by some part of the community. The term also carried a connotation, already obsolescent in England, of a republican form of government; the seventeenth-century British political writers with whose works the Americans were familiar had generally contrasted "state" with "monarchy" or "principality."

But the Declaration of Independence was, after all, the unanimous declaration of the *united* states. Although the Declaration proclaims that the states are "free and independent," they were not thereby made independent of one another. By the Declaration, the one American people assumes among the powers of the earth the separate and equal station to which it is entitled by natural and divine law. Thus is the American people declared to possess SOVEREIGNTY, and not the several states, although in the common usage, of the eighteenth as well as of the twentieth century, the term "state" refers to a sovereign entity.

The central paradox of American politics has always been, from the time of the Declaration and of the Constitution, the existence of ineradicable states within an indissoluble Union. The sovereignty of the people, from whom both the national and the state governments derive their just powers, is the basis for the distinctively American form of FEDERALISM. Neither is the central government the creature of the states nor do the states exist at the mercy of the central government, but both exercise those limited and delegate powers that are assigned them by the sovereign people.

Each of the original thirteen states had been founded and administered as a British colony prior to 1776. They had, therefore, established forms of government under their COLONIAL CHARTERS. During the Revolution, most of them adopted CONSTITUTIONS providing for government of the same persons and territory as the colonies had comprised. The fourteenth and fifteenth states, Vermont and Kentucky, had experienced provisional self-government before they were admitted to the Union. Before the ANNEXATION OF TEXAS, that state had revolted against Mexico and governed itself as an independent republic. California's brief existence as the "Bear Flag Republic" (1846) scarcely qualifies as independence or self-government; but, when the controversy over slavery prevented Congress from organizing the lands won in the Mexican War, California proceeded to adopt a constitution (1849) and to govern its own affairs until its admission to the Union (1850). Hawaii was an independent kingdom for centuries before American immigrants revolted against the native monarchy and engineered the annexation of those islands by the United States.

All of the rest of the states—thirty-two to date—have been formed out of the national dominion of the United States and have been admitted to the Union as states following a probationary period as TERRITORIES. The process by which the national dominion was to be settled and transformed into states was devised by THOMAS JEFFERSON and adopted by the CONTINENTAL CONGRESS as the ORDINANCE OF 1784, although that ordinance was never actually enforced. Essentially the same scheme was enacted in the NORTHWEST ORDINANCE (1787), which was the model for all subsequent treatment of the territories of the United States. At the CONSTITUTIONAL CONVENTION OF 1787 the delegates rejected GOUVERNEUR MORRIS's proposal that states formed from the western territories should have a status inferior to the original states, and they provided instead that new states should be admitted to the Union on terms of full equality with the existing states.

Under the ARTICLES OF CONFEDERATION the national government was entirely the creature of the state governments. The confederation derived its formal existence from a compact among the states, and the members of Congress were chosen by the state legislatures. Most of the delegates to the Constitutional Convention were convinced of the necessity of creating a national government directly responsible to the people of the nation. JAMES MADISON, for one, arrived in Philadelphia prepared to argue for a pure separation of state from national government, according to which the two tiers of government would be separately elected and separately responsible to the people in their respective spheres. But the Convention chose instead to give the institutions of the states a share in the government of the nation, and to provide, in the national constitution, for certain guarantees to the people of the states, including guarantees against their state governments.

In the Constitution, representatives in Congress are allocated to the states on the basis of population, and the state governments are left free to apportion them among districts and to provide for their election. Each state is allotted two senators, and until adoption of the SEVENTEENTH AMENDMENT (1913) the senators were chosen by the state legislatures. The President and vice-president are chosen by an ELECTORAL COLLEGE whose members are apportioned to, chosen by, and convened in the several states. The Constitution became effective only upon ratification by conventions in the several states, and amendment of the Constitution is impossible without the concurrence of the legislatures of (or conventions in) three-fourths of the states. And the TENTH AMENDMENT, adopted in 1791 as part of the BILL OF RIGHTS, reserves all governmental power not delegated to the national government by the Constitution to the states or the people.

On the other hand, Article I, section 10, prohibits the states from entering into treaties or alliances or granting LETTERS OF MARQUE AND REPRISAL; coining money, issuing BILLS OF CREDIT to circulate as currency, or making anything but gold or silver legal tender for payment of obligations; enacting EX POST FACTO laws or BILLS OF ATTAINDER, legislating to impair the OBLIGATION OF CONTRACTS, or conferring TITLES OF NOBILITY. The exercise of certain other powers by the states is made contingent upon the consent of Congress: taxation of imports or exports, maintenance of armies or navies, entering into INTERSTATE COMPACTS, and making war (unless actually invaded or imminently threatened by a foreign power). Moreover, the SUPREMACY CLAUSE subordinates the enactments of the states to the Constitution and to laws and treaties of the national government, and all state officers and judges are bound by oath to follow these, as the supreme law, whenever there is a conflict with state enactments or decisions.

But a proposal that the national Congress should have the power to review and "negative" state legislation failed to win a majority at the Constitutional Convention; and more drastic proposals that the states be abolished, or re-

Partnership for the Republic. San Francisco: Institute for Contemporary Studies.

MORLEY, FELIX 1959 *Freedom and Federalism.* Chicago: Henry Regnery Co.

SANFORD, TERRY 1967 *Storm over the States.* New York: McGraw-Hill.

VILE, M. J. C. 1961 *The Structure of American Federalism.* Oxford: Oxford University Press.

STATE ACTION

The phrase "state action," a term of art in our constitutional law, symbolizes the rule—or supposed rule—that constitutional guarantees of human rights are effective only against *governmental* action impairing those rights. (The word "state," in the phrase, denotes any unit or element of government, and not simply one of the American states, though the "state action" concept has been at its most active, and most problematic, with respect to these.) The problems have been many and complex; the "state action" doctrine has not reached anything near a satisfactory condition of rationality.

A best first step toward exploring the problems hidden in the "state action" phrase may be a look at its development in constitutional history. The development has revolved around the first section of the FOURTEENTH AMENDMENT, wherein the problem is in effect put forward by the words here italicized:

> All persons born or naturalized in the United States, and subject to the jurisdiction thereof, are citizens of the United States and of the State wherein they reside. *No State* shall make or enforce any law which shall abridge the privileges or immunities of citizens of the United States; *nor shall any State* deprive any person of life, liberty, or property, without due process of law; nor deny to any person within its jurisdiction the equal protection of the laws.

An early "state action" case under this section, *Ex parte Virginia* (1880), raised an audacious claim as to the limiting effect of the words emphasized above. A Virginia judge had been charged under a federal statute forbidding racial exclusion from juries. He was not directed by a state statute to perform this racial exclusion. The judge argued that the action was not that of the state of Virginia, but rather the act of an official, proceeding wrongfully on his own. On this theory, a "state" had not denied EQUAL PROTECTION. The Fourteenth Amendment, the judge contended, did not therefore forbid the conduct charged, or authorize Congress to make it criminal. The Supreme Court, however, declined to take such high ground.

"The constitutional provision," it said, ". . . must mean that no agency of the state, or of the officers or agents by whom its powers are exerted, shall deny . . . equal protection of the laws." But probably the only fully principled and maximally clear rule as to "state action" would have been that the "state," as a state, does not "act" except by its official enactments—and so does not "act" when one of its officers merely abuses his power. "Fully principled and maximally clear"—but, like so many such "rules," aridly formalistic, making practical nonsense of any constitutional rule it limits. There were gropings, around the year of this case, toward a "state action" requirement with bite, but the modern history of the concept starts with the CIVIL RIGHTS CASES of 1883, wherein many modern problems were foreshadowed. In the CIVIL RIGHTS ACT OF 1875, Congress had enacted "[t]hat all persons . . . shall be entitled to the full and equal enjoyment of the accommodations, advantages, facilities, and privileges of inns, public conveyances on land or water, theatres, and other places of public amusement . . . [regardless of race]."

Persons were indicted for excluding blacks from hotels, theaters, and railroads. The Court considered that the only possible source of congressional power to make such a law was section 5 of the Fourteenth Amendment: "The Congress shall have power to enforce, by appropriate legislation, the provisions of this article." This section the Court saw as authorizing only those laws which *directly* enforced the guarantees of the amendment's section 1 (quoted above), which in turn referred only to a *state*. The amendment therefore did not warrant, the Court held, any congressional dealing with racially discriminatory actions of individuals or CORPORATIONS.

Few judicial opinions seem to rest on such solid ground; at the end of Justice JOSEPH BRADLEY's performance, the reader is likely to feel, "Q.E.D." But this feeling of apparent demonstration is attained, as often it is, by the passing over in silence of disturbing facts and thoughts. Many of these were brought out in the powerful dissent of Justice JOHN MARSHALL HARLAN.

One of the cases involved racial discrimination by a railroad. The American railroads, while they were building, were generally given the power of EMINENT DOMAIN. Eminent domain is a sovereign power, enjoyed par excellence by the state, and given by the state to "private" persons for public purposes looked on as important to the state; the Fifth Amendment's language illustrates the firmness of the background assumption that "private property" shall be taken, even with JUST COMPENSATION, only for PUBLIC USE. The American railroads were, moreover, very heavily assisted by public subsidy from governmental units at all levels. Both these steps—the clothing of railroad corporations with eminent-domain power, and their subsidization out of public funds—were justified, both rhetorically and as a matter of law, on the grounds that the railroads were *public instrumentalities*, fulfilling the classic state function of furnishing a transportation system. Regulation of railroads was undertaken under the same theory.

Railroads and hotel-keepers, moreover, followed the so-called common callings, traditionally entailing an obligation to take and carry, or to accommodate, all well-behaved persons able to pay. The *withdrawal* of protection of such a right to equal treatment might be looked on as "state action," and Congress might well decide, as a practical matter, either that the right had been wholly withdrawn as to blacks (which was in many places the fact of the matter) or that the state action supporting these rights of access was insufficient and required supplementation; only the most purposefully narrow construction could deny to such supplementation the name of "enforcement."

Indeed, this line of thought, whether as to the *Civil Rights Cases* or as to all other "equal protection" cases, is fraught with trouble for the whole "state action" doctrine, in nature as in name. "Action" is an exceedingly inapt word for the "denial" of "protection." Protection against lynching was, for example, usually "denied" by "inaction." Inaction by the state is indeed the classic form of "denial of protection." The Civil Rights Cases majority did not read far enough, even for the relentless literalist; it read as far as "nor shall any Stat. . . ." but then hastily closed the book before reading what follows: ". . . *deny* to any person . . . the equal *protection* of the laws." Contrary to the majority's reading, the state's affirmative obligation of protection should have extended to the protection of the traditional rights of resort to public transport and common inns; it was notorious that the very people (blacks) whose "equal protection" was central to the Fourteenth Amendment were commonly the only victims of nominally "private" denial of these rights.

Justice Harlan pointed out that in its first sentence, conferring CITIZENSHIP on the newly emancipated slaves, the first section of the Fourteenth Amendment did not use any language in any way suggesting a "state action" requirement, so that there was not even the verbal support for the "state action" requirement that the Court had found in the other phrases of that section. The question then became, in Harlan's view, what the legal consequences of "citizenship" were; for purposes of the particular case at hand, he said:

But what was secured to colored citizens of the United States—as between them and their respective States—by the national grant to them of State citizenship? With what rights, privileges, or immunities did this grant invest them? There is one, if there be no other—exemption from race discrimination in respect of any civil right belonging to citizens of the white race in the same State. . . . Citizenship in this country necessarily imports at least equality of civil rights among citizens of every race in the same

State. It is fundamental in American citizenship that, in respect of such rights, there shall be no discrimination by the State, or its officers, or by individuals or corporations exercising public functions or authority, against any citizen because of his race or previous condition of servitude. . . .

There is a third, most interesting aspect to Harlan's dissent. The majority had summarily rejected the argument that under the THIRTEENTH AMENDMENT—forbidding SLAVERY and involuntary servitude and giving Congress enforcement power—racial exclusion from public places was one of the "badges and incidents" of slavery. Harlan argued that forced segregation in public accommodations was a BADGE OF SERVITUDE, and he pointed out that no "state action" requirement could be found in the words of the Thirteenth Amendment. This argument was plowed under and was heard from no more for many decades, but it is of great interest because it was revived and made the basis of decision in a leading case in the 1960s, JONES V. ALFRED H. MAYER CO. (1968).

The *Civil Rights Cases*, in the majority opinion, brushed past contentions that were in no way frivolous. Very many discriminatory actions of public scope are taken by persons or corporations enjoying special favor from government and heavily regulated by government; one cannot easily see their actions as isolated from public power. "Denial of equal protection," the central constitutional wrong in racial cases, seems to refer at least as naturally to inaction as it does to action. If any positive rights at all inhere in citizenship—and if there are no such rights, the citizenship clause is a mere matter of nomenclature—these rights are set up by the Fourteenth Amendment without limitation as to the source of their impairment. Nevertheless, the holdings and doctrine of the *Civil Rights Cases* fell on a thirstily receptive society. The "state action" doctrine became one of the principal reliances of a racist nation, North as well as South.

In a society where so much of access to goods and values is managed by nominally "private" persons and corporations—railroads, restaurants, streetcars, cinemas, even food and clothing—a protection that runs only against the government, strictly defined, can work out to very little effective protection. If the official justice system is hampered by inconvenient constitutional safeguards, the sheriff can play cards while the lynch mob forms, and there is "no state action." A nightclub may refuse to serve a black celebrity, and there is "no state action." The "state action" doctrine protected from constitutional scrutiny an enormous network of racial exclusion and humiliation, characterizing both North and South.

Paradoxically, the "state action" requirement may for a long time have been more important to the maintenance of northern racism than to that of the cruder racism of the South. The South developed SEGREGATION by law, in all phases of public life, and this regime was broadly validated by the notorious 1896 decision in PLESSY V. FERGUSON. For complex political reasons—and perhaps because of a faintly lingering adherence to scraps of CIVIL WAR idealism—segregation by official law was not widely imposed in the North. But the practices of real-estate agents, mortgage lenders, restaurant keepers, and a myriad of other "private" people and corporations added up to a pervasive custom of racial segregation in many phases of life, a custom less perfectly kept than the official legal dictates of the southern regime, but effectively barring most blacks from much of the common life of the communities they lived in.

A striking case in point was *Dorsey v. Stuyvesant Town Corporation* (1949–1950). The Metropolitan Life Insurance Company, having much money to invest, struck a complicated deal with the State and the City of New York. The contemplated end-result was the conversion of a large section of New York City—from 14th to 23rd Streets, and from Avenue A to the East River—into a vast complex of apartments, to be owned and run by a Metropolitan subsidiary. By formal statute and ordinance, the State and City acquiesced in this scheme, agreeing to use (and later using) the sovereign "eminent domain" power to acquire title to all the needed land, which was, as prearranged, later transferred to Metropolitan. Again by formal arrangement, a quarter-century tax exemption was granted on "improvements"—that is to say, on the immensely valuable apartment buildings. The public easement on certain streets was extinguished, and control over them turned over to Stuyvesant Town Corporation, a Metropolitan subsidiary; various water, sewage, and fire-protection arrangements were altered to suit the needs of the project. And all this was done, visibly and pridefully, as a joint effort of public and "private" enterprise; politicians as well as insurance men took bows. Then, when the whole thing was built, with "title" safely vested in "private" hands, Stuyvesant Town Corporation announced that no blacks need apply for apartments. The suit of a black applicant reached the highest court of New York, and that court held, 4–3, that there was not enough "state action" in all this to make applicable the Fourteenth Amendment prohibition of racial discrimination. The Supreme Court of the United States denied CERTIORARI.

The *Stuyvesant Town* case illustrates very well what could be done with the "state action" formula. With the fullest cooperation from government at all levels, as much of any city as might be desired (strictly public buildings alone excepted) could be turned into a "whites only" preserve. With the necessary cooperation, the process could be extended to a whole county, or a whole state. If they were prudent, the political partners in such deals would not put anything in writing about the racial exclusion contemplated.

But the essentiality of the "state action" formula to the success of northern racism must not obscure its considerable strategic importance even in the South. Segregation by law had in the main been validated, and this was the South's main reliance, but there were gaps, and the "state action" formula filled them in.

First, there was the role of nominally "private" violence against blacks, as the ultimate weapon of the racist regime—with lynching at the top of the arsenal's inventory. At this point the disregard of the Fourteenth Amendment's words, "nor shall any State *deny* . . . equal *protection* of the laws," is most surprising. But for a long time a whole lot of seemingly serious people saw no "denial of protection" in the de facto denial of protection to blacks against a great deal of "private" violence.

Second, outright racial residential zoning by law—just one form of segregation—had been struck down by the Supreme Court, in the 1917 case of BUCHANAN V. WARLEY. The opinion in that case does not adequately distinguish *Plessy v. Ferguson*, but it was the law, and nominally "private" methods of racial zoning had often to be resorted to in the South—just as they were, pervasively, in the North. Real-estate agents and mortgage banks played their accustomed part; until astonishingly recent times, the actually published codes of "ethics" of "realtors" forbade (under some transparent euphemism) actions tending toward spoiling the racial homogeneity of any neighborhood. But more was needed, and that more was found—South and North—in the "racially RESTRICTIVE COVENANT." These "covenants" were neither necessarily nor commonly mere casual contractual arrangements between parties dickering at random. Very commonly, when an "addition" was "subdivided," all the first deeds restricted ownership or occupancy, or both, to whites only—or to white Gentiles only, or to white Gentiles of northern European extraction. These covenants, recorded at the courthouse in a registry furnished by the State for this purpose, were ordained by many states' laws to "run with the land"—that is, they had to be put in all subsequent deeds forever, and usually were binding whether so inserted or not, since any buyer, examining title, could find them in the title-chain. These "covenants"—often functionally equivalent to racial zoning by law, enforced by court orders, and kept on file at the courthouse—were for a long time looked on as "merely private" action, in no way traceable to the state, and so not amenable to constitutional command.

A third and even more important use of the "state action" doctrine (or a doctrine closely akin) was peculiar to the South, and was the rotting-out base of southern politics for generations. The FIFTEENTH AMENDMENT forbade racial exclusions from voting—but, like the Fourteenth, it directed its prohibition at governments: "The right of citizens of the United States to vote shall not be denied or abridged by the United States or by any State on account of race, color, or previous condition of servitude."

The general response in the South to this politically inconvenient constitutional mandate was the all-white Democratic PRIMARY ELECTION. This primary was colloquially known as "the election"; its nominees virtually always won in the November balloting, when all the whites who had voted in the Democratic primary were expected to vote for its nominee, and enough did so to wipe out any scattered Republican votes, including the votes of those blacks who could surmount the other barriers to their voting—LITERACY TESTS, difficult registration procedures, and even more violent discouragements. This plain fraud on the Constitution did not rest wholly on the concept that the action of the Democratic party was not "state action," but the even bolder idea behind it—the idea, namely, that the practical substitution of a "party" election for the regular election could altogether escape the Fifteenth Amendment mandate, even when the State commanded the all-whiteness of the Party—was related in more than spirit to the "state action" doctrine as illustrated in the Stuyvesant Town case. Its basis was the thought that racial voting requirements were not "official" if a nominally "private" organization was put in as a buffer between the wrong done and state power. And the all-white primary in the end had to rely (vainly, as at last it turned out) on the "state action" requirement.

The "state action" doctrine is not a mere interesting footnote in constitutional law. It has served as an absolutely essential and broadly employed component in the means by which black equality, theoretically guaranteed by the post-Civil War amendments, was made to mean next to nothing. It could do this because of the fact that, in our society, vast powers over all of life are given to formally private organizations—the Democratic party, the realtors' association, the mortgage bank, the telephone company, and so on—and because, further and indispensably, the courts were (as is illustrated by a line of decisions from the *Civil Rights Cases* to the Stuyvesant Town case) willing in case after case to gloss over the fact that large organized enterprises can rarely if ever be successfully conducted without very considerable help from the government. Intermixed in these racial cases was, moreover, the disregard of the Fourteenth Amendment's textual condemnation of governmental *inaction*, where that inaction amounted to *denial of equal protection*, as inaction obviously may. And constitutional guarantees that were implicit rather than explicit as limits on government were mostly ignored. A doctrine that went to the length of seeming to make of lynching a thing untouched by the Constitution and (as in UNITED STATES V. CRUIKSHANK, 1875) untouchable by Congress was and could be again a powerful tool indeed for bringing national human rights, nationally enjoyed, to nothing, on the plane of life as lived.

The "state action" requirement thus served the major strategic goal of a nation to which racism, in practice, was utterly essential. But even outside the field of race, its incidence, though spotty, was wide-ranging. As late as 1951, in *Collins v. Hardyman*, the Supreme Court, obviously under the influence of the doctrine though not directly relying on it, forcibly construed a federal statute, in plain contradiction to the law's clear terms, as not to reach the "private" and violent breaking up of a political meeting of citizens.

But a strong countercurrent developed in the 1940s. Without entire consistency, the Supreme Court uttered a striking series of decisions that promised to clip the claws of the "state action" requirement. The Court declared the all-white Democratic primary unlawful in SMITH V. ALLWRIGHT (1944) and extended this ruling in TERRY V. ADAMS (1953) to a local primary serving the same function under another name and form. MARSH V. ALABAMA (1946) held that the FIRST AMENDMENT, as incorporated into the Fourteenth, forbade the barring of Jehovah's Witnesses from distributing leaflets in a company-owned town. And SHELLEY V. KRAEMER (1948) held that judicial enforcement of restrictive covenants was unlawful.

In the "white primary" cases the Court was doing no more than refusing to persevere in self-induced blindness to an obvious fraud on the Fifteenth Amendment. But *Marsh v. Alabama* suggested that the formality of "ownership" could not immunize from constitutional scrutiny the performance of a governmental function—an idea big with possibility. And the *Shelley* case even more profoundly stirred the foundations. Of course it was difficult to say that judicial enforcement of a racial-restrictive covenant, recorded at the courthouse, with the attendant implication that such covenants are not (as some others are) "against public policy," did not amount to "state action of some kind"—the requirement as worded in the fountainhead *Civil Rights Cases* of 1883. The difficulty in assimilation of *Shelley* arose from the fact that "state action of some kind" underpins and in one way or another enforces every nominally "private" action; the states had facilitated and lent their aid, indeed, to the very acts of discrimination considered in the 1883 cases. *Shelley*, therefore, forced a more searching analysis of the theory of "state action"; academic commentators became exceedingly eager and thorough, and in later decisions the Court became more willing to find "state action" and to move toward a fundamental doctrinal revision.

This process was accelerated by the civil rights movement that gained strength in the late 1950s, and grew to major force in the 1960s. In 1954, the famous case of BROWN V. BOARD OF EDUCATION had outlawed racial segregation in the public schools; a number of other decisions had extended this rule to all forms of segregation imposed by law or by uncontestable official action. Though enforcement of these decisions was to be difficult, the first of two principal jural supports of American racism—legal prohibition of participation by blacks in the common society—had crumbled. Naturally attention turned—whether with the aim of continuing racism or of completing its demolition—to the second of the pillars of American racism, the "state action" requirement.

Segregation and state action were now clearly seen to have a close functional similarity. Before the decisions following *Brown*, the blacks in a typical southern town could not eat in the good restaurants because state law commanded their exclusion. After these decisions, the proprietors of the restaurants, by and large, went on excluding blacks. (In this they were simply following a practice widely followed in the North already). There was a difference in legal theory, but no difference to the black people. The city-owned bus system could not make black people sit in the back—but most bus companies were "private" in form; seating in the back was "privately" commanded.

The resistance to this widespread public segregation under "private" form was led (actively in part and symbolically throughout) by Dr. MARTIN LUTHER KING, JR. Thousands of black people—most, but not all, young—defied the system by "sitting-in"—insisting upon service at "private" establishments open to the general public. They were in great numbers convicted of "crimes" selected with careful attention to the appearance of neutrality, such as "trespass after warning" or BREACH OF THE PEACE, and their cases reached the Supreme Court in some number.

The net result up to about 1965 was a considerable practical loosening up of the "state action" requirement, but no satisfactory theoretical reworking of that doctrine. A very few examples must be selected from the abundant case law.

The 1961 case of BURTON V. WILMINGTON PARKING AUTHORITY is an interesting example. The parking authority, a state agency, leased space in its parking building to a restaurateur, who forthwith refused to serve blacks. One might have thought it all but frivolous to contend that "state action of some kind" was absent here. The state had gone with open eyes into a transaction that empowered the restaurateur to insult and inconvenience citizens, in a public building owned by itself, and its police stood ready to make his rule stick. The state had done this—in effect certainly, if not in intent—for rent money. It had had the easy recourse of inserting in the lease a provision against racial discrimination; one has to wonder how the omission of that provision, obviously available under "the laws," can be anything but a "denial" of "equal protection of the laws," on the part of government. Yet the Court majority, though striking down the discrimination in the very case, roamed back and forth amongst the minutiae of facts— gas, service for the boiler-room, responsibility for struc-

tural repairs—and carefully confined its ruling to a lease of public property "in the manner and for the purpose shown to have been the case here. . . ." Still, the Wilmington case might have contributed toward some generality of constitutional theory.

As the "SIT-IN" issue heated up, however, the Court became even more evasive of the central issues. As cases reached the Court in great numbers, no "sit-in" conviction was ever affirmed. But neither the whole Court nor any majority ever reached and decided the central issue— whether *Shelley v. Kraemer* fairly implied that the knowing state use of state power to enforce discrimination, in publicly open facilities, constituted such action of the state as "denied equal protection of the laws." Instead the cases were decided on collateral grounds peculiar to each of them.

The culminating case was BELL V. MARYLAND (1964). Trespass convictions of Maryland civil-rights "sitters-in" were reversed, on the grounds (available by chance) that a newly enacted Maryland antidiscrimination statute might be held, in the state courts, to "abate" prosecution for prior attempts to get the service now guaranteed; nothing was actually decided on the more fundamental issues. Six Justices reached the "state action" issue, but of those six, three would have found it and three would not.

At this dramatic moment, with indefinite postponement of a major doctrinal decision seemingly impossible, Congress stepped in and solved the immediate problem, by passing the CIVIL RIGHTS ACT OF 1964, Title 2 of which made unlawful nearly all the discriminatory exclusions that had generated the sit-in prosecutions, making future prosecutions of sit-ins impossible. Then, in 1964, in *Hamm v. City of Rock Hill*, the Court held that the act compelled dismissal of all such prosecutions begun before its passage. Thus vanished the immediate problem of the sit-ins, and of many other claims to nondiscrimination previously based purely on the Constitution. It is noteworthy that Congress chose to base this Title 2, dealing with PUBLIC ACCOMMODATIONS, mainly on the COMMERCE CLAUSE rather than on the Fourteenth Amendment. This legislative decision reflected uncertainty as to whether the Court could be persuaded to overrule the 1883 *Civil Rights Cases*, which had severely limited congressional power to enforce the Fourteenth Amendment. In HEART OF ATLANTA MOTEL V. UNITED STATES (1964) and KATZENBACH V. MCCLUNG (1964) the Court construed the 1964 provisions broadly, and upheld them under the commerce clause theory that Congress had emphasized. The public accommodations crisis was over, and with it the really agonizing social crisis as to "state action."

Nevertheless, important problems continued to present themselves after 1964. It seemed for a time that, though no longer under the intense pressure of the public accommodations issue, the Court might be moving along the road toward relaxation of the state action requirement— a road along which travel had begun at least as early as the cases of *Smith v. Allwright* (1944—knocking out the all-white Democratic primary), *Marsh v. Alabama* (1946—the "company-town" case), and *Shelley v. Kraemer* (1948—the case of the racial-restriction covenants). (Indeed, no case actually denying relief on the "no-state-action" ground was decided by the Supreme Court from 1906 to 1970, except the 1935 case upholding the white primary, overruled nine years later).

In 1966 the Court held, in *Evans v. Newton*, that a huge public park in the center of Macon, Georgia, could no longer be operated as a park "for whites only," pursuant to the directions in the 1911 will of the man who had given it to the city, even though the city, for the purpose of seeing this all-white status maintained, had resigned as trustee, and had acquiesced in the appointment of a set of "private" trustees. In *Amalgamated Food Employees v. Logan Valley Plaza* (1968) the Court applied *Marsh v. Alabama* to hold a large SHOPPING CENTER subject to the First Amendment, and REITMAN V. MULKEY (1967) struck down under the Fourteenth Amendment a California constitutional amendment that would have forbidden state or local "fair" (i.e., antiracist) housing ordinances until such time as the state constitution might be amended again—a process substantially more difficult than the enactment of ordinary legislation. This opinion, by Justice BYRON R. WHITE, encouraged much hope, because it explicitly undertook to judge this state constitutional amendment "in terms of its "immediate objective,' its "ultimate effect,' and its "historical context and the conditions existing prior to its enactment." This attitude, if adhered to, would in every case bring the "state action" question down to the earth of reality. The Court would recognize the impact of formal state "neutrality" on the actual patterns of American racism, and would ask in each case whether such seeming "neutrality" operated as a *denial of equal protection* to the group principally marked for protection. This hope was further encouraged in 1969 in *Hunter v. Erickson* wherein the Court struck down an Akron, Ohio, requirement that fair-housing ordinances run an especially difficult gauntlet before they became effective; it was especially striking that Justices JOHN MARSHALL HARLAN and POTTER STEWART, who had dissented in *Reitman*, found the Akron provision too much, because on its face it discriminated against antiracist laws.

But the current of doctrine changed after President RICHARD M. NIXON made the most of his chance to put his stamp on the Court. The change was signaled by the 1970 decision in EVANS V. ABNEY, a follow-up to the first Macon park case, *Evans v. Newton*, above. After the Newton decision, the heirs of the donor of the park applied for a

reverter to them. The Court held this time that the state court's decision in their favor, in effect imposing a penalty on the citizens of Macon for their being unable under the Fourteenth Amendment to keep the park all-white, did not constitute "such state action" as to implicate the equal protection clause.

In 1971, in PALMER V. THOMPSON, the Court upheld the City of Jackson in its closing the city swimming pools and leasing one of them to the "private" YMCA, rather than having blacks swim in them. Here the Court found no state encouragement of discrimination, although the pools had been closed in response to a desegregation order. This was a total turn-about, in just four years, from the *Reitman v. Mulky* resolution to tie the operation of state-action law to the facts of life, and Justice White, the author of the *Reitman* opinion, dissented, with three other pre-Nixon Justices.

In 1974 the Court decided JACKSON V. METROPOLITAN EDISON COMPANY. A heavily regulated "private" electric company, enjoying a monopoly and a state-issued certificate of public convenience, terminated service to a customer without offering her any chance to be heard. This practice was allowed by a "tariff" on file with and at the least acquiesced in by the Public Utilities Commission. Justice WILLIAM H. REHNQUIST's opinion for the Court found insufficient "state action" in any of this to implicate the DUE PROCESS clause. This opinion and judgment, if adhered to in all their implications, would put us at least as far back as the 1883 Civil Rights Cases. Then, in 1976, HUDGENS V. NATIONAL LABOR RELATION BOARD explicitly overruled the *Logan Valley Shopping Center* case and made authoritative for the time being a very narrow view of *Marsh v. Alabama*.

Meanwhile, however, a new doctrinal thread had become visible. In the 1883 *Civil Rights Cases* the first Justice Harlan had argued that the Thirteenth Amendment, which contains no language to support a state-action requirement, proscribes all "badges and incidents" of slavery—which, historically, would mean a great many if not all racially discriminatory and degrading actions. This argument was a long time in coming into its own, but in 1968, in *Jones v. Alfred H. Mayer Co.*, the Court made it the ground of a decision upholding an old act of Congress which the Court interpreted to command nondiscrimination in the sale of housing. And in 1976, GRIFFIN V. BRECKENRIDGE, overruling *Collins v. Hardyman*, based decision solidly on the Thirteenth Amendment, holding that the amendment authorizes Congress to secure its beneficiaries against "racially discriminatory private action aimed at depriving them of . . . basic rights. . . ." Under the very formula of the 1883 *Civil Rights Cases* themselves—Congress may "enforce" only that which is substantively there—this should imply a large substantive content in the Thirteenth Amendment, far beyond literal "slavery." In RUNYON V. MCCRARY (1976) the Court extended much the same rationale to the condemnation of racial exclusion from a "private, commercially operated, nonsectarian" school.

"State action" doctrine has remained intractable to being made rational. What is wanted is attention to these points:

1. In almost any impingement by one person or more on another person or more, there is some contribution by the state: empowerment, support, or threatened support. Thus the presence or absence of "state action" is not a "test" at all; this has led to the spinning out of enormous series of subtests, hard to express and even harder to comprehend, none of which has much if any warrant in law.

2. Concomitantly, "state action" may not legitimately be confined—as the Supreme Court's recent opinions have confined it—to one or more neatly defined categories such as "command," "encouragement," or "public function." One may identify ten ways in which so infinitely complicated and subtle a being as the "state" may act—and the "state" may then act in an eleventh and then in a twelfth way—all "state action."

3. There is no warrant whatever in law for the assumption that "state action," to be significant, must be at a *high level* of involvement, or that a *very close* "nexus" must be found between "state action" and the wrong complained of.

4. Many constitutional guarantees do not explicitly require "state action" as a component. The modern "state action" requirement purported to draw its life from the words of the Fourteenth Amendment. Many rights and relationships set up by the Constitution and enforceable by Congress do not refer to the state at all, for example, the prohibition of slavery (and, as now held, its badges and incidents), the right to vote for congressmen and senators, the RIGHT TO TRAVEL. It is only custom-thought, which usually means half-thought, that would think it obvious that an impediment to INTERSTATE COMMERCE would be unconstitutional only if it were state-created.

5. A citizen of the United States should be regarded as having *relational* rights—rights of membership in the organized community—which nobody, state or private person, may interfere with. This principle has some life in the cases; in *Bewer v. Hoxie School District* (8th Cir. 1956), for example, an INJUNCTION was upheld that restrained private persons from interfering with state officials' attempts to comply with the national Constitution. But the principle deserves a greater generality. Anybody who tries forcibly to keep another person from getting his mail is interfering with a legitimate relation between citizen and government, even though the wrongdoer's own actions may not

be "state action" at all. (See also UNITED STATES V. GUEST, 1966.)

6. There is broad scope in the natural meaning of the Fourteenth Amendment's words: "deny to any person within its jurisdiction the equal protection of the laws." These words, even as a matter of "narrow verbal criticism," do not require "action."

7. Above all, while much of the defense of the "state action" requirement is conducted in the name of the private, personal lives of people whose conduct, it is said, ought not to be constitutionalized, it is very, very rare that any real "state action" case involves these values at all. The conduct of public transportation and restaurants, the operation of carnivals and parks, dealings with city swimming pools, the way the light company collects its bills, the character of a whole section of town—these are the usual stuff of "state action" problems in real life. If anybody ever files a lawsuit praying a mandatory injunction that he be included on somebody else's dinner list, that will be time enough to begin devising a well-founded "rule of reason" fencing constitutional prohibition out of the genuinely private life. This "genuinely private" life may be hard to define, but surely no harder to define than the "state action requirement" has turned out to be, and continues to be. And at least one would be trying to define the right thing.

CHARLES L. BLACK, JR.
(1986)

Bibliography

BLACK, CHARLES L., JR. 1962 The Constitution and Public Power. *Yale Review* 52:54–66.
——— 1967 "State Action," Equal Protection, and California's Proposition 14. *Harvard Law Review* 81:69–109.
HALE, ROBERT L. 1952 *Freedom through Law.* Chap. 11. New York: Columbia University Press.
HOROWITZ, HAROLD W. 1957 The Misleading Search for "State Action" under the Fourteenth Amendment. *Southern California Law Review* 30:208–221.
VAN ALSTYNE, WILLIAM W. 1965 Mr. Justice Black, Constitutional Review, and the Talisman of State Action. *Duke Law Journal* 1965:219–247.

STATE ACTION
(Update 1)

America's federal constitutional system generally protects individual rights only against violation by the national and state governments, their agencies, and officials. State action doctrine limits the scope of constitutional rights guarantees. If a state police officer arrests a criminal suspect without an ARREST WARRANT, for example, state action is clearly present and the Constitution's Fourth Amendment and Fourteenth Amendment SEARCH AND SEIZURE prohibitions apply. By contrast, if a private individual or organization infringes on another private person's constitutional liberties, the courts may well not find state action, and the federal Constitution will not provide a remedy. The more controversial extensions of the state action doctrine involve cases where constitutional injuries are caused in part by ostensibly private actors. At its furthest reaches, then, the doctrine depends on workable and principled standards for attributing the constitutionally harmful conduct of a private person to the public sector.

In Lugar v. Edmonson Oil Co. (1982) Edmonson had obtained an invalid attachment order from a state court clerk to sequester Lugar's property. Lugar contended that Edmonson had acted jointly with the state to deprive him of property in an unconstitutional manner. Justice BYRON R. WHITE's opinion in *Lugar* explained that in order for any constitutional rights claimant to attribute a private defendant's wrongful conduct to the federal or state government, the claimant must satisfy two independent inquiries. First, the private defendant must be sufficiently identified with the government to be fairly labeled a state actor. This might be called the "identity" inquiry. Second, the defendant's wrongful conduct must have been the direct and affirmative cause of a constitutional injury; the government will not be held liable for an error of omission or a failure to prevent constitutional injury. This might be called the "causality" inquiry. Because the state court official had assisted Edmonson in using the state's constitutionally defective procedures to sequester Lugar's property, the Court held that the identity and causality requirements were met.

Two critical decisions in the 1970s, JACKSON V. METROPOLITAN EDISON COMPANY (1974) and FLAGG BROTHERS, INC. V. BROOKS (1978), set extremely narrow terms for the current identity and causality standards. Even if a government delegates general law enforcement powers to a private individual (as in state self-help repossession statutes) or heavily regulates a private industry (as in state utility rate regulation), the private party will be identified with the government only if these powers and operations had been exercised traditionally and exclusively by the government. Even if the government knew, or should have known, of the private party's wrongdoing, causality now requires evidence that the government affirmatively compelled or specifically approved the practice that harmed a constitutional liberty.

Today the Supreme Court guards these narrow boundaries of the state action doctrine with a rigorous and sterile formalism. In two unusual cases emerging from the arena of amateur sports, the Court recently shielded private organizations from constitutional liability by discounting their functional relationships with the government. After the United States Olympic Committee refused to license use of the name Gay Olympic Games for a homosexual international athletic event, a Fifth Amendment challenge for discrimination in *San Francisco Arts & Athletics v. United States Olympic Committee* (1987) failed on the basis that the committee was not a governmental actor to whom constitutional prohibitions apply. Because the committee coordinated activities that were not traditional government functions, even Congress's unprecedented grant to the committee of exclusive regulatory authority over American athletic organizations and of unlimited trademark rights in the name Olympic did not satisfy the identity tests. Furthermore, because the committee's trademark enforcement decisions went unsupervised by any federal official, causality could not be attributed to the national government.

In National Collegiate Athletic Association v. Tarkanian (1988) the Court insulated the NCAA from liability for violation of a state university basketball coach's CIVIL RIGHTS, ruling that the university's voluntary compliance with NCAA disciplinary recommendations did not transform the NCAA's private conduct into state action. Although the NCAA's findings made at NCAA hearings of NCAA rules violations had influenced the university's decision to suspend Tarkanian in accord with its NCAA membership agreement, the Court reasoned that NCAA had neither imposed the sanction directly nor compelled the university to act within the meaning of the causality standards.

Theoretically, the state action doctrine may serve two important purposes. Jurists defend the doctrine as a safeguard of FEDERALISM : by preventing the federal judiciary from enforcing constitutional rights guarantees against private violators, the doctrine preserves the traditional realm of STATE POLICE POWER to regulate private civil rights. Additionally, the doctrine may promote liberal legal values: to the extent that it limits the Constitution's interference with private exercise of federal and state statutory or COMMON LAW rights, the doctrine fosters a realm of individual freedom of action.

To serve federalism and liberalism meaningfully, however, state action requires a dichotomy between public and private action that is both definite and defensible. The current standards for identity and causality could be challenged on both accounts. Given the highly bureaucratic state of modern America, characterized by government penetration into most private economic and social dealings, the integrated public and private venture is a commonplace. Yet, identity and causality demand the conceptual division of integrated operations into discrete practices that are traditionally governmental, governmentally compelled, and injury-causative. Practical rules for this division will be difficult for courts to formulate and apply; reliance on criteria such as tradition and government compulsion will result in line-drawing of the most arbitrary and unprincipled sort.

Moreover, the doctrine undermines its own raison d'être: with its narrow focus, it will not rip the veil away from nominally private actors who wield governmentally delegated powers to destroy individual rights. Although the Constitution permits government to "privatize" the functions that it otherwise would perform, the state action doctrine ought not to immunize the government from liability for private violations of its constitutional obligations.

However appropriate for federal constitutional purposes, the state action doctrine is often an anomaly in state constitutional law interpretation. The texts of many state bill of rights provisions do not explicitly target state action for their prohibitions; indeed, a number of state constitutions directly regulate specific transactions among private individuals and corporations. Because the states do not recognize county and municipal governments as coordinate sovereigns, state action need not reinforce federalism interests. State high courts might reject the conceptual limitations of the federal state action doctrine to provide stronger protection of CIVIL LIBERTIES under their state constitutions against private infringements.

DAVID M. SKOVER
(1992)

Bibliography

ALEXANDER, LARRY A. and HORTON, PAUL 1988 *Whom Does the Constitution Control?* Westport, Conn.: Greenwood Press.
CHEMERINSKY, ERWIN 1985 Rethinking State Action. *Northwestern University Law Review* 80:503–557.
SKOVER, DAVID M. 1992 State Action Doctrine. In Collins, Skover, Cogan, and Schuman, *State Constitutional Law and Individual Rights: Cases & Commentary.* Durham, N.C.: Carolina Academic Press.
SYMPOSIUM 1982 The Public/Private Distinction. *University of Pennsylvania Law Review* 130: 1289–1608
VAN ALSTYNE, WILLIAM and KARST, KENNETH L. 1961 State Action. *Stanford Law Review* 14: 3–58

STATE ACTION
(Update 2)

More than thirty years ago, legal scholar Charles L. Black, Jr., described the state action DOCTRINE as a "conceptual disaster area" and little has since changed. Indeed, surprisingly, the Supreme Court has paid little attention to state action issues in recent years. Major unresolved issues exist concerning when private action must comply with the Constitution. For example, when the government privatizes traditional government services, such as prisons or airports, does the action of the private operators constitute state action? In light of the tremendous growth in alternative dispute resolution, such as arbitration and mediation, should such private adjudication be regarded as state action, especially when required by law or court order? Thus far the Court has not confronted these issues. Rather, the Court's consideration of state action in recent years has been limited to two areas.

First, the Court has applied the state action doctrine to the exercise of PEREMPTORY JURY CHALLENGES by nongovernment litigants. Peremptory challenges allow litigants to excuse prospective jurors without showing cause. In BATSON V. KENTUCKY (1986), the Court held that EQUAL PROTECTION prohibits prosecutors from using peremptory challenges in a discriminatory fashion in criminal cases.

In *Edmonson v. Leesville Concrete Co.* (1991), the Court held that *Batson* applies in private civil litigation and found state action in private parties' exercise of peremptory challenges in a civil case in a manner reflective of RACIAL DISCRIMINATION. The Court explained that it is state and federal laws that authorize peremptory challenges in state and federal courts. Additionally, the Court emphasized the involvement of the government in jury selection, from subpoenaing individuals for JURY SERVICE to compelling completion of questionnaires to judicial supervision of the VOIR DIRE process. Moreover, juries function as a traditional and important government decisionmaking body. As a result, the Court found that discriminatory use of peremptory challenges denies equal protection, even if done by private litigants.

The Court took this reasoning a step further a year later in *Georgia v. McCollum* (1992), where the Court considered whether a criminal defendant's exercise of a peremptory challenge constitutes state action. If anyone is the antithesis of the government, it is a criminal defendant who is being prosecuted. Yet, for purposes of jury selection, the Court found that a criminal defendant is a state actor in exercising peremptory challenges. The Court followed exactly the same reasoning as in *Edmonson:* laws create peremptory challenges and jury selection is a government function accomplished through the power of the state and overseen by a judge.

The second major development concerning state action has been the Court's conclusion that CORPORATIONS created and managed by government must comply with the Constitution. In LEBRON V. NATIONAL RAILROAD PASSENGER CORP. (1995), the Supreme Court held that the National Railroad Passenger Corporation (Amtrak) must comply with the Constitution. Although the statute creating Amtrak declares that it "will not be an agency or establishment of the United States government," it is a corporation created by federal law, with a board appointed by the President, and it receives substantial federal funding.

An artist sued Amtrak after it refused to comply with a contractual commitment to display his art on a large billboard. The Court ruled that Amtrak is the government for state action purposes. The Court explained that where "the Government creates a corporation by special law, for the furtherance of governmental objectives, and retains for itself permanent authority to appoint a majority of the directors of that corporation, the corporation is part of the Government for purposes of the First Amendment." *Lebron* is significant in making it clear that such government-created corporations must comply with the Constitution.

ERWIN CHEMERINSKY
(2000)

(SEE ALSO: *Jury Discrimination; Privatization and the Constitution.*)

Bibliography

BLACK, CHARLES L., JR. 1967 State Action, Equal Protection, and California's Proposition 14. *Harvard Law Review* 81:69–109.

EULE, JULIAN N. and VARAT, JONATHAN D. 1998 Transporting First Amendment Norms to the Private Sector: With Every Wish There Comes a Curse. *UCLA Law Review* 45:1537–1634.

REUBEN, RICHARD C. 1996 Public Justice: Towards a State Action Theory of Alternative Dispute Resolution. *California Law Review* 85:577–641.

STATE ACTION—BEYOND RACE

For most of its century-long existence, the STATE ACTION limitation of the reach of the FOURTEENTH AMENDMENT and FIFTEENTH AMENDMENT has had its chief importance in cases involving RACIAL DISCRIMINATION. From the CIVIL RIGHTS CASES (1883) until the 1940s, the state action barrier impeded both judicial and congressional protection of CIVIL RIGHTS. As the civil rights movement gathered force in the years following WORLD WAR II, relaxation of the state action limitation was essential to the vindication of the rights of blacks and others who were making claims to constitutional equality. The WARREN COURT accelerated the erosion of the state action barrier, bringing more and more private conduct within the reach of the Fourteenth Amendment. ALEXANDER M. BICKEL accurately described the effects of the Court's decisions as "egalitarian, legalitarian, and centralizing." By the late 1960s some commentators were predicting the state action doctrine's early demise.

Those predictions missed the mark; today the state action limitation remains very much alive. Yet the doctrine's revival has not signaled a return to a restricted role for the national government in protecting rights of racial equality. By the time the BURGER COURT set about rebuilding the state action barrier, the Court had provided Congress with a firm basis for federal civil rights legislation in the THIRTEENTH AMENDMENT, which has never been interpreted to contain a state action limitation. Furthermore, the Court had generously interpreted various federal civil rights laws to forbid most types of private racial discrimination that had flourished behind the state action barrier in the prewar years.

Although the revival of the state action doctrine has offered little new support for private racial discrimination, that revival has diminished the "legalitarian" and "centralizing" effects of the Warren Court's decisions. Indeed, recent Supreme Court majorities have explicitly extolled the Court's use of the state action doctrine to promote the values of individual autonomy and FEDERALISM. The Warren Court had blurred the distinction between state and society, between what is "public" and what is "private." In so doing, the Court assumed that the force of law underlay all private dealings. It is only a short step from this assumption to the judicial creation of a great many constitutional rights of private individuals against other private individuals. Justice JOHN MARSHALL HARLAN, deploring the trend, argued in UNITED STATES V. GUEST (1966) that "[the] CONSTITUTIONAL CONVENTION was called to establish a nation, not to reform the COMMON LAW."

The Burger Court has viewed its revival of the state action barrier in precisely these terms, as a contraction of the reach of the Constitution—and especially the reach of the federal judiciary—with a corresponding expansion of both individual autonomy and state SOVEREIGNTY. The Court's recent majorities have drawn a sharp distinction between society's "public" and "private" spheres, and two implications have followed. First, the Constitution limits governmental, but not private, conduct. Second, if private conduct is to be regulated by government, the preferred regu-1737lator is the state government, and not Congress or the federal courts. The result has been a marked reduction in the Fourteenth Amendment's potential applications to private conduct, even when that conduct is carried on with what the Warren Court used to call "significant state involvement."

Indeed, the very search for "significant state involvement" has been replaced by a new analytical approach. Where the Warren Court determined the existence of state action by considering the totality of interconnections between government and private conduct, today's majority separately examines various arguments for finding state action underpinning private conduct—and typically, as in

JACKSON V. METROPOLITAN EDISON COMPANY (1974) and BLUM V. YARETSKY (1982), rejects those arguments one by one.

In doctrinal terms, the current majority of the Supreme Court has narrowed both of the principal avenues for finding state action in private conduct. First, the "public function" theory that informed the "white primary" cases from NIXON V. HERNDON (1927) to TERRY V. ADAMS (1953) and the "company town" decision in MARSH V. ALABAMA (1946) has been confined to cases in which the state has delegated to a private party a function traditionally performed exclusively by the state. In FLAGG BROTHERS, INC. V. BROOKS, (1978) the Court even tightened its rhetoric for such cases, referring to "the sovereign function doctrine."

Second, the various types of state support that previously contributed to findings of "significant state involvement" in private conduct, having been disaggregated in the Court's analysis, have been strictly limited in their separate meanings. Thus: heavy state financial aid to a private school was insufficient to establish state action in RENDELL-BAKER V. KOHN (1982); the theory of REITMAN V. MULKEY (1967) that the state had "encouraged" private racial discrimination has yet to be employed to find state action in another case; the state's licensing and comprehensive regulation of a public utility was insufficient to establish state action in *Jackson v. Metropolitan Edison Company;* the precedent of BURTON V. WILMINGTON PARKING AUTHORITY (1961) has been restricted to cases in which government and private actors are so intimately interconnected that their relationship can be called one of "symbiosis"—or, as in *Lugar v. Edmondson Oil Company* (1982), "joint participation"; and the RESTRICTIVE COVENANT precedent of SHELLEY V. KRAEMER (1948) has become a one-case category. Even a public defender, employed by the state to represent indigent defendants in criminal cases, was held in *Polk County v. Dodson* (1981) not to be acting under COLOR OF LAW as required by SECTION 1983, TITLE 42, U.S. CODE, statutory words that are interpreted to track the state action limitation.

The insight that law—and thus the coercive power of the state—provides the foundation for claims of right in human society is not new. Indeed, the proposition teeters on the edge of tautology. To say that a person owns land, for example, is mainly a shorthand statement about the readiness of state officials to employ force to protect that person's exercise of certain rights to control the use of that land. To speak of law itself is to speak of a power relationship. In a large and complex society the point may sometimes become diffused, but the potential application of coercive power, wielded by governmental officials, is one of the chief features differentiating interactions in nearly all human societies from those in a jungle. The publicprivate distinction may have its uses, but candid description is not one of them.

Nonetheless, Justice WILLIAM H. REHNQUIST, writing for the Supreme Court in the *Flagg Brothers* case, reaffirmed "the "essential dichotomy" between public and private acts" as a feature of American constitutional law. State action, for purposes of interpreting the Fourteenth Amendment, could not be found on the potential enforcement of law by state officials, but only on its actual enforcement. To rule otherwise, Rehnquist said, would "intolerably broaden" the notion of state action. Unquestionably, the publicprivate distinction is secure in American constitutional law.

The appeal of the public/private distinction for the judges and commentators who create constitutional DOCTRINE is readily identified. If any one value lies at the core of American CONSTITUTIONALISM, it is the protection of individual freedom against arbitrary exercises of governmental power. A central assumption in this value scheme is that a "neutral" body of law is no more than the playing field on which individuals autonomously pursue their own goals. The same assumption is also reassuring about autonomy itself—not just that autonomy is valuable, but that autonomy exists. It is hard to see how American constitutionalism could get along without some form of the publicprivate distinction, absent a fundamental transformation of the idea of constitutionalism.

Plainly, the publicprivate distinction would be compatible with a definition of state action much broader than the current one. The present restrictive interpretation of the state action limitation, in other words, serves purposes beyond the maintenance of a zone of individual freedom against arbitrary governmental interference. Those purposes are not far below the surface of the Supreme Court's recent state action opinions. The Supreme Court's current restrictive readings of the state action limitation are congenial to Justices who want to preserve state power against the intrusion of the federal government, and who want to restrict the role of the judiciary in second-guessing the political process. One's attitude toward the state action issue, as toward a great many constitutional issues in the last generation, will reflect one's general views about JUDICIAL ACTIVISM AND RESTRAINT. The consequences of these choices are not merely institutional; they affect substantive rights of liberty and equality. Every decision reinforcing the Fourteenth Amendment's state action barrier is a decision not to vindicate a claim of Fourteenth Amendment rights.

KENNETH L. KARST
(1986)

Bibliography

NOTE   1974   State Action: Theories for Applying Constitutional Restrictions to Private Activity. *Columbia Law Review* 74: 656–705.

SYMPOSIUM 1982 The Public/Private Distinction. *University of Pennsylvania Law Review* 130:1289–1608.

TRIBE, LAURENCE H. 1985 *Constitutional Choices.* Pages 246–268. Cambridge, Mass.: Harvard University Press.

STATE AID TO PAROCHIAL SCHOOLS

See: Government Aid to Religious Institutions

STATE AND LOCAL FISCAL ASSISTANCE ACT

See: Revenue Sharing

STATE AND LOCAL GOVERNMENT TAXATION

The Constitution contains only one provision explicitly restricting the general scope of state and local tax power. The Import-Export Clause provides that "no State shall, without the Consent of Congress, lay any Imposts or Duties on Imports or Exports, except what may be absolutely necessary for executing its inspection laws." For most of America's constitutional history, the Supreme Court construed this clause as forbidding any state tax on imports and exports, a question the Court resolved by asking whether the imported goods subject to tax were in their Original Package and whether the exported goods subject to tax were within the "stream" of exportation. In *Michelin Tire Company v. Administrator Of Wages* (1976), however, the Court dramatically revised its approach to import-export clause analysis by refocusing the constitutional inquiry on the question of whether the levy at issue was an "impost" or "duty," which the Court in essence defined as a tax discriminating against imports and exports. Hence, nondiscriminatory taxes, even though imposed on imports or exports, are constitutionally tolerable under contemporary doctrine.

Other restraints on state and local taxation derive from constitutional provisions directed at concerns much broader than the subject of taxation. The Court has construed the Commerce Clause as requiring that any tax affecting interstate commerce must satisfy four criteria: First, the tax must be applied to an activity that has a substantial nexus with the state. Second, the tax must be fairly apportioned to the activities carried on by the taxpayer in the taxing state. Third, the tax must not discriminate against Interstate Commerce. Fourth, the tax must be fairly related to services provided by the state. The commerce clause has been by far the most significant source for judicially developed restraints on state taxation of interstate business. The Court has decided hundreds of such cases delineating commerce clause restraints on state taxation.

The Court has interpreted the Due Process clause of the Fourteenth Amendment as restraining the territorial reach of the states' taxing powers. It has declared that there must be a minimum link between the state and the person, property, or transaction it seeks to tax. Furthermore, the due process clause requires a state, in taxing the property or income of an interstate enterprise, to include within the tax base only that portion of the taxpayer's property or income that is fairly apportioned to the taxpayer's activities in the state. Thus, there is considerable overlap between the restraints imposed by the commerce and due process clauses. However, the due process clause restrains state tax power under circumstances in which the commerce clause is inapplicable, either because the tax does not affect interstate commerce or because Congress has consented to state taxation under its power to regulate commerce.

The Court has interpreted the Equal Protection clause of the Fourteenth Amendment as prohibiting the states from making unreasonable classifications. The Court, however, has generally accorded the states considerable leeway in drawing classifications for tax purposes. Under current doctrine, a state tax classification will be sustained if the tax has a legitimate state purpose and if it was reasonable for state legislators to believe that the use of the challenged classification would promote that purpose.

The Supreme Court has relied on the Privileges And Immunities clause of Article IV to invalidate state taxes that discriminate against residents of other states. Thus, the Court has struck down license and other taxes that impose heavier burdens on nonresidents than on residents, and it has invalidated a taxing scheme that denied personal income tax exemptions to nonresidents. The scope of the privileges and immunities clause was significantly limited, however, by the Court's determination in the mid-nineteenth century that the clause, which technically protects only "citizens" of other states, did not apply to corporations.

In *Mcculloch v. Maryland* (1819) the Court held that the states are forbidden from taxing the federal government or its instrumentalities. Rooted in both the Supremacy Clause and the underlying structure of the federal system, this Intergovernmental Immunity doctrine was for many years interpreted broadly to exempt from state taxation not only the federal government itself but also private contractors who dealt with the government. Beginning in the late 1930s, however, the Court substantially cut back on the scope of the federal government's immunity from state taxation. Broadly speaking, modern case law has narrowed the immunity to a proscription against taxes whose legal incidence falls on the United States and to levies that discriminate against the federal government.

WALTER HELLERSTEIN
(1992)

(SEE ALSO: *Economic Due Process; Economic Equal Protection; Intergovernmental Tax Immunities; State Regulation of Commerce.*)

Bibliography

HELLERSTEIN, JEROME R. 1983 *State Taxation, I: Corporate Franchise and Income Taxes.* Boston, Mass.: Warren, Gorham & Lamont.

—— and HELLERSTEIN, WALTER 1988 *State and Local Taxation,* 5th ed. St. Paul, Minn.: West Publishing Co.

—— 1989 Cumulative Supplement to State Taxation, I: Corporate Franchise and Income Taxes. Boston, Mass.: Warren, Gorham & Lamont.

STATE AND LOCAL GOVERNMENT TAXATION
(Update)

When a court is forced to draw a line between permissible and impermissible activities, one of its main goals should be to ensure that substantially identical activities do not fall on opposite sides of that line. In the area of constitutional limitations on state taxation, the Justice best known for promoting that goal was HARLAN FISKE STONE. In an era when the Supreme Court's COMMERCE CLAUSE jurisprudence was marked by a rigid formalism, Stone's opinions stood apart as a fresh departure from the norm. In a series of decisions, Stone broke new ground by abandoning formalism and embracing a more pragmatic, less absolutist approach.

It should come as no surprise, then, that references to Stone's opinions figure prominently in the modern Court's state tax opinions. Ever since the 1977 decision in *Complete Auto Transit, Inc. v. Brady*, the Court's state tax opinions typically begin with a discussion and rejection of the Court's "old formalism" and the endorsement of a new, realistic, pragmatic approach. Despite the Court's rejection of "latter-day formalism," it is questionable whether the Court is truly being faithful to the antiformalist underpinnings of Stone's state tax jurisprudence. In fact, in a number of recent cases, the Court seems to have embraced a "new formalism," under which substantively identical state tax statutes can be either constitutional or unconstitutional, depending on the form they take.

In *West Lynn Creamery, Inc. v. Healy* (1994), the Court

rejected on commerce clause grounds a Massachusetts statutory scheme that combined an excise tax on milk dealers engaged in the sale of milk within Massachusetts and a subsidy—funded by the milk tax—to Massachusetts dairy farmers. The Court conceded that each of the two pieces of the statute would be constitutional if considered independently. Because the permissible tax was "conjoined" with a permissible subsidy, however, the Court held the statute to be unconstitutional. The Court's opinion seems to imply that the Massachusetts subsidy was unconstitutional because the source of funds was milk tax revenues. It did not take long for states to learn the lesson of *West Lynn Creamery* and, not surprisingly, Maine immediately amended its statute (which was identical to the Massachusetts statute) to incorporate the exact same features with two formal differences. First, the Maine statutes were enacted separately (one in January, one in February), so that the statute could not be considered to be "integrated" and thus subject to *West Lynn Creamery*– type analysis. Second, the subsidy was funded out of Maine's "general fund" (into which the milk tax revenues were paid), rather than out of a special milk tax fund. So, to avoid having a statute declared unconstitutional, it appears that a state need not change its policy, but merely reenact a "nonintegrated" statute in accordance with such formal requirements.

In *Oklahoma Tax Commission v. Jefferson Lines* (1995), the Court upheld an unapportioned Oklahoma tax on gross receipts derived from the sale of bus tickets for interstate travel. Nearly a half-century earlier, the Court had rejected a similar New York tax as violative of the commerce clause in *Central Greyhound Lines v. Mealey* (1948). The Oklahoma tax in *Jefferson Lines* had one important difference from the New York tax in *Central Greyhound*: Oklahoma called its tax a "sales tax" while New York called its tax a "gross receipts" tax. Under the Court's rationale in *Jefferson Lines*, this distinction was critical. While many states might justifiably assert jurisdiction to impose a tax upon a company's gross receipts, only one has the authority to impose a tax upon a sale. The detail that the Court seems to have neglected is that New York's tax, like Oklahoma's, extended only to gross receipts derived from sales within the state. So, in fact, there was no meaningful difference between the two taxes. The lesson from *Jefferson Lines* to state legislators seems to be that any tax based on a vendor's gross receipts derived from sales within a state must be labeled a "sales tax" and not a "gross receipts" tax in order to withstand constitutional scrutiny.

Finally, the Court's recent decision in *Camps Newfound/Owatonna, Inc. v. Town of Harrison, Maine* (1997), is another example of the Court's "new formalism." In this case, the Court considered Maine's property tax exemption for charitable organizations. Under the Maine statute, the exemption was not allowed for organizations serving principally nonresidents. The majority opinion suggests that there is nothing constitutionally impermissible about a town's favoring organizations that serve Maine residents over organizations that serve nonresidents, so long as the town does so through direct cash subsidies and not through discriminatory tax exemptions. Under the Court's approach, it would seem to be permissible for the town to disallow the exemption for all organizations (that is, impose the tax uniformly on all organizations) and then to enact a cash subsidy limited to charitable organizations that serve Maine residents. Once again, the Court appears to treat differently two statutes with little substantive difference.

Some commentators have suggested that the lines drawn in each of the cases described above are indeed meaningful, distinguishing between substantively different statutes. Thus, with regard to *West Lynn Creamery,* some have considered it constitutionally significant that the funds must be drawn from the general fund rather than a milk tax fund. Some have defended *Jefferson Lines,* noting the different legislative intent and design characteristics of sales taxes and gross receipts taxes and according these differences constitutional significance. And there is some scholarly support for a constitutional distinction between cash subsidies and "tax expenditures" of the sort at issue in *Camps Newfound/Owatonna.* Still, even if one concludes that the lines drawn by the Court in these cases make sense, it is ironic that the Court continues to praise Stone's rejection of the "old formalism" and then proceeds to articulate new formalistic requirements. The law concerning constitutional limitations on state taxing authority involves a delicate balancing of interests, including deference to state SOVEREIGNTY and some reasonable protection of INTERSTATE COMMERCE. Striking that balance may be impossible without resorting to some degree of formalism. Perhaps the Court could be more forthright in its articulation of new standards and confess that, in this complex area of law, maintaining formal distinctions is the best that the Court can do.

KIRK J. STARK
(2000)

STATE CONSTITUTIONAL LAW

American constitutionalism is more than the United States Constitution as interpreted by the United States Supreme Court. Each of the fifty states has its own constitution, which is the chief charter of government and of limitations on government in that state. State constitutions offer contrasts to common assumptions, based only on the United States Constitution, concerning both government and constitutional law.

STATE CONSTITUTIONS preceded the Constitution of the United States. State governments had to be formed when colonial governments were displaced in the move to American independence. The CONTINENTAL CONGRESS called upon each colony to establish its own government, but the Congress decided not to propose a single model for all. Eleven of the original thirteen states adopted written constitutions between 1776 and 1780; Connecticut and Rhode Island established their governing institutions without adopting constitutions until well into the nineteenth century. The generation that drafted the United States Constitution and the BILL OF RIGHTS first applied many of its political theories to forming the state constitutions.

One tradition dating from the early state constitutions is to place the declaration of rights at the beginning of the document. The rights so declared differed among the states, but together they covered virtually all of the guarantees later added to the United States Constitution. As to the structure of government, all states except Pennsylvania adopted bicameral legislatures (today only Nebraska's is unicameral), but they diverged on how and by whom representatives were elected. The theory of a separation of legislative, executive, and judicial powers was widely approved and expressly incorporated in Virginia's and other constitutional texts, but the legislatures were dominant in most states, electing governors, other executive officers, and judges.

By 1800 most of the original state constitutions had been replaced by revised documents. Nineteenth-century constitutions reflected the changing political concerns of old and new states as the nation expanded westward. Jeffersonian and Jacksonian views of democracy and equality broadened political participation and extended popular election from legislative to virtually all executive, administrative, and judicial offices. By mid-century, legislative profligacy with public credit in pursuit of economic development led to constitutional restraints on taxing and borrowing, on "lending the state's credit" or granting special PRIVILEGES OR IMMUNITIES to private persons, and on individual incorporation acts or other special or local laws. New governmental programs such as public education and regulation of banks, railroads, and public utilities were not left to ordinary legislation but were added to state constitutions, often to be administered by separately elected officials. State constitutions address such social problems as alcoholic beverages, gambling, and lotteries. The movement toward populist government reached its climax at the beginning of the twentieth century when many states provided for referenda on legislation and constitutional amendments upon petition by the requisite numbers of

tution. The revival was encouraged in a 1977 speech by Justice WILLIAM J. BRENNAN, himself a former member of the New Jersey Supreme Court. The theme was taken up by other Justices and state judges.

The result is a rapidly growing diversity of constitutional decisions among state and federal courts. The California court in SERRANO V. PRIEST (1977) and the New Jersey court in *Robinson v. Cahill* (1973) held that equal rights under their states' constitutions required equalization of financial support to public schools after the Supreme Court denied this claim under the Fourteenth Amendment in SAN ANTONIO SCHOOL DISTRICT V. RODRIGUEZ (1972). Similar holdings followed when the Supreme Court allowed the exclusion of abortion from state-paid medical services. After the United States Supreme Court limited rights of access to shopping centers in *Lloyd Corp., Ltd. v. Tanner* (1972), several state courts found such rights in their state constitutions, some on the far-reaching premise that their state's speech guarantees did not run only against government. State decisions have invalidated services to parochial school students that pass muster under the First Amendment. The Oregon Supreme Court in *Wheeler v. Green* (1979) forbade punitive damages for defamation, though the United States Supreme Court has indicated that they are permissible.

The most numerous and most controversial constitutional guarantees apply to criminal law. Their protection is not so generally valued by twentieth-century citizens as it was by those who gave them constitutional stature. State supreme courts have struck down the death penalty as cruel or unusual punishment and have departed from federal holdings on such issues as DOUBLE JEOPARDY, right to jury trial and to counsel for petty offenses, and SEARCHES INCIDENT TO ARREST. The response has included constitutional amendments by INITIATIVES to reinstate CAPITAL PUNISHMENT and to tie state provisions relating to police seizures to FOURTH AMENDMENT holdings of the United States Supreme Court.

Before the United States Supreme Court bound the states to most federal constitutional rights through the Fourteenth Amendment, courts had to decide only whether and how to apply each state's bill of rights. After the Supreme Court's incorporation doctrine decisions, most courts again applied only a single body of law, the federal case law. The revival of state constitutional guarantees raised problems inherent in the dual legal system of federalism that had long been forgotten. Some of these are procedural problems; others concern the substance of constitutional interpretation.

When state law, including state constitutional law, protects whatever right a person claims, it cannot logically be said that the state violates any federal guarantee that the person otherwise might invoke. Logical procedure, there-

fore, requires that the state's ordinary law and thereafter its constitutional law be determined before reaching any claim that the state falls short of federally mandated standards. This principle has been recognized by some state courts, for example Oregon's in *Sterling v. Cupp* (1981), Maine's in *State v. Cadman* (1984), and New Hampshire's in *State v. Ball* (1983). Other courts, however, apply their own state constitutions selectively when they perceive a reason to differ from federal doctrine or to insulate a decision from review by the United States Supreme Court, or they cite both federal and state constitutions for the same holding. These hybrid practices have been criticized as unprincipled because state constitutions are invoked only when necessary to diverge from less protective decisions of the United States Supreme Court, or because citation of both constitutions simultaneously prevents further review by the United States Supreme Court and discourages amendment of the state constitution. In 1983 the United States Supreme Court and some state courts called for "clear statements" whether the claimed right was grounded in the state or the federal constitution.

Many lawyers and judges routinely use contemporary Supreme Court pronouncements on federal constitutional law as benchmarks also for interpretation of state constitutions, particularly when similar texts are involved. But state courts need not regard these pronouncements as authoritative in state constitutional interpretation, whether or not the texts are the same. The fact that state and federal texts were adopted with the same intent or purpose does not make the federal interpretation presumptively correct; a difference in texts only makes this point easier to see. The principle is true both for results and for methodology; many state decisions do not follow the mid-century Supreme Court's formulas for analyzing and resolving constitutional issues, while others do so.

Responsible interpretation of state constitutions often presents problems unique to the state. Historical records are not readily available to lawyers; sometimes none were preserved. When old texts are repeated in successive constitutions, it is debatable which generation's understanding should matter. The uneven quality of opinions requires reliance on precedents to be selective yet not capricious. The ever present temptation held out to courts is to act as pragmatic policymakers in the guise of constitutional interpreters, without excessive scruple whether anyone placed the supposed principle of decision into the constitution, or whether the principle as stated can be given consistent application.

For many reasons constitutional law has long been equated with the decisions of the Supreme Court of the United States. The Court as an institution is the subject of extensive and continuing writings by social scientists and journalists as well as by legal scholars. Only its decisions apply throughout the nation. The Court's nationalization of individual rights in mid-twentieth century, coinciding with the development of dominant national news media and with the emphasis of professional education on national materials, obscures the fact that the federal system makes the states responsible for large and important areas of law over which the Supreme Court has no jurisdiction unless a state administers this responsibility in a manner contrary to the United States Constitution or laws.

The late-twentieth-century revival of state constitutions has served to remind the general public as well as legal professionals of the essentials of the federal system. Its importance is not measured by the instances in which state courts have enforced individual rights beyond decisions of the United States Supreme Court. Many important functions, problems, and innovations of state constitutions do not concern individual rights. Moreover, citizens sometimes were quick to repeal constitutional guarantees of rights when these were enforced by their courts. State constitutions provide no security for dispensing with the national guarantees of the Fourteenth Amendment.

Even debates over repealing guaranteed rights, however, brought citizen responsibility for these rights close to home as no United States Supreme Court decision could do. Although citizens in some states amended their constitutions to revive capital punishment and relinquish protections against police abuses, similar proposals were defeated in other states.

Experience in the states, in the conduct of state government as well as in state court decisions of constitutional issues, continues to offer alternative models and concepts by which to test, and sometimes to gain, ideas for the nation. After two centuries, independent constitutional thought and action in the states remains an essential strength of federalism as well as a guarantee of individual freedom.

HANS A. LINDE
(1986)

Bibliography

ABRAHAMSON, SHIRLEY S. 1982 Reincarnation of State Courts. *Southwestern Law Journal* 36:951–974.

BRENNAN, WILLIAM J. 1977 State Constitutions and the Protection of Individual Rights. *Harvard Law Review* 90:459–504.

DOUGLAS, CHARLES G. 1978 State Judicial Activism—The New Role for State Bills of Rights. *Suffolk University Law Review* 12:1123–1150.

ELAZAR, DANIEL J. and SCHECHTER, STEPHEN L., eds. 1982 State Constitutional Design in Federal Systems. *Publius* 12:1–185.

LINDE, HANS A. 1984 E Pluribus—Constitutional Theory and State Courts. *Georgia Law Review* 18:165–200.

McGRAW, BRADLEY D. 1984 *Developments in State Constitutional Law.* St. Paul, Minn.: West Publishing Co.

POLLOCK, STEWARD G. 1983 State Constitutions as Separate Sources of Fundamental Rights. *Rutgers Law Review* 35:705–722.

PORTER, STEWARD C. and TARR, G. ALAN, eds. 1982 *State Supreme Courts.* Westport, Conn.: Greenwood Press.

UTER, ROBERT F. 1984 Freedom and Diversity in a Federal System. *University of Puget Sound Law Review* 7:491–525.

STATE CONSTITUTIONS

When the American colonies broke with the mother country, several traditions led to the drafting of constitutions for the newly independent states. Steeped in the writings of JOHN LOCKE, Americans might have viewed themselves as being in a kind of state of nature; writing state constitutions would therefore be the adoption of social compacts. British constitutionalism offered a precedent; although Britain had, of course, no written constitution, the colonists, during the years up to the American Revolution, had become accustomed to relying upon "liberty documents" such as MAGNA CARTA. Americans could look as well to the example of their COLONIAL CHARTERS, whose guarantee of the "privileges, franchises, and immunities" of Englishmen they had invoked against British policies on revenue and other subjects during the 1760s and 1770s.

In 1775, Massachusetts proposed that Congress draft a model constitution for all the states. Congress chose not to take this step. In May 1776, Virginia's convention, meeting in Williamsburg, instructed its delegates in Congress to introduce a resolution declaring the colonies to be free and independent states. The Virginia resolves viewed the drafting of state constitutions as best left to the several states.

The drafting of a constitution was, in 1776, a new art, but drafters did not want for advice. As early as November 1775, JOHN ADAMS had offered his ideas on a constitution for Virginia in a letter to RICHARD HENRY LEE; Adams's plan was of a distinctly democratic flavor. Others, like Carter Braxton, looked to the British constitution, in the form it took after the Glorious Revolution of 1688–1689, as the best model for Americans. THOMAS JEFFERSON, then in Philadelphia, thought that the people ought to have a say if a state constitution was to be written. As early as 1776, work on, and thinking about, state constitutions foretold the emergence of comparative CONSTITUTIONALISM.

Virginia's convention set to work on two documents: a "declaration of rights" and a "plan of government." GEORGE MASON of Fairfax County had a central role in the drafting of both documents. The VIRGINIA DECLARATION OF RIGHTS became especially influential. It served as a model for the bill of rights subsequently adopted in other states, and it foreshadowed the BILL OF RIGHTS added to the United States Constitution in 1791. Indeed, French scholars have traced the influence of Mason's draft on their declaration of Rights of Man and Citizen, adopted in 1789.

In the 1770s the distinction between a constitution and ordinary laws was still imperfectly perceived. One thinks of a constitution as the ultimate act of the people, yet the first state constitutions were commonly drafted by revolutionary conventions or legislative assemblies and then enacted by the same bodies, without referendum. This pattern of enactment presented something of the paradox found in British notions of Magna Carta as a superstatute, yet, like other acts of the realm, subject to alteration or repeal by Parliament. Both Thomas Jefferson and JAMES MADISON argued that Virginia's 1776 convention had no authority to enact anything but ordinary legislation; by such reasoning, the 1776 constitution was only an ordinance. Jefferson called for a constitution resting "on a bottom which none will dispute."

It fell to Massachusetts to perfect the idea of a constitution based upon popular consent. In western Massachusetts, the Berkshire constitutionalists called for a "social Compact" so that there would be a clear distinction between FUNDAMENTAL LAW and the acts of the legislature. There must be, as an address from Pittsfield to the General Court put it, a foundation "from which the Legislature derives its authority." When the Commonwealth's leaders sought in 1779 to produce a constitution without full popular participation, western Massachusetts resisted. In 1780 a CONSTITUTIONAL CONVENTION was elected specifically to draft a constitution, which was then submitted to the voters for their approval. The political theory underlying the MASSACHUSETTS CONSTITUTION of 1780 is explicit in the document's declaration that it is "a social compact, by which the whole people covenants with each citizen, and each citizen with the whole people, that all shall be governed by certain laws for the common good."

The early state constitutions varied in important particulars. For example, in some states, legislatures were to be bicameral, and in others, unicameral. Notwithstanding such variations, however, the early state constitutions reflected certain shared assumptions. There was common ground, not simply in the tenets of political theory but more immediately in Americans' political and social experience during the colonial period, a gestation period for what became the framework of American constitutionalism. The first state constitutions bespoke a belief in LIMITED GOVERNMENT, the consent of the governed, and frequent elections. They were based, by and large, on a Whig tradition emphasizing direct, active, continuing popular control over the legislature in particular and of government in general.

In these constitutions, professions of theory sometimes conflicted with reality. A commitment to the SEPARATION OF POWERS was common, yet the early state constitutions in fact made the legislature the dominant branch of government. State governors were, by contrast, virtual ciphers. Only in New York and Massachusetts was the governor elected by the people. In the other states, he was elected by the legislature, lacked the power of veto, and executed the laws with the advice of a council of state chosen by the legislature. Jefferson criticized Virginia's 1776 constitution for disregarding its own proclamation of the separation of powers: "All the powers of government, legislative and judicial, result to the legislative body. The concentrating of these in the same hands is precisely the definition of despotic government."

State courts at the outset had little power or stature. The principle of JUDICIAL REVIEW—the power of a court to declare a legislative act unconstitutional—was not spelled out in the first state constitutions (just as it was not made explicit in the United States Constitution). After 1776, state judges gradually began to declare the power of judicial review. In a famous OBITER DICTUM in COMMONWEALTH V. CATON (1782), GEORGE WYTHE declared that should the legislature "attempt to overleap the bounds, prescribed to them by the people," he would be obliged to point to the Virginia constitution and say that "here is the limit of your authority; and hither, shall you go, but no further."

The states' experience with their constitutions between 1776 and 1787 was an important proving ground for constitutional principles and structure. The idea of a bill of rights proved especially powerful. The same George Mason who drafted Virginia's Declaration of Rights saw the CONSTITUTIONAL CONVENTION OF 1787 defeat his call for a bill of rights in the proposed federal Constitution. He and his fellow Anti-federalists came so close to thwarting ratification of the constitution, however, that the Federalists undertook to add a bill of rights as soon as the new federal government came into being—a pledge James Madison redeemed in drafting proposed amendments in 1789.

As to the frames of government created by the first state constituions, draftsmen of national constitutions were able to point to the states' documents as models to be imitated or avoided. The members of France's National Assembly, debating in 1789 what that nation's new constitution should look like, found the American precedents relevant. One faction, led by J. J. Mounier, argued for a bicameral legislature and an executive veto. The other faction, led by the Abbé Sieyès, saw such devices as being impediments to the popular will. The latter group, which ultimately prevailed, depended on POPULAR SOVEREIGNTY for a constitution's enforcement—rather like the path taken by the drafters of the first American state constitutions.

The delegates at the Convention of 1787 in Philadelphia read the state experience quite differently. Concerned that there were too few fetters on state legislative majorities, James Madison and others at Philadelphia looked to institutional safeguards to protect the constitutional order. Thus, the Madisonian constitution, relying on such devices as the separation of powers and CHECKS AND BALANCES, stands in striking contrast to the Whig constitutions found in the states.

In the two centuries since the founding era, the federal Constitution has only occasionally been amended (sixteen times since 1791). Most of what the Framers of 1787 wrote endures. State constitutions, by contrast, have seen frequent amendment and, in many states, periodic overhaul. Indeed, the people of most states seem to have honored Jefferson's advice that each generation ought to examine and revise the constitution so that laws and institutions will "go hand in hand with the progress of the human mind."

The evolution of the states' constitutions has mirrored the great movements and controversies of American history. The early years of the nineteenth century saw the rise of JEFFERSONIANISM and JACKSONIANISM. Growth and migration of population brought rising pressures to rewrite state constitutions that, in the older states, tended to insulate the existing order from change: reform brought the progressive abolition of property qualifications for voting, representation in state legislatures became more nearly equalized, governors gained power and status, limits began to be placed on LEGISLATIVE POWER (to protect against abuses by members of that branch), and explicit provisions were made for the revision and amendment of constitutions.

The era of CIVIL WAR and RECONSTRUCTION brought another period of great activity in the writing and rewriting of state constitutions. Between 1860 and 1875, eighteen states adopted new or revised constitutions. Reconstruction resulted in constitutions obliging the former Confederate states to respect the rights of the newly freed slaves. After federal troops left the South, Bourbon democracy emerged and southern states rewrote their constitutions yet again. This time the thrust was to institutionalize Jim Crow and to achieve widespread disenfranchisement of blacks through the POLL TAX, discriminatory registration requirements, and other devices.

The proponents of populism and progressivism used state constitutions to battle what they saw as the excessive power of corporations and other economic interests. Drafters sought to bypass legislatures by writing detailed provisions regarding the regulation of railroads and corporations. Oklahoma's 1907 constitution concerned itself with enumerating who would be permitted to ride on railroad passes and with legislating the eight-hour day in public employment. Opinions on such state constitutions

varied. WILLIAM HOWARD TAFT called Oklahoma's constitution a blend of "Bourbonism and despotism, flavored with socialism." William Jennings Bryan declared that Oklahoma had "the best constitution today of any state in this Union, and a better constitution than the Constitution of the United States." The resemblance of such constitutions to codes of law struck JAMES BRYCE, who concluded, "We find a great deal of matter which is in no distinctive sense constitutional law . . . matter which seems out of place in a constitution because [it is] fit to deal with in ordinary statutes."

Progressives pressed for forms of direct government—the initiative, the referendum, and recall, with Oregon leading the way. By the mid-1920s, nineteen states had adopted constitutional provisions providing for initiatives to enact legislation, fourteen states had provided for initiatives to approve constitutional amendments, twenty-one states had adopted the use of the referendum, and ten states had provided for recall measures.

As notions of the role of government expanded, including the delivery of services, some observers sought to recast state constitutions in a managerial mode. "Good government" groups sought to streamline state government. Emphasizing efficiency and rational administration, they argued that state constitutions should be revised to give more power to the government, make fewer offices elective (by way of the "short ballot," thus concentrating more power in the executive branch), and create a civil service. The paradigm of this kind of state charter is the National Municipal League's Model State Constitution (first drafted in 1921 and periodically updated).

Much of the mid-twentieth century was marked by a decline of interest in state constitutions. Several factors were at work. Too often state courts showed little interest in enforcing their own state charters. Moreover, state constitutional law tended to be eclipsed by the activism of the WARREN COURT. During those years of JUDICIAL ACTIVISM on the High Court, state judges could do little more than try to keep pace with advances in federal constitutional law. There seemed little time or opportunity for state courts to develop doctrine under state constitutions.

The passage of time brought a renaissance of interest in state constitutions. The BURGER COURT continued to plough new ground, but in some areas—notably in CRIMINAL JUSTICE opinions—a more conservative note was sounded. As the Supreme Court trimmed back earlier efforts to impose national standards on state criminal proceedings, litigants began to turn to state courts, asking them to use state constitutions to impose higher standards than those required by federal decisions.

After RONALD REAGAN became President in 1981, his efforts to cut back the role of the federal government was paralleled by the states' acceptance of enhanced responsibility. Indeed, partly because of federal mandates (ONE PERSON, ONE VOTE, decisions of the courts, and the operation of the VOTING RIGHTS ACT OF 1965), the states were healthier entities, better able to function as the social and political "laboratories" proclaimed by Justice LOUIS D. BRANDEIS.

There is ample evidence of state courts' taking state constitutions seriously. Leading state judges—Oregon's Hans Linde and New Jersey's Stewart Pollock, for example—have called for more reliance by lawyers and judges on state constitutions. Even Supreme Court Justice WILLIAM J. BRENNAN, a leading architect of the Warren Court's activism, joined the chorus of those urging greater use of state constitutions.

One key to understanding the independent role that state constitutions play in shaping American constitutional law is to recognize that the state and federal documents are separate documents, each to be enforced in its own right, independently of the other. A state judge is of course obliged to enforce the United States Constitution, just as is a federal judge. But, while a state court cannot do less than the federal Constitution requires, the court is free to look to the state constitution for imperatives quite beyond anything found in federal constitutional law. If a state court decides that a state law or other action violates the state constitution, the ruling in itself raises no FEDERAL QUESTION and the Supreme Court will decline review of the case (citing the "adequate and independent state ground" doctrine).

The Supreme Court has explicitly recognized the terrain thus left to state courts. The Supreme Court of California held that its state constitution gave right of access, for purposes of expression, to a privately owned shopping center, even though the United States Supreme Court had previously held that the FIRST AMENDMENT conferred no such right. Upholding California's action, Justice WILLIAM H. REHNQUIST saw nothing in the federal Supreme Court's prior rulings that would limit the state's authority "to adopt in its own constitution individual liberties more expansive than those conferred by the Federal Constitution."

State courts have sometimes used constitutions where the United States Constitution has little or nothing to say about the issue at hand. In other instances, a state court will use the state charter in areas in which federal doctrine exists but there is room for additional state interpretation. Examples include the following:

1. Economic regulation. Since the so-called constitutional revolution of 1937, the Supreme Court has abdicated the earlier practice of using the Fourteenth Amendment due process clause to second-guess state social or economic legislation. State courts, however, often use state constitutions to review economic measures. For example, a state court might invalidate a law restricting entry into a given trade (such as hairdressing) where it is evident that the purpose of the law is not to protect the public interest but to give special advantages to a favored group.

2. Environment. The federal courts have refused to recognize a federal constitutional right to a decent environment. State constitutions, however, often have provisions protecting the environment. State courts may, for example, give force to a "public trust" in state resources such as rivers and wetlands.

3. Education. The Supreme Court has refused to use the Fourteenth Amendment to require that states equalize expenditures for wealthy and poor school districts. Education is, however, dealt with at length in state constitutions. Courts in some states have used various state constitutional grounds to require more-equal funding of schools throughout the state.

4. Criminal justice. Through the INCORPORATION DOCTRINE, the Supreme Court has applied most of the provisions of the Bill of Rights to the states. Thus, federal constitutional standards regarding police practices (such as POLICE INTERROGATION AND CONFESSIONS and SEARCH AND SEIZURE) and criminal trials (such as the RIGHT TO COUNSEL) bind the states, as they do the federal government. Even in this highly federalized area of constitutional law, state constitutions play a role. For example, courts in some states have read the state constitutional ban on UNREASONABLE SEARCH and seizure as forbidding police actions that might be upheld under the Supreme Court's FOURTH AMENDMENT decisions.

If one were to review these and other uses state courts make of state constitutions, it would be difficult to label such decisions as being, in sum, liberal or conservative. Those who may benefit from a state court's decision may be as diverse as business enterprises, criminal defendants, or environmentalists.

State court interpretation of state constitutions raise questions about judicial role. The familiar debate over the legitimate bounds of judicial review by the federal courts applies in somewhat altered form to the state courts' displacement of judgments made by state legislatures or by other political forums.

State judges, no less than their federal counterparts, should be aware of the way that judicial review, state and federal, triggers a tension between two principles. One is the principle that in a democracy decisions are made by agents ultimately accountable to the people. The other principle, embodied in judicial review, is that the commands of the Constitution should be enforced, even in the face of a legislative or popular majority.

At the federal level, there are some potential checks on

judicial power, for example, the President's power to fill vacancies on the bench or Congress's Article III power to alter the Supreme Court's APPELLATE JURISDICTION. Practice among the states offers more opportunities for popular discontent with judicial decisions to be manifested. In particular, it is far easier to amend state constitutions than to amend the federal Constitution. Voters have used the amendment process to curb state courts' ability to decide when there had been illegal search and seizure (California and Florida) and to overturn court decisions invalidating CAPITAL PUNISHMENT on state constitutional grounds (Massachusetts and California).

No function of a constitution, state or federal, is more important than its use in defining a people's aspirations and fundamental values. The federal Constitution is, however, more concerned on its face with structure and process than with substantive outcomes. State constitutions, in the American tradition, tell us more of a people's values. It is in their state constitutions that the people of a state have recorded their definitions of justice, their moral values, and their hopes for the common good. A state constitution, in short, defines a way of life. In so doing, these state charters derive from the tradition given in George Mason's precept (in Virginia's Declaration of Rights) that "no free government, nor blessings of liberty, can be preserved to any people" but by a "frequent recurrence to fundamental principles."

A. E. DICK HOWARD
(1992)

Bibliography

ADAMS, WILLI PAUL   1980   *The First American Constitutions: Republican Ideology and the Making of the State Constitutions in the Revolutionary Era.* Chapel Hill: University of North Carolina Press.

HOWARD, A. E. DICK   1976   State Courts and Constitutional Rights in the Day of the Burger Court. *Virginia Law Review* 62:873–944.

MCGRAW, BRADLEY D., ed.   1985   *Developments in State Constitutional Law: The Williamsburg Conference.* St. Paul, Minn.: West Publishing Co.

PETERSON, MERRILL D.   1966   *Democracy, Liberty, and Property: The State Constitutional Conventions of the 1820s.* Indianapolis: Bobbs-Merrill.

SYMPOSIUM   1985   The Emergence of State Constitutional Law. *Texas Law Review* 63:959–976.

———   1987   New Developments in State Constitutional Law. *Publius: The Journal of Federalism* 17:1–179.

———   1988   State Constitutions in a Federal System. *Annals of the American Academy of Political and Social Science* 496: 1–191.

WILLIAMS, ROBERT F.   1988   *Understanding State Constitutional Law: Cases and Commentaries.* Washington, D.C.: United States Advisory Commission on Intergovernmental Relations.

STATE FREIGHT TAX CASE

See: *Philadelphia & Reading Railroad Co. v. Pennsylvania*

STATE IMMUNITY FROM FEDERAL LAW

By the end of the 1980s, Congress enjoyed virtually plenary power to create and enforce regulations of state governmental activities. The Supreme Court had interpreted the COMMERCE CLAUSE power of Congress quite expansively; had rejected claims that FEDERALISM principles (sometimes loosely but inaccurately labeled "TENTH AMENDMENT principles") prevent Congress from imposing generally applicable regulations on states; and had rejected claims that ELEVENTH AMENDMENT principles prevent Congress from enforcing those regulations by authorizing private suits against noncomplying states in federal court. In the 1990s, however, one of the hallmarks of the Court's jurisprudence has been a renewed commitment to securing states SOVEREIGN IMMUNITY from the application and federal court enforcement of certain forms of congressional dictates.

In addition to reminding Congress in UNITED STATES V. LÓPEZ (1995) that its commerce clause power is not plenary, the Court began to reimpose some limits on the regulatory authority of Congress over state activity. In the mid-1980s, the Court had declared in GARCÍA V. SAN ANTONIO METROPOLITAN TRANSIT AUTHORITY (1985) that the proper forum in which states should seek protection from direct regulation is Congress and not the courts. But in GREGORY V. ASHCROFT (1991), the Court altered the existing federal–state balance of power by employing a "clear statement rule" of STATUTORY INTERPRETATION. The Court announced that it would interpret federal statutes not to apply to traditional government functions unless Congress made its intent to do so "unmistakably clear." The next year, in NEW YORK V. UNITED STATES (1992), the Court held that while Congress may wield various sticks and carrots to encourage states to enact federally desired regulations, Congress may not simply "commandeer" states to enact regulations designed to accomplish national objectives. The Court then extended this anticommandeering rule in *Printz v. United States* (1997), holding that Congress may not conscript state executive officials to implement federal regulatory programs. In each of these three cases, the Court invoked the concept of "dual sovereignty" in justifying some limit on the authority of Congress to regulate the states directly, rather than merely to regulate persons and entities within the territorial boundaries of states.

Even where *García* still affords Congress regulatory authority over state activities as part of more generally applicable statutes, the Court has further protected the principle of state SOVEREIGNTY during the 1990s by refortifying the Eleventh Amendment. Ever since *Hans v. Louisiana* (1890) more than a century ago, the Court has interpreted the Eleventh Amendment to preclude federal courts from entertaining private suits that assert claims arising under federal law against unconsenting states. By the end of the 1980s, the Court had conceded that Congress retained the authority to override this erstwhile Eleventh Amendment immunity pursuant either to its power under the FOURTEENTH AMENDMENT, SECTION 5 to enforce the guarantees of that amendment, FITZPATRICK V. BITZER (1976), or its power to regulate INTERSTATE COMMERCE, *Pennsylvania v. Union Gas* (1989). In *Seminole Tribe v. Florida* (1996), however, the Court overruled *Union Gas* and held that Congress could not authorize private enforcement actions against states in federal court pursuant to its Article I grants of power. The Court felt that such a broad congressional authority was incompatible with the *Hans*-based tradition of state sovereign immunity. Thus, even when Congress may impose generally applicable regulatory burdens pursuant to its Article I powers on both state and private actors alike, Congress must rely primarily on state courts to vindicate private federal causes of action against the state. And while the Court did not disturb its previous conclusion in *Bitzer* that Congress may override state sovereign immunity pursuant to its section 5 power to enforce the FOURTEENTH AMENDMENT, the Court subsequently narrowed the substantive scope of this power in *Boerne (City of) v. Flores* (1997), thus circumscribing the *Bitzer* exception. To be sure, since EX PARTE YOUNG (1908) the Court has qualified the scope of the Eleventh Amendment by allowing private plaintiffs to seek prospective relief against state officials to rectify ongoing violations of federal law. The fiction here is that such suits are really against the officials rather than "the state." But in *Seminole Tribe* as well as *Idaho v. Coeur d'Alene Tribe* (1997), the Court somewhat narrowed this exception as well.

The Court's justifications for its recently renewed commitment to protecting state autonomy from some forms of direct congressional regulation and most forms of federal judicial enforcement have been criticized as excessively formalistic. Neither the regulatory nor JUDICIAL IMMUNITY doctrines are persuasively grounded in constitutional text; the regulatory immunity does not even purport to be text-based, and the Court has all but admitted that its broad interpretation of Eleventh Amendment immunity runs counter to the plain meaning of the words. The Court's various claims of support from historical intentions and understandings fare better by comparison, but are far from conclusive.

At bottom, the Court grounds both doctrines in what it calls the structural principle of "dual sovereignty" asserted to underlie our constitutional framework. This principle suggests that states and the federal government are coequal sovereigns, implying that each sovereign should be immune from regulation by the other. But this claim of coequal status ignores the competing constitutional principle of federal supremacy. Neither principle can be considered in isolation: as Chief Justice JOHN MARSHALL put it long ago, states are "members of one great empire— for some purposes sovereign, for some purposes subordinate." And as the *García* Court more recently conceded, "to say that the Constitution assumes the continued role of the States is to say little about the nature of that role." Thus the Court's recent formalist efforts to derive its regulatory and judicial immunity doctrines from the principle of dual sovereignty obscure various normative judgments that necessarily guide its decisions. And yet the Court has failed to provide a careful discussion of the various federalism values either served or disserved by its immunity doctrines.

These doctrines might plausibly be viewed as second-best methods of policing the general boundaries of the Article I regulatory authority of Congress. The Court has lamented the tremendous post–NEW DEAL expansion of the power of Congress to regulate interstate commerce, but has simultaneously found it difficult to limit this power through defensible doctrinal lines. The immunity doctrines, while not directly tailored to the concerns about congressional omnicompetence, at least provide readily enforceable mediating principles that constrain Congress to some degree and proclaim a resounding symbolic victory for state sovereignty.

EVAN H. CAMINKER
(2000)

(SEE ALSO: *Constitutional History, 1989–1998; Dual Federalism.*)

Bibliography

CAMINKER, EVAN H.   1995   State Sovereignty and Subordinacy: May Congress Commandeer State Officers to Implement Federal Law? *Columbia Law Review* 95:1001–1089.
——   1997   *Printz*, State Sovereignty, and the Limits of Formalism. *Supreme Court Review* 1997:199–248.
JACKSON, VICKI C.   1988   The Supreme Court, the Eleventh Amendment, and State Sovereign Immunity. *Yale Law Journal* 88:1–126.
MELTZER, DANIEL J.   1996   The *Seminole* Decision and State Sovereign Immunity. *Supreme Court Review* 1996:1–65.
POWELL, H. JEFFERSON   1993   The Oldest Question of Constitutional Law. *Virginia Law Review* 79:633–689.

PRAKASH, SAIKRISHNA B. 1993 Field Office Federalism. *Virginia Law Review* 79:1957–2037.

VÁSQUEZ, CARLOS MANUEL 1997 What Is Eleventh Amendment Immunity? *Yale Law Journal* 106:1683–1806.

STATE OF . . .

See entry under name of state

STATE OF EMERGENCY

See: Emergency Powers

STATE OF WAR

The existence of a "state of war" for various purposes of domestic and international law is not generally controlled by the existence or absence of a congressional DECLARATION OF WAR. The federal courts, including the Supreme Court, have often held that hostilities, not accompanied by any formal declaration of war (as has been the case in all but five of the approximately 160 occasions in which American armed forces have been committed to combat), were "war" and, conversely, that "peace" existed despite the fact that war had been declared and not terminated by a peace treaty or legislative action. Sometimes the same hostilities have been treated as "war" for one purpose and "peace" for another. Examples can describe the judicial approach better than generalities.

The undeclared naval combat with France in 1798–1799 was treated as war for the purpose of a statute rewarding those who recaptured American vessels "from the enemy" (*Bas v. Tingy*, 1800) but (many years later) as peace under the Franco American treaty of 1778 (*Gray v. United States*, 1884). The CIVIL WAR, though of course never declared by Congress, created a state of war under international law, so that neutral vessels running the Union blockade of Confederate ports could lawfully be captured and sold as prizes. (See PRIZE CASES.) American forces sent to China to help suppress the Boxer Uprising of 1900 were engaged in war under Article of War 58, which permitted courts-martial to try charges of murder only "in time of war" (*Hamilton v. McClaughry*, 1905). But although on June 10, 1949, a declared war still existed between the United States and Germany and Japan, the Supreme Court held that, since there were no hostilities, that date was "time of peace" under a similar Article of War (*Lee v. Madigan*, 1959; the decision effectively overruled *Kahn v. Anderson*, 1921). The COURT OF MILITARY APPEALS and at least one civilian court held that the Korean and Vietnam conflicts, though not declared wars, were nonetheless "war" under provisions of the Uniform Code of Military Justice, which suspended the statute of limitations and increased penalties for certain military offenses in wartime (*Broussard v. Patton*, 1972; *United States v. Bancroft*, 1953; *United States v. Anderson*, 1968). But the Court of Military Appeals and the COURT OF CLAIMS also held that only a declared war could trigger a provision of the Code which gives courts-martial JURISDICTION "in time of war [over] persons serving with or accompanying an armed force in the field." The principle that emerges from examination of these and many similar cases is that the existence of a "state of war" depends principally on the amount of violence, unless a holding that "war" existed would raise serious constitutional questions, as by giving courts-martial jurisdiction over civilians.

The question can, of course, be of profound importance, for war is chief among the great emergencies that may be held to justify actions of the executive and the legislature which would in normal times be plainly unconstitutional. The most extreme example is the Supreme Court's refusal to strike down the 1942 exclusion of American citizens of Japanese descent from the West Coast and their confinement in "relocation centers," under an EXECUTIVE ORDER of President FRANKLIN D. ROOSEVELT, which had been ratified by an act of Congress. (See Executive Order 9066; JAPANESE AMERICAN CASES.) As a general proposition it may be said that the Supreme Court's unwillingness to hold unconstitutional the actions of the President and Congress in such emergencies varies in inverse ratio to the size of the emergency and the decision's chronological closeness to it. It has been the practice of the Court to scrutinize emergency measures much more closely and to give the executive and legislature much less leeway if the case reaches the Court after the war is over. (See EX PARTE MILLIGAN; DUNCAN V. KAHANAMOKU.)

JOSEPH W. BISHOP, JR.
(1986)

Bibliography

BISHOP, JOSEPH W., JR. 1974 *Justice under Fire: A Study of Military Law.* Pages 178–180, 192–201. New York: Charterhouse.

RATNER, LEONARD G. 1971 The Coordinated Warmaking Power—Legislative, Executive and Judicial Roles. *Southern California Law Review* 44:461–489.

STATE POLICE POWER

The POLICE POWER of the STATES is one of the most important concepts in American constitutional history; yet, like PRIVACY or FREEDOM OF CONTRACT, its historic significance derives from usage and application, not from the language of the Constitution itself. Nowhere in the Constitution does the term appear.

In his *Commentaries on the Laws of England* (1769) WILLIAM BLACKSTONE provided a definition of public police as "the due regulation and domestic order of the kingdom, whereby the inhabitants of the State, like members of a well-governed family, are bound to conform their general behavior to the rules of propriety, good neighborhood, and good manners, and to be decent, industrious, and inoffensive in their respective stations." Some of the early American treatises quoted this definition, but in fact it serves badly as a guide to constitutional doctrine and governmental realities in the United States in the 1790s or the early nineteenth century. Nor was the Supreme Court much more effective in providing guidance as to the substance and limits of the police power. Chief Justice JOHN MARSHALL verged perilously near outright tautology in GIBBONS V. ODGEN (1824), when he referred to the police power of the states as "that immense mass of legislation, which embraces every thing within the territory of a State, not surrendered to the general [national] government," and as the "acknowledged power of a State to regulate its police, its domestic trade, and to govern its own citizens." Left entirely open, of course, was the matter of what indeed had not been "surrendered" in the way of state powers as well as the matter of what was "acknowledged" as a legitimate part of residual state SOVEREIGNTY in light of the Constitution. The Court itself, clearly, would acknowledge positive powers and define the terms of "surrender." As late as 1847, in his opinion in the LICENSE CASES, Chief Justice ROGER B. TANEY was referring to the state police power in terms that hardly improved upon Marshall's, so far as specificity was concerned, but that at least had a more positive (if not to say sweeping) rhetorical thrust: that power was, Taney declared, "nothing more or less than the powers of government inherent in every sovereignty to the extent of its dominions." Not until the post-CIVIL WAR years, when FOURTEENTH AMENDMENT litigation paraded state regulatory laws before the Supreme Court for review, did the Court begin to grapple more tellingly with the problem of definition. Even in contemporary times, however, fitting the police power into the constellation of constitutional ideas has remained one of the Court's most perplexing concerns. There was as much critical acumen as despair in Justice WILLIAM O. DOUGLAS's plaint, in *Berman v. Parker* (1954), that "an attempt to define its reach or trace its outer limits is fruitless, for each case must turn on its own facts." In the last analysis, Douglas contended, "the definition is essentially the product of legislative determinations. . . ."

The Marshall and Taney approach to definition of the police power was sufficient, in a sense, because it sought only to place some sort of label on the powers that remained with the states once the Court had determined the legitimate reach of the CONTRACT CLAUSE and of the COMMERCE CLAUSE; the police power was what the states had left when such determinations had been made. From the standpoint of state lawmakers, however, the approach of the two great Chief Justices was not at all sufficient. First, it did not make even the most basic conceptual distinctions among the fundamental types of governmental power; and so defining the police power as coextensive with sovereignty meant that police subsumed the powers of taxation and EMINENT DOMAIN. Second, the Marshall-Taney approach did not come to grips with power and its legitimate reach in a positive sense. What were the sources of state authority in its exercise of sovereign power? On what basis could a state court, for example, weigh the legitimacy of a regulatory law (even if clearly not beyond the bounds set by federal contract clause and commerce clause rules) against state constitutional limitations such as those prohibiting TAKINGS without JUST COMPENSATION?

It fell to one of the nation's greatest state judges, Chief Justice LEMUEL SHAW of Massachusetts, to produce a doctrinal exposition on the police power that would establish the framework for subsequent adjudication and debate. Shaw's formulation was set forth in *Commonwealth v. Alger* (1851), in which the Massachusetts high court upheld as a proper exercise of "the police power" (so explicitly called) a statute that forbade construction of any wharf in specified areas of Boston harbor. Shaw's great achievement was twofold. He broke out of the *cul de sac* to which Marshall and Taney had driven, addressing the legitimacy of the police power in terms liberated from boundaries set by commerce and contract clause doctrine; and he offered a jurisprudential foundation for positive governmental action.

Shaw conceded at the outset that the police power challenged head-on any efforts to tame it and bring it within bounds. Yet, while it was "not easy to mark its boundaries, or prescribe limits to its exercise," the police power must be acknowledged as superior in some reasoned way to private rights and claims. It was so, Shaw contended, as "a settled principle, growing out of the nature of well-ordered civil society." And so he turned to the task of giving substance to what the Supreme Court had lately termed "the police power belonging to the states, in virtue of their general sovereignty" (Justice JOSEPH STORY in PRIGG V. PENNSYLVANIA, 1842). One of the foundations of that power was the COMMON LAW rule *sic utere tuo ut alienum non laedas* (use your own property in such manner as not to injure that of another). Historically, the rule had been invoked to justify private nuisance and PUBLIC NUISANCE actions alike; in either way, however, it had been used in essentially defensive modes. Shaw linked the *sic utere* concept with a positive obligation of government to impose a system of reasonable restraints on private property uses. "Rights of property," he contended, are properly subject "to such reasonable restraints and regulations established by law, as the legislature, under the governing and controlling power vested in them by the Constitution, may think necessary and expedient." As Leonard W. Levy, the biographer of Shaw, has shown, Shaw thus advanced doctrine well beyond the old common law framework; although Shaw held out the possibility of judicial overturning of laws that were not "reasonable" and violated private VESTED RIGHTS, he stressed the propriety of the legislature's acting when necessary and expedient to impose restraints for the public good.

But Shaw also undertook to define a related, yet in some measure conceptually distinct, foundation for the police power: the concept of "rights of the public." Thus Shaw insisted on the "expediency and necessity of defining and securing the rights of the public," and elsewhere on "the acknowledged public right." Even acts not necessarily punishable by common law might properly be declared illegal by regulatory legislation, Shaw wrote, "for the sake of having a definitive, known and authoritative rule which all can understand and obey." Thus, from the Shaw court in 1851, American police power doctrine emerged in its essentials. As in an earlier decision in 1837 (*Commonwealth v. Blackington*), Shaw asserted the legislature's power to act for the public good to be "the general rule," whereas restraint of the legislature should be the "specific exception."

The next step in elaboration of police power doctrine was the specification of positive purposes, more detailed than the public good or "rights of the public" broadly stated, for which the power would justify regulatory legislation. Early efforts at specification along these lines, before Shaw reformulated the whole issue, had tended simply to codify the common law categories of behavior and property uses constituting nuisance. (Such, for example, is what one finds in Chancellor JAMES KENT's *Commentaries.*) Here again, the arsenal of the common law held an instrument potentially powerful—the principle *salus populi suprema lex* (the welfare of the people is the supreme law), which in the seventeenth and eighteenth centuries in England had often been invoked to assert the plenary powers of Parliament restricted only by accumulated constitutional liberties. In an influential Vermont decision, handed down three years after Shaw's great effort, Chief Justice Isaac Redfield declared that "the general comfort, health, and prosperity of the State" warranted state regulatory powers on the same basis of power as "resides in the British parliament, except where they are restrained by written constitutions" (*Thorpe v. Rutland Railroad*, 1855).

In some other state courts, judges proved reluctant to endorse wholly such broad definitions of legitimate intervention; yet even these more conservative jurists, while looking for principles on which to support JUDICIAL REVIEW, contributed to specification of the bases of positive authority. Thus one of the Michigan judges in *People v. Jackson & Co.* (1861) contended that powers "which can only be justified on [the] specific ground" of the police power or general legislative power must be "clearly necessary to the safety, comfort and well being of society." This line of reasoning was reflected in the 1877 decision of the Supreme Court in BOSTON BEER CO. V. MASSACHUSETTS, in which Justice JOSEPH P. BRADLEY stated for the Court that a PROHIBITION statute against sale of alcoholic beverages did not violate the rights of a brewery company, for clearly such legislation was warranted under the police power: "However difficult it may be to render a satisfactory definition of it," Bradley wrote, "there seems to be no doubt that it does extend to the protection of the lives, health, and property of the citizens, and to the preservation of good order and the public morals."

Two other doctrinal arguments found their way into antebellum state jurisprudence on the police power. The first, which was rooted in the notion that the power was part of the residuary sovereignty and of legislative authority comparable to that of Parliament, was that the police power was inalienable. That is, states could not bargain away their power—and obligation—to look after the public interest. (See INALIENABLE POLICE POWER.) The second, a pragmatic strain that would doubtless frighten those who believed that vested rights in property deserved more rigid protection, was the view that the police power needed to be consonant with the changing character and needs of the society. This latter, expansive view of the police power found vivid expression in decisions of the 1850s upholding new regulations which permitted railroads to use the public streets to gain access to urban centers. How the imperatives of material progress inspired this expansive doctrine was illustrated in the language of an Illinois decision in 1859 (*Moses v. Railroad*) declaring that to deny a railroad the use of public streets, "no matter how much the general good may require it, simply because streets were not so used in the days of Blackstone, would hardly comport with the advancement and enlightenment of the present age."

Although the antebellum state courts had provided them with a doctrinal foundation for expanded regulatory initiatives, the state legislatures in fact were slow to extend the range or increase the intensity of regulation. Still, grist for judicial mills was provided by laws that were challenged in the long-established areas of state intervention—that is, in such matters as the regulation of streams to protect navigation and fisheries, marketing regulations and standards, laws requiring the fencing-in of livestock, rudimentary safety legislation (especially against fire dangers), and the control of operations on public works such as bridges, highways, and canals. In the late 1840s and the 1850s, police-power measures proliferated as both the regulation of railroad operations and prohibition of alcoholic beverages became common. Astute lawyers were quick to resist expansive claims for the police power, especially when they limited the freedom that powerful economic interests enjoyed in the use of their property. Prior to 1833, challenges to the police power were often based on the Fifth Amendment as well as on comparable provisions of the state constitutions; but the decision of BARRON V. BALTIMORE cut off that line of defense for propertied interests. Still, lawyers continued to rely on the DUE PROCESS provisions of state constitutions; and they contended regularly that regulations took away the value of private property without just compensation—in other words, that the regulations effectively were "takings" and amounted to INVERSE CONDEMNATION. Despite the doctrinal contribution of Chief Justice Shaw and others in the 1850s, moreover, lawyers resorted commonly to the view that only uses of property that were actionable under the common law (as noxious uses, nuisances, or trespasses) could be reached by state regulations. In few cases did courts respond favorably to such arguments. Still, the intellectual and to some degree political groundwork was thereby laid for future attacks on the police power.

Adoption of the Fourteenth Amendment gave new impetus and hope to defenders of private property, who presented arguments in the courts that the PRIVILEGES AND IMMUNITIES clause and the due process clause alike afforded new protections against interventions under the police power. Simultaneously with adoption of the amendment, in 1868, came publication of THOMAS M. COOLEY's treatise, *Constitutional Limitations*, in its first edition. Of basic importance to Cooley's view of the limitations that ought to confine the power of state legislatures was his premise that the "due bounds of legislative power" were not set alone by "express constitutional provisions." The implied limitations that he believed ought to apply all hinged on a generalized "due process" concept. Due process, he contended, forbade enactment of what he termed "class legislation" (laws imposing burdens or granting privileges to specific groups or interests that were arbitrarily singled out instead of being "reasonably" classified). Moreover, his generous definition of due process would forbid laws that were "arbitrary and unusual [in] nature," and as such "unknown to the law of the land." The champions of laissez-faire, if given reason for optimism by the Fourteenth Amendment and the views in Cooley's treatise, were provided with a source of unbounded joy by publication in 1886 of CHRISTOPHER G. TIEDEMAN's *Limita-*

tions of the Police Power in the United States. Tiedeman's great contribution was his attempt to turn the clock back altogether, to negate the principal contribution the Shaw Court had made in *Alger,* by resurrecting wholesale the doctrine that the old common law limits also constituted the proper limits of the positive police power. In effect, Tiedeman attempted to fuse the concept of due process, in the Constitution, with the traditional common law limits of *sic utere.* By the late 1870s, the Supreme Court itself had become divided on the crucial question: how far could state regulation go in limiting the actions of private persons and corporations in the marketplace?

The subsequent battle was not confined to the courts; it extended to the legislatures and the political hustings. Indeed, the question of regulatory power was at the very vortex of the storm in both national and state politics for three-quarters of a century. Three issues were involved in the debates. The first was whether specific types of regulatory actions by government abridged, unconstitutionally, what came to be called FREEDOM OF CONTRACT. The second was whether the courts or, instead, the legislatures were supreme in determining whether specific regulations were constitutionally permissible. Finally, there was the issue of what standards the courts should apply generally—if indeed the judicial branch had the power to review specific regulatory measures—to distinguish constitutional measures from those that were unconstitutional. All these issues centered on the rights of property.

Supreme Court doctrine continued to echo pre-Civil War formulations, even expanding them (rhetorically, at least) at the height of conservative, property-minded influence on the Court. Thus in *Barbier v. Connolly* (1884) Justice STEPHEN J. FIELD declared that neither the Fourteenth Amendment nor any other "was designed to interfere with the power of the State, sometimes termed its police power, to prescribe regulations to promote the health, peace, morals, education, and good order of the people, and to legislate so as to increase the industries of the State, develop its resources, and to add to its wealth and prosperity." Going as far, but in terms perhaps even more open-ended and expansive, Justice JOHN MARSHALL HARLAN asserted in *Chicago, Burlington & Quincy Railway v. Commissioners* (1906) that the legitimate police power of the state "embraces regulations designed to promote the public convenience or the general prosperity, as well as regulations designed to promote the public health, the public morals or the public safety." Despite such assertions of legitimacy for regulatory power, virtually every new or proposed regulation threatening to impose costs or restraints on private interests met with resistance in the state legislatures and the courts. Regulation varied in scope and effectiveness, from one state to another. The latitude and potential for diversity within the legal system offered by FEDERALISM was never more apparent. Nonetheless, the emergent industrial order, the rapid growth of population and absorption of millions of immigrants, urbanization, and the social dislocations that attended the acceleration of technological change and the growth of large-scale firms with enormous leverage over their employees and markets all served to focus political and legislative attention on expansion of the states' regulatory activities. Soon the courts were crowded with cases challenging regulative innovations.

The threshold question, of course, was whether legislative discretion should be permitted or whether the courts should impose constitutional standards that went to questions of substance such as "reasonableness." Before the Civil War, "due process" had been understood as referring to procedural requirements (right to a FAIR HEARING, specification of procedural steps and forms, NOTICE, and the like). In the 1870s, counsel in both the SLAUGHTERHOUSE CASES of 1873 and *Munn v. Illinois* and the other GRANGER CASES of 1877 argued that state regulatory legislation should be overturned on grounds of "due process" deprivation now defined as deprivation of substantive rights in violation of the Fourteenth Amendment. However, the right to regulate private interests, the Court declared in *Munn*, is one "which may be abused," to be sure; but "for protection against abuses by legislatures the people must resort to the polls, not to the courts."

Within a short time, though, the Court reversed itself and began to review state legislation under the police power with a view toward deciding whether "abuse" had occurred. Expansion of the concepts of SUBSTANTIVE DUE PROCESS and freedom of contract, in the hands of a Court whose personnel and social philosophy had changed radically by the 1890s, brought the Court into the business of acting regularly as censor of legislation on substantive grounds. Despite the continued ascendancy in national politics of Republican and conservative-Democratic regimes that resisted pressures for sweeping social-reform legislation, still a flood of new state legislation came forth in such areas as municipal public health, franchise law affecting public utilities, factory and mining safety, maximum hours, child labor, building codes, and railroad safety and operating practices. Neither the state courts nor the Supreme Court lacked for opportunities to play the role of censor and apply the new substantive due process reading of the Fourteenth Amendment.

Thus the courts turned to the last of the great questions regarding constitutional definition of the police power and its limits in the post-Civil War era: the question of standards or formulae for determining constitutionality. One of those standards emerged early in the period—ironically, in *Munn v. Illinois*, in which the new Fourteenth Amendment claims were decisively rejected by the Court.

In deciding the case, however, the Court set forth the new principle of AFFECTATION WITH A PUBLIC INTEREST, asserting that warehouses and railroad companies were subject to regulation because they were virtual monopolies. They were comparable to bridges and ferries, long held by the common law to be a special category of business dedicated to service to the public, standing athwart essential lines of commerce and travel. Citizens were compelled, in effect, to resort to them; hence they were classified by the Court as being in the regulable category. The "affectation" doctrine was a Trojan horse. If there was a line to be drawn between businesses regulable because of their essential character—that is, because the public was compelled to use them for vital activities—then on the other side of that line were types of business immune from regulation. Such was the logic of *Munn*. In later years, the Court struck down a great variety of state regulatory laws on the grounds they were aimed at businesses not affected with a public interest. Indeed, not until 1934 in NEBBIA V. NEW YORK did the Court finally abandon the affectation distinction, ruling that a state could properly regulate any economic interest. "It is clear," the Court declared, "that there is no closed class or category of businesses affected with a public interest."

"Freedom of contract" similarly served as a standard for the Court to strike down regulatory legislation. Thus in LOCHNER V. NEW YORK (1905) and ADKINS V. CHILDREN'S HOSPITAL (1923), as well as in other decisions, the Court invalidated various state laws that regulated the terms of industrial employment. Like the "affectation" standard, however, the freedom of contract formulation as a restriction on the police power was destined to be discarded in the course of the New Deal period of the Court's history.

Other limitations on state exercise of the police power proved to be more enduring. They are, in part, the limitations rooted in the older, antebellum concept of due process as a procedural concept, reinforced by the terms of the EQUAL PROTECTION clause of the Fourteenth Amendment. Not only the Supreme Court but also the state courts—both in periods when many courts were inclined to invalidate social-reform legislation on the grounds of freedom of contract and in periods when they were more inclined to be deferential to legislatures—have contributed to the formulation of continuing restraints on the police power. Thoroughly accepted in American constitutional law, in recent decades, is Justice OLIVER WENDELL HOLMES's warning, in *Noble State Bank v. Haskell* (1911), that regulatory legislation by its definition will "more or less limit the liberty of the individual or . . . diminish property to a certain extent"—but government would be paralyzed if such limitations should regularly fall afoul of constitutional objections. Yet Holmes himself conceded in his opinion in the controversial case of *Pennsylvania Coal*

Company v. Mahon (1922) when the Court invalidated a Pennsylvania law curbing mining companies' property rights in an effort to save urban structures from collapsing, that there must be some definable "limits" to the police power: "While property may be regulated to a certain extent, if regulation goes too far it will be recognized as a taking." Thus a line must be drawn between the police power, which permits diminution of property or liberty, and the power of eminent domain, which authorizes a taking only for a public purpose and on payment of adequate compensation.

To this specific consideration of when regulation encroaches on the realm of eminent domain taking, the Supreme Court and state courts have welded the more traditional procedural concerns. Exemplary of the latter was the doctrine of the Tennessee high court in *Vanzant v. Waddel* (1829) to the effect that to be valid a regulation must be "a general public law, equally binding upon every member of the community ... under similar circumstances." Chief Justice Shaw of Massachusetts elaborated the theme in decisions upholding forfeiture of property deemed unwholesome or a PUBLIC NUISANCE, but requiring TRIAL BY JURY and judicial process. So long as the legislature established a precise statutory rule, applied it evenhandedly, and provided traditional procedural safeguards, the Shaw court would uphold police power regulation. Later, from the Supreme Court opinion in MUGLER V. KANSAS (1887), came the formulation that to be valid a police power regulation must have a "real or substantial relation" to public health, morals, safety, and welfare; and in 1936 (*Treigle v. Homestead Association*) the Court also declared that a regulation must be enacted "for an end which is in fact public and the means adopted must be reasonably adapted to the accomplishment of that end." These considerations of due process, too, have survived even though the restraining concepts to which they were once wedded—the "affectation" idea, and substantive due process concepts such as judicial determination of reasonableness—have largely been stripped from them.

In recent times, and particularly since the expansion of the positive state in the New Deal era, constitutional challenges to the police power have come to a focus on the question of how much administrative discretion ought to be allowed to state regulatory agencies. Agricultural marketing commissions, fish and game control agencies, mining-safety authorities, factory inspection boards, fire- and building-code enforcement agencies, air and water pollution control boards, and other regulatory agencies of government have been held to standards of administrative due process. Their substantive powers of regulation, however, have been generally upheld broadly by state and federal courts.

Emblematic of modern police power issues in the law is the history of land-use ZONING. Even prior to the decision in 1926 of EUCLID V. AMBLER REALTY, in which the Supreme Court upheld zoning that excluded industrial use, several of the states' appellate courts had validated such legislation. In each instance, they rejected claims that property owners had suffered from an effective "taking," hence ought to be compensated. As the Supreme Court itself noted in *Euclid*, such regulations a half century earlier "probably would have been rejected as arbitrary and oppressive"; now they were found necessary and valid because they were consonant with the magnitude of emergent industrial and urban problems. As the California Supreme Court declared in *Miller v. Board of Public Works* (1925), widely cited in other cases involving expansion of administrative discretion: "The police power, as such, is not confined within the narrow circumspection of precedents, resting upon past conditions which do not cover and control present-day conditions.... [It] is elastic and, in keeping with the growth of knowledge and the belief in the popular mind in the need for its application, capable of expansion...."

The presumption of constitutionality against claims based on due process was explicitly stated in opinions of the Supreme Court again in the 1930s, echoing the majority's views in *Munn*. In *Nebbia*, for example, the Court not only laid to rest "affectation with a public interest" as a limitation on the police power; it also held that a regulation should be accorded "every possible presumption ... in favor of its validity ... unless palpably in excess of legislative power." When the Court upheld a statute regulating prices charged by employment agencies, in OLSEN V. NEBRASKA (1941), it couched its holding in terms that made its new posture unmistakable: "We are not concerned," wrote Justice William O. Douglas, "with the wisdom, need, or appropriateness of the legislation.... There is no necessity for the state to demonstrate before us that evils persist." In FERGUSON V. SKRUPA (1963) the Court refused to strike down a state law that prohibited anyone from engaging in the business of debt-adjusting except as incidental to the practice of law. Justice HUGO L. BLACK, writing for the Court, acknowledged that good arguments doubtless could be made for the social utility of the activity thus restricted. But he concluded that though the regulation might be "wise or unwise," this substantive issue was not the Court's concern; it belonged to the state legislature. In *Agins v. Tiburon* (1980) a municipal zoning ordinance severely limited development of open-space lands; the Court again upheld a sweeping use of the police power and turned away due process arguments against the ordinance. So long as even a greatly reduced use of the land was permitted, the Court ruled, claims that "justice and fairness" had been denied would not be upheld. Although the Court still imposed commerce power limitations on the states' regulatory activities, by the 1980s it seemed that the presumption of constitutionality against due process, contract clause, and inverse condemnation claims was firmly entrenched.

A decision ostensibly on a narrow technical point yet vitally important for expansion of discretionary power's real-life effectiveness was *Morrissette v. United States* (1951). In this decision the Court reaffirmed state court rulings dating back to pre-Civil War years that when criminal penalties are used to enforce police power regulations regarding "public health, safety and welfare," the state is not constitutionally required to prove criminal intent, as in ordinary criminal cases.

In response to the emergence of the modern state police power, there has been abundant scholarly debate and legal controversy regarding its impact on private economic rights. Some have welcomed the enlarged regulatory power and administrative discretion, declaring them to be indispensable in the complex world of modern economic and social change. These same features of the modern police power have been condemned heatedly by others, however, as unfair in their application. That eminent domain takings, which do require compensation, and actions under the police power, which do not, are on a continuous spectrum of state power has long been recognized. Numerous scholarly formulations have been offered to distinguish the two powers. The classic distinction was given in ERNST FREUND's great treatise, *The Police Power: Public Policy and Constitutional Rights*, published in 1904. Freund contended that "the state takes property by eminent domain because it is useful to the public, and under the police power because it is harmful." Modern critics of the expanded police power and the positive state deplore restrictions upon uses of property that impose costs upon a private owner in order to benefit the public, rather than to prevent harm to the public; thus, the person prevented from building on his or her land where it stands in the flight path of an airport's runway is said by these critics to be harmed unfairly, forced in effect to bear alone the cost of a public benefit.

There are some, indeed, who take a hard-line position on the police power by arguing that virtually all restraints—but certainly those that deprive private property owners of what previously had been "reasonable expectations" of use and profit from regulated property—ought to be accompanied by reasonable compensation. Only the narrowest sort of regulation, based on common law nuisance and *sic utere* doctrine, would be exempt as these property-minded conservatives formulate their theory. The possibility that paralysis of the regulatory process might be caused by the sheer volume of government compensation payments required by this theory is a source of satisfaction rather than dismay to the most doctrinaire

proponents of this view. Posed against it, and in favor of a definition of police power broad in its terms and consonant with recent decisions, is a theory that when government undertakes the role of "enterpriser" (creating parks, building highways, sponsoring urban renewal projects) it ought to compensate owners whose property is taken or damaged; but in its role as "arbiter" of contending social interests, as Joseph Sax has written, its actions for regulation of private uses of property should require no compensation. Other commentators, taking a middle position, urge that courts should give fresh recognition to considerations of "fairness" in these matters—for example, guarding against the possibility of a property owner's becoming the victim of more or less systematic deprivation, and also distinguishing degrees of harm and damage to the private owners affected by a STATE ACTION. These commentators also urge that administrators and legislators should be aware of "demoralization costs" when no effort is made to ameliorate the suffering of those hit hardest by regulatory activities.

The conflict between claims of the public under the police power and the claims of private property thus constitutes one major area of constitutional adjudication and current debate. Another area, no less turbulent and controversial, is the conflict between the police power and personal freedoms. Virtually all confrontations between persons and the state on matters of SEPARATION OF CHURCH AND STATE, or discrimination based on sex or religion or race are confrontations involving the police power. The whole corpus of constitutional doctrine based on the BILL OF RIGHTS and on the Fourteenth Amendment, in this area, together with such federal statutes as the various CIVIL RIGHTS acts, serve as a comprehensive set of limitations upon exercise of the state police power. The states remain free, however, to impose a higher standard in regard to constitutional liberties than is required by prevailing Supreme Court doctrine based on the federal Constitution.

As the uses of the federal regulatory powers have expanded, especially since 1933, there has been increasing need for the courts to examine the question of PREEMPTION—that is, the supersession of state laws when federal regulation has occupied a given policy area. In cases such as PARKER V. BROWN in 1943, and *Florida Avocado Growers v. Paul* twenty years later, the Supreme Court has upheld state marketing regulations affecting agricultural products even though both federal antitrust regulation and federal farm policies presented serious preemption questions. In the fields of labor law and transportation regulation, however, the Court has been more inclined to curb the scope of state activity in fields regulated by federal statutes and administrative regulations. Since the mid-1960s, a wave of consumer-oriented, industrial safety, and environmental legislation enacted by Congress has brought national

for the courts. The question was whether the state interest in preventing injuries to railroad employees due to the slack action of cars on longer trains was outweighed by the burden the statute would have upon interstate commerce. The Court concluded that the state justification was weak and the burden heavy and so invalidated the statute. *Barnwell* was said to be different because it had dealt with the peculiarly local nature of state highways.

In recent years the Court has struggled with the question whether the *Barnwell* or the *Southern Pacific* approach should be used to judge state regulations of highways. In BIBB V. NAVAJO FREIGHT LINES, INC. (1959) the Court held invalid an Illinois statute requiring trucks to use contour mudguards when all other states permitted, and Arkansas required, straight mudflaps. The Court reaffirmed *Barnwell*, saying that courts should not engage in rebalancing the interests which the state legislature had, but added that this was "one of those cases—few in number—where local safety measures that are nondiscriminatory place an unconstitutional burden on interstate commerce." The Court has also dealt with state laws forbidding the use of trucks pulling double trailers as applied to interstate carriers. In RAYMOND MOTOR TRANSPORTATION, INC. V. RICE, (1978) the Court unanimously invalidated a Wisconsin statute, noting that extensive evidence showed the law's heavy burden on interstate commerce and that the state had made no effort to demonstrate any safety interest. In *Kassel v. Consolidated Freightways Corp.* (1981) the Court invalidated a similar Iowa statute but was unable to agree upon an opinion or upon the way in which such regulations should be judged. Only four Justices clearly applied the *Southern Pacific* approach in highway regulation cases; the others were willing to leave the matter to the states when the safety interests at stake were substantial.

Cases involving regulation of production and trade also give the Court difficulty in arriving at consistent standards. Some governing rules are fairly straightforward. A state cannot ban the importation of goods, except in the rare case when goods must be excluded to avoid substantial damage to persons or property. So the Court in GREAT ATLANTIC & PACIFIC TEA CO. V. COTTRELL (1976) held that Mississippi could not forbid the importation of milk from Louisiana which had refused to sign a reciprocity agreement with Mississippi. In PHILADELPHIA V. NEW JERSEY (1978) the Court held invalid a state law banning importation of garbage destined for private landfills. The Court said: "[W]here simple economic protectionism is effected by state legislation, a virtually *per se* rule of invalidity has been erected. . . . The clearest example of such legislation is a law that overtly blocks the flow of interstate commerce at a State's borders."

Nor can a state ban the exportation of goods, even for the purpose of conserving scarce goods for use by citizens of the state. Thus in *Hood & Sons v. Du Mond* (1949) the Court held that New York could not deny a milk dealer the right to purchase milk and ship it out of state, even though milk was short for a nearby city. In *Hughes v. Oklahoma* (1979) the Court said the commerce clause forbade the state from preventing the transportation or sale outside the state of minnows procured within the state. And an attempt by New Hampshire to make sure that electricity generated by water power served first the needs of local citizens, by forbidding the export of such power without permission of the state, was invalidated in *New England Power Co. v. New Hampshire* (1982). The Court said that the regulation was "precisely the sort of protectionist regulation that the COMMERCE CLAUSE declares off-limits to the States." However, *Sporhase v. Nebraska* (1982) suggests that a state restriction on the exportation of ground water may be upheld when done "to conserve and preserve for its own citizens this vital resource in times of severe shortage."

Regulations which discriminate against interstate commerce or otherwise operate to protect local commerce against competition are also invalidated. In *Baldwin v. G. A. F. Seelig, Inc.* (1935) the Court held unconstitutional a New York statute that made it unlawful to sell milk purchased from out-of-state producers at prices less than those paid local producers. The Court said: "If New York, in order to promote the economic welfare of her farmers, may guard them against competition with the cheaper prices of Vermont, the door has been opened to rivalries and reprisals that were meant to be averted by subjecting commerce between the states to the power of the nation." A Louisiana statute forbidding the export of shrimp unless the heads and hulls had been removed was held invalid in *Foster-Fountain Packing Co. v. Haydel* (1928) because the effect was to favor the canning of meat and the manufacture of bran in Louisiana.

Much more difficult for the Court have been cases that do not overtly discriminate against interstate commerce. In DEAN MILK CO. V. MADISON (1951) the Court invalidated a city ordinance forbidding the sale of milk as pasteurized unless it had been processed and bottled at an approved plant located within five miles of the center of Madison. Although the criterion excluded in-state as well as out-of-state milk, the Court said it discriminated against interstate commerce. The Court recognized that Madison had a legitimate interest in the purity of milk, but held it could not give an economic preference to local businesses if there were reasonable nondiscriminatory alternatives, such as inspection outside the state.

In *Pike v. Bruce Church, Inc.* (1970) the Court held unconstitutional, as applied to a grower with a substantial packing plant in California, an Arizona statute forbidding shipment of fruit out of the state unless it was packed in containers bearing the name of Arizona. The court set out a series of tests which have been frequently referred to in later cases: "Where the statute regulates even-handedly to effectuate a legitimate local public interest, and its effects on interstate commerce are only incidental, it will be upheld unless the burden imposed on such commerce is clearly excessive in relation to the putative local benefits. . . . If a legitimate local purpose is found, then the question becomes one of degree. And the extent of the burden that will be tolerated will of course depend on the nature of the local interest involved, and on whether it could be promoted as well with a lesser impact on interstate activities."

The Court has difficulty in applying the *Pike* formula. The major problem comes in deciding whether a case presents a nondiscriminatory statute with an incidental EFFECT ON COMMERCE or one which can be characterized as discriminatory, hence requiring the higher STANDARD OF REVIEW. In *Hunt v. Washington State Apple Advertising Commission* (1977) a North Carolina statute requiring all closed containers of apples sold in the state to bear no grade other than the applicable U.S. grade or standard was challenged by Washington, which marketed under its own grades which were equivalent or superior to the U.S. grades. Even though the statute applied equally to local and out-of-state shippers of apples, the Justices found that the statute discriminated against the Washington apples and held it invalid. The principal difficulty appeared to be that the statute took from Washington the market advantages it had earned through its own grading system.

The next year, in *Exxon Corp. v. Maryland* (1978), however, the Court upheld a state law forbidding a producer or refiner of petroleum products to operate any retail service station within the states. Maryland had no in-state oil production or refining. The Court said that the act did not affect the interstate transportation of gasoline—presumably the same volume would come in after the statute as before—but merely the structure of retailing. Further, since owners of multi-state chains of retail stations who did not produce gas could continue to compete, there was not even a preference for locally owned stations. The Court said that *Hunt* was different because there the statute favored in-state operators over out-of-state ones.

More recently, in *Minnesota v. Clover Leaf Creamery Co.* (1981), the Court upheld a Minnesota statute banning the retail sale of milk in plastic nonreturnable, nonrefillable containers while permitting such sale in other nonreturnable, nonrefillable containers such as paperboard milk cartons. The Court noted that the statute did not discriminate. The burden imposed on commerce was very slight since most dairies packaged their milk in various kinds of containers, and the shifts in the business would not be distributed on in-state, out-of-state lines.

Finally, the Court has held that when the state itself is in the market producing or selling goods, the commerce clause does not restrict the state. Thus in *Reeves, Inc. v. Stake* (1980) the Court upheld, 5–4, a decision by South Dakota to cease selling cement which the state manufactured to out-of-state customers in order to supply the needs of South Dakota customers. The Court said that the state, as a market participant, was free to prefer its own citizens, even though it could not order private businesses to do the same. The Court distinguished the manufacture of cement from regulating private use of natural resources such as coal, timber, wild game, or minerals. The cement was the end product of a complex process in which a physical plant and human labor of the state had acted on raw materials. The dissenters said the policy upheld was "precisely the kind of economic protectionism that the Commerce Clause was intended to prevent."

Today, as in 1824, the Court has great difficulty in defining its place with reference to state regulation of interstate commerce. States can regulate commerce in the absence of conflicting federal regulation so long as they do not go too far. The Court will strike down clear discriminations or economic preferences for local economic interests. But, when confronted with a nondiscriminatory regulation that imposes an incidental burden on commerce, the Court will sometimes let the regulation stand until Congress acts and in other cases will intervene to protect commerce. This uncertainty is likely to persist.

EDWARD L. BARRETT, JR.
(1986)

Bibliography

DOWLING, NOEL T. 1940 Interstate Commerce and State Power—Revised Version. *Virginia Law Review* 27:1–28.
NOWAK, JOHN E.; ROTUNDA, RONALD D.; and YOUNG, NELSON J. 1978 *Handbook on Constitutional Law.* Pages 243–266. St. Paul, Minn.: West Publishing Co.
RIBBLE, F. D. G. 1937 *State and National Power over Commerce.* New York: Columbia University Press.
TRIBE, LAURENCE H. 1978 *American Constitutional Law.* Pages 319–344. Mineola, N.Y.: Foundation Press.
VARAT, JONATHAN D. 1981 State "Citizenship" and Interstate Equality. *University of Chicago Law Review* 48:487–572.

STATE REGULATION OF COMMERCE
(Update 1)

In the period covered by this supplementary article, the Supreme Court has decided a case or two a year on state regulation of commerce. Considered individually, none of the cases through mid-1989 seeems destined to become a landmark in DORMANT COMMERCE CLAUSE doctrin. Collectively, however, the cases may indicate a decreasing emphasis on "balancing" and an increasing focus on preventing states from intentionally discriminating against out-of-state interests.

As Edward Barrett pointed out in the original article on this topic for this Encyclopedia, the Court has always recognized that state regulations discriminating against IN-TERSTATE COMMERCE are unconstitutional. But in 1970, in *Pike v. Bruce Church, Inc.*, the Court stated a BALANCING TEST, under which even a nondiscriminatory state regulation is unconstitutional if it affects interstate commerce and if the burdens imposed on such commerce by the regulation outweigh the local benefits. For the next fifteen years, balancing was treated as the central element in dormant commerce clause analysis, both by the Court and by scholars, who had taken up the cause of balancing long before the Court endorsed it explicitly.

Similarly, the first expressions of disaffection with balancing appeared, not in judicial opinions, but in the scholarly literature. Starting around 1980, some scholars began to question whether there was any warrant in the Constitution for judicial balancing of economic interests and to suggest that such balancing was a task courts were not well qualified for. These commentators suggested that courts would be more faithful to the Constitution—and would be doing something they were better qualified for—if they concentrated on identifying and overturning state regulations that discriminated against out-of-state interests.

Unfortunately, discrimination is a chameleon among concepts. The first proponents of the new antidiscrimination theory tended to think that a regulation was discriminatory if it would not have been adopted had all affected out-of-state interests been represented in the state legislature equally with the affected in-state interests. In application, this test leads right back to balancing. Furthermore, the test is theoretically suspect because it presupposes that out-of-state interests are entitled to virtual representation in the state's legislature, a notion that seems at odds with the genius of a federal system.

If we look for a narrower definition of discrimination, we are naturally led to a choice between defining it in terms of the effects of a regulation and defining it in terms of the regulation's purpose. Both possibilities have their advocates. It may seem at first that discriminatory effects are easier to identify than discriminatory purpose, so we should focus on effects. But it is clear that we cannot hold unconstitutional every state regulation that has any effect, however unintended, of (for example) moving business from out-of-state companies to their in-state competitors. Such a rule would plainly invalidate too much regulation. Thus, if we set out to focus on discriminatory effect, treating it as significant in itself and not just as evidence of discriminatory purpose, then whenever we find such an effect, we are led back to a version of balancing, as we try to decide whether the benefits of the regulation justify the discriminatory effect we have found.

The only test that does not lead back to balancing is a test that focuses on discriminatory purpose, invalidating a regulation when the legislature's motive was to prefer in-state over out-of-state interests. There is, of course, a long-standing debate, not limited to the dormant commerce clause, about whether the courts should review legislative motivation. The Court has spoken out of both sides of its mouth on this issue for two hundred years: on many occasions, the Court has said it would not engage in motive review, but on many others, it has engaged in it, covertly or openly. Motive review is now firmly ensconced in the SUSPECT CLASSIFICATIONS branch of equal protection doctrine and in the doctrine of the ESTABLISHMENT CLAUSE, and almost as firmly in the law on FREEDOM OF SPEECH. With regard to the dormant commerce clause, the Court explicitly reaffirmed the propriety, if not yet the centrality, of motive review in *Amerada Hess Corp. v. New Jersey* (1989).

To illustrate that there may be a trend away from balancing in the Court's opinions, one can compare the two most widely discussed recent cases, both involving statutes regulating corporate takeovers. In *Edgar v. MITE Corp.* (1982) the Court struck down an Illinois antitakeover statue. The statute applied only to corporations with significant Illinois connections, but even so, it covered some corporations that were incorporated outside Illinois and had mostly non-Illinois shareholders. Six Justices voted to overturn the statute, relying on three different theories (most of them relying on more than one of these theories). The theories were (1) that the statute was preempted by federal statutory law; (2) that the statute amounted to constitutionally forbidden extraterritorial regulation; and (3) that the statute failed the balancing test of *Pike v. Bruce Church, Inc.* (1970). Technically, the only theory supported by a majority of the Justices, and therefore the theory of the Court, was the *Pike* balancing theory, and *MITE* was widely read as a balancing case. Close reading would have cast doubt on this interpretation (as indeed close reading of the Court's other decisions, including *Pike* itself, raises doubt about whether the Court, whatever it has said, has ever actually engaged in balancing, except in cases involving regulation of the transportation system). In *MITE* the fifth vote for balancing, which made balancing the official theory of the Court, came from a Justice who seemingly disagreed with the result in the case and was voting with the sole object of making the holding of the case as little restrictive of state power as possible.

Five years later, in *CTS Corp. v. Dynamics Corp. of America* (1987), the Court reviewed an Indiana antitakeover statute. The most significant difference between it and the Illinois statute was that the Indiana statute was limited to businesses incorporated in Indiana. This difference is highly relevant to the extraterritoriality issue and arguably relevant to the preemption issue, but it is essentially irrelevant to the balancing approach. Therefore, the standard reading of *MITE* as a balancing case suggested the Indiana statute should be struck down. Instead, the Court upheld it. Writing for the Court, Justice LEWIS F. POWELL began his commerce clause analysis with the statement that "the principal objects of dormant Commerce Clause scrutiny are statutes that discriminate against interstate commerce." In his analysis of the case, Powell never cited *Pike*, the standard citation for the balancing approach since 1970. Justice ANTONIN SCALIA, concurring in the result in *CTS*, vehemently attacked balancing under the dormant commerce clause, as he has in many cases since.

Justice Scalia has not yet carried the day. He wrote for a unanimous Court in *New Energy Co. of Indiana v. Limbach* (1988) when he relied on "the cardinal requirement of nondiscrimination." But then, in *Bendix Autolite Corp. v. Midwesco Enterprises, Inc.* (1988), seven Justices reaffirmed the propriety of balancing and purported to invalidate the statute before them by balancing. The Court may have been right when it chose not to rely on a finding of discrimination in *Bendix Autolite,* but even so, it need not have claimed to balance. *Bendix Autolite* was one of those rare nontaxation cases like *Allenberg Cotton Co. v. Pittman* (1974), involving what we might categorize roughly as administrative requirements on businesses, that probably should be decided by a "multiple burdens" analysis similar to that used in state taxation cases.

As late as 1989, in *Northwest Central Pipeline Corp. v. State Corporation Commission of Kansas,* a unanimous Court cited *Pike* as authority for balancing. But many considerations suggest that this citation of *Pike* means little: the Court upheld the statute, the supposed balancing was a perfunctory coda to a long and complex discussion of statutory preemption, and even Justice Scalia did not bother to register disagreement. The Court as a body still seems much less confident about the role of balancing than it seemed ten years ago.

One other possible trend deserves mention. Since 1974, the Court has decided four cases under the dormant commerce clause that centrally involved EXTRATERRITORIALITY issues (the two cases on antitakeover statutes and two others on beer price-affirmation statutes). Extraterritoriality is a problem that has lurked in the background of many dormant commerce clause cases, but has rarely taken center stage. The Court has never produced anything like an adequate theory of when a regulation is impermissibly extraterritorial, and it is doubtful whether extraterritoriality should be viewed as a commerce clause problem at all. On the other hand, the Constitution undoubtedly prohibits extraterritorial state regulation, and this prohibition is not easily assignable to any particular clause of the Constitution. There is no harm in the Court's sometimes treating the prohibition as grounded in the commerce clause, provided the Court does not confuse extraterritoriality with other commerce clause issues. For the most part, the Court has treated extraterritoriality as a distinct issue, even when assigning it to the commerce clause. The Court may have taken a step down a dangerous path in *Healy v. The Beer Institute, Inc.* (1989), when it emphasized that the Connecticut price-affirmation statute would make it economically necessary for beer distributors setting a price for one state to consider market conditions in various states. In a multistate economy most state regulations have effects of this kind, and to treat such an effect as establishing a presumptive violation of the extraterritoriality prohibition would require some further step, presumably balancing, to decide when the presumptive violation was an actual violation. On the other hand, the Court also said in *Healy* that price-affirmation statutes "facially" violate the commerce clause, which means balancing is not required to identify the violation. There is work to be done here to develop a doctrine.

DONALD H. REGAN
(1992)

(SEE ALSO: *Economic Due Process; Economic Equal Protection; Economic Regulation; Legislative Intent; Legislative Purposes and Motives.*)

Bibliography

EULE, JULIAN N. 1982 Laying the Dormant Commerce Clause to Rest. *Yale Law Journal* 91:425–485.

REGAN, DONALD H. 1986 The Supreme Court and State Protectionism: Making Sense of the Dormant Commerce Clause. *Michigan Law Review* 84:1091–1287.

STATE REGULATION OF COMMERCE
(Update 2)

The Supreme Court has continued to decide cases involving challenges to state regulations of commerce at a rate of one or two each year. A few cases involve statutes that are clearly designed to promote local commerce at the expense of out-of-state commerce. A larger portion, however, seem to critics of the Court's work to involve statutes aimed at achieving socially beneficial goals without any design to harm out-of-state commerce. The decisions have increasingly focused on the presence of geographical terminology (local versus out-of-state) used to distinguish activities that are regulated from those that are not, even when it seems unlikely that the government used the terminology merely to disadvantage out-of-state commerce. There have been no significant majority opinions applying the BALANCING TEST in which the burdens on INTERSTATE COMMERCE are balanced against the benefits conferred by the statute, although some separate opinions have applied the test.

C & A Carbone, Inc. v. Clarkstown (1994) invalidated an ordinance directing that all solid WASTE generated within the town be delivered to a privately owned local recycling plant, rather than shipped out of the town or out of the state. The town planned to take over the plant after the private operator recouped the construction costs, and it adopted the flow-control ordinance to ensure that the recycling plant would be financially viable until the town took over the plant. The Court held that the ordinance discriminated against out-of-state plants that stood ready to accept solid waste from Clarkstown. Justice DAVID H. SOUTER, writing for three dissenters, argued that the ordinance was clearly not protectionist in any traditional sense.

The Court confronted an issue that had lurked in earlier cases when it invalidated a subsidy to Massachusetts milk producers in *West Lynn Creamery, Inc. v. Healy* (1994). Subsidies can serve the same protectionist purposes as discriminatory regulations: Instead of raising the prices out-of-state producers must charge to offset the cost of complying with a discriminatory regulation, a subsidy permits local producers to reduce their charges. The subsidy in *Healy* was paid to local milk producers from a fund created by a tax imposed on all milk sales in the state. Every producer, local and out-of-state, paid the tax, but only local producers received the subsidy. The Court rejected the argument that the statute should be upheld because both of its components were permissible when taken separately: The tax was nondiscriminatory, and the subsidy was a typical payment of state funds to state residents. Justice ANTONIN SCALIA, concurring in the judgment, asserted that a subsidy from general tax revenues would be constitutional, but the more focused Massachusetts system was not.

Carbone has been particularly troubling to commentators, who see the ordinance as a sensible attempt to deal with the problem that consumers ordinarily do not have strong financial incentives to engage in environmentally beneficial recycling. Consumers who generate solid waste will send it to the cheapest disposal site, which may make it impossible to create a financially viable recycling industry. Also, once Clarkstown takes the recycling plant over, acting as a market participant, presumably it could charge lower fees to local consumers who send it their solid wastes for recycling than it charges people from other towns or from out-of-state.

The Court's insistence that states and localities avoid drafting statutes that use geographical terminology may be justified, but not on the ground that using such terms definitively establishes that the state is attempting to discriminate against out-of-state commerce in a classic pro-

tectionist sense, that is, attempting to direct business away from out-of-state businesses and toward local ones. The Court's approach may be justified in two ways. First, the use of geographical terminology characterizes most protectionist legislation, and it rarely is necessary for nonprotectionist legislation. The Court must design rules that give clear guidance to legislatures and lowers courts, and barring the use of geographical terminology does so. The rule also invalidates most protectionist statutes and only a few nonprotectionist ones. A balancing test would make it too easy for legislators to enact, and lower courts to uphold, statutes that were truly protectionist. Second, a rule against using geographical terminology discourages legislators from thinking about commercial regulation in ways that lead them to treat out-of-state interests as irrelevant to their concerns. It thereby reinforces the thought underlying the Court's COMMERCE CLAUSE doctrine that the relevant economic unit is the nation, not the state or city.

Healy is easier to understand, because the separate fund device made it transparent that the subsidy was a substitute for discriminatory regulation. State and local subsidies to local businesses are quite widespread—to encourage construction of a sports stadium or location of a new manufacturing plant. The entire point of such subsidies is to discriminate in favor of local activities and against out-of-state ones. Full-fledged judicial action against discriminatory subsidies would be an ambitious program. This may be a situation in which Congress's power to preempt local regulations, or to specify a national regime for local subsidies, might offer a better solution than any judicial effort to police the use of these subsidies.

MARK TUSHNET
(2000)

(SEE ALSO: *State Tax Incentives and Subsidies to Business.*)

Bibliography

COENEN, DAN T. and HELLERSTEIN, WALTER 1997 Suspect Linkage: The Interplay of State Taxing and Spending Measures in the Application of Constitutional Antidiscrimination Rules. *Michigan Law Review* 95:2167–2233.
HEINZERLING, LISA 1995 The Commercial Constitution. *Supreme Court Review* 1995:217–276.

STATES' RIGHTS

"States' rights" is better understood not as a term of art denoting a constitutional principle but as a slogan with tactical value in political controversy. The slogan of states' rights has been raised at one time or another by advocates from every region of the country and by partisans of every political persuasion. The phrase emphasizes one element of FEDERALISM, but it is a serious error to equate federalism with states' rights.

Although the states' rights are often asserted in terms of state SOVEREIGNTY, the claim of states' rights is really a claim on behalf of the sovereignty of the people. No government, national or state, properly exercises any power that has not been delegated to it by the people. The assertion of states' rights is most often made by those who oppose a policy of the national government and who claim that the people have not delegated to the national government the power to implement the policy. Less often the assertion is made by those who believe that the states, or at least their own states, are more likely than the federal government to implement a desired policy.

The idea of states' rights is as old as the Republic. The jealousy with which the colonial legislatures guarded their limited local powers against the British Parliament and the royal government was carried over into ANTI-FEDERALIST CONSTITUTIONAL THOUGHT. To the extent that the argument for states' rights is one of principle, it is based on the classical notion that public virtue flourishes only in relatively small political communities. The French political philosopher Montesquieu, whom JAMES MADISON called the "oracle" for American constitutionalists of the Founding era, restated the classical view in modern terms and maintained that the best practical regime was a small republic confederated for military and commercial purposes with similar small republics. Many Anti-Federalists opposed the Constitution from a genuine fear of consolidation into a continental empire that only a despot could govern effectively.

But there was also a practical factor in the Anti-Federalist opposition. In the years between 1776 and 1789, the state governments had assumed responsibility for their internal affairs to a far greater degree than the colonial governments had ever done. Individual leaders, parties, cliques, and factions had arisen and assumed their places in state politics; creation of a national political environment was bound to reduce the power of most of them. Familiar ways of dealing with problems would be replaced with strange ones.

After the RATIFICATION OF THE CONSTITUTION, the erstwhile opponents of the new frame of government, along with some of its defenders, sought to interpret it in Anti-Federalist, or Montesquian, terms. The Constitution, according to this interpretation, was a compact between the people of each state and the people of the other states. When the Federalist-dominated national government adopted the ALIEN AND SEDITION ACTS (1798), "states' rights" became the battle cry of the Republican party, whose leaders, JAMES MADISON and THOMAS JEFFERSON, gave the slogan substantive expression in the VIRGINIA AND KENTUCKY RESOLUTIONS (1799).

In the nineteenth century the growing sectional rivalry between the commercial, and increasingly industrial, North and the agrarian South was reflected in competing THEORIES OF THE UNION. The states' rights position came to be identified in public discourse with the interest of the slave power. It found its champion in JOHN C. CALHOUN, who, in the South Carolina EXPOSITION AND PROTEST (1828–1829), announced the doctrine of NULLIFICATION as a logical consequence of the state compact theory. Nullification, of course, was an empty threat unless it was backed up by the possibility of SECESSION.

One attempt was made to implement Calhoun's doctrine, the SOUTH CAROLINA ORDINANCE OF NULLIFICATION directed against the TARIFF ACT OF 1828, and that was a failure. In 1861, when the election of ABRAHAM LINCOLN as President clearly signaled that slavery had been belatedly set upon its course of ultimate extinction, eleven southern states withdrew from the Union. Lincoln denied not only the legitimacy but also the very possibility of secession, and the victory of the Union in the CIVIL WAR vindicated his position for all practical purposes. Whatever rights the states have they have as members of the Union.

The FOURTEENTH AMENDMENT, adopted after the Civil War, proved an obstacle to state regulation of economic activity begun under the influence of the Populist and Progressive movements. Because the BILL OF RIGHTS applied only to the federal government, individuals whose rights were infringed by actions of the state governments (unless they were the victims of BILLS OF ATTAINDER, EX POST FACTO LAWS, or laws impairing the OBLIGATION OF CONTRACTS) previously had been able to rely only on the state constitution, political system, or courts for redress. In the late nineteenth and early twentieth centuries, however, the Supreme Court held the substantive guarantees (life, liberty, and property) of the Fourteenth Amendment's due process clause to be effective limitations on state legislative power. In the rhetoric of the reformers, the federal government (or at least its judicial branch) had infringed on the states' right to regulate their internal affairs.

In the 1920s the cry of "states' rights" was raised both by those who opposed federal intrusions into areas of state legislative concern and by those states that were frustrated in the attempt to expand state regulatory power. It is instructive that states' rights claims were raised in both MASSACHUSETTS V. MELLON (1923) and PIERCE V. SOCIETY OF SISTERS (1925), the first in the interest of less and the second in the interest of more governmental regulation.

Between the late 1940s and the late 1960s, the cause of states' rights became virtually identified with the cause of southern opposition to CIVIL RIGHTS legislation. The national commitment to abolishing racial SEGREGATION, first in publicly owned facilities and then in private establishments dealing with the public, aroused fierce opposition among those who were destined to lose their privileged position. Despite its long history of service to every shade of political opinion, the slogan of "states' rights" may have been permanently tarnished by its association with state-sponsored RACIAL DISCRIMINATION.

If the states, as states, have a valid claim of right to any particular field of legislation, that field would seem to be legislation concerning the internal workings of the governmental apparatus of the state. In the twentieth century the federal government undertook to regulate the compensation and working conditions of state employees, incidentally to its regulation of compensation and working conditions of private employees under the COMMERCE CLAUSE. In NATIONAL LEAGUE OF CITIES V. USERY (1976) the Supreme Court struck down such regulation insofar as the employees concerned were involved in the essential governmental operations of the states. The distinction was undermined in EQUAL EMPLOYMENT OPPORTUNITY COMMISSION V. WYOMING (1983), and discarded as unworkable in GARCIA V. SAN ANTONIO METROPOLITAN TRANSIT AUTHORITY (1985). In *Garcia* a 5–4 Supreme Court explicitly overruled *Usery*, and—unless the dissenters were accurate in predicting that the *Usery* doctrine would one day be revived—effectively put an end to the last vestige of states' rights in constitutional law.

DENNIS J. MAHONEY
(1986)

(SEE ALSO: *Tenth Amendment.*)

Bibliography

ELAZAR, DANIEL J.   1972   *American Federalism: A View from the States,* 2nd ed. New York: Thomas Y. Crowell Co.
GRODZINS, MORTON   1966   *The American System: A New View of Government in the United States,* ed. Daniel J. Elazar. Chicago: Rand-McNally.
SANFORD, TERRY   1967   *Storm over the States.* New York: McGraw-Hill.
VILE, M. J. C.   1961   *The Structure of American Federalism.* Oxford: Oxford University Press.

STATES' RIGHTS AMENDMENTS
(1963–1967)

The decisions of the WARREN COURT radically altered the constitutional balance of power to the disadvantage of the several states. In 1963, the Council of State Governments recommended three constitutional amendments that would, respectively, have established a third variation of the AMENDING PROCESS by which the states could alter the Constitution without the participation of Congress; denied the Supreme Court JURISDICTION over apportionment of

state legislatures; and created a Court of the Union, comprising all the state chief justices, with power to overrule the Supreme Court on questions of federal-state relations.

The amendments were introduced in Congress by Senator J. Strom Thurmond of South Carolina but were buried in committee. Supporters hoped to have two-thirds of the state legislatures petition Congress and thereby oblige Congress to call an amending convention. The first and third proposals encountered widespread opposition—including public denunciation by Chief Justice EARL WARREN. But the 1964 REAPPORTIONMENT decisions, REYNOLDS V. SIMS and *Lucas v. Forty-Fourth General Assembly,* spurred the legislatures to act on the remaining proposal. By the time the agitation ceased in 1967, thirty-three states (only one less than necessary) had petitioned for an amending convention on the apportionment issue.

DENNIS J. MAHONEY
(1986)

STATE SUICIDE THEORY

Massachusetts Senator CHARLES SUMNER, like most abolitionists and all Republicans before the Civil War, believed that the federal government lacked constitutional power to abolish slavery in the states. By early 1862, however, he and some other Republicans sought a theoretical basis for the exercise of congressional authority to govern occupied areas of the Confederacy and to eliminate slavery there. While other Republicans flirted with theories of territorialization or the CONQUERED PROVINCES concept of Representative THADDEUS STEVENS, Sumner developed his own unique amalgam of constitutional ideas for RECONSTRUCTION, which came to be known as the state suicide theory.

Sumner believed that the Confederate states, by seceding, had committed a sort of constitutional suicide, dissolving their "peculiar local institutions" (that is, slavery) and leaving their territory and inhabitants to be governed by Congress. This conception derived from three constitutional sources. The idea that the seceded states had reverted to the condition of TERRITORIES was widely discussed among Republicans after the outbreak of war. The belief that slavery, because it required positive law for its existence, would expire when that law expired, was derived from implications of the doctrine of SOMERSET'S CASE (1772) and had appeared in abolitionists' constitutional arguments before the war. Abolitionists also found a basis of congressional power to govern the states (including the power to abolish slavery there) in the clause of Article IV, section 4, that requires the United States to guarantee a REPUBLICAN FORM OF GOVERNMENT to each of the states. (See ABOLITIONIST CONSTITUTIONAL THEORY.)

Democrats, conservatives, and even moderate Republicans deplored the state suicide theory, regarding it as unconstitutional because it recognized the validity, or at least effectiveness, of SECESSION. Sumner abandoned his insistence on the constitutional death of the states but continued to maintain that Congress had plenary governmental power in the occupied states.

WILLIAM M. WIECEK
(1986)

Bibliography

DONALD, DAVID   1970   *Charles Sumner and the Rights of Man.* New York: Knopf.

STATE TAXATION OF COMMERCE

Since BROWN V. MARYLAND in 1827 the Supreme Court has decided hundreds of cases determining the extent to which the COMMERCE CLAUSE immunizes from state taxation property moving in INTERSTATE COMMERCE or businesses engaged in such commerce. From the outset, agreement has existed on one principle—state taxes that discriminate against interstate commerce are invalid. In *Welton v. Missouri* (1876) the Court held invalid a state tax on local sales because it applied only to goods produced outside the state. Recently, in *Boston Stock Exchange v. State Tax Commission* (1977), the Court stated that the "fundamental principle" that no state may impose a tax that discriminates against interstate commerce "follows inexorably from the basic purpose of the [Commerce] Clause. Permitting individual states to enact laws that favor local enterprises at the expense of out-of-state businesses "would invite a multiplication of preferential trade areas destructive' of the free trade which the Clause protects."

The Supreme Court recognized early, however, that even formally nondiscriminatory taxes might put interstate commerce at a competitive disadvantage. In PHILADELPHIA & READING RAILROAD V. PENNSYLVANIA (1873) a tax on transportation companies measured by cents per ton of freight carried within the state (but not apportioned to distance) was held invalid as applied to goods in interstate commerce even though local commerce paid the same tax. The Court noted that if one state could impose this tax all states could and commercial intercourse between states remote from each other might be destroyed. Interstate commerce could bear the imposition of a single tax but "it would be crushed under the load of many." To avoid such burdens the Court formulated broad prophylactic rules. States were not permitted to tax interstate commerce by laying taxes on property in transit in interstate commerce, the business which constituted such commerce, the privilege of engaging in it, or the receipts derived from it.

The Supreme Court did not go so far, however, as to hold that states could never secure revenue from interstate businesses. An immunity that broad would have placed the states in the position of being required to provide governmental services to interstate property and businesses within their borders without being able to secure from them any contribution to the costs of such governmental services. Hence the Court came to recognize a variety of avenues through which states could derive revenue from interstate commerce.

The principal state revenue producer in the last century was the *ad valorem* property tax. Although property taxes on goods actually moving in interstate commerce were forbidden (because of the risk that they would be applied by more states than one), states were permitted to impose property taxes upon railroad cars and barges if they were apportioned (usually by mileage) so as to apply, in effect, only to the average number of cars present in the state on any one day. The Supreme Court even went so far as to permit states to levy property taxes on the intangible values of interstate transportation companies by permitting the imposition of taxes upon the proportion of the total going-concern value of the companies that track mileage within the state bore to total track mileage.

In other cases activities were characterized as intrastate in order to permit state taxation. Manufacturing, mining, and PRODUCTION were held to be INTRASTATE COMMERCE and taxes upon such activities were permitted even though substantially all of the goods produced were shipped in interstate commerce. Sales involving the transfer of goods from seller to buyer within the state were regarded as intrastate while sales involving no more than solicitation of orders within the state followed by delivery from without were interstate sales. Hence, states could impose nondiscriminatory license taxes on peddlers who carried with them the goods they sold but not on drummers who merely took orders. Later, when modern sales taxes came into existence, the Court applied the same principles. A sales tax could not be imposed when the seller outside the state shipped goods to the purchaser inside the state, but it could be imposed upon the local retailer who brought the goods from outside and then sold and delivered them to customers. In order to protect local merchants from competition by out-of-state sellers, states imposed on purchasers a tax on the "first use" within the state of goods purchased, with an exemption for goods on which the sales tax had been paid. The Supreme Court sustained such taxes on the theory that they were imposed on a local transaction—the use—rather than upon the interstate sale.

Another major boost to the power of states to secure revenues from interstate commerce came in *United States Glue Co. v. Town of Oak Creek* (1918). The Supreme

Court upheld the power of a state to impose taxes measured by net income derived within the state, including net income from interstate activities. The Court distinguished earlier decisions forbidding the imposition of taxes on gross income from commerce by saying that such taxes burdened commerce directly while net income taxes, applied only to the taxpayers' net profits, bore only indirectly upon commerce. The power of the states to impose net INCOME TAXES was initially limited only by two principles. First, a net income tax could not be collected if the taxpayer did only interstate commerce within the state, because it would constitute an imposition on the privilege of engaging in interstate commerce—a privilege that the state did not grant. Second, the tax could be imposed only upon that portion of the net income fairly attributable to activities within the taxing state. A rational apportionment formula was required.

In *Western Livestock v. Bureau of Revenue* (1938), Justice HARLAN FISKE STONE sought to derive from the cases a general principle that would abrogate the general rule that interstate commerce itself could not be taxed. He said that it was not the purpose of the commerce clause "to relieve those engaged in interstate commerce from their just share of state tax burden even though it increases the cost of doing business." He noted that gross receipts taxes had often been held invalid. "The vice characteristic of those which have been held invalid is that they have placed on commerce burdens of such a nature as to be capable in point of substance, of being imposed . . . or added to . . . with equal right by every state which the commerce touches, merely because interstate commerce is being done, so that without the protection of the commerce clause it would bear cumulative burdens not imposed on local commerce."

The decision in *Western Livestock* did not mark an end to the older idea that interstate commerce itself could not be directly taxed. As recently as 1946 in *Freeman v. Hewit*, Justice FELIX FRANKFURTER speaking for the Court said:

> Nor is there any warrant in the constitutional principles heretofore applied by this Court to support the notion that a State may be allowed one single-tax-worth of direct interference with the free flow of commerce. An exaction by a State from interstate commerce falls not because of a proven increase in the cost of the product. What makes the tax invalid is the fact that there is interference by a State with the freedom of interstate commerce. . . . Trade being a sensitive plant, a direct tax upon it to some extent at least deters trade even if its effect is not precisely calculable.

For nearly three decades after *Western Livestock* the cases continued to reflect first one and then the other of these conflicting approaches.

Recently, however, the Supreme Court has cleared out most of the underbrush of the cases from the past and has established some relatively simple guidelines for the future. In *Complete Auto Transit, Inc. v. Brady* (1977) the Court said that it considers not the "formal language" of the tax statute but its "practical effect" and sustains "a tax against commerce clause challenge when the tax is applied to an activity with a substantial nexus with the taxing state, is fairly apportioned, does not discriminate against interstate commerce, and is fairly related to the services provided by the State."

With respect to *ad valorem* property taxation, the Court continues to forbid such taxes on goods moving in interstate commerce while reaffirming the rule that properly apportioned taxes may be imposed upon the instrumentalities of commerce such as railroad cars and airplanes. In *Japan Line, Ltd. v. County of Los Angeles* (1979), however, the Court limited this rule as applied to foreign-owned instrumentalities. It held that a country could not impose even an apportioned tax on the value of shipping containers owned by a Japanese shipping company because Japan was taxing the entire value of the containers. The Court said that its rule permitting apportioned property taxation was based on its ability to force apportionment on all potential taxing jurisdictions. Since Japan could not be required to apportion, the county could not tax at all even though it provided governmental services to the containers when they were in the state.

The distinction between taxes measured by gross income and those by net income has been abolished, along with the rule that states may not tax the privilege of engaging in interstate commerce. In the *Brady* case and in *Department of Revenue of Washington v. Association of Washington Stevedoring Companies* (1978) the Court upheld privilege taxes measured by gross receipts derived from exclusively interstate commerce within the taxing state. The Court indicated that the key is apportionment, which avoids multiple burdens. In *Washington Stevedoring*, for example, it upheld a tax on the gross receipts of a stevedoring company which had as its entire activity loading and unloading in Washington ships engaged in interstate and FOREIGN COMMERCE. It said that the state had "a significant interest in exacting from interstate commerce its fair share of the cost of state government. . . . The Commerce Clause balance tips against the tax only when it unfairly burdens commerce by exacting more than a just share from interstate activity."

A 1959 federal statute (section 381, Title 18, United States Code) provides that a state may not impose a net income tax if the taxpayer does no more within the state than solicit orders. Beyond that limit the major, current problems relate to the apportionment of an interstate business's income among the states having JURISDICTION TO TAX it. Nearly half of the states are adherents to the Multistate Tax Compact which calls for net income to be apportioned by a three-factor formula based on property, payroll, and sales. Most states, whether or not adherents to the Compact, utilize similar three-factor formulas. Iowa, however, applies a formula under which it taxes that proportion of net income that gross sales within the state bear to total gross sales. In *Moorman Manufacturing Co. v. Blair* (1978) a challenge to this formula was rejected. The taxpayer argued that to permit Iowa to use a single-factor formula when other states in which it did business used a three-factor formula would result in the taxation by Iowa of income that had been taxed in other states. The Supreme Court would go no further than to examine the particular formula to see that it is reasonable and does not allocate disproportionate amounts of income to the taxing state, leaving to Congress the question whether a uniform formula should be imposed on all states. The Court has also recently rejected challenges to the application of apportionment formulas to the entire net income of integrated companies engaged in production, refining, and distribution of petroleum products. In *Exxon Corporation v. Wisconsin Department of Revenue* (1980) the Court held that so long as the taxpayer is engaged in a "unitary business" any state in which it does business may apply its apportionment formula to the entire net income of the business without regard to how the taxpayer's own accounting system allocates profits and losses.

With respect to taxes on the sales transaction, existing doctrines permit the state in which goods are sold to tax through either a sales or a use tax. However, collection of the use tax is often impossible if the state cannot compel the seller to collect the tax from the purchaser and remit it to the state. Recent concern has been with the DUE PROCESS jurisdictional problem. The state must show some definite link, some minimum connection, between the seller and the state, before it can impose the duty of collection.

A century and a half after *Brown v. Maryland* the Supreme Court's approach to state taxation of interstate commerce is relatively simple: so long as the state taxes do not discriminate against such commerce or create a risk of multiplication of similar levies on the same property or activity, they will be upheld. States will be given wide latitude in devising formulas for apportioning income and allocating values. If more protection for commerce is desired, it will have to come from Congress.

EDWARD L. BARRETT, JR.
(1986)

(SEE ALSO: *Excise Tax; Import-Export Clause; Impost; Original Package Doctrine; State Regulation of Commerce.*)

Bibliography

BARRETT, EDWARD L., JR. 1953 "Substance" vs. "Form" in the Application of the Commerce Clause to State Taxation. *University of Pennsylvania Law Review* 101:740–791.
HARTMAN, PAUL J. 1953 *State Taxation of Interstate Commerce.* Buffalo, N.Y.: Dennis Co.
NOTE 1975 Developments in the Law: Federal Limitations on State Taxation of Interstate Business. *Harvard Law Review* 75:956–1036.

STATE TAX INCENTIVES AND SUBSIDIES TO BUSINESS

One significant impetus behind the CONSTITUTIONAL CONVENTION OF 1787 was concern over what Justice BENJAMIN N. CARDOZO described in *Baldwin v. G. A. F. Seeling, Inc.* (1935) as "the mutual jealousies and aggressions of the States, taking form in customs barriers and other economic retaliation." Among the weapons deployed by the Framers against this destructive economic rivalry was the COMMERCE CLAUSE, which the Supreme Court has consistently interpreted not only as a grant of power to Congress but also as a constraint on the authority of the states to interfere with the free flow of interstate economic activity.

In the latter part of the twentieth century, analogous interstate economic rivalry has resurfaced in the form of the proliferating use by states of tax incentives and subsidies to compete for business investment and jobs. This interstate competition has spawned a wide array of tools designed to attract businesses, ranging from property tax abatements to loan guarantees, and from investment tax credits to preferential methods of measuring taxable income. The competition has led to nationwide replication of many of these policies, and benefit packages offered to attract large new facilities often measure in the hundreds of millions of dollars. Business tax incentives have contributed substantially in many states to a sharp decline in business taxation's share of state revenues.

The question of whether state tax policies and incentives significantly influence business decisions about where to locate remains the subject of heated debate among the economists who study such issues. But there is little doubt that whatever influence these policies may exert affects only the location, and not the overall national magnitude, of business activity. The primary effects of the incentive competition are the depletion of state resources, the reduction of costs for mobile businesses, and the distortion of economic decisions away from the most efficient distribution of business investment. Nonetheless, no state can afford the political and economic risks of withdrawing from the competition while its neighbors continue.

The commerce clause offers a possible restraint on the

interstate competition over business tax incentives and subsidies. In a long line of cases, the Court has found that state policies, and especially state tax policies, which discriminate against out-of-state or interstate economic activity violate the commerce clause. In particular, the Court has repeatedly and consistently held that tax incentives that are restricted to transactions or businesses located in the granting state, and which thereby result in a comparatively heavier tax burden on interstate transactions or on interstate businesses, cannot survive the commerce clause's antidiscrimination standard.

While this case law has most commonly focused on protectionist measures that shelter local businesses from interstate competitors, many of the common types of location incentives provide precisely the same types of discriminatory advantages to those businesses that locate new economic activity within the state. Income tax credits or preferential deductions measured by, or conditioned upon, new investments or jobs located within the taxing jurisdiction appear particularly susceptible to the commerce clause's prohibition against discriminatory tax measures that give local commerce an advantage over out-of-state or interstate alternatives. Whether the Court will also extend the antidiscrimination standard to bar other forms of tax incentives, such as targeted property tax abatements or preferential rules for the apportionment of taxable income, raises more difficult questions of doctrinal evolution. Incentives provided by means of direct subsidies, rather than tax breaks, may be sheltered from commerce clause scrutiny by the market participant exception, although the Court's opinion in *Camps Newfound/Owatonna v. Town of Harrison* (1997) suggests that this "narrow exception" may be restricted to governmental involvement in a market in the role of buyer or seller, a characterization that does not naturally fit subsidy programs aimed generally at economic development.

PETER D. ENRICH
(2000)

(SEE ALSO: *Interstate Commerce; State Regulation of Commerce.*)

Bibliography

BARTIK, TIMOTHY J. 1991 *Who Benefits from State and Local Economic Development Policies?* Kalamazoo, Mich.: W. E. Upjohn Institute.

ENRICH, PETER D. 1996 Saving the States from Themselves: Commerce Clause Constraints on State Tax Incentives for Business. *Harvard Law Review* 110:377–468.

HELLERSTEIN, WALTER and COENEN, DAN T. 1996 Commerce Clause Restraints on State Business Development Incentives. *Cornell Law Review* 81:789–878.

HERZOG, HENRY W., JR., and SCHLOTTMAN, ALAN M., eds. 1991 *Industry Location and Public Policy.* Knoxville: University of Tennessee Press.

STATUS OF FORCES AGREEMENT

Following WORLD WAR II, as a consequence of entering into a series of mutual defense pacts, the United States established a continuing military presence in a number of foreign countries. To deal with the legal questions that inevitably arose because of this presence, the United States entered into a number of agreements—known as "status of forces agreements"—with the receiving (that is, host) countries involved.

Typically, status of forces agreements exempt visiting forces from the receiving state's passport and immigration regulations, and from its customs duties and taxes on personal property also. Further, the sending state is permitted to issue driving permits and licenses to members of its forces, to purchase goods locally for local consumption, and to employ indigenous civilian labor. In addition, provision usually is made for the settlement of claims for property damage allegedly caused by the visiting forces.

The heart of a status of forces agreement, however, is its allocation of JURISDICTION in respect of criminal offenses putatively committed by the members and accompanying civilians of the visiting forces. In general, the sending state and the receiving state retain exclusive jurisdiction over offenses not punishable by the laws of the other. Where an offense is punishable by the laws of both states, concurrent jurisdiction prevails, with either the sending state or the receiving state retaining the primary right to exercise criminal jurisdiction, depending on the nature of the offense and the circumstances of its occurrence. Where the receiving state exercises jurisdiction, it ordinarily guarantees a prompt and speedy trial, timely notice of charges, the right to confront hostile witnesses, satisfactory legal representation, and a competent interpreter. The accused is usually guaranteed the right to communicate with her or his governmental representatives and to have them present at trial, if possible.

BURNS H. WESTON
(1986)

(SEE ALSO: *North Atlantic Treaty; Treaty Power.*)

Bibliography

LAZAREFF, S. 1971 *Status of Military Forces under Current International Law.* Leyden, Netherlands: A. W. Sijthoff.

SNEE, J. and PYE, A. K. 1957 *Status of Forces Agreements and Criminal Jurisdiction.* Dobbs Ferry, N.Y.: Oceana Publications.

STATUTORY CONSTRUCTION

See: Legislation

STATUTORY INTERPRETATION

Much has been written of the circumstances under which courts should strike down LEGISLATION. The reluctance of Article III courts to strike down INTEREST GROUP legislation as unconstitutional finds its source in two seemingly irreconcilable components of American CONSTITUTIONAL THEORY, both derived from the SEPARATION OF POWERS embodied in Articles I, II, and III. The first is the system of CHECKS AND BALANCES, which is intended to raise the decision costs of government by requiring that the various branches share power. The second is the basic constitutional premise, embodied in Article I, that the legislature has the power to make law. These two constitutional principles, taken together, imply that judicial interpretation is consistent with the constitutional scheme only if two conditions are satisfied: the interpretive act (1) must result in making legislation more public-regarding by serving as a check on legislative excess and (2) must not intrude on the constitutional authority of the legislature to make law.

Condition 2 ensures that the Constitution's allocation of the lawmaking function to the legislature will remain intact, while Condition 1 reflects the constitutional premise that federal courts improve the operation of the democratic process by serving as a structural check on Congress's tendency to engage in factionalism. Condition 1 is justified by the need to mitigate the harmful effects of interest group domination of the political process. Condition 2 is justified by the basic principle of democratic theory that the power to make law ultimately should reside in representative institutions such as Congress.

While these conditions appear to be irreconcilable, they may be reconciled by recognizing that the constitutional requirement that the judiciary serve as a check on Congress's excesses often is fulfilled by the very act of statutory interpretation itself. The judiciary, using traditional methods of statutory interpretation, inevitably checks legislative excess by serving as a mechanism that encourages passage of public-regarding legislation and impedes passage of interest group bargains. In other words, there need not be overt confrontation between the judicial branch and the legislative branch in order for checking and balancing to take place. Checking legislative abuse is an institutional by-product of the judiciary's traditional role as interpreter of statutes in the resolution of specific legal disputes.

When called upon to interpret a statute, a court has three alternatives. First, it can look beyond the terms of the statute and seek to enforce the terms of the deal between the interest group and the legislature. This "legislation-as-contract" method of statutory interpretation is illegitimate because it violates Condition 1 described above. Specifically, it denies the federal judiciary its proper role in the constitutional scheme as a check on factionalism and legislative excess.

Conversely, a court can identify what it perceives to be a special interest group bargain and strike the deal down on constitutional grounds. While this approach satisfies the terms of Condition 1 by constraining the legislature, as ALEXANDER M. BICKEL observed, it violates Condition 2 by usurping the lawmaking prerogatives of Congress.

Finally, there is what is best called "the traditional approach" which, as the name implies, refers to the classic, time-honored methods of statutory interpretation that judges actually employ to decide cases. This method differs from the "legislation-as-contract" approach in that it counsels judges to interpret statutes based on what the statutes actually say, rather than on what the judges believe the bargain was between the interest group and the legislature. The traditional approach encourages more public-regarding legislation by frequently transforming statutes designed to benefit narrow interest groups into statues that in fact further the public's interests. Unlike the other two approaches, this one enables the judiciary to serve as a check on Congress without interfering with Congress's constitutionally granted authority to make law.

Important constraints on the legislature derive from aspects of the judicial process other than judicial nullification of legislative enactments on constitutional grounds. Although legislative acts are only infrequently declared unconstitutional, more subtle constraints are imposed upon the legislature by the judicial process itself. The very act of statutory construction often transforms statutes designed to benefit narrow interest groups into statutes that in fact further the public interest.

JONATHAN R. MACEY
(2000)

Bibliography

EASTERBROOK, FRANK H. 1983 Statutes' Domains. *University of Chicago Law Review* 50:533–552.

——— 1984 The Supreme Court, 1983 Term—Foreword: The Court and the Economic System. *Harvard Law Review* 98:4–60.

ESKRIDGE, WILLIAM N., JR. 1987 Dynamic Statutory Interpretation. *University of Pennsylvania Law Review* 135:1479–1555.

——— 1989 Public Values in Statutory Interpretation. *University of Pennsylvania Law Review* 137:1007–1095.

MACEY, JONATHAN R. 1986 Promoting Public-Regarding Legislation Through Statutory Interpretation: An Interest Group Model. *Columbia Law Review* 86:223–268.

SUNSTEIN, CASS R. 1989 Interpreting Statutes in the Regulatory State. *Harvard Law Review* 103:405–505.

STAY OF EXECUTION

A stay of execution is an order commanding that the enforcement (execution) of a lower court JUDGMENT be suspended (stayed) pending further proceedings before that court or an appeal of the judgment to a higher court. The entry of such an order is essentially a matter of judicial discretion, tempered by various principles developed in court rules and judicial precedents. In a civil case, a stay order may be conditioned on the posting of a bond to protect the interests of the prevailing party; in a criminal case a stay of a prison sentence raises the question of the defendant's entitlement to release or continued freedom, often conditioned on posting a BAIL bond.

In the federal court system, stays can be sought in district courts, courts of appeals, and ultimately in the Supreme Court. Generally speaking, a litigant must exhaust all possibilities of securing a stay from a lower court or courts before applying to a higher court. Stays are of two categories: a stay of a district court judgment pending an appeal to a court of appeals, and a stay of a court of appeals judgment or mandate pending application to the Supreme Court to review the judgment of the court of appeals. The Supreme Court or an individual Justice has statutory authority to grant both types of stays, provided that all efforts to secure a stay from the lower courts have failed.

Most stay applications in the Supreme Court are addressed to and resolved by individual Justices, acting in their capacity as circuit Justices "in chambers," although application can be made to the entire Court for reconsideration of an individual Justice's denial of a stay. Generally, a stay will be granted when there is a "reasonable probability" that four Justices, the minimum needed to grant review, will vote to review the case; that there is "a fair prospect" that the decision below will be reversed; that irreparable harm to the applicant will likely result if a stay is denied; and that the balance of equities, to the parties and to the public, favors a stay.

EUGENE GRESSMAN
(1986)

Bibliography

STERN, ROBERT L.; GRESSMAN, EUGENE; and SHAPIRO, STEPHEN M. 1986 *Supreme Court Practice*, 6th ed. Chap. 17. Washington, D.C.: Bureau of National Affairs.

STEAGALD v. UNITED STATES
451 U.S. 204 (1981)

A 7–2 Supreme Court extended to third parties the rule of PAYTON V. NEW YORK (1980) that, absent consent or exigent circumstances, law enforcement officers may not enter a home to make an arrest without a SEARCH WARRANT. Here the officers sought to execute an ARREST WARRANT for one person by entering the home of another and found EVIDENCE that served to convict that other party. The Court supported his contention that the FOURTH AMENDMENT required a warrant for the search of his home, reasoning that privacy, especially in one's home, outweighed the inconvenience to the officers of having to obtain a search warrant.

LEONARD W. LEVY
(1986)

STEEL SEIZURE CONTROVERSY

In the latter part of 1951, a dispute arose between the nation's steel companies and their employees over terms and conditions of employment. On December 18, the steelworkers union gave notice of intention to strike when existing agreements expired on December 31. On December 22, President HARRY S. TRUMAN referred the dispute to the federal Wage Stabilization Board and the strike was canceled. The Board's subsequent report produced no settlement. Early in April 1952, the United Steel Workers of America called a nationwide strike to begin April 9.

President Truman and his advisers feared that the interruption of production would jeopardize national defense, particularly in Korea. The President thus issued EXECUTIVE ORDER 10340 to Secretary of Commerce Charles Sawyer, instructing him to take possession and operate the steel mills in the name of the United States government. Truman's authority to take such action was not granted specifically by the statute, and he cited none, although the Selective Service Act of 1948 and the Defense Production Act of 1950 authorized the seizure of industrial plants failing to give priority to defense orders. Although the TAFT-HARTLEY ACT of 1947 had a procedure for injunctive relief in a strike situation affecting an entire industry, or imperiling the national health and safety, it did not contain seizure provisions. Truman preferred to act on the basis of what Department of Justice attorneys assured him was the INHERENT POWER in the office of the President, stemming from his authority as COMMANDER-IN-CHIEF and "in accordance with the Constitution and the laws of the United States."

The steel companies obeyed Secretary Sawyer's order

under protest but brought suit to enjoin the seizure in the District Court for the District of Columbia. There Judge David Pine granted a preliminary injunction restraining the secretary from continuing the seizure. Pine's ruling on the merits and the stay of the injunction by the United States Court of Appeals compelled the Supreme Court to face the constitutional issue also, on final appeal. (See YOUNGSTOWN STEEL AND TUBE V. SAWYER.)

PAUL L. MURPHY
(1986)

Bibliography

MARCUS, MAEVA 1977 *Truman and the Steel Seizure Case: The Limits of Presidential Power.* New York: Columbia University Press.

STEPHENS, ALEXANDER H.
(1812–1883)

A successful self-taught Georgia lawyer, Alexander Hamilton Stephens was a congressman (1843–1859, 1873–1882), vice-president of the Confederacy (1861–1865), and a lifelong defender of STATES' RIGHTS. As a southern Whig, Stephens sought to protect state SOVEREIGNTY and preserve the Union. These objectives led to apparent inconsistencies. Thus, he opposed JOHN C. CALHOUN and NULLIFICATION while arguing for the abstract right of SECESSION. Similarly, Stephens was a slaveowner who declared that "I am no defender of slavery in the abstract." He supported ANNEXATION OF TEXAS to preserve the balance of free and slave states, but he did not support slave extension generally. He opposed the Mexican War because of his unrelenting hatred of President JAMES K. POLK, his honest belief that the war was unjust, and his fear that it would reopen the divisive issue of SLAVERY IN THE TERRITORIES. But once the war was over he advocated opening the Mexican Cession to slavery. Ironically, he successfully moved to table the Clayton Compromise (1848), even though he supported its purpose, because he believed the Supreme Court would declare that existing Mexican law prohibited SLAVERY in the new territories.

Stephens opposed the COMPROMISE OF 1850, warning: "Whenever this Government is brought in hostile array against me and mine, I am for disunion—openly, boldly and fearlessly for *revolution.*" Nevertheless, once the compromise passed, Stephens supported it in Georgia, and at the state's secession convention of 1850 he helped write the Georgia Platform which denounced disunion. Stephens then joined ROBERT TOOMBS and Howell Cobb in organizing a Union Party in Georgia.

In 1854 Stephens became a Democrat. He was the floor manager for the KANSAS-NEBRASKA ACT (1854) and worked closely with STEPHEN A. DOUGLAS. As chairman of the House Committee on the Territories Stephens supported the LECOMPTON CONSTITUTION, unlike his Senate counterpart (Douglas). Despite Douglas's apostasy on this issue, Stephens supported his presidential nomination in 1860 and futilely campaigned for Douglas in Georgia.

In November 1860 Stephens opposed secession in Georgia, arguing that Southerners and northern Democrats could block any bill that threatened slavery or the South. His pro-Union speech, reprinted throughout the North, led to a brief correspondence with President-elect ABRAHAM LINCOLN. As a delegate to the Georgia secession convention (January 1861), Stephens supported the creation of a southern nation, provided that it adopted a CONSTITUTION similar to that of the United States. In the provisional Confederate Congress Stephens helped draft the CONFEDERATE CONSTITUTION, which owing in part to his influence resembled the Constitution of 1787. Stephens was then chosen vice-president of the Confederacy. As a moderate who had long opposed secession, Stephens gave the new government legitimacy. On slavery, Stephens was by this time quite "sound." As early as 1855 he had defended slavery on biological and biblical grounds, as well as its role in creating southern society, which Stephens believed was the greatest in history. By 1860 he owned more than thirty slaves. In March 1861 he told the South and the world, in his most famous speech, that slavery was the "cornerstone of the Confederacy."

Throughout the CIVIL WAR Stephens's relationship with JEFFERSON DAVIS was stormy. Stephens opposed CONSCRIPTION, martial law, and the suspension of the writ of HABEAS CORPUS. He accused Davis of becoming a dictator and advocated that Georgia seceded from the confederacy to seek peace and sovereignty on its own. Stephens urged that the Confederacy support George McClellan's presidential bid and then seek peace with the United States. He made numerous peace overtures, and in early 1865 met with Lincoln in an unrealistic attempt to negotiate a peace that would preserve a separate southern nation.

Arrested for TREASON in May 1865, Stephens was incarcerated at Fort Warren (Boston) until President ANDREW JOHNSON pardoned him in October. He then returned to Georgia where an unreconstructed state legislature elected him to the United States Senate. The Senate responded to this affront by denying Stephens his seat.

In a ponderous and tedious book, *A Constitutional View of the Late War Between the States* (2 vols., 1868, 1870), Stephens presented an elaborate and unconvincing defense of secession. He responded to his many hostile critics with an even duller book, *The Reviewers Reviewed* (1872). Reelected to Congress in 1873, Stephens remained for nearly a decade as an ineffectual and somewhat scorned relic of the past. He continued to defend slavery and states' rights, while opposing reconstruction and black rights.

PAUL FINKELMAN
(1986)

Bibliography

VON ABELE, RUDOLPH 1946 *Alexander H. Stephens: A Biography.* New York: Knopf.

STERILIZATION

Late in the nineteenth century, when simple and safe medical procedures for sterilization became available, the eugenics movement began to promote compulsory sterilization laws. A few laws were enacted specifying sterilization as punishment for sex crimes, but they were rarely enforced. In 1907 Indiana adopted a law authorizing sterilization of persons deemed "feebleminded," or, as one leading proponent put it, "socially defective." Other states soon followed. The Supreme Court lent both practical and moral support in its 1927 decision in BUCK V. BELL, upholding the constitutionality of Virginia's law. By 1935 more than thirty states had adopted forced sterilization laws, and 20,000 "eugenic" sterilizations had been performed. The victims of such laws tended to be poor; indeed, in the view of eugenics proponents, poverty and other forms of dependence were the marks of the "socially inadequate classes" that needed eradication.

Times have changed, and constitutional law has changed. Concurring in GRISWOLD V. CONNECTICUT (1965), Justice ARTHUR GOLDBERG said, "Surely the Government, absent a showing of a COMPELLING subordinating STATE INTEREST, could not decree that all husbands and wives must be sterilized after two children have been born to them." After SKINNER V. OKLAHOMA (1942) the point seems incontestable. Yet some state courts, following *Buck,* still uphold laws authorizing the involuntary sterilization of institutionalized mental patients. Although only fifteen years separated the *Buck* and *Skinner* decisions, their doctrinal foundations were worlds apart. *Skinner,* calling procreation "one of the basic civil rights of man," insisted on STRICT SCRUTINY by the Court of the justifications supporting a compulsory sterilization law. *Buck,* on the other hand, had employed a deferential form of RATIONAL BASIS review, analogizing forced sterilization to forced VACCINATION.

Skinner's crucial recognition was that sterilization was more than an invasion of the body; it was an irrevocable deprivation of the right to define one's life and one's identity as a biological parent. Vaccination implies no such con-

sequences for one's self-identification and social role. The constitutional issues presented by sterilization thus bear a strong analogy to the issues raised by laws restricting other forms of BIRTH CONTROL and abortion. (See FREEDOM OF INTIMATE ASSOCIATION.) The Supreme Court has characterized all these forms of state interference with REPRODUCTIVE AUTONOMY as invasions of FUNDAMENTAL INTERESTS, and has subjected them to close scrutiny in the name of both EQUAL PROTECTION, as in *Skinner,* and that form of SUBSTANTIVE DUE PROCESS that goes by the alias of a RIGHT OF PRIVACY, as in *Griswold* and ROE V. WADE (1973).

The issue of *Buck* seems certain to return to the Supreme Court one day, to be decided on the basis of a much heightened STANDARD OF REVIEW. Similarly, a state law requiring consent of a spouse before a person could be sterilized would surely be held invalid, on analogy to PLANNED PARENTHOOD OF MISSOURI V. DANFORTH (1976). If a law calling for involuntary sterilization must pass the test of strict scrutiny, and if a competent adult has a corresponding right to choose to be sterilized, then the critical ingredient is choice. An "informed consent" requirement thus seems defensible against constitutional attack, provided that the required "informing" procedure does not unreasonably burden the decision to be sterilized. (An informed consent requirement for abortion was upheld by the Supreme Court in *Danforth.*)

As Justice WILLIAM O. DOUGLAS noted in his *Skinner* opinion, sterilization in "evil or reckless hands" can be an instrument of genocide. Even the most devoted partisan of reproductive choice cannot be entirely comfortable knowing that the percentage of sterilized nonwhite women in the United States is almost triple that for white women, or that among public assistance recipients blacks are twice as likely to "choose" sterilization as are whites. Under current interpretations the Constitution has nothing to say about the bare fact of this disparity; yet it reflects a condition of constitutional dimension that deserves to be addressed, at least in the domain of PROCEDURAL DUE PROCESS. And if nonwhite women are led by government officers to believe that sterilization is voluntary in theory but somehow compulsory in fact, that form of "engineering of consent" appears reachable in actions for damages under SECTION 1983, TITLE 42, UNITED STATES CODE, based on the deprivation of substantive due process.

KENNETH L. KARST
(1986)

Bibliography

KELLY, MARY E. 1979 Sterilization Abuse: A Proposed Regulatory Scheme. *DePaul Law Review* 28:731–768.
KEVLES, DANIEL J. J. 1985 *In the Name of Eugenics: Genetics and the Uses of Human Heredity.* New York: Knopf.

PILPEL, HARRIET F. 1969 Voluntary Sterilization: A Human Right. *Columbia Human Rights Law Review* 7:105–119.

STETTLER v. O'HARA
243 U.S. 629 (1917)

An Oregon Supreme Court decision sustained that state's minimum wage law for women on the basis of the STATE POLICE POWER argument approved in MULLER V. OREGON (1908). A 4–4 Supreme Court affirmed that ruling in *Stettler*. Several state courts drew the inference that a properly drawn law regulating women's wages would be upheld and sustained such laws in reliance on *Stettler*. The DISTRICT OF COLUMBIA MINIMUM WAGE ACT nonetheless fell, 5–3, in ADKINS V. CHILDREN'S HOSPITAL (1923).

DAVID GORDON
(1986)

STEVENS, JOHN PAUL
(1920–   )

When President GERALD R. FORD named him to the Supreme Court in 1975, John Paul Stevens had all the conventional qualifications for the job. He had served for five years on the UNITED STATES COURT OF APPEALS for the Seventh Circuit, had been a distinguished antitrust law practitioner, a law school teacher, and a law clerk to Justice WILEY B. RUTLEDGE. But those who expected this conventional background to yield a conventional Justice soon learned better. Most new Justices write first for a unanimous Court; Justice Stevens's maiden effort, HAMPTON V. MOW SUN WONG (1976), included a combination of EQUAL PROTECTION and DELEGATION OF POWERS doctrine so novel that only four other Justices joined in it—and two of those added their own concurrence. In the terms that followed, Justice Stevens found it necessary to write separately far more often than any of his colleagues.

Many of his concurrences and dissents were sparked by disagreement with the substance of the BURGER COURT's decisions. He is the only Justice appointed since 1968 who does not regularly vote against criminal defendants, and his strong defense of PRISONERS' RIGHTS clearly runs counter to the majority's thinking. So too does his STRICT CONSTRUCTION of the ESTABLISHMENT OF RELIGION clause; and he is among the least receptive of the Justices when states assert local interests against the workings of a national economy, let alone the voice of Congress.

Overall, however, his moderate pragmatism puts him close to the center of the Court on most issues. What divides him from his colleagues is not so much substance as his fundamental dissatisfaction with the Court's judicial style. That style was summed up in UNITED STATES V. NIXON (1974), the year before Stevens's appointment. It is "emphatically the province and duty" of the judiciary, the Court quoted from MARBURY V. MADISON (1803), "to say what the law is." Left, right, and center, the Court he joined was nearly unanimous in wanting to say as much as possible about what the law is.

Stevens came from a different school. His first constitutional law professor, Nathaniel Nathanson, taught him that abstract talk about constitutional issues is usually misleading. In Nathanson's words, "we are the sworn enemies of the glittering half-truths, the over-simplified explanations. We are constantly at war with . . . the black-letter law, the restatements, the horn books." Another teacher soon reinforced the lesson; years after his clerkship, Stevens remembered: "Justice Rutledge exhibited great respect for experience and practical considerations. He was critical of broadly phrased rules which deceptively suggested that they would simplify the decision of difficult questions."

To a degree, this focus on the practical, the concrete, makes Stevens a spokesman for judicial restraint and narrow opinions. He can be relied upon, for example, to protest when the Court reaches out to decide constitutional issues on an insufficient record, as in *Globe Newspaper Co. v. Superior Court* (1982); when it leaps to interpret the Constitution despite a statute that would do the job, as in *Regents of the University of California v. Bakke* (1978); when it insists on reviewing for federal error a state court decision that will likely be restored on ADEQUATE STATE GROUNDS, as in *Michigan v. Long* (1983); or when it invokes the OVERBREADTH DOCTRINE to discuss facts not before the Court, as in *Metromedia, Inc. v. San Diego* (1981). And despite his reputation for unorthodox and strongly held views, some of Stevens's best work has been done in painstaking opinions such as *NAACP v. Claiborne Hardware Co.* (1982), where he held together a diverse group of Justices by saying no more than was necessary to resolve the case.

But Stevens's rejection of glittering half-truths and over-simplified explanations is no mere passive virtue. It has a radical side. In YOUNG V. AMERICAN MINI THEATRES, INC. (1976), for example, where Stevens defended the constitutionality of special ZONING for theaters showing sexually explicit movies, he did so by launching a frontal attack on that most glittering of half-truths—the assertion that government must ignore the content of the speech that it regulates. Only three other Justices joined him in *Mini Theatres*, but he persisted, pointing out in case after case that the principle of "content neutrality" was plainly too sweeping, that content-based distinctions had been employed for years in OBSCENITY, libel, and COMMERCIAL SPEECH cases. Ultimately he prevailed. In *New York v. Fer-*

ber (1982) the Court explicitly endorsed Stevens's *Mini Theatres* analysis in the course of making child PORNOGRAPHY a new class of unprotected speech. Perhaps characteristically, Stevens refused to join the Court's opinion; in his view, the *Ferber* Court had fallen victim to an equally egregious half-truth—the notion that some kinds of speech are wholly beyond the scope of the FIRST AMENDMENT's protection.

By stripping away the slogans that obscured the First Amendment, Justice Stevens left himself free to follow what he had so admired in Rutledge: he could seek "a practical solution to a practical problem," exercising "the faculty of judgment and not merely the logical application of unbending principles." Recognizing that even obscene speech is still speech, he looked at the practical effect of criminal obscenity prosecutions. In an analysis strikingly parallel to his CAPITAL PUNISHMENT opinions, he concluded that the Court's obscenity decisions had produced laws so vague that they supplied juries with little or no guidance. The result was that, for most pornography, criminal penalities were applied too arbitrarily to withstand scrutiny.

At the same time, it was plain to him that the reasons for restricting sexually offensive speech do not die at the indistinct boundary between the obscene and the merely indecent. Although speech bordering on obscenity cannot be wholly suppressed, Stevens concluded, the practical—and so the constitutionally permissible—solution was to confine such speech to contexts that minimize or even eliminate its offensiveness. Thus, in SCHAD V. VILLAGE OF MT. EPHRAIM (1981) he would have allowed the town to bar nude dancing from quiet shopping centers and neighborhoods—but apparently not from "a local replica of Place Pigalle." In FEDERAL COMMUNICATIONS COMMISSION V. PACIFICA FOUNDATION (1978) he would have let the government keep four-letter words off afternoon radio—but not out of the United States Reports.

This insistence that constitutional issues be examined context by context marks all of Stevens's campaigns against the artificiality of black-letter constitutional law. When he joined the Court, for example, EQUAL PROTECTION analysis had split into two tiers, each with its own set of incantations; the prevailing doctrinal dispute was whether and where to add yet a third, "intermediate" tier between STRICT SCRUTINY and RATIONAL BASIS review. Again Justice Stevens's solution was a striking doctrinal departure: not more tiers but fewer. "There is only one Equal Protection Clause," he wrote in CRAIG V. BOREN (1976), and so only one basic STANDARD OF REVIEW. By demanding that legislative classifications be genuinely relevant to a legitimate purpose, Justice Stevens produces results not unlike those that emerge from the clanking operation of two- or even three-tiered review. The difference is that Stevens candidly exercises judgment, taking account of the context, the offensiveness of the classification, and the credibility of the legislative purpose.

Though his approach pays dividends in candor and flexibility, it has its costs. Among the first casualties, ironically, are some of the pieties of judicial restraint. Stevens's equal protection analysis, for example, does not allow him to pretend that laws are invalidated by some brooding three-tiered omnipresence in the sky. Instead, it demands a far more skeptical and probing look at legislative politics than is usual for advocates of restraint. His First Amendment analysis, for example, would replace the discredited "content neutrality" standard with a narrower requirement that government not display bias against a particular viewpoint. This practical and pointed inquiry would save some laws that do not survive the Court's more abstract standard. But the price of this restraint is high. To uphold some lawmakers' actions, as in *FCC v. League of Women Voters* (1984), he must bluntly accuse others of actions "obviously directed at spokesmen for a particular point of view."

Perhaps it is a recognition of these costs that makes Stevens adroit at using such techniques as "legislative remand," particularly when federal policies are at stake. His opinion in *Hampton v. Mow Sun Wong* (1976), for example, struck down a civil service rule barring ALIENS from federal employment—not because the asserted federal purposes were insufficient but because they were none of the Civil Service Commission's business. If the President or Congress adopted the same rule, he suggested, it might well withstand review. Similarly, in FULLILOVE V. KLUTZNICK (1980) he would have invalidated a federal law reserving ten percent of certain construction grants for minority-owned businesses—not because such a set-aside was necessarily unconstitutional but because it raised profound constitutional questions that Congress had failed even to consider in its "slapdash" rush to enactment.

What does this unique mix of radicalism and restraint mean for Stevens's role on the Court? It seems clear, first, that his candor will always make him something of an outsider; it shows a glint of cheerful mischief too often for him to be a classic majority-building centrist. It may be true, as Stevens said in *Lakeside v. Oregon* (1978), that "most people formally charged with crime are guilty" or that "most people who remain silent in the face of serious accusations have something to hide and therefore are probably guilty." It may also be true, as Stevens wrote in *Fullilove*, that so-called benign racial preferences make it easier for "representatives of minority groups to disseminate patronage to their political backers." But as bracing as these unwelcome truths can be in the opinions of a single Justice, they will not, and probably should not, find their way soon into opinions of the Court.

More important over the long run is Stevens's campaign

to win back broad fields of constitutional judgment from the logicians and their half-truths. Here he has had occasional victories, but he is battling uphill. Justices write opinions that leave much unsaid only when they have faith in the wisdom of those who will finally fill the gaps—the lower courts, their colleagues, future Justices. So long as most members of the Court lack that faith, Stevens's campaign for institutional humility will face long odds. Even when the Court adopts his practical, contextual approach, as it essentially has in equal protection cases, its opinions are likely to cling to the words and forms of a more ME-CHANICAL JURISPRUDENCE.

Of course no Justice can expect to impose the full range of his or her views on the Supreme Court. It is when one looks at individual doctrines that the impact of Stevens's iconoclastic creativity becomes clear. At times the power of his attack has swept away entrenched dogma and cleared the way for new thinking, as it did in *Ferber*. More important still is his ability to come fresh to new constitutional problems and to tailor new solutions for them. This talent showed even on the Seventh Circuit, where, for example, he preceded the Court in declaring that the First Amendment is a safeguard against patronage dismissals and that state tort remedies are a way of providing due process to a prisoner deprived of his property. On the Court, by joining with other Justices in the center, Stevens has set new terms of constitutional debate in areas as diverse as the death penalty, SEARCH AND SEIZURE, and gerrymandering. As new Justices and new issues come to the Court, as the shock of his challenge to the old bromides fades, it is this practical creativity that will ultimately make his mark upon the law.

STEWART ABERCROMBIE BAKER
(1986)

Bibliography
STEVENS, J. P.   1956   Mr. Justice Rutledge. Pages 176–202 in Allison Dunham and Philip B. Kurland, eds., *Mr. Justice.* Chicago: University of Chicago Press.
———   1985   Judicial Restraint. *San Diego Law Review* 22: 437–452.

STEVENS, JOHN PAUL
(1920–   )
(Update 1)

In 1975, President GERALD R. FORD sought a "moderate conservative" of unimpeachable professional qualifications to fill the Supreme Court seat vacated by WILLIAM O. DOUGLAS. John Paul Stevens of Chicago, an intellectually gifted antitrust lawyer, former law clerk to Justice WILEY B. RUTLEDGE, occasional law professor, and federal court of appeals judge for the preceding five years, seemed to fit the bill. Justice Stevens in fact has more often been described as a "moderate liberal" of sometimes unpredictable or even idiosyncratic bent or as a "moderate pragmatist." A prolific writer of separate opinions frequently offering a different perspective, he generally is not a coalition builder. Even the common term "moderate" reflects his agreement in result with sometimes one and sometimes another more readily identifiable group of Justices on the Court or his balanced accommodation of community rights to govern and individual freedoms rather than his judicial substance or style.

Such labels usually mislead more than instruct, and in Justice Stevens's case conservative, moderate, and liberal strands of constitutional thought blend in a singular combination. He shares the judicial conservatism of Douglas's (and thus his) predecessor, Justice LOUIS D. BRANDEIS, who frequently urged the Court to reach constitutional questions only when necessary and to resolve constitutional disputes as narrowly as possible. He shares the moderate rationalist's antipathy to excessive generalization that Nathaniel Nathanson, Brandeis's law clerk and Stevens's admired constitutional law teacher, abhorred. He also shares the liberal substantive vision of Justice Rutledge, whom Stevens once admiringly described as a Justice who "exhibited great respect for experience and practical considerations," whose "concern with the importance of procedural safeguards was frequently expressed in separate opinions," and most importantly, who believed that "the securing and maintaining of individual freedom is the main end of society." Each of these elements of his intellectual lineage appear centrally in Justice Stevens's own constitutional writings.

His particular mixture of judicial restraint and vigorous judicial enforcement of individual liberty, although akin to those of Brandeis and Rutledge, sets Stevens apart from his contemporaries on both the BURGER COURT and the REHNQUIST COURT. His is not the judicial restraint of extreme deference to government authority, but the judicial restraint of limiting the occasions and the breadth of Supreme Court rulings, particularly when he concludes that a ruling is unnecessary to protect liberty. His adjudicative approach is to balance all the relevant factors in a particular context with thorough reasoning whose ultimate aim is resolving the particular dispute, not declaring broad propositions of law. Yet, because Stevens sees protection of liberty as a peculiarly judicial obligation, there is no conflict for him between judicial restraint and liberty-protecting judicial intervention, however narrow the basis of that intervention might be. Thus, his frequent criticism of "unnecessary judicial lawmaking" by his colleagues, although it extends to reliance on any intermediate doctrinal standard of review that is a judicial gloss on constitutional text, is most bitterly voiced when judge-made doctrines stand in the way of vindicating individual freedom. In *Rose v. Lundy* (1982), for example, his dissent objected to several judicially imposed procedural obstacles to federal HABEAS CORPUS review of claims of fundamental constitutional error in the conviction of state criminal defendants. In contrast, Stevens, always sensitive to matters of degree, expressed his inclination to address constitutional claims more readily the more fundamental they are and to husband scarce judicial resources for the occasions when judicial action is most acutely needed. Accordingly, he urged the Court to confine "habeas corpus relief to cases that truly involve fundamental fairness."

The same preference for employing JUDICIAL POWER to secure and maintain individual freedom, rather than to vindicate government authority, appears in other positions he has taken on the proper scope of the Court's institutional role. He has waged a lengthy, but largely unsuccessful, battle to convince the court to curtail its use of discretionary certiorari jurisdiction to review cases in which the claim of individual liberty prevailed in lower courts. In NEW JERSEY V. T.L.O. (1984) he inveighed against the Court's "voracious appetite for judicial activism in its Fourth Amendment jurisprudence, at least when it comes to restricting the constitutional rights of the citizen." To Stevens, the Court should not be concerned with legitimating prosecution practices or other governmental controls that lower courts have erroneously restricted through overly generous interpretations of federal law. In general, he sees dispersal of judicial power as a positive good, especially when state courts restrain state officials from interfering with individuals, even when those courts have applied the federal Constitution more stringently than the Supreme Court might. He has argued with respect to STARE DECISIS that the Court should adhere more readily to prior rulings that recognized a liberty claim than to those that rejected one. Similarly, he appears more likely to find a "case or controversy" calling for decision on the merits in an individual challenge to government action than in review of a claim that the government's prerogatives have been unreasonably limited. This distinction can be seen in a comparison of his dissents on the issue of standing in ALLEN V. WRIGHT (1984) and *Duke Power Co. v. Carolina Environmental Study Group* (1978). Similarly, he has argued for reduction in the Court's reliance on the doctrine of "HARMLESS ERROR," which allows convictions to be affirmed where arguably nonprejudicial error has occurred; in his view, saving convictions should have a low priority.

His substantive conception of the source and content of constitutional liberty is as distinctive as his view of the systemic judicial role in protecting it. Unlike protections for PROPERTY RIGHTS, which Stevens agrees originate in

positive law, he believes liberty stems from NATURAL LAW. His dissents in *Hewitt v. Helms* (1983) and *Meachum v. Fano* (1976) illustrate his belief that even justifiably confined inmates retain claims to liberty, including the right to be treated with dignity and impartiality. The source of that liberty "is not state law, nor even the Constitution itself." Rather, drawing on the DECLARATION OF INDEPENDENCE, he found it "self-evident that all men were endowed by their Creator with liberty as one of the cardinal inalienable rights." Not surprisingly, given this view, he has embraced judicial recognition of a wide spectrum of textually unenumerated fundamental liberties that cannot be infringed without strong justification, including those implicated by criminal and civil commitment proceedings, termination of parental rights, loss of CITIZENSHIP, restrictions on ABORTION and consensual sex, and laws limiting prisoners' rights to refuse antipsychotic drugs and terminal patients' rights to refuse unwanted, life-prolonging medical intervention. As to the last, his dissent in *Cruzan v. Missouri Department of Health* (1990) opined that "choices about death touch the core of liberty" and are "essential incidents of the unalienable rights to life and liberty endowed us by our Creator" and that the "Constitution presupposes respect for the personhood of every individual, and nowhere is strict adherence to that principle more essential than in the Judicial Branch." Stevens has been particularly distressed by the Court's rejection of a wide liberty to retain counsel in government-benefit disputes and the right to government-provided counsel in proceedings to terminate parental status, because he thinks these rulings substantially undervalue the fundamental liberty of legal representation. Of his general approach, he has written that judges are to use the common-law method of adjudication to ascertain the content of liberty: "The task of giving concrete meaning to the term 'liberty,' like the task of defining other concepts such as 'commerce among the States,' 'due process of law,' and 'unreasonable searches and seizures,' was a part of the work assigned to future generations of judges."

Contained in his conception of liberty are government obligations of impartiality, rational decision making, and procedural fairness. These obligations are tempered, however, by two factors. First, Justice Stevens is willing to search broadly for acceptable regulatory justifications, especially the justification that a particular regulation enhances rather than diminishes liberty. Second, he is a candid, interest balancer, willing to distinguish among degrees of liberty and degrees of regulatory interference, as well as among degrees of strength of governmental interests to be served. The result is to give government at least some leeway. Moreover, he would hold judges to at least the same level of obligation, a fact that sometimes enlarges the regulatory freedom of political actors. Thus, although

Justice Stevens starts from the presumption that government must justify its interference with liberty, rather than a presumption of judicial deference to regulation, he can be quite generous in accepting certain forms of regulation.

For Stevens, government treatment of individuals as equals with dignity and respect is a portion of their liberty, not just a derivation of the EQUAL PROTECTION clause of the FOURTEENTH AMENDMENT. His particular brand of equality analysis would eschew judicial searching for biased subjective motivations of decision makers in favor of an inquiry into whether a law's objectively identifiable purposes are legitimate and sufficiently served. His aversion to motive inquiry is founded largely on two concerns: judges lack capacity to assess motivation accurately and reliance on motive might mean that identical laws would be valid in one JURISDICTION and invalid in another, depending on their sponsors' motives. Lack of nationwide uniformity of federal constitutional restraints on regulatory power is anathema to Stevens because it tends to undermine the judicial obligation of evenhandedness.

Justice Stevens opposes the Court's longstanding articulation of different tiers of equal-protection review depending on the nature of the group disadvantaged. He also opposes sharply differentiating between discriminatory intent and disproportionate impact as the dividing line between permissible and impermissible laws. Sacrificing guidance to others for sensitive analysis—an easy accommodation for one who sees the judicial role as dispute resolution, not pronouncement of law—he would consider such factors relevant, but not determinative. Instead of categories, he insisted in CRAIG V. BOREN (1976) that there is "only one Equal Protection Clause" and that its requirement is "to govern impartially." To be impartial, classifications may not be based on insulting assumptions or allow "punishment of only one of two equally guilty wrongdoers," as he wrote in dissent in MICHAEL M. V. SUPERIOR COURT (1981). His version of impartiality requires that people be treated as equals in dignity and moral respect, not that they necessarily receive equal treatment; so that unlike the "insulting" law held invalid in *Craig*, which forbade young men, but not young women, from buying beer, and the statutory rape law that he would have invalidated in *Michael M.*, which punished only males, he voted in ROSTKER V. GOLDBERG (1981) to uphold Congress's male-only draft law—a law that did not assume greater moral culpability of males than females.

When assessing impartiality, Justice Stevens would also consider whether persons other than the complainants are disadvantaged and whether members of the complaining group could rationally support the disadvantaging classification. Thus, he refused to invalidate a veterans' preference for jobs in PERSONNEL ADMINISTRATOR OF MASSACHUSETTS V. FEENEY (1979), despite its disproportionately

disadvantageous effect on women, because the law also disadvantaged nonveteran men in large numbers. And in CLEBURNE V. CLEBURNE LIVING CENTER, INC. (1985) he left open the possibility that some restrictive regulations based on MENTAL RETARDATION might be permissible because a mentally retarded person, like an impartial lawmaker, could accept some regulation to protect himself or herself, or others.

Attention to the full composition of the disadvantaged group and to their views is related to political limits on discrimination and treatment with moral respect. In particular, adjusting judicial aggressiveness to the level of political protection that a constitutional challenger might otherwise have available pervades Justice Steven's jurisprudence. Most obviously, this view of the judicial function underlies his preference for reserving judicial power for vindicating the constitutional claims of individuals, not government. Less obviously, it is also reflected in his fervor for addressing the substance of unpopular claims, especially those raised by prisoners, to whose conditions politicians are seldom responsive. Conversely, Justice Steven is unlikely to overturn arrangements that disadvantage those with considerable political clout. His majority opinion in *Lying v. Catillo* (1986) upholding a food-stamp policy that disfavored close relatives in contrast to more distant relatives noted that families are hardly politically powerless. Outside the equal-protection arena, similar considerations explain his support of the current Court position that judicial enforcement of TENTH AMENDMENT limits on Congress's power to regulate the State is generally inappropriate given the states' ability to apply political pressure in Congress. On similar ground, he agreed in GOLDWATER V. CARTER (1979) that, given congressional power to protect its perogatives, whether the President may terminate a treaty with a foreign power without Senate consent is a nonjusticable "political question." Likewise in *United States v. Munoz-Flores* (1990) he argued unsuccessfully that the Court should not address a claimed violation of the constitutional provision requiring revenue bills to originate in the House of Representatives. It is the "weakest imaginable justification for judicial invaliadation of a statue" to contend "that the judiciary must intervene in order to protect a power of the most majoritarian body in the Federal Government, even though that body has absolute veto over any effort to unsurp that power." In yet another sphere he was the sole dissenter from the ruling in *Davis v. Michigan Department of Treasury* (1989) that a state may not extend a tax on employee retirement benefits to retired federal employees if the state and local retirees are exempt. So long as the state taxed retirement benefits of private sector employees—"the vast majority of the voters in the State"—he thought the tax on federal retirees was allowable.

The obligation of impartiality also embraces another theme that extends beyond the realm of equal protection: judges should not adopt constitutional standards that themselves risk arbitrary or uneven treatment. Evenhandedness does not mean equal concern for governmental power and individual liberty, but equal liberty for all. This is a judicial obligation that sometimes has led Justice Stevens to limit, and sometimes to approve, governmental regulation. For example, unlike his colleagues, who tend either to favor or disfavor *both* ESTABLISHMENT OF RELIGION and "free exercise of religion" arguments, he is simultaneously receptive to claims of strict SEPARATION OF CHURCH AND STATE, but unreceptive to claims that the free-exercise clause requires exemption from generally applicable laws for religiously motivated conduct. His singular stance appears grounded in an emphasis on evenhandedness. To Justice Stevens, preference for one religion over another or seeming endorsement of a limited set of religions that would offend others, violates the government's obligation of religious neutrality imposed by the ESTABLISHMENT CLAUSE. In contrast, neutral laws that apply generally do not impugn governmental evenhandedness, and religion-based claims to a selective exemption would reintroduce this problem. Accordingly, he concurred in decisions refusing to exempt the Amish from paying social-security taxes, an Orthodox Jew from an Air Force regulation barring headgear indoors, and members of the Native American Church from a ban on drug use, including peyote, which they smoked as part of a religious ceremony.

A similar emphasis on evenhandedness surfaces in his PUBLIC FORUM and other free-speech opinions, with alternately restrictive and permissive results. As with equal-protection standards of review, Justice Stevens doubts the value of public forum doctrine to resolve FIRST AMENDMENT issues of access to public property for free speech. But he is simultaneously intolerant of viewpoint discrimination and tolerant of broad but neutral exclusions of expression from public property. His majority opinion in *Los Angeles v. Taxpayers for Vincent* (1984) upheld an ordinance broadly banning posting of signs on public property after noting its viewpoint neutrality and its evenhanded enforcement. He rejected a claim for exemption of political signs because such an exemption "might create a risk of engaging in constitutionally forbidden content discrimination." Similarly, although he has adamantly opposed prohibitions on speech when the government's justification rests solely on the offensiveness of the message, he accepts restrictions designed to maintain government neutrality in the marketplace of ideas, even though the restrictions significantly lessen speech. This distinction is explained in *FCC v. League of Women Voters* (1984), where he dissented from the Court's invalidation of Congress's ban on all editorializing by publicly funded broad-

casters. Finally, he is particularly critical of the Court's judge-made standards for defining OBSCENITY unprotected by the First Amendment. As he wrote in his separate opinion in *Marks v. United States* (1977), those standards "are so intolerably vague that evenhanded enforcement of the law is a virtual impossibility," and "grossly disparate treatment of similar offenders is a characteristic of the criminal enforcement of obscenity law."

Justice Stevens's evenhandedness standard does not completely reject qualitative assessments of the comparative value of different kinds of speech. In particular, if speech is of limited social value, and its form, rather than its viewpoint, is found offensive—a distinction he, but not others, can perceive as viable—he would acknowledge government's right to regulate its nuisance effects, although probably not to ban it altogether. In accepting ZONING laws restricting the location of businesses offering "almost but not quite obscene" materials, and in permitting the Federal Communications Commission to declare that a profane radio broadcast during the day might be disciplined, Justice Stevens took explicit account of the low value of the speech, as well as of the limited nature of the governmental restriction. He concluded that the justification for both restrictions was offensiveness of the form of communication, not the message. In the profanity case, FEDERAL COMMUNICATIONS COMMISSION V. PACIFICA FOUNDATION (1978), he reasoned that it is "a characteristic of speech such as this that both its capacity to offend and its 'social value' . . . vary with the circumstances."

The moderating tendency of accepting regulation of limited intrusiveness into liberty of lesser dimension so long as discernible, nonrepressive governmental puposes are present has often led Justice Stevens to emphasize the validity of civil nuisance-type regulations where he might find criminalization unacceptable. Indeed, there is evidence that he would uphold innovative moderate forms of regulation as a means of accommodating the tension between individual freedom and the right of communities to protect against the harm that exercising such freedom may do to others. There is much of JOHN STUART MILL in Justice Stevens's severely limited view of government power to restrain individual liberty that does no tangible harm to others, but his more generous view of government's power to protect against the nuisance effects of unrestrained freedom. This view is evident not only in his obscenity opinions and opinions regarding civil DAMAGES for recovery for LIBEL such as *Philadelphia Newspapers, Inc. v. Hepps* (1986), but also in opinions addressing whether regulation of private property constitutes a deprivation of property without DUE PROCESS or a "TAKING OF PROPERTY" requiring payment of JUST COMPENSATION. In MOORE V. EAST CLEVELAND (1977), for example, he separately concurred in the Court's judgment invalidating the city's single-family zoning ordinance, which defined a family to exclude a grandmother and two grandsons who were cousins to each other. In that opinion he located the ordinance's constitutional defect in its interference with the grandmother's "right to use her own property as she sees fit" with respect to the "relationship of the occupants." He distinguished zoning ordinances forbidding unrelated individuals from living together as legitimately based on controlling transient living arrangements that arguably might impair a sense of permanence in the community. Stevens generously approaches zoning ordinances based on arguable external effects, but is unsympathetic to those that fail to accord the reciprocal advantages to all in the community that zoning regulations normally create. These views are reflected in his majority opinion allowing an uncompensated prohibition on coal mining that would cause subsidence of others' property in *Keystone Bituminous Coal Association v. DeBendictis* (1987), from which Chief Justice WILLIAM H. REHNQUIST dissented. The same views surely explain his joining of Rehnquist's dissent in PENN CENTRAL TRANSPORTATION CO. V. NEW YORK CITY (1978), which upheld a historic landmarks-preservation law as applied to prevent development in the airspace above Grand Central Terminal. Moreover, Stevens's tendency to allow moderate regulation of the use of property that affects others and his openness to a wide scope of legitimate, potentially innovative forms of regulation, underlies his dissenting view in *First English Evangelical Lutheran Church v. Los Angeles* (1987). He believed that the government should not be obligated to pay for the loss of property use during the temporary period that a land-use regulation is challenged as a compensable "taking." He was concerned that if government was required not only to lift its regulation, but also to pay for the loss during the period of the constitutional challenge, officials would be deterred from acting, and "the public interest in having important governmental decisions made in an orderly informed way" would be sacrificed.

A final distinctive theme of Justice Stevens—one he admired in Justice Rutledge—is that, even if government decision makers have broad latitude in choosing what goals to pursue and considerable discretion in choosing the means to achieve them, judges should carefully review the decision-making process to assure that the responsible officials sufficiently considered the rights of those whose constitutional interests are sacrificed. Moreover, his version of this "due process of lawmaking," which sometimes provides procedural safeguards in lieu of substantive limitations, tailors the intensity of the required process to the magnitude of the liberty and equality interests implicated by the decision or policy. His CAPITAL PUNISHMENT opinions illustrate this concern, as well as his reluctance to narrow government goals and his deep attachment to impartiality.

He would not prohibit imposition of the death penalty altogether, but he supports a variety of significant limitations on the process of its administration to limit arbitrariness. He insists on narrowing the category of those eligible for capital punishment, policing against its racially disproportionate infliction, and limiting, through defined and acceptable criteria, discretion of the prosecution to seek death sentences and discretion of the jury to impose them. He would not permit any death sentence not approved by a jury—in his view, the only acceptable voice for so irrevocable an expression of the community's sense of moral outrage. Furthermore, although he finds individualized guided jury discretion essential in all cases, he would preserve the jury's absolute discretion to spare life, as his powerful dissents in *Spaziano v. Florida* (1984) and *Walton v. Arizona* (1990) demonstrate.

Justice Stevens has expressed this preference for a calibrated review of process in a variety of circumstances. He readily protects the foundational rights of free and equal political participation against governmental action that would distort a fair political regime, just as he would broadly uphold governmental efforts to protect the purity of the political process. Not only do his influential and forceful opinions favoring constitutional limits on partisan gerrymandering and political patronage in cases like *Karcher v. Daggett* (1983), *Davis v. Bandemer* (1986), and BRANTI V. FINKEL (1980) reflect this; so do his concurring opinion favorable to government-imposed anticorruption limits on corporate expenditures to support candidates in AUSTIN V. MICHIGAN CHAMBER OF COMMERCE (1990), his dissent from the Court's refusal to extend the federal mail-fraud statute to cover deprivation of rights to honest government in *McNally v. United States* (1987), and his unwillingness in dissent in BROWN V. SOCIALIST WORKERS '74 CAMPAIGN COMMITTEE (1982) to require a First Amendment exemption for the Socialist Workers Party from a law mandating that political parties disclose their contributors. Not consistent judicial deference, but an overriding concern for a properly functioning political system, underlies his alternately restrictive or generous view of political efforts at domination or reform.

As many of these opinions suggest, he would require fair process for application as well as formulation of law, process whose demands increase the more fundamental the interest at issue. His dissent in BETHEL SCHOOL DISTRICT V. FRASER (1986) acknowledged that school officials could consider the content of vulgar speech in setting rules of student conduct, but especially since speech was involved, he would not have allowed a student who made sexually suggestive remarks at a school assembly to be suspended without sufficient warning that his speech would provoke punishment. He would also distinguish between the process fit for legislation and that suited for adjudication. Dissenting in *City of Eastlake v. Forest City Enterprises* (1976), he would have found "manifestly unreasonable" a requirement that zoning changes be approved by fifty-five percent of the vote in a city-wide referendum. He insisted that "[t]he essence of fair procedure is that the interested parties be given a reasonable opportunity to have their dispute decided on the merits by reference to articulable rules." Although he had "no doubt about the validity of the initiative or the referendum as an appropriate method of deciding questions of community policy," he thought it "equally clear that the popular vote is not an acceptable method of adjudicating the rights of individual litigants."

A distinctive element of Stevens's expectation of a rational decision-making process is found in his oft-noted inventive opinion in HAMPTON V. MOW SUN WONG (1976), which insisted that if questionable policies are to be implemented, at least the appropriate authority must adopt them. His plurality opinion invalidated a rule barring employment of aliens in the federal civil service, not because it violated equal protection, but because it was adopted by the Civil Service Commission to serve governmental interests that only the President or Congress could assert. More generally, he adheres closely to a constitutional vision in which all government officials, including judges, carry out the responsibilities particularly assigned to them. Several opinions aim to prevent Congress from abdicating its policymaking responsibilities. One is his separate concurrence in BOWSHER V. SYNAR (1986), arguing that although "Congress may delegate legislative power to independent agencies or to the Executive," if it elects to exercise lawmaking power itself, it cannot "authorize a lesser representative of the Legislative Branch to act on its behalf," but must follow the normal process of enactment by both Houses of Congress and presentment to the President. In that case, Congress had inappropriately given power under the GRAMM-RUDMAN-HOLLINGS ACT to the comptroller general, one of its own agents, to make important economic policy that binds the nation. Similarly, in his plurality opinion in *Industrial Union Department v. American Petroleum Institute* (1980), Stevens interpreted the Occupational Health and Safety Act to prohibit the secretary of labor from adopting standards for controlling potentially hazardous substances unless reasonably necessary to prevent significant harm in the workplace, rather than to achieve absolute safety. Construing Congress's intent more broadly would assume a delegation of "unprecedented power over American industry" that might constitute an unconstitutional transfer of legislative power—a conclusion that Justice Rehnquist's concurrence embraced.

Finally, Justice Stevens's vision of the minimal elements of an acceptably rational decision-making process builds on his presumption that government must justify its ac-

tions and entails a realistic appraisal of whether an identifiable and legitimate public purpose supports the challenged act, even if that purpose is not identified by the decision maker itself. Although broadly defining the legitimate goals that government may pursue—particularly including latitudinous conceptions of environmental or aesthetic improvements in the quality of community life and programs providing veterans benefits—he will not strain his imagination to prop up conduct that realistically could not have been aimed at legitimate objectives. Thus, he is not loath to ferret out protectionist state purposes that are invalid under the DORMANT COMMERCE CLAUSE or the absence of secular purposes for religion-connected decisions that are invalid under the establishment clause. Moreover, he condemns harmful classifications adopted out of "habit, rather than analysis," as he shows in several of his opinions involving sex discrimination and distinctions based on legitimacy of birth. Although he will not impose on legislative bodies a duty to articulate their "actual purposes" for legislation, he will not accept, as a majority of the Court does, any "plausible" or "conceivable" purpose. Rather, as he wrote in his separate concurrence in *United States Railroad Retirement Board v. Fritz* (1980), he demands "a correlation between the classification and either the actual purpose of the statute or a legitimate purpose that we may reasonably presume to have motivated an impartial legislature." As his lone dissenting opinion in *Delaware Tribal Business Committee v. Weeks* (1977) demonstrates, it is not enough for him that a disadvantaging classification is not invidious; it cannot be neglectful, purposeless, or unthinking.

Several of these themes coalesce in his otherwise seemingly inconsistent pattern of positions in the Court's AFFIRMATIVE ACTION cases. He dissented in FULLILOVE V. KLUTZNICK (1980) from the Court's sustaining of Congress's setting aside ten percent of public works employment funds for minority business enterprises, largely because Congress gave only "perfunctory consideration" to a racial classification of "profound constitutional importance." He detected a decision illegitimately based on pure racial politics, generally urged that "the procedural character of the decisionmaking process" should affect any constitutional assessment, and specifically insisted that "because classifications based on race are potentially so harmful to the entire body politic, it is especially important that the reasons for any such classification be clearly identified and unquestionably legitimate." He did not assume that all race classifications were impermissible, however, and in WYGANT V. JACKSON BOARD OF EDUCATION (1986) he dissented from the invalidation of a race-based preference for minority teachers contained in a lay-off provision of a COLLECTIVE BARGAINING agreement. Here he thought the interests of the disadvantaged white teachers were adequately represented and considered in the collective-bargaining process. He also urged that the validity of racial classifications must not be evaluated solely in relation to the justification of compensating for past discrimination, but also by considering their relevance to any valid public purposes, including achievement of the benefits of future diversity—a position subsequently adopted by the Court in METRO BROADCASTING, INC. V. FEDERAL COMMUNICATIONS COMMISSION (1990). In fact, he suggested in his concurring opinion in RICHMOND (CITY OF) V. J. A. CROSON COMPANY (1989), where he voted to nullify the city's *Fullilove*-style set-aside program, that "identifying past wrongdoers" and fashioning remedies for past discrimination is better suited to judicial than to legislative bodies.

Matching purposes to appropriate decision makers and requiring deliberation adequate to the liberty affected, yet remaining open to a multiplicity of valid governmental objectives, are essential characteristics of this rational, liberty-devoted and open-minded judge.

JONATHON D. VARAT
(1992)

Bibliography

BURRIS, SCOTT 1987 Death and a Rational Justice: A Conversation on the Capital Jurisprudence of Justice John Paul Stevens. *Yale Law Journal* 96:521–546.

CARLSON, JONATHAN C. and SMITH, ALAN D. 1976 The One Hundred and First Justice: An Analysis of the Opinions of Justice John Paul Stevens, Sitting as a Judge on the Seventh Circuit Court of Appeals. *Vanderbilt Law Review* 29:125–209.

——— 1978 The Emerging Constitutional Jurisprudence of Justice Stevens. *University of Chicago Law Review* 46:155–213.

——— 1987 Justice Stevens' Equal Protection Jurisprudence. *Harvard Law Review* 100:1146–1165.

O'BRIEN, DAVID M. 1989 Filling Justice William O. Douglas's Seat: President Gerald R. Ford's Appointment of Justice John Paul Stevens. *Supreme Court Historical Society Yearbook* 1989:20–39.

SICKELS, ROBERT JUDD 1988 *John Paul Stevens and the Constitution: The Search for Balance.* University Park and London: The Pennsylvania State University Press.

STEVENS, JOHN PAUL 1983 The Life Span of a Judge-Made Rule. *New York University Law Review* 58:1–21.

STEVENS, JOHN PAUL
(1920–   )
(Update 2)

With Justice HARRY A. BLACKMUN's retirement in 1994, Justice John Paul Stevens became the Supreme Court's second-most senior Justice, having served longer than any active member except Chief Justice WILLIAM H. REHNQUIST.

Stevens accordingly acquired the power to assign the Court's opinion or the principal dissent whenever he and Rehnquist were on opposite sides—which was not unusual in controversial cases.

Stevens soon made use of this prerogative. He wrote the majority opinion in *U.S. Term Limits v. Thorton* (1995). Stevens concluded that neither Congress nor the states could impose TERM LIMITS upon federal legislators. Much of his argument dwelled upon the ORIGINAL INTENT of the Framers. It is ironic that Stevens's first major statement as the Court's senior Associate Justice focused so heavily on the Framers. Originalist reasoning had not been especially prominent in Stevens's earlier opinions, and it seems an implausible foundation for his jurisprudence.

Yet, if Stevens's methodology in *U.S. Term Limits* was atypical, the principles he announced were paradigmatic of his approach. Stevens insisted on two points. First, he maintained that although "Members of Congress are chosen by separate consituencies, . . . they become, when elected, servants of the people of the United States." That position is consistent with Stevens's usual attitude toward FEDERALISM questions. He has never been especially friendly to claims of state SOVEREIGNTY.

Stevens's second key point in *U.S. Term Limits* provides a window on the foundations of his constitutional thought. He argued that the Constitution incorporates "an egalitarian ideal—that election to the National legislature should be open to all people of merit." Not everybody would describe this ideal as "egalitarian." Some popular conceptions of equality convert it into a leveling principle, under which all distinctions, including those supposedly based on "merit," are inherently suspect. For Stevens, though, equality presupposes neither sameness nor moral relativism. Equality entails instead the right to be held accountable as an individual for one's choices and actions. It is, in short, a right to be judged "on the merits," instead of on the basis of status, stereotypes, special privileges, or personal connections.

This idea reverberates through diverse branches of Stevens's jurisprudence. One can detect it in, for example, his views about the legal IMMUNITY OF PUBLIC OFFICIALS: he has looked skeptically on claims that public entities or persons should, by virtue of their status or importance, be exempt from the legal standards that govern everyone else. He has treated SOVEREIGN IMMUNITY as an anomalous ingredient in American law, and he has construed the ELEVENTH AMENDMENT narrowly. It is therefore fitting that Stevens spoke for the Court in CLINTON V. JONES (1997), which rejected the President's claim to immunity from private civil suits based on unofficial conduct.

Of course, the distinctive features of Stevens's conception of equality emerge most clearly in his decisions under the EQUAL PROTECTION clause. His interpretation of the guarantee of equal protection of the laws defies conventional political categories. On the one hand, he favors aggressive constitutional measures against prejudice and stereotyping. He has accordingly voted with liberal majorities in cases like ROMER V. EVANS (1996), which struck down Colorado's law limiting gay rights, and MISSISSIPPI UNIVERSITY FOR WOMEN V. HOGAN (1982), which required Mississippi to admit men to its nursing school.

On the other hand, when he sees no evidence of stereotypes or prejudice, Stevens has been willing to permit distinctions that other liberal Justices have condemned. Thus, for example, in *Miller v. Albright* (1998), Stevens voted to sustain the constitutionality of a CITIZENSHIP law that treated the foreign-born NONMARITAL CHILDREN of American mothers differently from those of American fathers. Conversely, Stevens has been willing to find equal protection clause violations even when no SUSPECT CLASSIFICATION is at issue. For example, in a DISSENTING OPINION in *Kadrmas v. Dickinson* (1988), Stevens argued that North Dakota had violated the equal protection clause by making an irrational geographic distinction in a law about school bus fees.

Stevens's views about equality have especially complex implications for AFFIRMATIVE ACTION. Stevens has preferred to see the government combat racial prejudice by using fair, merit-based procedures, rather than through reverse discrimination. Thus, he has voted to hold affirmative action programs unconstitutional in FULLILOVE V. KLUTZNICK (1980) and RICHMOND (CITY OF) V. J. A. CROSON CO. (1989). Yet, Stevens was always sympathetic to the ends of affirmative action policies, if not the means. He has recognized the need for government to root out racial prejudice, and he has accordingly drawn distinctions among affirmative action programs. Stevens has been willing, for example, to uphold such programs if their purpose was to supply role models for students, WYGANT V. JACKSON BOARD OF EDUCATION (1986), rather than to redistribute jobs.

More recently, Stevens joined the dissenters in ADARAND CONSTRUCTORS, INC. V. PEÑA (1995). *Adarand*, like *Fullilove* and *Croson*, involved an affirmative action plan applicable to government construction projects. The *Adarand* majority purported to follow Stevens's own dissent in *Fullilove*, but Stevens distinguished the two cases. He said that the affirmative action plan in *Fullilove* employed rigid racial criteria, whereas the plan in *Adarand* used racial presumptions as indicia of social and economic disadvantage. Certainly one can draw such a distinction. On the other hand, Stevens's tone seems more favorable to affirmative action in *Adarand* than in *Fullilove*. A reader of the two cases might conclude that Stevens's concerns about affirmative action had softened.

Stevens's view of equality presupposes that it is possible and desirable for government to draw objective, merit-based distinctions through the use of impartial, dispassionate procedures. This conviction has methodological entailments as well as substantive ones. Stevens believes that judges can reliably determine what is reasonable; he has therefore resisted the modern Court's tendency to confine its own judgment with rigid tests and bright-line rules. Most notably, he has rejected the "tiers of scrutiny" that other Justices have used in equal protection clause cases. In CRAIG V. BOREN (1976), where the Court developed a new tier of scrutiny to deal with SEX DISCRIMINATION, Stevens protested that "[t]here is only one equal protection clause." For Stevens, the question is always the same: has the government behaved impartially? Racial and gender-based distinctions flunk more frequently than do other classifications not because they must meet a stiffer test, but because they are less often reasonable.

Stevens has therefore consistently applied a demanding form of the RATIONAL BASIS test in equal protection cases. He has employed the same method in DUE PROCESS cases to protect substantive liberty interests, and his approach in other constitutional domains is similar. In FREEDOM OF SPEECH cases, for example, he has repudiated the Court's efforts to establish rigid categories through such constructions as the PUBLIC FORUM doctrine and content-neutrality. Stevens made this point a central theme of his dissent in R. A. V. V. CITY OF ST. PAUL (1992), where he voted to uphold a criminal law against HATE SPEECH.

Some political liberals were happy with Stevens's position in *R. A. V.*, but liberals have sometimes been displeased by his flexible FIRST AMENDMENT doctrine. Especially notable are his dissents in the two flag-burning cases, *Texas v. Johnson* (1989) and *United States v. Eichmann* (1990). Stevens argued that the government could prohibit FLAG DESECRATION in order to preserve the flag's unique symbolic value. According to Stevens, that value was useful to the government's critics, as well as to its supporters. He predicted that, if flag-burning ceased to be illegal, it would become a less meaningful form of protest. In Stevens's view, the benefits of preserving the flag's symbolic value had to be balanced against the "admittedly important interest in allowing every speaker to choose the method of expressing his or her ideas that he or she deems most effective and appropriate."

Few commentators have agreed with the way that Stevens struck this balance. Some of the criticism was unduly harsh: if Stevens's dissents in *Johnson* and *Eichmann* were unpersuasive, they were not unreasonable. One suspects that some observers were unsympathetic with Stevens's patriotism, finding it jingoistic. That is unfortunate, for the passion that shone through in *Johnson* and *Eichmann* reflects not intolerance but a heartfelt pride in American constitutional principles. If perhaps that passion colored Stevens's judgment in the flag-burning cases, it also inspired him to become one of the Court's most vigilant and independent defenders of liberty and equality.

CHRISTOPHER L. EISGRUBER
(2000)

Bibliography

STEVENS, JOHN PAUL 1986 The Third Branch of Liberty. *University of Miami Law Review* 41:277–93.
——— 1989 A Judge's Use of History. *Wisconsin Law Review* 1989:223–236.
——— 1992 The Bill of Rights: A Century of Progress. *University of Chicago Law Review* 59:13–38.
——— 1993 Is Justice Irrelevant? *Northwestern University Law Review* 87:1121–1130.
——— 1993 The Freedom of Speech. *Yale Law Journal* 102: 1293–1313.

STEVENS, THADDEUS
(1792–1868)

A Pennsylvania lawyer, state legislator (1833–1841), and congressman (1849–1853, 1859–1868), Thaddeus Stevens was the most powerful Republican congressman throughout the CIVIL WAR and beginning of RECONSTRUCTION. Stevens was the earliest and most consistent congressional supporter of black rights and opponent of slavery. Stevens initiated, sponsored, or helped pass all key Reconstruction acts from 1865 to 1868. More than any other individual, Stevens was responsible for making the ex-slaves citizens.

After reading law, Stevens began practicing in 1816. In 1817 his unsuccessful defense of an accused murderer with the then novel plea of insanity brought Stevens fame and clients. After an initial case in which he represented a master in regaining fugitive slaves, Stevens never again defended slavery. Throughout the rest of his career Stevens took numerous cases on behalf of fugitive slaves, free blacks, and abolitionists. As one congressman said after his death, Stevens "was an abolitionist before there was such a party name." By 1831 he was one of Pennsylvania's most successful lawyers and a national leader of the Anti-Masonic movement. In 1835 Stevens single-handedly convinced the legislature to create a system of free public education for Pennsylvania. His passionate defense of public education stemmed from his own poverty-stricken background.

In 1848 Stevens was elected to Congress as a Whig, campaigning against slavery in lands ceded by Mexico. In Congress he was an acerbic, sarcastic, unrelenting opponent of slavery. Opposing the COMPROMISE OF 1850, he predicted it would be "the fruitful mother of future rebellion,

disunion, and civil war." One of the first bloody fruits of the Compromise was the Christiana Riot, in Stevens's own county; a slaveowner was killed attempting to seize his fugitive slaves. Stevens helped organize the successful defense of Caster Hanway who was indicted for TREASON for refusing to help the master. A backlash against the riot and abolition cost Stevens his congressional seat the following year. After a short time in the Know-Nothing Party, he became a Republican in early 1855. In 1858 he was again elected to Congress, as a staunch opponent of his fellow Pennsylvanian, President JAMES BUCHANAN.

At the beginning of the Civil War Stevens became a leader of congressional Republicans. As chairman of the House Ways and Means Committee he influenced all legislation requiring appropriation of funds. Stevens was largely responsible for the Internal Revenue Act of 1862 and the Legal Tender Acts which were necessary to finance the war. As a member of the Joint Committee on the Conduct of the War Stevens helped insure that civilian, and not military, authority would be pre-eminent during the war. Stevens used this position, as well as his Ways and Means chairmanship, to press ABRAHAM LINCOLN's administration to stop the military from returning fugitive slaves and to allow blacks to enlist.

In 1861 Stevens was one of the few men in Washington who publicly recognized that slavery was the root cause of SECESSION and that the war required its destruction. In July 1861 he was one of two House members to oppose the Crittenden resolution, which declared that the North had no interest in interfering with slavery. In December 1861 Stevens helped defeat a reaffirmation of that resolution. From the outbreak of hostilities Stevens argued that the seceding states should be dealt with according to the "laws of war." He asserted that constitutional obligations and protections—such as those involving fugitive slaves, the protection of private property, or the writ of HABEAS CORPUS—should not be "binding on one party while they are repudiated by the other." Thus, he supported the creation of the new state of West Virginia on the theory that Virginia had ceased to exist as a state when it left the Union, so that it was unnecessary for Virginia to agree to the division of the state. Stevens's theory of STATE SUICIDE was never fully adopted by the Congress or the courts, but it was influential in persuading many congressmen to support his legislation during both the war and Reconstruction.

As early as August 1861 Stevens urged the abolition of slavery as a war measure. In 1862 he tried to secure legislation that would lead to the confiscation of plantations in the rebel states. He believed that such land could be constitutionally seized, not because it was owned by men who could be convicted of treason, but because it was the fruit of war. He subsequently introduced legislation to end slavery in the DISTRICT OF COLUMBIA, prevent the Army from returning fugitive slaves, and provide equal pay for black soldiers. He was a leader in securing other legislation that protected blacks and allowed them to serve in the military, even if they were owned by loyal masters.

During Reconstruction Stevens was the House Republican whip, a member of the Joint Committee on Reconstruction, and probably the most powerful politician in Washington. In early 1866 Stevens introduced legislation for the continuation of the FREEDMEN'S BUREAU, the adoption of the FOURTEENTH AMENDMENT to protect the freedmen, and the enfranchisement of blacks in Washington, D.C. President ANDREW JOHNSON's unexpected veto of the Freedmen's Bureau Bill, his subsequent attempts to prevent ratification of the Fourteenth Amendment, and his vehement opposition to voting by blacks led to congressional Reconstruction. Stevens sponsored legislation that prevented the former Confederate states from sending representatives to Congress without congressional approval. The legislation was specifically aimed at Johnson's home state of Tennessee, but applied to all the Confederate states.

During the election of 1866 Stevens openly argued for complete racial equality while campaigning for Republicans and against Andrew Johnson's administration. Johnson, meanwhile, publicly accused Stevens, CHARLES SUMNER, and the abolitionist Wendell Phillips of treason and suggested they ought to be hanged. The election gave the Republicans more than a two-thirds majority in both houses. Although ill through much of the Fortieth Congress, Stevens nevertheless sponsored the TENURE OF OFFICE ACT, which set the stage for Johnson's IMPEACHMENT, and the MILITARY RECONSTRUCTION ACT of 1867, which placed all former Confederate states, except Tennessee, under military rule. Stevens successfully backed many CIVIL RIGHTS measures introduced by others. He was the prime mover in requiring the former Confederate states to ratify the Fourteenth Amendment and enfranchise blacks. He supported legislation authorizing the army to protect the freedmen from white vigilantes. Virtually all this legislation was enacted over Johnson's veto, with Stevens, as majority whip, guiding it through Congress. Stevens failed, however, to persuade Congress to confiscate Southern plantations and provide land for the freedmen.

In 1866 and 1867 Stevens unsuccessfully supported Congressman James Ashley's motions for impeachment. In early 1868 Stevens himself sought Johnson's impeachment, but could not get committee support for it. However, after Johnson fired Secretary of War EDWIN M. STANTON, in violation of the Tenure of Office Act, an impeachment committee was quickly formed. Stevens, as a member of that committee, helped draft the ARTICLES OF IMPEACHMENT and later was a manager of the prosecution.

However, he was quite ill by then and took little part in the trial. Ten weeks after the trial Stevens died.

PAUL FINKELMAN
(1986)

Bibliography

BRODIE, FAWN M. 1959 *Thaddeus Stevens: Scourge of the South.* New York: Norton.
KORNGOLD, RALPH 1955 *Thaddeus Stevens.* New York: Harcourt Brace & World.

STEWARD MACHINE COMPANY v. DAVIS
301 U.S. 548 (1937)

Plaintiff, an employer, challenged the 1935 SOCIAL SECURITY ACT unemployment compensation provisions, which imposed a payroll tax on employers and directed that the tax receipts be paid to the general revenue. To offset part of this tax, the act granted employers a credit for taxes paid to a state unemployment fund conforming to federal benefit and solvency requirements. One such requirement was that state funds be held for safekeeping by the secretary of the treasury and invested in federal government securities. Plaintiff invoked UNITED STATES V. BUTLER (1936), which had invalidated AGRICULTURAL ADJUSTMENT ACT price support provisions that enabled the secretary of agriculture to contract with farmers to reduce agricultural production in exchange for payments funded by a federal tax levied on agricultural commodity processing. *Butler* had generally addressed the scope of Congress's power "to lay and collect taxes . . . to . . . provide . . . for the GENERAL WELFARE of the United States." While ostensibly rejecting the narrowest reading of the clause, originally proposed by JAMES MADISON, that the taxation power could be exercised only to carry out specifically ENUMERATED POWERS, and purporting to adopt a broader, though undefined, interpretation of the TAXING AND SPENDING POWER, *Butler* nevertheless had treated the TENTH AMENDMENT as a limitation on the federal taxation power. In *Steward Machine Co.*, plaintiff argued that the unemployment taxation scheme, like the agricultural price support provisions, exceeded congressional powers because it infringed the Tenth Amendment's reservation to the states of power not delegated by the Constitution to the United States.

The unemployment compensation scheme was sustained, 5–4. Justice BENJAMIN N. CARDOZO, writing for the majority, distinguished *United States v. Butler* on two grounds: the unemployment tax proceeds were to be used for the "general welfare" because they were not earmarked for any special group; and the unemployment compensation plan did not infringe state prerogatives because state participation in this cooperative federal-state program was entirely voluntary. The Court described unemployment as a "problem . . . national in area and dimensions." Many states wished to develop unemployment compensation programs but feared economic competition from those states without such plans. Hence a federal tax was necessary to enable states to accomplish their general welfare goals.

In its permissive, though vague, interpretation of the term "general welfare," *Steward Machine Co.* and its companion case, HELVERING V. DAVIS (1937), seem to repudiate the *United States v. Butler* view that Congress, in exercising its power to tax for the general welfare, is required by the Tenth Amendment to eschew regulation of matters historically controlled by the states. *Steward Machine Co.* is also noteworthy for its sympathetic appraisal of joint federal-state welfare ventures. Justice Cardozo amply demonstrated that the competitive pressures of a national economy make it increasingly difficult for the states to perform traditional welfare functions without the national uniformity made possible by federal assistance and regulation.

GRACE GANZ BLUMBERG
(1986)

STEWART, POTTER J.
(1915–1985)

When DWIGHT D. EISENHOWER nominated Potter Stewart to the United States Supreme Court, the President was recognizing the perfect embodiment of Midwest Republican civic virtues. Born in Cincinnati, Stewart was the son of a popular reformist and Republican mayor who was later appointed to the Ohio Supreme Court. Stewart went from Cincinnati to Yale College where he was a class leader, then to Harvard for graduate study, and then back to Yale Law School. He returned to Cincinnati, after service in the Navy and on Wall Street to practice law and engage in civic affairs. In 1954, at the age of thirty-nine, he was named to the Court of Appeals for the Sixth Circuit. In October 1958, as a recess appointment, Stewart became an Associate Justice of the Supreme Court.

Stewart's tenure on the Court—more than twenty-three years—was atypically long. Only eighteen Justices have served a longer term. Yet Stewart did not seek to place a sharp imprint on the work of the Court, an imprint of the sort Justice HUGO L. BLACK or Justice FELIX FRANKFURTER had brought to their work. Nor did he seek to build a constituency within the Court or outside it. During two periods, at the outset of his tenure and shortly after the transition to the BURGER COURT, Stewart's vote was of great significance in determining the outcome of the Court's

work. Because he was not a member of a dominant and consistent majority, it would not be the case, under the customs of the Court, that the most significant cases of the quarter-century were his to write.

Stewart was guided in his decisions and his actions as a judge by a sense of decency and proportion. He believed in a nation in which order, partially derived from privately inculcated values, offered the opportunity for advancement, creativity, and freedom. His sense of propriety led him to decline the possibility of becoming Chief Justice, according to then-President RICHARD M. NIXON, because Stewart thought it inappropriate for a sitting Justice to aspire to a presidential elevation. Even his resignation was characteristic. Stewart resigned not out of illness, nor out of ambition, nor for alternative appointment, but merely because he felt that limited service was correct.

These themes of propriety, of respect for structure and rules, permeate the jurisprudence of Justice Stewart. He was a firm adherent to the principles of STARE DECISIS, even when its application led to a result varying from his own previously expressed view. In a 1974 DISSENTING OPINION he wrote: "A basic change in the law upon a ground no firmer than a change in our membership invites the popular misconception that this institution is little different from the two political branches of the Government. No misconception could do more lasting injury to this Court and to the system of law which it is our abiding mission to serve."

An elegant and careful treatment of the facts was often at the core of a Stewart opinion because an understanding of the facts was central to the way he approached the issues in a case. Regularly, he would indulge his belief that a decision should be of appropriately narrow scope by stating what the case was not about. For him, a deep understanding of context was a prophylactic against undue haste in constitutional decision making. Dissenting in ESTES V. TEXAS (1965), for example, Stewart sought to demonstrate that the use of television cameras in the courtroom in that criminal case did not provide the factual predicate for the sweeping pronouncements in the Court's opinion concerning rights of defendants. Context yielded DOCTRINE, and not the reverse. If the result of an understanding of the facts was increased doctrinal complexity, then that could not be helped. "The time is long past when men believed that development of the law must always proceed by the smooth incorporation of new situations into a single coherent analytical framework," he wrote in COOLIDGE V. NEW HAMPSHIRE (1971). He thought it wrong that doctrine, sometime encapsulated in a "sterile metaphor" should seem to substitute for careful analysis, a point he made in his dissenting opinion in ABINGTON SCHOOL DISTRICT V. SCHEMPP (1963).

Much of Stewart's most significant work dealt with

defining those rules, especially the FIRST AMENDMENT and the FOURTH AMENDMENT, which constrain the activities of government. There was a sharp tinge of the radical in Stewart's protection of the individual from government intervention. He celebrated the Fourth Amendment's warrant clause as a carefully conceived limitation on precipitate government searches and persistently opposed a reading that cheapened the clause. According to his colleague Justice LEWIS F. POWELL, Stewart's opinion in KATZ V. UNITED STATES (1967) "revitalized the fourth amendment" by rejecting the notion first espoused in OLMSTEAD V. UNITED STATES (1928) that the amendment applied only to physical trespass by police officers. In *Katz*, the court held that private conversations even outside the home must be secure from unwarranted police interception. "The Fourth Amendment," Stewart declared in characteristically pithy style, "protects people not places." Thus a Federal Bureau of Investigation microphone placed against the wall of a telephone booth was held to be an invasion of the RIGHT OF PRIVACY. Similarly, Stewart led the Court in a series of opinions that valued the doctrinal purity of a judicially sanctioned warrant requirement for a valid police search. Stewart sought to place the doctrine and its numerous exceptions in proper balance. At the same time, Stewart strongly recognized that in the field of ECONOMIC REGULATION legislatures should not be subject to similar constraints. He especially admired Justice ROBERT H. JACKSON and was fond of quoting Jackson's aphorism that "[t]he view of JUDICIAL SUPREMACY . . . has been its progressive closing of the avenues to peaceful and democratic conciliation of our social and economic conflicts."

Stewart's opinions gave important strength to the First Amendment guarantee of FREEDOM OF SPEECH and FREEDOM OF THE PRESS. He set as a task for himself a clearer and longer-lasting basis for the protection of the press so that it could monitor the government and inform the populace. In NEW YORK TIMES CO. V. UNITED STATES (1971) he wrote that only material that would cause "direct, immediate, and irreparable harm to the nation or its people" could be subject to prior restraint through court-ordered publication restrictions. In an early opinion for the Court, *Shelton v. Tucker* (1960), Stewart proclaimed that government cannot pursue even a legitimate end "by means that broadly stifle fundamental personal liberties when the end can be more narrowly achieved."

Stewart could be bold as well as forceful. It was his influence that led the Court to revitalize the THIRTEENTH AMENDMENT, validating Congress's power to establish a sweeping ban on RACIAL DISCRIMINATION in private housing. In JONES V. ALFRED H. MAYER CO. (1967) a land developer refused to sell a house to Joseph Lee Jones because Jones was black. By invoking the Thirteenth Amendment, Stewart's far-reaching opinion bypassed the limited and often confusing STATE ACTION requirement of the FOURTEENTH AMENDMENT and held that discrimination in private housing violated a previously dormant Reconstruction-era CIVIL RIGHTS statute, the CIVIL RIGHTS ACT OF 1866. In general, his civil rights opinions had a refreshing simplicity and directness that avoided temporizing and recognized statutory and constitutional imperatives.

Stewart was influential in other areas as well. For a time, his was one of the most original and radical views on the freakishness of the imposition of CAPITAL PUNISHMENT. It was his reconception of the criminal law in *Robinson v. California* (1962) that established new categories of thinking about sanctions and stigma. In *Carrington v. Rash* (1965) he broke new ground in his constitutional measure of state-imposed vote eligibility restrictions based on occupation, residency, and similar grounds.

Earlier than many of his colleagues Stewart brought to his analyses of the antitrust laws a keen sense of the economic impact of various approaches to the CLAYTON ACT and the SHERMAN ACT: his perceptions about the inappropriateness of a "per se" approach in vertical integration cases, stated in dissent in *United States v. Arnold, Schwinn & Co.* (1967), became the view of the Court in *Continental T.V., Inc. v. GTE Sylvania, Inc.* (1977); his scorn for mechanical reliance on market shares as a test for invalidating mergers, articulated in dissent in *United States v. Von's Grocery Co.* (1966), became the text of his majority opinion in *United States v. General Dynamics Corp.* (1973).

Stewart was a bridge, a point of continuity from the Court of the late 1950s to the Court of the 1980s. Throughout, he prized what he viewed as the qualities of being a judge. In HARRIS V. MCRAE (1980) he wrote—upholding the constitutionality of a law restricting federal funding for abortions—that it was not the mission of the Court to decide whether "the balance of competing interests" in that legislation, or any other, "is wise social policy." Citing one of his favorite cases, WILLIAMSON V. LEE OPTICAL, INC. (1955), Stewart concluded that "we cannot, in the name of the Constitution, overturn duly enacted statutes simply "because they may be unwise, inprovident, or out of harmony with a particular school of thought." Stewart's philosophy of law, his jurisprudence of appropriateness, his respect for the role of the Court, transcend categories as his devoted service on the Court transcended categorization.

MONROE E. PRICE
(1986)

Bibliography

FRIEDMAN, LEON   1978   Potter Stewart. In Leon Friedman and Fred L. Israel, eds., *The Justices of the United States Supreme Court: Their Lives and Major Opinions*, 2nd ed. New York: Chelsea House.

MERESMAN, BARNETT, MERESMAN, GOLDMAN & MORRIS 1982 A Lawyer's Lawyer, A Judge's Judge: Justice Potter Stewart and the Fourth Amendment. *University of Chicago Law Review* 51:509–544.

STEWART, POTTER 1975 Or of the Press. *Hastings Law Journal* 26:631–637.

STOCKHOLDER'S SUIT

Stockholders suing their CORPORATIONS rarely raise constitutional questions, although the Supreme Court accepted jurisdiction of a case involving such a suit as early as 1856. (See DODGE V. WOOLSEY.) Yet several celebrated constitutional decisions in review of acts of Congress have come in stockholder actions brought to prevent corporate compliance with tax or regulatory programs the stockholders deemed unconstitutional. Having failed to convince management to challenge the programs' constitutionality, dissenting stockholders have used the device of a stockholder's action to accomplish the same result. In most nonconstitutional cases, dissenting stockholders are not permitted to bypass the business judgment of corporate managers and sue on the corporation's behalf, but—ironically, and controversially—this rule has not always prevailed in constitutional cases. The device has not been used effectively since the New Deal era, but when it was used, the Supreme Court seemed eager to render major constitutional decisions, an orientation perennially opposed to the Court's professed practice.

Three celebrated examples tell the story. In POLLOCK V. FARMERS' LOAN & TRUST CO. (1895) the Supreme Court held a federal income tax law unconstitutional. The corporate taxpayer had planned to accept the tax obligation, and a federal statute prevented an INJUNCTION suit by the corporation, but the dissenting stockholders were permitted to seek an injunction preventing compliance. No one objected to the stockholders' right to sue; the plaintiff asserted that the suit was not a COLLUSIVE SUIT between the stockholder and the company; and the Court rendered its controversial decision on the merits—a decision subsequently overturned by the SIXTEENTH AMENDMENT (1913). In ASHWANDER V. TENNESSEE VALLEY AUTHORITY (1936) preferred stockholders of the Alabama Power Company sued to prevent their corporation from performing a contract with the TVA, claiming that Congress lacked constitutional power to authorize the TVA to develop and contract for the sale of electricity. The Supreme Court, over Justice LOUIS D. BRANDEIS's famous objection that the stockholders lacked STANDING to sue and that the Court generally should seek to avoid constitutional questions, permitted the suit. The Court held the TVA's action constitutional, thereby ending a major legal threat to an important New Deal program. A few months later, however, in CARTER V. CARTER COAL CO. (1936), another stockholder suit, the Court invalidated the Guffey Act of 1935, an important anti-Depression measure. The president of Carter Coal, whose parents were majority stockholders and who had set company policy in compliance with the act, initiated the suit as a dissenting stockholder the day after the law was enacted.

These stockholder actions raise several questions of JUSTICIABILITY. One is similar to that raised in taxpayers' and citizens' suits: are they suits to prevent individual injury, suits that incidentally necessitate constitutional interpretation, or are they public actions to assure constitutional governance for the whole citizenry? The allegation that corporate compliance with the questioned law will injure the corporation's (and therefore the stockholders') financial interests, may distinguish stockholder from taxpayer or citizen standing, despite a similar element of remoteness. A second question is raised by the possibility of a collusive suit, with both the dissenting stockholder and the corporate management desiring the same result. The possibility is real, but the drawbacks of collusive suits have not been a serious problem in stockholder suits. Despite the trumped-up appearance of *Carter v. Carter Coal Co.*, for example, the federal government vigorously opposed Carter. There was strongly adversary presentation, and, in a COMPANION CASE, another company directly challenged the government's enforcement of the new act. The most significant danger may be that the stockholder suit is really a request for a premature advisory opinion, because stockholder, corporation, and government all want a constitutional ruling when the corporation plans to comply with the law and no present controversy exists. The Court was eager to rule in *Pollock*, *Carter*, and *Ashwander*. The first two produced substantial interferences with congressional power, both subsequently overturned, and the last consciously legitimated government policy. Plainly, the stockholder suit has been used as an instrument of the Supreme Court's judicial activism in the exercise of JUDICIAL REVIEW.

JONATHAN D. VARAT
(1986)

STONE, HARLAN F.
(1872–1946)

After finishing Amherst College and Columbia Law School (where in 1906 he became dean), Harlan F. Stone divided his time between teaching and practice in New York City. In 1923, President CALVIN COOLIDGE, a former college mate from Amherst, appointed him attorney general of the United States. Less than a year later he became Associate Justice of the United States Supreme Court. In

PHY, who had joined Frankfurter in upholding the compulsory flag salute in *Gobitis,* changed their minds. Two new appointees, ROBERT H. JACKSON and WILEY B. RUTLEDGE, agreed with Stone's dissent in the earlier case, thus transforming a vote of 8–1 to uphold the compulsory salute to a vote of 6–3 striking it down. Speaking through Justice Jackson, the Court declared: "If there is any fixed star in our constitutional constellation, it is that no official, high or petty, can prescribe what shall be orthodox in politics, nationalism, religion, or other matters of opinion, or force citizens to confess by word or act their faith therein. If there are any circumstances which permit an exception, they do not occur to us."

Stone had initially expressed the "preferred freedoms" doctrine tentatively, merely raising the question whether in the case of legislation touching rights protected by the FIRST AMENDMENT there may be "narrower scope for the operation of the presumption of constitutionality" and whether such legislation might not be "subjected to more exacting judicial scrutiny." He first used the expression "preferred freedoms" in *Jones v. Opelika* (1942).

After Stone's death in 1946, the passing of Justices Murphy and Rutledge in 1949, and the intensification of the Cold War, the "preferred freedoms" doctrine fell into a constitutional limbo. Justice Frankfurter, still smarting from the second flag salute case, attacked the doctrine fiercely in KOVACS V. COOPER (1949) where, referring to "preferred freedoms," he wrote: "This is a phrase which has crept into some recent decisions of the Court. I deem it a mischievous phrase if it carries the thought, which it may subtly imply, that any law touching communication is infected with invalidity. . . . I say that the phrase is mischievous because it radiates a constitutional doctrine without avowing it."

DENNIS V. UNITED STATES (1951), a case involving the last stage of the 1949 trial of eleven leaders of the Communist party of the United States for violation of the Smith Act of 1940, dealt the doctrine a serious blow. Yet even after *Dennis* some substance of the doctrine remained. In dissent Justice Black expressed the hope "that in calmer times, when present pressure, passions, and fear subside, this or some later Court will restore the First Amendment liberties to the high preferred place where they belong in a free society."

Stone's guiding rule was judicial self-restraint, not self-abnegation. Before 1937 he criticized right-wing colleagues who equated what they considered economically undesirable legislation with unconstitutionality. After Roosevelt had reconstructed the Court, he was at loggerheads with judges on the left, equally intent, he thought, on reading their preferences into the constitution.

Repeated conflicts with Black and Douglas, who, he felt, were prone to resolve all doubt in labor's favor, alien-

ated him. Stone's creativity was confined by the boundaries of the known. Any marked departure from existing principles left him "a little hurt, a little bewildered and sometimes even a little angry." When in 1945 he found himself pitted against judicial activists on the left, he dolefully reminisced: "My more conservative brethren in the old days enacted their own economic prejudices into law. What they did placed in jeopardy a great and useful institution of government. The pendulum has now swung to the other extreme, and history is repeating itself. The Court is now in as much danger of becoming a legislative Constitution making body, enacting into law its own predilections, as it was then. The only difference is that now the interpretation of statutes, whether "over-conservative' or "over-liberal' can be corrected by Congress."

Stone's conception of judicial conduct was almost monastic. He strove against almost insuperable odds to keep the Court within what he considered appropriate bounds. A judge should limit himself precisely to the issue at hand. Contradictory precedents should usually be specifically overruled. The Court ought "to correct its own errors, even if I help in making them." Stone's judicial technique recognized complexity. "The sober second thought of the community," he urged, "is the firm base on which all law must ultimately rest."

Stone advocated restraint, not because he believed a judge's preference should not enter law, but precisely because it inevitably did. The sharp barbs of his thought were intended for the flesh of judges, both right and left, who, without weighing social values, prematurely enforced private convictions as law. He strove not to eliminate subjectivity but to tame it.

As Chief Justice he was less impressive. In 1929, when it was rumored that President HERBERT C. HOOVER might elevate Stone as Taft's successor, the Chief Justice had opposed it, saying that the Associate Justice was "not a great leader and would have a great deal of trouble in massing the Court." Years later, Taft's assessment proved true. The bench Stone headed was the most frequently divided, the most quarrelsome in history. If success be measured by the Chief's ability to maintain harmony, he was a failure. Solid convictions handicapped him. Nor would he resort to the high-pressure tactics of Chief Justices Taft and Hughes. Believing profoundly in freedom of expression for others, no less than himself, he was slow to cut off debate.

Stone had an abiding faith in free government and in JUDICIAL REVIEW as an essential adjunct to its operation. He believed that radical change was neither necessary not generally desirable. Drastic change could be avoided "if fear of legislative action, which Courts distrust or think unwise, is not overemphasized in interpreting the document." A free society needed continuity, "not of rules but of aims and ideals which will enable government in all the various crises of human affairs, to continue to function and to perform its appointed task within the bounds of reasonableness."

ALPHEUS THOMAS MASON
(1986)

Bibliography

DOUGLAS, WILLIAM O. 1946 Chief Justice Stone. *Columbia Law Review* 46:693–695.

DOWLING, NOEL T. 1941 The Methods of Mr. Justice Stone in Constitutional Cases. *Columbia Law Review* 41:1160–1181.

DOWLING, NOEL T. et al. 1936 Mr. Justice Stone and the Constitution. *Columbia Law Review* 36:351–381.

FRANK, JOHN P. 1957 Harlan Fiske Stone: An Estimate. *Stanford Law Review* 9:621–632.

HAND, LEARNED 1946 Chief Justice Stone's Conception of the Judicial Function. *Columbia Law Review* 46:696–699.

KONEFSKY, S. J. 1946 *Chief Justice Stone and the Supreme Court.* New York: Macmillan.

MASON, ALPHEUS THOMAS 1956 *Harlan Fiske Stone: Pillar of the Law.* New York: Viking.

WECHSLER, HERBERT 1946 Stone and the Constitution. *Columbia Law Review* 46:764–800.

STONE v. FARMERS' LOAN & TRUST CO.
116 U.S. 307 (1886)

This case marks a transition in our constitutional law from the Supreme Court's use of the CONTRACT CLAUSE as a bastion of VESTED RIGHTS protected by corporate charter to its use of SUBSTANTIVE DUE PROCESS as a check on state regulation of business. Here, however, the Court sustained the regulation before it even as it laid the basis for the new DOCTRINE. The facts seemingly constituted an open-and-shut case for a victory of the contract clause. A railroad company's charter explicitly authorized the railroad to set rates for carrying passengers and freight. Thirty-eight years after granting the charter, the state of Mississippi empowered a railroad commission to revise rates. The trust company, a stockholder of the railroad, sued to enjoin Stone and other members of the commission from enforcing the state rate regulations. In past rate cases, whenever the contract clause argument had lost, the RESERVED POLICE POWER doctrine had prevailed; in this case the state had reserved no power to alter the company's charter. The INALIENABLE POLICE POWER doctrine had defeated the contract clause argument only in cases involving the public health, safety, or morals. Yet the Court, by a vote of 7–2, held that the state had not violated the company's charter.

Chief Justice MORRISON R. WAITE, in his opinion for the Court, reasoned that the explicit grant of rate-making

powers to the railroad did not imply either a grant of exclusive powers or that the state had surrendered a power to revise rates set by the railroad. The state's power to regulate rates, Waite declared, cannot be "bargained away" except by a positive grant. Never before had the Court construed a contract so broadly in favor of the public and so strictly against a corporation.

Waite added, however, that the regulatory power was not unlimited: under pretense of regulating rates, the state could not require the railroad to carry persons or property free, and "neither can it do that which in law amounts to a taking of private property . . . without DUE PROCESS OF LAW. What would have this effect we need not now say, because no tariff has yet been fixed by the commission." Waite also declared that state rate-making does "not necessarily" deny due process. In effect he undercut his own proposition, asserted in *Munn v. Illinois* (1877), that the question of the reasonableness of rates is purely legislative in nature. (See GRANGER CASES.) In *Stone* the implied principle was that reasonableness was subject to JUDICIAL REVIEW. Moreover, the references to due process of law in effect reflected substantive due process, because a rate regulation could not violate due process except in a substantive sense. *Stone* heralded a new era in constitutional law, which the Court entered during the next decade.

LEONARD W. LEVY
(1986)

STONE v. GRAHAM

See: Religious Liberty

STONE v. MISSISSIPPI
101 U.S. 814 (1880)

Chief Justice MORRISON R. WAITE for a unanimous Supreme Court held that the state might revoke the chartered right of a lottery company to do business in the state, without violating the CONTRACT CLAUSE. Because the company was not subject to the state's reserved POLICE POWER to alter or repeal the contract, the Court relied on the doctrine of INALIENABLE POLICE POWER, here the power to protect the public morals by outlawing gambling.

LEONARD W. LEVY
(1986)

STONE v. POWELL
428 U.S. 465 (1976)

By act of Congress, a state prisoner may petition a federal court for a writ of HABEAS CORPUS on a claim that he was imprisoned in violation of his constitutional rights. In *Stone*, however, the Supreme Court ruled that federal courts should not entertain habeas corpus claims by prisoners who charge that they were convicted on unconstitutionally seized EVIDENCE, when the prisoner has had an opportunity for a full and fair hearing on the issue in the state courts.

The Court differentiated, for habeas corpus purposes, between the guarantees of the Fifth and Sixth Amendments, which are vital to the trustworthiness of the factfinding process, and the FOURTH AMENDMENT, which is not. Exclusion of evidence is not a personal right of the defendant but a judicial remedy designed to deter the police from unlawful searches. Thus the EXCLUSIONARY RULE is not an "absolute" but must be balanced against competing policies. Indiscriminate application of the rule, far from fostering respect for constitutional values, might generate disrespect for the judicial system. On the other hand, denying the right to raise SEARCH AND SEIZURE claims in habeas corpus proceedings would not seriously diminish the educational effect of the rule; it was scarcely likely that police would be deterred by the possibility that the legality of the search would be challenged in habeas corpus proceedings after the state courts had upheld it.

Dissenting Justices WILLIAM J. BRENNAN and THURGOOD MARSHALL averred that the exclusionary rule is a right of the defendant and not a "mere utilitarian tool" which turns on its deterrent value.

JACOB W. LANDYNSKI
(1986)

STONE v. WISCONSIN

See: Granger Cases

STONE COURT
(1941–1946)

When Associate Justice HARLAN FISKE STONE moved over to the central seat of the Chief Justice in October 1941, he presided over a bench seven of whose nine members had been appointed to the Court by President FRANKLIN D. ROOSEVELT. All seven, who were sympathetic to the mass of new regulatory laws and welfare measures sponsored by the President, could be expected to develop approvingly the constitutional revolution of 1937. Surely they would sustain vast congressional expansion of federal power under the COMMERCE CLAUSE and drastically curtail the scope of JUDICIAL REVIEW. Stone himself had been appointed Associate Justice by President CALVIN COOLIDGE, but he had long advocated newly dominant constitutional

principles in dissenting opinions. OWEN J. ROBERTS, now the senior Associate Justice, was a Republican appointed by President HERBERT C. HOOVER, but it was the shift of his vote, along with Chief Justice CHARLES EVANS HUGHES's, that had tipped the scales for change. Outside observers expected "a new unity in Supreme Court DOCTRINE, based upon a clearer philosophy of government than has yet been expressed in the swift succession of decisions rendered by a Court standing in the shadow of political changes."

But there was no unity. The new Chief Justice soon came to view his brethren as "a team of wild horses." DISSENTING OPINIONS and CONCURRING OPINIONS proliferated in numbers previously inconceivable. The controversies ranged from major jurisprudential differences to unworthy personal squabbles over such matters as the phrasing of the Court's letter to Justice Roberts upon his retirement.

The sources of disunity were both philosophical and temperamental. All but one or two of the Justices were highly individualistic, each was accustomed to speak his mind. All, with the possible exception of Justice Roberts, accepted the new regulatory and welfare state; but there were sharp differences over the proper pace and extent of change. The Chief Justice and Justices Roberts, STANLEY F. REED, JAMES F. BYRNES, and to a lesser degree Justices FELIX FRANKFURTER and ROBERT H. JACKSON, were more conservative in disposition than Justices HUGO L. BLACK, WILLIAM O. DOUGLAS, FRANK MURPHY, and Justice Byrnes's successor, WILEY B. RUTLEDGE. The temperamental differences were sometimes matched by differences in legal philosophy. The Chief Justice, Justice Frankfurter, and to a lesser degree Justice Jackson, were craftsmen of the law deeply influenced by a strong sense of the importance of the judge's loyalty to a growing, changing, but still coherent set of legal principles. For them, such institutional concerns were often more important than immediate, practical consequences. Justices Black, Douglas, and Murphy gave far more emphasis to the redistribution of social and economic power and to progressive reform. In conflicts between the individual and his government outside the economic area, the conservatives' instinct for order would often clash with the progressive liberals' enthusiasm for CIVIL LIBERTIES and CIVIL RIGHTS. The marked dissension indicates the difficulty any President of the United States faces in stamping one pattern upon the work of the Court.

Viewed in the sweep of constitutional history, the Stone years, 1941–1946, were the first part of a period of transition also encompassing the VINSON COURT, 1946–1953. By 1940 the main lines of CONSTITUTIONAL INTERPRETATION under the commerce clause and GENERAL WELFARE CLAUSE had been adapted to centralized ECONOMIC REGULATION and the welfare state. After 1953, when EARL WARREN became Chief Justice of the United States, the driving force would be a new spirit of libertarianism, egalitarianism, and emancipation. It remained for the Stone Court to complete the reinterpretation of the commerce clause and to pursue the philosophy of judicial deference to legislative determinations, whether state or federal. But harbingers of the new age of reform by constitutional adjudication also began to appear. The first explicit challenges to an across-the-board philosophy of judicial self-restraint were raised in the Stone Court. From the seeds thus scattered would grow the doctrinal principles supporting the subsequent vast expansion of constitutionally protected civil liberties and civil rights.

In interpreting the commerce clause, the Stone Court, whenever faced with a clear assertion of congressional intent to exercise such wide authority, did not shrink from pressing to its logical extreme the doctrine that Congress may regulate any local activities that in fact affect INTERSTATE COMMERCE. For example, in WICKARD V. FILBURN (1942) the Court sustained the imposition of a federal penalty upon the owner of a small family farm for sowing 11.9 acres of wheat in excess of his 11.1 acre federal allotment, upon the ground that Congress could rationally conclude that small individual additions to the total supply, even for home consumption, would cumulatively affect the price of wheat in interstate markets. The reluctance of the more conservative Justices to sanction unlimited expansion of federal regulation into once local affairs took hold when federal legislation was couched in terms sufficiently ambiguous to permit limitation. Decisions putting marginal limits upon the coverage of the federal wage and hour law are the best examples. Only a bare majority of four of the seven Justices participating could be mustered in UNITED STATES V. SOUTHEASTERN UNDERWRITERS ASSOCIATION (1944) for holding the insurance industry subject to the SHERMAN ANTITRUST ACT. In PAUL V. VIRGINIA (1879) the Court had first ruled that writing an insurance policy on property in another state was not interstate commerce. Later decisions and an elaborate structure of regulation in every state were built upon that precedent. Congress had essayed no regulation of insurance. The executive branch had not previously sought to apply the Sherman Act. Justices Black, Douglas, Murphy, and Rutledge seemed not to hesitate in sustaining the Department of Justice's novel assertion of federal power, a position supportable by the literal words of the statute and the logic of the expansive view of the commerce power. Respect for precedent and a strong sense of the importance of institutional continuity led the Chief Justice and Justices Frankfurter and Jackson to protest so sharp a departure from the status quo in the absence of a specific congressional directive: "it is the part of wisdom and self-restraint and good gov-

ernment to leave the initiative to Congress. . . . To force the hand of Congress is no more the proper function of the judiciary than to tie the hands of Congress." Congress responded to the majority by limiting the application of the Sherman Act to the insurance business, and by confirming the states' powers of regulation and taxation.

New constitutional issues that would lead to the next major phase in the history of constitutional adjudication began to emerge as wartime restrictions and the multiplication of government activities stirred fears for personal liberties. The war against Nazi Germany reinvigorated ideals of human dignity, equality, and democracy. As more civil liberties and civil rights litigation came upon the docket, a number of Justices began to have second thoughts about the philosophy of judicial deference to legislative determinations. That philosophy had well fitted the prevailing desire for progressive social and economic reform so long as the states and the executive and legislative branches of the federal government were engaged in the redistribution of power and the protection of the disadvantaged and distressed. The recollection of past judicial mistakes and the need for consistency of institutional theory cautioned against activist judicial ventures even in so deserving an area as civil liberty. On the other hand, continued self-restraint would leave much civil liberty at the mercy of executive or legislative oppression. The libertarian judicial activist could achieve a measure of logical consistency by elevating civil liberties to a preferred position justifying stricter standards of judicial review than those used in judging economic measures. The older dissenting opinions by Justices OLIVER WENDELL HOLMES and LOUIS D. BRANDEIS pleading for greater constitutional protection for FREEDOM OF SPEECH pointed the way even though they had failed to rationalize a double standard.

Stone himself, as an Associate Justice, had suggested one rationale in a now famous footnote in UNITED STATES V. CAROLENE PRODUCTS CO. (1938). Holding that the Court should indulge a strong presumption of constitutionality whenever the political processes of representative government were open, he nonetheless suggested that stricter judicial review might be appropriate when the challenge was to a statute that interfered with the political process— for example, a law restricting freedom of speech—or that was a result of prejudice against a DISCRETE AND INSULAR MINORITY—for example, a law discriminating against black people.

The issue was first drawn sharply under the FIRST and FOURTEENTH AMENDMENTS in the FLAG SALUTE CASES (1940, 1943). The substantive question was whether the constitutional guarantees of the freedom of speech and free exercise of religion permitted a state to expel from school and treat as truants the children of Jehovah's Witnesses, who refused to salute the United States flag. In the first case, the expulsions were sustained. Speaking for the Court, Justice Frankfurter invoked the then conventional rationale of judicial self-restraint. National unity and respect for national tradition, he reasoned, were permissible legislative goals. The compulsory flag salute could not be said to be an irrational means of seeking to secure those goals, even though the Court might be convinced that deeper patriotism would be engendered by refraining from coercing a symbolic gesture. To reject the legislative conclusion "would amount to no less than the pronouncement of pedagogical and psychological dogma in a field where courts possess no marked and certainly no controlling competence." The lone dissent came from Stone, who was still an Associate Justice.

Three years later the Court reversed itself. Justice Jackson, for the Court, summarized the core philosophy of the First Amendment: "If there is any fixed star in our constitutional constellation, it is that no official, high or petty, can prescribe what shall be orthodox in politics, nationalism, religion, or other matters of opinion or force citizens to confess by word or act their faith therein." First Amendment freedoms, the Court reasoned, rejecting Justice Frankfurter's plea for consistent application of the principle of judicial self-restraint, might not be curtailed for "such slender reasons" as would constitutionally justify restrictions upon economic liberty. Freedom of speech, of assembly, and of religion were susceptible of restriction "only to prevent grave and immediate danger to interests that the State may lawfully protect. We cannot because of modest estimates of our competence in such specialities as public education, withhold the judgment that history authenticates as the function of this Court when liberty is infringed."

Even in the 1980s, the deep and pervasive cleavage between the advocates of judicial self-restraint and the proponents of active judicial review in some categories of cases still divides both the Justices and constitutional scholars. It is now pretty clear, however, that judicial review will be stricter and there will be little deference to legislative judgments when restrictions upon freedom of expression, religion, or political association are at stake. (See JUDICIAL ACTIVISM AND RESTRAINT.)

In later years the Court would come also to scrutinize strictly, without deference to the political process, not only some laws challenged as denials of the EQUAL PROTECTION OF THE LAWS guaranteed by the Fourteenth Amendment but even statutes claimed to infringe FUNDAMENTAL RIGHTS in violation of the DUE PROCESS clauses of the Fifth and Fourteenth Amendments. The Stone Court broke the ground for STRICT SCRUTINY of statutory classifications prejudicing an "insular minority" in a opinion in one of the JAPANESE AMERICAN CASES declaring that "all legal restrictions which curtail the civil rights of a single racial group are immediately suspect . . . the courts must subject them to the most rigid scrutiny." In later years the constitutional standard thus declared became the basis for many decisions invalidating hostile RACIAL DISCRIMINATION at the hands of government, segregation laws, and other "invidious" statutory classifications.

Earlier the Stone Court opened the door to strict review in a second and still highly controversial class of cases under the equal protection clause. An Oklahoma statute mandated the STERILIZATION of persons thrice convicted of specified crimes, including grand larceny, but not of persons convicted of other crimes of much the same order and magnitude, such as embezzlement. The somewhat obscure opinion by Justice Douglas in SKINNER V. OKLAHOMA (1942), holding the differential treatment to violate the equal protection clause, emphasized the need for "strict scrutiny" of classifications made in a sterilization law, and referred to procreation as "a basic liberty." Later reforms by constitutional adjudication in the area of VOTING RIGHTS and legislative REPRESENTATION would be based upon the proposition that a legislative classification is subject to strict scrutiny not only when it is invidious but also when it differentiates among individuals in their access to a basic liberty. The precedent would also be invoked to support still later controversial decisions upholding claims of individual liberty in matters of sexual activity, childbirth, and abortion.

The Stone Court also sharpened the weapons for challenging crucial discrimination in the processes of representative government. In most of the states of the Old South, nomination as the candidate of the Democratic party still assured election to office. A political party was regarded as a private organization not subject to the equal protection clause of the Fourteenth Amendment or to the FIFTEENTH AMENDMENT's prohibition against denial or abridgment of VOTING RIGHTS by reason of race or color. Even after PRIMARY ELECTIONS regulated by state law became the standard method for nominating party candidates, "white primaries" remained an accepted method of excluding black citizens from participation in self government.

The first step in upsetting this neat device was taken in an opinion by Justice Stone just before he became Chief Justice. Interference with the right to cast an effective ballot in a primary held to nominate a party's candidate for election as senator or representative was held in UNITED STATES V. CLASSIC (1938) to interfere with the election itself and thus to be punishable under legislation enacted by Congress pursuant to its power to regulate the time, place, and manner of holding elections under Article I, section 4. Next, in SMITH V. ALLWRIGHT (1944) the Stone Court ruled that if black citizens are excluded because of race or color from a party primary prescribed and extensively regulated by state law, their "right . . . to vote" has been denied or abridged by the state in violation of the Fifteenth Amendment. Opening the polls to effective participation by racial minorities throughout the South, in accordance with the promise of the Fifteenth Amendment, would have to await the civil rights revolution and the enactment of the VOTING RIGHTS ACT OF 1965, but these decisions eliminating "white primaries" were the first major steps in that direction.

While marking its contributions to the mainstream of constitutional history, one should not forget that the Stone Court was a wartime court subject to wartime pressures as it faced dramatic cases posing the underlying and unanswerable question, "How much liberty and judicial protection for liberty may be sacrificed to ensure survival of the Nation?" Economic measures were uniformly upheld, even a scheme for concentrating the review of the legality of administrative price regulations in a special EMERGENCY COURT OF APPEALS, thus denying a defendant charged in an ordinary court with a criminal violation the right to assert the illegality of the regulation as a defense. Extraordinary deference to military commanders under wartime pressures alone can account for the Court's shameful decision sustaining the constitutionality of a military order excluding every person of Japanese descent, even American-born United States citizens, from most of the area along the Pacific Coast.

More often, the majority resisted the pressures when individual liberty was at stake. In DUNCAN V. KAHANAMOKU (1946), an opinion with constitutional overtones, the substitution of military tribunals for civilian courts in Hawaii was held beyond the statutory authority of Army commanders. Prosecution of a naturalized citizen of German descent who had befriended a German saboteur landed by German submarine and who took his funds for safekeeping was held in CRAMER V. UNITED STATES (1945) not to satisfy the constitutional definition of TREASON because the only overt acts proved by the testimony of two witnesses—meetings with the enemy saboteur in public places—were not shown to give aid and comfort to the enemy. In *Schneiderman v. United States* (1943) the Court held that proof that a naturalized citizen was an avowed Marxist and long-time active member, organizer, and officer of the Communist Party of the United States, both before and after his NATURALIZATION, was insufficient to warrant stripping him of CITIZENSHIP on the ground that, when naturalized, he had not been "attached to the principles of the Constitution . . . and well disposed to the good order and happiness of the United States."

The delicate balance that the Stone Court maintained between the effective prosecution of the war and the constitutional safeguards of liberty is perhaps best illustrated by the dramatic proceedings in EX PARTE QUIRIN (1942). In June 1942 eight trained Nazi saboteurs were put ashore in the United States by submarine, four on Long Island and four in Florida. They were quickly apprehended. President Roosevelt immediately appointed a military commission to try the saboteurs. The President was determined upon swift military justice. The proclamation declared the courts of the United States closed to subjects of any nation at war with the United States who might enter the United States and be charged with sabotage or attempt to commit sabotage. The trial was prosecuted with extraordinary speed and secrecy. Before the trial was complete, counsel for the saboteurs sought relief by petition for HABEAS CORPUS. By extraordinary procedure the case was rushed before the Supreme Court. The Justices broke their summer recess to hear oral argument. An order was promptly entered denying the petitions and promising a subsequent opinion. Within a few days the military tribunal passed sentence and six of the saboteurs were executed.

In the post-execution opinion the Court explained that the offense was triable by military commission; that the military commission was lawfully constituted; and that the proceedings were conducted without violation of any applicable provision of the Articles of War. The Justices were greatly troubled upon the last question. Some realized that in truth the swift and secret procedure ordained by the President left them with little ability to give meaningful protection to the saboteurs' legal rights in the military proceedings. Yet, even while recognizing that wartime pressures bent traditional legal safeguards in this as in other instances before the Stone Court, one should not conclude "inter arma silent leges." The hard core of the Court's decision was that judicial review of the saboteurs' constitutional contentions could not be barred even by the President as COMMANDER-IN-CHIEF. One may therefore hope that, if similar circumstances again arise, the Stone Court's basic defense of CONSTITUTIONALISM in time of war will prove more significant than its occasional yielding to the pressures of emergency.

ARCHIBALD COX
(1986)

Bibliography

MASON, ALPHEUS 1956 *Harlan Fiske Stone, Pillar of the Laws.* Chaps. 34–42. New York: Viking Press.

ROSTOW, EUGENE 1945 The Japanese American Cases: A Disaster. *Yale Law Journal* 54:489–533.

SWINDLER, WILLIAM F. 1970 *Court and Constitution in the Twentieth Century*, Vol. 2, chaps. 6–10. Indianapolis: Bobbs-Merrill.

WOODWARD, J. 1968 *Mr. Justice Murphy.* Chaps. 11–13. Princeton, N.J.: Princeton University Press.

STOP AND FRISK

Most courts recognize that a police officer has the authority to detain a person briefly for questioning even without PROBABLE CAUSE to believe that the person is guilty of a crime. The Supreme Court first addressed the "stop and frisk" issue in TERRY V. OHIO (1968). In *Terry*, an experienced police officer observed three unknown men conducting themselves in a manner that suggested the planning of an imminent robbery. With his suspicion aroused—but clearly without probable cause to make an ARREST—the officer stopped and patted the men down, finding weapons on two of them. The holders of the two guns were arrested and convicted of possession of a concealed weapon. The Supreme Court ruled that the officer's actions in stopping the suspects were constitutional.

Terry, therefore, authorized law enforcement officials, on the grounds of reasonable suspicion, to stop briefly a suspicious person in order to determine his identity or to maintain the status quo while obtaining more information. Such a "stop" is proper when: the police observe unusual conduct; the conduct raises reasonable suspicion that criminal activity may be afoot; and the police can point to specific and articulable facts that warrant that suspicion. A "frisk" is proper when the following prerequisites are met: a "frisk" cannot be justified on "inchoate and unparticularized suspicion or 'hunch'," but must be grounded on facts which, in light of the officer's experience, support "specific reasonable inferences" that justify the intrusion; a "frisk" is proper only after "reasonable inquiries" have been made, although such inquiries need not be extensive; and a "frisk" is authorized where an officer reaches a reasonable conclusion that the person stopped for questioning may be armed and presently dangerous.

Further clarifying the test permitting a valid "stop and frisk," the Supreme Court has stated that the totality of the circumstances must be taken into account. Looking at the whole picture, the detaining officers must have a particularized and objective basis for suspecting the particular person stopped of criminal activity. The Court has emphasized that the process of assessing all the circumstances often will not involve hard certainties but rather probabilities; the evidence to justify the stop must be weighed in accordance with the understanding and experience of law enforcement personnel.

Applying that standard in *United States v. Cortez* (1981), the Court upheld the propriety of stopping a defendant whose camper van was observed late at night near a suspected pick-up point for illegal ALIENS. The size of the vehicle, the lateness of the hour, and the remoteness of the spot all combined to make the stop reasonable.

Moreover, in *Adams v. Williams* (1972) the Supreme Court extended the *Terry* DOCTRINE in the following ways:

(1) a "stop and frisk" is authorized for such offenses as possession of illegal drugs or a concealed weapon; (2) an informant's tip may provide reasonable cause for a "stop and frisk" even where no unusual conduct has been observed by an officer; and (3) the "identification" and "reasonable inquiries" requirements of the *Terry* decision are no longer absolute prerequisites. The *Terry* doctrine was again extended in *Michigan v. Long* (1983) where a "frisk" for weapons was not restricted to the person but was extended to any area that might contain a weapon posing danger to the police. A search of the passenger compartment of a car was held reasonable due to the observance of a hunting knife, the intoxicated state of the defendant, and the fact that the encounter took place at night in an isolated rural area.

In *Pennsylvania v. Mimms* (1977) the Court held that, whenever a vehicle is lawfully detained for a traffic violation, the police officer may order the driver out of the vehicle for questioning without violating the proscriptions of the FOURTH AMENDMENT.

In SIBRON V. NEW YORK (1968) a patrolman observed Sibron with a group of known drug addicts. The officer approached Sibron in a restaurant and ordered him outside. During a brief conversation with the officer, Sibron reached into his pocket. The patrolman promptly thrust his hand into the same pocket and found several glassine envelopes containing heroin.

The Supreme Court found the search to be unlawful on several grounds, including the fact that the "mere act of talking with a number of known addicts" was not enough to produce a reasonable inference that a person was armed and dangerous. The officer's motive, which was clearly to search for drugs, not for a weapon, invalidated the search as well. The *Sibron* decision is important because it made clear that *Terry* established only a narrow power to search on less than probable cause to arrest, and that the right to frisk is not an automatic concomitant to a lawful stop. *Sibron* also established proper motive as a prerequisite to a proper frisk.

In *Peters v. New York* (1968), *Sibron*'s companion case, an off-duty policeman saw through the peephole of his apartment door two strangers tiptoeing down the hallway. After calling the police station, dressing, and arming himself, the officer pursued the men and questioned Peters. Peters said he was visiting a married girlfriend but would not identify her. The officer then patted down Peters and felt in his pocket a hard, knife-like object. He removed the object, which turned out to be a plastic envelope containing burglar's tools. Peters was charged with unlawful possession of burglar's tools. The search was held proper as incident to a lawful arrest because the circumstantial EVIDENCE available to the officer reached the level of probable cause to arrest Peters for attempted burglary.

After *Sibron* and *Peters*, the issue arises as to the legal consequences when a police officer pats down a suspect, reaches into the suspect's pocket, and pulls out evidence of a crime but not a weapon. The questions are whether the officer could reasonably have believed the item was a weapon, and whether the item was visible even without removing it. Using *Sibron* and *Peters* as models, a box of burglar's tools would satisfy the test (*Peters*), while a soft bag of heroin would not be admissible (*Sibron*).

The lower courts have expanded the scope of a constitutionally permissible frisk beyond a limited pat-down of a suspect's outer clothing. Courts have included within the scope of a permissible frisk the area under a suspect's car seat, after the suspect appeared to hide something there, and a glove compartment within the reach of a suspect. In addition, the lower courts have relaxed their supervision over police judgments concerning objects that seem to be weapons when suspects are frisked, allowing officers to search after they have touched objects such as razor blades, cigarette lighters, and even lipstick containers.

The Supreme Court has declined to impose a rigid time limit for stop and frisk situations. In *United States v. Sharpe* (1985), where a pickup truck involved in drug trafficking was detained for twenty minutes, the Court determined that the length of the stop was reasonable by considering the purpose of the stop, the reasonableness of the time in effectuating the purpose, and the reasonableness of the means of investigation. In *United States v. Hensley* (1985) the Court widened the application of permissible investigative stops to include investigations of completed crimes. The Court also articulated that a police officer's reliance on a "wanted flyer" issued by another police department provided reasonable basis to conduct a stop if the flyer was based on "specific and articulable facts."

Finally, courts have handled the special case of airport "stop and frisk" situations in three ways. The first treats the problem through a straightforward application of the *Terry* test. The second method involves courts lowering the *Terry* level of "reasonable suspicion" to a less stringent standard. The third approach overtly abandons the *Terry* formula, opting for an ADMINISTRATIVE SEARCH consent rationale which does not even require reasonable suspicion. Today, the use of electronic scanning devices at most airports has diminished this area of "stop and frisk" concern.

CHARLES H. WHITEBREAD
(1986)

(SEE ALSO: *Body Search*.)

Bibliography

WHITEBREAD, CHARLES H. 1980 *Criminal Procedure*. Mineola, N.Y.: Foundation Press.

STORING, HERBERT J.
(1928–1977)

Herbert Storing established the American Founding as a special field of study, both in his teaching at the University of Chicago and in his scholarship. Storing's monumental work, *The Complete Anti-Federalist*, contains introductions to and annotated, accurate texts of all substantial ANTI-FEDERALIST writings, along with the essay, "What the Anti-Federalists were *For*." This material plus his essay on "The 'Other' Federalist Papers," facilitates a full study of the dialogue over RATIFICATION OF THE CONSTITUTION in 1787–1788. It also explains why the Constitution's opponents "must be seen as playing an indispensable, if subordinate, part in the founding process." Storing argued that the Anti-Federalists lost the debate, ultimately, because they could not reconcile the contradiction of supporting union while opposing adequate powers for the federal government, but he regarded as well taken their criticism of the Constitution as not providing for, and even undermining, republican virtue.

Elsewhere, in essays on slavery, CIVIL DISOBEDIENCE, the political thought of black Americans, and statesmanship, and in congressional testimony concerning the ELECTORAL COLLEGE, Storing demonstrated the continuing relevance of the founding dialogue for American politics.

MURRAY DAY
(1986)

Bibliography

STORING, HERBERT J. 1976 "The 'Other' Federalist Papers." *Political Science Reviewer* 6:215–247.

——— 1981 *The Complete Anti-Federalist*. 7 Vols. Chicago: University of Chicago Press. (Volume 1 was also published separately under the title, *What the Anti-Federalists were For*.)

STORY, JOSEPH
(1779–1845)

Joseph Story's contributions to American nationalism were as great as those of any other figure in American judicial history. The record of his career—his thirty-four years as an associate Justice of the Supreme Court, his hundreds of opinions delivered from the First Circuit Court (of Appeals), his many influential *Commentaries*, his contributions to the creation of admiralty and commercial law and EQUITY jurisprudence, his re-creation of the Harvard Law School—is more abundant, more distinguished, and more fertile than that of any jurist of his generation. Imbued with a deep pride in the American nation, Story believed that nationalism should proclaim itself in the might of the government and the majesty of the law, and in the expression of this philosophy he was articulate beyond any of his fellow jurists. Ceaselessly—in Congress, on the bench, from the professor's podium and the speaker's platform, in his study, and through his voluminous correspondence—he admonished the American people to exalt the nation and to preserve the Constitution and adapt it to the exigencies of history.

Born in Marblehead, Massachusetts, in 1779, Story graduated from Harvard College in 1798, read law, and began legal practice in Salem in 1801. In 1807 New England land speculators retained him to protect their interests in the notorious Yazoo lands controversy; his argument before the Supreme Court in their behalf was accepted by Chief Justice JOHN MARSHALL for the Court in FLETCHER V. PECK (1810).

A conservative Republican in a predominantly Federalist state, Story served for three years (1805–1808) in the Massachusetts legislature and then briefly (1808–1809) in the national House of Representatives. Though nominally a Republican, Story early displayed his independence by openly challenging President THOMAS JEFFERSON's policies on naval preparedness and on the Embargo; Jefferson blamed the "pseudo-Republican," Story, for the repeal of that Embargo, which he had hoped would be a substitute for war. On returning to Massachusetts, Story reentered the state legislature and in 1811 was elected its speaker. When Justice WILLIAM CUSHING of Massachusetts died in 1810, Story was one of four candidates proposed to President JAMES MADISON as Cushing's successor. Not having forgiven Story's opposition to the Embargo, Jefferson protested to Madison that Story was "unquestionably a tory . . . and too young." Only after three other prospective nominees—LEVI LINCOLN, Alexander Wolcott, and JOHN QUINCY ADAMS—had declined the nomination or were rejected by the Senate did Madison turn to Story. At thirty-two, he was—and remains—the youngest appointee in the history of the Court.

When Story took his seat on the Bench in 1812, he was already an ardent nationalist. From the beginning he endorsed that BROAD CONSTRUCTION of the Constitution that we associate with Marshall, and throughout Marshall's life he was not so much a disciple of as a collaborator with the Chief Justice. For the next quarter century, these two magisterial jurists presented a united front on most major constitutional issues; only on the issue of PRESIDENTIAL POWERS in wartime, raised in Brown v. United States (1814), and a few issues of admiralty, international, and prize law did they ever disagree. Yet throughout his judicial career, Story's was an independent and original mind different in style if not in philosophy from Marshall's. Story respected and even venerated the Chief Justice, and the respect was mutual. If Story looked to Marshall for

authoritative exposition of the Constitution, Marshall looked to Story for the substantiation of his logic and for help in other areas of law—notably in admiralty, conflict of laws, and equity. And when Story spoke on constitutional issues, it was in no mere imitative tones; frequently he pointed the way that Marshall later followed, as when his great opinion in MARTIN V. HUNTER'S LESSEE (1816) anticipated Marshall's opinion in COHENS V. VIRGINIA (1821). Although in some areas—such as the interpretation of the COMMERCE, NECESSARY AND PROPER, and CONTRACT CLAUSES of the Constitution—Marshall blazed the way, in others—notably those concerning the proper realms of executive and judicial power, issues of concurrent state and national power, and the creation of a uniform national commercial law—Story's was the greater overall achievement.

What emerges most strikingly from a study of Story's constitutional opinions is his passionate commitment to the authority of the national government in the federal system. He was quick to counter any attack or limitation upon its powers; he was alert to the potentialities of the concept of IMPLIED POWERS; he was ambitious to extend federal JURISDICTION by judicial opinion, legislation, or doctrinal writing. His ambitions were chiefly for the judiciary, for whose authority he was acquisitive and even belligerent, but he made bold claims for the national executive and legislative powers as well.

Story's solicitude for national executive authority was early asserted in Brown v. United States (1814), one of the few constitutional cases where he and Marshall disagreed. The issue presented was the validity of the confiscation of enemy property during the War of 1812 by the local United States district attorney without express legislative authority. Marshall, speaking for the Court, held such seizures illegal absent express authority granted by Congress. Story claimed that under the WAR POWER, the executive had full authority to direct such seizures, for in the absence of legislation he was bound only by international law, which countenanced such action. Not content to vindicate the executive power merely under the rules of international law, Story rested his case upon the doctrine of implied powers in the Constitution, here anticipating Marshall's statement of that doctrine in MCCULLOCH V. MARYLAND (1819). Story later seized the opportunity to restate and expand on his views on the implied powers of the executive in national emergencies in MARTIN V. MOTT (1827), which established the constitutional authority of the President to use his discretion as to the exigency that justified calling out the militia.

Though Story was not as jealous for legislative as for executive authority, in cases where the distribution of powers in the federal system was at issue he ranged himself strongly on the nationalist side. Thus, in PRIGG V. PENNSYLVANIA (1842), which presented the grave question whether authority to enforce the FUGITIVE SLAVE ACT of 1793 was vested exclusively in the national government or concurrently in the national and state governments, the Court held unconstitutional a Pennsylvania statute setting up parallel state enforcement machinery and imposing heavy penalties on any person who should seize or remove from the state anyone who had not been adjudged a fugitive from service. Story held for the Court that Congress had preempted the field by passing the 1793 act. This general argument was nothing new, being derived from Marshall's statement of the PREEMPTION doctrine in GIBBONS V. OGDEN (1824), but Story went further, arguing in dictum that the Constitution's fugitive slave clause did not impose upon the states any obligation to carry it into effect. Congressional authority was exclusive, so that the states not only could not cooperate with it through parallel legislation but might even prohibit their officials from acting under it. This was nationalism with a vengeance—as well as an escape hatch for northern states' PERSONAL LIBERTY LAWS. Only Justice JAMES M. WAYNE accepted Story's reasoning entirely; Chief Justice ROGER B. TANEY and Justices PETER V. DANIEL and HENRY BALDWIN agreed that the state statute was unconstitutional but denied that a state could release its officers from the obligation to enforce a federal law, while Justice JOHN MCLEAN dissented *in toto*, upholding the state statute's constitutionality.

Story's ambiguous views on slavery, exemplified by his opinion in *Prigg*, merit special discussion. Story detested slavery and denounced it in charges to federal GRAND JURIES, and it was the source of his sole extrajudicial public statement on political issues—his condemnation of the MISSOURI COMPROMISE. Yet he generally yielded to the countervailing pull of his belief in the necessity to support and sustain the authority of the legal system. Thus, his opinion in *The Amistad* (1841), while upholding the claims for freedom of Africans who had liberated themselves from captivity and seized control of the slave ship carrying them to Latin America, rested solidly upon principles of international law, not on the noble rhetoric of John Quincy Adams's argument in the Africans' behalf. And while his OBITER DICTUM in *Prigg* might be read as flowing from hostility to slavery, his appeals in his lectures at the Harvard Law School that all citizens faithfully obey the Fugitive Slave Act indicate that it was his zeal for the RULE OF LAW and for exclusive national authority rather than sympathy for the fugitive slave that dictated the ingenious reasoning in *Prigg*.

Story's support for exclusive congressional authority extended to other areas as well. In *Houston v. Moore* (1820) he argued (in dissent) that by providing for the trial and punishment of offenses against the federal militia act, Congress had preempted the field, thereby precluding the states from making similar provisions; it followed that the criminal jurisdiction of the United States in this area could not be delegated in whole or in part to state tribunals. In his dissent in MAYOR OF NEW YORK V. MILN (1837) Story asserted that congressional authority to regulate commerce was supreme and exclusive and that a state law requiring the master of a foreign vessel to supply elaborate information about his passengers was an unconstitutional regulation of commerce rather than a constitutional exercise of the STATE POLICE POWER. Similarly, in *United States v. Coombs* (1838), he expanded the reach of federal power under the commerce clause, holding for the Court that a federal statute prohibiting as a crime against the United States the theft of goods from wrecked or stranded ships was a constitutional regulation of commerce, even though it might not fall within federal admiralty jurisdiction.

Ready as Story was to vindicate national executive and legislative powers, it was the judicial prerogative that was closest to his heart. In his eyes the judiciary was the bulwark of the Constitution, and the courts' role in maintaining the balance of the departments and the federal system was of supreme importance.

Key to this balance was Section 25 of the JUDICIARY ACT OF 1789, which provided for APPEALS from state to federal courts, guaranteeing the harmonious interpretation of the Constitution throughout the United States. In *Martin v. Hunter's Lessee* (1816), Story upheld the constitutionality of Section 25. In one form or another, this case had dragged its tortuous way through the courts for almost a quarter of a century. While the legal issues were complicated, the constitutional question was comparatively simple: was the authoritative interpretation of the Constitution lodged finally in the Supreme Court or did it share this prerogative with the highest state courts? The Court had already decided the legal issues in *Fairfax v. Hunter's Lessee* (1813), but the Virginia courts refused to be bound by that decision. Marshall disqualified himself from the case for reasons of judicial propriety, so Story spoke for the Court in his first great opinion. To him the case presented the simple question of national versus state supremacy, and his answer was equally simple, in contrast to his opinion's verbosity: the national government was supreme. Appeals from state to national courts did not involve any infringement upon the SOVEREIGNTY of the state, for the people of the state, acting in their sovereign capacity, had already provided for such appeals through their ratification of the Constitution. Building on *Martin*, Marshall later seized his chance to vindicate Section 25 anew in *Cohens v. Virginia*.

Story's other efforts to expand federal judicial power were to prove no less significant than *Martin*. While early in his judicial career he had unsuccessfully advocated common-law jurisdiction for the federal courts, Story achieved that goal indirectly in SWIFT V. TYSON (1842). In *Swift*, Story held that Section 34 of the Judiciary Act of

1789, which provided that "the laws of the several States, except where the Constitution, treaties, or statutes of the United States shall otherwise require or provide, shall be regarded as rules of decision in trials at common law in the courts of the United States," did not always bind federal courts to follow the decisions of state courts. He contended rather that Section 34 required federal courts to follow state court decisions only in strictly state matters, and that federal courts were free in cases posing "questions of general commercial law" to follow "the general principles and doctrines of commercial jurisprudence."

Swift was the entering wedge for the gradual creation of a FEDERAL COMMON LAW, but the decision had a troubled history until, after repeated challenge and criticism, the Court overruled it in ERIE RAILROAD CO. V. TOMPKINS (1938). Despite *Erie*, the need for uniformity of interpretation in contracts, sales, commercial paper, secured transactions, and other branches of commercial law resulted in the gradual though somewhat disorderly creation of a common commercial law. Through federal legislation, uniform state laws (such as the Uniform Commercial Code), the American Law Institute's promulgation of Restatements of the various branches of the law, and the publication of authoritative treatises and reports of decisions, Story's dream of a national commercial law has been substantially vindicated.

Story helped to establish uniformity in many areas of commercial law. Almost single-handed, he shaped American admiralty law in his opinions on the First Circuit Court and the Supreme Court. More important, however, were his many authoritative *Commentaries*, which he composed as part of his responsibilities as Dane Professor of Law at Harvard, a position which he held from 1829 until his death. Story was "driven to accept" this post by his old friend Nathan Dane, who conditioned his gift to the near moribund Harvard Law School on Story's acceptance of the chair. His lectures gave rise to commentaries on *Bailments* (1832), the *Constitution* (3 vols., 1833), *Conflict of Laws* (1834), *Equity Jurisprudence* (1836), *Equity Pleading* (1838), *Agency* (1839), *Partnership* (1841), *Bill of Exchange* (1843), and *Promissory Notes* (1845), which together comprise the most impressive body of scholarship on commercial law ever to come from the pen of one scholar. These commentaries, together with his authority and prestige, made the Harvard Law School the largest and most distinguished in the nation.

To three fields particularly Story's contributions were of outstanding importance. His *Commentaries on the Constitution* molded constitutional law and history for half a century; in light of their influence on DANIEL WEBSTER and ABRAHAM LINCOLN, it might be said that it was Story who triumphed in the Civil War and the FOURTEENTH AMENDMENT. His works on equity established its popularity in the American legal system by giving equity (in the words of an English commentator) "a philosophical character with which it never had been invested by any preceding author." His *Conflict of Laws*, the most original and learned of all his books, opened up a relatively new subject and revealed the possibilities of Continental to American and—even more remarkable—of American to English and Continental law, as well as winning for Story a distinguished international reputation.

Equally characteristic of Story's zeal for national authority and uniformity was his legal and judicial conservatism. His belief in natural law—that laws are discovered rather than made—was part and parcel of the thinking of his generation, as of that earlier generation which had fought the American Revolution and framed state and national constitutions. Of the talismanic trio of life, liberty, and property, Story emphasized property—an emphasis peculiarly congenial to his temperament. The society in which Story lived was acquisitive and speculative—more fully so than the society that produced Marshall and Taney—and Story, along with JAMES KENT, came to be its most persuasive legal representative.

TERRETT V. TAYLOR (1816) gave Story his first opportunity to uphold property rights from the bench; writing for the Court, he struck down Virginia's attempt to revoke grants of glebe lands to the Episcopal Church, on the HIGHER LAW ground that legislative grants of land could not constitutionally be revoked by a subsequent legislative act. Similarly, Story's learned concurring opinion in DARTMOUTH COLLEGE V. WOODWARD (1819) supported Marshall's conclusion that the Constitution's contract clause forbade the revision or revocation by a state legislature of a college's charter. In the hands of Marshall and Story, the contract clause proved a powerful weapon for the maintenance of the status quo and the frustration of legislative experiments.

Marshall's death in 1835 and his replacement by Taney created a situation in which Story was increasingly uncomfortable. In three cases in the 1837 Term—*Mayor of New York v. Miln* (discussed above), CHARLES RIVER BRIDGE CO. V. WARREN BRIDGE, and BRISCOE V. BANK OF KENTUCKY—Story found himself in lonely and eloquent dissent, mourning the passing of the "old law." In *Charles River Bridge*, Story's most famous dissent, he bitterly countered the Court's decision upholding the Massachusetts legislature's grant of a permit to a new bridge company to build a bridge across the Charles River in competition with an existing bridge authorized by an earlier charter. Story's opinion ransacked the history of the COMMON LAW to establish that public grants were to be construed in the same manner as private grants—against the grantor; thus, the earlier grant of permission to build the first bridge should be read as granting an irrevocable monopoly. In *Briscoe*, Story dissented from a decision upholding Kentucky's creation of a state bank authorized to issue bank notes.

Invoking the departed Marshall, Story argued that because a state could not do through an agent what it was barred from doing directly, Kentucky had violated the constitutional prohibition against the issuing by a state of BILLS OF CREDIT. These three cases dramatized the contrast between the Story-Marshall interpretation of the Constitution and that advanced by Taney and his colleagues; they illustrate the TANEY COURT's modification of the MARSHALL COURT's earlier positions to favor the states' police powers and a greater exercise of judicial continence.

Although Story died suddenly in 1845, leaving unwritten his projected works on admiralty and insurance and his memoirs, he had in large part succeeded in his determination to create a rounded system of law not only through judicial opinions but also through systematic treatises and teaching. His judicial opinions helped to formulate our constitutional, equity, COPYRIGHT, admiralty, insurance, and commercial law. His *Commentaries* did more than those of any other expositor until our own day to mold popular ideas about the American constitutional system and to influence professional ideas about law, while they all but created the fields of commercial law and conflict of laws. And from the great law school which was so largely of his making and the extension of his shadow, he sent forth lawyers, judges, and teachers imbued with his nationalist philosophy of law and politics. Nor, indeed, did his influence end here; through such disciples as CHARLES SUMNER, TIMOTHY WALKER, and FRANCIS LIEBER, he handed on a vital and persistent tradition.

HENRY STEELE COMMAGER
RICHARD B. BERNSTEIN
(1986)

Bibliography

COMMAGER, HENRY STEELE 1953 Joseph Story. In *Caspar G. Bacon Lectures on the Constitution of the United States, 1940–1950.* Boston: Boston University Press.

DUNNE, GERALD T. 1970 *Justice Joseph Story and the Rise of the Supreme Court.* New York: Simon & Schuster.

McCLELLAN, JAMES 1971 *Joseph Story and the American Constitution: A Study in Political and Legal Thought.* Norman: University of Oklahoma Press.

NEWMYER, R. KENT 1985 *Supreme Court Justice Joseph Story: Statesman of the Old Republic.* Chapel Hill: University of North Carolina Press.

STORY, WILLIAM W. 1851 *Life and Letters of Joseph Story,* 2 vols. Boston: Little, Brown.

STRADER v. GRAHAM
10 Howard (51 U.S.) 83 (1851)

In a suit under a Kentucky statute making an abettor of fugitive slaves liable to the master for their value, defendant attempted to evade liability by arguing that the slaves, who had previously been permitted by their master, the plaintiff, to sojourn in free states, became free there and retained that status upon their return to their slave-state domicile. Defendant sought a reversal of the Kentucky Court of Appeals' determination that their slave status reattached.

On the central question, Chief Justice ROGER B. TANEY held that a state court's determination of the status of blacks was conclusive on federal courts. But he went on to assert in dictum that every state had the right to determine the status of persons within its territory "except in so far as the powers of the states in this respect are restrained, or duties and obligations imposed on them" by the federal Constitution, thus suggesting that the Constitution might somehow invalidate northern abolition statutes or statutes regulating the permissible stay of sojourning slaves. He also insisted that the NORTHWEST ORDINANCE was defunct, its famous sixth article no longer a basis for the exclusion of slavery from the five states of the former Northwest Territory, thus suggesting that Congress might not be able to impose an enforceable antislavery condition on a territory's admission as a state.

Had the United States Supreme Court in 1857 wished to evade the controversial question raised in DRED SCOTT V. SANDFORD of the constitutionality of congressional prohibition of SLAVERY IN THE TERRITORIES, it might have used *Strader* to hold that the determination of Scott's status by the Missouri Supreme Court was binding on federal courts. Justice SAMUEL NELSON's concurrence in *Dred Scott*, originally intended to be the opinion for the Court, did in fact adopt this approach.

WILLIAM M. WIECEK
(1986)

STRATEGIC LAWSUITS AGAINST PUBLIC PARTICIPATION IN GOVERNMENT

Citizen activism on public issues since the 1960s has been confronted by a new genre of civil litigation: lawsuits claiming injury from others' communications to government. A National Science Foundation–sponsored study at the University of Denver has found that citizens, nonprofit organizations, and businesses are being sued for exercising the basic FIRST AMENDMENT right to "petition the government for a redress of grievances." Lawsuits, typically with multimillion-dollar claims, have been filed against citizens and groups for testifying against real estate developments at city ZONING hearings; reporting public official and police misconduct; filing consumer or CIVIL RIGHTS complaints; writing letters to the President opposing political APPOINTMENTS; reporting violations of ENVIRONMENTAL REGULATION; complaining to school boards about incompetent teachers;

or testifying before Congress or state legislatures on pending bills.

Although the lawsuits make various claims—most typically defamation, business torts, process violations, and conspiracy—they have come to be collectively viewed by courts and commentators as "SLAPPs" for "strategic lawsuits against public participation" in government, an acronym that captures both their cause and their effect; namely, sanctioning political opponents' participation in government decisionmaking. SLAPPs are a classic example of "dispute transformation," a unilateral changing of the nature of the dispute, the forum, and the issues so that, for example, a public, political-forum, policy controversy over zoning is transformed into a private, judicial-forum, legalistic controversy over slander, to the perceived advantage of the lawsuit filer.

The University of Denver study found these attempts to "privatize" public debate typically arise when a party's civically or politically motivated communications to a government official, body, or the electorate threaten the private economic interests of another party, thus provoking a tension between the twin cultural values of democracy and capitalism. While the overwhelming majority of SLAPPs are eventually dismissed in court, the study found that they nevertheless have serious emotional, financial, and political consequences and have a CHILLING EFFECT on targets' and other observers' willingness to participate politically.

Because the American legal tradition encourages public participation as a cornerstone of representative democracy and recognizes, as NEW YORK TIMES V. SULLIVAN (1964) put it "a profound national commitment to the principle that debate on public issues should be uninhibited, robust, and wide-open," SLAPPs have met with strong condemnation. "Short of a gun to the head, a greater threat to First Amendment expression can scarcely be imagined," one judge has inveighed, while another likened these suits to "the *auto da fe*" threatening "the most protected and encouraged form of expression known in this country."

The Supreme Court, state courts, legislatures, attorneys general, and government agencies have taken a dim view of this litigation tactic, favoring early dismissal. The Court's jurisprudence is muddled at the confluence of two different lines of authority, both creating a "qualified immunity" for government petitioning. On the one hand, in defamation-based SLAPPs, such as *McDonald v. Smith* (1985), the Court has applied the *New York Times v. Sullivan* LIBEL doctrine requiring dismissal unless "actual malice" (knowledge of falsity or reckless disregard of the truth) is shown. On the other hand, in SLAPPs alleging ANTITRUST or business torts, such as *City of Columbia v. Omni Outdoor Advertising, Inc.* (1991), it has applied the more protective *Noerr–Pennington* doctrine requiring dismissal unless it is shown that the petitioning was "not genuinely aimed at procuring favorable government action at all," regardless of the defendant's intent or purpose.

More than a dozen states, including New York, California, Massachusetts, Minnesota, and Georgia, have adopted "anti-SLAPP laws," generally based on the qualified immunity approach of one or the other of the two Supreme Court lines of authority. In the absence of LEGISLATION, a few state courts have gone further and applied state law "absolute immunity" doctrines to protect SLAPP defendants, but the weight of court opinions favors the qualified immunity approaches.

In a number of cases, countersuits have been filed against SLAPP filers and their attorneys, once the SLAPP is dismissed. Typically based on malicious prosecution, abuse of process, and civil rights claims, these "SLAPP-backs," as they have come to be called, have resulted in jury awards in the multimillions of dollars.

GEORGE W. PRING
PENELOPE CANAN
(2000)

(SEE ALSO: *Freedom of Petition.*)

Bibliography

PRING, GEORGE W. and CANAN, PENELOPE 1996 *SLAPPs: Getting Sued for Speaking Out.* Philadelphia: Temple University Press.

STRAUDER v. WEST VIRGINIA
100 U.S. 303 (1880)

VIRGINIA v. RIVES
100 U.S. 313 (1880)

EX PARTE VIRGINIA
100 U.S. 339 (1880)

On a day in 1880 the Supreme Court handed down three opinions that fixed the constitutional law of JURY DISCRIMINATION for over half a century. The effect of the three, taken collectively, barred overt state denial of the rights of blacks to serve on juries and effectively barred blacks from jury service in the South. Anything so crude as an announced and deliberate effort to exclude persons on ground of race was unconstitutional; but if official policy did not refer to race and yet blacks were systematically excluded by covert practices, the Constitution's integrity remained unimpaired. No estimate can be made of the miscarriages of justice that occurred in the South and border states where only whites sat in judgment in civil cases involving the property of blacks or in criminal cases involving their life and liberty over a period of at least fifty-five years.

Strauder was a case in which official state policy was overtly discriminatory on racial grounds. West Virginia by statute declared that only whites might serve on juries. Justice WILLIAM STRONG, for the Court, holding the act to be a violation of the EQUAL PROTECTION clause of the FOURTEENTH AMENDMENT, declared that denying citizens the right to participate in the administration of justice solely for racial reasons "is practically a brand upon them, affixed by law; an assertion of their inferiority, and a stimulant to that race prejudice which is an impediment to securing to individuals of the race that equal justice which the law aims to secure to all others." The Court also sustained the constitutionality of a section of the CIVIL RIGHTS ACT OF 1866 by which Congress authorized the removal of a case from a state court to a federal court in order to prevent the denial of CIVIL RIGHTS by the state court. Justice STEPHEN J. FIELD and NATHAN CLIFFORD dissented without opinion.

In *Ex Parte Virginia and J. D. Coles,* the Court sustained the constitutionality of an act of Congress which provided that no qualified person should be disqualified because of race for service as a grand or petit juror in any court, state or federal. Coles, a county court judge of Virginia charged with selecting jurors, excluded from jury lists all black persons. He was indicted by the United States and was liable to be fined $5,000. On petition for a writ of HABEAS CORPUS, he alleged that the federal court had no JURISDICTION over him and that the act of Congress was unconstitutional. Strong declared that under the Fourteenth Amendment, Congress could reach any act of a state that violated the right of black citizens to serve on juries or their right to be tried by juries impartially selected without regard to race. The act of Judge Coles was the act of the state of Virginia, for a state acts through its officers and agents, none of whom may deny the equal protection of the laws. By so ruling, the Court prepared the ground for the doctrine of STATE ACTION. Field and Clifford, again dissenting, thought the act of Congress regulated purely local matters and destroyed state autonomy.

The effects of *Strauder* and *Ex Parte Virginia* were vitiated by the *Rives* decision. Two black men, indicted for the murder of a white man, sought to have their cases removed from a state court to a federal court on the ground that the GRAND JURY that indicted them and the PETIT JURY summoned to try them were composed entirely of whites. The prisoners claimed that the jury lists should include one third blacks, in proportion to the population, and, most important, that no blacks had ever been allowed to serve on juries in the county where they were to be tried. In this case the record did not show, as it did in the

other two, overt and direct exclusion of blacks. Strong, for the Court, this time supported by Field and Clifford concurring separately, simply stated, without further ado, that the "assertions" that no blacks ever served on juries in the county "fall short" of showing the denial of a civil right or the existence of racial discrimination. The defendants might still be tried impartially. Similarly, they had no right to a jury composed in part of members of their race. A mixed jury, said the Court, is not essential to the equal protection of the laws. There was no "unfriendly legislation" in this case. In effect the Court placed upon black prisoners the burden of proving deliberate and systematic exclusion on ground of race. As a result, blacks quickly disappeared from jury service in the South.

LEONARD W. LEVY
(1986)

(SEE ALSO: *Neal v. Delaware; Norris v. Alabama.*)

Bibliography

SCHMIDT, BENNO C.   1983   Juries, Jurisdiction, and Race Discrimination: The Lost Promise of *Strauder v. West Virginia.* *Texas Law Review* 61:1401–1499.

STREAM OF COMMERCE DOCTRINE

The Supreme Court introduced the "stream" or "current" metaphor in SWIFT & CO. V. UNITED STATES (1905) to represent the movement of goods in INTERSTATE COMMERCE. The DOCTRINE is significant because it marks the Court's first recognition that commercial markets ignored state lines; the Justices departed from decades of CONSTITUTIONAL INTERPRETATION in which economic reality had yielded to formal legal discrimination. The doctrine itself may be stated as follows: what appears, when out of context, to be INTRASTATE COMMERCE comes within the reach of the interstate commerce power if that commerce is but an incident related to an interstate continuum. Thus Congress can regulate the local aspects of commerce that are inseparably related to the current of interstate commerce, even though the flow has been temporarily interrupted by a kind of whirlpool or eddy while the product goes through some stage in the transformation of the raw material into the finished goods before being shipped again in the interstate stream to reach its final destination.

In *Swift* the government charged the nation's largest meat packers with conspiring to monopolize interstate commerce in violation of the SHERMAN ANTITRUST ACT. The packers asserted that their activities took place at the stockyards—solely within the boundaries of a single state—and thus involved only local or intrastate com-

structionist. The impoundment of funds appropriated by Congress, the invasion of Cambodia, the assertion of EXECUTIVE PRIVILEGE, and many of Nixon's domestic security measures all suggest an expansive, nonstrict view of a president's constitutional authority.

Finally, "strict construction" may have other sensible meanings that do not refer to narrow interpretations. Justice HUGO BLACK may have thought himself to be construing the Constitution strictly when he applied it literally, as in First Amendment cases. Another plausible meaning is strict adherence to the letter and spirit of the Constitution. Under this view, everyone can claim to be a strict constructionist, adhering to what he or she ascertains to be the principles embodied in the Constitution. Strict construction also may characterize a passive judiciary. For example, many believe legislative apportionment to be a POLITICAL QUESTION, a matter of concern only for the legislative and executive branches. A judge who invades the area is deemed active and, therefore, not a strict constructionist. Judge LEARNED HAND may have used strict construction in this sense when he stated that the Supreme Court's failure to define political questions is "a stench in the nostrils of strict constructionists."

THEODORE EISENBERG
(1986)

Bibliography

BLACK, CHARLES L., JR. 1960 *The People and the Court*. New York: Macmillan.

KELLY, ALFRED H.; HARBISON, WINFRED A.; and BELZ, HERMAN 1983 *The American Constitution*, 6th ed. New York: Norton.

KOHLMEIER, LOUIS M., JR. 1972 *God Save This Honorable Court*. New York: Scribner's.

MURPHY, WILLIAM P. 1967 *The Triumph of Nationalism*. Chicago: Quadrangle Books.

STRICT SCRUTINY

In its modern use, "strict scrutiny" denotes JUDICIAL REVIEW that is active and intense. Although the "constitutional revolution" of the late 1930s aimed at replacing JUDICIAL ACTIVISM with a more restrained review using the RATIONAL BASIS formula, even that revolution's strongest partisans recognized that "a more exacting judicial scrutiny" might be appropriate in some cases. Specific prohibitions of the BILL OF RIGHTS, for example, might call for active judicial defense, and legislation might be entitled to a diminished presumption of validity when it interfered with the political process itself or was directed against DISCRETE AND INSULAR MINORITIES. (See UNITED STATES V. CAROLENE PRODUCTS CO.) The term "strict scrutiny" appears to have been used first by Justice WILLIAM O. DOUGLAS in

his opinion for the Supreme Court in SKINNER V. OKLAHOMA (1942), in a context suggesting special judicial solicitude both for certain rights that were "basic" and for certain persons who seemed the likely victims of legislative prejudice.

Both these concerns informed the WARREN COURT's expansion of the reach of the EQUAL PROTECTION clause. "Strict scrutiny" was required for legislation that discriminated against the exercise of FUNDAMENTAL INTERESTS or employed SUSPECT CLASSIFICATIONS. In practice, as Gerald Gunther put it, the Court's heightened scrutiny was "strict' in theory and fatal in fact." The Court took a hard look at both the purposes of the legislature and the means used for achieving them. To pass the test of strict scrutiny, a legislative classification must be "necessary to achieve a COMPELLING STATE INTEREST." Thus the state's objectives must be not merely legitimate but of compelling importance, and the means used must be not merely rationally related to those purposes but necessary to their attainment.

The same demanding standard of review has emerged in other areas of constitutional law. Thus even some "indirect" regulations of the FREEDOM OF SPEECH—that is, regulations that do not purport to regulate message content—must be strictly scrutinized. Similarly, strict scrutiny is appropriate for general legislation whose application is attacked as a violation of the right of free exercise of religion. (See RELIGIOUS LIBERTY.) And in those places where SUBSTANTIVE DUE PROCESS has made a comeback—notably in defense of liberties having to do with marriage and family relations, abortion and contraception, and more generally the FREEDOM OF INTIMATE ASSOCIATION—the same strict judicial scrutiny is the order of the day.

The Court has developed intermediate STANDARDS OF REVIEW falling between the rational basis and strict scrutiny standards. Not every heightening of the intensity of judicial review, in other words, implies strict scrutiny. Most critics of the Supreme Court's modern activism reject not only its employment of the strict scrutiny standard but also its use of any heightened standard of review. For these critics, there is little room in the Constitution for any judicial inquiry into the importance of governmental goals or the utility of governmental means. Some action by the state is forbidden by the Constitution, more or less explicitly. Beyond these prohibitions, say these critics, lie no principled guides to judicial behavior.

Yet strict judicial scrutiny of legislation is almost as old as the Constitution itself. From one season to another, the special objects of the judiciary's protection have varied, but from JOHN MARSHALL's day to our own the courts have always found *some* occasions for "a more exacting judicial scrutiny" of the political branches' handiwork. It is hard to imagine what our country would be like if they had not done so.

KENNETH L. KARST
(1986)

Bibliography

GUNTHER, GERALD 1972 The Supreme Court, 1971 Term—Foreword: In Search of Evolving Doctrine on a Changing Court: A Model for a Newer Equal Protection. *Harvard Law Review* 86:1–48.

STROMBERG v. CALIFORNIA
283 U.S. 359 (1931)

A California law made it a crime to display a red flag or banner "as a sign, symbol or emblem of opposition to organized government or as an invitation or stimulus to anarchistic action or as an aid to propaganda that is of a seditious character. . . ." A member of the Young Communist League who ran a summer camp where the daily ritual included the raising of "the workers' red flag" was convicted for violating the statute, although a state appellate court noted that the prohibition contained in the first clause—"opposition to organized government"—was so vague as to be constitutionally questionable. That court nonetheless upheld the conviction on the grounds that the defendant had been found guilty of violating the entire statute and that the other two clauses relating to "anarchistic action" and "seditious character" were sufficiently definite.

Chief Justice CHARLES EVANS HUGHES and six other members of the Supreme Court reversed the conviction. In his opinion, Hughes pointed out that, the jury having rendered a general verdict, it was impossible to know under which clause or clauses the defendant had been convicted. If any of the three clauses were invalid, the conviction could not stand. The Court found the first clause "so vague and indefinite" that it violated the DUE PROCESS clause of the FOURTEENTH AMENDMENT because it prohibited not only violent, illegal opposition to organized government but also "peaceful and orderly opposition to government by legal means. . . ." Justices JAMES C. MCREYNOLDS and PIERCE BUTLER dissented.

MICHAEL E. PARRISH
(1986)

STRONG, WILLIAM
(1808–1895)

Strong was a learned, able, hard-working Supreme Court Justice who competently handled the tedious routine of COMMON LAW, admiralty, PATENT, and revenue law cases. Except for sustaining legal tenders and invalidating state-authorized exclusion of blacks from jury service, he rarely spoke for the Court in constitutional matters during his ten-year career. Strong's appointment in 1870 was viewed as part of an alleged court-packing scheme to reverse a recent decision invalidating legal tender legislation. But President ULYSSES S. GRANT had decided to nominate Strong and JOSEPH P. BRADLEY in January 1870, a month before an eight-man court, including a Justice who already had resigned, narrowly decided *Hepburn v. Griswold*. Grant, meanwhile, was well aware that Strong had written an opinion for the Pennsylvania Supreme Court sustaining the laws.

Strong did not disappoint Grant. In May 1871, he wrote the majority opinion in *Knox v. Lee* and *Parker v. Davis*, reversing *Hepburn*. He largely based his argument on the NECESSARY AND PROPER clause, finding the legal tender legislation a necessary concomitant to the WAR POWER. He also refuted the *Hepburn* argument that the laws violated the "spirit of the Constitution" because they impaired the OBLIGATION OF CONTRACTS. All contracts, Strong contended, had to anticipate the rightful exercise of congressional power.

Strong generally defended vested contractual and property rights, the LEGAL TENDER CASES notwithstanding. He joined Justice STEPHEN J. FIELD's dissent in *Munn v. Illinois* (1877). In his own dissent in the SINKING FUND CASES (1879), he maintained that the government could not require railroads to divert part of their earnings into a special fund for payment of their federal debts. The original railroad grant contained no such provision, but Congress had reserved the right to alter, amend, or repeal the act. Strong nevertheless insisted that the new requirement was "plainly transgressive of legislative power" for it violated an implied contractual promise not to call for debt payment before 1897. Strong's dissent, along with those by JOSEPH BRADLEY and Field, heralded the procorporation, antistatist tendencies that dominated the Court for several decades.

The Court's concern with state economic regulation inevitably provoked operations of national authority. In the *State Freight Tax Case* (1873) (see PHILADELPHIA AND READING R.R. CO. V. PENNSYLVANIA) Strong offered a significant commentary on the scope of the COMMERCE CLAUSE when it conflicted with traditional state power. Pennsylvania had imposed a tonnage tax on railroad freight carried within and out of the state, but Strong held that the transportation of goods was a "constituent of commerce" and the tax's "effect" unduly burdened INTERSTATE COMMERCE. In a comparison case, Strong held valid a tax on corporate gross receipts irrespective of whether they came from interstate or intrastate businesses (*State Tax on Railway Gross Receipts*, 1873). In effect, the commerce clause was not a shield for private enterprise against STATE TAXATION.

Strong's record on CIVIL RIGHTS was mixed. He joined the Court's majority in the SLAUGHTERHOUSE CASES (1873) to restrict the scope of the FOURTEENTH AMENDMENT. Similarly, he voted to limit federal guarantees for voting and civil rights. In BLYEW V. UNITED STATES (1872), he wrote the Court's first opinion restricting the CIVIL RIGHTS ACT OF 1866. The act authorized federal trials for crimes "affecting persons" denied rights secured by law. Strong held, however, that federal courts lacked JURISDICTION over a defendant accused of murdering three blacks on the ground that the dead persons could not be affected by any prosecution. Although Strong favored upholding a state statute requiring equal access in public transportation, he silently acquiesced when the Court held that the law unduly burdened interstate commerce (HALL V. DECUIR, 1878). But he spoke for the Court in a series of cases that marked some exceptional, however limited, victories for blacks.

In STRAUDER V. WEST VIRGINIA (1880) the Court invalidated a state statute excluding blacks from juries. Strong conceded that blacks were not entitled to have other blacks sit on their juries, but he held that they had a right to have juries selected impartially. The protection of one's life and liberty against racial prejudice was, Strong contended, a "legal right" under the Fourteenth Amendment and therefore the state's exclusion law constituted a denial of EQUAL PROTECTION OF THE LAWS. In a companion case, *Ex parte Virginia* (1880), Strong upheld a section of the 1875 CIVIL RIGHTS ACT which prohibited RACIAL DISCRIMINATION in jury selection. Although state law forbade such discrimination, a state judge had refused to call blacks as jurors. Strong brushed aside arguments that the judge's refusal was not the same as STATE ACTION, which Congress concededly could prohibit. The judge, he insisted, held state office and acted for the state; as such he was obligated to obey the federal constitution and law. But in a third case decided that day, *Virginia v. Rives* (1880), Strong denied a plea for removal of a cause to a federal court on the ground of JURY DISCRIMINATION. Here blacks had been excluded as a result of discretionary action by jury commissioners, not as a result of state law as in *Strauder*. The decision in effect condoned the practical exclusion of blacks from southern juries for the next seventy-five years. Nevertheless, Strong's opinion in *Ex Parte Virginia* preserved a vestige of federal power that was revived in the CIVIL RIGHTS ACT OF 1957, the first such legislation since Reconstruction.

Strong did not have the domineering intellectual force of a Bradley, Field, or Miller, but he performed capably during his career. He was admired and respected by his diverse colleagues, and he managed to avoid the intense personal and ideological conflicts that characterized the period. He abruptly resigned in 1880. Strong was in good health, but he supposedly stepped down as an example to NATHAN CLIFFORD, WARD HUNT, and NOAH SWAYNE who were ill and frequently absent from the bench. Within two years, the three resigned. In retirement, Strong publicized the Court's burdensome workload, and his efforts contributed to the creation of new courts of appeal in 1891. (See CIRCUIT COURTS OF APPEALS ACT.)

STANLEY I. KUTLER
(1986)

Bibliography

KUTLER, STANLEY I. 1969 William Strong. In Friedman, Leon, and Israel, Fred L., eds., *The Justices of the United States Supreme Court, 1789–1969: Their Lives and Major Opinions*, pages 1153–1178. New York: Chelsea House.

STUART v. LAIRD
1 Cranch 299 (1803)

The JUDICIARY ACT OF 1802, having repealed the JUDICIARY ACT OF 1801 before it could go into operation, abolished the new CIRCUIT COURTS and returned the Justices of the Supreme Court to circuit duty under the JUDICIARY ACT OF 1789. The *Stuart* case raised the constitutionality of the repeal act of 1802. Although Chief Justice JOHN MARSHALL despised the repeal act and believed it to be unconstitutional, on circuit duty he sidestepped the constitutional issue. When the case came before the Court on a WRIT OF ERROR, Justice WILLIAM PATERSON for the Court, with Marshall abstaining, ruled that the practice of riding circuit had begun under the act of 1789 and that long acquiescence "has fixed the construction. It is a contemporary interpretation of the most forcible nature." Thus the Court avoided holding unconstitutional an act of THOMAS JEFFERSON's administration.

LEONARD W. LEVY
(1986)

(SEE ALSO: *Marbury v. Madison.*)

STUDENTS CHALLENGING REGULATORY AGENCY PROCEDURES (SCRAP), UNITED STATES v.
412 U.S. 669 (1973)

Environmentalists sued to force the Interstate Commerce Commission to suspend a freight rate surcharge announced by the nation's railroads. Plaintiffs claimed the surcharge would raise the cost of transporting recyclable materials and thus injure their recreational and aesthetic use of areas around Washington, D.C., by increasing pollution from waste disposal and causing greater consumption of natural resources.

In one of its most generous rulings on STANDING, the Court held that environmental advocates could raise a statutory claim that, according to three dissenters, was based on injuries that were too remote, speculative, and insubstantial to confer standing. Justice POTTER J. STEWART followed the implications of SIERRA CLUB V. MORTON (1972): environmental harm, however widespread, satisfies the "injury in fact" requirement of standing, and the case will be heard if those who complain allege harm to themselves. The harm need not be "substantial." Nor did it matter that the line of causation between the challenged government act and the asserted environmental harm was "attenuated." Several subsequent decisions, such as *Warth v. Seldin* (1975) and SIMON V. EASTERN KENTUCKY WELFARE RIGHTS ORGANIZATION (1976), differ from *SCRAP*, insisting that the causal link between act and harm be more clearly shown. *SCRAP's* relaxed view of causal nexus in standing may reflect a special judicial receptivity to environmental litigation.

JONATHAN D. VARAT
(1986)

STUMP v. SPARKMAN
435 U.S. 349 (1978)

This decision confirmed judges' absolute immunity from damage suits for alleged constitutional violations. At the request of a mother who was displeased with her "somewhat retarded" fifteen-year-old daughter's behavior, and in EX PARTE proceeding in which the child was not represented, Judge Stump ordered the child to be sterilized. The girl was told she was having an appendectomy, and she discovered some years later she had been sterilized. In an action brought by the sterilization victim and her husband, the Supreme Court held, 5–3, that the judge was immune from liability. Because signing the sterilization order was a judicial act, and because there was no express statement in state law that judges lacked JURISDICTION to entertain sterilization requests, the judge's behavior was covered by the doctrine of JUDICIAL IMMUNITY. In the name of judicial independence, the majority immunized conduct that the three dissenters aptly called "lawless," "beyond the pale of anything that could sensibly be called a judicial act."

THEODORE EISENBERG
(1986)

STURGES v. CROWNINSHIELD
4 Wheaton 122 (1819)

This was the first of the very rare CONTRACT CLAUSE cases decided by the Supreme Court involving private executory contracts. The case arose during a depression, when many states had enacted bankruptcy or insolvency statutes. Chief Justice JOHN MARSHALL, for a unanimous Court, agreed that the states possessed a concurrent power to enact such statutes in the absence of the exercise by Congress of its power to establish uniform bankruptcy laws but held that New York's act violated the contract clause. Crowninshield had declared his bankruptcy under that state's act to protect himself from paying a debt contracted before its passing. The doctrine of the case is that a state act cannot operate retroactively on previously existing contracts; a statute that relieves the debtor from imprisonment is valid but not one that cancels the obligation of his contract. The case left uncertain the constitutionality of bankruptcy acts that operate prospectively on contracts formed after their enactment. (See OGDEN V. SAUNDERS.)

LEONARD W. LEVY
(1986)

SUBJECTS OF COMMERCE

A chief purpose of the COMMERCE CLAUSE of the federal Constitution is to assure the free movement of the subjects of commerce among the several states. What are these subjects? Essentially, the term refers to things sold or transported in INTERSTATE COMMERCE. But they need not be articles of trade or even of value. Nor are they confined to objects as such. They may include PERSONS. All are included as subjects or articles of commerce when they begin to move from one state to another. They remain articles of commerce until they fall into the possession of the ultimate buyer or reach their final stage of repose within a given state. Thus, at any point between the beginning and the end of their journey among the states, they are legitimate candidates for congressional regulation. With respect to these subjects, as with interstate commerce generally, Congress may, in the words of GIBBONS V. OGDEN (1824), "prescribe the rule by which commerce is to be governed."

Congress ordinarily exerts its power over the subjects of commerce in order to protect their free movement across state borders. But this power has also been construed to permit Congress to divest some subjects of their interstate character. Divestment occurs when Congress prohibits the interstate transportation of certain goods or persons. Examples of such subjects are stolen automobiles, intoxicating beverages, forged checks, convict-made goods, explosives, prostitutes, firearms, lottery tickets, and kidnaped children. Federal laws prohibiting commerce in such subjects are usually designed to assist the states in fighting crime or protecting their citizens against social, moral, or economic harm. (See NATIONAL POLICE POWER.) But Congress has also banned the interstate shipment of ordinary objects of trade, like lumber, in opposition to state policy. Any such federal law must of course bear a reasonable relationship to interstate commerce. Thus, according to UNITED STATES V. DARBY (1941), Congress may validly bar the interstate shipment of goods produced in violation of a federal MAXIMUM HOUR AND MINIMUM WAGE law so that "interstate commerce [does not become] the instrument of competition in the distribution of goods produced under substandard labor conditions."

The commerce clause, however, is not merely an authorization to Congress to enact laws for the protection of the subjects of commerce. It serves also by its own force to prevent the states from erecting trade barriers or passing any legislation that would obstruct the movement of goods from state to state. As a practical matter the states, not Congress, regulate most subjects (and aspects) of commerce. They may do so out of a legitimate concern for the health, welfare, and safety of their own citizens. Yet, the exercise of this valid STATE POLICE POWER is often in tension with the value of free and open borders that informs the commerce clause. (See STATE REGULATION OF COMMERCE; STATE TAXATION OF COMMERCE.)

A central development in modern commerce clause jurisprudence is the Supreme Court's identification as legitimate articles of commerce many subjects historically regarded as the exclusive preserve of the states. Such subjects include insurance contracts, natural resources, fish and wild game, and even valueless material such as solid and liquid wastes. Prevailing DOCTRINE holds that the shipment in and out of the states of these subjects of commerce is protected by the commerce clause unless Congress ordains otherwise. Most recently, in *Sporkase v. Nebraska* (1982), the Supreme Court added ground water to its list of legitimate subjects of commerce. As the Court noted in PHILADELPHIA V. NEW JERSEY (1978), no object of interstate trade is excluded by definition from this list.

Still the tension between state power and the commerce clause remains. In the watershed case of COOLEY V. BOARD OF WARDENS (1851) the Court tried to resolve this tension by declaring that states may not regulate a subject of commerce the *nature* of which requires a single (national) uniform plan of regulation, even in the absence of any federal law. The *Cooley* rule has not yielded a long list of particular subjects requiring exclusive national regulation. It has been applied mainly to identify subjects whose number and diversity might require, when regulated, local

knowledge and experience. State or local regulation of such subjects, whether justified to facilitate trade or to protect the public, is valid unless it conflicts with a law of Congress. *Cooley* itself upheld state regulation of harbor traffic, over commerce clause objections, because of the local peculiarities of port facilities.

Today, however, the Court rarely finds the *Cooley* rule applicable. The modern approach to commerce clause analysis applies a "balancing" test that weighs the interest served by a local regulation of a subject of commerce against the regulation's burden upon interstate commerce. If the burden substantially outweighs the local benefit, even if the legislation is nondiscriminatory, the regulation is unlikely to survive constitutional analysis. (If the *Cooley* rule forbids state regulation there is of course no balancing.) Generally, an article of commerce, although it may be taxed or regulated by the state, may not be so burdened as to prevent or seriously to obstruct its transportation in interstate commerce.

Yet the states do bar some "subjects of commerce" from entering their borders. Local inspection laws, for example, may exclude goods such as diseased cattle, adulterated food, and infectious plants. Such articles do not fall within the Court's classification of *legitimate* subjects of commerce. Correspondingly, the states may validly prevent some goods from leaving their borders. Certain natural resources, like rare birds and fish, may be withheld from commercial exploitation altogether. Such resources assume the character of subjects of commerce, however, when they are permitted legally to be sold or are reduced to personal possession. At that point, even though the private acquisition of such resources may be regulated by law in the interest of their preservation, the states are generally forbidden to restrict their use or sale to their own citizens.

DONALD P. KOMMERS
(1986)

Bibliography

BENSON, PAUL R., JR. 1970 *The Supreme Court and the Commerce Clause, 1937–1970.* Cambridge, Mass.: Dunnellen.

CORWIN, EDWARD S. 1936 *The Commerce Power Versus States Rights.* Princeton, N.J.: Princeton University Press.

SCHWARTZ, BERNARD 1979 Commerce, the States, and the Burger Court. *Northwestern University Law Review* 74:409–439.

SUBPOENA

A subpoena is a court order that compels a person to appear for the purpose of giving testimony at a trial or a pretrial proceeding, such as a preliminary examination or pretrial deposition. A court also can issue a subpoena for documents or other items of tangible EVIDENCE. Parties to civil suits, and the prosecution in criminal cases, had a COMMON LAW right to compel testimony before the creation of the Constitution. The Sixth Amendment provides defendants in criminal cases a basis for fairly presenting their defense by giving them the power to subpoena witnesses. The government in some circumstances may have an affirmative duty to help a defendant find a witness, such as a government informer, or to refrain from restricting the defendant's ability to locate a witness essential to the presentation of a defense.

The Sixth Amendment, in part, provides that accused persons have the right of witnesses and the right "to have compulsory process" for obtaining witnesses in their behalf. The confrontation and compulsory process clauses permit the defendant to use the power of the courts to obtain witnesses and they limit governmental interference with the defendant's ability to examine witnesses at trial. These clauses have been incorporated into the FOURTEENTH AMENDMENT by the Supreme Court; thus they govern both federal and state prosecutions.

A defendant may compel a person to testify in a court proceeding by applying to the court for a subpoena ordering the person to appear in court or at a pretrial hearing. However, the defendant's ability to use the court's subpoena power is not unlimited. A court can require a defendant to provide it with information that justifies the production of the witness.

When a defendant has a court issue a subpoena to a witness, the witness normally is entitled to a statutory fee to offset his expenses for attendance at the judicial proceeding. An INDIGENT defendant may use the court's subpoena power to compel witnesses to testify in his behalf even though he cannot pay the witness fee. In these circumstances, however, a court may require the indigent defendant to show that the persons whom he subpoenas are likely to give testimony relevant to the charge.

An indigent defendant may try to use the subpoena power to compel an expert (such as a psychiatrist or a ballistics expert) to attend court to testify on the defendant's behalf. Whether the government must pay the cost for providing the defendant with an expert witness is primarily a DUE PROCESS, rather than a subpoena power, issue. However the issue be phrased, courts must determine whether, under the circumstances of the case, a fair trial depends on government provision of the expert witness.

The Sixth Amendment's confrontation clause, together with the compulsory process clause, restricts the government's ability to limit the testimony of potential defense witnesses and the cross-examination of prosecution witnesses. If a person who has received a subpoena to give testimony believes that his testimony would not be relevant to the trial, or that his testimony is subject to an EVIDENTIARY PRIVILEGE, he may move to quash the subpoena. A witness may assert a constitutionally based privilege, such as the RIGHT AGAINST SELF-INCRIMINATION, or a common law or statutory privilege, such as a doctor-patient privilege. One who has no such privilege may not refuse to respond to the subpoena or refuse to give testimony.

JOHN E. NOWAK
(1986)

Bibliography

LaFave, Wayne R. and Israel, Jerold H. 1984 *Criminal Procedure*. Section 23.3. St. Paul, Minn.: West Publishing.
Wright, Charles Alan and Graham, K. 1980 *Federal Practice and Procedure: Evidence*. Section 5436. St. Paul, Minn.: West Publishing.

SUBSIDIES TO BUSINESS

See: State Tax Incentives and Subsidies to Business

SUBSIDIZED SPEECH

Americans customarily view FREEDOM OF SPEECH as a matter of personal right. A FIRST AMENDMENT thus conceived serves both the individual and the community—at least in the context of traditional command and control regulation. In this context, a person may wish to speak but the government commands him not to do so, on pain of punishment if that order is ignored. The person's right to speak, though, countermands the order. With this countermand, the individual gains as his or her will to speak is secured. As for the community, it gains as it receives the speech.

But consider personal rights in a context apart from that of traditional command and control regulation. This other context is that of our large public sector, wherein government-controlled wealth amounts to about one-third of the national economy. In this context, the government, instead of ordering a person not to speak, may "buy him off" by offering him some benefit for not speaking. Should a person accept the payment, and not speak, his "right" to speak will not have been taken, the reason being that personal rights are as a rule alienable. A person may transfer or forgo a personal right as he or she wishes, the object being, as Thomas Hobbes said, "some good to himself." To view a right as other than alienable would, as many have noted, be contrary to the principles of free choice and autonomy that underlie individual rights.

No personal right may be taken, but the community's interest is; as the speaker is bought off, the community is denied the speech. For instance, in RUST V. SULLIVAN (1991), federal funds were provided to family planning and maternal health clinics, but only on the condition that these clinics and their doctors not provide counseling to their clients about ABORTION. To a claim that these conditions violated the free speech rights of the clinics and their private sponsors, the Court responded that the clinics were not forced to forgo abortion counseling; rather, they might refuse the federal aid and speak as they wished. No free speech rights were taken by the government "offering that choice." Still in all, speech for a particular community, that of the clientele of the family clinics, had surely diminished.

The predicament, then, is that subsidized speech breaks the tie between the rights of the speaker and the interests of the community. This disconnect is one of the greater problems of modern First Amendment jurisprudence, for which problem there is, unfortunately, presently no reliable solution. There are, however, various approaches that may be discerned in the case law. One such approach has been a formal observation of the relation of rights, wherein the courts characterize government attempts to buy up speech not as an inducement (which would leave choice and free will intact) but as an order (coercion) that binds the speaker and thus amounts to a taking of personal speech. In SPEISER V. RANDALL (1958), the Supreme Court reviewed a state law under which veterans might claim a tax exemption, but only on the condition that they forswear certain types of political association. The Court overturned that arrangement by characterizing the inducement respecting speech as a coercive taking of speech rather than as a matter of incentive and choice. As explained in the MAJORITY OPINION, "the denial of tax exemption for engaging in certain speech necessarily will have the effect of coercing the claimants to refrain from the proscribed speech." But at other times, as in *Grove City College v. Bell* (1984), the courts have instead characterized a benefit conditioned on forgoing speech as offering the speaker a choice that in no sense violates the right to speak. This rights-oriented approach to subsidized speech has not yielded consistent results for it has required the courts to engage in psychological speculation as to when inducement shades over into coercion. Indeed, as noted by Justice ANTONIN SCALIA, the decisions seem more the result of "idiosyncratic discretion."

Another, more promising approach, is that of rereading the First Amendment so that it does not establish free speech as solely a matter of personal right. Instead, the amendment impersonally provides that "Congress shall make no law . . . abridging the freedom of speech." In light of this text, we may plausibly view the First Amendment as establishing free speech as a common good, as a state of lively and unfettered discourse among the people that advances knowledge, politics, and culture to the benefit of

all. The First Amendment simply precludes the government from "abridging" this good, whether by command or by purchase. The Supreme Court has approached this position in a number of cases by assessing whether a government benefit conditioned on speech might diminish speech as a common good. For instance, in ROSENBERGER V. RECTORS AND VISITORS OF THE UNIVERSITY OF VIRGINIA (1995), the Court held that an award of public funds could not be conditioned on the recipients' refraining from religiously oriented speech, because that condition "risks the suppression of free speech and inquiry in one of the vital centers for the nation's intellectual life, its college and university campuses." When Congress conditioned subsidies to public broadcasters on the stations' agreement to refrain from editorials, the Court, in *Federal Communications Commission v. League of Women Voters* (1984), overturned that arrangement on the grounds that "debate on public issues should be uninhibited, robust, and wide-open."

A third approach has to do not with speech per se, but with FREEDOM OF THE PRESS. The First Amendment provides that Congress shall not abridge "the freedom of speech, or of the press." This specific reference to the press may plausibly be taken as marking the press as a constitutionally protected business, independent and free of the government by virtue of being a for-profit enterprise. Consistent with this view, several decisions of the Supreme Court (mostly involving the print media) have struck down government subsidies (often in the form of special tax exemptions or other tax breaks); such subsidies would have diminished the independence of the press by making it beholden to the government. In these opinions, there is no talk of speech as a personal right that might appropriately be bought by the government. Instead, the focus is elsewhere, to how a subsidy might amount to a governmental derangement of the free-market basis of a free press.

WILLIAM T. MAYTON
(2000)

Bibliography

KREIMER, SETH F. 1984 Allocational Sanctions: The Problem of Negative Rights in a Positive State. *University of Pennsylvania Law Review* 132:1293–1397.

MAYTON, WILLIAM T. 1994 "Buying-Up Speech": Active Government and the Terms of the First and Fourteenth Amendments. *William & Mary Bill of Rights Journal* 3:373–418.

POST, ROBERT C. 1996 Subsidized Speech. *Yale Law Journal* 106:151–195.

VAN ALSTYNE, WILLIAM W. 1968 The Demise of the Right-Privilege Doctrine in Constitutional Law. *Harvard Law Review* 81:1439–1464.

SUBSTANTIVE DUE PROCESS

To say that governmental action violates "substantive due process" is to say that the action, while adhering to the forms of law, unjustifiably abridges the Constitution's fundamental constraints upon the content of what government may do to people in the name of "law." As the Supreme Court put the matter most succinctly in HURTADO V. CALIFORNIA (1884), "Law is something more than mere will exerted as an act of power. . . . [It] exclud[es], as not due process of law, acts of attainder, bills of pains and penalties, acts of confiscation . . . and other similar special, partial and arbitrary exertions of power under the forms of legislation. Arbitrary power, enforcing its edicts to the injury of the persons and property of its subjects, is not law, whether manifested as the decree of a personal monarch or of an impersonal multitude."

Substantive due process thus restricts government power, requiring coercive actions of the state to have public as opposed to merely private ends, defining certain means that government may not employ absent the most compelling necessity, and identifying certain aspects of behavior which it may not regulate without a clear showing that no less intrusive means could achieve government's legitimate public aims.

The phrase DUE PROCESS OF LAW derives from King John's promise in MAGNA CARTA to abide "by the law of the land," as translated four centuries later by Sir EDWARD COKE. But the belief that even the sovereign must follow a HIGHER LAW can be traced further back still. Even before the Middle Ages, kings symbolically acknowledged their limitations when they accepted their crowns; royal coronations were religious rites in which the rulers supposedly received power directly from God. The medieval notion of a divine law that even the sovereign might not transgress lay at the heart of English COMMON LAW and of the barons' demands at Runnymede. By the eighteenth century, the idea was phrased in terms of a natural law philosophy of SOCIAL COMPACT between sovereign and citizen. Although individuals were thought to surrender certain freedoms to the state, other rights were considered so much a part of personhood that they lay outside the scope of the social compact. Indeed, protection of such rights had to be the aim of any valid government; a state would abrogate its essential function were it to deny its citizens these fundamental freedoms.

The most famous articulation of that social compact philosophy in American history is the statement in the DECLARATION OF INDEPENDENCE that "all men . . . are endowed by their Creator with certain unalienable Rights . . . among these are Life, Liberty and the Pursuit of Happiness . . . to secure these Rights, Governments are instituted among Men, deriving their just Powers from the Consent of the Governed." Although the Declaration of Independence does not, of course, use the words "due process," the notion that substantive limits may be implied from the character of our society and from our reasons for ceding coercive authority to the state underlies both that document and the system of law and politics structured by our Constitution. The Fifth and FOURTEENTH AMENDMENTS to the Constitution provide, respectively, that neither the federal government nor the states may deprive persons "of life, liberty, or property, without due process of law." The Supreme Court has long recognized that STATE ACTION that follows fair procedures and thus satisfies PROCEDURAL DUE PROCESS may nonetheless violate substantive due process by exceeding the limits of the proper sphere of government. In the name of substantive due process, the Supreme Court has accordingly struck down hundreds of statutes governing matters ranging from wages and hours to sexual conduct.

Some commentators have called "substantive due process" a contradiction in terms. But a dismissal on semantic grounds of the very notion of substantive due process is unwarranted. First, the very idea of "process" has often been taken to include concerns as to the nature of the body taking an action, and legislatures have at times been understood as structurally improper sources of particular kinds of public actions. Second, the Constitution guarantees "due process *of law*," and, as the passage quoted above from *Hurtado* suggests, the term "law" can itself be taken to imply various normative requirements. Third, even the purest "procedural" norms inevitably embody substantive choices. Finally, the choice of the constitutional phrase on which substantive review has been pinned is to a large degree accidental; the Fourteenth Amendment's "privileges or immunities" clause might have been a happier selection—but the real question is whether and how individual rights not explicitly guaranteed by the Constitution should be protected under that document taken as a whole, not whether courts have picked a felicitous phrase to describe that protective task.

The Constitution, however, does not specify the essential rights of personhood; the BILL OF RIGHTS lists only certain rights that particularly warranted articulation in 1791, and the NINTH AMENDMENT makes clear that the list is not to be taken as exhaustive. It is on a largely open landscape that courts, including the Supreme Court, have had to mark out our fundamental freedoms. The process has necessarily been one of continual redefinition, responding to the changing—one hopes evolving—values and concerns of the Justices and the nation. Due process, as FELIX FRANKFURTER noted, has a "blessed versatility."

Not until the adoption of the Fourteenth Amendment in 1868 did the Constitution explicitly require state deprivations of liberty or property to comply with "due process of law"; BARRON V. BALTIMORE (1833) had interpreted the parallel Fifth Amendment bar to limit only the federal government. Well before 1868, however, both the Supreme Court and various state courts had begun to articulate inherent, judicially enforceable bounds on governmental interference with individual autonomy. Insofar as these limits were announced and enforced by federal judges, such holdings occurred in cases not involving specific provisions of the United States Constitution but falling within the DIVERSITY JURISDICTION of federal courts because the opposing parties were citizens of different states. The liberties the courts protected were almost exclusively economic: the ability to contract as one wished and to do as one pleased with one's own property.

Thus, as early as 1798, Justice SAMUEL CHASE wrote in CALDER V. BULL that any law that "takes property from A. and gives it to B." is invalid as contrary to "general principles of law and reason," even if it is not "expressly restrained" by the Constitution. Justice Chase reasoned that such a law would usurp judicial authority if intended to correct an injustice A had done to B, and, if intended simply to improve matters, would not be "law" at all but would instead transgress limitations implied by the very notion of representative government: "the nature, and ends of legislative power will limit the exercise of it."

From time to time throughout the nineteenth century, the Supreme Court struck down state statutes it judged to exceed these inherent limits on legislative power. Typically, however, the Court left unclear whether the limits derived from the purpose and character of legislatures, as Justice Chase had argued; or from an ahistorical body of natural law; or from specific, if unnamed, provisions of the Constitution. In FLETCHER V. PECK (1810), for example, the Supreme Court invalidated a Georgia statute that attempted to revoke state land grants. Writing for the Court, Chief Justice JOHN MARSHALL explained only that the statute was rendered invalid "either by general principles which are common to our free institutions, or by the particular provisions of the Constitution." Similarly, when the Supreme Court in TERRETT V. TAYLOR (1815) struck down Virginia's attempt to divest the Episcopal Church of its property, it rested its holding on "principles of natural justice" and "fundamental laws of every free government," as well as on the "spirit and letter" of the Constitution.

Within a decade or so after the Civil War, however, the Supreme Court more clearly embraced a theory of implied limitations. When, in LOAN ASSOCIATION V. TOPEKA (1875), the Court invalidated a tax designed to finance a bonus for local industry, it did not mention the Constitution at all; exercising the common law power of a federal court sitting in a diversity case, the Court simply found the tax "purely in aid of private or personal objects" and hence "beyond the legislative power and . . . an unauthorized invasion of private right." Echoing *Calder v. Bull*, the *Loan Association* Court declared that there are "rights in every free government beyond the control of the state" and that limitations on sovereign power "grow out of the essential nature of free governments."

Ironically, it was a notion of intrinsic limits on proper government action, including judicial action—a notion similar to that underlying the Court's invalidation of state and local laws in *Fletcher v. Peck*, *Terrett v. Taylor*, and *Loan Association v. Topeka*—that initially constrained substantive review of state legislation under the Fourteenth Amendment. By prohibiting state laws that "abridge the PRIVILEGES OR IMMUNITIES of citizens of the United States," the amendment's framers may have intended to provide federal protection against state encroachment of fundamental rights, but the Supreme Court in the SLAUGHTERHOUSE CASES (1873) construed the clause narrowly to safeguard only rights peculiarly associated with national CITIZENSHIP, such as the right to vote in national elections. In the Court's view, the clause did not protect the essential freedoms traditionally protected by the states themselves in intrastate disputes and protected by federal courts under Article IV, section 2, only from state laws unjustly discriminating against out-of-staters. Upholding the constitutionality of a state-granted monopoly on slaughterhouses around New Orleans, the *Slaughterhouse* Court held that the right to pursue one's trade was a right of state not national citizenship.

Writing for the Court in *Slaughterhouse*, Justice SAMUEL F. MILLER—who two years later penned the majority opinion in *Loan Association v. Topeka*—made clear that the main motivation for the *Slaughterhouse* decision lay in the Court's fear that a more expansive interpretation of the Fourteenth Amendment would allow the federal government to exceed the proper bounds of its authority and to intrude on the regulatory domain of the states. Construing the amendment's privileges or immunities clause or its due process clause to protect all fundamental rights, Miller explained, "would constitute this Court a perpetual censor upon all legislation of the states" and, by virtue of the affirmative enforcement power granted Congress in section 5 of the Fourteenth Amendment, would allow Congress to "pass laws in advance, limiting and restricting the exercise of legislative power by the states in their most ordinary and useful functions." In contrast, the largely nonconstitutional review carried out in *Fletcher*, *Terrett*, and *Loan* was seen by the Court as guided and constrained by well-developed common law notions of the inherent limits of legitimate state action, gave no affirmative power to Congress, and fell within one of the federal government's clearly proper roles: adjudicating cases in which diversity of citizenship cast doubt on the impartiality of state tribunals.

But the doctrinal distinction between constitutional and common law review of the substantive legitimacy of state legislation was internally unstable: if natural law limitations on government could guide and constrain the Court in diversity-of-citizenship cases, they could do the same in cases brought pursuant to the Fourteenth Amendment. Moreover, the Court could apply common law principles to invalidate any congressional attempt under the guise of the Fourteenth Amendment to prohibit perfectly legitimate state activity.

Partly because of this doctrinal instability, and partly because of strong pressure from the organized bar for a more expansive review of state ECONOMIC REGULATION, the Court moved rapidly in the years following *Loan Association* and *Slaughterhouse* toward substantive review of state legislation under the Fourteenth Amendment's due process clause. Throughout the last quarter of the nineteenth century, the Court often warned in OBITER DICTA that the due process clause prohibited states from transgressing common law limitations on legitimate governmental action. In particular, the Court gave notice that unreasonable state deprivations of property or of the FREEDOM OF CONTRACT would be struck down as unconstitutional. In ALLGEYER V. LOUISIANA (1897) this line of dicta finally ripened into a landmark HOLDING: the Court there invalidated a Louisiana restriction on insurance contracts as substantively incompatible with due process of law. By barring companies not licensed by the state from insuring Louisiana property, the Court held, Louisiana had exceeded its STATE POLICE POWER and had unconstitutionally impaired the freedom of contract.

In the four decades following *Allgeyer*, the Supreme Court scrutinized socioeconomic legislation more aggressively and persistently than ever before or since, striking down scores of federal and state statutes as violative of substantive due process. The period from 1897 to 1937 has come to be known as "the *Lochner* era," after its most infamous product, LOCHNER V. NEW YORK (1905). *Lochner* invalidated a New York law limiting the work week of bakery employees to sixty hours; the Court found the statute an unreasonable infringement of the freedom of contract. In dissent, Justice OLIVER WENDELL HOLMES protested that "[t]he fourteenth amendment does not enact Mr. Herbert Spencer's *Social Statics*."

Throughout the *Lochner* era, the Court closely examined both the means and the ends of socioeconomic legislation. The Court required that the relationship between a statute and its legitimate objectives be "real and substantial," and it repeatedly invalidated laws that it deemed to burden individual economic liberty more than strictly necessary to accomplish the goals of such laws. Thus, the majority in *Lochner* reasoned that regulation of bakery work hours exceeded the proper bounds of the police power in part because the state could protect the health of bakery employees without infringing so fundamentally on contractual freedom. Similarly, ADKINS V. CHILDREN'S HOSPITAL (1923) struck down minimum wage laws for women partly because the Court deemed narrower wage regulations sufficient to achieve the legislature's legitimate ends, and *Liggett Co. v. Baldridge* (1928), which invalidated Pennsylvania restrictions on corporate ownership of pharmacies, noted less objectionable regulatory means the state could employ to protect the same interests in public health.

In addition to demanding a tight fit between ends and means, the *Lochner* Court required that the statutory ends themselves fit its sense of the proper aims of lawmaking. Informed by earlier doctrines of implied limitations, as well as by the popular notions of social Darwinism and the writings of conservative legal COMMENTATORS ON THE CONSTITUTION such as THOMAS M. COOLEY and CHRISTOPHER G. TIEDEMAN, the Court viewed protection of individual common law rights and advancement of the general health, safety, and moral welfare to be the only valid objectives of government regulation. Laws aimed at redistributing economic and social power—giving A's property to B—by their very nature fell outside the realm of legitimate legislative action. Thus, for example, in *Adair v. United States* (1908) and COPPAGE V. KANSAS (1915), the Court invalidated prohibitions against YELLOW DOG CONTRACTS that conditioned employment on workers' promises not to join unions. Writing for the majority in *Coppage*, Justice MAHLON PITNEY rejected the argument that inequality of bargaining power could justify infringing contractual liberty: it is "impossible to uphold freedom of contract and the right of private property without at the same time recognizing as legitimate those inequalities of fortune that are the necessary result of the exercise of those rights."

Although the Court in the *Lochner* era struck down close to 200 statutes under the due process clauses, it upheld even more. Many of the laws sustained were distinguished from invalidated statutes only by subtle factual differences supporting findings that they served the Court's narrow vision of the general welfare. After repeatedly striking down price controls, for example, the Court in NEBBIA V. NEW YORK (1934) upheld regulation of milk prices, concluding that the regulation was plausibly connected to public health on the theory that price competition encouraged suppliers to cut corners on sanitation. Other statutes, however, were sustained for a more specific reason: the Court exempted from its general liberty-of-contract approach statutes designed to protect especially disadvantaged or vulnerable groups. Thus, in HOLDEN V. HARDY (1897), the Court upheld restrictions on the hours worked by coal miners; the Court stressed the ultrahazardous nature of coal mining and the ability of coal companies in company-run towns virtually to dictate the terms of employment. Similarly, the Court in MULLER V. OREGON (1908), moved in part by the supposed physical vulnerability of women and by sexist notions of their maternal mission, permitted Oregon to limit women's hours of work outside the home.

Just as prior doctrinal instabilities had helped to usher in the *Lochner* era, so these exceptions to the regime of laissez-faire presaged the era's close. By acknowledging that a state could protect at least some groups at the expense of others, *Holden* and *Muller* made available in every substantive due process case the argument that the legislature might reasonably have determined that the class protected by the challenged statute was unable to, or should not be forced to, fend for itself. Indeed, *Lochner v. New York* was itself drastically limited *sub silentio* in 1917, when the Court in BUNTING V. OREGON (1917) relied on *Muller* in upholding a state law limiting to ten hours the work day of manufacturing employees.

With the onset of the Depression, moreover, it became progressively more difficult to view the relative wealth of A and B as a matter of purely private concern, outside the domain of proper governmental authority. Increasingly, economic transactions were seen as interrelated, and the general welfare was understood as intimately linked to the welfare of disadvantaged groups. The Supreme Court's persistent invalidation of redistributive legislation was sharply criticized by labor unions, the liberal press, and NEW DEAL politicians, all of whom argued that extensive economic regulation, both state and federal, was necessary to alleviate the Depression. The perceived legitimacy of such regulation was further bolstered by the work of "realist" legal scholars such as MORRIS R. COHEN and Robert Hale, who portrayed distributions of private wealth and power as the results of public choices expressed, for example, in the law of property and contract.

After much outcry, the Supreme Court parted dramatically with *Lochner* in WEST COAST HOTEL V. PARRISH (1937), which abandoned earlier precedent and upheld a statutory minimum wage for women as reasonable in light of women's vulnerability to economic exploitation and the public interest in minimizing the number of workers requiring government relief. In the years that followed, the Court confirmed its abandonment of *Lochner* by repeatedly rejecting challenges to expansive New Deal regulation of private economic arrangements, and in 1949 the Court unanimously and explicitly rejected the "*Allgeyer Lochner-Adair-Coppage* constitutional doctrine."

Never, however, did the Supreme Court explicitly abandon *Lochner*'s substantive theory of what constitutes legitimate legislation; it remains the official dogma to this day that regulatory power may not be exercised solely to transfer property from one private party to another. Instead, the Court relaxed the STANDARD OF REVIEW it applied to socioeconomic regulation: the close scrutiny of the *Lochner* era was replaced with extreme deference to legislative determinations. Thus, in UNITED STATES V. CAROLENE PRODUCTS CO. (1938) the Court promised to uphold socioeconomic legislation if any known or reasonably inferable state of facts supported the legislature's judgment.

In the intervening decades, this extreme deference has become virtually complete judicial abdication. Although substantive scrutiny has occasionally been smuggled in through the privileges or immunities clause of Article IV or the CONTRACT CLAUSE, in due process review the Court has required of economic regulation only "minimum rationality" and has shown itself willing to uphold laws on the basis of purely hypothetical facts or objectives, or on blind trust in legislative rationality. Justice WILLIAM H. REHNQUIST carried the Court's approach to its logical extreme in his opinion for the majority in *Railroad Retirement Board v. Fritz* (1980). Rejecting a due process challenge to legislation that phased out the eligibility of long-retired railroad employees to receive both social security and railroad retirement benefits, but preserved the similar eligibility of more recently retired employees of equally long (or longer) tenure, the majority reasoned that the statute was clearly a rational way to accomplish its precise result: cutting off the dual benefits of the very employees adversely affected by the law. "The plain language" of the statute, Justice Rehnquist wrote, "marks the beginning and end of our inquiry."

The Supreme Court has not been entirely without textual guidance in its post-1937 effort to define the fundamental freedoms protected by the Fourteenth Amendment's due process clause. Although the Bill of Rights formally applies only to the federal government, the Court has relied heavily on the first eight amendments in determining which rights—both procedural and substantive—are so essential that governmental action abrogating them violates due process of law. Most of the guarantees in the Bill of Rights have now been "selectively incorporated" into the Fourteenth Amendment, although the Court has decisively repudiated the view, espoused by Justice HUGO L. BLACK, that the Fourteenth Amendment applies the Bill of Rights to the states *in toto*.

At the close of the *Lochner* era, the Justices laid down a fairly restrictive rule for determining which provisions of the Bill of Rights were "incorporated." Writing for the Court in PALKO V. CONNECTICUT (1937), Justice BENJAMIN N. CARDOZO limited incorporation to those rights "implicit in the concept of ORDERED LIBERTY." Eventually recognizing the irrelevance of an inquiry into whether "a civilized system could be imagined that would not accord the particular protection," the Court in the late 1960s adopted a more contextual approach, asking whether a particular right was essential to the American political order. Thus, in DUNCAN V. LOUISIANA (1968) the Court held that criminal trial safeguards provided by the Bill of Rights are absorbed by the Fourteenth Amendment if they are "fundamental in the context of the criminal processes maintained by the American states." Over time, *Duncan* has come to stand for the more general proposition that guarantees in the Bill of Rights should be incorporated—and guarantees not expressly mentioned should be added—if they are necessary to protect values basic to our society. (See IN-CORPORATION DOCTRINE.)

Although substantive due process protection of implied rights to contractual liberty virtually vanished with the close of the *Lochner* era, judicial solicitude has grown in the ensuing years for a different set of liberties not expressly protected by the Constitution—a diverse group of claims to personal autonomy that have been collectively labeled the RIGHT OF PRIVACY. In contrast to the narrow contractual liberty to which the *Lochner* Court devoted the bulk of its concern, the right of privacy has come to embrace a wide array of freedoms, including rights of association and reproduction as well as of seclusion and intellectual independence. Some of these freedoms have been derived by extrapolation (or, perhaps, excavation) from the Bill of Rights or other clauses of the Fifth and Fourteenth Amendments. Yet the stirring rhetoric that has typically accompanied the elaboration of these personal freedoms testifies to a judicial perception that they are in some way more fundamental than the textual provisions to which they are pegged.

The Supreme Court made clear the essential nature of these "privacy" or "personhood" rights when it gave them their earliest articulation during the *Lochner* era itself. Striking down a state law that forbade the teaching of foreign languages before the eighth grade, the Court in MEYER V. NEBRASKA (1923) stressed the importance of allowing teachers to pursue their calling and parents to raise their children as they saw fit. Justice JAMES C. MCREYNOLDS's majority opinion gave broad scope to the liberty protected by the due process clauses: "Without doubt, [it] denotes not merely freedom from bodily restraint but also the right of the individual to contract, to engage in any of the common occupations of life, to acquire useful knowledge, to marry, establish a home and bring up children, to worship God according to the dictates of his own conscience, and generally to enjoy those privileges long recognized at common law as essential to the orderly pursuit of happiness by free men." Two years later, in PIERCE V. SOCIETY OF SISTERS (1925), the Court marshaled similar rhetoric in invalidating a state requirement that all students attend public schools. Still more sweeping—and perhaps of more lasting influence—was Justice LOUIS D. BRANDEIS's formulation in his dissent in OLMSTEAD V. UNITED STATES (1928):

"The makers of our Constitution . . . sought to protect Americans in their beliefs, their thoughts, their emotions, and their sensations. They conferred, as against the government, the right to be let alone—the most comprehensive of rights and the right most valued by civilized men."

Despite the broad language of these early opinions, *Meyer* and *Pierce* evinced special judicial solicitude primarily for family autonomy—freedom from government intrusion into the traditionally intimate realms of marriage, reproduction, and child-rearing. That emphasis, along with recognition of personal autonomy rights as fundamental, was furthered by the watershed case of SKINNER V. OKLAHOMA (1942), the Supreme Court's first important privacy decision following the demise of *Lochner*. Invalidating a state statute providing for the STERILIZATION of persons convicted two or more times of "felonies involving moral turpitude," the Court termed the right to reproduce "one of the basic civil rights of man." Part of the Court's concern stemmed from fear of the invidious and possibly genocidal ways in which government control over reproduction might be exercised: the Court observed that the "power to sterilize, . . . [i]n evil or reckless hands . . . can cause races or types which are inimical to the dominant group to wither and disappear."

The right to REPRODUCTIVE AUTONOMY recognized in *Skinner* has since been elaborated and considerably expanded. As recently as 1978, the Court in ZABLOCKI V. REDHAIL "reaffirm[ed] the fundamental character of the right to marry," holding that a state may not forbid marriage of parents unable to meet their child support obligations. More controversial has been the extension of *Skinner* to BIRTH CONTROL practices. In GRISWOLD V. CONNECTICUT (1965) the Supreme Court ruled that a married couple's decision to purchase and use contraceptives is a private matter beyond the proper reach of government authority. Perhaps not surprisingly, Justice WILLIAM O. DOUGLAS's majority opinion focused on the intimacy of marital choices, invoking "a right of privacy older than the Bill of Rights" and defending the "sacred precincts of marital bedrooms." The freedom to practice contraception was not freed of its familial trappings until 1972, when Justice WILLIAM J. BRENNAN wrote for the Court in EISENSTADT V. BAIRD that, if "the right of privacy means anything, it is the right of the *individual*, married or unmarried, to be free from unwarranted governmental intrusions into matters so fundamentally affecting a person as the decision whether to bear or beget a child." That *Baird* singled out as decisive in *Griswold* the element of reproductive autonomy was made clear by CAREY V. POPULATION SERVICES INTERNATIONAL (1977), which invalidated a state statute allowing contraceptives to be sold only by licensed pharmacists and only to persons over sixteen.

When the Court assessed the constitutionality of ABOR-

TION laws in ROE V. WADE (1973), its commitment to reproductive autonomy collided with an equally basic concern for the sanctity of human life. Writing for the majority, Justice HARRY L. BLACKMUN reasoned that the liberty protected by the due process clauses includes a woman's fundamental right to decide, with her physician, whether to end or to continue a pregnancy, but that certain state interests are sufficiently compelling to override that right. During the final trimester of pregnancy, the state's interest in preserving the fetus, by then viable, justifies a ban on abortions; before the third trimester, however, abortions may not be prohibited and may be regulated only as necessary to protect the woman's health; and, before the second trimester, the state may require only that abortions be performed by licensed physicians.

As an element of substantive due process, the right to privacy has received its doctrinally purest exposition in reproductive autonomy cases. Equally important rights to personal autonomy, however, have been found in the "penumbras" of constitutional provisions less abstract than the requirement of "due process of law," most notably the FIRST AMENDMENT. In *West Virginia State Board of Education v. Barnette* (1943) the Court construed the First Amendment, along with the Fifth and the Fourteenth, to establish for each individual a sphere of intellectual and spiritual independence. Striking down a compulsory flag salute in public schools, Justice ROBERT H. JACKSON wrote for the Court that, "[i]f there is any fixed star in our constitutional constellation, it is that no official, high or petty, can prescribe what shall be orthodox in politics, nationalism, religion, or other matters of opinion or force citizens to confess by word or act their faith therein." The Court appealed to the same notion when it held, in *Wooley v. Maynard* (1977), that New Hampshire could not punish a person for obscuring the words "Live Free or Die" on his license plate because he found it religiously or philosophically repugnant to display the state's slogan on his car. The Court reasoned that the state had impermissibly invaded the private "sphere of intellect and spirit" by requiring individuals "to use their private property as a "mobile billboard' for the State's ideological message."

In NAACP V. ALABAMA (1958) and *Talley v. California* (1960) the Court found in the First Amendment guarantees of associational and expressive freedom correlative rights to anonymity. And in MOORE V. CITY OF EAST CLEVELAND (1977) the Court protected a special right to familial association by invalidating a single-family zoning ordinance that prevented a woman from living with her son and two grandsons. Renewing its special commitment to traditional visions of family autonomy, the Court distinguished the zoning law upheld in *Village of Belle Terre v. Boraas* (1974) on the basis that "the ordinance there affected only *unrelated* individuals," whereas East Cleve-

land had "chosen to regulate the occupancy of its housing by slicing deeply into the family itself."

Other penumbral rights to personal autonomy have been found in the intersection of several textual provisions, or in the constitutional system taken as a whole. In SHAPIRO V. THOMPSON (1969), for example, the Court alluded to the COMMERCE CLAUSE, the privileges or immunities clause of the Fourteenth Amendment, and the similar language in Article IV, section 2, as well as to the Fifth Amendment's due process clause and "the nature of our Federal Union" in finding that "our constitutional concepts of personal liberty" imposed a general requirement that "all citizens be free to travel throughout the length and breadth of our land uninhibited by statutes, rules, or regulations which unreasonably burden or restrict this movement." The newly vitalized RIGHT TO TRAVEL had earlier been recognized in the context of international mobility, at least when other First Amendment rights were also at stake: the Court in APTHEKER V. SECRETARY OF STATE (1964) had struck down a congressional denial of passports to members of the Communist party. In HAIG V. AGEE (1981) the Court sustained revocation of the passport of a former intelligence agent who was engaged in exposing undercover agents stationed abroad. In *Haig* the Court distinguished sharply between the "right" of inter*state* travel and the "freedom" of inter*national* travel, refusing to extend to congressional regulation of the latter the close scrutiny it had given state regulation of the former.

The Supreme Court attempted to unify some of these disparate doctrinal threads in WHALEN V. ROE (1976), its most comprehensive treatment thus far of the right of privacy. Writing for a unanimous Court, Justice JOHN PAUL STEVENS upheld a carefully crafted state scheme for maintaining computerized records of prescriptions for certain dangerous drugs, but only after examining the statute's implications for what he described as the two components of the right to privacy: an interest in confidentiality—"avoiding disclosure of personal matters"—and an interest in free choice—"independence in making certain kinds of important decisions."

Despite this seemingly broad formulation, the Court has resisted the creation of a generic right to choose how one lives. In *Kelley v. Johnson* (1976), for example, the Court upheld police department rules regulating officers' hair styles and prohibiting them from having beards. Writing for the majority, Justice Rehnquist argued that the rules did not violate the right of privacy recognized in *Roe, Baird,* and *Griswold;* he distinguished those cases as involving "substantial claims of infringement on the individual's freedom of choice with respect to certain basic matters of procreation, marriage, and family life." Nor is the Court apparently prepared to protect even all intimate decisions central to one's self-definition; the Justices have, for example, passed up several opportunities to review statutes punishing or burdening private homosexual activity between consenting adults. (See FREEDOM OF INTIMATE ASSOCIATION.)

Some lower courts have been more willing to expand the protected sphere of personal autonomy, recognizing broad rights of lifestyle choice as well as, in some cases, freedom to decide how and when one will die. The Supreme Court, however, appears unlikely to follow very quickly. Not only are some Justices concerned about the open-ended and potentially radical nature of such decisions, but the Court has repeatedly dropped unsubtle hints that there are fairly sharp limits to its tolerance. The "blessed versatility" of substantive due process is limited by the Justices' awareness that the Supreme Court is an institution of government.

LAURENCE H. TRIBE
(1986)

Bibliography

BLACK, CHARLES L.   1969   *Structure and Relationship in Constitutional Law.* Baton Rouge: Louisiana State University Press.

BREST, PAUL and LEVINSON, SANFORD   1983   *Processes of Constitutional Decisionmaking: Cases and Materials.* Boston: Little, Brown.

CHOPER, JESSE H.   1980   *Judicial Review and the National Political Process: A Functional Reconsideration of the Role of the Supreme Court.* Chicago: University of Chicago Press.

ELY, JOHN HART   1980   *Democracy and Distrust: A Theory of Judicial Review.* Cambridge, Mass.: Harvard University Press.

GUNTHER, GERALD   1975   *Cases and Materials on Constitutional Law.* Mineola, N.Y.: Foundation Press.

KENNEDY, DUNCAN   1980   Toward an Historical Understanding of Legal Consciousness: The Case of Classical Legal Thought in America 1850–1940. *Research in Law & Sociology* 3:3–57.

LOCKHART, WILLIAM B.; KAMISAR, YALE; and CHOPER, JESSE H. (1964) 1980   *Constitutional Law: Cases—Comments—Questions.* St. Paul, Minn.: West Publishing Co.

PENNOCK, ROLAND J. and CHAPMAN, JOHN W., eds.   1977   *Due Process.* New York: New York University Press.

TRIBE, LAURENCE H.   1978   *American Constitutional Law.* Mineola, N.Y.: Foundation Press.

———   1985   *Constitutional Choices.* Cambridge, Mass.: Harvard University Press.

SUBSTANTIVE DUE PROCESS
(Update 1)

In the period preceding the NEW DEAL, DUE PROCESS OF LAW meant more than a guaranty of procedural regularity; it also embodied a substantive dimension that curtailed the role of the state in altering the outcomes of private marketplace decisions. This was the era of LOCHNER V. NEW YORK (1905), in which the Supreme Court decreed that government could intervene only to aid parties deemed in special need of paternalistic measures, such as minors and women, or to address externalities (where private bargains impose uncompensated costs on third parties). During a time of considerable social unrest, Lochnerian jurisprudence imposed sharp limits on the domain of ordinary politics while, in many quarters, also placing in question the very legitimacy of JUDICIAL REVIEW.

With the onset of the Great Depression, the growing political demands on government to curb instability in markets, to reduce widespread unemployment, and to bolster consumer demand forced the Court to alter its conception of the role of the state. Thus, in NEBBIA V. NEW YORK (1934) and WEST COAST HOTEL CO. V. PARRISH (1937), the Court rejected *Lochner*'s narrow definition of permissible governmental goals. Legislative efforts to redistribute wealth through social programs or enhance the bargaining positions of weaker parties were now legitimate exercises of power. With the permissible ends of government thus broadened, the Court soon indicated in UNITED STATES V. CAROLENE PRODUCTS CO. (1938) that *Lochner*'s rigorous insistence on a close fit of "ends" and "means" in ECONOMIC REGULATION had to yield to a policy of judicial deference to reasonably debatable economic measures. The hands-off approach to economic regulations with a RATIONAL BASIS also extended to decisions narrowly construing the reach of the CONTRACT CLAUSE and the takings clause.

This policy of judicial deference would not necessarily extend beyond the economic sphere, however. Justice HARLAN FISKE STONE, in his famous footnote four to *Carolene Products*, explained that regulations interfering with fundamental personal liberties and burdening disadvantaged minority groups would be subjected to a more demanding level of scrutiny. This dual standard for review allowed the Court in a number of decisions that culminated in ROE V. WADE (1973) to apply STRICT SCRUTINY to government action interfering with private decisions within a "zone of privacy" that included the intimate realms of marriage, reproduction, and child rearing.

In the years since 1985, without rejecting this dual framework, the Court has confined the privacy interests protected by substantive due process to those that reflect deeply entrenched, widely held traditional values. In *Michael H. v. Gerald D.* (1989) the state's traditional interest in the "unitary family" prevailed over a natural father's paternity claim where the child was born into an extant marital family. Most prominently, in BOWERS V. HARDWICK (1986) the Court held that Georgia could criminalize the act of homosexual sodomy between consenting adults committed in the privacy of the home. Justice BYRON R. WHITE's opinion for the majority explained that the right

life support, contrary to the wishes of her parents and a court-appointed guardian, in the absence of clear and convincing evidence of her own preferences expressed when competent. Yet five Justices plainly stated that the Constitution requires compliance with the terms of a "living will" executed by a competent adult. Similarly, in *Glucksberg*, while the Court unanimously rejected the argument that terminally ill patients possess a constitutional right to commit suicide with physician assistance, a majority of five Justices intimated that the Constitution would not permit a state to forbid physicians from prescribing drugs for terminally ill patients suffering great pain, even if those drugs were likely to induce death.

Glucksberg sheds light on the status of substantive due process in the late 1990s. The open-ended discretion to right perceived wrongs afforded by such a doctrine is too attractive for the Justices entirely to repudiate it. At the same time, however, the lesson that the Court seems to have derived from a quarter-century's worth of criticism in the face of *Roe v. Wade* is that it must be more cautious in applying the doctrine. *Roe* effectively nullified the abortion statutes of forty-six states. In *Glucksberg*, the Court was unwilling to invalidate the laws of the forty-nine states that, as of 1997, continued to criminalize physician-assisted suicide. How substantive due process doctrine evolves in the future with regard to the right to die will depend, as CONSTITUTIONAL INTERPRETATION generally does, on changes in social mores.

MICHAEL J. KLARMAN
(2000)

Bibliography

CORWIN, EDWARD S. 1911 The Doctrine of Due Process Before the Civil War. *Harvard Law Review* 24:366–385; 460–479.

ELY, JOHN HART 1973 The Wages of Crying Wolf: A Comment on *Roe v. Wade*. *Yale Law Journal* 82:920–949.

GILLMAN, HOWARD 1993 *The Constitution Besieged: The Rise and Demise of Lochner Era Police Powers Jurisprudence.* Durham, N.C.: Duke University Press.

GREY, THOMAS 1978 Origins of the Unwritten Constitution. *Stanford Law Review* 30:843–893.

PERRY, MICHAEL 1976 Abortion, the Public Morals and the Police Power: The Ethical Function of Substantive Due Process. *UCLA Law Review* 23:689–736.

SHERRY, SUZANNA 1987 The Founders' Unwritten Constitution. *University of Chicago Law Review* 54:1127–1177.

SUNSTEIN, CASS R. 1997 The Right to Die. *Yale Law Journal* 106:1123–1163.

SUBVERSIVE ACTIVITIES CONTROL BOARD

The INTERNAL SECURITY ACT of 1950 created the Subversive Activities Control Board (SACB). This agency was to determine, on request of the ATTORNEY GENERAL, whether a particular organization was a communist-action, communist-front, or communist-infiltrated organization. After SACB had issued an order so designating an organization and after the order had been sustained by the courts, various disabilities and sanctions could be imposed on the group and its members. These included being barred from federal jobs, being denied employment in defense-related industries, and being prohibited from using United States passports.

Eleven years after SACB's creation, the Supreme Court sustained its findings that the Communist party was a communist-action organization as defined by the act and upheld an order requiring the party to register. (See COMMUNIST PARTY V. SACB, 1961.) The Court subsequently declared unconstitutional attempts to implement the sanctions of the act, and in 1965 (ALBERTSON V. SACB) it ruled that the forced registration of individual members of the party would violate the RIGHT AGAINST SELF-INCRIMINATION. By the late 1960s, SACB was moribund. Congress, attempting salvage, gave it authority to register with the attorney general the names of persons it had determined were members of communist organizations, and SACB eventually declared seven persons to be in this category. Such limited action, as well as a 1967 decision holding unconstitutional provisions barring members of registered organizations from jobs in defense-related industries, further limited SACB's utility. In 1974, the RICHARD M. NIXON administration, bowing to SACB's critics, requested no further funding, effectively ending its life.

PAUL L. MURPHY
(1986)

Bibliography

MURPHY, PAUL L. 1972 *The Constitution in Crisis Times, 1918–1969.* New York: Harper & Row.

SUBVERSIVE ACTIVITY

Activity is "subversive" if it is directed toward the overthrow of the existing form of government by force or other unlawful means. Subversive activity comprises SEDITION, insurrection, and sabotage, as well as other unlawful acts committed with the requisite intent. Although individuals may engage in subversive activity, concerted or organized subversion is more common and excites more public concern. Active, purposive membership in subversive organizations—such as the Communist party, the American Nazi party, or the Ku Klux Klan—is a federal crime, and between 1950 and 1974 the ATTORNEY GENERAL'S LIST was maintained as an official catalog of such groups.

In twentieth-century America, the suppression of subversion has been controversial where the "activity" has seemed to consist primarily of SUBVERSIVE ADVOCACY. But the controversy should not obscure the fact that there is such a thing as subversive activity and that the survival of constitutional government requires that such activity be controlled.

The critical distinction is not between words and deeds, speech and action. Even the staunchest defenders of CIVIL LIBERTIES agree that INCITEMENT TO UNLAWFUL CONDUCT may be punished by law, at least when the speaker has the intention and capability of inducing his hearers to engage in insurrection, riot, or disobedience of law. Some forms of subversive activity—for example, the attack on the House of Representatives by Puerto Rican nationalists in 1954—are extreme forms of SYMBOLIC SPEECH, known in revolutionary jargon as "propaganda of the deed." The political goal toward which it is aimed is precisely what distinguishes subversive activity.

Because the government of the United States is one of limited and ENUMERATED POWERS, its authority to define and punish subversive activities as crimes is not entirely clear. Treason is defined in Article III, section 2, of the Constitution, and as the same section limits the range of punishment for treason, it implies the power of Congress to prescribe punishment within the permitted range. The Constitution does not define any lesser degree of subversive activity, nor does it expressly grant to Congress the power to define and punish such crimes. Instead, the power must be an IMPLIED POWER incidental to the power to punish treason or else NECESSARY AND PROPER for the carrying out of one or more of the enumerated powers.

In the absence of statutes against insurrection or rebellion, the perpetrators of FRIES' REBELLION and the WHISKEY REBELLION were tried for treason. The prosecutors argued that an armed rising to prevent the execution of federal law—the normal definition of insurrection—was at least a constructive treason as the COMMON LAW had understood the term. Similarly, when AARON BURR assembled an armed force in the Western territories, for purposes that are still not entirely clear, the only federal offense for which he could be tried was treason. But a charge of treason seems manifestly to have been inappropriate in each of these cases.

On the other hand, the ALIEN AND SEDITION ACTS, enacted when the country was on the brink of war with France, generously defined offenses against the United States. Although section 2, defining SEDITIOUS LIBEL, is more famous, section 1 of the Sedition Act proscribed certain subversive activities: combination or conspiracy to impede the operation of law or to intimidate government officials, procuring or counseling riot or insurrection—whether or not the activity was successful. The ESPIONAGE ACT OF 1917, enacted while the country was fighting World War I, treated as criminal any attempt to procure draft evasion or to interfere with military recruitment while the Sedition Act of 1918 proscribed all advocacy of revolution, however remote the prospect of success.

In the latter half of the twentieth century, the phenomenon of political terrorism raised new problems. Frequently directed from outside the United States, terrorist activity, like the extreme forms of subversive activity, employs politically motivated violence. Although the aim of terrorism may not be the overthrow of the American government, terrorism shares with the more extreme forms of subversive activity the substitution of violence for public deliberation and constitutional government.

DENNIS J. MAHONEY
(1986)

Bibliography

GRODZINS, MORTON 1956 *The Loyal and the Disloyal: Social Boundaries of Patriotism and Treason.* Chicago: University of Chicago Press.

HURST, JAMES WILLARD 1971 *The Law of Treason in the United States.* Westport, Conn.: Greenwood Press.

SUBVERSIVE ADVOCACY

The quest for NATIONAL SECURITY has placed strains on the FIRST AMENDMENT when the country has been at war, or threatened by war, or torn by fear of an external enemy or domestic social unrest. Federal and state governments have sought to silence those regarded as "subversives" and internal enemies because they supported a foreign cause or advocated revolutionary change in American institutions.

The ALIEN AND SEDITION ACTS, passed only seven years after ratification of the First Amendment, were the most extreme of these measures in our history. President JOHN ADAMS and the Federalist Congress used them to stifle the opposition Republicans who were accused of being "servile minions" of France, with which war seemed imminent in early 1798. Seventeen prosecutions were instituted against Republican newspaper editors, officeholders, and adherents, with only one acquittal.

The constitutionality of the Sedition Act was never tested in the Supreme Court, which then had no JURISDICTION to review federal criminal convictions. But the act was sustained by the lower federal courts, including three Supreme Court Justices sitting as trial judges. The modern Supreme Court, in NEW YORK TIMES CO. V. SULLIVAN (1964), has stated that the First Amendment bars prosecution for SEDITIOUS LIBEL. Opposition to the government in power, accompanied by criticism of official policy and conduct, cannot constitutionally be proscribed as "seditious" or "subversive."

During the nineteenth century there was no federal legislation limiting FREEDOM OF SPEECH or FREEDOM OF THE PRESS. No official efforts were made to silence the Federalist denunciation of the War of 1812. Abolitionist sentiment did not fare so well in the succeeding decades of bitter controversy over slavery. Southern states passed laws limiting the freedom to criticize slavery. During the CIVIL WAR no sedition act was passed to suppress the widespread opposition to the war in the North. But President ABRAHAM LINCOLN suspended the writ of HABEAS CORPUS, controlled the mails, telegraph, and passports, and approved military detention of thousands of persons accused of disloyalty.

The rapid industrialization and urbanization of the country after the Civil War was accompanied by social unrest. The Haymarket Square bombing in Chicago in 1886, the violent Homestead and Pullman strikes in the 1890s, the assassination of President WILLIAM MCKINLEY in 1901 by a presumed "anarchist," and the militant tactics of the Industrial Workers of the World led to the passage of the first state Criminal Anarchy Law in New York in 1902. By 1921, thirty-three states had enacted similar laws making it a crime to advocate the overthrow of existing government by force or violence. Unlike the Sedition Act of 1798, these laws forbade only the advocacy of illegal means to effect political change.

Together with the federal ESPIONAGE ACT of 1917, these state laws were used to suppress opposition to WORLD WAR I voiced by pacifists, sympathizers with Germany, and international socialists. The 1917 act made it criminal to obstruct recruiting, cause insubordination in the armed forces, or interfere with military operations. Amendments to the Espionage Act (the SEDITION ACT of 1918) made it an offense, among other things, to say or do anything that would favor any country at war with the United States, oppose the cause of the United States in the war, or incite contempt for the American form of government or the uniform of the Army or Navy. Under the Espionage Act 877 people were convicted, almost all for expressing opinions about the merits and conduct of the war. The Supreme Court sustained these convictions, rejecting the contention that they violated the First Amendment.

SCHENCK V. UNITED STATES (1919) was the first of the Espionage Act cases to reach the Supreme Court. Justice OLIVER WENDELL HOLMES wrote the Court opinion affirming the conviction and, for the first time, enunciated the CLEAR AND PRESENT DANGER test to determine when advocacy of unlawful conduct is protected by the First Amendment. Holmes also wrote the opinions of the Court in FROHWERK V. UNITED STATES (1919) and DEBS V. UNITED STATES (1919), sustaining the convictions of a newspaper editor for questioning the constitutionality of the draft and charging that Wall Street had dragged the country into the war, and of Eugene V. Debs, the railroad union and Socialist party leader, for denouncing the war as a capitalist plot. Just what the "clear and present danger" was in these cases was doubtful, and Holmes and Brandeis soon began to dissent from the way the majority used the test.

Their first great dissent came in ABRAMS V. UNITED STATES (1919). In his dissenting opinion, which Brandeis joined, Holmes gave new content to the clear and present danger test by emphasizing the immediacy of the danger that must exist. Although Holmes would have softened this requirement, permitting punishment of speech with the specific intent to bring about the danger even if the danger itself was not "immediate," he did not think the necessary intent had been shown in *Abrams*.

The Red Scare of 1919 and 1920 was induced not only by fear of the Bolshevik revolution and the Communist International but also by the economic and social insecurity that accompanied demobilization after World War I. The PALMER RAIDS expressed the federal government's fears and antiradical sentiments. The states resorted to their criminal anarchy laws and the Supreme Court sustained convictions under these laws in GITLOW V. NEW YORK (1925) and WHITNEY V. CALIFORNIA (1927).

In *Gitlow* the Court assumed that freedom of speech and press, protected by the First Amendment from abridgment by Congress, was a "liberty" protected by the DUE PROCESS clause of the FOURTEENTH AMENDMENT against state impairment. In both *Gitlow* and *Whitney* the Court refused to apply the clear and present danger test because the state legislatures had prohibited a particular class of speech—the advocacy of the doctrine that the government should be overthrown by violence. Gitlow's advocacy of violent revolution violated the law even if there were no clear and present danger of revolution. The legislature might reasonably seek "to extinguish the spark without waiting until it has enkindled the flame or blazed into the conflagration."

Dissenting in *Gitlow*, Holmes argued for application of the clear and present danger test, but did not confront the majority's position. But Brandeis, concurring in *Whitney*, insisted that courts and juries must be free to decide whether, under the circumstances of each case, "the evil apprehended is [relatively serious and its incidence] so imminent that it may befall before there is opportunity for full discussion. . . . Only an emergency can justify repression."

From the end of the Red Scare to the outbreak of WORLD WAR II, federal action against alleged subversives was limited to deportation of alien communists. State prosecutions under criminal anarchy laws were infrequent after the middle 1920s. The Sedition Act of 1918 was repealed in 1921 and has never been revived.

The Smith Act of 1940 was modeled on the New York Criminal Anarchy law. During World War II, twenty-eight pro-Nazi individuals were prosecuted under it for conspiring to cause insubordination in the armed forces, but the judge died and the prosecution was dropped. Eighteen members of the Trotskyist Socialist Workers party, which opposed the war, were convicted of conspiracy to cause insubordination in the armed forces and to advocate violent overthrow of the government.

On the whole, the country supported World War II. After the Nazi invasion of the Soviet Union, in June 1941, communists became the staunchest supporters of the war. But as soon as the war was won, the activities of the international communist movement resumed. In 1949 eleven leaders of the Communist party were convicted under the Smith Act for conspiring to advocate violent overthrow of the United States government and establishment of a dictatorship of the proletariat, and to organize the Communist party to advocate these goals. The Supreme Court affirmed the convictions, 6–2, in DENNIS V. UNITED STATES (1951).

In 1948 the Soviet Union had blockaded Berlin and engineered the communist coup that overthrew the parliamentary regime in Czechoslovakia. By the time the Supreme Court decided *Dennis*, several Soviet spy rings in the West had been exposed, the communists had taken control in China, and Americans were dying in the KOREAN WAR. The domestic and foreign policies of the American Communist party were consistent with Soviet policies and directives. In light of these events, a plurality of four Justices, speaking through Chief Justice FRED M. VINSON, reformulated the clear and present danger test into a BALANCING TEST that weighed the seriousness of the danger, discounted by its improbability, against the degree of invasion of freedom of speech.

Justice FELIX FRANKFURTER concurred, deferring to Congress's judgment regarding the extent of the danger posed by the Communist party and the world communist movement. With the experience of the Nuremberg war crimes trials still fresh in his memory, Justice ROBERT H. JACKSON also concurred, joining Frankfurter in rejecting the appropriateness of the clear and present danger test to the communist conspiracy.

Though not purporting to overrule *Dennis*, the Supreme Court, in YATES V. UNITED STATES (1957), reversed convictions of the officers of the Communist party in California. Justice JOHN MARSHALL HARLAN's plurality opinion read the Smith Act as requiring proof that the defendants had advocated "unlawful action" and not merely "abstract doctrine" that the United States government should be overthrown. *Yates* did not represent a return to the Holmes-Brandeis version of the clear and present danger test. It emphasized the content of the advocacy, not its consequences. On this view, advocacy of unlawful action was punishable, irrespective of the immediacy of the danger.

After *Yates* was decided, the government concluded that it could not satisfy the requirements of proof demanded by the Supreme Court and abandoned all prosecutions under the Smith Act. Altogether twenty-nine communists were convicted under that act, including the leaders involved in *Dennis* and the only person convicted under the provision proscribing membership in the Communist party. His conviction was upheld in SCALES V. UNITED STATES (1961) because he was an "active member" who knew of the Party's unlawful goals and had a "specific intent" to achieve them.

In 1950, shortly after the outbreak of the Korean War, Congress enacted the SUBVERSIVE ACTIVITIES CONTROL ACT, which required communist organizations to register with the ATTORNEY GENERAL. When the Communist party failed to register, the attorney general asked the Subversive Activities Control Board to order it to register and list its members. In COMMUNIST PARTY V. SUBVERSIVE ACTIVITIES CONTROL BOARD (1961) the Court upheld the board's finding that the party was a communist-action organization and its order requiring the party to register. Only Justice HUGO L. BLACK dissented from the majority view that the First Amendment did not prohibit Congress from removing the party's "mask of anonymity."

The Supreme Court in 1961 did not pass upon the contention that compulsory registration would violate the RIGHT AGAINST SELF-INCRIMINATION afforded by the Fifth Amendment because it would subject party members to prosecution under the Smith Act and the 1954 COMMUNIST CONTROL ACT. This contention was eventually sustained in ALBERTSON V. SUBVERSIVE ACTIVITIES CONTROL BOARD (1965). As a result, neither the Communist party nor any of its members ever registered under the act, and no organization ever registered as a communist front. In 1968, Congress removed the registration obligation. Instead, the Subversive Activities Control Board was authorized to keep records, open to public inspection, of the names and addresses of communist organizations and their members. But in 1969 and 1970 the courts held that mere membership in the party was protected by the First Amendment, and the board was disbanded in 1973.

The Communist Control Act of 1954 purported to deprive the Communist party of the "rights, privileges, and immunities attendant upon legal bodies." It was not clear whether Congress intended this provision to dissolve the party as a legal organization or only to bar it from the ballot and benefits such as mailing privileges. Though the Supreme Court has not passed upon its constitutionality, the act has become a dead letter.

Although the Espionage Act and the Smith Act remained in force during the VIETNAM WAR, no prosecutions were brought under either measure. In *Bond v. Floyd* (1966) the Supreme Court assumed that opposition to the war and the draft was protected by the First Amendment.

In 1967 a Ku Klux Klan leader was convicted of violating the Ohio CRIMINAL SYNDICALISM LAW by making a speech at a Klan rally to which only television newsmen had been invited. The speech was derogatory of blacks and Jews and proclaimed that if the white race continued to be threatened, "it's possible that there might have to be some revengence [sic] taken." In a PER CURIAM opinion in BRANDENBURG V. OHIO (1969) the Supreme Court reversed the conviction and held the Ohio statute unconstitutional. In so doing, it overruled *Whitney v. California* and again reformulated the clear and present danger doctrine: "constitutional guarantees of free speech and free press do not permit a State to forbid or proscribe advocacy of the use of force or of law violation except where such advocacy is directed to inciting or producing such action." Although the Court purported to follow *Dennis*, commentators generally conclude that *Brandenburg* overruled *Dennis*. In *Communist Party of Indiana v. Whitcomb* (1974) the Supreme Court held that it was unconstitutional for Indiana to refuse a place on the ballot to the Communist party of Indiana because its officers had refused to submit an oath that the party "does not advocate the overthrow of local, state or national government by force or violence."

The *Brandenburg* formula, the most speech-protective standard yet evolved by the Supreme Court, has been criticized from opposing sides. Concurring in *Brandenburg*, Justices WILLIAM O. DOUGLAS and Black would have abandoned the clear and present danger test in favor of a distinction between ideas and overt acts. Some critics reject even this concession on the ground that an incitement-of-overt-acts test can be manipulated by the courts to cut off speech just when it comes close to being effective.

Others argue that advocacy of the forcible overthrow of the government, or of any unlawful act, is not protected by the First Amendment. Such advocacy is not political speech because it is a call to revoke the results that political speech has produced; violent overthrow destroys the premises of our system. An organization that seeks power through illegal means refuses to abide by the legitimate conditions of party competition in a democracy.

Furthermore, in suppressing totalitarian movements, even if they purport to reject illegal means, a democratic society is not acting to protect the status quo but the very

same interest which freedom of speech itself seeks to secure—the possibility of peaceful progress under freedom. In this view, the *Brandenburg* formula would deny our democracy the constitutional right to act until it might be too late to prevent a totalitarian victory.

Although one may disagree with the view that the problem of a totalitarian party's competing for political power in a democracy is solely one of "freedom of expression," the reasons for toleration—to keep even the freedom of expression open to challenge lest it become a "dead dogma," and to allow extremist groups to advocate revolution because they may represent real grievances that deserve to be heard—must be seriously considered by legislators in determining whether suppression is a wise policy. But if wisdom may sometimes dictate toleration, that conclusion does not imply that the Constitution gives the enemies of freedom the right to organize to crush it.

CARL A. AUERBACH
(1986)

Bibliography

GUNTHER, GERALD   1975   Learned Hand and the Origins of Modern First Amendment Doctrine: Some Fragments of History. *Stanford Law Review* 27:719–773.

LEVY, LEONARD W.   1985   *Emergence of a Free Press.* New York: Oxford University Press.

LINDE, HANS A.   1970   "Clear and Present Danger" Reexamined: Dissonants in the Brandenburg Concerto. *Stanford Law Review* 22:1163–1186.

NATHANSON, NATANIEL L.   1950   The Communist Trial and the Clear-and-Present-Danger Test. *Harvard Law Review* 63: 1167–1175.

SUFFRAGE

See: Alien Suffrage; Woman Suffrage;
Woman Suffrage Movement

SUGARMAN v. DOUGALL
413 U.S. 634 (1973)

GRIFFITHS, IN RE
413 U.S. 717 (1973)

In *Sugarman*, the Supreme Court held, 8–1, that New York's law making ALIENS ineligible for civil service employment was unconstitutional. In *Griffiths*, the Court held, 7–2, that Connecticut could not constitutionally bar resident aliens from the practice of law. Both decisions rested on EQUAL PROTECTION grounds. Justice LEWIS F. POWELL, writing for the Court in *Griffiths*, concluded that the state had not shown that excluding aliens from law practice was necessary to serve an interest sufficiently substantial to justify the rule. In *Sugarman*, Justice HARRY A. BLACKMUN wrote for the Court, repeating what he had said in GRAHAM V. RICHARDSON (1971), that discrimination against aliens must survive STRICT SCRUTINY by the courts. Here the bar to aliens was not necessary to achieve any substantial interest. Justice Blackmun added that some discrimination against aliens would be justified in the name of "political community": the right to vote or to hold high public office, for example, might be limited to citizens. These OBITER DICTA assumed importance in the later cases of FOLEY V. CONNELIE (1978) and AMBACH V. NORWICK (1979).

KENNETH L. KARST

(1986)

SUGAR TRUST CASE

See: *Knight Company, E. C., United States v.*

SULLIVAN, UNITED STATES v.
332 U.S. 689 (1948)

In no other case has the Supreme Court more sweepingly construed the COMMERCE CLAUSE. To protect consumers the Federal Food, Drug, and Cosmetic Act of 1938, passed under the NATIONAL POLICE POWER, prohibited the misbranding of drugs "held for sale after interstate shipment." Nine months after a bottle of sulfathiazole tablets had been shipped from Chicago to Atlanta, a retail druggist in Columbus, Georgia, who had purchased the bottle, properly labeled with a warning that the drug could be toxic, sold twelve tablets in a box without the mandatory warning. The local druggist thereby committed a federal crime. A federal court of appeals reversed his conviction on the ground that the words "held for sale after interstate shipment" extended only to the first intrastate sale and could not apply to all subsequent local sales after any lapse of time.

The Supreme Court, in an opinion by Justice HUGO L. BLACK for a bare majority, reversed and sustained the constitutionality of the statute. Black declared that it prohibited misbranding no matter when the drug was sold and without regard to how many local sales intervened; the statute remained in force "to the moment of . . . delivery to the ultimate consumer" in an intrastate transaction. Sullivan, the druggist, had contended that the statute so construed exceeded the commerce power and invaded powers reserved to the states under the TENTH AMENDMENT. Black replied merely that a 1913 precedent, *McDermott v. Wisconsin*, which had sustained the misbranding provision of

the PURE FOOD AND DRUG ACT of 1906, controlled the case. He thought that the "variants" between the two cases were "not sufficient" to distinguish *McDermott*, although he conceded that the retailer in *McDermott* had been the direct consignee of an interstate shipment. That fact should have made the precedent inapplicable. Black did not take notice that in *McDermott* the Court had reversed the state conviction of a grocer who misbranded under state law but complied with federal law. Black did not consider that under the ORIGINAL PACKAGE DOCTRINE the druggist sold local merchandise. Justice WILEY RUTLEGE concurred without reaching the constitutional issue and like the three dissenters wrote only on the construction of the statute.

After *Sullivan* the commerce power seemed to have no stratable limits, though the rationale of the decision is unclear. The transaction involved in *Sullivan* was neither INTRASTATE COMMERCE that affected INTERSTATE COMMERCE, nor the PRODUCTION of goods for interstate commerce. The reach of the national police power, which began with CHAMPION V. AMES (1903), seems to have no end.

LEONARD W. LEVY

(1986)

SUMNER, CHARLES
(1811–1874)

In 1833 Charles Sumner, a protege of JOSEPH STORY, graduated from Harvard Law School. Until 1851 he practiced law, taught at Harvard Law School, annotated Vesey's Chancery Reports, and became a well-known lecturer advocating, among other reforms, world peace and abolition of SLAVERY. In 1848 Sumner was an unsuccessful Free Soil candidate for Congress, campaigning against the "lords of the lash and the lords of the loom." In ROBERTS V. BOSTON (1849) Sumner unsuccessfully challenged government compulsion of SEGREGATION in Boston schools, arguing that racially separate schools denied equality. In upholding segregation, Massachusetts Chief Justice LEMUEL SHAW enunciated, for the first time, the doctrine of SEPARATE BUT EQUAL.

In 1851 Sumner won the SENATE seat once held by DANIEL WEBSTER. In his first speech, "Freedom National, Slavery Sectional," Sumner attacked the fugitive slave law and congressional support of slavery for nearly four hours. In an 1856 speech, "The Crime Against Kansas," Sumner vilified senators who had supported the KANSAS-NEBRASKA ACT. He described STEPHEN A. DOUGLAS as "the squire of slavery, its very Sancho Panza, ready to do all its humiliating offices." South Carolina's Andrew Butler was, in Sumner's view, the Don Quixote of slavery who had "chosen a mistress to whom he has made his vows, and who, though ugly to others . . . is chaste in his sight; I mean the harlot slavery." Two days later Congressman Preston Brooks, a relative of Butler, repaid Sumner for these remarks by beating him insensible with a cane. Many Northerners viewed this incident as a symbol of a violent slavocracy which threatened the Constitution and the nation. After a three-and-a-half-year convalescence Sumner returned to the Senate in 1860, renewing his crusade against bondage with a four-hour oration, "The Barbarism of Slavery." This speech became a Republican campaign document in 1860.

From the beginning of the CIVIL WAR Sumner urged the abolition of slavery. He argued that secession was STATE SUICIDE, that the Confederate States had reverted to territorial status, and that, despite the decision in DRED SCOTT V. SANDFORD, Congress had the power to end slavery in these TERRITORIES. On a less theoretical level Sumner successfully sponsored legislation to repeal the fugitive slave laws and to allow black witnesses to testify in federal courts. Sumner was unsuccessful, however, in his attempts to gain congressional support for the integration of Washington's street railroads and other facilities. As chairman of the Senate Foreign Relations Committee, Sumner was constantly at odds with Secretary of State WILLIAM SEWARD, and often served as President ABRAHAM LINCOLN's unofficial adviser on foreign policy. Sumner exploited that position to gain diplomatic recognition for Haiti and Liberia and to secure a passport for a black constituent. As chairman of the Select Committee on Slavery and Freedmen, Sumner laid the groundwork for the FREEDMEN'S BUREAU.

During Reconstruction, Sumner was the Senate's most vociferous advocate of black rights and an early opponent of ANDREW JOHNSON. Sumner's increasingly moralistic and uncompromising posture undermined his legislative effectiveness during Reconstruction. Sumner initially opposed the THIRTEENTH and FOURTEENTH AMENDMENTS because they failed to give blacks enough rights. He gave little support to the FIFTEENTH AMENDMENT because he believed the Constitution embodied the highest moral principles and thus enabled Congress under existing constitutional powers to enfranchise blacks. After 1870 Sumner devoted himself to a comprehensive CIVIL RIGHTS bill, which would give the freedmen complete equality. Its passage, in a somewhat truncated form, as the CIVIL RIGHTS ACT OF 1875 was a posthumous tribute to Sumner's integrity and his passionate devotion to racial equality.

PAUL FINKELMAN
(1986)

Bibliography

DONALD, DAVID HERBERT 1960 *Charles Sumner and the Coming of the Civil War.* New York: Knopf.
——— 1970 *Charles Sumner and the Rights of Man.* New York: Knopf.

SUNDAY CLOSING LAWS

The first compulsory Sunday observance law in what is now the United States was promulgated in Virginia in 1610. It made absence from church services punishable by death for the third offense. Although there is no record of any person suffering the death penalty, lesser penalties, including whipping, were in effect in all the colonies and were continued after independence. Implicit constitutional recognition of Sunday observance is found in Article I, section 7, which excepts Sundays from the ten days wherein the President is required to exercise his veto of bills adopted by Congress.

Before the Supreme Court ruled that the FIRST AMENDMENT was applicable to the states, it held, in *Hennington v. Georgia* (1896), that Georgia had not unconstitutionally burdened INTERSTATE COMMERCE by regulating the movement of freight trains on Sundays. Four years later, it held, in *Petit v. Minnesota* (1900), that the state had not denied DUE PROCESS in refusing to classify barbering as an act of necessity or charity that could legally be performed on Sundays.

In 1961, after the Court had ruled the First Amendment applicable to the states, it considered the constitutionality of three state Sunday closing laws under that Amendment in four cases, known collectively as the Sunday Closing Law Cases. Two, *McGowan v. Maryland* and *Two Guys from Harrison-Allentown, Inc. v. McGinley,* concerned owners of highway discount stores that were open for business seven days a week. The other two, *Gallagher v. Crown Kosher Super Market* and *Braunfeld v. Brown,* involved stores owned by Orthodox Jews, who, by reason of religious convictions, abstained from all business activities on Saturdays.

In these cases the statutes were challenged on three principal grounds: that the laws violated the ban on the ESTABLISHMENT OF RELIGION; that the statutes' crazy-quilt pattern of exemptions was arbitrary, constituting a denial of due process and the EQUAL PROTECTION OF THE LAWS (for example, in one of the states it was legal to sell fish and food stuffs wholesale, but not at retail; in another, merchandise customarily sold at beaches and amusement parks might be sold there, but not elsewhere); that, at least in respect to Jews, Seventh-Day Adventists, and others whose religions required rest on Saturday, the laws violated the constitutional protection of RELIGIOUS LIBERTY by making it economically difficult if not impossible for them to observe their own Sabbath when their competitors operated six days each week.

In all four cases the Court upheld the constitutionality of the challenged laws, with all the prevailing opinions written by Chief Justice EARL WARREN. He recognized that the laws challenged in these cases had been enacted in colonial times with the purpose of ensuring observance of the majoritarian Christian Sabbath as a religious obligation. However, he said, the religious origin of these statutes did not require their invalidation if their present purpose was secular.

Warren said that the modern purpose of the challenged statutes was to set aside a day for "rest, repose, relaxation, tranquillity"; the purpose was therefore secular rather than religious. The Maryland statutes, for example, permitted such Sunday activities as the operation of bathing beaches, amusement parks, and even pinball and slot machines, as well as the sale of alcoholic beverages and the performance of professional sports. That such exemptions are directly contrary to the religiosity of the Sabbath indicated clearly that the Sunday laws' present purpose was not religious.

Viewed as welfare legislation, the Sunday laws presented little constitutional difficulty. The Chief Justice noted in *McGowan* that numerous federal and state laws affecting public health, safety, conditions of labor, weekend diversion at parks and beaches, and cultural activities of various kinds, had long been upheld. To forbid a state from prescribing Sunday as a day of rest solely because centuries ago such laws had their genesis in religion would be a CONSTITUTIONAL INTERPRETATION based on hostility to the public welfare rather than the SEPARATION OF CHURCH AND STATE.

The Court had more difficulty in sustaining laws applied against persons observing a day other than Sunday as their divinely ordained day of rest. Six Justices agreed that state legislatures, if they so elected, could constitutionally exempt Sabbatarians from complying with Sunday law restrictions, but the free exercise clause did not mandate that they do so. However, a majority of the Court could not agree upon one opinion to that effect. The Chief Justice, speaking for a plurality of four, noted that while the clause secured freedom to hold any belief, it did not forbid regulation of secular practices merely because some persons might suffer economically if they obeyed the dictates of their religion. Income tax laws, for example, did not violate the clause even though they limited the amount of deductions for religious contributions. If a state regulated conduct by a general law, the purpose and effect of which were to advance secular goals, its action was valid despite its indirect burden on the exercise of religion unless the purpose could practicably be otherwise accomplished. A sabbatarian exemption would be hard to enforce, and would interfere with the goal of providing a uniform day of rest that as far as possible eliminated the atmosphere of commercial activity. The laws thus did not violate the free exercise clause.

In THORNTON V. CALDOR, INC. (1985) the Court went even further. It ruled unconstitutional, under the effect aspect of the purpose-effect-entanglement test of constitutionality under the establishment clause, a Connecticut law that accorded employees an absolute right not to work on their chosen Sabbath.

LEO PFEFFER
(1986)

Bibliography

PFEFFER, LEO (1953) 1967 *Church, State and Freedom.* Boston: Beacon Press.

STOKES, ANSON PHELPS 1950 *Church and State in the United States.* New York: Harper & Brothers.

SUPERMAJORITY RULES

A supermajority rule is a rule that requires a legislative body to pass a class of legislative enactments, such as treaties or bills of certain types, by more than a bare majority. Supermajority rules are created either by the legislature or by the Constitution. An example of a legislative supermajority rule is the requirement first adopted by the U.S. HOUSE OF REPRESENTATIVES in the 104th Congress that three-fifths of those voting are needed to pass an increase in income tax rates. Examples of constitutional supermajority rules include the clause requiring that two-thirds of the U.S. SENATE approve treaties and the provision allowing Congress to propose constitutional amendments only if two-thirds of the House and the Senate approve.

Supermajority rules have a number of justifications. Some matters such as constitutional amendments are thought to be so important that they require a greater-than-majority consensus. For other matters, supermajority rules are justified as necessary to offset what is thought to be the disproportionate power of special interests in a legislature governed by majority rule. For example, proposals to require supermajorities for tax increases has been based on the view that the power of special interests would otherwise lead to higher taxes than the majority of citizens actually prefers.

Controversy over federal legislative supermajority rules centers on whether Congress has the constitutional authority to enact them. Defenders of the constitutionality of such rules have argued (1) that the clause authorizing "each House [to] determine the Rules of its Proceedings" allows either house to pass whatever rules it chooses unless they violate a constitutional provision and (2) that no constitutional provision precludes supermajority rules. Those who attack the constitutionality of legislative supermajority rules argue that the constitutional clause allowing Congress to pass bills should be read to mean "pass by a majority." Defenders counter that neither constitutional history nor structure support this reading. One proposition accepted by both sides of the debate is that neither house may prevent a majority from repealing supermajority rules. This proposition, however, raises questions about the utility of such rules. If simple legislative majorities can undo legislative supermajority rules, they may not greatly restrain such majorities.

Constitutional supermajority rules, however, are more entrenched political norms and cannot be so easily undone. Constitutional supermajority rules represent a compromise between the two other principal forms of constitutional governance: rule by legislative majority and absolute constitutional limitations, such as those contained in the BILL OF RIGHTS. Like rule by legislative majority, supermajority rules allow Congress to make the decision whether to pass a bill. Like absolute constitutional limitations, however, supermajority rules restrain a simple majority from passing certain types of laws.

Proponents of constitutional supermajority rules argue that, as a third distinct form of constitutional governance, such rules will under certain circumstances be preferable to both legislative majority rule and absolute limitations. Supermajority rules will be superior to legislative majority rule when special interests (or other defects) undermine the majoritarian process. In these circumstances, supermajority rules may act as a constitutional filter, blocking more undesirable LEGISLATION than desirable legislation. Supermajority rules will function better than absolute limitations in areas where there is no determinate principle for judges to enforce or where it is inappropriate to give judges the authority that absolute limitations generally provide.

Opponents of supermajority rules suggest that they are inconsistent with democracy because they detract from majority rule and the principle that citizens should have equal influence on legislation. Proponents of constitutional supermajority rules respond that all constitutional limitations constrain simple democracy, and say that the question is whether these limitations will work well. Moreover, if supermajority rules are employed to limit special interests, proponents argue that such rules will in fact advance the democratic goal of equal influence.

MICHAEL B. RAPPAPORT
JOHN O. MCGINNIS
(2000)

Bibliography

AMAR, AKHIL REED et al. 1995 An Open Letter to Congressman Gingrich. *Yale Law Journal* 104:1539–1544.
McGINNIS, JOHN O. and RAPPAPORT, MICHAEL B. 1995 The Constitutionality of Supermajority Rules: A Defense. *Yale Law Journal* 105:470–483.
—— 1997 The Rights of Legislators and the Wrongs of Interpretation: A Further Defense of the Constitutionality of Legislative Supermajority Rules. *Duke Law Journal* 47:327–349.
—— 1999 Supermajority Rules as a Constitutional Solution. *William and Mary Law Review* 40:365–470.
RUBENFELD, JED 1996 Rights of Passage: Majority Rule in Congress. *Duke Law Journal* 46:73–90.

SUPREMACY CLAUSE

The supremacy clause of Article VI, clause 2, declares: "This Constitution and the Laws of the United States which shall be made in Pursuance thereof; and all Treaties made, or which shall be made, under the authority of the United States, shall be the supreme law of the Land." This principle of national supremacy was a radical departure from the constitutional order that prevailed under the ARTICLES OF CONFEDERATION. Whereas the Articles created a short-lived confederation of states—according to its terms a mere "league of friendship" founded on the good faith of sovereign states—the Constitution established a federal union designed to last in perpetuity. The distinguishing feature of the "more perfect union" created by the Constitution was a strong national government capable of dealing with the problems and complexities of a growing nation and strong state governments acting within their sphere of authority. The Constitution does not establish the supremacy of the national government in all things. National supremacy is limited to laws made Pursuant to the Constitution. What is not granted to the national government under its ENUMERATED POWERS is, as a general rule, reserved to the people or to the states under the TENTH AMENDMENT.

The supremacy clause may truly be regarded as the linchpin of American FEDERALISM. It holds the republic together by providing a principle for the resolution of conflicts between the states and the nation. Valid national law is clearly paramount in the face of conflicting state law. But whether a state law conflicts with federal law or a federal constitutional provision is not always clear. When doubts exist over the compatibility of federal and state law, and a real controversy arises from these doubts, the judiciary is usually called upon to work out the implications of the supremacy clause through interpretation. The outcome of such cases often depends on inferences drawn by the courts from the structure of the federal system and the values it represents.

The problems of interpretation generated by the supremacy clause have taken two forms epitomized by the celebrated cases of MCCULLOCH V. MARYLAND (1819) and GIBBONS V. OGDEN (1824). In the first Maryland taxed a national bank doing business within its borders; in the second New York granted a monopoly over steamboat navigation on its internal waterways. The supremacy clause operated to invalidate both measures. *McCulloch* stands for the principle that even a power reserved to the states—here the ordinary and indispensable power of taxation—may not be exercised in such a way as to impede or unduly burden a federal agency or activity; *Gibbons* stands for the principle that the state's regulation of a subject matter within its territory, and normally under its control, must give way before a conflicting, and valid, federal statute. "It is of the very essence of [national] supremacy," wrote Chief Justice JOHN MARSHALL, "to remove all obstacles to its action within its own sphere, and to so modify every power vested in subordinate governments as to exempt its own operation from . . . their influence." In both cases, Marshall underscored the plenary nature of the enumerated powers of Congress; they admit of no limitations save those prescribed in the Constitution. When combined with *McCulloch*'s doctrine of IMPLIED POWERS, fortified by the NECESSARY AND PROPER CLAUSE, the reach of federal power cuts a potentially deep furrow into the field of state SOVEREIGNTY.

This expansive view of federal power was for almost a century strongly contested by the doctrine of DUAL FEDERALISM. It held that nation and states were essentially equal in their respective spheres of influence. The doctrine did not hold that the states could decide for themselves the extent of their sovereign powers. Once again this was a judicial task, for dual federalism was an axiom of CONSTITUTIONAL INTERPRETATION. Beginning roughly in 1835, shortly after ROGER B. TANEY replaced Marshall as Chief Justice, the Supreme Court deployed and developed the concept of STATE POLICE POWER—broadly characterized as the power of a state to provide for the general welfare of its people—to limit the reach of national law. This movement attained its apogee in the first third of the twentieth century when the Supreme Court used the Tenth Amendment to invalidate numerous federal laws, all of them regulating various aspects of the economy. Most of these decisions supported the ideology of individualism and capitalism. The national statutes struck down by the Court were deemed to interfere with state police power yet arguably enacted pursuant to the delegated powers of Congress and clearly not expressly forbidden by the Constitution.

The year 1937 marks the collapse of the doctrine that state sovereignty constitutes a limitation on the exercise of power delegated by the Constitution to Congress. Since then the Supreme Court has returned and held steadfastly to the spirit of *McCulloch* and *Gibbons*. Even activities sponsored or operated by the state are subject to federal regulation when imposed pursuant to a delegated power. NATIONAL LEAGUE OF CITIES V. USERY (1976) is the only exception to this principle: in striking down a federal wage and hour provision as applied to state and local public employees, a closely divided Supreme Court ruled that such power—in this instance the federal commerce power—may not be exercised to interfere with "functions essential to the separate and independent existence" of the "states as states." The ghost of dual federalism lurks in *Usery*. In 1985, however, a closely divided Court overruled *Usery* in GARCIA V. SAN ANTONIO METROPOLITAN TRANSIT AUTHORITY.

In interpreting the supremacy clause today, the Supreme Court has given up the search for bright lines separating federal and state authority. The two levels of government are no longer perceived as antagonistic rivals, whatever the tensions between them. The supremacy clause once operated to immunize persons closely related to the federal government from most forms of state taxation. The pre-1937 doctrine of federal tax immunity, based on the generalized notion of federal supremacy rooted in *McCulloch*, was construed to invalidate such levies as state or local taxes on the income of federal employees, on interest income from federal bonds, on income derived from property leased by the federal government, and on sales to the United States. Since 1937, however, the Supreme Court with the help of Congress has wiped out most of this RECIPROCAL TAX IMMUNITY. The prevailing doctrine today, particularly after *United States v. New Mexico* (1982), is that a nondiscriminatory state tax even upon private contractors with close and intricate relationships with the federal government will not violate the supremacy clause unless the tax is imposed *directly* upon the United States.

In the field of regulation, too, sharp lines between federal and state authority are often difficult to find. Modern government is complex, involving the entanglement of federal and state policy in fields once regarded as exclusively state concerns. Education, conservation, aid to the poor and the handicapped, and environmental protection are prominent examples of such fields. The relationship between levels of government in all these areas today is one of cooperation and reciprocity. By means of FEDERAL GRANTS-IN-AID and other funding programs the national government, pursuant to its power of taxing and spending for the GENERAL WELFARE, has actually encouraged the states to pass laws and adopt policies in response to local needs. This new context of COOPERATIVE FEDERALISM does not mean, however, that the supremacy clause has lost its bite. Indeed, it has operated to establish the primacy of the national government even in some of the aforementioned fields. An example is *Blum v. Bacon* (1982), where the Supreme Court invalidated a New York law excluding recipients of a federal program aiding poor families with dependent children from receiving aid under the state's federally funded emergency welfare program. (*Blum* involved a state statutory policy that conflicted with a federal administrative regulation.)

As the preceding suggests, contemporary supremacy clause analysis is largely a matter of statutory interpretation. The supremacy clause has not been interpreted to prevent federal and state governments from regulating the same subject, partly out of the judiciary's recognition of the reality of cooperative federalism. The nature of some subjects (e.g., IMMIGRATION and NATURALIZATION, bankruptcy, PATENTS, and some articles of commerce) may require national uniform legislation. But most problems of American national life are valid topics of both national and state legislation (e.g., air and water pollution, motor carrier transportation, labor relations, consumer protection, and CIVIL RIGHTS). States and nation may legislate on these topics for similar or different reasons. The key to the validity of such concurrent or parallel legislation is whether both federal and state regulations can be enforced without impairing federal superintendence of the field. Even apparently conflicting state legislation may survive supremacy clause analysis if the state law deals with a field traditionally occupied by the state and the state's interest is substantial enough to offset any presumption that Congress may have intended to occupy the field all by itself. A principle of comity has thus replaced the earlier antagonism between nation and states characteristic of dual federalism. Today, as a general rule, unless Congress statutorily declares its intent to occupy a field, federal regulation preempts state law only where the latter seriously impedes the former.

Jones v. Roth Packing Company (1977) is a leading example of a case in which federal policy displaced state law notwithstanding the absence of explicit preemptive language in the congressional statute. Here the federal Fair Packaging and Labeling Act, enacted under the COMMERCE CLAUSE, was construed to conflict with a state consumer protection law dealing with the weight of certain goods packaged for sale. The Supreme Court read into the federal statute a congressional intent to supersede state law. Supersession was inferred from the supremacy clause because the enforcement of the state law was an obstacle to the full accomplishment and execution of the congressional purpose. In other cases federal PREEMPTION has been inferred because "[t]he scheme of federal regulation may be so pervasive as to make reasonable the inference that Congress left no room for the states to supplement it" or because "the Act of Congress may touch a field in which the federal interest is so dominant that the federal system will be assumed to preclude enforcement of state laws on the same subject." The supremacy clause thus remains a vital operative principle of American constitutional law even though the Supreme Court tends to presume the validity of concurrent state legislation, barring proof of its interference with federal policy.

DONALD P. KOMMERS
(1986)

Bibliography

CORWIN, EDWIN S. 1913 *National Supremacy: Treaty Power versus State Power.* New York: Holt.
SCHMIDHAUSER, JOHN R. 1958 *The Supreme Court as Final Arbiter of Federal-State Relations.* Chapel Hill: University of North Carolina Press.

SUPREME COURT
(History)

The only court whose existence is mandated by the Constitution is the Supreme Court. Article III states: "The judicial power of the United States shall be vested in one supreme court, and in such inferior courts as the Congress may from time to time ordain and establish." Besides its existence, a few attributes are constitutionally entrenched by Article III. The tenure of the judges is to be "during GOOD BEHAVIOR," and their compensation "shall not be diminished during their continuance in office." These provisions, modeled on English law and made applicable to all federal judges, were obviously intended to assure the independence of a judiciary appointed, pursuant to Article II, by the President with the ADVICE AND CONSENT of the SENATE.

Other features having a bearing on the character and independence of the Court were not addressed, presumably to be left at large or determined from time to time by Congress. Qualifications for membership on the Court were not specified; nor were the size of the Court, the period of its TERMS, or the level of the judges' compensation. The Court was to have both ORIGINAL JURISDICTION and APPELLATE JURISDICTION, but the latter was subject to "such exceptions, and under such regulations, as the Congress shall make." Nothing was said concerning the relation of the Supreme Court to the courts of the STATES.

Thus from the outset the Court was only partially sheltered from the politics of republican government. The status of the Court was one of those creative ambiguities that have marked the Constitution as no less an organism than a mechanism, Darwinian as well as Newtonian. The position of the Court may have been in the mind of an eminent modern foreign-born mathematician who, contemplating American CITIZENSHIP, regretted that he could not swear allegiance to the Constitution because "it is full of inconsistencies." In a self-governing nation, to be sure, the Court is detached but not disengaged, distant but not remote. Therein lay its potential either for popular neglect and scorn or for power and prestige.

The need for a federal judiciary, and so for an ultimate tribunal, was felt by the Framers as part of the transition from a confederation to a federal union. The ARTICLES OF CONFEDERATION supplied no such institution, except a supreme tribunal for prize and admiralty cases. A system of federal courts, parallel to those of the states, was one of the innovative conceptions of 1787. Their function was to serve as impartial tribunals, free of local bias, in suits between states, or controversies involving citizens of different states or a foreign country; to establish a uniform interpretation of federal laws; and to maintain the supremacy of federal law in cases where a state law conflicted with the Constitution, federal statutes, or treaties of the United States. In sum, the JURISDICTION OF THE FEDERAL COURTS could rest on the nature of the parties or of the question presented. Only in cases where a state, or a foreign country or its diplomatic representative, was a party was the Supreme Court given original (nonappellate) jurisdiction.

These skeletal provisions of Article III were fleshed out by Congress in the JUDICIARY ACT OF 1789. That act set the number of Supreme Court Justices at five associate Justices and one CHIEF JUSTICE, with salaries of $3,500 and $4,000, respectively. (The monetary differential remained at $500 until 1969, when it was increased to $2,500.) Three provisions of the act led to developments that proved to be of seminal importance for the prestige and power of the Supreme Court: a requirement that the Justices serve on regional CIRCUIT COURTS ("circuit riding"); a provision in section 13 that seemed to grant original jurisdiction to the Court to issue WRITS OF MANDAMUS; and a grant of power in section 25 to review the decisions of state supreme courts in cases turning on the Constitution, laws, or treaties of the United States. Each of these merits attention.

The circuit duties meant sitting with a federal district judge to form a circuit court, which heard appeals from district courts and had original jurisdiction in diversity of citizenship cases. In the early years circuit riding consumed the greater part of a Justice's time and surely his energy; travel by carriage or horseback over rough roads and stopovers at uncomfortable inns resulted in a weariness of flesh and spirit, against which the Justices complained bitterly, but which they forbore to resist. Yet these excursions into the local courthouses brought them into touch with lawyers, journalists, and townspeople, and gave a reality to the Supreme Court that its functioning in the capital city could not match. Moreover, the assignment of each Justice to a particular circuit affected significantly the appointments to the Court, for a vacancy on the Court would normally be filled by an appointment from the same circuit, and so at any time the practical range of nominees was limited and the influence of a small group of senators was proportionately great. Not until 1891, with the passage of the CIRCUIT COURTS OF APPEALS ACT, were the Justices fully relieved of circuit-riding duties. Thereafter geography played a decreasing role in appointments. A striking instance was the widely acclaimed appointment by President HERBERT C. HOOVER in 1932 of Judge BENJAMIN N. CARDOZO of New York to succeed Justice OLIVER WENDELL HOLMES of Massachusetts, although two New Yorkers, Chief Justice CHARLES EVANS HUGHES and Justice HARLAN FISKE STONE, were already on the Court. A comparable instance was the appointment by President Reagan in 1981 of Judge SANDRA DAY O'CONNOR of Arizona to succeed Justice POTTER STEWART of Ohio even though another Arizonan, Justice WILLIAM H. REHNQUIST, was already serving.

As circuit riding was a cardinal factor in gaining popular recognition of the Court (at considerable cost to the Justices) and in determining appointments, so did the practice furnish an early opportunity for the Court to judge the validity of an act of Congress. In the waning days of the Federalist administration, Congress passed the JUDICIARY ACT OF 1801, compounded of partisanship and principle, which created new judgeships and abolished circuit riding. When the Jeffersonians took office, however, they countered with the Judiciary Act of 1802, which abolished the judgeships and restored circuit riding. Chief Justice JOHN MARSHALL, sensing a political crisis for the Court, solicited the opinions of his brethren on the question of complying with the law or treating it as beyond the authority of Congress. The Justices had serious doubts about the law's validity, and a strong distaste for the resumption of the burden it imposed, yet a majority counseled compliance, in accord with Marshall's own inclination. But a private litigant, defeated in a circuit court in Virginia at which Marshall himself presided, appealed to the Supreme Court, arguing the unconstitutionality of the 1802 act. The Congress, fearing a judgment voiding the act, had abolished the 1802 term of the Supreme Court. When the case, STUART V. LAIRD, was decided, in February of 1803, the Court, with Marshall not participating, surprised and gratified the Jeffersonians by upholding the act, in a brief opinion which simply declared that acquiescence by the Court in circuit duty for twelve years under the Judiciary Act of 1789 had given a practical construction of the Constitution that would not now be disturbed. That the Court would at least consider the validity of an act of Congress had been resolved just six days earlier in the landmark case of MARBURY V. MADISON (1803).

That case, establishing the power of JUDICAL REVIEW of acts of Congress, marked the second of the three germinal developments from the Judiciary Act of 1789. Section 13, which gave the Court power to issue mandamus and other writs, might have been read simply as conferring the power where the jurisdiction of the Court rested on one of the grounds specified in Article III. But the Court was not of a mind for so narrow a reading. When William Marbury of Maryland invoked the original jurisdiction of the Court to enforce a right to an office of justice of the peace pursuant to an appointment by President JOHN ADAMS, and sought a mandamus to compel Secretary of State JAMES MADISON to deliver his commission, the Court regarded section 13 as conferring jurisdiction, and as so construed beyond the ambit of original jurisdiction defined in Article III. The suit for mandamus was therefore dismissed, again to the gratification of the Jeffersonians, but in the process the Court had declared the far more significant principle that in the decision of a case where a federal law was arguably incompatible with the Constitution, the Court, in deciding what "the law" was, must, if necessary, vindicate the HIGHER LAW and treat the legislative act as ineffectual.

Despite some provocative language in Marshall's opinion (the executive branch cannot "sport away" the rights of others), the Jeffersonians focused on the immediate result and regarded it as a victory at the hands of a still-Federalist Court. Indeed, judicial review was not then the divisive party issue; the Jeffersonians would have welcomed a Supreme Court decision holding the Sedition Act of 1798 unconstitutional. Whether Marshall's doctrine of judicial review was a usurpation later became a subject of heated debate, scholarly and unscholarly. Although the Constitution contains no specific mention of the power, and although Marshall's opinion, resting on the logic of the decisional process, can be said to beg the question of who is to decide, the debates in the CONSTITUTIONAL CONVENTION do indicate obliquely an acceptance of the power, in explaining the rejection of attempts to involve judges in an extrajudicial power of veto of legislation. But the debates were not cited in *Marbury*; MADISON'S NOTES, the most authoritative source, pursuant to the policy of secrecy, were not published until fifty years after the Convention.

The third of the salient projections from the Judiciary Act of 1789, involving section 25, produced more immediate partisan repercussions. Section 25 empowered the Court to review decisions of state courts that denied rights claimed under the federal Constitution, statutes, or treaties. Again, no constitutional provision explicitly conferred such power on the Supreme Court, although Article VI does declare the supremacy of federal law: "the judges in every state shall be bound thereby." By their silence, the Framers may have sought to avoid confrontations in the ratifying process, as in forbearing to be explicit about a national power to issue paper money or to establish a national bank.

The storm over the Court's power to review state court decisions was precipitated by its decision in MARTIN V. HUNTER'S LESSEE (1816) sustaining the validity of section 25. The case was a contest over title to the extensive Fairfax estate in the northern neck of Virginia, turning on the intricate interrelations of Virginia land law and treaties of the United States with Great Britain concerning ownership of land by British nationals. Holding that the Virginia court had misapplied both Virginia and federal law, the Supreme Court in 1813, through Justice JOSEPH STORY, reversed the state court's judgment and remanded the case to that court. A number of factors weakened the force of the decision. Story's opinion controverted the state court's even on points of the interpretation of state law, although section 25 itself limited review to federal questions. At a time when seven Justices constituted the Court, only four participated in the decision; the vote was 3–1, and the mandate to the Virginia court was unfortunately in the traditional form addressed to an inferior court, "you are hereby commanded, etc." The Virginia court was outraged and refused to obey the mandate. On a new WRIT OF ERROR to the Supreme Court, Story elaborated the justification of Supreme Court review in terms of the need for uniformity and supremacy of national law. The nature of the cause, not the court, was determinative of the Supreme Court's power to review (though critics wondered, no doubt unfairly, if the Supreme Court could then be given authority to review certain decisions of the House of Lords). John Marshall could not have uttered a pronouncement more nationalistic than that of the New England Republican appointed by President JAMES MADISON. (Marshall had excused himself because of his family's ownership of part of the land. Story, appointed in 1811 at the age of thirty-two, one of the most learned and powerful of Justices and a firm ally of Marshall, had been Madison's fourth choice to succeed WILLIAM CUSHING of Massachusetts: LEVI LINCOLN declined the nomination, Alexander Wolcott was rejected by the Senate, and JOHN QUINCY ADAMS also declined. Thus are the inevitabilities of history determined.)

In a sequel to the decision, the Court took the further step of sustaining its power to review even criminal judgments of state courts where a federal question, such as the interpretation of a federal law, was implicated. The opinion by Chief Justice Marshall in COHENS V. VIRGINIA (1821) was the climactic realization of the Court's vision of a uniform federal law and a Constitution that was supreme in reality as well as in principle.

Reaction to the *Cohens* decision by Jeffersonians, particularly in Virginia, was intense. Judge SPENCER ROANE, who instead of Marshall would probably have become Chief Justice if OLIVER ELLSWORTH had not resigned before Jefferson took office, published a series of bitter letters under pseudonyms, paying his respects to "A most monstrous and unexampled decision. It can only be accounted for from that love of power which all history informs us infects and corrupts all who possess it, and from which even the upright and eminent Judges are not exempt." The Court's "extravagant pretension" reached "the zenith of despotic power." In the following years a series of bills were introduced in Congress to repeal, in whole or in part, the appellate jurisdiction of the Supreme Court. Under these genial auspices was thus established a particularly sensitive and probably the most crucial power of the highest court in our federal union: the review of decisions of state courts in the interest of vindicating rights secured by the Constitution.

Conflicts between the Supreme Court, on the one hand, and the executive or legislative branches, or both, on the other, have occurred continually. The other branches have utilized the full spectrum of measures made available by the constitution. The most drastic of these, IMPEACHMENT, was the first to be tried; indeed it was designed as a trial run by Jefferson to prepare the way for a similar attack on Chief Justice Marshall. The immediate target was Justice SAMUEL CHASE, ardent Federalist, whose partisan outbursts in charges to the grand jury in Maryland furnished the occasion. The attempt misfired, however; Chase was narrowly acquitted in the Senate, owing probably to comparable overreaching by the fiery JOHN RANDOLPH, who managed the case for the Jeffersonians.

A milder form of resistance to the Court was the doctrine of departmental independence, whereby the President was as free to act on his view of constitutional authority as the Court was to act on its own. Despite the prospect of endless oscillation that this theory implied, it was espoused in some form by Jefferson, ANDREW JACKSON, and ABRAHAM LINCOLN. President JACKSON'S VETO OF THE BANK BILL (1832) was based partly on grounds of unconstitutionality, although the earlier law creating the bank had been sustained by the Supreme Court. In his message justifying the veto, Jackson had the advice and aid of his attorney general, ROGER B. TANEY. By an irony of history, when President Lincoln in his first inaugural address dealt with Taney's opinion in DRED SCOTT V. SANDFORD (1857), he adopted something of the Jackson-Taney philosophy, maintaining that although he offered no resistance to the decision as a settlement of the lawsuit he could not regard it as binding on the political branches for the future.

The indeterminate size of the Court became a weapon in the contest between President ANDREW JOHNSON and Congress over RECONSTRUCTION. By successive statutory changes, following the admission of new states and the creation of new circuits, the authorized membership of the Court had been increased to ten. A radical Congress, distrustful of Johnson and wishing to deprive him of the power to make new appointments to the Court, reduced the number of seats prospectively to seven. (Contributing to the move was a plan of Chief Justice SALMON P. CHASE to induce a reluctant Congress to increase the Justices' salaries in return for a decrease in the number to be compensated. That plan failed, but Chase did succeed in having the title of his office changed from Chief Justice of the Supreme Court to Chief Justice of the United States.) The actual number of Justices did not fall below eight, and in 1869 the number was fixed at nine.

More famous is the action of the same Congress in withdrawing the appellate jurisdiction of the Supreme Court in cases under a HABEAS CORPUS act, giving rise to the decision in EX PARTE MCCARDLE in 1869. While the immediate issue in the case was whether a military commission in Mississippi could try a newspaper editor for inflammatory writings urging citizens not to cooperate with the military government, Congress was fearful that a politically minded majority on the Court would hold the entire plan of Reconstruction unconstitutional. The Court, which had already heard argument in the case, bowed to the withdrawal of jurisdiction, but carefully pointed out that another appellate route remained unaffected by the repealing statute. Consequently the value of *McCardle* as a PRECEDENT, which is the centerpiece of constitutional argument on the extent of congressional power to limit the Court's jurisdiction, is at best doubtful.

The post-Reconstruction Court alienated labor and progressives by decisions taking a narrow view of state power to regulate and tax business; the COMMERCE CLAUSE and FREEDOM OF CONTRACT protected by SUBSTANTIVE DUE PROCESS served as shields for industry. The Progressive party platform in 1912, under the aegis of THEODORE ROOSEVELT, advocated the RECALL of judges and judicial decisions by popular vote. Although this thrust was aimed at state courts rather than the Supreme Court, the latter had set a tone for judicial review in a triad of decisions in 1895. UNITED STATES V. E. C. KNIGHT CO. held that a combination of sugar refiners controlling ninety percent of sugar production in the nation was not subject to the SHERMAN ANTITRUST ACT because processing is not commerce. IN RE DEBS held that a labor leader could be imprisoned for violating a federal court's INJUNCTION in a railroad labor strike, without judicial reliance on any statutorily defined offense. POLLOCK V. FARMERS LOAN AND TRUST CO. held the federal income tax law unconstitutional as applied to income from real property, stocks, and bonds, though valid as applied to wages, because an income tax is tantamount to a tax on

ment occurred at a time of rising totalitarianism abroad. FREEDOM OF THE PRESS and FREEDOM OF ASSOCIATION AND ASSEMBLY were unmistakably put under the protection of the liberty secured by the Fourteenth Amendment in NEAR V. MINNESOTA (1931) and DEJONGE V. OREGON (1937), respectively. The principle that a conviction in a state court following the use of a coerced confession is a violation of DUE PROCESS OF LAW was announced for the first time BROWN V. MISSISSIPPI (1936). A state's duty to afford racial equality in education was sharpened in MISSOURI EX REL. GAINES V. CANADA (1938): it could not be satisfied by resort to a neighboring state. Mayors and governors were subjected to the reach of federal judicial process in HAGUE V. CIO (1939) and *Sterling v. Constantin* (1932), an accountability that came to be important in later contests over desegregation.

If the drama of these seminal developments was largely overlooked, the same cannot be said of the great expansion of civil liberties and CIVIL RIGHTS by the WARREN COURT. The leading decisions have become familiar landmarks. BAKER V. CARR (1962), requiring substantial equality of population in electoral districts within a state, asserted judicial power over what had previously been deemed a POLITICAL QUESTION; Chief Justice Warren regarded it as the most important decision of his tenure, because of its potential for redistributing basic political power. BROWN V. BOARD OF EDUCATION (1954, 1955) was both the culmination and the beginning in the long drive against RACIAL DISCRIMINATION: doctrinally a climax, practically a starting point in the devising of remedies. MIRANDA V. ARIZONA (1966), limiting POLICE INTERROGATION of suspects in custody and giving suspects the RIGHT TO COUNSEL during interrogation, has become a symbol of the Court's intense concern for standards of CRIMINAL PROCEDURE, a concern that has sometimes been viewed as an index to a society's civilization. The EQUAL PROTECTION guarantee, which Justice Holmes in 1927 could call the last refuge of a constitutional lawyer, was revitalized in the service not only of racial minorities but of other stereotyped groups: ALIENS, illegitimates, and women. Freedom of the press was extended well beyond freedom from restraint on publication: In actions for LIBEL brought by PUBLIC FIGURES following NEW YORK TIMES V. SULLIVAN (1964), the defendant publisher would be liable only if he acted with legal malice, that is, with knowledge of the publication's falsity or with reckless disregard for its truth or falsity.

A constitutional RIGHT OF PRIVACY, of uncertain scope, extending beyond the explicit SEARCH AND SEIZURE guarantee to encompass at least certain conjugal intimacies, was established in GRISWOLD V. CONNECTICUT (1965). The religion clauses of the FIRST AMENDMENT were given new vitality in decisions rejecting organized prayer in the public schools, such as ENGEL V. VITALE (1962).

On any measure, it is an impressive performance. The momentum was somewhat slackened during the first decade and a half of Chief Justice WARREN E. BURGER's tenure, particularly in the areas of criminal procedure and nonestablishment of religion; yet during this period the Court reached the high-water mark of constitutionally protected autonomy in ROE V. WADE (1973), upholding freedom of choice respecting abortion in the first two trimesters of pregnancy.

Criticism of the modern Court has taken diverse directions. Some critics have complained that the Court has been unfaithful to the historic meaning of constitutional provisions. But the argument begs the question of "meaning." If the term signifies denotative meaning, the particular instances that the Framers envisioned as comprehended in the text, the original meaning has indeed been departed from. If, however, the purposive meaning is accepted, and the application does not contradict the language of the text, there is no infidelity. Such an analysis will not disapprove, for example, the "meaning" ascribed to the freedom of the press in the First Amendment.

Another criticism charges defenders of the Court with a double standard: the modern Court is a mirror image of the pre-1937 Court, the judicial vetoes coming now from the left instead of the right. The asserted parallel, however, is inexact. The problem is to identify the appropriate role for judicial review in a representative democracy. The older Court set aside such products of the political process as minimum wage, price control, and tax legislation. The modern Court, by and large, has given its intensive scrutiny to two areas of law that are of peculiarly legitimate concern to the judiciary. One is the field of procedure, in a large sense, civil and criminal. The other is the set of issues concerning representation of interests in the formation of public opinion and lawmaking. This category would include FREEDOM OF SPEECH and press and association, VOTING RIGHTS, education, and the interests of groups underrepresented in the formulation of public policy. This approach gives a certain coherence to constitutional theory: as the commerce clause protects out-of-state enterprise against hostility, open or covert, the Bill of Rights and the Civil War amendments especially protect the political, social, or ethnic "outsider" against official neglect or ostracism.

A more qualified criticism is addressed to two tendencies of the modern Court. One is a perceived disposition to carry a constitutional safeguard to excessive lengths, as in BUCKLEY V. VALEO (1976), which held invalid, in the name of freedom of expression, statutory limits on expenditures by or on behalf of candidates for federal offices. The other, illustrated by the abortion and police interrogation cases, is an inclination, when holding a state law or practice invalid, to prescribe only a single form of corrective that will not offend constitutional standards.

A problem faced by the Court throughout much of its history, one that has again become acute, is the burden of an expanding caseload. In the last hundred years two statutory jurisdictional revisions brought temporary relief. The Circuit Courts of Appeals Act of 1891, by establishing a system of regional appellate courts, assured litigants of one opportunity for review without resort to the Supreme Court. The JUDICIARY ACT OF 1925, sponsored by the Justices themselves and promoted by Chief Justice WILLIAM HOWARD TAFT, made discretionary review by WRIT OF CERTIORARI, instead of APPEAL as of right, the normal mode of access to the Supreme Court.

Each solution, however, has in time become part of the problem. With thirteen courts of appeals, and the burgeoning of federal statutory law, there is a growing incidence of conflicting decisions calling for review. Moreover, the disposition of petitions for certiorari has occupied an increasing amount of the Justices' time, with more than 4,000 filed each term. Of these, approximately 175 are granted and the cases decided with full opinion after oral argument.

A study group appointed under the auspices of the Federal Judicial Center reported in 1972 that the caseload was reaching the saturation point. Certain ameliorative measures had already been taken. The normal time allowed for oral argument had been reduced from an hour to a half hour for each side. The number of law CLERKS had been increased in stages from one to four for each Justice. The study group expressed disquiet at what it viewed as a bureaucratic movement, and recommended the creation of a national court of appeals to review decisions that warranted review but not necessarily by the Supreme Court. Others proposed variations on this plan, notably one or more courts of appeals having specialized jurisdiction, in tax or criminal or regulatory cases. Sixty years after the 1925 act, the problem has not been resolved. And yet without adequate time for reflection, collegial discussion, critical scrutiny, mutual accommodation, and persuasive exposition, the Court cannot function at its best.

At its best, the Court can recall the legal profession and the people to an appreciation of their constitutional heritage, by translating the ideals and practices embodied in an eighteenth-century charter of the Enlightenment into the realities of a modern industrial democracy.

PAUL A. FREUND
(1986)

Bibliography

BICKEL, ALEXANDER M. 1962 *The Least Dangerous Branch.* Indianapolis: Bobbs-Merrill.

CONGRESSIONAL QUARTERLY 1981 *The Supreme Court and Its Work.* Washington, D.C.: Congressional Quarterly.

FREUND, PAUL A. 1961 *The Supreme Court of the United States.* Cleveland and New York: Meridian Books.

FREUND, PAUL A. and SCHMIDT, BENNO C., JR. 1984 *The Judiciary and Responsible Government, 1910–1921.*

FRIEDMAN, LEON and ISRAEL, FRED L., eds. 1969–1978 *The Justices of the United States Supreme Court, 1789–1969.* 5 Vols. New York: Chelsea House.

LEWIS, ANTHONY 1964 *Gideon's Trumpet.* New York: Random House.

POLLAK, LOUIS H., ed. 1966 *The Constitution and the Supreme Court: A Documentary History.* 2 Vols. Cleveland: World Publishing Co.

SWINDLER, WILLIAM F. 1970 *Court and Constitution in the Twentieth Century: The New Legality, 1932–1968.* Indianapolis: Bobbs-Merrill.

WARREN, CHARLES 1926 *The Supreme Court in United States History.* 2 Vols. Boston: Little, Brown.

WESTIN, ALAN, ed. 1961 *The Supreme Court: Views from Inside.* New York: Norton.

SUPREME COURT
(Role in American Government)

The Supreme Court is the only court in the United States whose existence is mandated by the Constitution, yet the Constitution designates no number of judges for the Supreme Court and sets no qualifications for judicial service. So far as the Constitution is concerned, the Supreme Court could as readily consist of two or of twenty-two judges, rather than of nine as has been the case since 1870. And so undemanding is the Constitution in setting qualifications for appointment to the Supreme Court that its members could consist entirely of persons not qualified to serve in either House of Congress, for which at least a few minimum standards of eligibility (of age and of CITIZENSHIP) are constitutionally prescribed. The Constitution speaks simply to the vesting of the JUDICIAL POWER OF THE UNITED STATES in "one supreme court, and in such inferior Courts as the Congress may from time to time ordain and establish," but it leaves much else to discretion and a great deal to chance.

The role of the Supreme Court in American government is much like this overall. Some impressions of what the Court's role was meant to be can be gained from what the Constitution says and from the immediate history of 1789, as well as from the categories of JURISDICTION assigned to the Court by Article III. But much of that role is also the product of custom and of practice about which the Constitution itself is silent.

The constitutional text itself suggests several ways of describing the Supreme Court's role, in conformity with Article III's prescriptions of the Court's jurisdiction. The useful jurisdictional distinctions are of four principal kinds, each providing some insight into what the Court was originally expected to do.

First mentioned is the Supreme Court's jurisdiction as a trial court, an ORIGINAL JURISDICTION invocable by certain parties in particular (states and representatives of foreign states) but by no one else. Second is that branch of its appellate jurisdiction applicable also solely because of who the parties are, irrespective of the nature of the dispute between them. Third is the Court's appellate jurisdiction that attaches solely because the case involves a federal statute or treaty of the United States, or arises under ADMIRALTY AND MARITIME LAW, without regard to who the parties may be and whether or not any constitutional question may be involved. Finally, the Court may exercise an appellate jurisdiction over "all cases arising under [the] Constitution," a phrase construed broadly to include any case in which the outcome may be affected by a question of constitutional law. It is the application of this phrase, of course, that tends to fix the Supreme Court's most important role, but as can be seen from the foregoing larger enumeration, it is not by any means the sole business to which the Court was expected to attend.

The role of the Supreme Court as a court of original jurisdiction has been useful but minor. Ordinarily, the Court's small complement of original jurisdiction has merely expedited its speedy examination of certain legal issues raised by states against other states (typically involving boundary or interstate river claims) or against the national government, as in OREGON V. MITCHELL—a 1970 decision holding unconstitutional one portion of an act of Congress that sought to override state voting age restrictions. Because Congress can provide for expedited Supreme Court review of cases originating in other courts, however, it is doubtful whether this feature of Article III has been terribly vital. Its one theoretical importance may be that the original jurisdiction it provides to the states is guaranteed against elimination by Congress—for unlike the Court's appellate jurisdiction, its original jurisdiction is not subject to the "exceptions" clause of Article III.

Dwarfing the Court's role as a court of original jurisdiction is its much larger and more familiar role as the ultimate appellate court in the United States for a vastly greater number and variety of disputes, although the Court is not obliged to review all such cases and in fact hears but a small fraction of those eligible for review. The cases eligible for review, some on APPEAL and a larger number on petition for a WRIT OF CERTIORARI, are divisible into two principal categories: those in which the character of the contesting parties makes the case reviewable, and those in which the nature of the legal issue raised by the case makes the case reviewable.

In the first category of cases within the Court's appellate jurisdiction there are many that raise no constitutional questions and indeed need not raise any kind of federal question. As these cases are within the Court's power of review solely because of the parties, regardless of the subject in dispute between them, they may involve very ordinary legal issues (for example, of contract, tort, or property law) as to which there is no special expertise in the Supreme Court and no obvious reason why they need be considered there. And in practice, they are not reviewed.

Part of the original interest in providing the Supreme Court as the ultimate appellate tribunal in the United States reflected the Framers' desire to provide an appellate court for litigants likely to be sued in hostile jurisdictions—cases, for instance, arising in state courts which nonresident defendants might fear would be inclined to favor local parties as against outsiders. Since the furnishing of lower federal courts (to hear such cases) was left entirely optional with Congress to provide or not provide as it liked, the Supreme Court's appellate jurisdiction even from state court diversity cases was directly provided for in Article III. Nonetheless, in the course of 200 years the felt need for such cases to be heard in the Supreme Court has never materialized—although such cases remain a staple of lower federal court jurisdiction. (Efforts in Congress to repeal this entire category of lower federal court jurisdiction are more than a half-century old, but they have been only partly successful, largely in restricting such cases to those involving sums in excess of $10,000.) In the meantime, however, the Supreme Court does not review such cases and, by act of Congress, it is under no obligation to take them. This particular anticipated role of the Supreme Court, as an active court in hearing appeals in ordinary diversity cases presenting no federal question and implicating no general interest of the United States, has never been significant in fact.

In contrast, the second branch of the Supreme Court's appellate jurisdiction—identified not by the parties but by the nature of the legal questions—remains intensely active. Indeed, the principal role the Court plays today as an appellate court undoubtedly arises almost entirely from this subject matter assignment of appellate jurisdiction of cases involving disputes of national law. In these cases the Court interprets acts of Congress and treaties of the United States as well as the Constitution as the ultimate source of governing law in the United States.

Specifically, these cases may raise any of the following four kinds of basic conflicts: conflicts between claims relying upon mutually exclusive interpretations of concededly valid acts of Congress or treaties of the United States; between constitutional claims of state power and claims of federal power (FEDERALISM conflicts); between constitutional claims by Congress and claims by the President or claims by the judiciary (SEPARATION OF POWERS conflicts); or between constitutional claims of personal right and claims of either state or of national power (personal rights conflicts). A principal function of Article III was to establish the Supreme Court as the ultimate national court of appeals to provide finality and consistency of result in the interpretation and application of all federal and constitutional law in the United States, within the full range of these four fundamental and enduring concerns.

For nearly the first hundred years (1789–1875), almost all appeals to the Supreme Court on such federal questions as these came from state courts rather than from lower federal courts. Not until 1875, in the aftermath of the CIVIL WAR, were lower federal courts given any significant original (trial) jurisdiction over private civil cases arising under acts of Congress or treaties of the United States. Since 1875, moreover, many federal question cases still proceed from state courts to the Supreme Court, because reliance on some federal law or on the Constitution often arises only in answer to some claim filed in a state court and thus emerges only by way of defense rather than as the basis of complaint.

The fact that this arrangement of the Court's appellate jurisdiction places the Supreme Court in appellate command over all other courts in the United States in all federal question cases is exactly what makes the Supreme Court supreme. In constitutional matters, for instance, this fact is the basis of Justice ROBERT H. JACKSON's observation, in speaking of the Court, that "[w]e are not final because we are infallible, but we are infallible only because we are final," that is, superior in constitutional authority to review the determinations of other courts and in turn unreviewable by any other court. It likewise animates the 1907 observation by CHARLES EVANS HUGHES (later Chief Justice of the United States). "We are under a Constitution," Hughes acknowledged, "but the Constitution is what the judges say it is," since it is their view and, most important, the Supreme Court's view, that ultimately controls in each case. And even when no constitutional issue is present, but the issue is how an act of Congress shall be interpreted and applied, the finality of the Supreme Court's appellate jurisdiction is equally pivotal; it is the Americanized version of Bishop Hoadley's observation in 1717, in reference to the power of the English courts in interpreting acts of Parliament. "Whoever hath an absolute authority to interpret any written or spoken laws," Hoadley observed, "it is he who is truly the lawgiver, to all intents and purposes, and not the person who first spoke or wrote them." From an early time Americans seem to have believed in the wisdom of reposing in the courts—and ultimately in the Supreme Court—the responsibility of substantive constitutional review, and it seems clear (despite some scholars' qualified doubts) that the Supreme Court was indeed meant to exercise that responsibility. (See JUDICIAL REVIEW.) It is unquestionably this role of substantive constitutional review that marks the special position of the Supreme Court.

The Supreme Court's decisions in constitutional cases may be roughly divided into three kinds, according to which its role in American government is occasionally assessed or described. The three kinds of decisions are these: legitimizing, braking, and catalytic.

A decision is said to be legitimizing whenever the Court examines any act of government on constitutional grounds and finds it not wanting. In holding that the act as applied is in fact authorized by the Constitution and not offensive to any of its provisions (for example, the BILL OF RIGHTS or the FOURTEENTH AMENDMENT), the Court thus vouches for its constitutional legitimacy. A decision may be called a braking decision whenever its immediate effect is necessarily to arrest the further application of an act of Congress because the Court holds the act either inapplicable or unconstitutional, or whenever OBITER DICTA accompanying the decision serve notice of constitutional barriers in the way of similar legislation. Finally, a decision may be called catalytic when its immediate practical effect is to compel highly significant action of a sort not previously forthcoming from national or state government.

A significant and controversial example of the legitimizing sort is PLESSY V. FERGUSON (1896), the case sustaining certain state racial SEGREGATION laws as not inconsistent with the Fourteenth Amendment, despite intense argument to the contrary. A modern example of the same sort may be FULLILOVE V. KLUTZNICK (1980), a case sustaining a limited form of RACIAL DISCRIMINATION in favor of certain minority contractors as not inconsistent with the Fifth Amendment, despite intense argument as well. In each case, the Court considered a previously untested kind of race-related law. In each, the Supreme Court's decision could be said effectively to have impressed the operative law with a judicial imprimatur of constitutional legitimacy, given that in each case the challenged statute was sustained.

Examples of the braking sort may be found in the Court's early NEW DEAL decisions holding Congress unauthorized by the COMMERCE CLAUSE to supplant state laws with its own much more sweeping and detailed ECONOMIC REGULATIONS. In this instance, the critical decisions of the Court forced a momentary pause in the onrush of legislation, compelling more deliberate attention to what the nation had been and what it meant to become. As it happened, the braking effect of these cases was eventually overcome, but it is nonetheless true that in the meantime the position taken by the Court played a sobering role. In a few other instances, the braking effect of equivalent cases was overcome by formal amendment of the Constitution itself: the SIXTEENTH AMENDMENT, for instance, was adopted principally to overcome the effect of the Court's decision in POLLOCK V. FARMERS' LOAN & TRUST (1895); the Thirteenth Amendment and Fourteenth Amendment displaced the Court's decision in DRED SCOTT V. SANDFORD (1857); and the TWENTY-SIXTH AMENDMENT displaced the decision in *Oregon v. Mitchell.* These reactions are by themselves not an indication that the Court has erred, of course, since the Constitution itself separates the role of the Court from the formal processes of constitutional modification. (See AMENDING PROCESS.) Any decision in the Supreme Court holding a statute unconstitutional may provide occasion to activate the AMENDING PROCESS provided for in Article V. Amendments by themselves are not proof that the decisions they effectively overrule were necessarily poorly conceived. They may, rather, but mark new Cambrian rings in what is meant to be a living constitution.

An example of a catalytic decision would be one holding certain prison conditions to be so inadequate as to constitute a form of CRUEL AND UNUSUAL PUNISHMENT, such that either the prisoners must be released (which public authorities are loath to do), or large sums must be raised and less congested prisons must be built. The change-forcing nature of the Court's catalytic decision is but descriptive of its practical implications. By itself it thus carries no suggestion that the Court acted from impulse rather than from obligation, in ruling as it did. The same observation may apply equally to the other two categories of decisions.

Thus, in the "legitimizing" decision there is no necessary insinuation that the measure that has been sustained is on that account also necessarily desirable or well-taken legislation; such questions are ordinarily regarded as no proper part of the judicial business. Adjudicated constitutionality properly vouches solely for an act's consistency with the Constitution, which consistency may still leave much to be desired, depending upon one's own point of view and one's feeling of constitutional adequacy. Similarly, it does not follow that an act's adjudicated unconstitutionality necessarily implies its undesirability or, indeed, that there would be anything terribly wrong were the Constitution amended so that similar legislation might subsequently be reenacted and sustained. It means merely that the act does not pass muster under the Constitution as it is and as the judges are oath-bound to apply it until it is altered.

So also with catalytic decisions: such forced change as a particular decision may produce is required simply to bring the conduct of government back within constitutional lines as they are, and not as they need be. As conscientiously applied by the Court, the Constitution thus speaks to such constitutional boundaries as were put in place sometime in the past, from a considered political judgment of the time that such boundaries would be important. The judgment is wholly an inherited one, however, and contemplates the possibility of amendment to cast off such restraints as subsequent extraordinary majorities may find unendurable. Viewed in this way, the Constitution is a device by means of which past generations signal to subsequent generations their cumulative assessment of what sorts of restraints simple majoritarianism needs most. The Supreme Court is the ultimate judicial means by which the integrity of those restraints is secured against the common tendency to think them ill-conceived or obsolete, sustaining them when pressed by proper litigants with suitable standing, until instructed by amendment to acknowledge the change. It is a signal responsibility and an unusual power—one which few other national supreme courts have been given.

On the other hand, the phrases "legitimizing," "braking," and "catalytic" are not always used so descriptively, however well they capture the by-products of the Court's work. Rather, they are sometimes used prescriptively, and thus in an entirely different sense. In this different usage they presume to provide a more jurisprudential blueprint for the role of the Supreme Court: that it is appropriate for the Court actively to serve these three functions politically as it were, and to involve the Constitution only instrumentally in their service. Employed in this different locution, they are phrases used to express faith in a specific kind of judicial activism, according to which the right role of the Court is to identify the needs of efficient and humane government and to adjust its own adjudications accordingly.

In this view, it is in fact the proper role of the Supreme Court to legitimate (by holding constitutional) such laws as circumstances persuade it ought not be disapproved, to brake (by adverse construction or by holding unconstitutional) such developments as it determines to have been precipitously taken or otherwise to have been ill-advised, and to catalyze (by artful action) such changes it deems highly desirable but unlikely to be forthcoming from government unless the Court so requires. The persuasive justification for the Supreme Court lies in what it can do best as a distinct institution, in this view, and only secondarily in adhering to the Constitution. And what the Supreme Court can do better than others is to compensate for such gaps as it finds in the Constitution or in the political process, and to take such measured steps as it can to repair them. Accordingly, the more appropriate role of the Supreme Court is to conduct itself institutionally as best it can to contribute actively to a better political quality of life in the United States: in deciding which cases to hear, when to hear them, on what grounds to decide them, and how to make them come out in ways most in keeping with these three vital functions of granting legitimacy to the good, putting brakes on the bad, and compelling such changes as are overdue.

As an original jurisprudence of proposed judicial role, this perspective on the Supreme Court has had considerable occasional support. In the concrete, moreover, there is good reason to believe that certain Justices—probably a nontrivial number—have embraced it in selected aspects of their own work. At the least, there are a large number of constitutional decisions that appear to reflect its view of what judges should seek to do, as indeed some Justices have virtually absorbed it as an articulate feature of proper judicial review; their decisions seem sometimes to be based on little else.

Still, and for obvious reasons, it remains deeply problematic, for at bottom it would have the judges struggle against the obligation of their oaths. Insofar as cases such as *Plessy* or *Fullilove* were to any extent self-conscious efforts by a Supreme Court majority simply to legitimate race-based arrangements it thought desirable, and not decisions reporting a difficult judicial conclusion respecting the lack of constitutional restrictions on the legislative acts at issue, for instance, it is doubtful whether the "legitimacy" thus established was appropriate or, indeed, constitutionally authorized. Likewise, insofar as the early New Deal cases were to any extent simply a deliberate institutional attempt by the majority Justices to arrest what they thought to be ill-advised varieties of market intervention, and not decisions reflecting an attentive interpretation respecting the limits of Congress's commerce power, it is debatable whether the "braking" thus applied was appropriate or authorized. So, too, with such decisions as may be catalytic, but which may be driven more by a judicial desire to see changes made than by a mere firm resolve that the Constitution shall be obeyed.

Without doubt, however, the tendency to urge the Supreme Court to compose its interpretations of the Constitution in subordination to allegedly significant social tasks remains widespread. Moreover, the malleability of many constitutional clauses invites it, and the political staffing mechanism (provided by Article III) for selecting the judges may appear obliquely to legitimate it. The tendency to rationalize its propriety is deeply entrenched.

Even so, the conscious treatment of constitutional clauses as but textual or pretextual occasions for judicial legitimation, braking, or social catalysis, does tend to pit the Court against itself in its disjunction of fundamentally incompatible roles. The resulting tension has split the Court virtually from the beginning. It divides it even now: between these two visions of the Court, as a professional court first of all or as a political court first of all, lie two centuries of unsteady swings of actual judicial review. The history of the Supreme Court in this respect but reiterates a classic antinomy in American constitutional law. It

doubtless reflects the conflicts Americans tend to sense within themselves—as to what role they genuinely wish this Court to fulfill.

With certain highly notable exceptions (including West Germany, Japan, Australia, and most recently Canada), the written CONSTITUTIONS of most modern nation-states serve merely as each nation's explanation of itself as a government. Such a constitution typically presents a full plan of government, a statement of its purposes and powers, and an ample declaration of rights. Yet, unlike the Constitution of the United States, such a constitution cannot be invoked by litigants and does not require or even permit courts of law to use it as against which all other laws may be examined. It is, rather, a nonjusticiable document. It is intended to be taken seriously (at least this is the case generally), but only in the political sense that legislative and executive authorities are meant to reconcile their actions with the constitution at the risk of possible popular disaffection should they stray too far from what the constitution provides. Whether the authorities have thus strayed, however, and what consequences shall follow if they have, is not deemed to be the appropriate business of courts of law.

The enormous distinction of American constitutional law has thus rested in the very different and exceptional role of the judiciary, from the most unprepossessing county courts through the hierarchy of the entire federal court system. The unique role of the Supreme Court has been its own role as the ultimate appellate court in reference to that judiciary, most critically in all constitutional cases. The arrangement thus established does not lessen the original obligation of other government officials separately to take care that their own actions are consistent with the Constitution, but it is meant to provide—as effectively as human institutions can arrange—an additional and positive check. When official action is not consistent with the Constitution, as ultimately determined under the Supreme Court's authority, the courts are given both the power and the obligation to intercede: to interpose such authority as they have and to provide such redress as appears to be due. Judged even by international standards, this is an ample role. It is not this role that now appears fairly open to question, moreover, but rather the definition of role that would assume something more or accept something less.

WILLIAM W. VAN ALSTYNE
(1986)

Bibliography

ABRAHAM, HENRY J. 1986 *The Judicial Process*, 5th ed. New York: Oxford University Press.

AGRESTO, JOHN 1984 *The Supreme Court and Constitutional Democracy*. Ithaca, N.Y.: Cornell University Press.

BICKEL, ALEXANDER M. 1962 *The Least Dangerous Branch: The Supreme Court at the Bar of Politics*. Indianapolis, Ind.: Bobbs-Merrill.

COX, ARCHIBALD 1976 *The Role of the Supreme Court in American Government*. New York: Oxford University Press.

ELY, JOHN HART 1980 *Democracy and Distrust: A Theory of Judicial Review*. Cambridge, Mass.: Harvard University Press.

FREUND, PAUL 1961 *The Supreme Court of the United States*. Cleveland, Ohio: World Publishing Company.

HOROWITZ, DONALD L. 1977 *The Courts and Social Policy*. Washington, D.C.: The Brookings Institution.

JACKSON, ROBERT H. 1955 *The Supreme Court in the American System of Government*. New York: Harper & Row.

MASON, ALPHEUS THOMAS 1979 *The Supreme Court from Taft to Burger*, 3d ed. Baton Rouge: Louisiana State University Press.

McCLOSKEY, ROBERT G. 1960 *The American Supreme Court*. Chicago: University of Chicago Press.

WOLFE, CHRISTOPHER 1986 *The Rise of Modern Judicial Review*. New York: Basic Books.

SUPREME COURT, 1789–1801

On January 8, 1801, twelve days before President JOHN ADAMS appointed JOHN MARSHALL as Chief Justice, a Jeffersonian newspaper reported: "JOHN JAY, after having thru' decay of age become incompetent to discharge the duties of Governor, has been appointed to the sinecure of Chief Justice of the United States. That the Chief Justiceship is a sinecure needs no other evidence than that in one case the duties were discharged by one person who resided at the same time in England, and by another during a year's residence in France." The one in France was OLIVER ELLSWORTH, sent there by President Adams as a special ambassador to negotiate peace. Ellsworth had recently resigned, and Jay, whose appointment as Ellsworth's successor had been confirmed by the Senate, had himself been the first Chief Justice, whom President GEORGE WASHINGTON had sent to England to negotiate a treaty that bore Jay's name. The chief justiceship was no sinecure: although the Supreme Court then met for only two short terms a year, the Justices also served as circuit court judges, and riding circuit was extremely arduous. When Jay was offered the position again, he declined it because of the circuit responsibilities and because the Court had neither "the energy, weight and dignity" necessary for it to support the national government nor "the public confidence and respect."

Jay's judgment was harsh although the Court did have problems, some of its own making. All the Justices were Federalists; their decisions EN BANC or on circuit seemed partisan—pro-Administration, pro-English, or procreditor—and they presided at trials under the infamous Sedition Act, whose constitutionality they affirmed. But the Court was not responsible for most of its difficulties. It had no official reporter (ALEXANDER J. DALLAS's unofficial reports first appeared in 1798) and the press publicized only a few of the Court's decisions. The public knew little about the Court, and even members of its own bar were unfamiliar with its decisions. Nothing better symbolizes the nation's neglect of the Court than the fact that when the United States government moved to Washington, D.C., in late 1800, the Court had been forgotten. Not only did it lack a building; it had no courtroom. Congress hastily provided a small committee room in the basement of the Senate wing of the Capitol for the Court to meet.

The Court's beginnings were hardly more auspicious, however distinguished its membership. At its first term in February 1790 it had nothing to do except admit attorneys to its bar, and it shortly adjourned. It began as a court without a reporter, litigants, a docket, appeals, or decisions to make. It was chiefly an appellate court whose APPELLATE JURISDICTION scarcely matched the breadth of the JUDICIAL POWER OF THE UNITED STATES stated in Article III. Congress in the JUDICIARY ACT OF 1789 had authorized the Court to review state court decisions that denied claims based on federal law, including the Constitution. Review was not authorized when the state court upheld a claim of federal right. The system of appellate jurisdiction thus permitted the Supreme Court to maintain federal law's supremacy but not its uniform interpretation. The Court's review of civil decisions of the lower federal courts was limited to cases involving more than $2,000 in controversy, and it could not review criminal cases from those courts. Congress had stingily authorized the Court to hear cases in its appellate capacity in order to keep it weak, to prevent centralization of judicial powers, to preserve the relative importance of state courts, and to insulate the Court from many matters that concerned ordinary citizens. For its first two years it heard no cases, and it made no substantive decisions until 1793. Its docket never got crowded. Dallas reported less than seventy cases for the pre-Marshall Court, and fewer than ten percent of them involved constitutional law. The Court was then first a COMMON LAW court, second a court of ADMIRALTY AND MARITIME JURISDICTION.

Although its members were able, the pre-Marshall Court had difficulty attracting and keeping them. When Marshall became Chief Justice, only WILLIAM CUSHING of the original six Justices appointed by Washington remained. Robert H. Harrison, one of the original six, was confirmed but declined appointment, preferring instead the chancellorship of Maryland. JAMES IREDELL accepted Harrison's place, so that the first Court consisted of Chief Justice Jay and Justices Cushing, JOHN BLAIR, JOHN RUTLEDGE, JAMES WILSON, and Iredell. Rutledge performed his circuit duties but had never attended a session of the

Court when he resigned after two years to become chief justice of South Carolina. CHARLES C. PINCKNEY and Edward Rutledge declined appointment to John Rutledge's seat, preferring to serve in their state legislature. THOMAS JOHNSON accepted that seat but resigned it in less than two years because circuit riding was too strenuous. WILLIAM PATERSON succeeded him. The February 1794 term was Jay's last. That he reentered New York politics after negotiating JAY'S TREATY says something about the Court's prestige at the time. So too does the fact that ALEXANDER HAMILTON preferred private practice to the chief justiceship. At that point, John Rutledge, who had quit the Court, applied for the post vacated by Jay. Washington appointed Rutledge, who attended the August 1795 term of the Court when it decided only two cases. The Senate, having reconvened, rejected him because of his opposition to Jay's Treaty. Washington offered the chief justiceship to PATRICK HENRY who declined it. The President then named Justice Cushing, whom the Senate confirmed; but he too declined, preferring to remain Associate Justice. In 1796, Oliver Ellsworth became Chief Justice but quit after four years. John Blair retired early in 1796 and Washington again had to fill a vacancy on the Court. After EDMUND RANDOLPH refused the position, SAMUEL CHASE accepted. In 1798, Wilson became the first Justice to die in office. RICHARD PETERS refused to be considered for the position, and John Marshall also declined. Adams then appointed BUSHROD WASHINGTON, and after Iredell died in 1798, he appointed ALFRED MOORE, who resigned within five years. When Ellsworth resigned and Jay declined reappointment, even though the Senate confirmed him, Adams turned to Marshall. The rapid turnover in personnel during the Court's first decade did not ease its work or enhance its reputation.

Jeffersonians grumbled about the Court's Federalist constitutional theories, but Jay kept his Court out of politics and established its independence from the other branches of the government. That achievement and the Court's identification of its task as safeguarding the supreme law of the land kept the Court a viable institution, despite its many problems during the first decade, and laid the groundwork for the achievements of the MARSHALL COURT.

Late in 1790, Virginia's legislature denounced as unconstitutional the bill for national assumption of state debts. Washington allowed Hamilton to send a copy of the Virginia resolves to Jay and to inquire whether the various branches of the government should employ their "collective weight . . . in exploding [Virginia's STRICT CONSTRUCTION] principles." Hamilton warned that Virginia had shown "the first symptom of a spirit which must either be killed or it will kill the Constitution of the United States." However, Jay, who privately advised Washington and drafted his PROCLAMATION OF NEUTRALITY, recognized the difference between a judicial pronouncement and an extrajudicial one. The Court, strongly believing in the principle of SEPARATION OF POWERS, would not express ex officio opinions except in judicial cases before it. Jay calmly declined the executive's invitation.

Similar principles motivated the Justices when confronted by Congress's Invalid Pensioners' Act of 1792 which required the circuit courts to pass on the pension applications of disabled veterans, subject to review by the secretary of war and Congress. Justices Wilson and Blair together with Judge Peters on circuit in the district of Pennsylvania, having refused to pass on an application from one Hayburn, explained their conduct in a letter to the President. They could not proceed because first, the business directed by the statute was not judicial in nature, there being no constitutional authority for it, and second, because the possible revision of the Court's judgment by the other branches of government would be "radically inconsistent with the independence" of the judiciary. In their circuits, Jay, Cushing, and Iredell similarly explained that a judicial decision must be a final decision. HAYBURN'S CASE (1792), which was not really a "case" and in which nothing was judicially decided, was important because the Court, in Wilson's words, affirmed "a principle important to freedom," that the judicial branch must be independent of the other branches.

Similarly, Jay established another principle vital to the Court's independent, judicial, and nonpolitical character when he declined Washington's request for an ADVISORY OPINION. That request arose out of apparent conflicts between American treaty obligations to France and the Proclamation of Neutrality. The French commissioned privateers in American ports and established prize courts to condemn vessels captured by those privateers. Washington sought the Court's opinion on twenty-nine questions involving international law and treaty interpretation, in connection with the French practices. Jay, relying again on the principle of separation of powers, observed that the Court should not "extra-judicially" decide questions that might come before it in litigation. Thus, by preserving its purely judicial character, the Court was free to decide some of those questions when real cases posed them. From the beginning, the Court staked its power and prestige on its special relationship to the supreme law of the land, which it safeguarded, expounded, and symbolized.

The pre-Marshall Court also exercised the power of JUDICIAL REVIEW. The Justices on circuit quickly held state acts unconstitutional for violating the supreme law of the land. Jay and Cushing on circuit in the district of Connecticut held that that state, by adversely affecting debts owed to British creditors, had violated the treaty of peace with Britain; Iredell in Georgia and Paterson in South Carolina made similar decisions. The Justices held that

United States treaties were superior to state laws. The Supreme Court confronted the issue in WARE V. HYLTON (1796). With Iredell alone dissenting, the Court rejected the arguments of John Marshall, making his only appearance before the Justices, as counsel for the debtor interests of Virginia. He opposed "those who wish to impair the sovereignty of Virginia" and contended first that the Constitution had not authorized the Court to question the validity of state statutes and, second, that a treaty could not annul them. Seriatim opinions by Chase, Paterson, Wilson, and Cushing held otherwise.

In *Clarke v. Harwood* (1797) the Court ruled that *Ware* "settled" the question before it. *Clarke* was the Court's first decision against the validity of a state act in a case arising on a WRIT OF ERROR to a state court under section 25 of the Judiciary Act of 1789. Section 25 authorized the Court to reverse or affirm state decisions that denied rights claimed under United States treaties. Maryland's high court, relying on a state statute sequestering debts owed to British creditors, had barred a claim based on the treaty of peace with Britain. By reversing the Maryland court, the Supreme Court in effect voided the state act. However, the Court rarely heard cases on a writ of error to a state court. Indeed, it had not decided its first such case until shortly before *Clarke*. In *Olney v. Arnold* (1796) the Court had reversed a Rhode Island decision that misconstrued a revenue act of Congress. The Court's power of reviewing state decisions under Section 25 did not become controversial until 1814. (See MARTIN V. HUNTER'S LESSEE, 1816.) During the Court's first decade, judicial review of state legislation was uncontested, and it was exercised.

On circuit the Justices also struck down state acts as violating the CONTRACT CLAUSE of the Constitution. The first such decision occurred in 1792 in CHAMPION AND DICKASON V. CASEY, which voided a Rhode Island state law. Given the hullaballoo in that state when its own judiciary was suspected of having voided a state act in TREVETT V. WEEDEN (1787), the meek acceptance of the 1792 decision showed the legitimacy of judicial review over the states.

In HYLTON V. UNITED STATES (1796) the Court for the first time determined the constitutionality of an act of Congress, ruling that an EXCISE on carriages, not being a DIRECT TAX, was valid even if not apportioned among the states. Those hoping for the Court to hold the federal excise unconstitutional were Jeffersonians; they did not then or at any time during the Court's first decade challenge the legitimacy of the Court's power to refuse to enforce an unconstitutional statute. Until the debate on the repeal of the JUDICIARY ACT OF 1801 (see JUDICIARY ACTS OF 1802), scarcely anyone opposed judicial review, whether over state or over congressional legislation. *Hayburn's Case* in 1792 was misunderstood throughout the nation. Not only did Attorney General Randolph believe that the Court had annulled an act of Congress; so did Congress. The House established an investigating committee, "this being the first instance in which a Court of Justice had declared a law of Congress unconstitutional." Jeffersonians gleefully praised the Justices and hoped the Court would extend the precedent by holding unconstitutional other congressional legislation that promoted Hamilton's economic programs. Later, Jeffersonians in Sedition Act trials sought to persuade the Justices on circuit that they should declare the statute void. Repeatedly during the first decade, bills arose in Congress that provoked members in both houses to state that the Court should and would hold them unconstitutional. The way to the doctrine of judicial review announced in MARBURY V. MADISON (1803) was well paved, and the opposition to the Court's opinion did not derive from its assumption of a power to void an act of Congress.

Another major theme in the work of the Court during its first decade was nationalism. Once again, the Marshall Court built on what the Jay and Ellsworth Courts had first shaped. The early Courts helped vindicate the national character of the United States government, maintain the supremacy of the nation over the states, and keep the states from undermining the new constitutional system. On circuit duty the Justices frequently lectured federal GRAND JURIES, inculcating doctrines from THE FEDERALIST, and these grand jury charges were well publicized in the newspapers. In one of his charges, Jay, in 1790, having declared, "We had become a Nation," explained why national tribunals became necessary for the interpretation and execution of national law, especially in a nation accustomed only to state courts and state policies. Circuit court opinions striking down state laws in violation of the contract clause or federal treaties preached nationalism and national supremacy. Many of the criminal prosecutions before the federal circuit courts during the first decade were connected with national suppression of the WHISKEY REBELLION and the FRIES REBELLION. Similarly, prosecutions under the Sedition Act were intended to vindicate the reputations of Congress and the President.

The development of a FEDERAL COMMON LAW OF CRIMES, expanding the jurisdiction of the national courts, fit the nationalist pattern. Whether the courts could try nonstatutory offenses was a question that first arose in Henfield's case (1793). Wilson maintained that an American citizen serving on a French privateer commissioned in an American port and attacking ships of England, with whom the United States was at peace, had committed an indictable offense under the Proclamation of Neutrality, the law of nations, and the treaty with England, even though Congress had not made his act a crime.

The same nationalist pattern unified several of the Court's opinions in cases dealing with various issues. In

CHISHOLM V. GEORGIA (1793) the Court's holding, that its jurisdiction extended to suits against a state by citizens of another state, was founded on nationalist principles as well as on the text of Article III. Wilson, for example, began with the principles that the people of the United States form a nation, making ridiculous the "haughty notions of state independence, state SOVEREIGNTY, and state supremacy." "As to the purposes of the Union," he said, "therefore, Georgia is not a sovereign state." Jay's opinion also stressed "the national character" of the United States and the "inexpediency" of allowing state courts to decide questions that involved the performance of national treaties. The denunciation of the Court for its "consolidation of the Union" and its "annihilation of the sovereignty of the States" led to the ELEVENTH AMENDMENT, which was intended to nullify *Chisholm.*

In *Glass v. Sloop Betsy* (1794) the Court supported the government's neutrality policy by ruling that France, after capturing a neutral ship, could not hold or award her as a prize in an American port. Only the United States courts could determine the lawfulness of prizes brought into its ports, and no foreign nation controlled its admiralty law or could subvert American rights under international law. In *Penhallow v. Doane* (1795) the Court resolved an old dispute over the ownership of a prize. One party's claims relied on decisions of a New Hampshire court, the other's on a decision of a prize court established by the old Congress of the Confederation. Paterson, in the Supreme Court's principal opinion, upheld the lower federal courts, which had decided against the state court and claimed jurisdiction. No nation, he said, had recognized the states as sovereign for the purpose of awarding prizes. The old Congress had been the supreme council of the nation and center of the Union, he claimed, whose sovereignty was approved by the people of America and recognized by foreign nations. The federal courts succeeded to that sovereignty in prize matters. New Hampshire angrily remonstrated against the "destruction" of its sovereignty but the Court's ruling prevailed.

Its decision in *Hylton v. United States* gave life to the government's revenue powers. When the Court upheld federal treaties as paramount to state laws, in *Ware v. Hylton* (1796), Chase, in the principal opinion for the Court, indulged in fanciful nationalism when declaring, "There can be no limitation on the power of the people of the United States. By their authority the State Constitutions were made."

Other notable cases of the first decade were VAN HORNE'S LESSEE V. DORRANCE (1794) and CALDER V. BULL (1798), in which the Court laid the foundation for the judicial doctrine of VESTED RIGHTS, which it developed further in contract clause and HIGHER LAW decisions during Marshall's chief justiceship. Although the Court was left out of the

planning for the new national capital, it had been enunciating doctrines—of judicial review, national supremacy, and vested rights—that helped shape the United States and would in time make the judicial branch of government impossible to ignore.

LEONARD W. LEVY
(1986)

Bibliography

CURRIE, DAVID P. 1981 The Constitution in the Supreme Court: 1789–1801. *University of Chicago Law Review* 48: 819–885.
GOEBEL, JULIUS 1971 *Antecedents and Beginnings.* Vol. I of the *Oliver Wendell Holmes Devise History of the Supreme Court,* ed. Paul Freund. New York: Macmillan.
HAINES, CHARLES GROVE 1944 *The Role of the Supreme Court in American Government and Politics, 1789–1835.* Berkeley: University of California Press.
HENDERSON, DWIGHT F. 1971 *Courts for a New Nation.* Washington, D.C.: Public Affairs Press.
WARREN, CHARLES 1923 *The Supreme Court in United States History.* Vol. I. Boston: Little, Brown.

SUPREME COURT AT WORK

In its first decade, the Supreme Court had little business, frequent turnover in personnel, no chambers or staff, no fixed customs, and no institutional identity. When the Court initially convened on February 1, 1790, only Chief Justice JOHN JAY and two other Justices arrived at the Exchange Building in New York City. They adjourned until the next day, when Justice JOHN BLAIR arrived. With little to do other than admit attorneys to practice before its bar, the Court concluded its first sessions in less than two weeks. When the capital moved from New York City to Philadelphia in the winter of 1790, the Court met in Independence Hall and in the Old City Hall for ten years, until the capital again moved to Washington, D.C. Most of the first Justices' time, however, was spent riding circuit. Under the JUDICIARY ACT OF 1789, they were required twice a year to hold CIRCUIT COURT, in the company of district judges, to try some types of cases and to hear appeals from the federal district courts. Hence, the Justices resided primarily in their circuits rather than in Washington and often felt a greater allegiance to their circuits than to the Supreme Court.

When the capital moved to Washington, D.C., in 1800, no courtroom was provided. Between 1801 and 1809, the Justices convened in various rooms in the basement of the Capitol. In 1810, they shared a room in the capitol with the Orphans' Court of the DISTRICT OF COLUMBIA. This room was destroyed when the British burned the Capitol on August 24, 1814, and for two years, the Court met in the Bell Tavern. In 1817, the Court moved back into the Capitol, holding sessions in a small dungeonlike room for two years. In 1819, it returned to its restored courtroom, where it met for almost half a century.

For most of the nineteenth century, the Justices resided in their circuits and stayed in boardinghouses during the Court's terms. Chief Justice ROGER BROOKE TANEY (1836–1864) was the first to reside in the Federal City, and as late as the 1880s most Justices did not maintain homes there. Lacking offices and sharing the law library of Congress, the Justices relied on a single clerk to answer correspondence, collect fees, and to locate boardinghouse rooms for them.

Coincident with the 1801 move into the Capitol, JOHN MARSHALL assumed the Chief Justiceship. During his thirty-four years on the Court, Marshall established regularized procedures and a tradition of collegiality. He saw to it that the Justices roomed in the same boardinghouse and, thereby, turned the disadvantage of transiency into strategic opportunity for achieving unanimity in decision making. After a day of hearing ORAL ARGUMENTS, the Justices would dine together, and around 7:00 p.m. they would discuss cases.

After 1860, the Court met upstairs in the old Senate Chamber, between the new chambers of the Senate and those of the House of Representatives. The Justices still had no offices or staff of their own. After the CIVIL WAR, however, the caseload steadily grew, the Court's terms lengthened, and the Justices deserted boardinghouses for fashionable hotels along Pennsylvania Avenue. Instead of dining together and discussing cases after dinner, they held CONFERENCES on Saturdays and announced decisions on Monday.

By the turn of the century, the Justices resided in the capitol and for the most part worked at home, where each had a library and employed a messenger and a secretary. The Court's collegial procedures had evolved into institutional norms based on majority rule. The CHIEF JUSTICE assumed a special role in scheduling and presiding over conferences and oral arguments. But the Court's deliberative process was firmly rooted in the Justices' interaction as equals. Each Justice was considered a sovereign in his or her own right, even though the Justices decided cases together and strove for institutional opinions.

After becoming Chief Justice in 1921, WILLIAM HOWARD TAFT persuaded four Justices to support his lobbying Congress for the construction of a building for the Court. Taft envisioned a marble temple symbolizing the modern Court's prestige and independence. Yet, when the building that houses the Court was completed in 1935, none of the sitting Justices moved in, although sessions and conferences were held there in the later years of the HUGHES COURT (1930–1941). Upon his appointment in 1937, HUGO L. BLACK was the first to move in, leading the way for President FRANKLIN D. ROOSEVELT's other appointees. Even when HARLAN FISKE STONE was elevated from Associate to Chief Justice, he still worked at home. The VINSON COURT (1946–1953) was the first to see all nine Justices regularly working in the Supreme Court building.

The marble temple stands for more than a symbol of the modern Court. Once again, the institutional life of the Court changed. As Taft hoped, the building buttressed the Court's prestige and reinforced the basic norms of secrecy, tradition, and collegiality that condition the Court's work. The Justices continued to function independently, but the work of the Court grew more bureaucratic. Along with the rising caseload in the decades following WORLD WAR II, the number of law clerks more than tripled and the number of other employees dramatically increased as well. The Justices in turn delegated more and incorporated modern office technology and managerial practices into their work. The WARREN COURT (1953–1969) started delivering opinions on any day of open session, and the BURGER COURT (1969–1986) moved conferences back to Fridays.

When POTTER STEWART joined the Court in 1958, he expected to find "one law firm with nine partners, if you will, the law clerks being the associates." But Justice JOHN MARSHALL HARLAN told him, "No, you will find here it is like nine firms, sometimes practicing law against one another." Even today, each Justice and his or her staff works in rather secluded chambers with little of the direct daily interaction that occurs in some appellate courts. Nor do recent Justices follow FELIX FRANKFURTER's practice of sending clerks ("Felix's happy hotdogs") scurrying around the building to lobby other clerks and Justices.

A number of factors isolate the Justices, but most important is the caseload. The Justices, in Justice BYRON R. WHITE's view, "stay at arm's length" and rely on formal printed communications because the workload discourages them "from going from chamber to chamber to work things out." Each chamber averages about seven: the Justice, three to four law clerks, two secretaries, and a messenger. As managing chambers and supervising paperwork consumes more time, the Justices talk less to each other and read and write more memoranda and opinions. Each chamber now has a photocopying machine and four to five terminals for word processing and legal research.

Law CLERKS became central to the work of the Court. In 1882, Justice HORACE GRAY initiated the practice of hiring a "secretary" or law clerk. When OLIVER WENDELL HOLMES, JR. succeeded Gray, he continued the practice, and other Justices gradually followed. By Chief Justice Stone's time it was well established for each Justice to have one clerk. During the chief justiceships of FRED M. VINSON and

EARL WARREN, the number increased to two. In the 1970s, the number grew to three and to four. The number of secretaries likewise increased—initially, in place of adding clerks and, later, to assist the growing number of clerks. A Legal Office, staffed by two attorneys, was created in 1975 to assist with cases in the Court's ORIGINAL JURISDICTION and with expedited appeals.

Although the duties and functions of clerks vary with each chamber, all share certain commonly assigned responsibilities. Most notably, Justices have delegated to them the task of initially screening all filings for writs of CERTIORARI. This practice originated with the handling of INDIGENTS' petitions by Chief Justice CHARLES EVANS HUGHES and his clerks. Unlike the "paid" petitions that are filed in multiple copies, an indigent's petition is typically a handwritten statement. Except when an unpaid petition raised important legal issues or involved a capital case, Hughes neither circulated the petitions to the other Justices nor discussed them at conference. Stone, Vinson, and Warren, however, circulated to the chambers their clerks' memoranda, which summarized the facts and questions presented, and recommended whether the case should be denied, dismissed, or granted a review. But Chief Justice WARREN E. BURGER refused to have his clerks shoulder the entire burden of screening these petitions. And in 1972, a majority of the Justices began to pool their clerks, dividing up all paid and unpaid filings and having a single clerk's certiorari memo circulate to those Justices participating in what is called "the cert. pool." With more than a hundred filings each week, even those Justices who objected to the "cert. pool" have found it necessary to give their clerks considerable responsibility for screening petitions. Justice JOHN PAUL STEVENS describes his practice: "[The clerks] examine them all and select a small minority that they believe I should read myself. As a result, I do not even look at the papers in over 80 percent of the cases that are filed."

Law clerks have also assumed responsibility for the preliminary drafting of the Justices' opinions. Chief Justice WILLIAM H. REHNQUIST's practice, for instance, is to have one of his clerks do a first draft, without bothering about style, in about ten days. Before beginning work on an opinion, Rehnquist goes over the conference discussion with the clerk and explains how he thinks "an opinion can be written supporting the result reached by the majority." Once the clerk finishes a draft and Rehnquist works the draft into his own opinion, it circulates three or four times among the other clerks in the chambers before it circulates to the other chambers.

In addition to law clerks, five officers and their staffs also assist the Justices. Central to the Court's work is the Office of the Clerk. For most of the Court's history, the clerk earned no salary, but this changed in 1921 when Taft lobbied for legislation making the clerk a salaried employee. The clerk's office collects filing and admission fees; receives and records all motions, petitions, BRIEFS, and other documents; and circulates those necessary items to each chamber. The clerk also establishes the oral-argument calendar and maintains the order list of cases granted or denied review and final judgments. In 1975, the office acquired a computer system that automatically notifies counsel in over ninety-five percent of all cases of the disposition of their filings.

There was no official reporter of decisions during the first quarter-century of the Court, and not until 1835 were the Justices' opinions given to the clerk. Early reporters worked at their own expense and for their own profit. In 1922, Congress established the present arrangement (at Chief Justice Taft's request): the reporter's salary is fixed by the Justices and paid by the government, and the Government Printing Office publishes the *United States Reports*. The reporter has primary responsibility for supervising the publication of the Court's opinions, writing headnotes or syllabi that accompany each opinion, and for making editorial suggestions subject to the Justices' approval.

Order in the courtroom was preserved by U.S. marshals until 1867, when Congress created the Office of Marshal of the Supreme Court. The Marshal not only maintains order in the courtroom and times oral arguments but also oversees building maintenance and serves as business manager for the more than two hundred Court employees, including messengers, carpenters, police and workmen, a nurse, physiotherapist, barber, seamstress, and cafeteria workers.

The Justices acquired their first small library in 1832. It was run by the clerk until the marshal's office took over in 1884. In 1948, Congress created the Office of the Librarian, which employs several research librarians to assist the Justice.

Unlike other members of the Court, the Chief Justice has special administrative duties. Over fifty statutes confer duties ranging from chairing the JUDICIAL CONFERENCE and the Federal Judicial Center to supervising the Administrative Office of the U.S. Courts and serving as chancellor of the Smithsonian Institution. Unlike Taft and Hughes, Stone felt overwhelmed by these duties. His successor, Vinson, appointed a special assistant to deal with administrative matters, whereas Warren delegated such matters to his secretary. By contrast, Burger became preoccupied with administrative matters and pushed for judicial reforms. In historical perspective, he brought Taft's marble temple into the world of modern technology and managerial practices. Burger also lobbied Congress to create a fifth legal officer of the Court, the administrative assistant to the Chief Justice. While also employing an administrative assistant, Chief Justice Rehnquist has less interest in judicial administration, and his assistant is less occupied with liaison work with organizations outside the Court.

The caseload remains the driving force behind the Court's work; its increase has changed the Court's operations. After Taft campaigned for relief for the Court, Congress passed the JUDICIARY ACT OF 1925, which enlarged the Court's discretionary JURISDICTION and enabled it to deny cases review. Subsequently, on a piecemeal basis, the Court's discretion over its jurisdiction was further expanded, and in 1988, virtually all mandatory appeals were eliminated. As a result, the Court has the power to manage its docket and set its agenda for decision making.

The cornerstone of the modern Court's operation, in Justice John Harlan's words, "is the control it possesses over the amount and character of its business." The overwhelming majority of all cases are denied review; less than three percent of the more than 5,000 cases on the Court's annual docket are granted and decided by fully written opinion.

When a petition is filed at the Court, the clerk's staff determines whether it satisfies the rules as to form, length, and fees. After receiving opposing papers from respondents, the clerk circulates to the chambers a list of cases ready for consideration and a set of papers for each case. For much of the Court's history, every Justice reviewed every case, but this practice no longer prevails. Since the creation of the "cert. pool" in 1972, most of the Justices have delegated to their clerks much of this initial screening task. Moreover, the Court has found it necessary to hold its initial conference in the last week of September, before the formal opening of its term. At this conference, the Justices dispose of more than 1,000 cases, discussing less than two hundred. Before the start of the term, the Court has thus disposed of approximately one-fifth of its entire docket, with more than four-fifths of those cases effectively screened out by law clerks and never collectively considered by the Justices.

In conference, attended only by the Justices, the Court decides which cases to accept and discusses the merits of argued cases. During the weeks in which the Court hears oral arguments, conferences are held on Wednesday afternoons to take up the four cases argued on Monday, and then on Fridays to discuss new filings and the eight cases argued on Tuesday and Wednesday. In May and June, when oral arguments are not heard, conferences are held on Thursdays, from 10:00 a.m. to 4:00 p.m., with a forty-five-minute lunch break around 12:30 p.m.

Summoned by a buzzer five minutes before the hour, the Justices meet in their conference room, located directly behind the courtroom itself. Two conference lists circulate to each chamber by noon on the Wednesday before a conference. On the first list are those cases deemed worth discussing; typically, the discuss list includes about fifty cases. Attached is a second list, the "Dead List," containing those cases considered unworthy of discussion. Any Justice may request that a case be discussed, but over seventy percent of the cases on the conference lists are denied review without discussion.

For a case to be heard by the Court, at least four Justices must agree that it warrants consideration. This informal RULE OF FOUR was adopted when the Justices were trying to persuade Congress that important cases would still be decided after the Court was given discretionary controll over much of its jurisdiction under the Judiciary Act of 1925, Unanimity in case selection, nevertheless, remains remarkably high becaues the Justices agree that only a limited number of cases may be taked. "As a rule of thumb," Justice White explains, "the Court should not be expected to produce more than 150 opinions per term in argued cases." The rule of four, however, also permits an ideological bloc to grant review in cases it wants to hear and thus to influence the Court's agenda.

Since the Chief Justice presides over conferences, he has significant opportunities for structuring and influencing the Court's work. Chief Justices, however, vary widely in their skills, style, and ideological orientations. Hughes is widely considered to be the greatest Chief Justice in this century because of his photographic memory and ability to state concisely the relative importance of each case. "Warren was closer to Hughes than any others," in Justice WILLIAM O. DOUGLAS's view, and "Burger was closer to Vinson. Stone was somewhere in between." Rehnquist, by all accounts, is an effective Chief Justice because he moves conferences along quickly and has the intellectual and temperamental wherewithal to be a leader.

For a case to be heard by the Court, at least four Justices must agree that it warrants consideration. This informal RULE OF FOUR was adopted when the Justices were trying to persuade Congress that important cases would still be decided after the Court was given discretionary control over much of its jurisdiction under the Judiciary Act of 1925. Unanimity in case selection, nevertheless, remains remarkably high because the Justices agree that only a limited number of cases may be taken. "As a rule of thumb," Justice White explains, "the Court should not be expected to produce more than 150 opinions per term in argued cases." The rule of four, however, also permits an ideological bloc to grant review in cases it wants to hear and, thus, to influence the Court's agenda.

Immediately after conference, the Chief Justice traditionally had the task of reporting to the clerk which cases were granted review, which were denied review, and which were ready to come down. Burger, however, delegated this task to the junior Justice. The clerk then notifies both sides in a case granted review that they have thirty days to file briefs on merits and supporting documents. Once all briefs (forty copies of each) are submitted, cases are scheduled for oral argument.

The importance of oral argument, Chief Justice Charles Evans Hughes observed, lies in the fact that often "the impression that a judge has at the close of a full oral argument accords with the conviction which controls his final vote." Because the Justices vote in conference within a day or two of hearing arguments, oral arguments come at a crucial time. Still, oral arguments were more prominent in the work of the Court in the nineteenth century. Unlimited time was allowed, until the Court began cutting back on oral argument in 1848, allowing eight hours per case. The time has been reduced periodically, and since 1970, arguments have been limited to thirty minutes per side. The argument calendar permits hearing no more than 180 cases a year. For fourteen weeks each term, from the first Monday in October until the end of April, the Court hears arguments from 10:00 to 12:00 and 1:00 to 3:00 on Monday, Tuesday, and Wednesday about every two weeks.

Justices differ in their preparation for oral arguments. Douglas insisted that "oral arguments win or lose a case," but Chief Justice Earl Warren claimed that they were "not highly persuasive." Most Justices come prepared with "bench memos" drafted by their law clerks, identifying the central facts, issues, and possible questions. On the bench, they also vary in their style and approach toward questioning attorneys. Justices SANDRA DAY O'CONNOR and ANTONIN SCALIA, for example, are aggressive and relentless in the questioning of attorneys, while Justices WILLIAM J. BRENNAN and HARRY A. BLACKMUN tend to sit back and listen.

Conference discussions following oral arguments no longer play the role they once did. When the docket was smaller, conferences were integral to the Court's work. Cases were discussed in detail, differences hammered out, and the Justices strove to reach agreement on an institutional opinion for the Court. As the caseload grew, conferences became largely symbolic of past collective deliberations. They currently serve only to discover consensus. "In fact," Justice Scalia points out, "to call our discussion of a case a conference is really something of a misnomer. It's much more a statement of the views of each of the nine Justices."

Most of the time spent in conference is consumed by the Justices deciding which cases should be granted review. Moreover, less time is spent in conference (now about 108 hours) each term. The caseload and conference schedule permits on average only about six minutes for each case on the discuss list and about twenty-nine minutes for those granted full consideration. Perhaps as a result, the Justices agree less often on the opinion announcing the Court's decision and file a greater number of separate opinions. In short, the combination of more cases and less collective deliberation discourages the compromises necessary for institutional opinions and reinforces the tendency of the Justices to function independently.

All votes at conference are tentative until the final opinion comes down. Voting thus presents each Justice with opportunities to negotiate which issues are to be decided and how they are to be resolved. Before, during, and after conference, Justices may use their votes in strategic ways to influence the outcome of a case. At conference, a Justice may vote with others who appear to constitute a majority, even though the Justice may disagree with their reasoning. The Justice may then suggest changes in draft opinions to try to minimize the damage, from his or her perspective, of the Court's decision.

Because conference votes are tentative, the assignment, drafting, and circulation of opinions is crucial to the Court's work. Opinions justify or explain votes at conference. The OPINION OF THE COURT is the most important and most difficult to write because it represents a collective judgment. Writing the Court's opinion, as Justice Holmes put it, requires that a "judge can dance the sword dance; that is he can justify an obvious result without stepping on either blade of opposing fallacies." Because Justices remain free to switch votes and to write separate opinions, concurring in or dissenting from the Court's decision, they continue after conference to compete for influence on the final decision and opinion.

The power of opinion assignment is the Chief Justice's "single most influential function," observed Justice TOM C. CLARK, and an exercise in "judicial-political discretion." By tradition, when the Chief Justice votes with the majority, he assigns the Court's opinion. If the Chief Justice is not with the majority, then the senior Associate Justice in the majority either writes the opinion or assigns it to another Justice.

Chief Justices may keep the Court's opinion for themselves, especially when a case is unanimously decided. Since Vinson, however, Chief Justices have generally sought parity in their opinion assignments. Opinions may be assigned to pivotal Justices to ensure or expand the size of the majority joining the opinion for the Court. But the Chief Justice may also take other factors into account, such as a Justice's expertise or what kind of reaction a ruling may engender. Hughes, for example, was inclined to assign the opinions in "liberal" decisions to "conservative" Justices.

The circulation of draft opinions among the chambers has added to the Supreme Court's workload and changed its deliberative process. The practice of circulating draft

largely responded by deleting or substituting joint resolutions for one-House veto provisions. However, in the
year following *Chadha,* Congress passed no less than
thirty new provisions for LEGISLATIVE VETOES.

Congress indubitably has the power to delay and undercut implementation of the Court's rulings. On major
issues of public policy, Congress is likely to prevail or at
least temper the impact of the Court's rulings.

The Court has often been the focus of presidential campaigns and power struggles as well. Presidents rarely
openly defy particular decisions by the Court, and in major
confrontations, they have tended to yield. Still, presidential reluctance to enforce rulings may thwart implementation of the Court's rulings. In the short and long run,
Presidents may undercut the Court's work by issuing contradictory directives to federal agencies and assigning low
priority for enforcement by the Department of Justice.
Presidents may also make broad moral appeals in response
to the Court's rulings, and those appeals may transcend
their limited time in office. The Court put school DESEG-
REGATION and ABORTION on the national political agenda.
Yet JOHN F. KENNEDY's appeal for CIVIL RIGHTS captivated a
generation and encouraged public acceptance of the
Court's ruling in *Brown v. Board of Education.* Similarly,
RONALD REAGAN's opposition to abortion focused attention
on "traditional family values" and served to legitimate resistance to the Court's decisions.

Presidential influence over the Court in the long run
remains contingent on appointments to the Court. Vacancies occur on the average of one every twenty-two months,
and there is no guarantee as to how a Justice will vote or
whether that vote will prove the key to limiting or reversing past rulings with which a President disagrees. Yet
through their appointments, Presidents leave their mark
on the Court and possibly align it and the country or precipitate later confrontations.

The Supreme Court at work is unlike any other. It has
virtually complete discretion to select which cases are reviewed, to control its work load, and to set its own substantive agenda. From the thousands of cases arriving each
year, less than two hundred are accepted and decided. The
Court thus functions like a superlegislature. But the
Justices' chambers also work like nine separate law offices,
competing for influence when selecting and deciding
those cases. The Justices no longer spend time collectively
deliberating cases at conference. Instead, they simply tally
votes and then hammer out differences, negotiating and
compromising on the language of their opinions during
the postconference period when drafts are circulated
among the chambers. When the final opinions come down,
the Court remains dependent on the cooperation of other
political branches and public acceptance for compliance
with its rulings. The work of the Court, in Chief Justice
EDWARD D. WHITE's words, "rests solely upon the approval
of a free people."

DAVID M. O' BRIEN
(1992)

(SEE ALSO: *Jeffersonianism.*)

Bibliography

ABRAHAM, HENRY J.   1986   *The Judicial Process,* 5th ed. New
    York: Oxford University Press.
CHOPER, JESSE   1980   *Judicial Review and the National Demo-
    cratic Process.* Chicago: University of Chicago Press.
CONGRESSIONAL QUARTERLY   1989   *Guide to the U.S. Supreme
    Court,* 2nd ed. Washington, D.C.: Congressional Quarterly
    Press.
DIAMOND, PAUL   1989   *The Supreme Court & Judicial Choice:
    The Role of Provisional Judicial Review.* Ann Arbor: Univer-
    sity of Michigan Press.
FISHER, LOUIS   1988   *Constitutional Dialogues.* Princeton, N.J.:
    Princeton University Press.
JOHNSON, CHARLES and CANNON, BRADLEY   1984   *Judicial Poli-
    cies: Implementation and Impact.* Washington, D.C.: Con-
    gressional Quarterly Press.
O'BRIEN, DAVID M.   1990   *Storm Center: The Supreme Court in
    American Politics,* 2nd ed. New York: W. W. Norton.
STERN, ROBERT and GRESSMAN, EUGENE   1987   *Supreme Court
    Practice,* 6th ed. Washington, D.C.: Bureau of National Af-
    fairs.

SUPREME COURT BAR

The bar of the Supreme Court is not cohesive, and it is
not active in any organizational sense. The number of lawyers admitted to practice before the Supreme Court is
greatly in excess of the number who actually appear there.

The first rule of the Supreme Court with respect to
admissions was adopted on February 5, 1790, three days
after the Court opened in New York. The Court then made
the provision, which continues to this day, that applicants
for admission shall have been admitted "for three years
past in the Supreme Courts of the State to which they
respectively belong." The formula also provided, then and
throughout the nineteenth century, that the private and
professional character of the applicants "shall appear to
be fair." As the American language evolved, the word
"fair" acquired a dual meaning, and the use of the phrase
in oral motions sometimes produced a laugh in the courtroom. So the wording was changed, and for most of the
twentieth century the sponsor was required to say that he
"vouched" for the applicant. Under the rule as it stands
now, he affirms "that the applicant is of good moral and
professional character." All motions for admissions were

made in open court until about 1970. Now the whole procedure can be done by mail.

Under the first rule for admission, the applicant was required to elect whether he would practice as an attorney (office lawyer) or as a counselor (appearing in court), and he could not practice as both. If this rule had remained in effect (it was eliminated in 1801), the long-established division in England between solicitors and barristers would have been perpetuated in the United States and the bar of the Supreme Court would have been drawn from a much narrower group.

There is no published list of the members of the bar of the Supreme Court. Indeed, no one knows how many members there are. The clerk of the Supreme Court maintains a list of those admitted since October 1925. In early 1990 the number of those who had been admitted was about 185,000. But there is no record of those who have died or retired from active practice (though the list does record 800 names of lawyers who have been disbarred). By an estimate there are now 75,000 lawyers in the United States who have been admitted to practice before the Supreme Court and thus are members of its bar. No more than 300 of these actually present arguments before the Supreme Court in any year, and there are probably fewer than 5,000 living lawyers in the country (out of a total of close to 700,000 lawyers altogether) who have ever made a personal appearance before the Court.

The first member of the bar of the Supreme Court was Elias Boudinot of New Jersey, who was admitted to practice in February 1790. There was, of course, no one to move his admission. No procedure had yet been established for the filing of credentials. After a short interval, the Court turned to the attorney general, EDMUND RANDOLPH. Though he was never admitted to practice before the Court, he was treated as an officer of the Court. Before long, the practice was established of admission to the bar on motions of persons already admitted.

During the first ten years of its existence, the Supreme Court heard very few cases. ALEXANDER HAMILTON made his sole appearance before the Court in the case of HYLTON V. UNITED STATES in 1796. JOHN MARSHALL made his sole appearance before the Court in WARE V. HYLTON (1796). This was the famous British debts case, and Marshall was unsuccessful.

As time passed, and the country developed, the number of cases before the Court steadily increased. Thomas A. Emmet arrived in New York from Ireland in 1804 and was soon established as a leading lawyer. He appeared before the Supreme Court for the first time in 1815. The culmination of his career was his argument in the famous steamboat case of GIBBONS V. OGDEN (1824). Another of the early leaders was Littleton W. Tazewell of Virginia, who specialized in criminal law and admiralty. DANIEL WEBSTER

wrote of him, "He is a correct, fluent, easy & handsome speaker and a learned, ingenuous & *subtle* lawyer"—a standard to which any Supreme Court lawyer might aspire. Others who appeared during the early years of the nineteenth century were LUTHER MARTIN, WILLIAM PINKNEY, and Francis Scott Key of Maryland; Roger Griswold of Connecticut; Edmund J. Lee and WILLIAM WIRT of Virginia; JOHN QUINCY ADAMS, Samuel Dexter, LEVI LINCOLN, and Rufus G. Amory of Massachusetts; JARED INGERSOLL and HORACE BINNEY of Pennsylvania; and Edward Livingston of New York and Louisiana.

Daniel Webster made his first appearance in 1814. Early in his career he argued DARTMOUTH COLLEGE V. WOODWARD (1818). The decision of the Court in this case, announced in 1819, relied on the OBLIGATION OF CONTRACTS clause in the Constitution to uphold the charter of Dartmouth College against efforts of the legislature of New Hampshire to change it. The argument in *Dartmouth College* lasted for three days and was a great social event in Washington. Webster concluded with an emotional peroration that has become part of American folklore. He is supposed to have said, "It is . . . a small college. And yet *there are those who love it.*" But there is no contemporaneous record of this passage. It first appeared in a eulogy on Webster spoken by Rufus Choate in July 1853, thirty-five years after the argument. Choate's source was a letter written to him in 1852 by Chauncey Goodrich, a professor at Yale University, who attended the March 1818 argument.

Webster (perhaps aided by geography and travel limitations of the times) was for more than thirty years the acknowledged leader of the Supreme Court bar. Indeed, he still holds the record for arguing the most cases before the Court—more than three hundred of them. The second largest total of cases argued was also achieved at this time by a little-known figure, Walter Jones, a District of Columbia lawyer. He appeared in more than two hundred cases before the Court. The next highest total of arguments, and the highest total in the twentieth century, was made by JOHN W. DAVIS, who was active from about 1910 to 1954. He argued a total of 141 cases. Davis was SOLICITOR GENERAL of the United States from 1913 to 1918 and in 1924 was the Democratic presidential candidate. Today no one makes such a high number of arguments unless he is a solicitor general or a member of the staff of the solicitor general's office.

The first black lawyer to be admitted to the bar of the Supreme Court was Dr. John S. Rock, who was born of free parents in New Jersey in 1825. He was admitted on February 1, 1865, just short of his fortieth birthday. Before then, he had been a teacher, a dentist, and a doctor. He had moved to Boston in 1853 and was one of the founders of the Republican party in Massachusetts. In 1858 he wanted to go to France for medical treatment, but he was refused a passport on the ground that he was not a citizen. The Massachusetts legislature then passed a law providing for state passports, and this was accepted in France.

A year or so later, Dr. Rock returned to Boston where he read law. He was admitted to practice in Massachusetts in September 1861 and in the Supreme Court in 1865, shortly after the appointment of SALMON P. CHASE as Chief Justice. It is interesting to note that this came before the termination of the CIVIL WAR and before the adoption of the Thirteenth, Fourteenth and Fifteenth amendments—and with DRED SCOTT V. SANDFORD (1857) still on the books. As the *New York Times* reported, "By Jupiter the sight was good." Rock's admission was moved by Senator CHARLES SUMNER. The newspaper reporter observed that the "assenting nod" of the Chief Justice "dug . . . the grave to bury the Dred Scott decision."

The next of these significant events was the admission of the first woman to the Supreme Court bar. In BRADWELL V. ILLINOIS (1873) the Supreme Court refused to interfere with the action of the supreme court of Illinois, which denied admission to Myra Bradwell, publisher of a successful legal newspaper in Chicago. Bradwell relied in the Supreme Court on the PRIVILEGES AND IMMUNITIES clause of the recently adopted Fourteenth Amendment, but persuaded only Chief Justice Chase.

Less than seven years later, however, Belva A. Lockwood became the first woman admitted to practice before the Supreme Court. This was on March 3, 1879. So quick was the change of view that this action evoked no opinion from any member of the Court. Indeed, Myra Bradwell herself, who had been denied admission in 1872, was finally admitted when she applied again in 1892.

Despite this opening of the door, it took fifty years, or until 1929, before the number of women admitted to the bar of the Supreme Court reached a total of one hundred. Some of the early admittees had distinguished careers in the law. These included Florence Allen, who became the first woman judge of a constitutional federal court; Mabel Walker Willebrandt, who was assistant attorney general under President HERBERT C. HOOVER; and Helen Carloss, who had a long and distinguished career in the Tax Division of the Department of Justice. The great increase in the number of women lawyers, however, has occurred in the past fifteen years. In another fifteen years, if present trends continue, they will constitute perhaps thirty percent of the members of the bar of the Supreme Court.

There have been periods when relatively few lawyers were widely recognized as leaders of the bar practicing before the Supreme Court. There were the orators of the nineteenth century, starting with Daniel Webster and continuing through John G. Johnson of Pennsylvania. There was such a bar in the 1920s and the 1930s, when CHARLES EVANS HUGHES, Owen D. Roberts, John W. Davis, George Wharton Pepper, and William D. Mitchell made frequent appearances before the Court. By this time, oratory had become passé. The presentations were less flowery, but they were mellifluous. Davis showed great skill in persuasion, though his record of wins over losses was not especially high, reflecting the fact that the cases in which he was retained were often especially difficult. There is one case that brought together three of these giants. In *United States v. George Otis Smith* (1932) the question was whether the Senate could reconsider its confirmation of a presidential nomination after the President had acted on it by making the appointment. The Senate retained Davis as its counsel. Attorney General William D. Mitchell appeared for the United States, essentially representing the President, and George Wharton Pepper represented Smith, the nominee. That argument was one of the high points of advocacy in this century.

One group has long provided the backbone of the Supreme Court bar: the solicitor general and his staff, and his associates in the Department of Justice. This office has long maintained a high standard and a great tradition. It appears, in one way or another, in nearly half the cases heard on the merits by the Court and in a high percentage of all applications for review.

A considerable number of cases are now brought to the Supreme Court by parties representing particular interests. The National Association for the Advancement of Colored People was first represented by one of the country's great lawyers, CHARLES H. HOUSTON—work carried on with great ability by THURGOOD MARSHALL. Other similar work has been done by lawyers representing groups interested in the rights of women, in other civil rights, in the environment, and in other causes.

The bar of the Supreme Court can never be assembled, nor is it possible to take a consensus of the bar. It is clear that it plays an important role in the work of the Court. Yet the demands on the Court are such that the bar has difficulty in making its full contribution. In 1935, arguments were heard five days a week for a total of about seventy-five days a year. Now the Court hears arguments on about forty-five days during the year. Fifty years ago, the time made available for oral argument was an hour on each side, and there were frequent substantial allowances of additional time. Now the time allotted is thirty minutes on a side, and additional time is rarely granted. This inevitably presents problems for oral arguments and requires a wholly different type of argument from that customary even fifty years ago. The advocate today can rarely present his case as a case. He has to pick out certain salient points and hope that with questioning by the justices he will still have time to deal with the matters he regards as vital. The printed briefs filed by counsel today appear to be much better than they were fifty years ago, probably more greatly improved than is commonly recognized. But oral argument remains a difficult and tantalizing field.

The Supreme Court moved into its new building in 1935. According to newspaper articles, the first words spoken by Chief Justice Hughes in the new courtroom were "Are there any admissions?" Thus was the bar recognized, and thus has it been recognized at every session since.

The bar of the Supreme Court, diverse and divided as it is, plays an important part in the work of the third branch of American constitutional government. Though Alexander Hamilton called the judiciary "the least dangerous branch," its role is central to the effective operation of our federal system. If the work of the Court is central to American government, the efforts of the Supreme Court bar may well be regarded as an essential buttress to the Court.

ERWIN N. GRISWOLD
(1992)

(SEE ALSO: *Supreme Court's Work Load; Women in Constitutional History.*)

Bibliography

CONTEE, CLARENCE G. 1976 The Supreme Court Bar's First Black Member. Pages 82–85 in *Supreme Court Historical Society Year Book, 1976.* Washington, D.C.: Supreme Court Historical Society.

HARBAUGH, WILLIAM H. 1973 *Lawyer's Lawyer.* New York: Oxford University Press.

O'DONNELL, ALICE L. 1977 Women and Other Strangers Before the Bar. Pages 59–62 in *Supreme Court Historical Society Year Book, 1977.* Washington, D.C.: Supreme Court Historical Society.

WARREN, CHARLES (1908) 1970 *History of the Harvard Law School and of Early Legal Conditions in America.* New York: DaCapo.

——— (1911) 1980 *A History of the American Bar.* Boston: Longwood.

WHITE, EDWARD G. 1988 *The Marshall Court and Cultural Change, 1815–34.* New York: Macmillan.

SUPREME COURT DECISIONS, IMPACT OF

The Supreme Court's DECISIONS have regularly embroiled it in controversy. Its rulings have considerable impact. In its early years, the Court, over strenuous objection from the states, shaped our federal system and helped establish the national government's supremacy. The Court also had substantial effects on the ECONOMY, aiding in the creation of an American economic common market and providing opportunities for the private sector to develop. The Court's major effects on FEDERALISM and the economy subsided after the 1930s. However, its effect on CIVIL RIGHTS, visible earlier with respect to SLAVERY and its emasculation of RECONSTRUCTION civil rights statutes, again became apparent as questions such as school DESEGREGATION came to the fore in the 1950s.

The Supreme Court's impact includes ways in which federal and state agencies and lower federal and state courts carry out the Court's decisions, but it also includes the ways in which the agencies and courts delay, circumvent, misunderstand, and erode them. It includes the response to decisions by different "populations"—those who explain or elaborate its rulings, those supposed to apply or implement them, those for whom the rulings are intended, and the general population. Because the Court, "the least dangerous branch," lacks the capacity to enforce its rulings directly, assistance from those at whom a ruling is directed or from others (legislatures, executive agencies, courts) is required. The Court is now recognized to be a political actor, but one must abandon the tacit assumption held by earlier scholars that Supreme Court decisions are self-executing and recognize that the law is what the judges say it is only after all others have had their say.

Impact and compliance are not identical but are related. Compliance, the process by which individuals accept a decision prior to its impact or effect, cannot occur unless a person knows of the ruling and is required to take or abstain from a certain action. Compliance means an individual's intentionally conforming behavior to the ruling's dictates, that is, doing what the decision commands because of the ruling. Because noncompliance, or refusal to obey, occurs relatively seldom despite the attention it receives, it is important to pay heed to implementation of decisions, the process by which they are put into effect. Short-run resistance may blend into longer-run obedience, as resulted in the aftermath of the REAPPORTIONMENT decisions.

Impact includes all effects, direct and indirect, resulting from a ruling of the Court, regardless of whether those affected knew about the decision; it includes the results of rulings permitting but not requiring the adoption of certain policies. When effects of a ruling indirectly induce behavior congruent with the ruling, that behavior is better viewed as impact than as compliance. Impact encompasses actions neither directly defiant nor clearly obedient, such as attempts at evasion coupled with technical obedience and efforts to anticipate the Court's decisions ("anticipatory compliance"). Impact also includes both short-term and long-run consequences of a decision, for example, massive resistance to school desegregation rulings and the rulings' arguable contribution to "white flight" to the suburbs. There will also be situations in which no response occurs, that is, where there is an absence of obvious impact.

The Supreme Court's effect on the President has generally been one of support and reinforcement. The Court has been least willing to overturn his acts in time of war, when presidential resistance to Court decisions would be most likely. Although limiting somewhat the President's authority to remove certain government employees, the Court, since the NEW DEAL, has sustained DELEGATIONS OF POWER to the President and the executive branch and has generally been deferential to the REGULATORY COMMISSIONS since WORLD WAR II. Confrontations between Court and President have been relatively infrequent; when the Court invalidates policies the President had espoused, for example, WIRETAPPING, it is not attacking the presidency as an institution. Presidents may have been reluctant to assist in enforcing the Court's decisions, but direct defiance is rare indeed. Both President HARRY S. TRUMAN and President RICHARD M. NIXON complied with orders when their actions (seizure of the steel mills and withholding of tapes) were ruled improper. In those situations, as with IMPOUNDMENT of appropriated funds, the Court insisted that the President follow the law as interpreted by the courts rather than determine for himself whether he should be subject to it; in the case of the STEEL SEIZURE, the Court insisted that he follow a course of action legislated by Congress.

The Court has had considerable impact on Congress's internal processes—its authority to exclude members, LEGISLATIVE INVESTIGATIONS, and the CONTEMPT POWER. Congressional reaction to the Court's decisions has been manifested in a number of ways. After the Court has engaged in statutory interpretation or, less frequently, has invalidated statutes for VAGUENESS, Congress has often rewritten or reenacted the laws to reestablish its "legislative intent," in effect establishing a continuing dialogue between Court and Congress. Congress has also shown negative reaction to the Court's ruling through proposals to eliminate APPELLATE JURISDICTION in particular classes of cases, for example, internal security, abortions, and school prayer, but these attempts have been less frequent and far less successful than those to rewrite statutes. Efforts to overturn the Court's rulings have also resulted in introduction of numerous proposals to amend the Constitution, but most such proposals die. Only a few—the ELEVENTH AMENDMENT, CIVIL WAR amendments, SIXTEENTH AMENDMENT, and TWENTY-SIXTH AMENDMENT—have been both submitted and ratified.

The impact of the Supreme Court's decisions extends well beyond the other branches of the national government. Controversial Supreme Court rulings have affected public opinion and have produced divided editorial reaction on a wide range of decisions. Changes in the public's feelings of trust or confidence in the Court have paralleled changes in feeling about the presidency and Congress but generally have been somewhat more positive. Such ratings have changed rapidly, but shifts in the Court's doctrine on controversial topics (such as CRIMINAL PROCEDURE) in the direction of public opinion usually are not immediately reflected in changed public opinion ratings.

The public generally supports the Court's work. Those giving the Court general (or "diffuse") support, however, outnumber those giving the Court specific support (for particular rulings) by a large ratio. The proportion of the public that feels the Court may legitimately produce structural political change is quite small. Acquiescence in the Court's rulings, which helps produce compliance, has been more common than active approval of the decisions.

The public also has little information about the Court. Even many controversial decisions fail to penetrate the general public's consciousness. The greater the knowledge, however, the greater the *dis*approval, but those reporting negative views on specific cases outnumber those whose general view of the Court is negative. Those with negative views also tend to hold them more intensely, but seldom would most members of the public do more than write letters of protest; demonstrations and other overt protest are atypical. Negative views about the Court are usually accounted for by reactions to the few specific decisions that catch the attention of large proportions of the public. Those salient decisions change with considerable rapidity, shifting in the 1960s from civil rights and school prayer to criminal procedure.

The Supreme Court's impact on the states and local communities is varied. Effectuating many decisions involves little controversy, and implementation may be prompt and complete, particularly if actions of only a few public officials are necessary. Other rulings, such as those on school DESEGREGATION, school prayer, and criminal procedure, produce a disproportionate amount both of resistance or attempts to evade and of critical rhetoric— rhetoric at times not matched by reality. Despite claims that the warnings required by MIRANDA V. ARIZONA (1966) would have a negative impact on police work, suspects and defendants often talk to police after being "read their rights." However, even these criticized rulings have definite impacts, for example, more professional police work as a result of criminal procedure rulings. Although opponents of the rule that improperly seized evidence should be excluded (the EXCLUSIONARY RULE of MAPP V. OHIO, 1961) have claimed that the rule does not deter illegal seizures and is too costly because guilty defendants are set free, some studies have suggested that the rule might be having some of its intended effect. At least in some cities, few cases were dropped after motions to suppress evidence and a higher proportion of searches conducted after the rule was promulgated were constitutional.

If people are to comply with Supreme Court rulings or if the rulings are to have an impact, they must be communicated to those expected to implement or adhere to them. One cannot, however, assume that effective communication takes place. A ruling may have to be transmitted through several levels, at each of which distortion can be introduced, before reaching its ultimate audience. Lawyers may be accustomed to easy access to the Court's published opinions, but many others, such as police or school officials, often do not receive the opinions or have such direct access to them and must therefore rely on other means of communication through which to learn of them.

The mass media, with the exception of a few newspapers, provide only sketchy information about the Court's decisions. Specialized media, for example, trade publications, provide only erratic coverage even of decisions relevant to the groups for which they are published. Most newspapers and radio and television stations must rely on the wire services for information about Supreme Court rulings. Disproportionate nationwide emphasis is given to decisions the wire services emphasize, with little or no coverage given to other rulings. The media also have different patterns of coverage ("profiles"). Newspapers, for example, give more attention to postdecision events, while the wire services and television pay more attention to cases before they are decided. All the media, however, generally convey much information about immediate reaction to, or impact of, decisions instead of emphasizing the content of, or rationale for, the Court's rulings.

The lower courts do not constitute a bureaucratic structure through which decisions are fully communicated downward. Lawyers thus become particularly important in transmitting the Court's rulings, as they are in transmitting any law. Lower court judges who do not routinely follow the Court's decisions may find out about them only if lawyers arguing cases cite the decisions, which they do not always do accurately. Lawyers, either individually or through their bar associations, do little to inform the general public about developments in the law. Some state attorneys general and local prosecutors undertake to inform state and local officials of recent rulings affecting their work. The failure of these officials to do so in most locations has led some local agencies, which can afford to do so, to hire their own lawyers, for example, police department "police legal advisers," to monitor the Court's rulings, provide appropriate information to the agency, and arrange for implementation.

Training programs—effective because they combine printed materials with oral presentation—can be particularly important in the transmission of rulings. They are especially necessary because the educational system has generally done little to educate students, later to be members of the general public, about the Court's functioning or its rulings. Training programs are, however, not available to all those expected to be cognizant or familiar with the Court's rulings. Many members of some important occupational groups such as the police do not receive adequate legal training about the Court's decisions. Even if initially well-trained, they are less likely to receive adequate follow-up through in-service training.

The impact of the Court's decisions is, of course, affected by far more than deficiencies and distortions in the lengthy, often convoluted process by which the decisions are communicated. Numerous other factors affect both the communication process, thus indirectly affecting impact, and impact itself. One is the legitimacy attributed to the Court and its work. If a particular audience, for example, the police during the WARREN COURT's "criminal procedure revolution," feels that the Court is not acting fairly or lacks appropriate information on which to base its decisions, that audience will heed the Court's word less carefully even when the opinions are fully communicated. Characteristics of the Court's rulings, such as their relative unanimity and relative clarity or ambiguity, are also important, as both unanimity and clarity are thought to produce greater compliance. In new and sensitive areas of policy such as civil rights and criminal procedure, the lower courts can exercise power over the Supreme Court by their resistance. Rulings by lower court judges applying and extending (or narrowing) the Court's decisions are particularly important in such situations and in those where gaps in doctrinal development—a result of case-by-case development of the law—leave unanswered questions. In many, perhaps most, areas of the law, however, lower court judges enforce Supreme Court rulings because those rulings are a matter of relative personal indifference for the judges, because they have been socialized to follow those rulings, and because they wish to avoid being reversed.

Whether someone follows up a decision, who that "someone" is, and how they act, also affect a decision's impact. Elites' support for a decision may be able to calm negative public reaction. The likelihood that desegregation would be accepted in either the short or long run was decreased because southern elites were not favorably disposed toward either the result of BROWN V. BOARD OF EDUCATION (1954) or the Court's opinion. Because most rulings of the Court are not self-enforcing, follow-up by government agencies is often crucial for effective implementation. Officials not committed to the values in the Court's rulings are less likely to be assiduous in their follow-up; thus the attitudes of individual decision makers, particularly those in key policymaking or enforcement positions, are of considerable importance.

The situation into which a Supreme Court ruling is "injected"—whether in a crisis or in normal times—also affects the ruling's impact. A local community's belief system and its past history both are part of that situation. So are community pressures on the individuals expected to carry out the Court's dictates. Often a wide variety of enforcement mechanisms must be used before compliance is achieved. Incentive systems in organizations can lead individuals either to follow the Court's rulings or to continue existing practices. Because organizations have considerable interest in maintaining such practices, externally imposed penalties may be insufficient to produce required change.

To overcome problems of communicating Supreme Court rulings so that they reach the appropriate audience might seem insuperable. The Court's rulings are, however, often complied with and do have widespread impact. Were it otherwise, we should not hear so much about the problems occurring in particularly sensitive areas of the law such as civil rights and CIVIL LIBERTIES. The difficulties in implementing the Court's decisions to achieve their greatest impact should remind us that, as an active policymaker, the Supreme Court faces many of the same problems faced by other policymaking institutions.

STEPHEN L. WASBY
(1986)

Bibliography

BECKER, THEODORE L. and FEELEY, MALCOLM, eds. 1973 *The Impact of Supreme Court Decisions: Empirical Studies*, 2nd ed. New York: Oxford University Press.

JOHNSON, CHARLES A. and CANON, BRADLEY C. 1984 *Judicial Policies: Implementation and Impact*. Washington D.C.: Congressional Quarterly Press.

KRISLOV, SAMUEL, ed. 1972 *Compliance and the Law: A Multidisciplinary Approach*. Beverly Hills, Calif.: Sage Publications.

WASBY, STEPHEN L. 1970 *The Impact of the United States Supreme Court: Some Perspectives*. Homewood, Ill.: Dorsey Press.

SUPREME COURT OPINIONS

See: Advisory Opinion; Concurring Opinion; Dissenting Opinion; Grounds of Opinion; Opinion of the Court; Plurality Opinion; Public Understanding of Supreme Court Opinions

SUPREME COURT PRACTICE

The SUPREME COURT is the only judicial body created by the Constitution. Article III, Section 1, specifies that "The JUDICIAL POWER OF THE UNITED STATES, shall be vested in one supreme Court, and in such inferior Courts as the Congress may from time to time ordain and establish." The judges of that "one supreme Court," like the judges of the inferior courts created by Congress, are to hold their offices "during GOOD BEHAVIOUR" and to suffer no diminution of compensation during their continuance in office. Supreme Court Justices can be impeached, however. And it is not constitutionally clear that their "good Behaviour" term of office is the equivalent of a life term, as generally thought.

In practice, this "one supreme Court" has always acted as a unitary body. That means that the Court never divides into panels or groups of Justices for purposes of resolving matters submitted to the Court. All petitions and briefs are circulated to, and considered by, all participating Justices; and all Court decisions are rendered on behalf of the Court as a unit of nine Justices.

Article III of the Constitution, in establishing the judicial institution known as the Supreme Court, vests in the Court two basic kinds of jurisdiction: ORIGINAL JURISDICTION and APPELLATE JURISDICTION. The Court's original jurisdiction is its power to decide certain cases and controversies in the first instance. Its appellate jurisdiction is its power to review certain cases and controversies decided in the first instance by lower courts.

In COHENS V. VIRGINIA (1821), Chief Justice JOHN MARSHALL stated that the Court "must decide" a case before it that is properly within one of these two areas of jurisdiction, and that the Court has "no more right to decline the exercise of jurisdiction which is given, than to usurp that which is not given . . . [either of which] would be treason to the Constitution." But in the Court's judicial world, Marshall's proposition is no longer universally true, if it ever was. The modern need to control and limit the voluminous number of cases clamoring for review has forced the Court to resist demands that every facet of the Court's vested jurisdiction be exercised. Limitations of time and human energy simply do not permit the luxury of resolving every dispute that comes before the Court. Notions of judicial prudence and sound discretion, given these limitations, have thus become dominant in the Court's selection of those relatively few cases it feels it can afford to review in a plenary fashion and to resolve the merits. Such factors are evident in the Court's control of both its original docket and its appellate docket.

Section 2 of Article III specifies that the Supreme Court "shall have original jurisdiction" in all cases "affecting Ambassadors, other public Ministers and Consuls, and those in which a State shall be Party." Compared with cases on the appellate docket, cases on the original docket are quite few in number. Indeed, cases involving ambassadors, ministers, and consuls have never been common and have virtually disappeared from the original docket. The typical original case has thus become that in which a state is the plaintiff or defendant; most frequent are suits between two or more states over boundaries and water rights, suits that cannot appropriately be handled by any other tribunal. States have also sued each other over state financial obligations, use of natural resources, multistate domiciliary and escheat problems, breaches of contracts between states, and various kinds of injuries to the public health and welfare of the complaining state.

States can also invoke the Court's original jurisdiction to sue private nonresident citizens, or ALIENS, for alleged injuries to the sovereign interests of the complaining state. And a state may bring such suits on behalf of all its citizens to protect the economy and natural resources of the state, as well as the health and welfare of the citizens. The ELEVENTH AMENDMENT bars an original action against a defendant state brought by a private plaintiff who is a citizen of another state; and the sovereign immunity principle recognized by that Amendment also bars such an action by a citizen of the defendant state. Because that amendment does not apply to the federal sovereign as plaintiff, the United States can bring an original action in the Supreme Court against a defendant state. All cases brought by a state against a private party defendant, however, fall within the nonexclusive category of the Court's original jurisdiction; such suits can alternatively be brought in some other federal or state court. The Court in recent years has sought to reduce its original docket workload by rejecting some nonexclusive causes of action and requiring the parties to proceed in an available alternative forum.

Original cases often involve factual disputes. In processing such cases, the Court considers itself the equivalent of a federal trial court, though with significant differences. The Court's rules and procedures in this respect are not very specific, and practices may vary from case to case. The case starts with a motion for leave to file a complaint, a requirement that permits the Court to consider and resolve jurisdictional and prudential objections. If the Court denies the motion for leave to file, the case terminates. If the motion is granted, the complaint is ordered filed, the defendant files an answer, and in most instances a trial ensues.

The Justices themselves do not conduct trials in original cases. Instead, they appoint a member of the bar or a retired lower court judge to serve as a special master. The special master then takes evidence, hears witnesses, makes fact-findings, and recommends legal conclusions.

But all rulings, findings, and conclusions of the special master are subject to review by the Court. That review occurs after parties aggrieved by the special master's actions have filed exceptions thereto; all parties then brief and orally argue the exceptions before the entire Court, which decides the case by written opinion. A complicated case may require more than one hearing before the special master and more than one opinion by the Court, prolonging the case for years.

The Court itself has admitted that it is "ill-equipped for the task of factfinding and so forced, in original cases, awkwardly to play the role of factfinder without actually presiding over the introduction of evidence." Original cases take away valuable time and attention from the Court's main mission, the exercise of its appellate jurisdiction, where the Court serves as the prime overseer of important matters of federal constitutional and statutory law. The Court is thus increasingly disposed to construe its original jurisdiction narrowly, exercising that jurisdiction only where the parties cannot secure an initial resolution of their controversy in another tribunal. If there is such an alternative proceeding, the Court prefers to REMAND the parties to the lower court and to deal with any important issues in the case on review of the lower court's determination.

The Court's appellate jurisdiction is also defined and vested by Article III, section 2. That jurisdiction extends to all categories of CASES AND CONTROVERSIES, decided in the first instance by lower federal courts or state courts, that fall within the JUDICIAL POWER OF THE UNITED STATES. Those categories include: cases arising under the Constitution, laws, and treaties of the United States; cases affecting ambassadors, ministers, and consuls; cases of ADMIRALTY AND MARITIME JURISDICTION; controversies to which the United States is a party; controversies between two or more states; and controversies between a state and citizens of another state, between citizens of different states, between citizens of the same state claiming lands under grants of different states, or between a state or its citizens and foreign states or citizens. The Court's appellate jurisdiction extends "both as to Law and Fact, with such Exceptions, and under such Regulations as the Congress shall make."

The exceptions clause in section 2 contains within it a constitutional enigma, as yet unsolved. The problem is the extent of Congress's power to control and limit the Supreme Court's appellate jurisdiction. The Court has never held that its appellate jurisdiction is coterminous with the section 2 categories of judicial power. Consistently since *Wiscart v. Dauchy* (1796) the Court has said, albeit often by way of OBITER DICTUM, that it can exercise appellate jurisdiction only to the extent permitted by acts of Congress, and that a legislative denial of jurisdiction may be implied from a failure by Congress to make an affirmative grant of jurisdiction. The Court, in other words, assumes that its appellate jurisdiction comes from statutes, not directly from section 2 of Article III. The assumption is that Congress cannot add to the constitutional definitions of appellate jurisdiction, but that Congress can subtract from or make exceptions to those definitions.

It is clear that Congress has made broad statutory grants of jurisdiction to the Court, though not to the full extent permitted by section 2. These affirmative grants have always been sufficient to permit the Court to fulfill its essential function of interpreting and applying the Constitution and of insuring the supremacy of federal law. So far, the statutory omissions and limitations have not hobbled the performance of that function.

At the same time, periodic proposals have been made in Congress to use the exceptions clause to legislate certain exclusions from the appellate jurisdiction previously granted by Congress. Such proposals usually spring from displeasure with Court decisions dealing with specific constitutional matters. The proponents would simply excise those areas of appellate jurisdiction that permit the Court to render the objectionable decisions. Many commentators contend that the exceptions clause was not designed to authorize Congress to strip the Court of power to perform its essential function of overseeing the development of constitutional doctrines and guarantees. Objections are also raised that such legislative excisions are mere subterfuges for overruling constitutional rights established by the Court, a most serious infringement of the separation of powers doctrine. Because no jurisdictional excisions of this broad nature have been enacted, the Court has yet to speak to this constitutional conundrum. (See JUDICIAL SYSTEM.)

Whatever the outer limits of the exceptions clause, Congress since 1789 has vested in the Court broad appellate power to review lower court decisions that fall within the constitutional "case or controversy" categories. Statutes permit the Court to review virtually all decisions of lower federal appellate courts, as well as a limited number of decisions of federal trial courts. And Congress has from the start given the Court jurisdiction to review decisions of the highest state courts that deal with federal constitutional, treaty, or statutory matters.

An ingredient of most jurisdictional statutes are legislative directions as to the mode by which the Court's appellate powers are to be invoked. In modern times, most lower court decisions are made reviewable by way of WRIT OF CERTIORARI or, in a declining number of specialized instances, by way of APPEAL. Congress permits the Court to issue its own extraordinary writs, such as HABEAS CORPUS or MANDAMUS, and to review certain matters not otherwise reviewable on certiorari or appeal; and there is a rarely used authorization for lower federal appellate court CERTIFICATION of difficult questions to be answered by the Supreme Court.

At COMMON LAW, the term "certiorari" means an original writ commanding lower court judges or officers to certify and transfer the record of the lower court proceedings in a case under review by a higher court. In the Supreme Court lexicon, the common law meaning of the term has been modified and expanded. Certiorari refers generally to the entire process of discretionary review by the Supreme Court of a lower court decision. Such review is sought by filing a petition for writ of certiorari. That document sets forth in short order the reasons why the questions presented by the decision below are so nationally important that the Court should review the case and resolve those questions on the merits. In most cases, the record in the court below is not routinely filed in the Court along with the petition.

Each Justice, after reviewing the petition for certiorari, the brief in opposition, and the opinion below, makes his or her own subjective assessment as to the appropriateness of plenary review by the entire Court. Such review is granted only if at least four Justices vote to grant the petition, a practice known as the RULE OF FOUR. If the petition is granted, a formal order to that effect is entered; copies of the order are sent to the parties and to the court below, which is then requested to transmit a certified copy of the record. But at no time does any writ of certiorari issue from the Court. The parties proceed thereafter to brief and argue orally the questions presented in the petition.

An appeal, on the other hand, refers to a theoretically obligatory type of review by the Supreme Court. That means that once the appeal is properly filed and docketed, the Court must somehow consider and dispose of the case on its merits. There is said to be no discretion to refuse to make such a decision on the merits of the appeal, which serves to distinguish an appeal from a certiorari case.

To invoke the Court's review powers by way of appeal, the aggrieved party first files a short notice of appeal in the lower court and then dockets the appeal in the Supreme Court by filing a document entitled "jurisdictional statement." Apart from the different title, a jurisdictional statement is remarkably like a petition for writ of certiorari. Like a petition, the jurisdictional statement sets forth briefly the reasons why the issues are so substantial, or important, "as to require plenary consideration, with briefs on the merits and oral argument, for their resolution." The Rule of Four is followed in considering whether to grant plenary consideration of an appeal. Such a grant takes the form of an order to the effect that "probable jurisdiction is noted," although if there remains any question as to whether the case complies with the technical jurisdictional requirements of an appeal, the order is changed to read: "further consideration of the question of jurisdiction is postponed to the hearing of the case on the merits." The appeal then follows the pattern of a certiorari case with respect to obtaining the record from the lower court(s), briefing the questions presented, and arguing orally before the Court.

As if to underscore the similarity between a jurisdictional statement and a petition for writ of certiorari, Congress has directed the Court, in situations where a party has "improvidently" taken an appeal "where the proper mode of review is by petition for certiorari," to consider and act on the jurisdictional statement as if it were a petition for writ of certiorari, and then either granting or denying certiorari. Thus a party cannot be prejudiced by seeking the wrong mode of Supreme Court review.

There is, however, one historical and confusing difference in the Court's summary disposition of certiorari cases and appeals, a difference springing from the notion that the Court is obliged to dispose of all appeals on their merits. When a petition for writ of certiorari is denied, the order denying the petition has no precedential value. It means only that fewer than four Justices, or perhaps none at all, want to hear and decide the merits of the questions presented. That is the end of the case.

But when fewer than four Justices wish to hear an appeal in a plenary manner, the long-held theory is that the Court is still compelled to dispose of the appeal on the merits of the questions presented. To comply with this theory, which is judge-made and not dictated by Congress, the Court has constructed a number of one-line orders, any one of which can be used to dismiss or dispose of the appeal without further briefing or oral argument. A typical order of this nature, used particularly in appeals from state court decisions, reads: "the appeal is dismissed for want of a substantial FEDERAL QUESTION." Such summary orders, which are devoid of explanation of the insubstantiality of the question involved, consistently have been held to be precedents. The Court has said that they must be understood and followed by state and lower federal courts.

In 1978, all nine Justices publicly conceded to the Congress that, while these summary dispositions of appeals are decisions on the merits, experience has shown that they "often are uncertain guides to the courts bound to follow them and not infrequently create more confusion than clarity." The Justices accordingly asked Congress to eliminate virtually all appeals, thereby recognizing formally that the Court's appellate jurisdiction is almost wholly discretionary. Congress has yet to respond.

At the start in 1789 and for a century thereafter, the Court was authorized to exercise only mandatory jurisdiction, either by way of appeal or a closely related process known as WRIT OF ERROR. But as the nation expanded and matured, litigation proliferated. It became evident toward the end of the nineteenth century that the Court could not keep up with its growing docket if it had to continue resolving the merits of every case that was filed. Gradually, Congress began to withdraw some of this mandatory jurisdiction from the Court, replacing it with discretionary jurisdiction by way of certiorari. But it was not until 1925 that Congress decreed a major shift toward discretionary review powers. At that time the dockets of the Court were so clogged with mandatory appeals and writs of error that litigants had to wait two and three years to have their cases decided. In the JUDICIARY ACT OF 1925, written largely at the suggestion of the Court, Congress transferred large segments of appellate jurisdiction from the obligatory to the discretionary category. Fully eighty percent of the Court's docket thereafter was of the certiorari variety.

But the 1925 transfer proved insufficient. During the 1970s, Congress eliminated many of the remaining appeals that could be taken from lower federal courts, leaving only a handful within the federal sector of Supreme Court jurisdiction. The largest pocket of mandatory appeals left untouched consists of appeals from state court decisions validating state statutes in the face of federal constitutional challenges. The caseload explosions in the 1970s and 1980s, which saw the Court's annual case filings rising near the 5,000 mark, created pressure to eliminate all significant remnants of mandatory appeal jurisdiction.

Nearly one-half of these filed cases are petitions and applications filed by prisoners, petitions that are often frivolous and thus quickly disposed of. But from the overall pool of some 5,000 cases the Justices select about 150 cases each term for plenary review and resolution. The Justices feel that time limitations do not permit them to dispose of many more than 150 important and complex controversies, although they do manage to dispose of another 200 or so cases in a summary fashion, without briefs or oral arguments. In any event, the number of cases granted full review has hovered around the 150 mark for many of the last fifty years. This constancy is largely the product of the discretion and the docket control inherent in the certiorari jurisdiction. Without discretion to deny review to more than ninety-five percent of the certiorari petitions filed each year, the Court's ability to function efficiently would soon cease.

The procedures by which the Court achieves this docket control and makes this vital selection of cases for plenary review are simple but not well understood by the public. And some of the processes change as workloads increase and issues tend to become more difficult of resolution. As of the 1980s, the procedures may be summarized as follows:

By law, the Supreme Court begins its annual TERM, or working session, on the first Monday in October. Known as the October Term, this session officially runs for a full year, eliminating the prior practice of convening special sessions during the summer to hear urgent matters. But for most administrative purposes, each term continues for about nine months, October through June, or until all cases considered ready for disposition have been resolved. At that point, the Court normally recesses without formally adjourning until the following October.

The Court usually disposes of requests for review, hears oral arguments, and issues written opinions only during the nine-month working portion of the term. But the Court never closes for purposes of accepting new cases, as well as briefs and motions in pending cases. That means that filing time requirements are never waived during the summer recess; parties must respect those requirements in all seasons. In most civil cases, certiorari petitions and jurisdictional statements must be filed within ninety days from the entry of judgment, or from the denial of rehearing, in the court below. This filing period is only sixty days in criminal cases, federal or state.

As soon as opposing parties have filed briefs or motions in response to a certiorari petition or jurisdictional statement, these documents are circulated to all nine Justices. These circulations occur on a weekly basis all year round. The circulated cases are then scheduled by the Court's clerk for disposition by the Justices at the next appropriate CONFERENCE. Cases circulated during the summer recess accumulate for consideration at a lengthy conference held just before the opening of the new October term. Cases circulated during term time are considered at a conference held about two weeks after a given weekly circulation.

The massive numbers of case filings make it impossible for every Justice personally to examine these thousands of documents, although some may try. Most are aided in this task by law CLERKS, each Justice being entitled to employ four. The clerks often have the task of reading these documents and reducing them to short memoranda for the convenience of their respective Justices. In recent years, a number of Justices have used a "cert pool" system, whereby law clerk resources in several chambers are pooled to produce memoranda for the joint use of all the participating Justices. But whether a Justice reads all these matters or is assisted by law clerk memoranda, the ultimate discretionary judgments made respecting the grant or denial of review are necessarily those of each Justice. Law clerks simply do not make critical judgments or cast votes.

Law clerks are selected personally by each Justice, a practice dating back to 1882 when Justice HORACE GRAY first employed a top Harvard Law School graduate. In modern times, clerks are invariably selected from among recent law school graduates with superior academic re-

cords. And many Justices require that their clerks also have clerked for lower court judges. The clerks normally stay with their Justices for one term only, though some have served longer. Many law clerks have gone on to distinguished legal careers of their own. Three of them have become Supreme Court Justices: Justices BYRON R. WHITE, WILLIAM H. REHNQUIST, and JOHN PAUL STEVENS.

An important element of each Justice's workload is to act in the capacity of Circuit Justice, a vestigial remnant of the earlier circuit-riding tasks. For this purpose, each Justice is assigned one or more federal judicial circuits, which divide the nation into twelve geographical areas. The Justice assigned to a particular circuit handles a variety of preliminary motions and applications in cases originating in the area covered by the circuit. Included are such matters as applications for stays of lower court judgments pending action on a petition for certiorari, applications in criminal cases for bail or release pending such action, and applications to extend the time for filing certiorari or appeal cases. Law clerks frequently assist in processing these applications, and on occasion an application may be disposed of by a written "in chambers" opinion of the Circuit Justice.

The Court no longer discusses every certiorari petition at conference. The excessive number of petitions makes it necessary and appropriate to curtail collegial discussion of petitions at the formal conferences of the Justices. At present, the Chief Justice circulates a "discuss list," a list of cases in a given weekly circulation deemed worthy of discussion and formal voting at conference. All appeals are discussed at conference, but rarely more than thirty percent of the certiorari cases are listed for discussion. Any Justice may add an omitted case to the list, however. Review is then automatically denied to any unlisted case, without conference consideration.

Decisions whether to grant or deny review of cases on the "discuss list" are reached at one of the periodic secret conferences. During term time, conferences are normally held each Friday during the weeks when oral arguments are heard, and on the Friday just before the commencement of each two-week oral argument period. Conferences can be held on other days as well. Only the Justices are present at these conferences; no law clerks or secretaries are permitted to attend.

Conferences are held in a well-appointed room adjacent to the Chief Justice's chambers, which are to the rear of the courtroom. The conference begins with exchanges of handshakes among the Justices, a custom originating in 1888. Coffee is available from a silver urn. The typical conference begins with discussion and disposition of the "discuss list" cases, appeals being considered first. The Chief Justice leads the discussion of each case, followed by each associate Justice in order of seniority. Any formal voting takes place in reverse order of seniority. Then, if there are argued cases to be decided, a similar order of discussion and voting is followed. Argued cases, however, may be discussed at other conferences scheduled immediately after a day or two of oral arguments, thus making the Friday conferences less lengthy.

Using the Rule of Four at these conferences, the Court selects from the pool of "discuss list" cases those that it will review and resolve on the merits, following full briefs and oral argument. A few cases, however, may be granted review and then resolved immediately in a summary manner without briefs or oral argument, by way of a PER CURIAM written opinion. Such summary disposition has been much criticized by those who lose their cases without being fully heard, but the practice has been codified in the Court's rules. The important point is that it is the cases that are selected at these conferences for plenary review that account for the 150 or so cases at the core of the Court's workload each term.

The cases thus selected for full review reflect issues that, in the Justices' view, are of national significance. It is not enough that the issues are important to the parties to the case; they must be generally important. But the Court rarely if ever explains why review is denied, or why the issues were not deemed important enough to warrant plenary attention. There are occasional written explanatory dissents from the denial of review, but these can only express the views of a minority. Review is granted only when four or more Justices are subjectively convinced that there are special and important reasons for reviewing the questions presented, which may or may not involve a conflict among lower courts as to how to resolve such questions. It bears emphasis that the exercise of this kind of discretionary judgment enables the Court to control its docket and to limit the extent of its plenary workload.

When a "discuss list" case is granted review, the petitioning party has forty-five days in which to file a brief on the merits, together with a printed record appendix. The opposing party then has thirty days to file a brief on the merits. Briefs of intervening parties and AMICI CURIAE, if there are any in a given case, are filed during these periods. When all briefs are in, the case is ready to be scheduled for oral argument.

Oral argument before the Justices occurs only on Monday, Tuesday, and Wednesday of a scheduled week of argument, leaving the other weekdays available for work and conferences. Usually, fourteen weeks of oral argument are scheduled, in two-week segments from October through April. One hour of argument is allowed in most cases, one-half hour for each side. Arguments start promptly at 10 a.m. and end at 3 p.m., with a lunch adjournment from noon to 1 p.m. The Justices are well prepared, having read the briefs. Some may also be aided by "bench memos" prepared by their law clerks, memoranda that outline the critical facts and the opposing arguments. Counsel arguing a case may thus expect sharp and penetrating questions from the bench; and counsel are warned by the Court's rules not to read arguments from a prepared text.

Sometime during the week in which a particular case has been argued, the Court meets in secret conference to decide the merits of that case. With the Chief Justice presiding and leading the discussion, the normal pattern of collegial discussion and voting takes place. But the vote reached at conference is necessarily tentative and subject to change as work begins on opinion writing. Shortly after the vote is taken, the case is assigned to one of the Justices to draft an opinion for the Court. The assignment is made by the senior Justice in the majority, if the vote is split. Normally, the assignment is made by the Chief Justice, unless he is in dissent.

The Justice assigned to write an opinion for the Court then begins work on a draft. This is essentially a lonely task. Following the conference discussion, there is little time for further collegial consultation among the Justices in the preparation of an opinion. Depending upon the work patterns of a particular Justice, the law clerks may engage in much of the research and analysis that underlie scholarly opinions; some clerks may be assigned the task of producing drafts of an opinion, while some Justices may do all the drafting themselves. Since 1981, drafting of opinions has been mechanically made easier by the installation of word processors in each Justice's chambers.

Once the draft of the majority opinion has been completed, it is circulated to all other members of the Court. The other Justices may suggest various changes or additions to the draft. To become an opinion of the Court, the draft opinion must attract the adherence and agreement of a majority of five Justices, which sometimes requires the author of the draft to accept modifications suggested by another Justice as the price of the latter's adherence. One or more of the Justices who cannot accept the reasoning or the result of the draft opinion then may produce their own drafts of CONCURRING or DISSENTING OPINIONS. The circulation of these separate opinion drafts may in turn cause the author of the majority draft to make further changes by way of answer to arguments made in a draft concurrence or dissent. Thus nothing is truly final until the collegial exchange of opinions is complete, the votes are set in concrete, and the result is considered ready for public announcement. Even then, there are cases in which the Court cannot reach a majority censensus, resulting in simply an announcement of the judgment of the Court accompanied by a number of PLURALITY, concurring, and dissenting opinions. The difficulty sometimes encountered in reaching a clear-cut majority result, while distressing to the bar and the lower courts, is generally reflective of the difficulty and complexity of some of the momentous issues that reach the Court.

The opinions and judgments of the Court in argued cases are announced publicly in the courtroom. At one time, opinions were uniformly announced on what became known as Opinion Monday. But the Court found that too many opinions announced on a Monday, particularly toward the end of a term, made it difficult for the press to give adequate media coverage to important Court rulings. The Court now announces opinions on any day it sits, thereby spreading out opinion announcements. In weeks in which oral arguments are scheduled for three days, the practice is to announce opinions only on a Tuesday or Wednesday, leaving Monday for the announcement of summary orders. Opinions may still be announced on a Monday, particularly if no oral arguments are scheduled for that day. After all oral arguments have been heard, usually by the end of April, opinions can be announced on any given Monday, when the Court sits to announce summary orders, or on any other day of the week that the Court wishes to sit solely to announce opinions.

The practices regarding the announcement of opinions in open court change from time to time. At one time, many opinions were read by the authors in full or in substantial part. More recently the Justices have tended merely to give short summaries save in the most important cases; in some less important cases only the result is announced. All opinions and orders are made available to the public and the news media a few moments after the courtroom announcements. Eventually, opinions and orders appear in bound volumes known as the United States Reports.

When the Court first convened in February of 1790, one of its first actions was to prescribe qualifications for lawyers wishing to practice before the Court. The original rule, in language very like that of the present rule, established two requirements: the attorney must have been admitted to practice in a state supreme court "for three years past," and the attorney's "private and professional character" must appear to be good.

Nearly 200,000 attorneys have been admitted to the Supreme Court bar since the Court was established. In recent times, as many as 6,000 have been admitted in a year. Prior to 1970, an attorney could be admitted only on motion of a sponsor in open court, before all the Justices. But the Court found that so much time was taken in listening to these routine motions and admissions and that it was often so expensive for a lawyer to travel to Washington from afar just to engage in this briefest of ceremonies, that an alternative "mail-order" procedure should be made available. Most attorneys today are admitted by mail, although some prefer to follow the earlier practice of being admitted in open court.

The modern Supreme Court bar has no formal structure or leadership. It is largely a heterogeneous collection of individual lawyers located in all parts of the nation. Many members of the bar never practice before the Court, and even fewer ever have the opportunity to argue orally. Most private practitioners who do have occasion to argue orally do so on a "once-in-a-lifetime" basis. Those who appear with some regularity before the Court are usually connected with an organization or governmental group specializing in Supreme Court litigation, such as the office of the SOLICITOR GENERAL of the United States. Gone are the days when private legal giants, such as DANIEL WEBSTER, were repeatedly employed specially by litigants to present oral arguments before the Court.

While a lay litigant may prepare and file petitions and briefs on the litigant's own behalf, without the aid of a member of the bar, the complexities and subtleties of modern practice make such self-help increasingly inadvisable. Only in the rarest of circumstances will the Court permit a lay litigant to present oral argument. Those imprisoned have frequently filed their own petitions for certiorari, seeking some sort of review of their criminal convictions. Indeed, about half of the nearly 5,000 case filings per year can be ascribed to prisoner petitions. The Court catalogues these petitions on its IN FORMA PAUPERIS docket but gives them the same careful treatment it gives petitions filed on behalf of clients who can afford to pay filing and printing costs.

The Court will, on application by an impecunious litigant or prisoner, appoint a member of the Court's bar to prepare briefs on the merits and to present oral arguments, once review has been granted in the case. But the Court will not appoint a lawyer to aid in preparing and filing a petition for certiorari or jurisdictional statement. Legal aid programs operating in most lower courts usually insure that a lawyer appointed or volunteering to represent a prisoner in the lower courts will be available to file such documents in the Supreme Court.

Such are the basic processes and procedures that enable the Court to perform its historic missions. As the Court approaches its third century, the Justices are deeply concerned with the Court's growing workload and the resulting effect upon the quality of its decision making. The Court's internal and external procedures have been streamlined and perfected about as much as possible. Some restructuring of its jurisdiction and functions seems necessary. Yet despite these perceived shortcomings, the Court has managed to maintain its prime role in the evolving history of the American legal system. The Court's effective performance of that role is due in no small part to the procedures and rules established for those who practice before it.

EUGENE GRESSMAN
(1986)

Bibliography

STERN, ROBERT L.; GRESSMAN, EUGENE; and SHAPIRO, STEPHEN M. 1986 *Supreme Court Practice*, 6th ed. Washington, D.C.: Bureau of National Affairs.

SUPREME COURT'S WORK LOAD

With the growth of population and the enormous expansion of federal law in the post-NEW DEAL period, the business of the federal courts has mushroomed. This increase is most striking in the first two tiers of the federal judicial pyramid. In the years 1960–1983, cases filed in UNITED STATES DISTRICT COURTS more than tripled, from 80,000 to 280,000, but cases docketed in the UNITED STATES COURTS OF APPEALS during the same period increased eightfold, from 3,765 to 25,580. To cope with this rise in appeals, Congress more than doubled the number of appellate judgeships. Not surprisingly, a similar growth can be found in Supreme Court filings: decade averages have increased in units of a thousand, from 1,516 per term in the 1950s to 2,639 in the 1960s, to 3,683 in the 1970s, to 4,422 in the 1981 term and 4,806 in the 1988 term.

The contrast between this explosion in federal judicial business and the fixed decisional capacity of the Supreme Court—the nine Justices sitting as a full bench hear an average of 150 argued cases per year—has led to persistent calls for enhancing the appellate capacity of the federal system. A number of proposals have emerged since 1970, none resulting in legislation. In 1971 the Study Commission on the Caseload of the Supreme Court, chaired by PAUL A. FREUND of the Harvard Law School, recommended creation of a National Court of Appeals (NCA) that would assume the Supreme Court's task of selecting cases for review. The Freund committee believed that the selection process consumed time and energy the Justices might better spend in deliberation and opinion writing. This proposal died at birth. In 1972, Congress created the Commission on Revision of the Federal Court Appellate System, chaired by Senator Roman Hruska. The Hruska commission envisioned a mechanism for national resolution of open intercircuit conflicts, recommending an NCA that would hear cases referred to it by the Supreme Court or the United States Courts of Appeals. This NCA was to be a permanent tribunal, with its own institutional identity and personnel. In 1983, Chief

Justice WARREN E. BURGER publicly endorsed proposed legislation to create on an experimental basis an Intercircuit Tribunal of the United State Courts of Appeals (ICT), which would decide cases referred to it by the Supreme Court. The ICT would be comprised of judges drawn from the current courts of appeals who would sit for a specified number of years. This proposal drew faint support.

Other proposals have sought to enhance national appellate capacity without establishing new tribunals. The most recent recommendation of this type can be found in the 1990 report of the Federal Courts Study Committee, chaired by Judge Joseph F. Weis, Jr. The report urges Congress to give the Supreme Court authority, for an experimental period, to refer cases presenting unresolved intercircuit conflicts to a randomly selected court of appeals for a ruling by that court's full bench. These EN BANC determinations would be binding on all other courts, save the Supreme Court.

Many of these proposals are conceived as measures to alleviate the Supreme Court's work load. The work load problem is, however, not one of obligatory jurisdiction; the Court's APPELLATE JURISDICTION has been largely discretionary as far back as the JUDICIARY ACT OF 1925, but even more so after 1988 legislation repealing virtually all mandatory appeals. The Justices do have to screen all of the petitions filed. It is doubtful, though, that any of the recent proposals promise much relief on this score. The Freund committee's NCA did, but received widespread criticism for suggesting delegation of the selection function. It is hard to believe referral to an NCA or a randomly selected court of appeals would reduce the Court's screening burden, for the losing party would still be free to appeal to the High Court. Moreover, the Justices will not likely tolerate nationally binding resolutions with which they disagree. Indeed, the Court's case selection process may be significantly complicated by adoption of any of these proposals.

If the Court's overload is not a function of its mandatory jurisdiction and if its selection burden cannot be alleviated (under current proposals), what function is the Court failing to perform that it ought to perform?

Critics claim that the Court is unable to ensure uniformity in federal law, because 150 appeals a year must leave unresolved an intolerable number of intercircuit conflicts. The evidence for this contention is largely anecdotal, and what little empirical work exists is sharply contested in the literature. Significant disagreement exists as to what constitutes a "conflict." Are conflicts clear disagreements over a governing issue of law or simply different approaches to a legal issue that are capable ultimately of being reconciled? Much also depends on one's view of the costs and benefits of leaving particular conflicts unresolved for a time. Does the absence of a rule of intercircuit STARE DE-CISIS in the federal system reflect a deliberate policy of allowing disagreements to percolate? The continuing conflicts may aid the Court's selection process by highlighting legal issues requiring national resolution. Through the process of multicourt consideration, the conflicts may improve the final decision of the Supreme Court when it does intervene. Moreover, some conflicts do not require immediate resolution, because they involve questions of local procedure, or do not frustrate planning concerns of multicircuit actors, or are not capable of being exploited by litigant forum shopping.

A broader claim, one not dependent upon the incidence of intercircuit conflict, is also made: that the problem is fundamentally one of insufficient supervision of the panel rulings of the courts of appeals. That conflicts are appropriately left unresolved does not matter, the argument goes. Given the sheer number of appeals, the practical inability of many of the circuits to engage in en banc review, and the infinitesimal probability of Supreme Court review, the panels operate as a law unto themselves. This version of the case for enhancing appellate capacity does have some force. It is undeniable that the Court can no longer engage in the kind of direct oversight of the courts of appeals that was possible in the 1920s, when it reviewed one in ten appellate rulings.

Whether this inability to supervise creates a problem requiring new institutional arrangements is, however, debatable. At present the Supreme Court appears not to have on its docket enough cases warranting plenary review to fill its argument calendar. Moreover, whether the panels operate as such wayward institutions is not clear. Many a circuit has, for example, adopted a "mini" en banc procedure to ensure uniformity of law within the circuit and to promote reconciliation of intercircuit splits. Even if one concedes that the Supreme Court has a work load problem (or that there is a need for additional appellate capacity), will the oversight benefits of an additional layer of review in, say, another 150 cases outweigh the attendant costs? Or will these otherwise nationally binding rulings be irresistible candidates for immediate plenary review by the Supreme Court—and hence a new category of practically mandatory jurisdiction?

The expansion of federal judicial business is the result of an explosion in federal law. Creating new layers of appeals creates more law, but not law enjoying the peculiar finality of a Supreme Court resolution. Improvements can be made. They are more likely to be found, however, in legislation reducing forum choice in federal statutes and imposing sanctions for unwarranted appeals; better management by the courts of appeals of panel disagreements and a greater willingness to reconsider circuit law in light of developments elsewhere; and strategic deployment by the High Court of its scarce decisional resources.

SAMUEL ESTREICHER
(1992)

Bibliography

BAKER, THOMAS E. and MCFARLAND, DOUGLAS D. 1987 The Need for a New National Court. *Harvard Law Review* 100: 1401–1416.

ESTREICHER, SAMUEL and SEXTON, JOHN E. 1986 *Redefining the Supreme Court's Role: A Theory of Managing the Federal Judicial Process.* New Haven, Conn.: Yale University Press.

GINSBURG, RUTH BADER and HUBER, PETER W. 1987 The Intercircuit Committee. *Harvard Law Review* 100:1417–1435.

POSNER, RICHARD 1985 *The Federal Courts: Crisis and Reform.* Cambridge, Mass.: Harvard University Press.

STRAUSS, PETER L. 1987 One Hundred Fifty Cases per Year: Some Implications of the Supreme Court's Limited Resources for Judicial Review of Agency Action. *Columbia Law Review* 87:1093–1136.

SUSPECT CLASSIFICATION

Long before the term "suspect classification" gained currency, Justice HARLAN FISKE STONE captured the idea in his opinion for the Supreme Court in UNITED STATES V. CAROLENE PRODUCTS CO. (1938). While insisting on RATIONAL BASIS as the appropriate STANDARD OF REVIEW for cases involving ECONOMIC REGULATION, Stone suggested that "prejudice against DISCRETE AND INSULAR MINORITIES [that is, religious, or national, or racial minorities] may be a special condition, which tends seriously to curtail the operation of those political processes ordinarily to be relied upon to protect minorities, and which may call for a correspondingly more searching judicial inquiry." In modern idiom, to call a legislative classification "suspect" is to suggest the possibility that it resulted from prejudice against the group it burdens, a possibility that justifies strict judicial scrutiny to assure that it is necessary to achieve a COMPELLING STATE INTEREST. In practice, most laws subject to this exacting standard are held invalid.

Irony attends the origins of the expression. Justice HUGO L. BLACK, writing for a majority in *Korematsu v. United States* (1944), one of the JAPANESE AMERICAN CASES, found no denial of EQUAL PROTECTION in an EXECUTIVE ORDER excluding American citizens of Japanese ancestry from the West Coast. Along the way to this extraordinary conclusion, however, he said: "all legal restrictions which curtail the civil rights of a single racial group are immediately suspect. That is not to say that all such restrictions are unconstitutional. It is to say that courts must subject them to the most rigid scrutiny." In *Korematsu* itself, the Court did no such thing; it paid the greatest deference to a "military" judgment that was chiefly political and steeped in racial prejudice. Yet *Korematsu's* main doctrinal legacy was that racial classifications were suspect.

In one view, this two-stage analysis, first identifying a classification as suspect and then subjecting it to STRICT SCRUTINY, is a roundabout way of addressing the issue of illicit legislative motives. (See LEGISLATION; WASHINGTON V. DAVIS.) Strict scrutiny is required in order to allay the suspicion that a law was designed to disadvantage a minority that lacked effective power in the legislature. That suspicion is laid to rest only by a showing that the law is well designed to achieve a legitimate purpose that has real importance. In another view, a classification based on race should be subjected to strict scrutiny because the immutable characteristic of race lends itself so well to a system thought dominated by stereotype, which automatically consigns a person to a general category, often implying inferiority. This concern for stigmatic harm is part of the substantive core of the equal protection clause, the principle of equal citizenship; the concern retains vitality even in an era when members of racial minorities have become electoral majorities in many of our major cities.

A number of egalitarian decisions in the later years of the WARREN COURT suggested a wide range of classifications that were candidates for inclusion by the Supreme Court in the "suspect" category: alienage, sex, ILLEGITIMACY, age, indigency. In the event, none of these candidates was accepted fully. Some classifications disadvantaging ALIENS were held "suspect," but many were not. The Court did significantly heighten the standard of review for most cases involving claimed denials of SEX DISCRIMINATION and gave some "bite" to the rational basis standard in cases involving illegitimacy. On the whole, however, the Court's behavior since the late 1970s suggests a determination to limit expansion of the list of suspect classifications, and thus to limit the occasions for active judicial supervision of legislation.

Some racial classifications are adopted as remedies for past societal discrimination based on race. Such an AFFIRMATIVE ACTION program presents neither of the principal dangers that have been said to require strict judicial scrutiny of racial classifications. There is less reason to suspect an illicit motive when a majoritarian body such as a legislature discriminates in favor of a historically disadvantaged minority, and the risk of stigmatic harm to a racial group is much reduced. Thus, varying majorities of the Supreme Court have consistently agreed that the appropriate standard of review for such remedial legislation, including RACIAL QUOTAS, is considerably less exacting than the strictest form of strict scrutiny.

The whole "suspect classifications" idea would seem to have outlived its usefulness. Surely the Supreme Court no longer needs the doctrine to justify its highest levels of intensity of judicial review. In race cases, for example, the Court needs no such locution in order to continue imposing on government a "heavy burden of justification" of laws imposing invidious racial discrimination. Abandonment of the rhetoric of suspect classifications would promote candor, by easing the way for open recognition of the sliding scale of standards of review now serving to cloak the Court's interest balancing. It would also remove a barrier, built into the very language of suspect "classifications," to doctrinal growth in the direction of affirmative governmental responsibility to alleviate those inequalities that prevent the realization of the principle of equal citizenship.

KENNETH L. KARST
(1986)

Bibliography

BREST, PAUL A. 1976 The Supreme Court, 1975 Term—Foreword: In Defense of the Antidiscrimination Principle. *Harvard Law Review* 90:1–54.
ELY, JOHN HART 1980 Democracy and Distrust: A Theory of Judicial Review. Cambridge, Mass.: Harvard University Press.

SUTHERLAND, GEORGE
(1862–1942)

George Sutherland, Supreme Court Justice from 1922 to 1938, was born in England in 1862. A year thereafter, he was brought by his parents to Brigham Young's Utah. Although he himself was never a Mormon, Sutherland attended a Mormon academy; in 1882–1883, he studied at the law school at the University of Michigan. On leaving the university, Sutherland was admitted to the Utah bar. He attained immediate prominence, both professionally and politically. He was elected to the HOUSE OF REPRESENTATIVES as a Republican in 1900 and to the SENATE in 1905, where he remained until 1917.

Sutherland's tenure in Congress forced him to confront issues in a political context that he would later deal with as a Supreme Court Justice. Generally he supported a conservative position. Yet his most enduring legislative achievements centered on improving conditions for seamen; advancing a federal WORKER'S COMPENSATION program; and promoting woman suffrage. Sutherland's congressional tenure enabled him as early as 1910 to establish his credentials for appointment to the Supreme Court. The 1920 election of Warren Harding, attributed in considerable part to Sutherland in his role of principal confidential adviser to the candidate, virtually assured him the nomination. The nomination was sent to an approving Senate on September 5, 1922.

Anyone interested in the new Justice's approach to legal and political problems had not far to look. In the five years since his retirement from the Senate, Sutherland had delivered major addresses setting forth his conservative philosophy. In his presidential address to the American Bar Association in 1917, he chose to speak on "Private Rights and Government Control." The message was clear. "Prying Commissions" and "governmental intermeddling" were unnecessary and at war with the "fundamental principle upon which our form of government depends, namely, that it is an empire of laws and not of men." Four years later Sutherland was telling the New York State Bar Association "that government should confine its activities, as a general rule, to preserving a free market and preventing fraud." He further explained that "fundamental social and economic laws" were beyond the "power of official control."

Once on the Court, Sutherland readily joined his conservative colleagues invoking SUBSTANTIVE DUE PROCESS to strike down exertions of governmental power. His first major opinion, in ADKINS V. CHILDREN'S HOSPITAL (1923), was directed at the minimum wage. Here, in the area of FREEDOM OF CONTRACT, no presumptive validity could be accorded to the exercise of legislative power. Rather, its legitimacy could be established only by "exceptional circumstances" and certainly not by considerations of a worker's needs or bargaining power. In short order, state attempts to regulate prices of gasoline, theater tickets, and employment agency services were similarly condemned. Other forms of state regulation fared no better. Nor was substantive due process the sole doctrinal reliance. In the Court's continuing battle with state legislatures, Sutherland led his colleagues in discovering hitherto unrealized prohibitions in the EQUAL PROTECTION, COMMERCE, and CONTRACT CLAUSES. And, under his hand, the PRIVILEGES AND IMMUNITIES clause of the FOURTEENTH AMENDMENT, neglected and forgotten for decades, sprang to life as a restraint on state power in COLGATE V. HARVEY (1935).

Eventually, of course, the Court repudiated the Sutherland approach to state legislative power and little of it remains. Yet, in at least two respects, his contribution in this area is of continuing significance. The first has to do with his seminal opinion in *Frost and Frost Trucking v. Railroad Commission* (1926) where he elaborated the theory of unconstitutional conditions. This theory destroyed the notion that a state's power to withhold a privilege somehow gives it authority to discriminate without check in granting the privilege. The second is his opinion for a divided court in EUCLID V. AMBLER REALTY (1926) which furnishes the constitutional foundation for the modern law of ZONING.

When Sutherland came to deal with the actions of Congress and the President, he exhibited the same jealousy of authority that characterized his response to state legislatures. Accordingly, he remained to the end unconvinced of the constitutionality of many of the New Deal enactments and in time was overwhelmed by the arrival of our modern-day Constitution of "powers." Even so, Sutherland's lasting impact will be found on close examination to have been highly significant. Particularly, he made highly personalized contributions to our *structural* Constitution; he had a distinctive role in shaping the Constitution as a guarantor of CIVIL RIGHTS; and he, more than anyone else, supplied the intellectual underpinnings for the FOREIGN AFFAIRS power.

As for the structural Constitution, Sutherland's opinion in *Massachusetts v. Mellon* (1923), and its companion case of FROTHINGHAM V. MELLON (1923), is still, despite scores of intervening qualifying decisions, the basic starting point in determining when a federal "taxpayer" has STANDING to raise a constitutional question in actions in the federal courts. Here plainly is one of the most telling limitations on federal judicial power. In a number of cases, Sutherland wrote opinions enforcing restraint on Supreme Court review of state decisions that were found to rest on independent and ADEQUATE STATE GROUNDS. In still others, he resisted effectively the pleas of reformers to whittle down guarantees of the right to TRIAL BY JURY, in civil as well as criminal cases. And in the highly technical matter of the relationship between state and federal courts, Sutherland's influence continues. Finally, Sutherland's views have been decisive in regard to the President's power to remove federal office holders. Early in his judicial career he concurred in Chief Justice WILLIAM HOWARD TAFT's unnecessarily wide-ranging opinion in MYERS V. UNITED STATES (1926), sanctioning a presidential power to remove without restraint. In HUMPHREY'S EXECUTOR V. UNITED STATES (1935) he started the Court on the way to new DOCTRINE. The removal power must take account of the nature of the office involved.

Sutherland's tenure on the Court spanned the years in which the Court began to take the BILL OF RIGHTS seriously as a check on STATE ACTION. His role in this development was not all of one piece. But he did write a leading opinion, in GROSJEAN V. AMERICAN PRESS COMPANY (1936), condemning a state tax on the press because of the levy's impermissible *motive* to make costly the criticism of public officials. And in POWELL V. ALABAMA (1932), he charted for the Court the first steps a state must take to assure counsel in legal proceedings. His problem there was counsel in a capital case. But Sutherland's opinion was not so confined in its implications and has proved influential even beyond the bounds of the criminal law.

Long before he went on the Court, Sutherland was

given to speculation about the foreign relations powers, producing in 1919 a book on the subject, *Constitutional Power and World Affairs*. In his book and elsewhere, Sutherland developed the theory that the powers of the United States in respect to foreign affairs were largely unrelated to any grant from the states and existed as an incident of SOVEREIGNTY devolved directly on the United States from Great Britain. Their employment and their distribution were to be governed by rules not applicable to the specific delegations of the Constitution. In 1936, in CURTISS-WRIGHT EXPORT CORP. V. UNITED STATES, Sutherland was able to incorporate these views in an opinion for a unanimous Court.

Sutherland retired from the Court in 1938. He died in 1942.

J. FRANCIS PASCHAL
(1986)

Bibliography
PASCHAL, JOEL FRANCIS 1951 *Mr. Justice Sutherland: A Man against the State.* Princeton, N.J.: Princeton University Press.

SWAIN v. ALABAMA
380 U.S. 202 (1965)

A 6–3 Court, speaking through Justice BYRON R. WHITE, rejected the claim of a black defendant to proportional representation of his race on grand and petit juries. Although blacks were substantially underrepresented on the jury panel, and although the prosecutor had used his peremptory challenges to exclude blacks in this case (there had been eight blacks on the venire), the Court found no evidence on the record of purposeful discrimination. The Court hinted that systematic use of peremptory challenges to exclude blacks from all juries would be unconstitutional, but it said that the record in *Swain* failed to show such systematic discrimination. In BATSON V. KENTUCKY (1986) the Court partially overruled *Swain*, holding that a prosecutor cannot constitutionally use peremptory challenges to exclude potential jurors solely on account of their race.

DENNIS J. MAHONEY
(1986)

(SEE ALSO: *Jury Discrimination.*)

SWANN v. CHARLOTTE-MECKLENBURG BOARD OF EDUCATION
402 U.S. 1 (1971)

Three years before *Swann* was decided, the Supreme Court had established a school board's affirmative duty to dismantle a school system that had been racially segregated by the command of law or by the board's deliberate actions. (See GREEN V. COUNTY SCHOOL BOARD.) In *Swann*, the Court was asked to apply this standard to a large metropolitan school district including the city of Charlotte, North Carolina, and its surrounding county. President RICHARD M. NIXON had made two appointments to the Court in the intervening years, and some observers expected the Justices' previous unanimity in school DESEGREGATION cases to be shattered in this case. In the event, no such thing happened; a unanimous Court affirmed a sweeping order by the federal district judge, James B. McMillan, calling for districtwide busing of children for the purpose of improving the schools' RACIAL BALANCE. (After issuing this order, Judge McMillan received death threats and was given police protection.) The *Swann* opinion was signed by Chief Justice WARREN E. BURGER. However, internal evidence strongly suggests that the opinion was a negotiated patchwork of drafts, and ivestigative journalists have asserted plausibly that Justice POTTER STEWART contributed its main substantive points.

Once a constitutional violation was found, the Court said, the school board had an obligation to take steps to remedy both present de jure segregation (see DE FACTO/DE JURE) and the present effects of past de jure segregation. These steps must achieve "the greatest possible degree of actual desegregation, taking into account the practicalities of the situation." The Court thus approved Judge McMillan's use of districtwide racial percentages as "a starting point" in shaping a remedy and placed on the school board the very difficult burden of showing that the continued existence of one-race schools was not the result of present or past de jure segregation. Finally, the Court approved the busing of children to schools not in their own neighborhoods as one permissible remedy within a court's discretion. The matter of busing, however, was not left to lower court discretion. In a COMPANION CASE from Mobile, Alabama, *Davis v. Board of School Commissioners*, the Court *required* busing the lower courts had not ordered.

Swann set the pattern for school desegregation litigation not only in southern cities but in the North and West as well. Once a court finds deliberate acts of segregation, *Swann's* affirmative duties arise.

KENNETH L. KARST
(1986)

(SEE ALSO: *Columbus Board of Education v. Penick; Keyes v. School District No. 1; School Busing.*)

Bibliography
FISS, OWEN M. 1974 School Desegregation: The Uncertain Path of the Law. *Philosophy & Public Affairs* 4:3–39.
WOODWARD, BOB and ARMSTRONG, SCOTT 1979 *The Brethren:*

Inside the Supreme Court. Pages 96–112. New York: Simon & Schuster.

SWAYNE, NOAH H.
(1804–1884)

Noah Haynes Swayne was the first of President ABRAHAM LINCOLN's five Supreme Court appointees. Geography, antislavery credentials, and support for the Union constituted Lincoln's chief criteria when he made his first appointments to the Court. Swayne fulfilled these qualifications.

Because of his hostility to SLAVERY, Swayne left his native Virginia and in 1823 moved to Ohio, where he served in the state legislature. In 1830 President ANDREW JACKSON named him United States Attorney. During the next several decades, he continued his active political career, and he appeared as counsel in a number of FUGITIVE SLAVERY cases. In 1855, he joined the fledgling Republican party and became a leading figure in the Ohio group. His close friend, Justice JOHN MCLEAN, had suggested Swayne as his successor. When McLean died early in 1861, Swayne quickly marshaled support from leading Ohio Republicans; Lincoln appointed him in January 1862.

On the Supreme Court, Swayne enthusiastically supported the administration, approving of Lincoln's blockade of southern ports in the PRIZE CASES (1862), upholding the Legal Tender Act of 1862 in *Roosevelt v. Meyer* (1863), and sustaining military trials in EX PARTE VALLANDIGHAM (1864). After the war, in EX PARTE MILLIGAN (1866), he joined the Court's minority faction which declined to discuss the question of congressionally authorized military tribunals.

During RECONSTRUCTION, Swayne again demonstrated consistent support for the congressional Republican program. For example, he dissented in the TEST OATH CASES (1867), and he voted to decline JURISDICTION in the unreported case of *Mississippi v. Stanton* (1868), when the Court divided evenly on whether to take another case that might have decided the fate of the Reconstruction program. Perhaps Swayne's clearest deference to congressional determination of Reconstruction was expressed in his dissent in TEXAS V. WHITE (1869). He rejected the majority fiction that Texas was not out of the Union and insisted that Texas's relationship to the Union must be determined by Congress. Swayne recognized that the FOURTEENTH AMENDMENT had been designed in part to benefit the freedmen, as evidenced by his vote in STRAUDER V. WEST VIRGINIA (1880), striking down RACIAL DISCRIMINATION in jury selection. Yet he repeatedly supported the Court's narrow construction of the FIFTEENTH AMENDMENT, thus limiting black VOTING RIGHTS.

After the CIVIL WAR, Swayne continued to back Republican programs. He dissented when the majority struck down the legal tender laws in 1870, but the next year he joined the new majority that reversed that decision. (See LEGAL TENDER CASES.) A decade later, just before his retirement, Swayne delivered the Court's opinion in SPRINGER V. UNITED STATES (1881) upholding the Civil War income tax. He impressively rejected arguments that the tax confiscated property without DUE PROCESS OF LAW and that it was a DIRECT TAX, and therefore need not be apportioned among the states according to population. That decision subsequently was temporarily overruled in POLLOCK V. FARMER'S LOAN AND TRUST (1895), but Swayne's opinion generally is regarded as the more historically valid.

In its time, Swayne's opinion in GELPCKE V. CITY OF DUBUQUE (1864) had enormous influence. Speaking for the Court, Swayne held that a state court could invalidate a lawfully controlled municipal bonding arrangement. The decision left countless municipalities responsible for maintaining railroad financing, despite popular protests against the practice as well as deceitful activities on the part of the railroads. Later, Swayne joined JOSEPH P. BRADLEY, STEPHEN J. FIELD, and SALMON P. CHASE in dissent in the SLAUGHTERHOUSE CASES (1873). Swayne's dissent lacked the elaborate rhetoric and logic of the Bradley and Field dissents, but he invoked the same mystical faith in the sanctity of property.

Swayne ranks as an ordinary Justice, not greatly appreciated even in his own time. His colleagues disapproved of his aggressive campaigning for the Chief Justiceship in 1864 and 1873, and he remained on the bench long after his physical and mental capacities had noticeably declined. He wrote few major opinions in his two decades on the bench.

STANLEY I. KUTLER
(1986)

Bibliography

FAIRMAN, CHARLES 1939 *Mr. Justice Miller and the Supreme Court, 1862–1890.* Cambridge, Mass.: Harvard University Press.

GILLETTE, WILLIAM 1969 Noah H. Swayne. In Leon Friedman and Fred L. Israel, eds., *The Justices of the Supreme Court*, Vol. 2:789–1010. New York: Chelsea House.

SWEATT v. PAINTER
339 U.S. 629 (1950)
MCLAURIN v. OKLAHOMA STATE REGENTS
339 U.S. 637 (1950)

Texas had established a separate law school for blacks; the state university law school thus rejected Sweatt, a black applicant. In *McLaurin*, the state university admitted a black to graduate study in education but made him sit in segregated classroom alcoves and at separate tables in the library and cafeteria. In both cases, state courts upheld the challenged SEGREGATION. In *Sweatt* the NAACP recruited some law professors to file a brief AMICUS CURIAE urging the Supreme Court to abandon the SEPARATE BUT EQUAL DOCTRINE and hold that state-sponsored segregation was unconstitutional. Eleven states supported the Texas position.

The Court unanimously held the practices of segregation in these cases unconstitutional, but it did not reach the broader issue. Chief Justice FRED M. VINSON wrote both opinions. In *Sweatt* he emphasized the intangibles of legal education: faculty reputation, influential alumni, traditions, prestige, and—most significant for the doctrinal future—a student body including members of a race that would produce an overwhelming majority of the judges, lawyers, witnesses, and jury members Sweatt might face. Assuming the continued vitality of "separate but equal," the new law school for blacks was not equal to the state university law school, and Sweatt must be admitted to the latter.

The *McLaurin* opinion, too, avoided direct attack on the separate-but-equal principle, but it sapped that principle's foundations: segregation impaired McLaurin's ability to study and learn, to discuss questions with other students and be accepted by them on his merits; thus the state must lift its restrictions on him.

In neither case did the Court discuss segregation's stigmatizing effects. In neither did the Court consider any asserted justifications for segregation. The only question was whether segregation produced significant inequality; affirmative answers to that question ended the Court's inquiries. Taken seriously, these decisions must lead—as they did, four years later—to the conclusion that racial segregation in public education is unconstitutional. (See BROWN V. BOARD OF EDUCATION.)

KENNETH L. KARST
(1986)

SWEEZY v. NEW HAMPSHIRE

See: *Watkins v. United States*

SWIFT v. TYSON
41 U.S. (16 Peters) 1 (1842)

In *Swift v. Tyson* the Supreme Court gave to the Rules of Decision Act (JUDICIARY ACT OF 1789, section 34) a construction that was to stand until ERIE RAILROAD CO. V. TOMPKINS (1938), almost a century later. As a result of this

construction, the federal courts came to exercise COMMON LAW authority over a wide variety of disputes, some of which involved matters outside the limits of federal legislative power. Because these federal court decisions did not purport to bind state courts, the result was often the parallel existence of two different rules of law applicable to the same controversy.

Proceeding on the basis of diversity of citizenship (see DIVERSITY JURISDICTION), Swift sued Tyson in a New York federal court on a bill of exchange. A critical question in the case was whether, in light of the particular facts, Swift was a "purchaser for value" of that bill. The Supreme Court, in an opinion by Justice JOSEPH STORY, held that he was, resolving the question on the basis of "general principles and doctrines of commercial jurisprudence," not on the basis of the decisional law of New York.

Tyson had argued that although there was no relevant state statute, the decisions of the New York state courts were controlling because the Rules of Decision Act provided that the "laws of the several states . . . shall be regarded as rules of decision . . . in cases where they apply." This provision, the Court replied, was limited in application to "the positive statutes of the state, and the construction thereof by the local tribunals, and to rights and titles to things having a permanent locality." It did not require adherence to state judicial decisions on such matters as "questions of general commercial law, where the state tribunals are called upon to perform the like functions as ourselves, that is, to ascertain, upon general reasoning and legal analogies . . . what is the just rule furnished by the principles of commercial law to govern the case."

Historians disagree on the justification and soundness of the *Swift* decision. But there is general agreement that in the years that followed, *Swift* was expanded well beyond its originally intended scope, and that its OVERRULING, in *Erie*, reflected a very different perception of the proper role of the federal courts.

DAVID L. SHAPIRO
(1986)

(SEE ALSO: *Federal Common Law, Civil.*)

SWIFT & COMPANY v. UNITED STATES
196 U.S. 375 (1905)

Justice OLIVER WENDELL HOLMES's opinion for a unanimous Supreme Court in *Swift* announced the STREAM OF COMMERCE doctrine, fundamental to constitutional COMMERCE CLAUSE adjudication ever since.

In 1902 Attorney General PHILANDER C. KNOX ordered that an EQUITY complaint be filed against the Beef Trust, the five largest meat-packing concerns in the country. The complaint alleged conspiracy and combination in restraint of interstate trade, suppression of competition, and price-fixing, all in violation of the SHERMAN ANTITRUST ACT. In 1903 federal district court judge PETER S. GROSSCUP issued a perpetual INJUNCTION against the packers. On appeal to the Supreme Court, the packers, though admitting the truth of the government allegations, contended that they were not involved in INTERSTATE COMMERCE. The entire transaction between the packers and those who purchased meat from them had occurred completely within the state where the packers slaughtered and prepared their meat. The sale had been consumated in-state and thus only IN-TRASTATE COMMERCE was involved. Knox's successor, WIL-LIAM H. MOODY, asserted that the restraint of trade directly affected interstate commerce even if no interstate acts were involved. Armed with the packers' admissions, Moody stressed the unity of the transactions, arguing that the operation had to be viewed as a whole.

The Court accepted Moody's view. The trust's "EFFECT UPON COMMERCE is not accidental, secondary, remote, or merely probable," Holmes declared, as he revised the Court's view of interstate commerce, affecting decisions for decades to come: "Commerce among the states is not a technical legal conception, but a practical one, drawn from the course of the business." Livestock moving from the range to the retailer, "with the only interruption necessary to find a purchaser at the stock yards," created "a current of commerce among the states, and the purchase of cattle is a part and incident of such commerce." Thus a local activity might be seen as part of interstate commerce. This stream of commerce doctrine fundamentally redirected the Court's examination of commerce clause questions and brought the Court face-to-face with economic reality, modifying the doctrinal effect of UNITED STATES V. E. C. KNIGHT COMPANY (1895).

DAVID GORDON
(1986)

Bibliography
GORDON, DAVID   1983   The Beef Trust: Antitrust Law and the Meat Packing Industry, 1902–1922. Ph.D. diss., Claremont Graduate School.

SWISHER, CARL BRENT
(1897–1968)

Carl Brent Swisher taught constitutional history for many years at Johns Hopkins University. A pioneer in the field of judicial biography, Swisher published *Stephen J. Field: Craftsman of the Law* (1930), still highly regarded. His *Roger B. Taney* (1935), the leading biography, and his posthumously published *The Taney Period, 1836–1864*

(1974; Vol. 5, Holmes Devise History of the Supreme Court) describe Taney's accomplishments as Chief Justice as well as his failures of judgment and proslavery bias, thereby rescuing Taney from the limbo to which most historians had consigned him in the wake of DRED SCOTT V. SANDFORD (1857). Swisher also published several general studies of constitutional law and the Supreme Court, including *American Constitutional Development* (1943; rev. ed. with E. M. Sait, 1954) and *The Supreme Court in Modern Role* (1958; rev. ed., 1965). In the most influential of these works, *The Growth of Constitutional Power in the United States* (1946; rev. ed., 1963), Swisher questioned the continuing usefulness of the doctrine of SEPARATION OF POWERS, fearing that it prevented government from achieving the ends which society increasingly expected government to achieve; he also urged government supervision of large corporations to check their political and economic power.

RICHARD B. BERNSTEIN
(1986)

SYMBOLIC SPEECH

Does communication by conduct rather than by words constitute "speech" within the FIRST AMENDMENT's guarantee of FREEDOM OF SPEECH? The status of communicative conduct, as with most free speech questions, is usually presented in an emotion-laden context: does the burning of a flag, or of a draft card, constitute a First-Amendment-protected activity? Is the act of marching in a public DEM-ONSTRATION (as distinguished from the placards which the marchers carry) a form of protected "speech?" Are school or other governmental regulations of hair styles an abridgment of freedom of speech? Does nude dancing constitute a form of First Amendment "speech?" Although the lower federal and state courts frequently have wrestled with all of these questions, the United States Supreme Court has yet to articulate a theoretical base that explains the status of symbolic speech under the First Amendment.

At least since STROMBERG V. CALIFORNIA (1931), the Supreme Court has assumed that "speech" within the meaning of the First Amendment's guarantee of "freedom of speech" includes more than merely verbal communications. In *Stromberg* the Court declared invalid a California statute that prohibited the public display of "any flag, badge, banner or device . . . as a sign, symbol or emblem of opposition to organized government." Among other decisions applying the First Amendment to nonverbal conduct, perhaps the most striking was TINKER V. DES MOINES INDEPENDENT COMMUNITY SCHOOL DISTRICT (1969). The Court there upheld the right of high school students to wear black armbands as a protest against American participation in the VIETNAM WAR, calling their conduct "the type of symbolic act that is within the Free Speech Clause of the First Amendment."

But if conduct sometimes constitutes protected "speech," sometimes it does not. UNITED STATES V. O'BRIEN (1968) affirmed a conviction for draft card burning. Chief Justice EARL WARREN, speaking for the Court, answered the defendant's symbolic speech defense by opining, "We cannot accept the view that an apparently limitless variety of conduct can be labeled "speech' whenever the person engaging in the conduct intends thereby to express an idea."

Any attempt to disentangle "speech" from conduct that is itself communicative will not withstand analysis. The speech element in symbolic speech is entitled to no lesser (and also no greater) degree of protection than that accorded to so-called pure speech. Indeed, in one sense all speech is symbolic. At this moment the reader is observing black markings on paper which curl and point in various directions. We call such markings letters, and in groups they are referred to as words. What is being said in this sentence is meaningful only because the reader recognizes these markings as symbols for particular ideas. The same is true of oral speech which is simply the use of symbolic sounds. Outside the science fiction realm of mind-to-mind telepathic communication, all communications necessarily involve the use of symbols.

But because all expression necessarily requires the use of symbols, it does not necessarily follow as a matter of logic that First Amendment protection is or should be available for all symbolic expressions. The "speech" protected by the First Amendment might be limited to expressions in which the symbols employed consist of conventional words. The Supreme Court has found so restrictive a reading of the First Amendment to be unacceptable. Significantly, in First Amendment cases, the Court often refers to "freedom of expression" as the equivalent of freedom of speech. Justice OLIVER WENDELL HOLMES's "free trade in ideas" may not be reduced to mere trade in words. It is the freedom to express ideas and feelings, not merely the freedom to engage in verbal locutions, that must be protected if the First Amendment's central values are to be realized.

In COHEN V. CALIFORNIA (1971) the Supreme Court held that the emotive form of speech is as entitled to First Amendment protection as is its cognitive content. Emotive expression can be fully as important as intellectual, or cognitive, content in the competition of ideas for acceptance in the marketplace. Of course, most communications encompass both cognitive and emotive content. But even if a communication is substantially devoid of all cognitive content, its emotive content surely lies within the First Amendment scope. Symphonic compositions or non-representational art are protected against governmental censorship, notwithstanding their lack of verbal or cognitive content.

Of course, not all conduct should be regarded as "speech" within the meaning of the First Amendment. Not even the most ardent free speech advocate would contend that all legislation regulating human conduct is subject to First Amendment restrictions. If, as the Court stated in the O'Brien opinion, the First Amendment is not to apply to a "limitless variety of conduct," what standards should be applied in determining whether given restrictions on conduct constitute First Amendment abridgment of symbolic speech?

If government's purpose in restricting is to suppress the message conveyed by the conduct, then the state should not be heard to deny the actor's claim that the conduct in question was intended to communicate a message. Such a message-restricting motivation by the state should also establish that the conduct in question constitutes symbolic speech. But such a conclusion does not necessarily imply that the speech is entitled to First Amendment protection. Even speech in words may in some circumstances be subordinated to a counter-speech interest. Likewise, no First Amendment ABSOLUTISM will protect communicative conduct. In some contexts symbolic speech may be overbalanced by counter-speech interests. If, however, the asserted or actual counter-speech interest is simply commitment to a particular view of the world—political, ethical, aesthetic, or otherwise—this interest will not justify abridgment of the right to express a contrary view, either by words or by conduct.

Just as First Amendment principles apply equally to expression in the symbols of the English or French languages, for example, the same principles govern when the symbols are of neither of these languages, nor of any conventional language. The crucial question under the First Amendment is whether meaningful symbols are being employed by one who wishes to communicate to others.

The courts have resisted equating symbolic speech with verbal speech because of a fear of immunizing all manner of conduct from the controls of the law. This fear is unjustifiable; it stems from a false premise as to the First Amendment protection accorded to verbal speech. In fact, speech in words is not immune from regulation. For example, an interest in excluding trespassers will justify abridging the verbal speech of those who wish to speak on property from which they may properly be excluded. Similarly, words that presage an imminent and likely BREACH OF THE PEACE will justify regulation just as much as if the idea be conveyed by nonverbal symbols. These are but two of many instances when verbal speech is subordinated to counter-speech interests.

According full and equal status to symbolic speech under the First Amendment will not open the floodgates to abuses, immunizing *O'Brien's* "apparently limitless variety of conduct" from legal regulation. Recognition of such equality of forms of expression would mean that no one will be penalized because he chooses to communicate—or is able to communicate—only in a language other than conventional words. We shall all be the richer for such recognition.

MELVILLE B. NIMMER
(1986)

Bibliography

NIMMER, MELVILLE B. 1973 The Meaning of Symbolic Speech to the First Amendment. *UCLA Law Review* 21:29–62.